2009 North American Discard

Coins & Prices

A GUIDE TO U.S., CANADIAN AND

18th Edition

David C. Harper, Editor

Harry Miller & Thomas Michael, Market Analysts

 The World's Best-Selling Coin Books

©2008 Krause Publications

Published by

krause publications

An Imprint of F+W Publications

700 East State Street • Iola, WI 54990-0001
715-445-2214 • 888-457-2873
www.krausebooks.com

Our toll-free number to place an order or obtain
a free catalog is (800) 258-0929.

ISSN 1935-0562
ISBN-13: 978-0-89689-705-2
ISBN-10: 0-89689-705-2

Designed by Sandra Morrison
Edited by George Cuhaj

Printed in the United States of America

Contents

HOW TO USE THE DVD

This DVD is PC and Macintosh® compatible when used with Adobe Acrobat Reader® version 6.0 or later. A step-by-step free download of Adobe Acrobat Reader® 8 is available at www.adobe.com. Adobe Reader® 8 was used in creating the instructions that follow.

To help you successfully navigate through the PDF document, several types of searches are available.

USING BOOKMARKS

Click on the Bookmarks icon to open the Bookmarks window. Use these links to go to specific points of interest. To scroll through pages in each section, use the arrows at the top of the screen (see next page for instructions to find page navigators).

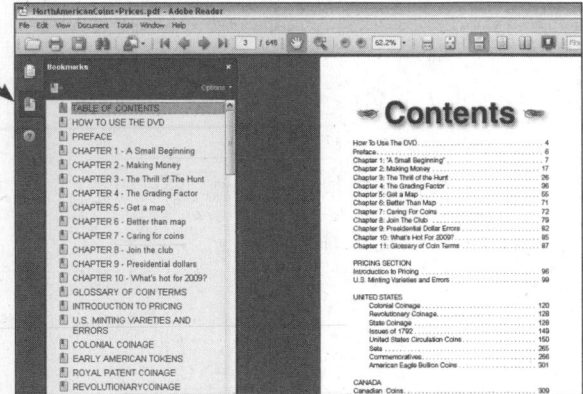

USING THE FIND BOX

Locate the find box in the tool bar and enter the word(s) you are searching for.

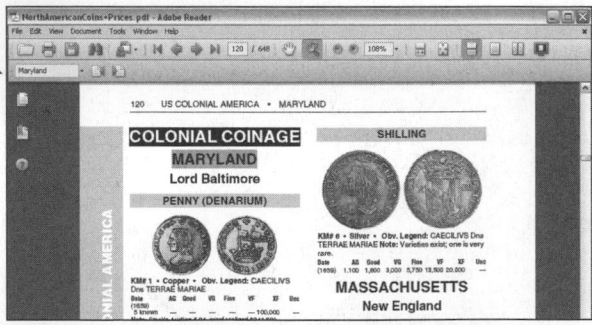

To navigate through the results of your search, use the Find Next icon.

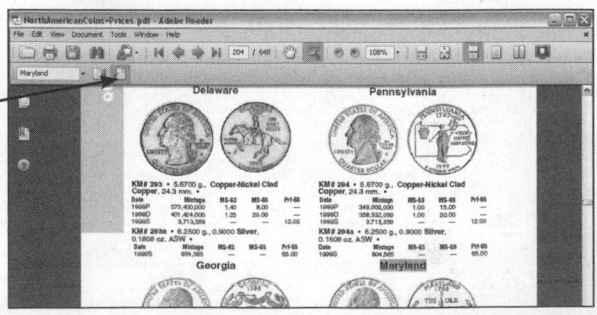

USING THE SEARCH OPTION

Locate the Search button by choosing Customize Toolbars in the Tools pull-down menu. Check Search (binocular icon) to have the Search option available in the toolbar.

Click on the Search icon to open the Search dialog box.

In the Search dialog box, enter the word(s) you are searching for and click on the Search button.

The list of results will appear in the dialog box. Click on the listings to view each page that contains your searched word(s).

To begin a new word search, click on the New Search button.

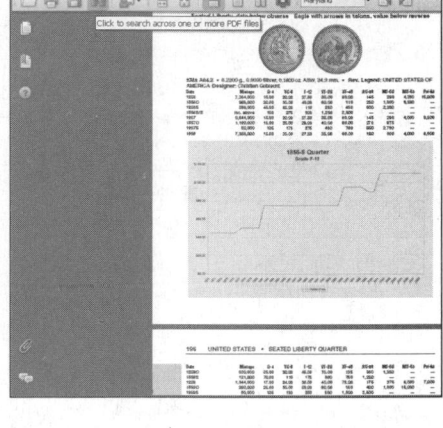

USING PAGE NAVIGATORS

Activate the Page Navigator Toolbar by choosing Customize Toolbars in the Tools pull-down menu. Check each tool as shown at right. You are now able to page through the PDF document by using the arrows at the top of the screen or by entering a page number you wish to view.

The Table of Contents is on page 3

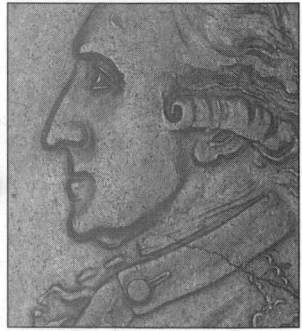

You may also enlarge the images of the coins up to 400% for easy viewing

≈ **Preface** ≈

Providing coin collectors with accurate, independently produced pricing information on collectible coins has become a trademark of F+W Publications' numismatic division in its 55 years of publishing. Visit our Web site at www.krausebooks.com for more information about us. We employ a full-time staff of market analysts who monitor auction results, trading on the Internet and trading at major shows.

This information is compiled by our analysts and they determine what price most accurately reflects the trading that has occurred for each date and mintmark in each grade listed in *North American Coins & Prices*. By studying this information and referring back to it repeatedly, a collector can arm himself with the necessary knowledge to go out in the market and make wise purchasing decisions. It must be remembered that these prices are intended solely as a guide. They are neither offers to buy or sell. Because prices do fluctuate, those that appear in this book may be in some cases obsolete by the time of publication. By checking the more than 40 price charts in the U.S. section, you can get a feel as to how price swings have occurred since 1972.

U.S. coins are the most popularly collected issues in the world. This is attributable in part to the popularity of coin collecting in the United States, but collectors in many other countries also covet collectible U.S. coins. After collecting U.S. coins for a while, many collectors in the United States branch out into issues of Canada and Mexico. These coins also enjoy a popular following in their countries of origin.

Thus, *North American Coins & Prices* brings together pricing information on all three of these countries. But this book also takes the price-guide concept a step further by providing information on the nuts and bolts of collecting coins: acquiring coins, grading them, organizing them into a collection, storing them properly and much more. Novice collectors can gain the necessary knowledge to collect coins enjoyably; veterans can pick up some pointers to add to their knowledge.

"A Small Beginning"
The U.S. Mint grew from a modest start

By Robert R. Van Ryzin

It was a "small beginning" but a significant one. In July 1792, a site for the new U.S. Mint not yet having been secured, 1,500 silver half dismes were struck on a small screw press nestled in the cellar of a Philadelphia building owned by sawmaker John Harper. Though some have since categorized these early emissions of the fledgling U.S. Mint as patterns, it is clear that first President George Washington – who is said to have deposited the silver from which the coins were struck – considered this small batch of half dismes the first official U.S. coins.

It is true that this limited coinage, the first since passage of the act establishing the Mint on April 2, 1792, pales by comparison to modern U.S. Mint presses. Today's machines can churn out up to 750 coins a minute, striking as many as four coins at a time and boasting yearly mintages in the billions. But it is also true that these first small pieces – struck from silver and stamped with a plump Liberty on the obverse and a scrawny eagle in flight on the reverse – have tremendous historical importance.

For within what Washington would declare in his 1792 address to Congress as a "small beginning" were the seeds of a monetary system that has lasted more than 200 years and has become the study and admiration of many.

Before the U.S. Mint

Collectors today can trace much of the nation's development and learn of its struggles and growth through its coinage: from a cumbersome system first proposed by Robert Morris, a Revolutionary War financier and first superintendent of finance, to the refinements tendered by Thomas Jefferson and Alexander Hamilton, which firmly placed the nation on an easily understood decimal system of coinage.

At first there was little coinage in circulation, except for foreign coins that arrived through trade or in the purses of the first settlers. Despite a dire need for coinage in the Colonies, Great Britain considered it a royal right and granted franchises sparingly. Much of the Colonial economy, therefore , revolved around barter, with food staples, crops, and goods serving as currency. Indian waupum or bead money also was used, first in the fur trade and later as a form of money for Colonial use.

Copper pieces were produced around 1616 for the Sommer Islands (now Bermuda), but coinage within the American Colonies apparently didn't begin until 1652, when John Hull struck silver threepence, sixpence and shillings under authority of the General Court of Massachusetts. This coinage continued, with design changes (willow, oak and pine trees), through 1682. Most of the coins were dated 1652, apparently to avoid problems with England.

In 1658 Cecil Calvert, second Lord Baltimore, commissioned coins to be struck in England for use in Maryland. Other authorized and unauthorized coinages – including those of Mark Newby, John Holt, William Wood, and Dr. Samuel Higley – all became part of the landscape of circulating coins. In the 1780s this hodgepodge of coinage was augmented by influxes of counterfeit British halfpenny coins and various state coinages.

In terms of the latter, the Articles of Confederation had granted individual states the right to produce copper coins. Many states found this to be appealing, and merchants in the mid-1780s traded copper coins of Vermont, Connecticut, Massachusetts, New Jersey, and New York. Not all were legal issues; various entrepreneurs used this as an invitation to strike imitation state coppers and British halfpence. Mutilated and worn foreign coins also circulated in abundance. Included among these were coins of Portugal, Great Britain and France, with the large majority of the silver arriving from Spain.

The accounting system used by the states was derived from the British system of pounds, shillings and pence. Each state was allowed to set its own rates at which foreign gold and silver coins would trade in relation to the British pound.

In 1782 Robert Morris, newly named superintendent of finance, was appointed to head a committee to determine the values and weights of the gold and silver coins in circulation. Asked simply to draw up a table of values, Morris took the opportunity to propose the establishment of a federal mint. In his Jan. 15, 1782, report (largely prepared by his assistant, Gouverneur Morris), Morris noted that the exchange rates between the states were complicated.

He observed that a farmer in New Hampshire would be hard-pressed if asked to determine the value of a bushel of wheat in South Carolina. Morris recorded that an amount of wheat worth four shillings in his home state of New Hampshire would be worth 21 shillings and eightpence under the accounting system used in South Carolina.

Robert Morris devised a complicated plan for a national coinage based on a common denominator of 1,440.

Morris claimed these difficulties plagued not only farmers, but that "they are perplexing to most Men and troublesome to all." Morris further pressed for the adoption of an American coin to solve the problems of the need for small change and debased foreign coinages in circulation.

In essence, what he was advocating was a monometallic system based on silver. He said that gold and silver had fluctuated throughout history. Because these fluctuations resulted in the more valuable metal leaving the country, any nation that adopted a bimetallic coinage was doomed to have its gold or silver coins disappear from circulation.

Gouverneur Morris calculated the rate at which the Spanish dollar traded to the British pound in the various states. Leaving out South Carolina, because it threw off his calculations, Gouverneur Morris arrived at a common denominator of 1,440. Robert Morris, therefore, recommended a unit of value of 1/1,440, equivalent to a quarter grain of silver. He suggested the striking of a silver 100-unit coin, or cent; a silver 500-unit coin, or quint; a silver 1,000-unit coin, or mark; and two copper coins, one of eight units and the other of five units.

On Feb. 21, 1782, the Grand Committee of Congress approved the proposal and directed Morris to press forward and report with a plan to establish a mint. Morris had already done so. Apparently feeling confident that Congress would like his coinage ideas, Morris (as shown by his diary) began efforts at the physical establishment prior to his January 1782 report. He had already engaged Benjamin Dudley to acquire necessary equipment for the mint and hoped to have sample coins available to submit with his original report to Congress.

Things went awry, however.

By Dec. 12, 1782, 10 months after Congress had approved his plan, Morris still could not show any samples of his coins. He was forced, ironically, to suggest that Congress draw up a table of rates for foreign coins to be used until his report was ready. It was not until April 2, 1783, that Morris was able to note in his diary that the first of his pattern coins were being struck.

"I sent for Mr. Dudley who delivered me a piece of Silver Coin," he wrote, "being the first that has been struck as an American Coin."

He also recorded that he had urged Dudley to go ahead with production of the silver patterns.

It wasn't until April 23, 1783, that Morris was able to send his Nova Constellatio patterns to Congress and suggest that he was ready to report on establishing a mint. Apparently nothing came of Morris' efforts. Several committees looked into the matter, but nothing was accomplished. Dudley was eventually discharged as Morris' hopes dimmed.

Thomas Jefferson was the next to offer a major plan. Jefferson liked the idea of a decimal system of coinage, but disliked Morris' basic unit of value. As chairman of the Currency Committee, Jefferson reviewed Morris' plan and formulated his own ideas.

To test public reaction, Jefferson gave his "Notes on Coinage" to The Providence Gazette, and Country Journal, which published his plan in its July 24, 1784, issue. Jefferson disagreed with Morris' suggestion for a 1/1,440 unit of value and instead proposed a decimal coinage based on the dollar, with the lowest unit of account being the mil, or 1/1,000.

"The most easy ratio of multiplication and division is that by ten," Jefferson wrote. "Every one knows the facility of Decimal Arithmetic."

Jefferson argued that although Morris' unit would have eliminated the unwanted fraction that occurred when merchants converted British farthings to dollars, this was of little significance. After all, the original idea of establishing a mint was to get rid of foreign currencies.

Morris' unit, Jefferson said, was too cumbersome for use in normal business transactions. According to Jefferson, under Morris' plan a horse valued at 80 Spanish dollars would require a notation of six figures and would be shown as 115,200 units.

Jefferson' coinage plan suggested the striking of a dollar, or unit; half dollar, or five-tenths; a double tenth, or fifth of a dollar, equivalent to a pistereen; a tenth, equivalent to a Spanish bit; and a one-fifth copper coin, relating to the British farthing. He also wanted a gold coin of $10, corresponding to the British double guinea; and a copper one-hundredth coin, relating to the British halfpence.

In reference to his coinage denominations, Jefferson said, it was important that the coins "coincide in value with some of the known coins so nearly, that the people may by quick reference in the mind, estimate their value."

Thomas Jefferson pro-posed that the United States adopt a decimal system of coinage.

More than a year, however, passed without any further action on his plan or that proposed by Morris. In a letter to William Grayson, a member of the Continental Congress, Washington expressed concern for the establishment of a national coinage system, terming it "indispensably necessary." Washington also complained of the coinage in circulation: "A man must travel with a pair of scales in his pocket, or run the risk of receiving gold at one-fourth less than it counts."

A plan at last

On May 13, 1785, the 13-member Grand Committee, to whom Jefferson's plan had been submitted, filed its report, generally favoring Jefferson's coinage system. The committee did, however, make slight alterations, including the elimination of the gold $10 coin, the addition of a gold $5 coin, and the dropping of Jefferson's double tenth, which it replaced with a quarter dollar. The committee also added a coin equal to 1/200th of a dollar (half cent). On July 6, 1785, Congress unanimously approved the Grand Committee's plan. It failed, however, to set a standard weight for the silver dollar or to order plans drawn up for a mint.

These two factors led to new proposals.

On April 8, 1786, the Board of Treasury, which had been reinstated after Morris' resignation as superintendent of finance two years prior, tendered three distinct coinage proposals based on varying weights and bimetallic ratios for the silver dollar. The first of these three plans (the one passed by Congress on Aug. 8, 1786) required the silver dollar to contain 375.64 grains of pure silver. The board's proposal varied from earlier coinage plans in that it advocated a higher bimetallic ratio of 15.256-to-1 and differing charges to depositors for coining of gold and silver. It called for minting of gold $5 and $10 coins, and silver denominations of the dime, double dime, half dollar, and dollar. In copper were a cent and half cent. The proposal came during the peak of state coinages and influxes of debased coppers, which, as the board reported, were being "Imported into or manufactured in the Several States."

Concerned over the need to control state coinages and foreign coppers, the board suggested that, within nine months of passage of its proposal, the legal-tender status of all foreign coppers be repealed and that values be set at which the state coppers would circulate. The board obviously expected immediate action and ordered a supply of copper that was being stored in Boston to be brought to New York in the hope that it might soon be coined. Their hopes, however, rested on the positive and quick action of Congress, something that hadn't occurred with the other proposals and would not occur this time.

Opposition to the mint was beginning to surface. Several members of Congress expressed their belief that the supply of foreign gold and silver coins in circulation was sufficient to preclude any need for a mint. They also argued that the problem with debased coppers could be solved by contracting with private individuals to strike the nation's cents and half cents.

Several proposals were offered for a contract coinage. On April 21, 1787, the board accepted a proposal by James Jarvis to strike 300 tons of copper coin at the federal standard. Jarvis, however, delivered slightly less than 9,000 pounds of his contract. The contract was voided the following year for his failure to meet scheduled delivery times, but helped to delay further action on a mint. Concerted action on a coinage system and a mint would wait until the formation of the new government.

Alexander Hamilton, named in September 1789 to head the new Treasury, offered three different methods by which the new nation could achieve economic stability, including the funding of the national debt, establishment of the Bank of North America, and the founding of the U.S. Mint. On Jan. 21, 1791, Hamilton submitted to Congress a "Report on the Establishment of a Mint." It was compiled through his study of European economic theories and the earlier works of Morris and Jefferson, along with the 1786 report of the Board of Treasury.

Hamilton agreed with Jefferson that the dollar seemed to be best suited to serve as the basic unit, but believed it necessary to establish a proper weight and fineness for the new coin. To do so, Hamilton had several Spanish coins assayed to determine the fine weight of the Spanish dollar. He also watched the rate at which Spanish dollars traded for fine gold (24 3/4 grains per dollar) on the world market.

From his assays and observations he determined that the Spanish dollar contained 371 grains of silver. He then multiplied 24 3/4 by 15 (the gold value of silver times his suggested bimetallic ratio) and arrived at 371 1/4 as the proper fine silver weight for the new silver dollar.

In regard to his findings, Hamilton admitted that Morris had made similar assays and had arrived at a weight of 373 grains for the Spanish dollar. Hamilton attributed the discrepancy to the differing equipment used in making the assays. He failed, however, to observe that silver coins were traded in the world market at actual weight rather than the weight at time of issue. The Spanish dollar contained 376 grains of pure silver when new, 4 3/4 grains more than Hamilton's proposed silver dollar.

Hamilton also wanted a bimetallic ratio of 15-to-1, in contrast to the Board of Treasury's 15.6-to-1 ratio. Hamilton said his ratio was closer to Great Britain's, which would be important for trade, and Holland's, which would be important for repaying loans from that country.

His report suggested the striking of a gold $10; gold dollar; silver dollar; silver tenth, or disme; and copper one-hundredth and half-hundredth. Hamilton felt the last of these, the half cent, was necessary because it would enable merchants to lower their prices, which would help the poor.

Congress passed the act establishing the U.S. Mint in April 1792. It reinstated several coin denominations left out by Hamilton and dropped his gold dollar. In gold, the act authorized at $10 coin, or "eagle"; a $5 coin, or "half eagle"; and a $2.50 coin, or "quarter eagle." In silver were to be a dollar, half dollar, quarter dollar, disme, and half disme, and in copper a cent and half cent.

Though it established a sound system of U.S. coinage, the act failed to address the problem of foreign coins in circulation. It was amended in February 1793 to cancel their legal-tender status within three years of the Mint's opening.

Coinage begins

Coinage totals at the first mint were understandably low. Skilled coiners, assayers and others who could handle the mint's daily operations were in short supply in the United States. Also in want were adequate equipment and supplies of metal for coinage. Much of the former had to be built or imported. Much of the latter was also imported or salvaged from various domestic sources, including previously struck tokens and coins, and scrap metal.

Coinage began in earnest in 1793 with the striking of half cents and cents at the new mint located at Seventh Street between Market and Arch streets in Philadelphia. Silver coinage followed in 1794, with half dimes, half dollars and dollars. Gold coinage did not begin until 1795 with the minting of the first $5 and $10 coins. Silver dimes and quarters and gold $2.50 coins did not appear until 1796.

Production at the first U.S. mint, in Philadelphia, was minuscule by today's standards.

Under the bimetallic system of coinage by which gold and silver served as equal representations of the unit of value, much of the success and failure of the nation's coinage to enter and remain in circulation revolved around the supply and valuation of precious metals. One need only to gain a cursory knowledge of such movements to understand what role precious metals played in development of U.S. coinage. That role, to a large extent, determined why some coins today are rare and why some passed down from generation to generation are still plentiful and of lower value to collectors.

From the Mint's beginning, slight miscalculations in the proper weight for the silver dollar and a proper bimetallic ratio led gold and silver to disappear from circulation. The U.S. silver dollar traded at par with Spanish and Mexican dollars, but because the U.S. coin was lighter, it was doomed to export.

A depositor at the first mint could make a profit at the mint's expense by sending the coins to the West Indies. There they could be traded at par for the heavier Spanish or Mexican eight reales, which were then shipped back to the United States for recoinage. As a result, few early silver dollars entered domestic circulation; most failed to escape the melting pots.

Gold fared no better. Calculations of the bimetallic ratio by which silver traded for gold on the world market were also askew at first and were always subject to fluctuations. Gold coins either disappeared quickly after minting or never entered circulation, languishing in bank vaults. These problems led President Jefferson to halt coinage of the gold $10 and silver dollar.

The gold $10 reappeared in 1838 at a new, lower-weight standard. The silver dollar, not coined for circulation since 1803, returned in 1836 with a limited mintage. Full-scale coinage waited until 1840.

Nor was the coinage of copper an easy matter for the first mint. Severe shortages of the metal led the Mint to explore various avenues of obtaining sufficient supplies for striking cents and half cents.

Witness, for example, the half-cent issues of 1795 and 1797 struck over privately issued tokens of the New York firm of Talbot, Allum & Lee because of a shortage of copper for the federal issue. Rising copper prices and continued shortages forced the Mint to lower the cent's weight from 208 grains to 168 grains in 1795.

By that same year Congress had begun to investigate the Mint. Complaints about high costs and low production had been raised. Suggestions that a contract coinage might be more suitable for the new nation surfaced again, despite bad experiences with previous attempts.

The Mint survived this and another investigation, but the problems of fluctuating metal supplies continued to plague the nation. In 1798, because of the coinage shortage, the legal-tender status of foreign coins was restored. Several more extensions were given during the 1800s, ending with the withdrawal of legal-tender status for Spanish coins in 1857.

In the 1830s great influxes of silver from foreign mints raised the value of gold in relation to silver, which made it necessary for the Mint to lower the standard weight of all gold coins in 1834. It also led to the melting of great numbers of gold coins of the old specifications.

By the 1850s discovery of gold in California had again made silver the dearer metal. All silver quickly disappeared from circulation. Congress reacted in 1853 by lowering the weight of the silver half dime, dime, quarter, and half dollar, hoping to keep silver in circulation. A new gold coin of $20 value was introduced to absorb a great amount of the gold from Western mines.

Not long after, silver was discovered in Nevada. By the mid-1870s the various mines that made up what was known as the Comstock Lode (after its colorful early proprietor, Henry P. Comstock) had hit the mother lode. Large supplies of silver from the Comstock, combined with European demonetization, caused a severe drop in its value, which continued through the close of the 19th century.

It was believed that the introduction of a heavier, 420-grain silver dollar in 1873, known as the Trade dollar, would create a market for much of the Comstock silver, bolster its price, and at the same time wrest control from Great Britain of lucrative trade with the Orient. It didn't. Large numbers of Trade dollars eventually flooded back into the United States, where they were, ironically, accepted only at a discount to the lesser-weight Morgan dollars.

The latter had been introduced in 1878 as a panacea to the severe economic problems following the Civil War. Those who proudly carried the banner of free silver contended that by taking the rich output of the Comstock mines and turning it into silver dollars, a cheaper, more plentiful form of money would become available. In its wake, they believed, would be a much needed economic recovery.

The Free Silver Movement gained its greatest support during the late 19th century when William Jennings Bryan attempted to gain the White House on a plank largely based on restoration of the free and unlimited coinage of the standard 412.5-grain silver dollar. He failed. Silver failed. Shortly thereafter the United States officially adopted a gold standard.

Silver continued to be a primary coinage metal until 1964, when rising prices led the Mint to remove it from the dime and quarter. Mintage of the silver dollar had ended in 1935. The half dollar continued to be coined through 1970 with a 40-percent-silver composition. It, too, was then debased.

Gold coinage ended in 1933 and exists today only in commemorative issues and American Eagle bullion coins with fictive face values. A clad composition of copper and nickel is now the primary coinage metal. Even the cent is no longer all copper; a copper-coated zinc composition has been used since 1982.

Precious-metal supplies were also linked to the opening of additional mints, which served the parent facility in Philadelphia. The impact of gold discoveries in the 1820s in the southern Appalachian Mountains was directly tied to the construction of branch mints in Dahlonega, Ga., and Charlotte, N.C., in 1838. These new mints struck only gold coins. New Orleans also became the site of a branch mint in the same year as Dahlonega and Charlotte. It took in some of the outflow of gold from Southern mines, but also struck silver coins.

Discovery of gold in California in the late 1840s created a gold rush, and from it sprang a great western migration. Private issues of gold coinage, often of debased quality, were prevalent, and the cost of shipping the metal eastward for coinage at Philadelphia was high. A call for an official branch mint was soon heard and heeded in 1852 with the authorization of the San Francisco Mint, which began taking deposits in 1854.

The discovery of silver in the Comstock Lode led to yet another mint. Located only a short distance via Virginia & Truckee Railroad from the fabulous Comstock Lode, the Carson City mint began receiving bullion in early 1870.

Denver, also located in a mineral-rich region, became the site of an assay office in 1863 when the government purchased the Clark, Gruber & Co. private mint. It became a U.S. branch mint in 1906. In addition to the Denver and Philadelphia mints, San Francisco and a facility in West Point, N.Y., continue to serve as U.S. mints, but the others have left behind a rich legacy.

The collector taking a more extended journey into the history of U.S. coinage can find plenty of interesting tales – some as tall as the day is long and others factually based – all of which are part of the rich and ever-changing panoply of U.S. coinage history. There are stories of denominations that failed, great discoveries, great rarities, great collectors, and, for those with an artistic bent, a rich field of pattern coins to be explored and a wealth of much-heralded designs by famous sculptors such as Augustus Saint-Gaudens, Adolph Weinman, James Earle Fraser, and others.

For those who are drawn to the hobby by the allure of age-old relics of days gone by, or by coins handed down through the family, or even by dreams of great wealth, coin collecting has much to offer. The history of the U.S. Mint, with its small but ever so important beginning, is the starting point.

Making Money
How coins are manufactured

By Alan Herbert

Just as printing is the process by which paper money is made, so is minting the method of manufacturing coins. The two are often confused by the public, but they are completely different.

The history of minting goes back several centuries before the birth of Christ. The Lydians are credited with making the first crude coins in the Middle East about 700 B.C., although the Chinese and Koreans trace their coinage back even further.

Some early coins were cast. That process continued in China into the 1900s, but only for low-value pieces. Here again the average person often assumes that all coins are cast, but as you will see, only a tiny fraction of a percent are – or were – actually made that way.

The methods developed by the Greeks and Romans centered on making dies that could be hammered by hand into the surface of a lump of metal, flattening it and impressing a design. Hammered coinage continued until after the end of the Middle Ages, about 1500. After that the first machines that could strike coins were invented. Today their successors can pound out 750 or more coins a minute.

From the early days when the fixed die was driven into a stump or a hole drilled in a rock, through fixing it in an anvil (the fixed die is still called the anvil die), to today's modern coin presses, the process is much the same. Force is applied to devices that impress or apply a design to a piece of material, which is transformed into a coin.

Early dies were made of wood. Then came copper, bronze, and finally iron as technology advanced. Today dies are made from exotic steels with special qualities that make them ideal for striking coins.

The history of coinage is fascinating. Interwoven into it are several familiar names: Leonardo da Vinci is credited with inventing one of the first coin presses.

James Watt, English inventor of the steam engine, was the first to incorporate steam power to drive the coin presses that earlier had depended on horses or human arms.

Whether the power comes from a hand holding a hammer or a mechanical ram, and whether it comes from above, below, or the side, the process is called "striking" a coin. Modern coin presses use a variety of methods in applying brute force to a piece of metal to turn it into a coin.

Another fable that traces to casting coins is the common belief that coins are made from liquid metal or at the least are red hot when they are struck. Neither is true. A coin's design is formed by the pressure that causes the metal to cold-flow into the pattern that you see on the coins in your pocket.

There are three basic parts of the minting process: (1) the making of the planchet, which is divided into the selection and processing of the metal and the preparation of the planchets, (2) the making of the dies, and (3) the use of the dies to strike the planchets. To help you remember these three parts, think of "P," "D" and "S" for planchet, die and striking.

Choosing a metal

Many different metals have and are being used for coins. The most popular coinage metals are those commonly found and relatively cheap, so they can be used for striking low-value coins. Precious metals – like silver, gold and platinum – are still used for commemorative coins.

A good coinage metal requires certain properties. The metal must be soft enough to be easily worked yet hard enough to withstand the wear and tear of a thousand pockets, a hundred thousand transactions. Few metals have all the right properties, so coin metals usually are an alloy, or mixture of two or more metals.

Copper is a favorite coin metal, either by itself or in an alloy. Zinc, nickel, iron, and aluminum are also found in coins struck by the United States and other countries. Silver and gold have to be alloyed with some metal, usually copper, to be hard enough to withstand commercial life. The so-called "pure" coins of silver or gold are known as "bullion coins," bought and sold primarily for their precious-metal content.

The metals chosen for a coin are melted and mixed together, and either poured into ingots or blocks, or extruded from furnaces that continuously cast a long strip of the metal. The ingots are passed several times between the big rolls in a rolling mill to reduce the ingot to the thickness of the blanks needed.

Once the strip is rolled to the correct thickness, it is sent to a blanking press. A gang of blunt-end punches are driven through the sheet, producing a dozen or more blanks with each stroke. The rough blanks are then ready to be processed.

Making the 'blanks'

The piece of metal (occasionally some other material, so it isn't always metal) that becomes a coin is known as a "blank." This is a usually round, flat piece that usually has been punched or cut from a sheet or strip of coin metal.

Strips of coin metal stand ready to be cut into "blanks."

A binful of blanks are ready for the coin press.

Before a blank can become a coin it has to be processed, cleaned, softened, and given what is known as an "upset edge" – a raised ridge or rim around both sides. The blank then becomes a "planchet" and is ready to be struck into a coin by the dies.

First they go through what looks like a monstrous cement mixer. A huge cylinder revolves slowly as the planchets are fed in at one end and spiral their way through. This is an annealing oven, which heats the planchets to soften them. When they come out the end, they fall into a bath where they are cleaned with a diluted acid or soap solution.

As the final step, they go through the upsetting mill, the machine that puts the raised rim on the blank and turns it into a planchet, ready to be struck. In a different department the process of making the dies used to strike the coins has already begun.

Preparing the dies

For those who haven't studied metallurgy, the concept of hard metal flowing about is pretty hard to swallow, but this is actually what happens. It is basically the same process as the one used in an auto plant to turn a flat sheet of steel into a fender with multiple curves and sharp bends. The cold metal is moved about by the pressure applied.

To make the metal move into the desired design, there has to be a die. Actually there has to be two dies, because one of the laws of physics is that for every action there has to be an equal and opposite reaction. You cannot hold a piece of metal in midair and strike one side of it. Instead you make two dies, fix one, and drive the other one against it – with a piece of metal in between to accept the design from each die.

A die is a piece of hard metal, like steel, with a design on its face that helps to form a mirror image on the struck coin. Early dies were made by hand. Engravers used hand tools to laboriously cut each letter, each digit, and each owl or eagle or whatever design was being used into the face of the die. Notice that this is "into" the surface of the die. Each part of the die design is a hole or cavity of varying shape and depth.

This is because we want a mirror image on the coin, but we want it raised, or in "relief." To make a relief image on a coin, the image on the die has to be into the face of the die, or "incuse." Of course, if we want an incuse image on the coin, such as the gold $2.50 and $5 coins of 1908-1929, the design on the die face would have to be in relief.

To fully understand this, take a coin from your pocket and a piece of aluminum foil. Press the foil down over the coin design and rub it with an eraser. When you take the foil off and look at the side that was in contact with the coin, you have a perfect copy of a die. Everywhere there is a relief design on the coin there is an incuse design on your foil "die."

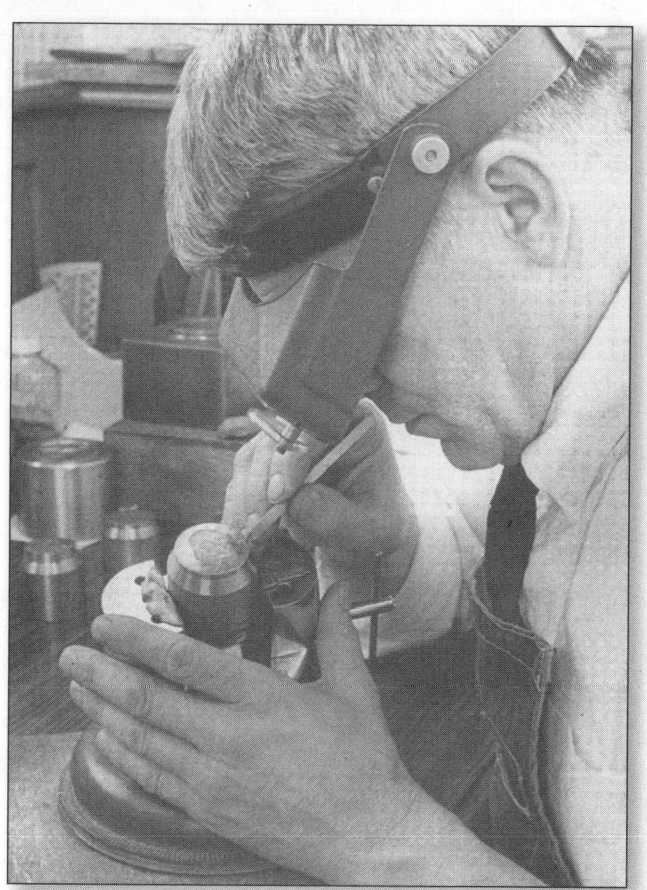

Edgar Steven, an engraver at the U.S. Mint puts the finishing touches on a die.

A galvano goes on the reducing lathe.

From sketchbook to coin

The design process begins with an artist's sketch. This is translated into a three-dimensional relief design that is hand-carved from plaster or, in recent years, from a form of plastic.

The plaster or plastic design is then transformed into a "galvano," which is an exact copy of the design that has been plated with a thin layer of copper. This is used as a template or pattern in a reducing lathe, which cuts the design into a die blank.

This die becomes the master die, from which all of the following steps descend. The process can be reversed so that the designs will be cut in relief, forming a tool called a "hub," which is simply a piece of steel with the design in relief, exactly the same as the relief design on the intended coin.

To make working dies, pieces of special steel are prepared, with one end shaped with a slight cone. The die blank is softened by heating it. Then the hub is forced into the face of the die, forming the incuse, mirror-image design in the face of the die.

The process usually has to be repeated because the die metal will harden from the pressure. The die is removed, softened, and returned to the hubbing press for a second impression from the hub. As you can imagine, it takes several hundred tons per square inch to force the hub into the die. Logically, this process is called "hubbing" a die.

The advantage of hubbing a die is that thousands of working dies can be made from a single hub, each one for all practical purposes as identical as the proverbial peas in a pod. This enables, for example, U.S. mints to strike billions of one-cent coins each year, each with the identical design.

Die making has come a long way from the early days when it took a skilled engraver a full day to carve a single letter into a die. The use of punches with the digits, letters or even parts of the design on the end reduced the amount of time required for the process. Today, thanks to the use of hubs, a complete die can be finished in a matter of hours.

Striking the coin

Yesterday's die might strike only a few hundred coins. Today it is not unusual for a die to strike well over a million coins.

The coin press used to strike modern coins is a complicated piece of equipment that consists basically of a feed system to place the planchets in position for the stroke of the hammer die to form a coin. This process takes only a fraction of a second, so the press has to operate precisely to spew out the hundreds of coins that are struck every minute.

The end of the early hammered coinage came with the introduction of the collar, which often is called the "third" die. The collar is nothing more than a steel plate with a hole in it. This hole is the exact diameter of the intended coin and

Rows of modern coin presses at the Philadelphia Mint turn out billions of coins a year.

A hopper is full of shiny new one-cent coins ready for shipment.

often is lined with carbide to prolong its life. It surrounds the lower, or fixed, die. Its sole purpose is to contain the coin metal to keep it from spreading sideways under the force of the strike.

If the intended coin has serrations, or "reeds," on the edge, then the collar has the matching design. The strike forces the coin metal against the serrations in the collar, forming the reeded edge at the same time that the two dies form the front and back, or obverse and reverse, of the coin.

Lettered-edge coins are produced usually by running the planchets through an edge-lettering die, or by using a segmented collar that is forced against the edge of the planchet during the strike by hydraulic pressure.

Several hundred tons were required to drive a hub into a die. Not as much but still significant amounts of force are needed to strike coins. A cent, for example, requires about 30 tons per square inch. One of the silver dollars took 150 tons. The other denominations fall in between.

Modern coin presses apply pressure in a variety of ways. A ram, carrying the moving or "hammer" die, is forced against the planchet. Most commonly this is with the mechanical advantage of a "knuckle" or connected pieces to which pressure is applied from the side. When the joint straightens – like straightening your finger – the ram at the end of the piece is driven into the planchet.

Once the strike is complete, at the final impact of the die pair, the coin has been produced. It is officially a coin now, and it's complete and ready to be spent.

The making of proof coins

While the high-speed coining presses are turning out billions of coins for commerce, there are other presses working at much slower speeds to produce collector coins, such as "proof" coins.

Proof coins started out as special presentation pieces. They were and still are struck on specially prepared planchets with specially prepared dies. Today the definition of a proof coin also requires that it be struck two or more times.

To make a proof coin, the planchets go through much the same process, but with some special care and some extra steps. Currently all proof versions of circulating U.S. coins are struck at the San Francisco Mint, but some of the proof commemorative coins have been struck at the other mints, including West Point.

After the proof blanks are punched from the strip, they go through the annealing oven, but on a conveyor belt rather than being tumbled in the revolving drum. After cleaning and upsetting they go into a huge vibrating machine where they are mixed with steel pellets that look like tiny footballs. The movement of the steel pellets against the planchets burnishes, or smooths, the surface so any scratches and gouges the planchets pick up during processing are smoothed over.

Proof dies get an extra polishing before the hubbing process. Like all other dies, they are made at Philadelphia and shipped to the branch mints.

When the proof dies arrive at San Francisco, they are worked on by a team of specialists who use diamond dust and other polishing agents to turn the fields of the proof dies into mirrorlike surfaces. The incuse design is sandblasted to make the surface rough, producing what is known as a "frosted" design.

Because collectors like the frosted proofs, the design is periodically swabbed with acid to keep the surface rough and increase the number of frosted proofs from each die. This is a relatively recent improvement, so frosted examples of earlier proofs are considerably scarcer.

The presses that strike proof coins usually are hand-operated rather than automatic. Some of the newer presses use equipment such as vacuum suction devices to pick up the planchets, place them in the coining chamber, and then remove the struck coins. This avoids handling the pieces any more than necessary.

On a hand-operated press, the operator takes a freshly washed and dried planchet and, using tongs, places it in the collar. The ram with the die descends two or more times before the finished coin is removed from the collar and carefully stored in a box for transport to storage or the packaging line. After each strike the operator wipes the dies to make sure that lint or other particles don't stick to the dies and damage the coins as they are struck.

Proof dies are used for only a short time before being discarded. Maximum die life is usually less than 10,000 coins, varying with the size of the coin and the alloy being struck.

Keeping up with demand

The minting process has come a long way from the first metal pellets that are barely recognizable as coins. Companies that manufacture equipment used in the world's mints are constantly researching to develop new methods of producing coins.

The purpose is to strike coins at as low a cost as possible and still retain the desired beauty in the design. Modern machines and new methods help the mints keep up with demand for coins.

The important point to remember is that the coins in your pocket are made no differently from the coins in the pocket of an English schoolchild or a Spanish police officer or an Italian opera singer. Mints around the world use the same methods, same equipment, and same common coin metals, with few if any variations from the basic methods. The minting process was shrouded in secrecy for centuries, but now has become common knowledge.

For the collector, knowing exactly how coins are minted can be some of the most valuable knowledge that can be learned. It often will make the difference between accepting a coin as a valuable addition to a collection or spotting it as a fake, counterfeit, or altered coin.

Because of the improvements in the making of coins, collecting the rare misstrikes and defective coins that escape quality control has become an important segment of the numismatic hobby. For a detailed description of over 400 categories of minting varieties, see the "U.S. Minting Varieties and Errors" section in this book.

The Thrill of The Hunt
How to aquire coins for your collection

By Al Doyle

Among the many pleasures coin collecting offers is the satisfaction of acquiring that long-sought piece that fills an important hole in a set or completes a collection. Many collectors say half the fun of pursuing the hobby is the thrill of the hunt — trying to find that needed coin in the condition desired and for a good price. Following are the main sources from which collectors acquire coins.

Circulation finds

Once the most popular method of building a collection, hunting through pocket change has declined substantially since 1965, when silver dimes and quarters were replaced by clad (base-metal) coinage.

Most collectors from 1935 into the 1960s got started in numismatics by searching through circulating coinage. It was worth the effort, as scarce and interesting coins such as the 1909-S VDB and 1914-D Lincoln cents, Liberty and Buffalo nickels, 1916-D and 1921 Mercury dimes, and Barber and Standing Liberty quarters were often found. Hobbyists who searched bank rolls and bags obtained at face value had no downside risk, and entire date collections of Lincoln cents were obtained in this manner.

Other denominations were also pursued in the treasure hunt. One Midwestern dealer found dozens of 1939-D Jefferson nickels (worth $1 to $30 each at the time, depending on condition) by searching through change obtained from parking meters of a nearby city. Another well-known numismatist put together a complete date and mintmark set of Walking Liberty half dollars in one afternoon by searching through coins obtained at his bank. Needless to say, those days are gone forever.

It's still possible to find collectible coins by searching large quantities of change, such as rolls.

What is available to pocket-change searchers today? Even the pre-1959 cents, with the Wheat-Ears reverse, are rare sights, but some interesting coins remain undiscovered.

Jefferson nickels can provide plenty of collecting enjoyment for virtually no financial commitment. A recent sampling of five rolls (200 coins, or $10) turned up 58 different date and mintmark combinations. Some of the highlights were a 1938-S (mintage 4.1 million) in grade fine, a 1947 in very fine, and a 1953-S. Looking through Jeffersons on a regular basis should lead to building the better part of a date and mintmark set.

Washington quarters experienced a circulation finds rebirth of sorts when the 50-state commemorative program began in 1999. Millions of Americans who had never collected coins before joined the hunt to acquire each of the new state designs as they were released at the rate of five per year.

Half dollars in your area may be another relatively untapped area in modern coinage. The 40-percent-silver pieces of 1965 to 1969 can sometimes be found in bank rolls. Half dollars seldom circulate, which means that older coins may be gathering dust in your local bank vault at this very moment.

Collecting Lincoln cents with the Memorial reverse, from 1959 to date, makes an excellent starter set. Many of the dates can be found in circulation.

What else might turn up in pocket change? Modern proofs enter circulation from time to time, and foreign coins are found occasionally. Canadian and U.S. coins frequently cross their respective borders.

Collectors of error coins sometimes find unusual pieces in circulation. What may be scorned as a reject by the average person is a valuable item to the error and variety specialist.

Start examining your pocket change. It's an inexpensive and pleasant way to get involved in the coin hobby.

Coin shops

Most medium-sized or larger cities and suburbs have at least one coin shop within driving distance, and a surprising number of small towns also boast of having a store that caters to local numismatists. Living in or near a metropolitan area is an advantage for the coin-shop enthusiast. For example, more than 15 dealers live in or near Cincinnati, and southern California and the New York area are home to hundreds of numismatic firms.

In some ways, a coin shop is similar to a small museum. All kinds of items from early coppers to gold coinage and other collectibles such as paper currency, stock certificates, and historic curiosities can be seen. A visit to a well-stocked shop is a visual treat.

It is likely that some of those coins in the display cases will appeal to you, and that means some comparison shopping and determining the value of your favorite coin are desirable. Prices do fluctuate, although collector-oriented coins tend to maintain steadier values than coins sought by investors.

If you are a casual collector, consider a subscription to Coins magazine. A monthly publication, Coins offers articles on a wide range of topics as well as a Coin Value Guide of retail prices for U.S. coins in most grades.

Serious collectors and others who want more frequent information will find Numismatic News to be a timely source of knowledge. Published weekly, the News includes coverage of recent market trends and reports from major coin conventions. World Coin News is published monthly and covers non-U.S. issues. All three publications also carry display advertisements from dozens of coin dealers.

Prices are determined by supply and demand as well as the grade, or state of preservation. Grading is often described as a subjective art rather than an exact science, and it does take some study and experience to become a competent grader (see Chapter 4).

Numismatic education is a never-ending process. Getting to know an experienced dealer who is enthusiastic about his product will certainly increase your knowledge of coins. Most shops carry a wide assortment of items, but dealers (like anyone else) have their personal favorites. If you find a dealer who is especially knowledgeable about a certain series, it could be to your advantage to do business with him or her if that also happens to be your favorite area too.

Strangely enough, doing business with a dealer who does not share your particular interest could work in your favor. Learning about collectible coins is a massive undertaking, and no one knows everything. Collectors of large cents and Bust half dollars are willing to pay substantial premiums for coins that have minor differences from other specimens struck during the same year, and specialists in those areas frequently "cherrypick" rare varieties that are offered at common-date prices.

Never be embarrassed to ask questions about coins or the dealer's experience in the hobby. As the old saying goes, "There is no such thing as a dumb question." A question asked at the right time could save you plenty of grief and money.

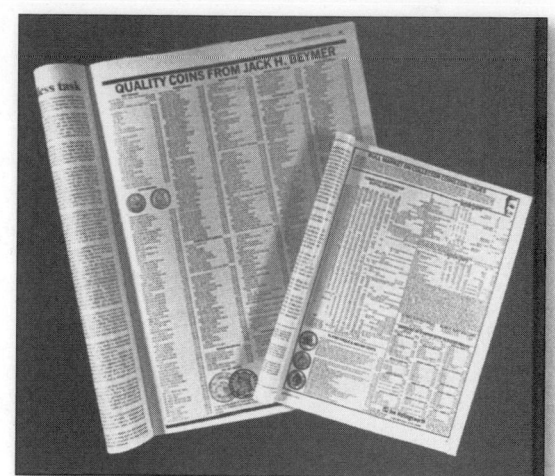

Advertisements in numismatic publications provide the convenience of shopping at home.

Mail order

This is one area that generates a fair amount of emotion among collectors. Many hobbyists swear by the convenience of shopping at home; others swear at mail-order firms that send overgraded and overpriced coins. Common sense and the same guidelines that apply to shopping for any other item should be used in selecting a mail-order coin dealer.

Look for someone who has a fair amount of experience in coins as well as enthusiasm for the hobby. Reputable dealers are willing to answer questions about their numismatic backgrounds and business practices. Word of mouth is often said to be one of the most effective forms of advertising, and it pays to ask other collectors about their favorite mail-order companies.

If several people agree that a firm provides accurately graded coins at fair prices, chances are excellent that you will also be a satisfied customer. How do you avoid being cheated? Collectors can be their own worst enemies and are often victimized by their own greed.

Take a coin that has a retail value in the $100 range in a particular grade. If that same coin is advertised at the same grade for $49.95, the savvy collector should immediately become suspicious. When a coin is offered at a price far under the going rate, remember these two sayings: "If it sounds too good to be true, it usually is," and "there is no Santa Claus in numismatics."

A dealer will generally pay $70 to $80 to acquire a popular coin with a retail value of $100. With that in mind, how can someone offer the same coin in the same grade at far less than wholesale cost? Wouldn't it be much easier to sell those coins to other dealers at a higher price and save on advertising expenses?

Obviously, the "underpriced" coins are not the same quality as their properly graded counterparts. It pays to keep up with current prices and grading standards. It is possible to find good deals at less than full retail cost, but don't expect to purchase decent coins for half price.

Does that mean all coins sold at real market prices are properly graded? Don't get complacent; overgraded coins are sometimes sold at full retail. But not everyone who sells an overgraded coin is intentionally fraudulent.

Grading standards are not carved in stone, which means that one person's MS-63 can be someone else's MS-64. Even though most dealers are extremely knowledgeable about coins, they can be fooled at times. The altered coin that a dealer bought as problem-free may be passed on to a collector in good faith, with no intention of deceit.

There is one important means of protection for consumers who buy through the mail: the return policy. Reputable firms allow buyers to return any unsatisfactory item for a full refund. The time allowed for returns varies widely from three working days to a month, but seven to ten days seems to be the most popular policy among mail-order dealers.

Look for "terms of sale" in dealer ads. Always read them before placing your order.

If you don't like coins received through the mail for any reason, send them back within the alloted time for a full refund. Companies might extend the deadline by a day or two if you call and ask for extra time.

What happens if you don't receive a refund or cannot satisfactorily resolve a problem with a mail-order dealer? There are several options:

The first step is to file a written complaint with the advertising department of any publication in which the dealer advertises. Include copies of invoices and other documentation. The publication cannot act on verbal complaints.

Written complaints can also be filed with a local or state chapter of the Better Business Bureau as well as any hobby-related organizations (the American Numismatic Association, Professional Numismatists Guild, and so on) in which the dealer holds membership. If you do business with a reputable dealer, it is unlikely that you will ever have to endure such a drawn-out complaint process, but be ready to take the proper steps if necessary.

For those who live in rural areas or prefer to shop at home, buying coins through the mail can be a rewarding experience and a convenient way to build a collection.

Coin shows

Dozens of shows are held every weekend across the nation. These events range from simple one-day shows with 10 to 20 tables to nationally known events such as the annual American Numismatic Association convention, Florida United Numismatists convention, the three-times-a-year shows held in Long Beach, Calif., Baltimore, Md. and the Central States Numismatic Society convention.

Admission to club-sponsored shows is usually free. Commercially sponsored shows oftentimes charge a nominal admission fee.

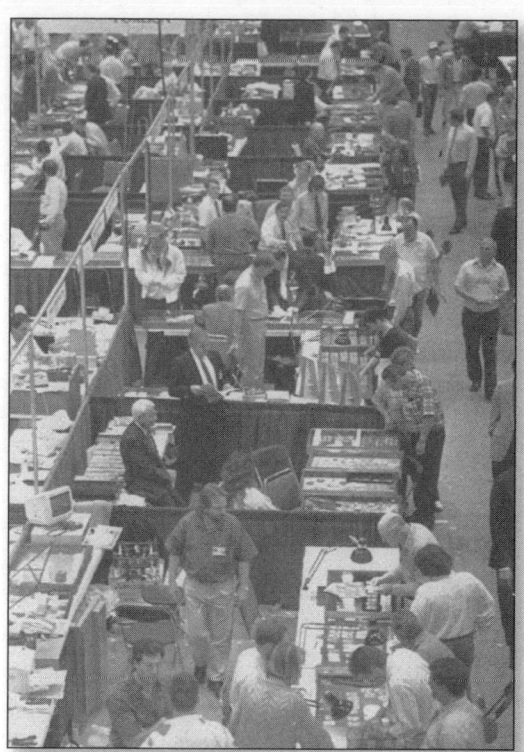

Shows big and small are held across the nation every weekend.

Somewhere between the show at the local VFW hall and the Baltimore show are state and regional conventions. Often sponsored by a club, these shows will have 40 to 100 dealer tables as compared to the 400 to 600 tables at a major convention. Tables at local and some regional conventions are often manned by part-time, or "vest pocket," dealers. Smaller shows tend to feature less expensive items; the larger shows will have a greater variety of scarce and expensive coins in addition to the more affordable pieces.

Major conventions will have a stunning array of merchandise ranging from coins of ancient Greece to major U.S. rarities. Even if you can't afford the expensive items, it doesn't cost anything to stroll the aisles and see some historic coins.

The big-ticket items are just part of the action at regional and major shows. A large assortment of affordable coins are available, and prices are often lower than at coin shops.

Dealers buy and sell thousands of coins among themselves at shows, and new purchases can often be had for a small markup. Good buys can sometimes be found later in the show when dealers are preparing to return home. A reasonable offer will often result in a new addition to your collection.

Speaking of offers, negotiating and dickering are as much a part of coin shows as silver dollars, but be reasonable. Tossing out an offer of $50 on a $200 coin is not shrewd; it's insulting.

If you make an offer on a coin and it is accepted, the coin is yours. Backing out of a deal is considered bad form. The coin business tends to be informal, and verbal offers carry serious weight. Your word is your bond on the bourse floor.

Purchases at a coin show do not carry a return policy. Unlike a mail-order transaction, you have ample opportunity to carefully examine the coin firsthand before making a financial commitment.

Why attend a show when you can acquire coins through the mail or from a local shop? There are many reasons to give the show circuit a try:

Conventions are an educational experience. Touring the bourse floor and talking to dealers and other collectors will increase your knowledge of numismatics, but there are other learning opportunities as well.

Many shows offer educational forums featuring speakers and presentations on various topics. These seminars cover everything from little-known specialties to advice on obtaining the best buys in a particular area of numismatics.

Exhibits will also add to your knowledge. Most medium-sized and major shows reserve a section of the bourse for collectors to display some of their holdings and compete for awards based on the educational value of their exhibit. The exhibit section offers an excellent opportunity to view something new and different.

You might be motivated to put together an exhibit yourself after a visit to a show. Keep in mind that it does not require a major collection to create a decent exhibit. Some of the most interesting displays incorporate low-priced coins and other collectibles.

Shows are excellent places to search for key-date coins and other material that may not be in stock at your local shop. Dealers do much of their shopping at shows, which should tell you something about the opportunities at a good-sized convention.

Want to introduce a friend or relative to coin collecting? Take them to a show and let them look around. Chances are excellent that the newcomer will become a fellow collector.

Looking for something different to collect? Paper money, world coins, tokens, medals, and medieval coins are often found at shows. You could find a new area of interest, and shows provide collectors with a chance to meet dealers and well-known hobbyists from across the country.

Have a game plan when you attend a show. Decide beforehand what you want to buy and how much money you plan to spend. Buying whatever looks nice will soon deplete your funds.

Coin shows offer something for everyone, so consider bringing the family. Jewelry (usually for much less than jewelry-store prices), baseball cards, antiques, and arts and crafts are also sometimes found at bourse tables.

One final note on coin-show etiquette: If you don't agree with a dealer's prices or grading, do not tell him that you can buy the same coin for less at another table or call him a crook. Just move on to the next table, and enjoy the rest of the show.

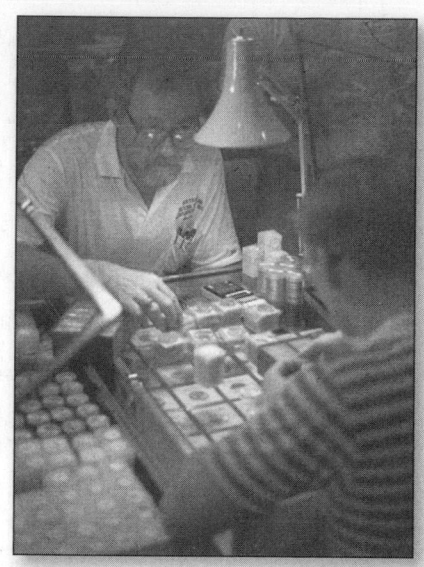

It's OK to bargain with a dealer at a show or shop, but collectors should be reasonable with their offers.

Information on upcoming shows in your area can be found in Coins and Numismatic News. Shows that feature a significant number of world coins are also listed in World Coin News. Coin-show advertising sometimes appears in local newspapers during the week prior to a show or in the paper's free listings of community events.

Auctions

Public auctions play an important role in the coin business. Prices realized at major auctions can indicate where the coin market is headed, as price fluctuations are a fact of life in numismatics. Important collections with major rarities are usually sold at a public auction. These sales are often held in conjunction with major shows.

However, affordable coins are often sold along with the rarities. A typical sale for a major auction firm will contain 1,000 to 6,000 lots, and most of those coins are not of the headline-grabbing variety. The larger the sale, the greater the likelihood that it will be broken into sessions conducted over a number of days.

The vast number of coins offered at a typical coin auction can work in favor of the collector who has a limited budget. Typical low- to medium-priced coins are often overlooked, as dealers and collectors focus on the trophy items. That may allow you to pick up some coins at reasonable prices. Internet auctions are another venue for lower priced items (See Chapter 13 for Web addresses and information.)

How can you participate in a public auction that is being held thousands of miles from your home? Catalogs are produced by auction companies for each sale, and mail, telephone and Internet bids are encouraged.

A typical auction catalog is illustrated with black and white as well as color photos of hundreds of coins. Descriptions of each lot give you an idea of the

A collector doesn't have to actually attend an auction to participate in it.

appearance of any coins that might be of interest. Many major firms post their catalogs on their Internet Web site.

If you are located near an auction site, it pays to examine your potential purchases at the pre-auction viewing session. The process is simple: Just visit the auction location (usually a major hotel or convention center) prior to the sale. The auction company sets up a room where the lots can be viewed. Long rows of tables with good lighting are provided. All you have to do is tell one of the attendants the lot numbers of the coins you want to view.

You can place written bids before you leave the premises, but it might pay to hang around for the auction and bid on coins in person. The action can be fast and furious at a major auction. Bidding increments of thousands of dollars are the rule when an expensive coin is being sold. It's an unforgettable sight to watch five or six serious competitors run up the price on a truly rare coin.

Keep several things in mind before you get involved in buying through auctions:

• You are legally responsible to honor all winning bids placed, so plan accordingly. It is unlikely that you will win every coin on which you bid, but placing too many bids could be hazardous to your financial health.

• Return policies vary among the major firms. Generally, floor bidders (those who personally attend the sale) do not have return privileges, as it is assumed that an adequate opportunity was provided to examine coins during the pre-auction viewing session.

One auction house does not allow any returns by mail bidders on certified coins, which are independently graded and encapsulated in a protective holder by an outside grading service. However, return privileges are the rule for all coins graded by the auction company's staff.

• Winning bids are generally subject to a 15 percent premium, or buyer's fee. If you successfully bid $300 on a coin, your final cost will be $345 plus postage and handling. Consider the buyer's fee when deciding on bids.

Getting started in buying through auctions requires a catalog of an upcoming sale. Typically priced at $10 to $25, auction catalogs can be excellent buys even if you don't participate in the sale, as they provide a wealth of numismatic information.

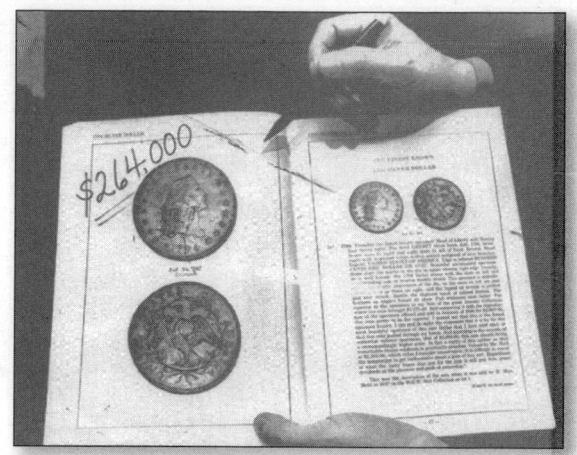

An auction catalog describes each lot offered.

Following are five major U.S. auction houses:

• Bowers and Merena Galleries, 18022 Cowan, Suite 200D. Irvine, CA 92614.

• Ira and Larry Goldberg Coins and Collectibles, Inc., 350 S. Beverly Drive, Suite 350, Beverly Hills, CA 90212.

• Heritage Numismatic Auctions, 3500 Maple Ave., 17th Floor, Dallas, TX 75219-3941.

• Stack's, 123 W. 57th St., New York, NY 10019.

• Superior Galleries, 9478 W Olympic Blvd., Beverly Hills, CA 90212-4246.

Smaller auctions will allow you to test the bidding process before you compete at a major sale. Local firms concentrate on less expensive coins, and a typical sale for these companies ranges from 250 to 1,000 lots. Catalogs are less elaborate, but they are also inexpensive. Prices range from free to $3, and mail bids are accepted.

Among the dozens of local companies that conduct coin auctions are the following:

• Michael Aron, P.O. Box 4388, San Clemente, CA 92674.

• Sonny Henry's Auction Service, 1510 Illinois Ave., Mendota, IL 61342.

Where to write for more information

Coins Magazine: 700 E. State St, Iola, WI 54990 or www.coinsmagazine.net
Numismatic News: 700 E. State St., Iola, WI 54990 or www.numismaticnews.net
World Coin News: 700 E. State St., Iola, WI 54990 or www.worldcoinnews.net
American Numismatic Association: 818 N. Cascade Ave.,
Colorado Springs, CO 80903-3279. Web address is http://www.money.org

Visit the Krause Publications Web site
http://www.krausebooks.com

The Grading Factor
How to classify a coin's condition

By Arlyn G. Sieber

Grading is one of the most important factors in buying and selling coins as collectibles. Unfortunately, it's also one of the most controversial. Since the early days of coin collecting in the United States, buying through the mail has been a convenient way for collectors to acquire coins. As a result, there has always been a need in numismatics for a concise way to classify the amount of wear on a coin and its condition in general.

A look back

In September 1888, Dr. George Heath, a physician in Monroe, Mich., published a four-page pamphlet titled *The American Numismatist*. Publication of subsequent issues led to the founding of the American Numismatic Association, and *The Numismatist*, as it's known today, is the association's official journal. Heath's first issues were largely devoted to selling world coins from his collection. There were no formal grades listed with the coins and their prices, but the following statement by Heath indicates that condition was a consideration for early collectors:

"The coins are in above average condition," Heath wrote, "and so confident am I that they will give satisfaction, that I agree to refund the money in any unsatisfactory sales on the return of the coins."

As coin collecting became more popular and The Numismatist started accepting paid advertising from others, grading became more formal. The February 1892 issue listed seven "classes" for the condition of coins (from worst to best): mutilated, poor, fair, good, fine, uncirculated, and proof. Through the years, the hobby has struggled with developing a grading system that would be accepted by all and could apply to all coins. The hobby's growth was accompanied by a desire for more grades, or classifications, to more precisely define a coin's condition. The desire for more precision, however, was at odds with the basic concept of grading: to provide a concise method for classifying a coin's condition.

For example, even the conservatively few classifications of 1892 included fudge factors.

"To give flexibility to this classification," *The Numismatist* said, "such modification of fine, good and fair, as 'extremely,' 'very,' 'almost,' etc., are used to express slight variations from the general condition."

The debate over grading continued for decades in *The Numismatist*. A number of articles and letters prodded the ANA to write grading guidelines and endorse them as the association's official standards. Some submitted specific suggestions for terminology and accompanying standards for each grade. But grading remained a process of "instinct" gained through years of collecting or dealing experience.

A formal grading guide in book form finally appeared in 1958, but it was the work of two individuals rather than the ANA, *A Guide to the Grading of United States Coins* by Martin R. Brown and John W. Dunn was a break-through in the great grading debate. Now collectors had a reference that gave them specific guidelines for specific coins and could be studied and restudied at home.

The first editions of Brown and Dunn carried text only, no illustrations. For the fourth edition, in 1964, publication was assumed by Whitman Publishing Co. of Racine, Wis., and line drawings were added to illustrate the text.

The fourth edition listed six principal categories for circulated coins (from worst to best): good, very good, fine, very fine, extremely fine, and about uncirculated. But again, the desire for more precise categories were evidenced. In the book's introduction, Brown and Dunn wrote, "Dealers will sometimes advertise coins that are graded G-VG, VG-F, F-VF, VF-XF. Or the description may be ABT. G. or VG plus, etc. This means that the coin in question more than meets minimum standards for the lower grade but is not quite good enough for the higher grade."

When the fifth edition appeared, in 1969, the "New B & D Grading System" was introduced. The six principal categories for circulated coins were still intact, but variances within those categories were now designated by up to four letters: "A," "B," "C" or "D." For example, an EF-A coin was "almost about uncirculated." An EF-B was "normal extra fine" within the B & D standards. EF-C had a "normal extra fine" obverse, but the reverse was "obviously not as nice as obverse due to poor strike or excessive wear." EF-D had a "normal extra fine" reverse but a problem obverse.

But that wasn't the end. Brown and Dunn further listed 29 problem points that could appear on a coin – from No. 1 for an "edge bump" to No. 29 for "attempted re-engraving outside of the Mint." The number could be followed by the letter "O" or "R" to designate whether the problem appeared on the obverse or reverse and a Roman numeral corresponding to a clock face to designate where the problem appears on the obverse or reverse. For example, a coin described as "VG-B-9-O-X" would grade "VG-B"; the "9" designated a "single rim nick"; the "O" indicated the nick was on the obverse; and the "X" indicated it appeared at the 10 o'clock position, or upper left, of the obverse.

The author's goal was noble – to create the perfect grading system. They again, however, fell victim to the age-old grading-system problem: Precision comes at the expense of brevity. Dealer Kurt Krueger wrote in the January 1976 issue of *The Numismatist*, "Under the new B & D system, the numismatist must contend with a minimum of 43,152 different grading combinations! Accuracy is apparent, but simplicity has been lost." As a result, the "New B & D Grading System" never caught on in the marketplace.

The 1970s saw two important grading guides make their debut. The first was *Photograde* by James F. Ruddy. As the title implies, Ruddy uses photographs instead of line drawings to show how coins look in the various circulated grades. Simplicity is also a virtue of Ruddy's book. Only seven circulated grades are listed (about good, good, very good, fine, very fine, extremely fine, and about uncirculated), and the designations stop there.

In 1977 the longtime call for the ANA to issue grading standards was met with the release of *The Official A.N.A. Grading Standards for United States Coins*. Like Brown and Dunn, the first edition of the ANA grading guide used line drawings to illustrate coins in various states of wear. But instead of using adjectival descriptions, the ANA guide adopted a numerical system for designating grades.

The numerical designations were based on a system used by Dr. William H. Sheldon in his book *Early American Cents*, first published in 1949. He used a scale of 1 to 70 to designate the grades of large cents.

"On this scale," Sheldon wrote, "1 means that the coin is identifiable and not mutilated – no more than that. A 70-coin is one in flawless Mint State, exactly as it left the dies, with perfect mint color and without a blemish or nick." (Sheldon's scale also had its pragmatic side. At the time, a No. 2 large cent was worth about twice a No. 1 coin; a No. 4 was worth about twice a No. 2, and so on up the scale.)

With the first edition of its grading guide, the ANA adopted the 70-point scale for grading all U.S. coins. It designated 10 categories of circulated grades: AG-3, G-4, VG-8, F-12, VF-20, VF-30, EF-40, EF-45, AU-50, and AU-55. The third edition, released in 1987, replaced the line drawings with photographs, and another circulated grade was added: AU-58. A fourth edition was released in 1991.

Grading circulated U.S. coins

Dealers today generally use either the ANA guide or Photograde when grading circulated coins for their inventories. (Brown and Dunn is now out of print.) Many local coin shops sell both books. Advertisers in *Numismatic News*, *Coins Maga-*

zine, and *Coin Prices* must indicate which standards they are using in grading their coins. If the standards are not listed, they must conform to ANA standards.

Following are some general guidelines, accompanied by photos, for grading circulated U.S. coins. Grading even circulated pieces can be subjective, particularly when attempting to draw the fine line between, for example, AU-55 and AU-58. Two longtime collectors or dealers can disagree in such a case.

But by studying some combination of the following guidelines, the ANA guide, and Photograde, and by looking at a lot of coins at shops and shows, collectors can gain enough grading knowledge to buy circulated coins confidently from dealers and other collectors. The more you study, the more knowledge and confidence you will gain. When you decide which series of coins you want to collect, focus on the guidelines for that particular series. Read them, reread them, and then refer back to them again and again.

AU-50

Indian cent

Lincoln cent

Buffalo nickel

Jefferson nickel

Mercury dime

Standing Liberty quarter

Washington quarter

Walking Liberty half dollar

Morgan dollar

Barber coins

AU-50 (about uncirculated): Just a slight trace of wear, result of brief exposure to circulation or light rubbing from mishandling, may be evident on elevated design areas. These imperfections may appear as scratches or dull spots, along with bag marks or edge nicks. At least half of the original mint luster generally is still evident.

XF-40

Indian cent

Lincoln cent

Buffalo nickel

Jefferson nickel

Mercury dime

Standing Liberty quarter

Washington quarter

Walking Liberty half dollar

Morgan dollar

Barber coins

XF-40 (extremely fine): The coin must show only slight evidence of wear on the highest points of the design, particularly in the hair lines of the portrait on the obverse. The same may be said for the eagle's feathers and wreath leaves on the reverse of most U.S. coins. A trace of mint luster may still show in protected areas of the coin's surface.

VF-20

Indian cent

Lincoln cent

Buffalo nickel

Jefferson nickel

Mercury dime

Standing Liberty quarter

Washington quarter

Walking Liberty half dollar

Morgan dollar

Barber coins

VF-20 (very fine): The coin will show light wear at the fine points in the design, though they may remain sharp overall. Although the details may be slightly smoothed, all lettering and major features must remain sharp.

Indian cent: All letters in "Liberty" are complete but worn. Headdress shows considerable flatness, with flat spots on the tips of the feathers.

Lincoln cent: Hair, cheek, jaw, and bow-tie details will be worn but clearly separated, and wheat stalks on the reverse will be full with no weak spots.

Buffalo nickel: High spots on hair braid and cheek will be flat but show some detail, and a full horn will remain on the buffalo.

Jefferson nickel: Well over half of the major hair detail will remain, and the pillars on Monticello will remain well defined, with the triangular roof partially visible.

Mercury dime: Hair braid will show some detail, and three-quarters of the detail will remain in the feathers. The two diagonal bands on the fasces will show completely but will be worn smooth at the middle, with the vertical lines sharp.

Standing Liberty quarter: Rounded contour of Liberty's right leg will be flattened, as will the high point of the shield.

Washington quarter: There will be considerable wear on the hair curls, with feathers on the right and left of the eagle's breast showing clearly.

Walking Liberty half dollar: All lines of the skirt will show but will be worn on the high points. Over half the feathers on the eagle will show.

Morgan dollar: Two-thirds of the hair lines from the forehead to the ear must show. Ear should be well defined. Feathers on the eagle's breast may be worn smooth.

Barber coins: All seven letters of "Liberty" on the headband must stand out sharply. Head wreath will be well outlined from top to bottom.

F-12

Indian cent

Lincoln cent

Buffalo nickel

Jefferson nickel

Mercury dime

Standing Liberty quarter

Washington quarter

Walking Liberty half dollar

Morgan dollar

Barber coins

F-12 (fine): Coins show evidence of moderate to considerable but generally even wear on all high points, though all elements of the design and lettering remain bold. Where the word "Liberty" appears in a headband, it must be fully visible. On 20th century coins, the rim must be fully raised and sharp.

VG-8

Indian cent

Lincoln cent

Buffalo nickel

Jefferson nickel

Mercury dime

Standing Liberty quarter

Washington quarter   *Walking Liberty half dollar*

Morgan dollar   *Barber coins*

VG-8 (very good): The coin will show considerable wear, with most detail points worn nearly smooth. Where the word "Liberty" appears in a headband, at least three letters must show. On 20th century coins, the rim will start to merge with the lettering.

SELL YOUR COINS & CURRENCY TO AN EXPERT!

Gary Adkins

Gary Adkins Associates, Inc. is one of the premier numismatic firms in the country. Our goal is to be the best company in the rare coin business. Not the biggest, but the best! We do that by providing personalized service and attention to every customer. Gary Adkins, our senior numismatist, has over 40 years in the business. As a board member & president of the Professional Numismatic Guild, he brings qualifications and credentials that insure our most important goal ... your complete satisfaction. We are proud to have a staff of very experienced numismatists who are qualified to help you with your coin purchases or sales, find coins that you need to complete your collection, and answer any of your numismatic questions.

We work with clients to provide whatever is best for each individual and we never lose sight of the fact that coins are not a necessity of life. They are a luxury meant to be enjoyed as objects of beauty, history, and pride of ownership. You can be assured that we will make every effort to give you the finest quality coins at the best possible price level for the grade you select. Our desire is to assist you in obtaining your objectives, both in portfolio selection and in the purchase or sale of your coins. Our company motto is, "If we wouldn't put it in our collection, we wouldn't ask you to put it in yours." We are here to build long-term relationships and help you enjoy your collecting to the fullest.

TEAR OUT AND MAIL IN TODAY

FREE INFORMATION! FREE APPRAISALS!*

Yes, I would like to know more about:

_____ Collecting rare coins

_____ Investing in rare coins

_____ Monthly collecting plans

_____ Having my coins appraised

_____ Selling my coins

Please send me your free information on the items checked above. I understand that I am under no obligation and that any information I provide will remain strictly confidential.

NAME _____

ADDRESS _____

_____

CITY _____ ST _____ ZIP _____

DAYTIME PHONE _____

EVENING PHONE _____

E-MAIL _____

Gary Adkins Associates, Inc.

NA2009

*Free appraisals are limited phone consultation or 1/2 hour off of billing for a formal written appraisal.

G-4

Indian cent

Lincoln cent

Buffalo nickel

Jefferson nickel

Mercury dime

Standing Liberty quarter

Washington quarter

Walking Liberty half dollar

Morgan dollar

Barber coins

G-4 (good): Only the basic design remains distinguishable in outline form, will all points of detail worn smooth. The word "Liberty" has disappeared, and the rims are almost merging with the lettering.

About good or fair: The coin will be identifiable by date and mint but otherwise badly worn, with only parts of the lettering showing. Such coins are of value only as fillers in a collection until a better example of the date and mintmark can be obtained. The only exceptions would be rare coins

Collectors have a variety of grading services to choose from. This set of Arkansas half dollars that appeared in an Early American History Auctions sale used two of the services.

Grading uncirculated U.S. coins

The subjectivity of grading and the trend toward more classifications becomes more acute when venturing into uncirculated, or mint-state, coins. A minute difference between one or two grade points can mean a difference in value of hundreds or even thousands of dollars. In addition, the standards are more difficult to articulate in writing and illustrate through drawings or photographs. Thus, the possibilities for differences of opinion on one or two grade points increase in uncirculated coins.

Back in Dr. George Heath's day and continuing through the 1960s, a coin was either uncirculated or it wasn't. Little distinction was made between uncirculated coins of varying condition, largely because there was little if any difference in value. When *Numismatic News* introduced its value guide in 1962 (the forerunner of today's *Coin Market* section in the *News*), it listed only one grade of uncirculated for Morgan dollars.

But as collectible coins increased in value and buyers of uncirculated coins became more picky, distinctions within uncirculated grade started to surface. In 1975 *Numismatic News* still listed only one uncirculated grade in *Coin Market*, but added this note: "Uncirculated and proof specimens in especially choice condition will also command proportionately higher premiums than these listed."

The first edition of the ANA guide listed two grades of uncirculated, MS-60 and MS-65, in addition to the theoretical but non-existent MS-70 (a flawless coin). MS-60 was described as "typical uncirculated" and MS-65 as "choice uncirculated." *Numismatic News* adopted both designations for *Coin Market*. In 1981, when the second edition of the ANA grading guide was released, MS-67 and MS-63 were added. In 1985 *Numismatic News* started listing six grades of uncirculated for Morgan dollars: MS-60, MS-63, MS-65, MS-65+, and MS-63 prooflike.

Then in 1986, a new entity appeared that changed the nature of grading and trading uncirculated coins ever since. A group of dealers led by David Hall of Newport Beach, Calif., formed the Professional Coin Grading Service. For a fee, collectors could submit a coin through an authorized PCGS dealer and receive back a professional opinion of its grade.

The concept was not new; the ANA had operated an authentication service since 1972 and a grading service since 1979. A collector or dealer could submit a coin directly to the service and receive a certificate giving the service's opinion on authenticity and grade. The grading service was the source of near constant debate among dealers and ANA officials. Dealers charged that ANA graders were too young and inexperienced, and that their grading was inconsistent.

Grading stability was a problem throughout the coin business in the early 1980s, not just with the ANA service. Standards among uncirculated grades would tighten during a bear market and loosen during a bull market. As a result, a coin graded MS-65 in a bull market may have commanded only MS-63 during a bear market.

PCGS created several innovations in the grading business in response to these problems:

1. Coins could be submitted through PCGS-authorized dealers only.

2. Each coin would be graded by at least three members of a panel of "top graders," all prominent dealers in the business. (Since then, however, PCGS does not allow its graders to also deal in coins.)

3. After grading, the coin would be encapsulated in an inert, hard-plastic holder with a serial number and the grade indicated on the holder.

4. PCGS-member dealers pledged to make a market in PCGS-graded coins and honor the grades assigned.

5. In one of the most far-reaching moves, PCGS said it would use all 11 increments of uncirculated on the 70-point numerical scale: MS-60, MS-61, MS-62, MS-63, MS-64, MS-65, MS-66, MS-67, MS-68, MS-69, and MS-70.

The evolution of more uncirculated grades had reached another milestone.

Purists bemoaned the entombment of classic coins in the plastic holders and denounced the 11 uncirculated grades as implausible. Nevertheless, PCGS was an immediate commercial success. The plastic holders were nicknamed "slabs," and dealers couldn't get coins through the system fast enough.

In subsequent years, a number of similar services have appeared. Among them, one of the original PCGS "top graders," John Albanese, left PCGS to found the Numismatic Guaranty Corp (NGC). The ANA grading service succumbed to "slab mania" and introduced its own encapsulated product.

There now are numerous other reputable private third-party grading services. PCGS and NGC are the oldest and remain the leaders. In 1990 the ANA sold its grading service to a private company. It operates under the ANACS acronym.

How should a collector approach the buying and grading of uncirculated coins? Collecting uncirculated coins worth thousands of dollars implies a higher level of numismatic expertise by the buyer. Those buyers without that level of expertise should cut their teeth on more inexpensive coins, just as today's experienced collectors did. Inexperienced collectors can start toward that level by studying the guidelines for mint-state coins in the ANA grading guide and looking at lots of coins at shows and shops.

Study the condition and eye appeal of a coin and compare it to other coins of the same series. Then compare prices. Do the more expensive coins look better? If so, why? Start to make your own judgments concerning relationships between condition and value.

According to numismatic legend, a collector walked up to a crusty old dealer at a show one time and asked the dealer to grade a coin the collector had with him. The dealer looked at the coin and said, "I grade it a hundred dollars." Such is the bottom line to coin grading.

Grading U.S. proof coins

Because proof coins are struck by a special process using polished blanks, they receive their own grading designation. A coin does not start out being a proof and then become mint state if it becomes worn. Once a proof coin, always a proof coin.

In the ANA system, proof grades use the same numbers as circulated and uncirculated grades, and the amount of wear on the coin corresponds to those grades. But the number is preceded by the word "proof." For example, Proof-65, Proof-55, Proof-45, and so on. In addition, the ANA says a proof coin with many marks, scratches or other defects should be called an "impaired proof."

Grading world coins

The state of grading non-U.S. issues is similar to U.S. coin grading before Brown and Dunn. There is no detailed, illustrated guide that covers the enormous scope and variety of world coins; collectors and dealers rely on their experience in the field and knowledge of the marketplace.

The *Standard Catalog of World Coins* gives the following guidelines for grading world coins, which apply to the Canadian and Mexican value listings in this book:

In grading world coins, there are two elements to look for: (1) overall wear and (2) loss of design details, such as strands of hair, feathers on eagles, designs on coats of arms, and so on. Grade each coin by the weaker of the two sides. Age, rarity or type of coin should not be considered in grading.

Grade by the amount of overall wear and loss of detail evident in the main design on each side. On coins with a moderately small design element that is prone to early wear, grade by that design alone.

In the marketplace, adjectival grades are still used for Mexican coins. The numerical system for Canadian coins is now commonplace:

Uncirculated, MS-60: No visible signs of wear or handling, even under a 30X microscope. Bag marks may be present.

Almost uncirculated, AU-50: All detail will be visible. There will be wear on only the highest points of the coin. There will often be half or more of the original mint luster present.

Extremely fine, XF-40: About 95 percent of the original detail will be visible. Or, on a coin with a design that has no inner detail to wear down, there will be light wear over nearly the entire coin. If a small design is used as the grading area, about 90 percent of the original detail will be visible. This latter rule stems from the logic that a smaller amount of detail needs to be present because a small area is being used to grade the whole coin.

Very fine, VF-20: About 75 percent of the original detail will be visible. Or, on a coin with no inner detail, there will be moderate wear over the entire coin. Corners of letters and numbers may be weak. A small grading area will have about 60 percent of the original detail.

Fine, F-12: About 50 percent of the original detail will be visible. Or, on a coin with no inner detail, there will be fairly heavy wear over the entire coin. Sides of letters will be weak. A typically uncleaned coin will often appear dirty or dull. A small grading area will have just under 50 percent of the original detail.

Very good, VG-8: About 25 percent of the original detail will be visible. There will be heavy wear on the entire coin.

Good, G-4: Design will be clearly outlined but with substantial wear. Some of the larger detail may be visible. The rim may have a few weak spots of wear.

About good, AG-3: Typically only a silhouette of a large design will be visible. The rim will be worn down into the letters, if any.

Where to write for more information

American Numismatic Association: 818 N. Cascade Ave., Colorado Springs, CO 80903-3279.

Independent Coin Grading Co.: 7901 E. Belleview Ave., Suite 50, Englewood, CO 80111.

Numismatic Guaranty Corp: P.O. Box 4776, Sarasota, FL 34230.

NTC (Numistrust Corp.): 2500 N. Military Trail, Suite 210, Boca Raton, FL 33431.

PCI, Inc.: P.O. Box 486, Rossville, GA 30741.

Professional Coin Grading Service: P.O. Box 9458, Newport Beach, CA 92658.

Sovereign Entities Grading Service: 401 Chestnut St., Suite 103, Chattanooga, TN 37402-4924.

Visit the Krause Publications Web site
http://www.numismaster.com

Get a map
How to organize a collection

By David C. Harper

Do you have a jar full of old coins? Did a favorite relative give you a few silver dollars over the years? Or did you just come across something unusual that you set aside?

All three circumstances make good beginnings for collecting coins. It may surprise you, but this is how just about everybody starts in the hobby. It is a rare collector who decides to start down the hobby road without first having come into a few coins one way or another.

What these random groupings lack is organization. It is organization that makes a collection. But think about it another way: Organization is the map that tells you where you can go in coin collecting and how you can get there.

Have you ever been at a large fair or a huge office building and seen the maps that say "you are here"? Did you ever consider that, over time, thousands of other people have stood on the same spot? This is true in numismatics also. Figuratively, you are standing on the same spot on which the writers of this book stood at some point in their lives.

At a fair, the map helps you consider various ways of seeing all the sights. In coin collecting, too, there are different ways to organize a collection. The method you choose helps you see the hobby sights you want to see.

It should be something that suits you. Remember, do what you want to do. See what you want to see. But don't be afraid to make a mistake; there aren't any. Just as one can easily retrace steps at a fair, one can turn around and head in another direction in the coin-collecting hobby. Besides, when you start off for any given point, often you see something along the way that was unplanned but more interesting. That's numismatics.

There are two major ways to organize a collection: by type, and by date and mintmark. These approaches work in basically the same fashion for coins of the United States, Canada and Mexico. Naturally, there are differences. But to establish the concepts, let's focus first on U.S. coins.

United States

Let's take collecting by type first. Look at your jar of coins, or take the change out of your pocket. You find Abraham Lincoln and the Lincoln Memorial on current cents. You find Thomas Jefferson and his home, Monticello, on the nickel. Franklin D. Roosevelt and a torch share the dime. George Washington and an eagle (or since 1999, designs honoring states) appear on the quarter. John F. Kennedy and the presidential seal are featured on the half dollar. Sacagawea and an eagle are on the dollar.

Each design is called a "type." If you took one of each and put the five coins in a holder, you would have a type set of the coins that are currently being produced for circulation by the U.S. Mint.

With just these six coins, you can study various metallic compositions. You can evaluate their states of preservation and assign a grade to each. You can learn about the artists who designed the coins, and you can learn of the times in which these designs were created.

As you might have guessed, many different coin types have been used in the United States over the years. You may remember seeing some of them circulating. These designs reflect the hopes and aspirations of people over time. Putting all of them together forms a wonderful numismatic mosaic of American history.

George Washington did not mandate that his image appear on the quarter. Quite the contrary. He would have been horrified. When he was president, he headed off those individuals in Congress who thought the leader of the country should have his image on its coins. Washington said it smacked of monarchy and would have nothing of it.

Almost a century and a half later, during the bicentennial of Washington's birth in 1932, a nation searching for its roots during troubled economic times decided that it needed his portrait on its coins as a reminder of his great accomplishments and as reassurance that this nation was the same place it had been in more prosperous days.

In its broadest definition, collecting coins by type requires that you obtain an example of every design that was struck by the U.S. Mint since it was founded in 1792. That's a tall order. You would be looking for denominations like the half cent, two-cent piece, three-cent piece, and 20-cent piece, which have not been produced in over a century. You would be looking for gold coins ranging in face value from $1 to $50.

But even more important than odd-sounding denominations or high face values is the question of rarity. Some of the pieces in this multi-century type set are rare and expensive. That's why type collectors often divide the challenge into more digestible units.

Type collecting can be divided into 18th, 19th, 20th and 21st century units. Obviously, a 21st century set is a short one. Just pull the change out of your pocket and ask the local bank for the half and dollar. Starting type collectors can focus on 20th century coin designs, which are easily obtainable. The fun and satisfaction of putting the 20th century set together then creates the momentum to continue backward in time.

In the process of putting a 20th century type set together, one is also learning how to grade, learning hobby jargon, and discovering how to obtain coins from dealers, the U.S. Mint, and other collectors. All of this knowledge is then refined as the collector increases the challenge to himself.

This book is designed to help. How many dollar types were struck in the 20th century? Turn to the U.S. price-guide section and check it out. We see the Morgan dollar, Peace dollar, Eisenhower dollar, and Anthony dollar. Hobbyists could also add the Ike dollar with the Bicentennial design of 1976 and the silver American Eagle bullion coin struck since 1986. One can also find out their approximate retail prices from the listings.

The beauty of type collecting is that one can choose the most inexpensive example of each type. There is no need to select a 1903-O Morgan when the 1921 will do just as well. With the 20th century type set, hobbyists can dodge some truly big-league prices.

As a collector's hobby confidence grows, he can tailor goals to fit his desires. He can take the road less traveled if that is what suits him. Type sets can be divided by denomination. You can choose over two centuries of one-cent coins. You can take just obsolete denominations or copper, silver or gold denominations.

You can even collect by size. Perhaps you would like to collect all coin types larger than 30 millimeters or all coins smaller than 20 millimeters. Many find this freedom of choice stimulating.

Type collecting has proven itself to be enduringly popular over the years. It provides a maximum amount of design variety while allowing collectors to set their own level of challenge.

The second popular method of collecting is by date and mintmark. What this means, quite simply, is that a collector picks a given type – Jefferson nickels, for example – and then goes after an example of every year, every mintmark, and every type of manufacture that was used with the Jefferson design.

Looking at this method of collecting brings up the subject of mintmarks. The "U.S. Mint" is about as specific as most non-collectors get in describing the government agency that provides everyday coins. Behind that label are the various production facilities that actually do the work.

In the more than two centuries of U.S. coinage, there have been eight such facilities. Four are still in operation. Those eight in alphabetical order are Carson City, Nev., which used a "CC" mintmark to identify its work; Charlotte, N.C. ("C"); Dahlonega, Ga. ("D"); Denver (also uses a "D," but it opened long after the

A basic type set of 20th century dollar coins would consist of (from top) a Morgan type, Peace type, Eisenhower type and Anthony type.

Dahlonega Mint closed, so there was never any confusion); New Orleans ("O"); Philadelphia (because it was the primary mint, it used no mintmark for much of its history, but currently uses a "P"); San Francisco ("S"); and West Point, N.Y. ("W").

A person contemplating the collecting of Jefferson nickels by date and mint-mark will find that three mints produced them: San Francisco, Denver and Phila-delphia. Because of first two are branch mints serving smaller populations, their output has tended over time to be smaller than that of Philadelphia. This fact, repeated in other series, has helped give mintmarks quite an allure to collectors. It provides one of the major attractions in collecting coins by date and mintmark.

The key date for Jeffersons is the 1950-D when using mintages as a guide. In that year, production was just 2.6 million pieces. Because collectors of the time were aware of the coin's low mintage, many examples were saved. As a result, prices are reasonable.

Jefferson nickels have been produced at the (from top) Philadephia, Denver and San Francisco Mints. Note the Denver and San Francisco mintmarks to the right of Monticello.

The wartime nickels of 1942-1945 marked the first time a "P" mintmark, for Philadelphia, was used.

The Depression-era 1939-D comes in as the most valuable regular-issue Jefferson nickel despite a mintage of 3.5 million – almost 1 million more than the 1950-D. The reason: Fewer were saved for later generations of coin collectors.

Date and mintmark collecting teaches hobbyists to use mintage figures as a guide but to take them with a grain of salt. Rarity, after all, is determined by the number of surviving coins, not the number initially created.

The Jefferson series is a good one to collect by date and mintmark, because the mintmarks have moved around, grown in size, and expanded in number.

When the series was first introduced, the Jefferson nickel was produced at the three mints previously mentioned. In 1942, because of a diversion of certain metals to wartime use, the coin's alloy of 75 percent copper and 25 percent nickel was changed. The new alloy was 35 percent silver, 56 percent copper, and 9 percent manganese.

To denote the change, the mintmarks were moved and greatly enlarged. The pre-1942 mintmarks were small and located to the right of Monticello; the wartime mintmarks were enlarged and placed over the dome. What's more, for the first time in American history, the Philadelphia Mint used a mintmark ("P").

The war's end restored the alloy and mintmarks to their previous status. The "P" disappeared. This lasted until the 1960s, when a national coin shortage saw all mintmarks removed for three years (1965-1967) and then returned, but in a different location. Mintmarks were placed on the obverse, to the right of Jefferson's portrait near the date in 1968. In 1980 the "P" came back in a smaller form and is still used.

Another consideration arises with date and mintmark collecting: Should the hobbyist include proof coins in the set? This can be argued both ways. Suffice to say that anyone who has the desire to add proof coins to the set will have a larger one. It is not necessary nor is it discouraged.

Some of the first proof coins to carry mintmarks were Jefferson nickels. When proof coins were made in 1968 after lapsing from 1965 to 1967, production occurred at San Francisco instead of Philadelphia. The "S" mintmark was placed on the proof coins of that year, including the Jefferson nickel, to denote the change. Since that time, mintmarks used on proof examples of various denominations have included the "P", "D", "S", and "W".

For all of the mintmark history that is embodied in the Jefferson series, prices

In 1968 the mintmarks reappeared on U.S. coins and production of proof coins resumed, this time at the San Francisco Mint. On the nickels, the mintmark moved from the reverse to the obverse below the date.

are reasonable. For a first attempt at collecting coins by date and mintmark, it provides excellent background for going on to the more expensive and difficult types. After all, if you are ever going to get used to the proper handling of a coin, it is far better to experiment on a low-cost coin than a high-value rarity.

As one progresses in date and mintmark collecting and type collecting, it is important to remember that all of the coins should be of similar states of preservation. Sets look slapdash if one coin is VG and another is MS-65 and still another is VF. Take a look at the prices of all the coins in the series before you get too far, figure out what you can afford, and then stick to that grade or range of grades.

Sure, there is a time-honored practice of filling a spot with any old example until a better one comes along. That is how we got the term "filler." But if you get a few placeholders, don't stop there. By assembling a set of uniform quality, you end up with a more aesthetically pleasing collection.

The date and mintmark method used to be the overwhelmingly dominant form of collecting. It still has many adherents. Give it a try if you think it sounds right for you.

Before we leave the discussion of collecting U.S. coins, it should be pointed out that the two major methods of organizing a collection are simply guidelines. They are not hard-and-fast rules that must be followed without questions. Collecting should be satisfying to the hobbyist. It should never be just one more item in the daily grind. Take the elements of these collecting approaches that you like or invent your own.

It should also be pointed out that U.S. coinage history does not start with 1792 nor do all of the coins struck since that time conform precisely to the two major organizational approaches. But these two areas are good places to start.

There are coins and tokens from the American Colonial period (1607-1776) that are just as fascinating and collectible as regular U.S. Mint issues. There are federal issues struck before the Mint was actually established. See the Colonial price-guide section in this book.

There are special coins called commemoratives, which have been struck by the U.S. Mint since 1892 to celebrate some aspect of American history or a contemporary event. They are not intended for circulation. There was a long interruption between 1954 and 1982, but currently annual commemoratives are being offered for sale directly to collectors by the Mint.

Collecting commemoratives has always been considered something separate from collecting regular U.S. coinage. It is, however, organized the same way. Commemoratives can be collected by date and mintmark or by type.

Current commemoratives can be purchased from the U.S. Mint. To get on its mailing list, write U.S. Mint, Customer Care Center, 801 Ninth St., N.W., Washington, D.C. 20220. Check the U.S. Mint Web site at www.usmint.gov. Once on the list, hobbyists will get the various solicitations for not only commemoratives, but regular proof sets and mint sets and proof American Eagle bullion coins. Hobbyists who order from the U.S. Mint's Web site receive notices of product availability by e-mail.

Buying coins from the Mint can be considered a hobby pursuit in its own right. Some collectors let the Mint organize their holdings for them. They buy complete sets and put them away. They never buy anything from anywhere else.

Admittedly, this is a passive form of collecting, but there are individuals around the world who enjoy collecting at this level without ever really going any deeper. They like acquiring every new issue as it comes off the Mint's presses.

Once done, there is a certain knowledge that one has all the examples of the current year. Obviously, too, collectors by date and mintmark of the current types would have to buy the new coins each year, but, of course, they do not stop there.

Varieties and errors make up another area. Under this heading come the coins the Mint did not intend to make. There are all kinds of errors. Many of them are inexpensive. Check out the U.S. Minting Varieties and Errors section in the price guide. If you want to pursue it further, there are specialty books that deal with the topic in more detail.

Canada

Starting point for the national coinage of Canada is popularly fixed at 1858. In that year a large cent was first produced for use in Upper and Lower Canada (Ontario and Quebec). These prices were intended to supplant local copper coinage, which in turn had been attempts to give various regions a medium of exchange.

What was circulating in Canada at the time was a hodgepodge of world issues. The large cent predates a unified national government by nine years, but it is considered the beginning of national issues nevertheless.

There are many similarities between the United States and Canada and their respective monetary systems. Both continent-sized nations thought in terms of taming the frontier, new settlements, and growth. Both came to use the dollar as the unit of account because of the pervasiveness of the Spanish milled dollar in trade. For each, the dollar divides into 100 cents.

However, Canada had a far longer colonial history. Many of its residents resisted the tide that carried the United States to independence and worked to preserve their loyalties to the British crown. As a result, Canada was firmly a part of the British Empire. So even today with its constitution (the British North America Act transferred from Westminster to Ottawa in 1982), parliamentary democracy, and a national consciousness perhaps best symbolized by the maple leaf, Canada retains a loyalty to the crown in the person of Queen Elizabeth II of the United Kingdom. Canada is a member of the British Commonwealth of Nations.

Canadian coins
have depicted (from
top) Queen Victoria,
King Edward VII,
King George V,
King George VI and
Queen Elizabeth II.

The effect of this on coins is obvious. Current issues carry the queen's effigy. How Canada got its coins in the past was also influenced. The fledgling U.S. government set about creating its own mint as one of its earliest goals, despite that better-quality pieces could be purchased abroad at lower cost. Canada found that ties to mints located in England were logical and comfortable.

The Royal Canadian Mint was not established until 1908, when it was called the Ottawa branch of the British Royal Mint, and it was not given its present name until 1931. Both events are within living memory. Canadian coins, therefore, have a unique mixture of qualities. They are tantalizingly familiar to U.S. citizens yet distinctly different.

The coinage of a monarchy brings its own logic to the organization of a collection. Type collecting is delineated by the monarch. United Canada has had six. The first was Queen Victoria, whose image appeared on those large cents of 1858. Her reign began in 1837 and lasted until 1901.

She was followed by Edward VII, 1901-1910; George V, 1910-1936; Edward VII, 1936; George VI, 1936-1952; and Queen Elizabeth II, 1952-present. All but Edward VIII had coins struck for circulation in Canada. The collectible monarchs, therefore, number five, but the longer reigns inspired changes of portraits over time to show the aging process at work. Legends also changed. When George VI ceased being emperor of India, Canada's coins were modified to recognize the change.

Like U.S. coins, sizes and alloys were altered to meet new demands placed on the coinage. However, the separateness of each nation might best be summed up this way: Though the United States abolished its large cent in 1857, Canada's was just getting under way in 1858. The United States put an end to the silver dollar in 1935, the very year Canada finally got its series going.

And Canada, the nickel-mining giant, used a small-sized silver five-cent coin until 1921, almost 50 years after the half dime was abolished in the United States. But whereas the Civil War was the major cause of the emergence of modern U.S. coinage as specified by the Coinage Act of 1873, World War I influenced the alterations that made Canada's coins what they are today.

It might be assumed that change in the monarch also signaled a change in the reverse designs of the various denominations. A check of the Canadian price guide section shows this is not necessarily the case. Current designs paired with Queen Elizabeth II basically date back to the beginning of her father's reign. The familiar maple-leaf cent, beaver five-cent piece, schooner 10-cent, caribou 25-cent, and coat-of-arms 50-cent have been running for over 50 years. Significant changes were made to the 50-cent coin in 1959, but the reverse design remains the coat of arms.

So where does that leave type collectors? It puts them in a situation similar to categorizing the various eagles on U.S. coins. They can be universalists and accept the broadest definitions of type, or they can narrow the bands to whatever degree suits them best.

By checking the price-guide section, date and mintmark collectors will quickly note that their method of organization more or less turns into collecting by date. Though currently there are three mints in Canada – Hull, Quebec; Ottawa, Ontario; and Winnipeg, Manitoba – they don't use mintmarks. Historically, few mintmarks were employed.

Ottawa used a "C" on gold sovereigns of 1908-1919 and on some exported colonial issues. The private Heaton Mint in Birmingham, England, used an "H" on coins it supplied to Canada from 1871 to 1907.

But the coins supplied to Canada by the British Royal Mint and later by its Ottawa branch did not carry any identifying mark. Collectors who confine their activities to the more recent issues need never think about a mintmark.

It would be easy to slant a presentation on Canadian issues to stress similarities or differences to U.S. issues. One should remember that the monetary structures of each evolved independently, but each was always having an impact on the other.

Common events, such as World War II, had a similar impact. For example, the Canadian five-cent coin changed in much the same way as the U.S. nickel. In Canada, nickel was removed and replaced first by a tombac (brass) alloy and then by chromium-plated steel. Peace brought with it a return to the prewar composition.

To see an example of differences between the United States and Canada, take the Canadian approach to the worldwide trend of removing silver from coinage. Canada made its move in 1968, three years after the United States. Instead of choosing a copper-nickel alloy as a substitute for silver, Canada looked to its own vast natural resources and employed pure nickel.

Canada also seems more comfortable with its coinage than the United States. Whereas the United States often feared confusion and counterfeiting from making the least little changes in its coins, Canada has long embraced coinage to communicate national events, celebrations and culture. Its silver-dollar series actually began as a celebration of George V's 25 years on the throne.

Succeeding years saw additional commemorative $1 designs interspersed with the regular Voyageur design. When the centennial of national confederation was observed in 1967, all of the denominations were altered for one year. The United States only reluctantly tried out the idea on three of its denominations for the nation's Bicentennial.

Ultimately, Canada began an annual commemorative dollar series in 1971. It issued coins for the 1976 Montreal Olympic Games and again in 1988 for the Calgary Olympic Games. Bullion coins were created to market its gold, silver and platinum output. A commemorative series of gold $100 coins was also undertaken. Canada, too, issues special proof, prooflike and specimen sets, similar to the United States.

Hobbyists who would like to be informed of new issues should write Royal Canadian Mint, P.O. Box 457, Station A, Ontario K1A 8V5, Canada. The mint also main-

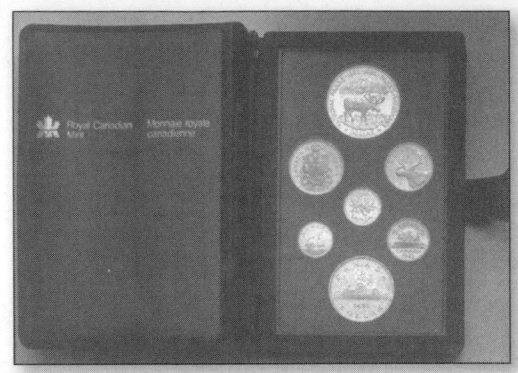

Like the U.S. Mint, the Royal Canadian Mint offers sets of coins in a variety of finishes to the collector market.

tains special toll-free lines. In the United States, hobbyists may telephone the Royal Canadian Mint at 1-800-268-6468. In Canada, the number is 1-800-267-1871. You can get on the mailing list by using these numbers and you can buy currently available coins. (See Chapter 6 for Web information.)

When collecting Canada, another thing to remember is the importance varieties play in the nation's various series. Certainly, a type collector has no need to dwell on this information, but the date and mintmark collector may puzzle over the many extra identifying abbreviations in the price guide for certain coins. These varieties should not be confused with the U.S. variety-and-error category.

Here the varieties are not mistakes; they are deliberately created and issued variations of the standard design. We see Voyageur dollars on which the number of water lines changes. Other dollars count the number of beads.

These differences are minor. Though they were deliberately done to meet varying mint needs, they were not intended to be set apart in the public mind. The hobby, however, likes to look at things under a microscope.

Some varieties were indeed intended to be deliberately and noticeably different. An example of this occurs with 1947-dated issues. A maple leaf was placed on the 1947-dated cent through 50-cent issues. This indicated the coin was struck after George VI lost his title of emperor of India, as proclaimed in the Latin legend, but that the design had not yet been altered to reflect this. All of these varieties are considered integral parts of the Canadian series, and they are listed as such.

Do not construe any of this to mean there is no collecting of varieties and errors of the type common in the United States. There is. Collecting Royal Canadian Mint mistakes is just as active, just as interesting, and just as rewarding. After all, mint errors are universal. The methods of manufacture are the same. So the mistakes can be classified in the same manner.

Canada's numismatic listings also include items from various provinces issued before they were part of the confederation. The largest portion of this section is devoted to Newfoundland, because it retained a separate status far longer than the other provinces – until 1949 in fact.

Advice given to collectors of U.S. coins also applies to collectors of Canadian coins: Do what interests you. Do what you can afford. Create sets of uniform grade.

The rules of rarity transcend national boundaries. The only thing to keep in mind is the relative size of the collecting population. Because Canada has only a tenth of the U.S. population, it stands to reason that the number of collectors in that nation is but a fraction of the U.S. number. A mintage that seems to indicate scarcity for U.S. coin, therefore, could indicate something quite common in Canada. Don't forget that mintage is just a guide. The same factors that caused loss of available specimens or preserved unusually large quantities were at work in Canada, too.

Mexico

Coinage produced in Mexico dates to the establishment of a mint in Mexico City in 1536, over 250 years before a federal mint was set up in the United States and more than 300 years before Canada circulated its own coins. The output of those extra centuries alone would make organizing a Mexican coin collection more challenging than a collection of U.S. or Canadian coins. But there are numerous other factors involved.

You say you like the kings and queens on Canada's coins? Mexico has kings, too – nearly 300 years' worth, plus a couple of emperors. You say the ideals of liberty embodied by the great men and women on U.S. coins is more your cup of tea? Mexico's coins also feature men and women committed to liberty.

In addition, Mexico is the crossroads of civilizations and empires. The great pyramid-building society of southern Mexico and Central America met its end at the hands of the Spanish conquistadors led initially by Hernando Cortez. The great Aztec empire was looted and overturned in 1519-1521 in the name of Spain.

The great natural resources of the area then supported successive Spanish kings in their grand dreams of dominating Europe. Through the doors of the Mexico City Mint and later facilities scattered about the country passed legendary quantities of silver. Even today the country ranks at the top of the list of silver producers.

But while Spain could dominate Mexico for a long time, the basic ideals of liberty and human dignity eventually motivated the people to throw off the foreign yoke. Unfortunately, victory was often neither complete nor wisely led. And in more recent years, the scourge of inflation had exacted a high toll on the currency itself. The numismatic consequences of a long history punctuated by periods of turmoil are an abundance of denominations, metals and types.

It is tempting for a would-be collector of Mexican coins to forget about anything that happened in the country prior to its monetary reform of 1905. By starting at that point, a hobbyist can happily overlook anything other than a decimal monetary system in which 100 centavos equal 1 peso. That system is as modern as any. The coins' striking quality is high. Legends are easy to read and understand, and the variety of issues is wide but not overwhelming.

There always is a certain logic to begin the collecting of any country with recent issues. The costs of learning are minimized, and as one becomes comfortable, a level of confidence can be built up sufficient to prompt diving further into the past.

One thousand of these equaled one new peso as 1993 began.

The issues of 1905 to date also more easily fit into the mold of type collecting and collecting by date and mintmark. To take type collecting, for example, let's look at the peso. In 1905 it was a silver-dollar-sized coin with a silver-dollar-sized quantity of bullion in it, 0.786 ounces. In 1918 it was reduced to 0.4663 ounces; in 1920, 0.3856 ounces; in 1947, 0.2250 ounces; 1950, 0.1285 ounces; 1957, 0.0514 ounces; and in 1970 silver was eliminated completely in favor of a copper-nickel alloy.

At almost every one of those steps, the design changed, too. After sinking to 3,300 to the U.S. dollar, monetary reform dropped three zeroes in 1993. The new peso, equal to 1,000 old ones, is now 10 to the U.S. dollar.

By beginning with 1905, a date and mintmark collector misses out on issues of the various branch mints that were located around the country. Regular issues were all struck in Mexico City. Yearly output was reasonably regular for the various denominations, so date sets are extensive.

There have been rumblings since the early 1980s that Mexico would abandon the peso because of its greatly reduced value. The government, however, has been working hard to retain it since the monetary reform. So far it has succeeded.

One thing the government cannot do, however, is turn the clock back to a time when the fractional denominations of 1, 2, 5, 10, 20, 25, and 50 centavos were relatively high face values. However, it is stimulating to assemble sets because they offer a range of rarities. They are neither so expensive that it would prevent a collector from acquiring them at some point, but neither are they so common that you can walk into a shop, write a check, and come away with all of the 20th century sets complete. Check out the price guide section and see.

Gold in the post-1905 era is basically so much bullion. There are some scarcer pieces and some strikingly beautiful designs, such as the Centenario, a gold 50-peso coin containing 1.2 ounces of bullion. It was first struck in 1921 to mark 100 years of independence. Because Mexico actively restruck its gold coins, however, it is virtually impossible to tell an original issue from the newer version.

The result is a retail price structure based on metallic content. Gold, however, does not conjure up the images that silver does. Silver is the magic word for Mexico. That, of course, means the peso.

The modern Mexico City Mint also strikes commemoratives and collector sets from time to time. These are generally marketed to collectors through private firms,

Mexico also strikes commemorative coins for the collector market. They are available through private firms in the United States.

details of which are published in hobby newspapers like World Coin News. Mexico, like the United States and Canada, also issues gold and silver bullion coins.

These also are marketed through arrangements with private firms. Interestingly, Mexico's many gold-coin restrikes were the bullion coins of their day. They had the advantage of ready identification, and they were legally tradable according to gold-coin regulations that existed in the United States from 1933 through 1974.

It is appropriate that we conclude discussion of the modern period on the concept of bullion, because bullion is at the root of Mexico's numismatic history. That is a period to which we now turn.

When Cortez toppled the Aztec Empire, for a time the wealth returning to Spain was merely that taken by the victors from the vanquished. But the business of permanently administering a vast area in the name of the Spanish king, exploiting its natural resources, and funneling the proceeds to Spain quite soon involved the establishment of a mint in Mexico City. This was undertaken in 1536, just 15 years after the end of Aztec dominion.

At first, the authorized coins were low denominations: silver quarter, half, 1, 2, 3, and 4 reales, and copper 2 and 4 maravedis. To understand their face values and how they related to each other, let's take the common reference point of a silver dollar. The silver dollar is 8 reales, and you might recognize the nickname for the denomination of "piece of eight" from pirate lore. The eighth part, the silver real, was divided into 34 copper maravedis. That means the 8 reales was worth 272 copper maravedis.

The copper coinage was hated and soon abolished, not to reappear until 1814. The silver coins were fine as far as they went. When the mines of Mexico began producing undreamed of quantities of metal, however, it was the 8 reales that took center stage. This occurred after 1572. The piece of eight became the standard form for shipping silver back to Spain.

Mexico City's output was prodigious. Minting standards were crude. All denominations produced are called "cobs," because they are basically little more than irregular-looking lumps of metal on which bits and pieces of design can be seen. The only constant was weight, fineness, and the appearance of assayer's initials (which guaranteed the weight and fineness). Not showing those initials was cause for severe punishment.

Designs showed the arms of the monarch on one side, a cross on the other, appropriate legends, and an indication of denomination. The period of cob issues lasted until 1732. Rulers of the period start with Charles and Johanna, 1516-1556; Philip II, 1556-1598; Philip III, 1598-1621; Philip IV, 1621-1665; Charles II, 1665-1700; Philip V, 1700-1724 and 1724-1746; and Luis I, 1724.

Modern mint machinery began turning out coins in 1732. Quality was similar to today. The arms design was continued. It was not until 1772 that the monarch's portrait began appearing. The honor of this numismatic debut belongs to Charles III. Kings of this period are Ferdinand VI, 1746-1759; Charles III, 1760-1788; Charles IV, 1788-1808; and Ferdinand VII, 1808-1821. *The Standard Catalog of Mexican Coins* by Colin R. Bruce II and Dr. George W. Vogt is recommended to those who want to study this period in greater depth.

The revolutionary period begins in 1810, when a parish priest, Miguel Hidalgo y Costilla, issued the call for independence. The first attempts to achieve this were violently suppressed. Hidalgo was executed, but independence did come in 1821.

With revolt against central authority came a dispersal of the right to strike coins. Mexico City continued as the major facility, but other operations began. The list of these over the next century is lengthy. Mintmarks and assayer initials proliferated.

The old colonial coinage standard survived the period. The 8 reales and its parts carried on. A slight reduction in bullion content had been ordered by the king in 1760, but otherwise things continued as they were. Gold was coined during the colonial period beginning in 1679 based on an 8-escudo piece, which divided into eighths just like the 8 reales. Gold, however, was not as important as silver.

Mexico's first emperor came shortly after independence. He was a leader in the struggle that set Mexico free from Spain. Augustin de Iturbide, originally an officer in the service of Spain, was proclaimed emperor in 1822. He abdicated in 1823 and was executed in 1824.

The second emperor had a reign almost as short as the first. Maximilian I, emperor only because he had a French army to secure the throne, reigned from 1863 to 1867. He was shot by a firing squad when the French left.

He is remembered numismatically because he decided to decimalize the coinage. The centavo and peso were born. Soon afterward, the republic was re-established. Further monetary changes were minor thereafter until 1905.

Collectors focusing on Mexico can devote much time to the study of the quasi-official issues of rebels during the periods of instability. They can look at hacienda tokens, which were issued by large farms or ranches that employed hundreds or thousands of people. Or they can pick whichever period in Mexico's history that fascinates them most. Whatever collectors of Mexico eventually settle on, they will find it rewarding.

Where to write for more information:

World Coin News: 700 E. State St., Iola, WI 54990.

Better than map
Three mints have Web sites

By David C. Kranz

Here's a handy electronic means of finding North American coinage.

The U.S. Mint's Web site, www.usmint.gov, has been most active, making several limited, exclusively online offers. These have involved small bags of the nation's 50 states quarter issues as well as numismatic-philatelic covers and Sacagawea dollars. The U.S. Mint also sells its traditional annual products such as mint sets and proof sets on the Web, along with commemorative coins and other Mint sales catalog items.

Online orders can be more convenient for many hobbyists. Shipping charges are currently the same between sets ordered online or by mail.

Canadian gold and silver, annual sets and commemoratives are available for purchase on the Royal Canadian Mint's site, www.mint.ca. Both French and English language versions of the RCM site are available. The site is set up for online orders (placed from Canada and the United States only), and the mint accepts Visa, Mastercard and American Express.

At the site of the Mexican Mint, www.cmonedam.com.mx/cmm, you can learn that it was the first mint in America, and that it has served without interruption since its inception by Spanish decree. The Mexican Mint site has Spanish and English language versions, with coinage history, current news, sales and promotions Web pages as well as technical information about the circulating coinage of Mexico. Telephone, fax, mail and e-mail information is provided for placing orders.

The fourth component of the North American continent, Greenland, has no mint within its borders and uses coins of Denmark in commerce. For more on these coins, see the *Standard Catalog of World Coins*, published by F+W Publications (www.krausebooks.com).

For a quick introduction to these countries' latest coinage, their Web sites can't be beat.

Caring for coins
How to store and preserve your collection

By Alan Herbert

From the day you acquire your first collectible coin, you have to consider where and how to store your collection. Often a shoebox or a small cardboard or plastic box of some kind will be the principal storage point as you start to gather coins, even before they can be considered a collection. Sooner or later you will outgrow that first box and need to think seriously about what to do with your coins to protect and preserve them.

All too often security takes precedence over preservation. We're more worried that the kids will dip into the coins for candy or ice cream or that burglars will somehow learn about your "valuable" collection and pay a visit. It often isn't until years later when you suddenly notice that your once beautiful coins are now dingy and dull, with spots and fingerprints all over them, that preservation becomes a primary consideration.

Learning good storage habits should be one of the first things to do right along with acquiring those first coins. There are a multitude of storage products on the market that are intended for more or less specific situations, so learning which to use and how to use them is vital to the health of your collection. Most if not all of the products mentioned here should be available at your nearest coin shop or hobby store.

Safe storage methods

The common impulse is to use what's available around the house; never allow that impulse to control your collecting. Plastic wrap, aluminum foil, cardboard, stationery envelopes, and other common household products are not designed for coin storage and never should be used for your collection. The same goes for soaps and cleansers found around the home.

Two-by-two cardboard holders are a common form of short-term, inexpensive coin storage.

Many dealers sell coins in 2-by-2 plastic "flips," but these should not be used for long-term storage.

There are specific products that have been designed, tested and found safe to use for coins. These are the media your collection deserves. The slight added expense will pay a thousand dividends years from now when you sell you collection or pass it on to your heirs.

The most common storage media are 2-inch by 2-inch cardboard holders with Mylar windows, 2-by-2 plastic "flips," coin tubes, hard-plastic holders, coin boards, and coin albums.

The 2-by-2 cardboard holders are the cheapest and most commonly used storage method. They are usually folded and stapled around the coin. They are intended for short-term general storage. They are not airtight or watertight, and staples driven too close to the coin can ruin it.

The 2-by-2 plastic flips come in good and bad varieties. The old, usually soft flips are made of plastics that contain polyvinyl chloride, a chemical found in many plastics. Over time it breaks down into substances that put a green slime on your coins, which attacks the surface and ruins them.

The good flips are made of Mylar, but they are brittle and prone to splitting. So they should not be used to mail coins or when the coins are moved about frequently. Mylar flips, too, are for short-term general storage.

Often you will find coins in PVC holders when you buy them from a dealer. Remove them immediately and put them in some better storage medium.

Coin tubes come in clear and cloudy, or translucent, plastic. These are made

Coin tubes are often used for bulk storage, but there is a proper technique to placing the coins in the tube.

of an inert plastic that will not harm your coins. Tubes are intended for bulk, medium- to long-term storage, with one caution: Use care when inserting the coins. Merely dropping one coin onto another in a tube can damage both coins. The best technique is to make a stack or pile of the coins, then slide the pile carefully into the tube while holding it at an angle.

Hard-plastic holders are the elite items for storing your collection. There are a number of varieties, some of which come in three parts that are screwed together. Some come in two pieces that fit together. Some of these are airtight and watertight. They are more expensive, but they deserve to be used for any really valuable coins in your collection.

Coins processed by the third-party grading services come in hard-plastic holders, most of which are at least semi-airtight. The hard-plastic holders used by the U.S. Mint for proof sets since 1968 are not airtight, so coins should be watched carefully for signs of problems. In recent years these holders have been improved, but you should check your proof sets periodically.

Any stored coins should be checked regularly, at least twice a year. Check coins for signs of spotting or discoloration. Check the storage media for any signs of deterioration, rust, mildew, or other problems.

The older mint sets and proof sets – issued from 1955 to 1964 – come in soft-plastic envelopes that are not intended for long-term storage. Coins in these envelopes should be put in better storage media for the long term. In recent years the Mint has switched to an inert, stiffer plastic for the mint sets. This plastic is safe.

A coin folder is frequently the first piece of equipment the beginning collector buys. It is simply a piece of cardboard with holes to hold the coins. The holder folds up for storage. It is intended for inexpensive circulated coins only.

Hard-plastic holders are the top of the line in coin storage.

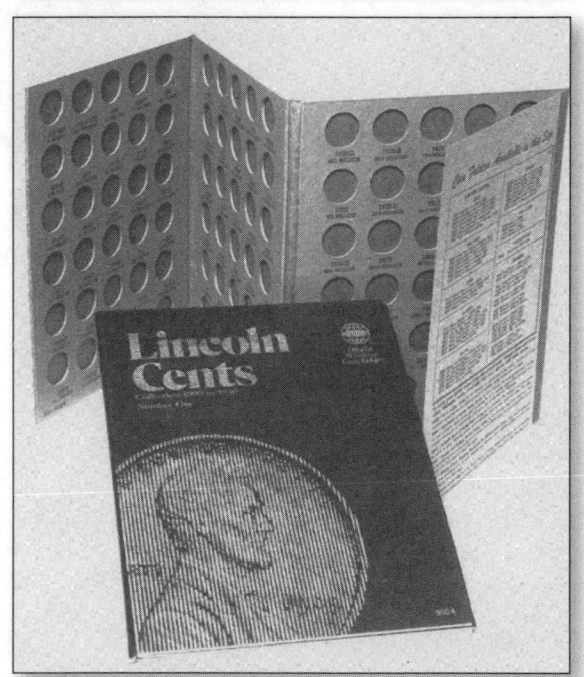

Coin folders are a low-cost and attractive way to store inexpensive circulated coins.

They give no protection from contamination or fingerprints. Worn coins will often fall out of the holes, which leads some novice collectors to tape the coins in the album. This is another example of misuse of a household product; tape can permanently damage a coin's surface.

Pride of ownership and the desire to show off a collection are the moving forces behind the sale of thousands of coin albums. They should also be used for inexpensive circulated coins only, with a couple of exceptions.

Some albums are merely coin boards mounted between covers. Others have pages with sliding plastic strips on both sides of the page so both sides of the coin can be seen.

The open-face albums are subject to fingerprints and contamination. Sneezing on your coins can do as much damage as gouging them with a knife. The

Coin albums also provide attractive storage for inexpensive circulated coins.

slides will rub on your coins, damaging the high points of the design over time. These two types of albums should never be used for expensive uncirculated or proof coins, although they are fine for circulated coins that you want to display.

Fairly new on the market are albums designed for coins in inert, airtight holders. This allows you to display your coins and still keep them safe from handling and contact with the atmosphere.

One more storage medium that deserves mention is the clear-plastic notebook page that has pockets for 2-by-2 holders or flips. Here again there are good and bad. Most old pocket sheets contain PVC, so they cannot be used to hold coins in non-airtight holders because the gases will migrate into the holders and damage the coins. The newer Mylar pages are brittle but will not generate damaging gases or liquids.

When buying storage media, make sure the dealer guarantees that his products are safe for coins. Many of the old albums, flips and pocket pages are still around, especially at flea markets. If you are in doubt, don't buy.

There are also thin, two-piece, inert plastic holders that many collectors use to protect coins put in flips or 2-by-2 cardboard holders, especially to protect them from moving about against the holder and getting scratched. They are virtually airtight, so they do offer some protection.

Coins need to be protected from burglars. A box under the bed or in the closet offers no protection. If you must keep coins at home, a good, fireproof safe is a must. Otherwise, rent a safe-deposit box at a bank, but read the fine print on your box contract to make sure a coin collection is covered.

Most homeowner's insurance policies will not cover a coin collection or will cover only a fraction of its value. Special riders are expensive, but if you keep most of your coins at the bank, this will cut costs. For details, consult your insurance agent. The American Numismatic Association also offers collection insurance to its members.

Where to store coins is often a problem. The commonest solution is to put them in the attic or basement. Those are the two worst places for your collection. Attics are notoriously hot. Heat can damage almost any storage media, and if there is the slightest hint of PVC, you've got trouble.

Basements are equally bad. They can flood, and humidity is high. Mildew can attack holders and other material stored with your coins.

So what's left? Ideally coins should be treated like a family member. They should be stored in some part of the house where temperature and humidity are relatively constant year round. If it's comfortable for you, it's probably much more comfortable for your coins than the basement or attic.

Protecting coins from humidity is always a good idea, even in areas where it is not a major health problem. For your coins, too much dampness can become a serious problem, often before you realize it. A good solution is to get several good-sized packets of silica gel and store them with your coins in your safe or a container of some kind that will isolate them from the general climate in the home.

To clean or not to clean

Before you store your coins, you should be aware that coins are like dishes: They should never be put away dirty. Ah, but you've probably already heard or read that you should never clean a coin. If you haven't, I'll say it now: Never clean a coin.

OK, so there are exceptions, but be careful of those exceptions and for good reason. Ignoring the exception can be excruciatingly and embarrassingly expensive.

Coins get dirty, just like anything else. The impulse is to shine them up – polish them to a brilliance that will dazzle the viewer. If you've already succumbed to the temptation to clean even a single coin, stand up, kick yourself, then sit back down and read on. The one exception is loose dirt, grease, oil, or something similar, and there are even exceptions to that rule.

Use a neutral solvent to dissolve the grease and oils that usually coat uncirculated coins as they come from the mint. Follow the instructions on the container exactly, and if the directions say to use the product outdoors, they mean it.

For circulated coins, lighter fluid will often dissolve the accumulated "gunk" that sticks to them, but I don't recommend it for uncirculated coins, especially copper alloy coins. Air dry the coins; don't rub or wipe them. Even the softest cloth or paper towel can pick up sharp-edged particles that will ruin a coin's surface. Proof coins are clean when they are packaged, so this should not be necessary and should be done only as a last resort if they have somehow picked up oil in handling.

Using dips, household cleansers, metal polish, and even soap can permanently damage a coin. Avoid acid-based cleaners at all costs. They work by eating away the coin's surface to remove the embedded dirt or discoloration. Cleaning a coin with any of these products will sharply reduce its collectible value. To put it simply, collectors do not want cleaned coins, so they are heavily discounted.

One of the reasons for this is that once a coin has been cleaned, it will discolor much more quickly, requiring fresh cleaning. Each time it is cleaned, the surface is further dulled, reducing the coin's appeal and reducing its value.

Obviously this advice applies especially to uncirculated and proof coins, but it applies to any coin that is or has the potential to become valuable. But if you clean it, its career ends right there.

There are products specifically designed for removing the green PVC slime from coins. They do not contain acid, so they are safe. They will stop but cannot reverse the damage that the PVC has already done to the coin. Read the label, and use exactly as directed.

I frequently am asked about ultrasonic cleaners. They fall under the same heading as the various cleaning products I've described. In other words, the apparatus should not be used for uncirculated, proof, or other valuable coins. If you do use one, do one coin at a time so there is no chance for the vibration to rub two coins together. Change or filter the cleaning solution frequently to keep abrasive particles from coming in contact with the vibrating coin.

Like anything else, cleaning can be carried to an extreme, so I'll give you one horror story and just such a mistake: Years ago I had a collector fly several hundred miles to bring his collection for me to sell for him. When he laid out the coins on the table, I was shocked to discover that the hundreds of coins had all been harshly cleaned.

When I questioned him he calmly recounted that he had decided that the coins needed cleaning, so he dumped them all into a rock tumbler and left it on for several hours. It ruined all his coins, reducing them to face value. With his passion for cleanliness he had destroyed several thousand dollars worth of collectible value, plus air fare, a rental car, and a motel bill.

The key to a long-term collection that might appreciate in value is to learn what not to do to your coins and what care they need to survive years of waiting in the wings. Learning to protect your coins with the best available storage methods and media is a key first step toward enjoying your collection for years to come.

A private firm, Numismatic Conservation Services, LLC, will clean coins that need it for a fee. The firm's Web site address is www.ncscoin.com.

Where to write for more information

American Numismatic Association: 818 N. Cascade Ave., Colorado Springs, CO 80903-3279. Web address is http://www.money.org.

Join the club

Coin collecting has lots of organizations

By David C. Harper

More than 160 years ago, Alexis de Tocqueville noted in his Democracy in America the penchant of people in the United States to create and voluntarily join public groups for a multitude of purposes. This urge to join carries over into coin collecting.

Whether it be a national organization or local coin club, groups have been organized in the United States, Canada and Mexico to help collectors enhance their hobby knowledge and enjoyment. They serve as clearinghouses for new information, maintain libraries, and bring collectors together in meetings to share their hobby experiences with each other. Clubs are so well defined that collectors can find one to serve any activity level and any degree of personal interaction with other collectors.

At the extreme, you can join a national organization by mail, spend a hobby lifetime utilizing its services, and yet never leave the privacy and comfort of home. At the other end, some areas offer such a multitude of clubs that you can find a meeting to attend on many nights of the week.

There are many ways to find a club. Some hobbyists inquire at the local coin shop to identify the organization nearest them. Numismatic News publishes news about clubs. Also, watch your local newspaper for listings of community events.

How does a collector match his needs with an appropriate club? The closest thing to a one-stop shopping place for an answer is the American Numismatic Association.

It is the United States' national coin-collecting organization and was granted a perpetual charter by Congress with a mission of education. It can be reached at 818 N. Cascade Ave., Colorado Springs, CO 80903-3279. Its Web address is www.money.org. It offers a wide array of personal hobby services, and its benefits cross national boundaries. In fact, when it was founded in 1891, it was expected that Canadians and Mexicans would be just as likely to join as U.S. citizens.

The most obvious benefit to an ANA member is a subscription to *The Numismatist*, the association's monthly magazine. In it you find news, historical features, membership information, and advertisements placed by dealers who are ready to fill every collector's want list.

More than 30,000 titles are available in the ANA library, and you don't have to walk into the ANA building to check them out. Any member anywhere can do that by mail. The ANA has called upon renowned numismatic authorities to create a correspondence course, which distills into 29 separate readings information that has taken many people a lifetime to learn. There are ANA educational seminars held in Colorado Springs and other sites across the United States.

The ANA sponsors two conventions annually. The early spring convention is usually held in March at locations across the country, selected and announced well in advance. The summer convention, which is so huge that it's billed as the "World's Fair of Money," is a tradition that dates back almost to the organization's founding.

Members also are offered a variety of optional services, ranging from coin-collection insurance to credit cards and car rental discounts. And if you do go to Colorado Springs, the ANA maintains its Money Museum at its headquarters. In it are some of the rarest and most famous coins in history.

Joining the ANA is easy. The membership fee is $36. Members over 65 years old get a $5 discount, and junior members (those under 18) are charged $20.

Beyond simply belonging to the ANA, though, are the doors that open to members. If you want to find a regional, state or local club, you can get help from the ANA. The important thing to remember is that you set your own level of involvement. If your profession is so hectic that you don't need another meeting to go to, the ANA is the place for you. If your hours are so regular that joining in the fun and camaraderie of a local club is just what you are looking for, the ANA can help you find that, too.

And just because the American Numismatic Association has "American" in its name, it doesn't mean that members are focused only on U.S. coins. Far from it. It is more accurate to say that if a coin was struck at any time anywhere in the world in the last 2,600 years, there are ANA members who collect it.

The ANA, if it connotes any exclusivity at all, is basically a regional designation based on where its members live. The farther one gets from the United States, the longer correspondence takes and the greater the possibility of a language barrier between the ANA staff and a potential member. It is therefore not surprising to find that 29,000 members are predominantly located in the United States.

The Canadian Numismatic Association dates to 1950. It publishes *The Canadian Numismatic Journal* 11 times a year. The CNA also sponsors an annual convention. Membership is considerably smaller than the ANA's, in line with the population difference between the United States and Canada. Membership fee is $35 a year. The mailing address is Canadian Numismatic Association, 5694 Hwy #7 East, Suite 432, Markham, ON, L3P 1B4, Canada.

The Sociedad Numismatica de Mexico A.C. was established in 1952. Basically, it oversees an annual convention in Mexico City. It may be contacted through its U.S. representative, Don Bailey, at PMB #139, 250 "D" South Lyon Ave., Hemet, CA 92543. A related group at the same address is the U.S. Mexican Numismatic Society.

That covers the national hobby umbrella groups. There are many more organizations of a national character that have somewhat narrower focus. Among these is the American Numismatic Society in New York City. It is older than the ANA, having been established in 1858. It maintains a superb collection of U.S. and world coins, and a world-class library. Emphasis of the ANS is on scholarly research.

Numismatics would be nothing if it were not for its research pioneers. If that is what appeals to you, you can write the ANS at 1 Hudson Square, New York, NY 10013, for information regarding its structure and various classes of membership.

Other national organizations focus on specific collectible areas, such as Seated Liberty coinage or the Token and Medal Society. These are popular and active. Many are member organizations of the ANA and hold meetings in conjunction with the ANA's conventions.

Coin dealers have organizations of their own. The Professional Numismatists Guild Inc. maintains high standards of membership qualification and conduct. Members are a who's who of the commercial sector of the hobby. All are ready to serve you in furthering your collecting goals. For a membership roster, contact Robert Brueggeman, Executive Director, 3950 Concordia Lane, Fallbrook, CA 92028.

This brief review merely puts you on the threshold of the organized numismatic world. It is up to you to open that door or walk away. Over the years, many collectors have found membership to be the most rewarding aspect of the hobby. They have benefited from working with others with a common interest to further their own knowledge and advance their collecting goals in an environment of mutual support and friendship.

Presidential dollars
Errors charge up market

By David C. Harper

It is as if someone at the Mint in early 2007 raised his arms and said, "Let there be errors." And there were errors and they were mighty good for the coin market. Hardly had the news broken that a Presidential dollar series was begun with a George Washington coin in February when reports reached Numismatic News that some of the edges, which were supposed to have the date, mintmark and two mottoes on them, were absolutely plain or smooth. This set off a mad dash by collectors to search for the new plain-edge errors. In the scramble, additional edge errors were reported. The hobby hasn't had this much error fun since the 1995 doubled-die cent was discovered in circulation.

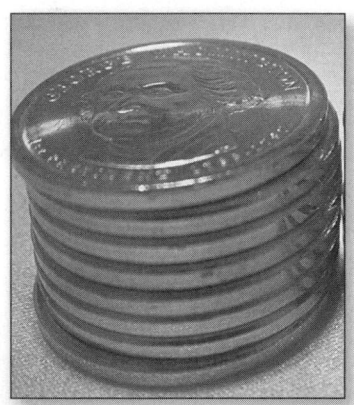

The nonhobby news media jumped aboard the phenomenon because one of the missing mottoes was "In God We Trust." This spawned a nickname, "the Godless dollar," for the error coins. This caused political outrage and legislation was introduced to move "In God We Trust" to either the obverse or reverse so that not even error coins could be called Godless.

All this occurred in just the first weeks of the new Presidential dollar coin program, which is going to issue four coins a year for at least 10 years.

When some Washington dollars without edge lettering were released in circulation in 2007, it set off a huge scramble by collectors to find them.
(Photos by Ken Potter)

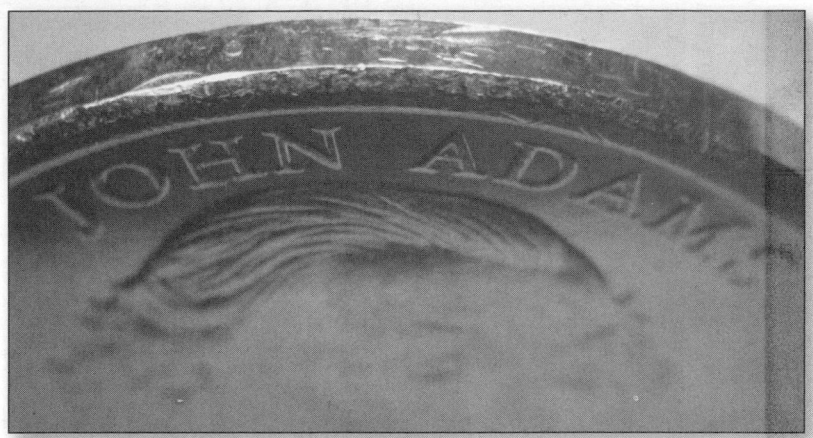

John Adams was not only the second President, but the second Presidential dollar coin to have an error version without the edge lettering. A normal edge features the date, mintmark, "In God We Trust" and "E Pluribus Unum.

When the second of the dollar series, the John Adams coin was introduced in May, the same kind of errors followed immediately. Some cried foul, thinking it was a deliberate scheme by the U.S. Mint to get people to accept a dollar coin when nobody really wanted to use it. In reality, the errors resulted from the fact that in order to apply the edge letters, normally struck coins have to be fed into a Schuler press to have the lettering impressed into the edge. It is not hard to imagine some of the struck coins missing their appointment for edge lettering and then escaping into circulation in the normal process of coin release through the Federal Reserve System. It is normal human error. Unfortunately, in this case, the Godless label made them very highly noticeable human error.

In all the hullabaloo, even normal coins were labeled errors at the start. This is because the edge lettering on a regular Presidential coin can have the tops of the letters nearer the obverse, or the tops could be nearer the reverse. It all depends on the random action of the coin when it is fed into the press. For a while there was confusion about these two possibilities and coins with upside down mottoes were proclaimed. In reality, there is no such thing as an upside down motto. Both are equally likely and collectors can collect one of each. But, this created a new kind of error, one in which the coin was fed into the edge letter press twice. For Adams coins, the result could be what looks like double impressions stretching out a date to look like 22000077, or they could have one set of lettering impressed and then the coin flipped over on the second time through and the second set of letters is upside down compared to the first. This creates a nice look of gobbledygook. See the photos on the following page. Nice, huh?

Then there is the old, plain vanilla error, the blank planchet. This occurs when a blank escapes the coining press completely but yet still gets packed into regular shipments leaving the Mint. It looks neat, but markets are not as hot about them

How do you like your edge lettering errors? Both upright as in the double edge lettering above or one set of letters upright and the other upside down as on the edge in the lower photo? In early market action, both were priced the same at around $125 each.

Blank planchets are visually dramatic, but they generally are not as rare and valuable as these other errors.

because blank planchets occur for virtually every denomination, so as errors go, they are rather common.

With the release of the Thomas Jefferson, James Madison and James Monroe dollars, new errors followed in their turn.

The Mint is trying to get a handle on the problem, but every success, such as eliminating plain edges, seems to be met by yet a new type of edge error.

The plain or smooth edge Washington dollar is trading on the market. For coins graded MS-64 by the top two grading services, the retail price as this is written is $250. For MS-65 it is $375. Both of these prices are higher than one year ago by $75 to $100. The Adams plain edge coins are nearly twice as expensive. Because of Mint actions to prevent their occurrence, they are rarer so far than plain-edge Washingtons.

The various kinds of Adams double edge letters are selling for about $125 each, with the market not making any price distinctions among the directional orientation. You can buy double edge letters up, double edge letters down, or one set of letters up and the other down all for the same price. These are early days and markets will continue to react as new information and/or new supplies enter the market.

For error collectors, this is the best of times. The search is on as each new Presidential dollar comes out. Happy hunting.

What's hot for 2009?

Look at the lowly cent before it disppears

By David C. Harper

Am I crazy to imply that the U.S. one-cent coin, a staple of the U.S. monetary system since it was first produced in 1793 and struck every single year since then except in 1815 might disappear? Perhaps.

But certainly there is good reason to worry about the cent's future. It costs 1.7 cents for the U.S. Mint to strike each one-cent coin and it doesn't take a rocket scientist to figure out that such economics ultimately will spell the cent's doom. Efforts are being made to find a cheaper material to make cents from. It is hard to believe that the current zinc planchet coated with a thin layer of copper is too expensive, but it is. More than 25 years of inflation have occurred since it was introduced in 1982.

Informed opinion in Washington, D.C., seems to believe an alloy of steel with a copper finish bonded to it will make a cheaper substitute. The problem is that it may not stay cheap enough for long enough to ensure the cent's future – certainly not the quarter century that the government has gotten out of the last alloy change.

Worse still, the cent is caught in a power struggle between Congress and the Treasury Department. The Treasury wants Congress to delegate its power to determine coin alloys to the Treasury secretary. Congress is saying "wait just a minute," and returning the favor by offering a bill that requires the Treasury secretary to wait five years after a cost problem occurs before he can act, and he can only do so with extensive consultations. If you think that is a recipe for inaction, you are right.

All of these headlines, though, are wonderful ways to implant the idea with the public that they had better get whatever cents they want now because what they are currently used to is about to change. Already on the coin market, Lincoln cent prices are on the rise. If you want to know what is the hottest, all you have to do is look at the key dates of 1909-S VDB, 1914-D, 1931-S and the 1955 doubled die. But any old Wheat-back cent of 1958 and before is selling for a mininum of five

Lincolns are 100 years old.

cents apiece. It doesn't sound like much, but it makes a roll of circulated coins a minimum of $2.50 each, or a $50 face value bag worth $250. If copper keeps rising in price, or if new collectors enter the market, these prices could rise higher still.

Also contributing to a growing buyer enthusiasm for the Lincoln cent is the fact that the year 2009 is the 200th anniversary of Abraham Lincoln's birth and the 100th anniversary of the Lincoln cent. To celebrate, four commemorative designs will appear on the reverse of the Lincoln cent. If the public is unaware of cent production costs, they can't miss the new designs when they receive them in change.

The four will be issued one each calendar quarter, beginning with one that marks Lincoln's early childhood in Kentucky. The second design will signify his formative years in Indiana. The third design will be for his professional life in Illinois. The fourth design will be honoring the Lincoln Presidency, 1861-1865.

Not only do collectors get four new designs in circulation, but they also get coins produced specifically for them made of the same 95-percent copper alloy that was used for the very first Lincoln cent in 1909. How creative the Mint can be with special sets including these new cents will further stoke buyer interest.

And as TV commercials often suggest, there is a bonus. Once 2009 passes into history, the 2010 cent might not look like the 2008 cent. The reverse is supposed to be emblematic of Lincoln's successful effort to preserve the United States as a united country. It is possible the Lincoln Memorial could meet that requirement, but if we use the Jefferson nickel as a guide to official intent, the odds are the Mint will come up with a new rendering for the cent's reverse just as it did for the Jefferson nickel obverse in 2006 following special designs in 2004 and 2005.

A potential alloy change to the cent and four or five new designs spell opportunity for coin collectors who wish to take advantage of growing interest in the denomination. You know what happened when the 50-state quarters program started in 1999. There was a tremendous rush into the hobby that led to greater interest in proof sets, mint sets and other special Mint offerings that included state quarters.

And that gets us right back to the question I asked at the beginning. Am I crazy to imply that the cent might be about to disappear after 216 or 217 years? I don't think so – and that spells the greatest opportunity of all for collectors. What's hot in 2009 might just stay hot for a long time to come. We can salute Lincoln and the previous cent designs for as long a there are collectors, but buy them now before the price goes up.

Glossary of coin terms

Adjustment marks: Marks made by use of a file to correct the weight of overweight coinage planchets prior to striking. Adjusting the weight of planchets was a common practice at the first U.S. Mint in Philadelphia and was often carried out by women hired to weigh planchets and do any necessary filing of the metal.

Altered coin: A coin that has been changed after it left the mint. Such changes are often to the date or mintmark of a common coin in an attempt to increase its value by passing to an unsuspecting buyer as a rare date or mint.

Alloy: A metal or mixture of metals added to the primary metal in the coinage composition, often as a means of facilitating hardness during striking. For example, most U.S. silver coins contain an alloy of 10 percent copper.

Anneal: To heat in order to soften. In the minting process planchets are annealed prior to striking.

Authentication: The act of determining whether a coin, medal, token or other related item is a genuine product of the issuing authority.

Bag marks: Scrapes and impairments to a coin's surface obtained after minting by contact with other coins. The term originates from the storage of coins in bags, but such marks can occur as coins leave the presses and enter hoppers. A larger coin is more susceptible to marks, which affect its grade and, therefore, its value.

Base metal: A metal with low intrinsic value.

Beading: A form of design around the edge of a coin. Beading once served a functional purpose of deterring clipping or shaving parts of the metal by those looking to make a profit and then return the debased coin to circulation.

Blank: Often used in reference to the coinage planchet or disc of metal from which the actual coin is struck. Planchets or blanks are punched out of a sheet of metal by what is known as a blanking press.

Business strike: A coin produced for circulation.

Beading →

Cast copy: A copy of a coin or medal made by a casting process in which molds are used to produce the finished product. Casting imparts a different surface texture to the finished product than striking and often leaves traces of a seam where the molds came together.

Center dot: A raised dot at the center of a coin caused by use of a compass to aid the engraver in the circular positioning of die devices, such as stars, letters, and dates. Center dots are prevalent on early U.S. coinage.

Chop: A mark used by Oriental merchants as a means of guaranteeing the silver content of coins paid out. The merchants' chop, or stamped insignia, often obliterated the original design of the host coin. U.S. Trade dollars,

Chop ✏

struck from 1873 through 1878 and intended for use in trade with China, are sometimes found bearing multiple marks.

Clash marks: Marks impressed in the coinage dies when they come together without a planchet between them. Such marks will affect coins struck subsequently by causing portions of the obverse design to appear in raised form on the reverse, and vice versa.

Clipping: The practice of shaving or cutting small pieces of metal from a coin in circulation. Clipping was prevalent in Colonial times as a means of surreptitiously extracting precious metal from a coin before placing it back into circulation. The introduction of beading and a raised border helped to alleviate the problem.

Coin alignment: U.S. coins are normally struck with an alignment by which, when a coin is held by the top and bottom edge and rotated from side-to-side, the reverse will appear upside down.

Collar: A ring-shaped die between which the obverse and reverse coinage dies are held during striking. The collar contains the outward flow during striking and can be used to produce edge reeding.

Commemorative: A coin issued to honor a special event or person. United States commemorative coins have historically been produced for sale to collectors and not placed in circulation, though the 50-states quarters are circulating commemoratives.

Copy: A replica of an original issue. Copies often vary in quality and metallic composition from the original. Since passage of the Hobby Protection Act (Public Law 93-167) of Nov. 29, 1973, it has been illegal to produce or import copies of coins or other numismatic items that are not clearly and permanently marked with the word "Copy."

Counterfeit: A coin or medal or other numismatic item made fraudulently, either for entry into circulation or sale to collectors.

Denticles: The toothlike pattern found around a coin's obverse or reverse border.

Die: A cylindrical piece of metal containing an incuse image that imparts a raised image when stamped into a planchet.

Die crack: A crack that develops in a coinage die after extensive usage, or if the die is defective or is used to strike harder metals. Die cracks, which often run through border lettering, appear as raised lines on the finished coin.

Device: The principal design element.

Double eagle: Name adopted by the Act of March 3, 1849, for the gold coin valued at 20 units or $20.

Rim

Field

Mintmark

Exergue

Obverse

Legend

Reverse

Eagle: Name adopted by the Coinage Act of 1792 for a gold coin valued at 10 units or $10. Also a name used to refer to gold, silver, and platinum coins of the American Eagle bullion coinage program begun in 1986.

Edge: The cylindrical surface of a coin between the two sides. The edge can be plain, reeded, ornamented, or lettered.

Electrotype: A copy of a coin, medal, or token made by electroplating.

Exergue: The lower segment of a coin, below the main design, generally separated by a line and often containing the date, designer initials, and mintmark.

Face value: The nominal legal-tender value assigned to a given coin by the governing authority.

Fasces: A Roman symbol of authority consisting of a bound bundle of rods and an axe.

Field: The flat area of a coin's obverse or reverse, devoid of devices or inscriptions.

Galvano: A reproduction of a proposed design from an artist's original model produced in plaster or other substance and then electroplated with metal. The galvano is then used in a reducing lathe to make a die or hub.

Glory: A heraldic term for stars, rays or other devices placed as if in the sky or luminous.

Grading: The largely subjective practice of providing a numerical or adjectival ranking of the condition of a coin, token, or medal. The grade is often a major determinant of value.

Gresham's law: The name for the observation made by Sir Thomas Gresham, 16th century English financier, that when two coins with the same face value but different intrinsic values are in circulation at the same time, the one with the lesser intrinsic value will remain in circulation while the other is hoarded.

Half eagle: Name adopted by the Coinage Act of 1792 for a gold coin valued at five units or $5.

Hub: A piece of die steel showing the coinage devices in relief. The hub is used to produce a die that, in contrast, has the relief details incuse. The die is then used to produce the final coin, which looks much the same as the hub. Hubs may be reused to make new dies.

Legend: A coin's principal lettering, generally shown along its outer perimeter.

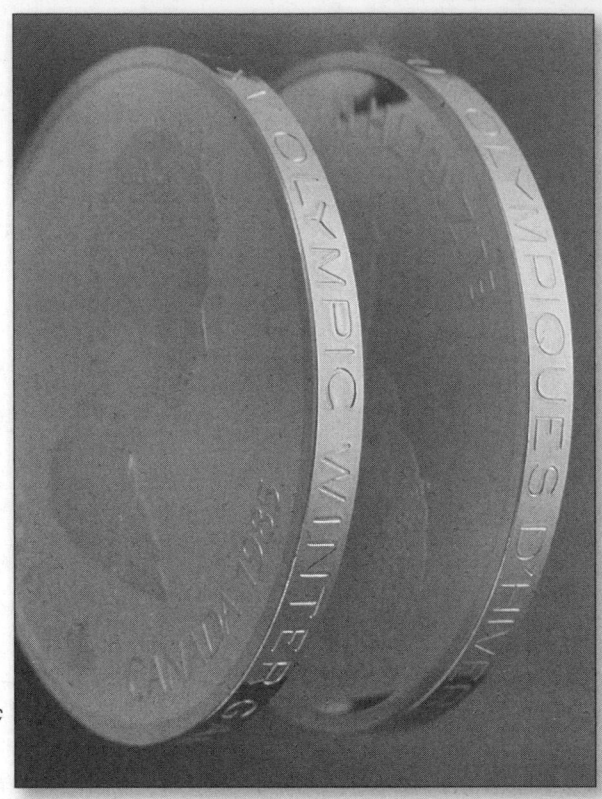

These Canadian Olympic commemoratives have lettered edges.

Lettered edge: Incuse or raised lettering on a coin's edge.

Matte proof: A proof coin on which the surface is granular or dull. On U.S. coins this type of surface was used on proofs of the early 20th century. The process has since been abandoned.

Magician's coin: A term sometimes used to describe a coin with two heads or two tails. Such a coin is considered impossible in normal production due to physical differences in obverse and reverse die mountings, though as of 2001 two have been certified as genuine by professional coin authenticators. The vast majority are products made outside the Mint as novelty pieces.

Medal: Made to commemorate an event or person. Medals differ from coins in that a medal is not legal tender and, in general, is not produced with the intent of circulating as money.

Medal alignment: Medals are generally struck with the coinage dies facing the same direction during striking. When held by the top and bottom edge and rotated from side-to-side, a piece struck in this manner will show both the obverse and reverse right side up.

A medal usually commemorates an event but has no monetary value. It can be issued by a private entity or a government.

Mintage: The total number of coins struck during a given time frame, generally one year.

Mintmark: A letter or other marking on a coin's surface to identify the mint at which the coin was struck.

Mule: The combination of two coinage dies not intended for use together.

Numismatics: The science, study or collecting of coins, tokens, medals, paper money, and related items.

Obverse: The front or "heads" side of a coin, medal, or token.

Overdate: Variety produced when one or more digits of the date are repunched over an old date on a die at the Mint, generally to save on dies or correct an error. Portions of the old date can still be seen under the new one.

Overmintmark: Variety created at the Mint when a different mintmark is punched over an already existing mintmark, generally done to make a coinage die already punched for one mint usable at another. Portions of the old mintmark can still be seen under the new one.

Overstrike: A coin, token or medal struck over another coin, token, or medal.

Pattern: A trial strike of a proposed coin design, issued by the Mint or authorized agent of a governing authority. Patterns can be in a variety of metals, thicknesses, and sizes.

Phrygian cap: A close-fitting, egg-shell-shaped hat placed on the head of a freed slave when Rome was in its ascendancy. Hung from a pole, it was a popular symbol of freedom during the French Revolution and in 18th century United States.

This U.S. Trade dollar has a reeded edge.

Planchet: A disc of metal or other material on which the image of the dies are impressed, resulting in a finished coin. Also sometimes called a blank.

Proof: A coin struck twice or more from specially polished dies and polished planchets. Modern proofs are prepared with a mirror finish. Early 20th century proofs were prepared with a matte surface.

Prooflike: A prooflike coin exhibits some of the characteristics of a proof despite having been struck by regular production processes. Many Morgan dollars are found with prooflike surfaces. The field will have a mirror background similar to that of a proof, and design details are frosted like some proofs.

Quarter eagle: Name adopted by the Coinage Act of 1792 for a gold coin valued at 2.5 units or $2.50.

Reeding: Serrated (toothlike) ornamentation applied to the coin's edge during striking.

Relief: The portion of a design raised above the surface of a coin, medal, or token.

Restrike: A coin, medal or token produced from original dies at a later date, often with the purpose of sale to collectors.

Reverse: The backside or "tails" side of a coin, medal or token, opposite from the principal figure of the design or obverse.

A token is issued by a private entity and can be redeemed for its face value in trade or service.

Rim: The raised area bordering the edge and surrounding the field.

Series: The complete group of coins of the same denomination and design and representing all issuing mints.

Token: A privately issued piece, generally in metal, with a represented value in trade or offer of service. Tokens are also produced for advertising purposes.

Type coin: A coin from a given series representing the basic design. A type coin is collected as an example of a particular design rather than for its date and mintmark.

Variety: Any coin noticeably different in dies from another of the same design, date and mint. Overdate and overmintmarks are examples of varieties.

Wire edge: Created when coinage metal flows between the coinage die and collar, producing a thin flange of coin metal at the outside edge or edges of a coin.

Introduction to pricing

The following value guide is divided into six sections:
1. U.S. minting varieties and errors.
2. Colonial coins, issued prior to the establishment of the United States
3. U.S. issues of 1792.
4. U.S. issues of 1793-present.
5. Canadian coins.
6. Mexican coins.

Value listings

Values listed in the following price guide are average retail prices. These are the approximate prices collectors can expect to pay when purchasing coins from dealers. They are not offers to buy or sell. The pricing section should be considered a guide only; actual selling prices will vary.

The values were compiled by Krause Publications' independent staff of market analysts. They derived the values listed by monitoring auction results, business on electronic dealer trading networks, and business at major shows, and in consultation with a panel of dealers. For rare coins, when only a few specimens of a particular date and mintmark are known, a confirmed transaction may occur only once every several years. In those instances, the most recent auction result is listed.

Grading

Values are listed for coins in various states of preservation, or grades. Standards used in determining grades for U.S. coins are those set by the American Numismatic Association. See Chapter 4 for more on grading.

Dates and mintmarks

The dates listed are the individual dates that appear on each coin. The letter that follows the date is the mintmark and indicates where the coin was struck: "C" — Charlotte, N.C. (1838-1861); "CC" — Carson City, Nev. (1870-1893); "D" — Dahlonega, Ga. (1838-1861), and Denver (1906-present); "O" New Orleans (1838-1909); "P" — Philadelphia (1793-present); "S" San Francisco (1854-present); and "W" — West Point, N.Y. (1984-present). Coins without mintmarks were struck at Philadelphia.

A slash mark in a date indicates an overdate. This means a new date was engraved on a die over an old date. For example, if the date is listed as "1899/8," an 1898 die had a 9 engraved over the last 8 in the date. Portions of the old numeral are still visible on the coin.

A slash mark in a mintmark listing indicates an overmintmark (example: "1922-P/D"). The same process as above occurred, but this time a new mintmark was engraved over an old.

See the "U.S. Minting Varieties and Errors" section for more information on overdates and overmintmarks.

Price charts

Pricing data for the selected charts in the U.S. section were taken from the January issues of *Coin Prices* for the years indicated.

Mexican coin mintages

Quantities minted of each date are indicated when that information is available.

Precious-metal content

Throughout this book precious-metal content is indicated in troy ounces. One troy ounce equals 480 grains, or 31.103 grams.

Abbreviations

AGW. Actual gold weight.

APW. Actual platinum weight.

ASW. Actual silver weight.

BV. Bullion value. This indicates the coin's current value is based on the amount of its precious-metal content and the current price for that metal.

Est. Indicates the exact mintage is not known and the figure listed is an estimate.

G. Grams.

Inc. Abv. Indicates the mintage for the date and mintmark listed is included in the previous listing.

KM#. Indicates "Krause-Mishler number." This sequential cataloging numbering system originated with the *Standard Catalog of World Coins* and provides collectors with a means for identifying coins.

Leg. Legend.

Mkt value. Market value.

MM. Millimeters.

Obv. Obverse.

P/L. Indicates "prooflike," a type of finish used on some Canadian coins.

Rev. Reverse.

Spec. Indicates "specimen," a type of finish used on some Canadian coins.

Pricing
Section

U.S. Minting Varieties and Errors

Introduction

By Alan Herbert

The P.D.S. cataloging system used here to list minting varieties was originally compiled by Alan Herbert in 1971. PDS stands for the three main divisions of the minting process, "planchet," "die" and "striking." Two more divisions cover collectible modifications after the strike, as well as non-collectible alterations, counterfeits and damaged coins.

This listing includes 445 classes, each a distinct part of the minting process or from a specific non-mint change in the coin. Classes from like causes are grouped together. The PDS system applies to coins of the world, but is based on U.S. coinage with added classes for certain foreign minting practices.

Price ranges are based on a U.S. coin in MS-60 grade (uncirculated.) The ranges may be applied in general to foreign coins of similar size or value although collector values are not usually as high as for U.S. coins. Prices are only a guide as the ultimate price is determined by a willing buyer and seller.

To define minting varieties, "A coin which exhibits a variation of any kind from the normal, as a result of any portion of the minting process, whether at the planchet stage, as a result of a change or modification of the die, or during the striking process. It includes those classes considered to be intentional changes, as well as those caused by normal wear and tear on the dies or other minting equipment and classes deemed to be "errors."

The three causes are represented as follows:
1. (I) = Intentional Changes
2. (W) = Wear and Tear
3. (E) = Errors
Note: A class may show more than one cause and could be listed as (IWE).

Rarity level

The rarity ratings are based on the following scale:
1 - Very Common. Ranges from every coin struck down to 1,000,000.
2 - Common. From 1,000,000 down to 100,000.
3 - Scarce. From 100,000 down to 10,000.
4 - Very Scarce. From 10,000 down to 1,000.
5 - Rare. From 1,000 down to 100.
6 - Very Rare. From 100 down to 10.
7 - Extremely Rare. From 10 down to 1.

Unknown: If there is no confirmed report of a piece fitting a particular class, it is listed as Unknown. Reports of finds by readers would be appreciated in order to update future presentations.

An Unknown does not mean that your piece automatically is very valuable. Even a Rarity 7 piece, extremely rare, even unique, may have a very low collector value because of a lack of demand or interest in that particular class.

Classes, definitions and price ranges are based on material previously offered in Alan Herbert's book, The Official Price Guide to Minting Varieties and Errors and in Coin Prices Magazine.

Pricing information has also been provided by John A. Wexler and Ken Potter, with special pricing and technical advice from Del Romines.

Also recommended is the Cherrypicker's Guide to Rare Die Varieties by Bill Fivaz and J.T. Stanton. Check your favorite coin shop, numismatic library or book seller for availability of the latest edition.

For help with your coin questions, to report significant new finds and for authentication of your minting varieties, include a loose first class stamp and write to Alan Herbert, 700 E. State St., Iola, WI 54990-0001. Don't include any numismatic material until you have received specific mailing instructions from me.

Quick check index

If you have a coin and are not sure where to look for the possible variety:
If your coin shows doubling, first check V-B-I.
Then try II-A, II-B, II-C, II-I (4 & 5), III-J, III-L, or IV-C.
If part of the coin is missing, check III-B, III-C, or III-D.
If there is a raised line of coin metal, check II-D, II-G.
If there is a raised area of coin metal, check II-E, II-F, or III-F.
If the coin is out of round, and too thin, check III-G.
If coin appears to be the wrong metal, check III-A, III-E, III-F-3 and III-G.
If the die appears to have been damaged, check II-E, II-G. (Damage to the coin itself usually is not a minting variety.)
If the coin shows incomplete or missing design, check II-A, II-E, III-B-3, III-B-5 or III-D.
If only part of the planchet was struck, check III-M.
If something was struck into the coin, check III-J and III-K.
If something has happened to the edge of the coin, check II-D-6, II-E-10, III-I, III-M and III-O.
If your coin shows other than the normal design, check II-A or II-C.
If a layer of the coin metal is missing, or a clad layer is missing, check III-B and III-D.
If you have an unstruck blank, or planchet, check I-G.
If your coin may be a restrike, check IV-C.
If your coin has a counterstamp, countermark, additional engraving or apparent official modifications, check
  IV-B and V-A-8.

Do not depend on the naked eye to examine your coins. Use a magnifying lens whenever possible, as circulation damage, wear and alterations frequently can be mistaken for legitimate minting varieties.

Division I: planchet varieties

The first division of the PDS System includes those minting varieties that occur in the manufacture of the planchet upon which the coins will ultimately be struck and includes classes resulting from faulty metallurgy, mechanical damage, faulty processing, or equipment or human malfunction prior to the actual coin striking.

Planchet alloy mix (I-A)

This section includes those classes pertaining to mixing and processing the various metals which will be used to make a coin alloy.
I-A-1 Improper Alloy Mix (WE), Rarity Level: 3-4 . . . . Values: $5 to $10
I-A-2 Slag Inclusion Planchet (WE), Rarity Level: 5-6. . . . . Values: $25 up

Damaged and defective planchets (I-B)

To be a class in this section the blank, or planchet, must for some reason not meet the normal standards or must have been damaged in processing. The classes cover the areas of defects in the melting, rolling, punching and processing of the planchets up to the point where they are sent to the coin presses to be struck.

I-B-1 Defective Planchet (WE), Rarity Level: 6 . . . . .Values: $25 up

I-B-2 Mechanically Damaged Planchet (WE), Rarity Level: – . . . . Values: No Value
(See values for the coin struck on a mechanically damaged planchet.)

I-B-3 Rolled Thin Planchet (WE), Rarity Level: 6 - *(Less rare on half cents of 1795, 1797 and restrikes of 1831-52.)* . . . . .Values: $10 up

I-B-4 Rolled Thick Planchet (WE), Rarity Level: 7 - *(Less rare in Colonial copper coins. Notable examples occur on the restrike half cents of 1840-52.)* . . . . .Values: $125 up

I-B-5 Tapered Planchet (WE), Rarity Level: 7 . . . . .Values: $25 up

I-B-6 Partially Unplated Planchet (WE), Rarity Level: 6. . . . . .Values: $15 up

I-B-7 Unplated Planchet (WE), Rarity Level: 6-7. . . . . .Values: $50 up

I-B-8 Bubbled Plating Planchet (WE), Rarity Level: 1 . . . . Values: No Value

I-B-9 Included Gas Bubble Planchet (WE), Rarity Level: 6-7. . . . . .Values: $50 up

I-B-10 Partially Unclad Planchet (WE), Rarity Level: 6 . . . . .Values: $20 up

I-B-11 Unclad Planchet (WE), Rarity Level: 6-7 . . . . .Values: $50 up

I-B-12 Undersize Planchet (WE), Rarity Level: 7 . . . . .Values: $250 up

I-B-13 Oversize Planchet (WE), Rarity Level: 7 . . . . .Values: $250 up

I-B-14 Improperly Prepared Proof Planchet (WE), Rarity Level: 7 . . . . .Values: $100 up

I-B-15 Improperly Annealed Planchet (WE), Rarity Level: - . . . . Values: No Value

I-B-16 Faulty Upset Edge Planchet (WE), Rarity Level: 5-6. . . . . .Values: $10 up

I-B-17 Rolled-In Metal Planchet (WE), Rarity Level: 6-7. . . . . .Values: $50 up

I-B-18 Weld Area Planchet (WE), Rarity Level: Unknown .Values: No Value Established
(See values for the coins struck on weld area planchets.)

I-B-19 Strike Clip Planchet (WE), Rarity Level: 7 . . . . .Values: $150 up

I-B-20 Unpunched Center-Hole Planchet (WE), Rarity Level: 5-7 . . . . Values: $5 and up

I-B-21 Incompletely Punched Center-Hole Planchet (WE), Rarity Level: 6-7. . . . . .Values. $15 up

I-B-22 Uncentered Center-Hole Planchet (WE), Rarity Level: 6-7. . . . . Values: $10 up

I-B-23 Multiple Punched Center-Hole Planchet (WE), Rarity Level: 7. .Values: $35 up

I-B-24 Unintended Center-Hole Planchet (WE), Rarity Level: Unknown . . . . .Values: -

I-B-25 Wrong Size or Shape Center-Hole Planchet (IWE), Rarity Level: 5-7 . . . . .Values: $10 up

Clipped planchets (I-C)

Clipped blanks, or planchets, occur when the strip of coin metal fails to move forward between successive strokes of the gang punch to clear the previously punched holes, in the same manner as a cookie cutter overlapping a previously cut hole in the dough. The size of the clip is a function of the amount of overlap of the next punch.

The overlapping round punches produce a missing arc with curve matching the outside circumference of the blanking punch. Straight clips occur when the punch overlaps the beginning or end of a strip which has had the end sheared or sawed off. Ragged clips occur in the same manner when the ends of the strip have been left as they were rolled out.

The term "clip" as used here should not be confused with the practice of clipping or shaving small pieces of metal from a bullion coin after it is in circulation.

I-C-1 Disc Clip Planchet (WE), Rarity Level: 3-5 . . . . .Values: $5 up

I-C-2 Curved Clip Planchet - (To 5%) (WE), Rarity Level: 5-6 . . . . .Values: $5 up

I-C-3 Curved Clip Planchet - (6 to 10%) (WE), Rarity Level: 6. . . . . .Values: $10 up

I-C-4 Curved Clip Planchet - (11 to 25%) (WE), Rarity Level: 5-6. . . . . Values: $15 up

I-C-5 Curved Clip Planchet - (26 to 60%) (WE), Rarity Level: 6-7. . . . . Values: $25 up

I-C-6 Double Curved Clip Planchet (WE), Rarity Level: 6. . . . . .Values: $10 up

I-C-7 Triple Curved Clip Planchet (WE), Rarity Level: 5-6 . . . . .Values: $25 up

I-C-8 Multiple Curved Clip Planchet (WE), Rarity Level: 6-7 . . . . .Values: $35 up

I-C-9 Overlapping Curved Clipped Planchet (WE), Rarity Level: 6-7 . . . . .Values: $50 up

I-C-10 Incompletely Punched Curved Clip Planchet (WE), Rarity Level: 6 . . . . .Values: $35 up

I-C-11 Oval Curved Clip Planchet (WE), Rarity Level: 6-7 . . . . .Values: $50 up

I-C-12 Crescent Clip Planchet - (61% or more) (WE), Rarity Level: 7 .Values: $200 up

I-C-13 Straight Clip Planchet (WE), Rarity Level: 6. . . . . .Values: $30 up

I-C-14 Incompletely Sheared Straight Clip Planchet (WE), Rarity Level: 6 . . . . .Values: $50 up

I-C-15 Ragged Clip Planchet (WE), Rarity Level: 6-7 . . . . .Values: $35 up

I-C-16 Outside Corner Clip Planchet (E), Rarity Level: - . . . . Values: No Value

I-C-17 Inside Corner Clip Planchet (E), Rarity Level: - . . . . Values: No Value

I-C-18 Irregularly Clipped Planchet (E) Rarity Level: - . . . . .Values: Value not established

I-C-19 Incompletely Punched Scalloped or Multi-Sided Planchet (E), Rarity Level: 7 . . . . .Values: $25 up

Laminated, split, or broken planchet (I-D)

For a variety of reasons the coin metal may split into thin layers (delaminate) and either split completely off the coin, or be retained. Common causes are included gas or alloy mix problems. Lamination cracks usually enter the surface of the planchet at a very shallow angle or are at right angles to the edge. The resulting layers differ from slag in that they appear as normal metal.

Lamination cracks and missing metal of any size below a split planchet are too common in the 35 percent silver 1942-1945 nickels to be collectible or have any significant value.

I-D-1 Small Lamination Crack Planchet (W), Rarity Level: 4-5 . . . . .Values: $1 up

I-D-2 Large Lamination Crack Planchet (W), Rarity Level: 3-4 . . . . .Values: $5 up

I-D-3 Split Planchet (W), Rarity Level: 5-6 . . . . .Values: $15 up

I-D-4 Hinged Split Planchet (W), Rarity Level: 6-7 . . . . .Values: $75 up

I-D-5 Clad Planchet With a Clad Layer Missing (W), Rarity Level: 5-6 . . . . .Values: $35 up

I-D-6 Clad Planchet With Both Clad Layers Missing (W), Rarity Level: 6-7 . . . . .Values: $75 up

I-D-7 Separated Clad Layer (W), Rarity Level: 5 . . . . .Values: $25 up

I-D-8 Broken Planchet (WE), Rarity Level: 3-4 . . . . .Values: $5 up

Wrong stock planchet (I-E)

The following classes cover those cases where the wrong coin metal stock was run through the blanking press, making blanks of the correct diameter, but of the wrong thickness, alloy or metal or a combination of the wrong thickness and the wrong metal.

I-E-1 Half Cent Stock Planchet (IE), Rarity Level: Unknown . . . . .Values: No Value Established

I-E-2 Cent Stock Planchet (IE), Rarity Level: Unknown . . . . .Values: No Value Established

I-E-3 Two Cent Stock Planchet (E), Rarity Level: Unknown .Values: No Value Established

I-E-4 Three Cent Silver Stock Planchet (E), Rarity Level: Unknown. . . . . .Values: No Value Established

I-E-5 Three Cent Nickel Stock Planchet (E), Rarity Level: Unknown . . . . .Values: No Value Established

I-E-6 Half Dime Stock Planchet (E), Rarity Level: Unknown . . . . .Values: No Value Established

I-E-7 Dime Stock Planchet (E), Rarity Level: 7 . . . . .Values: $200 up

I-E-8 Twenty Cent Stock Planchet (E), Rarity Level: Unknown. . . . . .Values: No Value Established

I-E-9 Quarter Stock Planchet (E), Rarity Level: Unknown . . . . .Values: No Value Established

I-E-10 Half Dollar Stock Planchet (E), Rarity Level: Unknown. . . . . .Values: No Value Established

I-E-11 Dollar Stock Planchet (E), Rarity Level: 7. . . . . .Values: $300 up

I-E-12 Token or Medal Stock Planchet (E), Rarity Level: Unknown . . . . .Values: No Value Established

I-E-13 Wrong Thickness Spoiled Planchet (IWE), Rarity Level: Unknown. . . . . . . .Values: No Value Established

I-E-14 Correct Thickness Spoiled Planchet (IWE), Rarity Level: Unknown . . . . . . .Values: No Value Established

I-E-15 Cut Down Struck Token Planchet (IWE), Rarity Level: Unknown . . . . .Values: No Value Established

I-E-16 Experimental or Pattern Stock Planchet (IE), Rarity Level: Unknown . . . . . .Values: No Value Established

I-E-17 Proof Stock Planchet (IE), Rarity Level: Unknown . . . . .Values: No Value Established

I-E-18 Adjusted Specification Stock Planchet (IE), Rarity Level: 7. . . . . .Values: $25 up

I-E-19 Trial Strike Stock Planchet (IE), Rarity Level: Unknown . . . . .Values: No Value Established

I-E-20 U.S. Punched Foreign Stock Planchet (E), Rarity Level: 7 . . . . .Values: $75 up

I-E-21 Foreign Punched Foreign Stock Planchet (E), Rarity Level: 7. .Values: $75 up

I-E-22 Non-Standard Coin Alloy Planchet (IE), Rarity Level: 7 . . . . .Values: Unknown

Extra metal on a blank, or planchet (I-F)

True extra metal is only added to the blank during the blanking operation. This occurs as metal is scraped off the sides of the blanks as they are driven down through the thimble, or lower die in the blanking press. The metal is eventually picked up by a blank passing through, welded to it by the heat of friction.

A second form of extra metal has been moved to this section, the sintered coating planchet, the metal deposited on the planchet in the form of dust during the annealing operation.

I-F-1 Extra Metal on a Type 1 Blank (W), Rarity Level: 7 . . . . .Values: $50 up
I-F-2 Extra Metal on a Type 2 Planchet (W), Rarity Level: 6-7 . . . . .Values: $75 up
I-F-3 Sintered Coating Planchet (W), Rarity Level: 7 . . . . .Values: $75 up

Normal or abnormal planchets (I-G)

This section consists of the two principal forms – the blank as it comes from the blanking press – and in the form of a planchet after it has passed through the upsetting mill. It also includes a class for purchased planchets and one for planchets produced by the mint.

I-G-1 Type I Blank (IWE), Rarity Level: 3-5 . . . . .Values: $2 up
I-G-2 Type II Planchet (IWE), Rarity Level: 3-4 . . . . .Values: 50 up
I-G-3 Purchased Planchet (I), Rarity Level: 1 . . . . Values: No Value
I-G-4 Mint Made Planchet (I), Rarity Level: 1 . . . . Values: No Value
I-G-5 Adjustment-Marked Planchet (I), Rarity Level: Unknown . . . . .Values: No Value
I-G-6 Hardness Test-Marked Planchet (I), Rarity Level: - . . . . .Values: No Value Established
Note: There are no classes between I-G-6 and I-G-23
I-G-23 Proof Planchet (IE), Rarity Level: 6-7 . . . . .Values: $1 up

Coin metal strip (I-H)

When the coin metal strip passes through the blanking press it goes directly to a chopper. This cuts the remaining web into small pieces to be sent back to the melting furnace. Pieces of the web or the chopped up web may escape into the hands of collectors.

I-H-1 Punched Coin Metal Strip (IWE), Rarity Level: 4-6 . . . . Values: $5 up,
    depending on size, denomination and number of holes showing
I-H-2 Chopped Coin Metal Strip (IE), Rarity Level: 3-5 . . . . .Values: $5 up

The die varieties

Division II

Die varieties may be unique to a given die, but will repeat for the full life of the die unless a further change occurs. Anything that happens to the die will affect the appearance of the struck coin. This includes all the steps of the die making:

- Cutting a die blank from a tool steel bar.
- Making the design.
- Transferring it to a model.
- Transferring it to the master die or hub.
- The hubbing process of making the die.
- Punching in the mintmark.
- Heat treating of the die.

The completed dies are also subject to damage in numerous forms, plus wear and tear during the striking process and repair work done with abrasives. All of these factors can affect how the struck coin looks.

Engraving varieties (II-A)

In all cases in this section where a master die, or master hub is affected by the class, the class will affect all the working hubs and all working dies descending from it.

Identification as being on a master die or hub depends on it being traced to two or more of the working hubs descended from the same master tools.

II-A-1 Overdate (IE), Rarity Level: 1-7 . . . . Values: $1 up
II-A-2 Doubled Date (IE), Rarity Level: 1-7 . . . . Values: $1 up
II-A-3 Small Date (IE), Rarity Level: 2-5 . . . . Values: $1 up
II-A-4 Large Date (IE), Rarity Level: 2-5 . . . . Values: $1 up
II-A-5 Small Over Large Date (IE), Rarity Level: 4-6 . . . . Values: $15 up
II-A-6 Large Over Small Date (IE), Rarity Level: 3-5 . . . . Values: $10 up
II-A-7 Blundered Date (E), Rarity Level: 6-7 . . . . Values: $50 up
II-A-8 Corrected Blundered Date (IE), Rarity Level: 3-5 . . . . Values: $5 up
II-A-9 Wrong Font Date Digit (IE), Rarity Level: 5-6 . . . . Values: Minimal
II-A-10 Worn, Broken or Damaged Punch (IWE), Rarity Level: 5-6 . . . . Values: $5 up
II-A-11 Expedient Punch (IWE), Rarity Level: 5-6 . . . . Values: $10 up
II-A-12 Blundered Digit (E), Rarity Level: 4-5 . . . . Values: $50 up
II-A-13 Corrected Blundered Digit (IE), Rarity Level: 3-6 . . . . Values: $10 up
II-A-14 Doubled Digit (IWE), Rarity Level: 2-6 . . . . Values: $2 up
II-A-15 Wrong Style or Font Letter or Digit (IE), Rarity Level: 3-5 . . . . Values: Minimal
II-A-16 One Style or Font Over Another (IE), Rarity Level: 4-6 . . . . Values: $10 up
II-A-17 Letter Over Digit (E), Rarity Level: 6-7 . . . . Values: $25 up
II-A-18 Digit Over Letter (E), Rarity Level: 6-7 . . . . Values: $25 up
II-A-19 Omitted Letter or Digit (IWE), Rarity Level: 4-6 . . . . Values: $5 up
II-A-20 Blundered Letter (E), Rarity Level: 6-7 . . . . Values: $50 up
II-A-21 Corrected Blundered Letter (IE), Rarity Level: 1-3 . . . . Values: $10 up
II-A-22 Doubled Letter (IWE), Rarity Level: 2-6 . . . . Values: $2 up
II-A-23 Blundered Design Element (IE), Rarity Level: 6-7 . . . . Values: $50 up
II-A-24 Corrected Blundered Design Element (IE), Rarity Level: 3-5 . . . . Values: $10 up
II-A-25 Large Over Small Design Element (IE), Rarity Level: 4-6 . . . . Values: $2 up
II-A-26 Omitted Design Element (IWE), Rarity Level: 5-7 . . . . Values: $10 up
II-A-27 Doubled Design Element (IWE), Rarity Level: 2-6 . . . . Values: $2 up
II-A-28 One Design Element Over Another (IE), Rarity Level: 3-6 . . . . Values: $5 up
II-A-29 Reducing Lathe Doubling (WE), Rarity Level: 6-7 . . . . Values: $50 up
II-A-30 Extra Design Element (IE), Rarity Level: 3-5 . . . . Values: $10 up
II-A-31 Modified Design (IWE), Rarity Level: 1-5 . . . . Values: No Value up
II-A-32 Normal Design (I), Rarity Level: 1 . . . . Values: No Extra Value
II-A-33 Design Mistake (IE), Rarity Level: 2-6 . . . . Values: $1 up
II-A-34 Defective Die Design (IWE), Rarity Level: 1 . . . . Values: No Value
II-A-35 Pattern (I), Rarity Level: 6-7 . . . . Values: $100 up
II-A-36 Trial Design (I), Rarity Level: 5-7 . . . . Values: $100 up
II-A-37 Omitted Designer's Initial (IWE), Rarity Level: 3-7 . . . . Values: $1 up
II-A-38 Layout Mark (IE), Rarity Level: 5-7 . . . . Values: Minimal
II-A-39 Abnormal Reeding (IWE), Rarity Level: 2-5 . . . . Values: $1 up
II-A-40 Modified Die or Hub (IWE), Rarity Level: 1-5 . . . . Values: No Value up
II-A-41 Numbered Die (I), Rarity Level: 3-5 . . . . Values: $5 up
II-A-42 Plugged Die (IW), Rarity Level: 5-6 . . . . Values: Minimal
II-A-43 Cancelled Die (IE), Rarity Level: 3-6 . . . . Values: No Value up
II-A-44 Hardness Test Marked Die (IE), Rarity Level: 7 . . . . Values: $100 up
II-A-45 Coin Simulation (IE), Rarity Level: 6-7 . . . . Values: $100 up, but may be illegal to own
II-A-46 Punching Mistake (IE), Rarity Level: 2-6 . . . . Values: $1 up
II-A-47 Small Over Large Design (IE), Rarity Level: 4-6 . . . . Values: $5 up
II-A-48 Doubled Punch (IE), Rarity Level: 5-7 . . . . Values: $5 up
II-A-49 Mint Display Sample (I) Rarity Level: 7 . . . . Values not established
II-A-50 Center Dot, Stud or Circle (IE) Rarity Level: 7, much more common on early cents . . Values not established

Hub doubling varieties (II-B)

Rotated hub doubling   *Hub break*

This section includes eight classes of hub doubling. Each class is from a different cause, described by the title of the class. At the latest count over 2,500 doubled dies have been reported in the U.S. coinage, the most famous being examples of the 1955, 1969-S and 1972 cent dies.

II-B-I Rotated Hub Doubling (WE), Rarity Level: 3-6 . . . . .Values: $1 up
II-B-II Distorted Hub Doubling (WE), Rarity Level: 3-6 . . . . .Values: $1 up
II-B-III Design Hub Doubling (IWE), Rarity Level: 3-6 . . . . Values: $1 up to five figure amounts
II-B-IV Offset Hub Doubling (WE), Rarity Level: 4-6 . . . . .Values: $15 up
II-B-V Pivoted Hub Doubling (WE), Rarity Level: 3-6 . . . . .Values: $10 up
II-B-VI Distended Hub Doubling (WE), Rarity Level: 2-5 . . . . .Values: $1 up
II-B-VII Modified Hub Doubling (IWE), Rarity Level: 2-5 . . . . .Values: $1 up
II-B-VIII Tilted Hub Doubling (WE), Rarity Level: 4-6 . . . . .Values: $5 up

Mintmark varieties (II-C)

Double   *Triple*

Mintmarks are punched into U.S. coin dies by hand (Up to 1985 for proof coins, to 1990 for cents and nickels and 1991 for other denominations). Variations resulting from mistakes in the punching are listed in this section. Unless exceptionally mispunched, values are usually estimated at 150 percent of numismatic value. Slightly tilted or displaced mintmarks have no value.

II-C-1 Doubled Mintmark (IE), Rarity Level: 2-6 . . . . Values: 50 cents up
II-C-2 Separated Doubled Mintmark (IE), Rarity Level: 5-6 . . . . .Values: $15 up
II-C-3 Over Mintmark (IE), Rarity Level: 3-6 . . . . .Values: $2 up
II-C-4 Tripled Mintmark (IE), Rarity Level: 3-5 . . . . .Values: 50 up
II-C-5 Quadrupled Mintmark (IE), Rarity Level: 4-6 . . . . .Values: $1 up
II-C-6 Small Mintmark (IE), Rarity Level: 2-5 . . . . Values: No Extra Value up
II-C-7 Large Mintmark (IE), Rarity Level: 2-5 . . . . Values: No Extra Value up
II-C-8 Large Over Small Mintmark (IE), Rarity Level: 2-5 . . . . .Values: $2 up
II-C-9 Small Over Large Mintmark (IE), Rarity Level: 3-6 . . . . .Values: $5 up
II-C-10 Broken Mintmark Punch (W), Rarity Level: 5-6 . . . . .Values: $5 up
II-C-11 Omitted Mintmark (IWE), Rarity Level: 4-7 . . . . .Values: $125 up
II-C-12 Tilted Mintmark (IE), Rarity Level: 5-7 . . . . .Values: $5 up
II-C-13 Blundered Mintmark (E), Rarity Level: 4-6 . . . . .Values: $5 up

II-C-14 Corrected Horizontal Mintmark (IE), Rarity Level: 4-6 ....Values: $5 up
II-C-15 Corrected Upside Down Mintmark (IE), Rarity Level: 4-6............................Values: $5 up
II-C-16 Displaced Mintmark (IE), Rarity Level: 4-6................................Values: $5 to $10
II-C-17 Modified Mintmark (IWE), Rarity Level: 1-4............................Values: No Extra Value up
II-C-18 Normal Mintmark (I), Rarity Level: 1....................................Values: No Extra Value
II-C-19 Doubled Mintmark Punch (I), Rarity Level: 6-7............................Values: No Extra Value up
II-C-20 Upside Down Mintmark (E) Rarity Level 6-7....................................Values: $5 up
II-C-21 Horizontal Mintmark (E) Rarity Level 6-7......................................Values: $5 up
II-C-22 Wrong Mintmark (E) Rarity Level 6-7..Values $15 up
(Example has a D mintmark in the date, but was used at Philadelphia.)

Die, collar and hub cracks (II-D)

Die cracks

Cracks in the surface of the die allow coin metal to be forced into the crack during the strike, resulting in raised irregular lines of coin metal above the normal surface of the coin. These are one of the commonest forms of die damage and wear, making them easily collectible.

Collar cracks and hub cracks are added to this section because the causes and effects are similar or closely associated.

Die cracks, collar cracks and hub cracks are the result of wear and tear on the tools, with intentional use assumed for all classes.

II-D-1 Die Crack (W), Rarity Level: 1-3........................Values: 10 to $1, $25 up on a proof coin
   with a rarity level of 6-7
II-D-2 Multiple Die Cracks (W), Rarity Level: 1-3................................Values: 25 cents to $2
II-D-3 Head-To-Rim Die Crack (Lincoln Cent) (W), Rarity Level: 2-6 .. Values: 25 to $10 for multiple die cracks
II-D-4 Split Die (W), Rarity Level: 5-6..Values: $10 up
II-D-5 Rim-To-Rim Die Crack (W), Rarity Level: 2-5....................................Values: $1 up
II-D-6 Collar Crack (W), Rarity Level: 4-6..Values: $10 up
II-D-7 Hub Crack (W), Rarity Level: 3-5 ....Values: $1-$2

Small die break II-E-2

Clogged letter II-E-1

Major die break, date missing, II-E-5

Rim die break II-E-4

Die breaks (II-E)

Breaks in the surface of the die allow coin metal to squeeze into the resulting holes, causing raised irregular areas above the normal surface of the coin. Die chips and small die breaks are nearly as common as the die cracks, but major die breaks, which extend in from the edge of the coin, are quite rare on the larger coins.

If the broken piece of the die is retained, the resulting design will be above or below the level of the rest of the surface.

II-E-1 Die Chip (W), Rarity Level: 1-2 . . . . Values: 10 to $1
II-E-2 Small Die Break (W), Rarity Level: 1-3 . . . . Values: 10 to $2
II-E-3 Large Die Break (W), Rarity Level: 3-5 . . . . Values: $1 to $50 and up
II-E-4 Rim Die Break (W), Rarity Level: 2-3 . . . . Values: 25 cents to $5
II-E-5 Major Die Break (WE), Rarity Level: 3-6 . . . . Values: $5 to $100 and up
II-E-6 Retained Broken Die (W), Rarity Level: 3-5 . . . . Values: $1 to $10 and up
II-E-7 Retained Broken Center of the Die (W), Rarity Level: 6-7 . . . . Values: $100 up
II-E-8 Laminated Die (W), Rarity Level: 3-5 . . . . Values: 10 cents to $5
II-E-9 Chipped Chrome Plating (W), Rarity Level: 4-5 . . . . Values: $10 to $25 on proofs
II-E-10 Collar Break (W), Rarity Level: 4-6 . . . . Values: $5 to $25 and up
II-E-11 Broken Letter or Digit on an Edge Die (W), Rarity Level: 4-6 . . . . Values: Minimal.
II-E-12 "Bar" Die Break (W), Rarity Level: 3-5 . . . . Values: 25 to $20
II-E-13 Hub Break (W), Rarity Level: 4-6 . . . . Values: 50 to $10 and up

"BIE" varieties (II-F)

A series of small die breaks or die chips in the letters of "LIBERTY" mostly on the wheat-reverse Lincoln cent are actively collected. The name results from the resemblance to an "I" between the "B" and "E" on many of the dies, but they are found between all of the letters in different cases. Well over 1,500 dies are known and cataloged. Numerous more recent examples are known.

II-F-1 ILI Die Variety (W), Rarity Level: 4-5 . . . . Values: 25 cents to $10
II-F-2 LII Die Variety (W), Rarity Level: 3-5 . . . . Values: 50 cents to $15
II-F-3 IIB Die Variety (W), Rarity Level: 3-5 . . . . Values: 50 cents to $15
II-F-4 BIE Die Variety (W), Rarity Level: 3-5 . . . . Values: $1 to $20
II-F-5 EIR Die Variety (W), Rarity Level: 3-5 . . . . Values: 50 to $15
II-F-6 RIT Die Variety (W), Rarity Level: 4-5 . . . . Values: $2 to $25
II-F-7 TIY Die Variety (W), Rarity Level: 4-5 . . . . Values: $5 to $30
II-F-8 TYI Die Variety (W), Rarity Level: 4-5 . . . . Values: $2 to $25

Worn and damaged dies, collars and hubs (II-G)

Many dies are continued deliberately in service after they have been damaged, dented, clashed or show design transfer, since none of these classes actually affect anything but the appearance ofthe coin. The root cause is wear, but intent or mistakes may enter the picture.

II-G-1 Dented Die, Collar or Hub (IWE), Rarity Level: 3-5 . . . . Values: 25 to $5
II-G-2 Damaged Die, Collar or Hub (IWE), Rarity Level: 3-5 . . . . Values: 25 to $5
II-G-3 Worn Die, Collar or Hub (IWE), Rarity Level: 2-3 . . . . Values: No Extra Value to Minimal Value
II-G-4 Pitted or Rusted Die, Collar or Hub (IWE), Rarity Level: 3-4 . . . . Values: No Extra Value, marker only
II-G-5 Heavy Die Clash (IWE), Rarity Level: 4-5 . . . . Values: $1 to $10 and up
II-G-6 Heavy Collar Clash (IWE), Rarity Level: 3-4 . . . . Values: $1 to $5 and up
II-G-7 Heavy Design Transfer (IWE), Rarity Level: 3-4 . . . . Values: 10 cents to $1

Die progressions (II-H)

The progression section consists of three classes. These are useful as cataloging tools for many different die varieties, but especially the die cracks and die breaks which may enlarge, lengthen or increase in number.

II-H-1 Progression (W), Rarity Level: 3-5 . . . . Values: $1 up

II-H-2 Die Substitution (IW), Rarity Level: 2-4 . . . . Values: No Extra Value to Minimal Value
II-H-3 Die Repeat (I), Rarity Level: 2-4 . . . . Values: No Extra Value to Minimal Value

Die scratches, polished and abraded dies (II-I)

This section consists of those classes having to do with the use of an abrasive in some form to intentionally polish proof dies, or repair the circulating die surface. Several classes which previously were referred to as "polished" now are listed as "abraded."

II-I-1 Die Scratch (IW), Rarity Level: 1-2 . . . . .Values: No Extra Value to 10 cents to 25 cents, as a marker
II-I-2 Polished (proof) Die (IW), Rarity Level: 1 . . . . .Values: No Extra Value
II-I-3 Abraded (Circulation) Die (IW), Rarity Level: 1-2 . . . . .Values: No Extra Value up to $10
II-I-4 Inside Abraded Die Doubling (IW), Rarity Level: 1-3 . . . . Values: No Extra Value to $1
II-I-5 Outside Abraded Die Doubling (IW), Rarity Level: 1-3 . . . . Values: No Extra Value to $1
II-I-6 Lathe Marks (IW), Rarity Level: 5-7 . . . . .Values: No Extra Value, marker only

Striking varieties

Division III

Once the dies are made and the planchets have been prepared, they are struck by a pair of dies and become a coin. In this division, we list the misstrikes resulting from human or mechanical malfunction in the striking process. These are one-of-a-kind varieties, but there may be many similar coins that fall in a given class.

Multiples and combinations of classes must be considered on a case by case basis. The first several sections match the planchet sections indicated in the title.

Struck on defective alloy mix planchets (III-A)

This section includes those classes of coins struck on planchets that were made from a defective alloy.

III-A-1 Struck on an Improper Alloy Mix Planchet (IE), Rarity Level: 2-3 . . . . Values: 10 cents to $2
III-A-2 Struck on a Planchet With Slag Inclusions(IE), Rarity Level: 5-6 . . . . .Values: $10 up

Struck on damaged, defective or abnormal planchet (III-B)

Struck on a defective planchet III-B-1   *Struck on a tapered planchet III-B-5*

Coins get struck on many strange objects. The more common of course are planchets which have been damaged in some way in the production process. In most of the classes in this section intent is at least presumed, if not specifically listed as a cause.

III-B-1 Struck on a Defective Planchet (IWE), Rarity Level: 4-6 . . . . Values: $5 to $10 and up
III-B-2 Struck on a Mechanically Damaged Planchet (IWE), Rarity Level: 5-6 . . . . . . .Values: $10 to $20 and up
III-B-3 Struck on a Rolled Thin Planchet (IWE), Rarity Level: 5-6 . . . . .Values: $2 to $5 and up
III-B-4 Struck on a Rolled Thick Planchet (IWE), Rarity Level: 5-6 . . . . Values: $35 to $50 and up
III-B-5 Struck on a Tapered Planchet (WE), Rarity Level: 4-6 . . . . Values: $2 to $5 and up
III-B-6 Struck on a Partially Unplated Planchet (WE), Rarity Level: 5 . . . . .Values: $10 up
III-B-7 Struck on an Unplated Planchet (WE), Rarity Level: 6-7 . . . . Values: $100 up
III-B-8 Struck on a Bubbled Plating Planchet (IWE), Rarity Level: 1 . . . . Values: No Value
III-B-9 Struck on an Included Gas Bubble Planchet (WE), Rarity Level: 5-6 . . . . .Values: $5 up
III-B-10 Struck on a Partially Unclad Planchet (WE), Rarity Level: 5-6 .Values: $5 up

III-B-11 Struck on an Unclad Planchet (WE), Rarity Level: 4-5 . . . . .Values: $5 and up
III-B-12 Struck on an Undersize Planchet (WF), Rarity Level: 4-6 . . . . .Values: Minimal
III-B-13 Struck on an Oversize Planchet (WE), Rarity Level: 6-7. . . . . Values: Minimal
III-B-14 Struck on an Improperly Prepared Proof Planchet (IWE), Rarity Level: 3-5 . . . . .Values: $5 up
III-B-15 Struck on an Improperly Annealed Planchet (IWE), Rarity Level: 4-5 . . . . .Values: $5 up
III-B-16 Struck on a Faulty Upset Edge Planchet (IWE), Rarity Level: 4-5 . . . . .Values: $1 to $2
III-B-17 Struck on a Rolled In Metal Planchet (WE), Rarity Level: 4-6. . . . . .Values: $2 up
III-B-18 Struck on a Weld Area Planchet (WE), Rarity Level: 6 . . . . .Values: $25 to $50
III-B-19 Struck on a Strike Clip Planchet (W), Rarity Level: 6-7 . . . . .Values: $25 up
III-B-20 Struck on an Unpunched Center Hole Planchet (WE), Rarity Level: 4-6. . . . . Values: $1 and up
III-B-21 Struck on an Incompletely Punched Center Hole Planchet (WE), Rarity Level: 6-7 . . . . . .Values: $5 up
III-B-22 Struck on an Uncentered Center Hole Planchet (WE), Rarity Level: 6-7. . . . . .Values: $10 up
III-B-23 Struck on a Multiple Punched Center Hole Planchet (WE), Rarity Level: 7. . . . . .Values: $25 up
III-B-24 Struck on an Unintended Center Hole Planchet (WE), Rarity Level: 6-7. . . . . Values: $25 and up
III-B-25 Struck on a Wrong Size or Shape Center Hole Planchet (WE), Rarity Level: 5-7 . . . . .Values: $5 up
III-B-26 Struck on Scrap Coin Metal (E), Rarity Level: 4-6 . . . . .Values: $10 up
III-B-27 Struck on Junk Non Coin Metal (E), Rarity Level: 4-6 . . . . .Values: $15 up
III-B-28 Struck on a False Planchet (E), Rarity Level: 3-5 . . . . .Values: $35 up
III-B-29 Struck on Bonded Planchets (E), Rarity Level: 6-7. . . . . .Values: $50 up

Struck on a clipped planchet (III-C)

Ragged edge clip III-C-15

Multiple clip III-C-8   *Incomplete curved clip III-C-10*

Coins struck on clipped blanks, or planchets, exhibit the same missing areas as they did before striking, modified by the metal flow from the strike which rounds the edges and tends to move metal into the missing areas. Values for blanks will run higher than planchets with similar clips.

III-C-1 Struck on a Disc Clip Planchet (WE), Rarity Level: 4-5 . . . . Values: $1 on regular coins,
    $20 and up for clad coins
III-C-2 Struck on a Curved Clip Planchet - to 5% (WE), Rarity Level: 3-5 . . . . Values: 50 cents up
III-C-3 Struck on a Curved Clip Planchet - (6 to 10%) (WE), Rarity Level: 4-5. . . . . Values: $1 up
III-C-4 Struck on a Curved Clip Planchet - (11 to 25%) (WE), Rarity Level: 4-5. . . . . .Values: $2 up
III-C-5 Struck on a Curved Clip Planchet - (26 to 60%) (WE), Rarity Level: 4-6 . . . . .Values: $10 up
III-C-6 Struck on a Double Curved Clip Planchet (WE), Rarity Level: 3-4. . . . . .Values: $2 up
III-C-7 Struck on a Triple Curved Clip Planchet (WE), Rarity Level: 4-5 . . . . .Values: $5 up
III-C-8 Struck on a Multiple Curved Clip Planchet (WE), Rarity Level: 4-6 . . . . .Values: $5 up
III-C-9 Struck on an Overlapping Curved Clipped Planchet (WE), Rarity Level: 5-6 . . . . .Values: $15 up
III-C-10 Struck on an Incomplete Curved Clip Planchet (WE), Rarity Level: 4-5. . . . . .Values: $10 up
III-C-11 Struck on an Oval Clip Planchet (WE), Rarity Level: 5-6 . . . . .Values: $20 up
III-C-12 Struck on a Crescent Clip Planchet - (61% or more) (WE), Rarity Level: 6-7 . . . . .Values: $100 up
III-C-13 Struck on a Straight Clip Planchet (E), Rarity Level: 4-6 . . . . .Values: $10 up

III-C-14 Struck on an Incomplete Straight Clip Planchet (WE), Rarity Level: 5-6 . . . . Values: $20 up
III-C-15 Struck on a Ragged Clip Planchet (E), Rarity Level: 4-6 . . . . Values: $15 up
III-C-16 Struck on an Outside Corner Clip Planchet (E), Rarity Level: 7 . . . . Values: $100 up
III-C-17 Struck on an Inside Corner Clip Planchet (E), Rarity Level: Unknown outside mint. . . . . Values:
III-C-18 Struck on an Irregularly Clipped Planchet (E), Rarity Level: 6-7 . . . . Values: $20 up.
III-C-19 Struck on an Incompletely Punched Scalloped or Multi-Sided Planchet (E), Rarity Level: 7
. . . . Values: $20 up.

Struck on a laminated, split or broken planchet (III-D)

Lamination crack III-D-1   *Layer peeled off III-D-2*   *Split planchet III-D-3*

This section has to do with the splitting, cracking or breaking of a coin parallel to the faces of the coin, or at least very nearly parallel, or breaks at right angles to the faces of the coin.

Lamination cracks and missing metal of any size below a split planchet are too common in the 35-percent silver 1942-1945 nickels to be collectible or have any significant value.

III-D-1 Struck on a Small Lamination Crack Planchet (W), Rarity Level: 3-4. . . . . Values: 10 up
III-D-2 Struck on a Large Lamination Crack Planchet (W), Rarity Level: 3-6. . . . . Values: $1 up
III-D-3 Struck on a Split Planchet (W), Rarity Level: 4-6. . . . . Values: $5 up
III-D-4 Struck on a Hinged Split Planchet (W), Rarity Level: 5-6. . . . . Values: $35 up
III-D-5 Struck on a Planchet With a Clad Layer Missing (W), Rarity Level: 4-5. . . . . Values: $15 up
III-D-6 Struck on a Planchet With Both Clad Layers Missing (W), Rarity Level: 4-5 . . . . Values: $25 up
III-D-7 Struck on a Separated Clad Layer or Lamination (W), Rarity Level: 6-7. . . . . Values: $75 up
III-D-8 Struck on a Broken Planchet Before the Strike (W), Rarity Level: 3-5 . . . . Values: $10 up
III-D-9 Broken Coin During or After the Strike (W), Rarity Level: 4-6 . . . . Values: $20 up
III-D-10 Struck Coin Fragment Split or Broken During or After the Strike (W), Rarity Level: 3-5. . . Values: $5 up
III-D-11 Reedless Coin Broken During or After the Strike (W), Rarity Level: Unknown . . . . Values: -

Struck on wrong stock planchets (III-E)

Quarter on dime stock
III-E-7 (lower coin edge)

These classes cover those cases where the wrong stock was run through the blanking press, making planchets of the correct diameter, but of the wrong thickness, alloy or metal or a combination of incorrect thickness and metal.

III-E-1 Struck on a Half Cent-Stock Planchet (IE), Rarity Level: Unknown. . . . . Values: No Value Established
III-E-2 Struck on a Cent-Stock Planchet (IE), Rarity Level: Unknown . . . . Values: No Value Established
III-E-3 Struck on a Two-Cent-Stock Planchet (E), Rarity Level: Unknown . . . . Values: -
III-E-4 Struck on a Three-Cent-Silver Stock Planchet (E), Rarity Level: Unknown . . . . Values: -
III-E-5 Struck on a Three-Cent-Nickel Stock Planchet (E), Rarity Level: Unknown . . . . Values: -
III-E-6 Struck on a Half Dime-Stock Planchet (E), Rarity Level: Unknown. . . . . Values: -
III-E-7 Struck on a Dime-Stock Planchet (E), Rarity Level: 5-6 . . . . Values: $20 up

III-E-8 Struck on a Twenty-Cent-Stock Planchet (E), Rarity Level: Unknown . . . . .Values: -
III-E-9 Struck on a Quarter-Stock Planchet (E), Rarity Level: 6 . . . . .Values: $50 up
III-E-10 Struck on a Half Dollar-Stock Planchet (E), Rarity Level: 6-7 .Values: $100 up
III-E-11 Struck on a Dollar-Stock Planchet (E), Rarity Level: 6-7 . . . . .Values: $300 up
III-E-12 Struck on a Token/Medal-Stock Planchet (E), Rarity Level: 7 . . . . .Values: No Value Established
III-E-13 Struck on a Wrong Thickness Spoiled Planchet (IWE), Rarity Level: 7 . . . . .Values: $50 up
III-E-14 Struck on a Correct Thickness Spoiled Planchet (IWE), Rarity Level: Unknown. Values: No Value Established
III-E-15 Struck on a Cut Down Struck Token (IWE), Rarity Level: 6-7 .Values: $50 up
III-E-16 Struck on an Experimental or Pattern-Stock Planchet (IE), Rarity Level: 7 . . . . .Values: $50 up
III-E-17 Struck on a Proof-Stock Planchet (IE), Rarity Level: 7 . . . . .Values: $100 up
III-E-18 Struck on an Adjusted Specification-Stock Planchet (IE), Rarity Level: 3-7. Values: No Value to $5 and up
III-E-19 Struck on a Trial Strike-Stock Planchet (IE), Rarity Level: Unknown. . . . . .Values: No Value Established
III-E-20 U.S. Coin Struck on a Foreign-Stock Planchet. (E), Rarity Level: 5 . . . . .Values: $35 up
III-E-21 Foreign Coin Struck on a Foreign-Stock Planchet (E), Rarity Level: 5-6 . . . . .Values: $25 up
III-E-22 Struck on a Non-Standard Coin Alloy (IE), Rarity Level: 4-7 .Values: $20 up

Extra metal (III-F)

Extra metal on a
struck coin (III-F-2)

Sintered coating III-F-3

The term "extra metal" for the purpose of this section includes both extra metal added to the blank during the blanking operation and metal powder added to the planchet during the annealing operation.

III-F-1 Struck on a Type 1 Blank With Extra Metal (W), Rarity Level: Unknown . . . . .Values: -
III-F-2 Struck on a Type 2 Planchet With Extra Metal (W), Rarity Level: 4-5 . . . . .Values: $10 up
III-F-3 Struck on a Sintered Coating Planchet (W), Rarity Level: 6-7 . . . . .Values: $35 up

Struck on normal or abnormal blanks, or planchets (III-G)

Half on dime
planchet III-G-10

Cent on dime
planchet III-G-10

Half on quarter
planchet III-G-10

This section includes coins struck on either a blank, as it comes from the blanking press, or as a planchet that has passed through the upsetting mill. Added to this section are those planchets which are normal until they are struck by the wrong dies. These differ from the wrong stock planchets because the wrong stock planchets are already a variety before they are struck.

III-G-1 Struck on a Type 1 Blank (IWE), Rarity Level: 4-6 . . . . .Values: $10 up
III-G-2 Struck on a Type 2 Planchet (I), Rarity Level: 1 . . . . .Values: No Extra Value
III-G-3 Struck on a Purchased Planchet (I), Rarity Level: 1 . . . . .Values: No Extra Value
III-G-4 Struck on a Mint-Made Planchet (I), Rarity Level: 1 . . . . .Values: No Extra Value
III-G-5 Struck on an Adjustment-Marked Planchet (I), Rarity Level: 4-7 . . . . Values: Minimal, and may
    reduce value of coin in some cases
III-G-6 Struck on a Hardness Test-Marked Planchet (I), Rarity Level: 6-7 . . . . .Values: $10 up

III-G-7 Wrong Planchet or Metal on a Half Cent Planchet (IE), Rarity Level: 5-7. . . . . .Values: $100 up
III-G-8 Wrong Planchet or Metal on a Cent Planchet (IE), Rarity Level: 3-6 . . . . .Values: $25 up
III-G-9 Wrong Planchet or Metal on a Nickel Planchet (E), Rarity Level: 4-6. . . . . .Values: $35 up
III-G-10 Wrong Planchet or Metal on a Dime Planchet (E), Rarity Level: 4-6 . . . . .Values: $50 up
III-G-11 Wrong Planchet or Metal on a Quarter Planchet (E), Rarity Level: 4-6. . . . . .Values: $100 up
III-G-12 Wrong Planchet or Metal on a Half Dollar Planchet (E), Rarity Level: 6-7 . . . . .Values: $500 up
III-G-13 Wrong Planchet or Metal on a Dollar Planchet (E), Rarity Level: 7 . . . . .Values: $500 up
III-G-14 Wrong Planchet or Metal on a Gold Planchet (E), Rarity Level: 7 . . . . .Values: $1000 up
III-G-15 Struck on a Wrong Series Planchet (IE), Rarity Level: 6-7. . . . . .Values: $1500 up
III-G-16 U.S. Coin Struck on a Foreign Planchet (E), Rarity Level: 5-7. . . . . .Values: $35 up
III-G-17 Foreign Coin Struck on a U.S. Planchet (E), Rarity Level: 6-7 . . . . .Values: $50 up
III-G-18 Foreign Coin Struck on a Wrong Foreign Planchet (E), Rarity Level: 6-7 . . . . .Values: $50 up
III-G-19 Struck on a Medal Planchet (E), Rarity Level: 6-7 . . . . .Values: $100 up
III-G-20 Medal Struck on a Coin Planchet (IE), Rarity Level: 3-5 . . . . .Values: $10 up
III-G-21 Struck on an Official Sample Planchet (IE), Rarity Level: Unknown . . . . . .Values: No Value Established
III-G-22 Struck Intentionally on a Wrong Planchet (I), Rarity Level: 6-7 . . Values: Mainly struck as Presentation
    Pieces, full numismatic value
III-G-23 Non-Proof Struck on a Proof Planchet (IE), Rarity Level: 6-7 . . . . .Values: $500 up

Struck on coin metal strip (III-H)

Pieces of the coin metal strip do manage at times to escape into the coin press.

III-H-1 (See I-H-1 Punched Coin Metal Strip), Rarity Level: Impossible. . . . . .Values: -
III-H-2 Struck on Chopped Coin Metal Strip (E), Rarity Level: 6-7 . . . . .Values: $25 up

Die adjustment strikes (III-I)

As the dies are set up and adjusted in the coin press, variations in the strike occur until the dies are properly set. Test strikes are normally scrapped, but on occasion reach circulation.

III-I-1 Die Adjustment Strike (IE), Rarity Level: 5-6. . . . . .Values: $35 up
III-I-2 Edge Strike (E), Rarity Level: 5-6 . . . . .Values: $10 to $20 and up
III-I-3 Weak Strike (W), Rarity Level: 1 . . . . .Values: No Extra Value
III-I-4 Strong Strike (IWE), Rarity Level: 1. . . . . .Values: No value except for the premium
    that might be paid for a well struck coin
III-I-5 Jam Strike (IE), Rarity Level: 7 . . . . .Values: $50 up
III-I-6 Trial Piece Strike (I), Rarity Level: 6-7. . . . . .Values: $100 up
III-I-7 Edge-Die Adjustment Strike (I), Rarity Level: 5-7 . . . . .Values: $5 up
III-I-8 Uniface Strike (I), Rarity Level 7 . . . . .Values: $50 up

Indented, brockage and counter-brockage strikes (III-J)

Indented strike   Counter-brockage strike   Capped die strike
III-J-1   III-J-11   III-J-15

Indented and uniface strikes involve an extra unstruck planchet between one of the dies and the planchet being struck. Brockage strikes involve a struck coin between one of the dies and the planchet and a counter-brockage requires a brockage coin between one of the dies and the planchet.

A cap, or capped die strike results when a coin sticks to the die and is squeezed around it in the shape of a bottle cap.

III-J-1 Indented Strike (W), Rarity Level: 3-6. . . . . .Values: $5 up
III-J-2 Uniface Strike (W), Rarity Level: 3-5 . . . . .Values: $15 up
III-J-3 Indented Strike By a Smaller Planchet (WE), Rarity Level: 5-7 . . . . .Values: $100 up

III-J-4 Indented Second Strike (W), Rarity Level: 3-5 . . . . Values: $10 up, about the same as a regular double strike of comparable size

III-J-5 Partial Brockage Strike (W), Rarity Level: 3-6. . . . . .Values: $15 up

III-J-6 Full Brockage Strike (W), Rarity Level: 3-6. . . . . .Values: $5 up

III-J-7 Brockage Strike of a Smaller Coin (WE), Rarity Level: 6-7 . . . . .Values: $200 up

III-J-8 Brockage Strike of a Struck Coin Fragment (WE), Rarity Level: 4-6 . . . . .Values: $5 up

III-J-9 Brockage Second Strike (WE), Rarity Level: 3-5. . . . . .Values: $5 up

III-J-10 Partial Counter-Brockage Strike (WE), Rarity Level: 3-5. . . . . .Values: $10 up

III-J-11 Full Counter-Brockage Strike (WE), Rarity Level: 5-7. . . . . .Values: $100 up

III-J-12 Counter-Brockage Second Strike (WE), Rarity Level: 4-6. . . . . .Values: $10 up

III-J-13 Full Brockage-Counter-Brockage Strike (WE), Rarity Level: 6-7. . . . . .Values: $150 up

III-J-14 Multiple Brockage or Counter-Brockage Strike (WE), Rarity Level: 5-7 . . . . .Values: $100 up

III-J-15 Capped Die Strike (WE), Rarity Level: 6-7 . . . . .Values: $500 up

III-J-16 Reversed Capped Die Strike (WE), Rarity Level: 7 . . . . .Values: $1,000 up

Struck through abnormal objects (III-K)

Struck through cloth
III-K-1

Struck through a filled die
III-K-4

Struck through a
dropped filling III-K-5

This section covers most of the objects or materials which might come between the planchet and the die and be struck into the surface of the coin. Unless noted, the materials - even the soft ones - are driven into the surface of the coin.

III-K-1 Struck Through Cloth (IWE), Rarity Level: 3-6. . . . . .Values: $35 up

III-K-2 Struck Through Wire (IWE), Rarity Level: 3-6 . . . . .Values: $5 up

III-K-3 Struck Through Thread (IWE), Rarity Level: 3-6. . . . . .Values: $5 up

III-K-4 Struck Through Dirt-and-Grease-Filled Die (IWE), Rarity Level: 1-4
. . . . Values: 10 cents to 25 cents up, but no value on a worn or circulated coin

III-K-5 Struck Through a Dropped Filling (IWE), Rarity Level: 5-6 . . . . Values: $10 up

III-K-6 Struck Through Wrong Metal Fragments (IWE), Rarity Level: 4-6 . . . . .Values: $1 up

III-K-7 Struck Through an Unstruck Planchet Fragment (IWE), Rarity Level: 3-5 . . . . .Values: $1 up

III-K-8 Struck Through a Rim Burr (IWE), Rarity Level: 3-5. . . . . Values: $1 to $2 and up

III-K-9 Struck Through plit-Off Reeding (IWE), Rarity Level: 5-6. . . . . .Values: $25 up

III-K-10 Struck Through a Feed Finger (IWE), Rarity Level: 5-7 . . . . Values: $25 to $50 and up

III-K-11 Struck Through Miscellaneous Objects (IWE), Rarity Level: 4-6 . . . . .Values: $1 up

III-K-12 Struck Through Progression (IWE), Rarity Level: 4-6 . . . . .Values: $1 up

Note: Some 1987 through 1994 quarters are found without mintmarks, classed as III-K-4, a Filled Die. Values depend on market conditions. Filled dies have value ONLY on current, uncirculated grade coins.

Double strikes (III-L)

Only coins which receive two or more strikes by the die pair fall in this section and are identified by the fact that both sides of the coin are affected. Unless some object interferes, an equal area of both sides of the coin will be equally doubled.

The exception is the second strike with a loose die, which will double only one side of a coin, but is a rare form usually occurring only on proofs. A similar effect is flat field doubling from die chatter.

III-L-1 Close Centered Double Strike (WE), Rarity Level: 4-6 . . . . .Values: $15 up

III-L-2 Rotated Second Strike Over a Centered First Strike (WE), Rarity Level: 4-6 . . . . .Values: $15 up

III-L-3 Off-Center Second Strike Over a Centered First Strike (WE), Rarity Level: 4-6. . . . . .Values: $15 up

Off-center second strike over centered first strike III-L-3

Non-overlapping double strike III-L-8

Multiple strike III-L-16

Chain strike III-L-10

III-L-4 Off-Center Second Strike Over an Off-Center First Strike (WE), Rarity Level: 4-6. . . . . . . .Values: $10 up
III-L-5 Off-Center Second Strike Over a Broadstrike (WE), Rarity Level: 5-6. . . . . .Values: $20 up
III-L-6 Centered Second Strike Over an Off-Center First Strike (WE), Rarity Level: 5-6. . . . . . . .Values: $50 up
III-L-7 Obverse Struck Over Reverse (WE), Rarity Level: 5-6. . . . . .Values: $25 up
III-L-8 Nonoverlapping Double Strike (WE), Rarity Level: 5-6. . . . . .Values: $20 up
III-L-9 Struck Over a Different Denomination or Series (WE), Rarity Level: 6 . . . . Values: $300 and up
III-L-10 Chain Strike (WE), Rarity Level: 6 . . . . . Values: $300 up for the pair of coins that were struck together
III-L-11 Second-Strike Doubling From a Loose Die (W), Rarity Level: 6-7 . . . . .Values: $200 up
III-L-12 Second-Strike Doubling From a Loose Screw Press Die (W), Rarity Level: 5-6 . . . . . .Values: $100 up
III-L-13 Second Strike on an Edge Strike (WE), Rarity Level: 5-6 . . . . .Values: $20 up
III-L-14 Folded Planchet Strike (WE), Rarity Level: 5-7. . . . . .Values: $100 up
III-L-15 Triple Strike (WE), Rarity Level: 6-7. . . . . .Values: $100 up
III-L-16 Multiple Strike (WE), Rarity Level: 6-7. . . . . .Values: $200 up
III-L-17 U.S. Coin Struck Over a Struck Foreign Coin (WE), Rarity Level: 6-7. . . . . .Values: $300 up
III-L-18 Foreign Coin Struck Over a Struck U.S. Coin (WE), Rarity Level: 6-7 . . . . .Values: $400 up
III-L-19 Foreign Coin Struck Over a Struck Foreign Coin (WE), Rarity Level: 7 . . . . .Values: $500 up
III-L-20 Double Strike on Scrap or Junk (E), Rarity Level: 6 . . . . .Values: $50 up
III-L-21 Struck on a Struck Token or Medal (E), Rarity Level: 5-6 . . . . .Values: $100 up
III-L-22 Double-Struck Edge Motto or Design (E), Rarity Level: 6-7 . . . . .Values: $200 up
III-L-23 One Edge Motto or Design Struck Over Another (E), Rarity Level: 7. . . . . .Values: $300 up
III-L-24 Flat Field Doubling (W), Rarity Level: 2-3 . . . . .Values: $1 to $5
III-L-25 Territorial Struck over Struck U.S. Coin: (I) Rarity Level: 6-7 . . . . .Values: $200 up
III-L-26 Pattern Struck over Struck U.S. Coin: (I) Rarity Level: 6-7 . . . . .Values: $200 up
III-L-27 Pattern Struck over Struck Pattern:(I) Rarity Level 6-7 . . . . .Values: $200 up
III-L-28 Pattern Struck Over Foreign Coin:(I) Rarity Level 6-7 . . . . Values - $200 up

Collar striking varieties (III-M)

The collar is often referred to as the "Third Die," and is involved in a number of forms of misstrikes. The collar normally rises around the planchet, preventing it from squeezing sideways between the dies and at the same time forming the reeding on reeded coins.

If the collar is out of position or tilted, a partial collar strike results; if completely missing, it causes a broadstrike; if the planchet is not entirely between the dies, an off-center strike.

Flanged partial collar III-M-1

Struck off center
10 to 30 percent III-M-7

Struck off center
31 to 70 percent III-M-8

Struck off center
71 percent or more
III-M-9

III-M-1 Flanged Partial Collar Strike (WE), Rarity Level: 5-6. . . . . Values: $20 up
III-M-2 Reversed Flanged Partial Collar Strike (WE), Rarity Level: 6-7 . . . . Values: $35 up
III-M-3 Tilted Partial Collar Strike (WE), Rarity Level: 5-6 . . . . Values: $20 up
III-M-4 Centered Broadstrike (WE), Rarity Level: 5-6 . . . . Values: $5 up
III-M-5 Uncentered Broadstrike (WE), Rarity Level: 5 . . . . Values: $3 up
III-M-6 Reversed Broadstrike (WE), Rarity Level: 6 . . . . Values: $10 up
III-M-7 Struck Off-Center 10-30% (W), Rarity Level: 3-6 . . . . Values: $3 up
III-M-8 Struck Off-Center 31-70% (W), Rarity Level: 4-6 . . . . Values: $5 up
III-M-9 Struck Off-Center 71% or More (W), Rarity Level: 3-5 . . . . Values: $2 up
III-M-10 Rotated Multi-sided Planchet Strike (W), Rarity Level: 5-6 . . . . Values: $10 up
III-M-11 Wire Edge Strike (IWE), Rarity Level: 1-2 . . . . Values: No Extra Value
III-M-12 Struck With the Collar Too High (WE), Rarity Level: 6-7. . . . . Values: $20 up
III-M-13 Off-Center Slide Strike (W), Rarity Level: 3-6 . . . . Values: $4 up

Misaligned and rotated (die) strike varieties (III-N)

Misaligned die III-N-1

Normal rotation   *90 degrees*   *180 degrees*

One (rarely both) of the dies may be Offset Misaligned, off to one side, or may be tilted (Vertically Misaligned). One die may either have been installed so that it is turned in relation to the other die, or may turn in the holder, or the shank may break allowing the die face to rotate in relation to the opposing die.

Vertical misaligned dies are rarely found, and like rotated dies, find only limited collector interest. Ninety and 180 degree rotations are the most popular. Rotations of 14 degrees or less have no value. The 1989-D Congress dollar is found with a nearly

180 degree rotated reverse, currently retailing for around $2,000. Only about 30 have been reported to date.

III-N-1 Offset Die Misalignment Strike (WE), Rarity Level: 3-5 . . . . .Values: $2 up

III-N-2 Vertical Die Misalignment Strike (WE), Rarity Level: 4-6 . . . . .Values: $1 up

III-N-3 Rotated Die Strike - 15 to 45 Degrees (IWE), Rarity Level: 4-6 . . . . .Values: $2 up

III-N-4 Rotated Die Strike - 46 to 135 Degrees (IWE), Rarity Level: 5-6 . . . . .Values: $10 up

III-N-5 Rotated Die Strike - 136 to 180 Degrees (IWE), Rarity Level: 5-6 . . . . .Values: $25 up

Lettered and design edge strike varieties (III-O)

Overlapping edge letters III-O-1

Early U.S. coins and a number of foreign coins have either lettered edges, or designs on the edge of the coin. Malfunctions of the application of the motto or design to the edge fall in this section.

III-O-1 Overlapping Edge Motto or Design (WE), Rarity Level: 3-4 . . . . Values: $5 to $10 and up

III-O-2 Wrong Edge Motto or Design (WE), Rarity Level: 5-6-7 . . . . .Values: $50 up

III-O-3 Missing Edge Motto, Design or Security Edge (IWE), Rarity Level: 5-6-7 . . . . .Values: $50 up

III-O-4 Jammed Edge Die Strike (W), Rarity Level: 6. . . . . .Values: $10 up

III-O-5 Misplaced Segment of an Edge Die (E), Rarity Level: 4-7 . . . . .Values: $25 up

III-O-6 Reeded Edge Struck Over a Lettered Edge (IE), Rarity Level: 3-6 . . . . Values: No Extra Value up

Defective strikes and mismatched dies (III-P)

The final section of the Striking Division covers coins which are not properly struck for reasons other than those in previous classes, such as coins struck with mismatched (muled) dies. The mismatched die varieties must be taken on a case by case basis, while the otherclasses presently have little collector demand or premium.

III-P-1 Defective Strike (WE), Rarity Level: 1. . . . . .Values: No Extra Value

III-P-2 Mismatched Die Strike (E), Rarity Level: 4-7 . . . . .Values: $25 up

III-P-3 Single-Strike Proof (WE), Rarity Level: 4-5 . . . . .Values: Minimal

III-P-4 Single Die-Proof Strike (IE), Rarity Level: 5-6 . . . . .Values: $100 up

III-P-5 Reversed Die Strike (I), Rarity Level: 4-5 . . . . .Values: No Extra Value to Minimal

Official Mint modifications
Division IV

Several mint produced varieties occur after the coin has been struck, resulting in the addition of the fourth division to my PDS System. Since most of these coins are either unique or are special varieties, each one must be taken on a case by case basis. All classes listed here are by definition intentional.

I have not listed values as the coins falling in these classes which are sold through regular numismatic channels, are cataloged with the regular issues or are covered in specialized catalogs in their particular area.

Matte proofs (IV-A)

Matte proofs IV-A-1

Matte proofs as a section include several of the forms of proof coins which have the striking characteristics of a mirror proof but have been treated AFTER striking to give them a grainy, non-reflective surface.

IV-A-1 Matte Proof (I), Rarity Level: 3-5 . . . . Values: Normal Numismatic Value
IV-A-2 Matte Proof on One Side (I), Rarity Level: 7 . . . . Values: Normal Numismatic Value
IV-A-3 Sandblast Proof (I), Rarity Level: 4-6 . . . . Values: Normal Numismatic Value

Additional engraving (IV-B)

Counterstamp IV-B-3

This section includes any added markings which are placed on the struck coin and struck coins which later were cut into pieces for various purposes. The warning is repeated: Anything done to a coin after the strike is extremely difficult t o authenticate and is much easier to fake than a die struck coin.

IV-B-1 Counterstamp and Countermark (I), Rarity Level: 3-6 . . . . Values: Normal Numismatic Value
IV-B-2 Perforated and Cut Coins (I), Rarity Level: 4-6 . . . . Values: Normal Numismatic Value

Restrikes (IV-C)

Restrike with new dies IV-C-7

Restrikes cover a complicated mixture of official use of dies from a variety of sources. Whether or not some were officially sanctioned is always a problem for the collector.

IV-C-1) Restrike on the Same Denomination Planchet (I), Rarity Level: 4-6. . .Values: Normal Numismatic Value

IV-C-2 Restrike on a Different Denomination or Series Planchet (I), Rarity Level: 4-6
. . . . .Values: Normal Numismatic Value

IV-C-3 Restrike on a Foreign Coin (I), Rarity Level: 6-7 . . . . .Values: Normal Numismatic Value

IV-C-4 Restrike on a Token or Medal (I), Rarity Level: 5-6 . . . . .Values: Normal Numismatic Value

IV-C-5 Restruck With the Original Dies (I), Rarity Level: 4-6 . . . . .Values: Normal Numismatic Value

IV-C-6 Restruck With Mismatched Dies (I), Rarity Level: 4-6 . . . . .Values: Normal Numismatic Value

IV-C-7 Copy Strike With New Dies (I), Rarity Level: 3-5 . . . . .Values: Normal Numismatic Value

IV-C-8 Fantasy Strike (I), Rarity Level: 4-6 . . . . .Values: Normal Numismatic Value

After strike modifications

Division V

This division includes both modifications that have value to collectors – and those that don't. I needed a couple of divisions to cover other things that happen to coins to aid in cataloging them. This avoids the false conclusion that an unlisted coin is quite rare, when the exact opposite is more likely to be the case.

Collectible modifications after strike (V-A)

Mint modification V-A-8

This section includes those classes having to do with deliberate modifications of the coin done with a specific purpose or intent which makes them of some value to collectors. Quite often these pieces were made specifically to sell to collectors, or at least to the public under the guise of being collectible.

V-A-1 Screw Thaler, Rarity Level: 5-6 . . . . .Values: Normal Numismatic Value
V-A-2 Love Token, Rarity Level: 3-6 . . . . .Values: $10 up
V-A-3 Satirical or Primitive Engraving, Rarity Level: 6-7 . . . . .Values: $5 up
V-A-4 Elongated Coin, Rarity Level: 2-7 . . . . Values: 50 cents to $1 and up
V-A-5 Coin Jewelry, Rarity Level: 2-5 . . . . .Values: $1 up
V-A-6 Novelty Coin, Rarity Level: 1-3 . . . . .Values: No Value up to $5 to $10
V-A-7 Toning, Rarity Level: 3-6 . . . . Values: No value up, depending on coloration. Easily faked
V-A-8 Mint Modification, Rarity Level: 4-7 . . . . Values: $5 up. Easily faked
V-A-9 Mint Packaging Mistake, Rarity Level: 5-7 . . . . Values: Nominal $1. Very easily faked

Alterations and damage after the strike (V-B)

Machine doubling damage V-B-1

This section includes those changes in a coin which have no collector value. In most cases their effect on the coin is to reduce or entirely eliminate any collector value - and in the case of counterfeits they are actually illegal to even own.

V -B-1 Machine Doubling Damage: *NOTE: Machine doubling damage is defined as: "Damage to a coin after the strike, due to die bounce or chatter or die displacement, showing on the struck coin as scrapes on the sides of the design elements, with portions of the coin metal in the relief elements either displaced sideways or downward, depending on the direction of movement of the loose die."* Machine doubling damage, or MDD, is by far the most common form of doubling found on almost any coin in the world.
Rarity Level: 0 . . . . Values: Reduces the coin's value
V-B-2 Accidental or Deliberate Damage, Rarity Level: 0 . . . . Values: Reduces the coin's value
V-B-3 Test Cut or Mark, Rarity Level: 0 . . . . .Values: Reduces value of coin to face or bullion value
V-B-4 Alteration, Rarity Level: 0 . . . . .Values: Reduces value to face or bullion value
V-B-5 Whizzing, Rarity Level: 0. . . . . . Values: Reduces value sharply and may reduce it to face or bullion value
V-B-6 Counterfeit, Copy, Facsimile, Forgery or Fake, Rarity Level: 0 . . Values: No Value and may be illegal to own
V-B-7 Planchet Deterioration. Very common on copper-plated zinc cents. Rarity level: 0 . . . . .Values: No Value

COLONIAL COINAGE

MARYLAND
Lord Baltimore

PENNY (DENARIUM)

KM# 1 • Copper • Obv. Legend: CAECILIVS Dns TERRAE MARIAE

Date	AG	Good	VG	Fine	VF	XF	Unc
(1659)							
5 known	—	—	—	—	—	100,000	—

Note: Stack's Auction 5-04, proof realized $241,500

4 PENCE (GROAT)

KM# 2 • Silver • Obv: Large bust **Obv. Legend:** CAECILIVS Dns TERRAE MARIAE **Rev:** Large shield

Date	AG	Good	VG	Fine	VF	XF	Unc
(1659)	1,250	1,850	3,500	6,250	13,500	20,000	—

KM# 3 • Silver • Obv: Small bust **Obv. Legend:** CAECILIVS Dns TERRAE MARIAE **Rev:** Small shield

Date	AG	Good	VG	Fine	VF	XF	Unc
(1659) unique	—	—	—	—	—	—	—

Note: Norweb $26,400

6 PENCE

KM# 4 • Silver • Obv: Small bust **Obv. Legend:** CAECILIVS Dns TERRAE MARIAE **Note:** Known in two other rare small-bust varieties and two rare large-bust varieties.

Date	AG	Good	VG	Fine	VF	XF	Unc
(1659)	850	1,400	2,400	4,900	9,000	15,000	—

SHILLING

KM# 6 • Silver • Obv. Legend: CAECILIVS Dns TERRAE MARIAE **Note:** Varieties exist; one is very rare.

Date	AG	Good	VG	Fine	VF	XF	Unc
(1659)	1,100	1,800	3,000	5,750	13,500	20,000	—

MASSACHUSETTS
New England

3 PENCE

KM# 1 • Silver • Obv: NE **Rev:** III

Date	AG	Good	VG	Fine	VF	XF	Unc
(1652) Unique	—	—	—	—	—	—	—

Note: Massachusetts Historical Society specimen

6 PENCE

KM# 2 • Silver • Obv: NE **Rev:** VI

Date	Good	VG	Fine	VF	XF	Unc
(1652)						
8 known	25,000	50,000	90,000	175,000	—	—

Note: Garrett $75,000

SHILLING

KM# 3 • Silver • Obv: NE **Rev:** XII

Date	Good	VG	Fine	VF	XF	Unc
(1652)	35,000	65,000	100,000	200,000	—	—

Oak Tree

2 PENCE

KM# 7 • Silver • Note: Small 2 and large 2 varieites exist

Date	AG	Good	VG	Fine	VF	XF	Unc
1662	—	500	900	2,000	3,850	6,500	15,000

3 PENCE

KM# 8 • Silver • Note: Two types of legends.

Date	AG	Good	VG	Fine	VF	XF	Unc
1652	350	600	1,000	2,500	5,500	9,000	—

6 PENCE

KM# 9 • Silver • Note: Three types of legends.

Date	AG	Good	VG	Fine	VF	XF	Unc
1652	400	900	1,100	2,700	6,400	9,500	25,000

SHILLING

KM# 10 • Silver • Note: Two types of legends.

Date	AG	Good	VG	Fine	VF	XF	Unc
1652	350	650	1,100	2,600	5,400	8,800	25,000

Pine Tree

3 PENCE

KM# 11 • Silver • Obv: Tree without berries

Date	AG	Good	VG	Fine	VF	XF	Unc
1652	250	500	700	1,650	3,000	5,600	17,500

KM# 12 • Silver • Obv: Tree with berries

Date	AG	Good	VG	Fine	VF	XF	Unc
1652	250	500	700	1,650	3,200	5,750	18,500

6 PENCE

KM# 13 • Silver • Obv: Tree without berries; "spiney tree"

Date	AG	Good	VG	Fine	VF	XF	Unc
1652	400	700	1,400	2,000	3,750	6,500	20,000

KM# 14 • Silver • Obv: Tree with berries

Date	AG	Good	VG	Fine	VF	XF	Unc
1652	300	500	800	1,750	3,500	6,250	18,000

SHILLING

KM# 15 • Silver • Note: Large planchet. Many varieties exist; some are very rare.

Date	AG	Good	VG	Fine	VF	XF	Unc
1652	350	600	950	2,000	4,350	7,500	20,000

KM# 16 • Silver • Note: Small planchet; large dies. All examples are thought to be contemporary fabrications.

Date	AG	Good	VG	Fine	VF	XF	Unc
1652	—	—	—	—	—	—	—

KM# 17 • Silver • Note: Small planchet; small dies. Many varieties exist; some are very rare.

Date	AG	Good	VG	Fine	VF	XF	Unc
1652	285	525	800	1,700	3,750	6,950	22,500

Willow Tree

3 PENCE

KM# 4 • Silver •

Date		AG	Good	VG	Fine	VF	XF	Unc
1652	3 known	—	—	—	—	—	—	—

6 PENCE

KM# 5 • Silver •

Date	AG	Good	VG	Fine	VF	XF
1652						
14 known	9,000	17,500	30,000	57,500	125,000	200,000

SHILLING

KM# 6 • Silver •

Date	AG	Good	VG	Fine	VF	XF
1652	9,800	18,000	34,000	80,000	150,000	225,000

NEW JERSEY
St. Patrick or Mark Newby

FARTHING

KM# 1 • Copper • Obv. Legend: FLOREAT
REX **Rev. Legend:** QUIESCAT PLEBS

Date	AG	Good	VG	Fine	VF	XF	Unc
(1682)	70.00	125	285	700	2,250	4,500	—

Note: One very rare variety is known with reverse legend:
QUIESAT PLEBS

KM# 1a • Silver • Obv. Legend: FLOREAT REX
Rev. Legend: QUIESCAT PLEBS

Date	AG	Good	VG	Fine	VF	XF	Unc
(1682)	800	1,500	2,200	4,500	8,000	12,500	—

HALFPENNY

KM# 2 • Copper • Obv. Legend: FLOREAT
REX **Rev. Legend:** ECCE GREX

Date	AG	Good	VG	Fine	VF	XF	Unc
(1682)	180	365	850	1,650	4,000	10,500	—

EARLY AMERICAN TOKENS
American Plantations

1/24 REAL

KM# Tn5.1 • Tin • Obv. Legend: ET HIB REX

Date	AG	Good	VG	Fine	VF	XF	Unc
(1688)	125	200	300	450	750	2,000	—

KM# Tn5.3 • Tin • Rev: Horizontal 4

Date	AG	Good	VG	Fine	VF	XF	Unc
(1688)	275	400	900	1,500	2,700	5,000	—

KM# Tn5.4 • Tin • Obv. Legend: ET HIB REX

Date	AG	Good	VG	Fine	VF	XF	Unc
(1688)	—	250	450	750	1,400	2,650	9,000

KM# Tn6 • Tin • Rev: Arms of Scotland left,
Ireland right

Date	AG	Good	VG	Fine	VF	XF	Unc
(1688)	450	750	1,250	2,000	3,000	6,500	—

KM# Tn5.2 • Tin • Obv: Rider's head left of "B" in
legend **Note:** Restrikes made in 1828 from two
obverse dies.

Date	AG	Good	VG	Fine	VF	XF	Unc
(1828)	75.00	110	175	275	500	1,000	—

Elephant

KM# Tn1.1 • 15.5500 g., Copper • Note: Thick
planchet.

Date	AG	Good	VG	Fine	VF	XF	Unc
(1664)	125	200	300	500	1,000	1,750	3,850

KM# Tn1.2 • Copper • Note: Thin planchet.

Date	AG	Good	VG	Fine	VF	XF	Unc
(1664)	175	300	500	850	3,000	5,500	11,750

KM# Tn2 • Copper • Rev: Diagonals tie shield

Date	AG	Good	VG	Fine	VF	XF	Unc
(1664)	250	450	650	2,250	6,500	10,000	17,500

KM# Tn3 • Copper • Rev: Sword right side of shield

Date	AG	Good	VG	Fine	VF	XF	Unc
(1664)							
3 known	—	—	—	—12,500	—	—	

Note: Norweb $1,320

KM# Tn4 • Copper • Rev. Legend: LON DON

Date	AG	Good	VG	Fine	VF	XF	Unc
(1684)	340	650	1,000	2,250	4,000	7,000	17,500

KM# Tn7 • Copper • Rev. Legend: NEW ENGLAND

Date	Good	VG	Fine	VF	XF	Unc
(1694)						
2 known	—	50,000	75,000	95,000	140,000	—

Note: Norweb $25,300

KM# Tn8.1 • Copper • Rev. Legend: CAROLINA (PROPRIETORS)

Date	Good	VG	Fine	VF	XF	Unc
(1694)						
5 known	—	4,750	6,500	14,000	22,500	—

Note: Norweb $35,200

KM# Tn8.2 • Copper • Rev. Legend: CAROLINA (PROPRIETORS, O over E)

Date	AG	Good	VG	Fine	VF	XF	Unc
1694	1,300	2,500	4,000	6,000	12,000	17,500	—

Note: Norweb $17,600

Gloucester

KM# Tn15 • Copper • Obv. Legend: GLOVCESTER COVRTHOVSE VIRGINIA **Rev. Legend:** RIGHAVLT DAWSON.ANNO.DOM.1714.

Date	AG	Good	VG	Fine	VF	XF	Unc
(1714)							
2 known	—	—	—	—	—	—	—

Note: Garrett $36,000

Hibernia-Voce Populi

FARTHING

KM# Tn21.1 • Copper • Note: Large letters

Date	AG	Good	VG	Fine	VF	XF	Unc
1760	125	200	325	600	1,600	3,000	8,500

KM# Tn21.2 • Copper • Note: Small letters

Date	AG	Good	VG	Fine	VF	XF	Unc
1760							
extremely rare	—	650	1,250	2,750	7,500	13,500	—

Note: Norweb $5,940.

HALFPENNY

KM# Tn22 • Copper •

Date	AG	Good	VG	Fine	VF	XF	Unc
1700							
Extremely rare	—	—	—	—	—	—	—

Note: Date is in error; ex-Roper $575. Norweb $577.50. Stack's Americana, VF, $2,900

Date	AG	Good	VG	Fine	VF	XF	Unc
1760	40.00	70.00	135	175	365	675	2,500
1760	50.00	80.00	135	195	425	775	3,500

Note: legend VOOE POPULI

Date	AG	Good	VG	Fine	VF	XF	Unc
1760 P below bust	65.00	100.00	185	350	700	1,750	8,000
1760 P in front of bust	55.00	90.00	170	325	600	1,400	6,500

Higley or Granby

KM# Tn16 • Copper • Obv. Legend:
CONNECTICVT **Note:** THE VALVE OF THREE
PENCE.

Date	AG	Good	VG	Fine	VF	XF	Unc
1737	—	10,000	18,000	40,000	80,000	—	—

Note: Garrett $16,000

KM# Tn17 • Copper • Obv. Legend: THE
VALVE OF THREE PENCE **Rev. Legend:** I AM
GOOD COPPER

Date	Good	VG	Fine	VF	XF	Unc
1737						
2 known	11,000	20,000	40,000	85,000	—	—

Note: ex-Norweb $6,875

KM# Tn18.1 • Copper • Obv. Legend: VALUE
ME AS YOU PLEASE **Rev. Legend:** I AM GOOD
COPPER

Date	AG	Good	VG	Fine	VF	XF
1737	6,500	10,000	18,000	40,000	80,000	—

KM# Tn18.2 • Copper • Obv. Legend:
VALVE.ME.AS.YOU.PLEASE. **Rev. Legend:** I AM
GOOD COPPER.

Date	AG	Good	VG	Fine	VF	XF	Unc
1737							
2 known	—	—	—	—	275,000	—	—

KM# Tn19 • Copper • Rev: Broad axe

Date	Good	VG	Fine	VF	XF	Unc
(1737)	10,000	18,000	35,000	125,000	—	—

Note: Garrett $45,000

1739						
5 known	—	—	—	—	—	—

Note: Eliasberg $12,650. Oechsner $9,900. Steinberg
(holed) $4,400.

KM# Tn20 • Copper • Obv. Legend: THE
WHEELE GOES ROUND **Rev:** J CUT MY WAY
THROUGH

Date	Good	VG	Fine	VF	XF	Unc
(1737) unique	—	—	150,000	—	—	—

Note: Roper $60,500

New Yorke

KM# Tn9 • Brass • Obv. Legend:
NEW.YORK.IN.AMERICA

Date	AG	Good	VG	Fine	VF	XF	Unc
1700	1,800	3,500	5,500	13,000	22,500	35,000	—

KM# Tn9a • White Metal • Obv. Legend:
NEW.YORK.IN.AMERICA

Date	Good	VG	Fine	VF	XF	Unc
1700						
4 known	—	6,000	15,000	28,000	50,000	—

Pitt

FARTHING

KM# Tn23 • Copper •

Date	Good	VG	Fine	VF	XF	Unc
1766	—	—	7,500	22,000	35,000	—

HALFPENNY

KM# Tn24 • Copper •

Date	AG	Good	VG	Fine	VF	XF	Unc
1766	140	250	400	700	1,500	2,750	7,500

KM# Tn24a • Copper Silvered •

Date	AG	Good	VG	Fine	VF	XF	Unc
1766	—	—	—	—	2,250	5,000	12,000

ROYAL PATENT COINAGE
Hibernia

FARTHING

KM# 20 • Copper • Note: Pattern.

Date	AG	Good	VG	Fine	VF	XF	Unc
1722	135	235	375	500	1,000	2,600	7,750

KM# 24 • Copper • Obv: 1722 obverse **Obv. Legend:** ...D:G:REX.

Date	AG	Good	VG	Fine	VF	XF	Unc
1723	20.00	40.00	60.00	90.00	150	350	—

KM# 25 • Copper • Obv. Legend: DEI • GRATIA • REX •

Date	AG	Good	VG	Fine	VF	XF	Unc
1723	25.00	45.00	60.00	180	300	550	950
1724	—	90.00	125	225	600	1,350	3,500

KM# 25a • Silver •

Date	AG	Good	VG	Fine	VF	XF	Unc
1723	—	—	1,600	2,250	4,000	5,500	10,000

HALFPENNY

KM# 21 • Copper • Obv: Bust right **Obv. Legend:** GEORGIUS.DEI . GRATIA.REX. **Rev:** Harp left, head left **Rev. Legend:** .HIBERNIA . 1722.

Date	AG	Good	VG	Fine	VF	XF	Unc
1722	50.00	90.00	110	160	325	700	1,750

KM# 22 • Copper • Obv: Bust right **Obv. Legend:** GEORGIVS D:G:REX **Rev:** Harp left, head right **Rev. Legend:** HIBERNIAE. **Note:** "Rocks Reverse" pattern.

Date	AG	Good	VG	Fine	VF	XF	Unc
1722	—	—	—	2,750	3,850	8,500	—

KM# 23.1 • Copper • Rev: Harp right

Date	AG	Good	VG	Fine	VF	XF	Unc
1722	35.00	60.00	80.00	120	285	600	1,400
1723	20.00	35.00	45.00	75.00	190	280	800
1723/22	35.00	60.00	80.00	150	375	750	1,750
1724	25.00	50.00	90.00	160	360	825	2,000

KM# 23.2 • Copper • Obv: DEII error in legend

Date	AG	Good	VG	Fine	VF	XF	Unc
1722	75.00	125	160	325	750	1,400	2,750

KM# 26 • Copper • Rev: Large head **Note:** Rare. Generally mint state only. Probably a pattern.

Date	AG	Good	VG	Fine	VF	XF	Unc
1723	—	—	—	—	—	—	—

KM# 27 • Copper • Rev: Continuous legend over head

Date	AG	Good	VG	Fine	VF	XF	Unc
1724	45.00	80.00	150	300	900	1,500	3,500

Rosa Americana

HALFPENNY

KM# 1 • **Copper** • **Obv. Legend:** D • G • REX •

Date	AG	Good	VG	Fine	VF	XF	Unc
1722	20.00	50.00	140	250	525	1,050	4,000

KM# 2 • **Copper** • **Obv:** Uncrowned rose **Obv. Legend:** DEI GRATIA REX. **Note:** Several varieties exist.

Date	AG	Good	VG	Fine	VF	XF	Unc
1722	50.00	90.00	135	250	450	950	3,500
1723	385	700	850	1,750	3,600	—	—

KM# 3 • **Copper** • **Rev. Legend:** VTILE DVLCI

Date	AG	Good	VG	Fine	VF	XF	Unc
1722	250	450	850	2,200	3,800	7,500	—

KM# 9 • **Copper** • **Rev:** Crowned rose

Date	AG	Good	VG	Fine	VF	XF	Unc
1723	45.00	85.00	110	165	425	1,000	4,500

PENNY

KM# 4 • **Copper** • **Rev. Legend:** UTILE DULCI **Note:** Several varieties exist.

Date	AG	Good	VG	Fine	VF	XF	Unc
1722	60.00	100.00	135	240	450	950	3,750

KM# 5 • **Copper** • **Note:** Several varieties exist. Also known in two rare pattern types with long hair ribbons, one with V's for U's on the obverse.

Date	AG	Good	VG	Fine	VF	XF	Unc
1722	18.00	35.00	150	275	750	1,350	5,600

KM# 10 • **Copper** • **Note:** Several varieties exist.

Date	AG	Good	VG	Fine	VF	XF	Unc
1723	40.00	75.00	110	175	425	900	3,600

KM# 12 • **Copper** • **Note:** Pattern.

Date	AG	Good	VG	Fine	VF	XF	Unc
1724 2 known	—	—	—	—	—	—	—

KM# 13 • **Copper** • **Rev. Legend:** ROSA:SINE:SPINA.

Date	AG	Good	VG	Fine	VF	XF	Unc
(1724) 5 known	—	—	—	—	—	—	—

Note: Norweb $2,035

KM# 14 • **Copper** • **Obv:** George II **Note:** Pattern.

Date	AG	Good	VG	Fine	VF	XF	Unc
1727 2 known	—	—	—	—	—	—	—

2 PENCE

KM# 6 • Copper • Rev: Motto with scroll

Date	AG	Good	VG	Fine	VF	XF	Unc
(1722)	80.00	150	200	425	700	1,200	6,250

KM# 7 • Copper • Rev: Motto without scroll

Date	AG	Good	VG	Fine	VF	XF	Unc
(1722) 3 known	—	—	—	—	—	—	—

KM# 8.1 • Copper • Obv: Period after REX **Rev:** Dated

Date	AG	Good	VG	Fine	VF	XF	Unc
1722	70.00	125	175	275	750	1,500	5,500

KM# 8.2 • Copper • Obv: Without period after REX

Date	AG	Good	VG	Fine	VF	XF	Unc
1722	70.00	125	175	275	775	1,600	6,000

KM# 11 • Copper • Obv: No stop after REX **Rev:** Stop after 1723 **Note:** Several varieties exist.

Date	AG	Good	VG	Fine	VF	XF	Unc
1723	65.00	120	160	285	550	1,200	3,500

KM# 15 • Copper • Note: Pattern. Two varieties exist; both extremely rare.

Date	AG	Good	VG	Fine	VF	XF	Unc
1724	—	—	—	—	—	—	—

Note: Stack's 5-05 choice AU realized $25,300. Ex-Garrett $5,775. Stack's Americana, XF, $10,925

KM# 16 • Copper • Obv: Bust left **Rev:** Crowned rose **Note:** Pattern.

Date	AG	Good	VG	Fine	VF	XF	Unc
1733							
4 known	—	—	—	—	—	—	—

Note: Norweb $19,800

Virginia Halfpenny

KM# Tn25.1 • Copper • Rev: Small 7s in date. **Note:** Struck on Irish halfpenny planchets.

Date	Good	VG	Fine	VF	XF	Unc	Proof
1773	—	—	—	—	—	—	22,000

KM# Tn25.2 • Copper • Obv: Period after GEORGIVS **Rev:** Varieties with 7 or 8 strings in harp

Date	AG	Good	VG	Fine	VF	XF	Unc
1773	30.00	50.00	70.00	110	235	425	1,000

KM# Tn25.3 • Copper • Obv: Without period after GEORGIVS **Rev:** Varieties with 6, 7 or 8 strings in harp

Date	AG	Good	VG	Fine	VF	XF	Unc
1773	35.00	60.00	75.00	135	275	500	1,250

KM# Tn25.4 • Copper • Obv: Without period after GEORGIVS **Rev:** 8 harp strings, dot on cross

Date	AG	Good	VG	Fine	VF	XF	Unc
1773	—	—	—	—	—	—	—

Note: ex-Steinberg $2,600

KM# Tn26 • **Silver** • **Note:** So-called "shilling" silver proofs.

Date	AG	Good	VG	Fine	VF	XF	Unc
1774 6 known	—	—	—	—	—	—	—

Note: Garrett $23,000

REVOLUTIONARY COINAGE
Continental "Dollar".

KM# EA5 • **Pewter** • **Obv. Legend:** CURENCY.

Date	Good	VG	Fine	VF	XF	Unc
1776	7,500	9,500	12,000	22,500	33,000	65,000

KM# EA5a • **Brass** • **Obv. Legend:** CURENCY. **Note:** Two varieties exist.

Date	Good	VG	Fine	VF	XF	Unc
1776	22,500	28,500	36,000	70,000	110,000	—

KM# EA5b • **Silver** • **Obv. Legend:** CURENCY.

Date	Good	VG	Fine	VF	XF	Unc
1776 unique	—	—	300,000	450,000	—	—

Note: Romano $99,000

KM# EA1 • **Pewter** • **Obv. Legend:** CURENCY.

Date	Good	VG	Fine	VF	XF	Unc
1776	7,500	9,350	12,000	21,000	32,500	70,000

KM# EA2 • **Pewter** • **Obv. Legend:** CURENCY, EG FECIT.

Date	Good	VG	Fine	VF	XF	Unc
1776	8,000	10,500	13,500	25,000	36,000	75,000

KM# EA2a • **Silver** • **Obv. Legend:** CURENCY, EG FECIT.

Date	Good	VG	Fine	VF	XF	Unc
1776 2 known	—	—	300,000	450,000	—	—

KM# EA3 • **Pewter** • **Obv. Legend:** CURRENCEY

Date	Good	VG	Fine	VF	XF	Unc
1776 extremely rare	—	—	—	—	100,000	—

KM# EA4 • **Pewter** • **Obv. Legend:** CURRENCY. **Rev:** Floral cross.

Date	Good	VG	Fine	VF	XF	Unc
1776 3 recorded	—	—	—	—	400,000	—

Note: Norweb $50,600. Johnson $25,300

STATE COINAGE
CONNECTICUT

KM# 1 • **Copper** • **Obv:** Bust facing right.

Date	AG	Good	VG	Fine	VF	XF	Unc
1785	35.00	55.00	90.00	200	650	1,750	—

KM# 2 • **Copper** • **Obv:** "African head."

Date	AG	Good	VG	Fine	VF	XF	Unc
1785	55.00	85.00	150	600	1,500	3,800	—

KM# 3.1 • Copper • Obv: Mailed bust facing left.

Date	AG	Good	VG	Fine	VF	XF	Unc
1785	125	220	375	750	1,800	3,850	—
1786	30.00	50.00	90.00	175	475	1,200	—
1787	30.00	50.00	85.00	160	450	1,350	—
1788	30.00	50.00	80.00	160	435	1,100	—

KM# 4 • Copper • Obv: Small mailed bust facing left. **Rev. Legend:** ETLIB INDE.

Date	AG	Good	VG	Fine	VF	XF	Unc
1786	45.00	75.00	150	350	900	2,100	—

KM# 5 • Copper • Obv: Small mailed bust facing right. **Rev. Legend:** INDE ET LIB.

Date	AG	Good	VG	Fine	VF	XF	Unc
1786	60.00	100.00	175	450	2,000	4,250	—

KM# 6 • Copper • Obv: Large mailed bust facing right.

Date	AG	Good	VG	Fine	VF	XF	Unc
1786	55.00	90.00	160	400	1,750	3,750	—

KM# 7 • Copper • Obv: "Hercules head."

Date	AG	Good	VG	Fine	VF	XF	Unc
1786	60.00	110	220	600	2,500	5,800	—

KM# 8.1 • Copper • Obv: Draped bust.

Date	AG	Good	VG	Fine	VF	XF	Unc
1786	50.00	90.00	175	475	1,150	2,750	—

KM# 9 • Copper • Obv: Small head. **Rev. Legend:** ETLIB INDE.

Date	AG	Good	VG	Fine	VF	XF	Unc
1787	65.00	110	180	375	1,500	3,750	—

KM# 10 • Copper • Obv: Small head. **Rev. Legend:** INDE ET LIB.

Date	AG	Good	VG	Fine	VF	XF	Unc
1787	75.00	135	200	450	2,000	4,000	—

KM# 11 • Copper • Obv: Medium bust. **Note:** Two reverse legend types exist.

Date	AG	Good	VG	Fine	VF	XF	Unc
1787	60.00	90.00	150	350	1,500	3,000	—

KM# 12 • Copper • Obv: "Muttonhead" variety. **Note:** Extremely rare with legend INDE ET LIB.

Date	AG	Good	VG	Fine	VF	XF	Unc
1787	60.00	90.00	175	500	2,200	4,500	—

KM# 3.3 • Copper • Obv: Perfect date. **Rev. Legend:** IN DE ET.

Date	AG	Good	VG	Fine	VF	XF	Unc
1787	50.00	80.00	125	350	750	1,500	—

KM# 13 • Copper • Obv: "Laughing head"

Date	AG	Good	VG	Fine	VF	XF	Unc
1787	35.00	60.00	120	240	650	1,800	—

KM# 14 • Copper • Obv: "Horned head"

Date	AG	Good	VG	Fine	VF	XF	Unc
1787	30.00	50.00	80.00	165	450	1,200	—

KM# 15 • Copper • Rev. Legend: IND ET LIB

Date	AG	Good	VG	Fine	VF	XF	Unc
1787/8	50.00	85.00	170	450	1,500	4,000	—
1787/1887	85.00	150	225	600	1,750	4,500	—

KM# 16 • Copper • Obv. Legend: CONNECT.
Rev. Legend: INDE ET LIB. **Note:** Two additional
scarce reverse legend types exist.

Date	AG	Good	VG	Fine	VF	XF	Unc
1787	35.00	50.00	120	240	550	1,500	—

KM# 8.2 • Copper • Obv: Draped bust. **Note:**
Many varieties.

Date	AG	Good	VG	Fine	VF	XF	Unc
1787	28.00	42.00	70.00	115	325	750	—

KM# 8.3 • Copper • Obv. Legend: AUCIORI.

Date	AG	Good	VG	Fine	VF	XF	Unc
1787	30.00	55.00	90.00	175	450	1,000	—

KM# 8.4 • Copper • Obv. Legend: AUCTOPI.

Date	AG	Good	VG	Fine	VF	XF	Unc
1787	35.00	65.00	110	200	650	1,650	—

KM# 8.5 • Copper • Obv. Legend: AUCTOBI.

Date	AG	Good	VG	Fine	VF	XF	Unc
1787	35.00	65.00	110	200	625	1,550	—

KM# 8.6 • Copper • Obv. Legend: CONNFC.

Date	AG	Good	VG	Fine	VF	XF	Unc
1787	32.00	60.00	90.00	160	475	1,000	—

KM# 8.7 • Copper • Obv. Legend: CONNLC.

Date	AG	Good	VG	Fine	VF	XF	Unc
1787	50.00	75.00	150	300	650	1,850	—

KM# 8.8 • Copper • Rev. Legend: FNDE.

Date	AG	Good	VG	Fine	VF	XF	Unc
1787	35.00	55.00	80.00	160	475	1,400	—

KM# 8.9 • Copper • Rev. Legend: ETLIR.

Date	AG	Good	VG	Fine	VF	XF	Unc
1787	32.00	50.00	75.00	150	440	1,175	—

KM# 8.10 • Copper • Rev. Legend: ETIIB.

Date	AG	Good	VG	Fine	VF	XF	Unc
1787	35.00	50.00	75.00	150	450	1,200	—

KM# 20 • Copper • Obv: Mailed bust facing
right.

Date	AG	Good	VG	Fine	VF	XF	Unc
1788	28.00	40.00	85.00	180	550	1,450	—

KM# 21 • Copper • Obv: Small mailed bust
facing right.

Date	AG	Good	VG	Fine	VF	XF	Unc
1788	850	1,500	2,950	4,150	9,500	18,500	—

KM# 3.4 • Copper • Obv. Legend: CONNLC.

Date	AG	Good	VG	Fine	VF	XF	Unc
1788	44.00	60.00	120	240	650	1,850	—

KM# 22.1 • Copper • Obv: Draped bust facing
left. **Rev. Legend:** INDE ET LIB.

Date	AG	Good	VG	Fine	VF	XF	Unc
1788	45.00	70.00	125	285	675	1,650	—

KM# 22.2 • Copper • Rev. Legend: INDLET
LIB.

Date	AG	Good	VG	Fine	VF	XF	Unc
1788	55.00	80.00	175	375	800	1,750	—

KM# 22.3 • Copper • Obv. Legend: CONNEC.
Rev. Legend: INDE ET LIB.

Date	AG	Good	VG	Fine	VF	XF	Unc
1788	58.00	85.00	190	400	875	1,850	—

KM# 22.4 • Copper • Obv. Legend: CONNEC.
Rev. Legend: INDL ET LIB.

Date	AG	Good	VG	Fine	VF	XF	Unc
1788	58.00	85.00	190	400	875	1,850	—

MASSACHUSETTS

HALFPENNY

KM# 17 • Copper •

Date	Good	VG	Fine	VF	XF	Unc
1776 unique	—	—	200,000	—	—	—

Note: Garrett $40,000

PENNY

KM# 18 • Copper •

Date	AG	Good	VG	Fine	VF	XF	Unc
1776 unique	—	—	—	—	—	—	—

HALF CENT

KM# 19 • Copper • Note: Varieties exist; some are rare.

Date	AG	Good	VG	Fine	VF	XF	Unc
1787	60.00	90.00	140	210	550	1,000	3,250
1788	70.00	110	175	260	585	1,100	3,500

CENT

KM# 20.1 • Copper • Rev: Arrows in right talon

Date	Good	VG	Fine	VF	XF	Unc
1787						
7 known	9,000	22,500	45,000	—	—	350,000

Note: Ex-Bushnell-Brand $8,800. Garrett $5,500

KM# 20.2 • Copper • Rev: Arrows in left talon

Date	AG	Good	VG	Fine	VF	XF	Unc
1787	60.00	90.00	165	240	650	1,250	6,800

KM# 20.3 • Copper • Rev: "Horned eagle" die break

Date	AG	Good	VG	Fine	VF	XF	Unc
1787	70.00	110	190	275	775	1,500	7,750

KM# 20.4 • Copper • Rev: Without period after Massachusetts

Date	AG	Good	VG	Fine	VF	XF	Unc
1788	70.00	105	190	260	675	1,600	6,250

KM# 20.5 • Copper • Rev: Period after Massachusetts, normal S's

Date	AG	Good	VG	Fine	VF	XF	Unc
1788	60.00	90.00	170	235	600	1,375	5,750

KM# 20.6 • Copper • Rev: Period after Massachusetts, S's like 8's

Date	AG	Good	VG	Fine	VF	XF	Unc
1788	50.00	75.00	135	200	575	1,250	5,400

NEW HAMPSHIRE

KM# 1 • Copper •

Date	Good	VG	Fine	VF	XF	Unc
1776 extremely rare	—	75,000	—	—	—	—

Note: Garrett $13,000

NEW JERSEY

KM# 8 • Copper • Obv: Date below draw bar.

Date	Good	VG	Fine	VF	XF	Unc
1786 extremely rare	—	48,000	110,000	—	—	—

Note: Garrett $52,000

KM# 9 • Copper • Obv: Large horse head, date below plow, no coulter on plow.

Date	AG	Good	VG	Fine	VF	XF	Unc
1786	450	750	1,450	2,350	7,500	20,000	—

KM# 10 • Copper • Rev: Narrow shield, straight beam.

Date	AG	Good	VG	Fine	VF	XF	Unc
1786	38.00	60.00	140	210	550	1,350	—

KM# 11.1 • Copper • Rev: Wide shield, curved beam. **Note:** Varieties exist.

Date	AG	Good	VG	Fine	VF	XF	Unc
1786	45.00	75.00	150	225	600	2,000	—

KM# 11.2 • Copper • Obv: Bridle variety (die break). **Note:** Reverse varieties exist.

Date	AG	Good	VG	Fine	VF	XF	Unc
1786	45.00	70.00	145	235	650	2,400	—

KM# 12.1 • Copper • Rev: Plain shield. **Note:** Small planchet. Varieties exist.

Date	AG	Good	VG	Fine	VF	XF	Unc
1787	35.00	55.00	110	200	500	1,050	—

KM# 12.2 • Copper • Rev: Shield heavily outlined. **Note:** Small planchet.

Date	AG	Good	VG	Fine	VF	XF	Unc
1787	38.00	60.00	120	215	550	1,150	—

KM# 13 • Copper • Obv: "Serpent head."

Date	AG	Good	VG	Fine	VF	XF	Unc
1787	55.00	85.00	200	375	1,500	3,750	—

KM# 14 • Copper • Rev: Plain shield. **Note:** Large planchet. Varieties exist.

Date	AG	Good	VG	Fine	VF	XF	Unc
1787	45.00	60.00	135	240	750	1,650	—

KM# 15 • Copper • Rev. Legend: PLURIBS.

Date	AG	Good	VG	Fine	VF	XF	Unc
1787	85.00	150	275	450	1,000	2,800	—

KM# 16 • Copper • Obv: Horse's head facing right. **Note:** Varieties exist.

Date	AG	Good	VG	Fine	VF	XF	Unc
1788	42.00	60.00	115	190	700	1,275	—

KM# 17 • Copper • Rev: Fox before legend. **Note:** Varieties exist.

Date	AG	Good	VG	Fine	VF	XF	Unc
1788	75.00	135	285	550	1,750	4,400	—

KM# 18 • Copper • Obv: Horse's head facing left. **Note:** Varieties exist.

Date	AG	Good	VG	Fine	VF	XF	Unc
1788	235	400	850	1,500	4,800	13,000	—

NEW YORK

KM# 1 • Copper • Obv: Bust right **Obv.**

Legend: NON VI VIRTUTE VICI. **Rev. Legend:** NEO-EBORACENSIS

Date	AG	Good	VG	Fine	VF	XF	Unc
1786	3,250	5,000	7,500	15,000	35,000	—	—

KM# 2 • Copper • Obv: Eagle on globe facing right. **Obv. Legend:** EXCELSIOR **Rev. Legend:** E. PLURIBUS UNUM

Date	AG	Good	VG	Fine	VF	XF	Unc
1787	1,400	2,250	3,850	7,000	17,500	32,500	—

KM# 3 • Copper • Obv: Eagle on globe facing left. **Obv. Legend:** EXCELSIOR **Rev. Legend:** E. PLURIBUS UNUM

Date	AG	Good	VG	Fine	VF	XF	Unc
1787	1,250	2,000	3,500	6,500	16,500	32,000	—

KM# 4 • Copper • Obv. Legend: EXCELSIOR **Rev:** Large eagle, arrows in right talon. **Rev. Legend:** E. PLURIBUS UNUM

Date	AG	Good	VG	Fine	VF	XF	Unc
1787	—	4,500	9,000	16,500	35,000	55,000	—

Note: Norweb $18,700

KM# 5 • Copper • Obv: George Clinton. **Rev. Legend:** EXCELSIOR

Date	AG	Good	VG	Fine	VF	XF	Unc
1787	4,500	7,500	14,500	26,000	48,500	125,000	

KM# 6 • Copper • Obv: Indian. Obv. Legend:
LIBERNATUS LIBERTATEM DEFENDO Rev: New
York arms. Rev. Legend: EXCELSIOR

Date	AG	Good	VG	Fine	VF	XF	Unc
1787	4,500	7,000	10,000	17,500	40,000	90,000	—

KM# 7 • Copper • Obv: Indian. Obv. Legend:
LIBERNATUS LIBERTATEM DEFENDO Rev:
Eagle on globe. Rev. Legend: NEO EBORACUS
EXCELSIOR

Date	AG	Good	VG	Fine	VF	XF
1787	6,000	11,000	15,000	27,500	55,000	120,000

KM# 8 • Copper • Obv: Indian. Rev: George III.

Date	Good	VG	Fine	VF	XF	Unc
1787	3 Known	—	60,000	—	—	—

Machin's Mill

KM# 13 • Copper • Note: Crude, lightweight
imitations of the British Halfpenny were struck at
Machin's Mill in large quantities bearing the
obverse legends: GEORGIVS II REX, GEORGIVS
III REX, and GEORGIUS III REX, with the
BRITANNIA reverse. There are many different
mulings. Plain crosses in the shield of Britannia
are noticeable on high grade pieces, unlike
common British made imitations, which usually
have outlined crosses in the shield. Some
Machin's Mill varieties are very rare.

Date	AG	Good	VG	Fine	VF	XF
(1747-1788)	40.00	70.00	120	250	750	2,200

Note: Prices are for most common within date ranges.
Examples are dated: 1747, 1771, 1772, 1774, 1775, 1776,
1777, 1778, 1784, 1785, 1786, 1787 and 1788. Other dates
may exist

Nova Eboracs

KM# 1 • Copper • Obv: Bust right Obv.
Legend: NON VI VIRTUTE VICI. Rev. Legend:
NEO-EBORACENSIS

Date	AG	Good	VG	Fine	VF	XF
1786	3,250	5,000	7,500	15,000	35,000	—

KM# 2 • Copper • Obv: Eagle on globe facing
right. Obv. Legend: EXCELSIOR Rev. Legend: E.
PLURIBUS UNUM

Date	AG	Good	VG	Fine	VF	XF	Unc
1787	1,400	2,250	3,850	7,000	17,500	32,500	—

KM# 3 • Copper • Obv: Eagle on globe facing
left. Obv. Legend: EXCELSIOR Rev. Legend: E.
PLURIBUS UNUM

Date	AG	Good	VG	Fine	VF	XF	Unc
1787	1,250	2,000	3,500	6,500	16,500	32,000	—

KM# 4 • Copper • Obv. Legend: EXCELSIOR
Rev: Large eagle, arrows in right talon. Rev.
Legend: E. PLURIBUS UNUM

Date	Good	VG	Fine	VF	XF	Unc
1787	4,500	9,000	16,500	35,000	55,000	—

Note: Norweb $18,700

KM# 5 • Copper • Obv: George Clinton. **Rev. Legend:** EXCELSIOR

Date	AG	Good	VG	Fine	VF	XF
1787	4,500	7,500	14,500	26,000	48,500	125,000

KM# 6 • Copper • Obv: Indian. **Obv. Legend:** LIBERNATUS LIBERTATEM DEFENDO **Rev:** New York arms. **Rev. Legend:** EXCELSIOR

Date	AG	Good	VG	Fine	VF	XF
1787	4,500	7,000	10,000	17,500	40,000	90,000

KM# 7 • Copper • Obv: Indian. **Obv. Legend:** LIBERNATUS LIBERTATEM DEFENDO **Rev:** Eagle on globe. **Rev. Legend:** NEO EBORACUS EXCELSIOR

Date	AG	Good	VG	Fine	VF	XF
1787	6,000	11,000	15,000	27,500	55,000	120,000

KM# 8 • Copper • Obv: Indian. **Rev:** George III.

Date	Good	VG	Fine	VF	XF	Unc
1787	3 Known	— 60,000	—	—	—	—

KM# 9 • Copper • Obv: Bust right **Obv. Legend:** NOVA EBORAC. **Rev:** Figure seated right. **Rev. Legend:** VIRT.ET.LIB.

Date	AG	Good	VG	Fine	VF	XF	Unc
1787	75.00	115	220	360	1,150	2,700	—

KM# 10 • Copper • Obv: Bust right **Obv. Legend:** NOVA EBORAC **Rev:** Figure seated left. **Rev. Legend:** VIRT.ET.LIB.

Date	AG	Good	VG	Fine	VF	XF	Unc
1787	60.00	100.00	200	325	825	1,750	—

KM# 11 • Copper • Obv: Small head, star above. **Obv. Legend:** NOVA EBORAC. **Rev:** Figure seated left **Rev. Legend:** VIRT.ET.LIB.

Date	AG	Good	VG	Fine	VF	XF	Unc
1787	2,450	3,500	5,200	7,500	20,000	55,000	—

KM# 12 • Copper • Obv: Large head, two quatrefoils left. **Obv. Legend:** NOVA EBORAC. **Rev:** Figure seated left **Rev. Legend:** VIRT.ET.LIB.

Date	AG	Good	VG	Fine	VF	XF	Unc
1787	350	600	1,250	2,250	7,500	15,000	—

VERMONT

KM# 1 • Copper • Rev. Legend: IMMUNE COLUMBIA.

Date	AG	Good	VG	Fine	VF	XF	Unc
(1785)	3,750	5,500	9,000	12,750	32,000	—	—

KM# 2 • **Copper** • **Obv:** Sun rising over field with plow **Obv. Legend:** VERMONTIS. RES. PUBLICA. **Rev:** Eye, with rays and stars **Rev. Legend:** QUARTA. DECIMA. STELLA.

Date	AG	Good	VG	Fine	VF	XF	Unc
1785	120	290	650	1,450	4,500	11,000	—

KM# 3 • **Copper** • **Obv:** Sun rising over field with plow **Obv. Legend:** VERMONTS. RES. PUBLICA. **Rev:** Eye, with rays and stars **Rev. Legend:** QUARTA. DECIMA. STELLA.

Date	AG	Good	VG	Fine	VF	XF	Unc
1785	150	275	600	1,250	3,100	7,500	—

KM# 4 • **Copper** • **Obv:** Sun rising over field with plow **Obv. Legend:** VERMONTENSIUM.RES.PUBLICA **Rev:** Eye, with pointed rays and stars **Rev. Legend:** QUARTA. DECIMA. STELLA.

Date	AG	Good	VG	Fine	VF	XF	Unc
1786	140	235	400	750	2,000	4,400	—

KM# 5 • **Copper** • **Obv:** "Baby head." **Obv. Legend:** AUCTORI: VERMON: **Rev:** Seated figure left **Rev. Legend:** ET:LIB: INDE

Date	AG	Good	VG	Fine	VF	XF	Unc
1786	200	350	650	1,750	4,800	12,500	—

KM# 6 • **Copper** • **Obv:** Bust facing left. **Obv. Legend:** VERMON: AUCTORI: **Rev:** Seated figure left **Rev. Legend:** INDE ETLIB

Date	AG	Good	VG	Fine	VF	XF
1786	115	175	350	800	2,800	4,750
1787 extremely rare	—	—	4,500	11,000	27,500	44,000

KM# 7 • **Copper** • **Obv:** Bust facing right. **Obv. Legend:** VERMON. AUCTORI. **Rev:** Seated figure left **Rev. Legend:** INDE ETLIB **Note:** Varieties exist.

Date	AG	Good	VG	Fine	VF	XF	Unc
1787	—	150	260	575	1,450	3,000	—

KM# 8 • **Copper** • **Obv:** Bust right **Obv. Legend:** VERMON AUCTORI **Rev:** Seated figure left **Note:** Britannia mule.

Date	AG	Good	VG	Fine	VF	XF	Unc
1787	65.00	110	150	275	650	1,650	—

KM# 9.2 • **Copper** • **Obv:** Bust right. "C" backward in AUCTORI. **Rev:** Seated figure left

Date	Good	VG	Fine	VF	XF
1788 extremely rare	4,200	7,000	17,500	38,000	—

Note: Stack's Americana, Fine, $9,775

KM# 10 • Copper • Obv: Bust right **Rev:** Seated figure left **Rev. Legend:** .ET LIB. .INDE.

Date	AG	Good	VG	Fine	VF	XF	Unc
1788	200	325	625	1,250	4,000	13,500	—

KM# 11 • Copper • Obv: Bust right **Rev:** Seated figure left **Note:** George III Rex mule.

Date	AG	Good	VG	Fine	VF	XF	Unc
1788	300	550	900	2,250	4,500	12,000	—

KM# 9.1 • Copper • Obv: Bust right **Obv. Legend:** VERMON. AUCTORI. **Rev:** Seated figure left **Rev. Legend:** INDE . ET LIB. **Note:** Varieties exist.

Date	AG	Good	VG	Fine	VF	XF	Unc
1788	200	325	625	1,350	4,000	11,500	—

EARLY AMERICAN TOKENS

Albany Church "Penny"

KM# Tn54.1 • Copper • Obv: Without "D" above church. **Note:** Uniface.

Date	Good	VG	Fine	VF	XF	Unc
5 known	—	10,000	25,000	75,000	—	—

KM# Tn54.2 • Copper • Obv: With "D" above church. **Note:** Uniface.

Date	AG	Good	VG	Fine	VF	XF	Unc
rare	—	—	9,000	22,500	67,500	—	—

Auctori Plebis

KM# Tn50 • Copper • Obv: Bust left **Obv. Legend:** AUCTORI: PLEBIS: **Rev:** Seated figure left **Rev. Legend:** INDEP: ET. LIBER

Date	AG	Good	VG	Fine	VF	XF	Unc
1787	—	100.00	165	340	800	2,100	15,000

Bar "Cent"

KM# Tn49 • Copper • Obv: USA monogram **Rev:** Horizontal bars

Date	AG	Good	VG	Fine	VF	XF	Unc
(1785)	—	1,400	1,750	3,100	6,250	9,500	27,500

Castorland "Half Dollar"

KM# Tn87.1 • Silver • Obv. Legend: FRANCO.AMERICANA COLONIA **Edge:** Reeded.

Date	AG	Good	VG	Fine	VF	XF	Unc
1796	—	—	—	—	—	5,000	13,500

KM# Tn87.1a • Copper • Obv. Legend:
FRANCO.AMERICANA COLONIA **Edge:** Reeded.

Date	AG	Good	VG	Fine	VF	XF	Unc
1796 3 known	—	—	—	—	—	2,850	

KM# Tn87.1b • Brass • Obv. Legend:
FRANCO.AMERICANA COLONIA **Edge:** Reeded.

Date	AG	Good	VG	Fine	VF	XF	Unc
1796	—	—	—	—	—	200	650

KM# Tn87.2 • Copper • Obv. Legend:
FRANCO.AMERICANA COLONIA **Edge:** Plain.
Note: Thin planchet.

Date	AG	Good	VG	Fine	VF	XF	Unc
1796 unique	—	—	—	—	—	—	—

KM# Tn87.3 • Silver • Obv. Legend:
FRANCO.AMERICANA COLONIA **Edge:** Reeded.
Note: Thin planchet. Restrike.

Date	Good	VG	Fine	VF	XF	Unc	Proof
1796	—	—	—	—	—	500	—

KM# Tn87.4 • Silver • Obv. Legend:
FRANCO.AMERICANA COLONIA **Edge:** Lettered.
Edge Lettering: ARGENT. **Note:** Thin planchet.
Restrike.

Date	Good	VG	Fine	VF	XF	Unc	Proof
1796	—	—	—	—	—	200	—

KM# Tn87.3a • Copper • Obv. Legend:
FRANCO.AMERICANA COLONIA **Edge:** Reeded.
Note: Thin planchet. Restrike.

Date	Good	VG	Fine	VF	XF	Unc	Proof
1796	—	—	—	—	—	450	—

KM# Tn87.5 • Copper • Obv. Legend:
FRANCO.AMERICANA COLONIA **Edge:** Lettered.
Edge Lettering: CUIVRE. **Note:** Thin planchet.
Restrike.

Date	Good	VG	Fine	VF	XF	Unc	Proof
1796	—	—	—	—	—	150	—

Chalmers

3 PENCE

KM# Tn45 • Silver •

Date	AG	Good	VG	Fine	VF	XF	Unc
1783	650	1,100	1,750	3,250	6,500	13,500	—

6 PENCE

KM# Tn46.1 • Silver • Rev: Small date

Date	AG	Good	VG	Fine	VF	XF	Unc
1783	900	1,600	2,500	6,000	12,500	22,500	—

KM# Tn46.2 • Silver • Rev: Large date

Date	AG	Good	VG	Fine	VF	XF	Unc
1783	775	1,450	2,250	6,000	11,500	18,500	—

SHILLING

KM# Tn47.1 • Silver • Rev: Birds with long worm

Date	AG	Good	VG	Fine	VF	XF	Unc
1783	450	750	1,250	2,400	5,500	10,000	—

KM# Tn47.2 • Silver • Rev: Birds with short worm

Date	AG	Good	VG	Fine	VF	XF	Unc
1783	450	750	1,250	2,350	5,000	10,000	—

KM# Tn48 • Silver • Rev: Rings and stars

Date	Good	VG	Fine	VF	XF	Unc
1783 4 known	—	—	—	200,000	—	—

Note: Garrett $75,000

Copper Company of Upper Canada

HALFPENNY

KM# Tn86 • Copper • Obv. Legend: BRITISH
SETTLEMENT KENTUCKY

Date	Good	VG	Fine	VF	XF	Unc	Proof
1796	—	—	—	—	—		—10,500

Franklin Press

KM# Tn73 • Copper • Obv: Printing press **Obv.
Legend:** SIC ORITUR DOCTRINA SURGETQUE
LIBERTAS **Edge:** Plain.

Date	AG	Good	VG	Fine	VF	XF	Unc
1794	30.00	75.00	110	150	250	425	1,350

Kentucky Token

KM# Tn70.1 • Copper • Obv. Legend:
UNANIMITY IS THE STRENGTH OF SOCIETY
Rev. Legend: E. PLURIBUS UNUM **Edge:** Plain.
Note: 1793 date is circa.

Date	AG	Good	VG	Fine	VF	XF	Unc
(1793)	12.00	25.00	40.00	150	200	375	1,210

KM# Tn70.2 • Copper • Obv. Legend:
UNANIMITY IS THE STRENGTH OF SOCIETY
Rev. Legend: E. PLURIBUS UNUM **Edge:**
Engrailed.

Date	AG	Good	VG	Fine	VF	XF	Unc
(1793)	35.00	75.00	125	200	500	950	3,400

KM# Tn70.3 • Copper • Obv. Legend:
UNANIMITY IS THE STRENGTH OF SOCIETY
Rev. Legend: E. PLURIBUS UNUM **Edge:**
Lettered. **Edge Lettering:** PAYABLE AT
BEDWORTH.

Date	AG	Good	VG	Fine	VF	XF	Unc
(1793) unique	—	—	—	—	—	1,980	—

KM# Tn70.4 • Copper • Obv. Legend:
UNANIMITY IS THE STRENGTH OF SOCIETY
Rev. Legend: E. PLURIBUS UNUM **Edge:**
Lettered. **Edge Lettering:** PAYABLE AT
LANCASTER.

Date	AG	Good	VG	Fine	VF	XF	Unc
(1793)	14.00	28.00	45.00	65.00	225	400	1,250

KM# Tn70.5 • Copper • Obv. Legend:
UNANIMITY IS THE STRENGTH OF SOCIETY
Rev. Legend: E. PLURIBUS UNUM **Edge:**
Lettered. **Edge Lettering:** PAYABLE AT
I.FIELDING.

Date	Good	VG	Fine	VF	XF	Unc
(1793) unique	—	—	—	—	—	—

KM# Tn70.6 • Copper • Obv. Legend:
UNANIMITY IS THE STRENGTH OF SOCIETY
Rev. Legend: E. PLURIBUS UNUM **Edge:**
Lettered. **Edge Lettering:** PAYABLE AT W.
PARKERS.

Date	Good	VG	Fine	VF	XF	Unc
(1793) unique	—	—	—	20,000	—	—

KM# Tn70.7 • Copper • Obv. Legend:
UNANIMITY IS THE STRENGTH OF SOCIETY
Rev. Legend: E. PLURIBUS UNUM **Edge:**
Ornamented branch with two leaves.

Date	Good	VG	Fine	VF	XF	Unc
(1793) unique	—	—	—	—	—	—

Mott Token

KM# Tn52.1 • Copper • Obv: Clock **Rev:** Eagle
with shield **Note:** Thin planchet.

Date	AG	Good	VG	Fine	VF	XF	Unc
1789	50.00	80.00	150	250	400	750	1,750

KM# Tn52.2 • Copper • Obv: Clock **Rev:** Eagle
with shield **Note:** Thick planchet. Weight generally
about 170 grams.

Date	AG	Good	VG	Fine	VF	XF	Unc
1789	60.00	95.00	175	325	550	1,250	—

KM# Tn52.3 • Copper • Obv: Clock **Rev:** Eagle
with shield **Edge:** Fully engrailed. **Note:** Specimens
struck with perfect dies are scarcer and generally
command higher prices.

Date	AG	Good	VG	Fine	VF	XF	Unc
1789	90.00	160	325	450	700	1,750	4,800

Myddelton Token

KM# Tn85 • Copper • Obv. Legend: BRITISH
SETTLEMENT KENTUCKY **Rev. Legend:**
PAYABLE BY P.P.P.MYDDELTON.

Date	Good	VG	Fine	VF	XF	Unc	Proof
1796	—	—	—	—	—	—	37,500

KM# Tn85a • Silver •

Date	Good	VG	Fine	VF	XF	Unc	Proof
1796	—	—	—	—	—	—	12,000

New York Theatre

KM# Tn90 • Copper • Obv: Theater building
Obv. Legend: THE.THEATRE.AT.NEW.YORK.

AMERICA **Rev:** Ships at sea, viewed from dock
Rev. Legend: MAY.COMMERCE.FLOURISH
Note: 1796 date is circa.

Date	AG	Good	VG	Fine	VF	XF	Unc
1796	—	—	—	—	7,000	9,500	25,000

North American

HALFPENNY

KM# Tn30 • **Copper** • **Obv:** Seated figure left, with harp **Obv. Legend:** NORTH AMERICAN TOKEN **Rev:** Ship **Rev. Legend:** COMMERCE

Date	AG	Good	VG	Fine	VF	XF	Unc
1781	32.00	50.00	65.00	130	300	750	3,250

Rhode Island Ship

KM# Tn27a • **Brass** • **Obv:** Without wreath below ship.

Date	AG	Good	VG	Fine	VF	XF	Unc
1779	—	—	325	550	1,000	2,000	7,500

KM# Tn27b • **Pewter** • **Obv:** Without wreath below ship.

Date	AG	Good	VG	Fine	VF	XF	Unc
1779	—	—	—	—	5,000	8,500	18,500

KM# Tn28a • **Brass** • **Obv:** Wreath below ship.

Date	AG	Good	VG	Fine	VF	XF	Unc
1779	—	—	—	675	1,100	2,100	7,750

KM# Tn28b • **Pewter** • **Obv:** Wreath below ship.

Date	AG	Good	VG	Fine	VF	XF	Unc
1779	—	—	—	—	5,500	9,000	20,000

KM# Tn29 • **Brass** • **Obv:** VLUGTENDE below ship

Date	Good	VG	Fine	VF	XF	Unc
1779 unique	—	—	—	—	35,000	—

Note: Garrett $16,000

Standish Barry

3 PENCE

KM# Tn55 • **Silver** • **Obv:** Bust left **Obv. Legend:** BALTIMORE.TOWN.JULY.4.90. **Rev:** Denomination **Rev. Legend:** STANDISH BARRY.

Date	Good	VG	Fine	VF	XF	Unc
1790	—	15,000	22,500	50,000	—	—

Talbot, Allum & Lee

CENT

KM# Tn71.1 • **Copper** • **Rev:** NEW YORK above ship **Edge:** Lettered. **Edge Lettering:** PAYABLE AT THE STORE OF

Date	AG	Good	VG	Fine	VF	XF	Unc
1794	32.00	50.00	85.00	165	275	550	2,000

KM# Tn71.2 • **Copper** • **Rev:** NEW YORK above ship **Edge:** Plain. **Note:** Size of ampersand varies on obverse and reverse dies.

Date	Good	VG	Fine	VF	XF	Unc
1794 4 known	—	—	—	10,000	24,000	—

KM# Tn72.1 • **Copper** • **Rev:** Without NEW YORK above ship **Edge:** Lettered. **Edge Lettering:** PAYABLE AT THE STORE OF

Date	AG	Good	VG	Fine	VF	XF	Unc
1794	200	375	600	3,500	6,500	10,500	22,000

KM# Tn72.2 • **Copper** • **Edge:** Lettered. **Edge Lettering:** WE PROMISE TO PAY THE BEARER ONE CENT.

Date	AG	Good	VG	Fine	VF	XF	Unc
1795	30.00	50.00	75.00	135	240	375	1,200

KM# Tn72.3 • **Copper** • **Edge:** Lettered. **Edge Lettering:** CURRENT EVERYWHERE.

Date	Good	VG	Fine	VF	XF	Unc
1795 unique	—	—	—	—	—	—

KM# Tn72.4 • Copper • Edge: Olive leaf.

Date	Good	VG	Fine	VF	XF	Unc
1795 unique	—	—	—	— 15,000	—

Note: Norweb $4,400

KM# Tn72.5 • Copper • Edge: Plain.

Date	Good	VG	Fine	VF	XF	Unc
1795 plain edge; 2 known	—	—	—	—	—	—
1795 Lettered edge; unique	—	—	—	— 15,000	—

Note: Edge: Cambridge Bedford Huntington.X.X.; Norweb, $3,960

Washington Pieces

KM# Tn35 • Copper • Obv. Legend: GEORGIVS TRIUMPHO.

Date	AG	Good	VG	Fine	VF	XF	Unc
1783	—	95.00	125	260	325	750	—

KM# Tn36 • Copper • Obv: Large military bust. **Note:** Varieties exist.

Date	AG	Good	VG	Fine	VF	XF	Unc
1783	—	—	50.00	85.00	180	450	2,600

KM# Tn37.1 • Copper • Obv: Small military bust. **Edge:** Plain.

Date	AG	Good	VG	Fine	VF	XF	Unc
1783	—	—	70.00	95.00	220	525	3,600

Note: One proof example is known. Value: $25,000

KM# Tn37.2 • Copper • Obv: Small military bust. **Edge:** Engrailed.

Date	AG	Good	VG	Fine	VF	XF	Unc
1783	—	75.00	110	150	300	750	4,250

KM# Tn38.1 • Copper • Obv: Draped bust, no button on drapery, small letter.

Date	AG	Good	VG	Fine	VF	XF	Unc
1783	—	40.00	60.00	90.00	180	400	2,200

KM# Tn38.2 • Copper • Obv: Draped bust, button on drapery, large letter.

Date	AG	Good	VG	Fine	VF	XF	Unc
1783	—	85.00	110	150	325	600	4,000

KM# Tn38.4 • Copper • Edge: Engrailed. **Note:** Restrike.

Date	Good	VG	Fine	VF	XF	Unc	Proof
1783	—	—	—	—	—	—	800

KM# Tn38.4a • Copper • Note: Bronzed. Restrike.

Date	Good	VG	Fine	VF	XF	Unc	Proof
1783	—	—	—	—	—	—	—

KM# Tn83.3 • Copper • Obv: Large modern lettering. **Edge:** Plain. **Note:** Restrike.

Date	Good	VG	Fine	VF	XF	Unc	Proof
1783	—	—	—	—	—	—	900

KM# Tn83.4b • Silver • Note: Restrike.

Date	Good	VG	Fine	VF	XF	Unc	Proof
1783	—	—	—	—	—	—	1,600

KM# Tn83.4c • Gold AGW • **Note:** Restrike.

Date	Good	VG	Fine	VF	XF	Unc
1783 2 known	—	—	—	—	—	—

KM# Tn60.1 • Copper • Obv. Legend: WASHINGTON PRESIDENT. **Edge:** Plain.

Date	AG	Good	VG	Fine	VF	XF	Unc
1792	850	1,450	3,000	7,500	16,000	—	—

Note: Steinberg $12,650. Garrett $15,500

KM# Tn60.2 • Copper • Obv. Legend: WASHINGTON PRESIDENT. **Edge:** Lettered. **Edge Lettering:** UNITED STATES OF AMERICA.

Date	AG	Good	VG	Fine	VF	XF	Unc
1792	—	—	—	—	—	—	—

KM# Tn61.1 • Copper • Obv. Legend: BORN VIRGINIA. **Note:** Varieties exist.

Date	AG	Good	VG	Fine	VF	XF	Unc
(1792)	500	1,000	2,000	4,000	7,500	12,000	—

KM# Tn61.2 • Silver • Edge: Lettered. **Edge Lettering:** UNITED STATES OF AMERICA.

Date	Good	VG	Fine	VF	XF	Unc
(1792) 2 known	—	—	—	—	—	—

KM# Tn61.1a • Silver • Edge: Plain.

Date	Good	VG	Fine	VF	XF	Unc
(1792) 4 known	—	—	—	—	200,000	—

Note: Roper $16,500

KM# Tn62 • Silver • Rev: Heraldic eagle. 1792 half dollar. **Note:** Mule.

Date	Good	VG	Fine	VF	XF	Unc
(1792) 3 known	—	—	—	50,000	75,000	—

KM# Tn77.1 • Copper • Obv. Legend: LIBERTY AND SECURITY. **Edge:** Lettered. **Note:** "Penny."

Date	AG	Good	VG	Fine	VF	XF	Unc
(1795)	70.00	110	165	300	525	1,100	3,500

KM# Tn77.2 • Copper • Edge: Plain. **Note:** "Penny."

Date	Good	VG	Fine	VF	XF	Unc
(1795) extremely rare	—	—	—	—	—	—

KM# Tn77.3 • Copper • Note: "Penny." Engine-turned borders.

Date	AG	Good	VG	Fine	VF	XF	Unc
(1795) 12 known	—	275	450	650	1,250	2,400	7,500

KM# Tn78 • Copper • Note: Similar to "Halfpenny" with date on reverse.

Date	AG	Good	VG	Fine	VF	XF	Unc
1795 very rare	—	—	—	—	—	—	—

Note: Roper $6,600

HALFPENNY

KM# Tn56 • Copper • Obv. Legend: LIVERPOOL HALFPENNY

Date	AG	Good	VG	Fine	VF	XF	Unc
1791	40.00	70.00	1,000	125	300	550	3,250

KM# Tn66.1 • Copper • Rev: Ship **Edge:** Lettered.

Date	AG	Good	VG	Fine	VF	XF	Unc
1793	20.00	30.00	60.00	200	425	800	3,400

KM# Tn66.2 • Copper • Rev: Ship **Edge:** Plain.

Date	Good	VG	Fine	VF	XF	Unc
1793 5 known	—	—	—	15,000	—	—

KM# Tn75.1 • Copper • Obv: Large coat buttons **Rev:** Grate **Edge:** Reeded.

Date	AG	Good	VG	Fine	VF	XF	Unc
1795	—	—	70.00	110	200	400	900

KM# Tn75.2 • Copper • Rev: Grate **Edge:** Lettered.

Date	AG	Good	VG	Fine	VF	XF	Unc
1795	90.00	140	210	275	400	800	2,800

KM# Tn75.3 • Copper • Obv: Small coat buttons **Rev:** Grate **Edge:** Reeded.

Date	AG	Good	VG	Fine	VF	XF	Unc
1795	50.00	75.00	120	190	275	585	2,650

KM# Tn76.1 • **Copper** • **Obv. Legend:**
LIBERTY AND SECURITY. **Edge:** Plain.

Date	AG	Good	VG	Fine	VF	XF	Unc
1795	18.00	35.00	60.00	160	350	700	3,250

KM# Tn76.2 • **Copper** • **Edge:** Lettered. **Edge Lettering:** PAYABLE AT LONDON ...

Date	AG	Good	VG	Fine	VF	XF	Unc
1795	40.00	65.00	90.00	140	300	625	2,850

KM# Tn76.3 • **Copper** • **Edge:** Lettered. **Edge Lettering:** BIRMINGHAM ...

Date	AG	Good	VG	Fine	VF	XF	Unc
1795	55.00	85.00	115	165	340	775	3,600

KM# Tn76.4 • **Copper** • **Edge:** Lettered. **Edge Lettering:** AN ASYLUM ...

Date	AG	Good	VG	Fine	VF	XF	Unc
1795	18.00	35.00	60.00	275	600	1,600	6,500

KM# Tn76.5 • **Copper** • **Edge:** Lettered. **Edge Lettering:** PAYABLE AT LIVERPOOL ...

Date	AG	Good	VG	Fine	VF	XF	Unc
1795	unique	—	—	—	—	—	—

KM# Tn76.6 • **Copper** • **Edge:** Lettered. **Edge Lettering:** PAYABLE AT LONDON-LIVERPOOL.

Date	AG	Good	VG	Fine	VF	XF	Unc
1795	unique	—	—	—	—	—	—

KM# Tn81.1 • **Copper** • **Rev. Legend:** NORTH WALES **Edge:** Plain.

Date	AG	Good	VG	Fine	VF	XF	Unc
(ca.1795)	60.00	110	175	265	625	1,750	—

KM# Tn82 • **Copper** • **Rev:** Four stars at bottom **Rev. Legend:** NORTH WALES

Date	AG	Good	VG	Fine	VF	XF	Unc
(1795)	1,250	2,000	4,500	7,500	21,000	—	—

KM# Tn81.2 • **Copper** • **Rev. Legend:** NORTH WALES **Edge:** Lettered.

Date	AG	Good	VG	Fine	VF	XF	Unc
	350	550	1,150	1,750	5,500	9,500	—

CENT

KM# Tn39 • **Copper** • **Obv:** Draped Bust left **Obv. Legend:** WASHINGTON & INDEPENDENCE **Rev:** Denomination in wreath **Rev. Legend:** UNITY STATES OF AMERICA

Date	AG	Good	VG	Fine	VF	XF	Unc
1783	30.00	50.00	70.00	100.00	250	500	2,250

KM# Tn40 • **Copper** • **Note:** Double head.

Date	AG	Good	VG	Fine	VF	XF	Unc
(1783)	25.00	45.00	60.00	90.00	225	450	2,750

KM# Tn41 • **Copper** • **Obv:** "Ugly head." **Note:** 3 known in copper, 1 in white metal.

Date	AG	Good	VG	Fine	VF	XF	Unc
1784	—90,000	—	—	—	—	—	—

Note: Roper $14,850

KM# Tn57 • **Copper** • **Obv:** Military bust left **Obv. Legend:** WASHINGTON PRESIDENT. **Rev:** Small eagle

Date	AG	Good	VG	Fine	VF	XF	Unc
1791	—	—	350	500	725	1,000	4,750

KM# Tn58 • **Copper** • **Obv:** Military bust left **Obv. Legend:** WASHINGTON PRESIDENT **Rev:** Large eagle

Date	AG	Good	VG	Fine	VF	XF	Unc
1791	—	200	325	475	650	900	2,850

KM# Tn65 • **Copper** • **Obv:** "Roman" head **Obv. Legend:** WASHINGTON PRESIDENT.

Date	AG	Good	VG	Fine	VF	XF	Unc
1792	—	—	—	—	—	—	—

HALF DOLLAR

KM# Tn59.1 • **Copper** • **Edge:** Lettered. **Edge Lettering:** UNITED STATES OF AMERICA

Date	AG	Good	VG	Fine	VF	XF	Unc
1792 2 known	—	—	—	—	—75,000	—	

Note: Roper $2,860. Benson, EF, $48,300

KM# Tn59.2 • **Copper** • **Edge:** Plain.

Date	Good	VG	Fine	VF	XF
1792 3 known	—	—	—	125,000	200,000

KM# Tn59.1a • **Silver** • **Edge:** Lettered. **Edge Lettering:** UNITED STATES OF AMERICA

Date	Good	VG	Fine	VF	XF	Unc
1792 rare	—	—	—	40,000	65,000	—

Note: Roper $35,200

KM# Tn59.2a • **Silver** • **Edge:** Plain.

Date	AG	Good	VG	Fine	VF	XF	Unc
1792 rare	—	—	—	—	—	—	—

KM# Tn59.1b • **Gold** AGW • **Edge:** Lettered. **Edge Lettering:** UNITED STATES OF AMERICA

Date	Good	VG	Fine	VF	XF	Unc
1792 unique	—	—	—	—	—	—

KM# Tn63.1 • **Silver** • **Rev:** Small eagle **Edge:** Plain.

Date	AG	Good	VG	Fine	VF	XF	Unc
1792	—	—	—	—	200,000	300,000	—

KM# Tn63.2 • **Silver** • **Edge:** Ornamented, circles and squares.

Date	Good	VG	Fine	VF	XF	Unc
1792 5 known	—	—	—	100,000	175,000	400,000

KM# Tn63.1a • **Copper** • **Edge:** Plain.

Date	Good	VG	Fine	VF	XF	Unc
1792	4,000	6,500	12,500	32,000	65,000	—

Note: Garrett $32,000

KM# Tn63.3 • **Silver** • **Edge:** Two olive leaves.

Date	Good	VG	Fine	VF	XF	Unc
1792 unique	—	—	—	—	—	—

KM# Tn64 • **Silver** • **Rev:** Large heraldic eagle

Date	Good	VG	Fine	VF	XF	Unc
1792 unique	—	—	—	100,000	—	—

Note: Garrett $16,500

EARLY AMERICAN PATTERNS
Confederatio

KM# EA22 • **Copper** • **Obv:** Standing figure with bow & arrow **Obv. Legend:** INIMICA TYRANNIS.AMERICANA. **Rev. Legend:** .CONFEDERATIO.

Date	AG	Good	VG	Fine	VF	XF	Unc
1785	—	—	—	—	50,000	95,000	—

KM# EA23 • Copper • Obv: Standing figure with bow & arrow **Obv. Legend:** INIMICA TYRANNIS.AMERICANA. **Rev:** Large circle of stars. **Rev. Legend:** .CONFEDERATIO. **Note:** The Confederatio dies were struck in combination with 13 other dies of the period. All surviving examples of these combinations are extremely rare.

Date	Good	VG	Fine	VF	XF	Unc
extremely rare	—	—	—	50,000	100,000	—

Immune Columbia

KM# EA20 • Copper • Obv: George III. **Obv. Legend:** GEORGIVS III.REX. **Rev. Legend:** IMMUNE COLUMBIA.

Date	AG	Good	VG	Fine	VF	XF	Unc
1785	3,500	5,000	7,500	9,500	22,500	—	—

KM# EA21 • Copper • Obv: Head right **Obv. Legend:** VERMON AUCTORI **Rev. Legend:** IMMUNE COLUMBIA.

Date	AG	Good	VG	Fine	VF	XF	Unc
1785	—	5,500	8,500	11,500	35,000	—	—

KM# EA17a • Silver • Obv. Legend: IMMUNE COLUMBIA. **Rev:** Eye, with pointed rays & stars **Rev. Legend:** NOVA CONSTELLATIO

Date	AG	Good	VG	Fine	VF	XF	Unc
	—	—	—	—	45,000	90,000	—

KM# EA19a • Gold AGW • **Obv. Legend:** IMMUNE COLUMBIA. **Rev:** Blunt rays **Rev. Legend:** NOVA CONSTELATIO.

Date	AG	Good	VG	Fine	VF	XF	Unc
1785 unique	—	—	—	—	—	—	—

Note: In the Smithsonian Collection

KM# EA17 • Copper • Obv. Legend: IMMUNE COLUMBIA. **Rev:** Eye, with pointed rays & stars **Rev. Legend:** NOVA CONSTELLATIO

Date	AG	Good	VG	Fine	VF	XF	Unc
1785	—	—	—	—	22,500	40,000	—

KM# EA18 • Copper • Obv. Legend: IMMUNE COLUMBIA. **Rev:** Eye, with pointed rays & stars. Extra star in reverse legend **Rev. Legend:** NOVA . CONSTELLATIO *

Date	AG	Good	VG	Fine	VF	XF	Unc
1785	—	—	—	—	22,500	40,000	—

Note: Caldwell $4,675

KM# EA19 • Copper • Obv. Legend: IMMUNE COLUMBIA. **Rev:** Blunt rays. **Rev. Legend:** NOVA CONSTELATIO

Date	Good	VG	Fine	VF	XF	Unc
1785 2 known	—	—	—	—	100,000	—

Note: Norweb $22,000

KM# EA28 • Copper • Obv. Legend: IMMUNIS COLUMBIA **Rev:** Eagle. **Rev. Legend:** *E*PLURIBUS*UNUM*

Date	Good	VG	Fine	VF	XF	Unc
1786 3 known	—	—	—	50,000	90,000	—

KM# EA24 • Copper • Obv: Washington. **Rev:** Stars in rayed circle **Rev. Legend:** CONFEDERATIO

Date	Good	VG	Fine	VF	XF	Unc
1786 3 known	—	—	—	50,000	—	—

Note: Garrett $50,000. Steinberg $12,650

KM# EA25 • **Copper** • **Obv:** Eagle, raw shield. **Obv. Legend:** *E.PLURIBUS UNUM. **Rev:** Shield **Rev. Legend:** *E*PLURIBUS*UNUM*

Date	Good	VG	Fine	VF	XF	Unc
1786 unique	—	—	—	—	—	—

Note: Garrett $37,500

KM# EA26 • **Copper** • **Obv:** Washington. **Obv. Legend:** GEN.WASHINGTON. **Rev:** Eagle.

Date	Good	VG	Fine	VF	XF	Unc
1786 2 known	—	—	—	—	—	—

KM# EA27 • **Copper** • **Obv. Legend:** IMMUNIS COLUMBIA. **Rev:** Shield **Rev. Legend:** *E*PLURIBUS*UNUM*

Date	Good	VG	Fine	VF	XF	Unc
1786 extremely rare	—	—	—	40,000	—	—

Note: Rescigno, AU, $33,000. Steinberg, VF, $11,000

Nova Constellatio

KM# EA6.1 • **Copper** • **Obv:** Pointed rays. **Obv. Legend:** CONSTELLATIO. **Rev:** Small "US".

Date	AG	Good	VG	Fine	VF	XF	Unc
1783	50.00	70.00	100.00	225	440	950	3,750

KM# EA6.2 • **Copper** • **Obv:** Pointed rays. **Obv. Legend:** CONSTELLATIO. **Rev:** Large "US".

Date	AG	Good	VG	Fine	VF	XF	Unc
1783	55.00	75.00	110	250	600	1,400	6,000

KM# EA7 • **Copper** • **Obv:** Blunt rays. **Obv. Legend:** CONSTELATIO.

Date	AG	Good	VG	Fine	VF	XF	Unc
1783	50.00	75.00	110	250	575	1,300	5,000

KM# EA8 • **Copper** • **Obv:** Blunt rays. **Obv. Legend:** CONSTELLATIO.

Date	AG	Good	VG	Fine	VF	XF	Unc
1785	50.00	75.00	110	260	625	1,500	6,500

KM# EA9 • **Copper** • **Obv:** Pointed rays. **Obv. Legend:** CONSTELLATIO.

Date	AG	Good	VG	Fine	VF	XF	Unc
1785	—	—	100.00	225	450	1,000	3,600

KM# EA10 • **Copper** • **Note:** Contemporary circulating counterfeit. Similar to previously listed coin.

Date	Good	VG	Fine	VF	XF	Unc
1786 extremely rare	—	—	—	—	—	—

5 UNITS

KM# EA12 • **Copper** • **Obv:** Eye, with pointed rays & stars **Obv. Legend:** NOVA CONSTELLATIO **Rev. Legend:** .LIBERTAS. JUSTITIA.

Date	Good	VG	Fine	VF	XF	Unc
1783 unique	—	—	—	—	—	—

100 (BIT)

KM# EA13.1 • **Silver** • **Obv:** Eye, with pointed rays & stars **Obv. Legend:** NOVA CONSTELLATIO **Rev. Legend:** .LIBERTAS. JUSTITIA. **Edge:** Leaf.

Date	Good	VG	Fine	VF	XF	Unc
1783 2 known	—	—	—	—	—	—

Note: Garrett $97,500. Stack's auction, May 1991, $72,500

KM# EA13.2 • **Silver** • **Obv:** Eye, with pointed rays & stars **Obv. Legend:** NOVA CONSTELLATIO **Rev. Legend:** .LIBERTAS. JUSTITIA. **Edge:** Plain.

Date	Good	VG	Fine	VF	XF	Unc
1783 unique	—	—	—	—	—	—

500 (QUINT)

KM# EA14 • **Silver** • **Obv:** Eye with pointed rays & stars **Obv. Legend:** NOVA CONSTELLATIO **Rev. Legend:** .LIBERTAS. JUSTITIA.

Date	Good	VG	Fine	VF	XF	Unc
1783 unique	—	—	—	—	250,000	—

Note: Garrett $165,000

KM# EA15 • **Silver** • **Obv:** Eye, with rays & stars, no legend **Rev. Legend:** .LIBERTAS. JUSTITIA.

Date	Good	VG	Fine	VF	XF	Unc
1783 unique	—	—	75,000	—	—	—

Note: Garrett $55,000

1000 (MARK)

KM# EA16 • **Silver** • **Obv:** Eye, with pointed rays & stars **Obv. Legend:** *NOVA CONSTELLATIO **Rev. Legend:** .LIBERTAS. JUSTITIA.

Date	Good	VG	Fine	VF	XF	Unc
1783 unique	—	—	—	350,000	—

Note: Garrett $190,000

EARLY FEDERAL COINAGE

Brasher

KM# Tn51.1 • **Gold** AGW • **Obv:** Sunrise over mountains. **Rev:** Displayed eagle with shield on breast, EB counterstamp on wing.

Date	AG	Good	VG	Fine	VF	XF	Unc
1787 6 known	—	—	—	—	—	—	—

Note: Heritage FUN Sale, January 2005, AU-55, $2.415 million.

KM# Tn51.2 • Gold AGW • **Obv:** Sun rise over mountains **Rev:** Displayed eagle with sheild on breast. EB counterstamp on breast.

Date	Good	VG	Fine	VF	XF	Unc
1787 unique	—	—	—	—	—	—

Note: Heritage FUN Sale, January 2005, XF-45, $2.99 million. Foreign gold coins with the EB counterstamp exist. These are valued at over $5,000, with many much higher.

Fugio "Cent"

KM# EA30.1 • Copper • Obv: Club rays, round ends.

Date	AG	Good	VG	Fine	VF	XF	Unc
1787	225	325	450	850	2,000	3,850	—

KM# EA30.2 • Copper • Obv: Club rays, concave ends.

Date	AG	Good	VG	Fine	VF	XF	Unc
1787	1,500	2,500	3,500	8,000	20,000	—	—

KM# EA30.3 • Copper • Obv. Legend: FUCIO.

Date	AG	Good	VG	Fine	VF	XF	Unc
1787	—	2,000	3,000	7,000	25,000	35,000	—

KM# EA31.1 • Copper • Obv: Pointed rays. **Rev:** UNITED above, STATES below.

Date	AG	Good	VG	Fine	VF	XF	Unc
1787	600	950	1,400	3,000	7,750	10,000	—

KM# EA31.2 • Copper • Rev: UNITED STATES at sides of ring.

Date	AG	Good	VG	Fine	VF	XF	Unc
1787	110	175	275	550	850	1,600	3,500

KM# EA31.3 • Copper • Rev: STATES UNITED at sides of ring.

Date	AG	Good	VG	Fine	VF	XF	Unc
1787	110	190	275	550	800	1,500	3,500

KM# EA31.4 • Copper • Rev: Eight-pointed stars on ring.

Date	AG	Good	VG	Fine	VF	XF	Unc
1787	150	285	450	650	1,200	2,500	9,000

KM# EA31.5 • Copper • Rev: Raised rims on ring, large lettering in center.

Date	AG	Good	VG	Fine	VF	XF	Unc
1787	185	325	500	900	2,400	5,250	17,500

KM# EA32.1 • Copper • Obv: No cinquefoils, cross after date. **Obv. Legend:** UNITED STATES.

Date	AG	Good	VG	Fine	VF	XF	Unc
1787	300	485	750	1,450	3,500	6,500	—

KM# EA32.2 • Copper • Obv: No cinquefoils, cross after date. **Obv. Legend:** STATES UNITED.

Date	AG	Good	VG	Fine	VF	XF	Unc
1787	—	—	750	1,500	3,750	6,800	—

KM# EA32.3 • Copper • Obv: No cinquefoils, cross after date. **Rev:** Raised rims on ring.

Date	AG	Good	VG	Fine	VF	XF	Unc
1787	—	—	—	—	22,500	—	—

KM# EA33 • Copper • Obv: No cinquefoils, cross after date. **Rev:** With rays. **Rev. Legend:** AMERICAN CONGRESS.

Date	Good	VG	Fine	VF	XF	Unc
1787 extremely rare	—	—	— 275,000	—	—	

Note: Norweb $63,800

KM# EA34 • Brass • Note: New Haven restrike.

Date	AG	Good	VG	Fine	VF	XF	Unc
1787	—	—	—	—	—	450	1,000

KM# EA34a • Copper • Note: New Haven restrike.

Date	AG	Good	VG	Fine	VF	XF	Unc
1787	—	—	—	—	450	750	1,000

KM# EA34b • Silver • Note: New Haven restrike.

Date	AG	Good	VG	Fine	VF	XF	Unc
1787 (ca.1858)	—	—	—	—	1,500	4,000	

KM# EA34c • Gold AGW • **Note:** New Haven restrike.

Date	Good	VG	Fine	VF	XF	Unc
1787 (ca.1858) 2 known	—	—	—	—	—	—

Note: Norweb (holed) $1,430

ISSUES OF 1792

CENT

KM# PnE1 • Copper Around Silver • Note: Silver plug in center.

Date	Good	VG	Fine	VF	XF	Unc
1792						
12 known	—	—	175,000	300,000	450,000	—

Note: Norweb, MS-60, $143,000.

KM# PnF1 • Copper • Note: No silver center.

Date	Good	VG	Fine	VF	XF	Unc
1792						
8 known	—	—	250,000	500,000	750,000	—

Note: Norweb, EF-40, $35,200; Benson, VG-10, $57,500

KM# PnG1 • Copper • Edge: Plain **Note:** Commonly called "Birch cent."

Date	Good	VG	Fine	VF	XF	Unc
1792 unique	—	—	—	—	500,000	—

KM# PnH1 • Copper • Obv: One star in edge legend **Note:** Commonly called "Birch cent."

Date	Good	VG	Fine	VF	XF	Unc
1792						
2 known	—	—	150,000	350,000	450,000	—

Note: Norweb, EF-40, $59,400

KM# PnI1 • Copper • Obv: Two stars in edge legend **Note:** Commonly called "Birch cent."

Date	Good	VG	Fine	VF	XF	Unc
1792 6 known	—	—	—	—	—	—

Note: Hawn, strong VF, $57,750

KM# PnJ1 • White Metal • Rev: "G.W.Pt." below wreath tie **Note:** Commonly called "Birch cent."

Date	Good	VG	Fine	VF	XF	Unc
1792 unique	—	—	—	—	550,000	—

Note: Garrett, $90,000

HALF DISME

KM# 5 • Silver •

Date	AG	VG	Fine	VF	XF	Unc
1792	25,000	35,000	55,000	90,000	125,000	450,000

KM# PnA1 • Copper •

Date	Good	VG	Fine	VF	XF	Unc
1792 unique	—	—	—	—	—	—

DISME

KM# PnB1 • Silver •

Date	VG	Fine	VF	XF	Unc
1792 3 known	—	—	700,000	1,000,000	—

Note: Norweb, EF-40, $28,600

KM# PnC1 • Copper • Edge: Reeded

Date	VG	Fine	VF	XF	Unc
1792 14 known	—	—	150,000	250,000	500,000

Note: Hawn, VF, $30,800; Benson, EF-45, $109,250

KM# PnD1 • Copper • Edge: Plain

Date	VG	Fine	VF	XF	Unc
1792 2 known	—	—	450,000	750,000	—

Note: Garrett, $45,000

QUARTER

KM# PnK1 • Copper • Edge: Reeded **Note:** Commonly called "Wright quarter."

Date	Good	VG	Fine	VF	XF	Unc
1792 2 known	—	—	—	—	—	—

KM# PnL1 • White Metal • Edge: Plain **Note:** Commonly called "Wright quarter."

Date	Good	VG	Fine	VF	XF	Unc
1792 2 known	—	—	—	—	—	—

Note: Norweb, VF-30 to EF-40, $28,600

KM# PnM1 • White Metal • Note: Commonly called "Wright quarter."

Date	Good	VG	Fine	VF	XF	Unc
1792 die trial	—	—	—	—	—	—

Note: Garrett, $12,000

UNITED STATES

CIRCULATION COINAGE

HALF CENT

Liberty Cap
Head facing left obverse

KM# 10 • 6.7400 g., **Copper**, 22 mm. • **Designer:** Henry Voigt

Date	Mintage	G-4	VG-8	F-12	VF-20	XF-40	MS-60
1793	35,334	2,200	3,400	6,750	10,000	17,000	35,000

Head facing right obverse

KM# 14 • **Copper**, 6.74 g. 1794-95 and 5.44 g. 1795-97, 23.5 mm. • **Designer:** Robert Scot 1794 and John Smith Gardner 1795 **Notes:** The "lettered edge" varieties have "Two Hundred for a Dollar" inscribed around the edge. The "pole" varieties have a pole upon which the cap is hanging, resting on Liberty's shoulder. The "punctuated date" varieties have a comma after the 1 in the date. The 1797 "1 above 1" variety has a second 1 above the 1 in the date.

Date	Mintage	G-4	VG-8	F-12	VF-20	XF-40	MS-60
1794	81,600	400	650	900	1,600	3,500	18,000
1795 lettered edge, pole	25,600	450	700	950	1,500	4,250	17,500
1795 plain edge, no pole	109,000	375	475	800	1,400	3,500	16,000
1795 lettered edge, punctuated date	Inc. above	475	700	1,000	1,600	3,750	20,000
1795 plain edge, punctuated date	Inc. above	350	450	750	1,200	3,000	27,500
1796 pole	5,090	16,000	20,000	23,500	30,000	35,000	—
1796 no pole	1,390	27,000	32,500	47,500	90,000	—	—
1797 plain edge	119,215	400	575	950	1,900	6,000	27,500
1797 lettered edge	Inc. above	1,700	2,700	4,000	8,000	25,000	—
1797 1 above 1	Inc. above	375	475	950	1,600	3,250	20,000
1797 gripped edge	Inc. above	16,000	37,500	48,000	60,000	70,000	—

Draped Bust Half Cent
Draped bust right, date at angle below obverse   Value within thin wreath reverse

Stemless   Stems

KM# 33 • 5.4400 g., **Copper**, 23.5 mm. • **Obv. Legend** LIBERTY **Rev. Legend:** UNITED STATES OF AMERICA **Designer:** Robert Scot **Notes:** The wreath on the reverse was redesigned slightly in 1802, resulting in "reverse of 1800" and "reverse of 1802" varieties. The "stems" varieties have stems extending from the wreath above and on both sides of the fraction on the reverse. On the 1804 "crosslet 4" variety, a serif appears at the far right of the crossbar on the 4 in the date. The "spiked chin" variety appears to have a spike extending from Liberty's chin, the result of a damaged die. Varieties of the 1805 strikes are distinguished by the size of the 5 in the date. Varieties of the 1806 strikes are distinguished by the size of the 6 in the date.

Date	Mintage	G-4	VG-8	F-12	VF-20	XF-40	MS-60
1800	211,530	50.00	75.00	100.00	200	500	2,500
1802/0 rev. 1800	14,366	15,000	22,000	30,000	—	—	—
1802/0 rev. 1802	Inc. above	800	1,400	2,750	6,500	17,000	—
1803	97,900	45.00	70.00	125	275	950	7,000
1804 plain 4, stemless wreath	1,055,312	50.00	60.00	85.00	130	250	1,400
1804 plain 4, stems	Inc. above	45.00	75.00	125	250	1,500	12,000
1804 crosslet 4, stemless	Inc. above	50.00	75.00	85.00	125	250	1,350
1804 crosslet 4, stems	Inc. above	47.00	75.00	110	175	300	1,200
1804 spiked chin	Inc. above	60.00	90.00	125	175	325	1,200
1805 small 5, stemless	814,464	50.00	75.00	90.00	135	400	3,500
1805 small 5, stems	Inc. above	800	1,200	2,400	4,500	8,000	—
1805 large 5, stems	Inc. above	49.00	65.00	85.00	125	400	3,000
1806 small 6, stems	356,000	200	325	600	1,000	2,750	—
1806 small 6, stemless	Inc. above	50.00	65.00	85.00	125	235	1,350
1806 large 6, stems	Inc. above	50.00	65.00	85.00	125	250	1,200
1807	476,000	50.00	80.00	120	175	300	1,400
1808/7	400,000	300	400	600	1,200	6,000	27,500
1808	Inc. above	50.00	65.00	90.00	135	350	5,000

Classic Head Half Cent

Classic head left, flanked by stars, date below obverse   Value within wreath reverse

KM# 41 • 5.4400 g., **Copper**, 23.5 mm. • **Rev. Legend:** UNITED STATES OF AMERICA **Designer:** John Reich **Notes:** Restrikes listed were produced privately in the mid-1800s. The 1831 restrikes have two varieties with different-size berries in the wreath on the reverse. The 1828 strikes have either 12 or 13 stars on the obverse.

Date	Mintage	G-4	VG-8	F-12	VF-20	XF-40	MS-60
1809/6	1,154,572	60.00	80.00	110	150	215	1,000
1809	Inc. above	32.00	40.00	55.00	80.00	215	800
1809 circle in 0	—	35.00	45.00	60.00	110	250	2,100
1810	215,000	45.00	60.00	120	200	600	3,250
1811	63,140	225	375	750	1,800	4,000	—
1811 restrike, reverse of 1802, uncirculated	—	—	—	—	—	—	27,500
1825	63,000	45.00	60.00	75.00	110	200	950

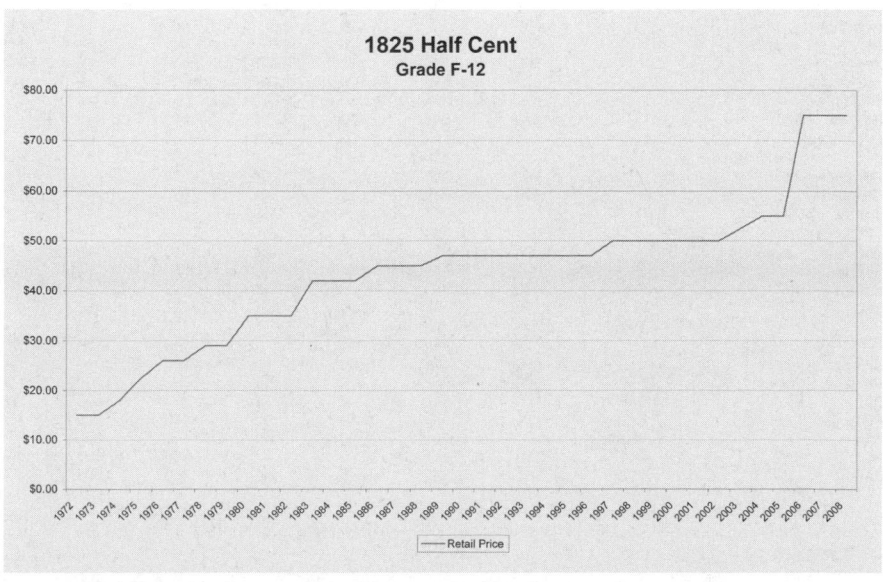

1825 Half Cent
Grade F-12

Retail Price

HALF CENT

Date	Mintage	G-4	VG-8	F-12	VF-20	XF-40	MS-60
1826	234,000	40.00	55.00	75.00	90.00	200	750
1828 13 stars	606,000	40.00	60.00	75.00	85.00	110	300
1828 12 stars	Inc. above	50.00	80.00	120	175	250	850
1829	487,000	40.00	55.00	70.00	100.00	150	500
1831 original	2,200	5,500	7,500	11,000	16,500	22,500	—
1831 1st restrike, lg. berries, reverse of 1836	—	—	—	—	—	—	6,500
1831 2nd restrike, sm. berries, reverse of 1840, proof	—	—	—	—	—	—	25,000
1832	154,000	39.00	50.00	70.00	95.00	130	350
1833	120,000	39.00	50.00	70.00	95.00	130	350
1834	141,000	39.00	50.00	70.00	95.00	130	350
1835	398,000	39.00	50.00	70.00	95.00	130	350
1836 original, proof	—	—	—	—	—	—	6,000
1836 restrike, reverse of 1840, proof	—	—	—	—	—	—	20,000

Braided Hair Half Cent
Head left, braided hair, within circle of stars, date below obverse
Value within wreath reverse

KM# 70 • 5.4400 g., **Copper**, 23 mm. • **Rev. Legend:** UNITED STATES OF AMERICA **Designer:**
Christian Gobrecht **Notes:** 1840-1849 and 1852 strikes, both originals and restrikes, are known in proof only;
mintages are unknown. The small-date varieties of 1849, both originals and restrikes are known in proof only.
The Restrikes were produced clandestinely by Philadelphia Mint personnel in the mid-1800s.

Date	Mintage	G-4	VG-8	F-12	VF-20	XF-40	MS-60	Prf-60
1840 original	—	1,000	1,200	1,500	2,000	3,000	—	5,500
1840 1st restrike	—	1,000	1,200	1,500	2,000	3,000	—	6,500
1840 2nd restrike	—	1,000	1,200	1,500	2,000	3,000	—	5,500
1841 original	—	1,000	1,200	1,500	2,000	3,000	—	5,500
1841 1st restrike	—	1,000	1,200	1,500	2,000	3,000	—	6,500
1841 2nd restrike	—	1,000	1,200	1,500	2,000	3,000	—	6,000
1842 original	—	1,000	1,200	1,500	2,000	3,000	—	6,000
1842 1st restrike	—	1,000	1,200	1,500	2,000	3,000	—	6,000
1842 2nd restrike	—	1,000	1,200	1,500	2,000	3,000	—	6,000
1843 original	—	1,000	1,200	1,500	2,000	3,000	—	6,500
1843 1st restrike	—	1,000	1,200	1,500	2,000	3,000	—	6,000
1843 2nd restrike	—	1,000	1,200	1,500	2,000	3,000	—	6,500
1844 original	—	1,000	1,200	1,500	2,000	3,000	—	6,000
1844 1st restrike	—	1,000	1,200	1,500	2,000	3,000	—	6,000
1844 2nd restrike	—	1,000	1,200	1,500	2,000	3,000	—	6,000
1845 original	—	1,000	1,200	1,500	2,000	3,000	—	6,000
1845 1st restrike	—	1,000	1,200	1,500	2,000	3,000	—	6,000
1845 2nd restrike	—	1,000	1,200	1,500	2,000	3,000	—	6,000
1846 original	—	1,000	1,200	1,500	2,000	3,000	—	6,000
1846 1st restrike	—	1,000	1,200	1,500	2,000	3,000	—	6,500
1846 2nd restrike	—	1,000	1,200	1,500	2,000	3,000	—	6,000
1847 original	—	1,000	1,200	1,500	2,000	3,000	—	6,000
1847 1st restrike	—	3,000	4,000	4,500	5,000	5,500	—	8,000
1847 2nd restrike	—	1,000	1,200	1,500	2,000	3,000	—	6,000
1848 original	—	1,000	1,200	1,500	2,000	3,000	—	6,000
1848 1st restrike	—	1,000	1,200	1,500	2,000	3,000	—	6,000
1848 2nd restrike	—	1,000	1,200	1,500	2,000	3,000	—	6,000
1849 original, small date	—	1,000	1,200	1,500	2,000	3,000	—	6,500
1849 1st restrike small date	—	1,000	1,200	1,500	2,000	3,000	—	6,000
1849 large date	39,864	50.00	70.00	90.00	125	175	325	—
1850	39,812	45.00	60.00	90.00	150	200	400	—
1851	147,672	45.00	60.00	75.00	90.00	120	175	—
1852 original	—	12,000	25,000	30,000	35,000	40,000	—	90,000
1852 1st restrike	—	1,000	1,200	1,500	2,000	3,000	—	5,000
1852 2nd restrike	—	1,000	1,200	1,500	2,000	3,000	—	7,000
1853	129,694	50.00	75.00	90.00	125	160	300	—
1854	55,358	50.00	75.00	90.00	125	160	300	—
1855	56,500	50.00	75.00	90.00	125	160	300	—
1856	40,430	50.00	75.00	90.00	125	160	300	—
1857	35,180	80.00	100.00	200	250	300	500	—

CENT

Flowing Hair Cent
Chain reverse

KM# 11 • 13.4800 g., **Copper**, 26-27 mm. • **Designer:** Henry Voigt

Date	Mintage	G-4	VG-8	F-12	VF-20	XF-40	MS-60
1793 "AMERI"	36,103	9,750	13,750	24,500	43,500	77,500	175,000
1793 "AMERICA"	Inc. above	7,750	10,000	16,750	32,500	55,000	115,000
1793 periods after "LIBERTY"	Inc. above	8,650	10,750	17,850	34,500	56,500	118,000

Flowing Hair Cent
Wreath reverse

KM# 12 • 13.4800 g., **Copper**, 26-28 mm. • **Designer:** Henry Voigt

Date	Mintage	G-4	VG-8	F-12	VF-20	XF-40	MS-60
1793 vine and bars edge	63,353	1,950	2,950	4,750	7,500	12,500	30,000
1793 lettered edge	Inc. above	2,100	3,250	5,200	8,000	14,000	—
1793 strawberry leaf; 4 known	—	—	—	600,000	—	—	—

Liberty Cap Cent

KM# 13 • **Copper**, 13.48 g. 1793-95 and 10.89 g. 1795-96, 29 mm. • **Designer:** Joseph Wright 1793-1795 and John Smith Gardner 1795-1796 **Notes:** The heavier pieces were struck on a thicker planchet. The Liberty design on the obverse was revised slightly in 1794, but the 1793 design was used on some 1794 strikes. A 1795 "lettered edge" variety has "One Hundred for a Dollar" and a leaf inscribed on the edge.

Date	Mintage	G-4	VG-8	F-12	VF-20	XF-40	MS-60
1793 cap	11,056	3,500	6,500	11,500	36,500	67,500	—
1794 head '93	918,521	1,350	2,600	4,000	7,900	12,000	—
1794 head '94	Inc. above	425	485	750	1,200	3,750	9,000
1794 head '95	Inc. above	—	—	—	—	—	—
1794 starred rev.	Inc. above	10,500	17,500	35,000	—	—	—
1795 plain edge	501,500	350	485	650	1,000	2,000	4,750
1795 reeded edge	Inc. above	—	—	—	—	—	—
1795 Jefferson head	Inc. above	—	—	—	—	—	—

Liberty Cap Cent

KM# 13a • 10.8900 g., **Copper**, 29 mm. • **Designer:** Joseph Wright 1793-1795 and John Smith Gardner 1795-1796

Date	Mintage	G-4	VG-8	F-12	VF-20	XF-40	MS-60
1795 lettered edge, "One Cent" high in wreath	37,000	400	550	900	1,750	4,000	15,000
1796	109,825	350	500	800	1,400	3,750	21,000

Draped Bust Cent
Draped bust right, date at angle below obverse   Value within wreath reverse

Stemless   Stems

KM# 22 • 10.9800 g., **Copper**, 29 mm. • **Obv. Legend** LIBERTY **Rev. Legend:** UNITED STATES OF AMERICA **Designer:** Robert Scot **Notes:** The 1801 "3 errors" variety has the fraction on the reverse reading "1/000," has only one stem extending from the wreath above and on both sides of the fraction on the reverse, and "United" in "United States of America" appears as "linited."

Date	Mintage	G-4	VG-8	F-12	VF-20	XF-40	MS-60
1796 Rev. of 1794	363,375	350	600	850	1,800	3,400	—
1796 Rev. of 1796	Inc. above	—	—	—	—	—	—
1796 Rev. of 1797	Inc. above	—	—	—	—	—	—
1796 Liberty error	Inc. above	—	—	—	—	—	—
1797	897,510	130	175	250	335	1,150	3,300
1797 stemless	Inc. above	300	495	600	910	3,200	—
1798	1,841,745	90.00	130	200	350	1,300	3,100
1798/7	Inc. above	200	300	375	1,200	3,900	—
1799	42,540	3,500	5,000	8,500	16,000	35,000	—

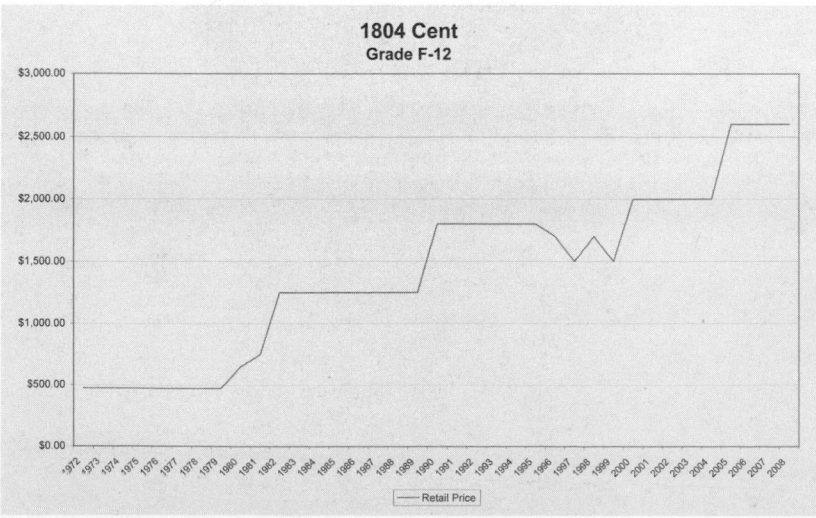

1804 Cent
Grade F-12

Date	Mintage	G-4	VG-8	F-12	VF-20	XF-40	MS-60
1800	2,822,175	50.00	95.00	200	400	1,750	—
1801	1,362,837	60.00	87.00	180	325	1,000	—
1801 3 errors	Inc. above	225	500	925	1,750	5,500	—
1802	3,435,100	50.00	75.00	150	250	775	2,250
1803	2,471,353	50.00	80.00	150	250	775	2,250
1804	96,500	1,400	2,000	2,600	3,200	7,000	—
1804 Restrike of 1860	—	400	500	700	900	1,100	1,500
1805	941,116	60.00	90.00	160	300	875	2,450
1806	348,000	70.00	100.00	150	375	1,100	4,700
1807	727,221	60.00	80.00	160	300	800	2,250
1807/6 large 7/6	—	60.00	80.00	160	350	1,275	—
1807/6 small 7/6	—	1,900	2,900	4,200	6,000	19,000	—

Classic Head Cent

Classic head left, flanked bt stars, date below obverse   Value within wreath reverse

KM# 39 • 10.8900 g., **Copper**, 29 mm. • **Rev. Legend:** UNITED STATES OF AMERICA **Designer:** John Reich

Date	Mintage	G-4	VG-8	F-12	VF-20	XF-40	MS-60
1808	1,109,000	85.00	150	250	575	1,450	3,600
1809	222,867	135	250	450	1,050	2,650	6,300
1810/09	1,458,500	—	—	—	—	—	—
1810	Inc. above	75.00	95.00	210	550	1,100	3,850
1811/10	218,025	130	200	440	1,200	2,200	—
1811	Inc. above	110	175	400	1,000	1,500	7,000
1812	1,075,500	54.00	88.00	215	550	975	2,800
1813	418,000	60.00	175	400	800	1,200	—
1814 Plain 4	357,830	54.00	93.00	225	530	975	2,800
1814 Crosslet 4	Inc. above	54.00	88.00	215	550	975	—

Coronet Cent

Coronet head left, within circle of stars, date below obverse   Value within wreath reverse

KM# 45 • 10.8900 g., **Copper**, 28-29 mm. • **Rev. Legend:** UNITED STATES OF AMERICA **Designer:** John Reich **Notes:** The 1817 strikes have either 13 or 15 stars on the obverse.

Date	Mintage	G-4	VG-8	F-12	VF-20	XF-40	MS-60
1816	2,820,982	31.00	37.00	51.00	98.00	175	420
1817 13 stars	3,948,400	29.00	34.00	45.00	75.00	145	500
1817 15 stars	Inc. above	35.00	50.00	90.00	225	500	1,600
1818	3,167,000	29.00	33.00	40.00	72.00	125	270
1819	2,671,000	29.00	33.00	40.00	72.00	120	285
1820	4,407,550	29.00	33.00	40.00	72.00	120	300
1821	389,000	40.00	75.00	250	400	1,500	6,000
1822	2,072,339	31.00	35.00	50.00	100.00	195	750
1823 Included in 1824 mintage	—	90.00	200	310	690	2,750	—
1823/22 Included in 1824 mintage	—	80.00	110	300	675	2,450	—
1823 Restrike	—	600	750	850	1,000	1,200	2,000
1824	1,262,000	31.00	35.00	38.00	180	350	950
1824/22	Inc. above	35.00	45.00	100.00	400	975	3,600
1825	1,461,100	300	35.00	50.00	110	300	960
1826	1,517,425	30.00	35.00	40.00	84.00	175	750
1826/25	Inc. above	30.00	40.00	75.00	175	600	2,000
1827	2,357,732	29.00	33.00	40.00	91.00	125	750

Date	Mintage	G-4	VG-8	F-12	VF-20	XF-40	MS-60
1828	2,260,624	29.00	33.00	40.00	81.00	150	450
1829	1,414,500	29.00	33.00	40.00	91.00	130	475
1830	1,711,500	25.00	29.00	36.00	68.00	120	400
1831	3,359,260	25.00	29.00	36.00	68.00	115	315
1832	2,362,000	25.00	29.00	36.00	68.00	120	380
1833	2,739,000	25.00	29.00	38.00	68.00	113	300
1834	1,855,100	25.00	29.00	36.00	68.00	125	375
1834 Large 8 & stars, small letters	Inc. above	75.00	120	145	250	625	—
1835	3,878,400	25.00	29.00	36.00	68.00	105	300
1836	2,111,000	25.00	29.00	38.00	68.00	105	350
1837	5,558,300	25.00	29.00	38.00	68.00	105	300
1838	6,370,200	25.00	29.00	36.00	68.00	105	300
1839	3,128,661	29.00	33.00	40.00	72.00	110	350
1839/36	Inc. above	300	600	1,250	2,450	4,900	—

Braided Hair Cent
Head left, braided hair, within circle of stars, date below obverse
Value within wreath reverse

KM# 67 • 10.8900 g., **Copper**, 27.5 mm. • **Rev. Legend:** UNITED STATES OF AMERICA **Designer:** Christian Gobrecht **Notes:** 1840 and 1842 strikes are known with both small and large dates, with little difference in value. 1855 and 1856 strikes are known with both slanting and upright 5s in the date, with little difference in value. A slightly larger Liberty head and larger reverse lettering were used beginning in 1843. One 1843 variety uses the old obverse with the new reverse.

Date	Mintage	G-4	VG-8	F-12	VF-20	XF-40	MS-60
1840	2,462,700	25.00	28.00	31.00	36.00	69.00	475
1841	1,597,367	25.00	28.00	31.00	39.00	79.00	440
1842	2,383,390	25.00	28.00	31.00	36.00	69.00	425
1843	2,425,342	25.00	28.00	31.00	36.00	69.00	445
1843 obverse 1842 with reverse of 1844	Inc. above	27.00	30.00	33.00	38.00	79.00	400
1844	2,398,752	25.00	28.00	31.00	36.00	69.00	300
1844/81	Inc. above	40.00	50.00	60.00	100.00	225	700
1845	3,894,804	25.00	28.00	31.00	36.00	69.00	250
1846	4,120,800	23.00	26.00	29.00	34.00	69.00	250
1847	6,183,669	23.00	26.00	29.00	34.00	69.00	250
1847/7	Inc. above	32.00	50.00	90.00	150	385	1,350
1848	6,415,799	25.00	28.00	31.00	36.00	61.00	250
1849	4,178,500	25.00	28.00	31.00	36.00	61.00	325
1850	4,426,844	25.00	28.00	31.00	36.00	61.00	250
1851	9,889,707	23.00	26.00	29.00	34.00	59.00	165
1851/81	Inc. above	36.00	45.00	55.00	85.00	175	600
1852	5,063,094	23.00	26.00	29.00	34.00	59.00	600
1853	6,641,131	23.00	26.00	29.00	34.00	59.00	165
1854	4,236,156	23.00	26.00	29.00	34.00	59.00	165
1855 Slanted 5's	1,574,829	43.00	56.00	66.00	71.00	96.00	200
1855 Upright 5's	—	23.00	26.00	29.00	34.00	59.00	165
1855 Slanted 5's Knob on Ear	—	29.00	34.00	41.00	52.00	99.00	—
1856 Slanted 5	2,690,463	23.00	26.00	29.00	34.00	59.00	165
1856 Upright 5	—	43.00	56.00	69.00	—	—	—
1857 Lg. Date	333,456	125	150	175	225	300	600
1857 Sm. Date	—	85.00	110	140	190	265	—

Flying Eagle Cent
Flying eagle above date obverse   Value within wreath reverse

Large letters AM touch at bottom

Small letters Space between AM

KM# 85 • 4.6700 g., **Copper-Nickel**, 19 mm. • **Obv. Legend** UNITED STATES OF AMERICA **Designer:** James B. Longacre **Notes:** On the large-letter variety of 1858, the "A" and "M" in "America" are connected at their bases; on the small-letter variety, the two letters are separated.

Date	Mintage	G-4	VG-8	F-12	VF-20	XF-40	AU-50	MS-60	MS-65	Prf-65
1856	Est. 2,500	6,250	7,250	9,000	10,750	12,850	1,350	16,500	100,000	28,500
1857	17,450,000	27.50	39.00	40.00	47.00	125	165	320	4,000	29,000
1858/7	—	65.00	92.50	175	380	760	1,500	3,300	60,000	—
1858 large letters	24,600,000	27.50	41.00	43.50	56.00	150	220	340	4,000	24,500
1858 small letters	Inc. above	26.00	39.00	42.00	47.00	135	175	300	3,850	30,000

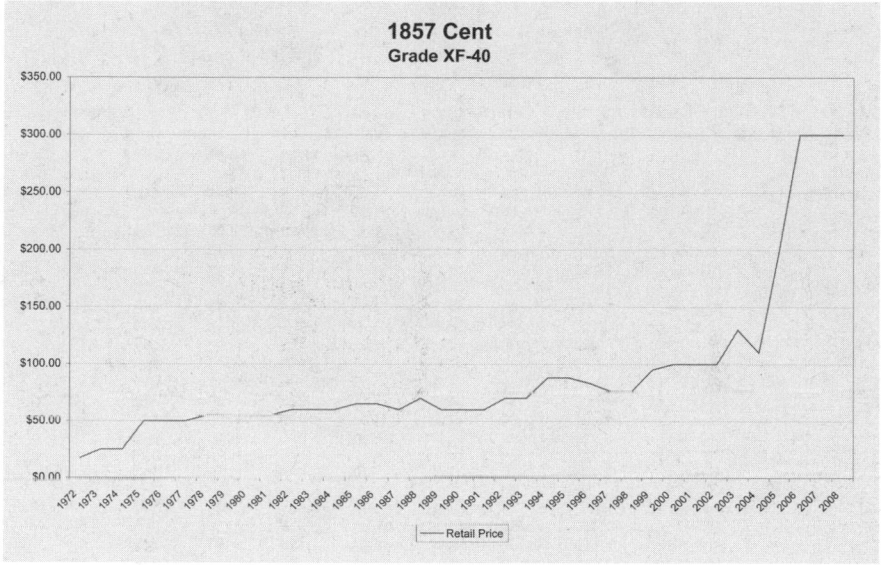

1857 Cent
Grade XF-40

Indian Head Cent
Indian head with headdress left above date obverse   Value within wreath reverse

KM# 87 • 4.6700 g., **Copper-Nickel**, 19 mm. • **Obv. Legend** UNITED STATES OF AMERICA **Designer:** James B. Longacre

Date	Mintage	G-4	VG-8	F-12	VF-20	XF-40	AU-50	MS-60	MS-65	Prf-65
1859	36,400,000	13.00	16.00	22.50	48.00	100.00	175	230	3,500	5,200

Indian Head Cent
Indian head with headdress left above date obverse
Value within wreath, shield above reverse

KM# 90 • 4.6700 g., **Copper-Nickel**, 19 mm. • **Obv. Legend** UNITED STATES OF AMERICA **Designer:** James B. Longacre

Date	Mintage	G-4	VG-8	F-12	VF-20	XF-40	AU-50	MS-60	MS-65	Prf-65
1860 Rounded Bust	20,566,000	11.00	15.00	22.00	46.00	68.00	110	190	965	3,600
1860	1,000	—	—	—	—	—	—	—	—	—
1860 Pointed Bust	Inc. above	20.00	30.00	42.00	60.00	100.00	160	300	6,000	—
1861	10,100,000	20.00	30.00	42.00	58.00	95.00	160	180	975	7,250
1862	28,075,000	11.00	11.50	12.50	15.00	28.00	60.00	80.00	975	2,350
1863	49,840,000	7.50	9.00	11.00	12.50	25.00	58.00	75.00	1,025	3,100
1864	13,740,000	16.00	28.00	35.00	72.00	125	175	220	1,300	3,200

Indian Head Cent
Indian head with headdress left above date obverse
Value within wreath, shield above reverse

  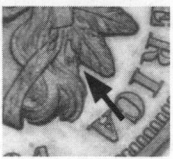

1864 "L"

KM# 90a • 3.1100 g., **Bronze**, 19 mm. • **Obv. Legend** UNITED STATES OF AMERICA **Designer:** James B. Longacre **Notes:** The 1864 "L" variety has the designer's initial in Liberty's hair to the right of her neck.

Date	Mintage	G-4	VG-8	F-12	VF-20	XF-40	AU-50	MS-60	MS-65	Prf-65
1864	39,233,714	8.00	20.00	25.00	45.00	70.00	80.00	110	375	4,300
1864 L pointed bust	Inc. above	52.50	72.50	139	185	275	325	410	1,750	110,000
1865 plain 5	35,429,286	7.00	11.00	20.00	25.00	45.00	60.00	90.00	450	1,550
1865 fancy 5	Inc. above	6.00	10.50	18.50	23.00	40.00	55.00	85.00	—	—
1866	9,826,500	46.00	66.00	80.00	115	195	240	285	1,900	950
1867	9,821,000	52.00	72.00	110	120	195	240	285	1,900	1,050
1867/1867	—	60.00	85.00	130	190	275	385	565	—	—
1868	10,266,500	37.50	50.00	77.00	120	180	245	265	1,200	985
1869/9	6,420,000	190	375	525	750	865	1,000	1,250	2,500	—
1869	Inc. above	90.00	125	230	335	450	560	625	1,750	950
1870	5,275,000	62.00	118	225	285	410	510	600	1,750	1,075
1871	3,929,500	88.00	125	280	310	420	510	610	3,000	1,100
1872	4,042,000	90.00	180	390	425	625	750	840	4,100	1,100
1873 closed 3	11,676,500	30.00	52.00	95.00	135	235	300	400	1,500	850
1873 open 3	Inc. above	20.00	34.00	65.00	82.00	175	215	250	—	—
1873 Double Liberty die 1	Inc. above	275	450	950	1,500	2,400	4,250	7,500	—	—
1873 Double Liberty die 2	Inc. above	—	—	450	900	1,650	2,800	4,500	—	—
1874	14,187,500	15.00	22.50	46.00	65.00	112	150	225	800	800
1875	13,528,000	16.00	29.00	56.00	72.00	120	165	215	800	1,500
1876	7,944,000	27.00	38.50	74.00	130	230	295	335	1,500	925
1877	852,500	950	1,250	1,650	2,250	2,850	3,250	3,750	13,500	6,750
1878	5,799,850	26.00	35.00	68.00	135	245	290	350	1,000	490
1879	16,231,200	7.00	10.00	16.50	33.00	75.00	90.00	100.00	450	450
1880	38,964,955	3.50	5.50	6.50	11.00	28.00	48.00	66.00	450	435
1881	39,211,575	3.50	4.25	6.50	8.00	22.00	30.00	43.00	350	425
1882	38,581,100	3.50	4.25	5.00	10.00	22.00	30.00	40.00	350	425
1883	45,589,109	3.00	4.00	4.50	7.50	17.50	30.00	42.00	350	425
1884	23,261,742	3.50	4.50	7.00	12.50	29.00	40.00	60.00	500	425
1885	11,765,384	6.50	8.00	12.00	27.00	62.00	82.00	105	750	425

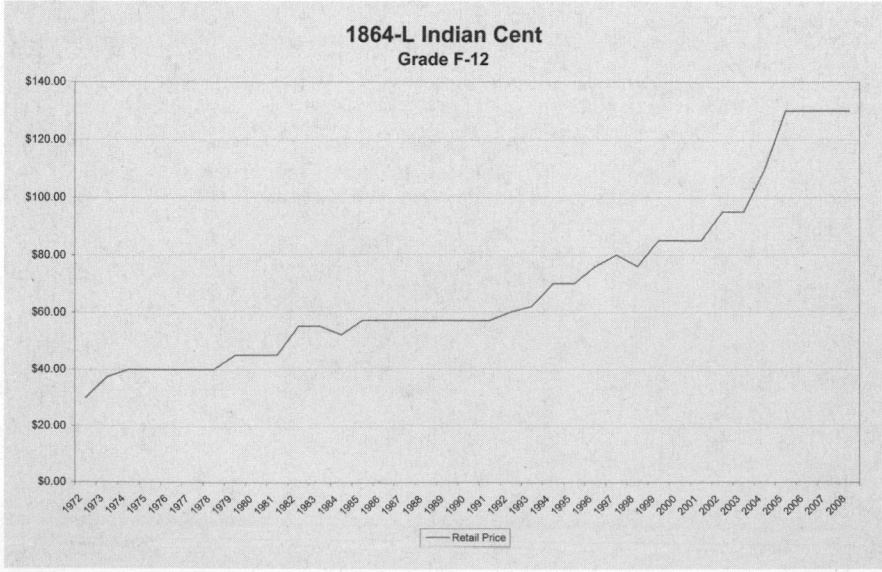

1864-L Indian Cent
Grade F-12

Date	Mintage	G-4	VG-8	F-12	VF-20	XF-40	AU-50	MS-60	MS-65	Prf-65
1886 Type 1 obverse	17,654,290	3.75	6.60	19.75	56.00	148	170	190	1,250	500
1886 Type 2 obverse	Inc. above	7.00	10.00	35.00	90.00	200	250	325	—	—
1887	45,226,483	2.50	3.00	4.00	7.00	19.00	28.00	50.00	400	475
1888	37,494,414	2.75	3.25	5.00	8.00	21.00	28.00	48.00	950	525
1889	48,869,361	2.25	2.75	3.50	6.00	12.00	26.00	40.00	450	450
1890	57,182,854	2.10	2.50	3.00	5.50	10.00	23.00	37.50	400	500
1891	47,072,350	2.25	2.75	3.25	5.50	13.00	23.00	37.00	400	520
1892	37,649,832	2.40	3.25	4.40	6.00	18.50	25.00	35.00	400	525
1893	46,642,195	2.10	2.75	3.25	5.50	10.00	22.00	30.00	350	540
1894	16,752,132	5.00	6.00	13.00	20.00	50.00	65.00	85.00	375	525
1894/94	Inc. above	24.00	34.00	80.00	150	275	440	800	—	—
1895	38,343,636	2.10	2.40	3.50	4.50	11.00	22.00	32.00	275	475
1896	39,057,293	1.95	2.50	3.25	4.75	13.00	26.00	34.00	275	425
1897	50,466,330	1.95	2.40	2.75	4.00	10.00	22.00	30.00	175	425
1898	49,823,079	1.95	2.40	2.75	4.00	10.00	22.00	30.00	275	425
1899	53,600,031	1.95				1	10.00	22.00	30.00	175	415
1900	66,833,764	1.95				10	12.00	23.00	28.00	225	425
1901	79,611,143	1.85	2.10	2.	.30	11.00	22.00	28.00	200	425
1902	87,376,722	1.85	2.20	2.50	.00	10.00	22.00	28.00	200	425
1903	85,094,493	1.85	2.20	2.50	.00	10.00	21.00	28.00	200	425
1904	61,328,015	1.75	2.20	2.50	4.00	10.00	21.00	28.00	200	475
1905	80,719,163	1.75	2.20	2.50	3.50	9.00	20.00	28.00	175	475
1906	96,022,255	1.75	2.20	2.50	3.50	9.00	21.00	28.00	175	395
1907	108,138,618	1.75	2.20	2.50	3.50	8.50	20.00	28.00	175	485
1908	32,327,987	1.75	2.20	2.50	3.50	9.00	20.00	28.00	145	395
1908S	1,115,000	58.00	61.00	70.00	83.00	160	185	285	2,650	—
1909	14,370,645	15.00	15.25	15.50	15.90	18.50	30.00	38.00	150	400
1909S	309,000	500	540	585	630	720	750	840	1,650	—

Lincoln Cent
Wheat Ears reverse

KM# 132 • 3.1100 g., **Bronze**, 19 mm. • **Designer:** Victor D. Brenner **Notes:** The 1909 "VDB" varieties have the designer's initials inscribed at the 6 o'clock position on the reverse. The initials were removed until 1918, when they were restored on the obverse • MS60 prices are for Brown coins and MS65 prices are for coins that are at least 90% original red.

Date	Mintage	G-4	VG-8	F-12	VF-20	XF-40	AU-50	MS-60	MS-65	Prf-65
1909 VDB	27,995,000	12.00	12.50	12.75	13.00	14.00	16.00	21.00	125	—
1909 VDB Doubled Die Obverse	Inc. above	—	—	55.00	75.00	100.00	120	150	1,900	—
1909S VDB	484,000	760	895	1,010	1,150	1,290	1,450	1,650	6,900	—
1909	72,702,618	4.25	4.40	4.75	5.00	6.00	12.00	15.00	85.00	520
1909S	1,825,000	115	120	130	170	245	265	360	1,325	—
1909S/S S over horizontal S	Inc. above	125	132	145	190	280	325	385	1,600	—
1910	146,801,218	.50	.60	.75	1.50	4.50	10.00	17.50	250	700
1910S	6,045,000	17.00	19.00	21.50	29.00	49.00	75.00	105	800	—
1911	101,177,787	.60	.80	2.00	2.50	7.00	11.50	20.00	375	600
1911D	12,672,000	5.25	6.00	10.00	18.50	54.00	74.00	92.00	1,550	—
1911S	4,026,000	45.00	48.00	51.00	55.00	80.00	112	180	3,300	—
1912	68,153,060	1.75	2.00	2.50	6.00	14.00	26.00	34.00	550	950
1912D	10,411,000	7.00	9.50	12.00	27.00	74.00	112	165	2,800	—
1912S	4,431,000	23.00	25.00	30.00	42.00	83.00	120	185	4,400	—
1913	76,532,352	1.00	1.20	1.75	3.40	18.50	29.50	36.00	400	550
1913D	15,804,000	3.00	3.50	4.00	11.00	50.00	65.00	98.00	2,100	—
1913S	6,101,000	13.50	17.50	20.00	32.00	56.00	108	195	6,650	—
1914	75,238,432	.75	1.10	2.25	6.50	19.00	40.00	47.50	415	600
1914D	1,193,000	220	260	4,000	495	975	1,475	1,975	24,000	—
1914S	4,137,000	24.50	27.00	28.00	39.00	92.00	170	295	11,500	—
1915	29,092,120	1.65	2.85	4.10	18.50	60.00	73.00	84.00	1,150	600
1915D	22,050,000	1.75	2.40	3.60	6.75	24.00	44.00	70.00	1,350	—
1915S	4,833,000	20.00	23.00	27.00	30.00	82.00	98.00	175	4,800	—
1916	131,833,677	.35	.60	1.25	2.60	8.00	13.00	18.00	385	1,650
1916D	35,956,000	1.75	2.25	3.00	6.00	15.50	36.00	72.00	3,300	—
1916S	22,510,000	2.25	3.25	4.50	7.00	25.00	38.00	84.00	8,500	—

2 CENTS

**Shield in front of crossed arrows, banner above, date below obverse
Value within wheat wreath reverse**

Small motto   Large motto

KM# 94 • 6.2200 g., **Copper-Tin-Zinc**, 23 mm. • **Rev. Legend:** UNITED STATES OF AMERICA
Designer: James B. Longacre **Notes:** The motto "In God We Trust" was modified in 1864, resulting in small-motto and large-motto varieties for that year.

Date	Mintage	G-4	VG-8	F-12	VF-20	XF-40	AU-50	MS-60	MS-65	Prf-65
1864 small motto	19,847,500	125	185	265	400	595	675	900	3,000	45,000
1864 large motto	Inc. above	15.00	16.00	22.00	28.50	38.50	67.50	85.00	520	1,400
1865	13,640,000	15.00	16.00	22.00	28.50	38.50	67.50	85.00	520	850
1866	3,177,000	15.00	19.00	23.00	28.50	38.50	67.50	85.00	660	850
1867	2,938,750	17.50	22.00	36.00	46.00	60.00	96.00	130	550	850
1868	2,803,750	17.50	22.00	37.50	47.50	62.50	100.00	145	625	850
1869	1,546,000	18.50	23.00	40.00	50.00	71.00	120	160	650	850
1870	861,250	25.00	32.50	46.00	65.00	115	160	255	775	850
1871	721,250	34.00	41.50	55.00	82.50	130	195	270	750	850
1872	65,000	325	375	470	650	850	960	1,400	4,300	900
1873 proof	Est. 1,100	1,250	1,350	1,500	1,600	1,750	2,000	—	—	4,350

SILVER 3 CENTS

Silver 3 Cents - Type 1

**Shield within star, no outlines in star obverse
Roman numeral in designed C, within circle of stars reverse**

KM# 75 • 0.8000 g., 0.7500 **Silver**, 0.0193 oz. ASW, 14 mm. • **Obv. Legend** UNITED STATES OF
AMERICA **Designer:** James B. Longacre

Date	Mintage	G-4	VG-8	F-12	VF-20	XF-40	AU-50	MS-60	MS-65	Prf-65
1851	5,447,400	25.00	41.50	42.50	45.00	65.00	155	185	975	—
1851O	720,000	38.50	47.50	55.00	100.00	160	250	340	2,600	—
1852	18,663,500	25.00	41.50	42.50	45.00	65.00	155	180	975	—
1853	11,400,000	25.00	41.50	42.50	45.00	65.00	155	180	975	—

Silver 3 Cents - Type 2

**Shield within star, three outlines in star obverse
Roman numeral in designed C, within circle of stars reverse**

KM# 80 • 0.7500 g., 0.9000 **Silver**, 0.0217 oz. ASW, 14 mm. • **Obv. Legend** UNITED STATES OF
AMERICA **Designer:** James B. Longacre

Date	Mintage	G-4	VG-8	F-12	VF-20	XF-40	AU-50	MS-60	MS-65	Prf-65
1854	671,000	26.00	42.50	44.00	50.00	105	230	350	3,450	33,500
1855	139,000	44.00	57.50	75.00	125	205	340	550	8,500	15,000
1856	1,458,000	30.00	45.00	46.00	65.00	125	205	275	4,500	15,500
1857	1,042,000	28.50	42.50	45.00	62.50	130	240	300	3,300	13,500
1858	1,604,000	27.50	42.50	44.00	55.00	110	200	240	3,300	6,400

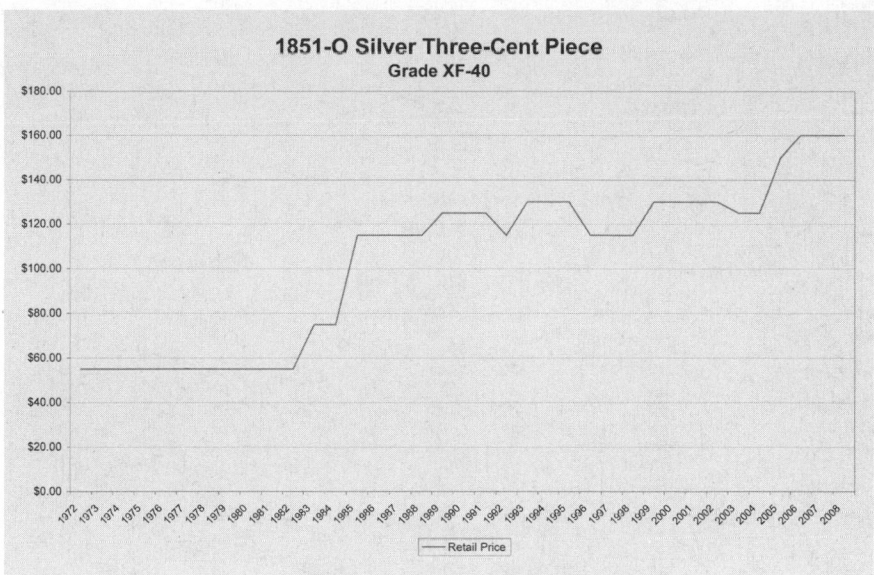

1851-O Silver Three-Cent Piece
Grade XF-40

Silver 3 Cents - Type 3
Shield within star, two outlines in star obverse
Roman numeral in designed C, within circle of stars reverse

KM# 88 • 0.7500 g., 0.9000 **Silver**, 0.0217 oz. ASW, 14 mm. • **Obv. Legend** UNITED STATES OF
AMERICA **Designer:** James B. Longacre

Date	Mintage	G-4	VG-8	F-12	VF-20	XF-40	AU-50	MS-60	MS-65	Prf-65
1859	365,000	30.00	44.00	50.00	62.50	82.50	170	195	975	2,150
1860	287,000	30.00	44.00	45.00	60.00	80.00	170	195	975	4,000
1861	498,000	30.00	44.00	45.00	60.00	80.00	170	195	975	1,800
1862	343,550	38.50	51.00	50.00	70.00	82.50	195	230	975	1,400
1863	21,460	340	375	400	445	480	625	780	2,250	1,350
1863/62 proof only; Rare	Inc. above	—	—	—	—	—	—	—	—	5,400
1864	12,470	340	375	400	445	480	625	780	1,700	1,350
1865	8,500	400	440	475	520	550	600	750	1,700	1,350
1866	22,725	340	375	400	445	495	550	650	1,900	1,325
1867	4,625	400	440	475	520	550	600	720	2,750	1,300
1868	4,100	400	445	480	520	575	625	740	5,750	1,400
1869	5,100	400	445	480	520	575	625	720	2,350	1,400
1869/68 proof only; Rare	Inc. above	—	—	—	—	—	—	—	—	—
1870	4,000	420	450	495	550	595	670	900	5,500	1,350
1871	4,360	400	440	480	520	575	625	750	1,700	1,450
1872	1,950	420	450	495	550	595	675	795	5,500	1,350
1873 proof only	600	650	685	730	800	890	980	—	—	2,500

NICKEL 3 CENTS

Coronet head left, date below obverse   Roman numeral value within wreath reverse

KM# 95 • 1.9400 g., **Copper-Nickel**, 17.9 mm. • **Obv. Legend** UNITED STATES OF AMERICA
Designer: James B. Longacre

Date	Mintage	G-4	VG-8	F-12	VF-20	XF-40	AU-50	MS-60	MS-65	Prf-65
1865	11,382,000	15.50	16.50	17.50	22.50	37.50	60.00	100.00	650	6,500

Date	Mintage	G-4	VG-8	F-12	VF-20	XF-40	AU-50	MS-60	MS-65	Prf-65
1866	4,801,000	15.50	16.50	17.50	22.50	37.50	60.00	100.00	650	1,725
1867	3,915,000	15.50	16.50	17.50	22.50	37.50	60.00	100.00	770	1,575
1868	3,252,000	15.50	16.50	17.50	22.50	37.50	60.00	100.00	650	1,450
1869	1,604,000	16.50	17.50	19.50	25.50	40.50	61.00	120	795	1,050
1870	1,335,000	17.50	18.50	20.50	26.50	41.50	62.00	135	795	2,250
1871	604,000	17.50	19.00	22.50	27.50	42.50	64.00	155	800	1,200
1872	862,000	19.00	22.50	24.50	28.50	43.50	68.00	175	1,075	910
1873	1,173,000	16.50	18.50	22.50	25.50	40.50	62.00	145	1,375	1,125
1874	790,000	17.50	20.50	22.50	27.50	42.50	66.00	160	1,050	950
1875	228,000	19.00	22.50	27.50	30.50	45.50	80.00	190	850	1,500
1876	162,000	20.50	23.50	26.50	34.50	49.50	95.00	225	1,550	1,025
1877 proof	Est. 900	1,100	1,150	1,175	1,250	1,300	1,350	—	—	3,750
1878 proof	2,350	615	645	720	770	795	830	—	—	1,200
1879	41,200	65.00	75.00	96.00	110	115	180	320	850	690
1880	24,955	100.00	115	130	165	185	235	375	800	700
1881	1,080,575	15.50	16.50	19.00	23.50	39.50	60.00	100.00	670	680
1882	25,300	130	150	180	225	300	325	425	1,100	700
1883	10,609	200	225	260	305	375	425	480	4,850	690
1884	5,642	400	445	550	600	645	730	800	6,250	700
1885	4,790	470	520	645	700	745	775	900	2,300	720
1886 proof	4,290	320	330	345	385	385	420	—	—	715
1887/6 proof	7,961	350	390	415	450	460	515	—	—	940
1887	Inc. above	305	355	395	440	455	500	540	1,350	1,125
1888	41,083	54.00	63.00	70.00	80.00	100.00	170	315	725	690
1889	21,561	90.00	115	140	180	220	255	320	800	690

HALF DIME

Flowing Hair Half Dime

KM# 15 • 1.3500 g., 0.8920 **Silver**, 0.0387 oz. ASW, 16.5 mm. • **Designer:** Robert Scot

Date	Mintage	G-4	VG-8	F-12	VF-20	XF-40	MS-60
1794	86,416	1,325	1,625	2,150	3,125	7,325	19,850
1795	Inc. above	1,050	1,350	1,875	2,850	5,750	13,850

Draped Bust Half Dime
Small eagle reverse

KM# 23 • 1.3500 g., 0.8920 **Silver**, 0.0387 oz. ASW, 16.5 mm. • **Designer:** Robert Scot **Notes:** Some 1796 strikes have "Liberty" spelled as "Likerty." The 1797 strikes have either 13, 15 or 16 stars on the obverse.

Date	Mintage	G-4	VG-8	F-12	VF-20	XF-40	MS-60
1796	10,230	1,435	1,550	3,000	4,700	8,700	19,550
1796 "Likerty"	Inc. above	1,485	1,600	3,050	4,750	8,750	19,600
1796/5	Inc. above	1,555	1,700	3,150	4,850	8,850	19,700
1797 13 stars	44,527	2,100	2,650	4,100	5,800	9,800	32,750
1797 15 stars	Inc. above	1,385	1,500	2,950	4,650	8,650	19,500
1797 16 stars	Inc. above	1,535	1,750	3,200	4,900	8,900	19,750

Draped Bust Half Dime

Draped bust right, flanked by stars, date at angle below obverse   Heraldic eagle reverse

KM# 34 • 1.3500 g., 0.8920 **Silver**, 0.0387 oz. ASW, 16.5 mm. • **Obv. Legend** LIBERTY **Rev. Legend:** UNITED STATES OF AMERICA **Designer:** Robert Scot

Date	Mintage	G-4	VG-8	F-12	VF-20	XF-40	MS-60
1800	24,000	1,000	1,250	1,875	2,350	6,750	13,850
1800 "Libekty"	Inc. above	1,000	1,250	1,875	2,350	7,250	15,400
1801	33,910	1,225	1,500	2,125	2,600	7,000	18,100

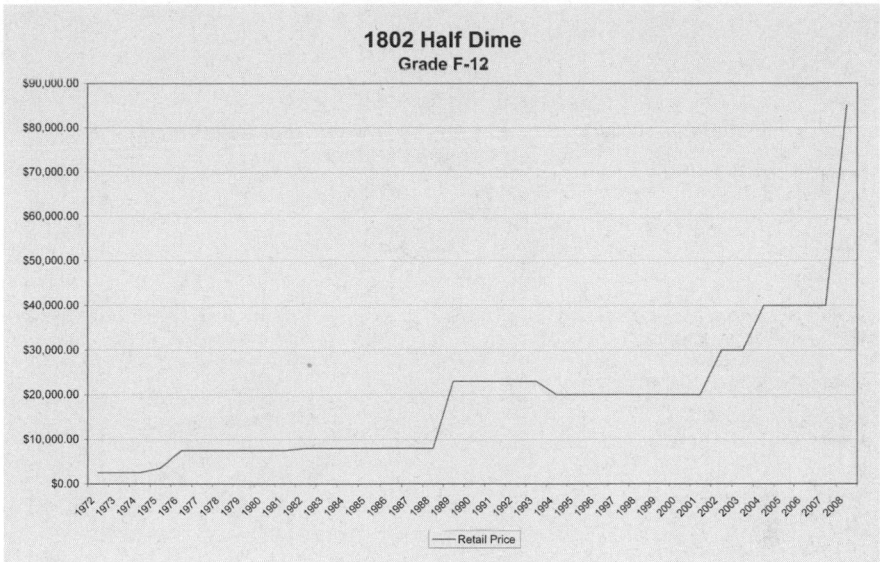

1802 Half Dime
Grade F-12

— Retail Price

Date	Mintage	G-4	VG-8	F-12	VF-20	XF-40	MS-60
1802	3,060	44,500	65,000	95,000	135,000	300,000	—
1803 Large 8	37,850	1,100	1,375	2,000	2,475	6,875	13,975
1803 Small 8	Inc. above	1,325	1,625	2,250	2,725	7,125	16,200
1805	15,600	1,225	1,525	2,350	2,825	10,150	31,350

Liberty Cap Half Dime
Classic head left, flanked by stars, date below obverse
Eagle with arrows in talons, banner above reverse

KM# 47 • 1.3500 g., 0.8920 **Silver**, 0.0387 oz. ASW, 15.5 mm. • **Rev. Legend:** UNITED STATES OF AMERICA **Designer:** William Kneass **Notes:** Design modifications in 1835, 1836 and 1837 resulted in variety combinations with large and small dates, and large and small "5C." inscriptions on the reverse.

Date	Mintage	G-4	VG-8	F-12	VF-20	XF-40	AU-50	MS-60	MS-65
1829	1,230,000	55.00	60.00	72.00	125	185	275	365	3,300
1830	1,240,000	47.50	52.50	62.00	95.00	155	215	350	3,150
1831	1,242,700	47.50	52.50	62.00	95.00	155	215	350	3,150
1832	965,000	47.50	52.50	62.00	95.00	155	215	350	3,150
1833	1,370,000	47.50	52.50	62.00	95.00	155	215	350	3,150
1834	1,480,000	47.50	52.50	62.00	95.00	155	215	350	3,150
1835 lg. dt., lg. 5C.	2,760,000	47.50	60.00	74.00	110	170	235	350	3,150
1835 lg. dt., sm. 5C	Inc. above	47.50	52.50	62.00	95.00	155	215	410	4,350
1835 sm. dt., lg. 5C	Inc. above	47.50	52.50	62.00	95.00	155	215	375	4,050
1835 sm. dt., sm. 5C	Inc. above	47.50	52.50	62.00	95.00	155	215	350	3,150
1836 lg. 5C.	1,900,000	47.50	52.50	62.00	95.00	155	215	350	3,150
1836 sm. 5C.	Inc. above	47.50	52.50	66.00	105	167	227	362	3,650
1837 lg. 5C.	2,276,000	47.50	52.50	70.00	113	170	235	395	4,350
1837 sm. 5C.	Inc. above	54.50	62.50	77.00	125	235	465	950	11,000

Seated Liberty Half Dime
Seated Liberty, no stars around border, date below obverse   Value within wreath reverse

KM# 60 • 1.3400 g., 0.9000 **Silver**, 0.0388 oz. ASW, 15.5 mm. • **Rev. Legend:** UNITED STATES OF AMERICA **Designer:** Christian Gobrecht **Notes:** A design modification in 1837 resulted in small-date and large-date varieties for that year.

HALF DIME

Date	Mintage	G-4	VG-8	F-12	VF-20	XF-40	AU-50	MS-60	MS-65
1837 small date	Inc. above	35.00	46.50	75.00	135	220	485	770	4,450
1837 large date	Inc. above	39.00	49.50	82.00	150	235	435	640	3,650
1838O	70,000	110	130	250	475	975	1,450	2,500	29,500

Seated Liberty Half Dime

Seated Liberty, stars around top 1/2 of border, date below obverse
Value within wreath reverse

KM# 62.1 • 1.3400 g., 0.9000 **Silver**, 0.0388 oz. ASW, 15.5 mm. • **Rev. Legend:** UNITED STATES OF AMERICA **Designer:** Christian Gobrecht **Notes:** The two varieties of 1838 are distinguished by the size of the stars on the obverse. The 1839-O with reverse of 1838-O was struck from rusted reverse dies. The result is a bumpy surface on this variety's reverse.

Date	Mintage	G-4	VG-8	F-12	VF-20	XF-40	AU-50	MS-60	MS-65
1838 large stars	2,255,000	21.50	25.50	29.00	36.00	88.00	173	280	2,475
1838 small stars	Inc. above	25.50	31.50	46.00	115	189	274	610	3,950
1839	1,069,150	22.50	26.50	30.00	37.00	93.00	178	280	2,400
1839O	1,034,039	26.50	30.50	34.00	41.00	88.00	173	730	6,850
1839O reverse 1838O	—	500	700	1,200	1,750	3,000	—	—	—
1840	1,344,085	23.50	27.50	31.00	38.00	80.00	165	270	2,275
1840O	935,000	28.50	32.50	38.00	48.00	138	343	1,250	—

Seated Liberty Half Dime

Seated Liberty, stars around top 1/2 of border, date below obverse

KM# 62.2 • 1.3400 g., 0.9000 **Silver**, 0.0388 oz. ASW, 15.5 mm. • **Rev. Legend:** UNITED STATES OF AMERICA **Designer:** Christian Gobrecht **Notes:** In 1840 drapery was added to Liberty's left elbow. Varieties for the 1848 Philadelphia strikes are distinguished by the size of the numerals in the date.

Date	Mintage	G-4	VG-8	F-12	VF-20	XF-40	AU-50	MS-60	MS-65
1840	Inc. above	20.00	18.00	75.00	135	210	350	490	3,850
1840O	Inc. above	51.00	60.00	115	225	650	1,350	6,500	—

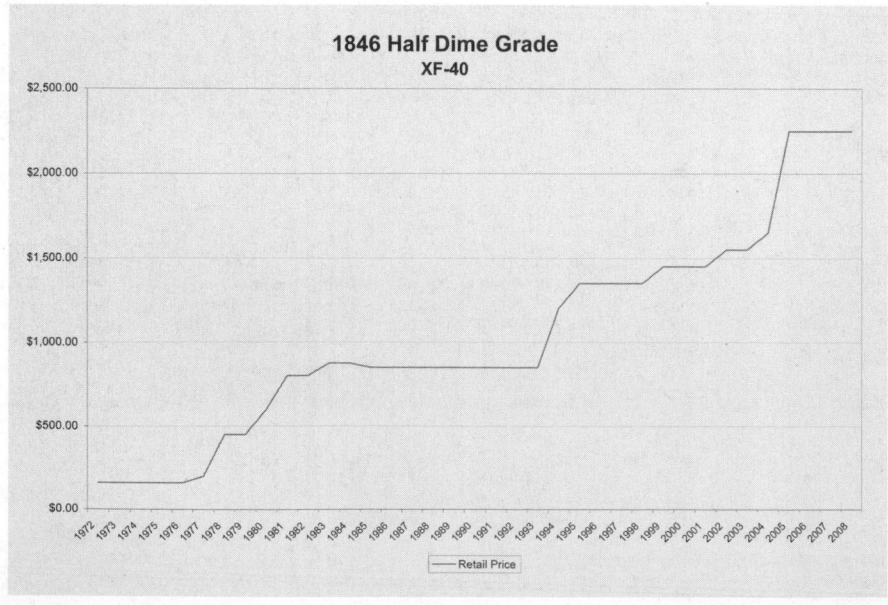

1846 Half Dime Grade
XF-40

Date	Mintage	G-4	VG-8	F-12	VF-20	XF-40	AU-50	MS-60	MS-65
1841	1,150,000	17.00	21.50	23.50	31.00	58.00	125	180	1,325
1841O	815,000	20.00	24.50	30.00	50.00	125	300	650	6,750
1842	815,000	16.00	21.50	23.50	28.00	55.00	125	175	1,850
1842O	350,000	38.00	45.00	75.00	225	550	1,050	2,250	16,500
1843	1,165,000	16.00	21.50	23.50	28.00	55.00	120	175	1,365
1844	430,000	19.00	24.50	26.50	34.00	58.00	125	180	1,250
1844O	220,000	80.00	110	210	600	1,300	2,650	5,400	27,500
1845	1,564,000	16.00	21.50	23.50	35.00	58.00	120	175	1,250
1845/1845	Inc. above	19.00	24.50	26.50	38.00	85.00	130	190	1,300
1846	27,000	410	550	850	1,250	2,475	3,600	11,500	—
1847	1,274,000	16.00	21.50	23.50	28.00	55.00	125	175	1,250
1848 medium date	668,000	19.00	24.50	26.50	34.00	65.00	135	215	3,150
1848 large date	Inc. above	22.50	28.00	48.00	65.00	145	275	635	4,250
1848O	600,000	20.00	25.50	33.00	62.00	135	265	450	2,450
1849/8	1,309,000	28.50	35.00	47.50	67.50	140	250	785	2,950
1849/6	Inc. above	24.00	26.00	30.00	56.50	110	200	425	2,900
1849	Inc. above	19.00	18.50	27.50	52.50	65.00	135	190	1,925
1849O	140,000	29.00	40.00	95.00	225	540	1,100	2,350	—
1850	955,000	19.00	24.50	26.50	34.00	60.00	125	190	1,400
1850O	690,000	20.00	24.50	35.00	65.00	125	280	685	4,450
1851	781,000	16.00	21.50	23.50	28.00	57.00	120	175	1,450
1851O	860,000	19.00	24.50	26.50	41.50	110	220	500	4,350
1852	1,000,500	16.00	21.50	23.50	28.00	57.00	120	175	1,250
1852O	260,000	25.00	44.50	79.00	135	275	475	885	11,500
1853	135,000	40.00	60.00	90.00	175	300	525	850	2,850
1853O	160,000	285	325	450	850	1,800	3,500	6,450	27,500

Seated Liberty Half Dime
Seated Liberty, stars around top 1/2 of border, arrows at date obverse
Value within wreath reverse

KM# 76 • 1.2400 g., 0.9000 **Silver**, 0.0359 oz. ASW • **Rev. Legend:** UNITED STATES OF AMERICA
Designer: Christian Gobrecht

Date	Mintage	G-4	VG-8	F-12	VF-20	XF-40	AU-50	MS-60	MS-65	Prf-65
1853	13,210,020	16.00	19.00	22.50	28.00	58.00	135	200	2,100	—
1853O	2,200,000	19.00	27.00	30.50	36.00	66.00	143	315	3,950	—
1854	5,740,000	16.00	19.00	24.50	30.00	60.00	137	210	2,100	15,000
1854O	1,560,000	17.00	20.00	32.50	38.00	88.00	165	240	4,250	—
1855	1,750,000	17.00	20.00	24.50	30.00	60.00	137	205	2,500	15,000
1855O	600,000	21.00	25.00	38.50	54.00	140	220	545	4,950	—

Seated Liberty Half Dime
Seated Liberty, stars around top 1/2 of border, date below obverse
Value within wreath reverse

KM# A62.2 • 1.2400 g., 0.9000 **Silver**, 0.0359 oz. ASW • **Rev. Legend:** UNITED STATES OF AMERICA
Designer: Christian Gobrecht **Notes:** On the 1858/inverted date variety, the date was engraved into the die upside down and then re-engraved right side up. Another 1858 variety has the date doubled.

Date	Mintage	G-4	VG-8	F-12	VF-20	XF-40	AU-50	MS-60	MS-65	Prf-65
1856	4,880,000	16.00	21.00	23.00	27.00	52.50	115	175	1,400	15,000
1856O	1,100,000	17.00	22.00	26.00	28.00	97.50	260	470	2,350	—
1857	7,280,000	16.00	21.00	23.00	27.00	52.50	115	175	1,250	5,600
1857O	1,380,000	17.00	22.00	24.00	28.00	62.50	185	320	1,950	—
1858	3,500,000	16.00	21.00	23.00	27.00	52.50	115	175	1,350	5,500
1858 inverted date	Inc. above	30.00	43.50	62.50	100.00	225	300	675	3,950	—
1858 double date	Inc. above	45.00	60.00	90.00	175	285	425	800	—	—
1858O	1,660,000	17.00	22.00	24.00	28.00	71.50	137	245	1,850	—
1859	340,000	18.00	23.00	25.00	29.00	54.50	117	225	1,550	4,000
1859O	560,000	19.00	24.00	26.00	42.00	128.5	200	285	2,050	—

HALF DIME

Seated Liberty Half Dime
Seated Liberty, date below obverse   Value within wreath reverse

KM# 91 • 1.2400 g., 0.9000 **Silver**, 0.0359 oz. ASW • **Obv. Legend** UNITED STATES OF AMERICA **Designer:** Christian Gobrecht **Notes:** In 1860 the legend "United States of America" replaced the stars on the obverse.

Date	Mintage	G-4	VG-8	F-12	VF-20	XF-40	AU-50	MS-60	MS-65	Prf-65
1860	799,000	16.00	20.00	23.00	26.00	47.00	77.00	145	1,025	1,550
1860O	1,060,000	16.00	20.00	23.00	29.00	49.00	79.00	170	1,375	—
1861	3,361,000	16.00	20.00	22.00	25.00	45.00	75.00	145	1,025	1,600
1861/0	Inc. above	25.00	32.50	59.00	125	260	435	560	3,650	—
1862	1,492,550	20.00	25.00	34.00	44.00	64.00	94.00	154	1,025	1,550
1863	18,460	200	250	300	400	485	550	800	1,575	1,550
1863S	100,000	35.00	45.00	70.00	95.00	165	300	750	3,450	—
1864	48,470	375	475	575	750	950	1,100	1,375	2,350	1,600
1864S	90,000	60.00	75.00	115	175	250	450	785	3,750	—
1865	13,500	375	475	575	750	950	1,100	1,350	1,950	1,550
1865S	120,000	29.00	40.00	60.00	85.00	145	375	975	5,450	—
1866	10,725	350	475	550	700	875	1,000	1,225	2,575	1,550
1866S	120,000	29.00	40.00	60.00	85.00	145	285	485	5,000	—
1867	8,625	550	650	775	900	1,100	1,200	1,375	2,350	1,550
1867S	120,000	29.00	40.00	60.00	85.00	150	325	850	3,850	—
1868	89,200	60.00	90.00	190	225	300	425	625	2,400	1,550
1868S	280,000	20.00	25.00	35.00	42.00	59.00	125	325	3,250	—
1869	208,600	20.00	25.00	35.00	42.00	59.00	135	200	1,375	1,560
1869S	230,000	18.00	24.00	30.00	35.00	55.00	125	310	4,150	—
1870	536,600	18.00	24.00	30.00	35.00	55.00	125	185	975	1,550
1870S unique	—	—	—	—	—	—	—	—	—	—

Note: 1870S, Superior Galleries, July 1986, brilliant uncirculated, $253,000.

Date	Mintage	G-4	VG-8	F-12	VF-20	XF-40	AU-50	MS-60	MS-65	Prf-65
1871	1,873,960	16.00	20.00	22.00	25.00	45.00	75.00	135	975	1,550
1871S	161,000	25.00	30.00	45.00	60.00	90.00	175	320	2,425	—
1872	2,947,950	16.00	20.00	22.00	25.00	45.00	75.00	135	975	1,550
1872S mint mark in wreath	837,000	16.00	20.00	22.00	25.00	45.00	75.00	135	975	—
1872S mint mark below wreath	Inc. above	17.00	21.00	24.00	27.00	47.00	80.00	135	975	—
1873	712,600	16.00	20.00	22.00	25.00	45.00	75.00	135	1,375	1,550
1873S	324,000	20.00	25.00	30.00	42.00	62.00	90.00	150	975	—

5 CENTS

Shield Nickel
Draped garland above shield, date below obverse
Value within center of rays between stars reverse

KM# 96 • 5.0000 g., **Copper-Nickel**, 20.5 mm. • **Obv. Legend** IN GOD WE TRUST **Rev. Legend:** UNITED STATES OF AMERICA **Designer:** James B. Longacre

Date	Mintage	G-4	VG-8	F-12	VF-20	XF-40	AU-50	MS-60	MS-65	Prf-65
1866	14,742,500	27.50	38.50	50.00	75.00	155	235	260	2,700	3,850
1867	2,019,000	37.50	50.00	67.50	100.00	200	295	350	4,150	75,000

Shield Nickel
Draped garland above shield, date below obverse   Value within circle of stars reverse

KM# 97 • 5.0000 g., **Copper-Nickel** • **Obv. Legend** IN GOD WE TRUST **Rev. Legend:** UNITED STATES OF AMERICA

Date	Mintage	G-4	VG-8	F-12	VF-20	XF-40	AU-50	MS-60	MS-65	Prf-65
1867	28,890,500	18.00	21.00	28.00	37.50	60.00	120	160	900	3,450
1868	28,817,000	18.00	21.00	28.00	37.50	60.00	120	160	975	1,500
1869	16,395,000	18.00	21.00	28.00	37.50	60.00	120	160	775	1,000
1870	4,806,000	27.00	34.00	52.00	65.00	90.00	145	200	1,700	1,250
1871	561,000	70.00	90.00	125	170	265	325	375	2,100	1,100
1872	6,036,000	35.00	42.00	70.00	80.00	115	150	235	1,350	820
1873 Open 3	4,550,000	28.00	36.00	52.00	65.00	80.00	135	200	2,400	840
1873 Closed 3	—	34.00	42.00	65.00	90.00	150	220	350	3,250	—
1874	3,538,000	29.00	39.00	70.00	82.00	105	140	225	1,500	1,000
1875	2,097,000	40.00	55.00	80.00	110	145	190	250	2,000	1,650
1876	2,530,000	38.00	50.00	74.00	100.00	135	175	230	1,900	900
1877 proof	Est. 900	1,500	1,650	1,750	2,000	2,150	2,300	—	—	4,300
1878 proof	2,350	800	875	900	1,100	1,300	1,450	—	—	2,150
1879	29,100	415	520	625	675	750	825	970	2,000	840
1870/8	—	—	—	—	—	—	—	—	—	850
1880	19,995	560	620	775	950	1,300	1,750	3,450	47,500	700
1881	72,375	270	340	445	500	600	730	800	1,900	660
1882	11,476,600	18.00	20.00	27.00	36.00	58.00	115	150	750	660
1883	1,456,919	18.00	21.00	32.00	37.50	60.00	118	160	750	660
1883/2	—	210	285	425	650	850	1,000	1,400	4,000	—

Liberty Nickel
Liberty head left, within circle of stars, date below obverse
Roman numeral value within wreath, without "cents" below reverse

KM# 111 • 5.0000 g., **Copper-Nickel**, 21.2 mm. • **Rev. Legend:** UNITED STATES OF AMERICA
Designer: Charles E. Barber

Date	Mintage	G-4	VG-8	F-12	VF-20	XF-40	AU-50	MS-60	MS-65	Prf-65
1883	5,479,519	5.50	6.50	7.00	7.50	8.00	12.50	26.00	310	1,100

Liberty Nickel
Liberty head left, within circle of stars, date below obverse
Roman numeral value within wreath, "Cents" below reverse

KM# 112 • 5.0000 g., **Copper-Nickel** • **Rev. Legend:** UNITED STATES OF AMERICA

Date	Mintage	G-4	VG-8	F-12	VF-20	XF-40	AU-50	MS-60	MS-65	Prf-65
1883	16,032,983	16.00	27.50	41.50	57.50	90.00	130	170	720	675
1884	11,273,942	21.00	35.00	41.50	60.00	93.50	135	200	2,000	660

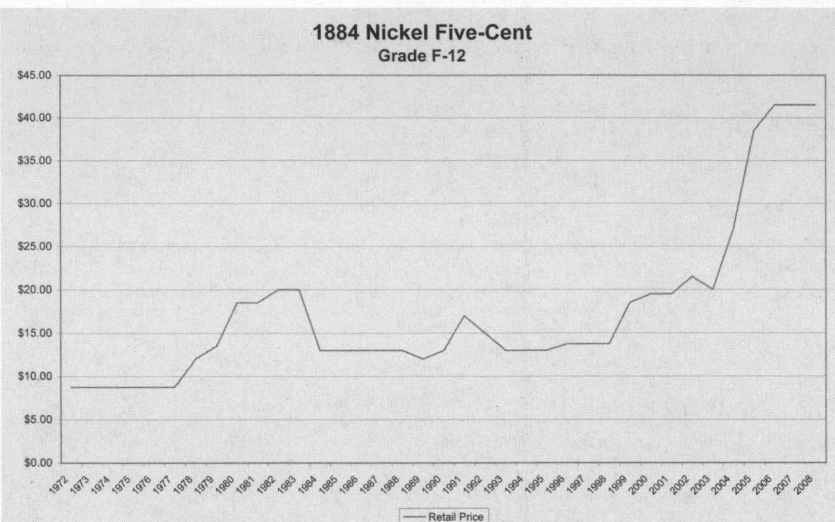

1884 Nickel Five-Cent
Grade F-12

Date	Mintage	G-4	VG-8	F-12	VF-20	XF-40	AU-50	MS-60	MS-65	Prf-65
1885	1,476,490	600	650	900	1,100	1,350	1,700	2,050	8,400	3,350
1886	3,330,290	290	345	425	520	715	875	1,100	9,000	1,950
1887	15,263,652	12.50	22.00	32.50	45.00	82.50	115	150	1,450	675
1888	10,720,483	30.00	45.00	70.00	130	185	250	305	2,200	765
1889	15,881,361	11.00	16.00	31.00	55.00	82.50	125	160	1,000	675
1890	16,259,272	8.00	20.00	27.50	41.50	68.50	115	170	1,875	685
1891	16,834,350	6.00	11.00	22.00	38.50	62.50	125	160	1,100	675
1892	11,699,642	7.00	11.00	23.00	41.50	65.00	125	165	1,500	675
1893	13,370,195	5.50	11.00	25.00	38.50	62.50	125	155	1,400	675
1894	5,413,132	17.50	31.00	100.00	165	240	315	375	1,600	800
1895	9,979,884	5.75	8.00	25.00	46.00	70.00	125	150	2,900	690
1896	8,842,920	9.50	20.00	41.50	68.50	100.00	160	215	2,500	750
1897	20,428,735	3.00	4.50	12.50	27.50	44.00	74.00	100.00	1,250	675
1898	12,532,087	2.35	4.50	11.00	23.50	41.50	72.00	140	1,250	675
1899	26,029,031	1.85	2.00	8.50	20.00	34.00	69.00	96.00	725	675
1900	27,255,995	1.85	2.50	8.50	19.50	34.00	72.00	90.00	725	675
1901	26,480,213	1.85	2.50	7.50	15.00	34.00	69.00	88.00	720	675
1902	31,480,579	1.85	2.50	4.50	15.00	31.00	69.00	94.00	720	675
1903	28,006,725	1.85	2.50	5.00	15.00	31.00	69.00	85.00	725	675
1904	21,404,984	1.85	2.50	5.00	12.50	29.00	69.00	88.00	750	700
1905	29,827,276	1.85	2.50	4.50	12.50	29.00	69.00	88.00	720	675
1906	38,613,725	1.85	2.50	4.50	12.50	29.00	69.00	88.00	950	675
1907	39,214,800	1.85	2.25	4.50	12.50	29.00	69.00	88.00	1,400	675
1908	22,686,177	1.85	2.25	4.50	12.50	29.00	69.00	93.00	1,300	675
1909	11,590,526	2.20	2.50	4.50	13.50	32.00	85.00	105	1,350	675
1910	30,169,353	1.85	2.25	4.50	11.00	29.00	55.00	72.00	720	675
1911	39,559,372	1.85	2.25	4.50	11.00	29.00	55.00	72.00	720	675
1912	26,236,714	1.85	2.25	4.50	11.00	29.00	55.00	72.00	720	675
1912D	8,474,000	2.70	4.00	12.00	38.00	74.00	175	290	2,600	—
1912S	238,000	175	245	280	500	850	1,350	1,550	7,500	—
1913 5 known	—	—	—	—	—	—	—	—	—	—

Note: 1913, Superior Sale, March 2001, Proof, $1,840,000.

Buffalo Nickel
Buffalo standing on a mound reverse

KM# 133 • 5.0000 g., Copper-Nickel, 21.2 mm. • Designer: James Earle Fraser

Date	Mintage	G-4	VG-8	F-12	VF-20	XF-40	AU-50	MS-60	MS-65	Prf-65
1913	30,993,520	8.00	11.00	11.75	12.50	18.50	25.00	32.50	200	3,500
1913D	5,337,000	16.00	19.50	21.00	25.00	35.00	57.00	62.50	330	—
1913S	2,105,000	43.00	47.00	50.00	60.00	75.00	100.00	125	725	—

Buffalo Nickel
American Bison standing on a line reverse

1937D 3-legged

1918/17D

KM# 134 • 5.0000 g., **Copper-Nickel**, 21.2 mm. • **Designer:** James Earle Fraser **Notes:** In 1913 the reverse design was modified so the ground under the buffalo was represented as a line rather than a mound. On the 1937D 3-legged variety, the buffalo's right front leg is missing, the result of a damaged die.

Date	Mintage	G-4	VG-8	F-12	VF-20	XF-40	AU-50	MS-60	MS-65	Prf-65
1913	29,858,700	8.00	11.00	11.50	12.50	18.50	25.00	34.00	375	2,600
1913D	4,156,000	125	155	180	190	205	240	285	1,575	—
1913S	1,209,000	365	425	445	475	575	675	850	4,300	—
1914	20,665,738	17.00	21.00	22.00	23.00	27.50	37.50	49.00	450	2,250
1914/3	Inc. above	150	300	425	525	700	1,050	2,750	24,000	—
1914D	3,912,000	92.00	130	155	220	315	395	450	1,850	—
1914/3D	Inc. above	—	—	—	—	—	—	—	—	—
1914S	3,470,000	26.00	37.50	45.00	62.50	90.00	145	160	2,350	—
1914/3S	Inc. above	250	500	750	1,000	1,450	2,200	4,300	—	—
1915	20,987,270	5.50	7.00	7.75	11.00	21.50	38.50	50.00	325	2,100
1915D	7,569,500	21.50	31.00	41.50	66.00	115	150	225	2,500	—
1915S	1,505,000	47.00	74.00	105	185	320	490	625	3,400	—
1916	63,498,066	5.00	6.40	7.00	8.00	13.50	21.00	43.50	350	3,650
1916/16	Inc. above	2,000	4,250	8,000	12,000	17,000	38,000	55,000	395,000	—
1916D	13,333,000	15.00	26.50	29.00	38.50	82.50	110	150	2,500	—
1916S	11,860,000	11.00	13.50	20.00	35.00	75.00	125	175	2,650	—
1917	51,424,029	5.00	7.00	8.00	10.00	16.00	32.50	60.00	580	—
1917D	9,910,800	20.00	31.00	55.00	80.00	135	255	345	3,750	—
1917S	4,193,000	23.00	42.00	80.00	110	180	285	395	5,250	—
1918	32,086,314	5.00	6.50	8.00	15.00	31.00	48.50	110	1,700	—
1918/17D	8,362,314	1,150	1,650	2,850	6,250	10,000	11,800	28,500	365,000	—
1918D	Inc. above	22.50	39.00	66.00	135	220	330	430	5,000	—
1918S	4,882,000	14.00	27.50	55.00	100.00	175	300	495	28,500	—
1919	60,868,000	2.20	3.40	3.80	7.00	16.00	32.00	60.00	595	—
1919D	8,006,000	15.50	31.00	66.00	115	235	335	570	7,750	—
1919S	7,521,000	8.00	20.00	50.00	110	225	360	540	26,000	—
1920	63,093,000	1.50	2.75	3.25	8.00	16.00	30.00	59.00	850	—
1920D	9,418,000	8.50	19.00	35.00	125	275	340	555	7,600	—
1920S	9,689,000	4.50	12.75	30.00	100.00	200	300	525	28,500	—
1921	10,663,000	3.75	6.25	8.50	25.00	53.50	73.00	125	850	—
1921S	1,557,000	67.50	120	200	545	845	1,100	1,500	8,000	—
1923	35,715,000	1.70	3.25	4.25	7.00	14.00	37.50	60.00	750	—
1923S	6,142,000	8.00	11.00	27.00	125	275	335	595	12,500	—
1924	21,620,000	1.25	2.40	4.50	10.00	19.00	41.00	73.50	950	—
1924D	5,258,000	8.00	12.00	30.00	90.00	215	315	375	5,600	—
1924S	1,437,000	16.50	32.00	96.00	455	1,100	1,700	2,300	13,500	—

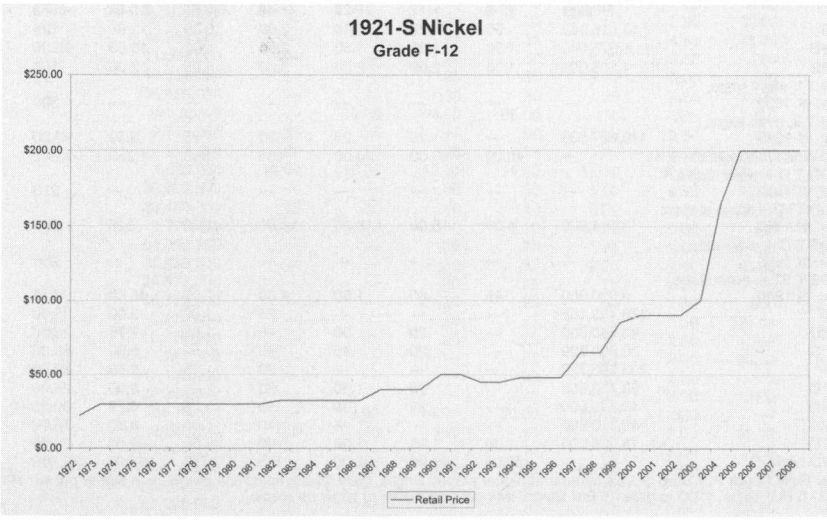

1921-S Nickel
Grade F-12

Jefferson large profile - Bison Reverse

Thomas Jefferson large profile right obverse American Bison right reverse

KM# 368 • 5.0000 g., **Copper Nickel**, 21.2 mm. • **Obv. Designer:** Joe Fitzgerald and Don Everhart II **Rev. Designer:** Jamie Franki and Norman E. Nemeth

Date	Mintage	MS-65	Prf-65
2005P	448,320,000	1.00	—
2005D	487,680,000	1.00	—
2005S	—	—	7.50

Jefferson - Pacific Coastline

Pacific coastline reverse

KM# 369 • 5.0000 g., **Copper Nickel**, 21.2 mm. • **Obv. Designer:** Joe Fitzgerald and Don Everhart **Rev. Designer:** Joe Fitzgerald and Donna Weaver

Date	Mintage	MS-65	Prf-65
2005P	394,080,000	1.00	—
2005D	411,120,000	1.00	—
2005S	—	—	6.50

Jefferson large facing portrait - Enhanced Monticello Reverse

Jefferson head facing obverse Monticello, enhanced design reverse

KM# 381 • 5.0000 g., **Copper-Nickel**, 21 mm. • **Obv. Designer:** Jamie N. Franki and Donna Weaver **Rev. Designer:** Felix Schlag and John Mercanti

Date	Mintage	MS-65	Prf-65
2006P	693,120,000	1.00	—
2006D	809,280,000	1.00	—
2006S	—	—	4.00
2007P	—	1.00	—
2007D	—	1.00	—
2007S	—	—	4.00
2008P	—	1.00	—
2008D	—	1.00	—
2008S	—	—	4.00

DIME

Draped Bust Dime

Small eagle reverse

KM# 24 • 2.7000 g., 0.8920 **Silver**, 0.0774 oz. ASW, 19 mm. • **Designer:** Robert Scot **Notes:** 1797 strikes have either 13 or 16 stars on the obverse.

Date	Mintage	G-4	VG-8	F-12	VF-20	XF-40	MS-60
1796	22,135	2,850	3,450	5,500	7,650	12,500	28,500
1797 13 stars	25,261	1,600	2,650	3,650	4,900	8,000	57,500
1797 16 stars	Inc. above	1,650	2,550	3,500	4,700	7,350	29,000

Draped Bust Dime
Draped bust right, date at angle below obverse Heraldic eagle reverse

KM# 31 • 2.7000 g., 0.8920 **Silver**, 0.0774 oz. ASW, 19 mm. • **Obv. Legend** LIBERTY **Rev. Legend:** UNITED STATES OF AMERICA **Designer:** Robert Scot **Notes:** The 1805 strikes have either 4 or 5 berries on the olive branch held by the eagle.

Date	Mintage	G-4	VG-8	F-12	VF-20	XF-40	MS-60
1798 large 8	27,550	775	1,135	1,375	1,875	3,350	9,650
1798 small 8	Inc. above	1,075	1,385	1,700	2,550	4,400	12,500
1798/97 13 stars	Inc. above	1,850	3,250	4,850	7,500	13,500	70,000
1798/97 16 stars	Inc. above	825	1,085	1,450	2,025	4,450	12,000

Note: The 1798 overdates have either 13 or 16 stars on the obverse; Varieties of the regular 1798 strikes are distinguished by the size of the 8 in the date

Date	Mintage	G-4	VG-8	F-12	VF-20	XF-40	MS-60
1800	21,760	800	1,160	1,700	2,500	5,100	32,500
1801	34,640	900	1,285	1,900	3,450	5,900	47,500
1802	10,975	1,500	2,000	3,000	4,200	7,500	52,500
1803	33,040	825	1,235	1,900	2,575	5,450	—
1804 13 stars	8,265	2,350	4,150	8,650	19,500	38,500	—
1804 14 stars	Inc. above	4,850	6,250	9,800	19,500	46,500	—
1805 4 berries	120,780	875	1,185	1,650	2,175	3,600	10,400
1805 5 berries	Inc. above	625	935	1,200	1,425	2,750	7,650
1807	165,000	625	935	1,200	1,425	2,750	7,650

Liberty Cap Dime
Draped bust left, flanked by stars, date below obverse
Eagle with arrows in talons, banner above, value below reverse

KM# 42 • 2.7000 g., 0.8920 **Silver**, 0.0774 oz. ASW, 18.8 mm. • **Rev. Legend:** UNITED STATES OF AMERICA **Designer:** John Reich **Notes:** Varieties of the 1814, 1821 and 1828 strikes are distinguished by the size of the numerals in the dates. The 1820 varieties are distinguished by the size of the 0 in the date. The 1823 overdates have either large E's or small E's in "United States of America" on the reverse.

Date	Mintage	G-4	VG-8	F-12	VF-20	XF-40	AU-50	MS-60	MS-65
1809	51,065	140	220	450	700	1,500	2,850	4,500	24,500
1811/9	65,180	110	175	275	650	1,350	2,000	4,000	33,500
1814 small date	421,500	60.00	80.00	145	300	650	1,250	2,000	19,500
1814 large date	Inc. above	43.00	52.00	75.00	135	435	670	1,175	15,000
1814 STATESOF	Inc. above	70.00	88.00	160	335	750	1,400	2,350	24,500
1820 large O	942,587	42.00	50.00	71.00	122	430	665	1,160	12,750
1820 small O	Inc. above	43.00	52.00	75.00	137	450	750	1,425	15,250
1820 STATESOF	Inc. above	43.00	52.00	75.00	135	435	670	1,175	14,500
1821 large date	1,186,512	42.00	50.00	71.00	122	430	665	1,160	12,750
1821 small date	Inc. above	43.00	52.00	75.00	137	450	750	1,425	17,000
1822	100,000	1,000	1,850	3,250	4,500	6,250	7,850	13,500	70,000
1823/22 large E's	440,000	42.00	50.00	71.00	130	450	685	1,210	14,850
1823/22 small E's	Inc. above	42.00	50.00	71.00	130	450	685	1,210	13,600
1824/22 mintage undetermined	—	50.00	80.00	145	300	650	1,250	2,000	19,500
1825	510,000	39.00	46.00	65.00	112	410	625	1,100	12,850
1827	1,215,000	39.00	46.00	65.00	112	410	625	1,100	12,500
1827/7	Inc. above	250	—	—	750	1,100	1,500	—	—
1828 large date	125,000	70.00	110	175	375	750	1,250	2,850	6,850

Liberty Cap Dime
Draped bust left, flanked by stars, date below obverse
Eagle with arrows in talons, banner above, value below reverse

KM# 48 • **Silver**, 18.5 mm. • **Rev. Legend:** UNITED STATES OF AMERICA **Designer:** John Reich
Notes: The three varieties of 1829 strikes and two varieties of 1830 strikes are distinguished by the size of
"10C." on the reverse. On the 1833 "high 3" variety, the last 3 in the date is higher than the first 3. The two
varieties of the 1834 strikes are distinguished by the size of the 4 in the date.

Date	Mintage	G-4	VG-8	F-12	VF-20	XF-40	AU-50	MS-60	MS-65
1828 small date	Inc. above	40.00	48.00	80.00	155	425	625	1,250	12,500
1829 very large 10C.	770,000	60.00	75.00	120	235	550	800	1,500	—
1829 large 10C.	—	54.00	65.00	110	200	400	600	1,150	9,250
1829 medium 10C.	Inc. above	36.00	42.00	54.00	85.00	255	375	775	6,850
1829 small 10C.	Inc. above	36.00	42.00	56.00	90.00	270	395	795	7,050
1829 curl base 2	—	7,750	10,500	16,500	27,500	38,500	44,000	—	—
1830 large 10C.	510,000	36.00	42.00	56.00	85.00	255	375	775	6,850
1830 small 10C.	Inc. above	36.00	42.00	54.00	90.00	270	400	825	8,850
1830/29	Inc. above	52.00	75.00	120	220	430	750	1,500	—
1831	771,350	36.00	42.00	54.00	85.00	255	375	775	6,850
1832	522,500	36.00	42.00	54.00	85.00	255	375	775	6,850
1833	485,000	36.00	42.00	54.00	85.00	260	390	790	6,850
1833 lastt 3 high	Inc. above	36.00	42.00	54.00	85.00	260	390	820	9,350
1834 small 4	635,000	36.00	42.00	54.00	85.00	255	375	775	7,000
1834 large 4	Inc. above	36.00	42.00	54.00	85.00	255	375	775	6,850
1835	1,410,000	36.00	42.00	54.00	85.00	255	375	775	6,850
1836	1,190,000	36.00	42.00	54.00	85.00	255	375	775	6,850
1837	1,042,000	36.00	42.00	56.00	90.00	270	395	795	7,000

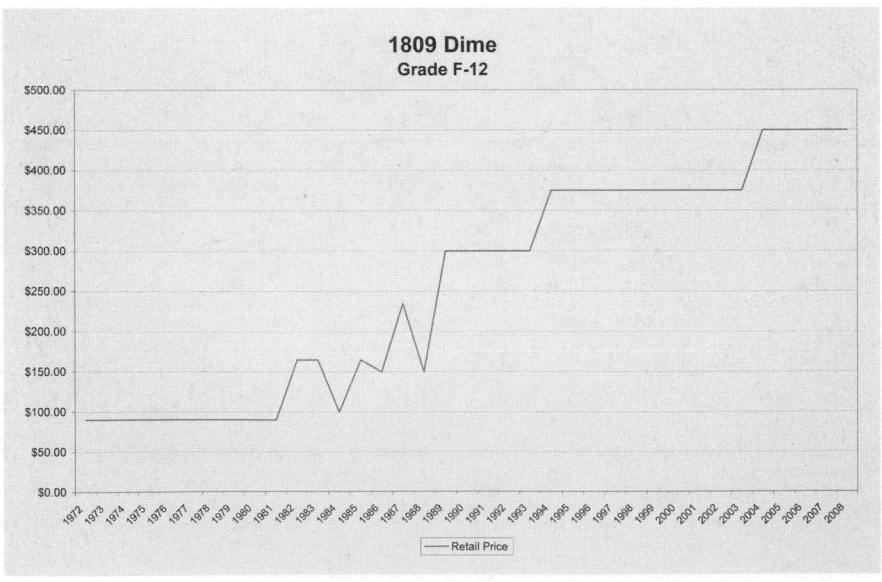

1809 Dime
Grade F-12

Seated Liberty Dime
Seated Liberty, date below obverse   Value within wreath reverse

KM# 61 • 2.6700 g., 0.9000 **Silver**, 0.0773 oz. ASW, 17.9 mm. • **Rev. Legend:** UNITED STATES OF AMERICA **Designer:** Christian Gobrecht **Notes:** The two 1837 varieties are distinguished by the size of the numerals in the date.

Date	Mintage	G-4	VG-8	F-12	VF-20	XF-40	AU-50	MS-60	MS-65
1837 small date	Inc. above	40.00	50.00	85.00	290	550	750	1,100	6,500
1837 large date	Inc. above	40.00	50.00	85.00	290	550	750	1,100	6,500
1838O	406,034	40.00	60.00	110	375	725	1,250	3,500	21,000

Seated Liberty Dime
Seated Liberty, stars around top 1/2 of border, date below obverse
Value within wreath reverse

No drapery at elbow

KM# 63.1 • 2.6700 g., 0.9000 **Silver**, 0.0773 oz. ASW, 17.9 mm. • **Obv. Designer:** Christian Gobrecht **Rev. Legend:** UNITED STATES OF AMERICA **Notes:** The two 1838 varieties are distinguished by the size of the stars on the obverse. The 1838 "partial drapery" variety has drapery on Liberty's left elbow. The 1839-O with reverse of 1838-O variety was struck from rusted dies. This variety has a bumpy surface on the reverse.

Date	Mintage	G-4	VG-8	F-12	VF-20	XF-40	AU-50	MS-60	MS-65
1838 small stars	1,992,500	25.00	30.00	50.00	80.00	165	350	600	—
1838 large stars	Inc. above	17.50	20.00	30.00	37.50	110	215	280	8,500
1838 partial drapery	Inc. above	35.00	50.00	85.00	150	225	350	550	—
1839	1,053,115	16.00	18.50	25.00	35.00	105	195	280	3,000
1839O	1,323,000	18.50	22.50	35.00	60.00	150	365	1,250	6,000
1839O reverse 1838O	—	165	225	375	550	1,150	—	—	—
1840	1,358,580	16.00	18.50	25.00	35.00	105	195	300	4,000
1840O	1,175,000	18.50	22.50	40.00	70.00	165	365	975	6,500

Seated Liberty Dime
Seated Liberty, stars around top 1/2 of border, date below obverse
Value within wreath reverse

Drapery at elbow

KM# 63.2 • 2.6700 g., 0.9000 **Silver**, 0.0773 oz. ASW, 17.9 mm. • **Rev. Legend:** UNITED STATES OF AMERICA **Designer:** Christian Gobrecht **Notes:** Drapery added to Liberty's left elbow

Date	Mintage	G-4	VG-8	F-12	VF-20	XF-40	AU-50	MS-60	MS-65
1840	Inc. above	35.00	50.00	95.00	185	350	1,250	—	—
1841	1,622,500	16.00	18.50	21.50	27.50	50.00	175	260	2,700
1841O	2,007,500	18.50	22.50	28.50	45.00	75.00	250	1,500	5,000
1841O large O	Inc. above	600	900	1,200	2,500	—	—	—	—
1842	1,887,500	15.00	17.50	21.50	26.00	45.00	175	260	2,700
1842O	2,020,000	18.50	23.50	30.00	75.00	225	1,350	2,900	—
1843	1,370,000	15.00	17.50	21.50	26.00	45.00	175	260	3,000
1843/1843	—	16.00	18.50	22.50	30.00	75.00	200	295	—
1843O	150,000	50.00	80.00	135	325	1,100	2,250	—	—
1844	72,500	275	350	550	800	1,450	2,200	3,000	—
1845	1,755,000	16.00	18.50	21.50	27.50	45.00	120	260	2,600
1845/1845	Inc. above	17.00	20.00	35.00	55.00	100.00	175	—	—
1845O	230,000	25.00	35.00	95.00	250	750	1,750	—	—
1846	31,300	250	350	500	950	1,750	2,750	5,500	—
1847	245,000	19.00	25.00	40.00	85.00	150	350	950	9,000
1848	451,500	18.50	21.50	25.00	50.00	95.00	250	750	7,000
1849	839,000	17.50	19.50	23.50	33.50	60.00	140	500	4,000
1849O	300,000	21.50	30.00	50.00	135	275	750	2,200	—

DIME

Date	Mintage	G-4	VG-8	F-12	VF-20	XF-40	AU-50	MS-60	MS-65
1850	1,931,500	17.50	19.50	23.50	32.50	55.00	120	260	5,900
1850O	510,000	21.50	25.00	40.00	90.00	175	475	1,250	—
1851	1,026,500	17.50	20.00	22.50	30.00	60.00	120	325	5,000
1851O	400,000	21.50	25.00	40.00	90.00	175	500	1,850	—
1852	1,535,500	15.00	16.00	18.50	23.50	50.00	120	290	2,550
1852O	430,000	22.50	30.00	45.00	125	235	550	1,800	—
1853	95,000	95.00	125	200	295	425	575	800	—

Seated Liberty Dime

Seated Liberty, stars around top 1/2 of border, arrows at date obverse
Value within wreath reverse

KM# 77 • 2.4900 g., 0.9000 **Silver**, 0.0720 oz. ASW • **Rev. Legend:** UNITED STATES OF AMERICA
Designer: Christian Gobrecht

Date	Mintage	G-4	VG-8	F-12	VF-20	XF-40	AU-50	MS-60	MS-65	Prf-65
1853	12,078,010	8.00	9.00	10.00	14.00	45.00	125	330	2,500	31,500
1853O	1,100,000	11.00	14.00	20.00	45.00	145	400	900	—	—
1854	4,470,000	8.75	9.25	10.00	15.00	45.00	125	330	2,500	31,500
1854O	1,770,000	10.00	11.00	14.00	25.00	75.00	175	600	—	—
1855	2,075,000	8.75	9.25	14.00	20.00	55.00	150	350	3,800	31,500

Seated Liberty Dime

Seated Liberty, stars around top 1/2 of border, date below obverse
Value within wreath reverse

KM# A63.2 • 2.4900 g., 0.9000 **Silver**, 0.0720 oz. ASW • **Rev. Legend:** UNITED STATES OF AMERICA
Designer: Christian Gobrecht **Notes:** The two 1856 varieties are distinguished by the size of the numerals in the date.

Date	Mintage	G-4	VG-8	F-12	VF-20	XF-40	AU-50	MS-60	MS-65	Prf-65
1856 small date	5,780,000	14.00	15.00	18.00	22.00	37.50	115	250	7,050	38,000
1856 large date	Inc. above	16.00	18.50	19.50	25.00	65.00	175	475	—	—
1856O	1,180,000	16.00	18.50	19.50	35.00	85.00	215	625	5,250	—
1856S	70,000	160	225	375	550	1,200	1,750	—	—	—
1857	5,580,000	14.00	15.50	16.50	22.50	37.50	110	260	2,600	3,400
1857O	1,540,000	14.00	16.00	18.50	27.50	70.00	200	375	2,600	—
1858	1,540,000	14.00	15.50	16.50	22.50	55.00	145	260	2,600	3,400
1858O	290,000	19.00	25.00	40.00	85.00	165	280	800	5,000	—
1858S	60,000	150	200	325	475	1,000	1,500	—	—	—
1859	430,000	16.00	20.00	25.00	45.00	70.00	140	350	—	3,400
1859O	480,000	16.00	20.00	25.00	45.00	80.00	225	550	—	—
1859S	60,000	160	225	375	550	1,350	3,000	—	—	—
1860S	140,000	40.00	55.00	75.00	145	325	800	—	—	—

Seated Liberty Dime

"United States of America" replaced stars obverse   Value within wreath reverse

KM# 92 • 2.4900 g., 0.9000 **Silver**, 0.0720 oz. ASW • **Obv. Legend** UNITED STATES OF AMERICA **Obv. Designer:** Christian Gobrecht **Notes:** The 1873 "closed-3" and "open-3" varieties are distinguished by the amount of space between the upper left and lower left serifs of the 3 in the date.

Date	Mintage	G-4	VG-8	F-12	VF-20	XF-40	AU-50	MS-60	MS-65	Prf-65
1860	607,000	15.00	22.00	29.00	31.00	55.00	125	275	1,350	1,400
1860O	40,000	450	600	1,000	1,950	3,500	5,500	8,500	—	—
1861	1,884,000	15.00	17.00	20.00	23.00	34.00	85.00	150	1,250	1,400

Date	Mintage	G-4	VG-8	F-12	VF-20	XF-40	AU-50	MS-60	MS-65	Prf-65
1861S	172,500	55.00	90.00	165	275	400	900	1,400	—	—
1862	847,550	16.00	17.50	19.50	25.00	45.00	77.50	165	1,250	1,400
1862S	180,750	45.00	65.00	95.00	185	375	775	1,000	—	—
1863	14,460	425	500	650	900	950	1,100	1,300	—	1,400
1863S	157,500	40.00	55.00	80.00	145	275	650	1,200	—	—
1864	11,470	425	500	650	750	900	1,000	1,200	—	1,400
1864S	230,000	35.00	45.00	75.00	110	225	425	1,200	—	—
1865	10,500	475	575	700	875	1,000	1,200	1,350	—	1,400
1865S	175,000	45.00	55.00	85.00	145	325	850	—	—	—
1866	8,725	500	600	775	950	1,100	1,200	1,800	—	1,750
1866S	135,000	50.00	65.00	100.00	150	325	700	1,900	—	—
1867	6,625	600	700	950	1,100	1,450	1,600	1,800	—	1,750
1867S	140,000	50.00	60.00	90.00	150	325	700	1,200	—	—
1868	464,000	18.00	22.00	29.00	39.00	85.00	175	300	—	1,400
1868S	260,000	30.00	35.00	50.00	85.00	165	300	600	—	—
1869	256,600	25.00	35.00	45.00	80.00	135	250	600	—	1,400
1869S	450,000	25.00	30.00	40.00	55.00	85.00	175	400	—	—
1870	471,000	18.00	22.00	30.00	40.00	50.00	80.00	150	—	1,400
1870S	50,000	300	375	500	650	850	1,200	2,000	—	—
1871	907,710	16.00	20.00	25.00	33.00	55.00	175	300	—	1,400
1871CC	20,100	2,500	3,500	4,500	6,500	10,000	—	—	—	—
1871S	320,000	35.00	55.00	75.00	130	195	350	900	—	—
1872	2,396,450	12.00	15.00	17.00	20.00	31.00	95.00	175	—	1,400
1872CC	35,480	950	1,250	1,850	3,000	6,500	—	—	—	—
1872S	190,000	40.00	65.00	85.00	150	250	450	1,100	—	—
1873 closed 3	1,568,600	12.50	15.00	18.00	22.00	50.00	100.00	200	—	1,400
1873 open 3	Inc. above	28.00	35.00	50.00	75.00	125	250	650	—	—
1873CC	12,400	—	—	—	—	—	—	—	—	—

Note: 1873 CC, Heritage Sale, April 1999, MS-64, $632,500.

Seated Liberty Dime

Seated Liberty, arrows at date obverse   Value within wreath reverse

KM# 105 • 2.5000 g., 0.9000 **Silver**, 0.0723 oz. ASW • **Obv. Legend** UNITED STATES OF AMERICA
Designer: Christian Gobrecht

Date	Mintage	G-4	VG-8	F-12	VF-20	XF-40	AU-50	MS-60	MS-65	Prf-65
1873	2,378,500	15.00	18.50	25.00	55.00	150	350	500	4,500	4,500
1873CC	18,791	2,350	3,250	4,250	6,500	10,000	—	—	—	—
1873S	455,000	20.00	30.00	40.00	70.00	190	400	1,500	—	—
1874	2,940,700	13.50	17.50	22.50	50.00	150	315	500	4,500	4,500
1874CC	10,817	5,000	6,500	8,000	12,500	25,000	—	—	—	—
1874S	240,000	60.00	75.00	100.00	160	250	450	1,500	—	—

Seated Liberty Dime

Seated Liberty, date below obverse   Value within wreath reverse

KM# A92 • 2.5000 g., 0.9000 **Silver**, 0.0723 oz. ASW • **Obv. Legend** UNITED STATES OF AMERICA
Designer: Christian Gobrecht **Notes:** On the 1876-CC doubled-obverse variety, doubling appears in the words "of America" in the legend.

Date	Mintage	G-4	VG-8	F-12	VF-20	XF-40	AU-50	MS-60	MS-65	Prf-65
1875	10,350,700	14.00	16.00	17.50	20.00	30.00	75.00	125	2,250	4,600
1875CC mint mark in wreath	4,645,000	15.00	19.00	22.50	35.00	47.50	90.00	190	2,700	—
1875CC mint mark under wreath	Inc. above	15.00	19.00	27.50	45.00	75.00	165	235	3,000	—
1875S mint mark in wreath	9,070,000	20.00	25.00	30.00	43.00	65.00	125	225	3,100	—
1875S mint mark under wreath	Inc. above	12.50	15.50	17.50	20.00	27.50	72.50	125	1,100	—
1876 Type 1 rev	11,461,150	14.00	16.00	17.50	20.00	30.00	75.00	125	1,100	1,200
1876 Type 2 rev	Inc. above	20.00	25.00	30.00	40.00	60.00	120	200	—	—
1876CC Type 1 rev	8,270,000	20.00	25.00	30.00	40.00	65.00	125	225	—	—
1876CC Type 2 rev	Inc. above	25.00	35.00	48.00	65.00	90.00	175	300	—	—

DIME

Date	Mintage	G-4	VG-8	F-12	VF-20	XF-40	AU-50	MS-60	MS-65	Prf-65
1876CC doubled die obverse	Inc. above	20.00	26.00	44.00	100.00	185	340	600	—	—
1876S Type 1 rev	10,420,000	14.00	16.00	17.50	20.00	30.00	75.00	125	1,750	—
1876S Type 2 rev	Inc. above	18.00	20.00	24.00	30.00	40.00	90.00	150	—	—
1877 Type 1 rev	7,310,510	14.00	16.00	17.50	20.00	30.00	75.00	125	1,100	1,200
1877 Type 2 rev	Inc. above	18.00	20.00	24.00	30.00	40.00	90.00	150	—	—
1877CC Type 1 rev	7,700,000	25.00	35.00	48.00	65.00	90.00	175	300	1,100	—
1877CC Type 2 rev	Inc. above	20.00	25.00	30.00	40.00	65.00	125	225	—	—
1877S Type 1 rev	2,340,000	—	—	—	—	—	—	—	—	—
1877S Type 2 rev	Inc. above	14.00	18.00	20.00	30.00	50.00	105	225	—	—
1878 Type 1 rev	1,678,800	28.00	35.00	50.00	65.00	100.00	175	—	—	—
1878 Type 2 rev	Inc. above	14.00	16.00	20.00	30.00	36.00	72.50	125	1,500	1,200
1878CC Type 1 rev	200,000	100.00	135	175	285	450	700	—	—	—
1878CC Type 2 rev	Inc. above	65.00	90.00	125	225	370	500	900	3,500	—
1879	15,100	275	310	375	425	500	575	675	1,750	1,500
1880	37,335	250	275	315	350	400	450	550	1,750	1,500
1881	24,975	265	300	350	400	475	550	650	2,500	1,600
1882	3,911,100	14.00	16.00	17.50	20.00	30.00	75.00	125	1,100	1,200
1883	7,675,712	14.00	16.00	17.50	20.00	30.00	75.00	125	1,100	1,200
1884	3,366,380	14.00	16.00	17.50	20.00	30.00	75.00	125	1,100	1,200
1884S	564,969	30.00	35.00	45.00	55.00	125	280	650	—	—
1885	2,533,427	14.00	16.00	17.50	20.00	30.00	75.00	125	1,100	1,200
1885S	43,690	450	650	950	1,750	2,400	3,600	5,000	—	—
1886	6,377,570	12.50	15.00	17.00	20.00	27.50	72.50	125	1,100	1,200
1886S	206,524	50.00	70.00	80.00	125	175	280	600	—	—
1887	11,283,939	14.00	16.00	17.50	20.00	30.00	75.00	125	1,100	1,200
1887S	4,454,450	12.50	15.00	17.00	20.00	38.00	80.00	125	1,100	—
1888	5,496,487	14.00	16.00	17.50	20.00	30.00	75.00	125	1,100	1,200
1888S	1,720,000	12.50	15.00	17.00	25.00	40.00	95.00	200	—	—
1889	7,380,711	14.00	16.00	17.50	20.00	30.00	75.00	125	1,100	1,200
1889S	972,678	14.00	18.00	25.00	45.00	70.00	150	475	4,500	—
1890	9,911,541	14.00	16.00	17.50	20.00	30.00	75.00	125	1,100	1,200
1890S	1,423,076	14.00	15.00	22.50	50.00	85.00	155	400	4,900	—
1891	15,310,600	14.00	16.00	17.50	20.00	30.00	75.00	125	1,100	1,200
1891O	4,540,000	12.50	15.00	17.00	20.00	27.50	72.50	175	1,750	—
1891O /horizontal O	Inc. above	65.00	95.00	125	175	225	400	—	—	—
1891S	3,196,116	13.50	15.00	17.50	20.00	30.00	75.00	225	1,650	—
1891S/S	Inc. above	25.00	30.00	40.00	85.00	135	250	—	—	—

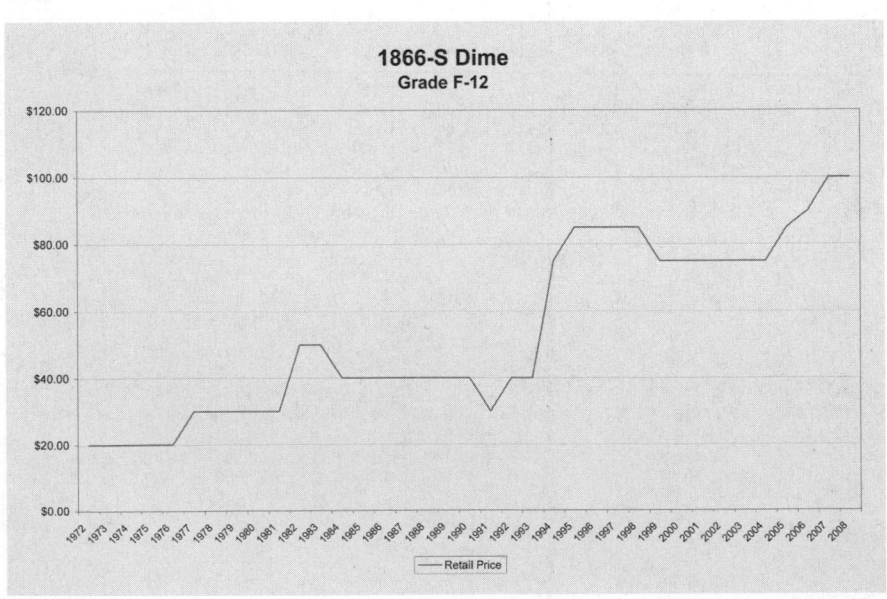

1866-S Dime
Grade F-12

Barber Dime
Laureate head right, date at angle below obverse   Value within wreath reverse

KM# 113 • 2.5000 g., 0.9000 **Silver**, 0.0723 oz. ASW, 17.9 mm. • **Obv. Legend** UNITED STATES OF AMERICA **Designer:** Charles E. Barber

Date	Mintage	G-4	VG-8	F-12	VF-20	XF-40	AU-50	MS-60	MS-65	Prf-65
1892	12,121,245	5.00	7.00	16.00	23.50	27.50	70.00	110	750	1,450
1892O	3,841,700	11.00	15.00	32.50	54.00	75.00	96.00	160	1,275	—
1892S	990,710	66.00	115	200	235	285	335	425	4,000	—
1893	3,340,792	8.25	12.50	20.00	30.00	46.00	82.50	160	1,000	1,450
1893O	1,760,000	31.00	45.00	115	150	190	250	330	3,250	—
1893S	2,491,401	14.00	25.00	37.50	45.00	85.00	155	300	4,350	—
1894	1,330,972	25.00	45.00	115	155	190	235	320	1,200	1,450
1894O	720,000	70.00	105	205	275	445	650	1,550	15,500	—
1894S	24	—	—	—	—	—	—	—1,300,000		—

Note: 1894S, Eliasberg Sale, May 1996, Prf-64, $451,000.

Date	Mintage	G-4	VG-8	F-12	VF-20	XF-40	AU-50	MS-60	MS-65	Prf-65
1895	690,880	85.00	180	345	480	575	650	775	2,800	2,000
1895O	440,000	385	575	880	1,250	2,500	3,800	6,000	19,500	—
1895S	1,120,000	43.50	60.00	130	185	240	320	500	7,800	—
1896	2,000,762	11.50	23.00	55.00	90.00	100.00	120	160	1,500	1,450
1896O	610,000	80.00	155	295	375	480	715	1,000	9,400	—
1896S	575,056	85.00	160	280	325	400	525	770	4,600	—
1897	10,869,264	2.50	3.45	8.00	15.00	32.50	76.00	130	700	1,450
1897O	666,000	69.50	115	280	375	480	615	975	4,700	—
1897S	1,342,844	21.00	45.00	96.00	125	185	275	450	4,250	—
1898	16,320,735	2.50	3.45	8.00	15.00	32.50	76.00	130	720	1,450
1898O	2,130,000	13.00	27.50	85.00	140	205	285	450	4,150	—
1898S	1,702,507	8.50	15.00	32.50	47.50	80.00	160	370	3,850	—
1899	19,580,846	2.50	2.80	7.50	11.50	26.00	70.00	115	700	1,450
1899O	2,650,000	9.75	19.50	70.00	100.00	150	230	415	4,850	—
1899S	1,867,493	8.50	16.00	26.00	34.00	47.50	110	300	4,600	—
1900	17,600,912	2.80	4.00	7.00	11.00	27.50	780	100.00	825	1,450
1900O	2,010,000	19.50	38.50	110	150	225	355	595	6,000	—
1900S	5,168,270	4.75	6.25	12.50	19.50	31.50	75.00	155	1,900	—
1901	18,860,478	2.50	3.75	6.50	10.00	27.50	65.00	110	850	1,450
1901O	5,620,000	3.75	5.25	16.00	27.50	67.50	180	450	4,500	—
1901S	593,022	80.00	150	360	450	520	675	1,000	5,500	—
1902	21,380,777	3.00	3.75	5.50	8.00	23.00	65.00	100.00	700	1,450
1902O	4,500,000	3.45	5.25	15.00	32.50	62.50	135	340	4,650	—
1902S	2,070,000	8.00	21.00	55.00	85.00	135	200	385	4,000	—

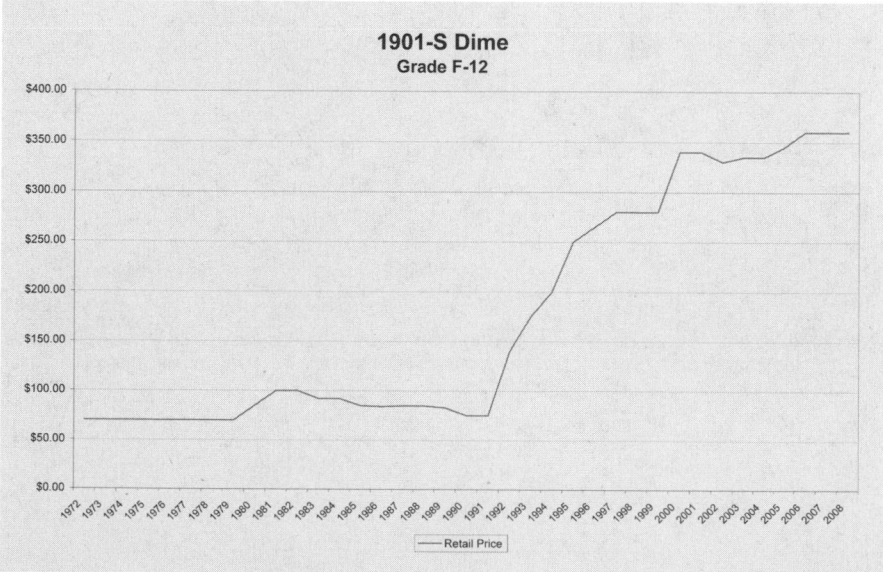

1901-S Dime
Grade F-12

DIME

Date	Mintage	G-4	VG-8	F-12	VF-20	XF-40	AU-50	MS-60	MS-65	Prf-65
1903	19,500,755	2.50	3.75	4.40	8.00	25.00	65.00	110	1,150	1,450
1903O	8,180,000	3.50	5.00	13.50	23.50	50.00	110	250	5,100	—
1903S	613,300	84.00	130	340	490	770	845	1,150	3,750	—
1904	14,601,027	2.50	3.75	6.25	9.50	25.00	65.00	110	1,950	1,450
1904S	800,000	45.00	75.00	160	240	345	480	750	4,500	—
1905	14,552,350	2.80	3.45	5.60	8.00	25.00	65.00	110	700	1,450
1905O	3,400,000	4.00	10.00	34.00	57.50	96.00	155	285	1,900	—
1905S	6,855,199	3.50	3.85	9.00	18.50	45.00	100.00	220	800	—
1906	19,958,406	1.75	2.20	3.75	6.75	22.00	62.50	100.00	700	1,450
1906D	4,060,000	2.75	3.85	7.00	15.00	36.00	80.00	175	1,600	—
1906O	2,610,000	5.50	13.00	47.50	75.00	100.00	135	200	1,300	—
1906S	3,136,640	2.80	5.25	12.50	22.00	46.00	115	240	1,300	—
1907	22,220,575	1.75	2.20	3.40	6.75	22.00	62.50	110	700	1,450
1907D	4,080,000	2.50	4.00	8.50	17.50	45.00	115	280	4,600	—
1907O	5,058,000	3.45	6.75	31.50	47.50	62.50	110	210	1,350	—
1907S	3,178,470	3.45	5.50	16.00	27.50	67.50	150	420	2,500	—
1908	10,600,545	2.20	2.50	3.40	6.75	22.00	62.50	110	700	1,450
1908D	7,490,000	2.15	2.50	4.65	9.50	30.00	62.50	130	1,150	—
1908O	1,789,000	5.00	11.00	42.50	61.00	96.00	150	300	1,700	—
1908S	3,220,000	3.45	5.25	11.50	22.00	47.50	175	325	2,750	—
1909	10,240,650	2.20	2.50	3.40	6.75	22.00	62.50	110	700	1,700
1909D	954,000	7.50	19.50	60.00	96.00	135	230	500	3,600	—
1909O	2,287,000	4.00	7.50	12.50	22.00	50.00	96.00	190	2,000	—
1909S	1,000,000	9.00	20.00	85.00	125	190	330	535	3,200	—
1910	11,520,551	1.85	2.20	3.40	9.50	23.00	62.50	110	700	1,450
1910D	3,490,000	2.50	4.00	8.50	19.50	47.50	110	220	1,550	—
1910S	1,240,000	5.25	10.00	50.00	71.00	110	200	435	2,600	—
1911	18,870,543	1.75	2.10	3.40	6.75	22.00	62.50	110	700	1,700
1911D	11,209,000	1.75	2.10	3.40	6.75	25.00	62.50	110	750	—
1911S	3,520,000	2.80	3.75	8.50	19.00	41.50	110	200	1,300	—
1912	19,350,700	1.75	2.10	3.40	6.75	22.00	62.50	110	700	1,700
1912D	11,760,000	1.75	2.10	3.75	6.75	22.00	62.50	110	700	—
1912S	3,420,000	2.20	2.75	5.60	12.50	34.00	96.00	160	850	—
1913	19,760,622	1.75	2.10	3.00	6.50	22.00	62.50	110	700	1,450
1913S	510,000	30.00	47.50	110	170	240	330	480	1,350	—
1914	17,360,655	1.75	2.10	3.00	6.50	22.00	62.50	110	700	1,700
1914D	11,908,000	1.75	2.10	3.40	6.50	22.00	62.50	110	700	—
1914S	2,100,000	3.00	4.00	8.00	17.50	41.50	80.00	150	1,350	—
1915	5,620,450	2.20	2.50	3.00	7.00	22.00	62.50	110	700	2,000
1915S	960,000	7.00	12.00	32.50	47.50	70.00	135	250	1,600	—
1916	18,490,000	1.75	2.15	3.40	8.00	22.00	62.50	110	700	—
1916S	5,820,000	1.75	2.65	4.00	8.00	23.50	65.00	110	850	—

Mercury Dime

Mint mark   1942/41

Full split bands

KM# 140 • 2.5000 g., 0.9000 **Silver**, 0.0723 oz. ASW, 17.9 mm. • **Designer:** Adolph A. Weinman **Notes:** All specimens listed as -65FSB are for fully struck MS-65 coins with fully split and rounded horizontal bands on the fasces.

Date	Mintage	G-4	VG-8	F-12	VF-20	XF-40	MS-60	MS-65	Prf-65	-65FSB
1916	22,180,080	3.45	4.70	6.25	7.00	12.00	30.00	110	—	120
1916D	264,000	1,000	1,600	2,700	3,850	6,200	13,750	26,500	—	44,500
1916S	10,450,000	4.00	5.50	9.75	15.00	25.00	46.00	210	—	600
1917	55,230,000	1.85	2.25	2.50	5.50	8.00	28.00	155	—	400
1917D	9,402,000	4.00	6.00	11.00	26.00	51.00	120	1,100	—	6,000
1917S	27,330,000	1.80	2.40	3.50	6.50	14.00	64.00	470	—	1,150
1918	26,680,000	2.50	3.20	5.75	12.00	34.00	70.00	420	—	1,150
1918D	22,674,800	2.65	3.25	5.00	12.00	32.00	105	600	—	33,500

Date	Mintage	G-4	VG-8	F-12	VF-20	XF-40	MS-60	MS-65	Prf-65	-65FSB
1918S	19,300,000	2.40	3.00	3.85	10.00	24.00	96.00	660	—	6,600
1919	35,740,000	1.90	2.50	3.00	5.50	12.00	37.00	315	—	700
1919D	9,939,000	3.50	6.50	12.00	25.00	46.00	180	2,100	—	38,500
1919S	8,850,000	2.90	3.25	8.00	17.00	42.00	180	1,250	—	13,000
1920	59,030,000	1.50	1.75	2.25	4.00	8.50	28.00	235	—	515
1920D	19,171,000	2.50	2.85	4.50	8.00	24.00	110	750	—	4,000
1920S	13,820,000	2.40	2.75	4.00	8.50	21.00	110	1,300	—	8,000
1921	1,230,000	60.00	75.00	125	280	550	1,175	3,100	—	4,400
1921D	1,080,000	78.00	125	205	380	675	1,325	3,250	—	5,600
1923	50,130,000	1.50	2.00	2.25	4.00	7.00	28.00	115	—	295
1923S	6,440,000	2.60	3.00	7.50	18.00	75.00	160	1,150	—	6,900
1924	24,010,000	1.50	2.00	2.75	4.50	13.50	42.00	175	—	520
1924D	6,810,000	3.00	4.25	6.50	22.00	63.00	175	1,050	—	1,400
1924S	7,120,000	2.90	3.75	4.25	12.00	60.00	170	1,100	—	14,000
1925	25,610,000	1.50	1.75	2.35	4.00	9.00	28.00	210	—	1,000
1925D	5,117,000	4.00	4.25	12.00	44.00	135	350	1,750	—	3,500
1925S	5,850,000	2.50	2.75	7.00	14.00	85.00	185	1,400	—	4,400
1926	32,160,000	1.50	1.75	2.00	3.00	6.00	25.00	240	—	525
1926D	6,828,000	2.90	4.00	5.00	10.00	32.00	125	550	—	2,650
1926S	1,520,000	10.50	12.50	29.00	70.00	290	900	3,000	—	6,500
1927	28,080,000	1.50	1.75	2.00	3.50	6.00	26.00	138	—	400
1927D	4,812,000	2.90	5.00	7.50	21.00	88.00	175	1,285	—	8,500
1927S	4,770,000	2.25	3.75	5.00	9.00	32.00	285	1,400	—	7,700
1928	19,480,000	1.50	1.75	1.85	3.50	4.50	27.50	120	—	300
1928D	4,161,000	3.75	4.00	9.00	22.00	55.00	175	875	—	2,500
1928S Large S	7,400,000	2.75	3.25	4.50	10.00	30.00	200	640	—	—
1928S Small S	Inc. above	2.00	2.25	3.00	6.50	19.00	125	425	—	1,900
1929	25,970,000	1.50	1.75	2.10	3.00	4.50	21.00	60.00	—	265
1929D	5,034,000	2.00	3.00	4.00	8.00	15.00	27.00	75.00	—	225
1929S	4,730,000	1.50	1.85	2.25	5.00	7.00	32.50	90.00	—	525
1929S Doubled Die Obv	Inc. above	5.00	9.00	16.00	25.00	40.00	90.00	275	—	—
1930	6,770,000	1.50	1.75	2.10	3.75	7.00	26.00	120	—	525
1930S	1,843,000	2.50	3.50	4.80	6.50	19.00	82.00	200	—	565
1931	3,150,000	2.25	3.00	3.35	4.25	12.50	33.00	135	—	—
1931D	1,260,000	9.00	11.00	15.00	18.00	45.00	100.00	285	—	350
1931 Doubled Die Obv & Rev	Inc. above	—	—	—	50.00	70.00	135	485	—	—
1931S	1,800,000	4.00	5.00	5.50	11.00	22.00	96.00	275	—	2,100
1931S Doubled Die Obv	—	7.50	10.00	13.00	25.00	35.00	140	425	—	—
1934	24,080,000	—	1.45	1.75	3.00	6.50	29.00	42.00	—	150
1934D	6,772,000	1.60	2.10	3.25	7.50	14.00	50.00	78.00	—	360
1935	58,830,000	—	1.35	1.50	2.15	4.25	10.00	30.00	—	70.00
1935D	10,477,000	1.50	1.90	2.85	6.50	13.00	37.00	84.00	—	600
1935S	15,840,000	1.35	1.65	2.00	3.00	5.50	24.00	37.00	—	500
1936	87,504,130	—	—	1.50	2.50	3.50	9.00	26.50	1,950	90.00
1936 Doubled Die Obv	Inc. above	—	—	8.00	15.00	25.00	50.00	165	—	—
1936D	16,132,000	—	1.65	2.10	4.25	8.50	28.00	53.00	—	295
1936S	9,210,000	—	1.50	1.90	3.00	6.00	20.00	33.00	—	85.00

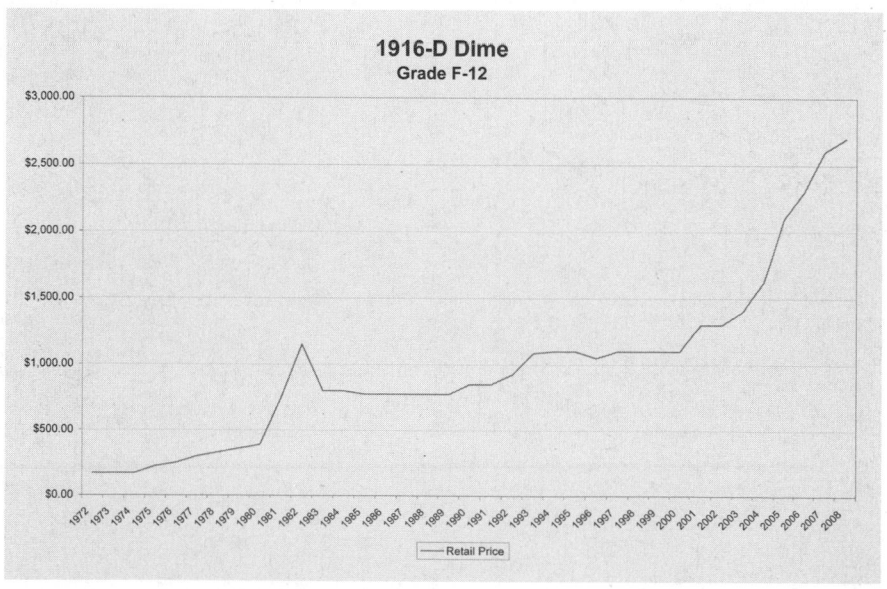

1916-D Dime
Grade F-12

DIME

Date	Mintage	G-4	VG-8	F-12	VF-20	XF-40	MS-60	MS-65	Prf-65	-65FSB
1937	56,865,756	—	—	1.50	2.00	3.75	8.00	24.00	800	42.00
1937 Doubled Die Obv	Inc. above	—	—	—	6.00	9.00	20.00	60.00	—	—
1937D	14,146,000	—	1.40	1.80	3.00	6.00	22.00	43.00	—	100.00
1937S	9,740,000	—	1.50	2.00	3.00	5.50	22.00	36.00	—	195
1937S Doubled Die Obv	Inc. above	—	—	—	5.00	7.00	24.00	80.00	—	—
1938	22,198,728	—	—	1.50	2.25	3.75	13.00	25.00	480	80.00
1938D	5,537,000	1.75	2.25	3.25	5.00	6.00	18.00	34.00	—	65.00
1938S	8,090,000	1.50	2.00	2.75	3.25	5.00	21.00	37.00	—	135
1939	67,749,321	—	—	1.50	2.00	3.25	9.00	25.00	425	170
1939 Doubled Die Obv	Inc. above	—	—	—	4.00	6.00	14.00	35.00	—	—
1939D	24,394,000	—	1.25	1.50	2.00	3.50	7.50	26.00	—	45.00
1939S	10,540,000	1.50	1.75	2.25	3.50	6.75	25.00	50.00	—	750
1940	65,361,827	—	—	—	1.25	2.50	6.00	30.00	325	57.50
1940D	21,198,000	—	—	—	1.40	3.00	8.00	32.00	—	55.00
1940S	21,560,000	—	—	—	1.40	3.00	8.50	32.00	—	95.00
1941	175,106,557	—	—	—	1.25	1.60	6.00	30.00	325	42.00
1941 Doubled Die Obv	Inc. above	—	—	—	10.00	16.00	55.00	140	—	—
1941D	45,634,000	—	—	—	1.40	2.00	8.00	23.00	—	40.00
1941D Doubled Die Obv	Inc. above	—	—	—	9.00	14.00	30.00	90.00	—	—
1941S Small S	43,090,000	—	—	—	1.40	2.00	7.00	30.00	—	50.00
1941S Large S	Inc. above	2.50	4.00	8.00	15.00	25.00	110	250	—	—
1941S Doubled Die Rev	—	1.75	2.50	3.00	4.00	5.00	18.00	50.00	—	—
1942	205,432,329	—	—	—	1.25	1.60	6.00	24.00	325	52.50
1942/41	Inc. above	525	525	625	735	800	2,250	12,500	—	38,500
1942D	60,740,000	—	—	—	1.40	2.00	8.00	27.50	—	40.00
1942/41D	Inc. above	500	595	680	840	920	2,650	7,000	—	19,500
1942S	49,300,000	—	—	—	1.40	2.00	9.50	24.00	—	140
1943	191,710,000	—	—	—	1.25	1.60	6.00	31.00	—	50.00
1943D	71,949,000	—	—	—	1.40	2.00	7.75	30.00	—	40.00
1943S	60,400,000	—	—	—	1.40	2.00	9.00	26.50	—	66.00
1944	231,410,000	—	—	—	1.25	1.60	6.00	23.00	—	80.00
1944D	62,224,000	—	—	—	1.40	2.00	7.50	23.00	—	40.00
1944S	49,490,000	—	—	—	1.40	2.00	7.50	30.00	—	50.00
1945	159,130,000	—	—	—	1.25	1.60	6.00	23.00	—	8,000
1945D	40,245,000	—	—	—	1.40	2.00	6.50	24.00	—	40.00
1945S	41,920,000	—	—	—	1.40	2.00	7.00	24.00	—	135
1945S micro S	Inc. above	3.00	4.00	6.00	9.00	13.00	28.00	115	—	650

Roosevelt Dime

Mint mark 1946-64

KM# 195 • 2.5000 g., 0.9000 Silver, 0.0723 oz. ASW, 17.9 mm. • Designer: John R. Sinnock

Date	Mintage	G-4	VG-8	F-12	VF-20	XF-40	AU-50	MS-60	MS-65	Prf-65
1946	225,250,000	—	—	—	—	1.50	2.00	2.00	14.00	—
1946D	61,043,500	—	—	—	—	1.50	2.20	2.25	15.00	—
1946S	27,900,000	—	—	—	—	1.50	2.25	2.35	17.00	—
1947	121,520,000	—	—	—	—	1.50	2.00	4.00	15.00	—
1947D	46,835,000	—	—	—	—	1.70	2.25	5.00	17.00	—
1947S	34,840,000	—	—	—	—	1.50	2.00	5.00	16.00	—
1948	74,950,000	—	—	—	—	1.60	2.00	4.50	15.00	—
1948D	52,841,000	—	—	—	—	1.90	2.50	6.00	17.00	—
1948S	35,520,000	—	—	—	—	1.80	2.25	5.00	14.00	—
1949	30,940,000	—	—	1.50	2.00	3.00	8.00	16.00	50.00	—
1949D	26,034,000	—	—	1.35	1.75	2.25	5.00	9.00	22.00	—
1949S	13,510,000	—	1.60	2.00	3.50	7.50	14.00	40.00	65.00	—
1950	50,181,500	—	—	—	1.75	2.25	3.50	10.00	25.00	55.00
1950D	46,803,000	—	—	—	—	—	2.50	5.00	12.00	—
1950S	20,440,000	—	1.20	1.80	2.00	3.75	9.00	32.00	60.00	—
1951	102,937,602	—	—	—	—	—	2.10	2.50	10.00	60.00
1951D	56,529,000	—	—	—	—	—	2.00	2.50	8.00	—
1951S	31,630,000	—	—	—	1.70	2.00	4.00	10.00	26.00	—
1952	99,122,073	—	—	—	—	—	1.90	2.50	9.00	40.00
1952D	122,100,000	—	—	—	—	—	1.90	2.50	10.00	—
1952S	44,419,500	—	—	—	1.75	1.90	2.75	5.50	15.00	—
1953	53,618,920	—	—	—	—	—	1.90	2.25	8.00	45.00
1953D	136,433,000	—	—	—	—	—	1.90	2.45	8.00	—
1953S	39,180,000	—	—	—	—	—	2.30	3.00	15.00	—
1954	114,243,503	—	—	—	—	—	1.90	2.10	7.00	20.00
1954D	106,397,000	—	—	—	—	—	1.90	2.10	7.00	—
1954S	22,860,000	—	—	—	—	—	1.90	2.20	10.00	—
1955	12,828,381	—	—	—	1.75	1.50	2.30	2.75	10.00	18.00
1955D	13,959,000	—	—	—	1.75	1.60	2.45	2.75	10.00	—
1955S	18,510,000	—	—	—	1.75	1.55	2.35	2.25	9.00	—

Date	Mintage	G-4	VG-8	F-12	VF-20	XF-40	AU-50	MS-60	MS-65	Prf-65
1956	109,309,384	—	—	—	—	—	1.90	2.10	9.00	8.00
1956D	108,015,100	—	—	—	—	—	1.90	2.20	10.00	—
1957	161,407,952	—	—	—	—	—	1.90	2.10	8.00	6.00
1957D	113,354,330	—	—	—	—	—	1.90	2.10	8.00	—
1958	32,785,652	—	—	—	—	—	1.90	2.10	8.50	6.00
1958D	136,564,600	—	—	—	—	—	1.90	2.10	9.00	—
1959	86,929,291	—	—	—	—	—	1.90	2.10	8.00	5.00
1959D	164,919,790	—	—	—	—	—	1.90	2.10	8.00	—
1960	72,081,602	—	—	—	—	—	1.90	2.10	7.50	5.00
1960D	200,160,400	—	—	—	—	—	1.90	2.10	7.50	—
1961	96,758,244	—	—	—	—	—	1.90	2.10	6.50	4.50
1961D	209,146,550	—	—	—	—	—	1.90	2.10	6.50	—
1962	75,668,019	—	—	—	—	—	1.90	2.10	7.00	4.50
1962D	334,948,380	—	—	—	—	—	1.90	2.10	7.00	—
1963	126,725,645	—	—	—	—	—	1.90	2.10	6.50	4.00
1963D	421,476,530	—	—	—	—	—	1.90	2.10	6.50	—
1964	933,310,762	—	—	—	—	—	1.90	2.10	6.00	4.00
1964D	1,357,517,180	—	—	—	—	—	1.90	2.10	6.00	—

Roosevelt Dime

1982 No mint mark

Mint mark
1968-present

KM# 195a • 2.2700 g., **Copper-Nickel Clad Copper**, 17.9 mm. • **Designer:** John R. Sinnock **Notes:** The 1979-S and 1981-S Type II proofs have clearer mint marks than the Type I proofs of those years. On the 1982 no-mint-mark variety, the mint mark was inadvertently left off.

Date	Mintage	MS-65	Prf-65	Date	Mintage	MS-65	Prf-65
1965	1,652,140,570	1.00	—	1981D	712,284,143	1.00	—
1966	1,382,734,540	1.00	—	1981S type I	—	—	1.00
1967	2,244,007,320	1.50	—	1981S type II	—	—	2.00
1968	424,470,000	1.00	—	1982P	519,475,000	8.50	—
1968D	480,748,280	1.00	—	1982 no mint mark	—	300	—
1968S	3,041,506	—	1.00	1982D	542,713,584	3.00	—
1969	145,790,000	3.00	—	1982S	3,857,479	—	2.00
1969D	563,323,870	1.00	—	1983P	647,025,000	7.00	—
1969S	2,934,631	—	0.80	1983D	730,129,224	2.50	—
1970	345,570,000	1.00	—	1983S	3,279,126	—	2.00
1970S No S	—	—	1,300	1984P	856,669,000	1.00	—
1970D	754,942,100	1.00	—	1984D	704,803,976	2.00	—
1970S	2,632,810	—	1.00	1984S	3,065,110	—	2.00
1971	162,690,000	2.00	—	1985P	705,200,962	1.00	—
1971D	377,914,240	1.00	—	1985D	587,979,970	1.00	—
1971S	3,220,733	—	1.00	1985S	3,362,821	—	1.00
1972	431,540,000	1.00	—	1986P	682,649,693	2.00	—
1972D	330,290,000	1.00	—	1986D	473,326,970	2.00	—
1972S	3,260,996	—	1.00	1986S	3,010,497	—	2.75
1973	315,670,000	1.00	—	1987P	762,709,481	1.00	—
1973D	455,032,426	1.00	—	1987D	653,203,402	1.00	—
1973S	2,760,339	—	1.00	1987S	4,227,728	—	1.00
1974	470,248,000	1.00	—	1988P	1,030,550,000	1.00	—
1974D	571,083,000	1.00	—	1988D	962,385,488	1.00	—
1974S	2,612,568	—	1.00	1988S	3,262,948	—	3.00
1975	585,673,900	1.00	—	1989P	1,298,400,000	1.00	—
1975D	313,705,300	1.00	—	1989D	896,535,597	1.00	—
1975S	2,845,450	—	2.00	1989S	3,220,194	—	4.00
1976	568,760,000	1.50	—	1990P	1,034,340,000	1.00	—
1976D	695,222,774	1.00	—	1990D	839,995,824	1.00	—
1976S	4,149,730	—	1.00	1990S	3,299,559	—	2.00
1977	796,930,000	1.00	—	1991P	927,220,000	1.00	—
1977D	376,607,228	1.00	—	1991D	601,241,114	1.00	—
1977S	3,251,152	—	2.00	1991S	2,867,787	—	3.00
1978	663,980,000	1.00	—	1992P	593,500,000	1.00	—
1978D	282,847,540	1.00	—	1992D	616,273,932	1.00	—
1978S	3,127,781	—	1.00	1992S	2,858,981	—	4.00
1979	315,440,000	1.00	—	1993P	766,180,000	1.00	—
1979D	390,921,184	1.00	—	1993D	750,110,166	1.50	—
1979 type I	—	—	1.00	1993S	2,633,439	—	7.00
1979S type I	3,677,175	—	1.00	1994P	1,189,000,000	1.00	—
1979S type II	Inc. above	—	2.00	1994D	1,303,268,110	1.00	—
1980P	735,170,000	1.00	—	1994S	2,484,594	—	5.00
1980D	719,354,321	.70	—	1995P	1,125,500,000	1.50	—
1980S	3,554,806	—	1.00	1995D	1,274,890,000	2.00	—
1981P	676,650,000	1.00	—	1995S	2,010,384	—	20.00

DIME

Date	Mintage	MS-65	Prf-65
1996P	1,421,163,000	1.00	—
1996D	1,400,300,000	1.00	—
1996W	1,457,949	25.00	—
1996S	2,085,191	—	2.50
1997P	991,640,000	2.00	—
1997D	979,810,000	1.00	—
1997S	1,975,000	—	11.00
1998P	1,163,000,000	1.00	—
1998D	1,172,250,000	1.25	—
1998S	2,078,494	—	4.00
1999P	2,164,000,000	1.00	—
1999D	1,397,750,000	1.00	—
1999S	2,557,897	—	4.00
2000P	1,842,500,000	1.00	—
2000D	1,818,700,000	1.00	—
2000S	3,097,440	—	1.00
2001P	1,369,590,000	1.00	—
2001D	1,412,800,000	1.00	—
2001S	2,249,496	—	1.00
2002P	1,187,500,000	1.00	—
2002D	1,379,500,000	1.00	—
2002S	2,268,913	—	2.00
2003P	1,085,500,000	1.00	—
2003D	986,500,000	1.00	—
2003S	2,076,165	—	2.00
2004P	1,328,000,000	1.00	—
2004D	1,159,500,000	1.00	—
2004S	1,804,396	—	4.75
2005P	1,412,000,000	1.00	—

Date	Mintage	MS-65	Prf-65
2005D	1,423,500,000	1.00	—
2005S	—	—	2.25
2006P	1,381,000,000	1.00	—
2006D	1,447,000,000	1.00	—
2006S	—	—	2.25
2007P	—	1.00	—
2007D	—	1.00	—
2007S	—	—	2.25

Roosevelt Dime

KM# A195 • Silver •

Date	Mintage	Prf-65
1992S	1,317,579	5.00
1993S	761,353	9.00
1994S	785,329	9.00
1995S	838,953	25.00
1996S	830,021	9.00
1997S	821,678	25.00
1998S	878,792	9.00
1999S	804,565	6.50
2000S	965,921	4.00
2001S	849,600	5.00
2002S	888,826	5.00
2003S	1,090,425	4.00
2004S	—	4.50
2005S	—	3.50
2006S	—	3.50
2007S	—	3.50

20 CENTS

Seated Liberty within circle of stars, date below obverse
Eagle with arrows in talons, value below reverse

KM# 109 • 5.0000 g., 0.9000 **Silver**, 0.1447 oz. ASW, 22 mm. • **Rev. Legend:** UNITED STATES OF
AMERICA **Designer:** William Barber

Date	Mintage	G-4	VG-8	F-12	VF-20	XF-40	AU-50	MS-60	MS-65	Prf-65
1875	39,700	165	210	270	325	415	550	835	5,500	9,500
1875S	1,155,000	100.00	110	120	175	210	320	500	4,900	—
Note: 1875-S exists as a branch mint proof										
1875 Clear S	—	110	120	135	200	235	350	600	5,500	—
1875 S over horizontal S	—	100.00	110	120	175	210	320	500	4,900	—
1875 $ Sign var.	—	—	120	130	150	225	260	375	1,300	—
1875CC	133,290	335	385	475	600	775	1,150	1,650	10,000	—
1876	15,900	185	225	285	350	410	535	800	5,600	9,400
1876CC	10,000	20,000	25,000	30,000	35,000	50,000	60,000	—	—	175,000
Note: 1876CC, Eliasberg Sale, April 1997, MS-65, $148,500. Heritage 1999 ANA, MS-63, $86,500.										
1877 proof only	510	—	—	2,700	2,900	3,300	3,500	—	—	10,000
1878 proof only	600	—	—	2,000	2,300	2,400	2,800	—	—	9,500

DIME

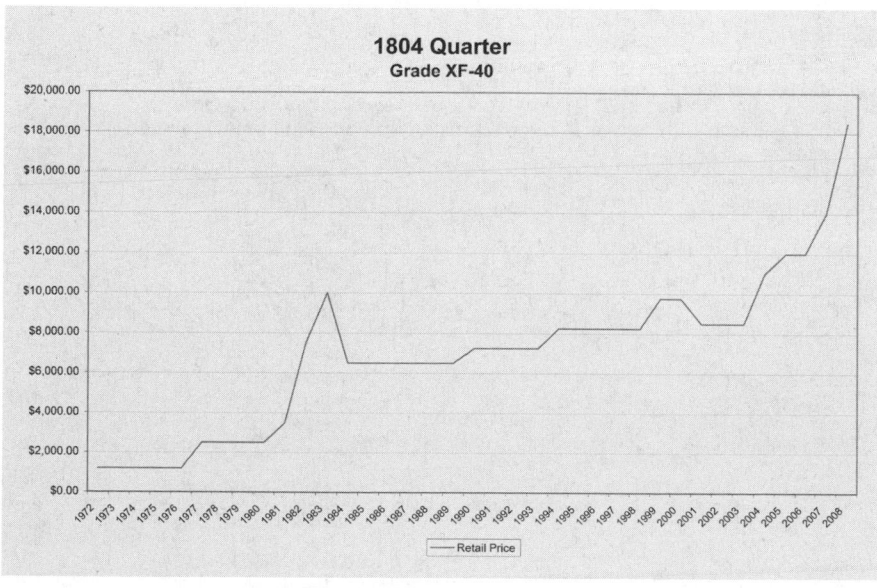

20 CENTS

QUARTER

Draped Bust Quarter
Small eagle reverse

KM# 25 • 6.7400 g., 0.8920 **Silver**, 0.1933 oz. ASW, 27.5 mm. • **Designer:** Robert Scot

Date	Mintage	G-4	VG-8	F-12	VF-20	XF-40	AU-50	MS-60	MS-65
1796	6,146	9,250	16,500	28,000	36,500	42,500	68,000	82,500	235,000

Draped Bust Quarter
Draped bust right, flanked by stars, date at angle below obverse   Heraldic eagle reverse

KM# 36 • 6.7400 g., 0.8920 **Silver**, 0.1933 oz. ASW, 27.5 mm. • **Obv. Legend** LIBERTY **Rev. Legend:** UNITED STATES OF AMERICA **Designer:** Robert Scot

Date	Mintage	G-4	VG-8	F-12	VF-20	XF-40	AU-50	MS-60	MS-65
1804	6,738	3,250	5,400	7,500	10,500	18,500	31,000	52,500	225,000
1805	121,394	230	285	520	960	2,500	4,450	6,600	62,000
1806/5	206,124	250	375	650	1,400	2,850	5,000	7,150	72,000
1806	Inc. above	220	275	500	900	2,350	4,250	6,300	56,000
1807	220,643	220	275	500	925	2,350	4,250	6,300	58,000

Liberty Cap Quarter
Draped bust left, flanked by stars, date below obverse
Eagle with arrows in talons, banner above, value below reverse

KM# 44 • 6.7400 g., 0.8920 **Silver**, 0.1933 oz. ASW, 27 mm. • **Rev. Legend:** UNITED STATES OF AMERICA **Designer:** John Reich **Notes:** Varieties of the 1819 strikes are distinguished by the size of the 9 in the date. Varieties of the 1820 strikes are distinguished by the size of the 0 in the date. One 1822 variety and one 1828 variety have "25" engraved over "50" in the denomination. The 1827 restrikes were produced privately using dies sold as scrap by the U.S. Mint.

Date	Mintage	G-4	VG-8	F-12	VF-20	XF-40	AU-50	MS-60	MS-65
1815	89,235	100.00	135	200	425	1,375	1,750	3,250	30,000
1818/15	361,174	100.00	130	190	450	1,350	1,850	3,200	28,500
1818	Inc. above	95.00	125	180	410	1,200	1,600	2,850	19,500
1819 small 9	144,000	95.00	125	180	410	1,225	1,659	2,900	23,500
1819 large 9	Inc. above	95.00	130	185	435	1,300	1,750	3,100	25,000
1820 small O	127,444	95.00	125	180	420	1,300	1,700	3,100	34,500
1820 large O	Inc. above	95.00	125	180	415	1,225	1,600	2,900	32,500
1821	216,851	100.00	130	185	420	1,275	1,650	2,875	20,000
1822	64,080	110	135	200	440	1,225	2,750	4,200	—
1822 25/50C.	Inc. above	1,650	3,350	4,350	6,800	12,500	20,000	33,000	125,000

Date	Mintage	G-4	VG-8	F-12	VF-20	XF-40	AU-50	MS-60	MS-65
1823/22	17,800	30,000	35,000	48,500	58,500	68,000	100,000	175,000	—
Note: 1823/22, Superior, Aug. 1990, Proof, $62,500.									
1824/2 mintage unrecorded	—	275	425	600	1,650	4,200	7,000	14,500	—
1825/22	168,000	125	175	260	500	1,550	2,100	3,000	—
1825/23	Inc. above	115	150	235	450	1,400	1,850	3,400	25,000
1825/24	Inc. above	100.00	135	210	420	1,325	1,700	3,150	22,000
1827 original curl base 2	4,000	—	—	—	70,000	75,000	80,000	—	—
Note: Eliasberg, April 1997, VF-20, $39,600.									
1827 restrike, square base 2	Inc. above	—	—	—	—	—	—	—	—
Note: 1827 restrike, Eliasberg, April 1997, Prf-65, $77,000.									
1828	102,000	90.00	120	180	400	1,100	1,650	3,000	26,000
1828 25/50C.	Inc. above	165	320	550	1,250	2,650	4,250	9,500	—

Liberty Cap Quarter
Draped bust left, flanked by stars, date below obverse
Eagle with arrows in talons, value below reverse

KM# 55 • 0.8920 **Silver**, 24.3 mm. • **Rev. Legend:** UNITED STATES OF AMERICA **Designer:** William Kneass **Notes:** Varieties of the 1831 strikes are distinguished by the size of the lettering on the reverse.

Date	Mintage	G-4	VG-8	F-12	VF-20	XF-40	AU-50	MS-60	MS-65
1831 small letter	398,000	70.00	95.00	115	160	400	850	1,175	19,500
1831 large letter	Inc. above	70.00	90.00	110	150	385	775	1,100	17,000
1832	320,000	70.00	90.00	110	150	385	775	1,075	22,750
1833	156,000	75.00	100.00	115	170	420	855	1,400	20,500
1834	286,000	70.00	90.00	110	150	385	775	1,100	17,000
1834 0 over O	—	—	—	—	—	—	—	—	—
1835	1,952,000	70.00	90.00	110	150	385	775	1,100	23,750
1836	472,000	70.00	90.00	110	150	385	775	1,100	18,850
1837	252,400	70.00	90.00	110	150	385	775	1,100	17,000
1838	832,000	70.00	90.00	110	150	385	775	1,100	19,500

Seated Liberty Quarter
Seated Liberty, stars around top 1/2 of border, date below obverse
Eagle with arrows in talons, value below reverse

KM# 64.1 • 6.6800 g., 0.9000 **Silver**, 0.1933 oz. ASW, 24.3 mm. • **Rev. Legend:** UNITED STATES OF AMERICA **Designer:** Christian Gobrecht

Date	Mintage	G-4	VG-8	F-12	VF-20	XF-40	AU-50	MS-60	MS-65
1838	Inc. above	42.00	50.00	60.00	110	360	550	1,250	30,000
1839	491,146	36.00	44.00	52.00	85.00	350	550	1,250	34,000
1840O	425,200	46.00	54.00	75.00	135	375	575	1,350	38,500

Seated Liberty Quarter

**Drapery added to Liberty's left elbow, stars around top 1/2 of border obverse
Eagle with arrows in talons, value below reverse**

KM# 64.2 • 6.6800 g., 0.9000 **Silver**, 0.1933 oz. ASW, 24.3 mm. • **Rev. Legend:** UNITED STATES OF
AMERICA **Designer:** Christian Gobrecht **Notes:** Two varieties for 1842 and 1842-O are distinguished by the
size of the numerals in the date. 1852 obverse dies were used to strike the 1853 no-arrows variety, with the 2
being recut to form a 3.

Date	Mintage	G-4	VG-8	F-12	VF-20	XF-40	AU-50	MS-60	MS-65
1840	188,127	27.00	52.00	75.00	125	225	350	950	12,000
1840O	Inc. above	29.00	39.00	70.00	115	250	450	1,000	—
1841	120,000	65.00	90.00	125	170	275	385	750	11,000
1841O	452,000	21.50	27.50	50.00	85.00	165	350	700	10,000
1842 small date	88,000	—	—	—	—	—	—	—	—
Note: 1842 small date, Eliasberg, April 1997, Prf-63, $66,000.									
1842 large date	Inc. above	100.00	125	190	275	375	850	1,850	—
1842O small date	769,000	425	650	1,200	1,950	4,000	—	—	—
1842O large date	Inc. above	28.00	42.00	55.00	70.00	135	300	900	—
1843	645,600	22.00	26.00	34.00	45.00	75.00	175	400	6,750
1843O	968,000	25.00	31.50	55.00	125	250	750	2,000	11,000
1844	421,200	20.00	25.00	31.50	50.00	80.00	160	450	5,500
1844O	740,000	25.00	28.50	40.00	75.00	140	280	1,000	6,000
1845	922,000	20.00	25.00	31.50	45.00	70.00	150	465	5,000
1846	510,000	20.00	25.00	36.50	55.00	85.00	175	475	6,000
1847	734,000	20.00	25.00	31.50	50.00	70.00	150	450	5,000
1847O	368,000	30.00	45.00	70.00	135	300	750	1,900	—
1848	146,000	40.00	60.00	110	185	225	375	1,000	10,000
1849	340,000	20.00	30.00	45.00	65.00	125	275	750	9,000
1849O	—	550	750	1,150	1,850	3,250	5,750	—	—
1850	190,800	40.00	50.00	80.00	125	175	275	800	—
1850O	412,000	20.00	30.00	60.00	110	175	450	1,300	—
1851	160,000	60.00	75.00	125	225	285	400	850	8,500
1851O	88,000	185	275	425	700	1,250	2,250	4,000	—
1852	177,060	50.00	60.00	100.00	185	225	350	500	4,800
1852O	96,000	195	275	475	800	1,350	3,500	8,000	—
1853 recut date	44,200	450	650	900	1,100	1,350	1,800	2,600	9,000

Seated Liberty Quarter

Seated Liberty, arrows at date obverse   Rays around eagle reverse

KM# 78 • 6.2200 g., 0.9000 **Silver**, 0.1800 oz. ASW, 24.3 mm. • **Rev. Legend:** UNITED STATES OF
AMERICA **Designer:** Christian Gobrecht

Date	Mintage	G-4	VG-8	F-12	VF-20	XF-40	AU-50	MS-60	MS-65	Prf-65
1853	15,210,020	20.00	23.00	32.00	46.00	150	275	950	16,500	100,000
1853/4	Inc. above	40.00	65.00	100.00	200	275	750	1,750	—	—
1853O	1,332,000	18.00	35.00	50.00	100.00	275	1,100	2,750	—	—

Seated Liberty Quarter
Seated Liberty, arrows at date obverse   Eagle with arrows in talons, value below reverse

KM# 81 • 6.6800 g., 0.9000 **Silver**, 0.1933 oz. ASW, 24.3 mm. • **Rev. Legend:** UNITED STATES OF AMERICA **Designer:** Christian Gobrecht **Notes:** The 1854-O "huge O" variety has an oversized mint mark.

Date	Mintage	G-4	VG-8	F-12	VF-20	XF-40	AU-50	MS-60	MS-65	Prf-65
1854	12,380,000	15.00	20.00	27.50	35.00	75.00	225	440	7,500	17,500
1854O	1,484,000	17.00	24.00	35.00	60.00	125	300	1,750	—	—
1854O huge O	Inc. above	800	1,350	2,850	4,750	7,500	12,500	17,000	—	—
1855	2,857,000	15.00	20.00	27.50	35.00	75.00	225	440	8,500	18,500
1855O	176,000	50.00	75.00	110	240	475	950	2,750	—	—
1855S	396,400	40.00	60.00	80.00	225	500	1,250	2,000	—	—

Seated Liberty Quarter
Seated Liberty, date below obverse   Eagle with arrows in talons, value below reverse

KM# A64.2 • 6.2200 g., 0.9000 **Silver**, 0.1800 oz. ASW, 24.3 mm. • **Rev. Legend:** UNITED STATES OF AMERICA **Designer:** Christian Gobrecht

Date	Mintage	G-4	VG-8	F-12	VF-20	XF-40	AU-50	MS-60	MS-65	Prf-65
1856	7,264,000	15.00	20.00	27.50	35.00	60.00	145	290	4,250	15,000
1856O	968,000	20.00	30.00	40.00	60.00	110	250	1,000	8,500	—
1856S	286,000	45.00	65.00	110	250	450	900	2,200	—	—
1856S/S	Inc. above	150	275	500	1,250	2,000	—	—	—	—
1857	9,644,000	15.00	20.00	27.50	35.00	60.00	145	290	4,000	9,500
1857O	1,180,000	15.00	20.00	29.00	40.00	80.00	275	975	—	—
1857S	82,000	125	175	275	450	700	950	2,750	—	—
1858	7,368,000	15.00	20.00	27.50	35.00	60.00	160	300	4,000	6,500

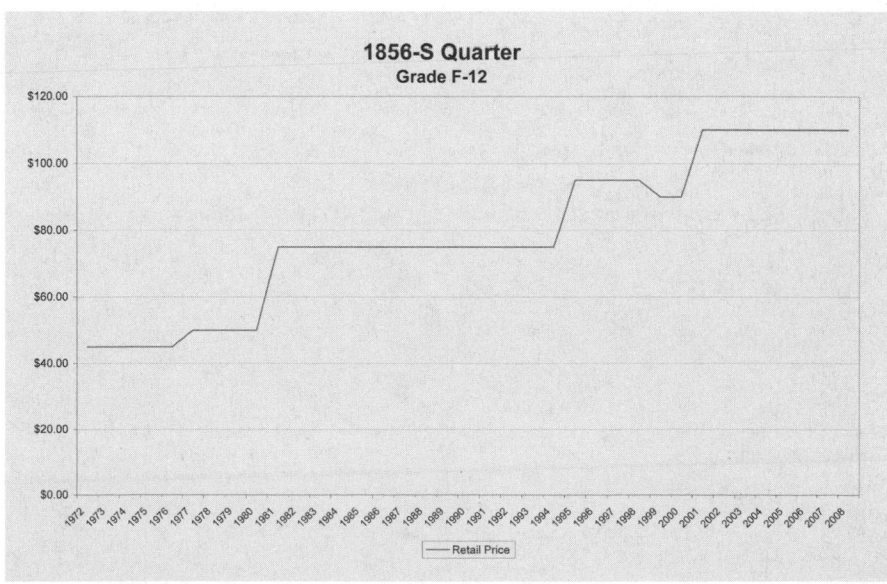

1856-S Quarter
Grade F-12

Date	Mintage	G-4	VG-8	F-12	VF-20	XF-40	AU-50	MS-60	MS-65	Prf-65
1858O	520,000	25.00	30.00	45.00	70.00	135	360	1,350	—	—
1858S	121,000	70.00	110	175	300	750	1,250	—	—	—
1859	1,344,000	17.00	24.00	30.00	40.00	75.00	175	375	6,000	7,000
1859O	260,000	25.00	30.00	50.00	80.00	150	400	1,000	15,000	—
1859S	80,000	125	150	250	500	1,500	2,500	—	—	—
1860	805,400	18.00	22.00	28.00	33.00	60.00	160	500	—	5,250
1860O	388,000	20.00	30.00	40.00	55.00	100.00	275	1,200	—	—
1860S	56,000	200	350	600	975	4,000	6,000	—	—	—
1861	4,854,600	16.00	19.00	27.00	32.00	55.00	150	290	4,200	5,500
1861S	96,000	90.00	145	235	400	1,250	2,750	—	—	—
1862	932,550	18.00	22.00	33.00	40.00	65.00	165	300	4,350	5,350
1862S	67,000	80.00	125	200	325	700	1,600	2,750	—	—
1863	192,060	30.00	45.00	60.00	120	185	300	650	4,350	5,500
1864	94,070	90.00	120	160	245	345	400	650	5,000	5,500
1864S	20,000	400	600	900	1,350	2,350	3,750	7,000	—	—
1865	59,300	85.00	115	150	235	325	375	875	9,500	5,500
1865S	41,000	125	175	250	425	750	1,250	2,350	11,500	—
1866 unique	—	—	—	—	—	—	—	—	—	—

Seated Liberty Quarter

Seated Liberty, date below obverse   "In God We Trust" above eagle reverse

KM# 98 • 6.2200 g., 0.9000 **Silver**, 0.1800 oz. ASW, 24.3 mm. • **Rev. Legend:** UNITED STATES OF AMERICA **Designer:** Christian Gobrecht **Notes:** The 1873 closed-3 and open-3 varieties are distinguished by the amount of space between the upper left and lower left serifs in the 3.

Date	Mintage	G-4	VG-8	F-12	VF-20	XF-40	AU-50	MS-60	MS-65	Prf-65
1866	17,525	475	600	750	1,000	1,200	1,500	2,250	7,500	3,000
1866S	28,000	325	375	675	1,050	1,450	2,000	3,000	—	—
1867	20,625	250	325	500	675	850	975	1,200	—	2,450
1867S	48,000	275	385	600	900	1,350	1,700	—	—	—
1868	30,000	200	250	325	400	500	650	900	7,000	3,450
1868S	96,000	95.00	110	195	300	625	1,350	2,000	—	—
1869	16,600	350	450	600	800	900	1,000	1,275	—	2,500
1869S	76,000	110	135	225	375	700	1,400	2,400	16,000	—
1870	87,400	55.00	80.00	145	245	295	425	850	6,000	2,750
1870CC	8,340	4,500	6,500	9,500	15,000	—	—	—	—	—
1871	119,160	40.00	65.00	75.00	150	195	350	650	6,000	2,500
1871CC	10,890	3,500	4,500	7,500	12,500	18,000	—	—	—	—
1871S	30,900	375	500	700	950	1,200	1,850	3,000	10,000	—
1872	182,950	30.00	40.00	80.00	110	155	300	600	6,500	2,500
1872CC	22,850	1,100	1,500	2,250	3,750	6,500	7,500	14,000	—	—
1872S	83,000	900	1,250	1,750	2,400	3,500	4,500	7,500	—	—
1873 closed 3	212,600	250	350	475	800	1,200	1,800	2,800	—	2,600
1873 open 3	Inc. above	30.00	42.50	80.00	120	175	250	450	5,000	—
1873CC 6 known	4,000	—	75,000	—	—	—	—	—	—	—

Note: 1873CC, Heritage, April 1999, MS-62, $106,375.

Seated Liberty Quarter

Seated Liberty, arrows at date obverse   "In God We Trust" above eagle reverse

KM# 106 • 6.2500 g., 0.9000 **Silver**, 0.1808 oz. ASW, 24.3 mm. • **Rev. Legend:** UNITED STATES OF AMERICA **Designer:** Christian Gobrecht

Date	Mintage	G-4	VG-8	F-12	VF-20	XF-40	AU-50	MS-60	MS-65	Prf-65
1873	1,271,700	16.00	23.00	30.00	60.00	200	400	775	4,250	8,000
1873CC	12,462	3,500	4,500	8,000	11,000	17,000	—	—	—	—
1873S	156,000	25.00	40.00	85.00	140	275	550	1,200	8,000	—
1874	471,900	20.00	26.00	40.00	70.00	220	420	850	4,000	6,750
1874S	392,000	23.00	30.00	50.00	110	240	425	900	4,500	—

Seated Liberty Quarter
Seated Liberty, date below obverse "In God We Trust" above eagle reverse

KM# A98 • 6.2500 g., 0.9000 **Silver**, 0.1808 oz. ASW, 24.3 mm. • **Rev. Legend:** UNITED STATES OF AMERICA **Designer:** Christian Gobrecht **Notes:** The 1876-CC fine-reeding variety has a more finely reeded edge.

Date	Mintage	G-4	VG-8	F-12	VF-20	XF-40	AU-50	MS-60	MS-65	Prf-65
1875	4,293,500	14.00	17.00	25.00	30.00	50.00	135	225	1,600	2,300
1875CC	140,000	75.00	110	225	350	550	850	1,600	15,000	—
1875S	680,000	25.00	36.00	67.00	110	175	275	575	3,200	—
1876	17,817,150	14.00	17.00	25.00	30.00	50.00	135	225	1,600	2,250
1876CC	4,944,000	30.00	40.00	50.00	65.00	90.00	150	325	3,600	—
1876CC fine reeding	Inc. above	30.00	40.00	50.00	65.00	90.00	150	325	3,600	—
1876S	8,596,000	16.00	19.00	25.00	30.00	50.00	135	225	2,000	—
1877	10,911,710	14.00	17.00	25.00	30.00	50.00	135	225	1,600	2,250
1877CC	4,192,000	30.00	40.00	50.00	65.00	90.00	150	325	2,000	—
1877S	8,996,000	14.00	17.00	25.00	30.00	50.00	135	225	1,600	—
1877S /horizontal S	Inc. above	45.00	60.00	95.00	175	250	375	650	—	—
1878	2,260,800	16.00	18.00	28.00	34.00	55.00	145	250	2,750	2,300
1878CC	996,000	35.00	45.00	55.00	80.00	110	150	450	3,500	—
1878S	140,000	165	200	300	400	650	875	1,450	—	—
1879	14,700	190	235	285	325	400	485	575	1,700	2,250
1880	14,955	190	235	285	325	400	485	575	1,600	2,250
1881	12,975	200	250	300	350	425	500	600	1,650	2,200
1882	16,300	200	250	300	350	425	500	600	1,850	2,200
1883	15,439	210	265	315	365	435	525	625	2,450	2,200
1884	8,875	375	450	550	650	750	750	850	1,900	2,200
1885	14,530	210	265	315	365	435	525	625	2,600	2,200
1886	5,886	500	600	700	800	900	1,000	1,250	2,600	2,400
1887	10,710	300	350	450	550	650	750	850	2,350	2,200
1888	10,833	275	325	425	500	600	700	800	2,000	2,350
1888S	1,216,000	15.00	20.00	27.50	30.00	60.00	160	245	2,450	—
1889	12,711	250	300	375	425	500	575	675	1,750	2,350
1890	80,590	65.00	85.00	100.00	125	200	300	425	—	2,350
1891	3,920,600	15.00	20.00	27.50	30.00	60.00	160	245	1,750	2,350
1891O	68,000	150	225	325	550	950	1,250	3,000	14,500	—
1891S	2,216,000	16.00	22.00	29.00	65.00	52.50	185	275	2,400	—

Barber Quarter
Laureate head right, flanked by stars, date below obverse Heraldic eagle reverse

KM# 114 • 6.2500 g., 0.9000 **Silver**, 0.1808 oz. ASW, 24.3 mm. • **Obv. Legend** IN GOD WE TRUST **Rev. Legend:** UNITED STATES OF AMERICA **Designer:** Charles E. Barber

Date	Mintage	G-4	VG-8	F-12	VF-20	XF-40	AU-50	MS-60	MS-65	Prf-65
1892	8,237,245	5.25	8.50	25.00	46.00	75.00	120	220	1,300	2,000
1892O	2,640,000	13.50	21.50	41.50	55.00	96.00	150	300	1,650	—
1892S	964,079	30.00	50.00	80.00	125	190	300	480	4,850	—
1893	5,484,838	6.25	8.50	27.50	41.50	75.00	120	210	1,750	2,000
1893O	3,396,000	8.00	13.50	30.00	55.00	100.00	160	275	1,900	—
1893S	1,454,535	18.00	34.00	62.50	110	160	300	480	8,400	—
1894	3,432,972	5.50	9.50	34.00	50.00	93.50	150	250	1,550	2,000
1894O	2,852,000	8.50	16.00	41.50	67.50	125	225	340	3,000	—
1894S	2,648,821	8.25	12.50	38.00	62.50	115	205	315	3,000	—
1895	4,440,880	6.00	9.00	31.50	41.50	80.00	135	230	1,900	2,000
1895O	2,816,000	11.00	18.00	46.00	75.00	135	225	400	2,750	—
1895S	1,764,681	18.00	27.50	60.00	100.00	150	285	445	4,150	—
1896	3,874,762	5.00	7.00	25.00	41.50	80.00	135	235	1,600	2,000
1896O	1,484,000	26.00	48.50	115	250	425	750	850	7,750	—

QUARTER

Date	Mintage	G-4	VG-8	F-12	VF-20	XF-40	AU-50	MS-60	MS-65	Prf-65
1896S	188,039	750	1,300	1,850	2,750	4,300	5,500	8,000	56,000	—
1897	8,140,731	5.00	6.25	21.50	33.50	75.00	120	220	1,300	2,000
1897O	1,414,800	18.00	38.50	115	235	395	640	1,000	4,150	—
1897S	542,229	85.00	120	275	300	440	700	1,000	7,000	—
1898	11,100,735	5.00	6.25	22.50	33.50	75.00	120	220	1,300	2,000
1898O	1,868,000	13.00	27.50	75.00	150	295	435	650	10,000	—
1898S	1,020,592	12.00	18.50	47.50	65.00	96.00	210	400	7,200	—
1899	12,624,846	5.00	6.25	22.50	33.50	75.00	120	215	1,300	2,000
1899O	2,644,000	11.00	19.00	35.00	60.00	130	275	415	3,400	—
1899S	708,000	17.00	28.50	70.00	85.00	135	275	440	3,800	—
1900	10,016,912	6.00	8.00	21.50	35.00	71.50	135	215	1,300	2,000
1900O	3,416,000	11.00	25.00	62.50	100.00	150	345	585	3,800	—
1900S	1,858,585	8.00	15.00	38.00	55.00	80.00	135	385	5,400	—
1901	8,892,813	11.00	13.00	25.00	41.50	80.00	135	215	2,250	2,200
1901O	1,612,000	40.00	60.00	135	275	470	685	900	5,750	—
1901S	72,664	7,000	11,000	16,500	21,000	28,500	38,000	42,000	100,000	—
1902	12,197,744	6.00	8.00	19.50	33.50	70.00	125	220	1,300	2,100
1902O	4,748,000	8.50	16.00	52.50	82.50	150	245	485	5,000	—
1902S	1,524,612	13.50	22.00	55.00	95.00	170	260	540	3,600	—
1903	9,670,064	6.75	8.00	19.00	33.50	66.00	115	215	2,600	2,000
1903O	3,500,000	8.00	12.50	41.50	65.00	125	260	450	5,800	—
1903S	1,036,000	15.50	25.00	46.00	80.00	145	285	450	2,900	—
1904	9,588,813	8.00	9.75	20.00	36.00	72.50	125	225	1,475	2,000
1904O	2,456,000	11.00	21.50	62.50	100.00	225	460	850	3,250	—
1905	4,968,250	11.00	13.00	27.50	41.50	75.00	125	215	1,650	2,000
1905O	1,230,000	18.50	32.50	82.50	160	260	375	515	6,600	—
1905S	1,884,000	11.00	15.00	43.50	66.00	115	225	350	3,650	—
1906	3,656,435	6.75	8.00	19.00	33.50	70.00	115	215	1,300	2,000
1906D	3,280,000	7.00	8.00	25.00	42.50	71.50	155	220	2,200	—
1906O	2,056,000	7.00	9.00	41.50	60.00	105	200	300	1,400	—
1907	7,192,575	5.25	8.00	17.50	33.50	66.00	115	215	1,300	2,000
1907D	2,484,000	6.00	9.00	29.00	52.50	80.00	180	250	2,750	—
1907O	4,560,000	5.25	8.00	19.00	38.50	70.00	135	220	2,600	—
1907S	1,360,000	10.00	18.50	47.50	75.00	135	275	480	3,500	—
1908	4,232,545	5.00	6.25	18.50	33.50	70.00	115	215	1,300	2,200
1908D	5,788,000	5.00	6.25	17.50	32.50	70.00	120	250	1,750	—
1908O	6,244,000	5.00	8.50	17.50	38.50	75.00	125	215	1,300	—
1908S	784,000	20.00	40.00	92.50	160	320	520	775	5,100	—
1909	9,268,650	5.00	6.25	17.50	33.50	66.00	115	215	1,300	2,000
1909D	5,114,000	6.25	8.00	22.00	41.50	90.00	160	215	2,350	—
1909O	712,000	25.00	60.00	175	400	900	1,250	1,700	9,000	—
1909S	1,348,000	8.00	11.00	37.50	57.50	96.00	200	300	2,400	—
1910	2,244,551	7.75	10.00	30.00	46.00	80.00	140	215	1,300	2,000
1910D	1,500,000	8.00	11.00	47.50	75.00	130	260	375	2,250	—
1911	3,720,543	5.25	8.00	17.50	33.50	72.50	125	215	1,300	2,000
1911D	933,600	8.00	19.00	95.00	215	330	500	700	6,250	—
1911S	988,000	7.00	12.00	51.50	80.00	160	300	400	1,500	—

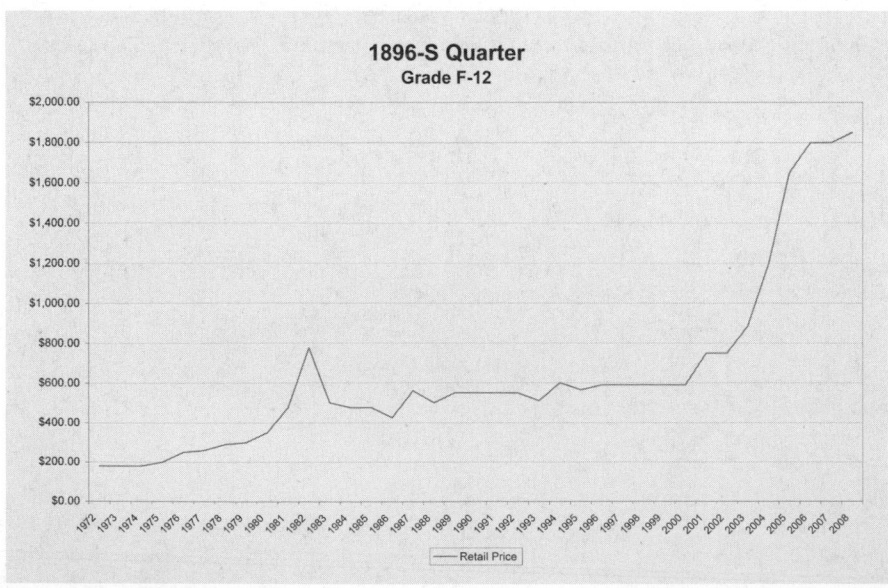

1896-S Quarter
Grade F-12

Date	Mintage	G-4	VG-8	F-12	VF-20	XF-40	AU-50	MS-60	MS-65	Prf-65
1912	4,400,700	5.75	8.00	17.50	33.50	70.00	115	215	1,300	2,000
1912S	708,000	10.00	13.00	46.00	77.50	125	230	390	2,750	—
1913	484,613	15.00	25.00	75.00	185	415	535	960	5,000	2,200
1913D	1,450,800	12.50	13.50	38.50	58.50	94.00	185	275	1,400	—
1913S	40,000	1,500	2,150	4,000	5,600	6,500	7,000	9,000	24,000	—
1914	6,244,610	5.00	6.25	17.50	30.00	57.50	115	215	1,300	2,200
1914D	3,046,000	5.00	6.25	17.50	30.00	57.50	115	215	1,300	—
1914S	264,000	70.00	105	200	315	520	700	940	3,550	—
1915	3,480,450	5.00	6.25	17.50	30.00	66.00	115	215	1,300	2,200
1915D	3,694,000	5.00	6.25	17.50	30.00	66.00	115	215	1,300	—
1915S	704,000	9.00	13.00	35.00	57.50	110	220	285	1,300	—
1916	1,788,000	5.00	9.50	17.50	27.50	57.50	115	215	1,300	—
1916D	6,540,800	5.00	6.25	17.50	30.00	57.50	115	215	1,300	—
1916D/D	—	15.00	22.00	30.00	50.00	125	—	—	—	—

Standing Liberty Quarter
Right breast exposed; Type 1 obverse

Right breast exposed

KM# 141 • 6.2500 g., 0.9000 **Silver**, 0.1808 oz. ASW, 24.3 mm. • **Designer:** Hermon Λ. MacNeil

Date	Mintage	G-4	VG-8	F-12	VF-20	XF-40	AU-50	MS-60	MS-65	-65FH
1916	52,000	3,500	6,350	9,500	13,000	14,500	16,500	18,500	30,000	37,500
1917	8,792,000	24.00	40.00	52.00	70.00	95.00	175	200	750	1,500
1917D	1,509,200	28.00	42.00	55.00	85.00	125	195	235	950	2,550
1917S	1,952,000	30.00	44.00	60.00	90.00	160	210	240	1,200	4,100

QUARTER

QUARTER

Standing Liberty Quarter

Right breast covered; Type 2 obverse   Three stars below eagle reverse

Right breast covered   Mint mark

KM# 145 • 6.2500 g., 0.9000 **Silver**, 0.1808 oz. ASW, 24.3 mm. • **Designer:** Hermon A. MacNeil

Date	Mintage	G-4	VG-8	F-12	VF-20	XF-40	AU-50	MS-60	MS-65	-65FH
1917	13,880,000	22.00	33.00	42.50	54.00	75.00	105	165	575	950
1917D	6,224,400	40.00	45.00	65.00	78.00	110	160	225	1,325	3,500
1917S	5,522,000	40.00	45.00	63.00	75.00	108	155	215	1,100	3,650
1918	14,240,000	17.00	21.00	29.00	35.00	46.00	80.00	135	560	1,750
1918D	7,380,000	26.00	36.00	66.00	78.00	122	195	250	1,485	4,850
1918S	11,072,000	17.00	21.00	32.00	35.00	48.00	95.00	185	1,250	13,500
1918/17S	Inc. above	1,550	2,250	3,850	5,200	7,500	13,500	17,850	110,000	320,000
1919	11,324,000	33.00	44.00	55.00	74.00	80.00	118	175	600	1,650
1919D	1,944,000	85.00	110	195	345	565	695	825	2,950	28,500
1919S	1,836,000	80.00	105	185	285	510	585	750	4,200	30,000
1920	27,860,000	15.00	18.00	25.00	37.00	51.00	90.00	165	600	2,100
1920D	3,586,400	48.00	65.00	88.00	120	160	215	325	2,250	7,200
1920S	6,380,000	19.00	25.00	30.00	37.00	57.00	110	235	2,650	24,000
1921	1,916,000	185	220	450	625	750	1,100	1,500	3,850	5,500
1923	9,716,000	15.00	18.00	35.00	37.00	55.00	95.00	155	620	4,000
1923S	1,360,000	300	425	675	985	1,250	1,650	2,300	4,750	6,500
1924	10,920,000	15.00	18.00	25.00	34.00	45.00	90.00	170	585	1,650
1924D	3,112,000	56.00	68.00	108	135	185	220	300	610	5,750
1924S	2,860,000	27.00	32.00	43.00	57.00	105	220	315	1,850	6,500
1925	12,280,000	4.00	4.75	7.00	18.50	44.00	90.00	150	575	950
1926	11,316,000	3.50	4.00	6.00	14.00	37.00	80.00	140	585	2,250
1926D	1,716,000	6.50	10.00	20.00	40.00	75.00	118	170	545	22,500
1926S	2,700,000	4.50	5.40	11.00	30.00	110	225	325	2,175	28,000
1927	11,912,000	3.50	4.00	6.00	12.00	32.00	70.00	105	550	1,300
1927D	976,400	14.00	19.00	32.00	70.00	140	210	250	600	2,650
1927S	396,000	35.00	48.00	110	285	1,000	2,650	4,750	12,000	165,000
1928	6,336,000	3.50	4.75	6.00	12.00	32.00	65.00	100.00	540	2,150
1928D	1,627,600	4.75	6.00	7.50	20.00	42.50	90.00	135	540	5,650
1928S Large S	2,644,000	6.00	7.50	10.00	25.00	65.00	115	200	—	—
1928S Small S	Inc. above	4.50	5.50	6.50	16.50	38.00	79.00	125	560	900
1929	11,140,000	3.50	4.75	6.00	12.00	32.00	65.00	100.00	540	900
1929D	1,358,000	4.25	5.50	6.75	16.00	38.50	79.00	135	540	5,850
1929S	1,764,000	4.00	5.50	6.50	15.00	34.00	75.00	120	540	875
1930	5,632,000	3.50	4.00	6.00	12.00	32.00	65.00	100.00	540	875
1930S	1,556,000	4.00	5.50	6.50	15.00	34.00	70.00	115	550	925

Washington Quarter

Mint mark 1932-64

KM# 164 • 6.2000 g., **Silver**, 24.3 mm. • **Designer:** John Flanagan

Date	Mintage	G-4	VG-8	F-12	VF-20	XF-40	AU-50	MS-60	MS-65	Prf-65
1932	5,404,000	4.00	5.20	6.00	7.50	9.75	15.00	26.00	435	—
1932D	436,800	165	180	205	240	345	500	1,000	24,500	—
1932S	408,000	195	200	205	240	285	300	500	7,000	—
1934 Medium Motto	31,912,052	4.40	4.80	5.40	6.30	6.80	10.00	27.50	110	—
1934 Heavy Motto	Inc. above	4.50	5.75	7.00	12.50	18.00	30.00	50.00	225	—
1934 Light motto	Inc. above	4.00	5.00	6.00	10.00	15.00	26.00	45.00	400	—
1934 Doubled Die Obverse	Inc. above	75.00	100.00	165	200	320	450	800	8,000	—
1934D Medium Motto	3,527,200	5.00	6.00	8.50	13.50	28.00	95.00	245	1,550	—
1934D Heavy Motto	Inc. above	6.00	8.00	11.00	16.00	37.00	110	295	1,900	—
1935	32,484,000	4.10	4.20	4.40	4.80	5.00	10.00	21.50	145	—
1935D	5,780,000	4.40	4.90	7.50	14.00	30.00	130	255	975	—
1935S	5,660,000	4.40	4.90	5.00	7.50	15.00	38.50	100.00	465	—
1936	41,303,837	4.10	4.20	4.40	4.80	4.80	9.50	22.50	115	1,950

Date	Mintage	G-4	VG-8	F-12	VF-20	XF-40	AU-50	MS-60	MS-65	Prf-65
1936D	5,374,000	5.00	6.50	8.50	22.00	55.00	275	625	1,850	—
1936S	3,828,000	4.40	4.90	4.40	6.25	13.50	52.50	115	420	—
1937	19,701,542	4.10	4.20	4.40	4.80	4.50	16.00	23.50	94.00	665
1937D	7,189,600	4.40	4.90	5.00	6.25	13.50	34.00	67.00	175	—
1937S	1,652,000	4.00	5.00	7.00	15.00	34.00	100.00	170	415	—
1938	9,480,045	4.00	4.75	5.25	6.25	16.00	46.00	94.00	250	405
1938S	2,832,000	4.75	5.25	6.00	9.75	22.50	57.50	112	300	—
1939	33,548,795	4.10	4.20	4.40	4.80	4.00	7.00	16.00	56.00	345
1939D	7,092,000	4.40	4.90	4.50	5.25	11.00	20.00	45.00	125	—
1939S	2,628,000	4.00	4.40	5.25	9.00	22.00	60.00	110	375	—
1940	35,715,246	4.10	4.20	4.40	4.80	4.00	5.50	18.50	57.50	250
1940D	2,797,600	3.50	4.25	7.00	12.50	27.50	70.00	135	350	—
1940S	8,244,000	4.40	4.90	5.00	6.50	9.00	18.00	28.00	62.50	—
1941	79,047,287	—	—	—	—	4.00	4.40	9.75	45.00	205
1941D	16,714,800	—	—	—	3.50	4.50	15.00	35.00	70.00	—
1941S	16,080,000	—	—	—	3.50	6.50	12.50	31.00	70.00	—
1942	102,117,123	—	—	—	—	4.00	4.10	5.50	37.50	190
1942D	17,487,200	—	—	—	3.50	6.00	11.00	19.00	45.00	—
1942S	19,384,000	—	—	—	3.75	9.00	24.00	80.00	180	—
1943	99,700,000	—	—	—	—	4.00	4.10	5.00	44.00	—
1943D	16,095,600	—	—	—	3.75	8.00	16.50	31.00	52.50	—
1943S	21,700,000	—	—	3.00	5.00	7.50	15.00	28.00	60.00	—
1943S Double Die Obv.	Inc. above	40.00	75.00	125	175	225	275	500	3,500	—
1944	104,956,000	—	—	—	—	4.00	4.10	5.00	37.50	—
1944D	14,600,800	—	—	—	3.50	4.25	10.00	20.00	37.50	—
1944S	12,560,000	—	—	—	3.50	4.00	9.00	15.00	37.50	—
1945	74,372,000	—	—	—	—	4.00	4.10	5.00	45.00	—
1945D	12,341,600	—	—	—	3.50	6.50	11.50	19.00	47.50	—
1945S	17,004,001	—	—	—	3.50	3.75	6.00	9.00	38.50	—
1946	53,436,000	—	—	—	—	4.00	4.10	5.00	47.50	—
1946D	9,072,800	—	—	—	3.50	4.25	5.50	10.00	46.00	—
1946S	4,204,000	—	—	—	3.50	4.00	5.00	9.00	40.00	—
1947	22,556,000	—	—	—	—	4.30	5.00	11.50	47.50	—
1947D	15,338,400	—	—	—	3.50	4.10	4.50	11.00	44.00	—
1947S	5,532,000	—	—	—	3.50	4.10	4.50	10.00	40.00	—
1948	35,196,000	—	—	—	3.50	4.00	4.00	5.50	45.00	—
1948D	16,766,800	—	—	—	3.50	4.10	7.00	13.50	56.00	—
1948S	15,960,000	—	—	—	3.50	4.00	5.00	8.00	50.00	—
1949	9,312,000	—	—	—	3.50	6.50	15.00	38.50	65.00	—
1949D	10,068,400	—	—	—	3.40	5.00	10.00	18.00	51.00	—
1950	24,971,512	—	—	—	—	4.00	4.10	5.50	32.00	65.00
1950D	21,075,600	—	—	—	—	4.00	4.10	5.00	34.00	—
1950D/S	Inc. above	30.00	33.00	40.00	60.00	140	215	275	3,400	—
1950S	10,284,004	—	—	—	—	3.50	4.50	9.00	42.00	—
1950S/D	Inc. above	32.00	36.00	44.00	70.00	180	315	400	850	—
1950S/S	Inc. above	—	—	—	—	—	—	—	—	—

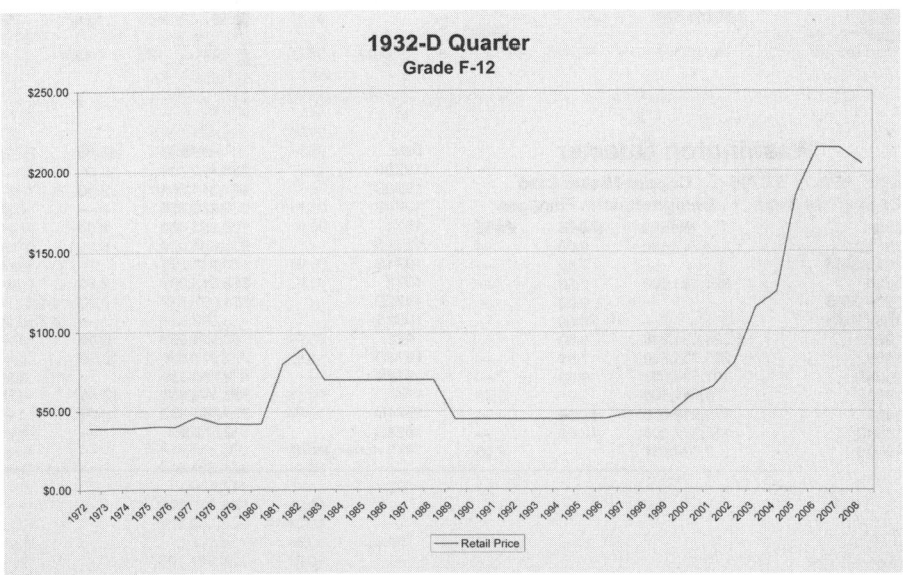

1932-D Quarter
Grade F-12

Retail Price

50 State Quarters

Connecticut

KM# 297 • Copper-Nickel Clad Copper •

Date	Mintage	MS-63	MS-65	Prf-65
1999P	688,744,000	1.00	10.00	—
1999D	657,480,000	1.00	9.00	—
1999S	3,713,359	—	—	12.00

KM# 297a • 6.2500 g., 0.9000 Silver, 0.1808 oz. ASW

Date	Mintage	MS-63	MS-65	Prf-65
1999S	804,565	—	—	65.00

Delaware

KM# 293 • 5.6700 g., Copper-Nickel Clad Copper, 24.3 mm. •

Date	Mintage	MS-63	MS-65	Prf-65
1999P	373,400,000	1.40	8.00	—
1999D	401,424,000	1.25	20.00	—
1999S	3,713,359	—	—	12.00

KM# 293a • 6.2500 g., 0.9000 Silver, 0.1808 oz. ASW •

Date	Mintage	MS-63	MS-65	Prf-65
1999S	804,565	—	—	65.00

Georgia

KM# 296 • Copper-Nickel Clad Copper •

Date	Mintage	MS-63	MS-65	Prf-65
1999P	451,188,000	1.20	14.00	—
1999D	488,744,000	1.20	14.00	—
1999S	3,713,359	—	—	12.00

KM# 296a • 6.2500 g., 0.9000 Silver, 0.1808 oz. ASW •

Date	Mintage	MS-63	MS-65	Prf-65
1999S	804,565	—	—	65.00

New Jersey

KM# 295 • Copper-Nickel Clad Copper •

Date	Mintage	MS-63	MS-65	Prf-65
1999P	363,200,000	1.00	10.00	—
1999D	299,028,000	1.00	9.00	—
1999S	3,713,359	—	—	12.00

KM# 295a • 6.2500 g., 0.9000 Silver, 0.1808 oz. ASW •

Date	Mintage	MS-63	MS-65	Prf-65
1999S	804,565	—	—	65.00

Pennsylvania

KM# 294 • 5.6700 g., Copper-Nickel Clad Copper, 24.3 mm. •

Date	Mintage	MS-63	MS-65	Prf-65
1999P	349,000,000	1.00	15.00	—
1999D	358,332,000	1.00	20.00	—
1999S	3,713,359	—	—	12.00

KM# 294a • 6.2500 g., 0.9000 Silver, 0.1808 oz. ASW •

Date	Mintage	MS-63	MS-65	Prf-65
1999S	804,565	—	—	65.00

Maryland

KM# 306 • Copper-Nickel Clad Copper •

Date	Mintage	MS-63	MS-65	Prf-65
2000P	678,200,000	1.00	11.00	—
2000D	556,526,000	1.00	11.00	—
2000S	4,078,747	—	—	3.50

KM# 306a • 6.2500 g., 0.9000 Silver, 0.1808 oz. ASW •

Date	Mintage	MS-63	MS-65	Prf-65
2000S	965,921	—	—	5.50

Massachusetts

KM# 305 • Copper-Nickel Clad Copper •

Date	Mintage	MS-63	MS-65	Prf-65
2000P	629,800,000	1.00	10.00	—
2000D	535,184,000	1.00	12.00	—
2000S	4,078,747	—	—	3.50

KM# 305a • 6.2500 g., 0.9000 Silver, 0.1808 oz. ASW •

Date	Mintage	MS-63	MS-65	Prf-65
2000S	965,921	—	—	5.50

New Hampshire

KM# 308 • Copper-Nickel Clad Copper •

Date	Mintage	MS-63	MS-65	Prf-65
2000P	673,040,000	1.00	12.50	—
2000D	495,976,000	1.00	10.00	—
2000S	4,078,747	—	—	3.50

KM# 308a • 6.2500 g., 0.9000 Silver, 0.1808 oz. ASW •

Date	Mintage	MS-63	MS-65	Prf-65
2000S	965,921	—	—	5.50

South Carolina

KM# 307 • Copper-Nickel Clad Copper •

Date	Mintage	MS-63	MS-65	Prf-65
2000P	742,756,000	1.40	9.00	—
2000P	742,756,000	1.40	9.00	—
2000D	566,208,000	1.40	12.00	—
2000D	566,208,000	1.40	12.00	—
2000S	4,078,747	—	—	3.50
2000S	4,078,747	—	—	3.50

KM# 307a • 6.2500 g., 0.9000 Silver, 0.1808 oz. ASW •

Date	Mintage	MS-63	MS-65	Prf-65
2000S	965,921	—	—	5.50

Virginia

KM# 309 • Copper-Nickel Clad Copper •

Date	Mintage	MS-63	MS-65	Prf-65
2000P	943,000,000	1.00	8.00	—
2000D	651,616,000	1.00	8.00	—
2000S	4,078,747	—	—	3.35

KM# 309a • 6.2500 g., 0.9000 Silver, 0.1808 oz. ASW •

Date	Mintage	MS-63	MS-65	Prf-65
2000S	965,921	—	—	5.50

Kentucky

KM# 322 • Copper-Nickel Clad Copper •

Date	Mintage	MS-63	MS-65	Prf-65
2001P	353,000,000	1.20	7.00	—
2001D	370,564,000	1.00	8.00	—
2001S	3,009,800	—	—	11.00

KM# 322a • 6.2500 g., 0.9000 Silver, 0.1808 oz. ASW •

Date	Mintage	MS-63	MS-65	Prf-65
2001S	849,500	—	—	21.00

New York

KM# 318 • Copper-Nickel Clad Copper •

Date	Mintage	MS-63	MS-65	Prf-65
2001P	655,400,000	1.00	8.50	—
2001D	619,640,000	1.00	8.50	—
2001S	3,009,800	—	—	11.00

KM# 318a • 6.2500 g., 0.9000 Silver, 0.1808 oz. ASW •

Date	Mintage	MS-63	MS-65	Prf-65
2001S	849,600	—	—	24.00

QUARTER

QUARTER

North Carolina

KM# 319 • Copper-Nickel Clad Copper •

Date	Mintage	MS-63	MS-65	Prf-65
2001P	627,600,000	1.00	7.50	—
2001D	427,876,000	1.00	8.50	—
2001S	3,009,800	—	—	11.00

KM# 319a • 6.2500 g., 0.9000 Silver, 0.1808 oz. ASW •

Date	Mintage	MS-63	MS-65	Prf-65
2001S	849,600	—	—	22.00

Rhode Island

KM# 320 • 5.6000 g., Copper-Nickel Clad Copper •

Date	Mintage	MS-63	MS-65	Prf-65
2001P	423,000,000	1.00	6.50	—
2001D	447,100,000	1.00	8.00	—
2001S	3,009,800	—	—	11.00

KM# 320a • 6.2500 g., 0.9000 Silver, 0.1808 oz. ASW •

Date	Mintage	MS-63	MS-65	Prf-65
2001S	849,600	—	—	19.00

Vermont

KM# 321 • Copper-Nickel Clad Copper •

Date	Mintage	MS-63	MS-65	Prf-65
2001P	423,400,000	1.20	7.00	—
2001D	459,404,000	1.00	7.00	—
2001S	3,009,800	—	—	11.00

KM# 321a • 6.2500 g., 0.9000 Silver, 0.1808 oz. ASW •

Date	Mintage	MS-63	MS-65	Prf-65
2001S	849,600	—	—	19.00

Indiana

KM# 334 • 5.6700 g., Copper-Nickel Clad Copper •

Date	Mintage	MS-63	MS-65	Prf-65
2002P	362,600,000	1.00	6.00	—
2002D	327,200,000	1.00	6.50	—
2002S	3,084,185	—	—	4.00

KM# 334a • 6.2500 g., 0.9000 Silver, 0.1808 oz. ASW •

Date	Mintage	MS-63	MS-65	Prf-65
2002S	892,229	—	—	9.00

Louisiana

KM# 333 • Copper-Nickel Clad Copper •

Date	Mintage	MS-63	MS-65	Prf-65
2002P	362,000,000	1.00	6.50	—
2002D	402,204,000	1.00	7.00	—
2002S	3,084,185	—	—	4.00

KM# 333a • 6.2500 g., 0.9000 Silver, 0.1808 oz. ASW •

Date	Mintage	MS-63	MS-65	Prf-65
2002S	892,229	—	—	9.00

Mississippi

KM# 335 • 5.6700 g., Copper-Nickel Clad Copper •

Date	Mintage	MS-63	MS-65	Prf-65
2002P	290,000,000	1.00	5.00	—
2002D	289,600,000	1.00	6.00	—
2002S	3,084,185	—	—	4.00

KM# 335a • 6.2500 g., 0.9000 Silver, 0.1808 oz. ASW •

Date	Mintage	MS-63	MS-65	Prf-65
2002S	892,229	—	—	9.00

Ohio

KM# 332 • **Copper-Nickel Clad Copper** •

Date	Mintage	MS-63	MS-65	Prf-65
2002P	217,200,000	1.00	6.50	—
2002D	414,832,000	1.00	7.00	—
2002S	3,084,185	—	—	4.00

KM# 332a • 6.2500 g., 0.9000 **Silver**, 0.1808 oz. ASW •

Date	Mintage	MS-63	MS-65	Prf-65
2002S	892,229	—	—	9.00

Tennessee

KM# 331 • **Copper-Nickel Clad Copper** •

Date	Mintage	MS-63	MS-65	Prf-65
2002P	361,600,000	1.40	6.50	—
2002D	286,468,000	1.40	7.00	—
2002S	3,084,185	—	—	4.00

KM# 331a • 6.2500 g., 0.9000 **Silver**, 0.1808 oz. ASW •

Date	Mintage	MS-63	MS-65	Prf-65
2002S	892,229	—	—	9.00

Alabama

KM# 344 • 5.6700 g., **Copper-Nickel Clad Copper** •

Date	Mintage	MS-63	MS-65	Prf-65
2003P	225,000,000	1.00	7.00	—
2003D	232,400,000	1.00	7.00	—
2003S	3,270,603	—	—	3.50

KM# 344a • 6.2500 g., 0.9000 **Silver**, 0.1808 oz. ASW •

Date	Mintage	MS-63	MS-65	Prf-65
2003S	—	—	—	5.25

Arkansas

KM# 347 • **Copper-Nickel Clad Copper** •

Date	Mintage	MS-63	MS-65	Prf-65
2003P	228,000,000	1.00	7.00	—
2003D	229,800,000	1.00	7.00	—
2003S	3,270,603	—	—	3.50

KM# 347a • 6.2500 g., 0.9000 **Silver**, 0.1808 oz. ASW •

Date	Mintage	MS-63	MS-65	Prf-65
2003S	—	—	—	5.25

Illinois

KM# 343 • 5.6700 g., **Copper-Nickel Clad Copper** •

Date	Mintage	MS-63	MS-65	Prf-65
2003P	225,800,000	1.10	7.00	—
2003D	237,400,000	1.10	6.00	—
2003S	3,270,603	—	—	3.50

KM# 343a • 6.2500 g., 0.9000 **Silver**, 0.1808 oz. ASW •

Date	Mintage	MS-63	MS-65	Prf-65
2003S	—	—	—	5.25

Maine

KM# 345 • **Copper-Nickel Clad Copper** •

Date	Mintage	MS-63	MS-65	Prf-65
2003P	217,400,000	1.00	6.50	—
2003D	213,400,000	1.00	8.00	—
2003S	3,270,603	—	—	3.50

KM# 345a • 6.2500 g., 0.9000 **Silver**, 0.1808 oz. ASW •

Date	Mintage	MS-63	MS-65	Prf-65
2003S	—	—	—	5.25

QUARTER

QUARTER

Missouri

KM# 346 • **Copper-Nickel Clad Copper** •

Date	Mintage	MS-63	MS-65	Prf-65
2003P	225,000,000	1.00	7.00	—
2003D	228,200,000	1.00	7.00	—
2003S	3,270,603	—	—	3.50

KM# 346a • 6.2500 g., 0.9000 **Silver**, 0.1808 oz. ASW •

Date	Mintage	MS-63	MS-65	Prf-65
2003S	—	—	—	5.25

Florida

KM# 356 • 5.6700 g., **Copper-Nickel Clad Copper** •

Date	Mintage	MS-63	MS-65	Prf-65
2004P	240,200,000	.75	6.50	—
2004D	241,600,000	.75	7.00	—
2004S	—	—	—	5.00

KM# 356a • 6.2500 g., 0.9000 **Silver**, 0.1808 oz. ASW •

Date	Mintage	MS-63	MS-65	Prf-65
2004S	—	—	—	6.00

Iowa

KM# 358 • 5.6700 g., **Copper-Nickel Clad Copper** •

Date	Mintage	MS-63	MS-65	Prf-65
2004P	213,800,000	.75	6.50	—
2004D	251,800,000	.75	7.00	—
2004S	—	—	—	5.00

KM# 358a • 6.2500 g., 0.9000 **Silver**, 0.1808 oz. ASW •

Date	Mintage	MS-63	MS-65	Prf-65
2004S	—	—	—	6.00

Michigan

KM# 355 • 5.6700 g., **Copper-Nickel Clad Copper** •

Date	Mintage	MS-63	MS-65	Prf-65
2004P	233,800,000	.75	6.50	—
2004D	225,800,000	.75	6.50	—
2004S	—	—	—	5.00

KM# 355a • 6.2500 g., 0.9000 **Silver**, 0.1808 oz. ASW •

Date	Mintage	MS-63	MS-65	Prf-65
2004S	—	—	—	6.00

Texas

KM# 357 • 5.6700 g., **Copper-Nickel Clad Copper** •

Date	Mintage	MS-63	MS-65	Prf-65
2004P	278,800,000	.75	7.00	—
2004D	263,000,000	.75	7.00	—
2004S	—	—	—	5.00

KM# 357a • 6.2500 g., 0.9000 **Silver**, 0.1808 oz. ASW •

Date	Mintage	MS-63	MS-65	Prf-65
2004S	—	—	—	6.00

Wisconsin

KM# 359 • 5.6700 g., **Copper-Nickel Clad Copper** •

Date	Mintage	MS-63	MS-65	Prf-65
2004P	226,400,000	1.00	8.00	—
2004D	226,800,000	1.00	10.00	—
2004D Extra Leaf Low	Est. 9,000	300	600	—
2004D Extra Leaf High	Est. 3,000	400	900	—
2004S	—	—	—	5.00

KM# 359a • 6.2500 g., 0.9000 **Silver**, 0.1808 oz. ASW •

Date	Mintage	MS-63	MS-65	Prf-65
2004S	—	—	—	6.00

California

KM# 370 • 5.7000 g., **Copper-Nickel Clad Copper** •

Date	Mintage	MS-63	MS-65	Prf-65
2005P	257,200,000	.75	5.00	—
2005P Satin Finish	Inc. above	3.50	6.00	—
2005D	263,200,000	.75	5.00	—
2005D Satin Finish	Inc. above	3.50	6.00	—
2005S	—	—	—	3.00

KM# 370a • 6.2500 g., 0.9000 **Silver**, 0.1808 oz. ASW •

Date	Mintage	MS-63	MS-65	Prf-65
2005S	—	—	—	5.50

Kansas

KM# 373 • **Copper-Nickel Clad Copper** •

Date	Mintage	MS-63	MS-65	Prf-65
2005P	263,400,000	.75	5.00	—
2005P Satin Finish	Inc. above	3.50	6.00	—
2005D	300,000,000	.75	5.00	—
2005D Satin Finish	Inc. above	3.50	6.00	—
2005S	—	—	—	3.00

KM# 373a • 6.2500 g., 0.9000 **Silver**, 0.1808 oz. ASW •

Date	Mintage	MS-63	MS-65	Prf-65
2005S	—	—	—	5.50

Minnesota

KM# 371 • 5.7000 g., **Copper-Nickel Clad Copper** •

Date	Mintage	MS-63	MS-65	Prf-65
2005P	226,400,000	.75	5.00	—
2005P Satin Finish	Inc. above	3.50	6.00	—
2005D	226,800,000	.75	5.00	—
2005D Satin Finish	Inc. above	3.50	6.00	—
2005S	—	—	—	3.00

KM# 371a • 6.2500 g., 0.9000 **Silver**, 0.1808 oz. ASW •

Date	Mintage	MS-63	MS-65	Prf-65
2005S	—	—	—	5.50

Oregon

KM# 372 • 5.6700 g., **Copper-Nickel Clad Copper** •

Date	Mintage	MS-63	MS-65	Prf-65
2005P	316,200,000	.75	5.00	—
2005P Satin Finish	Inc. above	3.50	6.00	—
2005D	404,000,000	.75	5.00	—
2005D Satin Finish	Inc. above	3.50	6.00	—
2005S	—	—	—	3.00

KM# 372a • 6.2500 g., 0.9000 **Silver**, 0.1808 oz. ASW •

Date	Mintage	MS-63	MS-65	Prf-65
2005S	—	—	—	5.50

West Virginia

KM# 374 • 5.6700 g., **Copper-Nickel Clad Copper** •

Date	Mintage	MS-63	MS-65	Prf-65
2005P	365,400,000	.75	5.00	—
2005P Satin Finish	Inc. above	3.50	6.00	—
2005D	356,200,000	.75	5.00	—
2005D Satin Finish	Inc. above	3.50	6.00	—
2005S	—	—	—	3.00

KM# 374a • 6.2500 g., 0.9000 **Silver**, 0.1808 oz. ASW •

Date	Mintage	MS-63	MS-65	Prf-65
2005S	—	—	—	5.50

Colorado

KM# 384 • 5.6400 g., **Copper-Nickel Clad Copper** •

Date	Mintage	MS-63	MS-65	Prf-65
2006P	274,800,000	.75	5.00	—
2006P Satin Finish	Inc. above	3.00	5.00	—
2006D	294,200,000	.75	5.00	—
2006D Satin Finish	Inc. above	3.00	5.00	—
2006S	—	—	—	5.00

KM# 384a • 6.2500 g., 0.9000 **Silver**, 0.1808 oz. ASW •

Date	Mintage	MS-63	MS-65	Prf-65
2006S	—	—	—	5.75

Nebraska

KM# 383 • 5.7300 g., **Copper-Nickel Clad Copper** •

Date	Mintage	MS-63	MS-65	Prf-65
2006P	318,000,000	.75	6.00	—
2006P Satin Finish	Inc. above	3.00	5.00	—
2006D	273,000,000	.75	6.00	—
2006D Satin Finish	Inc. above	3.00	5.00	—
2006S	—	—	—	5.00

KM# 383a • 6.2500 g., 0.9000 **Silver,** 0.1808 oz. ASW •

Date	Mintage	MS-63	MS-65	Prf-65
2006S	—	—	—	5.75

Nevada

KM# 382 • 5.6800 g., **Copper-Nickel Clad Copper** •

Date	Mintage	MS-63	MS-65	Prf-65
2006P	277,000,000	.75	6.00	—
2006P Satin Finish	Inc. above	3.00	5.00	—
2006D	312,800,000	.75	6.00	—
2006D Satin Finish	Inc. above	3.00	5.00	—
2006S	—	—	—	5.00

KM# 382a • 6.2500 g., 0.9000 **Silver,** 0.1808 oz. ASW •

Date	Mintage	MS-63	MS-65	Prf-65
2006S	—	—	—	5.75

North Dakota

KM# 385 • 5.6100 g., **Copper-Nickel Clad Copper** •

Date	Mintage	MS-63	MS-65	Prf-65
2006P	305,800,000	.75	5.00	—
2006P Satin Finish	Inc. above	3.00	5.00	—
2006D	359,000,000	.75	5.00	—
2006D Satin Finish	Inc. above	3.00	5.00	—
2006S	—	—	—	5.00

KM# 385a • 6.2500 g., 0.9000 **Silver,** 0.1808 oz. ASW •

Date	Mintage	MS-63	MS-65	Prf-65
2006S	—	—	—	5.75

South Dakota

KM# 386 • 5.6400 g., **Copper-Nickel Clad Copper** •

Date	Mintage	MS-63	MS-65	Prf-65
2006P	245,000,000	.75	5.00	—
2006P Satin Finish	Inc. above	3.00	5.00	—
2006D	265,800,000	.75	5.00	—
2006D Satin Finish	Inc. above	3.00	5.00	—
2006S	—	—	—	5.00

KM# 386a • 6.2500 g., 0.9000 **Silver,** 0.1808 oz. ASW •

Date	Mintage	MS-63	MS-65	Prf-65
2006S	—	—	—	5.75

Idaho

KM# 398 • **Copper-Nickel Clad Copper** •

Date	Mintage	MS-63	MS-65	Prf-65
2007P	294,600,000	.75	8.00	—
2007D	286,800,000	.75	8.00	—
2007S	—	—	—	4.00

KM# 398a • 6.2500 g., 0.9000 **Silver,** 0.1808 oz. ASW •

Date	Mintage	MS-63	MS-65	Prf-65
2007S	Inc. above	—	—	6.50

Montana

KM# 396 • **Copper-Nickel Clad Copper** •

Date	Mintage	MS-63	MS-65	Prf-65
2007P	257,000,000	.75	8.00	—
2007D	256,240,000	.75	5.00	—
2007S	—	—	—	4.00

KM# 396a • 6.2500 g., 0.9000 **Silver,** 0.1808 oz. ASW •

Date	Mintage	MS-63	MS-65	Prf-65
2007S	Inc. above	—	—	6.50

Utah

KM# 400 • Copper-Nickel Clad Copper •

Date	Mintage	MS-63	MS-65	Prf-65
2007P	—	.75	8.00	—
2007D	—	.75	8.00	—
2007S	—	—	—	4.00

KM# 400a • 6.2500 g., 0.9000 Silver, 0.1808 oz. ASW •

Date	Mintage	MS-63	MS-65	Prf-65
2007S	Inc. above	—	—	6.50

Washington

KM# 397 • Copper-Nickel Clad Copper •

Date	Mintage	MS-63	MS-65	Prf-65
2007P	265,200,000	.75	8.00	—
2007D	280,000,000	.75	8.00	—
2007S	—	—	—	4.00

KM# 397a • 6.2500 g., 0.9000 Silver, 0.1808 oz. ASW •

Date	Mintage	MS-63	MS-65	Prf-65
2007S	Inc. above	—	—	6.50

Wyoming

KM# 399 • Copper-Nickel Clad Copper •

Date	Mintage	MS-63	MS-65	Prf-65
2007P	—	.75	8.00	—
2007D	—	.75	8.00	—
2007S	—	—	—	4.00

KM# 399a • 6.2500 g., 0.9000 Silver, 0.1808 oz. ASW •

Date	Mintage	MS-63	MS-65	Prf-65
2007S	Inc. above	—	—	6.50

Alaska

KM# 424 • Copper-Nickel Clad Copper •

Date	Mintage	MS-63	MS-65	Prf-65
2008P	—	.75	8.00	—
2008D	—	.75	8.00	—
2008S	—	—	—	4.00

KM# 424a • 6.2500 g., 0.9000 Silver, 0.1808 oz. ASW •

Date	Mintage	MS-63	MS-65	Prf-65
2008S	—	—	—	6.50

Arizona

KM# 423 • Copper-Nickel Clad Copper •

Date	Mintage	MS-63	MS-65	Prf-65
2008P	—	.75	8.00	—
2008D	—	.75	8.00	—
2008S	—	—	—	4.00

KM# 423a • 6.2500 g., 0.9000 Silver, 0.1808 oz. ASW •

Date	Mintage	MS-63	MS-65	Prf-65
2008S	—	—	—	6.50

Hawaii

KM# 425 • Copper-Nickel Clad Copper •

Date	Mintage	MS-63	MS-65	Prf-65
2008P	—	.75	8.00	—
2008D	—	.75	8.00	—
2008S	—	—	—	4.50

KM# 425a • 6.2500 g., 0.9000 Silver, 0.1808 oz. ASW •

Date	Mintage	MS-63	MS-65	Prf-65
2008S	—	—	—	6.50

QUARTER

HALF DOLLAR

New Mexico

KM# 422 • Copper-Nickel Clad Copper •

Date	Mintage	MS-63	MS-65	Prf-65
2008P	—	.75	8.00	—
2008D	—	.75	8.00	—
2008S	—	—	—	4.00

KM# 422a • 6.2500 g., 0.9000 Silver, 0.1808 oz. ASW •

Date	Mintage	MS-63	MS-65	Prf-65
2008S	—	—	—	6.50

Oklahoma

KM# 421 • Copper-Nickel Clad Copper •

Date	Mintage	MS-63	MS-65	Prf-65
2008P	—	.75	8.00	—
2008D	—	.75	8.00	—
2008S	—	—	—	4.00

KM# 421a • 6.2500 g., 0.9000 Silver, 0.1808 oz. ASW •

Date	Mintage	MS-63	MS-65	Prf-65
2008S	—	—	—	6.50

HALF DOLLAR
Flowing Hair Half Dollar

KM# 16 • 13.4800 g., 0.8920 **Silver**, 0.3866 oz. ASW, 32.5 mm. • **Designer:** Robert Scot **Notes:** The 1795 "recut date" variety had the date cut into the dies twice, so both sets of numbers are visible on the coin. The 1795 "3 leaves" variety has three leaves under each of the eagle's wings on the reverse.

Date	Mintage	G-4	VG-8	F-12	VF-20	XF-40	MS-60
1794	23,464	2,650	5,200	7,750	19,500	35,000	125,000
1795	299,680	650	900	1,600	2,750	8,500	25,000
1795 recut date	Inc. above	700	950	1,650	2,900	9,000	29,500
1795 3 leaves	Inc. above	2,600	3,000	4,400	6,850	13,500	50,000

Draped Bust Half Dollar
Small eagle reverse

KM# 26 • 13.4800 g., 0.8920 **Silver**, 0.3866 oz. ASW, 32.5 mm. • **Designer:** Robert Scot **Notes:** The 1796 strikes have either 15 or 16 stars on the obverse.

Date	Mintage	G-4	VG-8	F-12	VF-20	XF-40	MS-60
1796 15 stars	3,918	29,000	36,500	60,000	87,500	108,000	175,000
1796 16 stars	Inc. above	30,500	38,500	67,500	92,000	115,000	205,000
1797	Inc. above	28,500	36,000	70,000	89,500	110,000	175,000

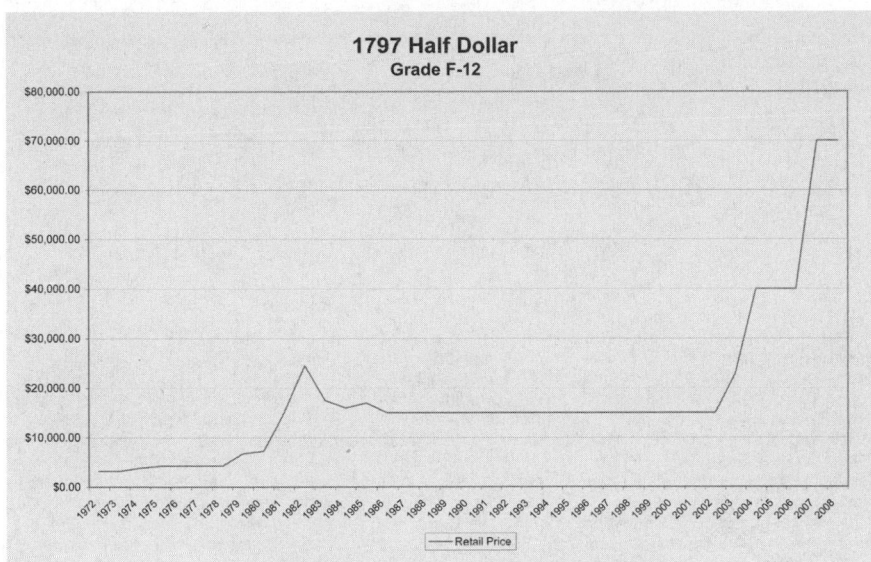

1797 Half Dollar
Grade F-12

Draped Bust Half Dollar
Draped bust right, flanked by stars, date at angle below obverse   Heraldic eagle reverse

KM# 35 • 13.4800 g., 0.8920 **Silver**, 0.3866 oz. ASW, 32.5 mm. • **Obv. Legend** LIBERTY **Rev. Legend:** UNITED STATES OF AMERICA **Designer:** Robert Scot **Notes:** The two varieties of the 1803 strikes are distinguished by the size of the 3 in the date. The several varieties of the 1806 strikes are distinguished by the style of 6 in the date, size of the stars on the obverse, and whether the stem of the olive branch held by the reverse eagle extends through the claw.

Date	Mintage	G-4	VG-8	F-12	VF-20	XF-40	MS-60
1801	30,289	850	1,100	2,350	3,600	8,100	36,500
1802	29,890	775	1,000	2,250	3,500	7,750	45,000
1803 small 3	188,234	160	185	325	600	1,850	10,750
1803 large 3	Inc. above	150	175	250	450	1,250	8,900
1805	211,722	150	175	250	425	1,200	7,900
1805/4	Inc. above	190	300	500	850	2,200	30,000
1806 knobbed 6, large stars	839,576	150	175	250	385	1,150	—
1806 knobbed 6, small stars	Inc. above	150	175	250	385	1,150	7,750
1806 knobbed 6, stem not through claw	Inc. above	20,000	35,000	42,000	57,500	90,000	—
1806 pointed-top 6, stem not through claw	Inc. above	170	210	285	465	1,325	7,950
1806 pointed-top 6, stem through claw	Inc. above	150	185	250	385	1,150	7,500
1806/5	Inc. above	165	200	285	450	1,650	10,500
1806 /inverted 6	Inc. above	185	350	550	1,000	2,850	25,000
1807	301,076	150	175	250	365	1,150	7,250

Capped Bust

Draped bust left, flanked by stars, date at angle below obverse   "50 C." below eagle reverse

KM# 37 • 13.4800 g., 0.8920 **Silver**, 0.3866 oz. ASW, 32.5 mm. **• Rev. Legend:** UNITED STATES OF AMERICA **Designer:** John Reich **Notes:** There are three varieties of the 1807 strikes. Two are distinguished by the size of the stars on the obverse. The third was struck from a reverse die that had a 5 cut over a 2 in the "50C" denomination. Two varieties of the 1811 are distinguished by the size of the 8 in the date. A third has a period between the 8 and second 1 in the date. One variety of the 1817 has a period between the 1 and 7 in the date. Two varieties of the 1819/18 overdate are distinguished by the size of the 9 in the date. Two varieties of the 1820 are distinguished by the size of the date. On the 1823 varieties, the "broken 3" appears to be almost separated in the middle of the 3 in the date; the "patched 3" has the error repaired; the "ugly 3" has portions of its detail missing. The 1827 "curled-2" and "square-2" varieties are distinguished by the numeral's base -- either curled or square. Among the 1828 varieties, "knobbed 2" and "no knob" refers to whether the upper left serif of the digit is rounded. The 1830 varieties are distinguished by the size of the 0 in the date. The four 1834 varieties are distinguished by the sizes of the stars, date and letters in the inscriptions. The 1836 "50/00" variety was struck from a reverse die that had "50" recut over "00" in the denomination.

Date	Mintage	G-4	VG-8	F-12	VF-20	XF-40	AU-50	MS-60	MS-65
1807 small stars	750,500	125	175	325	550	1,150	3,500	5,900	54,000
1807 large stars	Inc. above	100.00	165	275	475	800	2,500	4,800	—
1807 50/20 C.	Inc. above	85.00	115	185	300	575	2,850	4,600	30,000
1807 bearded goddess	—	350	550	900	1,800	3,450	7,500	—	—
1808	1,368,600	75.00	85.00	100.00	135	325	600	1,800	15,000
1808/7	Inc. above	90.00	110	135	240	425	1,150	2,400	—
1809 Normal edge	1,405,810	75.00	85.00	100.00	135	275	525	1,600	15,000
1809 XXXX edge	Inc. above	80.00	105	130	185	290	540	2,450	—
1809 IIIIIII edge	Inc. above	85.00	110	140	210	325	560	3,200	—
1810	1,276,276	72.00	83.00	95.00	130	245	475	1,550	14,000
1811 small 8	1,203,644	74.00	85.00	95.00	125	190	450	1,250	12,800
1811 large 8	Inc. above	74.00	85.00	95.00	130	200	500	1,300	13,500
1811 dated 18.11	Inc. above	85.00	95.00	110	180	375	700	1,900	—
1812	1,628,059	72.00	83.00	95.00	130	200	385	1,450	9,800
1812/1 small 8	Inc. above	85.00	95.00	125	200	300	700	2,400	16,000
1812/1 large 8	Inc. above	1,550	2,100	3,950	6,000	8,800	21,000	—	—
1812 Single leaf below wing	Inc. above	750	950	1,250	2,400	4,000	6,800	12,500	—
1813	1,241,903	72.00	83.00	95.00	130	200	460	1,575	11,000
1813 50/UNI reverse	1,241,903	85.00	95.00	125	175	350	900	1,900	—
1814	1,039,075	72.00	83.00	95.00	130	200	500	1,475	10,500
1814/3	Inc. above	100.00	135	190	285	475	1,100	2,350	16,500
1814 E/A in States	Inc. above	85.00	95.00	125	160	300	675	1,850	—
1814 Single leaf below wing	Inc. above	75.00	90.00	160	235	575	1,350	2,600	—
1815/2	47,150	1,100	1,450	1,850	2,850	4,200	6,000	11,500	85,000
1817	1,215,567	72.00	83.00	95.00	130	200	400	11,500	1,500
1817/3	Inc. above	125	185	280	450	800	1,800	3,750	43,500
1817/4	—	60,000	80,000	150,000	200,000	250,000	340,000	—	—
1817 dated 181.7	Inc. above	90.00	100.00	130	130	240	650	1,500	12,500
1817 Single leaf below wing	Inc. above	85.00	95.00	120	175	400	900	2,200	—
1818	1,960,322	60.00	68.00	85.00	105	185	420	1,300	10,500
1818/7 Large 8	Inc. above	90.00	100.00	115	140	240	760	1,600	15,500
1818/7 Small 8	Inc. above	90.00	100.00	115	140	240	760	1,600	15,500
1819	2,208,000	60.00	35.00	52.00	105	175	400	1,250	11,000
1819/8 small 9	Inc. above	57.50	62.50	75.00	100.00	200	550	1,300	1,150
1819/8 large 9	Inc. above	57.50	62.50	75.00	100.00	200	550	1,300	11,500
1820 Curl Base 2, small date	751,122	67.00	85.00	100.00	145	280	650	1,350	13,000
1820 Square Base 2 with knob, large date	Inc. above	67.00	85.00	100.00	145	280	650	1,350	13,000
1820 Square Base 2 without know, large date	Inc. above	67.00	85.00	100.00	145	280	650	1,350	13,000
1820 E's without Serifs	Inc. above	260	320	425	650	950	2,200	4,800	—
1820/19 Square Base 2	Inc. above	95.00	115	140	200	340	875	2,000	25,000
1820/19 Curled Base 2	Inc. above	95.00	115	140	200	350	900	2,100	30,000
1821	1,305,797	58.00	67.00	80.00	98.00	165	525	1,200	10,000
1822	1,559,573	58.00	67.00	80.00	98.00	165	385	1,150	9,000
1822/1	Inc. above	80.00	90.00	125	190	290	750	1,650	12,000
1823	1,694,200	55.00	64.00	75.00	90.00	150	350	1,050	8,600

Date	Mintage	G-4	VG-8	F-12	VF-20	XF-40	AU-50	MS-60	MS-65
1823 broken 3	Inc. above	74.00	88.00	115	165	400	1,050	2,800	—
1823 patched 3	Inc. above	70.00	80.00	105	145	250	600	1,500	15,000
1823 ugly 3	Inc. above	66.00	76.00	98.00	135	225	900	1,700	14,000
1824	3,504,954	55.00	64.00	75.00	90.00	150	350	1,050	8,600
1824/21	Inc. above	60.00	70.00	84.00	100.00	170	450	1,250	10,850
1824/4	Inc. above	60.00	70.00	88.00	110	190	500	1,350	11,250
1824 1824/various dates	Inc. above	70.00	85.00	100.00	145	240	875	1,850	15,000
1825	2,943,166	55.00	64.00	75.00	90.00	150	350	1,050	8,600
1826	4,004,180	55.00	64.00	75.00	90.00	150	350	1,050	8,600
1827 curled 2	5,493,400	70.00	80.00	95.00	130	190	500	1,350	12,500
1827 square 2	Inc. above	55.00	64.00	75.00	90.00	150	350	1,050	8,600
1827/6	Inc. above	85.00	95.00	120	155	235	450	1,250	11,500
1828 curled-base 2, no knob	3,075,200	55.00	64.00	75.00	90.00	150	350	1,050	8,600
1828 curled-base 2, knobbed 2	Inc. above	65.00	75.00	95.00	125	165	375	1,350	9,800
1828 small 8s, square-base 2, large letters	Inc. above	55.00	64.00	75.00	90.00	150	350	1,050	8,600
1828 small 8s, square-base 2, small letters	Inc. above	60.00	75.00	100.00	140	250	750	1,350	10,000
1828 large 8s, square-base 2	Inc. above	55.00	64.00	75.00	90.00	150	350	1,100	9,250
1829	3,712,156	52.00	60.00	65.00	75.00	140	340	1,050	9,000
1829 Large letters	Inc. above	56.00	67.00	75.00	85.00	160	420	1,250	10,500
1829/7	Inc. above	70.00	80.00	95.00	125	200	385	1,250	12,000
1830 Small O rev	4,764,800	52.00	60.00	65.00	75.00	140	340	1,000	8,500
1830 Large O	Inc. above	55.00	65.00	70.00	80.00	150	375	1,150	9,000
1830 Large letter rev	Inc. above	1,500	2,250	3,000	3,750	4,800	9,800	—	—
1831	5,873,660	52.00	60.00	65.00	75.00	140	340	1,000	8,500
1832 small letters	4,797,000	52.00	60.00	65.00	75.00	140	340	1,000	8,500
1832 large letters	Inc. above	52.00	60.00	70.00	95.00	165	360	1,150	8,850
1833	5,206,000	52.00	60.00	65.00	75.00	140	340	1,000	8,500
1834 small date, large stars, small letters	6,412,004	52.00	60.00	65.00	75.00	140	340	1,000	8,500
1834 small date, small stars, small letters	Inc. above	52.00	60.00	65.00	75.00	140	340	1,000	8,500
1834 large date, small letters	Inc. above	52.00	60.00	65.00	75.00	140	340	1,000	8,500
1834 large date, large letters	Inc. above	52.00	60.00	65.00	75.00	140	340	1,000	8,500
1835	5,352,006	52.00	60.00	65.00	75.00	140	340	1,000	9,000
1836	6,545,000	52.00	60.00	65.00	75.00	140	340	1,000	8,500
1836 50/00	Inc. above	80.00	85.00	110	185	300	800	1,750	15,000

Bust Half Dollar

**Draped bust left, flanked by stars, date at angle below obverse
"50 Cents" below eagle reverse**

KM# 58 • 13.3600 g., 0.9000 **Silver**, 0.3866 oz. ASW, 30 mm. • **Rev. Legend:** UNITED STATES OF AMERICA **Designer:** Christian Gobrecht **Edge Desc:** Reeded.

Date	Mintage	G-4	VG-8	F-12	VF-20	XF-40	AU-50	MS-60	MS-65
1836	1,200	850	1,075	1,550	1,950	2,800	3,900	7,250	58,000
1837	3,629,820	55.00	65.00	80.00	120	195	350	1,000	15,000

Bust Half Dollar

Draped bust left, flanked by stars, date below obverse   "Half Dol." below eagle reverse

KM# 65 • 13.3600 g., 0.9000 **Silver**, 0.3866 oz. ASW, 30 mm. • **Rev. Legend:** UNITED STATES OF AMERICA **Designer:** Christian Gobrecht

Date	Mintage	G-4	VG-8	F-12	VF-20	XF-40	AU-50	MS-60	MS-65
1838	3,546,000	55.00	65.00	80.00	120	195	350	1,000	18,500
1838O proof only	Est. 20	—	—	—	—	250,000	300,000	—	—
1839	1,392,976	60.00	70.00	100.00	145	225	390	1,100	30,000
1839O	178,976	240	320	425	650	900	1,350	2,850	40,000

Seated Liberty Half Dollar

Seated Liberty, date below obverse   "Half Dol." below eagle reverse

KM# 68 • 13.3600 g., 0.9000 **Silver**, 0.3866 oz. ASW, 30.6 mm. • **Rev. Legend:** UNITED STATES OF AMERICA **Designer:** Christian Gobrecht **Notes:** The 1839 varieties are distinguished by whether there's drapery extending from Liberty's left elbow. One variety of the 1840 strikes has smaller lettering; another used the old reverse of 1838. Varieties of 1842 and 1846 are distinguished by the size of the numerals in the date.

Date	Mintage	G-4	VG-8	F-12	VF-20	XF-40	AU-50	MS-60	MS-65
1839 no drapery from elbow	Inc. above	45.00	80.00	150	340	800	1,850	6,000	178,000
1839 drapery	Inc. above	38.00	50.00	59.00	86.00	165	265	1,000	25,000
1840 small letters	1,435,008	36.00	46.00	60.00	84.00	150	325	600	7,500
1840 reverse 1838	Inc. above	150	200	275	350	650	1,350	3,400	30,000
1840O	855,100	36.00	48.00	57.00	90.00	140	275	450	—
1841	310,000	50.00	65.00	100.00	150	235	325	1,200	6,850
1841O	401,000	30.00	44.00	56.00	82.00	180	230	600	7,000
1842 small date	2,012,764	38.00	55.00	75.00	120	175	325	1,300	13,500
1842 medium date	Inc. above	30.00	41.00	51.00	64.00	115	220	750	8,800
1842O small date	957,000	650	850	1,400	2,450	4,650	7,750	16,500	—
1842O medium date	Inc. above	35.00	42.00	55.00	90.00	185	500	1,250	10,500
1843	3,844,000	28.00	39.00	51.00	65.00	110	225	500	4,500
1843O	2,268,000	30.00	41.00	51.00	65.00	120	240	550	—
1844	1,766,000	30.00	41.00	51.00	65.00	110	210	440	4,500
1844O	2,005,000	30.00	41.00	51.00	70.00	110	225	550	—
1844/1844O	Inc. above	500	775	1,000	1,300	2,500	5,750	10,000	—
1845	589,000	35.00	45.00	65.00	125	210	325	850	12,000
1845O	2,094,000	30.00	41.00	51.00	70.00	135	240	550	9,400
1845O no drapery	Inc. above	35.00	47.00	70.00	115	185	375	750	—
1846 medium date	2,210,000	30.00	41.00	51.00	70.00	110	200	500	9,000
1846 tall date	Inc. above	35.00	47.00	70.00	85.00	145	250	650	12,000
1846 /horizontal 6	Inc. above	175	250	325	450	625	1,000	2,500	—
1846O medium date	2,304,000	30.00	41.00	51.00	65.00	110	225	550	12,000
1846O tall date	Inc. above	165	285	365	620	1,050	1,250	6,650	—
1847/1846	1,156,000	2,000	2,750	3,750	5,250	7,700	12,500	21,000	—
1847	Inc. above	35.00	45.00	54.00	67.00	105	250	480	9,000
1847O	2,584,000	30.00	41.00	51.00	65.00	120	275	640	7,000
1848	580,000	45.00	65.00	95.00	185	265	485	1,000	9,000
1848O	3,180,000	30.00	41.00	51.00	70.00	110	285	750	9,000
1849	1,252,000	35.00	45.00	54.00	67.00	108	365	1,250	15,000
1849O	2,310,000	30.00	41.00	51.00	70.00	110	250	650	9,000
1850	227,000	275	325	400	550	675	1,000	1,500	—
1850O	2,456,000	35.00	28.00	45.00	80.00	135	275	650	9,000

Date	Mintage	G-4	VG-8	F-12	VF-20	XF-40	AU-50	MS-60	MS-65
1851	200,750	335	450	550	850	950	1,200	2,250	—
1851O	402,000	40.00	55.00	95.00	120	185	300	700	9,000
1852	77,130	425	500	700	925	1,100	1,350	1,700	—
1852O	144,000	75.00	125	200	350	600	1,250	3,850	26,000
1853O mintage unrecorded	—	—	250,000	—	—	450,000	—	—	—

Note: 1853O, Eliasberg Sale, 1997, VG-8, $154,000.

Seated Liberty Half Dollar
Seated Liberty, arrows at date obverse   Rays around eagle reverse

KM# 79 • 12.4400 g., 0.9000 **Silver**, 0.3599 oz. ASW • **Rev. Legend:** UNITED STATES OF AMERICA
Designer: Christian Gobrecht

Date	Mintage	G-4	VG-8	F-12	VF-20	XF-40	AU-50	MS-60	MS-65	Prf-65
1853	3,532,708	28.00	10.00	47.00	90.00	250	590	1,650	21,500	175,000
1853O	1,328,000	38.00	48.00	57.00	125	310	750	2,350	27,500	—

Seated Liberty Half Dollar
Seated Liberty, arrows at date obverse   "Half Dol." below eagle reverse

KM# 82 • 12.4400 g., 0.9000 **Silver**, 0.3599 oz. ASW • **Rev. Legend:** UNITED STATES OF AMERICA
Designer: Christian Gobrecht

Date	Mintage	G-4	VG-8	F-12	VF-20	XF-40	AU-50	MS-60	MS-65	Prf-65
1854	2,982,000	28.00	38.00	47.00	60.00	100.00	270	675	8,000	37,500
1854O	5,240,000	28.00	38.00	47.00	60.00	100.00	270	600	8,000	—
1855	759,500	30.00	40.00	49.00	63.00	120	325	700	9,000	39,500
1855/4	Inc. above	65.00	84.00	160	250	375	600	2,000	17,500	37,000
1855O	3,688,000	28.00	38.00	47.00	60.00	100.00	270	650	8,000	—
1855S	129,950	350	475	800	1,500	3,150	6,850	19,500	—	—

Seated Liberty Half Dollar
Seated Liberty, date below obverse   "Half Dol." below eagle reverse

KM# A68 • 12.4400 g., 0.9000 **Silver**, 0.3599 oz. ASW • **Rev. Legend:** UNITED STATES OF AMERICA
Designer: Christian Gobrecht

Date	Mintage	G-4	VG-8	F-12	VF-20	XF-40	AU-50	MS-60	MS-65	Prf-65
1856	938,000	32.00	38.00	50.00	70.00	110	195	425	6,500	12,500
1856O	2,658,000	28.00	38.00	52.00	60.00	100.00	190	385	12,500	—
1856S	211,000	85.00	120	160	260	500	1,250	3,500	19,000	—

HALF DOLLAR

Date	Mintage	G-4	VG-8	F-12	VF-20	XF-40	AU-50	MS-60	MS-65	Prf-65
1857	1,988,000	28.00	38.00	50.00	60.00	100.00	190	385	5,150	12,500
1857O	818,000	33.00	40.00	52.00	85.00	135	275	885	12,500	—
1857S	158,000	100.00	120	145	285	575	975	3,500	19,000	—
1858	4,226,000	28.00	38.00	47.00	60.00	90.00	190	385	6,500	12,500
1858O	7,294,000	28.00	38.00	47.00	60.00	90.00	190	385	12,500	—
1858S	476,000	38.00	48.00	62.00	110	215	400	950	12,500	—
1859	748,000	30.00	41.00	51.00	70.00	120	200	650	6,600	5,500
1859O	2,834,000	28.00	38.00	47.00	60.00	100.00	190	450	6,500	—
1859S	566,000	38.00	44.00	59.00	100.00	215	375	750	12,500	—
1860	303,700	38.00	42.00	51.00	100.00	150	350	1,000	6,500	5,500
1860O	1,290,000	30.00	41.00	52.00	70.00	100.00	190	450	5,150	—
1860S	472,000	38.00	40.00	51.00	85.00	135	245	850	12,500	—
1861	2,888,400	30.00	40.00	49.00	65.00	100.00	190	440	5,150	5,500
1861O	2,532,633	30.00	41.00	53.00	86.00	125	235	450	5,150	—
1861S	939,500	35.00	44.00	53.00	70.00	120	195	975	9,500	—
1862	253,550	38.00	51.00	57.00	120	200	295	750	5,150	5,500
1862S	1,352,000	30.00	41.00	52.00	75.00	120	195	460	9,000	—
1863	503,660	35.00	48.00	57.00	85.00	135	250	750	5,150	5,500
1863S	916,000	33.00	45.00	52.00	70.00	120	195	460	9,000	—
1864	379,570	30.00	48.00	57.00	120	195	250	750	5,150	5,500
1864S	658,000	33.00	45.00	51.00	70.00	125	215	675	9,000	—
1865	511,900	28.00	47.00	55.00	90.00	150	275	750	5,150	5,500
1865S	675,000	35.00	45.00	52.00	70.00	120	235	500	9,000	—
1866 proof, unique	—	—	—	—	—	—	—	—	—	—
1866S	60,000	460	575	850	1,250	2,550	3,350	5,400	68,000	—

1855-S Half Dollar
Grade XF-40

Seated Liberty Half Dollar
Seated Liberty, date below obverse   "In God We Trust" above eagle reverse

KM# 99 • 12.4400 g., 0.9000 **Silver**, 0.3599 oz. ASW • **Rev. Legend:** UNITED STATES OF AMERICA
Designer: Christian Gobrecht **Notes:** In 1866 the motto "In God We Trust" was added to the reverse. The "closed-3" and "open-3" varieties are distinguished by the amount of space between the upper and lower left serifs of the 3.

Date	Mintage	G-4	VG-8	F-12	VF-20	XF-40	AU-50	MS-60	MS-65	Prf-65
1866	745,625	35.00	45.00	53.00	80.00	120	225	350	4,800	3,750
1866S	994,000	33.00	43.00	51.00	70.00	110	275	650	5,000	—
1867	449,925	38.00	48.00	59.00	110	165	250	350	4,800	3,750
1867S	1,196,000	32.00	42.00	51.00	70.00	110	250	350	7,000	—
1868	418,200	48.00	55.00	95.00	185	225	300	525	7,100	3,750
1868S	1,160,000	32.00	42.00	51.00	70.00	110	250	350	7,000	—
1869	795,900	35.00	45.00	49.00	70.00	110	190	385	4,600	3,750
1869S	656,000	35.00	47.00	51.00	70.00	120	265	600	7,000	—
1870	634,900	35.00	45.00	50.00	80.00	125	250	475	7,000	3,750
1870CC	54,617	900	1,500	1,900	3,900	12,500	30,000	100,000	—	—
1870S	1,004,000	31.00	43.00	53.00	85.00	150	275	575	7,000	—
1871	1,204,560	32.00	42.00	52.00	75.00	120	165	350	7,000	3,750
1871CC	153,950	225	325	600	1,200	1,950	10,000	15,000	—	—
1871S	2,178,000	30.00	41.00	49.00	70.00	110	215	400	7,000	—
1872	881,550	32.00	40.00	49.00	75.00	120	195	430	2,850	3,750
1872CC	272,000	85.00	125	275	400	1,500	4,000	8,000	50,000	—
1872S	580,000	31.00	47.00	67.00	135	225	375	975	7,000	—
1873 closed 3	801,800	35.00	46.00	64.00	98.00	135	250	545	4,500	3,750
1873 open 3	Inc. above	2,650	3,400	4,350	5,500	7,900	13,500	30,000	—	—
1873CC	122,500	225	320	425	950	1,900	6,500	12,000	80,000	—
1873S no arrows	5,000	—	—	—	—	—	—	—	—	—

Note: 1873S no arrows, no specimens known to survive.

Seated Liberty Half Dollar

Seated Liberty, arrows at date obverse   "In God We Trust" above eagle reverse

KM# 107 • 12.5000 g., 0.9000 **Silver,** 0.3617 oz. ASW • **Rev. Legend:** UNITED STATES OF AMERICA
Designer: Christian Gobrecht

Date	Mintage	G-4	VG-8	F-12	VF-20	XF-40	AU-50	MS-60	MS-65	Prf-65
1873	1,815,700	32.00	49.00	60.00	90.00	230	400	850	17,500	9,000
1873CC	214,560	150	275	375	850	2,000	2,400	5,700	42,000	—
1873S	233,000	55.00	78.00	130	245	425	675	2,200	40,000	—
1874	2,360,300	32.00	42.00	56.00	85.00	210	400	850	12,750	9,000
1874CC	59,000	400	575	1,000	1,750	3,600	5,600	10,500	—	—
1874S	394,000	43.00	65.00	85.00	185	365	685	1,850	20,000	—

Seated Liberty Half Dollar

Seated Liberty, date below obverse   "In God We Trust" above eagle reverse

KM# A99 • 12.5000 g., 0.9000 **Silver,** 0.3617 oz. ASW • **Rev. Legend:** UNITED STATES OF AMERICA
Designer: Christian Gobrecht

Date	Mintage	G-4	VG-8	F-12	VF-20	XF-40	AU-50	MS-60	MS-65	Prf-65
1875	6,027,500	28.00	38.00	47.00	56.00	88.00	180	420	3,500	3,375
1875CC	1,008,000	50.00	56.00	75.00	125	200	325	650	8,350	—
1875S	3,200,000	28.00	38.00	47.00	63.00	100.00	165	360	2,700	—
1876	8,419,150	28.00	38.00	47.00	56.00	88.00	165	360	5,300	3,775
1876CC	1,956,000	50.00	56.00	75.00	115	180	275	560	4,200	—
1876S	4,528,000	28.00	38.00	47.00	56.00	88.00	165	360	2,700	—
1877	8,304,510	28.00	38.00	47.00	56.00	88.00	165	360	2,700	3,825
1877CC	1,420,000	50.00	56.00	75.00	115	180	275	630	3,250	—
1877S	5,356,000	28.00	38.00	47.00	56.00	88.00	165	360	2,700	—
1878	1,378,400	35.00	46.00	67.00	80.00	120	165	425	3,650	3,900

Date	Mintage	G-4	VG-8	F-12	VF-20	XF-40	AU-50	MS-60	MS-65	Prf-65
1878CC	62,000	450	600	1,000	1,500	3,150	4,850	7,000	43,500	—
1878S	12,000	23,500	37,500	45,000	47,500	52,000	60,000	70,000	175,000	—
1879	5,900	275	310	360	400	465	575	700	3,650	3,150
1880	9,755	260	280	315	355	410	535	700	3,750	3,150
1881	10,975	270	300	335	385	455	565	700	4,000	3,150
1882	5,500	340	365	385	450	525	600	750	3,850	3,150
1883	9,039	325	340	365	435	500	575	775	3,950	3,150
1884	5,275	385	375	415	500	560	635	800	3,850	3,150
1885	6,130	390	425	475	550	625	700	825	3,850	3,150
1886	5,886	400	500	600	700	775	875	1,000	3,900	3,150
1887	5,710	500	525	650	775	875	950	1,100	3,900	3,150
1888	12,833	280	300	365	400	485	550	800	3,900	3,150
1889	12,711	275	315	350	400	485	550	800	3,900	3,150
1890	12,590	285	310	365	415	500	550	800	3,850	3,150
1891	200,600	55.00	60.00	94.00	122	155	260	480	3,850	3,150

1878-S Half Dollar
Grade F-12

Retail Price

Barber Half Dollar
Laureate head right, flanked by stars, date below obverse   Heraldic eagle reverse

Mint mark

KM# 116 • 12.5000 g., 0.9000 **Silver**, 0.3617 oz. ASW, 30.6 mm. • **Obv. Legend** IN GOD WE TRUST
Rev. Legend: UNITED STATES OF AMERICA **Designer:** Charles E. Barber

Date	Mintage	G-4	VG-8	F-12	VF-20	XF-40	AU-50	MS-60	MS-65	Prf-65
1892	935,245	28.50	40.00	65.00	115	180	295	450	3,600	3,500
1892O	390,000	310	400	515	575	630	690	850	4,500	—
1892O micro O	—	2,000	3,750	4,500	7,000	10,000	17,500	24,000	64,000	—
1892S	1,029,028	250	325	425	530	600	700	940	5,350	—
1893	1,826,792	20.00	31.00	75.00	135	205	325	520	5,350	3,500
1893O	1,389,000	36.00	62.50	130	220	360	435	625	10,000	—
1893S	740,000	185	220	300	500	635	725	1,275	28,500	—
1894	1,148,972	32.50	50.00	118	200	290	375	500	3,850	3,500

Date	Mintage	G-4	VG-8	F-12	VF-20	XF-40	AU-50	MS-60	MS-65	Prf-65
1894O	2,138,000	22.00	34.00	95.00	170	290	365	525	7,250	—
1894S	4,048,690	19.00	28.00	70.00	125	230	335	490	11,500	—
1895	1,835,218	18.00	25.00	72.00	150	235	335	595	3,900	3,500
1895O	1,766,000	23.00	39.00	115	210	285	395	595	7,500	—
1895S	1,108,086	33.00	54.00	130	235	310	410	575	8,650	—
1896	950,762	21.50	28.00	90.00	160	265	365	565	6,000	3,500
1896O	924,000	42.00	56.00	185	290	475	750	1,500	15,500	—
1896S	1,140,948	105	145	210	350	495	750	1,400	11,250	—
1897	2,480,731	12.50	15.00	47.50	100.00	160	345	485	4,150	3,500
1897O	632,000	170	230	495	835	1,100	1,350	1,750	9,750	—
1897S	933,900	155	215	385	550	840	1,050	1,500	8,500	—
1898	2,956,735	12.50	15.00	38.50	96.00	165	345	485	3,850	3,500
1898O	874,000	37.50	75.00	225	355	525	625	1,250	10,500	—
1898S	2,358,550	27.50	52.50	87.50	175	335	440	950	10,250	—
1899	5,538,846	13.50	16.00	39.50	100.00	170	350	475	4,150	3,500
1899O	1,724,000	26.00	37.50	80.00	170	300	420	675	8,350	—
1899S	1,686,411	23.00	40.00	80.00	140	225	360	660	6,900	—
1900	4,762,912	13.50	15.50	37.50	94.00	155	310	485	4,000	3,500
1900O	2,744,000	17.50	22.50	62.00	165	285	375	860	16,500	—
1900S	2,560,322	15.00	18.50	46.50	100.00	200	310	640	10,500	—
1901	4,268,813	13.50	16.00	38.50	96.00	180	300	510	4,400	3,500
1901O	1,124,000	16.50	26.50	80.00	205	350	475	1,350	16,500	—
1901S	847,044	34.00	55.00	160	355	610	1,050	1,850	19,500	—
1902	4,922,777	12.50	13.50	32.50	86.00	175	295	475	4,850	3,500
1902O	2,526,000	13.50	17.00	52.50	105	225	360	725	12,500	—
1902S	1,460,670	16.00	19.00	62.50	150	260	420	750	8,400	—
1903	2,278,755	13.50	16.00	47.50	100.00	200	325	500	11,000	3,500
1903O	2,100,000	13.00	17.00	54.00	115	210	335	665	10,000	—
1903S	1,920,772	15.00	18.00	55.00	125	235	380	610	8,800	—
1904	2,992,670	12.00	13.50	34.00	85.00	155	300	475	6,000	3,500
1904O	1,117,600	20.00	32.50	80.00	220	385	590	1,100	12,500	—
1904S	553,038	38.50	70.00	260	565	1,075	1,775	6,250	38,500	—
1905	662,727	22.50	29.50	95.00	180	270	345	565	7,500	3,500
1905O	505,000	30.00	50.00	125	235	340	440	760	5,250	—
1905S	2,494,000	15.50	18.00	50.00	125	230	365	615	9,800	—
1906	2,638,675	11.75	13.25	31.00	85.00	165	290	475	3,800	3,500
1906D	4,028,000	11.75	13.25	32.50	85.00	160	300	485	4,500	—
1906O	2,446,000	11.75	13.25	44.00	100.00	185	310	600	6,500	—
1906S	1,740,154	13.00	16.50	57.50	110	215	310	610	6,500	—
1907	2,598,575	11.75	13.25	30.00	85.00	155	300	470	3,650	3,500
1907D	3,856,000	11.75	13.25	30.00	78.50	155	300	470	3,600	—
1907O	3,946,000	11.75	13.25	32.00	93.50	165	325	575	3,700	—
1907S	1,250,000	16.00	22.00	80.00	170	310	650	1,275	13,500	—
1908	1,354,545	11.75	13.25	30.00	83.00	155	285	470	4,350	3,500
1908D	3,280,000	11.75	13.25	30.00	83.00	155	295	485	3,700	—
1908O	5,360,000	11.75	13.25	30.00	93.50	155	315	540	3,600	—
1908S	1,644,828	18.50	27.00	75.00	160	285	435	850	6,600	—
1909	2,368,650	12.50	16.00	32.50	84.00	160	275	470	3,600	3,500
1909O	925,400	16.00	23.50	58.00	140	300	510	775	4,950	—
1909S	1,764,000	12.00	13.50	37.50	100.00	190	395	600	4,650	—
1910	418,551	20.00	28.50	90.00	170	330	415	610	3,900	3,500
1910S	1,948,000	13.50	16.50	37.50	100.00	190	350	650	6,850	—
1911	1,406,543	11.75	13.25	30.00	83.00	155	290	475	3,600	3,500
1911D	695,080	13.00	16.00	41.00	94.00	195	285	550	3,800	—
1911S	1,272,000	13.50	16.50	41.00	98.00	180	325	580	6,100	—
1912	1,550,700	11.75	13.25	30.00	83.00	160	295	480	4,350	3,500
1912D	2,300,800	13.00	13.50	30.00	83.00	155	310	470	3,600	—
1912S	1,370,000	15.00	20.00	41.50	100.00	195	330	535	6,250	—
1913	188,627	78.00	90.00	235	420	600	850	1,150	5,250	3,500
1913D	534,000	17.00	21.00	44.00	100.00	200	300	485	5,250	—
1913S	604,000	20.00	25.00	53.50	110	225	365	610	4,850	—
1914	124,610	155	175	325	550	775	1,025	1,400	8,500	3,500
1914S	992,000	15.00	19.00	41.00	98.00	190	315	575	5,000	—
1915	138,450	118	175	285	380	575	900	1,250	6,400	3,500
1915D	1,170,400	11.75	13.25	30.00	80.00	155	285	470	3,600	—
1915S	1,604,000	15.50	20.00	41.50	99.00	170	295	485	3,675	—

HALF DOLLAR

Walking Liberty Half Dollar

Obverse mint mark   Reverse mint mark

KM# 142 • 12.5000 g., **Silver**, 30.6 mm. • **Designer:** Adolph A. Weinman **Notes:** The mint mark appears on the obverse below the word "Trust" on 1916 and some 1917 issues. Starting with some 1917 issues and continuing through the remainder of the series, the mint mark was changed to the reverse, at about the 8 o'clock position near the rim.

Date	Mintage	G-4	VG-8	F-12	VF-20	XF-40	AU-50	MS-60	MS-65	Prf-65
1916	608,000	45.00	52.50	100.00	180	250	285	350	1,800	—
1916D	1,014,400	45.00	52.50	80.00	140	225	265	375	2,400	—
1916S	508,000	110	130	285	470	650	750	1,100	6,250	—
1917D obv. mint mark	765,400	22.00	31.50	80.00	160	235	350	640	8,000	—
1917S obv. mint mark	952,000	27.50	44.00	135	375	720	1,225	2,300	19,500	—
1917	12,292,000	7.40	7.60	9.00	20.00	44.00	75.00	135	1,000	—
1917D rev. mint mark	1,940,000	10.00	16.50	45.00	135	275	575	975	18,500	—
1917S rev. mint mark	5,554,000	7.40	8.00	16.50	33.00	65.00	160	345	13,000	—
1918	6,634,000	7.40	8.00	16.00	70.00	160	275	580	3,800	—
1918D	3,853,040	8.00	13.00	36.00	96.00	235	500	1,350	25,000	—
1918S	10,282,000	7.40	7.60	15.00	35.00	65.00	200	525	18,000	—
1919	962,000	19.00	32.50	78.50	275	550	920	1,350	7,500	—
1919D	1,165,000	18.00	38.50	100.00	325	765	1,550	6,250	130,000	—
1919S	1,552,000	17.50	30.00	75.00	325	850	1,800	3,450	20,500	—
1920	6,372,000	7.40	7.60	16.00	44.00	75.00	160	350	5,250	—
1920D	1,551,000	12.00	20.00	70.00	250	475	960	1,550	12,000	—
1920S	4,624,000	7.40	8.00	20.00	80.00	235	520	850	12,500	—
1921	246,000	185	225	350	780	1,550	2,750	4,350	18,000	—
1921D	208,000	315	39.00	550	940	2,200	3,400	5,300	27,500	—
1921S	548,000	46.00	70.00	220	750	4,800	8,600	14,000	105,000	—
1923S	2,178,000	8.50	11.50	27.50	115	315	700	1,400	15,000	—
1927S	2,392,000	7.40	8.00	13.50	47.50	160	415	1,050	10,000	—
1928S	1,940,000	10.00	12.50	24.00	110	300	600	1,650	—	—
1928S	Inc. above	6.75	7.25	15.00	70.00	195	450	1,000	10,750	—
1929D	1,001,200	8.00	12.00	19.00	60.00	110	210	415	3,500	—
1929S	1,902,000	7.40	8.00	12.50	28.50	115	230	425	3,550	—
1933S	1,786,000	8.50	11.00	12.50	20.00	60.00	260	625	4,500	—
1934	6,964,000	7.10	7.60	7.70	8.00	11.00	26.00	85.00	625	—
1934D	2,361,400	7.40	8.00	8.10	10.00	29.00	90.00	155	1,700	—
1934S	3,652,000	7.10	7.80	8.10	8.50	27.00	105	395	5,200	—

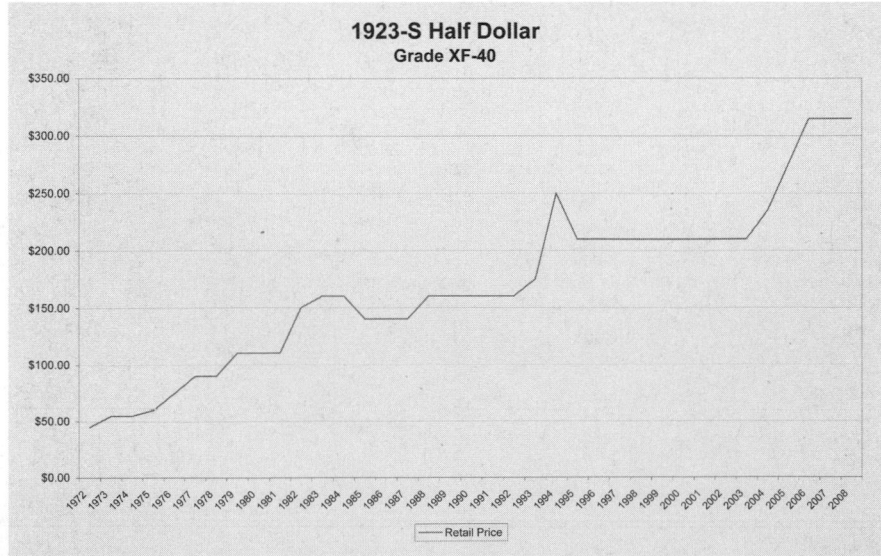

1923-S Half Dollar
Grade XF-40

Date	Mintage	G-4	VG-8	F-12	VF-20	XF-40	AU-50	MS-60	MS-65	Prf-65
1935	9,162,000	7.10	7.60	7.70	8.00	8.50	22.50	45.00	585	—
1935D	3,003,800	7.10	7.80	8.10	10.00	32.50	70.00	140	3,150	—
1935S	3,854,000	7.10	7.80	8.10	8.50	29.00	100.00	295	3,700	—
1936	12,617,901	7.10	7.60	7.70	8.00	8.50	21.50	38.50	300	6,600
1936D	4,252,400	7.10	7.80	8.10	8.50	20.00	55.00	80.00	700	—
1936S	3,884,000	7.10	7.80	8.10	8.50	21.50	62.50	135	1,050	—
1937	9,527,728	7.10	7.60	7.70	8.00	8.50	22.50	40.00	335	1,700
1937D	1,676,000	7.10	8.00	8.50	14.00	33.50	110	225	850	—
1937S	2,090,000	7.10	7.80	8.10	8.50	25.50	65.00	175	850	—
1938	4,118,152	7.10	7.80	8.10	8.50	9.50	41.50	70.00	550	1,275
1938D	491,600	90.00	100.00	115	135	220	260	525	1,550	—
1939	6,820,808	7.10	7.30	6.50	7.00	8.50	22.50	42.50	230	1,150
1939D	4,267,800	7.10	7.60	7.70	8.00	8.50	26.00	47.50	275	—
1939S	2,552,000	7.10	7.80	8.10	9.00	25.00	80.00	150	370	—
1940	9,167,279	7.10	7.30	7.00	7.50	9.00	11.00	30.00	210	1,000
1940S	4,550,000	7.10	7.60	7.70	8.00	12.00	22.00	52.50	420	—
1941	24,207,412	7.10	7.30	7.00	7.50	9.00	11.00	32.50	160	850
1941D	11,248,400	7.10	7.60	7.70	8.00	10.00	18.00	38.50	200	—
1941S	8,098,000	7.10	7.60	7.70	8.00	12.00	27.50	75.00	1,175	—
1942	47,839,120	7.10	7.30	7.00	7.50	9.00	11.00	32.50	150	850
1942D	10,973,800	7.10	7.60	7.70	8.00	10.00	19.00	38.50	345	—
1942S	12,708,000	7.10	7.60	7.70	8.00	10.00	17.50	38.50	700	—
1943	53,190,000	7.10	7.30	7.00	7.50	9.00	11.00	33.50	150	—
1943D	11,346,000	7.10	7.60	7.70	8.00	10.00	25.00	43.50	330	—
1943D Double Die Obverse	—	7.30	7.50	9.00	12.00	15.00	30.00	55.00	450	—
1943S	13,450,000	7.10	7.60	7.70	8.00	10.00	18.50	43.50	485	—
1944	28,206,000	7.10	7.30	7.00	7.50	9.00	11.00	33.50	220	—
1944D	9,769,000	7.10	7.60	7.70	8.00	10.00	20.00	37.50	240	—
1944S	8,904,000	7.10	7.60	7.70	8.00	10.00	16.00	38.50	490	—
1945	31,502,000	7.10	7.30	7.00	7.50	9.00	11.00	32.50	160	—
1945D	9,966,800	7.10	7.60	7.70	8.00	10.00	19.00	34.00	160	—
1945S	10,156,000	7.10	7.60	7.70	8.00	10.00	17.50	35.00	220	—
1946	12,118,000	7.10	7.30	7.00	7.50	9.00	11.00	32.50	250	—
1946D	2,151,000	7.10	7.80	7.70	8.00	25.50	38.50	50.00	150	—
1946S	3,724,000	7.10	7.60	7.70	8.00	12.00	19.00	43.50	165	—
1947	4,094,000	7.10	7.25	7.75	8.00	11.00	22.00	52.50	230	—
1947D	3,900,600	7.10	7.80	7.70	8.00	14.00	31.50	52.50	150	—

Franklin Half Dollar

Mint mark

KM# 199 • 12.5000 g., 0.9000 **Silver**, 0.3617 oz. ASW, 30.6 mm. • **Designer:** John R. Sinnock

Date	Mintage	G-4	VG-8	F-12	VF-20	XF-40	AU-50	MS-60	MS-65	-65FBL	-65CAM
1948	3,006,814	—	5.00	6.00	7.00	8.50	11.50	15.50	75.00	190	—
1948D	4,028,600	—	5.00	6.00	7.00	8.00	11.00	15.00	125	260	—
1949	5,614,000	—	—	—	—	8.00	12.00	38.50	145	300	—
1949D	4,120,600	—	—	—	—	8.00	25.00	43.50	900	1,750	—
1949S	3,744,000	—	—	—	7.00	11.00	30.00	62.50	155	650	—
1950	7,793,509	—	—	—	—	8.00	10.00	26.00	110	250	3,700
1950D	8,031,600	—	—	—	—	9.00	11.50	22.00	425	1,150	—
1951	16,859,602	—	—	—	—	—	8.00	11.00	75.00	235	2,200
1951D	9,475,200	—	—	—	—	12.00	17.50	26.00	170	525	—
1951S	13,696,000	—	—	—	—	—	15.00	23.50	125	775	—
1952	21,274,073	—	—	—	—	—	8.00	8.50	80.00	200	1,100
1952D	25,395,600	—	—	—	—	—	8.00	8.50	135	450	—
1952S	5,526,000	—	—	6.00	12.00	20.00	32.00	50.00	100.00	1,500	—
1953	2,796,920	—	—	—	—	10.00	16.00	25.00	125	850	475
1953D	20,900,400	—	—	—	—	—	8.00	15.00	160	400	—
1953S	4,148,000	—	—	—	—	—	15.00	25.00	65.00	16,000	—
1954	13,421,503	—	—	—	—	—	8.00	8.50	80.00	250	250
1954D	25,445,580	—	—	—	—	—	8.00	8.50	110	200	—
1954S	4,993,400	—	—	—	—	—	8.50	13.50	105	425	—
1955	2,876,381	—	18.00	20.00	21.00	22.00	23.00	24.00	65.00	185	195
1955 Bugs Bunny	—	—	20.00	22.00	23.00	25.00	26.00	28.00	100.00	750	—
1956	4,701,384	—	7.25	7.50	7.75	8.00	8.50	13.50	50.00	95.00	75.00
1957	6,361,952	—	—	—	—	—	8.00	8.50	62.50	95.00	135
1957D	19,966,850	—	—	—	—	—	8.00	8.50	65.00	100.00	—
1958	4,917,652	—	—	—	—	—	8.00	8.50	60.00	100.00	250

HALF DOLLAR

Date	Mintage	G-4	VG-8	F-12	VF-20	XF-40	AU-50	MS-60	MS-65	-65FBL	-65CAM
1958D	23,962,412	—	—	—	—	—	8.00	8.50	62.50	75.00	—
1959	7,349,291	—	—	—	—	—	8.00	8.50	105	250	475
1959D	13,053,750	—	—	—	—	—	8.00	8.50	135	190	—
1960	7,715,602	—	—	—	—	—	8.00	8.50	135	350	75.00
1960D	18,215,812	—	—	—	—	—	8.00	8.50	475	1,250	—
1961	11,318,244	—	—	—	—	—	8.00	8.50	145	1,750	75.00
1961D	20,276,442	—	—	—	—	—	8.00	8.50	200	875	—
1962	12,932,019	—	—	—	—	—	8.00	8.50	160	1,850	50.00
1962D	35,473,281	—	—	—	—	—	8.00	8.50	225	775	—
1963	25,239,645	—	—	—	—	—	8.00	8.50	55.00	775	50.00
1963D	67,069,292	—	—	—	—	—	8.00	8.50	70.00	125	—

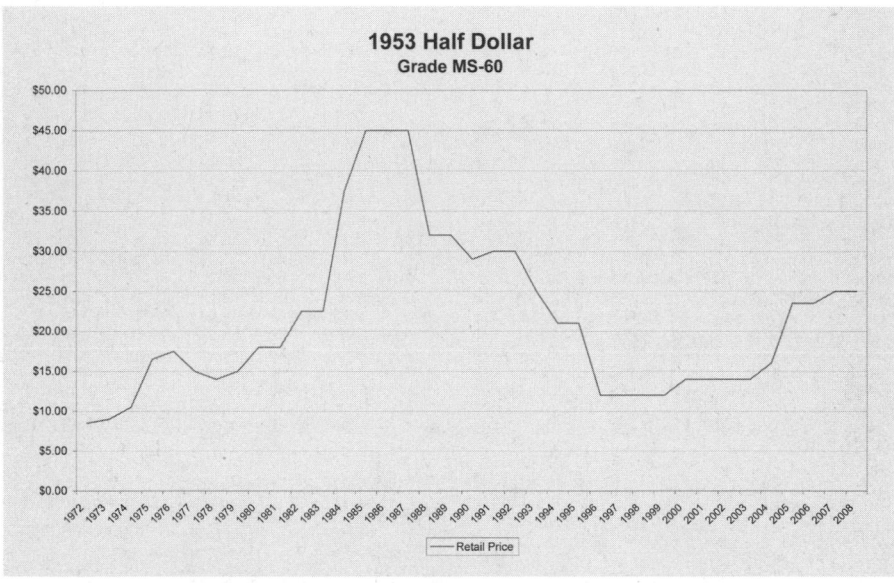

1953 Half Dollar
Grade MS-60

— Retail Price

Kennedy Half Dollar

Mint mark 1964

KM# 202 • 12.5000 g., 0.9000 **Silver**, 0.3617 oz. ASW, 30.6 mm. • **Obv. Designer:** Gilroy Roberts
Rev. Designer: Frank Gasparro

Date	Mintage	MS-60	MS-65	Prf-65
1964	277,254,766	7.50	20.00	12.00
1964 Accented Hair	Inc. above	—	—	40.00
1964D	156,205,446	7.50	24.00	—

Kennedy Half Dollar

Mint mark 1968 - present

KM# 202a • 11.5000 g., **Silver**, 30.6 mm. •
Obv. Designer: Gilroy Roberts **Rev. Designer:**
Frank Gasparro

Date	Mintage	MS-60	MS-65	Prf-65
1965	65,879,366	3.00	18.00	—
1965 SMS	2,360,000	—	15.00	—
1966	108,984,932	3.00	14.00	—
1966 SMS	2,261,583	—	17.00	—
1967	295,046,978	3.00	22.00	—
1967 SMS	18,633,440	—	18.00	—
1968D	246,951,930	3.00	18.00	—
1968S	3,041,506	—	—	7.00
1969D	129,881,800	3.00	20.00	—
1969S	2,934,631	—	—	7.50
1970D	2,150,000	13.00	38.00	—
1970S	2,632,810	—	—	20.00

Kennedy Half Dollar

KM# 202b • 11.3400 g., **Copper-Nickel Clad
Copper**, 30.6 mm. • **Obv. Designer:** Gilroy
Roberts **Rev. Designer:** Frank Gasparro

Date	Mintage	MS-60	MS-65	Prf-65
1971	155,640,000	1.00	15.00	—
1971D	302,097,424	1.00	15.00	—
1971S	3,244,183	—	—	8.00
1972	153,180,000	1.00	20.00	—
1972D	141,890,000	1.00	14.00	—
1972S	3,267,667	—	—	7.00
1973	64,964,000	1.00	14.00	—
1973D	83,171,400	—	12.00	—
1973S	2,769,624	—	—	7.00
1974	201,596,000	1.00	18.00	—
1974D	79,066,300	1.00	20.00	—
1974S	2,617,350	—	—	5.00
1975 none minted	—	—	—	—
1975D none minted	—	—	—	—
1975S none minted	—	—	—	—

Kennedy Half Dollar
Bicentennial design,
Independence Hall reverse

KM# 205 • 11.1000 g., **Copper Nickel** • **Rev.
Designer:** Seth Huntington

Date	Mintage	MS-60	MS-65	Prf-65
1976	234,308,000	1.00	22.00	—
1976D	287,565,248	1.00	9.00	—
1976S	7,059,099	—	—	4.00

Kennedy Half Dollar
Bicentennial design,
Independence Hall reverse

KM# 205a • 11.5000 g., 0.4000 **Silver**, 0.1479 oz.
ASW • **Rev. Designer:** Seth Huntington

Date	Mintage	MS-60	MS-65	Prf-65
1976S	4,908,319	—	12.00	—
1976S	3,998,625	—	—	6.00

Kennedy Half Dollar
Regular design resumed reverse

KM# A202b • 11.3400 g., **Copper-Nickel Clad
Copper**, 30.6 mm. • **Notes:** KM#202b design and
composition resumed. The 1979-S and 1981-S
Type II proofs have clearer mint marks than the
Type I proofs of those years.

Date	Mintage	MS-65	Prf-65
1977	43,598,000	18.00	—
1977D	31,449,106	20.00	—
1977S	3,251,152	—	4.50
1978	14,350,000	12.00	—
1978D	13,765,799	10.00	—
1978S	3,127,788	—	6.00
1979	68,312,000	11.00	—
1979D	15,815,422	9.00	—
1979S type I	3,677,175	—	6.00
1979S type II	Inc. above	—	20.00
1980P	44,134,000	9.00	—
1980D	33,456,449	6.50	—
1980S	3,547,030	—	6.00
1981P	29,544,000	8.00	—
1981D	27,839,533	8.50	—
1981S type I	4,063,083	—	5.00
1981S type II	Inc. above	—	17.50
1982P	10,819,000	10.00	—
1982P no initials FG	Inc. above	40.00	—
1982D	13,140,102	9.00	—
1982S	38,957,479	—	6.50
1983P	34,139,000	20.00	—
1983D	32,472,244	10.00	—
1983S	3,279,126	—	6.50
1984P	26,029,000	10.00	—
1984D	26,262,158	15.00	—
1984S	3,065,110	—	7.00
1985P	18,706,962	10.00	—
1985D	19,814,034	12.00	—
1985S	3,962,138	—	6.00
1986P	13,107,633	25.00	—
1986D	15,336,145	17.00	—
1986S	2,411,180	—	8.00
1987P	2,890,758	14.00	—
1987D	2,890,758	10.00	—
1987S	4,407,728	—	6.50
1988P	13,626,000	16.00	—
1988D	12,000,096	12.00	—
1988S	3,262,948	—	6.00
1989P	24,542,000	18.00	—
1989D	23,000,216	14.00	—
1989S	3,220,194	—	8.00
1990P	22,780,000	20.00	—
1990D	20,096,242	15.00	—
1990S	3,299,559	—	7.00
1991P	14,874,000	15.00	—
1991D	15,054,678	18.00	—
1991S	2,867,787	—	16.00
1992P	17,628,000	18.00	—
1992D	17,000,106	8.00	—
1992S	2,858,981	—	8.00
1993P	15,510,000	15.00	—
1993D	15,000,006	14.00	—
1993S	2,633,439	—	14.00
1994P	23,718,000	8.00	—
1994D	23,828,110	8.00	—
1994S	2,484,594	—	11.00

HALF DOLLAR

Date	Mintage	MS-65	Prf-65
1995P	26,496,000	9.00	—
1995D	26,288,000	8.00	—
1995S	2,010,384	—	35.00
1996P	24,442,000	11.00	—
1996D	24,744,000	8.00	—
1996S	2,085,191	—	16.00
1997P	20,882,000	14.00	—
1997D	19,876,000	10.00	—
1997S	1,975,000	—	34.00
1998P	15,646,000	14.00	—
1998D	15,064,000	14.00	—
1998S	2,078,494	—	22.00
1999P	8,900,000	9.00	—
1999D	10,682,000	9.00	—
1999S	2,557,897	—	24.00
2000P	22,600,000	9.00	—
2000D	19,466,000	7.00	—
2000S	3,082,944	—	8.00
2001P	21,200,000	9.00	—
2001D	19,504,000	9.00	—
2001S	2,235,000	—	10.00
2002P	3,100,000	10.00	—
2002D	2,500,000	10.00	—
2002S	2,268,913	—	8.00
2003P	2,500,000	14.00	—
2003D	2,500,000	14.00	—
2003S	2,076,165	—	6.00
2004P	2,900,000	14.00	—
2004D	2,900,000	14.00	—
2004S	1,789,488	—	13.00
2005P	3,800,000	9.00	—
2005P Satin finish	1,160,000	8.00	—
2005D	3,500,000	9.00	—
2005D Satin finish	1,160,000	10.00	—
2005S	2,275,000	—	7.00
2006P	2,400,000	12.00	—
2006P Satin finish	847,361	12.00	—
2006D	2,000,000	20.00	—
2006D Satin finish	847,361	14.00	—
2006S	1,934,965	—	10.00

Date	Mintage	MS-65	Prf-65
2007P	—	7.00	—
2007P Satin finish	—	—	—
2007D	—	7.00	—
2007D Satin finish	—	—	—
2007S	—	—	10.00

Kennedy Half Dollar

KM# B202b • Silver •

Date	Mintage	Prf-65
1992S	1,317,579	12.00
1993S	761,353	32.00
1994S	785,329	36.00
1995S	838,953	92.00
1996S	830,021	40.00
1997S	821,678	75.00
1998S	878,792	25.00
1998S Matte Proof	62,350	325
1999S	804,565	38.00
2000S	965,921	9.00
2001S	849,600	20.00
2002S	888,816	14.00
2003S	1,040,425	14.50
2004S	1,175,935	14.00
2005S	1,069,679	9.00
2006S	988,140	11.00
2007S	—	12.00

DOLLAR

Flowing Hair Dollar

KM# 17 • 26.9600 g., 0.8920 **Silver**, 0.7731 oz. ASW, 39-40 mm. • **Designer:** Robert Scot **Notes:** The two 1795 varieties have either two or three leaves under each of the eagle's wings on the reverse.

Date	Mintage	F-12	VF-20	XF-40	AU-50	MS-60	MS-63
1794	1,758	115,000	160,000	235,000	340,000	500,000	800,000
1795 2 leaves	203,033	3,350	5,500	12,850	22,500	54,000	110,000
1795 3 leaves	Inc. above	3,100	4,950	11,500	19,500	46,500	98,000
1795 Silver plug	—	10,500	14,500	30,000	—	—	—

Draped Bust Dollar
Small eagle reverse

KM# 18 • 26.9600 g., 0.8920 **Silver**, 0.7731 oz. ASW, 39-40 mm. • **Designer:** Robert Scot **Notes:** The 1796 varieties are distinguished by the size of the numerals in the date and letters in "United States of America." The 1797 varieties are distinguished by the number of stars to the left and right of the word "Liberty" and by the size of the letters in "United States of America." The 1798 varieties have either 13 or 15 stars on the obverse.

Date	Mintage	F-12	VF-20	XF-40	AU-50	MS-60	MS-63
1795 Off-center bust	Inc. above	2,550	4,250	8,400	13,500	36,500	74,000
1795 Centered bust	—	2,600	4,300	8,600	13,750	37,000	—
1796 small date, small letters	72,920	2,900	4,800	9,650	14,950	44,000	90,000
1796 small date, large letters	Inc. above	2,700	4,800	9,850	15,400	48,500	—
1796 large date, small letters	Inc. above	2,950	5,100	10,250	15,500	27,000	65,000
1797 9 stars left, 7 stars right, small letters	7,776	4,000	8,250	16,500	36,500	85,000	125,000
1797 9 stars left, 7 stars right, large letters	Inc. above	2,950	5,250	10,000	16,500	42,500	90,000
1797 10 stars left, 6 stars right	Inc. above	2,750	4,700	9,800	16,000	45,000	98,000
1798 13 stars	327,536	2,850	4,700	10,000	17,000	60,000	—
1798 15 stars	Inc. above	3,400	5,850	12,000	21,500	75,000	—

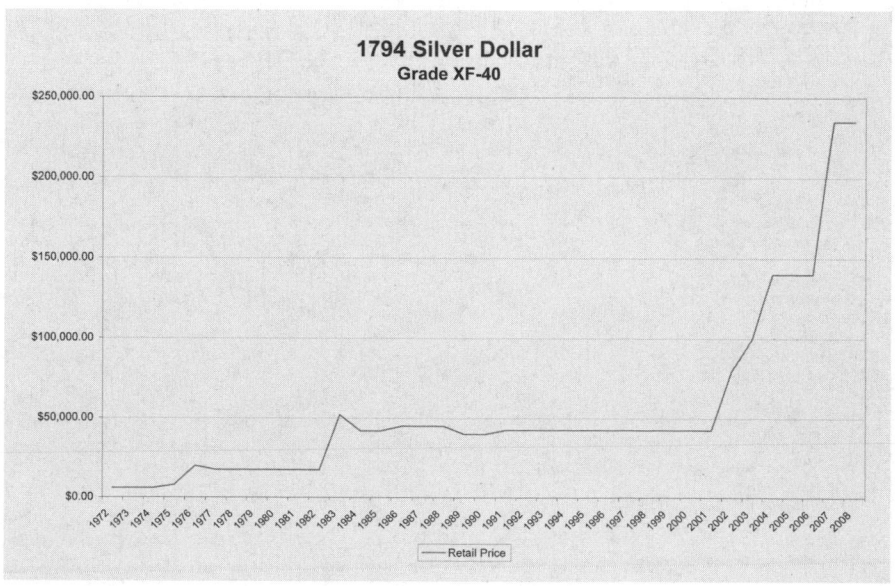

1794 Silver Dollar
Grade XF-40

Draped Bust Dollar
Draped bust right, flanked by stars, date below obverse   Heraldic eagle reverse

KM# 32 • 26.9600 g., 0.8920 **Silver**, 0.7731 oz. ASW, 39-40 mm. • **Obv. Legend** LIBERTY **Rev. Legend:** UNITED STATES OF AMERICA **Designer:** Robert Scot **Notes:** The 1798 "knob 9" variety has a serif on the lower left of the 9 in the date. The 1798 varieties are distinguished by the number of arrows held by the eagle on the reverse and the number of berries on the olive branch. On the 1798 "high-8" variety, the 8 in the date is higher than the other numerals. The 1799 varieties are distinguished by the number and positioning of the stars on the obverse and by the size of the berries in the olive branch on the reverse. On the 1700 "irregular date" variety, the first 9 in the date is smaller than the other numerals. Some varieties of the 1800 strikes had letters in the legend cut twice into the dies; as the dies became worn, the letters were touched up. On the 1800 "very wide date, low 8" variety, the spacing between the numerals in the date are wider than other varieties and the 8 is lower than the other numerals. The 1800 "small berries" variety refers to the size of the berries in the olive branch on the reverse. The 1800 "12 arrows" and "10 arrows" varieties refer to the number of arrows held by the eagle. The 1800 "Americai" variety appears to have the faint outline of an "I" after "America" in the reverse legend. The "close" and "wide" varieties of 1802 refer to the amount of space between the numerals in the date. The 1800 large-3 and small-3 varieties are distinguished by the size of the 3 in the date.

Date	Mintage	F-12	VF-20	XF-40	AU-50	MS-60	MS-63
1798 knob 9	Inc. above	1,225	2,075	3,950	8,250	21,750	43,500
1798 10 arrows	Inc. above	1,225	2,075	3,950	8,250	21,750	43,500
1798 4 berries	Inc. above	1,225	2,075	3,950	8,250	21,750	43,500
1798 5 berries, 12 arrows	Inc. above	1,225	2,075	3,950	8,250	21,750	43,500
1798 high 8	Inc. above	1,225	2,075	3,950	8,250	21,750	43,500
1798 13 arrows	Inc. above	1,225	2,075	3,950	8,250	21,750	45,000
1799/98 13-star reverse	423,515	1,450	2,350	4,300	8,600	23,500	45,000
1799/98 15-star reverse	Inc. above	1,325	2,125	4,000	8,300	24,500	47,500
1799 irregular date, 13-star reverse	Inc. above	1,300	2,150	3,900	8,200	23,500	45,000
1799 irregular date, 15-star reverse	Inc. above	1,275	2,125	3,950	8,250	21,500	42,500
1799 perfect date, 7- and 6-star obverse, no berries	Inc. above	1,200	2,050	3,850	8,150	18,500	42,500
1799 perfect date, 7- and 6-star obverse, small berries	Inc. above	1,200	2,050	3,850	8,150	18,500	42,500
1799 perfect date, 7- and 6-star obverse, medium large berries	Inc. above	1,225	2,050	3,850	8,150	18,500	42,500
1799 perfect date, 7- and 6-star obverse, extra large berries	Inc. above	1,225	2,050	3,850	8,150	18,500	51,500
1799 8 stars left, 5 stars right on obverse	Inc. above	1,300	2,150	3,900	8,200	24,000	45,000
1800 "R" in "Liberty" double cut	220,920	1,275	2,125	3,950	8,250	21,500	45,000
1800 first "T" in "States" double cut	Inc. above	1,275	2,125	3,950	8,250	21,500	45,000
1800 both letters double cut	Inc. above	1,275	2,125	3,950	8,250	21,500	45,000
1800 "T" in "United" double cut	Inc. above	1,275	2,125	3,950	8,250	21,500	45,000
1800 very wide date, low 8	Inc. above	1,275	2,125	3,950	8,250	21,500	—
1800 small berries	Inc. above	1,300	2,150	3,900	8,200	22,000	48,500
1800 dot date	Inc. above	150	2,350	4,300	8,600	21,500	45,000
1800 12 arrows	Inc. above	1,275	2,125	3,950	8,250	21,500	45,000
1800 10 arrows	Inc. above	1,275	2,125	3,950	8,250	21,500	48,500
1800 "Americai"	Inc. above	1,450	2,350	4,300	8,600	21,500	49,000
1801	54,454	1,400	2,400	4,000	8,300	25,000	—
1801 proof restrike	—	—	—	—	—	—	—
1802/1 close	Inc. above	1,450	2,350	4,300	8,600	20,500	—
1802/1 wide	Inc. above	1,450	2,350	4,300	8,600	20,500	—
1802 close, perfect date	Inc. above	1,300	2,150	3,900	8,200	20,500	—
1802 wide, perfect date	Inc. above	1,275	2,125	3,950	8,250	21,500	—
1802 proof restrike, mintage unrecorded	—	—	—	—	—	—	—
1803 large 3	85,634	1,325	2,225	4,000	8,300	20,500	47,500
1803 small 3	Inc. above	1,450	2,350	4,300	8,600	21,500	48,500
1803 proof restrike, mintage unrecorded	—	—	—	—	—	—	—
1804 15 known	—	—	—	—	3,000,000	—	—

Note: 1804, Childs Sale, Aug. 1999, Prf-68, $4,140,000.

Gobrecht Dollar

"C Gobrecht F." in base obverse
Eagle flying left amid stars reverse

KM# 59.1 • 26.7300 g., 0.9000 **Silver**, 0.7734 oz. ASW, 38.1 mm. • **Obv. Designer:** Christian Gobrecht **Rev. Legend:** UNITED STATES OF AMERICA **Edge Desc:** Plain.

Date	Mintage	VF-20	XF-40	AU-50	Prf-60
1836	1,000	11,500	14,850	—	25,500

"C. Gobrecht F." in base obverse
Eagle flying in plain field reverse

KM# 59.2 • 26.7300 g., 0.9000 **Silver**, 0.7734 oz. ASW, 38.1 mm. • **Obv. Designer:** Christian Gobrecht. **Edge Desc:** Plain.

Date	Mintage	VF-20	XF-40	AU-50	Prf-60
1836 Restrike	—	—	—	—	24,000

"C. Gobrecht F." in base obverse

KM# 59a.1 • 26.7300 g., 0.9000 **Silver**, 0.7734 oz. ASW, 38.1 mm. • **Obv. Legend** Eagle flying left amid stars. **Edge Desc:** Plain.

Date	Mintage	VF-20	XF-40	AU-50	Prf-60
1836	600	—	—	—	—

"C. Gobrecht F." in base obverse
Eagle flying left amid stars reverse

KM# 59a.2 • 26.7300 g., 0.9000 **Silver**, 0.7734 oz. ASW, 38.1 mm. • **Edge Desc:** Reeded.

Date	Mintage	VF-20	XF-40	AU-50	Prf-60
1836 Restrike	—	—	—	—	—

Designer's name omitted in base obverse
Eagle in plain field reverse

KM# 59a.3 • 26.7300 g., 0.9000 **Silver**, 0.7734 oz. ASW, 38.1 mm. • **Edge Desc:** Reeded.

Date	Mintage	VF-20	XF-40	AU-50	Prf-60
1839	300	—	—	—	38,000

Designer's name omitted in base obverse
Eagle in plain field reverse

KM# 59a.4 • 26.7300 g., 0.9000 **Silver**, 0.7734 oz. ASW, 38.1 mm. •

Date	Mintage	VF-20	XF-40	AU-50	Prf-60
1839 Restrike	—	—	—	—	36,500

Note: All other combinations are restrikes of the late 1850's.

Seated Liberty Dollar

Seated Liberty, date below obverse   No motto above eagle reverse

KM# 71 • 26.7300 g., 0.9000 **Silver**, 0.7734 oz. ASW, 38.1 mm. • **Rev. Legend:** UNITED STATES OF AMERICA **Designer:** Christian Gobrecht

Date	Mintage	G-4	VG-8	F-12	VF-20	XF-40	AU-50	MS-60	MS-63	MS-65	Prf-65
1840	61,005	240	275	325	385	600	900	5,500	16,500	—	62,500
1841	173,000	190	210	240	320	400	625	2,200	4,950	44,000	—
1842	184,618	190	210	240	320	400	600	2,150	4,650	—	90,000
1843	165,100	190	210	240	320	400	625	2,350	8,500	—	—
1844	20,000	220	240	300	395	535	840	4,200	12,500	47,000	—
1845	24,500	275	305	360	420	575	840	9,000	23,500	—	70,000
1846	110,600	205	230	275	350	480	600	2,600	5,900	—	85,000
1846O	59,000	215	250	315	400	560	1,000	17,500	17,500	37,500	—
1847	140,750	190	210	245	320	395	625	2,350	5,400	27,500	44,000
1848	15,000	285	350	480	590	800	1,250	3,750	8,250	40,000	96,000
1849	62,600	205	220	260	340	460	675	2,350	6,900	32,500	120,000
1850	7,500	360	475	650	800	1,100	1,800	6,250	13,000	50,000	47,500
1850O	40,000	295	450	450	670	1,125	3,550	12,500	22,500	60,000	—
1851	1,300	4,000	4,850	5,750	7,750	14,500	24,500	37,500	64,000	90,000	62,500
1851 Restrike	—	—	—	—	—	—	—	—	—	—	54,500
1852	1,100	3,500	4,150	5,200	7,000	13,750	24,000	35,000	60,000	71,500	62,500
1852 Restrike	—	—	—	—	—	—	—	—	—	—	56,500
1853	46,110	335	400	550	650	875	1,275	3,300	7,350	34,500	79,500
1854	33,140	1,000	1,300	1,850	2,600	3,750	4,950	8,000	11,000	2,800	47,500
1855	26,000	900	1,150	1,350	2,000	2,950	3,850	7,000	16,500	—	38,000
1856	63,500	345	425	600	650	1,050	1,900	4,000	8,250	—	27,000
1857	94,000	385	475	550	700	1,100	1,300	2,750	8,000	28,500	29,500
1858 proof only	Est. 800	3,200	3,600	4,000	4,800	5,500	7,300	—	—	—	27,000
Note: Proof Only restruck in later years.											
1859	256,500	275	320	390	575	650	900	2,000	6,000	—	13,000

Date	Mintage	G-4	VG-8	F-12	VF-20	XF-40	AU-50	MS-60	MS-63	MS-65	Prf-65
1859O	360,000	250	270	295	365	440	685	1,950	5,000	32,500	—
1859S	20,000	310	390	485	600	1,250	3,000	14,500	35,000	62,500	—
1860	218,930	250	290	375	460	550	600	1,850	3,900	27,500	13,500
1860O	515,000	240	270	295	365	440	675	1,750	4,600	16,500	—
1861	78,500	600	750	975	950	1,200	1,550	2,750	5,500	25,000	13,500
1862	12,090	440	600	875	925	1,100	1,450	2,700	5,600	37,500	13,500
1863	27,660	375	525	575	600	700	1,100	2,700	5,500	23,500	20,000
1864	31,170	350	410	500	530	640	1,050	2,700	6,000	22,000	13,000
1865	47,000	300	350	400	600	750	1,350	2,700	4,750	35,000	13,000
1866 2 known without motto	—	—	—	—	—	—	—	—	—	—	—

Seated Liberty Dollar
Seated Liberty, date below obverse   "In God We Trust" above eagle reverse

KM# 100 • 26.7300 g., 0.9000 **Silver**, 0.7734 oz. ASW, 38.1 mm. • **Rev. Legend:** UNITED STATES OF AMERICA **Designer:** Christian Gobrecht **Notes:** In 1866 the motto "In God We Trust" was added to the reverse above the eagle.

Date	Mintage	G-4	VG-8	F-12	VF-20	XF-40	AU-50	MS-60	MS-63	MS-65	Prf-65
1866	49,625	250	280	345	485	560	900	1,650	3,150	25,500	12,500
1867	47,525	230	260	325	430	525	875	1,500	3,250	27,500	11,000
1868	162,700	225	250	315	405	475	850	1,600	6,600	35,000	12,500
1869	424,300	230	240	295	395	450	650	1,450	3,550	32,500	11,000
1870	416,000	200	215	245	320	440	600	1,400	3,250	25,500	12,500
1870CC	12,462	420	500	720	1,050	1,700	3,000	10,250	20,500	42,500	—
1870S 12-15 known	—	50,000	44,000	65,000	125,000	250,000	500,000	750,000	1,250,000		
Note: 1870S, Eliasberg Sale, April 1997, EF-45 to AU-50, $264,000.											
1871	1,074,760	190	205	240	340	425	600	1,100	3,000	25,500	11,000
1871CC	1,376	2,000	2,750	4,000	6,000	9,750	18,500	50,000	175,000	300,000	—
1872	1,106,450	190	205	250	340	425	600	1,100	2,950	25,500	11,000
1872CC	3,150	900	1,300	2,200	3,250	5,300	10,000	19,000	47,500	—	—
1872S	9,000	250	325	450	650	1,100	2,750	8,500	23,500	62,500	—
1873	293,600	220	240	285	360	475	700	1,250	3,150	31,500	11,500
1873CC	2,300	3,450	4,750	6,500	10,000	17,000	35,000	80,000	135,000	—	—
1873S none known	700	—	—	—	—	—	—	—	—	—	—

Trade Dollar
Seated Liberty, "In God We Trust" in base above date obverse Trade Dollar below eagle reverse

KM# 108 • 27.2200 g., 0.9000 **Silver**, 0.7876 oz. ASW, 38.1 mm. • **Rev. Legend:** UNITED STATES OF AMERICA. **Designer:** William Barber

Date	Mintage	G-4	VG-8	F-12	VF-20	XF-40	AU-50	MS-60	MS-65	Prf-65
1873	397,500	100.00	125	144	200	250	360	1,050	12,500	11,000
1873CC	124,500	230	275	330	450	700	1,475	8,850	122,000	—
1873S	703,000	115	135	155	210	265	385	1,450	15,500	—

Date	Mintage	G-4	VG-8	F-12	VF-20	XF-40	AU-50	MS-60	MS-65	Prf-65
1874	987,800	100.00	130	150	185	250	365	1,150	13,850	10,800
1874CC	1,373,200	235	265	310	375	600	775	3,250	26,500	—
1874S	2,549,000	90.00	135	140	150	175	270	975	11,000	—
1875	218,900	160	185	375	460	590	850	2,450	13,000	10,700
1875CC	1,573,700	200	255	285	335	510	675	2,150	40,000	—
1875S	4,487,000	80.00	125	130	140	165	260	960	11,000	—
1875S/CC	Inc. above	220	285	375	560	925	1,450	4,650	65,000	—
1876	456,150	90.00	135	140	150	175	270	950	7,500	10,500
1876CC	509,000	235	265	300	365	525	720	6,000	78,500	—
1876S	5,227,000	80.00	125	130	140	165	260	940	11,000	—
1877	3,039,710	90.00	135	140	150	175	270	950	16,000	10,500
1877CC	534,000	235	275	320	410	700	800	2,450	60,000	—
1877S	9,519,000	80.00	125	130	140	165	260	940	11,000	—
1878 proof only	900	—	—	—	1,200	1,300	1,500	—	—	13,500
1878CC	97,000	425	525	710	1,050	2,400	4,200	12,000	112,000	—
1878S	4,162,000	80.00	125	130	140	165	260	940	11,000	—
1879 proof only	1,541	—	—	—	1,175	1,275	1,400	—	—	10,500
1880 proof only	1,987	—	—	—	1,150	1,250	1,350	—	—	10,500
1881 proof only	960	—	—	—	1,200	1,300	1,400	—	—	10,500
1882 proof only	1,097	—	—	—	1,175	1,275	1,375	—	—	10,500
1883 proof only	979	—	—	—	1,200	1,300	1,400	—	—	10,500
1884 proof only	10	—	—	—	—	—	100,000	—	—	—

Note: 1884, Eliasberg Sale, April 1997, Prf-66, $396,000.

1885 proof only	5	—	—	—	—	—	—	—	—	—

Note: 1885, Eliasberg Sale, April 1997, Prf-65, $907,500.

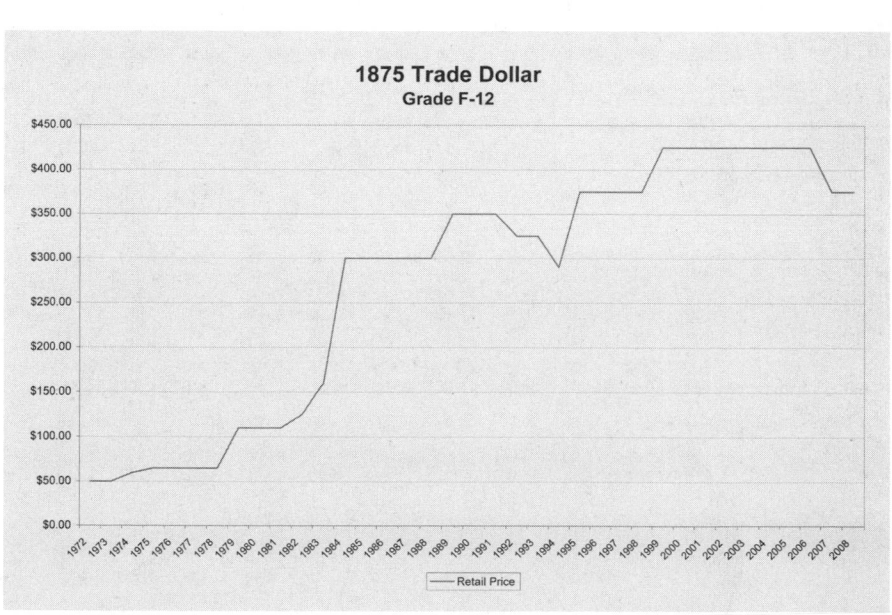

1875 Trade Dollar
Grade F-12

Morgan Dollar
Laureate head left, date below flanked by stars obverse   Eagle within 1/2 wreath reverse

8 Tail feathers   7 Tail feathers   7/8 Tail feathers

KM# 110 • 26.7300 g., 0.9000 **Silver**, 0.7734 oz. ASW, 38.1 mm. • **Obv. Legend** E.PLURIBUS.UNUM **Rev. Legend:** UNITED STATES OF AMERICA **Designer:** George T. Morgan **Notes:** "65DMPL" values are for coins grading MS-65 deep-mirror prooflike. The 1878 "8 tail feathers" and "7 tail feathers" varieties are distinguished by the number of feathers in the eagle's tail. On the "reverse of 1878" varieties, the top of the top feather in the arrows held by the eagle is straight across and the eagle's breast is concave. On the "reverse of 1879 varieties," the top feather in the arrows held by the eagle is slanted and the eagle's breast is convex. The 1890-CC "tail-bar variety has a bar extending from the arrow feathers to the wreath on the reverse, the result of a die gouge. The Pittman Act of 1918 authorized the melting of 270 Million pieces of various dates. They were not indivually recorded.

Date	Mintage	VG-8	F-12	VF-20	XF-40	AU-50	MS-60	MS-63	MS-64	MS-65	65DMPL	Prf-65
1878 8 tail feathers	750,000	29.00	32.00	37.50	46.00	74.00	128	175	385	1,375	19,500	7,500
1878 7 over 8 tail feathers	9,759,550	21.00	24.50	27.50	41.50	75.00	145	325	525	2,600	15,000	—
1878 7 tail feathers, reverse of 1878	Inc. above	20.50	22.00	23.00	25.00	40.00	74.00	105	260	1,375	10,200	11,500
1878 7 tail feathers, reverse of 1879	Inc. above	21.00	23.00	25.00	27.00	43.50	80.00	175	550	2,650	19,800	185,000
1878CC	2,212,000	98.50	100.00	110	125	150	225	390	625	1,650	9,500	—
1878S	9,744,000	20.00	21.00	22.50	27.00	37.50	60.00	74.00	115	310	8,250	—
1879	14,807,100	16.40	16.80	16.90	21.10	21.90	32.00	60.00	135	875	13,750	6,200
1879CC	756,000	165	185	285	735	1,900	4,150	7,500	10,500	28,000	48,750	—
1879CC capped CC	Inc. above	160	175	270	700	1,800	4,000	6,850	10,250	44,500	63,500	—
1879O	2,887,000	16.40	16.80	19.00	22.00	25.00	75.00	195	515	3,400	27,000	—
1879S reverse of 1878	9,110,000	22.50	23.50	25.00	30.00	47.50	125	400	1,450	7,300	24,000	—
1879S reverse of 1879	9,110,000	16.40	16.80	16.90	21.10	21.90	32.00	51.00	62.00	165	1,075	—
1880	12,601,335	16.40	16.80	16.90	21.10	21.90	32.00	55.00	145	775	5,350	6,000
1880CC reverse of 1878	591,000	175	210	245	300	355	575	660	1,265	2,800	19,200	
1880CC 80/79 reverse of 1878	Inc. above	190	230	270	335	410	640	850	1,700	4,000	—	—
1880CC 8/7 reverse of 1878	Inc. above	170	200	235	290	360	600	700	1,300	2,900	—	—
1880CC reverse of 1879	Inc. above	170	200	240	285	345	550	580	725	1,550	8,900	—
1880CC 8/7 high 7 reverse of 1879	Inc. above	175	205	245	290	355	575	620	800	1,850	—	—
1880CC 8/7 low 7 reverse of 1879	Inc. above	175	205	245	290	355	575	620	800	1,850	—	—
1880O	5,305,000	16.70	16.80	19.00	22.00	25.00	62.50	385	1,750	26,000	70,000	—
1880S	8,900,000	16.40	16.80	16.90	21.10	21.90	35.00	48.00	62.00	165	685	—
1881	9,163,975	16.40	16.80	16.90	21.10	21.90	32.00	63.00	150	820	20,000	6,300

Date	Mintage	VG-8	F-12	VF-20	XF-40	AU-50	MS-60	MS-63	MS-64	MS-65	65DMPL	Prf-65
1881CC	296,000	375	385	410	425	460	555	575	640	1,000	2,850	—
1881O	5,708,000	16.40	16.80	16.90	21.10	21.90	32.00	51.00	210	1,675	26,500	—
1881S	12,760,000	16.40	16.80	16.90	21.10	21.90	35.00	48.00	62.00	165	785	—
1882	11,101,100	16.40	16.80	16.90	21.10	21.90	32.00	51.00	67.00	515	5,950	6,000
1882CC	1,133,000	92.00	100.00	110	130	155	220	235	265	495	1,900	—
1882O	6,090,000	16.70	16.80	19.00	22.00	25.00	39.00	52.00	110	1,200	6,400	—
1882O/S	Inc. above	30.00	40.00	48.00	72.00	115	255	1,150	3,250	56,000	65,000	—
1882S	9,250,000	16.40	16.80	16.90	21.10	21.90	32.00	51.00	67.00	167	2,950	—
1883	12,291,039	16.40	16.80	16.90	21.10	21.90	32.00	48.00	65.00	210	1,625	6,150
1883CC	1,204,000	92.00	100.00	110	130	155	215	230	265	445	1,500	—
1883O	8,725,000	16.40	16.80	16.90	21.10	21.90	32.00	48.00	62.00	165	1,025	—
1883S	6,250,000	16.40	16.80	19.50	33.50	145	635	2,750	4,250	29,500	94,500	—
1884	14,070,875	16.40	16.80	16.90	21.10	21.90	32.00	51.00	62.00	275	3,400	6,000
1884CC	1,136,000	125	135	160	175	195	215	225	260	445	1,550	—
1884O	9,730,000	16.40	16.80	16.90	21.10	21.90	32.00	48.00	62.00	165	785	—
1884S	3,200,000	16.40	16.80	19.50	42.50	255	5,750	31,500	110,000	235,000	220,000	—
1885	17,787,767	16.40	16.80	16.90	21.10	21.90	32.00	51.00	62.00	165	725	6,000
1885CC	228,000	550	585	600	630	640	650	680	725	1,275	3,000	—
1885O	9,185,000	16.40	16.80	16.90	21.10	21.90	32.00	48.00	62.00	165	785	—
1885S	1,497,000	21.00	28.00	40.00	64.00	125	240	310	720	1,825	27,500	—
1886	19,963,886	16.40	18.00	19.00	21.10	21.90	32.00	48.00	62.00	165	1,050	6,000
1886O	10,710,000	16.40	16.80	21.00	23.00	78.00	685	3,750	10,500	240,000	300,000	—
1886S	750,000	47.50	62.50	85.00	90.00	180	320	465	775	3,150	24,000	—
1887	20,290,710	16.40	16.80	16.90	21.10	21.90	32.00	48.00	62.00	165	1,025	6,000
1887/6	Inc. above	23.00	26.00	34.00	55.00	165	425	725	1,300	4,650	39,500	—
1887O	11,550,000	16.40	16.80	21.00	23.00	25.00	52.00	110	460	3,200	10,500	—
1887/6O	—	24.00	30.00	39.00	65.00	190	450	2,600	7,950	32,000	—	—
1887S	1,771,000	18.00	19.00	22.00	24.00	44.00	110	285	700	3,100	29,500	—
1888	19,183,833	16.40	16.80	16.90	21.10	21.90	32.00	48.00	62.00	200	2,950	6,150
1888O	12,150,000	16.40	16.80	16.90	21.10	21.90	32.00	49.00	90.00	450	2,500	—
1888O Hot Lips	Inc. above	55.00	125	250	600	3,000	—	—	—	—	—	—
1888S	657,000	115	190	210	225	235	300	465	875	2,850	13,500	—
1889	21,726,811	16.40	16.80	16.90	21.10	22.00	32.00	48.00	65.00	335	3,750	6,000
1889CC	350,000	675	1,050	1,675	3,000	7,000	22,500	43,500	53,000	320,000	—	—
1889O	11,875,000	16.70	16.80	20.50	24.00	31.50	135	410	825	4,800	14,500	—
1889S	700,000	37.50	60.00	65.00	82.00	125	210	400	570	1,850	31,000	—
1890	16,802,590	16.40	16.80	16.90	21.10	21.90	32.00	48.00	160	2,000	18,500	6,000
1890CC	2,309,041	96.00	100.00	110	160	245	450	950	2,650	6,950	14,750	—
1890CC tail bar	Inc. above	155	175	225	400	700	1,450	3,600	5,500	—	—	—
1890O	10,701,000	19.00	20.00	21.00	23.00	29.50	63.00	115	365	1,600	8,500	—
1890S	8,230,373	16.70	16.80	19.00	23.10	25.00	56.00	110	270	975	11,000	—
1891	8,694,206	16.90	16.80	19.50	23.10	26.00	52.50	185	685	6,500	27,500	6,000
1891CC	1,618,000	96.00	98.50	110	150	220	360	800	1,450	4,850	24,500	—
1891CC Spitting Eagle	Inc. above	105	115	135	185	260	425	900	1,600	6,000	—	—
1891O	7,954,529	16.90	16.80	19.00	23.10	35.00	135	350	850	7,750	31,500	—
1891S	5,296,000	16.90	16.80	19.00	23.10	25.00	56.00	135	315	1,425	15,500	—

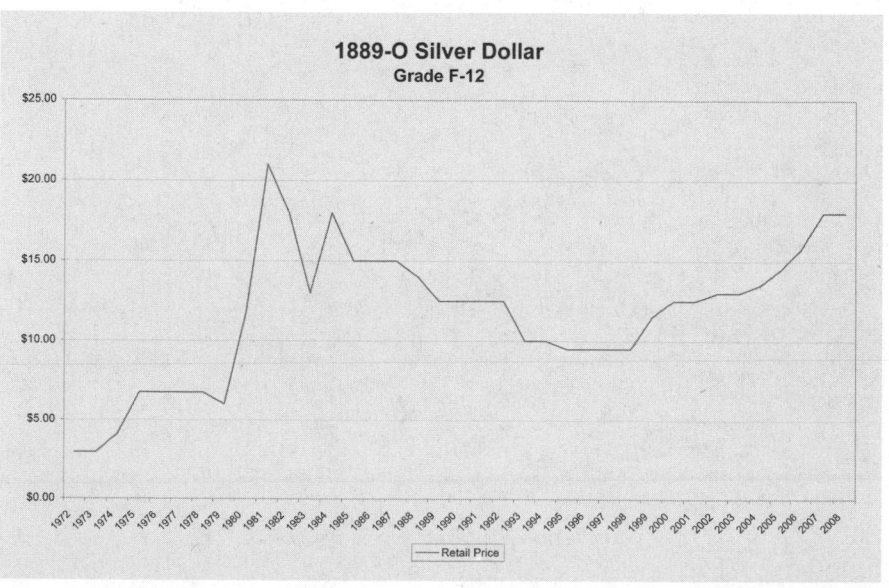

1889-O Silver Dollar
Grade F-12

Date	Mintage	VG-8	F-12	VF-20	XF-40	AU-50	MS-60	MS-63	MS-64	MS-65	65DMPL	Prf-65
1892	1,037,245	20.00	20.00	25.00	34.00	75.00	155	420	1,025	4,000	18,500	6,250
1892CC	1,352,000	195	220	315	535	800	1,650	2,450	3,450	9,750	33,500	—
1892O	2,744,000	20.00	21.00	22.00	32.00	62.50	160	325	825	5,350	41,500	—
1892S	1,200,000	26.00	32.00	135	365	1,950	34,500	63,500	100,000	190,000	195,000	—
1893	378,792	245	250	260	300	400	750	1,350	2,600	7,350	66,000	6,150
1893CC	677,000	265	345	725	1,850	2,350	3,700	6,800	14,000	67,500	85,000	—
1893O	300,000	205	250	380	620	975	2,250	7,500	17,850	210,000	215,000	—
1893S	100,000	380	4,950	7,250	10,500	27,500	85,000	150,000	250,000	485,000	445,000	—
1894	110,972	1,450	1,700	1,850	2,300	2,850	4,950	6,750	11,800	46,500	55,500	7,250
1894O	1,723,000	55.00	65.00	70.00	105	310	580	4,000	10,500	57,500	59,500	—
1894S	1,260,000	62.00	65.00	110	150	510	695	1,150	1,940	7,150	21,500	—
1895 proof only	12,880	21,500	27,500	29,000	33,500	37,500	—	—	—	—	—	79,000
1895O	450,000	335	415	595	725	1,450	17,000	57,500	94,000	225,000	—	—
1895S	400,000	450	510	775	1,175	1,875	4,150	7,000	9,100	22,750	42,500	—
1896	9,967,762	16.40	16.80	16.90	21.10	21.90	32.00	49.00	65.00	195	1,350	6,000
1896O	4,900,000	16.90	16.80	20.00	24.00	185	1,450	8,350	46,000	180,000	180,000	—
1896S	5,000,000	22.00	35.00	60.00	235	895	1,775	4,100	5,400	19,500	110,000	—
1897	2,822,731	16.40	16.80	16.90	21.10	21.90	32.00	49.00	69.00	305	3,950	6,000
1897O	4,004,000	16.90	19.50	21.00	25.00	110	735	4,850	15,500	51,500	58,500	—
1897S	5,825,000	16.90	16.80	19.00	23.10	24.00	58.00	115	175	620	26,500	—
1898	5,884,735	16.40	16.80	16.90	21.60	21.90	32.00	49.00	65.00	285	1,375	6,000
1898O	4,440,000	16.40	16.80	16.90	21.60	21.90	32.00	49.00	62.00	165	850	—
1898S	4,102,000	20.00	25.00	35.00	55.00	105	260	475	875	2,350	16,500	—
1899	330,846	170	185	215	240	275	320	370	515	1,010	2,775	6,000
1899O	12,290,000	16.40	16.80	16.90	20.00	21.90	32.00	48.00	62.00	165	1,325	—
1899S	2,562,000	21.00	26.00	37.50	62.50	125	320	480	800	1,875	19,000	—
1900	8,880,938	16.40	16.80	16.90	21.10	21.90	32.00	48.00	63.00	200	29,000	6,000
1900O	12,590,000	16.40	16.80	16.90	21.10	21.90	32.00	48.00	69.00	170	5,150	—
1900O/CC	Inc. above	37.50	47.50	62.50	100.00	190	350	925	1,400	3,250	19,000	—
1900S	3,540,000	16.40	21.00	25.00	37.50	85.00	325	420	600	1,525	29,000	—
1901	6,962,813	27.50	36.00	57.50	110	395	2,150	17,000	56,000	235,000	—	6,500
1901 doubled die reverse	Inc. above	275	450	900	2,000	3,850	—	—	—	—	—	—
1901O	13,320,000	16.40	16.80	16.90	21.10	21.90	32.00	48.00	65.00	205	9,200	—
1901S	2,284,000	19.50	21.00	31.50	46.00	220	470	700	1,075	3,750	16,850	—
1902	7,994,777	16.40	16.80	19.00	23.10	25.00	44.00	100.00	138	450	19,500	6,000
1902O	8,636,000	16.40	16.80	16.90	21.10	21.90	32.00	48.00	62.00	165	12,750	—
1902S	1,530,000	60.00	82.00	160	220	315	425	625	1,135	3,050	15,000	—
1903	4,652,755	48.00	50.00	52.00	58.00	60.00	75.00	92.00	125	320	29,750	6,000
1903O	4,450,000	325	350	375	400	415	425	450	475	735	5,800	—
1903S	1,241,000	95.00	130	215	425	2,100	4,400	7,000	8,500	10,850	40,000	—
1903S Micro S	Inc. above	135	225	450	1,150	3,000	—	—	—	—	—	—
1904	2,788,650	21.00	23.00	25.00	27.00	32.00	78.00	280	715	3,650	38,000	6,000
1904O	3,720,000	21.00	23.00	25.00	27.00	29.00	37.00	48.00	60.00	165	965	—
1904S	2,304,000	35.00	47.50	87.00	230	570	1,075	4,350	6,250	9,850	19,000	—
1921	44,690,000	15.40	15.80	15.90	19.10	19.90	23.00	35.00	44.00	175	11,000	—
1921D	20,345,000	15.40	15.80	15.90	19.60	21.00	45.00	56.00	155	420	10,000	—
1921S	21,695,000	15.40	15.80	15.90	19.10	20.00	34.00	69.00	170	965	31,000	—

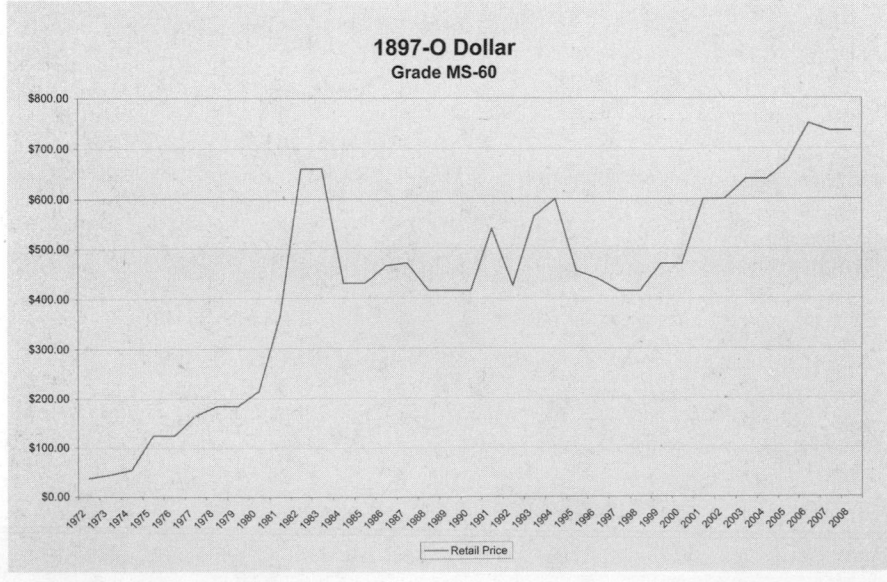

1897-O Dollar
Grade MS-60

DOLLAR

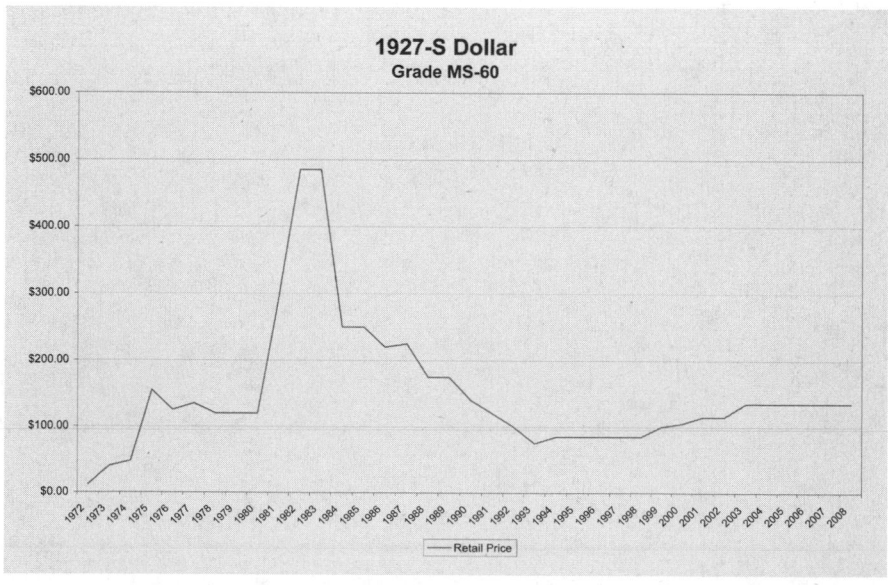

Peace Dollar

Liberty Head left obverse   Eagle facing right pearched on rock reverse

Mint mark

KM# 150 • 26.7300 g., 0.9000 **Silver**, 0.7734 oz. ASW, 38.1 mm. • **Designer:** Anthony DeFrancisci
Notes: Commonly called Peace dollars.

Date	Mintage	G-4	VG-8	F-12	VF-20	XF-40	AU-50	MS-60	MS-63	MS-64	MS-65
1921	1,006,473	100.00	125	135	140	150	170	245	545	850	2,450
1922	51,737,000	14.10	15.20	15.40	15.50	15.60	17.90	23.70	32.00	50.00	180
1922D	15,063,000	14.10	15.50	15.40	15.50	15.60	18.80	26.50	53.00	95.00	485
1922S	17,475,000	14.10	15.50	15.40	15.50	15.60	18.80	26.50	69.00	300	2,500
1923	30,800,000	14.10	15.20	15.40	15.50	1.60	17.90	23.70	32.00	50.00	170
1923D	6,811,000	14.10	16.00	16.50	17.00	18.00	22.00	52.00	135	290	1,300
1923S	19,020,000	14.10	15.50	15.40	15.50	15.60	18.80	28.50	74.00	375	6,850
1924	11,811,000	14.10	15.20	16.50	15.50	15.60	17.90	23.70	32.00	50.00	200
1924S	1,728,000	25.00	30.00	31.00	33.00	44.00	66.50	200	600	1,675	9,850
1925	10,198,000	14.10	15.20	16.50	15.50	15.60	17.90	23.00	32.00	50.00	200
1925S	1,610,000	15.00	19.50	21.00	25.00	29.00	46.00	75.00	210	1,050	21,500
1926	1,939,000	15.00	16.10	16.50	16.80	17.10	22.50	43.00	82.00	125	420
1926D	2,348,700	15.00	16.10	16.30	16.60	22.00	32.50	66.00	190	310	810
1926S	6,980,000	14.70	15.80	16.00	16.10	16.20	20.90	44.00	110	290	1,250
1927	848,000	25.00	29.00	32.00	33.00	38.00	50.00	70.00	185	440	3,650
1927D	1,268,900	24.00	28.00	30.00	31.00	34.00	80.00	145	365	1,000	5,150
1927S	866,000	24.00	28.00	31.00	32.00	35.00	80.00	135	445	1,575	11,350
1928	360,649	355	435	445	455	465	475	525	925	1,450	4,500
1928S Lg S	1,632,000	30.00	36.00	40.00	46.00	54.00	90.00	220	785	1,900	26,500
1928S Sm S	Inc. above	28.00	33.00	34.00	38.00	43.50	66.00	155	595	1,500	21,500
1934	954,057	15.00	19.50	20.00	21.00	22.50	46.00	120	245	465	965
1934D Lg D	1,569,500	17.00	20.00	21.00	23.00	26.00	60.00	165	600	900	3,000
1934D Sm D	Inc. above	15.00	16.10	19.50	21.00	22.00	46.00	135	500	725	1,925
1934S	1,011,000	26.00	31.00	48.00	85.00	200	500	1,750	3,850	6,250	8,650
1935	1,576,000	15.20	18.00	20.00	21.50	22.00	30.00	60.00	115	210	725
1935S	1,964,000	15.20	18.00	19.00	20.00	23.00	92.00	235	380	630	1,350

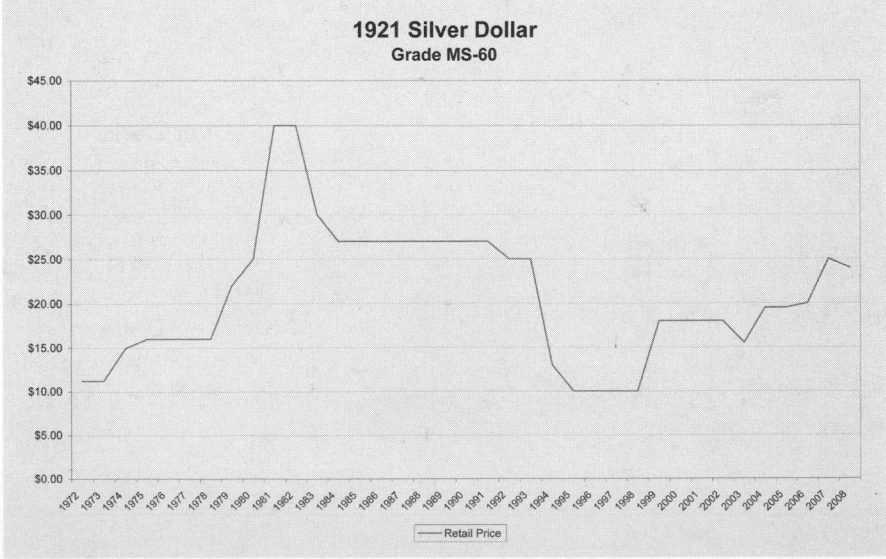

1921 Silver Dollar
Grade MS-60

Eisenhower Dollar

KM# 203 • 22.6800 g., **Copper-Nickel Clad Copper**, 38.1 mm. • **Designer:** Frank Gasparro

Date	Mintage	MS-63	Prf-65
1971	47,799,000	10.00	—
1971D	68,587,424	8.00	—
1972 Low Relief	75,890,000	6.50	—
1972 High Relief	Inc. above	175	—
1972 Modified High Relief	Inc. above	40.00	—
1972D	92,548,511	5.50	—
1973	2,000,000	14.00	—
1973D	2,000,000	15.00	—
1973S Proof	2,769,624	—	12.00
1974	27,366,000	5.50	—
1974D	35,466,000	7.00	—
1974S Proof	2,617,350	—	11.00

Eisenhower Dollar

KM# 203a • 24.5900 g., 0.4000 **Silver**, 0.3162 oz. ASW, 38.1 mm. • **Designer:** Frank Gasparro

Date	Mintage	MS-63	Prf-65
1971S	6,868,530	7.50	—
1971S Proof	4,265,234	—	11.00
1971S Peg Leg "R" Variety	Inc. above	—	17.00
1971S Partial Peg Leg "R" Variety	Inc. above	—	18.00
1972S	2,193,056	7.50	—
1972S Proof	1,811,631	—	14.00
1973S	1,833,140	8.50	—
1973S Proof	1,005,617	—	35.00
1974S	1,720,000	7.50	—
1974S Proof	1,306,579	—	14.00

Eisenhower Dollar
Bicentennial design, moon behind Liberty Bell reverse

Type I

Type II

KM# 206 • 22.6800 g., **Copper-Nickel Clad Copper**, 38.1 mm. • **Rev. Designer:** Dennis R. Williams **Notes:** In 1976 the lettering on the reverse was changed to thinner letters, resulting in the Type II variety for that year. The Type I variety was minted 1975 and dated 1976.

Date	Mintage	MS-63	Prf-65
1976 type I	117,337,000	9.00	—
1976 type II	Inc. above	5.00	—
1976D type I	103,228,274	6.00	—
1976D type II	Inc. above	5.00	—
1976S type I Proof	2,909,369	—	13.00
1976S type II Proof	4,149,730	—	9.00

Eisenhower Dollar
Bicentennial design, moon behind Liberty Bell reverse

KM# 206a • 24.5900 g., 0.4000 **Silver**, 0.3162 oz. ASW • **Rev. Designer:** Dennis R. Williams

Date	Mintage	MS-63	Prf-65
1976S	4,908,319	12.50	—
1976S Proof	3,998,621	—	20.00

Eisenhower Dollar
Regular design resumed reverse

KM# A203 • **Copper-Nickel Clad Copper**, 38.1 mm. •

Date	Mintage	MS-63	Prf-65
1977	12,596,000	7.00	—
1977D	32,983,006	7.00	—
1977S Proof	3,251,152	—	10.00
1978	25,702,000	5.00	—
1978D	33,012,890	5.00	—
1978S	—	—	12.00

Susan B. Anthony Dollar
**Susan B. Anthony bust right obverse
Eagle landing on moon, symbolic of Apollo
manned moon landing reverse**

KM# 207 • 8.1000 g., **Copper-Nickel Clad
Copper**, 26.5 mm. • **Designer:** Frank Gasparro
Edge Desc: Reeded **Notes:** The 1979-S and 1981-
S Type II coins have a clearer mint mark than the
Type I varieties for those years.

Date	Mintage	MS-63	Prf-65
1979P Near date	360,222,000	70.00	—
1979P	Inc. above	2.50	—
1979D	288,015,744	3.00	—
1979S Proof, Type I	3,677,175	—	8.00
1979S Proof, Type II	Inc. above	—	110
1979S	109,576,000	3.00	—
1980P	27,610,000	3.00	—
1980D	41,628,708	2.00	—
1980S	20,422,000	3.50	—
1980S Proof	3,547,030	—	8.00
1981P	3,000,000	7.50	—
1981D	3,250,000	7.50	—
1981S	3,492,000	7.50	—
1981S Proof, Type I	4,063,083	—	8.00
1981S Proof, Type II	Inc. above	—	230
1999P	29,592,000	4.00	—
1999P Proof; *maximum mintage	750,000	—	25.00
1999D	11,776,000	4.00	—

Sacagawea Dollar
**Sacagawea bust right,
with baby on back obverse
Eagle in flight left reverse**

KM# 310 • 8.0700 g., **Copper-Zinc-Manganese-
Nickel Clad Copper**, 26.4 mm. •

Date	Mintage	MS-63	Prf-65
2000P	767,140,000	2.00	—
2000D	518,916,000	2.00	—
2000S	4,048,865	—	10.00
2001P	62,468,000	2.00	—
2001D	70,909,500	2.00	—
2001S	3,084,600	—	100.00
2002P	3,865,610	2.00	—
2002D	3,732,000	2.00	—
2002S	3,157,739	—	28.50
2003P	3,090,000	3.00	—
2003D	3,090,000	3.00	—
2003S	3,116,590	—	20.00
2004P	2,660,000	2.50	—
2004D	2,660,000	2.50	—
2004S	—	—	22.50
2005P	2,520,000	2.50	—
2005D	2,520,000	2.50	—
2005S	—	—	22.50
2006P	4,900,000	2.50	—
2006D	2,800,000	5.00	—
2006S	—	—	22.50
2007P	—	2.50	—
2007D	—	2.50	—
2007S	—	—	22.50

GOLD

Liberty Head - Type 1
Liberty head left within circle of stars obverse   Value, date within 3/4 wreath reverse

KM# 73 • 1.6720 g., 0.9000 **Gold**, 0.0484 oz. AGW, 13 mm. • **Rev. Legend:** UNITED STATES OF
AMERICA **Designer:** James B. Longacre **Notes:** On the "closed wreath" varieties of 1849, the wreath on the
reverse extends closer to the numeral 1.

Date	Mintage	F-12	VF-20	XF-40	AU-50	MS-60
1849 open wreath	688,567	120	175	220	300	650
1849 small head, no L	—	—	—	—	—	—
1849 closed wreath	Inc. above	120	160	200	215	260
1849C closed wreath	11,634	800	950	1,450	2,400	8,850
1849C open wreath	Inc. above	135,000	240,000	320,000	475,000	600,000
1849D open wreath	21,588	1,050	1,300	1,875	2,600	6,000
1849O open wreath	215,000	140	185	265	335	800
1850	481,953	120	160	200	295	260
1850C	6,966	900	1,150	1,600	2,350	9,000
1850D	8,382	1,050	1,250	1,725	2,950	12,500
1850O	14,000	200	275	390	775	3,300
1851	3,317,671	120	160	200	215	260
1851C	41,267	840	1,150	1,500	1,700	3,150
1851D	9,882	1,000	1,250	1,675	2,500	5,650
1851O	290,000	160	195	240	265	775
1852	2,045,351	120	160	200	215	260
1852C	9,434	845	1,040	1,400	1,700	5,100

DOLLAR

Date	Mintage	F-12	VF-20	XF-40	AU-50	MS-60
1852D	6,360	1,025	1,250	1,675	2,300	10,000
1852O	140,000	130	175	260	385	1,400
1853	4,076,051	120	160	200	215	260
1853C	11,515	900	1,100	1,400	2,000	5,600
1853D	6,583	1,040	1,250	1,700	2,650	9,700
1853O	290,000	135	160	235	270	665
1854	736,709	120	160	200	215	260
1854D	2,935	1,050	1,400	2,350	6,000	13,000
1854S	14,632	260	360	525	775	2,450

Indian Head - Type 2

Indian head with headdress left obverse   Value, date within wreath reverse

KM# 83 • 1.6720 g., 0.9000 **Gold**, 0.0484 oz. AGW, 15 mm. • **Obv. Legend** UNITED STATES OF AMERICA **Designer:** James B. Longacre

Date	Mintage	F-12	VF-20	XF-40	AU-50	MS-60
1854	902,736	225	310	440	575	2,350
1855	758,269	225	310	440	575	2,350
1855C	9,803	975	1,450	3,750	11,500	33,000
1855D	1,811	3,250	4,750	9,800	22,000	48,000
1855O	55,000	345	440	600	1,500	7,800
1856S	24,600	525	820	1,325	2,500	8,650

Indian Head - Type 3

Indian head with headdress left obverse   Value, date within wreath reverse

KM# 86 • 1.6720 g., 0.9000 **Gold**, 0.0484 oz. AGW, 15 mm. • **Obv. Legend** UNITED STATES OF AMERICA **Designer:** James B. Longacre **Notes:** The 1856 varieties are distinguished by whether the 5 in the date is slanted or upright. The 1873 varieties are distinguished by the amount of space between the upper left and lower left serifs in the 3.

Date	Mintage	F-12	VF-20	XF-40	AU-50	MS-60	Prf-65
1856 upright 5	1,762,936	140	170	225	250	460	—
1856 slanted 5	Inc. above	135	160	200	215	310	55,000
1856D	1,460	2,350	3,650	5,800	8,000	32,000	—
1857	774,789	125	155	200	215	310	32,000
1857C	13,280	900	1,150	1,750	3,750	13,250	—
1857D	3,533	1,000	1,300	2,300	4,400	11,000	—
1857S	10,000	260	520	650	1,300	6,200	—
1858	117,995	125	155	200	215	310	28,500
1858D	3,477	1,025	1,250	1,600	2,850	10,000	—
1858S	10,000	300	400	575	1,450	5,350	—
1859	168,244	125	155	200	215	310	17,000
1859C	5,235	885	1,050	1,700	4,250	9,850	—
1859D	4,952	1,050	1,500	2,100	3,250	10,500	—
1859S	15,000	210	265	525	1,250	5,500	—
1860	36,668	125	155	200	215	310	16,500
1860D	1,566	2,150	2,500	4,200	7,000	13,500	—
1860S	13,000	300	380	500	750	1,650	—
1861	527,499	125	155	200	215	310	14,850
1861D mintage unrecorded	—	4,950	7,000	11,000	21,000	41,500	—
1862	1,361,390	125	155	200	215	310	15,000
1863	6,250	370	500	925	2,100	3,900	18,000
1864	5,950	290	370	475	825	1,050	18,000
1865	3,725	290	370	590	750	1,600	18,000
1866	7,130	300	385	470	685	1,025	18,000
1867	5,250	325	420	525	675	1,160	17,500
1868	10,525	265	290	415	500	1,025	19,000
1869	5,925	315	460	530	725	1,150	17,000
1870	6,335	255	290	410	500	875	16,000
1870S	3,000	300	475	785	1,250	2,650	—
1871	3,930	260	290	390	480	750	18,000
1872	3,530	260	295	400	480	975	18,500
1873 closed 3	125,125	325	425	825	950	1,650	—
1873 open 3	Inc. above	125	155	200	215	310	—
1874	198,820	125	155	200	215	310	30,000

Date	Mintage	F-12	VF-20	XF-40	AU-50	MS-60	Prf-65
1875	420	1,650	2,350	4,650	5,200	10,000	32,500
1876	3,245	240	300	360	475	725	16,750
1877	3,920	150	210	340	460	725	18,000
1878	3,020	195	250	365	480	675	15,500
1879	3,030	170	225	285	3,300	525	14,000
1880	1,636	150	180	215	245	425	14,000
1881	7,707	150	180	215	245	410	11,500
1882	5,125	160	185	215	245	410	10,500
1883	11,007	150	175	215	245	410	11,000
1884	6,236	150	175	215	245	410	10,000
1885	12,261	150	175	215	245	410	10,000
1886	6,016	150	175	215	245	410	10,000
1887	8,543	150	175	215	245	410	10,000
1888	16,580	150	175	215	245	410	10,000
1889	30,729	150	175	215	245	340	10,000

Presidents

George Washington

KM# 401 • 8.0700 g., **Copper-Zinc-Manganese-Nickel Clad Copper**, 26.4 mm. • **Edge Lettering:** "IN GOD WE TRUST" date and mint mark, "E PLURIBUS UNUM" **Notes:** Date and mint mark incuse on edge.

Date	Mintage	MS-63	MS-65	Prf-65
2007P	176,680,000	2.00	—	—
2007 Plain edge error	Inc. above	75.00	—	—
2007D	163,680,000	2.00	—	—
2007S	—	—	—	—

James Madison

KM# 404 • 8.0700 g., **Copper-Zinc-Manganese-Nickel Clad Copper**, 26.4 mm. • **Notes:** Date and mint mark incuse on edge.

Date	Mintage	MS-63	MS-65	Prf-65
2007P	—	2.00	3.00	—
2007D	—	2.00	3.00	—
2007S	—	—	—	—

John Adams

KM# 402 • 8.0700 g., **Copper-Zinc-Manganese-Nickel Clad Copper**, 26.4 mm. • **Notes:** Date and mint mark incuse on edge.

Date	Mintage	MS-63	MS-65	Prf-65
2007P	112,420,000	2.00	5.00	—
2007P Double edge lettering	Inc. above	250	—	—
2007D	102,810,000	2.00	5.00	—
2007S	—	—	—	8.00

Thomas Jefferson

KM# 403 • 8.0700 g., **Copper-Zinc-Manganese-Nickel Clad Copper**, 26.4 mm. • **Notes:** Date and mint mark incuse on edge.

Date	Mintage	MS-63	MS-65	Prf-65
2007P	—	2.00	3.00	—
2007D	—	2.00	3.00	—
2007S	—	—	—	—

Andrew Jackson

KM# 428 • 8.0700 g., **Copper-Zinc-Manganese-Nickel Clad Copper** •

Date	Mintage	MS-63	MS-65	Prf-65
2008P	—	2.00	3.00	—
2008D	—	2.00	3.00	—
2008S	—	2.00	3.00	—

James Monroe

KM# 426 • 8.0700 g., **Copper-Zinc-Manganese-Nickel Clad Copper** •

Date	Mintage	MS-63	MS-65	Prf-65
2008P	—	2.00	3.00	—
2008D	—	2.00	3.00	—
2008S	—	—	—	—

John Quincy Adams

KM# 427 • 8.0700 g., **Copper-Zinc-Manganese-Nickel Clad Copper** •

Date	Mintage	MS-63	MS-65	Prf-65
2008P	—	2.00	5.00	—
2008D	—	2.00	5.00	—
2008S	—	—	—	8.00

Martin van Buren

KM# 429 • 8.0700 g., **Copper-Zinc-Manganese-Nickel Clad Copper** •

Date	Mintage	MS-63	MS-65	Prf-65
2008P	—	2.00	5.00	—
2008D	—	2.00	5.00	—
2008S	—	—	—	8.00

DOLLAR

$2.50 QUARTER EAGLE

GOLD

Liberty Cap

Liberty cap on head, right, flanked by stars obverse   Heraldic eagle reverse

KM# 27 • 4.3700 g., 0.9160 **Gold**, 0.1287 oz. AGW, 20 mm. • **Obv. Legend** LIBERTY **Rev. Legend:** UNITED STATES OF AMERICA **Designer:** Robert Scot **Notes:** The 1796 "no stars" variety does not have stars on the obverse. The 1804 varieties are distinguished by the number of stars on the obverse.

Date	Mintage	F-12	VF-20	XF-40	MS-60
1796 no stars	963	30,000	42,000	70,000	165,000
1796 stars	432	28,000	40,000	63,000	140,000
1797	427	17,000	23,000	27,500	120,000
1798	1,094	4,750	10,000	12,500	55,000
1802/1	3,035	4,400	0,000	9,500	32,000
1804 13-star reverse	3,327	23,500	36,500	72,000	200,000
1804 14-star reverse	Inc. above	4,800	7,400	9,000	27,500
1805	1,781	6,000	7,500	9,000	21,000
1806/4	1,616	5,750	8,000	9,500	23,000
1806/5	Inc. above	6,000	8,000	18,000	77,000
1807	6,812	5,500	7,000	9.00	21,000

Turban Head

Turban on head left flanked by stars obverse   Banner above eagle reverse

KM# 40 • 4.3700 g., 0.9160 **Gold**, 0.1287 oz. AGW, 20 mm. • **Rev. Legend:** UNITED STATES OF AMERICA **Designer:** John Reich

Date	Mintage	F-12	VF-20	XF-40	MS-60
1808	2,710	22,500	31,000	45,000	125,000

Turban Head

Turban on head left within circle of stars obverse   Banner above eagle reverse

KM# 46 • 4.3700 g., 0.9160 **Gold**, 0.1287 oz. AGW, 18.5 mm. • **Rev. Legend:** UNITED STATES OF AMERICA **Designer:** John Reich

Date	Mintage	F-12	VF-20	XF-40	MS-60
1821	6,448	5,500	6,250	7,500	23,000
1824/21	2,600	5,500	6,250	7,250	22,000
1825	4,434	5,500	6,500	7,800	21,000
1826/25	760	6,000	7,000	8,500	36,000
1827	2,800	5,500	7,500	9,000	22,500

$2.50 GOLD

Turban Head
Turban on head left within circle of stars obverse   Banner above eagle reverse

KM# 49 • 4.3700 g., 0.9160 **Gold**, 0.1287 oz. AGW, 18.2 mm. • **Rev. Legend:** UNITED STATES OF AMERICA **Designer:** John Reich

Date	Mintage	F-12	VF-20	XF-40	MS-60
1829	3,403	4,900	5,850	6,700	12,500
1830	4,540	4,950	5,850	6,700	12,500
1831	4,520	4,950	5,850	6,700	12,500
1832	4,400	4,950	5,850	6,700	12,500
1833	4,160	4,950	5,850	6,800	12,750
1834	4,000	8,800	12,000	16,000	36,000

Classic Head
Classic head left within circle of stars obverse   No motto above eagle reverse

KM# 56 • 4.1800 g., 0.8990 **Gold**, 0.1208 oz. AGW, 18.2 mm. • **Rev. Legend:** UNITED STATES OF AMERICA **Designer:** William Kneass

Date	Mintage	VF-20	XF-40	AU-50	MS-60	MS-65
1834	112,234	475	675	965	3,300	27,000
1835	131,402	475	675	950	3,200	32,000
1836	547,986	475	675	940	3,100	29,000
1837	45,080	500	800	1,500	4,000	35,000
1838	47,030	500	625	1,100	3,200	30,000
1838C	7,880	1,700	3,000	8,000	27,000	55,000
1839	27,021	500	900	1,900	5,500	—
1839C	18,140	1,500	2,650	4,500	26,500	—
1839/8	Inc. above	—	—	—	—	—
1839D	13,674	1,750	3,450	8,000	24,000	—
1839O	17,781	700	1,100	2,500	7,250	—

Coronet Head
Coronet head left within circle of stars obverse   No motto above eagle reverse

1848 "Cal." reverse

KM# 72 • 4.1800 g., 0.9000 **Gold**, 0.1209 oz. AGW, 18 mm. • **Rev. Legend:** UNITED STATES OF AMERICA **Designer:** Christian Gobrecht **Notes:** Varieties for 1843 are distinguished by the size of the numerals in the date. One 1848 variety has "Cal." inscribed on the reverse, indicating it was made from California gold. The 1873 "closed-3" and "open-3" varieties are distinguished by the amount of space between the upper left and lower left serifs in the 3 in the date.

Date	Mintage	F-12	VF-20	XF-40	AU-50	MS-60	Prf-65
1840	18,859	160	190	900	2,950	6,000	—
1840C	12,822	975	1,400	1,600	6,000	13,000	—
1840D	3,532	2,000	3,200	8,700	15,500	35,000	—
1840O	33,580	250	400	825	2,100	11,000	—
1841	—	—	48,000	85,000	96,000	—	—
1841C	10,281	750	1,500	2,000	3,500	18,500	—
1841D	4,164	950	2,100	4,750	11,000	25,000	—
1842	2,823	500	900	2,600	6,500	20,000	140,000
1842C	6,729	700	1,700	3,500	8,000	27,000	—
1842D	4,643	900	2,100	4,000	11,750	38,000	—
1842O	19,800	240	370	1,200	2,500	14,000	—
1843	100,546	160	180	450	915	3,000	140,000
1843C small date, Crosslet 4	26,064	1,500	2,400	5,500	9,000	29,000	—
1843C large date, Plain 4	Inc. above	800	1,600	2,200	3,500	8,800	—

Date	Mintage	F-12	VF-20	XF-40	AU-50	MS-60	Prf-65
1843D small date, Crosslet 4	36,209	920	1,800	2,350	3,250	10,500	—
1843O small date, Crosslet 4	288,002	165	190	250	350	1,700	—
1843O large date, Plain 4	76,000	210	260	465	1,600	8,000	—
1844	6,784	225	365	850	2,000	7,500	140,000
1844C	11,622	700	1,600	2,600	7,000	20,000	—
1844D	17,332	785	1,650	2,200	3,200	7,800	—
1845	91,051	190	250	350	600	1,275	140,000
1845D	19,460	950	1,900	2,600	3,900	15,000	—
1845O	4,000	550	1,050	2,300	9,000	20,000	—
1846	21,598	200	275	500	950	6,000	140,000
1846C	4,808	725	1,575	3,500	8,950	18,750	—
1846D	19,303	800	1,400	2,000	3,000	12,000	—
1846O	66,000	170	280	400	1,150	6,500	—
1847	29,814	140	220	360	825	3,800	—
1847C	23,226	900	1,800	2,300	3,500	7,250	—
1847D	15,784	800	1,650	2,250	3,250	10,500	—
1847O	124,000	160	240	400	1,000	4,000	—
1848	7,497	315	500	850	2,400	7,000	125,000
1848 "Cal."	1,389	8,000	15,000	26,000	36,000	50,000	—
1848C	16,788	800	1,600	2,100	3,800	13,750	—
1848D	13,771	1,000	2,000	2,500	4,500	12,000	—
1849	23,294	180	275	475	1,000	2,600	—
1849C	10,220	800	1,475	2,150	5,150	23,500	—
1849D	10,945	950	2,000	2,500	4,500	18,000	—
1850	252,923	160	180	275	350	1,100	—
1850C	9,148	800	1,500	2,100	3,400	17,500	—
1850D	12,148	950	1,800	2,500	4,000	15,000	—
1850O	84,000	170	225	450	1,200	4,900	—
1851	1,372,748	145	180	200	225	325	—
1851C	14,923	900	1,750	2,300	4,800	13,000	—
1851D	11,264	950	1,700	2,600	4,200	13,000	—
1851O	148,000	160	200	220	1,000	4,650	—
1852	1,159,681	150	175	200	250	325	—
1852C	9,772	675	1,500	2,100	4,250	18,000	—
1852D	4,078	840	1,600	2,800	7,250	17,000	—
1852O	140,000	160	190	300	950	5,000	—
1853	1,404,668	150	180	200	225	350	—
1853D	3,178	950	2,100	3,400	4,900	18,000	—
1854	596,258	150	180	215	240	350	—
1854C	7,295	800	1,500	2,400	5,000	14,750	—
1854D	1,760	1,750	2,900	6,950	12,000	27,500	—
1854O	153,000	150	185	240	425	1,600	—
1854S	246	32,500	70,000	115,000	215,000	300,000	—
1855	235,480	145	180	225	250	360	—
1855C	3,677	800	1,675	3,300	6,500	25,000	—
1855D	1,123	1,750	3,250	7,500	24,000	46,000	—
1856	384,240	145	175	210	250	390	75,000
1856C	7,913	650	1,150	2,200	4,400	15,500	—
1856D	874	3,500	6,700	12,500	30,000	72,500	—
1856O	21,100	180	240	750	1,500	8,000	—
1856S	71,120	160	250	375	950	4,500	—
1857	214,130	150	190	205	230	380	75,000
1857D	2,364	875	1,750	2,900	3,850	13,000	—
1857O	34,000	155	210	350	1,100	4,600	—
1857S	69,200	160	210	340	900	5,500	—
1858	47,377	150	200	250	360	1,350	59,000
1858C	9,056	825	1,500	2,100	3,350	9,250	—
1859	39,444	150	185	265	400	1,250	61,000
1859D	2,244	1,000	1,900	3,300	4,900	20,000	—
1859S	15,200	200	350	1,000	2,800	7,000	—
1860	22,675	150	200	265	470	1,300	58,000
1860C	7,469	815	1,550	2,200	3,950	21,000	—
1860S	35,600	170	250	675	1,200	4,000	—
1861	1,283,878	150	180	210	230	325	31,500
1861S	24,000	200	400	1,000	3,700	7,400	—
1862	98,543	160	200	300	520	1,375	32,500
1862/1	Inc. above	450	950	2,000	4,000	8,000	—
1862S	8,000	500	1,000	2,100	4,500	17,000	—
1863	30	—	—	—	—	—	95,000
1863S	10,800	250	500	1,500	3,200	13,500	—
1864	2,874	2,500	5,500	8,800	21,500	37,500	27,000
1865	1,545	2,400	6,000	8,000	19,000	38,000	30,000
1865S	23,376	160	225	650	1,650	5,000	—
1866	3,110	650	1,300	3,500	6,000	11,500	25,000
1866S	38,960	180	300	650	1,600	6,250	—
1867	3,250	190	385	900	1,250	4,800	27,000
1867S	28,000	170	250	625	1,750	4,000	—
1868	3,625	170	235	400	675	1,600	27,000
1868S	34,000	150	200	300	1,100	4,000	—

$2.50 GOLD

Date	Mintage	F-12	VF-20	XF-40	AU-50	MS-60	Prf-65
1869	4,345	170	250	450	715	3,000	24,500
1869S	29,500	160	240	440	775	5,000	—
1870	4,555	165	225	425	740	3,800	22,750
1870S	16,000	155	215	400	800	4,900	—
1871	5,350	160	230	325	600	2,200	24,000
1871S	22,000	150	185	280	530	2,200	—
1872	3,030	200	400	750	1,100	4,650	22,000
1872S	18,000	155	225	415	900	4,500	—
1873 closed 3	178,025	155	170	210	260	535	22,500
1873 open 3	Inc. above	155	165	195	250	300	—
1873S	27,000	160	225	425	900	2,800	—
1874	3,940	170	240	380	720	2,100	32,000
1875	420	1,750	3,500	5,000	11,000	21,500	32,500
1875S	11,600	150	200	300	850	4,500	—
1876	4,221	170	275	675	925	3,200	22,000
1876S	5,000	170	225	525	980	3,300	—
1877	1,652	275	400	800	1,100	3,250	22,000
1877S	35,400	150	160	200	230	635	—
1878	286,260	150	160	200	225	275	26,000
1878S	178,000	150	160	200	235	340	—
1879	88,990	150	160	195	235	300	26,000
1879S	43,500	155	200	300	550	2,150	—
1880	2,996	170	210	335	600	1,300	20,250
1881	691	900	2,200	3,400	5,000	10,000	19,000
1882	4,067	160	210	290	400	700	15,000
1883	2,002	175	220	440	1,000	2,600	15,500
1884	2,023	175	225	420	600	1,600	16,000
1885	887	400	715	1,800	2,500	4,400	15,000
1886	4,088	170	190	270	425	1,100	16,500
1887	6,282	175	200	245	325	700	16,500
1888	16,098	160	180	240	285	340	15,000
1889	17,648	155	180	230	250	325	17,000
1890	8,813	170	190	240	280	500	13,750
1891	11,040	165	175	215	230	400	14,000
1892	2,545	170	180	250	325	765	15,000
1893	30,106	165	175	200	240	300	14,000
1894	4,122	170	180	225	325	800	13,500
1895	6,199	150	175	225	275	395	12,500
1896	19,202	150	175	225	235	285	12,500
1897	29,904	150	175	210	235	285	12,500
1898	24,165	150	175	210	235	285	12,500
1899	27,350	150	175	210	235	300	12,500
1900	67,205	150	175	240	320	415	12,500
1901	91,322	150	175	200	235	275	12,500
1902	133,733	150	170	200	235	275	12,500
1903	201,257	150	170	200	235	275	13,000
1904	160,960	150	170	200	240	275	12,500
1905	217,944	150	170	200	240	275	12,500
1906	176,490	150	170	200	240	275	12,500
1907	336,448	150	170	200	240	275	12,500

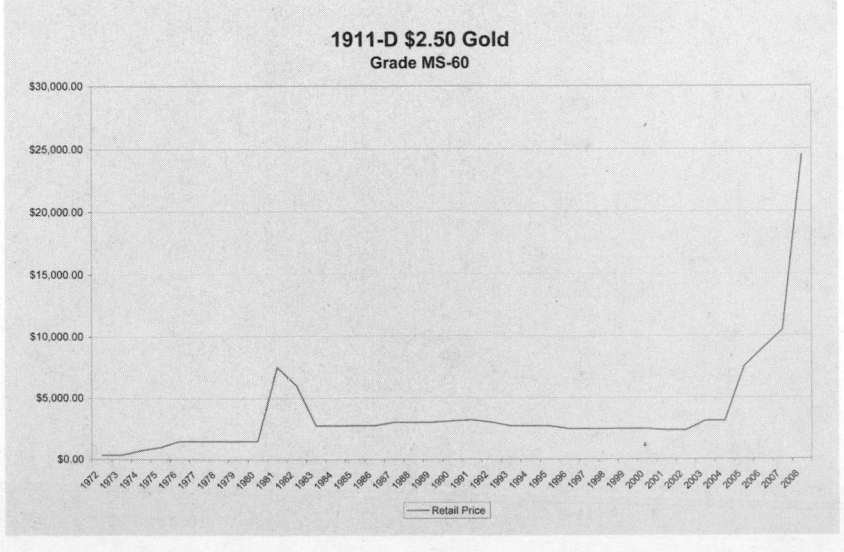

1911-D $2.50 Gold
Grade MS-60

— Retail Price

Indian Head

KM# 128 • 4.1800 g., 0.9000 **Gold**, 0.1209 oz. AGW, 18 mm. • **Designer:** Bela Lyon Pratt

Date	Mintage	VF-20	XF-40	AU-50	MS-60	MS-63	MS-65	Prf-65
1908	565,057	165	220	230	275	1,800	8,500	16,000
1909	441,899	175	220	230	275	2,600	11,000	30,000
1910	492,682	175	220	230	275	2,600	12,500	18,000
1911	704,191	175	220	230	280	1,600	12,500	16,000
1911D	55,680	2,500	3,650	5,000	9,850	24,500	90,000	16,000
1912	616,197	175	220	230	275	2,800	16,000	16,000
1913	722,165	175	220	230	280	1,725	14,000	16,500
1914	240,117	175	235	260	480	8,500	34,000	16,500
1914D	448,000	175	220	230	300	2,650	40,000	23,000
1915	606,100	175	220	230	275	1,650	13,500	15,250
1925D	578,000	175	220	230	275	1,450	7,000	—
1926	446,000	175	220	230	275	1,450	7,000	—
1927	388,000	175	220	230	275	1,450	7,000	—
1928	416,000	175	220	230	275	1,450	7,000	—
1929	532,000	180	230	250	340	1,600	10,000	—

$3

GOLD

Indian head with headdress, left obverse   Value, date within wreath reverse

KM# 84 • 5.0150 g., 0.9000 **Gold**, 0.1451 oz. AGW, 20.5 mm. • **Obv. Legend** UNITED STATES OF AMERICA **Designer:** James B. Longacre **Notes:** The 1873 "closed-3" and "open-3" varieties are distinguished by the amount of space between the upper left and lower left serifs of the 3 in the date.

Date	Mintage	VF-20	XF-40	AU-50	MS-60	MS-65	Prf-65
1854	138,618	850	1,100	2,000	3,400	18,000	125,000
1854D	1,120	8,300	15,000	29,000	65,000	—	—
1854O	24,000	1,000	2,000	4,000	20,000	—	—
1855	50,555	900	1,100	2,000	3,300	32,000	120,000
1855S	6,600	1,025	2,150	5,700	25,000	—	—
1856	26,010	880	1,100	2,150	3,500	27,000	—
1856S	34,500	900	1,500	2,350	10,000	—	—
1857	20,891	900	1,100	2,100	3,500	—	62,500
1857S	14,000	950	2,200	5,500	18,000	—	—
1858	2,133	950	1,800	3,000	9,000	—	62,500
1859	15,638	900	1,800	1,800	3,000	—	60,000
1860	7,155	900	1,600	2,000	3,600	21,000	46,000
1860S	7,000	950	2,000	7,000	17,000	—	—
1861	6,072	925	1,500	2,200	3,600	27,000	46,000
1862	5,785	925	1,850	2,200	3,600	28,000	46,500
1863	5,039	900	1,450	2,200	3,600	20,000	43,000
1864	2,680	950	1,500	2,300	3,600	29,000	42,000
1865	1,165	1,350	2,500	6,000	10,000	39,000	40,000
1866	4,030	970	1,100	2,000	3,600	27,500	42,000
1867	2,650	950	1,100	2,400	4,000	28,000	41,500
1868	4,875	740	1,100	2,100	3,000	22,000	42,000
1869	2,525	1,150	2,200	2,600	4,000	—	46,000
1870	3,535	1,000	1,500	2,400	5,000	—	47,000
1870S unique	—	—	—	—	—	—	—
Note: H. W. Bass Collection. AU50, cleaned. Est. value, $1,250,000.							
1871	1,330	1,000	1,500	2,000	4,000	27,500	47,000
1872	2,030	900	1,800	2,250	3,600	—	33,000
1873 open 3, proof only	25	3,300	5,000	8,700	—	—	—
1873 closed 3, mintage unknown	—	4,000	6,000	10,000	—	—	42,000
1874	41,820	800	1,300	1,900	3,000	16,000	42,000
1875 proof only	20	20,000	28,000	47,500	—	—	175,000
1876	45	6,000	10,000	16,500	—	—	60,000
1877	1,488	1,200	2,900	5,200	12,000	60,000	43,500

$3 GOLD

Date	Mintage	VF-20	XF-40	AU-50	MS-60	MS-65	Prf-65
1878	82,324	800	1,300	1,900	3,000	16,000	43,000
1879	3,030	850	1,300	2,000	2,650	19,000	32,000
1880	1,036	850	1,700	3,000	4,000	20,000	29,500
1881	554	1,400	2,750	5,500	8,000	24,000	25,000
1882	1,576	925	1,400	2,000	3,500	22,000	25,000
1883	989	1,000	1,600	3,500	3,600	24,000	25,000
1884	1,106	1,250	1,700	2,200	3,600	24,000	24,000
1885	910	1,300	1,800	2,850	3,900	24,000	25,000
1886	1,142	1,250	1,800	3,000	4,000	20,000	24,000
1887	6,160	900	1,300	2,000	3,000	18,000	21,000
1888	5,291	950	1,500	2,000	3,300	20,000	23,000
1889	2,429	925	1,300	1,700	3,100	18,000	22,000

$5 HALF EAGLE

GOLD
Liberty Cap
Liberty cap on head, right, flanked by stars obverse   Heraldic eagle reverse

KM# 19 • 8.7500 g., 0.9160 **Gold**, 0.2577 oz. AGW, 25 mm. • **Obv. Legend** LIBERTY **Rev. Legend:** UNITED STATES OF AMERICA **Designer:** Robert Scot **Notes:** From 1795 through 1798, varieties exist with either a "small eagle" or a "large heraldic eagle" on the reverse. After 1798, only the heraldic eagle was used. Two 1797 varieties are distinguished by the size of the 8 in the date. 1806 varieties are distinguished by whether the top of the 6 has a serif.

Date	Mintage	F-12	VF-20	XF-40	MS-60
1795 small eagle	8,707	11,500	17,000	19,000	47,000
1795 large eagle	Inc. above	8,800	14,000	20,000	75,000
1796/95 small eagle	6,196	12,000	17,500	24,000	75,000
1797/95 large eagle	3,609	8,600	14,000	22,000	150,000
1797 15 stars, small eagle	Inc. above	14,000	21,000	35,000	150,000
1797 16 stars, small eagle	Inc. above	13,000	17,500	34,000	145,000
1798 small eagle	—	90,000	155,000	275,000	—
1798 large eagle, small 8	24,867	3,300	4,500	6,000	21,000
1798 large eagle, large 8, 13-star reverse	Inc. above	3,000	3,700	4,500	17,500
1798 large eagle, large 8, 14-star reverse	Inc. above	3,000	4,200	7,000	35,000
1799	7,451	3,000	3,800	5,300	16,500
1800	37,628	3,000	3,800	5,000	8,800
1802/1	53,176	3,000	4,000	4,300	8,900
1803/2	33,506	3,000	3,800	4,300	8,700
1804 small 8	30,475	3,000	3,800	4,300	8,700
1804 large 8	Inc. above	3,000	3,800	4,300	9,600
1805	33,183	3,000	3,800	4,300	8,600
1806 pointed 6	64,093	3,200	3,700	4,300	9,000
1806 round 6	Inc. above	3,000	3,700	4,300	8,600
1807	32,488	3,000	3,800	4,300	8,700

Turban Head
Capped draped bust, left, flanked by stars obverse   Healdic eagle reverse

KM# 38 • 8.7500 g., 0.9160 **Gold**, 0.2577 oz. AGW, 25 mm. • **Rev. Legend:** UNITED STATES OF AMERICA **Designer:** John Reich **Notes:** The 1810 varieties are distinguished by the size of the numerals in the date and the size of the 5 in the "5D." on the reverse. The 1811 varieties are distinguished by the size of the 5 in the "5D." on the reverse.

Date	Mintage	F-12	VF-20	XF-40	MS-60
1807	51,605	2,400	3,000	4,300	8,400
1808	55,578	2,400	3,000	4,300	8,250

Date	Mintage	F-12	VF-20	XF-40	MS-60
1808/7	Inc. above	3,000	3,800	4,500	13,000
1809/8	33,875	2,500	3,000	3,750	8,500
1810 small date, small 5	100,287	9,600	22,500	32,000	95,000
1810 small date, large 5	Inc. above	2,300	3,000	3,800	8,500
1810 large date, small 5	Inc. above	13,500	24,000	32,000	115
1810 large date, large 5	Inc. above	2,600	3,000	3,750	8,500
1811 small 5	99,581	2,600	3,000	3,750	8,500
1811 large 5	Inc. above	2,500	2,900	38,000	9,000
1812	58,087	2,400	2,850	4,000	8,000

Turban Head
Capped head, left, within circle of stars obverse   Healdic eagle reverse

KM# 43 • 8.7500 g., 0.9160 **Gold**, 0.2577 oz. AGW, 25 mm. • **Rev. Legend:** UNITED STATES OF
AMERICA **Designer:** John Reich **Notes:** 1820 varieties are distinguished by whether the 2 in the date has a
curved base or square base and by the size of the letters in the reverse inscriptions. 1832 varieties are
distinguished by whether the 2 in the date has a curved base or square base and by the number of stars on
the reverse. 1834 varieties are distinguished by whether the 4 has a serif at its far right.

Date	Mintage	F-12	VF-20	XF-40	MS-60
1813	95,428	2,400	2,750	3,800	7,800
1814/13	15,454	2,500	2,800	3,500	10,000
1815	635	27,000	33,000	70,000	—
Note: 1815, private sale, Jan. 1994, MS-61, $150,000					
1818	48,588	2,475	3,100	4,000	8,250
1819	51,723	9,600	16,500	275,000	62,000
1820 curved-base 2, small letters	263,806	2,600	3,000	4,500	11,000
1820 curved-base 2, large letters	Inc. above	2,600	3,000	4,150	20,000
1820 square-base 2	Inc. above	2,600	3,000	3,800	14,000
1821	34,641	7,000	15,000	23,000	70,000
1822 3 known	—	—	—	—	1,000,000
Note: 1822, private sale, 1993, VF-30, $1,000,000.					
1823	14,485	2,500	3,400	5,000	16,000
1824	17,340	5,000	10,000	16,000	38,000
1825/21	29,060	5,150	9,500	12,000	38,000
1825/24	Inc. above	—	—	250,000	350,000
Note: 1825/4, Bowers & Merena, March 1989, XF, $148,500.					
1826	18,069	4,000	7,500	9,300	32,000
1827	24,913	6,000	10,000	12,250	34,000
1828/7	28,029	15,000	27,500	41,000	125,000
Note: 1828/7, Bowers & Merena, June 1989, XF, $20,900.					
1828	Inc. above	6,000	13,000	21,000	7,000
1829 large planchet	57,442	15,000	27,500	50,000	135,000
Note: 1829 large planchet, Superior, July 1985, MS-65, $104,500.					
1829 small planchet	Inc. above	37,500	50,000	82,500	140,000
Note: 1829 small planchet, private sale, 1992 XF-45, $89,000.					
1830 small "5D."	126,351	14,500	17,500	21,000	40,000
1830 large "5D."	Inc. above	14,500	17,500	21,000	40,000
1831	140,594	14,500	17,500	21,000	42,500
1832 curved-base 2, 12 stars	157,487	50,000	80,000	135,000	—
1832 square-base 2, 13 stars	Inc. above	14,500	17,500	21,000	40,000
1833	193,630	14,500	17,500	21,000	40,000
1834 plain 4	50,141	14,500	17,500	21,000	40,000
1834 crosslet 4	Inc. above	14,500	17,500	21,000	40,000

Classic Head
Classic head, left, within circle of stars obverse   No motto above eagle reverse

KM# 57 • 8.3600 g., 0.8990 **Gold**, 0.2416 oz. AGW, 22.5 mm. • **Rev. Legend:** UNITED STATES OF AMERICA **Designer:** William Kneass **Notes:** 1834 varieties are distinguished by whether the 4 has a serif at its far right.

Date	Mintage	VF-20	XF-40	AU-50	MS-60	MS-65
1834 plain 4	658,028	390	550	950	3,000	48,000
1834 crosslet 4	Inc. above	1,650	2,900	6,000	20,000	—
1835	371,534	390	560	1,000	3,150	70,000
1836	553,147	390	550	1,000	2,950	70,000
1837	207,121	390	585	1,200	3,500	75,000
1838	286,588	390	5,500	1,000	3,700	58,000
1838C	17,179	2,200	4,000	13,000	38,500	—
1838D	20,583	2,000	3,850	9,000	25,000	—

Coronet Head
Coronet head, left, within circle of stars obverse   No motto above eagle reverse

KM# 69 • 8.3590 g., 0.9000 **Gold**, 0.2419 oz. AGW, 21.6 mm. • **Rev. Legend:** UNITED STATES OF AMERICA **Designer:** Christian Gobrecht **Notes:** Varieties for the 1842 Philadelphia strikes are distinguished by the size of the letters in the reverse inscriptions. Varieties for the 1842-C and -D strikes are distinguished by the size of the numerals in the date. Varieties for the 1843-O strikes are distinguished by the size of the letters in the reverse inscriptions.

Date	Mintage	F-12	VF-20	XF-40	MS-60	Prf-65
1839	118,143	250	275	480	4,000	—
1839/8 curved date	Inc. above	275	325	700	2,250	—
1839C	17,205	1,250	2,300	2,900	24,000	—
1839D	18,939	1,125	2,200	3,200	22,000	—
1840	137,382	200	230	360	3,700	—
1840C	18,992	1,200	2,200	3,000	26,000	—
1840D	22,896	1,200	2,200	3,000	16,000	—
1840O	40,120	200	365	875	11,000	—
1841	15,833	200	400	875	5,500	—
1841C	21,467	1,200	1,850	2,400	20,000	—
1841D	30,495	1,400	1,800	2,350	15,000	—
1841O 2 known	50	—	—	—	—	—
1842 small letters	27,578	200	345	1,100	—	—
1842 large letters	Inc. above	350	750	2,000	11,000	—
1842C small date	28,184	4,500	10,000	23,000	110,000	—
1842C large date	Inc. above	900	1,800	2,200	18,000	—
1842D small date	59,608	1,000	2,000	2,300	15,000	—
1842D large date	Inc. above	1,400	2,350	6,500	48,000	—
1842O	16,400	550	1,000	3,400	22,000	—
1843	611,205	200	230	330	1,850	—
1843C	44,201	1,250	1,850	2,500	14,000	—
1843D	98,452	1,250	1,950	2,600	13,000	—
1843O small letters	19,075	300	660	1,700	26,000	—
1843O large letters	82,000	200	265	1,175	12,000	—
1844	340,330	200	230	330	2,000	—
1844C	23,631	1,300	1,900	3,000	24,000	—
1844D	88,982	1,500	1,950	2,400	12,000	—
1844O	364,600	220	250	375	4,700	—
1845	417,099	200	235	260	2,000	—
1845D	90,629	1,300	1,900	2,400	12,500	—
1845O	41,000	235	415	800	9,900	—
1846	395,942	200	230	330	2,400	—
1846C	12,995	1,350	1,900	3,000	24,000	—
1846D	80,294	1,250	1,800	2,400	13,000	—
1846O	58,000	215	375	1,000	11,500	—

Date	Mintage	F-12	VF-20	XF-40	MS-60	Prf-65
1847	915,981	200	230	250	1,650	—
1847C	84,151	1,350	1,800	2,400	13,000	—
1847D	64,405	1,400	2,000	4,000	10,000	—
1847O	12,000	550	2,200	6,750	28,000	—
1848	260,775	200	230	275	1,500	—
1848C	64,472	1,400	1,900	2,250	19,250	—
1848D	47,465	1,450	2,000	2,350	14,500	—
1849	133,070	200	230	280	2,800	—
1849C	64,823	1,500	1,900	2,400	14,000	—
1849D	39,036	1,550	2,000	2,600	16,500	—
1850	64,491	200	300	625	4,250	—
1850C	63,591	1,350	1,850	2,300	14,000	—
1850D	43,984	1,450	1,950	2,500	33,000	—
1851	377,505	200	230	250	2,800	—
1851C	49,176	1,300	1,900	2,350	17,500	—
1851D	62,710	1,400	1,950	2,400	15,000	—
1851O	41,000	280	590	1,500	13,000	—
1852	573,901	200	230	260	1,400	—
1852C	72,574	1,350	1,900	2,450	7,750	—
1852D	91,584	1,450	2,000	2,450	13,000	—
1853	305,770	200	230	250	1,400	—
1853C	65,571	1,500	1,950	2,350	8,500	—
1853D	89,678	1,550	2,000	2,500	11,000	—
1854	160,675	200	230	260	2,000	—
1854C	39,283	1,400	1,900	2,300	14,000	—
1854D	56,413	1,400	1,875	2,200	11,500	—
1854O	46,000	225	300	525	8,250	—
1854S	268	—	—	—	—	—
Note: 1854S, Bowers & Merena, Oct. 1982, AU-55, $170,000.						
1855	117,098	200	230	250	1,800	—
1855C	39,788	1,400	1,900	2,300	16,000	—
1855D	22,432	1,500	1,950	2,400	19,000	—
1855O	11,100	315	675	2,100	20,000	—
1855S	61,000	200	390	1,000	15,500	—
1856	197,990	200	230	240	2,300	—
1856C	28,457	1,450	1,875	2,400	20,000	—
1856D	19,786	1,475	1,950	2,600	15,000	—
1856O	10,000	370	650	1,600	14,000	—
1856S	105,100	200	300	700	6,750	—
1857	98,188	200	230	260	1,600	123,500
1857C	31,360	1,400	1,900	2,500	9,500	—
1857D	17,046	1,500	2,000	2,650	14,500	—
1857O	13,000	340	640	1,400	15,000	—
1857S	87,000	200	300	700	11,000	—
1858	15,136	200	240	550	3,850	190,000
1858C	38,856	1,400	1,900	2,350	11,000	—
1858D	15,362	1,500	2,000	2,450	12,500	—
1858S	18,600	400	825	2,350	31,000	—

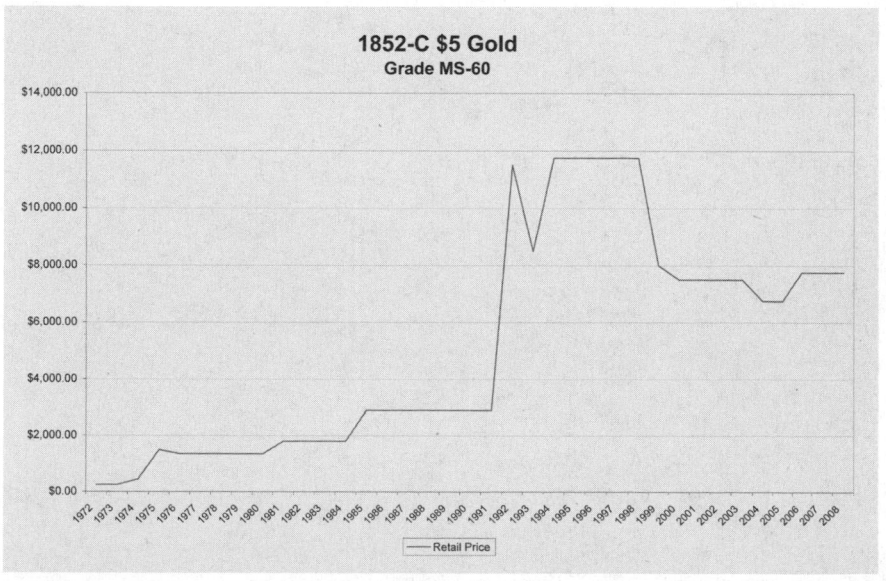

1852-C $5 Gold
Grade MS-60

Date	Mintage	F-12	VF-20	XF-40	MS-60	Prf-65
1859	16,814	200	325	625	7,000	—
1859C	31,847	1,400	1,900	2,450	16,000	—
1859D	10,366	1,600	2,150	2,600	16,000	—
1859S	13,220	615	1,800	4,150	30,000	—
1860	19,825	200	280	575	3,500	100,000
1860C	14,813	1,500	2,100	3,000	15,000	—
1860D	14,635	1,500	1,900	2,600	15,000	—
1860S	21,200	500	1,100	2,100	27,000	—
1861	688,150	200	230	245	1,450	100,000
1861C	6,879	1,500	2,400	3,900	25,000	—
1861D	1,597	3,000	4,700	7,000	50,000	—
1861S	18,000	500	1,100	4,500	36,500	—
1862	4,465	400	800	1,850	20,000	96,000
1862S	9,500	1,500	3,000	6,000	62,000	—
1863	2,472	450	1,200	3,750	27,500	90,000
1863S	17,000	600	1,450	4,100	35,500	—
1864	4,220	350	650	1,850	15,000	72,000
1864S	3,888	2,300	4,750	16,000	55,000	—
1865	1,295	500	1,450	4,100	20,000	82,500
1865S	27,612	475	1,400	2,400	20,000	—
1866S	9,000	750	1,750	4,000	40,000	—

Coronet Head

Coronet head, left, within circle of stars obverse   "In God We Trust" above eagle reverse

KM# 101 • 8.3590 g., 0.9000 **Gold**, 0.2419 oz. AGW, 21.6 mm. • **Rev. Legend:** UNITED STATES OF AMERICA **Designer:** Christian Gobrecht **Notes:** The 1873 "closed-3" and "open-3" varieties are known and are distinguished by the amount of space between the upper left and lower left serifs of the 3 in the date.

Date	Mintage	VF-20	XF-40	AU-50	MS-60	MS-63	MS-65	Prf-65
1866	6,730	800	1,650	3,500	16,500	—	—	70,000
1866S	34,920	900	2,600	8,800	25,000	—	—	—
1867	6,920	500	1,500	3,300	11,500	—	—	70,000
1867S	29,000	1,400	2,900	8,000	34,500	—	—	—
1868	5,725	650	1,000	3,500	11,500	—	—	70,000
1868S	52,000	400	1,550	4,000	20,000	—	—	—
1869	1,785	925	2,400	3,500	17,500	34,000	—	65,000
1869S	31,000	500	1,750	4,000	26,000	—	—	—
1870	4,035	800	2,000	2,850	18,000	—	—	75,000
1870CC	7,675	5,250	15,000	30,000	110,000	137,500	200,000	—
1870S	17,000	950	2,600	8,250	29,000	—	—	—
1871	3,230	900	1,700	3,300	12,500	—	—	70,000
1871CC	20,770	1,250	3,000	12,000	60,000	—	—	—
1871S	25,000	500	950	2,950	13,000	—	—	—
1872	1,690	850	1,925	3,000	15,000	18,000	—	60,000
1872CC	16,980	1,250	5,000	20,000	60,000	—	—	—
1872S	36,400	460	800	3,400	13,500	—	—	—
1873 closed 3	49,305	215	225	440	1,200	6,500	24,000	70,000
1873 open 3	63,200	215	220	350	850	3,650	—	—
1873CC	7,416	2,600	12,500	27,500	60,000	—	—	—
1873S	31,000	525	1,400	3,250	21,000	—	—	—
1874	3,508	660	1,675	2,500	13,000	26,000	—	66,000
1874CC	21,198	850	1,700	9,500	36,000	—	—	—
1874S	16,000	640	2,100	4,800	22,500	—	—	—
1875	220	34,000	45,000	60,000	190,000	—	—	185,000
1875CC	11,828	1,400	4,500	11,500	52,000	—	—	—
1875S	9,000	715	2,250	5,000	16,500	32,500	—	—
1876	1,477	1,100	2,500	4,125	11,000	14,500	55,000	60,000
1876CC	6,887	1,450	5,000	14,000	46,500	82,500	165,000	—
1876S	4,000	2,000	3,600	9,500	30,000	—	—	—
1877	1,152	900	2,750	4,000	13,750	29,000	—	75,000
1877CC	8,680	1,000	3,300	11,000	52,500	—	—	—
1877S	26,700	400	650	1,400	9,200	—	—	—
1878	131,740	215	220	240	425	2,000	—	50,000
1878CC	9,054	3,100	7,200	20,000	60,000	—	—	—
1878S	144,700	215	220	3,000	675	4,250	—	—
1879	301,950	215	220	225	400	2,000	12,000	55,000
1879CC	17,281	575	1,500	3,150	22,000	—	—	—
1879S	426,200	215	225	240	950	3,300	—	—
1880	3,166,436	215	225	225	235	840	7,500	54,000

Date	Mintage	VF-20	XF-40	AU-50	MS-60	MS-63	MS-65	Prf-65
1880CC	51,017	425	815	1,375	9,900	—	—	—
1880S	1,348,900	215	220	225	235	800	5,750	—
1881	5,708,802	215	220	225	235	775	4,800	54,000
1881/80	Inc. above	330	600	750	1,500	4,500	—	—
1881CC	13,886	550	1,500	7,000	22,500	60,000	—	—
1881S	969,000	215	220	225	235	775	7,150	—
1882	2,514,568	215	220	225	235	800	6,150	54,000
1882CC	82,817	415	625	900	7,500	40,000	—	—
1882S	969,000	215	220	225	235	800	4,500	—
1883	233,461	215	220	225	260	1,200	—	40,000
1883CC	12,958	460	1,100	3,200	18,000	—	—	—
1883S	83,200	215	240	315	1,000	2,950	—	—
1884	191,078	215	220	225	650	2,250	—	35,000
1884CC	16,402	550	975	3,000	17,000	—	—	—
1884S	177,000	215	220	225	345	2,000	—	—
1885	601,506	215	220	225	260	825	4,800	35,000
1885S	1,211,500	215	220	225	235	790	4,000	—
1886	388,432	215	220	225	235	1,125	5,600	44,000
1886S	3,268,000	215	220	225	235	815	4,500	—
1887	87	—	14,500	20,000	—	—	—	120,000
1887S	1,912,000	215	220	225	235	800	4,800	—
1888	18,296	215	230	300	550	1,500	—	29,000
1888S	293,900	215	220	320	1,200	4,000	—	—
1889	7,565	350	440	515	1,150	2,400	—	30,000
1890	4,328	400	475	550	2,200	6,500	—	27,000
1890CC	53,800	330	460	615	1,600	8,000	55,000	—
1891	61,413	215	220	230	450	1,900	5,400	29,000
1891CC	208,000	315	415	525	750	3,150	31,500	—
1892	753,572	215	220	225	235	880	7,000	30,000
1892CC	82,968	315	400	575	1,500	6,000	33,500	—
1892O	10,000	515	1,000	1,375	3,300	—	—	—
1892S	298,400	215	220	225	525	3,300	—	—
1893	1,528,197	215	220	225	235	800	3,900	34,000
1893CC	60,000	345	465	770	1,400	6,350	—	—
1893O	110,000	225	315	480	950	6,500	—	—
1893S	224,000	215	220	225	245	825	9,000	—
1894	957,955	215	220	225	235	800	2,600	35,000
1894O	16,600	200	360	570	1,300	5,500	—	—
1894S	55,900	240	375	575	2,900	10,000	—	—
1895	1,345,936	215	220	225	235	800	4,500	29,000
1895S	112,000	215	275	400	3,150	6,500	26,000	—
1896	59,063	215	220	225	235	9,750	4,500	30,000
1896S	155,400	215	220	240	300	1,150	6,000	24,500	—
1897	867,883	215	220	225	235	825	4,500	35,000
1897S	354,000	215	220	235	865	5,150	—	—
1898	633,495	215	220	225	235	885	6,000	30,000
1898S	1,397,400	215	220	225	230	950	—	—
1899	1,710,729	215	220	225	235	730	3,600	30,000
1899S	1,545,000	215	220	225	235	1,000	9,600	—
1900	1,405,730	215	220	225	235	790	3,600	30,000
1900S	329,000	215	220	230	245	900	14,000	—
1901	616,040	215	220	225	235	750	3,650	27,000
1901S	3,648,000	215	220	225	235	730	3,600	—
1902	172,562	215	220	225	235	730	4,400	27,000
1902S	939,000	215	220	225	235	730	3,600	—
1903	227,024	215	220	225	235	730	4,000	27,000
1903S	1,855,000	215	220	225	235	730	3,600	—
1904	392,136	215	220	225	235	730	3,600	27,000
1904S	97,000	215	240	285	900	3,850	9,600	—
1905	302,308	215	220	225	235	740	4,000	27,000
1905S	880,700	215	225	250	235	1,500	9,600	—
1906	348,820	215	220	225	235	745	3,600	26,000
1906D	320,000	215	220	225	235	930	3,200	—
1906S	598,000	215	220	230	240	900	4,400	—
1907	626,192	215	220	225	235	730	3,400	23,000
1907D	888,000	215	220	225	235	730	3,400	—
1908	421,874	215	220	225	235	730	3,400	—

Indian Head

KM# 129 • 8.3590 g., 0.9000 **Gold**, 0.2419 oz. AGW, 21.6 mm. • **Designer:** Bela Lyon Pratt

Date	Mintage	VF-20	XF-40	AU-50	MS-60	MS-63	MS-65	Prf-65
1908	578,012	330	355	385	460	4,350	25,000	25,500
1908D	148,000	330	355	385	460	4,350	27,500	—
1908S	82,000	330	415	430	1,275	4,350	24,000	—
1909	627,138	330	355	385	460	4,350	25,000	36,000
1909D	3,423,560	330	355	385	460	4,350	25,000	—
1909O	34,200	2,000	3,400	6,000	21,000	66,000	260,000	—
1909S	297,200	330	355	385	1,400	11,000	45,000	—
1910	604,250	330	355	385	460	4,350	25,000	37,000
1910D	193,600	330	355	385	460	4,350	42,500	—
1910S	770,200	330	355	385	1,000	6,000	44,000	—
1911	915,139	330	355	385	460	4,350	25,000	28,500
1911D	72,500	475	535	515	4,500	37,000	241,500	—
1911S	1,416,000	340	355	385	560	4,350	41,500	—
1912	790,144	330	355	385	460	4,350	25,000	28,500
1912S	392,000	330	365	400	1,700	13,500	93,500	—
1913	916,099	330	355	385	460	4,350	25,000	28,000
1913S	408,000	340	350	385	1,400	11,500	120,000	—
1914	247,125	330	355	385	460	4,350	25,000	28,500
1914D	247,000	335	355	385	460	4,350	26,000	—
1914S	263,000	340	365	400	1,375	13,500	100,000	—
1915	588,075	330	355	385	460	4,350	25,000	39,000
1915S	164,000	340	400	385	2,000	17,000	110,000	—
1916S	240,000	330	355	385	560	4,350	25,000	—
1929	662,000	4,200	9,600	10,500	13,250	17,500	45,000	—

$10 EAGLE

GOLD

Liberty Cap
Small eagle reverse

KM# 21 • 17.5000 g., 0.9160 **Gold**, 0.5154 oz. AGW, 33 mm. • **Designer:** Robert Scot

Date	Mintage	F-12	VF-20	XF-40	MS-60
1795 13 leaves	5,583	26,500	33,500	46,500	116,500
1795 9 leaves	Inc. above	30,000	45,000	73,500	250,000
1796	4,146	27,500	36,000	50,000	135,000
1797 small eagle	3,615	31,500	40,000	55,000	200,000

Liberty Cap
Liberty cap on head, right, flanked by stars obverse   Heraldic eagle reverse

KM# 30 • 17.5000 g., 0.9160 **Gold**, 0.5154 oz. AGW, 33 mm. • **Obv. Legend** LIBERTY **Rev. Legend:** UNITED STATES OF AMERICA **Designer:** Robert Scot **Notes:** The 1798/97 varieties are distinguished by the positioning of the stars on the obverse.

Date	Mintage	F-12	VF-20	XF-40	MS-60
1797 large eagle	10,940	9,800	12,850	20,500	58,500
1798/97CC 9 stars left, 4 right	900	13,500	19,000	34,500	127,500
1798/97 7 stars left, 6 right	842	28,500	38,500	87,500	235,000
1799 large star obv	37,449	9,350	10,750	17,300	37,500
1799 small star obv	Inc. above	9,350	10,750	17,300	37,500
1800	5,999	9,500	10,750	17,450	39,500
1801	44,344	9,250	10,900	16,500	37,500
1803 extra star	15,017	9,600	11,850	18,650	67,500
1803 large stars rev	Inc. above	9,250	11,400	16,900	37,500
1804 crosslet 4	3,757	16,500	22,750	31,500	92,500
1804 plain 4	—	—	—	—	400,000

Coronet Head
Old-style head, left, within circle of stars obverse   No motto above eagle reverse

KM# 66.1 • 16.7180 g., 0.9000 **Gold**, 0.4837 oz. AGW, 27 mm. • **Rev. Legend:** UNITED STATES OF AMERICA **Designer:** Christian Gobrecht

Date	Mintage	F-12	VF-20	XF-40	MS-60	Prf-65
1838	7,200	1,750	2,650	6,850	43,500	1,500,000
1839/8 Type of1838 obvious overdate	25,801	1,100	1,450	5,850	28,500	1,500,000
1839 large letters	Inc. above	800	1,150	2,150	32,000	—

Coronet Head
New-style head, left, within circle of stars obverse   No motto above eagle reverse

KM# 66.2 • 16.7180 g., 0.9000 **Gold**, 0.4837 oz. AGW, 27 mm. • **Rev. Legend:** UNITED STATES OF AMERICA **Designer:** Christian Gobrecht **Notes:** The 1842 varieties are distinguished by the size of the numerals in the date.

Date	Mintage	F-12	VF-20	XF-40	MS-60	Prf-65
1839 small letters	12,447	975	1,550	6,850	75,000	—
1840	47,338	504	534	774	11,500	—
1841	63,131	484	524	674	9,000	—
1841O	2,500	1,750	3,450	6,950	—	—
1842 small date	81,507	484	524	599	15,000	—

$10 GOLD

Date	Mintage	F-12	VF-20	XF-40	MS-60	Prf-65
1842 large date	Inc. above	484	524	589	9,500	—
1842O	27,400	484	534	904	22,500	—
1843	75,462	484	524	704	16,750	—
1843O	175,162	484	534	659	12,000	—
1844	6,361	800	1,350	3,200	16,750	—
1844O	118,700	44.00	534	844	15,000	—
1845	26,153	519	694	784	17,500	—
1845O	47,500	504	534	875	16,500	—
1845O repunched	Inc. above	579	894	3,850	—	—
1846	20,095	529	764	1,250	—	—
1846O	81,780	484	534	1,150	—	—
1846/5	Inc. above	579	894	1,135	—	—
1847	862,258	484	524	534	3,250	—
1847O	571,500	484	524	534	6,500	—
1848	145,484	484	524	599	5,000	—
1848O	38,850	559	714	1,850	17,750	—
1849	653,618	484	524	534	3,400	—
1849O	23,900	559	714	2,450	27,500	—
1850 large date	291,451	484	524	534	4,500	—
1850 small date	Inc. above	559	714	1,150	8,500	—
1850O	57,500	504	549	1,275	19,500	—
1851	176,328	484	524	534	5,150	—
1851O	263,000	484	534	589	6,650	—
1852	263,106	484	524	534	5,250	—
1852O	18,000	559	694	1,650	27,500	—
1853	201,253	504	534	534	3,600	—
1853/2	—	504	549	869	14,950	—
1853O	51,000	484	549	599	14,500	—
1854	54,250	484	524	559	6,250	—
1854O small date	52,500	504	549	839	11,000	—
1854O large date	Inc. above	559	689	925	9,450	—
1854S	123,826	484	524	559	10,500	—
1855	121,701	484	524	534	4,750	—
1855O	18,000	504	549	2,100	280,000	—
1855S	9,000	900	1,950	3,250	—	—
1856	60,490	484	524	534	4,250	—
1856O	14,500	559	849	2,150	18,500	—
1856S	68,000	484	524	609	9,000	—
1857	16,606	504	549	1,050	13,500	—
1857O	5,500	659	1,800	3,650	—	—
1857S	26,000	504	534	1,050	11,500	—
1858	2,521	3,000	5,200	8,250	35,000	—
1858O	20,000	484	524	859	10,000	—
1858S	11,800	900	1,600	3,950	—	—
1859	16,093	504	549	719	10,500	—
1859O	2,300	2,000	4,250	10,500	—	—
1859S	7,000	1,450	2,600	5,250	—	—
1860	15,105	529	589	769	8,450	175,000
1860O	11,100	549	689	1,850	13,750	—
1860S	5,000	1,400	2,950	6,400	—	—

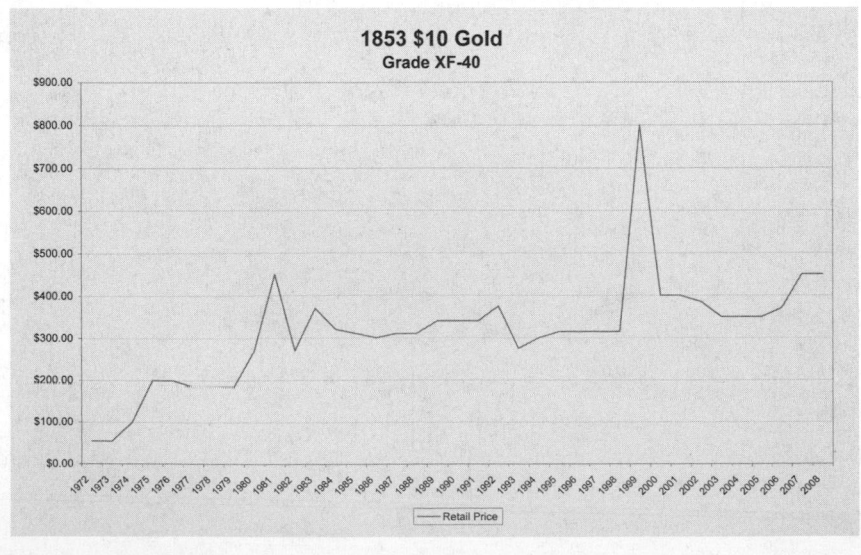

1853 $10 Gold
Grade XF-40

Date	Mintage	F-12	VF-20	XF-40	MS-60	Prf-65
1861	113,233	484	524	534	6,250	170,000
1861S	15,500	690	1,600	3,750	—	—
1862	10,995	559	679	1,200	—	170,000
1862S	12,500	700	2,000	3,450	—	—
1863	1,248	2,400	4,000	10,000	52,500	165,000
1863S	10,000	700	1,600	3,750	29,500	—
1864	3,580	775	1,800	4,950	18,000	165,000
1864S	2,500	2,600	5,100	17,500	—	—
1865	4,005	900	1,950	4,850	34,500	165,000
1865S	16,700	1,700	4,850	12,500	—	—
1865S /inverted 186	—	1,300	3,450	8,750	50,000	—
1866S	8,500	1,000	2,650	5,950	—	—

Coronet Head

New-style head, left, within circle of stars obverse   "In God We Trust" above eagle reverse

KM# 102 • 16.7180 g., 0.9000 **Gold**, 0.4837 oz. AGW, 27 mm. • **Rev. Legend:** UNITED STATES OF AMERICA **Designer:** Christian Gobrecht **Notes:** The 1873 "closed-3" and "open-3" varieties are distinguished by the amount of space between the upper left and lower left serifs of the 3 in the date.

Date	Mintage	VF-20	XF-40	AU-50	MS-60	MS-63	MS-65	Prf-65
1866	3,780	850	2,450	5,000	—	—	—	110,000
1866S	11,500	1,550	3,850	8,000	—	—	—	—
1867	3,140	1,500	2,600	5,000	33,000	—	—	—
1867S	9,000	2,350	6,650	9,850	—	—	—	—
1868	10,655	550	1,100	2,250	19,000	—	—	110,000
1868S	13,500	1,350	2,400	3,900	—	—	—	—
1869	1,855	1,550	3,000	5,650	36,000	—	—	—
1869S	6,430	1,500	2,700	6,250	25,000	—	—	—
1870	4,025	985	1,650	3,950	—	—	—	—
1870CC	5,908	13,000	30,000	52,500	—	—	—	—
1870S	8,000	1,150	2,850	7,400	33,500	—	—	—
1871	1,820	1,500	3,000	5,000	20,000	—	—	110,000
1871CC	8,085	2,600	6,400	22,500	65,000	—	—	—
1871S	16,500	1,300	2,200	6,000	30,000	—	—	—
1872	1,650	2,400	5,500	8,700	15,000	34,000	—	90,000
1872CC	4,600	2,850	9,850	24,500	—	—	—	—
1872S	17,300	675	1,175	1,900	—	—	—	—
1873 closed 3	825	4,500	9,750	17,500	55,000	—	—	—
1873CC	4,543	6,000	13,500	31,000	—	—	—	—
1873S	12,000	1,150	2,850	5,100	27,500	—	—	—
1874	53,160	491	510	517	2,100	7,250	42,500	110,000
1874CC	16,767	1,150	3,650	11,000	52,500	75,000	—	—
1874S	10,000	1,275	3,400	7,250	—	—	—	—
1875	120	40,000	67,500	80,000	—	—	—	—

Note: 1875, Akers, Aug. 1990, Proof, $115,000.

Date	Mintage	VF-20	XF-40	AU-50	MS-60	MS-63	MS-65	Prf-65
1875CC	7,715	4,250	9,850	25,000	71,500	—	—	—
1876	732	3,000	8,500	18,500	—	—	—	—
1876CC	4,696	3,600	7,750	21,500	—	—	—	—
1876S	5,000	1,300	2,950	7,500	—	—	—	—
1877	817	3,350	6,350	9,850	37,500	—	—	—
1877CC	3,332	2,400	6,750	15,000	—	—	—	—
1877S	17,000	550	1,250	2,450	33,500	—	—	—
1878	73,800	481	510	517	975	6,750	29,000	—
1878CC	3,244	3,850	10,000	19,000	—	—	—	—
1878S	26,100	521	775	2,150	16,500	29,500	—	—
1879	384,770	484	510	517	659	5,000	15,750	83,000
1879/78	Inc. above	491	522	802	1,250	2,850	—	—
1879CC	1,762	6,650	12,500	26,000	—	—	—	—
1879O	1,500	2,150	5,450	10,250	—	—	—	—
1879S	224,000	484	510	517	1,150	6,500	49,500	—
1880	1,644,876	466	472	479	514	3,650	—	—
1880CC	11,190	625	1,000	1,950	15,500	—	—	—
1880O	9,200	586	1,450	1,850	20,000	—	—	—
1880S	506,250	466	472	479	534	4,850	25,000	—
1881	3,877,260	466	472	479	514	1,325	16,500	63,000
1881CC	24,015	612	825	1,800	6,850	36,500	—	—

$10 GOLD

Date	Mintage	VF-20	XF-40	AU-50	MS-60	MS-63	MS-65	Prf-65
1881O	8,350	566	865	1,500	6,950	—	—	—
1881S	970,000	466	472	479	524	1,325	—	—
1882	2,324,480	466	472	479	514	1,325	19,500	63,000
1882CC	6,764	985	1,750	3,250	—	—	—	—
1882O	10,820	494	659	1,250	6,350	18,500	—	—
1882S	132,000	494	510	517	596	3,650	—	—
1883	208,740	466	472	479	524	3,100	—	63,000
1883CC	12,000	666	1,250	2,600	22,500	—	—	—
1883O	800	3,000	7,950	10,500	—	—	—	—
1883S	38,000	494	510	517	1,275	10,500	23,500	—
1884	76,905	494	510	517	694	5,100	15,000	53,000
1884CC	9,925	686	1,450	2,350	12,850	55,000	—	—
1884S	124,250	466	472	479	609	6,500	—	—
1885	253,527	466	472	479	514	4,850	—	53,000
1885S	228,000	466	472	479	514	4,400	—	—
1886	236,160	466	472	479	514	5,100	—	53,000
1886S	826,000	466	472	479	524	1,500	—	—
1887	53,680	494	510	517	800	4,750	—	53,000
1887S	817,000	466	472	479	524	3,500	—	—
1888	132,996	494	510	517	754	6,600	—	—
1888O	21,335	494	510	517	694	5,750	—	—
1888S	648,700	466	472	479	514	2,700	—	—
1889	4,485	524	699	1,100	2,700	—	—	53,000
1889S	425,400	466	472	479	524	1,500	18,500	—
1890	58,043	504	530	537	825	5,500	16,000	46,000
1890CC	17,500	606	692	935	3,850	18,500	—	—
1891	91,868	524	550	557	592	5,000	—	48,000
1891CC	103,732	606	652	840	1,300	7,150	—	—
1892	797,552	466	472	479	514	1,325	9,100	48,000
1892CC	40,000	606	652	825	3,800	22,500	—	—
1892O	28,688	524	510	517	572	11,000	—	—
1892S	115,500	494	534	541	576	4,500	—	—
1893	1,840,895	466	472	479	514	1,325	16,500	46,000
1893CC	14,000	606	692	1,800	8,500	—	—	—
1893O	17,000	494	510	559	794	5,300	—	—
1893S	141,350	494	510	517	552	5,250	19,500	—
1894	2,470,778	466	472	479	514	1,450	—	46,000
1894O	107,500	494	510	509	1,000	6,350	—	—
1894S	25,000	494	534	925	3,950	—	—	—
1895	567,826	466	472	479	514	1,325	17,500	43,500
1895O	98,000	494	510	529	664	8,000	—	—
1895S	49,000	494	522	675	2,400	9,500	—	—
1896	76,348	466	472	479	524	2,550	30,000	43,500
1896S	123,750	494	505	539	2,500	12,000	28,500	—
1897	1,000,159	466	472	479	514	1,450	10,000	—
1897O	42,500	494	510	517	800	5,850	27,500	—
1897S	234,750	494	505	512	870	5,750	22,500	—
1898	812,197	466	472	479	514	1,450	9,000	43,500
1898S	473,600	494	505	512	584	5,100	18,500	—
1899	1,262,305	466	472	479	514	1,325	7,900	43,500
1899O	37,047	494	510	519	694	8,450	—	—
1899S	841,000	466	472	479	524	3,650	12,850	—
1900	293,960	466	472	479	524	1,325	9,500	43,500
1900S	81,000	494	510	517	950	6,750	—	—
1901	1,718,825	466	472	479	514	1,325	7,900	43,500
1901O	72,041	494	510	517	634	3,750	12,500	—
1901S	2,812,750	466	472	479	514	1,325	7,900	—
1902	82,513	466	472	479	524	2,800	11,750	43,500
1902S	469,500	466	472	479	514	1,325	7,900	—
1903	125,926	466	472	479	524	2,450	13,500	43,500
1903O	112,771	494	510	517	624	3,250	18,000	—
1903S	538,000	466	472	479	524	1,350	7,900	—
1904	162,038	466	472	479	524	2,000	9,500	46,000
1904O	108,950	494	510	517	624	3,700	16,500	—
1905	201,078	466	472	479	514	1,450	8,500	43,500
1905S	369,250	494	505	544	1,100	5,600	22,500	—
1906	165,497	466	472	479	524	2,450	10,000	43,500
1906D	981,000	466	472	479	514	1,325	7,000	—
1906O	86,895	494	510	517	664	4,900	14,500	—
1906S	457,000	494	505	517	674	5,000	15,500	—
1907	1,203,973	466	472	479	514	1,325	7,900	43,500
1907D	1,030,000	466	472	479	524	2,250	—	—
1907S	210,500	494	505	539	714	5,450	17,000	—

Indian Head
No motto next to eagle reverse

KM# 125 • 16.7180 g., 0.9000 **Gold**, 0.4837 oz. AGW, 27 mm. • **Designer:** Augustus Saint-Gaudens
Notes: 1907 varieties are distinguished by whether the edge is rolled or wired, and whether the legend "E Pluribus Unum" has periods between each word.

Date	Mintage	VF-20	XF-40	AU-50	MS-60	MS-63	MS-65	Prf-65
1907 wire edge, periods before and after legend	500	9,500	14,900	16,900	22,000	36,500	65,000	—
1907 same, without stars on edge, unique	—	—	—	—	—	—	—	—
1907 rolled edge, periods	42	26,000	38,500	49,000	66,500	98,500	250,000	—
1907 without periods	239,406	580	600	630	775	3,100	11,450	—
1908 without motto	33,500	565	585	615	720	4,650	14,500	—
1908D without motto	210,000	565	585	615	760	6,250	38,500	—

Indian Head
"In God We Trust" left of eagle reverse

KM# 130 • 16.7180 g., 0.9000 **Gold**, 0.4837 oz. AGW, 27 mm. • **Designer:** Augustus Saint-Gaudens

Date	Mintage	VF-20	XF-40	AU-50	MS-60	MS-63	MS-65	Prf-65
1908	341,486	560	580	610	700	3,150	9,450	52,500
1908D	836,500	565	585	615	705	6,850	29,000	—
1908S	59,850	575	635	665	2,950	8,650	25,500	—
1909	184,863	560	580	610	700	3,500	12,750	54,500
1909D	121,540	565	585	615	775	4,650	34,500	—
1909S	292,350	565	585	615	775	5,350	13,900	—
1910	318,704	560	580	610	700	2,350	8,950	54,500
1910D	2,356,640	555	575	610	700	2,185	8,600	—
1910S	811,000	565	585	615	705	7,450	55,000	—
1911	505,595	555	575	605	695	2,185	8,800	52,500
1911D	30,100	610	675	950	4,200	21,500	120,000	—
1911S	51,000	595	555	645	1,050	7,950	14,500	—
1912	405,083	560	580	610	700	2,350	9,650	52,500
1912S	300,000	565	585	615	705	5,850	38,500	—
1913	442,071	560	580	610	700	2,350	8,800	52,500
1913S	66,000	610	600	775	3,900	28,500	100,000	—
1914	151,050	560	580	610	700	2,400	9,850	52,500
1914D	343,500	560	580	610	700	2,650	15,500	—
1914S	208,000	570	590	620	720	6,500	32,500	—
1915	351,075	560	580	610	700	2,350	9,850	55,000
1915S	59,000	610	725	775	3,150	14,850	65,000	—
1916S	138,500	595	615	645	735	5,150	18,500	—
1920S	126,500	7,800	11,000	14,500	28,500	71,500	275,000	—
1926	1,014,000	555	575	605	695	1,650	7,450	—
1930S	96,000	7,500	10,000	13,500	21,500	41,500	68,500	—
1932	4,463,000	555	575	605	695	1,650	7,500	—
1933	312,500	110,000	140,000	150,000	185,000	245,000	650,000	—

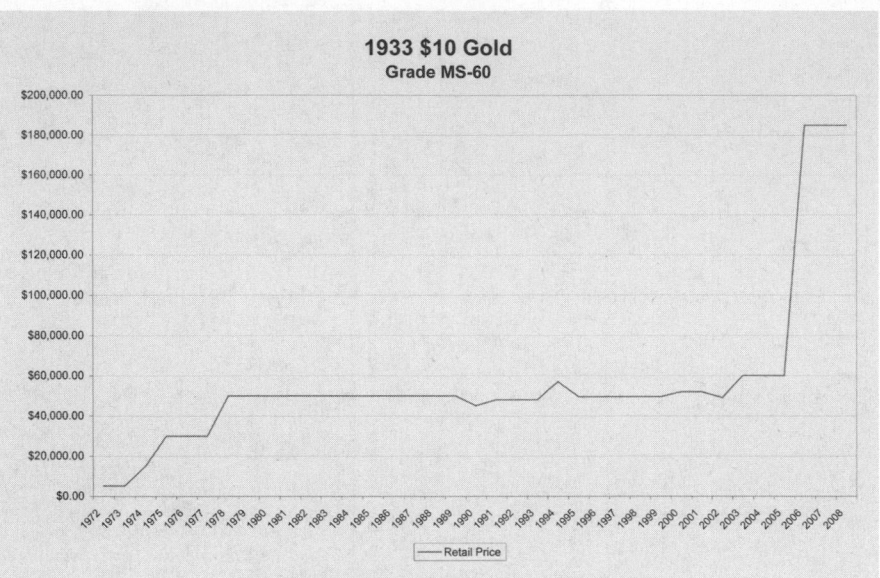

1933 $10 Gold
Grade MS-60

$20 DOUBLE EAGLE

GOLD

Liberty

Coronet head, left, within circle of stars obverse
"Twenty D." below eagle, no motto above eagle reverse

KM# 74.1 • 33.4360 g., 0.9000 **Gold**, 0.9675 oz. AGW, 34 mm. • **Rev. Legend:** UNITED STATES OF AMERICA **Designer:** James B. Longacre

Date	Mintage	VF-20	XF-40	AU-50	MS-60	MS-63	MS-65	Prf-65
1849 unique, in Smithsonian collection	1	—	—	—	—	—	—	—
1850	1,170,261	1,198	1,450	3,000	8,500	43,500	175,000	—
1850O	141,000	1,250	3,500	9,800	45,000	—	—	—
1851	2,087,155	1,098	1,188	1,388	3,850	19,500	—	—
1851O	315,000	1,100	2,250	3,650	23,000	58,500	—	—
1852	2,053,026	1,098	1,188	1,000	3,950	17,500	—	—
1852O	190,000	1,250	2,650	3,800	22,500	—	—	—
1853	1,261,326	1,098	1,188	1,000	5,000	27,500	—	—
1853/2	Inc. above	1,178	2,250	6,850	33,500	—	—	—
1853O	71,000	1,150	3,650	4,850	32,500	65,000	—	—
1854	757,899	1,098	1,188	1,050	6,000	26,500	—	—
1854	Inc. above	1,250	2,350	6,000	—	—	—	—
1854O	3,250	95,000	225,000	365,000	—	—	—	—
1854S	141,468	1,178	1,325	3,000	6,000	15,500	52,500	—
1855	364,666	1,098	1,188	1,450	8,250	65,000	—	—
1855O	8,000	3,650	19,500	24,500	110,000	—	—	—
1855S	879,675	1,078	1,188	1,400	7,200	19,500	—	—
1856	329,878	1,098	1,188	1,450	8,400	24,500	—	—
1856O	2,250	97,500	165,000	300,000	525,000	750,000	—	—

Date	Mintage	VF-20	XF-40	AU-50	MS-60	MS-63	MS-65	Prf-65
1856S	1,189,750	1,078	1,188	1,300	5,900	15,000	30,000	—
1857	439,375	1,098	1,188	1,288	3,400	26,500	—	—
1857O	30,000	1,300	2,950	6,400	31,000	115,000	—	—
1857S	970,500	1,078	1,188	1,200	4,500	7,750	14,000	—
1858	211,714	1,153	1,100	1,450	5,500	34,500	—	—
1858O	35,250	1,950	3,850	7,500	42,000	—	—	—
1858S	846,710	1,078	1,000	1,700	8,500	—	—	—
1859	43,597	1,153	2,450	4,400	28,000	—	—	280,000
1859O	9,100	6,400	16,500	44,000	110,000	—	—	—
1859S	636,445	1,078	1,188	1,650	5,000	35,000	—	—
1860	577,670	1,078	1,188	1,288	4,650	18,000	63,500	—
1860O	6,600	3,650	14,500	24,000	100,000	—	—	—
1860S	544,950	1,098	1,075	1,600	7,350	18,500	48,000	—
1861	2,976,453	1,078	1,188	1,263	2,750	12,850	41,500	275,000
1861O	17,741	5,650	17,500	24,000	88,000	—	—	—
1861S	768,000	1,098	1,125	2,250	10,500	31,500	—	—

Liberty
Coronet head, left, within circle of stars obverse
Paquet design, "Twenty D." below eagle reverse

KM# 93 • 33.4360 g., 0.9000 **Gold**, 0.9675 oz. AGW • **Rev. Legend:** UNITED STATES OF AMERICA
Notes: In 1861 the reverse was redesigned by Anthony C. Paquet, but it was withdrawn soon after its release. The letters in the inscriptions on the Paquet-reverse variety are taller than on the regular reverse.

Date	Mintage	VF-20	XF-40	AU-50	MS-60	MS-63	MS-65	Prf-65
1861 2 Known	—	—	—	—	—	—	—	—

Note: 1861 Paquet reverse, Bowers & Merena, Nov. 1988, MS-67, $660,000.

Date	Mintage	VF-20	XF-40	AU-50	MS-60	MS-63	MS-65	Prf-65
1861S	—	19,500	52,500	92,500	275,000	—	—	—

Note: Included in mintage of 1861S, KM#74.1

Liberty
Longacre design resumed reverse

KM# A74.1 • 33.4360 g., 0.9000 **Gold**, 0.9675 oz. AGW •

Date	Mintage	VF-20	XF-40	AU-50	MS-60	MS-63	MS-65	Prf-65
1862	92,133	1,000	2,250	4,900	16,500	34,000	—	250,000
1862S	854,173	1,063	1,350	2,100	12,400	36,000	—	—
1863	142,790	1,078	1,900	3,950	19,500	39,500	—	250,000
1863S	966,570	1,063	1,050	1,950	7,350	32,500	—	—
1864	204,285	1,078	1,150	2,450	14,500	40,000	—	250,000
1864S	793,660	1,063	1,050	1,950	8,600	32,000	—	—
1865	351,200	1,078	975	1,350	6,200	26,000	—	250,000
1865S	1,042,500	1,063	950	1,150	4,200	9,000	19,500	—
1866S	Inc. below	3,400	13,500	44,500	—	—	—	—

Liberty
Coronet head, left, within circle of stars obverse
"Twenty D." below eagle. "In God We Trust" above eagle reverse

KM# 74.2 • 33.4360 g., 0.9000 **Gold**, 0.9675 oz. AGW, 34 mm. • **Rev. Legend:** UNITED STATES OF AMERICA **Designer:** James B. Longacre **Notes:** The 1873 "closed-3" and "open-3" varieties are known and are distinguished by the amount of space between the upper left and lower left serif in the 3 in the date.

Date	Mintage	VF-20	XF-40	AU-50	MS-60	MS-63	MS-65	Prf-65
1866	698,775	1,048	950	1,750	6,950	28,500	—	200,000
1866S	842,250	1,048	985	2,100	15,500	—	—	—
1867	251,065	1,048	975	1,200	3,250	30,000	—	200,000
1867S	920,750	1,048	985	1,900	15,000	—	—	—
1868	98,600	1,088	1,250	2,250	11,500	50,000	—	200,000
1868S	837,500	1,048	1,000	1,650	10,000	—	—	—
1869	175,155	1,058	1,075	1,600	6,800	22,750	—	210,000
1869S	686,750	1,048	985	1,350	7,000	45,000	—	—
1870	155,185	1,068	1,140	1,925	9,250	50,000	—	215,000
1870CC	3,789	125,000	195,000	360,000	—	—	—	—
1870S	982,000	1,048	975	1,225	5,450	34,000	—	—
1871	80,150	1,058	1,075	1,800	4,500	24,500	—	—
1871CC	17,387	9,500	19,500	40,000	97,500	300,000	650,000	—
1871S	928,000	1,048	1,113	1,138	4,750	22,000	—	—
1872	251,880	1,048	1,143	1,168	3,750	24,500	—	—
1872CC	26,900	2,450	5,450	8,950	38,500	—	—	—
1872S	780,000	1,048	1,143	1,200	3,250	23,500	—	—
1873 closed 3	Est. 208,925	1,048	1,203	1,350	3,350	—	—	200,000
1873 open 3	Est. 1,500,900	1,048	1,143	1,065	1,225	12,000	85,000	—
1873CC	22,410	2,900	4,750	11,750	37,500	115,000	—	—
1873S closed 3	1,040,600	1,048	1,113	1,050	2,150	20,000	—	—
1873S open 3	Inc. above	1,048	1,143	1,500	5,900	29,500	—	—
1874	366,800	1,048	1,143	1,150	1,650	19,500	—	—
1874CC	115,085	1,400	1,950	3,000	10,500	—	—	—
1874S	1,214,000	1,045	1,113	1,010	1,550	24,000	—	—
1875	295,740	1,045	1,143	1,035	1,275	13,500	—	—
1875CC	111,151	1,300	1,550	1,950	3,750	24,500	—	—
1875S	1,230,000	1,048	1,113	1,010	1,250	16,850	—	—
1876	583,905	1,048	1,133	1,010	1,275	13,500	78,500	—
1876CC	138,441	1,300	1,500	1,950	6,750	38,500	—	—
1876S	1,597,000	1,048	1,113	1,010	1,250	12,400	90,000	—

Liberty
Coronet head, left, within circle of stars obverse   "Twenty Dollars" below eagle reverse

KM# 74.3 • 33.4360 g., 0.9000 **Gold**, 0.9675 oz. AGW • **Rev. Legend:** UNITED STATES OF AMERICA

Date	Mintage	VF-20	XF-40	AU-50	MS-60	MS-63	MS-65	Prf-65
1877	397,670	1,008	1,108	1,133	1,193	11,700	—	—
1877CC	42,565	1,500	1,900	3,350	19,500	—	—	—
1877S	1,735,000	998	1,043	1,093	1,163	15,000	—	—
1878	543,645	1,018	1,108	1,143	1,450	13,500	—	—

Date	Mintage	VF-20	XF-40	AU-50	MS-60	MS-63	MS-65	Prf-65
1878CC	13,180	2,450	3,950	8,400	30,000	—	—	—
1878S	1,739,000	998	1,018	1,028	1,163	20,500	—	—
1879	207,630	825	1,108	1,093	1,200	16,500	—	—
1879CC	10,708	3,000	4,850	8,850	34,000	77,500	—	—
1879O	2,325	12,500	21,500	32,000	75,000	127,500	—	—
1879S	1,223,800	998	1,018	1,028	1,750	30,000	—	—
1880	51,456	825	1,108	1,158	3,150	21,500	—	110,000
1880S	836,000	998	1,018	1,028	1,175	16,500	—	—
1881	2,260	6,800	12,500	21,500	79,000	—	—	110,000
1881S	727,000	998	1,018	1,028	1,063	19,500	—	—
1882	630	11,500	29,500	50,000	110,000	185,000	—	130,000
1882CC	39,140	1,350	1,750	2,200	7,950	65,000	—	—
1882S	1,125,000	998	1,018	1,028	1,233	18,500	—	—
1883 proof only	92	—	—	14,000	—	—	—	225,000
1883CC	59,962	1,350	1,600	2,000	5,250	21,000	—	—
1883S	1,189,000	998	1,018	1,028	1,163	8,250	—	—
1884 proof only	71	—	—	15,000	—	—	—	225,000
1884CC	81,139	1,250	1,550	1,900	4,250	23,500	—	—
1884S	916,000	998	1,018	1,028	1,103	5,950	43,500	—
1885	828	8,800	13,850	18,500	48,500	96,000	—	115,000
1885CC	9,450	2,500	3,850	6,200	21,500	44,500	—	—
1885S	683,500	998	1,018	1,028	1,103	5,900	29,500	—
1886	1,106	12,500	29,500	42,500	73,500	140,000	—	105,000
1887	121	—	—	26,500	—	—	—	142,500
1887S	283,000	998	1,018	1,028	1,163	18,500	35,000	—
1888	226,266	998	1,018	1,048	1,193	7,900	33,500	93,500
1888S	859,600	998	1,018	1,028	1,103	4,650	—	—
1889	44,111	1,138	1,238	1,333	1,150	12,750	32,500	105,000
1889CC	30,945	1,500	1,750	2,350	6,650	25,500	—	—
1889S	774,700	998	1,018	1,028	1,113	5,400	—	—
1890	75,995	998	1,043	1,063	1,163	10,000	—	115,000
1890CC	91,209	1,250	1,450	1,850	4,750	34,500	—	—
1890S	802,750	998	1,018	1,028	1,103	6,850	—	—
1891	1,442	3,500	5,750	9,500	52,000	98,500	—	108,000
1891CC	5,000	4,800	9,000	9,850	26,500	54,500	—	—
1891S	1,288,125	998	1,018	1,028	1,103	2,750	—	—
1892	4,523	1,350	2,250	2,650	7,400	19,500	—	90,000
1892CC	27,265	1,350	1,750	2,350	5,250	31,000	—	—
1892S	930,150	998	1,018	1,043	1,093	2,950	22,500	—
1893	344,339	998	1,033	1,053	1,133	1,950	—	95,000
1893CC	18,402	1,550	1,900	2,500	5,950	29,500	—	—
1893S	996,175	963	973	988	1,018	2,850	26,500	—
1894	1,368,990	963	973	988	1,018	1,650	26,500	85,000
1894S	1,048,550	963	973	988	1,018	2,450	24,500	—
1895	1,114,656	963	973	988	1,018	1,300	16,000	82,500
1895S	1,143,500	963	973	988	1,018	2,200	15,500	—
1896	792,663	963	973	988	1,018	1,850	16,500	82,500
1896S	1,403,925	963	973	988	—	1,975	26,500	—
1897	1,383,261	963	973	988	1,018	1,385	18,500	82,500
1897S	1,470,250	963	973	988	1,018	1,450	21,000	—
1898	170,470	968	1,003	1,038	1,325	4,500	—	82,500
1898S	2,575,175	963	973	988	1,018	1,300	9,250	—
1899	1,669,384	963	973	988	1,018	1,325	12,000	82,500
1899S	2,010,300	963	973	988	1,018	1,750	19,500	—
1900	1,874,584	963	973	988	1,018	1,180	6,000	82,500
1900S	2,459,500	963	973	988	1,018	2,100	23,000	50,000
1901	111,526	963	973	988	1,018	1,175	5,500	82,500
1901S	1,596,000	963	973	988	1,018	3,350	20,000	—
1902	31,254	1,063	1,173	1,050	1,400	11,250	37,500	95,000
1902S	1,753,625	963	973	988	1,018	2,900	24,000	—
1903	287,428	963	973	988	1,018	1,150	5,500	95,000
1903S	954,000	963	973	988	1,018	1,385	13,500	—
1904	6,256,797	963	973	988	1,018	1,150	4,650	95,000
1904S	5,134,175	963	973	988	1,018	1,175	5,400	—
1905	59,011	968	993	1,028	1,250	15,500	—	95,000
1905S	1,813,000	963	973	988	1,018	3,250	20,500	—
1906	69,690	968	978	993	1,118	6,850	22,500	82,500
1906D	620,250	963	973	988	1,018	3,250	19,000	—
1906S	2,065,750	963	973	988	1,018	2,350	19,500	—
1907	1,451,864	963	973	988	1,018	1,155	8,200	82,500
1907D	842,250	963	973	988	1,018	2,650	7,350	—
1907S	2,165,800	963	973	988	1,018	2,375	27,000	—

$20 GOLD

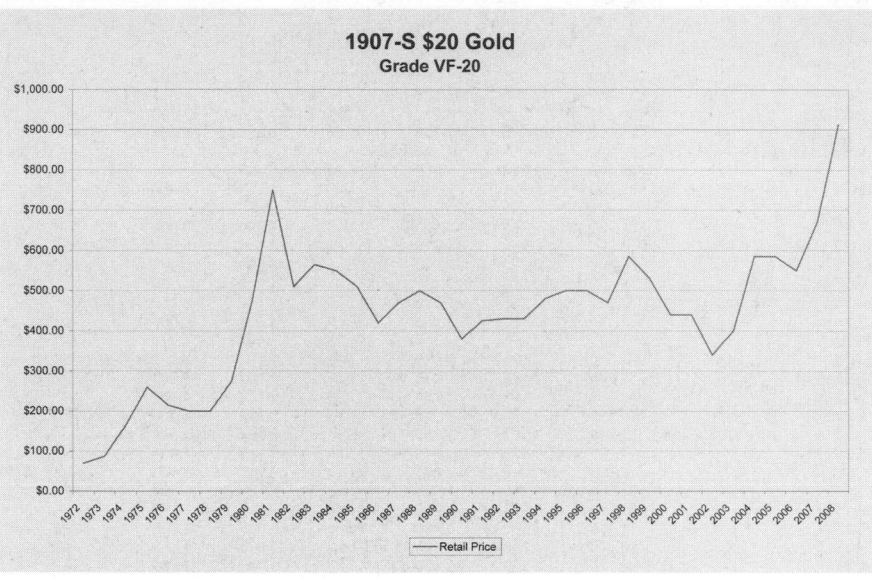

1907-S $20 Gold
Grade VF-20

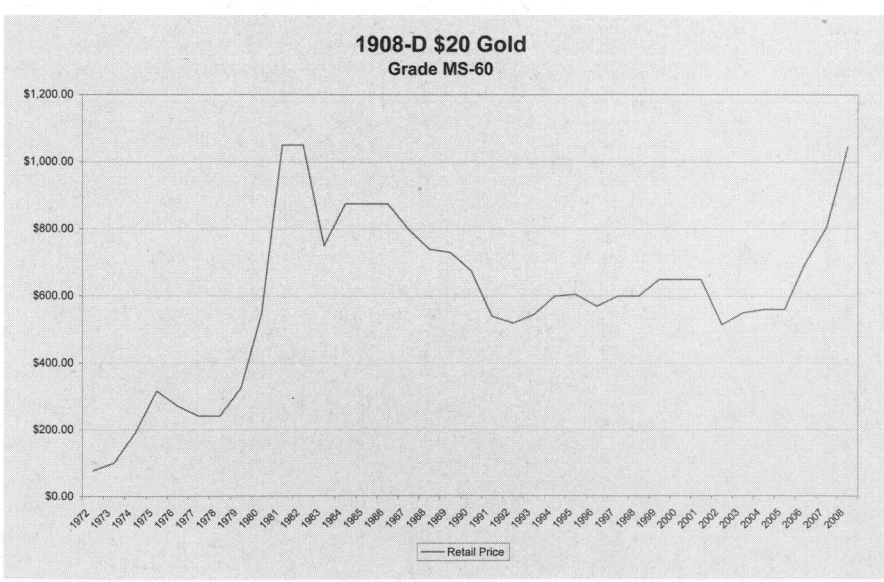

1908-D $20 Gold
Grade MS-60

Saint-Gaudens
Roman numerals in date obverse   No motto below eagle reverse

KM# 126 • 33.4360 g., 0.9000 **Gold**, 0.9675 oz. AGW, 34 mm. • **Designer:** Augustus Saint-Gaudens
Edge Desc: Plain.

Date	Mintage	VF-20	XF-40	AU-50	MS-60	MS-63	MS-65	Prf-65
MCMVII 1907 high relief, unique, AU-55, $150,000	—	—	—	—	—	—	—	—
MCMVII 1907 high relief, wire rim	11,250	7,500	8,500	10,800	13,500	21,700	46,500	—
MCMVII 1907 high relief, flat rim	Inc. above	7,750	8,850	11,250	15,000	24,650	49,500	—

Saint-Gaudens
Arabic numerals in date obverse   No motto below eagle reverse

KM# 127 • 33.4360 g., 0.9000 **Gold**, 0.9675 oz. AGW, 34 mm. • **Designer:** Augustus Saint-Gaudens
Edge Desc: Lettered; large letters.

Date	Mintage	VF-20	XF-40	AU-50	MS-60	MS-63	MS-65	Prf-65
1907 large letters on edge, unique	—	—	—	—	—	—	—	—
1907 small letters on edge	361,667	957	967	992	1,042	1,332	3,350	—
1908	4,271,551	947	957	972	1,002	1,222	1,750	—
1908D	663,750	957	967	982	1,027	1,332	9,000	—

Saint-Gaudens
Roman numerals in date obverse   No motto below eagle reverse

KM# Pn1874 • 33.4360 g., 0.9000 **Gold**, 0.9675 oz. AGW, 34 mm. • **Designer:** Augustus Saint-Gaudens
Edge Desc: Plain. **Notes:** The "Roman numerals" varieties for 1907 use Roman numerals for the date instead of Arabic numerals. The lettered-edge varieties have "E Pluribus Unum" on the edge, with stars between the words.

Date	Mintage	VF-20	XF-40	AU-50	MS-60	MS-63	MS-65	Prf-65
1907 extremely high relief, unique	—	—	—	—	—	—	—	—
1907 extremely high relief, lettered edge	—	—	—	—	—	—	—	—

Note: 1907 extremely high relief, lettered edge, Prf-68, private sale, 1990, $1,500,000

Saint-Gaudens
"In God We Trust" below eagle reverse

KM# 131 • 33.4360 g., 0.9000 **Gold**, 0.9675 oz. AGW, 34 mm. • **Designer:** Augustus Saint-Gaudens

Date	Mintage	VF-20	XF-40	AU-50	MS-60	MS-63	MS-65	Prf-65
1908	156,359	952	962	982	1,052	1,750	21,500	49,500
Note: 34500								
1908 Roman finish; Prf64 Rare	—	—	—	—	—	—	—	—
1908D	349,500	957	967	992	1,042	1,352	5,350	
1908S	22,000	1,450	2,050	4,650	10,500	22,500	43,000	—
1909/8	161,282	957	967	1,032	1,850	6,950	32,500	—
1909	Inc. above	967	987	1,002	1,102	3,350	42,500	49,000
1909D	52,500	997	1,007	1,127	3,100	8,850	39,500	—
1909S	2,774,925	957	967	992	1,022	1,307	5,500	—
1910	482,167	952	962	982	1,052	1,322	7,350	49,000
1910D	429,000	952	962	982	1,027	1,292	2,600	—
1910S	2,128,250	957	967	997	1,032	1,357	8,000	—
1911	197,350	957	967	1,002	1,042	1,875	15,500	39,500
1911D	846,500	952	962	982	1,027	1,292	1,850	—
1911S	775,750	952	962	982	1,032	1,292	6,200	—
1912	149,824	957	967	997	1,067	2,050	19,500	44,000
1913	168,838	957	967	997	1,072	2,850	33,000	44,000
1913D	393,500	952	962	982	1,027	1,332	6,500	—
1913S	34,000	1,007	1,017	1,032	2,000	4,350	36,500	—
1914	95,320	967	977	1,032	1,275	3,900	25,000	41,500
1914D	453,000	952	962	982	1,027	1,302	3,250	—
1914S	1,498,000	952	962	982	1,027	1,292	2,000	—
1915	152,050	957	967	992	1,032	2,200	28,500	47,500
1915S	567,500	952	962	982	1,027	1,292	2,000	—
1916S	796,000	957	967	992	1,067	1,322	2,700	—
1920	228,250	947	957	972	1,027	1,352	62,500	—
1920S	558,000	12,500	15,500	22,500	44,500	98,500	225,000	—
1921	528,500	17,500	29,500	43,500	100,000	240,000	950,000	—
1922	1,375,500	947	957	972	1,002	1,242	2,450	—
1922S	2,658,000	1,025	1,150	1,300	2,450	4,850	42,500	—
1923	566,000	947	957	972	1,002	1,242	4,750	—
1923D	1,702,250	957	967	982	1,012	1,242	1,850	—
1924	4,323,500	947	957	972	1,002	1,242	1,750	—
1924D	3,049,500	1,050	1,550	1,800	3,100	9,150	76,500	—
1924S	2,927,500	1,025	1,550	1,850	3,000	9,850	54,500	—
1925	2,831,750	947	957	972	1,002	1,222	1,950	—
1925D	2,938,500	1,550	2,100	2,375	4,450	11,500	96,000	—
1925S	3,776,500	1,350	1,950	3,450	9,000	24,500	105,000	—
1926	816,750	947	957	972	1,002	1,222	1,750	—
1926D	481,000	8,500	12,500	16,000	28,500	43,500	115,000	—
1926S	2,041,500	1,050	1,550	1,725	3,150	5,650	31,500	—
1927	2,946,750	947	957	972	1,002	1,242	1,750	—
1927D	180,000	155,000	220,000	265,000	340,000	1,500,000	2,100,000	—
1927S	3,107,000	5,850	8,250	12,750	26,500	57,500	130,000	—
1928	8,816,000	947	957	972	1,002	1,222	1,750	—
1929	1,779,750	5,750	9,000	12,500	18,500	39,500	105,000	—
1930S	74,000	15,500	26,500	30,000	39,000	125,000	235,000	—
1931	2,938,250	9,800	14,500	18,850	30,000	68,500	110,000	—
1931D	106,500	9,000	11,850	21,500	42,500	95,000	130,000	—
1932	1,101,750	8,000	14,500	16,850	26,500	72,500	110,000	—
1933	445,500	—	—	—	—	—	9,000,000	—

Note: Sotheby/Stack's Sale, July 2002. Thirteen known, only one currently available.

MINT SETS

Mint, or uncirculated, sets contain one uncirculated coin of each denomination from each mint produced for circulation that year. Values listed here are only for those sets sold by the U.S. Mint. Sets were not offered in years not listed. In years when the Mint did not offer the sets, some private companies compiled and marketed uncirculated sets. Mint sets from 1947 through 1958 contained two examples of each coin mounted in cardboard holders, which caused the coins to tarnish. Beginning in 1959, the sets have been packaged in sealed Pliofilm packets and include only one specimen of each coin struck for that year both P & D mints. Listings for 1965, 1966 and 1967 are for "special mint sets," which were of higher quality than regular mint sets and were prooflike. They were packaged in plastic cases. The 1970 large-date and small-date varieties are distinguished by the size of the date on the coin. The 1976 three-piece set contains the quarter, half dollar and dollar with the Bicentennial design. The 1971 and 1972 sets do not include a dollar coin; the 1979 set does not include an S-mint-marked dollar. Mint sets issued prior to 1959 were double sets containing two of each coin packaged in cardboard with a paper overlay. Original sets will always be toned and can bring large premiums if nicely preserved with good color.

Date	Sets Sold	Issue Price	Value	Date	Sets Sold	Issue Price	Value
1947 Est. 5,000	—	4.87	1,375	1976	1,892,513	6.00	10.50
1948 Est. 6,000	—	4.92	750	1977	2,006,869	7.00	8.00
1949 Est. 5,200	—	5.45	935	1978	2,162,609	7.00	6.75
1950 None issued	—	—	—	1979 Type I	2,526,000	8.00	6.75
1951	8,654	6.75	900	1980	2,815,066	9.00	7.25
1952	11,499	6.14	825	1981 Type I	2,908,145	11.00	14.00
1953	15,538	6.14	565	1982 & 1983 None issued	—	—	—
1954	25,599	6.19	265	1984	1,832,857	7.00	6.75
1955 flat pack	49,656	3.57	165	1985	1,710,571	7.00	6.50
1956	45,475	3.34	165	1986	1,153,536	7.00	13.50
1957	32,324	4.40	275	1987	2,890,758	7.00	6.50
1958	50,314	4.43	150	1988	1,646,204	7.00	6.25
1959	187,000	2.40	58.00	1989	1,987,915	7.00	6.75
1960 large date	260,485	2.40	31.00	1990	1,809,184	7.00	7.50
1961	223,704	2.40	49.00	1991	1,352,101	7.00	8.00
1962	385,285	2.40	28.00	1992	1,500,143	7.00	7.50
1963	606,612	2.40	28.00	1993	1,297,094	8.00	7.50
1964	1,008,108	2.40	28.00	1994	1,234,813	8.00	6.75
1965 Special Mint Set	2,360,000	4.00	7.50	1995	1,038,787	8.00	13.50
1966 Special Mint Set	2,261,583	4.00	7.25	1996	1,457,949	8.00	23.00
1967 Special Mint Set	1,863,344	4.00	15.00	1997	950,473	8.00	19.00
1968	2,105,128	2.50	6.00	1998	1,187,325	8.00	6.75
1969	1,817,392	2.50	7.00	1999	1,421,625	14.95	26.00
1970 large date	2,038,134	2.50	17.00	2000	1,490,160	14.95	10.00
1970 small date	Inc. above	2.50	72.00	2001	1,066,900	14.95	18.00
1971	2,193,396	3.50	4.90	2002	1,139,388	14.95	15.50
1972	2,750,000	3.50	4.90	2003	1,002,555	14.95	18.50
1973	1,767,691	6.00	15.50	2004	844,484	16.95	58.00
1974	1,975,981	6.00	6.00	2005	—	16.95	10.75
1975	1,921,488	6.00	8.75	2006	—	16.95	16.50
1976 3 coins	4,908,319	9.00	13.00	2007	—	—	22.95

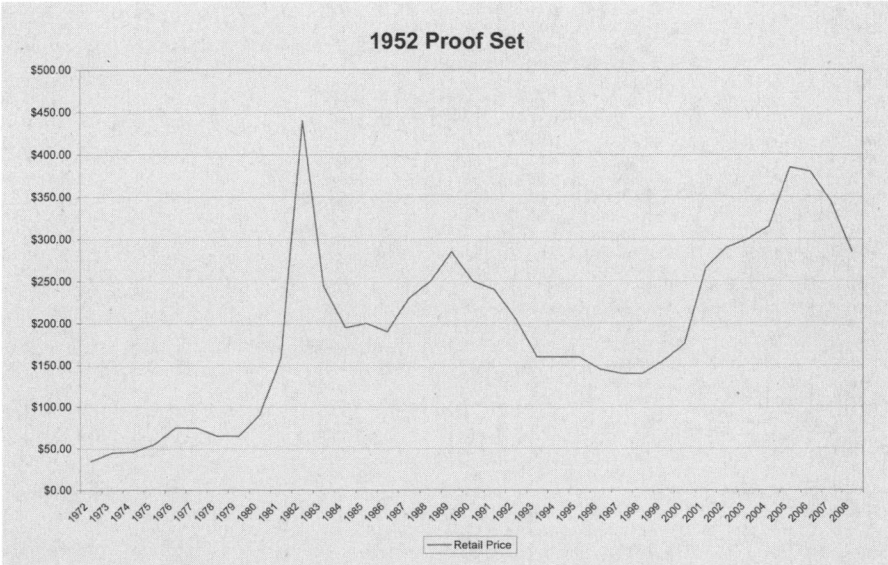

1952 Proof Set

PROOF SETS

Proof coins are produced through a special process involving specially selected, highly polished planchets and dies. They usually receive two strikings from the coin press at increased pressure. The result is a coin with mirrorlike surfaces and, in recent years, a cameo effect on its raised design surfaces. Proof sets have been sold off and on by the U.S. Mint since 1858. Listings here are for sets from what is commonly called the modern era, since 1936. Values for earlier proofs are included in regular date listings. Sets were not offered in years not listed. Since 1968, proof coins have been produced at the San Francisco Mint; before that they were produced at the Philadelphia Mint. In 1942 the five-cent coin was struck in two compositions. Some proof sets for that year contain only one type five-coin set; others contain both types. Two types of packaging were used in 1955 -- a box and a flat, plastic holder. The 1960 large-date and small-date sets are distinguished by the size of the date on the cent. Some 1968 sets are missing the mint mark on the dime, the result of an error in the preparation of an obverse die. The 1970 large-date and small-date sets are distinguished by the size of the date on the cent. Some 1970 sets are missing the mint mark on the dime, the result of an error in the preparation of an obverse die. Some 1971 sets are missing the mint mark on the five-cent piece, the result of an error in the preparation of an obverse die. The 1976 three-piece set contains the quarter, half dollar and dollar with the Bicentennial designs. The 1979 and 1981 Type II sets have clearer mint marks than the Type I sets for those years. Some 1983 sets are missing the mint mark on the dime, the result of an error in the preparation of an obverse die. Prestige sets contain the five regular-issue coins plus a commemorative silver dollar from that year. Sets issued prior to 1956 came in transparent envelopes stapled together in a small square box. In mid 1955 sets were changed to a flat clear cellophane envelope. In 1968 sets were changed to a clear hard plastic case as they still are currently issued.

Date	Sets Sold	Issue Price	Value	Date	Sets Sold	Issue Price	Value
1795 2006 XPn1-XPn3	—	—	—	1981S Type II	Inc. above	11.00	400
1836 2006 XPn4, 10-11	—	—	—	1982S	3,857,479	11.00	4.75
1863 2006 XPn12-14	—	—	—	1983S	3,138,765	11.00	7.00
1871 2006 XPn15-17	—	—	—	1983S Prestige Set	140,361	59.00	89.00
1879 2006 XPn18-20	—	—	—	1983S no mint mark dime	Inc. above	11.00	1,050
1879 2006 XPn21-23	—	—	—	1984S	2,748,430	11.00	6.00
1936	3,837	1.89	7,500	1984S Prestige Set	316,680	59.00	26.00
1937	5,542	1.89	4,350	1985S	3,362,821	11.00	5.75
1938	8,045	1.89	1,900	1986S	2,411,180	11.00	8.50
1939	8,795	1.89	1,800	1986S Prestige Set	599,317	48.50	28.50
1940	11,246	1.89	1,475	1987S	3,972,233	11.00	6.25
1941	15,287	1.89	1,450	1987S Prestige Set	435,495	45.00	23.00
1942 6 coins	21,120	1.89	1,475	1988S	3,031,287	11.00	7.00
1942 5 coins	Inc. above	1.89	1,375	1988S Prestige Set	231,661	45.00	30.50
1950	51,386	2.10	690	1989S	3,009,107	11.00	7.00
1951	57,500	2.10	565	1989S Prestige Set	211,087	45.00	39.50
1952	81,980	2.10	285	1990S	2,793,433	11.00	8.00
1953	128,800	2.10	250	1990S no S 1¢	3,555	11.00	6,650
1954	233,300	2.10	110	1990S Prestige Set	506,126	45.00	24.50
1955 box	378,200	2.10	115	1990S Prestige Set, no S 1¢	Inc. above	45.00	7,000
1955 flat pack	Inc. above	2.10	165	1991S	2,610,833	11.00	12.50
1956	669,384	2.10	68.00	1991S Prestige Set	256,954	59.00	58.50
1957	1,247,952	2.10	29.00	1992S	2,675,618	12.00	7.25
1958	875,652	2.10	54.00	1992S Prestige Set	183,285	59.00	72.00
1959	1,149,291	2.10	30.00	1992S Silver	1,009,585	21.00	16.50
1960 large date	1,691,602	2.10	23.50	1992S Silver premier	308,055	37.00	16.50
1960 small date	Inc. above	2.10	33.00	1993S	2,337,819	12.50	12.50
1961	3,028,244	2.10	15.25	1993S Prestige Set	224,045	57.00	34.00
1962	3,218,019	2.10	15.50	1993S Silver	570,213	21.00	34.00
1963	3,075,645	2.10	15.50	1993S Silver premier	191,140	37.00	34.00
1964	3,950,762	2.10	15.75	1994S	2,308,701	13.00	12.50
1968S	3,041,509	5.00	7.50	1994S Prestige Set	175,893	57.00	42.00
1968S no mint mark dime	Inc. above	5.00	17,500	1994S Silver	636,009	21.00	41.00
1969S	2,934,631	5.00	7.00	1994S Silver premier	149,320	37.50	41.00
1970S large date	2,632,810	5.00	10.00	1995S	2,010,384	12.50	32.50
1970S small date	Inc. above	5.00	100.00	1995S Prestige Set	107,112	57.00	128
1970S no mint mark dime	Inc. above	5.00	1,350	1995S Silver	549,878	21.00	87.00
1971S	3,224,138	5.00	4.75	1995S Silver premier	130,107	37.50	87.00
1971S no mint mark nickel Est. 1,655	1,655	5.00	1,850	1996S	2,085,191	16.00	15.00
1972S	3,267,667	5.50	4.75	1996S Prestige Set	55,000	57.00	475
1973S	2,769,624	7.00	9.25	1996S Silver	623,655	21.00	40.00
1974S	2,617,350	7.00	11.00	1996S Silver premier	151,366	37.50	40.00
1975S	2,909,369	7.00	12.00	1997S	1,975,000	12.50	29.00
1975S no mint mark dime	Inc. above	7.00	50,000	1997S Prestige Set	80,000	57.00	158
1976S 3 coins	3,998,621	12.00	17.00	1997S Silver	605,473	21.00	62.00
1976S	4,149,730	7.00	10.00	1997S Silver premier	136,205	37.50	62.00
1977S	3,251,152	9.00	8.50	1998S	2,078,494	12.50	19.50
1978S	3,127,788	9.00	9.50	1998S Silver	638,134	21.00	27.00
1979S Type I	3,677,175	9.00	8.50	1998S Silver premier	240,658	37.50	27.00
1979S Type II	Inc. above	9.00	120	1999S 9 piece	2,557,899	19.95	63.00
1980S	3,547,030	10.00	8.50	1999S 5 quarter set	1,169,958	13.95	50.00
1981S Type I	4,063,083	11.00	8.00	1999S Silver	804,565	31.95	330
				2000S 10 piece	3,097,442	19.95	16.50

Date	Sets Sold	Issue Price	Value	Date	Sets Sold	Issue Price	Value
2000S 5 quarter set	995,803	13.95	10.00	2004S Silver 5 quarter set	594,137	23.95	21.00
2000S Silver	965,421	31.95	32.00	2005S American Legacy	—	—	125
2001S 10 piece	2,249,498	19.95	98.00	2005S 11 piece	—	22.95	16.00
2001S 5 quarter set	774,800	13.95	52.00	2005S 5 quarter set	—	15.95	12.50
2001S Silver	849,600	31.95	148	2005S Silver 11 piece	—	37.95	32.00
2002S 10 piece	2,319,766	19.95	32.00	2005S Silver 5 quarter set	—	23.95	20.00
2002S 5 quarter set	764,419	13.95	19.00	2005S American Legacy	—	—	98.00
2002S Silver	892,229	31.95	61.00	2006S 10 piece clad	—	22.95	25.00
2003 X#207, 208, 209.2	—	44.00	28.75	2006S 5 quarter set	—	15.95	13.00
2003S 10 piece	2,175,684	19.95	22.00	2006S Silver 10 piece	—	37.95	32.00
2003S 5 quarter set	1,225,507	13.95	13.50	2006S Silver 5 quarter set	—	23.95	22.00
2003S Silver	1,142,858	31.95	29.50	2007S 5 quarter set	—	13.95	15.50
2004S 11 piece	1,804,396	22.95	36.00	2007S Silver 5 quarter set	—	22.95	25.50
2004S 5 quarter set	987,960	15.95	18.00	2007S 14 piece clad	—	—	44.00
2004S Silver 11 piece	1,187,673	37.95	32.00	2007S Silver 14 piece	—	—	55.00

UNCIRCULATED ROLLS

Listings are for rolls containing uncirculated coins. Large date and small date varieties for 1960 and 1970 apply to the one cent coins.

Date	Cents	Nickels	Dimes	Quarters	Halves
1938	485	540	1,100	3,200	1,850
1938D	510	500	1,075	—	—
1938S	385	365	1,350	3,250	—
1938D Buffalo	—	1,150	—	—	—
1939	180	160	620	1,040	1,250
1939D	360	4,200	515	1,875	1,975
1939S	240	2,750	1,850	3,200	2,400
1940	225	145	550	1,950	1,000
1940D	250	120	780	5,500	—
1940S	375	235	685	1,275	1,200
1941	170	215	440	775	750
1941D	335	270	750	2,750	1,200
1941S	360	280	560	2,500	3,000
1942	140	270	475	485	690
1942P	—	565	—	—	—
1942D	125	2,350	800	1,060	1,350
1942S	650	525	1,100	5,500	1,475
1943	100.00	275	490	420	725
1943D	160	265	640	2,250	1,775
1943S	425	315	675	2,450	1,365
1944	30.00	720	475	425	715
1944D	30.00	680	690	750	1,250
1944S	35.00	485	695	980	1,300
1945	125	410	450	365	730
1945D	120	325	530	1,050	1,050
1945S	26.50	270	525	640	965
1946	18.00	110	95.00	375	1,050
1946D	26.50	100.00	105	385	900
1946S	27.00	55.00	130	350	900
1947	145	58.00	260	750	1,000
1947D	26.50	70.00	285	660	1,000
1947S	30.00	70.00	230	475	—
1948	52.00	80.00	195	250	485
1948D	66.00	125	330	685	425
1948S	150	90.00	265	470	—
1949	110	325	1,360	2,650	1,450
1949D	72.00	215	550	1,350	1,475
1949S	140	138	2,400	—	2,325
1950	67.00	170	740	420	900
1950D	37.00	535	245	460	875
1950S	78.00	—	1,575	850	—
1951	70.00	265	170	435	425
1951D	23.00	355	80.00	365	800
1951S	60.00	280	735	1,450	925
1952	130	215	115	565	410
1952D	17.00	260	115	315	255
1952S	400	52.00	300	1,250	1,650
1953	26.50	26.00	120	660	490
1953D	21.00	19.00	82.00	180	285
1953S	32.00	52.00	82.00	320	875
1954	19.00	66.00	70.00	200	215
1954D	18.00	39.00	70.00	220	220
1954S	19.00	66.00	70.00	160	480
1955	21.00	26.00	70.00	150	365
1955D	15.50	9.00	70.00	145	—
1955S	27.50	—	70.00	—	—

UNCIRCULATED ROLLS

Date	Cents	Nickels	Dimes	Quarters	Halves
1956	13.00	8.50	70.00	175	320
1956D	12.00	8.50	70.00	165	—
1957	11.00	13.00	70.00	145	180
1957D	11.50	6.50	68.00	145	180
1958	11.00	8.00	68.00	145	165
1958D	11.00	6.50	68.00	145	160
1959	2.00	6.00	68.00	145	150
1959D	2.00	6.50	68.00	145	185
1960 large date	2.00	5.50	68.00	145	145
1960 small date	220	—	—	—	—
1960D large date	2.00	7.00	68.00	140	160
1960D small date	2.00	—	—	—	—
1961	2.00	5.50	68.00	140	144
1961D	2.00	5.50	68.00	140	144
1962	2.00	6.25	68.00	140	144
1962D	2.00	7.50	68.00	140	144
1963	2.00	5.50	68.00	140	140
1963D	2.00	6.00	68.00	140	140
1964	2.00	5.00	68.00	140	140
1964D	2.00	5.00	68.00	140	140
1965	2.25	6.00	9.00	27.00	59.00
1966	4.00	6.50	11.50	33.00	63.00
1967	4.25	10.50	10.25	27.00	59.00
1968	2.00	—	10.00	32.00	—
1968D	2.00	6.60	10.00	33.00	59.00
1968S	2.00	7.20	—	—	—
1969	5.00	—	44.00	100.00	—
1969D	2.00	7.00	23.00	95.00	59.00
1969S	2.00	7.50	—	—	—
1970	2.50	—	8.50	26.00	—
1970D	2.00	5.00	9.00	16.00	310
1970S	3.00	5.00	—	—	—
1970S small date	2,600	—	—	—	—
1971	5.00	29.00	16.50	42.00	28.00
1971D	3.00	8.00	10.00	24.00	17.00
1971S	3.50	—	—	—	—
1972	2.00	7.00	12.00	25.00	32.00
1972D	2.00	6.00	10.50	21.00	29.00
1972S	2.50	—	—	—	—
1973	2.00	4.50	11.50	22.00	31.00
1973D	2.00	7.00	10.00	24.00	21.00
1973S	3.00	—	—	—	—
1974	2.00	4.50	8.50	21.00	18.00
1974D	2.00	6.50	8.00	17.50	22.00
1974S	3.00	—	—	—	—
1975	2.00	13.00	10.00	—	—
1975D	2.00	5.50	12.50	—	—
1976	2.00	13.50	21.00	19.75	16.50
1976D	3.00	12.00	20.00	19.50	16.50
1977	2.00	5.50	10.50	16.50	26.00
1977D	2.50	6.00	9.75	17.50	29.00
1978	2.00	4.50	8.00	16.00	38.00
1978D	2.00	5.00	9.00	17.00	52.00
1979	2.00	4.75	8.75	17.00	24.50
1979D	2.00	5.75	8.00	23.00	26.00
1980	2.00	4.50	8.00	17.00	22.50
1980D	2.00	4.75	7.75	17.00	23.00
1981	2.00	4.25	7.50	16.50	24.50
1981D	2.00	4.75	8.00	16.50	24.50
1982	2.00	265	245	280	98.00
1982D	2.00	55.00	66.00	155	95.00
1983	3.75	80.00	235	1,075	108
1983D	11.00	37.00	39.00	410	116
1984	5.50	24.00	8.50	17.50	36.00
1984D	15.00	7.00	22.00	29.00	40.00
1985	4.00	10.00	10.00	31.00	76.00
1985D	3.50	8.00	9.50	22.00	66.00
1986	21.00	9.00	26.00	98.00	130
1986D	28.00	29.00	24.00	225	102
1987	3.00	6.50	7.75	16.00	65.00
1987D	3.50	4.50	9.00	16.00	55.00
1988	6.25	6.00	10.00	32.00	79.00
1988D	4.50	9.00	9.50	24.00	52.00
1989	3.75	6.00	13.50	22.50	44.00
1989D	3.75	8.75	13.50	21.00	34.00
1990	4.40	11.50	12.50	21.00	44.00
1990D	3.75	14.00	10.00	26.00	62.00
1991	2.75	12.50	10.00	31.00	58.00
1991D	3.50	12.50	13.00	35.00	52.00

Date	Cents	Nickels	Dimes	Quarters	Halves
1992	3.00	48.00	8.50	43.00	24.00
1992D	4.75	9.00	8.50	29.00	54.00
1993	3.50	13.50	9.75	40.00	62.00
1993D	4.00	17.50	14.00	37.50	24.00
1994	2.00	8.00	12.50	44.00	16.50
1994D	2.00	8.50	12.50	49.00	23.00
1995	2.25	11.00	17.50	47.00	16.00
1995D	2.25	20.00	21.00	41.00	16.00
1996	2.50	8.00	12.00	19.00	17.00
1996D	3.00	8.50	12.50	28.00	16.00
1997	2.75	14.50	31.00	23.00	17.00
1997D	3.25	62.00	12.50	40.00	16.00
1998	2.00	13.50	10.50	17.50	15.50
1998D	2.00	14.00	9.50	18.50	16.50
1999P	2.25	6.00	9.00	—	18.50
1999D	2.00	7.00	9.00	—	17.50
2000P	2.00	6.25	8.50	—	14.50
2000D	2.00	5.50	8.00	—	16.00
2001P	2.00	5.50	8.00	—	16.00
2001D	2.00	7.00	7.50	—	14.00
2002P	2.00	4.50	7.50	—	28.00
2002D	2.00	4.50	7.50	—	29.00
2003P	2.00	8.50	7.50	—	26.00
2003D	2.00	4.00	7.50	—	26.00
2004P Peace Medal Nickel	2.00	11.50	7.50	—	36.50
2004D Peace Medal Nickel	—	10.00	—	—	36.50
2004P Keelboat Nickel	2.00	4.25	7.50	—	—
2004D Keelboat Nickel	—	3.75	—	—	—
2005P Bison Nickel	2.00	4.00	7.50	—	23.50
2005D Bison Nickel	—	3.75	—	—	23.50
2005P Ocean in view Nickel	2.00	3.75	7.50	—	—
2005D Ocean in view Nickel	—	3.75	—	—	—
2006P	1.50	3.75	9.00	—	30.00
2006D	1.50	3.75	9.00	—	30.00
2007P	1.50	4.00	8.00	—	25.00
2007D	1.50	4.00	8.00	—	25.00
2008P	1.25	3.50	7.50	—	20.00
2008D	1.25	3.50	7.50	—	20.00

50 STATE QUARTERS UNCIRCULATED ROLLS

Listings are for rolls containing uncirculated coins.

State	Philadelphia	Denver	State	Philadelphia	Denver
1999 Delaware	19.75	19.75	2004 Florida	15.00	15.00
1999 New Jersey	17.50	17.50	2004 Texas	15.75	15.75
1999 Georgia	29.50	29.50	2004 Iowa	15.00	15.00
1999 Connecticut	19.50	19.25	2004 Wisconsin	14.50	15.00
2000 Massachusetts	16.00	16.75	2005 California	14.75	14.50
2000 Maryland	16.00	16.50	2005 Minnesota	15.25	15.00
2000 South Carolina	18.50	19.00	2005 Oregon	14.50	14.50
2000 New Hampshire	15.25	15.00	2005 Kansas	14.50	15.00
2000 Virginia	15.00	15.00	2005 West Virginia	14.50	14.50
2001 New York	14.50	14.50	2006 Nevada	14.50	14.50
2001 North Carolina	17.25	16.50	2006 Nebraska	15.00	14.75
2001 Rhode Island	17.25	16.00	2006 Colorado	14.50	14.50
2001 Vermont	17.50	15.00	2006 North Dakota	14.50	14.50
2001 Kentucky	19.50	19.75	2006 South Dakota	15.00	14.50
2002 Mississippi	16.50	16.50	2007 Montana	15.00	14.50
2002 Tennessee	35.00	35.00	2007 Washington	14.50	14.50
2002 Ohio	16.25	15.50	2007 Idaho	14.50	14.50
2002 Louisiana	15.00	15.25	2007 Wyoming	14.50	14.50
2002 Indiana	17.00	16.00	2007 Utah	14.50	14.50
2003 Illinois	16.50	17.75	2008 Oklahoma	15.00	15.00
2003 Alabama	17.00	17.00	2008 New Mexico	—	—
2003 Maine	17.00	15.50	2008 Arizona	—	—
2003 Missouri	15.75	15.50	2008 Alaska	—	—
2003 Arkansas	15.50	15.75	2008 Hawaii	—	—
2004 Michigan	15.00	15.00			

UNCIRCULATED ROLLS

COMMEMORATIVE COINAGE
1892 - 1954

All commemorative half dollars of 1892-1954 have the following specifications: diameter -- 30.6 millimeters; weight -- 12.5000 grams; composition -- 0.9000 silver, 0.3617 ounces actual silver weight. Values for PDS sets contain one example each from the Philadelphia, Denver and San Francisco mints. Type coin prices are the most inexpensive single coin available from the date and mint-mark combinations listed.

QUARTER

KM# 115 COLUMBIAN EXPOSITION
Weight: 6.2500 g. **Composition:** 0.9000 Silver, 0.1808 oz. ASW **Diameter:** 24.3mm.
Obv: Queen Isabella

Date	Mintage	AU-50	MS-60	MS-63	MS-64	MS-65
1893	24,214	590	665	875	1,400	4,200

HALF DOLLAR

KM# 117 COLUMBIAN EXPOSITION
Obv. Designer: Charles E. Barber
Rev. Designer: George T. Morgan

Date	Mintage	AU-50	MS-60	MS-63	MS-64	MS-65
1892	950,000	18.50	28.00	85.00	180	650
1893	1,550,405	15.50	28.00	80.00	195	875

KM# 135 PANAMA-PACIFIC EXPOSITION
Designer: Charles E. Barber

Date	Mintage	AU-50	MS-60	MS-63	MS-64	MS-65
1915S	27,134	465	550	825	1,550	2,650

KM# 143 LINCOLN-ILLINOIS
Obv. Designer: George T. Morgan
Rev. Designer: John R. Sinnock

Date	Mintage	AU-50	MS-60	MS-63	MS-64	MS-65
1918	100,058	135	155	170	250	525

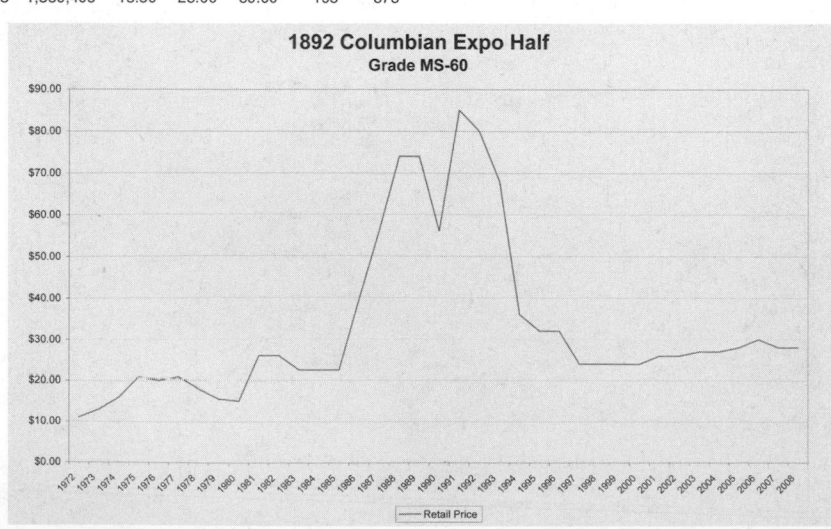

1892 Columbian Expo Half
Grade MS-60

Retail Price

KM# 146 MAINE CENTENNIAL
Designer: Anthony de Francisci

Date	Mintage	AU-50	MS-60	MS-63	MS-64	MS-65
1920	50,028	135	165	195	310	585

KM# 147.1 PILGRIM TERCENTENARY
Designer: Cyrus E. Dallin

Date	Mintage	AU-50	MS-60	MS-63	MS-64	MS-65
1920	152,112	85.00	110	122	160	465

2x2

KM# 148.1 ALABAMA CENTENNIAL
Obv: "2x2" at right above stars
Designer: Laura G. Fraser
Notes: "Fake 2x2" counterstamps exist.

Date	Mintage	AU-50	MS-60	MS-63	MS-64	MS-65
1921	6,006	315	330	600	950	1,975

KM# 148.2 ALABAMA CENTENNIAL
Obv. Designer: Laura G. Fraser

Date	Mintage	AU-50	MS-60	MS-63	MS-64	MS-65
1921	59,038	190	215	525	685	1,800

KM# 149.1 MISSOURI CENTENNIAL
Designer: Robert Aitken

Date	Mintage	AU-50	MS-60	MS-63	MS-64	MS-65
1921	15,428	410	725	925	1,775	5,000

2x4

KM# 149.2 MISSOURI CENTENNIAL
Obv: 2 star 4 in field at left
Designer: Robert Aitken
Notes: "Fake "2*4" counterstamps exist.

Date	Mintage	AU-50	MS-60	MS-63	MS-64	MS-65
1921	5,000	650	800	1,100	1,900	5,000

KM# 147.2 PILGRIM TERCENTENARY
Obv: 1921 date next to Pilgrim
Designer: Cyrus E. Dallin

Date	Mintage	AU-50	MS-60	MS-63	MS-64	MS-65
1921	20,053	175	200	225	285	600

KM# 151.1 GRANT MEMORIAL
Designer: Laura G. Fraser

Date	Mintage	AU-50	MS-60	MS-63	MS-64	MS-65
1922	67,405	115	125	160	290	800

COMMEMORATIVES

KM# 151.2 GRANT MEMORIAL Obv: Star above the word "Grant" Designer: Laura G. Fraser
Notes: "Fake star" counterstamps exist.

Date	Mintage	AU-50	MS-60	MS-63	MS-64	MS-65
1922	4,256	950	1,300	2,100	2,850	7,250

KM# 153 MONROE DOCTRINE CENTENNIAL
Designer: Chester Beach

Date	Mintage	AU-50	MS-60	MS-63	MS-64	MS-65
1923S	274,077	58.00	75.00	145	525	2,950

KM# 154 HUGUENOT-WALLOON TERCENTENARY Obv: Huguenot leader Gaspard de Coligny and William I of Orange Designer: George T. Morgan

Date	Mintage	AU-50	MS-60	MS-63	MS-64	MS-65
1924	142,080	135	155	175	250	550

KM# 155 CALIFORNIA DIAMOND JUBILEE
Designer: Jo Mora

Date	Mintage	AU-50	MS-60	MS-63	MS-64	MS-65
1925S	86,594	215	240	280	520	1,125

KM# 158 FORT VANCOUVER CENTENNIAL
Designer: Laura G. Fraser

Date	Mintage	AU-50	MS-60	MS-63	MS-64	MS-65
1925	14,994	335	415	475	600	1,450

KM# 156 LEXINGTON-CONCORD SESQUICENTENNIAL Designer: Chester Beach

Date	Mintage	AU-50	MS-60	MS-63	MS-64	MS-65
1925	162,013	96.00	110	120	185	485

KM# 157 STONE MOUNTAIN MEMORIAL
Designer: Gutzon Borglum

Date	Mintage	AU-50	MS-60	MS-63	MS-64	MS-65
1925	1,314,709	70.00	77.00	85.00	90.00	285

KM# 159 OREGON TRAIL MEMORIAL
Designer: James E. and Laura G. Fraser

Date	Mintage	AU-50	MS-60	MS-63	MS-64	MS-65
1926	47,955	140	170	190	210	335
1926S	83,055	140	170	185	205	335
Type coin	—	150	180	190	210	320
1928	6,028	220	245	280	290	390
1933D	5,008	375	400	410	420	540
1934D	7,006	205	220	230	240	365
1936	10,006	150	190	200	210	325
1936S	5,006	170	190	210	220	360
1937D	12,008	180	205	210	215	325

Date	Mintage	AU-50	MS-60	MS-63	MS-64	MS-65
1938	6,006	160	175	210	215	335
1938D	6,005	160	175	215	235	335
1938S	6,006	160	175	210	220	335
1939	3,004	525	620	630	655	720
1939D	3,004	525	620	640	675	735
1939S	3,005	525	620	630	655	725

KM# 160 U.S. SESQUICENTENNIAL
Designer: John R. Sinnock

Date	Mintage	AU-50	MS-60	MS-63	MS-64	MS-65
1926	141,120	88.00	115	150	600	4,400

KM# 162 VERMONT SESQUICENTENNIAL
Obv. Designer: Charles Keck

Date	Mintage	AU-50	MS-60	MS-63	MS-64	MS-65
1927	28,142	255	290	305	350	990

KM# 163 HAWAIIAN SESQUICENTENNIAL
Designer: Juliette M. Fraser **Notes:** Counterfeits exist.

Date	Mintage	AU-50	MS-60	MS-63	MS-64	MS-65
1928	10,008	1,750	2,650	3,500	4,500	6,850

KM# 165.1 DANIEL BOONE BICENTENNIAL
Designer: Augustus Lukeman

Date	Mintage	AU-50	MS-60	MS-63	MS-64	MS-65
1934	10,007	125	135	140	150	275
1935	10,010	118	120	125	130	275
1935D	5,005	133	140	145	152	325
1935S	5,005	133	140	145	152	325

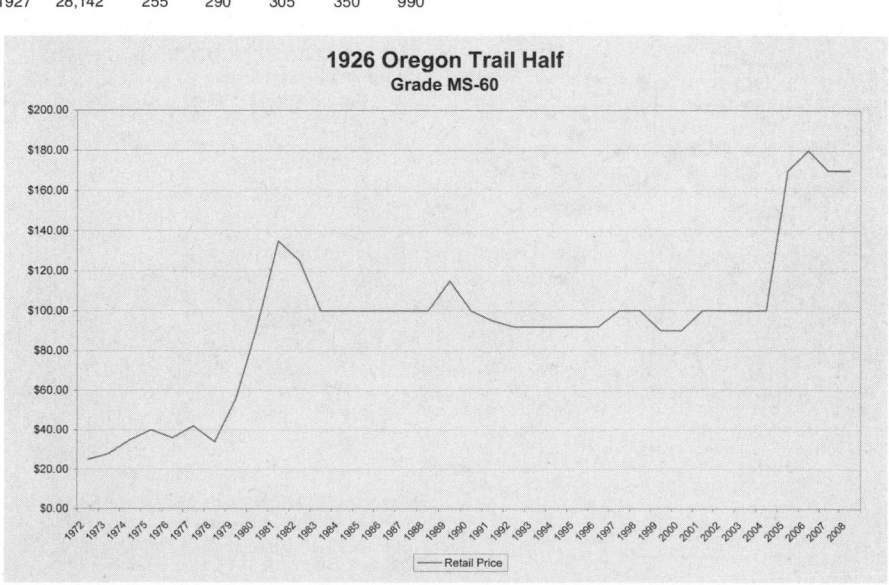

1926 Oregon Trail Half
Grade MS-60

COMMEMORATIVES

COMMEMORATIVES

KM# 165.2 DANIEL BOONE BICENTENNIAL
Rev: "1934" added above the word "Pioneer."
Designer: Augustus Lukeman

Date	Mintage	AU-50	MS-60	MS-63	MS-64	MS-65
1935	10,008	118	120	125	130	275
Type coin	—	130	135	145	150	240
1935D	2,003	375	415	430	485	860
1935S	2,004	375	415	430	450	890
1936	12,012	118	120	125	130	275
1936D	5,005	133	140	145	152	325
1936S	5,006	133	140	145	152	325
1937	9,810	125	130	135	980	285
1937D	2,506	285	385	390	385	560
1937S	2,506	285	385	390	415	590
1938	2,100	360	395	410	415	555
1938D	2,100	360	395	410	430	545
1938S	2,100	360	395	410	415	595

KM# 166 MARYLAND TERCENTENARY
Designer: Hans Schuler

Date	Mintage	AU-50	MS-60	MS-63	MS-64	MS-65
1934	25,015	160	180	195	215	350

KM# 167 TEXAS CENTENNIAL
Designer: Pompeo Coppini

Date	Mintage	AU-50	MS-60	MS-63	MS-64	MS-65
1934	61,463	140	145	155	160	290
Type coin	—	145	158	163	165	260
1935	9,994	140	145	155	160	290
1935D	10,007	140	145	155	160	290
1935S	10,008	140	145	155	160	290
1936	8,911	140	145	155	160	290
1936D	9,039	140	145	155	160	290
1936S	9,055	140	145	155	160	290
1937	6,571	142	148	160	165	295
1937D	6,605	142	148	160	165	295
1937S	6,637	142	148	160	165	295
1938	3,780	240	265	275	300	500
1938D	3,775	240	265	275	300	485
1938S	3,814	240	265	275	300	485

KM# 168 ARKANSAS CENTENNIAL
Designer: Edward E. Burr

Date	Mintage	AU-50	MS-60	MS-63	MS-64	MS-65
Type coin	—	110	115	125	130	210
1935	13,012	100.00	110	120	125	215
1935D	5,505	105	115	125	130	300
1935S	5,506	105	115	125	130	300
1936	9,660	100.00	110	120	125	230
1936D	9,660	100.00	110	120	125	230
1936S	9,662	100.00	110	120	125	230
1937	5,505	105	115	128	135	340
1937D	5,505	105	115	128	135	330
1937S	5,506	105	115	128	135	380
1938	3,156	165	190	210	210	620
1938D	3,155	165	190	195	210	610
1938S	3,156	165	190	195	210	675
1939	2,104	330	390	400	410	1,000
1939D	2,104	330	390	400	410	980
1939S	2,105	330	390	400	410	965

KM# 169 CONNECTICUT TERCENTENARY
Designer: Henry Kreiss

Date	Mintage	AU-50	MS-60	MS-63	MS-64	MS-65
1935	25,018	255	290	310	380	540

KM# 170 HUDSON, N.Y., SESQUICENTENNIAL
Designer: Chester Beach

Date	Mintage	AU-50	MS-60	MS-63	MS-64	MS-65
1935	10,008	750	925	1,250	1,675	2,250

KM# 172 OLD SPANISH TRAIL
Designer: L.W. Hoffecker **Notes:** Counterfeits exist.

Date	Mintage	AU-50	MS-60	MS-63	MS-64	MS-65
1935	10,008	1,250	1,375	1,700	1,900	2,250

KM# 171 SAN DIEGO, CALIFORNIA - PACIFIC EXPOSITION **Designer:** Robert Aitken

Date	Mintage	AU-50	MS-60	MS-63	MS-64	MS-65
1935S	70,132	105	130	145	150	170
1936D	30,092	105	135	150	160	170

KM# 173 ALBANY, N.Y., CHARTER ANNIVERSARY **Designer:** Gertrude K. Lathrop

Date	Mintage	AU-50	MS-60	MS-63	MS-64	MS-65
1936	17,671	320	330	380	385	470

KM# 187 ARKANSAS CENTENNIAL
Obv: Sen. Joseph T. Robinson **Obv. Designer:** Henry Kreiss **Rev. Designer:** Edward E. Burr

Date	Mintage	AU-50	MS-60	MS-63	MS-64	MS-65
1936	25,265	145	150	165	180	420

KM# 181 BATTLE OF GETTYSBURG 75TH ANNIVERSARY **Designer:** Frank Vittor

Date	Mintage	AU-50	MS-60	MS-63	MS-64	MS-65
1936	26,928	435	475	500	525	765

KM# 175 BRIDGEPORT, CONN., CENTENNIAL
Designer: Henry Kreiss

Date	Mintage	AU-50	MS-60	MS-63	MS-64	MS-65
1936	25,015	140	150	190	200	315

KM# 176 CINCINNATI MUSIC CENTER
Designer: Constance Ortmayer

Date	Mintage	AU-50	MS-60	MS-63	MS-64	MS-65
Type coin	—	335	345	375	560	700
1936	5,005	315	330	360	540	925
1936D	5,005	315	330	360	540	750
1936S	5,006	315	330	360	540	750

KM# 177 CLEVELAND-GREAT LAKES EXPOSITION **Designer:** Brenda Putnam

Date	Mintage	AU-50	MS-60	MS-63	MS-64	MS-65
1936	50,030	135	140	150	160	245

KM# 178 COLUMBIA, S.C., SESQUICENTENNIAL
Designer: A. Wolfe Davidson

Date	Mintage	AU-50	MS-60	MS-63	MS-64	MS-65
1936	9,007	275	280	300	310	415
Type coin	—	280	290	330	335	385
1936D	8,009	275	280	300	310	415
1936S	8,007	275	280	300	310	415

KM# 183 LYNCHBURG, VA., SESQUICENTENNIAL **Designer:** Charles Keck

Date	Mintage	AU-50	MS-60	MS-63	MS-64	MS-65
1936	20,013	235	265	280	295	365

KM# 179 DELAWARE TERCENTENARY
Designer: Carl L. Schmitz

Date	Mintage	AU-50	MS-60	MS-63	MS-64	MS-65
1936	20,993	310	325	365	385	490

KM# 184 NORFOLK, VA., BICENTENNIAL
Designer: William M. and Marjorie E. Simpson

Date	Mintage	AU-50	MS-60	MS-63	MS-64	MS-65
1936	16,936	535	565	590	610	650

KM# 180 ELGIN, ILL., CENTENNIAL
Designer: Trygve Rovelstad

Date	Mintage	AU-50	MS-60	MS-63	MS-64	MS-65
1936	20,015	245	265	280	295	355

KM# 185 RHODE ISLAND TERCENTENARY
Designer: Arthur G. Carey and John H. Benson

Date	Mintage	AU-50	MS-60	MS-63	MS-64	MS-65
1936	20,013	100.00	110	120	130	260
Type coin	—	105	110	125	128	290
1936D	15,010	100.00	110	120	130	275
1936S	15,011	100.00	110	120	130	290

KM# 182 LONG ISLAND TERCENTENARY
Designer: Howard K. Weinman

Date	Mintage	AU-50	MS-60	MS-63	MS-64	MS-65
1936	81,826	88.00	98.00	110	130	420

KM# 174 SAN FRANCISCO-OAKLAND BAY BRIDGE **Designer:** Jacques Schnier

Date	Mintage	AU-50	MS-60	MS-63	MS-64	MS-65
1936	71,424	170	180	220	225	375

KM# 188 WISCONSIN TERRITORIAL
CENTENNIAL Designer: David Parsons

Date	Mintage	AU-50	MS-60	MS-63	MS-64	MS-65
1936	25,015	230	255	275	315	400

KM# 189 YORK COUNTY, MAINE,
TERCENTENARY Designer: Walter H. Rich

Date	Mintage	AU-50	MS-60	MS-63	MS-64	MS-65
1936	25,015	135	170	195	300	590

KM# 190 BATTLE OF ANTIETAM 75TH
ANNIVERSARY Designer: William M. Simpson

Date	Mintage	AU-50	MS-60	MS-63	MS-64	MS-65
1937	18,028	725	760	790	850	985

KM# 186 ROANOKE ISLAND, N.C.
Designer: William M. Simpson

Date	Mintage	AU-50	MS-60	MS-63	MS-64	MS-65
1937	29,030	255	285	310	330	340

KM# 191 NEW ROCHELLE, N.Y.
Designer: Gertrude K. Lathrop

Date	Mintage	AU-50	MS-60	MS-63	MS-64	MS-65
1938	15,266	420	445	460	470	610

KM# 198 BOOKER T. WASHINGTON
Designer: Isaac S. Hathaway **Notes:** Actual
mintages are higher, but unsold issues were melted
to produce Washington Carver issues.

Date	Mintage	AU-50	MS-60	MS-63	MS-64	MS-65
1946	1,000,546	14.00	18.00	19.50	21.00	50.00
Type coin	—	15.00	16.00	17.50	18.50	56.00
1946D	200,113	16.00	20.00	21.00	30.00	64.00
1946S	500,729	14.00	18.00	19.50	21.00	50.00
1947	100,017	25.00	35.00	55.00	65.00	95.00
1947D	100,017	25.00	35.00	55.00	70.00	115
1947S	100,017	25.00	35.00	55.00	65.00	90.00
1948	8,005	38.00	58.00	85.00	86.00	100.00
1948D	8,005	38.00	58.00	85.00	86.00	94.00
1948S	8,005	38.00	58.00	85.00	95.00	98.00
1949	6,004	67.00	83.00	92.00	98.00	120
1949D	6,004	67.00	83.00	92.00	98.00	120
1949S	6,004	67.00	83.00	95.00	104	110
1950	6,004	45.00	65.00	78.00	88.00	98.00
1950D	6,004	45.00	65.00	75.00	88.00	96.00
1950S	512,091	15.00	20.00	24.00	28.00	52.00
1951	51,082	15.00	20.00	24.00	28.00	50.00
1951D	7,004	45.00	65.00	78.00	90.00	95.00
1951S	7,004	45.00	65.00	78.00	90.00	95.00

KM# 197 IOWA STATEHOOD CENTENNIAL
Designer: Adam Pietz

Date	Mintage	AU-50	MS-60	MS-63	MS-64	MS-65
1946	100,057	115	120	125	130	260

COMMEMORATIVES

KM# 200 BOOKER T. WASHINGTON AND GEORGE WASHINGTON CARVER
Designer: Isaac S. Hathaway

Date	Mintage	AU-50	MS-60	MS-63	MS-64	MS-65
1951	110,018	26.00	34.00	53.00	54.00	290
Type coin	—	14.00	16.00	18.50	20.00	52.50
1951D	10,004	35.00	43.00	60.00	58.00	140
1951S	10,004	35.00	43.00	60.00	58.00	140
1952	2,006,292	15.00	18.00	26.50	44.00	48.00
1952D	8,006	40.00	50.00	70.00	70.00	200
1952S	8,006	40.00	50.00	80.00	70.00	160
1953	8,003	35.00	47.00	75.00	85.00	260
1953D	8,003	35.00	47.00	75.00	85.00	175
1953S	108,020	26.00	33.00	50.00	55.00	120
1954	12,006	36.00	42.00	60.00	65.00	150
1954D	12,006	36.00	42.00	60.00	65.00	200
1954S	122,024	24.00	32.00	38.00	48.00	65.00

DOLLAR

KM# 118 LAFAYETTE Weight: 26.7300 g.
Composition: 0.9000 Silver, 0.7734 oz. ASW **Diameter:** 38.1mm. **Designer:** Charles E. Barber

Date	Mintage	AU-50	MS-60	MS-63	MS-64	MS-65
1900	36,026	675	1,025	2,150	3,700	10,850

KM# 120 LOUISIANA PURCHASE EXPOSITION
Weight: 1.6720 g. **Composition:** 0.9000 Gold, 0.0484 oz. AGW **Diameter:** 15mm. **Obv:** William McKinley **Obv. Designer:** Charles E. Barber

Date	Mintage	AU-50	MS-60	MS-63	MS-64	MS-65
1903	17,500	715	765	1,080	2,150	3,300

KM# 119 LOUISIANA PURCHASE EXPOSITION
Weight: 1.6720 g. **Composition:** 0.9000 Gold, 0.0484 oz. AGW **Diameter:** 15mm. **Obv:** Jefferson **Designer:** Charles E. Barber

Date	Mintage	AU-50	MS-60	MS-63	MS-64	MS-65
1903	17,500	700	765	1,160	1,900	3,100

KM# 121 LEWIS AND CLARK EXPOSITION
Weight: 1.6720 g. **Composition:** 0.9000 Gold, 0.0484 oz. AGW **Diameter:** 15mm. **Obv. Designer:** Charles E. Barber

Date	Mintage	AU-50	MS-60	MS-63	MS-64	MS-65
1904	10,025	1,050	1,350	2,550	5,900	12,250
1905	10,041	1,300	1,625	3,300	7,000	18,500

KM# 136 PANAMA-PACIFIC EXPOSITION
Weight: 1.6720 g. **Composition:** 0.9000 Gold, 0.0484 oz. AGW **Diameter:** 15mm. **Obv. Designer:** Charles Keck

Date	Mintage	AU-50	MS-60	MS-63	MS-64	MS-65
1915S	15,000	650	750	950	1,500	2,450

KM# 144 MCKINLEY MEMORIAL Weight:
1.6720 g. **Composition:** 0.9000 Gold, 0.0484 oz. AGW **Diameter:** 15mm. **Obv. Designer:** Charles E. Barber **Rev. Designer:** George T. Morgan

Date	Mintage	AU-50	MS-60	MS-63	MS-64	MS-65
1916	9,977	625	685	800	1,550	2,350
1917	10,000	785	800	1,325	2,200	3,800

KM# 152.1 GRANT MEMORIAL Weight: 1.6720
g. **Composition:** 0.9000 Gold, 0.0484 oz. AGW **Diameter:** 15mm. **Obv. Designer:** Laura G. Fraser **Notes:** Without an incuse "star" above the word GRANT on the obverse.

Date	Mintage	AU-50	MS-60	MS-63	MS-64	MS-65
1922	5,000	1,875	1,900	2,350	3,650	4,900

Star

KM# 152.2 GRANT MEMORIAL
Weight: 1.6720 g. **Composition:** 0.9000 Gold,

0.0484 oz. AGW **Diameter:** 15mm.
Obv. Designer: Laura G. Fraser **Notes:** Variety with an incuse "star" above the word GRANT on the obverse.

Date	Mintage	AU-50	MS-60	MS-63	MS-64	MS-65
1922	5,016	1,800	1,950	2,400	3,700	4,400

$2.50 QUARTER EAGLE

KM# 137 PANAMA-PACIFIC EXPOSITION
Weight: 4.1800 g. **Composition:** 0.9000 Gold,

0.1209 oz. AGW **Diameter:** 18mm. **Obv.**
Designer: Charles E. Barber **Rev. Designer:**
George T. Morgan

Date	Mintage	AU-50	MS-60	MS-63	MS-64	MS-65
1915S	6,749	1,750	2,100	4,350	6,300	8,000

KM# 161 PHILADELPHIA SESQUICENTENNIAL
Weight: 4.1800 g. **Composition:** 0.9000 Gold,
0.1209 oz. AGW **Diameter:** 18mm. **Obv.**
Designer: John R. Sinnock

Date	Mintage	AU-50	MS-60	MS-63	MS-64	MS-65
1926	46,019	525	565	850	1,700	4,200

$50

KM# 139 PANAMA-PACIFIC EXPOSITION OCTAGONAL   Weight: 83.5900 g. **Composition:** 0.9000
Gold, 2.4186 oz. AGW **Diameter:** 44mm. **Obv. Designer:** Robert Aitken

Date	Mintage	AU-50	MS-60	MS-63	MS-64	MS-65
1915S	645	52,500	55,000	80,000	99,500	148,000

KM# 138 PANAMA-PACIFIC EXPOSITION ROUND   Weight: 83.5900 g. **Composition:** 0.9000 Gold,
2.4186 oz. AGW **Diameter:** 44mm. **Obv. Designer:** Robert Aitken

Date	Mintage	AU-50	MS-60	MS-63	MS-64	MS-65
1915S	483	54,000	60,000	82,500	105,000	145,000

COMMEMORATIVE COINAGE
1982 - PRESENT

All commemorative silver dollar coins of 1982-present have the following specifications: diameter — 38.1 millimeters; weight — 26.7300 grams; composition — 0.9000 silver, 0.7736 ounces actual silver weight. All commemorative $5 coins of 1982-present have the following specificiations: diameter — 21.6 millimeters; weight — 8.3590 grams; composition: 0.9000 gold, 0.242 ounces actual gold weight.

Note: In 1982, after a hiatus of nearly 20 years, coinage of commemorative half dollars resumed. Those designated with a 'W' were struck at the West Point Mint. Some issues were struck in copper-nickel. Those struck in silver have the same size, weight and composition as the prior commemorative half-dollar series.

HALF DOLLAR

KM# 208 GEORGE WASHINGTON, 250TH BIRTH ANNIVERSARY Weight: 12.500 g. Composition: 0.9000 Silver, 0.3617 oz. ASW Diameter: 30.6mm. Obv. Designer: Elizabeth Jones

Date	Mintage	Proof	MS-65	Prf-65
1982D	2,210,458	—	6.50	—
1982S	—	4,894,044	—	6.50

KM# 228 MOUNT RUSHMORE 50TH ANNIVERSARY Weight: 11.3400 g. Composition: Copper-Nickel Clad Copper Obv. Designer: Marcel Jovine Rev. Designer: T. James Ferrell

Date	Mintage	Proof	MS-65	Prf-65
1991D	172,754	—	21.50	—
1991S	—	—	—	20.00

KM# 212 STATUE OF LIBERTY CENTENNIAL Weight: 11.3400 g. Composition: Copper-Nickel Clad Copper Obv. Designer: Edgar Z. Steever Rev. Designer: Sherl Joseph Winter

Date	Mintage	Proof	MS-65	Prf-65
1986D	928,008	—	5.50	—
1986S	—	6,925,627	—	5.50

KM# 233 1992 OLYMPICS Weight: 11.3400 g. Composition: Copper-Nickel Clad Copper Obv. Designer: William Cousins Rev. Designer: Steven M. Bieda

Date	Mintage	Proof	MS-65	Prf-65
1992P	161,607	—	8.50	—
1992S	—	519,645	—	8.50

KM# 224 BICENTENNIAL OF THE CONGRESS Weight: 11.3400 g. Composition: Copper-Nickel Clad Copper Obv. Designer: Patricia L. Verani Rev. Designer: William Woodward and Edgar Z. Steever

Date	Mintage	Proof	MS-65	Prf-65
1989D	163,753	—	8.00	—
1989S	—	—	—	8.00

KM# 237 500TH ANNIVERSARY OF COLUMBUS DISCOVERY Weight: 11.3400 g. Composition: Copper-Nickel Clad Copper Designer: T. James Ferrell

Date	Mintage	Proof	MS-65	Prf-65
1992D	135,702	—	11.50	—
1992S	—	390,154	—	11.50

KM# 240 JAMES MADISON AND BILL OF RIGHTS Weight: 12.5000 g. **Composition:** 0.9000 Silver, 0.3617 oz. ASW **Obv. Designer:** T. James Ferrell **Rev. Designer:** Dean McMullen

Date	Mintage	Proof	MS-65	Prf-65
1993W	173,224	—	20.00	—
1993S	—	559,758	—	16.50

KM# 243 WORLD WAR II 50TH ANNIVERSARY Weight: 11.3400 g. **Composition:** Copper-Nickel Clad Copper **Obv. Designer:** George Klauba **Rev. Designer:** William J. Leftwich

Date	Mintage	Proof	MS-65	Prf-65
1993P	192,968	—	29.00	—
1993P	—	290,343	—	26.50

KM# 246 1994 WORLD CUP SOCCER Weight: 11.3400 g. **Composition:** Copper-Nickel Clad Copper **Obv. Designer:** Richard T. LaRoche **Rev. Designer:** Dean McMullen

Date	Mintage	Proof	MS-65	Prf-65
1994D	168,208	—	9.75	—
1994P	122,412	—	10.25	—
1994P	—	609,354	—	8.50

KM# 257 ATLANTA OLYMPICS Weight: 11.3400 g. **Composition:** Copper-Nickel Clad Copper **Obv:** Basketball

Date	Mintage	Proof	MS-65	Prf-65
1995S	—	169,655	—	18.00
1995S	171,001	—	22.50	—

KM# 262 ATLANTA OLYMPICS Weight: 11.3400 g. **Composition:** Copper-Nickel Clad Copper **Obv:** Baseball **Obv. Designer:** Edgar Z. Steever

Date	Mintage	Proof	MS-65	Prf-65
1995S	164,605	—	22.50	—
1995S	—	118,087	—	19.00

KM# 254 CIVIL WAR Weight: 11.3400 g. **Comp.:** Copper-Nickel Clad Copper **Obv. Des.:** Don Troiani **Rev. Des.:** T. James Ferrell

Date	Mintage	Proof	MS-65	Prf-65
1995S	119,510	—	42.50	—
1995S	—	330,099	—	41.50

KM# 271 ATLANTA OLYMPICS Weight:
11.3400 g. **Composition:** Copper-Nickel Clad
Copper **Obv:** Soccer

Date	Mintage	Proof	MS-65	Prf-65
1996S	52,836	—	110	—
1996S	—	122,412	—	105

KM# 267 ATLANTA OLYMPICS Weight:
11.3400 g. **Composition:** Copper-Nickel Clad
Copper **Obv:** Swimming

Date	Mintage	Proof	MS-65	Prf-65
1996S	49,533	—	165	—
1996S	—	114,315	—	36.00

KM# 323 U. S. CAPITOL VISITOR CENTER
Weight: 11.3400 g. **Comp.:** Copper-Nickel Clad
Copper **Obv. Designer:** Dean McMullen **Rev.
Designer:** Alex Shagin and Marcel Jovine

Date	Mintage	Proof	MS-65	Prf-65
2001P	99,157	—	13.50	—
2001P	—	77,962	—	17.50

KM# 348 FIRST FLIGHT CENTENNIAL
Weight: 11.3400 g. **Composition:** Copper-Nickel
Clad Copper **Obv. Designer:** John Mercanti **Rev.
Designer:** Donna Weaver

Date	Mintage	Proof	MS-65	Prf-65
2003P	57,726	—	15.50	—
2003P	—	111,569	—	15.50

KM# 438 AMERICAN BALD EAGLE Weight:
11.3400 g. **Composition:** Copper-Nickel Clad
Copper **Diameter:** 30.6mm. **Obv:** Two eaglets in
nest with egg

Date	Mintage	Proof	MS-65	Prf-65
2008	750,000	—	—	—

DOLLAR

KM# 209 LOS ANGELES XXIII OLYMPIAD
Obv. Designer: Elizabeth Jones

Date	Mintage	Proof	MS-65	Prf-65
1983P	294,543	—	14.10	—
1983D	174,014	—	14.10	—
1983S	174,014	—	14.10	—
1983S	—	1,577,025	—	14.10

KM# 210 LOS ANGELES XXIII OLYMPIAD
Obv. Designer: Robert Graham

Date	Mintage	Proof	MS-65	Prf-65
1984P	217,954	—	14.10	—
1984D	116,675	—	14.40	—
1984S	116,675	—	14.40	—
1984S	—	1,801,210	—	14.10

KM# 214 STATUE OF LIBERTY CENTENNIAL
Obv. Designer: John Mercanti **Rev. Designer:** John Mercanti and Matthew Peloso

Date	Mintage	Proof	MS-65	Prf-65
1986P	723,635	—	14.10	—
1986S	—	6,414,638	—	14.10

KM# 222 OLYMPICS **Obv. Designer:** Patricia L. Verani **Rev. Designer:** Sherl Joseph Winter

Date	Mintage	Proof	MS-65	Prf-65
1988D	191,368	—	14.10	—
1988S	—	1,359,366	—	14.10

KM# 220 CONSTITUTION BICENTENNIAL
Obv. Designer: Patricia L. Verani

Date	Mintage	Proof	MS-65	Prf-65
1987P	451,629	—	14.10	—
1987S	—	2,747,116	—	14.10

KM# 225 BICENTENNIAL OF THE CONGRESS
Designer: William Woodward and Chester Y. Martin

Date	Mintage	Proof	MS-65	Prf-65
1989D	135,203	—	16.50	—
1989S	—	762,198	—	18.50

KM# 227 EISENHOWER CENTENNIAL Obv.
Designer: John Mercanti **Rev. Designer:** Marcel
Jovine and John Mercanti

Date	Mintage	Proof	MS-65	Prf-65
1990W	241,669	—	15.50	—
1990P	—	638,335	—	17.00

KM# 229 MOUNT RUSHMORE GOLDEN
ANNIVERSARY Obv. Designer: Marika Somogyi
Rev. Designer: Frank Gasparro

Date	Mintage	Proof	MS-65	Prf-65
1991P	133,139	—	32.50	—
1991S	—	738,419	—	30.00

KM# 231 KOREAN WAR Obv. Designer: John
Mercanti **Rev. Designer:** T. James Ferrell

Date	Mintage	Proof	MS-65	Prf-65
1991D	213,049	—	16.50	—
1991P	—	618,488	—	20.50

KM# 232 USO 50TH ANNIVERSARY
Obv. Designer: Robert Lamb **Rev. Designer:** John
Mercanti

Date	Mintage	Proof	MS-65	Prf-65
1991D	124,958	—	14.00	—
1991S	—	321,275	—	19.50

KM# 238 COLUMBUS QUINCENTENARY
Obv. Designer: John Mercanti **Rev. Designer:** Thomas D. Rogers, Sr.

Date	Mintage	Proof	MS-65	Prf-65
1992D	106,949	—	29.00	—
1992P	—	385,241	—	39.00

KM# 236 WHITE HOUSE BICENTENNIAL
Obv. Designer: Edgar Z. Steever **Rev. Designer:** Chester Y. Martin

Date	Mintage	Proof	MS-65	Prf-65
1992D	123,803	—	31.50	—
1992W	—	375,851	—	31.50

KM# 234 OLYMPICS
Obv. Designer: John R. Deecken and Chester Y. Martin **Rev. Designer:** Marcel Jovine

Date	Mintage	Proof	MS-65	Prf-65
1992D	187,552	—	24.50	—
1992S	—	504,505	—	26.00

KM# 241 JAMES MADISON AND BILL OF RIGHTS
Obv. Designer: William Krawczewicz and Thomas D. Rogers, Sr. **Rev. Designer:** Dean McMullen and Thomas D. Rogers, Sr.

Date	Mintage	Proof	MS-65	Prf-65
1993D	98,383	—	19.50	—
1993S	—	534,001	—	20.00

KM# 249 THOMAS JEFFERSON 250TH BIRTH ANNIVERSARY Designer: T. James Ferrell

Date	Mintage	Proof	MS-65	Prf-65
1993P	266,927	—	23.00	—
1993S	—	332,891	—	28.00

KM# 251 NATIONAL PRISONER OF WAR MUSEUM Obv. Designer: Thomas Nielson and Alfred Maletsky **Rev. Designer:** Edgar Z. Steever

Date	Mintage	Proof	MS-65	Prf-65
1994W	54,790	—	90.00	—
1994P	—	220,100	—	46.50

KM# 253 U.S. CAPITOL BICENTENNIAL

Date	Mintage	Proof	MS-65	Prf-65
1994D	68,352	—	20.00	—
1994S	—	279,416	—	25.00

KM# 244 WORLD WAR II 50TH ANNIVERSARY Designer: Thomas D. Rogers, Sr.

Date	Mintage	Proof	MS-65	Prf-65
1993D	94,708	—	31.50	—
1993W	—	322,422	—	40.00

KM# 250 VIETNAM VETERANS MEMORIAL
Obv. Designer: John Mercanti **Rev. Designer:** Thomas D. Rogers, Sr.

Date	Mintage	Proof	MS-65	Prf-65
1994W	57,317	—	85.00	—
1994P	—	226,262	—	69.00

KM# 247 WORLD CUP SOCCER Obv.
Designer: Dean McMullen and T. James Ferrell

Date	Mintage	Proof	MS-65	Prf-65
1994D	81,698	—	26.00	—
1994S	—	576,978	—	29.00

KM# 252 WOMEN IN MILITARY SERVICE
MEMORIAL   Obv. Designer: T. James Ferrell **Rev. Designer:** Thomas D. Rogers, Sr.

Date	Mintage	Proof	MS-65	Prf-65
1994W	53,054	—	39.50	—
1994P	—	213,201	—	36.00

KM# 260 ATLANTA OLYMPICS
Obv: Gymnastics

Date	Mintage	Proof	MS-65	Prf-65
1995D	42,497	—	75.00	—
1995P	—	182,676	—	58.00

COMMEMORATIVES

KM# 264 ATLANTA OLYMPICS Obv: Track and field **Obv. Designer:** John Mercanti

Date	Mintage	Proof	MS-65	Prf-65
1995D	24,796	—	98.00	—
1995P	—	136,935	—	53.00

KM# 259 ATLANTA OLYMPICS, PARALYMPICS Obv: Blind runner

Date	Mintage	Proof	MS-65	Prf-65
1995D	28,649	—	93.00	—
1995P	—	138,337	—	64.00

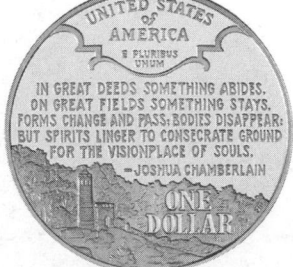

KM# 263 ATLANTA OLYMPICS Obv: Cycling **Obv. Designer:** John Mercanti

Date	Mintage	Proof	MS-65	Prf-65
1995D	19,662	—	150	—
1995P	—	118,795	—	47.50

KM# 255 CIVIL WAR Obv. Designer: Don Troiani and Edgar Z. Steever **Rev. Designer:** John Mercanti

Date	Mintage	Proof	MS-65	Prf-65
1995P	45,866	—	74.00	—
1995S	—	437,114	—	78.00

KM# 266 SPECIAL OLYMPICS WORLD GAMES
Obv. Designer: Jamie Wyeth and T. James Ferrell
Rev. Designer: Thomas D. Rogers, Sr.

Date	Mintage	Proof	MS-65	Prf-65
1995W	89,301	—	31.00	—
1995P	—	351,764	—	26.50

KM# 272 ATLANTA OLYMPICS Obv: Rowing
Rev. Designer: Thomas D. Rogers, Sr.

Date	Mintage	Proof	MS-65	Prf-65
1996D	16,258	—	345	—
1996P	—	151,890	—	75.00

KM# 269 ATLANTA OLYMPICS Obv: Tennis
Rev. Designer: Thomas D. Rogers, Sr.

Date	Mintage	Proof	MS-65	Prf-65
1996D	15,983	—	330	—
1996P	—	92,016	—	92.00

KM# 272A ATLANTA OLYMPICS Obv: High
jumper **Rev. Designer:** Thomas D. Rogers, Sr.

Date	Mintage	Proof	MS-65	Prf-65
1996D	15,697	—	400	—
1996P	—	124,502	—	60.00

COMMEMORATIVES

KM# 268 ATLANTA OLYMPICS, PARALYMPICS
Obv: Wheelchair racer **Rev. Designer:** Thomas D. Rogers, Sr.

Date	Mintage	Proof	MS-65	Prf-65
1996D	14,497	—	385	—
1996P	—	84,280	—	90.00

KM# 276 SMITHSONIAN INSTITUTION 150TH ANNIVERSARY **Obv. Designer:** Thomas D. Rogers, Sr. **Rev. Designer:** John Mercanti

Date	Mintage	Proof	MS-65	Prf-65
1996D	31,230	—	150	—
1996P	—	129,152	—	69.00

KM# 275 NATIONAL COMMUNITY SERVICE
Obv. Designer: Thomas D. Rogers, Sr. **Rev. Designer:** William C. Cousins

Date	Mintage	Proof	MS-65	Prf-65
1996S	23,500	—	235	—
1996S	—	101,543	—	82.00

KM# 279 JACKIE ROBINSON 50TH ANNIVERSARY **Obv. Designer:** Alfred Maletsky **Rev. Designer:** T. James Ferrell

Date	Mintage	Proof	MS-65	Prf-65
1997S	30,007	—	103	—
1997S	—	110,495	—	85.00

KM# 281 NATIONAL LAW ENFORCEMENT OFFICERS MEMORIAL Designer: Alfred Maletsky

Date	Mintage	Proof	MS-65	Prf-65
1997P	—	110,428	—	135
1997P	28,575	—	165	—

KM# 288 BLACK REVOLUTIONARY WAR PATRIOTS Obv: Crispus Attucks Obv. Designer: John Mercanti Rev. Designer: Ed Dwight

Date	Mintage	Proof	MS-65	Prf-65
1998S	37,210	—	175	—
1998S	—	75,070	—	123

KM# 287 ROBERT F. KENNEDY Obv. Designer: Thomas D. Rogers, Sr. Rev. Designer: James M. Peed and Thomas D. Rogers, Sr.

Date	Mintage	Proof	MS-65	Prf-65
1998S	106,422	—	32.50	—
1998S	—	99,020	—	43.00

KM# 278 U.S. BOTANIC GARDENS 175TH ANNIVERSARY Designer: Edgar Z. Steever

Date	Mintage	Proof	MS-65	Prf-65
1997P	57,272	—	45.00	—
1997P	—	264,528	—	44.00

COMMEMORATIVES

KM# 298 DOLLEY MADISON
Designer: Tiffany & Co.

Date	Mintage	Proof	MS-65	Prf-65
1999P	22,948	—	50.00	—
1999P	—	158,247	—	48.00

KM# 313 LEIF ERICSON Obv. Designer: John
Mercanti **Rev. Designer:** T. James Ferrell

Date	Mintage	Proof	MS-65	Prf-65
2000P	28,150	—	92.50	—
2000 Iceland	—	15,947	—	25.00
2000P	—	58,612	—	70.00

KM# 299 YELLOWSTONE Obv. Designer:
Edgar Z. Steever **Rev. Designer:** William C.
Cousins

Date	Mintage	Proof	MS-65	Prf-65
1999P	23,614	—	56.00	—
1999P	—	128,646	—	58.00

KM# 311 LIBRARY OF CONGRESS
BICENTENNIAL Obv. Designer: Thomas D.
Rogers, Sr. **Rev. Designer:** John Mercanti

Date	Mintage	Proof	MS-65	Prf-65
2000P	52,771	—	43.00	—
2000P	—	196,900	—	41.00

KM# 325 AMERICAN INDIAN - BISON
Designer: James E. Fraser

Date	Mintage	Proof	MS-65	Prf-65
2001D	197,131	—	260	—
2001P	—	272,869	—	290

KM# 338 WEST POINT MILITARY ACADEMY BICENTENNIAL Obv. Designer: T. James Ferrell
Rev. Designer: John Mercanti

Date	Mintage	Proof	MS-65	Prf-65
2002W	103,201	—	20.50	—
2002W	—	288,293	—	19.50

KM# 324 CAPITOL VISITOR CENTER
Obv. Designer: Marika Somogyi **Rev. Designer:** John Mercanti

Date	Mintage	Proof	MS-65	Prf-65
2001P	66,636	—	35.00	—
2001P	—	143,793	—	45.00

KM# 336   WINTER OLYMPICS - SALT LAKE CITY Obv. Designer: John Mercanti **Rev. Designer:** Donna Weaver

Date	Mintage	Proof	MS-65	Prf-65
2002P	35,388	—	35.00	—
2002P	—	142,873	—	42.00

KM# 349 FIRST FLIGHT CENTENNIAL Obv:
Orville and Wilbur Wright **Obv. Designer:** T. James Ferrell **Rev:** Wright Brothers airplane **Rev. Designer:** Norman E. Nemeth

Date	Mintage	Proof	MS-65	Prf-65
2003P	53,761	—	37.00	—
2003P	—	193,086	—	32.00

KM# 362 125TH ANNIVERSARY OF EDISON'S ELECTRIC LIGHT Obv. Designer: Donna
Weaver **Rev. Designer:** John Mercanti

Date	Mintage	Proof	MS-65	Prf-65
2004P	68,031	—	40.00	—
2004P	—	213,409	—	41.00

KM# 363 LEWIS AND CLARK CORPS OF DISCOVERY BICENTENNIAL

Date	Mintage	Proof	MS-65	Prf-65
2004P	90,323	—	35.00	—
2004P	—	288,492	—	33.00

KM# 376 U.S. MARINE CORPS, 230TH ANNIVERSARY

Date	Mintage	Proof	MS-65	Prf-65
2005P	130,000	—	47.00	—
2005P	—	370,000	—	54.00

KM# 375 CHIEF JUSTICE JOHN MARSHALL, 250TH BIRTH ANNIVERSARY Obv. Designer:
John Mercanti **Rev. Designer:** Donna Weaver

Date	Mintage	Proof	MS-65	Prf-65
2005P	48,953	—	37.50	—
2005P	—	141,993	—	40.00

KM# 387 BENJAMIN FRANKLIN, 300TH ANNIVERSARY OF BIRTH Obv: Youthful
Franklin flying kite **Obv. Designer:** Norman E. Nemeth **Rev:** Revolutionary era "Join or Die" snake cartoon illustration

Date	Mintage	Proof	MS-65	Prf-65
2006P	58,000	—	53.00	—
2006P	—	142,000	—	57.00

KM# 388 BENJAMIN FRANKLIN, 300TH ANNIVERSARY OF BIRTH Obv: Bust 3/4 right, signature in oval below **Rev:** Continental Dollar of 1776 in center

Date	Mintage	Proof	MS-65	Prf-65
2006P	58,000	—	52.00	—
2006P	—	142,000	—	54.00

KM# 394 SAN FRANCISCO MINT MUSEUM Obv: 3/4 view of building **Rev:** Reverse of 1880s Morgan silver dollar

Date	Mintage	Proof	MS-65	Prf-65
2006S	—	—	44.00	—
2006S	—	—	—	46.00

KM# 418 CENTRAL HIGH SCHOOL DESEGREGATION Obv: Childrens feet walking left with adult feet in military boots **Rev:** Little Rock's Central High School

Date	Mintage	Proof	MS-65	Prf-65
2007P	—	—	—	—
2007P	—	—	—	—

KM# 405 JAMESTOWN - 400TH ANNIVERSARY Obv: Two settlers and Native American **Rev:** Three ships

Date	Mintage	Proof	MS-65	Prf-65
2007P	—	—	—	—
2007P	—	—	—	—

KM# 439 AMERICAN BALD EAGLE Obv: Ealge with flight, mountain in background at right **Rev:** Great Seal of the United States

Date	Mintage	Proof	MS-65	Prf-65
2008P	500,000	—	—	—

$5 HALF EAGLE

KM# 215 STATUE OF LIBERTY CENTENNIAL
Designer: Elizabeth Jones

Date	Mintage	Proof	MS-65	Prf-65
1986W	95,248	—	226	—
1986W	—	404,013	—	226

KM# 221 CONSTITUTION BICENTENNIAL
Designer: Marcel Jovine

Date	Mintage	Proof	MS-65	Prf-65
1987W	214,225	—	226	—
1987W	—	651,659	—	226

KM# 223 OLYMPICS Obv. Designer: Elizabeth Jones **Rev. Designer:** Marcel Jovine

Date	Mintage	Proof	MS-65	Prf-65
1988W	62,913	—	226	—
1988W	—	281,456	—	226

KM# 226 BICENTENNIAL OF THE CONGRESS
Obv. Designer: John Mercanti

Date	Mintage	Proof	MS-65	Prf-65
1989W	46,899	—	226	—
1989W	—	164,690	—	226

KM# 230 MOUNT RUSHMORE 50TH ANNIVERSARY Obv. Designer: John Mercanti Rev. Designer: Robert Lamb and William C. Cousins

Date	Mintage	Proof	MS-65	Prf-65
1991W	31,959	—	285	—
1991W	—	111,991	—	226

KM# 239 COLUMBUS QUINCENTENARY Obv. Designer: T. James Ferrell Rev. Designer: Thomas D. Rogers, Sr.

Date	Mintage	Proof	MS-65	Prf-65
1992W	—	79,730	—	285
1992W	24,329	—	320	—

KM# 235 OLYMPICS Obv. Designer: James C. Sharpe and T. James Ferrell Rev. Designer: James M. Peed

Date	Mintage	Proof	MS-65	Prf-65
1992W	27,732	—	310	—
1992W	—	77,313	—	240

KM# 242 JAMES MADISON AND BILL OF RIGHTS Obv. Designer: Scott R. Blazek Rev. Designer: Joseph D. Peña

Date	Mintage	Proof	MS-65	Prf-65
1993W	—	78,651	—	265
1993W	22,266	—	325	—

KM# 245 WORLD WAR II 50TH ANNIVERSARY Obv. Designer: Charles J. Madsen Rev. Designer: Edward S. Fisher

Date	Mintage	Proof	MS-65	Prf-65
1993W	—	65,461	—	330
1993W	23,089	—	360	—

KM# 248 WORLD CUP SOCCER Obv. Designer: William J. Krawczewicz Rev. Designer: Dean McMullen

Date	Mintage	Proof	MS-65	Prf-65
1994W	22,464	—	325	—
1994W	—	89,619	—	265

KM# 256 CIVIL WAR Obv. Designer: Don Troiani Rev. Designer: Alfred Maletsky

Date	Mintage	Proof	MS-65	Prf-65
1995W	12,735	—	900	—
1995W	—	55,246	—	535

KM# 261 OLYMPICS Obv: Torch runner

Date	Mintage	Proof	MS-65	Prf-65
1995W	—	57,442	—	410
1995W	14,675	—	775	—

KM# 265 OLYMPICS Obv: Stadium

Date	Mintage	Proof	MS-65	Prf-65
1995W	—	43,124	—	535
1995W	10,579	—	1,200	—

KM# 270 1996 ATLANTA OLYMPICS
Obv: Cauldron

Date	Mintage	Proof	MS-65	Prf-65
1996W	—	38,555	—	600
1996W	9,210	—	1,000	—

KM# 274 OLYMPICS **Obv:** Flag bearer

Date	Mintage	Proof	MS-65	Prf-65
1996W	—	32,886	—	615
1996W	9,174	—	1,050	—

KM# 277 SMITHSONIAN INSTITUTION 150TH ANNIVERSARY **Obv. Designer:** Alfred Maletsky **Rev. Designer:** T. James Ferrell

Date	Mintage	Proof	MS-65	Prf-65
1996W	9,068	—	1,500	—
1996W	—	29,474	—	720

KM# 282 FRANKLIN DELANO ROOSEVELT
Obv. Designer: T. James Ferrell **Rev. Designer:** James M. Peed and Thomas D. Rogers, Sr.

Date	Mintage	Proof	MS-65	Prf-65
1997W	11,894	—	1,100	—
1997W	—	29,474	—	565

KM# 280 JACKIE ROBINSON 50TH ANNIVERSARY **Obv. Designer:** William C. Cousins **Rev. Designer:** James M. Peed

Date	Mintage	Proof	MS-65	Prf-65
1997W	5,202	—	5,750	—
1997W	—	24,546	—	900

KM# 300 GEORGE WASHINGTON DEATH BICENTENNIAL **Designer:** Laura G. Fraser

Date	Mintage	Proof	MS-65	Prf-65
1999W	22,511	—	475	—
1999W	—	41,693	—	475

KM# 326 CAPITOL VISITOR CENTER
Designer: Elizabeth Jones

Date	Mintage	Proof	MS-65	Prf-65
2001W	6,761	—	2,150	—
2001W	—	27,652	—	465

KM# 337 2002 SALT LAKE CITY WINTER OLYMPICS **Designer:** Donna Weaver

Date	Mintage	Proof	MS-65	Prf-65
2002W	10,585	—	555	—
2002W	—	32,877	—	510

KM# 395 SAN FRANCISCO MINT MUSEUM
Obv: Frontal view of entrance **Rev:** Eagle as on 1860's $5. Gold.

Date	Mintage	Proof	MS-65	Prf-65
2006	—	—	—	—

KM# 406 JAMESTOWN - 400TH ANNIVERSARY
Obv: Settler and Native American **Rev:** Jamestown Memorial Church ruins

Date	Mintage	Proof	MS-65	Prf-65
2007W	—	—	285	—
2007W	—	—	—	275

KM# 440 AMERICAN BALD EAGLE **Obv:** Two eagles on branch **Rev:** Eagle with shield

Date	Mintage	Proof	MS-65	Prf-65
2008W	100,000	—	—	—

$10 EAGLE

KM# 211 LOS ANGELES XXIII OLYMPIAD
Weight: 16.7180 g. **Composition:** 0.9000 Gold,
0.4837 oz. AGW **Diameter:** 27mm. **Obv.**
Designer: James M. Peed and John Mercanti **Rev.**
Designer: John Mercanti

Date	Mintage	Proof	MS-65	Prf-65
1984W	75,886	—	453	—
1984P	—	33,309	—	453
1984D	—	34,533	—	453
1984S	—	48,551	—	453
1984W	—	381,085	—	453

KM# 312 LIBRARY OF CONGRESS Weight:
16.2590 g. **Composition:** Platinum-Gold-Alloy **Obv.**
Designer: John Mercanti **Rev. Designer:** Thomas
D. Rogers, Sr. **Notes:** Composition is 48 percent
platinum, 48 percent gold, and 4 percent alloy.

Date	Mintage	Proof	MS-65	Prf-65
2000W	6,683	—	3,600	—
2000W	—	27,167	—	1,350

KM# 350   FIRST FLIGHT CENTENNIAL
Weight: 16.7180 g. **Composition:** 0.9000 Gold,
0.4837 oz. AGW **Designer:** Donna Weaver

Date	Mintage	Proof	MS-65	Prf-65
2003P	10,129	—	625	—
2003P	—	21,846	—	560

MODERN COMMEMORATIVE COIN SETS

Olympic, 1983-1984

Date	Price
1983 & 1984 3 coin set: 1983 and one 1984 uncirculated dollar and 1984W uncirculated gold $10; KM209, 210, 211.	455
1983S & 1984S 3 coin set: proof 1983 and 1984 dollar and 1984W gold $10; KM209, 210, 211.	455
1983 & 1984 6 coin set: 1983S and 1984S uncirculated and proof dollars, 1984W uncirculated and proof gold $10; KM209, 210, 211.	910
1983S & 1984S 2 coin set: proof dollars.	22.50
1983 collectors 3 coin set: 1983 PDS uncirculated dollars; KM209.	37.50
1984 collectors 3 coin set: 1984 PDS uncirculated dollars; KM210.	38.50

Statue of Liberty

Date	Price
1986 2 coin set: uncirculated silver dollar and clad half dollar; KM212, 214.	17.00
1986 2 coin set: proof silver dollar and clad half dollar; KM212, 214.	17.00
1986 3 coin set: uncirculated silver dollar, clad half dollar and gold $5; KM212, 214, 215.	225
1986 3 coin set: proof silver dollar, clad half dollar and gold $5; KM212, 214, 215.	225
1986 6 coin set: 1 each of the proof and uncirculated issues; KM212, 214, 215.	450

Constitution

Date	Price
1987 2 coin set: uncirculated silver dollar and gold $5; KM220, 221.	220
1987 2 coin set: proof silver dollar and gold $5; KM220, 221.	220
1987 4 coin set: silver dollar and $5 gold proof and uncirculated issues; KM220, 221.	445

Olympic, 1988

Date	Price
1988 2 coin set: uncirculated silver dollar and gold $5; KM222, 223.	220
1988 2 coin set: proof silver dollar and gold $5; KM222, 223.	220
1988 4 coin set: silver dollar and $5 gold proof and uncirculated issues; KM222, 223.	440

Congress

Date	Price
1989 2 coin set: uncirculated silver dollar and clad half dollar; KM224, 225.	20.00
1989 2 coin set: proof silver dollar and clad half dollar; KM224, 225.	21.00
1989 3 coin set: uncirculated silver dollar, clad half and gold $5; KM224, 225, 226.	220

Date	Price
1989 3 coin set: proof silver dollar, clad half and gold $5; KM224, 225, 226.	220
1989 6 coin set: 1 each of the proof and uncirculated issues; KM224, 225, 226.	440

Mt. Rushmore

Date	Price
1991 2 coin set: uncirculated half dollar and silver dollar; KM228, 229.	45.00
1991 2 coin set: proof half dollar and silver dollar; KM228, 229.	45.00
1991 3 coin set: uncirculated half dollar, silver dollar and gold $5; KM228, 229, 230.	300
1991 3 coin set: proof half dollar, silver dollar and gold $5; KM228, 229, 230.	225
1991 6 coin set: 1 each of proof and uncirculated issues; KM228, 229, 230.	495

Olympic, 1992

Date	Price
1992 2 coin set: uncirculated half dollar and silver dollar; KM233, 234.	28.00
1992 2 coin set: proof half dollar and silver dollar; KM233, 234.	28.00
1992 3 coin set: uncirculated half dollar, silver dollar and gold $5; KM233, 234, 235.	275
1992 3 coin set: proof half dollar, silver dollar and gold $5; KM233, 234, 235.	240
1992 6 coin set: 1 each of proof and uncirculated issues; KM233, 234, 235.	520

Columbus Quincentenary

Date	Price
1992 2 coin set: uncirculated half dollar and silver dollar; KM237, 238.	35.00
1992 2 coin set: proof half dollar and silver dollar; KM237, 238.	39.00
1992 3 coin set: uncirculated half dollar, silver dollar and gold $5; KM237, 238, 239.	320
1992 3 coin set: proof half dollar, silver dollar and gold $5; KM237, 238, 239.	265
1992 6 coin set: 1 each of proof and uncirculated issues; KM237, 238, 239.	780

Jefferson

Date	Price
1993 Jefferson: dollar, 1994 matte proof nickel and $2 note; KM249, 192.	100.00

Madison / Bill of Rights

Date	Price
1993 2 coin set: uncirculated half dollar and silver dollar; KM240, 241.	28.00
1993 2 coin set: proof half dollar and silver dollar; KM240, 241.	29.00
1993 3 coin set: uncirculated half dollar, silver dollar and gold $5; KM240, 241, 242.	320
1993 3 coin set: proof half dollar, silver dollar and gold $5; KM240, 241, 242.	250
1993 6 coin set: 1 each of proof and uncirculated issues; KM240, 241, 242.	550

World War II

Date	Price
1993 2 coin set: uncirculated half dollar and silver dollar; KM243, 244.	49.00
1993 2 coin set: proof half dollar and silver dollar; KM243, 244.	55.00
1993 3 coin set: uncirculated half dollar, silver dollar and gold $5; KM243, 244, 245.	345
1993 3 coin set: proof half dollar, silver dollar and gold $5; KM243, 244, 245.	335
1993 6 coin set: 1 each of proof and uncirculated issues; KM243, 244, 245.	665

World Cup

Date	Price
1994 2 coin set: uncirculated half dollar and silver dollar; KM246, 247.	32.00
1994 2 coin set: proof half dollar and silver dollar; KM246, 247.	37.00
1994 3 coin set: uncirculated half dollar, silver dollar and gold $5; KM246, 247, 248.	290
1994 3 coin set: proof half dollar, silver dollar and gold $5; KM246, 247, 248.	250
1994 6 coin set: 1 each of proof and uncirculated issues; KM246, 247, 248.	525

U.S. Veterans

Date	Price
1994 3 coin set: uncirculated POW, Vietnam, Women dollars; KM250, 251, 252.	170
1994 3 coin set: proof POW, Vietnam, Women dollars; KM250, 251, 252.	120

Olympic, 1995-96

Date	Price
1995 4 coin set: uncirculated basketball half, $1 gymnast & blind runner, $5 torch runner; KM257, 259, 260, 261.	715
1995 4 coin set: proof basketball half, $1 gymnast & blind runner, $5 torch runner; KM257, 259, 260, 261.	415
1995P 2 coin set: proof $1 gymnast & blind runner; KM259, 260.	105
1995P 2 coin set: proof $1 track & field, cycling; KM263, 264.	95.00
1995-96 4 coin set: proof halves, basketball, baseball, swimming, soccer; KM257, 262, 267, 271.	140
1995 & 96 8 coins in cherry wood case: proof silver dollars: blind runner, gymnast, cycling, track & field, wheelchair, tennis, rowing, high jump; KM259, 260, 263, 264, 268, 269, 272, 272A.	2,150
1995 & 96 16 coins in cherry wood case: bu and proof silver dollars: blind runner, gymnast, cycling, track & field, wheelchair, tennis, rowing, high jump; KM259, 260, 263, 264, 268, 269, 272, 272A.	2,350
1995 & 96 16 coins in cherry wood case: proof half dollars: basketball, baseball, swimming, soccer, KM257, 262, 267, 271. Proof silver dollars: blind runner, gymnast, cycling, track & field, wheelchair, tennis, rowing, high jump, KM259, 260, 263, 264, 268, 269, 272, 272A. Proof $5 gold: torch runner, stadium, cauldron, flag bearer, KM 261, 265, 270, 274.	2,400

COMMEMORATIVE SETS

Date	Price
1995 & 96 32 coins in cherry wood case: bu & proof half dollars: basketball, baseball, swimming, soccer, KM257, 262, 267, 271. BU & proof silver dollars: blind runner, gymnast, cycling, track & field, wheelchair, tennis, rowing, high jump, KM259, 260, 263, 264, 268, 269, 272, 272A. BU & proof $5 gold: torch runner, stadium, cauldron, flag bearer, KM261, 265, 270, 274.	6,600
1996P 2 coin set: proof $1 wheelchair & tennis; KM268, 269.	160
1996P 2 coin set: proof $1 rowing & high jump; KM272, 272A.	130

Civil War

Date	Price
1995 2 coin set: uncirculated half and dollar; KM254, 255.	90.00
1995 2 coin set: proof half and dollar; KM254, 255.	100.00
1995 3 coin set: uncirculated half, dollar and gold $5; KM254, 255, 256.	800
1995 3 coin set: proof half, dollar and gold $5; KM254, 255, 256.	500
1995 6 coin set: 1 each of proof and uncirculated issues; KM254, 255, 256.	1,275

Smithsonian

Date	Price
1996 2 coin set: proof dollar and $5 gold; KM276, 277.	615
1996 4 coin set: proof and B.U. ; KM276, 277.	2,100

Jackie Robinson

Date	Price
1997 2 coin set: proof dollar & $5 gold; KM279, 280.	800
1997 4 coin set: proof & BU; KM279, 280.	5,750
1997 legacy set.	850

Botanic Garden

Date	Price
1997 2 coin set: dollar, Jefferson nickel and $1 note; KM278, 192.	230

Franklin Delano Roosevelt

Date	Price
1997W 2 coin set: uncirculated and proof; KM282.	1,350

Kennedy

Date	Price
1998 2 coin set: proof; KM287.	70.00
1998 2 coin collectors set: Robert Kennedy dollar and John Kennedy half dollar; KM287, 202b. Matte finished.	325

Black Patriots

Date	Price
1998S 2 coin set: uncirculated and proof; KM288.	200

George Washington

Date	Price
1999 2 coin set: proof and uncirculated gold $5; KM300.	800

Dolley Madison

Date	Price
1999 2 coin set: proof and uncirculated silver dollars; KM298.	77.00

Yellowstone National Park

Date	Price
1999 2 coin set: proof and uncirculated silver dollars; KM299.	88.00

Millennium Coin & Currency

Date	Price
2000 2 coin set: uncirculated Sacagewea $1, silver Eagle & $1 note.	72.00

Leif Ericson

Date	Price
2000 2 coin set: proof and uncirculated silver dollars; KM313.	84.00

Capitol Visitor Center

Date	Price
2001 3 coin set: proof half, silver dollar, gold $5; KM323, 324, 326.	445

American Buffalo

Date	Price
2001 2 coin set: 90% silver unc. & proof $1.; KM325.	460
2001 coin & currency set 90% unc. dollar & replicas of 1899 $5 silver cert.; KM325.	240

Winter Olympics - Salt Lake City

Date	Price
2002 2 coin set: proof 90% silver dollar KM336 & $5.00 Gold KM337.	420
2002 4 coin set: 90% silver unc. & proof $1, KM336 & unc. & proof gold $5, KM337.	940

First Flight Centennial

Date	Price
2003 3 coin set: proof gold ten dollar KM350, proof silver dollar KM349 & proof clad half dollar KM348.	575

Lewis and Clark Bicentennial

Date	Price
2004 Coin and pouch set.	100.00
2004 coin and currency set: Uncirculated silver dollar, two 2005 nickels, replica 1901 $10 Bison note, silver plated peace medal, three stamps & two booklets.	85.00
2004 Westward Journey Nickel series coin and medal set: Proof Sacagawea dollar, two 2005 proof nickels and silver plated peace medal.	35.00

Thomas Alva Edison

Date	Price
2004 Uncirculated silver dollar and light bulb.	60.00

U.S. Marine Corps.

Date	Price
2005 Uncirculated silver dollar and stamp set.	75.00
2005 American Legacy: Proof Marine Corps dollar, Proof John Marshall dollar and 10 piece proof set.	180

Chief Justice John Marshall

Date	Price
2005 Coin and Chronicles set: Uncirculated silver dollar, booklet and BEP intaglio portrait.	60.00
2005 American Legacy: Proof Marine Corps dollar, Proof John Marshall dollar and 10 piece proof set.	180

Benjamin Franklin Tercentennary

Date	Price
2006 Coin and Chronicles set: Uncirculated "Scientist" silver dollar, four stamps, Poor Richards Almanac and intaglio print.	65.00

AMERICAN EAGLE BULLION COINS

SILVER DOLLAR

KM# 273 • 31.1010 g., 0.9993 **Silver**, 0.9992 oz. , 40.6mm. • **Obv. Designer:** Adolph A. Weinman
Rev. Designer: John Mercanti

Date	Mintage	Unc	Prf.	Date	Mintage	Unc	Prf.
1986	5,393,005	21.70	—	1996P	473,021	—	100.00
1986S	1,446,778	—	33.00	1997	4,295,004	21.20	—
1987	11,442,335	21.20	—	1997P	429,682	—	130
1987S	904,732	—	33.00	1998	4,847,549	22.20	—
1988	5,004,646	21.20	—	1998P	452,319	—	48.00
1988S	557,370	—	48.00	1999	7,408,640	23.20	—
1989	5,203,327	21.20	—	1999P	549,769	—	47.00
1989S	617,694	—	34.00	2000P	600,000	—	35.00
1990	5,840,210	21.20	—	2000	9,239,132	21.20	—
1990S	695,510	—	34.00	2001	9,001,711	21.20	—
1991	7,191,066	21.80	—	2001W	746,154	—	34.00
1991S	511,924	—	44.00	2002	10,539,026	21.20	—
1992	5,540,068	21.90	—	2002W	647,342	—	35.00
1992S	498,552	—	40.00	2003	8,495,008	21.20	—
1993	6,763,762	22.00	—	2003W	747,831	—	34.00
1993P	403,625	—	136	2004	8,882,754	21.20	—
1994	4,227,319	21.20	—	2004W	783,219	—	37.00
1994P	372,168	—	215	2005	8,891,025	21.20	—
1995	4,672,051	20.50	—	2005W	823,000	—	34.00
1995P	395,400	—	155	2006	10,676,522	21.20	—
1995W 10th Anniversary	30,125	—	4,350	2006W	—	—	40.00
1996	3,603,386	70.00	—	2006P Reverse Proof	250,000	—	300

Date	Mintage	Unc	Prf.	Date	Mintage	Unc	Prf.
2006W Burnished Unc.	470,000	105	—	2007	—	—	35.00
2007	9,028,036	21.20	—	2008	—	21.70	—
2007W	—	—	35.00	2008W	—	—	35.00

GOLD $5

KM# 216 • 3.3930 g., 0.9167 **Gold**, 0.1000 oz. , 16.5mm. • **Obv. Designer:** Augustus Saint-Gaudens
Rev. Designer: Miley Busiek

Date	Mintage	Unc	Prf.	Date	Mintage	Unc	Prf.
MCMLXXXVI 1986	912,609	111	—	1998W	39,653	—	123
MCMLXXXVII 1987	580,266	111	—	1999	2,750,338	110	—
MCMLXXXVIII 1988	159,500	200	—	1999W	48,426	—	165
MCMLXXXVIII 1988P	143,881	—	123	2000	569,153	118	—
MCMLXXXIX 1989	264,790	111	—	2000W	50,000	—	123
MCMLXXXIX 1989P	82,924	—	128	2001	269,147	111	—
MCMXC 1990	210,210	111	—	2001W	37,547	—	123
MCMXC 1990P	99,349	—	128	2002	230,027	111	—
MCMXCI 1991	165,200	115	—	2002W	40,864	—	123
MCMXCI 1991P	70,344	—	123	2003	245,029	111	—
1992	209,300	111	—	2003W	40,634	—	123
1992P	64,902	—	123	2004	250,016	111	—
1993	210,709	111	—	2004W	35,481	—	123
1993P	58,649	—	123	2005	300,043	110	—
1994	206,380	113	—	2005W	48,455	—	123
1994W	62,100	—	123	2006	285,006	112	—
1995	223,025	111	—	2006W	—	—	120
1995W	62,650	—	123	2006W Burnished Unc.	—	120	—
1996	401,964	111	—	2007	190,010	100.00	—
1996W	58,440	—	123	2007W	—	—	138
1997	528,515	110	—	2008	—	100.00	—
1997W	35,000	—	123	2008W	—	—	138
1998	1,344,520	111	—				

GOLD $10

KM# 217 • 8.4830 g., 0.9167 **Gold**, 0.2500 oz. , 22mm. • **Obv. Designer:** Augustus Saint-Gaudens
Rev. Designer: Miley Busiek

Date	Mintage	Unc	Prf.	Date	Mintage	Unc	Prf.
MCMLXXXVI 1986	726,031	266	—	1998W	29,733	—	283
MCMLXXXVII 1987	269,255	266	—	1999	564,232	266	—
MCMLXXXVIII 1988	49,000	266	—	1999W	34,416	—	283
MCMLXXXVIII 1988P	98,028	—	283	2000	128,964	281	—
MCMLXXXIX 1989	81,789	266	—	2000W	36,000	—	283
MCMLXXXIX 1989P	53,593	—	283	2001	71,280	266	—
MCMXC 1990	41,000	266	—	2001W	25,630	—	283
MCMXC 1990P	62,674	—	283	2002	62,027	266	—
MCMXCI 1991	36,100	375	—	2002W	29,242	—	283
MCMXCI 1991P	50,839	—	283	2003	74,029	266	—
1992	59,546	266	—	2003W	31,000	—	283
1992P	46,290	—	283	2004	72,014	266	—
1993	71,864	266	—	2004W	29,127	—	283
1993P	46,271	—	283	2005	72,015	266	—
1994	72,650	266	—	2005W	34,637	—	283
1994W	47,600	—	283	2006	60,004	266	—
1995	83,752	266	—	2006W	—	—	283
1995W	47,545	—	283	2006W Burnished Unc.	—	335	—
1996	60,318	266	—	2007	34,004	266	—
1996W	39,190	—	283	2007W	—	—	291
1997	108,805	266	—	2008	—	266	—
1997W	29,800	—	283	2008W	—	—	283
1998	309,829	266	—				

GOLD $25

KM# 218 • 16.9660 g., 0.9167 **Gold**, 0.5000 oz. , 27mm. • **Obv. Designer:** Augustus Saint-Gaudens
Rev. Designer: Miley Busiek

Date	Mintage	Unc	Prf.	Date	Mintage	Unc	Prf.
MCMLXXXVI 1986	599,566	516	—	1998	169,029	509	—
MCMLXXXVII 1987	131,255	509	—	1998W	25,896	—	485
MCMLXXXVII 1987P	143,398	—	543	1999	263,013	509	—
MCMLXXXVIII 1988	45,000	509	—	1999W	30,452	—	523
MCMLXXXVIII 1988P	76,528	—	543	2000	79,287	523	—
MCMLXXXIX 1989	44,829	550	—	2000W	32,000	—	543
MCMLXXXIX 1989P	44,264	—	543	2001	48,047	509	—
MCMXC 1990	31,000	750	—	2001W	23,261	—	475
MCMXC 1990P	51,636	—	543	2002	70,027	509	—
MCMXCI 1991	24,100	1,250	—	2002W	26,646	—	543
MCMXCI 1991P	53,125	—	543	2003	79,029	509	—
1992	54,404	509	—	2003W	29,000	—	543
1992P	40,982	—	543	2004	98,040	509	—
1993	73,324	509	—	2004W	27,731	—	543
1993P	43,319	—	543	2005	80,023	509	—
1994	62,400	509	—	2005W	33,598	—	543
1994W	44,100	—	543	2006	66,005	512	—
1995	53,474	509	—	2006W	—	—	450
1995W	45,511	—	543	2006W Burnished Unc.	—	700	—
1996	39,287	509	—	2007	47,002	512	—
1996W	35,937	—	543	2007W	—	—	543
1997	79,605	509	—	2008	—	509	—
1997W	26,350	—	475	2008W	—	—	543

GOLD $50

KM# 219 • 33.9310 g., 0.9167 **Gold**, 100000 oz. , 32.7mm. • **Obv. Designer:** Augustus Saint-Gaudens
Rev. Designer: Miley Busiek

Date	Mintage	Unc	Prf.	Date	Mintage	Unc	Prf.
MCMLXXXVI 1986	1,362,650	1,025	—	1994W	36,300	—	1,085
MCMLXXXVI 1986W	446,290	—	1,085	1995	200,636	1,025	—
MCMLXXXVII 1987	1,045,500	1,025	—	1995W	46,553	—	1,085
MCMLXXXVII 1987W	147,498	—	1,085	1996	189,148	1,025	—
MCMLXXXVIII 1988	465,000	1,025	—	1996W	37,302	—	1,085
MCMLXXXVIII 1988W	87,133	—	1,085	1997	664,508	1,025	—
MCMLXXXIX 1989	415,790	1,025	—	1997W	28,000	—	1,085
MCMLXXXIX 1989W	53,960	—	1,085	1998	1,468,530	1,025	—
MCMXC 1990	373,210	1,025	—	1998W	26,060	—	1,085
MCMXC 1990W	62,401	—	1,085	1999	1,505,026	1,025	—
MCMXCI 1991	243,100	1,025	—	1999W	31,446	—	1,085
MCMXCI 1991W	50,411	—	1,085	2000	433,319	1,025	—
1992	275,000	1,025	—	2000W	33,000	—	1,085
1992W	44,835	—	1,085	2001	143,605	1,025	—
1993	480,192	1,025	—	2001W	24,580	—	1,085
1993W	34,389	—	1,085	2002	222,029	1,025	—
1994	221,633	1,025	—	2002W	24,242	—	1,085

BULLION COINS

Date	Mintage	Unc	Prf.
2003	416,032	1,025	—
2003W	29,000	—	1,085
2004	417,019	1,025	—
2004W	28,731	—	1,085
2005	356,555	1,025	—
2005W	34,695	—	1,085
2006	237,510	1,025	—
2006W	—	—	1,085
2006W Reverse Proof	10,000	—	4,350
2007	140,016	1,025	—
2007W	—	—	1,085
2008	—	1,025	—
2008W	—	—	1,085

PLATINUM $10

KM# 283 • 3.1100 g., 0.9995 **Platinum**, 0.0999 oz. • **Obv. Designer:** John Mercanti
Rev. Designer: Thomas D. Rogers Sr

Date	Mintage	Unc	Prf.
1997	70,250	235	—
1997W	36,996	—	247
1998	39,525	235	—
1999	55,955	235	—
2000	34,027	235	—
2001	52,017	235	—
2002	23,005	235	—
2003	22,007	235	—
2004	15,010	240	—
2005	14,013	240	—
2006	11,001	235	—
2007	13,003	240	—
2008	—	240	—

KM# 289 • 3.1100 g., 0.9995 **Platinum**, 0.0999 oz. • **Obv. Designer:** John Mercanti

Date	Mintage	Unc	Prf.
1998W	19,832	—	247

KM# 301 • 3.1100 g., 0.9995 **Platinum**, 0.0999 oz. • **Obv. Designer:** John Mercanti

Date	Mintage	Unc	Prf.
1999W	19,123	—	247

KM# 314 • 3.1100 g., 0.9995 **Platinum**, 0.0999 oz. • **Obv. Designer:** John Mercanti

Date	Mintage	Unc	Prf.
2000W	15,651	—	247

KM# 327 • 3.1100 g., 0.9995 **Platinum**, 0.0999 oz. • **Obv. Designer:** John Mercanti

Date	Mintage	Unc	Prf.
2001W	12,193	—	247

KM# 339 • 3.1100 g., 0.9995 **Platinum**, 0.0999 oz. • **Obv. Designer:** John Mercanti

Date	Mintage	Unc	Prf.
2002W	12,365	—	247

KM# 351 • 3.1100 g., 0.9995 **Platinum**, 0.0999 oz. • **Obv. Designer:** John Mercanti
Rev. Designer: Al Maletsky

Date	Mintage	Unc	Prf.
2003W	8,161	—	300

KM# 364 • 3.1100 g., 0.9995 **Platinum**, 0.0999 oz. • **Obv. Designer:** John Mercanti

Date	Mintage	Unc	Prf.
2004W	6,846	—	900

KM# 377 • 3.1100 g., 0.9995 **Platinum**, 0.0999 oz. • **Obv. Designer:** John Mercanti
Rev. Designer: Donna Weaver

Date	Mintage	Unc	Prf.
2005W	8,000	—	410

KM# 389 • 3.1100 g., 0.9995 **Platinum**, 0.0999 oz. , 17mm. •

Date	Mintage	Unc	Prf.
2006W	—	—	225

KM# 414 • 3.1100 g., 0.9995 **Platinum**, 0.0999 oz. •

Date	Mintage	Unc	Prf.
2007W	—	—	245

KM# 434 • 3.1100 g., 0.9995 **Platinum**, 0.0999 oz. •

Date	Mintage	Unc	Prf.
2008W	—	—	245

PLATINUM $25

KM# 284 • 7.7857 g., 0.9995 **Platinum**, 0.2502 oz. • **Obv. Designer:** John Mercanti
Rev. Designer: Thomas D. Rogers Sr

Date	Mintage	Unc	Prf.
1997	27,100	578	—
1997W	18,628	—	603
1998	38,887	578	—
1999	39,734	578	—
2000	20,054	578	—
2001	21,815	578	—
2002	27,405	578	—
2003	25,207	578	—
2004	18,010	578	—
2005	12,013	578	—
2006	12,001	583	—
2006W Burnished Unc.	—	1,300	—
2007	8,402	578	—
2007W Burnished Unc.	—	1,100	—
2008	—	578	—

KM# 290 • 7.7857 g., 0.9995 **Platinum**, 0.2502 oz. • **Obv. Designer:** John Mercanti

Date	Mintage	Unc	Prf.
1998W	14,860	—	603

KM# 302 • 7.7857 g., 0.9995 **Platinum**, 0.2502 oz. • **Obv. Designer:** John Mercanti

Date	Mintage	Unc	Prf.
1999W	13,514	—	603

KM# 315 • 7.7857 g., 0.9995 **Platinum**, 0.2502 oz. • **Obv. Designer:** John Mercanti

Date	Mintage	Unc	Prf.
2000W	11,995	—	603

KM# 328 • 7.7857 g., 0.9995 **Platinum**, 0.2502 oz. • **Obv. Designer:** John Mercanti

Date	Mintage	Unc	Prf.
2001W	8,858	—	603

KM# 340 • 7.7857 g., 0.9995 **Platinum**, 0.2502 oz. • **Obv. Designer:** John Mercanti

Date	Mintage	Unc	Prf.
2002W	9,282	—	603

KM# 352 • 7.7857 g., 0.9995 **Platinum**, 0.2502 oz. • **Obv. Designer:** John Mercanti
Rev. Designer: Al Maletsky

Date	Mintage	Unc	Prf.
2003W	6,045	—	603

KM# 365 • 7.7857 g., 0.9995 **Platinum**, 0.2502 oz. • **Obv. Designer:** John Mercanti

Date	Mintage	Unc	Prf.
2004W	5,035	—	1,750

KM# 378 • 7.7857 g., 0.9995 **Platinum**, 0.2502 oz. • **Obv. Designer:** John Mercanti
Rev. Designer: Donna Weaver

Date	Mintage	Unc	Prf.
2005W	6,424	—	870

KM# 390 • 7.7857 g., 0.9995 **Platinum**, 0.2502 oz. , 22mm. •

Date	Mintage	Unc	Prf.
2006W	—	—	603

KM# 415 • 7.7857 g., 0.9995 **Platinum**, 0.2502 oz. •

Date	Mintage	Unc	Prf.
2007W	—	—	603

BULLION COINS

KM# 435 • 7.7857 g., 0.9995 **Platinum**, 0.2502 oz. •

Date	Mintage	Unc	Prf.
2008W	—	—	603

PLATINUM $50

KM# 285 • 15.5520 g., 0.9995 **Platinum**, 0.4997 oz. • **Obv. Designer:** John Mercanti
Rev. Designer: Thomas D. Rogers Sr

Date	Mintage	Unc	Prf.
1997	20,500	1,106	—
1997W	15,432	—	1,166
1998	32,415	1,106	—
1999	32,309	1,106	—
2000	18,892	1,106	—
2001	12,815	1,106	—
2002	24,005	1,106	—
2003	17,409	1,106	—
2004	98,040	1,106	—
2005	9,013	1,106	—
2006	9,602	1,106	—
2006W Burnished Unc.	—	1,650	—
2007	—	1,106	—
2007W Burnished Unc.	—	1,500	—
2008	—	1,106	—

KM# 291 • 15.5520 g., 0.9995 **Platinum**, 0.4997 oz. • **Obv. Designer:** John Mercanti

Date	Mintage	Unc	Prf.
1998W	13,821	—	1,166

KM# 303 • 15.5520 g., 0.9995 **Platinum**, 0.4997 oz. • **Obv. Designer:** John Mercanti

Date	Mintage	Unc	Prf.
1999W	11,098	—	1,166

KM# 316 • 15.5520 g., 0.9995 **Platinum**, 0.4997 oz. • **Obv. Designer:** John Mercanti

Date	Mintage	Unc	Prf.
2000W	11,049	—	1,166

KM# 329 • 15.5520 g., 0.9995 **Platinum**, 0.4997 oz. • **Obv. Designer:** John Mercanti

Date	Mintage	Unc	Prf.
2001W	8,268	—	1,166

KM# 341 • 15.5520 g., 0.9995 **Platinum**, 0.4997 oz. • **Obv. Designer:** John Mercanti

Date	Mintage	Unc	Prf.
2002W	8,772	—	1,166

KM# 353 • 15.5520 g., 0.9995 **Platinum**, 0.4997 oz. • **Obv. Designer:** John Mercanti **Rev. Designer:** Al Maletsky

Date	Mintage	Unc	Prf.
2003W	6,181	—	1,166

KM# 366 • 15.5520 g., 0.9995 **Platinum**, 0.4997 oz. • **Obv. Designer:** John Mercanti

Date	Mintage	Unc	Prf.
2004W	4,886	—	2,750

KM# 379 • 15.5520 g., 0.9995 **Platinum**, 0.4997 oz. • **Obv. Designer:** John Mercanti
Rev. Designer: Donna Weaver

Date	Mintage	Unc	Prf.
2005W	5,720	—	1,675

KM# 391 • 15.5520 g., 0.9995 **Platinum**,
0.4997 oz. , 27mm. •

Date	Mintage	Unc	Prf.
2006W	—	—	1,166

KM# 416 • 15.5520 g., 0.9995 **Platinum**,
0.4997 oz. •

Date	Mintage	Unc	Prf.
2007W	—	—	1,166

KM# 436 • 15.5520 g., 0.9995 **Platinum**,
0.4997 oz. •

Date	Mintage	Unc	Prf.
2008W	—	—	1,166

PLATINUM $100

KM# 286 • 31.1050 g., 0.9995 **Platinum**,
0.9995 oz. • **Obv. Designer:** John Mercanti
Rev. Designer: Thomas D. Rogers Sr

Date	Mintage	Unc	Prf.
1997	56,000	2,192	—
1997W	15,885	—	2,327
1998	133,002	2,192	—
1999	56,707	2,192	—
2000	18,892	2,192	—
2001	14,070	2,192	—
2002	11,502	2,192	—
2003	8,007	2,192	—
2004	7,009	2,192	—
2005	6,310	2,192	—
2006	6,000	2,192	—
2006W Burnished Unc.	—	2,550	—
2007	—	2,192	—
2007W Burnished Unc.	—	2,450	—
2008	—	2,192	—

KM# 292 • 31.1050 g., 0.9995 **Platinum**,
0.9995 oz. • **Obv. Designer:** John Mercanti

Date	Mintage	Unc	Prf.
1998W	14,203	—	2,307

KM# 304 • 31.1050 g., 0.9995 **Platinum**, 0.9995
oz. • **Obv. Designer:** John Mercanti

Date	Mintage	Unc	Prf.
1999W	—	—	2,307

KM# 317 • 31.1050 g., 0.9995 **Platinum**,
0.9995 oz. • **Obv. Designer:** John Mercanti

Date	Mintage	Unc	Prf.
2000W	—	—	2,307

KM# 330 • 31.1050 g., 0.9995 **Platinum**,
0.9995 oz. • **Obv. Designer:** John Mercanti

Date	Mintage	Unc	Prf.
2001W	8,990	—	2,307

KM# 342 • 31.1050 g., 0.9995 **Platinum**,
0.9995 oz. • **Obv. Designer:** John Mercanti

Date	Mintage	Unc	Prf.
2002W	9,834	—	2,307

KM# 354 • 31.1050 g., 0.9995 **Platinum**, 0.9995 oz. • **Obv. Designer:** John Mercanti **Rev. Designer:** Al Maletsky

Date	Mintage	Unc	Prf.
2003W	6,991	—	2,192

KM# 367 • 31.1050 g., 0.9995 **Platinum**, 0.9995 oz. • **Obv. Designer:** John Mercanti **Rev. Designer:** Donna Weaver

Date	Mintage	Unc	Prf.
2004W	5,833	—	3,500

KM# 380 • 31.1050 g., 0.9995 **Platinum**, 0.9995 oz. • **Obv. Designer:** John Mercanti **Rev. Designer:** Donna Weaver

Date	Mintage	Unc	Prf.
2005W	6,700	—	2,600

KM# 392 • 31.1050 g., 0.9995 **Platinum**, 0.9995 oz. , 33mm. •

Date	Mintage	Unc	Prf.
2006W	—	—	2,307

KM# 417 • 31.1050 g., 0.9995 **Platinum**, 0.9995 oz. •

Date	Mintage	Unc	Prf.
2007W	—	—	2,307

KM# 437 • 31.1050 g., 0.9995 **Platinum**, 0.9995 oz. •

Date	Mintage	Unc	Prf.
2008W	—	—	2,307

CANADA

CONFEDERATION

CIRCULATION COINAGE

CENT

KM# 1 Obv: Laureate head left **Obv. Legend:** VICTORIA DEI GRATIA REGINA.CANADA **Rev:** Denomination and date within beaded circle, chain of leaves surrounds **Weight:** 4.5400 g. **Composition:** Bronze

Date	Mintage	VG-8	F-12	VF-20	XF-40	MS-60	MS-63	Proof
1858	421,000	50.00	60.00	80.00	120	300	1,250	—
1859/8 Wide 9	Inc. above	25.00	35.00	60.00	90.00	250	1,350	—
1859 Narrow 9	9,579,000	2.25	3.00	5.00	7.00	35.00	250	—
1859 Double punched narrow 9 type I	Inc. above	175	250	350	540	1,150	4,750	—
1859 Double punched narrow 9 type II	Inc. above	55.00	70.00	95.00	150	500	2,800	—

KM# 7 Obv: Crowned head left within beaded circle **Obv. Legend:** VICTORIA DEI GRATIA REGINA. CANADA **Obv. Designer:** Leonard C. Wyon **Rev:** Denomination and date within beaded circle, chain of leaves surrounds **Edge:** Plain **Weight:** 4.5400 g. **Composition:** Bronze **Size:** 25.5 mm.

Date	Mintage	VG-8	F-12	VF-20	XF-40	MS-60	MS-63	Proof
1876H	4,000,000	2.00	2.75	4.00	7.50	45.00	250	—
1881H	2,000,000	3.00	4.00	9.00	14.00	60.00	300	—
1882H	4,000,000	2.00	2.75	4.00	7.50	32.00	250	—
1884	2,500,000	3.00	4.00	5.00	8.50	60.00	300	—
1886	1,500,000	3.75	5.00	10.00	20.00	90.00	350	—
1887	1,500,000	3.00	5.00	8.00	11.00	55.00	215	—
1888	4,000,000	2.00	3.00	5.00	7.50	35.00	160	—
1890H	1,000,000	6.00	8.00	14.00	25.00	100.00	400	—
1891 Large date	1,452,000	6.50	9.00	13.50	30.00	125	420	—
1891 S.D.L.L.	Inc. above	50.00	75.00	110	160	620	2,150	—
1891 S.D.S.L.	Inc. above	35.00	50.00	65.00	95.00	225	1,000	—
1892	1,200,000	4.50	8.00	12.00	13.50	55.00	220	—
1893	2,000,000	2.50	3.00	5.00	7.50	35.00	200	—
1894	1,000,000	8.00	12.00	18.00	30.00	90.00	265	—
1895	1,200,000	4.00	7.00	10.00	16.00	55.00	225	—
1896	2,000,000	3.00	4.00	5.00	7.50	40.00	150	—
1897	1,500,000	3.00	4.00	5.00	9.00	45.00	165	—
1898H	1,000,000	5.50	8.00	13.00	18.00	75.00	250	—
1899	2,400,000	2.25	3.00	4.00	7.00	35.00	150	—
1900	1,000,000	6.00	10.00	15.00	23.00	85.00	400	—
1900H	2,600,000	2.00	2.50	4.00	5.50	30.00	75.00	—
1901	4,100,000	2.25	4.50	3.00	8.50	35.00	85.00	—

KM# 8 Obv: Kings bust right within beaded circle **Obv. Designer:** G. W. DeSaulles **Rev:** Denomination above date within circle, chain of leaves surrounds **Edge:** Plain **Weight:** 4.5400 g. **Composition:** Bronze **Size:** 25.5 mm.

Date	Mintage	VG-8	F-12	VF-20	XF-40	MS-60	MS-63	Proof
1902	3,000,000	1.75	2.25	3.50	6.00	25.00	75.00	—
1903	4,000,000	1.75	2.25	3.00	6.00	30.00	80.00	—
1904	2,500,000	2.00	3.50	5.00	8.00	35.00	85.00	—
1905	2,000,000	3.50	6.00	7.50	12.00	45.00	150	—
1906	4,100,000	1.75	2.25	3.00	6.00	35.00	175	—
1907	2,400,000	2.00	3.50	4.50	9.00	35.00	200	—
1907H	800,000	12.00	24.00	30.00	50.00	175	550	—
1908	2,401,506	3.00	3.50	5.00	8.00	30.00	90.00	150
1909	3,973,339	1.75	2.50	3.00	6.00	30.00	100.00	—
1910	5,146,487	1.75	2.50	3.00	5.00	26.00	70.00	—

KM# 15 Obv: King's bust left **Obv. Designer:** E. B. MacKennal **Rev:** Denomination above date within beaded circle, chain of leaves surrounds **Edge:** Plain **Weight:** 4.5400 g. **Composition:** Bronze **Size:** 25.5 mm.

Date	Mintage	VG-8	F-12	VF-20	XF-40	MS-60	MS-63	Proof
1911	4,663,486	0.80	1.30	1.75	3.50	25.00	75.00	250

KM# 21 Obv: King's bust left **Obv. Designer:** E. B. MacKennal **Rev:** Denomination above date within beaded circle, chain of leaves surrounds **Edge:** Plain **Weight:** 4.5400 g. **Composition:** Bronze **Size:** 25.5 mm.

Date	Mintage	VG-8	F-12	VF-20	XF-40	MS-60	MS-63	Proof
1912	5,107,642	0.75	1.50	2.25	3.50	25.00	80.00	—
1913	5,735,405	0.75	1.50	2.25	4.00	23.00	80.00	—
1914	3,405,958	1.00	1.50	2.50	4.00	35.00	125	—
1915	4,932,134	0.75	2.25	3.00	4.00	30.00	100.00	—
1916	11,022,367	0.50	0.65	1.25	3.00	16.00	50.00	—
1917	11,899,254	0.50	0.65	0.90	2.25	13.00	45.00	—
1918	12,970,798	0.50	0.65	0.90	2.25	12.00	45.00	—
1919	11,279,634	0.50	0.65	0.90	2.25	12.00	45.00	—
1920	6,762,247	0.60	0.75	1.00	2.25	20.00	100.00	—

Dot below date

KM# 28 Obv: King's bust left **Obv. Designer:** E. B. MacKennal **Rev:** Denomination above date, leaves flank **Rev. Designer:** Fred Lewis **Edge:** Plain **Weight:** 3.2400 g. **Composition:** Bronze **Size:** 19.10 mm.

Date	Mintage	VG-8	F-12	VF-20	XF-40	MS-60	MS-63	Proof
1920	15,483,923	0.20	0.50	1.00	2.00	15.00	50.00	—
1921	7,601,627	0.50	0.75	1.75	5.00	35.00	200	—

CENT

Date	Mintage	VG-8	F-12	VF-20	XF-40	MS-60	MS-63	Proof
1922	1,243,635	13.00	16.00	21.00	35.00	200	1,200	—
1923	1,019,002	29.00	35.00	40.00	50.00	300	2,000	—
1924	1,593,195	5.00	6.50	8.50	15.00	125	850	—
1925	1,000,622	18.00	21.00	27.00	40.00	200	1,600	—
1926	2,143,372	3.50	4.50	7.00	11.00	100.00	650	—
1927	3,553,928	1.25	2.00	3.50	6.00	40.00	225	—
1928	9,144,860	0.15	0.30	0.65	1.50	20.00	90.00	—
1929	12,159,840	0.15	0.30	0.65	1.50	20.00	80.00	—
1930	2,538,613	2.00	2.50	4.50	8.50	50.00	225	—
1931	3,842,776	0.65	1.00	2.50	5.50	40.00	200	—
1932	21,316,190	0.15	0.20	0.50	1.50	14.00	45.00	—
1933	12,079,310	0.15	0.30	0.50	1.50	15.00	65.00	—
1934	7,042,358	0.20	0.30	0.75	1.50	14.00	45.00	—
1935	7,526,400	0.20	0.30	0.75	1.50	14.00	45.00	—
1936	8,768,769	0.15	0.30	0.75	1.50	14.00	45.00	—
1936 dot below date; Rare	678,823	—	—	—	—	—	—	—

Note: Only one possible business strike is known to exist. No other examples (or possible business strikes) have ever surfaced.

1936 dot below date, specimen, 3 known		—	—	—	—	—	—	—

Note: At the David Akers auction of the John Jay Pittman collection (Part 1, 10-97), a gem specimen realized $121,000. At the David Akers auction of the John Jay Pittman collection (Part 3, 10-99), a near choice specimen realized $115,000.

Maple leaf

KM# 32 Obv: Head left **Obv. Designer:** T. H. Paget **Rev:** Maple leaf divides date and denomination **Rev. Designer:** George E. Kruger-Gray **Edge:** Plain **Weight:** 3.2400 g. **Composition:** Bronze **Size:** 19.10 mm.

Date	Mintage	VG-8	F-12	VF-20	XF-40	MS-60	MS-63	Proof
1937	10,040,231	0.35	0.50	1.00	2.00	3.00	9.00	—
1938	18,365,608	0.15	0.20	0.35	0.75	3.00	13.00	—
1939	21,600,319	0.10	0.20	0.35	0.70	1.75	5.00	—
1940	85,740,532	0.10	0.15	0.25	0.50	2.25	5.50	—
1941	56,336,011	0.10	0.15	0.25	0.50	8.00	60.00	—
1942	76,113,708	0.10	0.15	0.25	0.50	8.00	60.00	—
1943	89,111,969	0.10	0.15	0.25	0.45	3.50	25.00	—
1944	44,131,216	0.10	0.15	0.30	0.60	12.00	100.00	—
1945	77,268,591	0.10	0.15	0.20	0.35	3.00	22.00	—
1946	56,662,071	0.10	0.15	0.20	0.35	3.00	7.50	—
1947	31,093,901	0.10	0.15	0.20	0.35	3.00	7.50	—
1947 maple leaf	47,855,448	0.10	0.15	0.20	0.35	3.00	5.00	—

KM# 41 Obv: Modified legend **Obv. Designer:** T. H. Paget **Rev. Designer:** George E. Kruger-Gray **Edge:** Plain **Weight:** 3.2400 g. **Composition:** Bronze **Size:** 19.10 mm.

Date	Mintage	VG-8	F-12	VF-20	XF-40	MS-60	MS-63	Proof
1948	25,767,779	—	0.15	0.25	0.70	4.00	35.00	—
1949	33,128,933	—	0.10	0.15	0.35	3.00	9.00	—
1950	60,444,992	—	0.10	0.15	0.25	2.00	9.00	—
1951	80,430,379	—	0.10	0.15	0.20	2.00	13.00	—
1952	67,631,736	—	0.10	0.15	0.20	2.00	7.00	—

No strap   With strap

KM# 49 Obv: Laureate bust right **Obv. Designer:** Mary Gillick **Rev:** Maple leaf divides date and denomination **Rev. Designer:** George E. Kruger-Gray **Weight:** 3.2400 g. **Composition:** Bronze **Size:** 19.10 mm.

Date	Mintage	VG-8	F-12	VF-20	XF-40	MS-60	MS-63	Proof
1953	67,806,016	0.10	0.10	0.10	0.35	0.65	1.50	—
Note: Without strap								
1953	Inc. above	0.50	1.00	1.50	2.50	12.00	55.00	—
Note: With strap								
1954	22,181,760	0.10	0.10	0.10	0.40	2.00	6.00	—
Note: With strap								
1954 Prooflike only	Inc. above	—	—	—	—	250	500	—
Note: Without strap								
1955	56,403,193	—	0.10	0.10	0.20	0.55	1.50	—
Note: With strap								
1955	Inc. above	85.00	125	150	250	600	1,800	—
Note: Without strap								
1956	78,658,535	—	—	—	0.15	0.50	0.90	—

CENT

Date	Mintage	VG-8	F-12	VF-20	XF-40	MS-60	MS-63	Proof
1957	100,601,792	—	—	—	0.10	0.30	0.60	—
1958	59,385,679	—	—	—	0.10	0.30	0.60	—
1959	83,615,343	—	—	—	0.10	0.15	0.30	—
1960	75,772,775	—	—	—	0.10	0.15	0.30	—
1961	139,598,404	—	—	—	—	0.15	0.30	—
1962	227,244,069	—	—	—	—	0.15	0.30	—
1963	279,076,334	—	—	—	—	0.15	0.30	—
1964	484,655,322	—	—	—	—	0.15	0.30	—

KM# 59.1 Obv: Queens bust right **Obv. Designer:** Arnold Machin **Rev:** Maple leaf divides date and denomination **Rev. Designer:** George E. Kruger-Gray **Edge:** Plain **Weight:** 3.2400 g. **Composition:** Bronze **Size:** 19.10 mm.

Date	Mintage	MS-60	MS-63	Proof
1965	304,441,082	1.00	4.00	—
Note: Small beads, pointed 5				
1965	Inc. above	0.10	0.20	—
Note: Small beads, blunt 5				
1965	Inc. above	18.00	35.00	—
Note: Large beads, pointed 5				
1965	Inc. above	0.10	0.20	—
Note: Large beads, blunt 5				
1966	184,151,087	0.10	0.20	—
1968	329,695,772	0.10	0.15	—
1969	335,240,929	0.10	0.15	—
1970	311,145,010	0.10	0.15	—
1971	298,228,936	0.10	0.15	—
1972	451,304,591	0.10	0.15	—
1973	457,059,852	0.10	0.15	—
1974	692,058,489	0.10	0.15	—
1975	642,318,000	0.10	0.15	—
1976	701,122,890	0.10	0.15	—
1977	453,762,670	0.10	0.15	—
1978	911,170,647	0.10	0.15	—

KM# 65 Subject: Confederation Centennial **Obv:** Queen's bust right **Obv. Designer:** Arnold Machin **Rev:** Dove with wings spread, denomination above, two dates below **Rev. Designer:** Alex Colville **Composition:** Bronze **Size:** 19.10 mm.

Date	Mintage	MS-60	MS-63	Proof
ND(1967)	345,140,645	0.10	0.20	1.00

KM# 59.2 Obv: Queen's bust right **Obv. Designer:** Arnold Machin **Rev:** Dove with wings spread, denomination above, dates below **Rev. Designer:** George E. Kruger-Gray **Edge:** Plain **Weight:** 3.2400 g. **Composition:** Bronze **Size:** 19.10 mm.

Date	Mintage	MS-60	MS-63	Proof
1979	754,394,064	0.10	0.15	—

KM# 127 Obv: Queen's bust right **Obv. Designer:** Arnold Machin **Rev. Designer:** George E. Kruger-Gray **Edge:** Plain **Weight:** 2.8000 g. **Composition:** Bronze **Size:** 19.10 mm. **Note:** Reduced weight.

Date	Mintage	MS-60	MS-63	Proof
1980	912,052,318	0.10	0.15	—
1981	1,209,468,500	0.10	0.15	—
1981 Proof	199,000	—	—	1.50

KM# 132 Obv: Queen's bust right **Obv. Designer:** Arnold Machin **Rev:** Maple leaf divides date and denomination **Rev. Designer:** George E. Kruger-Gray **Edge:** Plain **Weight:** 2.5000 g. **Composition:** Bronze **Size:** 19.10 mm. **Note:** Reduced weight.

Date	Mintage	MS-60	MS-63	Proof
1982	911,001,000	0.10	0.15	—
1982 Proof	180,908	—	—	1.50
1983	975,510,000	0.10	0.15	—
1983 Proof	168,000	—	—	1.50
1984	838,225,000	0.10	0.15	—
1984 Proof	161,602	—	—	1.50
1985	771,772,500	10.00	19.00	—
Note: Pointed 5				
1985	Inc. above	0.10	0.15	—
Note: Blunt 5				
1985 Proof	157,037	—	—	1.50
Note: Blunt 5				
1986	740,335,000	0.10	0.15	—
1986 Proof	175,745	—	—	1.50
1987	774,549,000	0.10	0.15	—
1987 Proof	179,004	—	—	1.50
1988	482,676,752	0.10	0.15	—
1988 Proof	175,259	—	—	1.50
1989	1,077,347,200	0.10	0.15	—
1989 Proof	170,928	—	—	1.50

KM# 181 Obv: Crowned Queen's head right **Obv. Designer:** Dora dePedery-Hunt **Rev:** Maple leaf divides date and denomination **Rev. Designer:** George E. Kruger-Gray **Edge:** Plain **Weight:** 2.5000 g. **Composition:** Bronze **Size:** 19.10 mm.

Date	Mintage	MS-60	MS-63	Proof
1990	218,035,000	0.10	0.15	—
1990 Proof	140,649	—	—	2.50
1991	831,001,000	0.10	0.15	—
1991 Proof	131,888	—	—	3.50
1993	752,034,000	0.10	0.15	—
1993 Proof	145,065	—	—	2.00
1994	639,516,000	0.10	0.15	—
1994 Proof	146,424	—	—	2.50
1995	624,983,000	0.10	0.15	—
1995 Proof	—	—	—	2.50
1996	445,746,000	0.10	0.15	—
1996 Proof	—	—	—	2.50

CENT

KM# 204 Subject: Confederation 125 **Obv:** Crowned Queen's head right **Obv. Designer:** Dora dePedery-Hunt **Rev:** Maple leaf divides date and denomination **Rev. Designer:** George E. Kruger-Gray **Composition:** Bronze **Size:** 19.10 mm.

Date	Mintage	MS-60	MS-63	Proof
ND(1992) Proof	147,061	—	—	2.50
ND(1992)	673,512,000	0.10	0.15	—

KM# 289 Obv: Crowned head right **Obv. Designer:** Dora dePédery-Hunt **Rev:** Maple twig design **Rev. Designer:** George E. Kruger-Gray **Edge:** Round and plain **Composition:** Copper Plated Steel **Size:** 19.1 mm.

Date	Mintage	MS-60	MS-63	Proof
1997	549,868,000	0.10	0.15	—
1997 Proof	—	—	—	2.75
1998	999,578,000	0.10	0.15	—
1998 Proof	—	—	—	3.00
1998W	—	—	1.75	—
1999P	—	—	6.00	—

Note: Plated planchet, set only

1999	1,089,625,000	0.10	0.15	—
1999W	—	—	—	—
1999 Proof	—	—	—	4.00
2000	771,908,206	0.10	0.15	—
2000 Proof	—	—	—	4.00
2000W	—	—	1.75	—
2001P Proof	—	—	—	5.00
2001	919,358,000	—	0.10	—
2003	92,219,775	—	0.10	—
2003P Proof	—	—	—	5.00
2003P	235,936,799	—	1.50	—

KM# 289a Composition: Bronze **Size:** 19.10 mm.

Date	Mintage	MS-60	MS-63	Proof
1998	—	—	0.75	—

Note: In Specimen sets only

KM# 309 Subject: 90th Anniversary Royal Canadian Mint - 1908-1998 **Obv. Designer:** Dora dePedery-Hunt **Rev. Designer:** G. W. DeSaulles **Weight:** 5.6700 g. **Composition:** 0.9250 Copper-Plated Silver 0.1686 oz.

Date	Mintage	MS-60	MS-63	Proof
ND(1998)	25,000	—	16.00	—

Note: Antique finish

| ND(1998) Proof | — | — | — | — |

KM# 332 Subject: 90th Anniversary Royal Canadian Mint - 1908-1998 **Obv:** Crowned Queen's head right, with "Canada" added to head **Obv. Designer:** Dora dePedery-Hunt **Rev:** Denomination above dates withn beaded circle, chain of leaves surrounds **Rev. Designer:** G. W. DeSaulles **Weight:** 5.6700 g. **Composition:** 0.9250 Silver 0.1686 oz. ASW

Date	Mintage	MS-60	MS-63	Proof
ND(2000) Proof	25,000	—	—	16.00

Note: Mirror finish

KM# 445 Subject: Elizabeth II Golden Jubilee **Obv:** Crowned head right, Jubilee commemorative dates 1952-2002 **Obv. Designer:** Dora dePédery-Hunt **Rev:** Denomination above maple leaves **Rev. Designer:** George E. Kruger-Gray **Edge:** Plain **Composition:** Copper Plated Steel **Size:** 19.1 mm.

Date	Mintage	MS-63	Proof
ND(2002)	716,366,000	0.75	—
ND(2002)P	114,212,000	1.00	—
ND(2002)P	32,642	—	5.00

Note: In Proof Sets only

KM# 445a Subject: Elizabeth II Golden Jubilee **Obv:** Crowned head right, Jubilee commemorative dates 1952-2002 **Obv. Designer:** Dora dePédery-Hunt **Rev:** Denomination above maple leaves **Rev. Designer:** George E. Kruger-Gray **Composition:** 0.9250 Silver

Date	Mintage	MS-63	Proof
ND(2002)	21,537	—	3.00

Note: In sets only

KM# 490 Obv: New effigy of Queen Elizabeth II right **Obv. Designer:** Susanna Blunt **Edge:** Plain **Composition:** Copper Plated Zinc **Size:** 19.1 mm.

Date	Mintage	MS-63	Proof
2003	56,877,144	0.25	—
2004	653,317,000	0.25	—
2004 Proof	—	—	2.50
2005	759,658,000	0.25	—
2005 Proof	—	—	2.50
2006	1,062,275,000	0.25	—
2006 Proof	—	—	2.50
2007(ml)	—	0.25	—
2007(ml) Proof	—	—	2.50

KM# 490a Composition: Acrylic **Size:** 19.1 mm.

Date	Mintage	MS-63	Proof
2003P	591,257,000	0.25	—
2003 WP	Inc. Above	0.25	—
2004P	134,906,000	0.25	—
2005P	30,525,000	0.25	—
2006P	137,733,000	0.25	—
2006(ml)	Inc. Above	0.25	—
2007(ml)	—	0.25	—

KM# 490b Composition: Copper Plated Zinc

Date	Mintage	MS-63	Proof
2004 Proof	7,746	—	—

Note: Bound into Annual Report

KM# 468 Subject: 50th Anniversary of the Coronation of Elizabeth II **Obv:** 1953 effigy of the Queen, Jubilee commemorative dates 1952-2002 **Obv. Designer:** Mary Gillick **Composition:** Copper

Date	Mintage	MS-63	Proof
ND(2002)	—	2.50	—

Note: In Coronation Proof sets only

CENT

3 CENTS

KM# 410 Subject: 1st Canadian Postage Stamp **Obv:** Crowned head right **Obv. Designer:** Dora dePédery-Hunt **Rev:** Partial stamp design **Rev. Designer:** Sandford Fleming **Edge:** Plain **Weight:** 3.1100 g. **Composition:** 0.9250 Gold Plated Silver 0.0925 oz. ASW AGW **Size:** 21.3 mm.

Date	Mintage	MS-63	Proof
2001 Proof	90,000	—	12.50

5 CENTS

Oval O's   Round O's

KM# 2   Obv: Head left **Obv. Legend:** VICTORIA DEI GRATIA REGINA. CANADA **Rev:** Denomination and date within wreath, crown above **Designer:** Leonard C. Wyon **Weight:** 1.1620 g. **Composition:** 0.9250 Silver 0.0346 oz. ASW

Date	Mintage	VG-8	F-12	VF-20	XF-40	MS-60	MS-63	Proof
1858 Small date	1,500,000	19.00	30.00	45.00	80.00	250	525	—
1858 Large date over small date	Inc. above	130	210	325	550	1,350	3,000	—
1870	2,800,000	13.50	22.50	40.00	60.00	250	650	—
Note: Flat rim								
1870	Inc. above	16.00	24.00	35.00	80.00	225	525	—
Note: Wire rim								
1871	1,400,000	13.50	22.50	40.00	70.00	275	600	—
1872H	2,000,000	13.00	20.00	35.00	80.00	250	1,250	—
1874H Plain 4	800,000	22.00	35.00	75.00	120	400	950	—
1874H Crosslet 4	Inc. above	14.00	30.00	60.00	120	450	1,100	—
1875H Large date	1,000,000	250	400	650	1,300	2,750	11,000	—
1875H Small date	Inc. above	95.00	175	300	500	1,750	4,550	—
1880H	3,000,000	6.00	12.00	27.00	65.00	250	600	—
1881H	1,500,000	9.00	15.00	30.00	70.00	265	650	—
1882H	1,000,000	12.00	18.00	27.00	80.00	275	700	—
1883H	600,000	23.00	35.00	70.00	150	750	3,000	—
1884	200,000	85.00	165	275	650	2,850	7,250	—
1885 Small 5	1,000,000	16.00	24.00	40.00	125	750	2,900	—
1885 Large 5	Inc. above	11.50	22.50	45.00	150	850	3,000	—
1885 Large 5 over small 5	Inc. above	65.00	125	200	450	2,850	—	—
1886 Small 6	1,700,000	7.00	15.00	25.00	50.00	300	1,300	—
1886 Large 6	Inc. above	9.00	16.00	28.00	60.00	350	1,500	—
1887	500,000	16.00	30.00	55.00	120	400	825	—
1888	1,000,000	6.00	9.00	18.00	50.00	165	425	—
1889	1,200,000	20.00	35.00	75.00	125	475	1,200	—
1890H	1,000,000	6.00	12.00	22.00	50.00	200	450	—
1891	1,800,000	6.00	9.00	15.00	30.00	150	385	—
1892	860,000	6.00	10.00	20.00	50.00	250	675	—
1893	1,700,000	6.00	9.00	14.00	30.00	175	400	—
1894	500,000	19.00	27.00	50.00	100.00	450	1,100	—
1896	1,500,000	6.00	9.00	14.00	35.00	175	375	—
1897	1,319,283	4.50	6.50	13.50	30.00	150	325	—
1898	580,717	10.00	20.00	35.00	70.00	350	750	—
1899	3,000,000	4.50	6.50	12.00	25.00	115	300	—
1900 Oval 0's	1,800,000	4.50	6.50	12.00	25.00	115	325	—
1900 Round 0's	Inc. above	17.50	37.50	55.00	120	450	800	—
1901	2,000,000	4.50	6.50	12.00	35.00	150	400	—

KM# 9   Obv. Designer: G. W. DeSaulles **Rev. Designer:** Leonard C. Wyon **Weight:** 1.1620 g. **Composition:** 0.9250 Silver 0.0346 oz. ASW

Date	Mintage	VG-8	F-12	VF-20	XF-40	MS-60	MS-63	Proof
1902	2,120,000	2.25	3.00	4.00	7.00	35.00	55.00	—
1902	2,200,000	2.25	3.25	5.50	11.00	35.00	60.00	—
Note: Large broad H								
1902	Inc. above	7.50	13.00	24.00	40.00	100.00	175	—
Note: Small narrow H								

KM# 13 Obv: King's bust right **Rev:** Denomination and date within wreath, crown at top **Weight:** 1.1620 g.
Composition: 0.9250 Silver 0.0346 oz. ASW

Date	Mintage	VG-8	F-12	VF-20	XF-40	MS-60	MS-63	Proof
1903	1,000,000	4.00	7.00	17.00	35.00	150	350	—
Note: 22 leaves								
1903H	2,640,000	1.75	3.00	7.00	16.00	100.00	300	—
Note: 21 leaves								
1904	2,400,000	2.75	4.50	7.00	23.00	175	500	—
1905	2,600,000	1.75	3.00	9.00	16.00	100.00	225	—
1906	3,100,000	2.25	3.00	6.00	13.00	85.00	225	—
1907	5,200,000	2.25	3.00	4.00	10.00	55.00	150	—
1908	1,220,524	6.00	10.00	23.00	35.00	100.00	175	—
1909	1,983,725	3.00	6.50	10.00	30.00	175	500	—
Note: Round leaves								
1909	Inc. above	12.00	18.00	35.00	95.00	550	1,300	—
Note: Pointed leaves								
1910	3,850,325	2.25	2.75	5.00	11.00	50.00	95.00	—
Note: Pointed leaves								
1910	Inc. above	15.00	17.00	30.00	85.00	400	1,300	—
Note: Round leaves								

KM# 16 Obv: King's bust left **Obv. Designer:** E. B. MacKennal **Rev:** Denomination and date within wreath, crown above **Rev. Designer:** Leonard C. Wyon **Weight:** 1.1620 g. **Composition:** 0.9250 Silver 0.0346 oz. ASW

Date	Mintage	VG-8	F-12	VF-20	XF-40	MS-60	MS-63	Proof
1911	3,692,350	2.00	3.00	6.00	9.00	60.00	100.00	—

KM# 22 Obv: King's bust left **Obv. Designer:** E. B. MacKennal **Rev:** Denomination and date within wreath, crown above **Rev. Designer:** Leonard C. Wyon **Weight:** 1.1620 g. **Composition:** 0.9250 Silver 0.0346 oz. ASW

Date	Mintage	VG-8	F-12	VF-20	XF-40	MS-60	MS-63	Proof
1912	5,863,170	2.00	3.00	5.00	9.00	50.00	150	—
1913	5,488,048	2.00	2.75	4.25	7.50	26.00	50.00	—
1914	4,202,179	2.00	3.00	5.00	9.00	50.00	125	—
1915	1,172,258	11.00	15.00	26.00	50.00	325	600	—
1916	2,481,675	2.75	7.50	13.00	22.00	100.00	250	—
1917	5,521,373	1.75	2.50	3.00	7.00	30.00	80.00	—
1918	6,052,298	1.75	2.50	3.00	6.50	30.00	65.00	—
1919	7,835,400	1.75	2.50	3.00	6.50	30.00	65.00	—

KM# 22a Obv. Designer: E. B. MacKennal **Rev. Designer:** Leonard C. Wyon **Weight:** 1.1664 g.
Composition: 0.8000 Silver 0.0300 oz. ASW **Size:** 15.48 mm.

Date	Mintage	VG-8	F-12	VF-20	XF-40	MS-60	MS-63	Proof
1920	10,649,851	1.75	2.50	3.00	6.50	26.00	50.00	—
1921	2,582,495	2,700	3,000	4,500	6,750	9,500	16,500	—

Note: Approximately 460 known; balance remelted. Stack's A.G. Carter Jr. Sale (12-89) choice BU, finest known, realized $57,200

Near 6   Far 6

KM# 29 Obv: King's bust left **Obv. Designer:** E. B. MacKennal **Rev:** Maple leaves divide denomination and date **Rev. Designer:** W. H. J. Blakemore **Weight:** 4.5200 g. **Composition:** Nickel **Size:** 21.2 mm.

Date	Mintage	VG-8	F-12	VF-20	XF-40	MS-60	MS-63	Proof
1922	4,794,119	0.35	1.00	1.75	7.00	45.00	95.00	—
1923	2,502,279	0.40	1.25	5.50	16.00	100.00	275	—
1924	3,105,839	0.50	1.00	3.75	10.00	85.00	200	—
1925	201,921	55.00	70.00	100.00	200	1,200	3,600	—
1926 Near 6	938,162	3.00	7.00	16.00	60.00	375	1,300	—
1926 Far 6	Inc. above	100.00	150	300	600	1,500	4,300	—
1927	5,285,627	0.35	0.65	2.75	15.00	60.00	125	—
1928	4,577,712	0.35	0.65	2.75	15.00	55.00	100.00	—
1929	5,611,911	0.35	0.65	2.75	15.00	60.00	150	—
1930	3,704,673	0.35	1.50	2.75	15.00	90.00	200	—
1931	5,100,830	0.35	1.50	3.25	18.00	175	475	—
1932	3,198,566	0.35	1.00	3.25	16.00	150	350	—
1933	2,597,867	0.40	1.50	6.00	18.00	175	650	—
1934	3,827,304	0.35	1.00	3.00	16.00	150	375	—
1935	3,900,000	0.35	1.00	2.75	11.00	95.00	250	—
1936	4,400,450	0.35	0.65	1.75	9.00	50.00	100.00	—

KM# 33 Obv: Head left **Obv. Designer:** T. H. Paget **Rev:** Beaver on rock divides denomination and date **Rev. Designer:** George E. Kruger-Gray **Weight:** 4.5000 g. **Composition:** Nickel **Size:** 21.2 mm.

Date	Mintage	VG-8	F-12	VF-20	XF-40	MS-60	MS-63	Proof
1937 Dot	4,593,263	0.25	0.35	1.25	2.50	9.00	22.00	—
1938	3,898,974	0.30	0.90	2.00	7.00	75.00	150	—
1939	5,661,123	0.25	0.35	1.25	3.00	45.00	80.00	—
1940	13,920,197	0.20	0.30	0.75	2.25	18.00	55.00	—
1941	8,681,785	0.20	0.30	0.75	2.25	23.00	70.00	—
1942 Round	6,847,544	0.20	0.30	0.75	1.75	18.00	35.00	—

KM# 39 Obv: Head left **Obv. Designer:** T. H. Paget **Rev:** Beaver on rock divides denomination and date **Rev. Designer:** George E. Kruger-Gray **Composition:** Tombac **Shape:** 12-sided **Size:** 21.2 mm.

Date	Mintage	VG-8	F-12	VF-20	XF-40	MS-60	MS-63	Proof
1942	3,396,234	0.40	0.65	1.25	1.75	3.00	14.00	—

KM# 40a Obv: Head left **Rev:** Torch on "V" divides date **Weight:** 4.4000 g. **Composition:** Chrome Plated Steel **Size:** 21.2 mm.

Date	Mintage	VG-8	F-12	VF-20	XF-40	MS-60	MS-63	Proof
1944	11,532,784	0.10	0.35	0.50	0.90	2.00	7.00	—
1945	18,893,216	0.10	0.20	0.40	0.80	2.00	7.00	—

5 CENTS

Dot   Maple leaf

KM# 39a **Obv:** Head left **Obv. Designer:** T. H. Paget **Rev:** Beaver on rock divides denomination and date
Rev. Designer: George E. Kruger-Gray **Weight:** 4.5000 g. **Composition:** Nickel **Size:** 21.2 mm.

Date	Mintage	VG-8	F-12	VF-20	XF-40	MS-60	MS-63	Proof
1946	6,952,684	0.10	0.30	0.50	2.00	14.00	32.00	—
1947	7,603,724	0.20	0.30	0.50	1.25	10.00	25.00	—
1947 Dot	Inc. above	12.00	20.00	27.00	60.00	175	300	—
1947 Maple leaf	9,595,124	0.20	0.30	0.45	1.25	10.00	25.00	—

KM# 42 **Obv:** Head left, modified legend **Obv. Designer:** T. H. Paget **Rev:** Beaver on rock divides date and
denomination **Rev. Designer:** George E. Kruger-Gray **Weight:** 4.5400 g. **Composition:** Nickel **Size:** 21.2 mm.

Date	Mintage	VG-8	F-12	VF-20	XF-40	MS-60	MS-63	Proof
1948	1,810,789	0.40	0.50	1.00	3.00	18.00	35.00	—
1949	13,037,090	0.20	0.30	0.50	0.75	6.00	12.00	—
1950	11,970,521	0.20	0.30	0.50	0.75	6.00	12.00	—

KM# 42a **Obv:** Head left **Obv. Designer:** T. H. Paget **Rev:** Beaver on rock divides date and denomination
Rev. Designer: George E. Kruger-Gray **Composition:** Chromium And Nickel-Plated Steel **Size:** 21.2 mm.

Date	Mintage	VG-8	F-12	VF-20	XF-40	MS-60	MS-63	Proof
1951	4,313,410	0.10	0.25	0.50	0.80	3.50	11.00	—
Note: Low relief; Second "A" in GRATIA points between denticles								
1951	Inc. above	350	525	700	1,000	1,900	3,100	—
Note: High relief; Second "A" in GRATIA points to a denticle								
1952	10,891,148	0.10	0.20	0.45	0.80	3.00	7.50	—

KM# 48 **Subject:** Nickel Bicentennial **Obv:** Head left **Obv. Designer:** T. H. Paget **Rev:** Buildings with center
tower divide dates and denomination **Rev. Designer:** Stephen Trenka **Weight:** 4.5500 g. **Composition:** Nickel
Shape: 12-sided **Size:** 21.2 mm.

Date	Mintage	VG-8	F-12	VF-20	XF-40	MS-60	MS-63	Proof
ND(1951)	9,028,507	0.20	0.30	0.35	0.45	1.75	5.50	—

KM# 50 **Obv:** Laureate queen's bust, right **Obv. Designer:** Mary Gillick **Rev:** Beaver on rock divides date
and denomination **Rev. Designer:** George E. Kruger-Gray **Composition:** Chromium And Nickel-Plated Steel
Shape: 12-sided **Size:** 21.2 mm.

Date	Mintage	VG-8	F-12	VF-20	XF-40	MS-60	MS-63	Proof
1953	16,635,552	0.10	0.20	0.40	0.90	3.00	7.00	—
Note: Without strap								
1953	Inc. above	300	500	750	900	1,300	2,300	—
Note: Without strap, near leaf								
1953	Inc. above	150	225	300	475	1,100	2,300	—
Note: With strap, far leaf								
1953	Inc. above	0.10	0.20	0.40	0.90	3.50	7.00	—
Note: With strap								
1954	6,998,662	0.10	0.25	0.50	1.00	4.00	8.00	—

KM# 50a Obv: Laureate queen's bust right **Obv. Designer:** Mary Gillick **Rev:** Beaver on rock divides date and denomination **Rev. Designer:** George E. Kruger-Gray **Weight:** 4.5900 g. **Composition:** Nickel **Size:** 21.2 mm.

Date	Mintage	VG-8	F-12	VF-20	XF-40	MS-60	MS-63	Proof
1955	5,355,028	0.20	0.25	0.40	0.75	3.50	4.50	—
1956	9,399,854	—	0.20	0.30	0.45	2.25	5.00	—
1957	7,387,703	—	—	0.25	0.30	2.00	3.00	—
1958	7,607,521	—	—	0.25	0.30	2.00	3.00	—
1959	11,552,523	—	—	—	0.20	0.70	1.50	—
1960	37,157,433	—	—	—	0.20	0.75	1.50	—
1961	47,889,051	—	—	—	—	0.30	0.80	—
1962	46,307,305	—	—	—	—	0.30	0.80	—

KM# 57 Obv: Laureate queen's bust right **Obv. Designer:** Mary Gillick **Rev:** Beaver on rock divides date and denomination **Rev. Designer:** George E. Kruger-Gray **Composition:** Nickel **Shape:** Round **Size:** 21.2 mm.

Date	Mintage	MS-60	MS-63	Proof
1963	43,970,320	0.20	0.75	—
1964	78,075,068	0.20	0.75	—
1964	—	35.00	100.00	—

Note: Extra water line

KM# 60.1 Obv: Queen's bust right **Obv. Designer:** Arnold Machin **Rev:** Beaver on rock divides date and denomination **Rev. Designer:** George E. Kruger-Gray **Weight:** 4.5400 g. **Composition:** Nickel **Size:** 21.2 mm.

Date	Mintage	MS-60	MS-63	Proof
1965	84,876,018	0.20	0.30	—
1966	27,976,648	0.20	0.30	—
1968	101,930,379	0.20	0.30	—
1969	27,830,229	0.20	0.30	—
1970	5,726,010	0.35	0.75	—
1971	27,312,609	0.20	0.30	—
1972	62,417,387	0.20	0.30	—
1973	53,507,435	0.20	0.30	—
1974	94,704,645	0.20	0.30	—
1975	138,882,000	0.20	0.30	—
1976	55,140,213	0.20	0.30	—
1977	89,120,791	0.20	0.30	—
1978	137,079,273	0.20	0.30	—

KM# 66 Subject: Confederation Centennial **Obv:** Queen's bust right **Obv. Designer:** Arnold Machin **Rev:** Snowshoe rabbit bounding left divides dates and denomination **Rev. Designer:** Alex Coville **Composition:** Nickel **Size:** 21.2 mm.

Date	Mintage	MS-60	MS-63	Proof
ND(1967)	36,876,574	0.20	0.40	1.00

KM# 60.2 Obv: Queen's bust right **Obv. Designer:** Arnold Machin **Rev:** Beaver on rock divides date and denomination **Rev. Designer:** George E. Kruger-Gray **Composition:** Nickel **Size:** 21.2 mm.

Date	Mintage	MS-60	MS-63	Proof
1979	186,295,825	0.20	0.30	—
1980	134,878,000	0.20	0.30	—
1981	99,107,900	0.20	0.30	—
1981 Proof	199,000	—	—	1.50

KM# 60.2a Obv: Queen's bust right **Obv. Designer:** Arnold Machin **Rev:** Beaver on rock divides date and denomination **Rev. Designer:** George E. Kruger-Gray **Weight:** 4.6000 g. **Composition:** Copper-Nickel **Size:** 21.2 mm.

Date	Mintage	MS-60	MS-63	Proof
1982	64,924,400	0.20	0.30	—
1982 Proof	180,908	—	—	1.50
1983	72,596,000	0.20	0.30	—
1983 Proof	168,000	—	—	1.50
1984	84,088,000	0.20	0.30	—
1984 Proof	161,602	—	—	1.50
1985	126,618,000	0.20	0.30	—
1985 Proof	157,037	—	—	1.50
1986	156,104,000	0.20	0.30	—
1986 Proof	175,745	—	—	1.50
1987	106,299,000	0.15	0.30	—
1987 Proof	179,004	—	—	1.50
1988	75,025,000	0.15	0.30	—
1988 Proof	175,259	—	—	1.50
1989	141,570,538	0.15	0.30	—
1989 Proof	170,928	—	—	1.50

KM# 182 Obv: Crowned head right **Obv. Designer:** Dora dePedery-Hunt **Rev:** Beaver on rock divides dates and denomination **Rev. Designer:** George E. Kruger-Gray **Edge:** Plain **Weight:** 4.6000 g. **Composition:** Copper-Nickel **Size:** 19.55 mm.

Date	Mintage	MS-60	MS-63	Proof
1990	42,537,000	0.15	0.30	—
1990 Proof	140,649	—	—	2.50
1991	10,931,000	0.30	0.55	—
1991 Proof	131,888	—	—	7.00
1993	86,877,000	0.15	0.30	—
1993 Proof	143,065	—	—	2.50

5 CENTS

Date	Mintage	MS-60	MS-63	Proof
1994	99,352,000	0.15	0.30	—
1994 Proof	146,424	—	—	3.00
1995	78,528,000	0.15	0.30	—
1995 Proof	50,000	—	—	2.50
1996 Far 6	36,686,000	0.75	2.25	—
1996 Near 6	Inc. above	0.70	2.25	—
1996 Proof	—	—	—	6.00
1997	27,354,000	0.15	0.30	—
1997 Proof	—	—	—	5.00
1998	156,873,000	0.15	0.30	—
1998W	—	—	1.50	—
1998 Proof	—	—	—	5.00
1999	124,861,000	0.15	0.30	—
1999 Proof	—	—	—	5.00
1999W	—	—	—	—
2000	108,514,000	0.15	0.30	—
2000W	—	—	1.50	—
2000 Proof	—	—	—	5.00
2001	30,035,000	6.50	12.50	—
2001P Proof	—	—	—	10.00
2003	—	0.15	0.30	—

KM# 205 Subject: Confederation 125 **Obv:** Crowned head right **Obv. Designer:** Dora dePedery-Hunt **Rev:** Beaver on rock divides date and denomination **Rev. Designer:** George E. Kruger-Gray **Composition:** Copper-Nickel **Size:** 21.2 mm.

Date	Mintage	MS-60	MS-63	Proof
ND(1992)	53,732,000	0.15	0.30	—
ND(1992) Proof	147,061	—	—	4.00

KM# 182b Obv: Crowned head right **Obv. Designer:** Dora dePedery-Hunt **Rev:** Beaver on rock divides date and denomination **Rev. Designer:** George E. Kruger-Gray **Edge:** Plain **Weight:** 3.9000 g. **Composition:** Nickel Plated Steel **Size:** 21.2 mm.

Date	Mintage	MS-60	MS-63	Proof
1999 P	Est. 20,000	—	15.00	—
2000 P	Est. 2,300,000	1.50	3.50	—
2001 P	136,650,000	0.20	0.35	—
2003 P	31,388,921	—	0.35	—

KM# 182a Obv: Crowned head right **Obv. Designer:** Dora dePedery-Hunt **Rev:** Beaver on rock divides date and denomination **Rev. Designer:** George E. Kruger-Gray **Weight:** 5.3500 g. **Composition:** 0.9250 Silver 0.1591 oz. ASW **Size:** 21.2 mm.

Date	Mintage	MS-63	Proof
1996 Proof	—	—	5.00
1997 Proof	—	—	5.00
1998 Proof	—	—	5.00
1998O Proof	—	—	5.00
1999 Proof	—	—	5.00
2000 Proof	—	—	5.00
2001 Proof	—	—	5.00
2003 Proof	—	—	5.00

KM# 310 Subject: 90th Anniversary Royal Canadian Mint **Obv:** Crowned head right **Obv. Designer:** Dora dePedery-Hunt **Rev:** Denomination and date within wreath, crown above **Rev. Designer:** W. H. J. Blackmore **Weight:** 1.1670 g. **Composition:** 0.9250 Silver 0.0347 oz. ASW

Date	Mintage	MS-63	Proof
ND(1998)	25,000	12.00	—
ND(1998) Proof	25,000	—	12.00

KM# 400 Subject: First French-Canadian Regiment **Obv:** Crowned head right **Obv. Designer:** Dora dePedery-Hunt **Rev:** Regimental drums, sash and baton, denomination above, date at right **Rev. Designer:** R. C. M. Staff **Edge:** Plain **Composition:** 0.9250 Silver **Size:** 21.2 mm.

Date	Mintage	MS-63	Proof
2000 Proof	—	—	9.00

KM# 413 Subject: Royal Military College **Obv:** Crowned head right **Rev:** Marching cadets and arch **Rev. Designer:** Gerald T. Locklin **Edge:** Plain **Weight:** 5.3500 g. **Composition:** 0.9250 Silver 0.1591 oz. ASW **Size:** 21.2 mm.

Date	Mintage	MS-63	Proof
2001 Proof	25,834	—	7.00

KM# 446 Subject: Elizabeth II Golden Jubilee **Obv:** Crowned head right, Jubilee commemorative dates 1952-2002 **Obv. Designer:** Dora dePedery-Hunt **Rev. Designer:** George E. Kruger-Gray **Composition:** Nickel Plated Steel **Size:** 21.2 mm. **Note:** Magnetic.

Date	Mintage	MS-63	Proof
ND(2002)P	134,362,000	0.75	—
ND(2002)P Proof	32,642	—	10.00

KM# 446a Subject: Elizabeth II Golden Jubilee **Obv:** Queen, Jubilee commemorative dates 1952-2002 **Composition:** 0.9250 Silver **Size:** 21.2 mm.

Date	Mintage	MS-63	Proof
ND(2002)	21,573	—	11.50

Note: In proof sets only

KM# 453 Subject: Vimy Ridge - WWI **Obv:** Crowned head right **Rev:** Vimy Ridge Memorial, allegorical figure and dates 1917-2002 **Rev. Designer:** S. A. Allward **Composition:** 0.9250 Silver **Size:** 21.2 mm.

Date	Mintage	MS-63	Proof
ND(2002) Proof	22,646	—	11.50

5 CENTS

KM# 491 Obv: Crowned head right **Obv. Designer:** Susanna Blunt **Rev:** Beaver divides date and denomination **Rev. Designer:** George E. Kruger-Gray **Weight:** 3.9300 g. **Composition:** Nickel Plated Steel **Size:** 21.2 mm. **Note:** Magnetic.

Date	Mintage	MS-63	Proof
2003P	61,392,180	1.25	—
2004P	123,085,000	0.50	—
2004P Proof	—	—	2.50
2005P	—	0.50	—
2005P Proof	—	—	2.50
2006P	—	0.50	—
2006P Proof	—	—	2.50
2006(ml)	—	0.50	—
2006(ml) Proof	—	—	2.50

KM# 469 Subject: 50th Anniversary of the Coronation of Elizabeth II **Obv:** Crowned head right, Jubilee commemorative dates 1952-2002 **Obv. Designer:** Mary Gillick **Composition:** 0.9250 Silver **Size:** 21.2 mm.

Date	Mintage	MS-63	Proof
ND(2002)	30,000	11.50	—

Note: In Coronation Proof sets only

KM# 491a Obv: Crowned head right **Obv. Designer:** Susanna Blunt **Rev:** Beaver divides date and denomination **Edge:** Plain **Weight:** 5.3500 g. **Composition:** 0.9250 Silver 0.1591 oz. ASW **Size:** 21.1 mm.

Date	Mintage	MS-63	Proof
2004 Proof	—	—	3.50

KM# 506 Obv: Bare head right **Rev:** "Victory " design of the KM-40 reverse **Edge:** 12-sided plain **Weight:** 5.3500 g. **Composition:** 0.9250 Silver 0.1591 oz. ASW **Size:** 21.3 mm.

Date	Mintage	MS-63	Proof
ND(2004) Proof	20,019	—	15.00

KM# 627 Subject: 60th Anniversary, Victory in Europe 1945-2005 **Obv:** Head right **Rev:** Large V **Composition:** Nickel

Date	Mintage	MS-63	Proof
ND2005P	59,258,000	4.50	—

KM# 695 Obv: George VI head left **Rev:** Torch and large V **Composition:** Silver

Date	Mintage	MS-63	Proof
ND(1945-2005) Proof	47,792	—	70.00

KM# 695a Obv: George VI head left **Rev:** Torch and large V **Composition:** Silver

Date	Mintage	MS-63	Proof
ND(1945-2005) Proof	6,065	—	—

Note: Bound within cover of Annual Report

10 CENTS

KM# 3 Obv: Head left **Obv. Legend:** VICTORIA DEI GRATIA REGINA. CANADA **Rev:** Denomination and date within wreath, crown above **Designer:** Leonard C. Wyon **Edge:** Reeded **Weight:** 2.3240 g. **Composition:** 0.9250 Silver 0.0691 oz. ASW **Size:** 18.03 mm.

Date	Mintage	VG-8	F-12	VF-20	XF-40	MS-60	MS-63	Proof
1858/5	800	1,200	2,200	3,600	9,000	—	—	
1858	1,250,000	20.00	35.00	65.00	100.00	325	850	—
1870 Narrow 0	1,600,000	18.00	30.00	75.00	125	375	900	—
1870 Wide 0	Inc. above	25.00	50.00	100.00	200	500	2,100	—
1871	800,000	22.00	40.00	90.00	175	500	1,800	—
1871H	1,870,000	30.00	60.00	95.00	200	550	1,900	—
1872H	1,000,000	125	200	300	550	1,750	3,350	—
1874H	600,000	12.00	22.00	45.00	100.00	350	900	—
1875H	1,000,000	300	450	1,000	2,000	6,700	16,000	—
1880H	1,500,000	12.00	30.00	65.00	125	300	800	—
1881H	950,000	17.50	30.00	60.00	150	375	1,000	—
1882H	1,000,000	17.50	30.00	60.00	150	385	1,100	—
1883H	300,000	65.00	125	200	500	1,300	3,000	—
1884	150,000	250	500	950	1,500	5,150	12,000	—
1885	400,000	65.00	125	200	500	1,700	6,700	—
1886 Small 6	800,000	30.00	65.00	125	300	1,500	3,600	—
1886 Large 6	Inc. above	30.00	75.00	150	350	1,400	3,000	—
1887	350,000	65.00	85.00	175	375	1,700	3,000	—
1888	500,000	16.00	24.00	45.00	125	300	800	—
1889	600,000	500	900	1,550	3,200	10,000	31,000	—
1890H	450,000	20.00	35.00	80.00	175	425	950	—
1891 21 leaves	800,000	20.00	35.00	85.00	175	450	1,150	—
1891 22 leaves	Inc. above	20.00	35.00	85.00	175	435	1,000	—
1892/1	520,000	175	300	600	1,200	3,800	—	—
1892	Inc. above	20.00	35.00	75.00	145	425	950	—
1893 Flat-top 3	500,000	45.00	80.00	125	300	1,000	1,750	—
1893 Round-top 3	Inc. above	550	975	2,700	4,900	13,000	33,000	—
1894	500,000	45.00	80.00	150	250	750	1,800	—
1896	650,000	12.00	22.00	40.00	75.00	275	650	—
1898	720,000	12.00	24.00	45.00	80.00	300	700	—
1899 Small 9's	1,200,000	8.50	16.00	35.00	75.00	210	575	—
1899 Large 9's	Inc. above	16.00	28.00	60.00	120	400	1,100	—
1900	1,100,000	8.50	18.00	40.00	85.00	225	650	—
1901	1,200,000	8.50	18.00	40.00	85.00	225	650	—

KM# 10 Obv: Crowned bust right **Obv. Designer:** G. W. DeSaulles **Rev:** Denomination and date within wreath, crown above **Rev. Designer:** Leonard C. Wyon **Edge:** Reeded **Weight:** 2.3240 g. **Composition:** 0.9250 Silver 0.0691 oz. ASW **Size:** 18.03 mm.

Date	Mintage	VG-8	F-12	VF-20	XF-40	MS-60	MS-63	Proof
1902	720,000	8.00	16.00	30.00	80.00	325	1,100	—
1902H	1,100,000	4.00	8.00	18.00	40.00	100.00	250	—
1903	500,000	14.00	30.00	75.00	200	1,000	2,100	—
1903H	1,320,000	7.00	16.00	30.00	65.00	250	550	—
1904	1,000,000	11.00	24.00	45.00	100.00	325	700	—
1905	1,000,000	6.50	24.00	55.00	100.00	475	1,100	—
1906	1,700,000	6.50	12.00	30.00	60.00	275	750	—
1907	2,620,000	4.25	11.00	23.00	40.00	200	425	—
1908	776,666	8.00	24.00	55.00	95.00	200	400	—
1909	1,697,200	6.00	18.00	40.00	95.00	375	1,000	—
Note: "Victorian" leaves, similar to 1902-08 coins								
1909	Inc. above	10.00	27.00	55.00	125	500	1,300	—
Note: Broad leaves, similar to 1910-12 coins								
1910	4,468,331	4.00	8.00	18.00	35.00	125	300	—

KM# 17 Obv: Crowned bust left **Obv. Designer:** E. B. MacKennal **Rev:** Denomination and date within wreath, crown above **Rev. Designer:** Leonard C. Wyon **Edge:** Reeded **Weight:** 2.3240 g. **Composition:** 0.9250 Silver 0.0691 oz. ASW **Size:** 18.03 mm.

Date	Mintage	VG-8	F-12	VF-20	XF-40	MS-60	MS-63	Proof
1911	2,737,584	4.50	11.00	18.00	40.00	100.00	200	—

   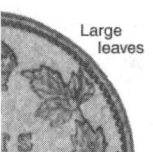

Small leaves   Large leaves

KM# 23 Obv: Crowned bust left **Obv. Designer:** E. B. MacKennal **Rev:** Denomination and date within wreath, crown above **Rev. Designer:** Leonard C. Wyon **Edge:** Reeded **Weight:** 2.3240 g. **Composition:** 0.9250 Silver 0.0691 oz. ASW **Size:** 18.03 mm.

Date	Mintage	VG-8	F-12	VF-20	XF-40	MS-60	MS-63	Proof
1912	3,235,557	1.75	4.25	9.00	30.00	175	500	—
1913	3,613,937	1.50	2.25	8.50	23.00	125	325	—
Note: Small leaves								
1913	Inc. above	95.00	175	350	900	5,600	20,000	—
Note: Large leaves								
1914	2,549,811	1.50	2.50	8.50	25.00	125	375	—
1915	688,057	6.00	15.00	30.00	100.00	325	650	—
1916	4,218,114	1.25	2.25	4.00	17.00	75.00	225	—
1917	5,011,988	1.25	1.50	3.00	10.00	50.00	95.00	—
1918	5,133,602	1.25	1.50	3.00	9.00	45.00	80.00	—
1919	7,877,722	1.25	1.50	3.00	9.00	45.00	80.00	—

KM# 23a Obv: Crowned bust left **Obv. Designer:** E. B. MacKennal **Rev:** Denomination and date within wreath, crown above **Edge:** Reeded **Weight:** 2.3328 g. **Composition:** 0.8000 Silver 0.0600 oz. ASW **Size:** 18.03 mm.

Date	Mintage	VG-8	F-12	VF-20	XF-40	MS-60	MS-63	Proof
1920	6,305,345	1.00	1.50	3.00	12.00	75.00	125	—
1921	2,469,562	1.25	2.00	6.00	20.00	80.00	225	—
1928	2,458,602	1.00	1.75	4.00	12.00	55.00	125	—

Date	Mintage	VG-8	F-12	VF-20	XF-40	MS-60	MS-63	Proof
1929	3,253,888	1.00	2.00	3.50	12.00	55.00	100.00	—
1930	1,831,043	1.00	2.50	4.50	14.00	60.00	125	—
1931	2,067,421	1.00	1.75	4.00	12.00	55.00	100.00	—
1932	1,154,317	1.50	2.50	9.00	23.00	90.00	225	—
1933	672,368	2.00	4.50	12.00	35.00	175	350	—
1934	409,067	3.00	6.00	22.00	60.00	250	500	—
1935	384,056	3.50	6.00	19.00	60.00	250	500	—
1936	2,460,871	1.00	1.25	3.00	9.00	45.00	80.00	—
1936 Dot on reverse	—	—	—	—	—	—	—	—

Note: Specimen, 4 known; David Akers sale of John Jay Pittman collection, Part 1, 10-97, a gem specimen realized $120,000

Maple leaf

KM# 34 Obv: Head left **Obv. Designer:** T. H. Paget **Rev:** Bluenose sailing left, date at right, denomination below **Rev. Designer:** Emanuel Hahn **Edge:** Reeded **Weight:** 2.3328 g. **Composition:** 0.8000 Silver 0.0600 oz. ASW **Size:** 18.03 mm.

Date	Mintage	VG-8	F-12	VF-20	XF-40	MS-60	MS-63	Proof
1937	2,500,095	BV	1.00	2.00	3.75	12.00	18.00	—
1938	4,197,323	0.85	1.75	3.25	6.50	40.00	90.00	—
1939	5,501,748	BV	1.25	2.50	5.00	45.00	90.00	—
1940	16,526,470	—	BV	1.50	3.00	15.00	30.00	—
1941	8,716,386	BV	1.25	2.50	6.00	35.00	90.00	—
1942	10,214,011	—	BV	1.25	4.00	30.00	50.00	—
1943	21,143,229	—	BV	1.25	4.00	18.00	35.00	—
1944	9,383,582	—	BV	1.50	4.50	25.00	45.00	—
1945	10,979,570	—	BV	1.25	4.00	18.00	27.00	—
1946	6,300,066	BV	1.00	2.00	4.50	30.00	50.00	—
1947	4,431,926	BV	1.25	2.50	6.00	30.00	50.00	—
1947	9,638,793	—	BV	1.50	3.00	10.00	15.00	—

Note: Maple leaf

KM# 43 Obv: Head left, modified legend **Obv. Designer:** T. H. Paget **Rev:** Bluenose sailing left, date at right, denomination below **Rev. Designer:** Emanuel Hahn **Weight:** 2.3328 g. **Composition:** 0.8000 Silver 0.0600 oz. ASW **Size:** 18.03 mm.

Date	Mintage	VG-8	F-12	VF-20	XF-40	MS-60	MS-63	Proof
1948	422,741	2.00	3.50	7.50	13.00	45.00	70.00	—
1949	11,336,172	—	BV	1.00	2.00	9.00	13.00	—
1950	17,823,075	—	—	BV	1.50	8.00	12.00	—
1951	15,079,265	—	—	BV	1.50	6.00	11.00	—
1951	—	—	1.50	2.50	7.00	35.00	60.00	—
Note: Doubled die								
1952	10,474,455	—	—	BV	1.50	5.00	9.00	—

KM# 51 Obv: Laureate bust right **Obv. Designer:** Mary Gllick **Rev:** Bluenose sailing left, date at right, denomination below **Rev. Designer:** Emanuel Hahn **Weight:** 2.3328 g. **Composition:** 0.8000 Silver 0.0600 oz. ASW **Size:** 18.03 mm.

Date	Mintage	VG-8	F-12	VF-20	XF-40	MS-60	MS-63	Proof
1953	Inc. above	—	BV	1.00	1.25	5.00	8.00	—
Note: With straps								
1953	17,706,395	—	BV	1.00	1.25	3.00	6.00	—
Note: Without straps								
1954	4,493,150	—	BV	1.00	2.25	10.00	17.00	—
1955	12,237,294	—	—	BV	1.00	4.50	7.00	—
1956	Inc. above	—	2.25	3.00	4.50	13.00	22.00	—
Note: Dot below date								
1956	16,732,844	—	—	BV	1.00	3.00	6.00	—
1957	16,110,229	—	—	—	BV	2.25	3.00	—

Date	Mintage	VG-8	F-12	VF-20	XF-40	MS-60	MS-63	Proof
1958	10,621,236	—	—	—	BV	2.25	3.00	—
1959	19,691,433	—	—	—	BV	2.25	3.00	—
1960	45,446,835	—	—	—	BV	1.50	2.25	—
1961	26,850,859	—	—	—	BV	1.00	2.25	—
1962	41,864,335	—	—	—	BV	1.00	1.50	—
1963	41,916,208	—	—	—	BV	1.00	1.50	—
1964	49,518,549	—	—	—	BV	1.00	1.50	—

KM# 61 **Obv:** Young bust right **Obv. Designer:** Arnold Machin **Rev:** Bluenose sailing left, date at right, denomination below **Weight:** 2.3328 g. **Composition:** 0.8000 Silver 0.0600 oz. ASW **Size:** 18.03 mm.

Date	Mintage	VG-8	F-12	VF-20	XF-40	MS-60	MS-63	Proof
1965	56,965,392	—	—	—	BV	1.00	1.50	—
1966	34,567,898	—	—	—	BV	1.00	1.50	—

KM# 67 **Subject:** Confederation Centennial **Obv:** Young bust right **Rev:** Atlantic mackeral left, denomination above, dates below **Rev. Designer:** Alex Colville **Weight:** 2.3328 g. **Composition:** 0.8000 Silver 0.0600 oz. ASW **Size:** 18.03 mm.

Date	Mintage	VG-8	F-12	VF-20	XF-40	MS-60	MS-63	Proof
ND(1967)	62,998,215	—	—	—	BV	1.00	1.50	2.00

KM# 67a **Subject:** Confederation Centennial **Obv:** Young bust right **Rev:** Fish left, denomination above dates below **Weight:** 2.3328 g. **Composition:** 0.5000 Silver 0.0375 oz. ASW **Size:** 18.03 mm.

Date	Mintage	VG-8	F-12	VF-20	XF-40	MS-60	MS-63	Proof
ND(1967)	Inc. above	—	—	—	BV	0.60	1.50	—

Ottawa

KM# 72 **Obv:** Young bust right **Obv. Designer:** Arnold Machin **Rev:** Bluenose sailing left, date at right, denomination below **Rev. Designer:** Emanuel Hahn **Weight:** 2.3328 g. **Composition:** 0.5000 Silver 0.0375 oz. ASW **Size:** 18.03 mm.

Date	Mintage	VG-8	F-12	VF-20	XF-40	MS-60	MS-63	Proof
1968	70,460,000	—	—	—	BV	0.60	1.25	—
Note: Ottawa reeding								

Ottawa

KM# 72a **Obv:** Young bust right **Obv. Designer:** Arnold Machin **Rev:** Bluenose sailing left, date at right, denomination below **Rev. Designer:** Emanuel Hahn **Composition:** Nickel **Size:** 18.03 mm.

Date	Mintage	VG-8	F-12	VF-20	XF-40	MS-60	MS-63	Proof
1968	87,412,930	—	—	—	0.15	0.20	0.35	—
Note: Ottawa reeding								

Philadelphia

KM# 73 **Obv:** Young bust right **Obv. Designer:** Arnold Machin **Rev:** Bluenose sailing left, date at right, denomination below **Rev. Designer:** Emanuel Hahn **Weight:** 2.3300 g. **Composition:** Nickel **Size:** 18.03 mm.

Date	Mintage	VG-8	F-12	VF-20	XF-40	MS-60	MS-63	Proof
1968	85,170,000	—	—	—	0.15	0.25	0.35	—
Note: Philadelphia reeding								
1969	—	—	6,100	8,300	11,000	19,000	—	—
Note: Large date, large ship, 10-20 known								

KM# 77.1 Obv: Young bust right **Obv. Designer:** Arnold Machin **Rev:** Redesigned smaller Bluenose sailing left, date at right, denomination below **Rev. Designer:** Emanuel Hahn **Weight:** 2.0700 g. **Composition:** Nickel **Size:** 18.03 mm.

Date	Mintage	MS-60	MS-63	Proof
1969	55,833,929	0.25	0.35	—
1970	5,249,296	0.40	0.90	—
1971	41,016,968	0.20	0.35	—
1972	60,169,387	0.20	0.35	—
1973	167,715,435	0.20	0.35	—
1974	201,566,565	0.20	0.35	—
1975	207,680,000	0.20	0.35	—
1976	95,018,533	0.20	0.35	—
1977	128,452,206	0.20	0.35	—
1978	170,366,431	0.20	0.35	—

KM# 77.2 Obv: Smaller young bust right **Obv. Designer:** Arnold Machin **Rev:** Redesigned smaller Bluenose sailing left, denomination below, date at right **Rev. Designer:** Emanuel Hahn **Weight:** 2.0700 g. **Composition:** Nickel **Size:** 18.03 mm.

Date	Mintage	MS-60	MS-63	Proof
1979	237,321,321	0.20	0.35	—
1980	170,111,533	0.20	0.35	—
1981	123,912,900	0.20	0.35	—
1981 Proof	199,000	—	—	1.50
1982	93,475,000	0.20	0.35	—
1982 Proof	180,908	—	—	1.50
1983	111,065,000	0.20	0.35	—
1983 Proof	168,000	—	—	1.50
1984	121,690,000	0.20	0.35	—
1984 Proof	161,602	—	—	1.50
1985	143,025,000	0.20	0.35	—
1985 Proof	157,037	—	—	1.50
1986	168,620,000	0.20	0.35	—
1986 Proof	175,745	—	—	1.50
1987	147,309,000	0.20	0.35	—
1987 Proof	179,004	—	—	1.50
1988	162,998,558	0.20	0.35	—
1988 Proof	175,259	—	—	1.50
1989	199,104,414	0.20	0.35	—
1989 Proof	170,528	—	—	1.50

KM# 183 Obv: Crowned head right **Obv. Designer:** Dora dePedery-Hunt **Rev:** Bluenose sailing left, date at right, denomination below **Rev. Designer:** Emanuel Hahn **Edge:** Reeded **Weight:** 2.1400 g. **Composition:** Nickel **Size:** 18.03 mm.

Date	Mintage	MS-60	MS-63	Proof
1990	65,023,000	0.20	0.35	—
1990 Proof	140,649	—	—	2.50
1991	50,397,000	0.30	0.45	—
1991 Proof	131,888	—	—	4.00
1993	135,569,000	0.20	0.35	—
1993 Proof	143,065	—	—	2.00
1994	145,800,000	0.20	0.35	—
1994 Proof	146,424	—	—	2.50
1995	123,875,000	0.20	0.35	—
1995 Proof	50,000	—	—	2.50
1996	51,814,000	0.20	0.35	—
1996 Proof	—	—	—	2.50
1997	43,126,000	0.20	0.35	—

Date	Mintage	MS-60	MS-63	Proof
1997 Proof	—	—	—	2.50
1998	203,514,000	0.20	0.35	—
1998 Proof	—	—	—	2.50
1998W	—	—	1.50	—
1999	258,462,000	0.20	0.35	—
1999 Proof	—	—	—	2.50
2000	159,125,000	0.20	0.35	—
2000 Proof	—	—	—	2.50
2000W	—	—	1.50	—

KM# 206 Subject: Confederation 125 **Obv:** Crowned head right **Rev:** Bluenose sailing left, date at right, denomination below **Composition:** Nickel **Size:** 18.03 mm.

Date	Mintage	MS-60	MS-63	Proof
ND(1992)	174,476,000	0.25	0.35	—
ND(1992) Proof	147,061	—	—	3.00

KM# 183a Obv: Crowned head right **Rev:** Bluenose sailing left, date at right, denomination below **Weight:** 2.4000 g. **Composition:** 0.9250 Silver 0.0714 oz. ASW **Size:** 18.03 mm.

Date	Mintage	MS-63	Proof
1996 Proof	—	—	5.50
1997 Proof	—	—	5.50
1998 Proof	—	—	4.00
1998O Proof	—	—	4.00
1999 Proof	—	—	5.00
2000 Proof	—	—	5.00
2001 Proof	—	—	5.00
2002 Proof	—	—	7.50
2003 Proof	—	—	7.50

KM# 299 Subject: John Cabot **Obv:** Crowned head right **Rev:** Ship with full sails divides dates, denomination below **Rev. Designer:** Donald H. Curley **Weight:** 2.4000 g. **Composition:** 0.9250 Silver 0.0714 oz. ASW **Size:** 18.03 mm.

Date	Mintage	MS-63	Proof
ND(1997) Proof	49,848	—	17.50

KM# 311 Subject: 90th Anniversary Royal Canadian Mint **Obv:** Crowned head right **Rev:** Denomination and date within wreath, crown above **Weight:** 2.3200 g. **Composition:** 0.9250 Silver 0.0690 oz. ASW **Size:** 18.03 mm.

Date	Mintage	MS-63	Proof
ND(1998) Proof	25,000	—	10.00
ND(1998) Matte	25,000	—	10.00

KM# 183b Obv: Crowned head right **Obv. Designer:** Dora dePedery-Hunt **Rev:** Bluenose sailing left, date at right, denomination below **Rev. Designer:** Emanuel Hahn **Edge:** Reeded **Composition:** Nickel Plated Steel **Size:** 18.03 mm.

Date	Mintage	MS-63	Proof
1999 P	Est. 20,000	15.00	—
2000 P	Est. 200	1,000	—
2001 P	266,000,000	0.45	—
2003 P	162,398,000	0.20	—

KM# 409 Subject: First Canadian Credit Union **Obv:** Crowned head right **Rev:** Alphonse Desjardins' house (founder of the first credit union in Canada), dates at right, denomination below **Edge:** Reeded **Weight:** 2.4000 g. **Composition:** 0.9250 Silver 0.0714 oz. ASW **Size:** 18.03 mm.

Date	Mintage	MS-63	Proof
ND(2000) Proof	66,336	—	8.00

KM# 412 Subject: Year of the Volunteer **Obv:** Crowned head right **Rev:** Three portraits left and radiant sun **Rev. Designer:** R. C. M. Staff **Edge:** Reeded **Weight:** 1.7700 g. **Composition:** Nickel Plated Steel **Size:** 18 mm.

Date	Mintage	MS-63	Proof
2001P Proof	—	—	8.50

KM# 412a Subject: Year of the Volunteer **Obv:** Crowned head right **Rev:** 3 portraits left above banner, radiant sun below **Edge:** Reeded **Weight:** 2.4000 g. **Composition:** 0.9250 Silver 0.0714 oz. ASW **Size:** 18 mm.

Date	Mintage	MS-63	Proof
2001P Proof	40,634	—	9.00

KM# 447 Subject: Elizabeth II Golden Jubilee **Obv:** Crowned head right, Jubilee commemorative dates 1952-2002 **Composition:** Nickel Plated Steel **Size:** 18 mm.

Date	Mintage	MS-63	Proof
ND(2002)P	251,278,000	1.00	—
ND(2002) Proof	32,642	—	2.50

KM# 447a Subject: Elizabeth II Golden Jubilee **Obv:** Crowned head right, Jubilee commemorative dates 1952-2002 **Comp:** 0.9250 Silver **Size:** 18 mm.

Date	Mintage	MS-63	Proof
ND(2002)	21,537	—	12.50
Note: In proof sets only			

KM# 492 Obv: Crowned head right **Obv. Designer:** Susanna Blunt **Composition:** Nickel Plated Steel **Size:** 18 mm.

Date	Mintage	MS-63	Proof
2003P	—	1.25	—
2004P	211,924,000	0.60	—
2004P Proof	—	—	2.50
2005P	—	0.60	—
2005P Proof	—	—	2.50
2006P	—	0.60	—
2006P Proof	—	—	2.50
2007(ml)	—	0.60	—
2007(ml) Proof	—	—	2.50

KM# 470 Subject: 50th Anniversary of the Coronation of Elizabeth II **Comp:** 0.9250 Silver

Date	Mintage	MS-63	Proof
ND(2003)	30,000	12.00	—
Note: In Coronation Proof sets only			

KM# 492a Obv: Crowned head right **Obv. Designer:** Susanna Blunt **Rev:** Sailboat **Edge:** Reeded **Weight:** 2.4000 g. **Composition:** 0.9250 Silver 0.0714 oz. ASW **Size:** 18 mm.

Date	Mintage	MS-63	Proof
2004 Proof	—	—	5.00

KM#524 Subject: Golf, Championship of Canada, Centennial. **Obv:** Head right **Weight:** 2.4000 g. **Comp:** 0.9250 Silver 0.0714 oz. ASW **Size:** 18 mm.

Date	Mintage	MS-63	Proof
2004	39,486	12.50	—

20 CENTS

KM# 4 Obv: Head left **Obv. Legend:** VICTORIA DEI GRATIA REGINA. CANADA **Rev:** Denomination and date within wreath, crown above **Weight:** 4.6480 g. **Composition:** 0.9250 Silver 0.1382 oz. ASW

Date	Mintage	VG-8	F-12	VF-20	XF-40	MS-60	MS-63	Proof
1858	750,000	45.00	60.00	90.00	170	725	1,950	—

25 CENTS

KM# 5 Obv: Crowned head left **Obv. Legend:** VICTORIA DEI GRATIA REGINA. CANADA **Obv. Designer:** Leonard C. Wyon **Rev:** Denomination and date within wreath, crown above **Weight:** 5.8100 g. **Composition:** 0.9250 Silver 0.1728 oz. ASW **Size:** 23.88 mm.

Date	Mintage	VG-8	F-12	VF-20	XF-40	MS-60	MS-63	Proof
1870	900,000	22.00	45.00	75.00	150	550	1,500	—
1871	400,000	22.00	40.00	125	225	800	2,100	—
1871H	748,000	25.00	70.00	115	250	1,100	1,650	—
1872H	Inc. above	—	—	—	—	2,500	6,000	—
Note: Inverted "A" for "V" in Victoria								
1872H	2,240,000	10.00	20.00	40.00	125	425	1,250	—
1874H	1,600,000	10.00	20.00	40.00	125	375	1,100	—
1875H	1,000,000	275	550	1,350	2,750	15,000	17,500	—
1880H Narrow 0	400,000	60.00	125	300	600	1,700	2,750	—
1880H Wide 0	Inc. above	125	300	600	1,400	4,500	4,750	—
1880H Narrow/wide 0	Inc. above	100.00	225	400	950	2,800	—	—
1881H	820,000	30.00	45.00	125	250	1,000	3,600	—
1882H	600,000	30.00	65.00	110	265	1,000	2,150	—
1883H	960,000	16.00	32.00	70.00	150	500	1,250	—
1885	192,000	150	300	450	950	3,500	7,500	—
1886/3	540,000	55.00	80.00	250	375	1,600	4,300	—
1886	Inc. above	30.00	65.00	110	285	1,600	4,300	—
1887	100,000	125	225	450	1,000	4,250	8,000	—
1888	400,000	20.00	40.00	80.00	185	650	1,550	—
1889	66,324	150	275	500	1,000	3,500	13,000	—
1890H	200,000	25.00	50.00	125	275	950	2,250	—
1891	120,000	70.00	130	320	650	1,600	2,500	—
1892	510,000	15.00	40.00	65.00	175	675	1,600	—
1893	100,000	125	185	375	700	1,750	3,000	—
1894	220,000	30.00	65.00	125	250	700	1,600	—
1899	415,580	11.00	20.00	55.00	150	600	1,350	—
1900	1,320,000	11.00	20.00	45.00	100.00	525	1,200	—
1901	640,000	12.00	22.00	50.00	150	550	1,200	—

KM# 11 Obv: Crowned bust right **Obv. Designer:** G. W. DeSaulles **Rev:** Denomination and date within wreath, crown above **Weight:** 5.8100 g. **Composition:** 0.9250 Silver 0.1728 oz. ASW **Size:** 23.4 mm.

Date	Mintage	VG-8	F-12	VF-20	XF-40	MS-60	MS-63	Proof
1902	464,000	10.00	27.00	65.00	175	750	1,900	—
1902H	800,000	6.50	16.00	45.00	100.00	250	500	—
1903	846,150	15.00	29.00	75.00	200	800	1,900	—
1904	400,000	20.00	55.00	150	350	1,600	5,000	—
1905	800,000	15.00	30.00	100.00	300	1,400	4,600	—
1906	1,237,843	8.00	21.00	55.00	225	750	1,700	—
Note: Large crown								
1906 Rare	Inc. above	2,500	3,900	6,000	7,500	—	16,000	—
Note: Small crown								
1907	2,088,000	6.50	16.00	55.00	125	425	1,200	—
1908	495,016	15.00	35.00	95.00	200	400	750	—
1909	1,335,929	12.00	26.00	70.00	175	600	1,700	—

KM# 11a Obv: Crowned bust right **Rev:** Denomination and date within wreath, crown above **Weight:** 5.8319 g. **Composition:** 0.9250 Silver 0.1734 oz. ASW

Date	Mintage	VG-8	F-12	VF-20	XF-40	MS-60	MS-63	Proof
1910	3,577,569	5.50	16.00	40.00	85.00	275	600	—

KM# 18 Obv: Crowned bust left **Obv. Designer:** E. B. MacKennal **Rev:** Denomination and date within wreath, crown above **Weight:** 5.8319 g. **Composition:** 0.9250 Silver 0.1734 oz. ASW

Date	Mintage	VG-8	F-12	VF-20	XF-40	MS-60	MS-63	Proof
1911	1,721,341	6.50	18.00	35.00	85.00	250	425	—

KM# 24 Obv: Crowned bust left **Obv. Designer:** E. B. MacKennal **Rev:** Denomination and date within wreath, crown above **Weight:** 5.8319 g. **Composition:** 0.9250 Silver 0.1734 oz. ASW **Size:** 23.5 mm.

Date	Mintage	VG-8	F-12	VF-20	XF-40	MS-60	MS-63	Proof
1912	2,544,199	5.50	9.00	20.00	55.00	350	1,200	—
1913	2,213,595	3.25	8.50	17.00	50.00	300	950	—
1914	1,215,397	5.00	10.00	23.00	60.00	500	1,600	—
1915	242,382	16.00	45.00	150	425	2,200	6,100	—
1916	1,462,566	3.00	7.50	18.00	40.00	225	700	—
1917	3,365,644	3.00	6.00	12.00	30.00	125	225	—
1918	4,175,649	3.00	5.00	12.00	26.00	95.00	175	—
1919	5,852,262	3.00	5.00	9.50	25.00	95.00	175	—

Dot below wreath

KM# 24a Obv: Crowned bust left **Obv. Designer:** E. B. MacKennal **Rev:** Denomination and date within wreath, crown below **Weight:** 5.8319 g. **Composition:** 0.8000 Silver 0.1500 oz. ASW

Date	Mintage	VG-8	F-12	VF-20	XF-40	MS-60	MS-63	Proof
1920	1,975,278	3.00	6.00	12.00	30.00	150	400	—
1921	597,337	11.00	24.00	80.00	225	1,100	2,700	—
1927	468,096	27.00	50.00	100.00	225	750	1,600	—
1928	2,114,178	3.00	6.00	13.00	35.00	125	325	—
1929	2,690,562	3.00	6.00	13.00	35.00	125	325	—
1930	968,748	3.00	6.00	18.00	40.00	200	500	—
1931	537,815	3.00	6.00	20.00	50.00	200	500	—
1932	537,994	3.00	6.00	25.00	50.00	200	500	—
1933	421,282	3.00	6.50	28.00	65.00	175	325	—
1934	384,350	3.50	9.00	30.00	70.00	225	500	—
1935	537,772	3.50	7.50	22.00	50.00	150	325	—
1936	972,094	3.00	5.00	12.00	21.00	95.00	175	—
1936 Dot	153,322	26.00	65.00	150	300	800	1,800	—

Note: David Akers John Jay Pittman sale Part Three, 10-99, nearly Choice Unc. realized $6,900; considered a possible specimen example

Maple leaf after date

KM# 35   Obv: Head left **Obv. Designer:** T. H. Paget **Rev:** Caribou left, denomination above, date at right
Rev. Designer: Emanuel Hahn **Weight:** 5.8319 g. **Composition:** 0.8000 Silver 0.1500 oz. ASW **Size:** 23.5 mm.

Date	Mintage	VG-8	F-12	VF-20	XF-40	MS-60	MS-63	Proof
1937	2,690,176	2.50	3.00	4.00	6.00	16.00	35.00	—
1938	3,149,245	2.50	3.00	5.00	10.00	65.00	125	—
1939	3,532,495	2.50	3.50	5.00	7.00	50.00	100.00	—
1940	9,583,650	—	BV	2.50	3.00	15.00	30.00	—
1941	6,654,672	—	BV	2.50	3.00	16.00	30.00	—
1942	6,935,871	—	BV	2.50	3.00	17.00	45.00	—
1943	13,559,575	—	BV	2.50	3.00	16.00	30.00	—
1944	7,216,237	—	BV	2.50	3.00	26.00	50.00	—
1945	5,296,495	—	BV	2.50	3.00	16.00	45.00	—
1946	2,210,810	BV	2.50	4.00	8.00	45.00	75.00	—
1947	1,524,554	—	BV	4.00	8.00	50.00	95.00	—
1947	Inc. above	30.00	40.00	70.00	150	250	500	—
Note: Dot after 7								
1947	4,393,938	—	BV	2.50	3.00	16.00	32.00	—
Note: Maple leaf								

KM# 44   Obv: Head left, modified legend **Obv. Designer:** T. H. Paget **Rev:** Caribou left, denomination above, date at right **Rev. Designer:** Emanuel Hahn **Weight:** 5.8319 g. **Composition:** 0.8000 Silver 0.1500 oz. ASW **Size:** 23.5 mm.

Date	Mintage	VG-8	F-12	VF-20	XF-40	MS-60	MS-63	Proof
1948	2,564,424	BV	2.50	3.00	13.00	55.00	75.00	—
1949	7,988,830	—	BV	2.50	3.00	10.00	20.00	—
1950	9,673,335	—	—	BV	2.50	8.00	15.00	—
1951	8,290,719	—	—	BV	2.50	7.00	12.00	—
1952	8,859,642	—	—	BV	2.50	6.00	11.00	—

KM# 52   Obv: Laureate bust right **Obv. Designer:** Mary Gillick **Rev:** Caribou left, denomination above, date at right **Rev. Designer:** Emanuel Hahn **Weight:** 5.8319 g. **Comp:** 0.8000 Silver 0.1500 oz. ASW **Size:** 23.8 mm.

Date	Mintage	VG-8	F-12	VF-20	XF-40	MS-60	MS-63	Proof
1953	10,546,769	—	—	BV	2.50	5.00	10.00	—
Note: Without strap								
1953	Inc. above	—	—	BV	2.50	6.50	18.00	—
Note: With strap								
1954	2,318,891	—	BV	2.50	7.00	25.00	40.00	—
1955	9,552,505	—	—	BV	2.50	6.00	15.00	—
1956	11,269,353	—	—	BV	2.50	3.25	6.50	—
1957	12,770,190	—	—	—	BV	BV	5.00	—
1958	9,336,910	—	—	—	BV	BV	5.00	—
1959	13,503,461	—	—	—	BV	BV	3.50	—
1960	22,835,327	—	—	—	BV	BV	3.50	—
1961	18,164,368	—	—	—	BV	BV	3.50	—
1962	29,559,266	—	—	—	BV	BV	3.50	—
1963	21,180,652	—	—	—	BV	BV	3.00	—
1964	36,479,343	—	—	—	BV	BV	3.00	—

KM# 62 Obv: Young bust right **Obv. Designer:** Arnold Machin **Rev:** Caribou left, denomination above, date at right **Rev. Designer:** Emanuel Hahn **Weight:** 5.8319 g. **Composition:** 0.8000 Silver 0.1500 oz. ASW **Size:** 23.8 mm.

Date	Mintage	MS-60	MS-63	Proof
1965	44,708,869	BV	BV	—
1966	25,626,315	BV	BV	—

KM# 62a Obv: Young bust right **Obv. Designer:** Machin **Rev:** Caribou left, denomination above, date at right **Weight:** 5.8319 g. **Composition:** 0.5000 Silver 0.0937 oz. ASW **Size:** 23.8 mm.

Date	Mintage	MS-60	MS-63	Proof
1968	71,464,000	1.50	2.25	—

KM# 62b Obv: Young bust right **Obv. Designer:** Machin **Rev:** Caribou left, denomination above, date at right **Weight:** 5.0600 g. **Composition:** Nickel **Size:** 23.8 mm.

Date	Mintage	MS-60	MS-63	Proof
1968	88,686,931	0.45	0.75	—
1969	133,037,929	0.45	0.75	—
1970	10,302,010	1.00	2.00	—
1971	48,170,428	0.45	0.75	—
1972	43,743,387	0.45	0.75	—
1973	135,958,589	0.50	1.00	—
Note: Small bust				
1973	Inc. above	150	500	—
Note: Large bust				
1974	192,360,598	0.45	0.75	—
1975	141,148,000	0.45	0.75	—
1976	86,898,261	0.45	0.75	—
1977	99,634,555	0.45	0.75	—
1978	176,475,408	0.45	0.75	—

KM# 68 Subject: Confederation Centennial **Obv:** Young bust right **Rev:** Lynx striding left divides dates and denomination **Rev. Designer:** Alex Colville **Weight:** 5.8319 g. **Composition:** 0.8000 Silver 0.1500 oz. ASW **Size:** 23.8 mm.

Date	Mintage	MS-60	MS-63	Proof
ND(1967)	48,855,500	BV	BV	—

KM# 68a Subject: Confederation Centennial **Obv:** Young bust right **Rev:** Lynx striding left divides dates and denomination **Weight:** 5.8319 g. **Composition:** 0.5000 Silver 0.0937 oz. ASW **Size:** 23.8 mm.

Date	Mintage	MS-60	MS-63	Proof
ND(1967)	Inc. above	1.50	2.50	—

KM#81.1 Subject: Royal Candian Mounted Police Centennial **Obv:** Young bust right **Rev:** Mountie divides dates, denomination above **Rev. Designer:** Paul Cedarberg **Composition:** Nickel **Size:** 23.8 mm. **Note:** 120 beads.

Date	Mintage	MS-60	MS-63	Proof
ND(1973)	134,958,587	0.55	1.00	—

KM#81.2 Subject: RCMP Centennial **Obv:** Young bust right **Rev:** Mountie divides dates, denomination above **Composition:** Nickel **Size:** 23.8 mm. **Note:** 132 beads.

Date	Mintage	MS-60	MS-63	Proof
ND(1973)	Inc. above	100.00	200	—

KM# 74 Obv: Small young bust right **Obv. Designer:** Machin **Rev. Designer:** Emanuel Hahn **Weight:** 5.0700 g. **Composition:** Nickel **Size:** 23.88 mm.

Date	Mintage	MS-60	MS-63	Proof
1979	131,042,905	0.45	0.75	—
1980	76,178,000	0.45	0.75	—
1981	131,580,272	0.45	0.75	—
1981 Proof	199,000	—	—	2.00
1982	171,926,000	0.45	0.75	—
1982 Proof	180,908	—	—	2.00
1983	13,162,000	0.75	1.50	—
1983 Proof	168,000	—	—	3.00
1984	121,668,000	0.45	0.75	—
1984 Proof	161,602	—	—	2.00
1985	158,734,000	0.45	0.75	—
1985 Proof	157,037	—	—	2.00
1986	132,220,000	0.45	0.75	—
1986 Proof	175,745	—	—	2.00
1987	53,408,000	0.60	1.25	—
1987 Proof	179,004	—	—	2.00
1988	80,368,473	0.45	1.00	—
1988 Proof	175,259	—	—	2.00
1989	119,796,307	0.45	0.75	—
1989 Proof	170,928	—	—	2.00

KM# 184 Obv: Crowned head right **Obv. Designer:** Dora dePedery-Hunt **Rev:** Caribou left, denomination above, date at right **Rev. Designer:** Emanuel Hahn **Weight:** 5.0700 g. **Composition:** Nickel **Size:** 23.88 mm.

Date	Mintage	MS-60	MS-63	Proof
1990	31,258,000	0.45	0.90	—
1990 Proof	140,649	—	—	2.50
1991	459,000	6.00	12.00	—
1991 Proof	131,888	—	—	20.00
1993	73,758,000	0.35	0.70	—

Date	Mintage	MS-60	MS-63	Proof
1993 Proof	143,065	—	—	2.00
1994	77,670,000	0.35	0.70	—
1994 Proof	146,424	—	—	3.00
1995	89,210,000	0.35	0.70	—
1995 Proof	50,000	—	—	3.00
1996	28,106,000	—	0.70	—
1996 Proof	—	—	—	6.00
1997 Proof	—	—	—	6.00
1997	—	—	0.70	—
1998W	—	—	5.00	—
1999 Proof	—	—	—	6.00
1999	258,888,000	—	0.75	—
2000	434,087,000	—	0.75	—
2000 Proof	—	—	—	6.00
2000W	—	—	5.00	—
2001	8,415,000	3.00	5.00	—
2001 Proof	—	—	—	7.50

KM# 207 Subject: Confederation 125 **Obv:** Crowned head right **Obv. Designer:** Dora dePedery-Hunt **Rev:** Caribou left, denomination above, date at right **Rev. Designer:** Emanuel Hahn **Composition:** Nickel **Size:** 23.8 mm.

Date	Mintage	MS-60	MS-63	Proof
ND(1992)	442,986	—	12.50	—
ND(1992) Proof	147,061	—	—	20.00

KM# 203 Subject: 125th Anniversary of Confederation, New Brunswick **Obv:** Crowned head right **Rev:** Covered bridge in Newton, denomination below **Rev. Designer:** Ronald Lambert **Composition:** Nickel **Size:** 23.8 mm.

Date	Mintage	MS-60	MS-63	Proof
ND(1992)	12,174,000	0.35	0.70	—

KM# 203a Subject: 125th Anniversary of Confederation, New Brunswick **Obv:** Crowned head right **Rev:** Covered bridge in Newton, denomination below **Weight:** 5.8319 g. **Composition:** 0.9250 Silver 0.1734 oz. ASW **Size:** 23.8 mm.

Date	Mintage	MS-60	MS-63	Proof
ND(1992) Proof	149,579	—	—	5.50

KM# 212 Subject: 125th Anniversary of Confederation, Northwest Territories **Obv:** Crowned head right **Rev. Designer:** Beth McEachen **Composition:** Nickel **Size:** 23.8 mm.

Date	Mintage	MS-60	MS-63	Proof
ND(1992)	12,582,000	0,35	0.70	—

KM# 212a Subject: 125th Anniversary of Confederation, Northwest Territories **Obv:** Crowned head right **Weight:** 5.8319 g. **Composition:** 0.9250 Silver 0.1734 oz. ASW **Size:** 23.8 mm.

Date	Mintage	MS-60	MS-63	Proof
ND(1992) Proof	149,579	—	—	5.50

KM# 213 Subject: 125th Anniversary of Confederation, Newfoundland **Rev:** Fisherman rowing a dory, denomination below **Rev. Designer:** Christopher Newhook **Composition:** Nickel **Size:** 23.8 mm.

Date	Mintage	MS-60	MS-63	Proof
ND(1992)	11,405,000	0.35	0.70	—

KM# 213a Subject: 125th Anniversary of Confederation, Newfoundland **Rev:** Fisherman rowing a dory, denomination below **Weight:** 5.8319 g. **Composition:** 0.9250 Silver 0.1734 oz. ASW **Size:** 23.8 mm.

Date	Mintage	MS-60	MS-63	Proof
ND(1992) Proof	149,579	—	—	5.50

KM# 214 Subject: 125th Anniversary of Confederation, Manitoba **Obv:** Crowned head right **Rev. Designer:** Muriel Hope **Composition:** Nickel **Size:** 23.8 mm.

Date	Mintage	MS-60	MS-63	Proof
ND(1992)	11,349,000	0.35	0.70	—

KM# 214a Subject: 125th Anniversary of Confederation, Manitoba **Obv:** Crowned head right **Weight:** 5.8319 g. **Composition:** 0.9250 Silver 0.1734 oz. ASW **Size:** 23.8 mm.

Date	Mintage	MS-60	MS-63	Proof
ND(1992) Proof	149,579	—	—	5.50

KM# 220 Subject: 125th Anniversary of Confederation, Yukon **Obv:** Crowned head right **Rev. Designer:** Libby Dulac **Composition:** Nickel **Size:** 23.8 mm.

Date	Mintage	MS-60	MS-63	Proof
ND(1992)	10,388,000	0.35	0.70	—

KM# 220a Subject: 125th Anniversary of Confederation, Yukon **Obv:** Crowned head right **Weight:** 5.8319 g. **Composition:** 0.9250 Silver 0.1734 oz. ASW **Size:** 23.8 mm.

Date	Mintage	MS-60	MS-63	Proof
ND(1992) Proof	149,579	—	—	5.50

KM# 221 Subject: 125th Anniversary of Confederation, Alberta **Obv:** Crowned head right **Rev:** Rock formations in the badlands near Drumhelter, denomination below **Rev. Designer:** Mel Heath **Composition:** Nickel **Size:** 23.8 mm.

Date	Mintage	MS-60	MS-63	Proof
ND(1992)	12,133,000	0.35	0.70	—

KM# 221a Subject: 125th Anniversary of Confederation, Alberta **Obv:** Crowned head right **Rev:** Rock formations in the badlands near Drumhelter, denomination below **Rev. Designer:** Mel Heath **Weight:** 5.8319 g. **Composition:** 0.9250 Silver 0.1734 oz. ASW **Size:** 23.8 mm.

Date	Mintage	MS-60	MS-63	Proof
ND(1992) Proof	—	—	—	5.50

KM# 222 Subject: 125th Anniversary of Confederation, Prince Edward Island **Obv:** Crowned head right **Rev. Designer:** Nigel Roe **Composition:** Nickel **Size:** 23.8 mm.

Date	Mintage	MS-60	MS-63	Proof
ND(1992)	13,001,000	0.35	0.70	—

KM# 222a Subject: 125th Anniversary of Confederation, Prince Edward Island **Obv:** Crowned head right **Rev. Designer:** Nigel Roe **Weight:** 5.8319 g. **Composition:** 0.9250 Silver 0.1734 oz. ASW **Size:** 23.8 mm.

Date	Mintage	MS-60	MS-63	Proof
ND(1992) Proof	149,579	—	—	5.50

KM# 223 Subject: 125th Anniversary of Confederation, Ontario **Obv:** Crowned head right **Rev:** Jack pine, denomination below **Rev. Designer:** Greg Salmela **Composition:** Nickel **Size:** 23.8 mm.

Date	Mintage	MS-60	MS-63	Proof
ND(1992)	14,263,000	0.35	0.70	—

KM# 223a Subject: 125th Anniversary of Confederation, Ontario **Obv:** Crowned head right **Rev:** Jack pine, denomination below **Rev. Designer:** Greg Salmela **Weight:** 5.8319 g. **Composition:** 0.9250 Silver 0.1734 oz. ASW **Size:** 23.8 mm.

Date	Mintage	MS-60	MS-63	Proof
ND(1992) Proof	149,579	—	—	5.50

KM# 231 Subject: 125th Anniversary of Confederation, Nova Scotia **Obv:** Crowned head right **Rev:** Lighthouse, denomination below **Rev. Designer:** Bruce Wood **Weight:** 5.0300 g. **Composition:** Nickel **Size:** 23.8 mm.

Date	Mintage	MS-60	MS-63	Proof
ND(1992)	13,600,000	0.35	0.70	—

KM# 231a Subject: 125th Anniversary of Confederation, Nova Scotia **Obv:** Crowned head right **Rev:** Lighthouse, denomination below **Rev. Designer:** Bruce Wood **Weight:** 5.8319 g. **Comp:** 0.9250 Silver 0.1734 oz. ASW **Size:** 23.8 mm.

Date	Mintage	MS-60	MS-63	Proof
ND(1992) Proof	149,579	—	—	5.50

KM# 232 Subject: 125th Anniversary of Confederation, British Columbia **Obv:** Crowned head right, dates below **Rev:** Large rock, whales, denomination below **Rev. Designer:** Carla Herrera Egan **Composition:** Nickel **Size:** 23.8 mm.

Date	Mintage	MS-60	MS-63	Proof
ND(1992)	14,001,000	0.35	0.70	—

KM# 232a Subject: 125th Anniversary of Confederation, British Columbia **Obv:** Crowned head right, dates below **Rev:** Large rock, whales, denomination below **Rev. Designer:** Carla Herrera Egan **Weight:** 5.8319 g. **Composition:** 0.9250 Silver 0.1734 oz. ASW **Size:** 23.8 mm.

Date	Mintage	MS-60	MS-63	Proof
ND(1992) Proof	149,579	—	—	5.50

KM# 233 Subject: 125th Anniversary of Confederation, Saskatchewan **Obv:** Crowned head right **Rev:** Buildings behind wall, grain stalks on right, denomination below **Rev. Designer:** Brian Cobb **Composition:** Nickel **Size:** 23.8 mm.

Date	Mintage	MS-60	MS-63	Proof
ND(1992)	14,165,000	0.35	0.70	—

KM# 233a Subject: 125th Anniversary of Confederation, Saskatchewan **Obv:** Crowned head right **Rev:** Buildings behind wall, grain stalks on right, denomination below **Rev. Designer:** Brian Cobb **Weight:** 5.8319 g. **Composition:** 0.9250 Silver 0.1734 oz. ASW **Size:** 23.8 mm.

Date	Mintage	MS-60	MS-63	Proof
ND(1992) Proof	149,579	—	—	5.50

KM# 234 Subject: 125th Anniversary of Confederation, Quebec **Obv:** Crowned head right **Rev:** Boats on water, large rocks in background, denomination below **Rev. Designer:** Romualdas Bukauskas **Composition:** Nickel **Size:** 23.8 mm.

Date	Mintage	MS-60	MS-63	Proof
ND(1992)	13,607,000	0.35	0.70	—

KM# 234a Subject: 125th Anniversary of Confederation, Quebec **Obv:** Crowned head right **Rev:** Boats on water, large rocks in background, denomination below **Rev. Designer:** Romualdas Bukauskas **Weight:** 5.8319 g. **Composition:** 0.9250 Silver 0.1734 oz. ASW **Size:** 23.8 mm.

Date	Mintage	MS-60	MS-63	Proof
ND(1992) Proof	149,579	—	—	5.50

KM# 184a Obv: Crowned head right **Rev:** Caribou left, denomination above, date at right **Weight:** 5.9000 g. **Composition:** 0.9250 Silver 0.1755 oz. ASW **Size:** 23.88 mm.

Date	Mintage	MS-63	Proof
1996 Proof	—	—	6.50
1997 Proof	—	—	6.50
1998 Proof	—	—	5.50
1998O Proof	—	—	5.50
1999 Proof	—	—	5.50
2001 Proof	—	—	6.50
2003 Proof	—	—	6.50

25 CENTS

KM# 312 Subject: 90th Anniversary Royal Canadian Mint **Obv:** Crowned head right **Rev:** Denomination and date within wreath, crown above **Size:** 23.8 mm.

Date	Mintage	MS-60	MS-63	Proof
ND(1998) Matte	25,000	—	—	15.00
ND(1998) Proof	—	—	—	15.00

KM# 184b Obv: Crowned head right **Rev:** Caribou left, denomination above, date at right **Composition:** Nickel Plated Steel **Size:** 23.88 mm.

Date	Mintage	MS-60	MS-63	Proof
1999 P	Est. 20,000	—	20.00	—
2000 P	—	3,350	5,500	—
Note: 3-5 known				
2001 P	55,773,000	1.25	2.50	—
2001 P Proof	—	—	—	5.00
2002 P	—	—	2.50	—
2002 P Proof	—	—	—	5.00
2003 P	15,905,090	—	2.50	—
2003 p Proof	—	—	—	5.00

KM# 342 Subject: Millennium, January - A Country Unfolds **Obv:** Crowned head right **Rev:** Totem pole, portraits **Rev. Designer:** P. Ka-Kin Poon **Composition:** Nickel **Size:** 23.8 mm.

Date	Mintage	MS-60	MS-63	Proof
1999	12,181,200	0.50	0.65	—

KM# 342a Subject: Millennium, January **Obv:** Crowned head right **Rev:** Totem pole, portraits **Rev. Designer:** P. Ka-kin Poon **Weight:** 5.8319 g. **Composition:** 0.9250 Silver 0.1734 oz. ASW **Size:** 23.8 mm.

Date	Mintage	MS-60	MS-63	Proof
1999 Proof	113,645	—	—	8.00

KM# 343 Subject: Millennium, February - Etched in Stone **Obv:** Crowned head right **Rev:** Native petroglyphs **Rev. Designer:** L. Springer **Weight:** 5.0900 g. **Composition:** Nickel **Size:** 23.8 mm.

Date	Mintage	MS-60	MS-63	Proof
1999	14,469,250	0.50	0.65	—

KM# 343a Subject: Millennium, February **Obv:** Crowned head right **Rev:** Native petroglyphs **Rev. Designer:** L. Springer **Weight:** 5.8319 g. **Composition:** 0.9250 Silver 0.1734 oz. ASW **Size:** 23.8 mm.

Date	Mintage	MS-60	MS-63	Proof
1999 Proof	113,645	—	—	8.00

KM# 344 Subject: Millennium, March - The Log Drive **Obv:** Crowned head right **Rev:** Lumberjack **Rev. Designer:** M. Lavoie **Composition:** Nickel **Size:** 23.8 mm.

Date	Mintage	MS-60	MS-63	Proof
1999	15,033,500	0.50	0.65	—

KM# 344a Subject: Millennium, March **Obv:** Crowned head right **Rev:** Lumberjack **Rev. Designer:** M. Lavoie **Weight:** 5.8319 g. **Composition:** 0.9250 Silver 0.1734 oz. ASW **Size:** 23.8 mm.

Date	Mintage	MS-60	MS-63	Proof
1999 Proof	113,645	—	—	8.00

KM# 345 Subject: Millennium, April - Our Northern Heritage **Obv:** Crowned head right **Rev:** Owl, polar bear **Rev. Designer:** Ken Ojnak Ashevac **Weight:** 5.0500 g. **Composition:** Nickel **Size:** 23.8 mm.

Date	Mintage	MS-60	MS-63	Proof
1999	15,446,000	0.50	0.65	—

KM# 345a Subject: Millennium, April **Obv:** Crowned head right **Rev:** Owl, polar bear **Rev. Designer:** Ken Ojnak Ashevac **Weight:** 5.8319 g. **Composition:** 0.9250 Silver 0.1734 oz. ASW **Size:** 23.8 mm.

Date	Mintage	MS-60	MS-63	Proof
1999 Proof	113,645	—	—	8.00

KM# 346 Subject: Millennium, May - The Voyageures **Obv:** Crowned head right **Rev:** Voyageurs in canoe **Rev. Designer:** S. Mineok **Composition:** Nickel **Size:** 23.8 mm.

Date	Mintage	MS-60	MS-63	Proof
1999	15,566,100	0.50	0.65	—

KM# 346a Subject: Millennium, May **Obv:** Crowned head right **Rev:** Voyageurs in canoe **Rev. Designer:** S. Mineok **Weight:** 5.8319 g. **Composition:** 0.9250 Silver 0.1734 oz. ASW **Size:** 23.8 mm.

Date	Mintage	MS-60	MS-63	Proof
1999 Proof	113,645	—	—	8.00

KM# 347 Subject: Millennium, June - From Coast to Coast **Obv:** Crowned head right **Rev:** 19th-century locomotive **Rev. Designer:** G. Ho **Weight:** 5.0300 g. **Composition:** Nickel **Size:** 23.8 mm.

Date	Mintage	MS-60	MS-63	Proof
1999	20,432,750	0.50	0.65	—

KM# 347a Subject: Millennium, June **Obv:** Crowned head right **Rev:** 19th-century locomotive **Rev. Designer:** G. Ho **Weight:** 5.8319 g. **Composition:** 0.9250 Silver 0.1734 oz. ASW **Size:** 23.8 mm.

Date	Mintage	MS-60	MS-63	Proof
1999 Proof	113,645	—	—	8.00

KM# 348 Subject: Millennium, July - A Nation of People **Obv:** Crowned head right **Rev:** 6 stylized portraits **Rev. Designer:** M. H. Sarkany **Composition:** Nickel **Size:** 23.8 mm.

Date	Mintage	MS-60	MS-63	Proof
1999	17,321,000	0.50	0.65	—

KM# 348a Subject: Millennium, July **Obv:** Crowned head right **Rev:** 6 stylized portraits **Rev. Designer:** M.H. Sarkany **Weight:** 5.8319 g. **Composition:** 0.9250 Silver 0.1734 oz. ASW **Size:** 23.8 mm.

Date	Mintage	MS-60	MS-63	Proof
1999 Proof	113,645	—	—	8.00

KM# 349 Subject: Millennium, August - The Pioneer Spirit **Obv:** Crowned head right **Rev:** Hay harvesting **Rev. Designer:** A. Botelho **Weight:** 5.1000 g. **Composition:** Nickel **Size:** 23.8 mm.

Date	Mintage	MS-60	MS-63	Proof
1999	18,153,700	0.50	0.65	—

KM# 349a Subject: Millennium, August **Obv:** Crowned head right **Rev:** Hay harvesting **Rev. Designer:** A. Botelho **Weight:** 5.8319 g. **Composition:** 0.9250 Silver 0.1734 oz. ASW **Size:** 23.8 mm.

Date	Mintage	MS-60	MS-63	Proof
1999 Proof	113,645	—	—	8.00

KM# 350 Subject: Millennium, September - Canada Through a Child's Eye **Obv:** Crowned head right **Rev:** Childlike artwork **Rev. Designer:** Claudia Bertrand **Composition:** Nickel **Size:** 23.8 mm.

Date	Mintage	MS-60	MS-63	Proof
1999	31,539,350	0.50	0.65	—

KM# 350a Subject: Millennium, September **Obv:** Crowned head right **Rev:** Childlike artwork **Rev. Designer:** Claudia Bertrand **Weight:** 5.8319 g. **Composition:** 0.9250 Silver 0.1734 oz. ASW **Size:** 23.8 mm.

Date	Mintage	MS-60	MS-63	Proof
1999 Proof	113,645	—	—	8.00

KM# 351 Subject: Millennium, October - Tribute to the First Nations **Obv:** Crowned head right **Rev:** Aboriginal artwork **Rev. Designer:** J. E. Read **Weight:** 5.1000 g. **Composition:** Nickel **Size:** 23.8 mm.

Date	Mintage	MS-60	MS-63	Proof
1999	32,136,650	0.50	0.65	—

KM# 351a Subject: Millennium, October **Obv:** Crowned head right **Rev:** Aboriginal artwork **Rev. Designer:** J.E. Read **Weight:** 5.8319 g. **Composition:** 0.9250 Silver 0.1734 oz. ASW **Size:** 23.8 mm.

Date	Mintage	MS-60	MS-63	Proof
1999 Proof	113,645	—	—	8.00

KM# 352 Subject: Millennium, November - The Airplane Opens the North **Obv:** Crowned head right **Rev:** Bush plane with landing skis **Rev. Designer:** B. R. Brown **Composition:** Nickel **Size:** 23.8 mm.

Date	Mintage	MS-60	MS-63	Proof
1999	27,162,800	0.50	0.65	—

KM# 352a Subject: Millennium, November **Obv:** Crowned head right **Rev:** Bush plane with landing skis **Rev. Designer:** B.R. Brown **Weight:** 5.8319 g. **Composition:** 0.9250 Silver 0.1734 oz. ASW **Size:** 23.8 mm.

Date	Mintage	MS-60	MS-63	Proof
1999 Proof	113,645	—	—	8.00

KM# 353 Subject: Millennium, December - This is Canada **Obv:** Crowned head right **Rev:** Eclectic geometric design **Rev. Designer:** J. L. P. Provencher **Weight:** 5.0900 g. **Composition:** Nickel **Size:** 23.8 mm.

Date	Mintage	MS-60	MS-63	Proof
1999	43,339,200	0.50	0.70	—

KM# 353a Subject: Millennium, December **Obv:** Crowned head right **Rev:** Eclectic geometric design **Rev. Designer:** J.L.P. Provencher **Weight:** 5.8319 g. **Composition:** 0.9250 Silver 0.1734 oz. ASW **Size:** 23.8 mm.

Date	Mintage	MS-60	MS-63	Proof
1999 Proof	113,645	—	—	8.00

KM# 373 Subject: Health **Obv:** Crowned head right, denomination below **Rev:** Ribbon and caduceus, date above **Rev. Designer:** Anny Wassef **Composition:** Nickel **Size:** 23.8 mm.

Date	Mintage	MS-60	MS-63	Proof
2000	35,470,900	0.50	0.65	—

KM# 373a Subject: Health **Obv:** Crowned head right, denomination below **Rev:** Ribbon and caduceus, date above **Rev. Designer:** Anny Wassef **Composition:** 0.9250 Silver **Size:** 23.8 mm.

Date	Mintage	MS-60	MS-63	Proof
2000 Proof	76,956	—	—	8.00

KM# 374 Subject: Freedom **Obv:** Crowned head right, denomination below **Rev:** 2 children on maple leaf and rising sun, date above **Rev. Designer:** Kathy Vinish **Weight:** 5.1000 g. **Composition:** Nickel **Size:** 23.8 mm.

Date	Mintage	MS-60	MS-63	Proof
2000	35,188,900	0.50	0.65	—

KM# 374a Subject: Freedom **Obv:** Crowned head right, denomination below **Rev:** 2 children on maple leaf and rising sun, date above **Rev. Designer:** Kathy Vinish **Composition:** 0.9250 Silver **Size:** 23.8 mm.

Date	Mintage	MS-60	MS-63	Proof
2000 Proof	76,956	—	—	6.00

KM# 375 Subject: Family **Obv:** Crowned head right, denomination below **Rev:** Wreath of native carvings, date above **Rev. Designer:** Wade Stephen Baker **Composition:** Nickel **Size:** 23.8 mm.

Date	Mintage	MS-60	MS-63	Proof
2000	35,107,700	0.50	0.65	—

KM# 375a Subject: Family **Obv:** Crowned head right, denomination below **Rev:** Wreath of native carvings, date above **Rev. Designer:** Wade Stephen Baker **Composition:** 0.9250 Silver **Size:** 23.8 mm.

Date	Mintage	MS-60	MS-63	Proof
2000 Proof	76,956	—	—	6.00

KM# 376 Subject: Community **Obv:** Crowned head right, denomination below **Rev:** Map on globe, symbols surround, date above **Rev. Designer:** Michelle Thibodeau **Weight:** 5.0800 g. **Composition:** Nickel **Size:** 23.8 mm.

Date	Mintage	MS-60	MS-63	Proof
2000	35,155,400	0.50	0.65	—

KM# 376a Subject: Community **Obv:** Crowned head right, denomination below **Rev:** Map on globe, symbols surround, date above **Rev. Designer:** Michelle Thibodeau **Composition:** 0.9250 Silver **Size:** 23.8 mm.

Date	Mintage	MS-60	MS-63	Proof
2000 Proof	76,956	—	—	6.00

25 CENTS

KM# 377 Subject: Harmony **Obv:** Crowned head right, denomination below **Rev:** Maple leaf, date above **Rev. Designer:** Haver Demirer **Composition:** Nickel **Size:** 23.8 mm.

Date	Mintage	MS-60	MS-63	Proof
2000	35,184,200	0.50	0.65	—

KM#377a Subject: Harmony **Obv:** Crowned head right, denomination below **Rev:** Maple leaf **Rev. Designer:** Haver Demirer **Composition:** 0.9250 Silver **Size:** 23.8 mm.

Date	Mintage	MS-60	MS-63	Proof
2000 Proof	76,956	—	—	6.00

KM# 378 Subject: Wisdom **Obv:** Crowned head right, denomination below **Rev:** Man with young child, date above **Rev. Designer:** Cezar Serbanescu **Composition:** Nickel **Size:** 23.8 mm.

Date	Mintage	MS-60	MS-63	Proof
2000	35,123,950	0.50	0.65	—

KM# 378a Subject: Wisdom **Obv:** Crowned head right, denomination below **Rev:** Man with young child **Rev. Designer:** Cezar Serbanescu **Composition:** 0.9250 Silver **Size:** 23.8 mm.

Date	Mintage	MS-60	MS-63	Proof
2000 Proof	76,956	—	—	6.00

KM# 379 Subject: Creativity **Obv:** Crowned head right, denomination below **Rev:** Canoe full of children, date above **Rev. Designer:** Kong Tat Hui **Composition:** Nickel **Size:** 23.8 mm.

Date	Mintage	MS-60	MS-63	Proof
2000	35,316,770	0.50	0.65	—

KM# 379a Subject: Creativity **Obv:** Crowned head right, denomination below **Rev:** Canoe full of children **Rev. Designer:** Kong Tat Hui **Composition:** 0.9250 Silver **Size:** 23.8 mm.

Date	Mintage	MS-60	MS-63	Proof
2000 Proof	76,956	—	—	6.00

KM# 380 Subject: Ingenuity **Obv:** Crowned head right, denomination below **Rev:** Crescent-shaped city views, date above **Rev. Designer:** John Jaciw **Composition:** Nickel **Size:** 23.8 mm.

Date	Mintage	MS-60	MS-63	Proof
2000	36,078,360	0.50	0.65	—

KM#380a Subject: Ingenuity **Obv:** Crowned head right, denomination below **Rev:** Crescent-shaped city views **Rev. Designer:** John Jaciw **Composition:** 0.9250 Silver **Size:** 23.8 mm.

Date	Mintage	MS-60	MS-63	Proof
2000 Proof	76,956	—	—	6.00

KM# 381 Subject: Achievement **Obv:** Crowned head right, denomination below **Rev:** Rocket above jagged design, date above **Rev. Designer:** Daryl Dorosz **Composition:** Nickel **Size:** 23.8 mm.

Date	Mintage	MS-60	MS-63	Proof
2000	35,312,750	0.50	0.65	—

KM# 381a Subject: Achievement **Obv:** Crowned head right, denomination below **Rev:** Rocket above jagged design **Rev. Designer:** Daryl Dorosz **Composition:** 0.9250 Silver **Size:** 23.8 mm.

Date	Mintage	MS-60	MS-63	Proof
2000 Proof	76,956	—	—	6.00

KM# 382 Subject: Natural legacy **Obv:** Crowned head right, denomination below **Rev:** Environmental elements, date above **Rev. Designer:** Randy Trantau **Composition:** Nickel **Size:** 23.8 mm.

Date	Mintage	MS-60	MS-63	Proof
2000	36,236,900	0.50	0.65	—

KM#382a Subject: Natural legacy **Obv:** Crowned head right, denomination below **Rev:** Environmental elements **Rev. Designer:** Randy Trantau **Composition:** 0.9250 Silver **Size:** 23.8 mm.

Date	Mintage	MS-60	MS-63	Proof
2000 Proof	76,956	—	—	6.00

KM# 383 Subject: Celebration **Obv:** Crowned head right, denomination below **Rev:** Fireworks, children behind flag, date above **Rev. Designer:** Laura Paxton **Composition:** Nickel **Size:** 23.8 mm.

Date	Mintage	MS-60	MS-63	Proof
2000	35,144,100	0.50	0.65	—

25 CENTS

KM# 383a **Subject:** Celebration **Obv:** Crowned head right, denomination below **Rev:** Fireworks, children behind flag **Rev. Designer:** Laura Paxton **Composition:** 0.9250 Silver **Size:** 23.8 mm.

Date	Mintage	MS-60	MS-63	Proof
2000 Proof	76,956	—	—	6.00

KM# 384.1 **Subject:** Pride **Obv:** Crowned head right, denomination below **Rev:** Large ribbon 2 in red with 3 small red maple leaves on large maple leaf, date above **Rev. Designer:** Donald F. Warkentin **Edge:** Reeded **Composition:** Nickel **Size:** 23.8 mm. **Note:** Colorized version.

Date	Mintage	MS-60	MS-63	Proof
2000	49,399	—	6.50	—

KM# 384.2 **Subject:** Pride **Obv:** Crowned head right, denomination below **Rev:** Large ribbon 2 with three small maple leaves on large maple leaf, date above **Rev. Designer:** Donald F. Warkentin **Composition:** Nickel **Size:** 23.8 mm.

Date	Mintage	MS-60	MS-63	Proof
2000	50,666,800	0.50	0.65	—

KM# 384.2a **Subject:** Pride **Obv:** Crowned head right, denomination below **Rev:** Ribbon 2 with 3 small maple leaves on large maple leaf **Rev. Designer:** Donald F. Warkentin **Composition:** 0.9250 Silver **Size:** 23.8 mm.

Date	Mintage	MS-60	MS-63	Proof
2000 Proof	76,956	—	—	6.00

KM# 419 **Subject:** Canada Day **Obv:** Crowned head right **Rev:** Maple leaf at center, children holding hands below **Rev. Designer:** Silke Ware **Edge:** Reeded **Weight:** 5.0600 g. **Composition:** Nickel Plated Steel **Size:** 23.9 mm.

Date	Mintage	MS-63	Proof
2001	96,352	7.00	—

KM# 448 **Subject:** Elizabeth II Golden Jubilee **Obv:** Crowned head right **Composition:** Nickel Plated Steel **Size:** 23.9 mm. **Note:** Double-dated 1952-2002.

Date	Mintage	MS-63	Proof
ND(2002)P	152,485,000	2.00	—
ND(2002)P Proof	32,642	—	6.00

KM# 448a **Subject:** Elizabeth II Golden Jubilee **Obv:** Crowned head right, Jubilee commemorative dates 1952-2002 **Composition:** 0.9250 Silver **Size:** 23.9 mm.

Date	Mintage	MS-63	Proof
ND(2002) Proof	100,000	—	12.50

KM# 451 **Rev:** Small Human figures supporting large maple leaf **Composition:** Nickel Plated Steel

Date	Mintage	MS-63	Proof
ND(1952-2002)P	30,627,000	5.00	—

KM# 451a **Subject:** Canada Day **Obv:** Crowned head right **Rev:** Human figures with large red maple leaf **Edge:** Reeded **Weight:** 4.4000 g. **Composition:** Nickel Plated Steel **Size:** 23.88 mm.

Date	Mintage	MS-63	Proof
ND2002P	49,903	6.00	—

KM# 493 **Obv:** Crowned head right **Obv. Designer:** Susanna Blunt **Weight:** 4.4500 g. **Composition:** Nickel Plated Steel **Size:** 23.9 mm.

Date	Mintage	MS-63	Proof
2003W	—	—	—
2003P	66,861,633	2.00	—
2004P	159,465,000	2.50	—
2004P Proof	—	—	5.00
2005P	—	2.50	—
2005P Proof	—	—	5.00
2006P	—	2.50	—
2006P Proof	—	—	5.00
2007(ml)	—	2.50	—
2007(ml) Proof	—	—	5.00

KM# 471 **Subject:** 50th Anniversary of the Coronation of Elizabeth II **Obv:** 1953 effigy of the Queen, Jubilee commemorative dates 1952-2002 **Obv. Designer:** Mary Gillick **Composition:** 0.9250 Silver **Size:** 23.9 mm.

Date	Mintage	MS-63	Proof
ND(2002)	30,000	12.50	—

Note: In Coronation Proof sets only

KM# 474 **Subject:** Canada Day **Obv:** Queens head right **Rev:** Polar bear and red colored maple leaves **Composition:** 0.9250 Silver **Size:** 23.9 mm.

Date	Mintage	MS-63	Proof
2003 Proof	—	—	7.50

25 CENTS

KM# 510 Obv: Crowned head right **Rev:** Red Poppy in center of maple leaf **Edge:** Reeded **Weight:** 4.4000 g. **Composition:** Nickel Plated Steel **Size:** 23.9 mm.

Date	Mintage	MS-63	Proof
2004	28,500,000	5.00	—

KM# 510a Obv: Crowned head right **Rev:** Gold-plated poppy in maple leaf **Edge:** Reeded **Composition:** 0.9250 Silver **Size:** 23.9 mm.

Date	Mintage	MS-63	Proof
2004 Proof	12,677	—	20.00

Note: Encased in cover of Annual Report

KM# 525 Obv: Crowned head right **Rev:** Maple leaf, colorized **Weight:** 4.4300 g. **Composition:** Nickel Plated Steel

Date	Mintage	MS-63	Proof
2004	16,028	8.00	—

KM# 493a Obv: Crowned head right **Obv. Designer:** Suanne Blunt **Rev:** Caribou **Edge:** Reeded **Weight:** 5.9000 g. **Composition:** 0.9250 Silver 0.1755 oz. ASW **Size:** 23.9 mm.

Date	Mintage	MS-63	Proof
2004 Proof	—	—	6.50

KM# 696 Rev: Santa, colorized **Composition:** Nickel Plated Steel

Date	Mintage	MS-63	Proof
2004	—	5.00	—

KM# 697 Subject: Canada Day, **Rev:** Moose head, humorous **Composition:** Nickel Plated Steel

Date	Mintage	MS-63	Proof
2004	—	5.00	—

KM# 628 Subject: First Settlement, Ile Ste Croix 1604-2004 **Obv:** Crowned head right **Rev:** Sailing ship Bonne-Renommee **Weight:** 4.4600 g. **Composition:** Nickel Plated Steel

Date	Mintage	MS-63	Proof
ND2004P	15,400,000	5.00	—

KM# 529 Subject: WWII, 60th Anniversary **Obv:** Head right **Rev:** Three soldiers and flag **Weight:** 4.4300 g. **Composition:** Nickel Plated Steel **Size:** 23.9 mm.

Date	Mintage	MS-63	Proof
2005	3,500	20.00	—

KM# 530 Subject: Alberta **Obv:** Head right **Weight:** 4.4300 g. **Composition:** Nickel Plated Steel **Size:** 23.9 mm.

Date	Mintage	MS-63	Proof
2005P	20,640,000	7.00	—

KM# 531 Subject: Canada Day **Obv:** Head right **Rev:** Beaver, colorized **Weight:** 4.4300 g. **Composition:** Nickel Plated Steel **Size:** 23.9 mm.

Date	Mintage	MS-63	Proof
2005P	58,370	8.50	—

KM# 532 Subject: Saskatchewan **Obv:** Head right **Weight:** 4.4300 g. **Composition:** Nickel Plated Steel **Size:** 23.9 mm.

Date	Mintage	MS-63	Proof
2005P	19,290,000	7.00	—

KM# 533 Obv: Head right **Rev:** Stuffed bear in Christmas stocking, colorized **Weight:** 4.4300 g. **Composition:** Nickel Plated Steel **Size:** 23.9 mm.

Date	Mintage	MS-63	Proof
2005P	72,831	10.00	—

KM# 535 Subject: Year of the Veteran **Obv:** Head right **Rev:** Profile of young and old soldier **Weight:** 4.4300 g. **Composition:** Nickel Plated Steel **Size:** 23.9 mm.

Date	Mintage	MS-63	Proof
2005P	29,390,000	7.00	—

KM# 534 Subject: Toronto Maple Leafs **Obv:** Head right **Rev:** Colorized team logo **Weight:** 4.4300 g. **Composition:** Nickel Plated Steel **Size:** 23.9 mm.

Date	Mintage	MS-63	Proof
2006P	—	12.50	—

KM# 575 Subject: Montreal Canadiens **Obv:** Head right **Rev:** Colorized logo **Weight:** 4.4300 g. **Composition:** Nickel Plated Steel **Size:** 23.9 mm.

Date	Mintage	MS-63	Proof
2006P	—	12.50	—

KM# 576 Subject: Quebec Winter Carnival **Obv:** Head right **Rev:** Snowman, colorized **Weight:** 4.4300 g. **Composition:** Nickel Plated Steel **Size:** 23.9 mm.

Date	Mintage	MS-63	Proof
2006	8,095	10.00	—

KM# 632 Subject: Queen Elizabeth II 80th Birthday **Rev:** Crown, colorized **Weight:** 12.6100 g. **Composition:** Nickel Plated Steel

Date	Mintage	MS-63	Proof
2006	—	25.00	—

KM# 633 Subject: Canada Day **Obv:** Crowned head right **Rev:** Boy marching with flag, colorized **Weight:** 4.4300 g. **Composition:** Nickel Plated Steel

Date	Mintage	MS-63	Proof
2006P	29,760	6.00	—

KM# 634 Subject: Breast Cancer **Rev:** Ribbons, all colorized **Weight:** 4.4300 g. **Composition:** Nickel Plated Steel **Note:** Sold housed in a bookmark.

Date	Mintage	MS-63	Proof
2006P	40,911	10.00	—

KM# 637 Subject: Wedding **Rev:** Colorized flowers **Weight:** 4.4300 g. **Composition:** Nickel Plated Steel

Date	Mintage	MS-63	Proof
2007(ml)	—	5.00	—

KM# 642 Subject: Ottawa Senators **Obv:** Head right **Rev:** Logo **Weight:** 4.4300 g. **Composition:** Nickel Plated Steel

Date	Mintage	MS-63	Proof
2006P	—	12.50	—

KM# 644 Subject: Calgary Flames **Obv:** Head right **Rev:** Logo **Weight:** 4.4300 g. **Composition:** Nickel Plated Steel

Date	Mintage	MS-63	Proof
2007(ml)	—	12.50	—

KM# 645 Subject: Edmonton Oilers **Obv:** Head right **Rev:** Logo **Weight:** 4.4300 g. **Composition:** Nickel Plated Steel

Date	Mintage	MS-63	Proof
2007(ml)	—	12.50	—

KM# 647 Subject: Santa and Rudolph **Rev:** Colorized Santa in sled, lead by Rudolph **Weight:** 4.4300 g. **Composition:** Nickel Plated Steel

Date	Mintage	MS-63	Proof
2006P	99,258	5.00	—

KM# 629 Subject: Bravery Medal **Obv:** Crowned head right **Weight:** 4.4300 g. **Composition:** Nickel Plated Steel

Date	Mintage	MS-63	Proof
2006P	24,845	20.00	—

KM# 698 Subject: 80th Birthday **Composition:** Nickel Plated Steel

Date	Mintage	MS-63	Proof
ND (2006)	—	5.00	—

KM# 638 Subject: Birthday **Rev:** Colorized baloons **Weight:** 4.4300 g. **Composition:** Nickel Plated Steel

Date	Mintage	MS-63	Proof
2006(ml)	—	5.00	—

KM# 639 Subject: Baby birth **Rev:** Colorized baby rattle **Weight:** 4.4300 g. **Composition:** Nickel Plated Steel

Date	Mintage	MS-63	Proof
2006(ml)	—	5.00	—

KM# 640 Subject: Oh Canada **Obv:** Head right **Rev:** Maple leaf, colorized **Weight:** 4.4300 g. **Composition:** Nickel Plated Steel

Date	Mintage	MS-63	Proof
2006(ml)	—	8.50	—

KM# 641 Subject: Congratulations **Obv:** Head right **Weight:** 4.4300 g. **Composition:** Nickel Plated Steel

Date	Mintage	MS-63	Proof
2006(ml)	—	8.00	—

KM# 643 Subject: Vancouver Canucks **Obv:** Head right **Rev:** Logo **Weight:** 4.4300 g. **Composition:** Nickel Plated Steel

Date	Mintage	MS-63	Proof
2007(ml)	—	12.50	—

KM# 682 Subject: Curling **Obv:** Head right **Weight:** 4.4300 g. **Composition:** Nickel Plated Steel

Date	Mintage	MS-63	Proof
2007	—	7.50	—

KM# 683 Subject: Ice Hockey **Obv:** Head right **Weight:** 4.4300 g. **Composition:** Nickel Plated Steel

Date	Mintage	MS-63	Proof
2007	—	7.50	—

KM# 684 Subject: Paraolympic Winter Games **Obv:** Head right **Rev:** Wheelchair curling **Weight:** 4.4300 g. **Composition:** Nickel Plated Steel

Date	Mintage	MS-63	Proof
2007	—	7.50	—

KM# 685 Subject: Biathlon **Obv:** Head right **Weight:** 4.4300 g. **Composition:** Nickel Plated Steel

Date	Mintage	MS-63	Proof
2007	—	7.50	—

KM# 686 Subject: Alpine Skiing **Obv:** Head right **Weight:** 4.4300 g. **Composition:** Nickel Plated Steel

Date	Mintage	MS-63	Proof
2007	—	7.50	—

KM# 693 Obv: Elizabeth II **Rev:** Multicolor Ruby-throated Hummingbird and flower **Edge:** Plain **Weight:** 12.6100 g. **Composition:** Nickel Plated Steel **Size:** 35 mm.

Date	Mintage	MS-63	Proof
2007	25,000	25.00	—

KM# 694 Subject: Red-breasted Nuthatch **Obv:** Head right **Obv. Legend:** ELIZABETH II - D • G • REGINA **Obv. Designer:** Susanna Blunt **Rev:** Nuthatch perched on pine branch multicolor **Rev. Legend:** CANADA **Rev. Designer:** Arnold Nogy **Edge:** Plain **Weight:** 12.6100 g. **Composition:** Nickel Plated Steel **Size:** 35.0 mm.

Date	Mintage	MS-63	Proof
2007(ml)	—	25.00	—

KM# 699 Subject: Oh Canada, **Rev:** Mountie, colorized **Composition:** Nickel Plated Steel

Date	Mintage	MS-63	Proof
2007(ml)	—	5.00	—

KM# 700 Rev: Montreal Canadians logo, colorized **Composition:** Nickel Plated Steel

Date	Mintage	MS-63	Proof
2007(ml)	—	5.00	—

KM# 701 Rev: Toronto Maple Leaf logo, colorized **Composition:** Nickel Plated Steel

Date	Mintage	MS-63	Proof
2007(ml)	—	5.00	—

KM# 702 Rev: Ottawa Senators logo, colorized **Composition:** Nickel Plated Steel

Date	Mintage	MS-63	Proof
2007(ml)	—	5.00	—

25 CENTS

50 CENTS

KM# 6 Obv: VICTORIA DEI GRATIA REGINA. CANADA **Obv. Designer:** Leonard C. Wyon **Rev:** Denomination and date within wreath, crown above **Weight:** 11.6200 g. **Composition:** 0.9250 Silver 0.3456 oz. ASW

Date	Mintage	VG-8	F-12	VF-20	XF-40	MS-60	MS-63	Proof
1870	450,000	800	1,300	2,000	3,400	25,000	38,500	—
1870 LCW	Inc. above	45.00	75.00	165	375	3,500	10,000	—
1871	200,000	50.00	120	250	500	7,000	11,500	—
1871H	45,000	90.00	175	375	850	6,700	22,000	—
1872H	80,000	45.00	75.00	175	400	3,800	10,250	—
1872H Inverted A for V in Victoria	Inc. above	250	600	1,300	3,300	19,000	—	—
1881H	150,000	45.00	85.00	200	450	4,250	16,000	—
1888	60,000	175	300	600	1,100	9,500	22,000	—
1890H	20,000	1,000	1,900	3,200	6,000	28,000	65,000	—
1892	151,000	50.00	95.00	320	500	6,000	21,000	—
1894	29,036	350	700	1,100	2,100	13,000	31,000	—
1898	100,000	75.00	120	350	750	9,000	26,000	—
1899	50,000	150	300	700	1,600	14,000	35,000	—
1900	118,000	45.00	75.00	165	375	4,000	10,500	—
1901	80,000	55.00	150	225	550	5,700	15,000	—

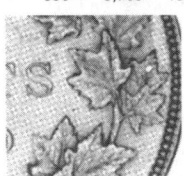

Victorian leaves

KM# 12 Obv: Crowned bust right **Obv. Designer:** G. W. DeSaulles **Rev:** Denomination and date within wreath, crown above **Weight:** 11.6200 g. **Composition:** 0.9250 Silver 0.3456 oz. ASW

Date	Mintage	VG-8	F-12	VF-20	XF-40	MS-60	MS-63	Proof
1902	120,000	15.00	35.00	100.00	250	1,300	3,500	—
1903H	140,000	22.00	45.00	175	450	1,500	3,700	—
1904	60,000	150	200	600	1,000	3,300	9,500	—
1905	40,000	150	275	600	1,400	6,000	15,000	—
1906	350,000	12.00	35.00	95.00	250	1,300	3,500	—
1907	300,000	12.00	35.00	95.00	250	1,400	3,900	—
1908	128,119	21.00	65.00	175	375	1,000	2,000	—
1909	302,118	17.00	60.00	175	475	2,400	7,600	—
1910	649,521	22.00	45.00	175	400	1,600	6,000	—

Note: Victorian leaves

Edwardian leaves

KM# 12a Obv: Crowned bust right **Obv. Designer:** G. W. DeSaulles **Rev:** Denomination and date within wreath **Weight:** 11.6638 g. **Composition:** 0.9250 Silver 0.3469 oz. ASW

Date	Mintage	VG-8	F-12	VF-20	XF-40	MS-60	MS-63	Proof
1910	Inc. above	8.00	29.00	85.00	250	1,200	3,300	—

Note: Edwardian leaves

KM# 19 Obv: Crowned bust left **Obv. Designer:** E. B. MacKennal **Rev:** Denomination and date within wreath, crown above **Weight:** 11.6638 g. **Composition:** 0.9250 Silver 0.3469 oz. ASW

Date	Mintage	VG-8	F-12	VF-20	XF-40	MS-60	MS-63	Proof
1911	209,972	18.00	70.00	250	550	1,400	3,200	—

KM# 25 Obv: Crowned bust left, modified legend **Obv. Designer:** E. B. MacKennal **Rev:** Denomination and date within wreath, crown above **Weight:** 11.6638 g. **Composition:** 0.9250 Silver 0.3469 oz. ASW

Date	Mintage	VG-8	F-12	VF-20	XF-40	MS-60	MS-63	Proof
1912	285,867	9.00	24.00	100.00	225	1,100	2,900	—
1913	265,889	9.00	24.00	150	300	1,400	4,800	—
1914	160,128	22.00	55.00	225	550	2,800	7,800	—
1916	459,070	6.00	14.00	55.00	175	650	2,100	—
1917	752,213	5.50	11.00	40.00	100.00	475	1,100	—
1918	754,989	5.50	10.00	30.00	90.00	400	1,000	—
1919	1,113,429	5.50	10.00	30.00	90.00	375	1,200	—

KM# 25a Obv: Crowned bust left **Obv. Designer:** E. B. MacKennal **Rev:** Denomination and date within wreath, crown below **Weight:** 11.6638 g. **Composition:** 0.8000 Silver 0.3000 oz. ASW

Date	Mintage	VG-8	F-12	VF-20	XF-40	MS-60	MS-63	Proof
1920	584,691	5.00	13.00	35.00	125	500	1,800	—
1921	—	22,000	24,000	28,000	32,000	50,000	90,000	—
Note: 75 to 100 known; David Akers John Jay Pittman sale, Part Three, 10-99, Gem Unc. realized $63,250								
1929	228,328	5.00	13.00	35.00	100.00	475	1,100	—
1931	57,581	11.00	29.00	80.00	225	800	1,800	—
1932	19,213	150	185	375	800	3,600	8,300	—
1934	39,539	15.00	30.00	100.00	225	650	1,300	—
1936	38,550	15.00	29.00	100.00	175	500	1,000	—

KM# 36   Obv: Head left **Obv. Designer:** T. H. Paget **Rev:** Crowned arms with supporters, denomination above, date below **Rev. Designer:** George E. Kruger-Gray **Weight:** 11.6638 g. **Composition:** 0.8000 Silver 0.3000 oz. ASW **Size:** 30 mm.

Date	Mintage	VG-8	F-12	VF-20	XF-40	MS-60	MS-63	Proof
1937	192,016	BV	5.00	7.00	10.00	30.00	85.00	—
1938	192,018	BV	5.50	10.00	25.00	90.00	400	—
1939	287,976	BV	5.00	8.00	17.00	60.00	250	—
1940	1,996,566	—	—	BV	6.00	27.00	60.00	—
1941	1,714,874	—	—	BV	6.00	27.00	60.00	—
1942	1,974,164	—	—	BV	6.00	27.00	60.00	—
1943	3,109,583	—	—	BV	6.00	27.00	60.00	—
1944	2,460,205	—	—	BV	6.00	27.00	60.00	—
1945	1,959,528	—	—	BV	6.00	30.00	90.00	—
1946	950,235	—	BV	5.00	8.00	60.00	175	—
1946	Inc. above	15.00	28.00	45.00	150	1,100	2,800	—
Note: hoof in 6								
1947	424,885	—	5.00	8.00	12.00	65.00	175	—
Note: straight 7								
1947	Inc. above	—	5.00	9.00	22.00	100.00	300	—
Note: curved 7								
1947	38,433	18.00	23.00	45.00	70.00	160	275	—
Note: maple leaf, straight 7								
1947	Inc. above	1,000	1,300	1,700	2,200	3,900	7,000	—
Note: maple leaf, curved 7								

KM# 45   Obv: Head left, modified legend **Obv. Designer:** T. H. Paget **Rev:** Crowned arms with supporters, denomination above, date below **Rev. Designer:** George E. Kruger-Gray **Weight:** 11.6638 g. **Composition:** 0.8000 Silver 0.3000 oz. ASW

Date	Mintage	VG-8	F-12	VF-20	XF-40	MS-60	MS-63	Proof
1948	37,784	65.00	85.00	100.00	150	250	350	—
1949	858,991	—	—	BV	7.00	35.00	150	—
1949	Inc. above	10.00	18.00	35.00	60.00	325	750	—
Note: hoof over 9								
1950	2,384,179	6.00	10.00	11.00	35.00	125	225	—
Note: no lines								
1950	Inc. above	—	—	BV	5.00	9.00	30.00	—
Note: lines in 0								
1951	2,421,730	—	—	—	BV	9.00	26.00	—
1952	2,596,465	—	—	—	BV	6.00	18.00	—

KM# 53 Obv: Laureate bust right **Obv. Designer:** Mary Gillick **Rev:** Crowned arms with supporters, denomination above, date below **Weight:** 11.6638 g. **Composition:** 0.8000 Silver 0.3000 oz. ASW

Date	Mintage	MS-60	MS-63	Proof
1953	1,630,429	7.00	15.00	—
Note: small date				
1953	Inc. above	22.00	35.00	—
Note: lg. date, straps				
1953	Inc. above	75.00	150	—
Note: lg. date without straps				
1954	506,305	18.00	35.00	—
1955	753,511	15.00	30.00	—
1956	1,379,499	6.00	14.00	—
1957	2,171,689	5.00	10.00	—
1958	2,957,266	5.00	8.50	—

KM# 56 Obv: Luareate bust right **Obv. Designer:** Mary Gillick **Rev:** Crown divides date above arms with supporters, denomination at right **Rev. Designer:** Thomas Shingles **Weight:** 11.6638 g. **Composition:** 0.8000 Silver 0.3000 oz. ASW **Size:** 30 mm.

Date	Mintage	MS-60	MS-63	Proof
1959	3,095,535	5.00	6.00	—
Note: horizontal shading				
1960	3,488,897	BV	5.00	—
1961	3,584,417	BV	5.00	—
1962	5,208,030	BV	5.00	—
1963	8,348,871	BV	5.00	—
1964	9,377,676	BV	5.00	—

KM# 63 Obv: Young bust right **Obv. Designer:** Arnold Machin **Rev:** Crown divides date above arms with supporters, denomination at right **Rev. Designer:** Thomas Shingles **Weight:** 11.6638 g. **Composition:** 0.8000 Silver 0.3000 oz. ASW

Date	Mintage	MS-60	MS-63	Proof
1965	12,629,974	BV	5.00	—
1966	7,920,496	BV	5.00	—

KM# 69 Subject: Confederation Centennial **Obv:** Young bust right **Rev:** Seated wolf howling divides denomination at top, dates at bottom **Rev. Designer:** Alex Colville **Weight:** 11.6638 g. **Composition:** 0.8000 Silver 0.3000 oz. ASW **Size:** 29.5 mm.

Date	Mintage	MS-60	MS-63	Proof
ND(1967)	4,211,392	5.00	6.50	9.00

KM# 75.1 Obv: Young bust right **Obv. Designer:** Arnold Machin **Rev:** Crown divides date above arms with supporters, denomination at right **Rev. Designer:** Thomas Shingles **Composition:** Nickel **Size:** 27.1 mm.

Date	Mintage	MS-60	MS-63	Proof
1968	3,966,932	0.65	1.00	—
1969	7,113,929	0.65	1.00	—
1970	2,429,526	0.65	1.00	—
1971	2,166,444	0.65	1.00	—
1972	2,515,632	0.65	1.00	—
1973	2,546,096	0.65	1.00	—
1974	3,436,650	0.65	1.00	—
1975	3,710,000	0.65	1 00	—
1976	2,940,719	0.65	1.00	—

KM# 75.2 Obv: Small young bust right **Obv. Designer:** Arnold Machin **Rev:** Crown divides date above arms with supporters, denomination at right **Rev. Designer:** Thomas Shingles **Weight:** 8.1000 g. **Composition:** Nickel **Size:** 27 mm.

Date	Mintage	MS-60	MS-63	Proof
1977	709,839	1.35	2.00	—

KM# 75.3 Obv: Young bust right **Obv. Designer:** Arnold Machin **Rev:** Crown divides date above arms with supporters, denomination at right, redesigned arms **Rev. Designer:** Thomas Shingles **Weight:** 8.1000 g. **Composition:** Nickel **Size:** 27 mm.

Date	Mintage	MS-60	MS-63	Proof
1978	3,341,892	0.65	1.00	—
Note: square jewels				
1978	Inc. above	4.50	6.00	—
Note: round jewels				
1979	3,425,000	0.65	1.00	—
1980	1,574,000	0.65	1.00	—

Date	Mintage	MS-60	MS-63	Proof
1981	2,690,272	0.65	1.00	—
1981 Proof	199,000	—	—	3.00
1982	2,236,674	65.00	100.00	—
Note: small beads				
1982 Proof	180,908	—	—	3.00
Note: small beads				
1982	Inc. above	0.65	1.00	—
Note: large beads				
1983	1,177,000	0.65	1.00	—
1983 Proof	168,000	—	—	3.00
1984	1,502,989	0.65	1.00	—
1984 Proof	161,602	—	—	3.00
1985	2,188,374	0.65	1.00	—
1985 Proof	157,037	—	—	3.00
1986	781,400	1.00	1.25	—
1986 Proof	175,745	—	—	3.00
1987	373,000	1.00	1.25	—
1987 Proof	179,004	—	—	3.50
1988	220,000	1.00	1.25	—
1988 Proof	175,259	—	—	3.00
1989	266,419	1.00	1.25	—
1989 Proof	170,928	—	—	3.00

KM# 185 Obv: Crowned head right **Obv. Designer:** Dora dePedery-Hunt **Rev:** Crown divides date above arms with supporters, denomination at right **Rev. Designer:** Thomas Shingles **Composition:** Nickel **Size:** 27 mm.

Date	Mintage	MS-60	MS-63	Proof
1990	207,000	1.00	1.25	—
1990 Proof	140,649	—	—	5.00
1991	490,000	0.85	1.00	—
1991 Proof	131,888	—	—	7.00
1993	393,000	0.85	1.00	—
1993 Proof	143,065	—	—	3.00
1994	987,000	0.75	1.00	—
1994 Proof	146,424	—	—	4.00
1995	626,000	0.75	1.00	—
1995 Proof	50,000	—	—	4.00
1996 Proof	—	—	—	—
1996	458,000	0.65	1.00	—

KM# 208 Subject: Confederation 125 **Obv:** Crowned head right **Obv. Designer:** Dora dePedery-Hunt **Rev:** Crown divides date above arms with supporters, denomination at right **Rev. Designer:** Thomas Shingles **Composition:** Nickel **Size:** 27 mm.

Date	Mintage	MS-60	MS-63	Proof
ND(1992)	445,000	0.75	1.00	—
ND(1992) Proof	147,061	—	—	5.00

KM# 261 Obv: Crowned head right **Rev:** Atlantic Puffin, denomination and date at right **Rev. Designer:** Sheldon Beveridge **Weight:** 11.6638 g. **Composition:** 0.9250 Silver 0.3469 oz. ASW

Date	Mintage	MS-63	Proof
1995 Proof	—	—	24.00

KM# 262 Obv: Crowned head right **Rev:** Whooping crane left, denomination and date at right **Rev. Designer:** Stan Witten **Weight:** 11.6638 g. **Composition:** 0.9250 Silver 0.3469 oz. ASW

Date	Mintage	MS-63	Proof
1995 Proof	—	—	24.00

KM# 263 Obv: Crowned head right **Rev:** Gray Jays, denomination and date at right **Rev. Designer:** Sheldon Beveridge **Weight:** 11.6638 g. **Composition:** 0.9250 Silver 0.3469 oz. ASW

Date	Mintage	MS-63	Proof
1995 Proof	—	—	24.00

KM# 264 Obv: Crowned head right **Rev:** White-tailed ptarmigans, date and denomination at right **Rev. Designer:** Cosme Saffioti **Weight:** 11.6638 g. **Composition:** 0.9250 Silver 0.3469 oz. ASW

Date	Mintage	MS-63	Proof
1995 Proof	—	—	22.00

KM# 185a   Obv: Crowned head right **Obv. Designer:** Dora dePedery-Hunt **Rev:** Crown divides date above arms with supporters, denomination at right **Rev. Designer:** Thomas Shingles **Weight:** 11.6380 g. **Comp:** 0.9250 Silver 0.3461 oz. ASW

Date	Mintage	MS-63	Proof
1996 Proof	—	—	9.00

KM# 283   Obv: Crowned head right **Rev:** Moose calf left, denomination and date at right **Rev. Designer:** Ago Aarand **Weight:** 11.6638 g. **Composition:** 0.9250 Silver 0.3469 oz. ASW

Date	Mintage	MS-63	Proof
1996 Proof	—	—	20.00

KM# 284   Obv: Crowned head right **Rev:** Wood ducklings, date and denomination at right **Rev. Designer:** Sheldon Beveridge **Weight:** 11.6638 g. **Composition:** 0.9250 Silver 0.3469 oz. ASW

Date	Mintage	MS-63	Proof
1996 Proof	—	—	20.00

KM# 285   Obv: Crowned head right **Rev:** Cougar kittens, date and denomination at right **Rev. Designer:** Stan Witten **Weight:** 11.6638 g. **Composition:** 0.9250 Silver 0.3469 oz. ASW

Date	Mintage	MS-63	Proof
1996 Proof	—	—	20.00

KM#286   Obv: Crowned head right **Rev:** Bear cubs standing, date and denomination at right **Rev. Designer:** Sheldon Beveridge **Weight:** 11.6638 g. **Composition:** 0.9250 Silver 0.3469 oz. ASW

Date	Mintage	MS-63	Proof
1996 Proof	—	—	20.00

KM# 290   Obv: Crowned head right **Obv. Designer:** Dora dePedery-Hunt **Rev:** Redesigned arms **Rev. Designer:** Cathy Bursey-Sabourin **Weight:** 6.9000 g. **Comp:** Nickel **Size:** 27.13 mm.

Date	Mintage	MS-63	Proof
1997	387,000	1.00	—
1997 Proof	—	—	5.00
1998	308,000	1.00	—
1998 Proof	—	—	—
1998W	—	2.00	—
1999	496,000	1.00	—
1999 Proof	—	—	5.00
2000	559,000	1.00	—
2000 Proof	—	—	5.00
2000W	—	1.50	—
2001P	—	1.50	—
2001P Proof	—	—	5.00
2003P	—	1.50	—
2003P Proof	—	—	5.00

KM# 292   Obv: Crowned head right **Rev:** Duck Toling Retriever, date and denomination at right **Rev. Designer:** Stan Witten **Weight:** 11.6638 g. **Composition:** 0.9250 Silver 0.3469 oz. ASW

Date	Mintage	MS-63	Proof
1997 Proof	—	—	17.00

KM# 293   Obv: Crowned head right **Rev:** Labrador leaping left, date and denomination at right **Rev. Designer:** Sheldon Beveridge **Weight:** 11.6638 g. **Composition:** 0.9250 Silver 0.3469 oz. ASW

Date	Mintage	MS-63	Proof
1997 Proof	—	—	17.00

KM# 294   Obv: Crowned head right **Rev:** Newfoundland right, date and denomination at right **Rev. Designer:** William Woodruff **Weight:** 11.6638 g. **Comp:** 0.9250 Silver 0.3469 oz. ASW

Date	Mintage	MS-63	Proof
1997 Proof	—	—	17.00

50 CENTS

KM# 295 Obv: Crowned head right **Rev:** Eskimo dog leaping forward, date and denomination at right **Rev. Designer:** Cosme Saffioti **Weight:** 11.6638 g. **Composition:** 0.9250 Silver 0.3469 oz. ASW

Date	Mintage	MS-63	Proof
1997 Proof	—	—	17.00

KM# 290a Obv: Crowned head right **Obv. Designer:** Dora dePedery-Hunt **Rev:** Redesigned arms **Rev. Designer:** Cathy Bursey-Sabourin **Weight:** 11.6380 g. **Composition:** 0.9250 Silver 0.3461 oz. ASW **Size:** 27.13 mm.

Date	Mintage	MS-63	Proof
1997 Proof	—	—	10.00
1998 Proof	—	—	10.00
1999 Proof	—	—	10.00
2000 Proof	—	—	10.00
2001 Proof	—	—	10.00
2003 Proof	—	—	10.00

KM# 313 Subject: 90th Anniversary Royal Canadian Mint **Obv:** Crowned head right **Rev:** Denomination and date within wreath, crown above **Rev. Designer:** W. H. J. Blakemore **Weight:** 11.6638 g. **Composition:** 0.9250 Silver 0.3469 oz. ASW

Date	Mintage	MS-63	Proof
ND(1998) Matte	25,000	—	15.00
ND(1998) Proof	25,000	—	15.00

KM# 314 Subject: 110 Years Canadian Speed and Figure Skating **Obv:** Crowned head right **Rev:** Speed skaters, dates below, denomination above **Rev. Designer:** Sheldon Beveridge **Weight:** 11.6638 g. **Composition:** 0.9250 Silver 0.3469 oz. ASW

Date	Mintage	MS-63	Proof
ND(1998) Proof	—	—	9.00

KM# 315 Subject: 100 Years Canadian Ski Racing **Obv:** Crowned head right **Rev:** Skiers, dates below, denomination upper left **Rev. Designer:** Ago Aarand **Weight:** 11.6638 g. **Composition:** 0.9250 Silver 0.3469 oz. ASW

Date	Mintage	MS-63	Proof
ND(1998) Proof	—	—	9.00

KM# 318 Obv: Crowned head right **Rev:** Killer Whales, date and denomination at right **Rev. Designer:** William Woodruff **Weight:** 11.6638 g. **Composition:** 0.9250 Silver 0.3469 oz. ASW

Date	Mintage	MS-63	Proof
1998 Proof	—	—	17.00

KM# 319 Obv: Crowned head right **Rev:** Humpback whale, date and denomination at right **Rev. Designer:** Sheldon Beveridge **Weight:** 11.6638 g. **Composition:** 0.9250 Silver 0.3469 oz. ASW

Date	Mintage	MS-63	Proof
1998 Proof	—	—	17.00

KM# 320 Obv: Crowned head right **Rev:** Beluga whales, date and denomination at right **Rev. Designer:** Cosme Saffioti **Weight:** 11.6638 g. **Composition:** 0.9250 Silver 0.3469 oz. ASW

Date	Mintage	MS-63	Proof
1998 Proof	—	—	17.00

KM# 321 Obv: Crowned head right **Rev:** Blue whale, date and denomination at right **Rev. Designer:** Stan Witten **Weight:** 11.6638 g. **Composition:** 0.9250 Silver 0.3469 oz. ASW

Date	Mintage	MS-63	Proof
1998 Proof	—	—	17.00

KM# 327 Subject: 110 Years Canadian Soccer **Obv:** Crowned head right **Rev:** Soccer players, dates above, denomination at right **Rev. Designer:** Stan Witten **Weight:** 11.6638 g. **Composition:** 0.9250 Silver 0.3469 oz. ASW

Date	Mintage	MS-63	Proof
ND(1998) Proof	—	—	9.00

KM# 328 Subject: 20 Years Canadian Auto Racing **Obv:** Crowned head right **Rev:** Race car divides date and denomination **Rev. Designer:** Cosme Saffioti **Weight:** 11.6638 g. **Composition:** 0.9250 Silver 0.3469 oz. ASW

Date	Mintage	MS-63	Proof
ND(1998) Proof	—	—	9.00

KM# 290b Obv: Crowned head right **Obv. Designer:** Dora dePedery-Hunt **Rev:** Redesigned arms **Rev. Designer:** Cathy Bursey-Sabourin **Weight:** 6.9000 g. **Composition:** Nickel Plated Steel **Size:** 27.13 mm.

Date	Mintage	MS-63	Proof
1999 P	Est. 20,000	15.00	—
2000 P	Est. 50	3,500	—
Note: Available only in RCM presentation coin clocks			
2001 P	389,000	1.50	—
2003 P	—	5.00	—

KM# 333 Subject: 1904 Canadian Open **Obv:** Crowned head right **Rev:** Golfers, date at right, denomination below **Rev. Designer:** William Woodruff **Weight:** 11.6638 g. **Composition:** 0.9250 Silver 0.3469 oz. ASW

Date	Mintage	MS-63	Proof
ND(1999) Proof	—	—	13.50

KM# 334 Subject: First U.S.-Canadian Yacht Race **Obv:** Crowned head right **Rev:** Yachts, dates at left, denomination below **Rev. Designer:** Stan Witten **Weight:** 11.6638 oz. **Composition:** 0.9250 Silver 0.3469 oz. ASW

Date	Mintage	MS-63	Proof
ND(1999) Proof	—	—	9.00

KM#335 Subject: Canadian Cats, **Obv:** Crowned head right **Rev:** Cymric cat, date below, denomination at bottom **Rev. Designer:** Susan Taylor **Weight:** 11.6638 g. **Composition:** 0.9250 Silver 0.3469 oz. ASW

Date	Mintage	MS-63	Proof
1999 Proof	—	—	20.00

KM#336 Subject: Canadian Cats, **Obv:** Crowned head right **Rev:** Tonkinese cat, date below, denomination at bottom **Rev. Designer:** Susan Taylor **Weight:** 11.6638 g. **Composition:** 0.9250 Silver 0.3469 oz. ASW

Date	Mintage	MS-63	Proof
1999 Proof	—	—	20.00

KM# 337 Subject: Canadian Cats, **Obv:** Crowned head right **Rev:** Cougar, date and denomination below **Rev. Designer:** Susan Taylor **Weight:** 11.6638 g. **Composition:** 0.9250 Silver 0.3469 oz. ASW

Date	Mintage	MS-63	Proof
1999 Proof	—	—	20.00

KM#338 Subject: Canadian Cats, **Obv:** Crowned head right **Rev:** Lynx, date and denomination below **Rev. Designer:** Susan Taylor **Weight:** 11.6638 g. **Composition:** 0.9250 Silver 0.3469 oz. ASW

Date	Mintage	MS-63	Proof
1999 Proof	—	—	20.00

KM#371 Subject: Basketball **Obv:** Crowned head right **Rev:** Basketball players **Rev. Designer:** Sheldon Beveridge **Edge:** Reeded **Weight:** 9.3600 g. **Composition:** 0.9250 Silver 0.2783 oz. ASW **Size:** 27.1 mm.

Date	Mintage	MS-63	Proof
ND(1999) Proof	—	—	9.00

KM# 372 Obv: Crowned head right **Rev:** Football players **Rev. Designer:** Cosme Saffioti **Edge:** Reeded **Weight:** 9.3600 g. **Composition:** 0.9250 Silver 0.2783 oz. ASW **Size:** 27.1 mm.

Date	Mintage	MS-63	Proof
ND(1999) Proof	—	—	9.00

KM# 385 Subject: Ice Hockey **Obv:** Crowned head right **Rev:** 4 hockey players **Rev. Designer:** Stanley Witten **Composition:** 0.9250 Silver

Date	Mintage	MS-63	Proof
ND(2000) Proof	—	—	12.00

KM# 386 Subject: Curling **Obv:** Crowned head right **Rev:** Motion study of curlers, dates and denomination below **Rev. Designer:** Cosme Saffioti **Composition:** 0.9250 Silver

Date	Mintage	MS-63	Proof
ND(2000) Proof	—	—	9.00

KM# 389 Obv: Crowned head right **Rev:** Great horned owl, facing, date and denomination at right **Rev. Designer:** Susan Taylor **Weight:** 9.3500 g. **Composition:** 0.9250 Silver 0.2781 oz. ASW

Date	Mintage	MS-63	Proof
2000 Proof	—	—	20.00

KM# 390 Obv: Crowned head right **Rev:** Red-tailed hawk, dates and denomination at right **Weight:** 9.3500 g. **Composition:** 0.9250 Silver 0.2781 oz. ASW

Date	Mintage	MS-63	Proof
2000 Proof	—	—	20.00

KM# 391 Obv: Crowned head right **Rev:** Osprey, dates and denomination at right **Rev. Designer:** Susan Taylor **Weight:** 9.3500 g. **Composition:** 0.9250 Silver 0.2781 oz. ASW

Date	Mintage	MS-63	Proof
2000 Proof	—	—	20.00

KM# 392 Obv: Crowned head right **Rev:** Bald eagle, dates and denomination at right **Rev. Designer:** William Woodruff **Weight:** 9.3500 g. **Composition:** 0.9250 Silver 0.2781 oz. ASW

Date	Mintage	MS-63	Proof
2000 Proof	—	—	20.00

KM# 393 Subject: Steeplechase **Obv:** Crowned head right **Rev:** Steeplechase, dates and denomination below **Rev. Designer:** Susan Taylor **Composition:** 0.9250 Silver

Date	Mintage	MS-63	Proof
2000 Proof	—	—	9.00

KM# 394 Subject: Bowling **Obv:** Crowned head right **Rev. Designer:** William Woodruff **Composition:** 0.9250 Silver

Date	Mintage	MS-63	Proof
2000 Proof	—	—	9.00

KM# 420 Subject: Festivals - Quebec, **Obv:** Crowned head right **Rev:** Snowman and Chateau Frontenac **Rev. Designer:** Sylvie Daigneault **Edge:** Reeded **Weight:** 9.3000 g. **Composition:** 0.9250 Silver 0.2766 oz. ASW **Size:** 27.13 mm.

Date	Mintage	MS-63	Proof
2001 Proof	58,123	—	8.50

KM# 421 Subject: Festivals - Nunavut, **Obv:** Crowned head right **Rev:** Dancer, dog sled and snowmobiles **Rev. Designer:** John Mardon **Edge:** Reeded **Weight:** 9.3000 g. **Composition:** 0.9250 Silver 0.2766 oz. ASW **Size:** 27.13 mm.

Date	Mintage	MS-63	Proof
2001 Proof	58,123	—	8.50

KM# 422 Subject: Festivals - Newfoundland, **Obv:** Crowned head right **Rev:** Sailor and musical people **Rev. Designer:** David Craig **Edge:** Reeded **Weight:** 9.3000 g. **Composition:** 0.9250 Silver 0.2766 oz. ASW **Size:** 27.13 mm.

Date	Mintage	MS-63	Proof
2001 Proof	58,123	—	8.50

KM# 423 Subject: Festivals - Prince Edward Island, **Obv:** Crowned head right **Rev:** Family, juggler and building **Rev. Designer:** Brenda Whiteway **Edge:** Reeded **Weight:** 9.3000 g. **Comp:** 0.9250 Silver 0.2766 oz. ASW **Size:** 27.13 mm.

Date	Mintage	MS-63	Proof
2001 Proof	58,123	—	8.50

KM# 424 Subject: Folklore - The Sled, **Obv:** Crowned head right **Rev:** Family scene **Rev. Designer:** Valentina Hotz-Entin **Edge:** Reeded **Weight:** 9.3000 g. **Composition:** 0.9250 Silver 0.2766 oz. ASW **Size:** 27.13 mm.

Date	Mintage	MS-63	Proof
2001 Proof	28,979	—	9.00

KM# 425 Subject: Folklore - The Maiden's Cave, **Obv:** Crowned head right **Rev:** Woman shouting **Rev. Designer:** Peter Kiss **Edge:** Reeded **Weight:** 9.3000 g. **Composition:** 0.9250 Silver 0.2766 oz. ASW **Size:** 27.13 mm.

Date	Mintage	MS-63	Proof
2001 Proof	28,979	—	9.00

KM# 426 Subject: Folklore - The Small Jumpers, **Obv:** Crowned head right **Rev:** Jumping children on seashore **Rev. Designer:** Miynki Tanobe **Edge:** Reeded **Weight:** 9.3000 g. **Composition:** 0.9250 Silver 0.2766 oz. ASW **Size:** 27.13 mm.

Date	Mintage	MS-63	Proof
2001 Proof	28,979	—	9.00

KM# 509 Obv: Crowned head right **Rev:** National arms **Edge:** Reeded **Weight:** 6.9000 g. **Composition:** Nickel Plated Steel **Size:** 27.13 mm.

Date	Mintage	MS-63	Proof
ND(2001) P	—	1.50	—

KM# 444 Subject: Queen's Golden Jubilee **Obv:** Coronation crowned head right and monogram **Rev:** Canadian arms **Rev. Designer:** Bursey Sabourin **Edge:** Reeded **Weight:** 6.9000 g. **Composition:** Nickel Plated Steel **Size:** 27.13 mm.

Date	Mintage	MS-63	Proof
ND(2002)P	1,440,000	2.50	—

KM# 444a Subject: Elizabeth II Golden Jubilee **Obv:** Crowned head right, Jubilee commemorative dates 1952-2002 **Weight:** 9.3000 g. **Composition:** 0.9250 Silver 0.2766 oz. ASW **Size:** 27.13 mm.

Date	Mintage	MS-63	Proof
ND(2002)	100,000	—	17.50

   Note: In proof sets only

KM# 444b Subject: Queen's Golden Jubilee **Obv:** Crowned head right and monogram **Rev:** Canadian arms **Edge:** Reeded **Weight:** 9.3000 g. **Composition:** 0.9250 Gold Plated Silver 0.2766 oz. ASW AGW **Size:** 27.13 mm. **Note:** Special 24 karat gold plated issue of KM#444.

Date	Mintage	MS-63	Proof
ND(2002) Proof	32,642	—	35.00

KM# 454 Subject: Nova Scotia Annapolis Valley Apple Blossom Festival **Obv:** Crowned head right **Rev. Designer:** Bonnie Ross **Weight:** 9.3000 g. **Composition:** 0.9250 Silver 0.2766 oz. ASW **Size:** 27.13 mm.

Date	Mintage	MS-63	Proof
2002 Proof	59,998	—	8.50

KM# 455 Subject: Stratford Festival **Obv:** Crowned head right **Rev:** Couple with building in background **Rev. Designer:** Laurie McGaw **Weight:** 9.3000 g. **Composition:** 0.9250 Silver 0.2766 oz. ASW **Size:** 27.13 mm.

Date	Mintage	MS-63	Proof
2002 Proof	59,998	—	8.50

KM# 456 Subject: Folklorama **Obv:** Crowned head right **Rev. Designer:** William Woodruff **Weight:** 9.3000 g. **Composition:** 0.9250 Silver 0.2766 oz. ASW **Size:** 27.13 mm.

Date	Mintage	MS-63	Proof
2002 Proof	59,998	—	8.50

KM# 457 Subject: Calgary Stampede **Obv:** Crowned head right **Rev. Designer:** Stan Witten **Weight:** 9.3000 g. **Composition:** 0.9250 Silver 0.2766 oz. ASW **Size:** 27.13 mm.

Date	Mintage	MS-63	Proof
2002 Proof	59,998	—	8.50

KM# 458 Subject: Squamish Days Logger Sports **Obv:** Crowned head right **Rev. Designer:** Jose Osio **Weight:** 9.3000 g. **Composition:** 0.9250 Silver 0.2766 oz. ASW **Size:** 27.13 mm.

Date	Mintage	MS-63	Proof
2002 Proof	59,998	—	8.50

KM# 459 Subject: Folklore and Legends, **Obv:** Crowned head right **Rev:** The Shoemaker in Heaven **Rev. Designer:** Francine Gravel **Weight:** 9.3000 g. **Composition:** 0.9250 Silver 0.2766 oz. ASW **Size:** 27.13 mm.

Date	Mintage	MS-63	Proof
2002 Proof	19,267	—	9.50

KM# 460 Subject: Folklore and Legends, The Ghost Ship **Obv:** Crowned head right **Rev. Designer:** Colette Boivin **Weight:** 9.3000 g. **Comp:** 0.9250 Silver 0.2766 oz. ASW **Size:** 27.13 mm.

Date	Mintage	MS-63	Proof
2002 Proof	19,267	—	9.50

KM# 461 Subject: Folklore and Legends, The Pig That Wouldn't Get Over the Stile **Obv:** Crowned head right **Rev. Designer:** Laura Jolicoeur **Weight:** 9.3000 g. **Composition:** 0.9250 Silver 0.2766 oz. ASW **Size:** 27.13 mm.

Date	Mintage	MS-63	Proof
2002 Proof	19,267	—	9.50

KM# 494 Obv: Crowned head right **Obv. Designer:** Susanna Blunt **Rev. Designer:** Cathy Bursey-Sabourin **Weight:** 6.9000 g. **Composition:** Nickel Plated Steel **Size:** 27.13 mm.

Date	Mintage	MS-63	Proof
2003W	—	5.00	—
2003W Proof	—	—	7.50
2004P	—	5.00	—
2004P Proof	—	—	7.50
2005P	—	1.50	—
2005P Proof	—	—	5.00
2006P	—	1.50	—
2006P Proof	—	—	5.00
2006(ml)	—	1.50	—
2007(ml) Proof	—	—	5.00

KM# 472 Subject: 50th Anniversary of the Coronation of Elizabeth II **Obv:** Crowned head right, Jubilee commemorative dates 1952-2002 **Obv. Designer:** Mary Gillick **Weight:** 11.6200 g. **Comp:** 0.9250 Silver 0.3456 oz. ASW **Size:** 27.13 mm.

Date	Mintage	MS-63	Proof
ND(2003)	30,000	15.00	—

   Note: In coronation proof sets only

KM# 475 Obv: Crowned head right **Obv. Designer:** Dora dePédery-Hunt **Rev:** Golden daffodil **Rev. Designer:** Christie Paquet, Stan Witten **Comp:** 0.9250 Silver **Size:** 27.13 mm.

Date	Mintage	MS-63	Proof
2003 Proof	55,000	—	15.00

KM# 476 Subject: Yukon International Storytelling Festival **Obv:** Crowned head right **Obv. Designer:** Dora dePédery-Hunt **Rev. Designer:** Ken Anderson, Jose Oslo **Weight:** 9.3000 g. **Comp:** 0.9250 Silver 0.2766 oz. ASW **Size:** 27.13 mm.

Date	Mintage	MS-63	Proof
2003 Proof	—	—	11.00

KM# 477 Subject: Festival Acadien de Caraquet **Obv:** Crowned head right **Obv. Designer:** Dora dePédery-Hunt **Rev:** Sailboat and couple **Rev. Designer:** Susan Taylor, Hudson Design Group **Weight:** 9.3000 g. **Composition:** 0.9250 Silver 0.2766 oz. ASW **Size:** 27.13 mm.

Date	Mintage	MS-63	Proof
2003 Proof	—	—	11.00

KM#478 Subject: Back to Batoche **Obv:** Crowned head right **Obv. Designer:** Dora dePédery-Hunt **Rev. Designer:** David Hannan, Stan Witten **Weight:** 9.3000 g. **Composition:** 0.9250 Silver 0.2766 oz. ASW **Size:** 27.13 mm.

Date	Mintage	MS-63	Proof
2003 Proof	—	—	11.00

KM# 479 Subject: Great Northern Arts Festival **Obv:** Crowned head right **Obv. Designer:** Dora dePédery-Hunt **Rev. Designer:** Dawn Oman, Susan Taylor **Weight:** 9.3000 g. **Composition:** 0.9250 Silver 0.2766 oz. ASW **Size:** 27.13 mm.

Date	Mintage	MS-63	Proof
2003 Proof	—	—	11.00

KM# 526 Subject: Moose **Obv:** Head right **Rev:** Moose head facing right **Weight:** 1.2700 g. **Comp:** 0.9999 Gold 0.0408 oz. AGW **Size:** 14 mm.

Date	Mintage	MS-63	Proof
2004 Proof	—	—	85.00

KM# 494a Obv: Crowned head right **Obv. Designer:** Susanna Blunt **Rev:** Canadian coat of arms **Edge:** Reeded **Weight:** 9.3000 g. **Comp:** 0.9250 Silver 0.2766 oz. ASW **Size:** 27.13 mm.

Date	Mintage	MS-63	Proof
2004 Proof	—	—	7.50

KM# 703 Rev: Tiger Swallowtail Butterfly **Composition:** Silver

Date	Mintage	MS-63	Proof
2004	—	—	25.00

KM# 606 Obv: Head right **Obv. Designer:** Susanna Blunt **Rev:** Clouded Sulphur Butterfly, hologram **Rev. Designer:** Susan Taylor **Weight:** 9.3000 g. **Composition:** 0.9250 Silver 0.2766 oz. ASW **Size:** 27.13 mm.

Date	Mintage	MS-63	Proof
2004 Proof	15,281	—	37.50

KM# 536 Subject: Golden rose **Obv:** Head right **Obv. Designer:** Susanna Blunt **Rev. Designer:** Christie Paquet **Weight:** 9.3000 g. **Composition:** 0.9250 Silver With Partial Gold Plating 0.2766 oz. **Size:** 27.13 mm.

Date	Mintage	MS-63	Proof
2005 Proof	17,418	—	19.00

KM# 537 Subject: Great Spangled Fritillary butterfly, hologram **Obv:** Head right **Obv. Designer:** Susanna Blunt **Rev. Designer:** Jianping Yan **Weight:** 9.3000 g. **Composition:** 0.9250 Silver 0.2766 oz. ASW **Size:** 27.13 mm.

Date	Mintage	MS-63	Proof
2005 Proof	20,000	—	37.50

KM# 538 Subject: Toronto Maple Leafs **Obv:** Head right **Obv. Designer:** Susanna Blunt **Rev:** Darryl Sittler **Weight:** 9.3000 g. **Composition:** 0.9250 Silver 0.2766 oz. ASW **Size:** 27.13 mm.

Date	Mintage	MS-63	Proof
2005	25,000	17.50	—

KM# 539 Subject: Toronto Maple Leafs **Obv:** Head right **Obv. Designer:** Susanna Blunt **Rev:** Dave Keon **Weight:** 9.3000 g. **Composition:** 0.9250 Silver 0.2766 oz. ASW **Size:** 27.13 mm.

Date	Mintage	MS-63	Proof
2005	25,000	17.50	—

KM# 540 Subject: Toronto Maple Leafs **Obv:** Head right **Obv. Designer:** Susanna Blunt **Rev:** Jonny Bover **Weight:** 9.3000 g. **Composition:** 0.9250 Silver 0.2766 oz. ASW **Size:** 27.13 mm.

Date	Mintage	MS-63	Proof
2005	25,000	17.50	—

KM# 541 Subject: Toronto Maple Leafs **Obv:** Head right **Obv. Designer:** Susanna Blunt **Rev:** Tim Horton **Weight:** 9.3000 g. **Composition:** 0.9250 Silver 0.2766 oz. ASW **Size:** 27.13 mm.

Date	Mintage	MS-63	Proof
2005	25,000	17.50	—

KM# 542 Subject: Voyageurs **Obv:** Head right **Weight:** 1.2700 g. **Composition:** 0.9999 Gold 0.0408 oz. AGW

Date	Mintage	MS-63	Proof
2005 Proof	—	—	65.00

KM# 543 Subject: WWII - Battle of Britain **Obv:** Head right **Rev:** Fighter plane in sky **Composition:** Silver

Date	Mintage	MS-63	Proof
2005	—	22.50	—

KM# 544 Subject: WWII - Battle of Scheldt **Obv:** Head right **Obv. Designer:** Susanna Blunt **Rev:** Four soldiers walking down road **Rev. Designer:** Peter Mossman **Weight:** 9.3000 g. **Composition:** 0.9250 Silver 0.2766 oz. ASW **Size:** 27.13 mm.

Date	Mintage	MS-63	Proof
2005	20,000	19.00	—

KM# 545 Subject: WWII - Battle of the Atlantic **Obv:** Head right **Obv. Designer:** Susanna Blunt **Rev:** Merchant ship sinking **Rev. Designer:** Peter Mossman **Weight:** 9.3000 g. **Composition:** 0.9250 Silver 0.2766 oz. ASW **Size:** 27.13 mm.

Date	Mintage	MS-63	Proof
2005	20,000	19.00	—

KM# 546 Subject: WWII - Conquest of Sicily **Obv:** Head right **Obv. Designer:** Susanna Blunt **Rev:** Tank among town ruins **Rev. Designer:** Peter Mossman **Weight:** 9.3000 g. **Composition:** 0.9250 Silver 0.2766 oz. ASW **Size:** 27.13 mm.

Date	Mintage	MS-63	Proof
2005	20,000	19.00	—

KM# 547 Subject: WWII - Liberation of the Netherlands **Obv:** Head right **Obv. Designer:** Susanna Blunt **Rev:** Soldiers in parade, one holding flag **Rev. Designer:** Peter Mossman **Weight:** 9.3000 g. **Composition:** 0.9250 Silver 0.2766 oz. ASW **Size:** 27.13 mm.

Date	Mintage	MS-63	Proof
2005	20,000	19.00	—

KM# 548 Subject: WWII - Raid of Dieppe **Obv:** Head right **Obv. Designer:** Susanna Blunt **Rev:** Three soldiers exiting landing craft **Rev. Designer:** Peter Mossman **Weight:** 9.3000 g. **Composition:** 0.9250 Silver 0.2766 oz. **ASW Size:** 27.13 mm.

Date	Mintage	MS-63	Proof
2005	20,000	19.00	—

KM# 577 Subject: Montreal Canadiens **Obv:** Head right **Obv. Designer:** Susanna Blunt **Rev:** Guy LaFleur **Weight:** 9.3000 g. **Composition:** 0.9250 Silver 0.2766 oz. **ASW Size:** 27.13 mm.

Date	Mintage	MS-63	Proof
2005	25,000	17.50	—

KM# 578 Subject: Montreal Canadiens **Obv:** Head right **Obv. Designer:** Susanna Blunt **Rev:** Jaque Plante **Weight:** 9.3000 g. **Composition:** 0.9250 Silver 0.2766 oz. **ASW Size:** 27.13 mm.

Date	Mintage	MS-63	Proof
2005	25,000	17.50	—

KM# 579 Subject: Montreal Canadiens **Obv:** Head right **Obv. Designer:** Susanna Blunt **Rev:** Jean Beliveau **Weight:** 9.3000 g. **Composition:** 0.9250 Silver 0.2766 oz. **ASW Size:** 27.13 mm.

Date	Mintage	MS-63	Proof
2005	25,000	17.50	—

KM# 580 Subject: Montreal Canadiens **Obv:** Head right **Obv. Designer:** Susanna Blunt **Rev:** Maurice Richard **Weight:** 9.3000 g. **Composition:** 0.9250 Silver 0.2766 oz. **ASW Size:** 27.13 mm.

Date	Mintage	MS-63	Proof
2005	25,000	17.50	—

KM# 599 Subject: Monarch Butterfly, colorized **Obv:** Head right **Obv. Designer:** Susanna Blunt **Rev. Designer:** Susan Taylor **Weight:** 9.3000 g. **Composition:** 0.9250 Silver 0.2766 oz. ASW **Size:** 27.13 mm.

Date	Mintage	MS-63	Proof
2005 Proof	20,000	—	37.50

KM# 648 Subject: Golden Daisy **Obv:** Head right **Weight:** 9.3000 g. **Composition:** 0.9250 Silver 0.2766 oz. ASW

Date	Mintage	MS-63	Proof
2006	17,771	10.00	—

KM# 649 Subject: Short tailed swallotail **Obv:** Head right **Rev:** Colorized butterfly **Weight:** 9.3000 g. **Composition:** 0.9250 Silver 0.2766 oz. ASW

Date	Mintage	MS-63	Proof
2006	20,000	10.00	—

KM# 650 Subject: Butterfly hologram **Obv:** Head right **Rev:** Silvery blue hologram **Weight:** 9.3000 g. **Composition:** 0.9250 Silver 0.2766 oz. ASW

Date	Mintage	MS-63	Proof
2006	16,000	10.00	—

KM# 651 Subject: Cowboy **Obv:** Head right **Weight:** 9.3000 g. **Composition:** 0.9250 Silver 0.2766 oz. ASW

Date	Mintage	MS-63	Proof
2006		17.50	—

KM# 704 Rev: Forget-me-not flower **Composition:** Silver

Date	Mintage	MS-63	Proof
2007	—	—	40.00

SOVEREIGN

KM# 14 Rev: St. George slaying dragon, mint mark below horse's rear hooves **Weight:** 7.9881 g. **Composition:** 0.9170 Gold 0.2355 oz. AGW

Date	Mintage	F-12	VF-20	XF-40	AU-50	MS-60	MS-63
1908C	636	1,250	1,850	2,350	2,600	2,850	4,000
1909C	16,273	200	225	250	285	500	1,600
1910C	28,012	BV	200	225	265	500	3,000

KM# 20 Rev: St. George slaying dragon, mint mark below horse's rear hooves **Weight:** 7.9881 g. **Composition:** 0.9170 Gold 0.2355 oz. AGW

Date	Mintage	F-12	VF-20	XF-40	AU-50	MS-60	MS-63
1911C	256,946	—	—	BV	BV	200	250
1911C Specimen	—	—	—	—	—	—	—
1913C	3,715	550	700	950	1,200	1,500	3,000
1914C	14,871	200	225	350	450	600	950
1916C About 20 known	—	8,000	12,500	15,750	17,750	20,000	27,500
Note: Stacks' A.G. Carter Jr. Sale 12-89 Gem BU realized $82,500							
1917C	58,845	—	—	BV	BV	200	750
1918C	106,514	—	—	BV	BV	200	1,100
1919C	135,889	—	—	BV	BV	200	750

DOLLAR

KM# 30 Subject: Silver Jubilee **Obv:** Bust left **Obv. Designer:** Percy Metcalfe **Rev:** Voyager, date and denomination below **Rev. Designer:** Emanuel Hahn **Weight:** 23.3276 g. **Composition:** 0.8000 Silver 0.6000 oz. ASW

Date	Mintage	F-12	VF-20	XF-40	AU-50	MS-60	MS-63	Proof
1935	428,707	12.00	18.00	28.00	32.00	37.50	60.00	4,500

KM# 31 Obv: Crowned bust left **Obv. Designer:** E. B. MacKennal **Rev:** Voyageur, date and denomination below **Rev. Designer:** Emanuel Hahn **Weight:** 23.3276 g. **Composition:** 0.8000 Silver 0.6000 oz. ASW

Date	Mintage	F-12	VF-20	XF-40	AU-50	MS-60	MS-63	Proof
1936	339,600	12.50	14.50	26.00	30.00	35.00	75.00	5,000

Pointed 7   Blunt 7

Maple leaf

KM# 37 Obv: Head left **Obv. Designer:** T. H. Paget **Rev:** Voyageur, date and denomination below **Rev. Designer:** Emanuel Hahn **Weight:** 23.3276 g. **Composition:** 0.8000 Silver 0.6000 oz. ASW

Date	Mintage	F-12	VF-20	XF-40	AU-50	MS-60	MS-63	Proof
1937	207,406	9.50	10.00	12.00	22.00	25.00	100.00	—
1937 Mirror Proof	1,295	—	—	—	—	—	—	650
1937 Matte Proof	Inc. above	—	—	—	—	—	—	250
1938	90,304	25.00	35.00	65.00	80.00	100.00	175	6,000
1945	38,391	75.00	150	175	225	300	475	2,000
1946	93,055	15.00	25.00	35.00	45.00	95.00	300	1,800
1947		60.00	80.00	150	125	265	1,400	3,500
Note: Pointed 7								
1947	65,595	45.00	60.00	80.00	95.00	125	250	4,500
Note: Blunt 7								
1947	21,135	125	150	175	200	250	475	1,800
Note: Maple leaf								

DOLLAR

KM# 38   Subject: Royal Visit **Obv:** Head left **Obv. Designer:** T. H. Paget **Rev:** Tower at center of building, date and denomination below **Rev. Designer:** Emanuel Hahn **Weight:** 23.3276 g. **Composition:** 0.8000 Silver 0.6000 oz. ASW

Date	Mintage	F-12	VF-20	XF-40	AU-50	MS-60	MS-63	Proof
1939	1,363,816	—	BV	9.50	10.00	12.00	30.00	—
1939	—	—	—	—	—	—	—	475
Note: Matte specimen								
1939 Proof	—	—	—	—	—	—	—	750
Note: Mirror specimen								

KM# 46   Obv: Head left, modified left legend **Obv. Designer:** T. H. Paget **Rev:** Voyageur, date and denomination below **Rev. Designer:** Emanuel Hahn **Weight:** 23.3276 g. **Composition:** 0.8000 Silver 0.6000 oz. ASW

Date	Mintage	F-12	VF-20	XF-40	AU-50	MS-60	MS-63	Proof
1948	18,780	500	600	1,000	1,100	1,300	1,900	3,000
1950	261,002	BV	9.50	10.00	12.00	16.00	50.00	800
Note: With 3 water lines								
1950 Matte Proof	—	—	—	—	—	—	—	—
Note: With 4 water lines, 1 known								
1950	Inc. above	11.00	14.00	21.00	28.00	40.00	90.00	1,500
Note: Arnprior with 2-1/2 water lines								
1951	416,395	BV	9.50	10.00	11.00	13.00	23.00	650
Note: With 3 water lines								
1951	Inc. above	35.00	50.00	60.00	100.00	175	400	2,000
Note: Arnprior with 1-1/2 water lines								
1952	406,148	BV	9.50	10.00	11.00	12.00	23.00	1,000
Note: With 3 water lines								
1952	Inc. above	11.00	12.00	22.00	30.00	40.00	100.00	1,250
Note: Arnprior type								
1952	Inc. above	BV	9.50	10.00	11.00	16.50	45.00	—
Note: Without water lines								

KM# 47 Subject: Newfoundland **Obv:** Head left **Obv. Designer:** T. H. Paget **Rev:** The "Matthew", John Cabot's ship, date and denomination below **Rev. Designer:** Thomas Shingles **Weight:** 23.3276 g. **Composition:** 0.8000 Silver 0.6000 oz. ASW

Date	Mintage	F-12	VF-20	XF-40	AU-50	MS-60	MS-63	Proof
1949	672,218	10.00	13.00	16.50	18.50	22.50	27.50	—
1949 Specimen proof	—	—	—	—	—	—	—	1,200

KM# 54 Obv: Laureate bust right **Obv. Designer:** Mary Gillick **Rev:** Voyageur, date and denomination below **Rev. Designer:** Emanuel Hahn **Weight:** 23.3276 g. **Composition:** 0.8000 Silver 0.6000 oz. ASW **Note:** All genuine circulation strike 1955 Arnprior dollars have a die break running along the top of TI in the word GRATIA on the obverse.

Date	Mintage	F-12	VF-20	XF-40	AU-50	MS-60	MS-63	Proof
1953	1,074,578	—	—	BV	9.50	10.00	25.00	400
Note: Without strap, wire rim								
1953	Inc. above	—	—	BV	9.50	10.00	25.00	—
Note: With strap, flat rim								
1954	246,606	BV	9.50	10.00	11.00	16.00	35.00	—
1955	268,105	BV	9.50	10.00	11.00	15.00	29.00	—
Note: With 3 water lines								
1955	Inc. above	45.00	65.00	90.00	100.00	125	175	—
Note: Arnprior with 1-1/2 water lines* and die break								
1956	209,092	BV	9.50	13.00	16.00	20.00	50.00	—
1957	496,389	—	—	—	BV	9.50	16.00	—
Note: With 3 water lines								
1957	Inc. above	—	BV	9.50	10.00	15.00	35.00	—
Note: With 1 water line								
1959	1,443,502	—	—	—	—	BV	11.00	—
1960	1,420,486	—	—	—	—	BV	11.00	—
1961	1,262,231	—	—	—	—	BV	11.00	—
1962	1,884,789	—	—	—	—	BV	11.00	—
1963	4,179,981	—	—	—	—	BV	9.50	—

KM# 55 Subject: British Columbia **Obv:** Laureate bust right **Obv. Designer:** Mary Gillick **Rev:** Totem Pole, dates at left, denomination below **Rev. Designer:** Stephan Trenka **Weight:** 23.3276 g. **Composition:** 0.8000 Silver 0.6000 oz. ASW

Date	Mintage	F-12	VF-20	XF-40	AU-50	MS-60	MS-63	Proof
ND(1958)	3,039,630	—	—	BV	9.50	10.00	15.00	—

KM# 58 Subject: Charlottetown **Obv:** Laureate bust right **Rev:** Design at center, dates at outer edges, denomination below **Rev. Designer:** Dinko Voldanovic **Weight:** 23.3276 g. **Composition:** 0.8000 Silver 0.6000 oz. ASW **Size:** 36 mm.

Date	Mintage	F-12	VF-20	XF-40	AU-50	MS-60	MS-63	Proof
ND(1964)	7,296,832	—	—	—	—	BV	9.50	—
ND(1964) Specimen proof	Inc. above	—	—	—	—	—	—	250

Small beads

Medium beads

Large beads

KM# 64.1 Obv: Young bust right **Obv. Designer:** Arnold Machin **Rev:** Voyageur, date and denomination below **Rev. Designer:** Emanual Hahn **Weight:** 23.3276 g. **Composition:** 0.8000 Silver 0.6000 oz. ASW **Size:** 36 mm.

Date	Mintage	F-12	VF-20	XF-40	AU-50	MS-60	MS-63	Proof
1965	10,768,569	—	—	—	—	DV	9.50	—
Note: Small beads, pointed 5								
1965	Inc. above	—	—	—	—	BV	9.50	—
Note: Small beads, blunt 5								
1965	Inc. above	—	—	—	—	BV	9.50	—
Note: Large beads, blunt 5								
1965	Inc. above	—	—	—	—	BV	11.00	—
Note: Large beads, pointed 5								

Date	Mintage	F-12	VF-20	XF-40	AU-50	MS-60	MS-63	Proof
1965	Inc. above	—	BV	9.50	10.00	12.00	35.00	—
Note: Medium beads, pointed 5								
1966	9,912,178	—	—	—	—	BV	9.50	—
Note: Large beads								
1966	485	—	—	1,200	1,500	1,800	3,300	—
Note: Small beads								

KM# 70 Subject: Confederation Centennial **Obv:** Young bust right **Obv. Designer:** Arnold Machin **Rev:** Goose left, dates below, denomination above **Rev. Designer:** Alex Colville **Weight:** 23.3276 g. **Composition:** 0.8000 Silver 0.6000 oz. ASW **Size:** 36 mm.

Date	Mintage	MS-63	Proof
ND(1967)	6,767,496	11.00	12.00

KM# 76.1 Obv: Young bust right **Obv. Designer:** Arnold Machin **Rev:** Voyageur, date and denomination below **Rev. Designer:** Emanuel Hahn **Composition:** Nickel **Size:** 32 mm.

Date	Mintage	MS-63	P/L	Proof
1968	5,579,714	1.25	—	—
1968	—	8.50	—	—
Note: Small island				
1968	1,408,143	—	1.75	—
1968	—	—	4.00	—
Note: No island				
1968	—	—	25.00	—
Note: Doubled die; exhibits extra water lines				
1969	4,809,313	1.25	—	—
1969	594,258	—	2.00	—
1972	2,676,041	1.50	—	—
1972	405,865	—	2.50	—

KM# 78 Subject: Manitoba **Obv:** Young bust right **Rev:** Pasque flower divides dates and denomination **Rev. Designer:** Raymond Taylor **Composition:** Nickel **Size:** 32 mm.

Date	Mintage	MS-63	P/L	Proof
1970	4,140,058	2.00	—	—
1970	645,869	—	2.50	—

KM# 79 Subject: British Columbia **Obv:** Young bust right **Rev:** Shield divides dates, denomination below, flowers above **Rev. Designer:** Thomas Shingles **Composition:** Nickel **Size:** 32 mm.

Date	Mintage	MS-63	P/L	Proof
1971	4,260,781	2.00	—	—
1971	468,729	—	2.25	—

KM# 80 Subject: British Columbia **Obv:** Young bust right **Rev:** Crowned arms with supporters divide dates, maple at top divides denomination, crowned lion atop crown on shield **Rev. Designer:** Patrick Brindley **Weight:** 23.3276 g. **Composition:** 0.5000 Silver 0.3750 oz. ASW **Size:** 36 mm.

Date	Mintage	MS-63	P/L	Proof
1971	585,674	—	—	—

KM# 64.2a Obv: Smaller young bust right **Obv. Designer:** Arnold Machin **Rev:** Voyageur **Rev. Designer:** Emanuel Hahn **Weight:** 23.3276 g. **Comp:** 0.5000 Silver 0.3750 oz. ASW **Size:** 36 mm.

Date	Mintage	MS-63	P/L	Proof
1972	341,598	—	—	8.50
Note: Specimen $5.50.				

KM# 82 Subject: Prince Edward Island **Obv:** Young bust right **Rev:** Building, inscription below divides dates, denomination above **Rev. Designer:** Terry Manning **Composition:** Nickel **Size:** 32 mm.

Date	Mintage	MS-63	P/L	Proof
1973	3,196,452	2.00	—	—
1973 (c)	466,881	—	2.50	—

KM# 83 Obv: Young bust right **Rev:** Mountie left, dates below, denomination at right **Rev. Designer:** Paul Cedarberg **Weight:** 23.3276 g. **Composition:** 0.5000 Silver 0.3750 oz. ASW **Size:** 36 mm.

Date	Mintage	MS-63	P/L	Proof
1973	1,031,271	—	—	—

KM# 83v Note: Mountie Dollar in blue case with R.C.M.P. crest.

Date	Mintage	MS-63	P/L	Proof
1973	Inc. above	—	—	—

KM# 88a Subject: Winnipeg Centennial **Obv:** Young bust right **Rev:** Zeros frame pictures, dates below, denomination at bottom **Rev. Designer:** Paul Pederson and Patrick Brindley **Composition:** 0.5000 Silver **Size:** 36 mm.

Date	Mintage	MS-63	P/L	Proof
1974	728,947	—	—	—

KM# 76.2 Obv: Smaller young bust right **Obv. Designer:** Arnold Machin **Rev:** Voyageur **Rev. Designer:** Emanuel Hahn **Weight:** 15.6200 g. **Composition:** Nickel **Size:** 32 mm.

Date	Mintage	MS-63	P/L	Proof
1975	3,256,000	1.50	—	—
1975	322,325	—	2.50	—
1976	2,498,204	1.50	—	—
1976	274,106	—	2.50	—

KM# 76.3 Obv: Young bust right **Obv. Designer:** Arnold Machin **Rev:** Voyageur **Rev. Designer:** Emanuel Hahn **Composition:** Nickel **Size:** 32 mm. **Note:** Only known in prooflike sets with 1976 obverse slightly modified.

Date	Mintage	MS-63	P/L	Proof
1975	Inc. above	—	3.00	—
Note: mule with 1976 obv.				

KM# 97 Subject: Calgary **Obv:** Youmg bust right **Rev:** Figure on bucking horse, dates divided below, denomination above **Rev. Designer:** Donald D. Paterson **Weight:** 23.3276 g. **Composition:** 0.5000 Silver 0.3750 oz. ASW **Size:** 36 mm.

Date	Mintage	MS-63	P/L	Proof
1975	930,956	—	—	—

KM# 88 Subject: Winnipeg Centennial **Obv:** Young bust right **Rev:** Zeros frame pictures, dates below, denomination at bottom **Rev. Designer:** Paul Pederson and Patrick Brindley **Composition:** Nickel **Size:** 32 mm.

Date	Mintage	MS-63	P/L	Proof
1974	2,799,363	2.00	—	—
1974 (c)	363,786	—	2.50	—

KM# 106 Subject: Parliament Library **Obv:** Young bust right **Rev:** Library building, dates below, denomination above **Rev. Designer:** Walter Ott and Patrick Brindley **Weight:** 23.3276 g. **Composition:** 0.5000 Silver 0.3750 oz. ASW **Size:** 36 mm.

Date	Mintage	MS-63	P/L	Proof
1976	578,708	—	—	—
1976	Inc. above	—	—	—

Note: Blue case VIP

KM# 117 Obv: Young bust right **Obv. Designer:** Arnold Machin **Rev:** Voyageur modified **Rev. Designer:** Emanuel Hahn **Composition:** Nickel **Size:** 32 mm.

Date	Mintage	MS-63	P/L	Proof
1977	1,393,745	2.25	—	—
1977	—	—	2.50	—

KM# 118 Subject: Silver Jubilee **Obv:** Young bust right, dates below **Rev:** Throne, denomination below **Rev. Designer:** Raymond Lee **Weight:** 23.3276 g. **Composition:** 0.5000 Silver 0.3750 oz. ASW **Size:** 36 mm.

Date	Mintage	MS-63	P/L	Proof
1977	744,848	—	—	—
1977	Inc. above	—	—	—

Note: red case VIP

KM# 120.1 Obv: Young bust right **Obv. Designer:** Arnold Machin **Rev:** Voyageur, date and denomination below **Rev. Designer:** Emanuel

Hahn **Weight:** 15.6200 g. **Composition:** Nickel **Size:** 32.13 mm. **Note:** Modified design.

Date	Mintage	MS-63	Proof
1978	2,948,488	1.50	—
1979	2,954,842	1.50	—
1980	3,291,221	1.50	—
1981	2,778,900	1.50	—
1981 Proof	—	—	—
1982	1,098,500	1.50	—
1982 Proof	180,908	—	5.25
1983	2,267,525	1.50	—
1983 Proof	166,779	—	5.25
1984	1,223,486	1.50	—
1984 Proof	161,602	—	6.00
1985	3,104,092	1.50	—
1985 Proof	153,950	—	7.00
1986	3,089,225	2.00	—
1986 Proof	176,224	—	7.50
1987	287,330	3.50	—
1987 Proof	175,686	—	7.50

KM# 121 Subject: XI Commonwealth Games **Obv:** Young bust right **Rev:** Commonwealth games, logo at center **Rev. Designer:** Raymond Taylor **Weight:** 23.3276 g. **Composition:** 0.5000 Silver 0.3750 oz. ASW **Size:** 36 mm.

Date	Mintage	MS-63	P/L	Proof
1978	709,602	—	—	—

KM# 124 Subject: Griffon **Obv:** Young bust right **Rev:** Ship, dates below, denomination above **Rev. Designer:** Walter Schluep **Weight:** 23.3276 g. **Composition:** 0.5000 Silver 0.3750 oz. ASW **Size:** 36 mm.

Date	Mintage	MS-63	P/L	Proof
1979	826,695	—	—	—

KM# 128 **Subject:** Arctic Territories **Obv:** Young bust right **Rev:** Bear right, date below, denomination above **Rev. Designer:** Donald D. Paterson **Weight:** 23.3276 g. **Composition:** 0.5000 Silver 0.3750 oz. ASW **Size:** 36 mm.

Date	Mintage	MS-63	P/L	Proof
1980	539,617	—	—	—

KM# 130 **Subject:** Transcontinental Railroad **Obv:** Young bust right **Rev:** Train engine and map, date below, denomination above **Rev. Designer:** Christopher Gorey **Weight:** 23.3276 g. **Comp:** 0.5000 Silver 0.3750 oz. ASW **Size:** 36 mm.

Date	Mintage	MS-63	P/L	Proof
1981	699,494	8.50	—	—
1981 Proof	—	—	—	13.50

KM# 133 **Subject:** Regina **Obv:** Young bust right **Rev:** Cattle skull divides dates and denomination below **Rev. Designer:** Huntley Brown **Weight:** 23.3276 g. **Composition:** 0.5000 Silver 0.3750 oz. ASW **Size:** 36 mm.

Date	Mintage	MS-63	P/L	Proof
1982	144,930	8.50	—	—
1982 Proof	758,958	—	—	8.50

KM# 134 **Subject:** Constitution **Obv:** Young bust right **Rev:** Meeting of Government **Rev. Designer:** Ago Aarand **Weight:** 15.4200 g. **Composition:** Nickel **Size:** 32 mm.

Date	Mintage	MS-63	P/L	Proof
1982	9,709,422	3.00	6.00	—

KM# 138 **Subject:** Edmonton University Games **Obv:** Young bust right **Rev:** Athlete within game logo, date and denomination below **Rev. Designer:** Carola Tietz **Weight:** 23.3276 g. **Composition:** 0.5000 Silver 0.3750 oz. ASW **Size:** 36 mm.

Date	Mintage	MS-63	P/L	Proof
1983	159,450	8.50	—	—
1983 Proof	506,847	—	—	8.50

KM# 140 **Subject:** Toronto Sesquicentennial **Obv:** Young bust right **Rev. Designer:** D. J. Craig **Weight:** 23.3276 g. **Composition:** 0.5000 Silver 0.3750 oz. ASW **Size:** 36 mm.

Date	Mintage	MS-63	P/L	Proof
1984	133,610	8.50	—	—
1984 Proof	732,542	—	—	8.50

KM# 141 **Subject:** Jacques Cartier **Obv:** Young bust right **Rev:** Cross with shield above figures **Rev. Designer:** Hector Greville **Weight:** 15.6400 g. **Composition:** Nickel **Size:** 32 mm.

Date	Mintage	MS-63	P/L	Proof
1984	7,009,323	2.25	—	—
1984 Proof	87,760	—	—	6.00

Date	Mintage	MS-63	Proof
1988	138,893,539	2.25	—
1988 Proof	175,259	—	6.75
1989	184,773,902	3.00	—
1989 Proof	170,928	—	6.75

KM# 154 Subject: John Davis **Obv:** Young bust right **Rev:** Ship "John Davis" with masts, rock in background, dates below, denomination at bottom **Rev. Designer:** Christopher Gorey **Weight:** 23.3276 g. **Composition:** 0.5000 Silver 0.3750 oz. ASW **Size:** 36 mm.

Date	Mintage	MS-63	P/L	Proof
1987	118,722	8.50	—	—
1987 Proof	602,374	—	—	9.00

KM# 143 Subject: National Parks **Obv:** Young bust right **Rev:** Moose right, dates above, denomination below **Rev. Designer:** Karel Rohlicek **Weight:** 23.3276 g. **Composition:** 0.5000 Silver 0.3750 oz. ASW **Size:** 36 mm.

Date	Mintage	MS-63	P/L	Proof
1985	163,314	8.50	—	—
1985 Proof	733,354	—	—	10.00

KM# 161 Subject: Ironworks **Obv:** Young bust right **Rev:** Ironworkers, date and denomination below **Rev. Designer:** Robert R. Carmichael **Weight:** 23.3276 g. **Composition:** 0.5000 Silver 0.3750 oz. ASW **Size:** 36 mm.

Date	Mintage	MS-63	P/L	Proof
1988	106,872	8.50	—	—
1988 Proof	255,013	—	—	16.00

KM# 149 Subject: Vancouver **Obv:** Young bust right **Rev:** Train left, dates divided below, denomination above **Rev. Designer:** Elliot John Morrison **Weight:** 23.3276 g. **Composition:** 0.5000 Silver 0.3750 oz. ASW **Size:** 36 mm.

Date	Mintage	MS-63	P/L	Proof
1986	125,949	8.50	—	—
1986 Proof	680,004	—	—	8.50

KM# 168 Subject: MacKenzie River **Obv:** Young bust right **Rev:** People in canoe, date above, denomination below **Rev. Designer:** John Mardon **Weight:** 23.3276 g. **Composition:** 0.5000 Silver 0.3750 oz. ASW **Size:** 36 mm.

Date	Mintage	MS-63	P/L	Proof
1989	99,774	14.00	—	—
1989 Proof	244,062	—	—	16.00

KM# 157 Obv: Young bust right **Obv. Designer:** Arnold Machin **Rev:** Loon right, date and denomination below **Rev. Designer:** Robert R. Carmichael **Weight:** 7.0000 g. **Composition:** Aureate-Bronze Plated Nickel **Shape:** 11-sided **Size:** 26.5 mm.

Date	Mintage	MS-63	Proof
1987	205,405,000	2.25	—
1987 Proof	178,120	—	8.00

DOLLAR

KM# 186 Obv: Crowned head right
Obv. Designer: Dora dePedery-Hunt **Rev:** Loon right, date and denomination **Rev. Designer:** Robert R. Carmichael **Weight:** 7.0000 g.
Composition: Aureate-Bronze Plated Nickel **Shape:** 11-sided **Size:** 26.5 mm.

Date	Mintage	MS-63	Proof
1990	68,402,000	1.75	—
1990 Proof	140,649	—	7.00
1991	23,156,000	1.75	—
1991 Proof	—	—	13.00
1993	33,662,000	2.00	—
1993 Proof	—	—	6.00
1994	16,232,530	2.00	—
1994 Proof	—	—	7.00
1995	27,492,630	3.00	—
1995 Proof	—	—	7.00
1996	17,101,000	2.00	—
1996 Proof	—	—	7.50
1997	—	5.00	—
1997 Proof	—	—	8.00
1998	—	2.50	—
1998 Proof	—	—	10.00
1998W	—	—	—
1999	—	2.00	—
1999 Proof	—	—	8.00
2000	—	2.00	—
2000 Proof	—	—	8.00
2001	—	2.50	—
2001 Proof	—	—	8.00
2002	—	4.50	—
2002 Proof	—	—	7.50
2003	—	5.50	—
2003 Proof	100,000	—	12.00

KM# 170 Subject: Henry Kelsey **Obv:** Crowned head right **Rev:** Kelsey with natives, dates below, denomination above **Rev. Designer:** D. J. Craig
Weight: 23.3276 g. **Composition:** 0.5000 Silver 0.3750 oz. ASW **Size:** 36 mm.

Date	Mintage	MS-63	P/L	Proof
1990	99,455	8.50	—	—
1990 Proof	254,959	—	—	18.00

KM# 179 Subject: S.S. Frontenac **Obv:** Crowned head right **Rev:** Ship,"Frontenac", date and denomination below **Rev. Designer:** D. J. Craig
Weight: 23.3276 g. **Composition:** 0.5000 Silver 0.3750 oz. ASW **Size:** 36 mm.

Date	Mintage	MS-63	P/L	Proof
1991	73,843	8.50	—	—
1991 Proof	195,424	—	—	24.00

KM# 210 Subject: Stagecoach service **Obv:** Crowned head right **Rev:** Stagecoach, date and denomination below **Rev. Designer:** Karsten Smith **Weight:** 25.1750 g. **Composition:** 0.9250 Silver 0.7487 oz. ASW **Size:** 36 mm.

Date	Mintage	MS-63	P/L	Proof
1992	78,160	16.50	—	—
1992 Proof	187,612	—	—	16.50

KM# 209 Subject: Loon right, dates and denomination **Obv:** Crowned head right
Rev. Designer: Robert R. Carmichael
Composition: Aureate **Size:** 26.5 mm.

Date	Mintage	MS-63	Proof
ND(1992)	4,242,085	2.00	—
ND(1992) Proof	—	—	8.00

KM# 218 Subject: Parliament **Obv:** Crowned head right, dates below **Rev:** Backs of three seated figures in front of building, denomination below **Rev. Designer:** Rita Swanson **Composition:** Aureate **Size:** 26 mm.

Date	Mintage	MS-63	Proof
ND(1992)	23,915,000	2.25	—
ND(1992) Proof	24,227	—	9.00

KM# 235 Subject: Stanley Cup hockey **Obv:** Crowned head right **Rev:** Hockey players between cups, dates below, denomination above **Rev. Designer:** Stewart Sherwood **Weight:** 25.1750 g. **Composition:** 0.9250 Silver 0.7487 oz. ASW **Size:** 36 mm.

Date	Mintage	MS-63	P/L	Proof
1993	88,150	16.50	—	—
1993 Proof	294,314	—	—	16.50

KM# 251 Subject: Last RCMP sled-dog patrol **Obv:** Crowned head right **Rev:** Dogsled, denomination divides dates below **Rev. Designer:** Ian Sparks **Weight:** 25.1750 g. **Composition:** 0.9250 Silver 0.7487 oz. ASW **Size:** 36 mm.

Date	Mintage	MS-63	P/L	Proof
1994	61,561	16.50	—	—
1994 Proof	170,374	—	—	25.00

KM# 248 Subject: War Memorial **Obv:** Crowned head right, date below **Rev:** Memorial, denomination at right **Rev. Designer:** R. C. M. Staff **Composition:** Aureate **Size:** 26 mm.

Date	Mintage	MS-63	Proof
1994	20,004,830	2.25	—
1994 Proof	54,524	—	7.50

KM# 258 Subject: Peacekeeping Monument in Ottawa **Obv:** Crowned head right, date below **Rev:** Monument, denomination above right **Rev. Designer:** J. K. Harmon, R. G. Henriquez and C. H. Oberlander **Weight:** 7.0000 g. **Composition:** Aureate **Size:** 26 mm. **Note:** Mintage included with KM#186.

Date	Mintage	MS-63	Proof
1995	18,502,750	2.25	—
1995 Proof	43,293	—	7.50

KM#259 Subject: Hudson Bay Co. **Obv:** Crowned head right **Rev:** Explorers and ship, date and denomination below **Rev. Designer:** Vincent McIndoe **Weight:** 25.1750 g. **Composition:** 0.9250 Silver 0.7487 oz. ASW **Size:** 36 mm.

Date	Mintage	MS-63	P/L	Proof
1995	61,819	16.50	—	—
1995 Proof	166,259	—	—	30.00

KM# 274 Subject: McIntosh Apple **Obv:** Crowned head right **Rev:** Apple, dates and denomination below **Rev. Designer:** Roger Hill **Weight:** 25.1750 g. **Composition:** 0.9250 Silver 0.7487 oz. ASW **Size:** 36 mm.

Date	Mintage	MS-63	P/L	Proof
1996	58,834	16.50	—	—
1996 Proof	133,779	—	—	24.00

KM# 282 Subject: 25th Anniversary Hockey Victory **Obv:** Crowned head right **Rev:** The winning goal by Paul Aenderson. Based on a painting by Andre l'Archeveque, dates at right, denomination at bottom **Rev. Designer:** Walter Burden **Weight:** 25.1750 g. **Composition:** 0.9250 Silver 0.7487 oz. ASW **Size:** 36 mm.

Date	Mintage	MS-63	P/L	Proof
ND(1997)	155,252	16.50	—	—
ND(1997) Proof	184,965	—	—	24.00

KM# 291 Subject: Loon Dollar 10th Anniversary **Obv:** Crowned head right **Rev:** Loon in flight left, dates above, denomination below **Rev. Designer:** Jean-Luc Grondin **Comp:** Aureate **Size:** 26 mm.

Date	Mintage	MS-63	P/L	Proof
1997	—	—	22.00	—

KM# 296 Subject: Loon Dollar 10th Anniversary **Obv:** Crowned head right **Rev:** Loon in flight left, dates above, denomination below **Rev. Designer:** Jean-Luc Grondin **Weight:** 25.1750 g. **Comp:** 0.9250 Silver 0.7487 oz. ASW **Size:** 36 mm.

Date	Mintage	MS-63	P/L	Proof
1997 Proof	24,995	—	—	75.00

KM# 306 Subject: 120th Anniversary Royal Canadian Mounted Police **Obv:** Crowned head right **Rev:** Mountie on horseback, dates at left, denomination above **Rev. Designer:** Adeline Halvorson **Weight:** 25.1750 g. **Composition:** 0.9250 Silver 0.7487 oz. ASW **Size:** 36 mm. **Note:** Individually cased prooflikes, proofs or specimens are from broken-up prooflike or specimen sets.

Date	Mintage	MS-63	P/L	Proof
1998	79,777	—	16.50	—
1998 Proof	120,172	—	—	20.00

KM# 355 Subject: International Year of Old Persons **Obv:** Crowned head right **Rev:** Figures amid trees, date and denomination below **Rev. Designer:** S. Armstrong-Hodgson **Weight:** 25.1750 g. **Composition:** 0.9250 Silver 0.7487 oz. ASW **Size:** 36 mm.

Date	Mintage	MS-63	P/L	Proof
1999 Proof	24,976	—	—	40.00

KM# 356 Subject: Discovery of Queen Charlotte Isle **Obv:** Crowned head right **Rev:** Ship and three boats, dates at right, denomination below **Rev. Designer:** D. J. Craig **Weight:** 25.1750 g. **Comp:** 0.9250 Silver 0.7487 oz. ASW **Size:** 36 mm.

Date	Mintage	MS-63	P/L	Proof
ND(1999) Proof	126,435	—	—	22.50
ND(1999)	67,655	—	16.50	—

KM# 401 Subject: Voyage of Discovery **Obv:** Crowned head right **Rev:** Human and space shuttle, date above, denomination below **Rev. Designer:** D. F. Warkentine **Weight:** 25.1750 g. **Composition:** 0.9250 Silver 0.7487 oz. ASW **Size:** 36 mm.

Date	Mintage	MS-63	P/L	Proof
2000	60,100	—	16.50	—
2000 Proof	114,130	—	—	22.50

KM# 443 Subject: Queen's Golden Jubilee **Obv:** Crowned head right, with anniversary date at left **Obv. Designer:** Dora dePédery-Hunt **Rev:** Queen in her coach and a view of the coach, denomination

below **Edge:** Reeded **Weight:** 25.1750 g. **Comp:** 0.9250 Silver 0.7487 oz. ASW **Size:** 36 mm.

Date	Mintage	MS-63	P/L	Proof
ND(2000) Proof	—	—	—	20.00
ND(2002)	65,140	—	16.50	—
ND(2002) Proof	29,688	—	—	21.50

KM# 414 Subject: National Ballet **Obv:** Crowned head right **Rev:** Ballet dancers **Rev. Designer:** Scott McKowen **Edge:** Reeded **Weight:** 25.1750 g. **Composition:** 0.9250 Silver 0.7487 oz. ASW **Size:** 36 mm.

Date	Mintage	MS-63	P/L	Proof
2001	65,000	9.00	16.50	—
2001 Proof	225,000	—	—	21.50

KM# 434 Obv: Crowned head right **Rev:** Recycled 1911 pattern dollar design: denomination, country name and dates in crowned wreath. **Edge:** Reeded. **Weight:** 25.1750 g. **Composition:** 0.9250 Silver 0.7487 oz. ASW **Size:** 36 mm.

Date	Mintage	MS-63	P/L	Proof
ND(2001) Proof	24,996	—	—	55.00

KM# 186a Subject: Olympic Win **Composition:** Gold Plated **Size:** 26.5 mm.

Date	Mintage	MS-63	Proof
2002 Proof	—	—	40.00

KM# 443a Subject: Queen's Golden Jubilee **Obv:** Crowned head right with anniversary date **Rev:** Queen in her coach and a view of the coach **Edge:** Reeded **Weight:** 25.1800 g. **Composition:** 0.9250 Gold Plated Silver 0.7488 oz. ASW AGW **Size:** 36 mm. **Note:** Special 24 karat gold plated issue of KM#443.

Date	Mintage	MS-63	Proof
ND(2002) Proof	32,642	—	40.00

KM# 462 Obv: Commemorative dates 1952-2002 **Obv. Designer:** Dora dePédery-Hunt **Rev:** Family of Loons **Weight:** 7.0000 g. **Composition:** Aureate-Bronze Plated Nickel

Date	Mintage	MS-63	Proof
ND(2002)	67,672	10.00	—
Note: In Specimen Sets only			

KM# 467 Subject: Elizabeth II Golden Jubilee **Obv:** Crowned head right, Jubilee commemorative dates 1952-2002 **Obv. Designer:** Dora dePédery-Hunt **Weight:** 7.0000 g. **Composition:** Aureate-Bronze Plated Nickel

Date	Mintage	MS-63	Proof
ND(2002)	—	2.50	—
ND(2002) Proof	—	—	8.00

KM# 503 Subject: Queen Mother **Obv:** Crowned head right **Obv. Designer:** Dora de Pedery-Hunt **Rev:** Queen Mother facing **Weight:** 25.1750 g. **Composition:** 0.9250 Silver 0.7487 oz. ASW **Size:** 36 mm.

Date	Mintage	MS-63	Proof
2002 Proof	9,994	—	300

KM# 450 Subject: Cobalt Mining Centennial **Obv:** Queens portrait right **Obv. Designer:** Dora dePédery-Hunt **Rev:** Mine tower and fox **Edge:** Reeded **Weight:** 25.1750 g. **Composition:** 0.9999 Silver 0.8093 oz. ASW **Size:** 36 mm.

Date	Mintage	MS-63	Proof
ND(2003)	51,130	20.00	—
ND(2003) Proof	88,536	—	28.00

KM# 495 Obv: Crowned head right **Obv. Designer:** Susanna Blunt **Rev. Designer:** Robert R. Carmichael **Weight:** 7.0000 g. **Composition:** Aureate-Bronze Plated Nickel **Size:** 26.5 mm.

Date	Mintage	MS-63	Proof
2003	5,102,000	5.50	—
2003	—	—	7.50
2003W	—	7.50	—
2004	3,409,000	3.00	—
2004 Proof	—	—	12.00
2005	—	3.00	—
2005 Proof	—	—	7.50
2006	—	3.00	—
2006 Proof	—	—	7.50
2006(ml)	—	3.00	—
2006(ml) Proof	—	—	7.50

KM# 473 Subject: 50th Anniversary of the Coronation of Elizabeth II **Obv:** 1953 effigy of the Queen, Jubilee commemorative dates 1953-2003 **Obv. Designer:** Mary Gillick **Rev:** Voyageur, date and denomination below **Weight:** 25.1750 g. **Composition:** 0.9999 Silver 0.8093 oz. ASW

Date	Mintage	MS-63	Proof
ND(2003)	29,586	35.00	—

Note: In Coronation Proof sets only

KM# 480 Subject: Coronation of Queen Elizabeth II **Obv:** Head right **Rev:** Voyaguers **Rev. Designer:** Emanuel Hahn **Weight:** 25.1750 g. **Composition:** 0.9999 Silver 0.8093 oz. ASW

Date	Mintage	MS-63	Proof
ND2003 Proof	21,400	—	38.00

KM# 507 Obv: Bare head right, date below **Obv. Designer:** Susanna Blunt **Rev:** Loon **Edge:** Plain **Weight:** 7.0000 g. **Comp:** Aureate-Bronze Plated Nickel **Shape:** 11-sided **Size:** 26.5 mm.

Date	Mintage	MS-63	Proof
2004 Proof	12,550	—	12.50

KM# 513 Subject: Olympics **Obv:** Crowned head right **Rev:** Maple leaf, Olympic flame and rings above loon **Edge:** Plain **Weight:** 7.0000 g. **Composition:** Aureate-Bronze Plated Nickel **Shape:** 11-sided **Size:** 26.5 mm.

Date	Mintage	MS-63	Proof
2004	6,526,000	8.00	—

KM# 513a Subject: Olympics **Obv:** Crowned head right **Rev:** Multicolor maple leaf, Olympic flame and rings above loon **Edge:** Plain **Weight:** 9.3100 g. **Composition:** 0.9250 Silver 0.2769 oz. ASW **Shape:** 11-sided **Size:** 26.5 mm.

Date	Mintage	MS-63	Proof
2004 Proof	19,994	—	50.00

KM# 512 Subject: First French Settlement in America **Obv:** Crowned head right **Rev:** Sailing ship **Edge:** Reeded **Weight:** 25.1750 g. **Composition:** 0.9999 Silver 0.8093 oz. ASW **Size:** 36 mm.

Date	Mintage	MS-63	Proof
2004	42,582	30.00	—
2004 Fleur-dis-lis	8,315	50.00	—
2004 Proof	106,974	—	40.00

KM# 552 Subject: Terry Fox **Obv:** Head right **Weight:** 7.0000 g. **Composition:** Aureate-Bronze Plated Nickel

Date	Mintage	MS-63	Proof
2005	1,290,900	3.50	—

KM# 549 Subject: 40th Anniversary of National Flag **Obv:** Head right **Obv. Designer:** Susanna Blunt **Rev. Designer:** William Woodruff **Weight:** 25.1750 g. **Comp:** 0.9250 Silver 0.7487 oz. ASW

Date	Mintage	MS-63	Proof
2005	50,948	22.50	—
2005 Proof	95,431	—	32.50

KM# 549a Subject: 40th Anniversary of National Flag **Obv:** Head right **Weight:** 7.0000 g. **Composition:** 0.9250 Silver With Partial Gold Plating 0.2082 oz.

Date	Mintage	MS-63	Proof
2005	62,483	65.00	—

KM# 553 Subject: Tuffed Puffin **Obv:** Head right **Obv. Designer:** Susanna Blunt **Weight:** 7.0000 g. **Composition:** Aureate-Bronze Plated Nickel

Date	Mintage	MS-63	Proof
2005	40,000	30.00	—

Note: In Specimen sets only

KM# 581 Subject: Lullabies Loonie **Obv:** Head right **Obv. Designer:** Susanna Blunt **Rev:** Loon and moon, teddy bear in stars **Weight:** 7.0000 g. **Composition:** 0.9250 Silver 0.2082 oz. ASW

Date	Mintage	MS-63	Proof
2006	—	3.50	—

KM# 582 Subject: Snowy owl **Obv:** Head right **Obv. Designer:** Susanna Blunt **Rev:** Snowy owl with year above **Weight:** 7.0000 g. **Composition:** Aureate-Bronze Plated Nickel

Date	Mintage	MS-63	Proof
2006	40,000	30.00	—

Note: In specimen sets only

KM# 653 Subject: Thayendanegea **Obv:** Head right **Weight:** 25.1750 g. **Composition:** 0.9250 Silver 0.7487 oz. ASW

Date	Mintage	MS-63	Proof
2006(ml)	35,000	30.00	—
2006(ml) Proof	65,000	—	40.00

KM# 656 Subject: Medal of Bravery **Obv:** Head right **Weight:** 28.1750 g. **Composition:** 0.9250 Silver 0.8379 oz. ASW

Date	Mintage	MS-63	Proof
2006	7,846	20.00	—

KM# 656a Subject: Medal of Bravery **Obv:** Head right **Rev:** Maple leaf within wreath. Colorized. **Weight:** 28.1750 g. **Composition:** 0.9250 Silver And Multi-Color Enamel 0.8379 oz.

Date	Mintage	MS-63	Proof
2006	4,951	20.00	—

KM#630 Subject: Olympic Games **Obv:** Crowned head right **Weight:** 7.0000 g. **Composition:** 0.9250 Silver And Multi-Color Enamel 0.2082 oz.

Date	Mintage	MS-63	Proof
2006	19,956	30.00	—

KM# 583 Subject: Victoria Cross **Obv:** Head right **Weight:** 25.1750 g. **Composition:** 0.9250 Silver 0.7487 oz. ASW

Date	Mintage	MS-63	Proof
2006	27,254	26.50	—
2006 Proof	54,835	—	35.00

KM# 583a Subject: Victoria Cross **Obv:** Head right **Weight:** 25.1750 g. **Composition:** 0.9250 Silver With Partial Gold Plating 0.7487 oz.

Date	Mintage	MS-63	Proof
2006 Proof	—	—	60.00

KM# 654 Obv: Head right **Rev:** Snowflake, colorized **Weight:** 7.0000 g. **Composition:** 0.9250 Silver 0.2082 oz. ASW **Note:** Sold in a CD package.

Date	Mintage	MS-63	Proof
2006(ml)	—	30.00	—

KM# 655 Subject: Baby Rattle **Obv:** Head right **Rev:** Baby rattle, colorized **Weight:** 7.0000 g. **Composition:** 0.9250 Silver 0.2082 oz. ASW

Date	Mintage	MS-63	Proof
2006	—	20.00	—

KM# 687 Subject: Joseph Brant **Obv:** Head right **Weight:** 28.1750 g. **Composition:** 0.9250 Silver With Partial Gold Plating 0.8379 oz.

Date	Mintage	MS-63	Proof
2007	—	20.00	—

KM# 688 Subject: Trumpeter Swan **Obv:** Head right **Rev:** Loon **Weight:** 7.0000 g. **Composition:** Aureate-Bronze Plated Nickel

Date	Mintage	MS-63	Proof
2007(ml)	40,000	20.00	—

KM# 705 Rev: Alphabet Letter Blocks **Composition:** Silver

Date	Mintage	MS-63	Proof
2007	—	—	25.00

KM# 706 Subject: Celebration of the Arts **Composition:** Silver

Date	Mintage	MS-63	Proof
2007	—	—	50.00

KM# 707 Rev: Vancouver Olympics "stone man" logo **Composition:** Aureate Bonded Bronze

Date	Mintage	MS-63	Proof
2010 (2007)	—	5.00	—

2 DOLLARS

KM# 270 Obv: Crowned head right within circle, date below **Obv. Designer:** Dora dePedery-Hunt **Rev:** Polar bear right within circle, denomination below **Rev. Designer:** Brent Townsend **Weight:** 7.3000 g. **Composition:** Bi-Metallic **Size:** 28 mm.

Date	Mintage	MS-63	Proof
1996	375,483,000	3.25	—
1996 Proof	—	—	10.00
1997	16,942,000	3.25	—
1998	4,926,000	3.25	—
1998W	—	3.25	—
1999	25,130,000	3.25	—
2000	29,847,000	3.25	—
2000W	—	3.25	—
2001	27,008,000	5.00	—
2001 Proof	—	—	12.50
2002	11,910,000	5.00	—
2002 Proof	—	—	12.50
2003	—	5.00	—
2003 Proof	—	—	12.50

KM# 270b Obv: Crowned head right within circle, date below **Rev:** Polar bear right within circle, denomination below **Edge:** 4.5mm thick **Weight:** 25.0000 g. **Composition:** Bi-Metallic Gold And Silver **Size:** 28 mm.

Date	Mintage	MS-63	P/L	Proof
1996 Proof	10,000	—	—	55.00
1998 Proof	—	—	—	—

KM# 270c Obv: Crowned head right within circle, date below **Rev:** Polar bear right within circle, denomination below **Edge:** 1.8mm thickness **Weight:** 8.8300 g. **Composition:** 0.9250 Silver 0.2626 oz. ASW **Size:** 28 mm.

Date	Mintage	MS-63	Proof
1996 Proof	10,000	—	12.00
1997 Proof	—	—	10.00
1998O Proof	—	—	12.00
1999 Proof	—	—	12.00
2000 Proof	—	—	12.00
2001 Proof	—	—	12.00

KM# 270a Obv: Crowned head right within circle, date below **Rev:** Polar bear right within circle, denomination below **Weight:** 10.8414 g. **Composition:** Bi-Metallic **Size:** 28 mm.

Date	Mintage	MS-63	P/L	Proof
1996 Proof	5,000	—	—	145

KM# 357 Subject: Nunavut **Obv:** Crowned head right within circle, date below **Rev:** Inuit person with drum, denomination below **Rev. Designer:** G. Arnaktavyok **Weight:** 7.3000 g. **Composition:** Bi-Metallic **Size:** 28 mm.

Date	Mintage	MS-63	P/L	Proof
1999	—	3.50	—	—

KM# 357a Subject: Nunavut **Obv:** Crowned head right **Rev:** Drum dancer **Edge:** Interrupted reeding **Weight:** 8.5200 g. **Composition:** 0.9250 Gold Plated Silver 0.2534 oz. ASW AGW **Size:** 28 mm.

Date	Mintage	MS-63	P/L	Proof
1999 Proof	—	—	—	15.00

KM# 357b Subject: Nunavut **Obv:** Crowned head right **Rev:** Drum dancer **Composition:** Gold

Date	Mintage	MS-63	P/L	Proof
1999 Proof	10,000	—	—	175

KM# 399 Subject: Knowledge **Obv:** Crowned head right within circle, denomination below **Rev:** Polar bear and 2 cubs right within circle, date above **Rev. Designer:** Tony Bianco **Edge:** Reeded and plain sections **Weight:** 7.3000 g. **Composition:** Bi-Metallic **Size:** 28 mm.

Date	Mintage	MS-63	Proof
2000	—	3.50	—

KM# 399a Subject: Knowledge **Obv:** Crowned head right within circle, denomination below **Rev:** Polar bear and 2 cubs within circle, date above **Composition:** 0.9250 Gold Plated Silver

Date	Mintage	MS-63	P/L	Proof
2000 Proof	40,000	—	—	15.00

KM# 399b Subject: Knowledge **Obv:** Crowned head right within circle, denomination below **Rev:** Polar bear and two cubs right within circle, date above **Weight:** 6.3100 g. **Composition:** 0.9160 Gold 0.1858 oz. AGW

Date	Mintage	MS-63	P/L	Proof
2000 Proof	—	—	—	175

KM# 449 Subject: Elizabeth II Golden Jubilee **Obv:** Crowned head right, jubilee commemorative dates 1952-2002 **Weight:** 7.3000 g. **Composition:** Bi-Metallic

Date	Mintage	MS-63	Proof
ND(2002)	27,008,000	4.00	—

KM# 449a Subject: Elizabeth II Golden Jubilee **Obv:** Crowned head right, jubilee commemorative dates 1952-2002 **Weight:** 8.8300 g. **Composition:** 0.9250 Silver 0.2626 oz. ASW

Date	Mintage	MS-63	Proof
ND(2002) Proof	100,000	—	14.00

KM# 496 Obv: Head right **Obv. Designer:** Susanna Blunt **Rev. Designer:** Brent Townsend **Weight:** 7.3000 g. **Composition:** Bi-Metallic

Date	Mintage	MS-63	Proof
2003	—	5.00	—
2003W	—	—	18.00
2004	—	5.00	—
2004 Proof	—	—	12.50
2005	—	5.00	—
2005 Proof	—	—	12.50
2006	—	5.00	—
2006 Proof	—	—	12.50

KM# 270d Subject: 100th Anniversary of the Cobalt Silver Strike **Obv:** Crowned head right, within circle, date below **Rev:** Polar bear right, within circle, denomination below **Composition:** Bi-Metallic

Date	Mintage	MS-63	Proof
2003 Proof	100,000	—	25.00

KM# 631a Subject: 10th Anniversary of $2 coin **Obv:** Crowned head right **Rev:** Polar bear **Composition:** Bi-Metallic

Date	Mintage	MS-63	Proof
ND(2006) Proof	3,000	—	385

KM# 631 Subject: 10th Anniversary of $2 coin **Obv:** Crowned head right **Composition:** Bi-Metallic

Date	Mintage	MS-63	Proof
ND(2006)(ml)	—	25.00	—
ND(2006)(ml) Proof	—	—	40.00

KM# 708 Rev: Proud Polar Bear advancing right **Composition:** Silver

Date	Mintage	MS-63	Proof
2004	21,607	—	50.00

KM# 709 Subject: 10th Anniversary, 2 dollar coin **Rev:** "Churchill" Polar Bear, northern lights **Composition:** Bi-Metallic

Date	Mintage	MS-63	Proof
ND (1996-2006)(ml)	—	7.50	—

KM# 710 Obv: Bust left, date at top **Rev:** Polar Bear advancing right **Composition:** Bi-Metallic

Date	Mintage	MS-63	Proof
2006(ml)	—	750	—
2007(ml)	—	750	—

3 DOLLARS

KM# 657 Rev: Beaver within wreath **Composition:** 0.9250 Gold Plated Silver **Shape:** Square **Size:** 27x27 mm.

Date	Mintage	MS-63	Proof
2006	19,963	—	200

5 DOLLARS

KM# 26 Obv: Crowned bust left **Obv. Designer:** E. B. MacKennal **Rev:** Arms within wreath, date and denomination below **Rev. Designer:** W. H. J. Blakemore **Weight:** 8.3592 g. **Composition:** 0.9000 Gold 0.2419 oz. AGW

Date	Mintage	F-12	VF-20	XF-40	AU-50	MS-60	MS-63
1912	165,680	BV	225	250	275	325	800
1913	98,832	BV	225	250	275	325	900
1914	31,122	225	—	350	425	650	3,000

KM# 84 Subject: 1976 Montreal Olympics **Obv:** Young bust right, small maple below, date at right **Rev:** Sailboat "Kingston", date at left, denomination below **Rev. Designer:** Georges Huel **Weight:** 24.3000 g. **Composition:** 0.9250 Silver 0.7226 oz. ASW **Size:** 38 mm. **Note:** Series I.

Date	Mintage	MS-63	Proof
1973	—	11.50	—
1973 Proof	165,203	—	11.50

KM# 85 Subject: 1976 Montreal Olympics **Obv:** Young bust right, small maple leaf below, date at right **Rev:** North American map, denomination below **Rev. Designer:** Georges Huel **Composition:** 0.9250 Silver **Note:** Series I.

Date	Mintage	MS-63	Proof
1973	—	11.50	—
1973 Proof	165,203	—	11.50

KM# 89 Subject: 1976 Montreal Olympics **Obv:** Young bust right, small maple leaf below, date at right **Rev:** Olympic rings, denomination below **Rev. Designer:** Anthony Mann **Weight:** 24.3000 g. **Composition:** 0.9250 Silver 0.7226 oz. ASW **Size:** 38 mm. **Note:** Series II.

Date	Mintage	MS-63	Proof
1974	—	11.50	—
1974 Proof	97,431	—	11.50

KM# 90 Subject: 1976 Montreal Olympics **Obv:** Young bust right, small maple leaf below, date at right **Rev:** Athlete with torch, denomination below **Rev. Designer:** Anthony Mann **Weight:** 24.3000 g. **Composition:** 0.9250 Silver 0.7226 oz. ASW **Size:** 38 mm. **Note:** Series II.

Date	Mintage	MS-63	Proof
1974	—	11.50	—
1974 Proof	97,431	—	11.50

KM# 91 Subject: 1976 Montreal Olympics **Obv:** Young bust right, small maple leaf below, date at right **Rev:** Rower, denomination below **Rev. Designer:** Ken Danby **Weight:** 24.3000 g. **Composition:** 0.9250 Silver 0.7226 oz. ASW **Size:** 38 mm. **Note:** Series III.

Date	Mintage	MS-63	Proof
1974	—	11.50	—
1974 Proof	104,684	—	11.50

KM# 92 Subject: 1976 Montreal Olympics **Obv:** Young bust right, small maple leaf below, date at right **Rev:** Canoeing, denomination below **Rev. Designer:** Ken Danby **Weight:** 24.3000 g. **Composition:** 0.9250 Silver 0.7226 oz. ASW **Size:** 38 mm. **Note:** Series III.

Date	Mintage	MS-63	Proof
1974	—	11.50	—
1974 Proof	104,684	—	11.50

KM# 100 Subject: 1976 Montreal Olympics **Obv:** Young bust right, small maple leaf below, date at right **Rev:** Swimmer, denomination below **Rev. Designer:** Lynda Cooper **Weight:** 24.3000 g. **Composition:** 0.9250 Silver 0.7226 oz. ASW **Size:** 38 mm. **Note:** Series V.

Date	Mintage	MS-63	Proof
1975	—	11.50	—
1975 Proof	89,155	—	11.50

KM# 98 Subject: 1976 Montreal Olympics **Obv:** Young bust right, small maple leaf below, date at right **Rev:** Marathon, denomination below **Rev. Designer:** Leo Yerxa **Weight:** 24.3000 g. **Composition:** 0.9250 Silver 0.7226 oz. ASW **Size:** 38 mm. **Note:** Series IV.

Date	Mintage	MS-63	Proof
1975	—	11.50	—
1975 Proof	89,155	—	11.50

KM# 101 Subject: Montreal 1976 - 21st Summer Olympic Games **Obv:** Young bust right, small maple leaf below, date at right **Rev:** Platform Diver, denomination below **Rev. Designer:** Lynda Cooper **Weight:** 24.3000 g. **Composition:** 0.9250 Silver 0.7226 oz. ASW **Size:** 38 mm. **Note:** Series V.

Date	Mintage	MS-63	Proof
1975	—	11.50	—
1975 Proof	89,155	—	11.50

KM# 99 Subject: Montreal 1976 - 21st Summer Olympic Games **Obv:** Young bust right, small maple leaf below, date at right **Rev:** Women's javelin event, denomination below **Rev. Designer:** Leo Yerxa **Weight:** 24.3000 g. **Composition:** 0.9250 Silver 0.7226 oz. ASW **Size:** 38 mm. **Note:** Series IV.

Date	Mintage	MS-63	Proof
1975	—	11.50	—
1975 Proof	89,155	—	11.50

KM# 107 Subject: 1976 Montreal Olympics **Obv:** Young bust right, small maple leaf below, date at right **Rev:** Fencing, denomination below **Rev. Designer:** Shigeo Fukada **Weight:** 24.3000 g. **Composition:** 0.9250 Silver 0.7226 oz. ASW **Size:** 38 mm. **Note:** Series VI.

Date	Mintage	MS-63	Proof
1976	—	11.50	—
1976 Proof	82,302	—	11.50

KM# 108 Subject: 1976 Montreal Olympics **Obv:**
Young bust right, small maple leaf below, date at
right **Obv. Legend:** Boxing **Rev:** Boxers,
denomination below **Rev. Designer:** Shigeo
Fukada **Weight:** 24.3000 g. **Comp:** 0.9250 Silver
0.7226 oz. ASW **Size:** 38 mm. **Note:** Series VI.

Date	Mintage	MS-63	Proof
1976	—	11.50	—
1976 Proof	82,302	—	11.50

KM# 109 Subject: 1976 Montreal Olympics **Obv:**
Young bust right, small maple leaf below, date at
right **Rev:** Olympic village, denomination below
Rev. Designer: Elliot John Morrison **Weight:**
24.3000 g. **Composition:** 0.9250 Silver 0.7226 oz.
ASW **Size:** 38 mm. **Note:** Series VII.

Date	Mintage	MS-63	Proof
1976	—	11.50	—
1976 Proof	76,908	—	11.50

KM# 110 Subject: 1976 Montreal Olympics **Obv:**
Young bust right, maple leaf below, date at right
Rev: Olympic flame, denomination below
Rev. Designer: Elliot John Morrison **Weight:**
24.3000 g. **Composition:** 0.9250 Silver 0.7226 oz.
ASW **Size:** 38 mm. **Note:** Series VII.

Date	Mintage	MS-63	Proof
1976	—	11.50	—
1976 Proof	79,102	—	11.50

KM# 316 Subject: Dr. Norman Bethune **Obv:**
Young bust right **Rev:** Bethune and party, date at
upper right **Rev. Designer:** Harvey Chan **Weight:**
31.3900 g. **Comp:** 0.9999 Silver 1.0091 oz. ASW

Date	Mintage	MS-63	Proof
1998 Proof	61,000	—	30.00

KM# 398 Obv: Young bust right **Rev:** Viking ship
under sail **Rev. Designer:** Donald Curley
Composition: Copper-Zinc-Nickel **Note:** Sold in
sets with Norway 20 kroner, KM#465.

Date	Mintage	MS-63	Proof
1999 Proof	—	—	18.50

KM# 435 Subject: Guglielmo Marconi **Obv:**
Crowned head right **Rev:** Gold-plated cameo
portrait of Marconi **Rev. Designer:** Cosme Saffioti
Edge: Reeded **Weight:** 16.8600 g. **Composition:**
0.9250 Silver 0.5014 oz. ASW **Size:** 28.4 mm.
Note: Only issued in two coin set with British 2
pounds KM#1014a.

Date	Mintage	MS-63	Proof
ND(2001) Proof	30,000	—	22.00

KM# 519 Obv: Crowned head right **Rev:** National
arms **Edge:** Reeded **Weight:** 8.3600 g. **Comp:**
0.9000 Gold 0.2419 oz. AGW **Size:** 21.6 mm.

Date	Mintage	MS-63	Proof
ND (2002) Proof	2,002	—	245

KM# 518 Subject: F.I.F.A. World Cup Soccer ,
Germany 2006 **Obv:** Crowned head right,
denomination **Rev:** Goalie on knees **Edge:** Reeded
Weight: 31.1200 g. **Composition:** 0.9999 Silver
1.0004 oz. ASW **Size:** 38 mm.

Date	Mintage	MS-63	Proof
2003 Proof	21,542	—	29.00

KM# 514 Obv: Crowned head right **Rev:** Moose
Edge: Reeded **Weight:** 31.1200 g. **Composition:**
0.9999 Silver 1.0004 oz. ASW **Size:** 38 mm.

Date	Mintage	MS-63	Proof
2004 Proof	25,555	—	120

KM#527 Subject: Golf, Championship of Canada,
Centennial **Obv:** Head right **Weight:** 31.1200 g.
Composition: 0.9999 Silver 1.0004 oz. ASW

Date	Mintage	MS-63	Proof
2004 Proof	18,750	—	25.00

KM# 607 Obv: Head right **Rev:** Maple leaf, winter
colors **Weight:** 31.1200 g. **Composition:** 0.9999
Silver 1.0004 oz. ASW

Date	Mintage	MS-63	Proof
2004	—	35.00	—

KM# 556.1 Subject: WWII Veterans **Obv:** Head
right **Rev:** Large V and three portraits **Weight:**
31.1200 g. **Composition:** 0.9990 Silver 0.9995 oz.
ASW **Size:** 38 mm.

Date	Mintage	MS-63	Proof
2005	25,000	35.00	—

KM# 554 Subject: Alberta **Obv. Designer:** Head
right **Rev. Designer:** Michelle Grant **Weight:**
31.1200 g. **Composition:** 0.9999 Silver 1.0004 oz.
ASW

Date	Mintage	MS-63	Proof
2005 Proof	20,000	—	35.00

KM#555 Subject: Saskatchewan **Obv:** Head right
Obv. Designer: Susanna Blunt **Rev. Designer:**
Paulett Sapergia **Weight:** 31.1200 g.
Composition: 0.9999 Silver 1.0004 oz. ASW

Date	Mintage	MS-63	Proof
2005 Proof	20,000	—	35.00

Reeded **Weight:** 31.1200 g. **Composition:** 0.9990
Silver 0.9995 oz. ASW **Size:** 38 mm.

Date	Mintage	MS-63	Proof
2005	10,000	50.00	—

KM# 557 Subject: Walrus and calf **Obv:** Head
right **Obv. Designer:** Susanna Blunt **Rev:** Two
walrusus and calf **Rev. Designer:** Pierre Leduc
Weight: 31.1200 g. **Composition:** 0.9999 Silver
1.0004 oz. ASW

Date	Mintage	MS-63	Proof
2005 Proof	5,519	—	35.00

KM# 558 Subject: White tailed deer **Obv:** Head
right **Obv. Designer:** Susanna Blunt **Rev:** Two deer
standing **Rev. Designer:** Xerxes Irani **Weight:**
31.1200 g. **Composition:** 0.9999 Silver 1.0004 oz.
ASW

Date	Mintage	MS-63	Proof
2005 Proof	6,439	—	35.00

KM# 585 Obv: Head right **Obv. Designer:**
Susanna Blunt **Rev:** Peregrine Falcon feeding
young ones **Rev. Designer:** Dwayne Harty **Weight:**
31.1200 g. **Comp:** 0.9999 Silver 1.0004 oz. ASW

Date	Mintage	MS-63	Proof
2006 Proof	6,145	—	40.00

KM#586 Subject: Sable Island horses **Obv:** Head
right **Obv. Designer:** Susanna Blunt **Rev:** Horse
and foal standing **Rev. Designer:** Christie Paquet
Weight: 31.1200 g. **Composition:** 0.9999 Silver
1.0004 oz. ASW

Date	Mintage	MS-63	Proof
2006 Proof	7,589	—	40.00

KM# 658 Subject: Breast Cancer Awareness
Rev: Colorized pink ribbon **Weight:** 31.1200 g.
Composition: 0.9999 Silver 1.0004 oz. ASW

Date	Mintage	MS-63	Proof
2006 Proof	11,048	—	50.00

KM#659 Subject: C.A.F. Snowbirds Acrobatic Jet
Flying Team **Weight:** 31.1200 g. **Composition:**
0.9999 Silver 1.0004 oz. ASW

Date	Mintage	MS-63	Proof
2006 Proof	7,896	—	50.00

8 DOLLARS

KM# 556.2 Subject: WW II **Obv:** Elizabeth II **Rev:**
Three military portraits and letter V on large maple
leaf flanked by two small maple leaves **Edge:**

KM# 515 Obv: Head right **Obv. Designer:**
Susanna Blunt **Rev:** Grizzly bear walking left **Edge:**
Reeded **Weight:** 28.8000 g. **Composition:** 0.9250
Silver 0.8565 oz. ASW **Size:** 39 mm.

Date	Mintage	MS-63	Proof
2004 Proof	12,942	—	60.00

KM# 597 Subject: Canadian Pacific Railway, 120th Anniversary **Obv:** Head right **Obv. Designer:** Susanna Blunt **Rev:** Railway bridge **Weight:** 32.1500 g. **Comp:** 0.9999 Silver 1.0335 oz. ASW

Date	Mintage	MS-63	Proof
2005 Proof	12,942	—	50.00

KM#598 Subject: Canadian Pacific Railway, 120th Anniversary **Obv:** Head right **Rev:** Railway memorial to the Chinese workers **Weight:** 32.1500 g. **Composition:** 0.9999 Silver 1.0335 oz. ASW

Date	Mintage	MS-63	Proof
2005 Proof	9,892	—	50.00

10 DOLLARS

KM# 27 Obv: Crowned bust left **Obv. Designer:** E. B. MacKennal **Rev:** Arms within wreath, date and denomination below **Rev. Designer:** W. H. J. Blakemore **Weight:** 16.7185 g. **Composition:** 0.9000 Gold 0.4837 oz. AGW

Date	Mintage	F-12	VF-20	XF-40	AU-50	MS-60	MS-63
1912	74,759	BV	BV	450	500	800	3,000
1913	149,232	BV	BV	450	500	800	3,000
1914	140,068	BV	450	500	550	1,000	4,000

KM# 86.1 Subject: 1976 Montreal Olympics **Obv:** Young bust right, maple leaf below, date at right **Rev:** World map, denomination below **Rev. Designer:** Georges Huel **Weight:** 48.6000 g. **Composition:** 0.9250 Silver 1.4453 oz. ASW **Size:** 45 mm. **Note:** Series I.

Date	Mintage	MS-63	Proof
1973 Proof	165,203	—	23.00
1973	103,426	23.00	—

KM# 87 Subject: 1976 Montreal Olympics **Obv:** Young bust right, small maple leaf below, date at right **Rev:** Montreal skyline, denomination below **Rev. Designer:** Georges Huel **Weight:** 48.6000 g. **Composition:** 0.9250 Silver 1.4453 oz. ASW **Size:** 45 mm. **Note:** Series I.

Date	Mintage	MS-63	Proof
1973	—	23.00	—
1973 Proof	165,203	—	23.00

KM# 86.2 Subject: 1976 Montreal Olympics **Obv:** Young bust right, small maple leaf below, date at right **Rev:** World map **Rev. Designer:** Georges Huel **Weight:** 48.6000 g. **Composition:** 0.9250 Silver 1.4453 oz. ASW **Size:** 45 mm. **Note:** Series I.

Date	Mintage	MS-63	Proof
1974	320	275	—

Note: Error: mule

KM# 93 Subject: 1976 Montreal Olympics **Obv:** Young bust right, small maple leaf below, date at right **Rev:** Head of Zeus, denomination below **Rev. Designer:** Anthony Mann **Weight:** 48.6000 g. **Composition:** 0.9250 Silver 1.4453 oz. ASW **Size:** 45 mm. **Note:** Series II.

Date	Mintage	MS-63	Proof
1974 Proof	104,684	—	23.00
1974	—	23.00	—

KM# 94 **Subject:** 1976 Montreal Olympics **Obv:**
Young bust right, small maple leaf below, date at
right **Rev:** Temple of Zeus, denomination below
Rev. Designer: Anthony Mann **Weight:** 48.6000 g.
Composition: 0.9250 Silver 1.4453 oz. ASW **Size:**
45 mm. **Note:** Series II.

Date	Mintage	MS-63	Proof
1974	—	23.00	—
1974 Proof	104,684	—	23.00

KM# 95 **Subject:** 1976 Montreal Olympics **Obv:**
Young bust right, small maple leaf below, date at
right **Rev:** Cycling, denomination below
Rev. Designer: Ken Danby **Weight:** 48.6000 g.
Composition: 0.9250 Silver 1.4453 oz. ASW **Size:**
45 mm. **Note:** Series III.

Date	Mintage	MS-63	Proof
1974	—	23.00	—
1974 Proof	97,431	—	23.00

KM# 96 **Subject:** 1976 Montreal Olympics **Obv:**
Young bust right, small maple leaf below, date at
right **Rev:** Lacrosse, denomination below

Rev. Designer: Ken Danby **Weight:** 48.6000 g.
Composition: 0.9250 Silver 1.4453 oz. ASW **Size:**
45 mm. **Note:** Series III.

Date	Mintage	MS-63	Proof
1974	—	23.00	—
1974 Proof	97,431	—	23.00

KM# 102 **Subject:** 1976 Montreal Olympics **Obv:**
Young bust right, small maple leaf below, date at
right **Rev:** Men's hurdles, denomination below
Rev. Designer: Leo Yerxa **Weight:** 48.6000 g.
Composition: 0.9250 Silver 1.4453 oz. ASW **Size:**
45 mm. **Note:** Series IV.

Date	Mintage	MS-63	Proof
1975	—	23.00	—
1975 Proof	82,302	—	23.00

KM# 103 **Subject:** Montreal 1976 - 21st Summer
Olympic Games **Obv:** Young bust right, small maple
leaf below, date at right **Rev:** Women's shot put,
denomination below **Rev. Designer:** Leo Yerxa
Weight: 48.6000 g. **Composition:** 0.9250 Silver
1.4453 oz. ASW **Size:** 45 mm. **Note:** Series IV.

Date	Mintage	MS-63	Proof
1975	—	23.00	—
1975 Proof	82,302	—	23.00

KM# 104 Subject: 1976 Montreal Olympics **Obv:** Young bust right, small maple leaf below, date at right **Rev:** Sailing, denomination below **Rev. Designer:** Lynda Cooper **Weight:** 48.6000 g. **Composition:** 0.9250 Silver 1.4453 oz. ASW **Size:** 45 mm. **Note:** Series V.

Date	Mintage	MS-63	Proof
1975	—	23.00	—
1975 Proof	89,155	—	23.00

KM# 105 Subject: 1976 Montreal Olympics **Obv:** Young bust right, small maple leaf below, date at right **Rev:** Canoeing, denomination below **Rev. Designer:** Lynda Cooper **Weight:** 48.6000 g. **Composition:** 0.9250 Silver 1.4453 oz. ASW **Size:** 45 mm. **Note:** Series V.

Date	Mintage	MS-63	Proof
1975	—	23.00	—
1975 Proof	89,155	—	23.00

KM# 111 Subject: 1976 Montreal Olympics **Obv:** Young bust right, small maple leaf below, date at right **Rev:** Football, denomination below

Rev. Designer: Shigeo Fukada **Weight:** 48.6000 g. **Composition:** 0.9250 Silver 1.4453 oz. ASW **Size:** 45 mm. **Note:** Series VI.

Date	Mintage	MS-63	Proof
1976 Proof	76,908	—	23.00
1976	—	23.00	—

KM# 112 Subject: 1976 Montreal Olympics **Obv:** Young bust right, small maple leaf below, date at right **Rev:** Field hockey **Rev. Designer:** Shigeo Fukada **Weight:** 48.6000 g. **Composition:** 0.9250 Silver 1.4453 oz. ASW **Size:** 45 mm. **Note:** Series VI.

Date	Mintage	MS-63	Proof
1976	—	23.00	—
1976 Proof	76,908	—	23.00

KM# 113 Subject: 1976 Montreal Olympics **Obv:** Young bust right, small maple leaf below, date at right **Rev:** Olympic Stadium, denomination below **Rev. Designer:** Elliot John Morrison **Weight:** 48.6000 g. **Composition:** 0.9250 Silver 1.4453 oz. ASW **Size:** 45 mm. **Note:** Series VII.

Date	Mintage	MS-63	Proof
1976	—	23.00	—
1976 Proof	79,102	—	23.00

10 DOLLARS

KM# 114 Subject: 1976 Montreal Olympics **Obv:**
Young bust right, small maple leaf below, date at
right **Rev:** Olympic Velodrome, denomination below
Rev. Designer: Elliot John Morrison **Weight:**
48.6000 g. **Composition:** 0.9250 Silver 1.4453 oz.
ASW **Size:** 45 mm. **Note:** Series VII.

Date	Mintage	MS-63	Proof
1976	—	23.00	—
1976 Proof	79,102	—	23.00

KM# 520 Obv: Crowned head right **Rev:** National
arms **Edge:** Reeded **Weight:** 16.7200 g. **Comp:**
0.9000 Gold 0.4838 oz. AGW **Size:** 26.92 mm.

Date	Mintage	MS-63	Proof
ND (2002) Proof	2,002	—	475

KM# 559 Subject: Pope John Paul II **Obv:** Head
right **Weight:** 25.1750 g. **Composition:** 0.9999
Silver 0.8093 oz. ASW

Date	Mintage	MS-63	Proof
2005 Proof	24,716	—	35.00

KM# 661 Subject: National Historic Sites **Obv:**
Head right **Rev:** Fortress of Louisbourg **Weight:**
25.1750 g. **Comp:** 0.9999 Silver 0.8093 oz. ASW

Date	Mintage	MS-63	Proof
2006	15,000	35.00	—

15 DOLLARS

KM# 215 Subject: 1992 Olympics **Obv:** Crowned
head right, date at left, denomination below **Rev:**
Coaching track **Rev. Designer:** Stewart Sherwood
Weight: 33.6300 g. **Composition:** 0.9250 Silver
1.0000 oz. ASW **Size:** 39 mm.

Date	Mintage	MS-63	Proof
1992 Proof	275,000	—	28.00

KM# 216 Subject: 1992 Olympics **Obv:** Crowned
head right, date at left, denomination below **Rev:**
High jump, rings, speed skating **Rev. Designer:**
David Craig **Weight:** 33.6300 g. **Composition:**
0.9250 Silver 1.0000 oz. ASW

Date	Mintage	MS-63	Proof
1992 Proof	275,000	—	28.00

KM#304 Subject: Year of the Tiger **Obv:** Crowned head right **Rev:** Tiger within octagon at center, animal figures surround **Rev. Designer:** Harvey Chan **Composition:** Bi-Metallic **Size:** 40 mm.

Date	Mintage	MS-63	Proof
1998 Proof	68,888	—	275

KM# 331 Subject: Year of the Rabbitt **Obv:** Crowned head right **Rev:** Rabbit within octagon at center, animal figures surround **Rev. Designer:** Harvey Chan **Composition:** Bi-Metallic

Date	Mintage	MS-63	Proof
1999 Proof	—	—	35.00

KM# 387 Subject: Year of the Dragon **Obv:** Crowned head right **Rev. Designer:** Harvey Chan **Composition:** Bi-Metallic

Date	Mintage	MS-63	Proof
2000 Proof	—	—	125

KM# 415 Subject: Year of the Snake **Obv:** Crowned head right **Rev:** Snake within circle of lunar calendar signs **Rev. Designer:** Harvey Chain **Edge:** Reeded **Weight:** 33.6300 g. **Composition:** 0.9250 Silver 1.0000 oz. ASW **Size:** 40 mm.

Date	Mintage	MS-63	Proof
2001 Proof	60,754	—	35.00
2001 Proof	60,754	—	35.00

KM# 463 Subject: Year of the Horse **Obv:** Crowned head right **Obv. Designer:** Dora dePédery-Hunt **Rev:** Horse in center with Chinese Lunar calendar around **Rev. Designer:** Harvey Chain **Weight:** 33.6300 g. **Composition:** 0.9250 Silver 1.0000 oz. ASW

Date	Mintage	MS-63	Proof
2002 Proof	59,395	—	65.00

KM# 481 Subject: Year of the Sheep **Obv:** Crowned head right **Rev:** Sheep in center with Chinese Lunar calendar around **Rev. Designer:** Harvey Chain **Weight:** 33.6300 g. **Composition:** 0.9250 Silver 1.0000 oz. ASW **Size:** 40 mm.

Date	Mintage	MS-63	Proof
2003 Proof	53,714	—	60.00

KM# 610 Subject: Year of the Monkey **Obv:** Crowned head right **Rev:** Monkey in center with Chinese Lunar calendar around **Weight:** 33.6300 g. **Composition:** 0.9250 Silver 1.0000 oz. ASW

Date	Mintage	MS-63	Proof
2004 Proof	46,175	—	75.00

KM# 560 Subject: Year of the Rooster **Obv:** Crowned head right **Rev:** Rooster in center with Chinese Lunar calendar around **Weight:** 33.6300 g. **Composition:** 0.9250 Silver 1.0000 oz. ASW

Date	Mintage	MS-63	Proof
2005 Proof	44,690	—	75.00

KM# 587 Subject: Year of the Dog **Obv:** Crowned head left **Rev:** Dog in center with Chinese Lunar calendar around **Weight:** 33.6300 g. **Composition:** 0.9250 Silver 1.0000 oz. ASW

Date	Mintage	MS-63	Proof
2006 Proof	41,617	—	65.00

KM# 662 Subject: Year of the Pig **Obv:** Crowned head right **Rev:** Pig in center with Chinese Lunar calendar around **Weight:** 33.6300 g. **Composition:** 0.9250 Silver 1.0000 oz. ASW

Date	Mintage	MS-63	Proof
2006 Proof	48,888	—	80.00

20 DOLLARS

KM#71 Subject: Centennial **Obv:** Crowned head right **Rev:** Crowned and supported arms **Edge:** Reeded **Weight:** 18.2733 g. **Composition:** 0.9000 Gold 0.5287 oz. AGW **Size:** 27.05 mm.

Date	Mintage	MS-63	Proof
1967 Proof	337,688	—	450

KM# 147 Subject: 1988 Calgary Olympics **Obv:** Young bust right, small maple leaf below, date at right **Rev:** Biathlon, denomination below **Rev. Designer:** John Mardon **Edge:** Lettered **Weight:** 33.6300 g. **Composition:** 0.9250 Silver 1.0000 oz. ASW **Size:** 40 mm.

Date	Mintage	MS-63	Proof
1986 Proof	308,086	—	21.50
1986 Proof	Inc. above	—	175
Note: Plain edge			

KM# 145 Subject: 1988 Calgary Olympics **Obv:** Young bust right, maple leaf below, date at right **Rev:** Downhill skier, denomination below **Rev. Designer:** Ian Stewart **Edge:** Lettered **Weight:** 33.6300 g. **Composition:** 0.9250 Silver 1.0000 oz. ASW **Size:** 40 mm.

Date	Mintage	MS-63	Proof
1985 Proof	406,360	—	21.50
1985 Proof	Inc. above	—	175
Note: Plain edge			

KM# 148 Subject: 1988 Calgary Olympics **Obv:** Young bust right, small maple leaf below, date at right **Rev:** Hockey, denomination below **Rev. Designer:** Ian Stewart **Edge:** Lettered **Weight:** 33.6300 g. **Composition:** 0.9250 Silver 1.0000 oz. ASW **Size:** 40 mm.

Date	Mintage	MS-63	Proof
1986 Proof	396,602	—	21.50
1986 Proof	Inc. above	—	175
Note: Plain edge			

KM# 146 Subject: 1988 Calgary Olympics **Obv:** Young bust right, small maple leaf below, date at right **Rev:** Speed skater, denomination below **Rev. Designer:** Friedrich Peter **Edge:** Lettered **Weight:** 33.6300 g. **Composition:** 0.9250 Silver 1.0000 oz. ASW **Size:** 40 mm.

Date	Mintage	MS-63	Proof
1985 Proof	354,222	—	21.50
1985 Proof	Inc. above	—	175
Note: Plain edge			

KM# 150 Subject: Calgary 1988 - 15th Winter Olympic Games **Obv:** Young bust right, small maple leaf below, date at right **Rev:** Cross-country skier, denomination below **Rev. Designer:** Ian Stewart **Edge:** Lettered **Weight:** 33.6300 g. **Composition:** 0.9250 Silver 1.0000 oz. ASW **Size:** 40 mm.

Date	Mintage	MS-63	Proof
1986 Proof	303,199	—	21.50

KM# 151 Subject: 1988 Calgary Olympics **Obv:** Young bust right, small maple leaf below, date at right **Rev:** Free-style skier, denomination below **Rev. Designer:** Walter Ott **Edge:** Lettered **Weight:** 33.6300 g. **Composition:** 0.9250 Silver 1.0000 oz. ASW **Size:** 40 mm.

Date	Mintage	MS-63	Proof
1986 Proof	294,322	—	21.50
1986 Proof	Inc. above	—	175

Note: Plain edge

KM# 159 Subject: 1988 Calgary Olympics **Obv:** Young bust right, small maple leaf below, date at right **Rev:** Ski jumper, denomination below **Rev. Designer:** Raymond Taylor **Edge:** Lettered **Weight:** 34.1070 g. **Composition:** 0.9250 Silver 1.0143 oz. ASW **Size:** 40 mm.

Date	Mintage	MS-63	Proof
1987 Proof	290,954	—	21.50

KM# 155 Subject: Calgary 1988 - 15th Winter Olympic Games **Obv:** Young bust right, small maple leaf below, date at right **Rev:** Figure skating pairs event, denomination below **Rev. Designer:** Raymond Taylor **Edge:** Lettered **Weight:** 34.1070 g. **Composition:** 0.9250 Silver 1.0143 oz. ASW **Size:** 40 mm.

Date	Mintage	MS-63	Proof
1987 Proof	334,875	—	21.50

KM# 160 Subject: 1988 Calgary Olympics **Obv:** Young bust right, maple leaf below, date at right **Rev:** Bobsled, denomination below **Rev. Designer:** John Mardon **Edge:** Lettered **Weight:** 34.1070 g. **Comp:** 0.9250 Silver 1.0143 oz. ASW **Size:** 40 mm.

Date	Mintage	MS-63	Proof
1987 Proof	274,326	—	21.50

KM# 156 Subject: 1988 Calgary Olympics **Obv:** Young bust right, small maple leaf below, date at right **Rev:** Curling, denomination below **Rev. Designer:** Ian Stewart **Edge:** Lettered **Weight:** 34.1070 g. **Composition:** 0.9250 Silver 1.0143 oz. ASW **Size:** 40 mm.

Date	Mintage	MS-63	Proof
1987 Proof	286,457	—	21.50

KM# 172 Subject: Aviation **Obv:** Crowned head right, date below **Rev:** Lancaster, Fauquier in cameo, denomination below **Rev. Designer:**

Robert R. Carmichael **Weight:** 31.1030 g. **Comp:** 0.9250 Silver 0.9249 oz. ASW **Size:** 38 mm.

Date	Mintage	MS-63	Proof
1990 Proof	43,596	—	100
1990 Proof	43,596	—	100

KM# 196 Subject: Aviation **Obv:** Crowned head right, date below **Rev:** Silver Dart, John A. D. McCurdy and F. W. "Casey" Baldwin in cameo, denomination below **Rev. Designer:** George Velinger **Weight:** 31.1030 g. **Composition:** 0.9250 Silver 0.9249 oz. ASW **Size:** 38 mm.

Date	Mintage	MS-63	Proof
1991 Proof	28,791	—	30.00
1991 Proof	28,791	—	30.00

KM# 197 Subject: Aviation **Obv:** Crowned head right, date below **Rev:** de Haviland Beaver, Philip C. Garratt in cameo, denomination below **Rev. Designer:** Peter Massman **Weight:** 31.1030 g. **Composition:** 0.9250 Silver 0.9249 oz. ASW **Size:** 38 mm.

Date	Mintage	MS-63	Proof
1991 Proof	29,399	—	30.00
1991 Proof	29,399	—	30.00

KM# 224 Subject: Aviation **Obv:** Crowned head right, date below **Rev:** Curtiss JN-4 Canick ("Jenny"), Sir Frank W. Baillie in cameo, denomination below **Rev. Designer:** George Velinger **Weight:** 31.1030 g. **Composition:** 0.9250 Silver 0.9249 oz. ASW **Size:** 38 mm.

Date	Mintage	MS-63	Proof
1992 Proof	33,105	—	30.00
1992 Proof	33,105	—	30.00

KM# 225 Subject: Aviation **Obv:** Crowned head right, date below **Rev:** de Haviland Gypsy Moth, Murton A. Seymour in cameo, denomination below **Rev. Designer:** John Mardon **Weight:** 31.1030 g. **Comp:** 0.9250 Silver 0.9249 oz. ASW **Size:** 38 mm.

Date	Mintage	MS-63	Proof
1992 Proof	32,537	—	30.00
1992 Proof	32,537	—	30.00

KM# 237 Subject: Aviation **Obv:** Crowned head right, date below **Rev:** Lockheed 14, Zebulon Lewis Leigh in cameo, denomination below **Rev. Designer:** Robert R. Carmichael **Weight:** 31.1030 g. **Composition:** 0.9250 Silver 0.9249 oz. ASW **Size:** 38 mm.

Date	Mintage	MS-63	Proof
1993 Proof	32,550	—	30.00
1993 Proof	32,550	—	30.00

KM# 247 Subject: Aviation **Obv:** Crowned head right, date below **Rev:** Vickers Vedette, Wilfred T. Reid in cameo, denomination below **Rev. Designer:** Robert R. Carmichael **Weight:** 31.1030 g. **Composition:** 0.9250 Silver 0.9249 oz. ASW **Size:** 38 mm.

Date	Mintage	MS-63	Proof
1994 Proof	30,880	—	30.00
1994 Proof	30,880	—	30.00

KM# 271 Subject: Aviation **Obv:** Crowned head right, date below **Rev:** C-FEA1 Fleet Cannuck, denomination below **Rev. Designer:** Robert Bradford **Weight:** 31.1030 g. **Composition:** 0.9250 Silver 0.9249 oz. ASW **Size:** 38 mm.

Date	Mintage	MS-63	Proof
1995 Proof	17,438	—	30.00
1995 Proof	17,438	—	30.00

KM# 272 Subject: Aviation **Obv:** Crowned head right, date below **Rev:** DHC-1 Chipmunk, denomination below **Rev. Designer:** Robert Bradford **Weight:** 31.1030 g. **Composition:** 0.9250 Silver 0.9249 oz. ASW **Size:** 38 mm.

Date	Mintage	MS-63	Proof
1995 Proof	17,722	—	30.00
1995 Proof	17,722	—	30.00

KM# 276 Subject: Aviation **Obv:** Crowned head right, date below **Rev:** CF-100 Cannuck, denomination below **Rev. Designer:** Jim Bruce **Weight:** 31.1030 g. **Composition:** 0.9250 Silver 0.9249 oz. ASW **Size:** 38 mm.

Date	Mintage	MS-63	Proof
1996 Proof	18,508	—	32.50
1996 Proof	18,508	—	32.50

KM# 277 Subject: Aviation **Obv:** Crowned head right, date below **Obv. Legend:** CF-105 Arrow, denomination below **Rev. Designer:** Jim Bruce **Weight:** 31.1030 g. **Composition:** 0.9250 Silver 0.9249 oz. ASW **Size:** 38 mm.

Date	Mintage	MS-63	Proof
1996 Proof	27,163	—	65.00
1996 Proof	27,163	—	65.00

KM# 297 Subject: Aviation **Obv:** Crowned head right, date below **Rev:** Canadair F-86 Sabre, denomination below **Rev. Designer:** Ross Buckland **Weight:** 31.1030 g. **Composition:** 0.9250 Silver 0.9249 oz. ASW **Size:** 38 mm.

Date	Mintage	MS-63	Proof
1997 Proof	14,389	—	30.00
1997 Proof	14,389	—	30.00

KM# 329 Subject: Aviation **Obv:** Crowned head, right, date below **Rev:** CP-107 Argus, denomination below **Weight:** 31.1030 g. **Composition:** 0.9250 Silver 0.9249 oz. ASW **Size:** 38 mm.

Date	Mintage	MS-63	Proof
1998 Proof	Est. 50,000	—	37.50
1998 Proof	Est. 50,000	—	37.50

KM# 330 Subject: Aviation **Obv:** Crowned head right, date below **Rev:** CP-215 Waterbomber, denomination below **Rev. Designer:** Peter Mossman **Weight:** 31.1030 g. **Composition:** 0.9250 Silver 0.9249 oz. ASW **Size:** 38 mm.

Date	Mintage	MS-63	Proof
1998 Proof	Est. 50,000	—	37.50
1998 Proof	Est. 50,000	—	37.50

KM# 395 Subject: First Canadian locomotive **Obv:** Crowned head right, date below **Rev:** Locomotive below multicolored cameo, denomination below **Composition:** 0.9250 Silver **Size:** 38 mm.

Date	Mintage	MS-63	Proof
2000 Proof	—	—	40.00

KM# 339 Subject: Aviation **Obv:** Crowned head right, date below **Rev:** DHC-6 Twin Otter, denomination below **Rev. Designer:** Neil Aird **Weight:** 31.1030 g. **Composition:** 0.9250 Silver 0.9249 oz. ASW **Size:** 38 mm.

Date	Mintage	MS-63	Proof
1999 Proof	Est. 50,000	—	37.50
1999 Proof	Est. 50,000	—	37.50

KM# 396 Subject: First Canadian self-propelled car **Obv:** Crowned head right, date below **Rev:** Car below multicolored cameo, denomination below **Composition:** 0.9250 Silver **Size:** 38 mm.

Date	Mintage	MS-63	Proof
2000 Proof	—	—	40.00

KM# 340 Subject: Aviation **Obv:** Crowned head right, date below **Rev:** DHC-8 Dash 8, denomination below **Weight:** 31.1030 g. **Composition:** 0.9250 Silver 0.9249 oz. ASW **Size:** 38 mm.

Date	Mintage	MS-63	Proof
1999 Proof	50,000,000	—	37.50
1999 Proof	50,000,000	—	37.50

KM# 397 Subject: Bluenose sailboat **Obv:** Crowned head right, date below **Rev:** Bluenose sailing left below multicolored cameo, denomination below **Composition:** 0.9250 Silver **Size:** 38 mm.

Date	Mintage	MS-63	Proof
2000 Proof	—	—	150

KM# 411 Subject: Transportation - Steam Locomotive **Obv:** Crowned head right **Obv. Designer:** Dora dePédery-Hunt **Rev:** First Canadian Steel Steam Locomotive and cameo hologram **Rev. Designer:** Don Curely **Edge:** Reeded and plain sections **Weight:** 31.1035 g. **Composition:** 0.9250 Silver 0.9250 oz. ASW **Size:** 38 mm.

Date	Mintage	MS-63	Proof
2001 Proof	15,000	—	35.00

KM# 427 Subject: Transportation - The Marco Polo, **Obv:** Crowned head right **Rev:** Sailship with hologram cameo **Rev. Designer:** J. Franklin Wright **Edge:** Reeded and plain sections **Weight:** 31.1030 g. **Composition:** 0.9250 Silver 0.9249 oz. ASW **Size:** 38 mm.

Date	Mintage	MS-63	Proof
2001 Proof	15,000	—	35.00

KM# 428 Subject: Transportation - Russell Touring Car, **Obv:** Crowned head right **Rev:** Russell touring car with hologram cameo **Rev. Designer:** John Mardon **Edge:** Reeded and plain sections **Weight:** 31.1030 g. **Composition:** 0.9250 Silver 0.9249 oz. ASW **Size:** 38 mm.

Date	Mintage	MS-63	Proof
2001 Proof	15,000	—	35.00

KM# 464 Obv: Crowned head right **Obv. Designer:** Dora dePédery-Hunt **Rev:** Gray-Dort Model 25-SM with cameo hologram **Rev. Designer:** John Mardon **Weight:** 31.1030 g. **Composition:** 0.9250 Silver 0.9249 oz. ASW

Date	Mintage	MS-63	Proof
2002 Proof	15,000	—	40.00

KM# 465 Obv: Crowned head right **Obv. Designer:** Dora dePédery-Hunt **Rev:** Sailing ship William D. Lawrence **Rev. Designer:** Bonnie Ross **Weight:** 31.1030 g. **Composition:** 0.9250 Silver 0.9249 oz. ASW

Date	Mintage	MS-63	Proof
2002 Proof	15,000	—	40.00

KM# 484 Subject: Canadian National FA-1 diesel-electric locomotive **Obv:** Crowned head right **Obv. Designer:** Dora dePédery-Hunt **Rev. Designer:** John Mardon, William Woodruff **Composition:** 0.9250 Silver

Date	Mintage	MS-63	Proof
2003 Proof	15,000	—	40.00

KM# 485 Obv: Crowned head right **Obv. Designer:** Dora dePédery-Hunt **Rev:** The Bricklin SV-1 **Rev. Designer:** Brian Hughes, José Oslo **Weight:** 31.1030 g. **Composition:** 0.9250 Silver With Partial Gold Plating 0.9249 oz.

Date	Mintage	MS-63	Proof
2003 Proof	15,000	—	45.00

KM# 482 Obv: Crowned head right **Obv. Designer:** Dora dePédery-Hunt **Rev:** Niagara Falls hologram **Rev. Designer:** Gary Corcoran **Weight:** 31.3900 g. **Composition:** 0.9999 Silver 1.0091 oz. ASW

Date	Mintage	MS-63	Proof
2003 Proof	29,967	—	65.00

KM# 483 Subject: The HMCS Bras d'or (FHE-400) **Obv:** Crowned head right **Obv. Designer:** Dora dePédery-Hunt **Rev:** Ship in water **Rev. Designer:** Donald Curley, Stan Witten **Weight:** 31.1030 g. **Composition:** 0.9250 Silver 0.9249 oz. ASW

Date	Mintage	MS-63	Proof
2003 Proof	15,000	—	40.00

KM# 523 Subject: Canadian Rockies, colorized **Obv:** Crowned head right **Obv. Designer:** Dora dePédery-Hunt **Rev:** Canadian Rockies **Weight:** 31.3900 g. **Comp:** 0.9990 Silver 1.0082 oz. ASW

Date	Mintage	MS-63	Proof
2003 Proof	29,967	—	50.00

KM# 611 Obv: Head right **Obv. Designer:** Susanna Blunt **Rev:** Iceburg, hologram **Weight:** 31.3900 g. **Comp:** 0.9999 Silver 1.0091 oz. ASW

Date	Mintage	MS-63	Proof
2004 Proof	24,879	—	55.00

KM# 561 Subject: Three-masted sailing ship, hologram **Obv:** Head right **Obv. Designer:** Susanna Blunt **Rev. Designer:** Bonnie Ross **Weight:** 31.3900 g. **Composition:** 0.9999 Silver 1.0091 oz. ASW

Date	Mintage	MS-63	Proof
2005 Proof	18,276	—	55.00

20 DOLLARS

KM# 562 Subject: Northwest Territories Diamonds **Obv:** Head right **Obv. Designer:** Susanna Blunt **Rev:** Multicolor diamond hologram on landscape **Rev. Designer:** José Oslo **Edge:** Reeded **Weight:** 31.3900 g. **Composition:** 0.9999 Silver 1.0091 oz. ASW **Size:** 38 mm.

Date	Mintage	MS-63	Proof
2005 Proof	35,000	—	45.00

KM# 563 Subject: Mingan Archepelago **Obv:** Head right **Obv. Designer:** Susanna Blunt **Rev:** Cliffs with whale tail out of water **Rev. Designer:** Pierre Leduc **Weight:** 31.3900 g. **Composition:** 0.9999 Silver 1.0091 oz. ASW

Date	Mintage	MS-63	Proof
2005 Proof	—	—	60.00

KM# 564 Subject: Rainforests of the Pacific Northwest **Obv:** Head right **Rev:** Open winged bird **Designer:** Susanna Blunt **Weight:** 31.3900 g. **Composition:** 0.9999 Silver 1.0091 oz. ASW

Date	Mintage	MS-63	Proof
2005 Proof	—	—	55.00

KM# 565 Subject: Toronto Island National Park **Obv:** Head right **Rev:** Toronto Island Lighthouse **Composition:** Silver

Date	Mintage	MS-63	Proof
2005 Proof	—	—	62.50

KM# 588 Subject: Georgian Bay National Park **Obv:** Head right **Rev:** Canoe and small trees on island **Weight:** 31.3900 g. **Composition:** 0.9999 Silver 1.0091 oz. ASW

Date	Mintage	MS-63	Proof
2006 Proof	—	—	60.00

KM#589 Subject: Notre Dame Basilica, Montreal, as a hologram **Obv:** Head right **Weight:** 31.1000 g. **Composition:** 0.9999 Silver 0.9997 oz. ASW

Date	Mintage	MS-63	Proof
2006 Proof	15,000	—	60.00

KM# 663 Subject: Nahanni National Park **Obv:** Head right **Rev:** Bear walking along sream, cliff in background **Weight:** 31.3900 g. **Composition:** 0.9999 Silver 1.0091 oz. ASW

Date	Mintage	MS-63	Proof
2006 Proof	—	—	60.00

KM# 664 Subject: Jasper National Park **Obv:** Head right **Rev:** Cowboy on horseback in majestic scene **Weight:** 31.3900 g. **Composition:** 0.9999 Silver 1.0091 oz. ASW

Date	Mintage	MS-63	Proof
2006 Proof	—	—	60.00

KM# 665 Subject: CN Tower, Toronto **Obv:** Head right **Rev:** Holographic rendering of CN Tower **Weight:** 31.1000 g. **Composition:** 0.9999 Silver 0.9997 oz. ASW

Date	Mintage	MS-63	Proof
2006 Proof	15,000	—	70.00

KM# 666 Subject: Pengrowth (Calgary Saddledome) **Obv:** Head right **Rev:** Holographic view of Saddledome **Weight:** 31.1000 g. **Composition:** 0.9999 Silver 0.9997 oz. ASW

Date	Mintage	MS-63	Proof
2006 Proof	15,000	—	70.00

KM# 667 Subject: Tall Ship **Obv:** Head right **Rev:** Ketch and holographic image **Weight:** 31.3900 g. **Composition:** 0.9999 Silver 1.0091 oz. ASW

Date	Mintage	MS-63	Proof
2006 Proof	10,299	—	70.00

30 DOLLARS

KM# 590 Subject: Pacific Northwest Wood Carvings **Obv:** Head right **Rev:** Welcome figure totem pole **Weight:** 31.5000 g. **Composition:** 0.9250 Silver 0.9368 oz. ASW

Date	Mintage	MS-63	Proof
2006 Proof	9,904	—	65.00

KM#668 Subject: Canadarm and Col. C. Hadfield **Obv:** Head right **Rev:** Hologram of Canadarm **Weight:** 31.5000 g. **Composition:** 0.9250 Silver 0.9368 oz. ASW

Date	Mintage	MS-63	Proof
2006 Proof	9,357	—	60.00

KM# 669 Subject: National War Memorial **Obv:** Head right **Weight:** 31.5000 g. **Composition:** 0.9250 Silver 0.9368 oz. ASW

Date	Mintage	MS-63	Proof
2006 Proof	15,000	—	80.00

KM# 670 Subject: Beaumont Hamel Newfoundland **Obv:** Head right **Weight:** 31.5000 g. **Composition:** 0.9250 Silver 0.9368 oz. ASW

Date	Mintage	MS-63	Proof
2006 Proof	15,000	—	80.00

KM# 671 Subject: Dog Sled Team **Obv:** Head right **Rev:** Colorized **Weight:** 31.5000 g. **Composition:** 0.9250 Silver 0.9368 oz. ASW

Date	Mintage	MS-63	Proof
2006 Proof	6,797	—	80.00

50 DOLLARS

KM# 566 Subject: WWII **Obv:** Head right **Rev:** Large V and three portraits **Weight:** 12.0000 g. **Composition:** 0.5833 Gold 0.2250 oz. AGW

Date	Mintage	MS-63	Proof
2005 Proof	4,000	—	275

KM# 672 Subject: Constellation Spring **Rev:** Large Bear at top **Weight:** 31.1600 g. **Composition:** 0.9995 Palladium 1.0013 oz.

Date	Mintage	MS-63	Proof
2006 Proof	297	—	1,200

KM# 673 Subject: Constellation Summer **Rev:** Large Bear at left. **Weight:** 31.1600 g. **Composition:** 0.9995 Palladium 1.0013 oz.

Date	Mintage	MS-63	Proof
2006 Proof	296	—	1,200

KM# 674 Subject: Constellation Autumn **Rev:** Large Bear towards bottom **Weight:** 31.1600 g. **Composition:** 0.9995 Palladium 1.0013 oz.

Date	Mintage	MS-63	Proof
2006 Proof	296	—	1,200

KM# 675 Subject: Constellation Winter **Rev:** Large Bear towards right. **Weight:** 31.1600 g. **Composition:** 0.9995 Palladium 1.0013 oz.

Date	Mintage	MS-63	Proof
2006 Proof	293	—	1,200

75 DOLLARS

KM# 567 Subject: Pope John Paul II **Obv:** Head right **Weight:** 31.4400 g. **Composition:** 0.4166 Gold 0.4211 oz. AGW

Date	Mintage	MS-63	Proof
2005 Proof	1,870	—	415

100 DOLLARS

KM# 115 Subject: 1976 Montreal Olympics **Obv:** Young bust right, maple leaf below, date at right, beaded borders **Rev:** Past and present Olympic figures, denomination at right **Rev. Designer:** Dora dePedery-Hunt **Weight:** 13.3375 g. **Composition:** 0.5830 Gold 0.2500 oz. AGW **Size:** 27 mm.

Date	Mintage	MS-63	Proof
1976	650,000	215	—

KM# 116 Subject: 1976 Montreal Olympics **Obv:** Young bust right, maple leaf below, date at right, plain borders **Rev:** Past and present Olympic figures, denomination at right **Rev. Designer:** Dora dePedery-Hunt **Weight:** 16.9655 g. **Composition:** 0.9170 Gold 0.5002 oz. AGW **Size:** 25 mm.

Date	Mintage	MS-63	Proof
1976 Proof	337,342	—	425

KM# 119 Subject: Queen's silver jubilee **Obv:** Young bust right **Rev:** Bouquet of provincial flowers, denomination below **Rev. Designer:** Raymond Lee **Weight:** 16.9655 g. **Composition:** 0.9170 Gold 0.5002 oz. AGW

Date	Mintage	MS-63	Proof
ND(1977) Proof	180,396	—	425

KM# 122 Subject: Canadian unification **Obv:** Young bust right, denomination at left, date upper right **Rev:** Geese (representing the provinces) in flight formation **Rev. Designer:** Roger Savage **Weight:** 16.9655 g. **Composition:** 0.9170 Gold 0.5002 oz. AGW

Date	Mintage	MS-63	Proof
1978 Proof	200,000	—	425

KM# 126 Subject: International Year of the Child **Obv:** Young bust right **Rev:** Children with hands joined divide denomination and date **Rev. Designer:** Carola Tietz **Weight:** 16.9655 g. **Composition:** 0.9170 Gold 0.5002 oz. AGW

Date	Mintage	MS-63	Proof
1979 Proof	250,000	—	425

KM# 129 Subject: Arctic Territories **Obv:** Young bust right, denomination at left, date above right **Rev:** Kayaker **Rev. Designer:** Arnaldo Marchetti **Weight:** 16.9655 g. **Composition:** 0.9170 Gold 0.5002 oz. AGW

Date	Mintage	MS-63	Proof
1980 Proof	300,000	—	425

KM# 131 Subject: National anthem **Obv:** Young bust right, denomination at left, date above right **Rev:** Music score on map **Rev. Designer:** Roger Savage **Weight:** 16.9655 g. **Composition:** 0.9170 Gold 0.5002 oz. AGW

Date	Mintage	MS-63	Proof
1981 Proof	102,000	—	425

100 DOLLARS

KM# 137   Subject: New Constitution **Obv:** Young bust right, denomination at left **Rev:** Open book, maple leaf on right page, date below **Rev. Designer:** Friedrich Peter **Weight:** 16.9655 g. **Composition:** 0.9170 Gold 0.5002 oz. AGW

Date	Mintage	MS-63	Proof
1982 Proof	121,708	—	425

KM# 139   Subject: 400th Anniversary of St. John's, Newfoundland **Obv:** Young bust right **Rev:** Anchor divides building and ship, denomination below, dates above **Rev. Designer:** John Jaciw **Weight:** 16.9655 g. **Comp:** 0.9170 Gold 0.5002 oz. AGW

Date	Mintage	MS-63	Proof
ND(1983) Proof	83,128	—	425

KM# 142   Subject: Jacques Cartier **Obv:** Young bust right **Rev:** Cartier head on right facing left, ship on left, date lower right, denomination above **Rev. Designer:** Carola Tietz **Weight:** 16.9655 g. **Composition:** 0.9170 Gold 0.5002 oz. AGW

Date	Mintage	MS-63	Proof
ND(1984) Proof	67,662	—	425

KM# 144   Subject: National Parks **Obv:** Young bust right **Rev:** Bighorn sheep, denomination divides dates below **Rev. Designer:** Hector Greville **Weight:** 16.9655 g. **Composition:** 0.9170 Gold 0.5002 oz. AGW

Date	Mintage	MS-63	Proof
ND(1985) Proof	61,332	—	425

KM# 152   Subject: Peace **Obv:** Young bust right **Rev:** Maple leaves and letters intertwined, date at right, denomination below **Rev. Designer:** Dora dePedery-Hunt **Weight:** 16.9655 g. **Composition:** 0.9170 Gold 0.5002 oz. AGW

Date	Mintage	MS-63	Proof
1986 Proof	76,409	—	425

KM# 158   Subject: 1988 Calgary Olympics **Obv:** Young bust right, maple leaf below, date at right **Rev:** Torch and logo, denomination below **Rev. Designer:** Friedrich Peter **Edge:** Lettered in English and French **Weight:** 13.3375 g. **Composition:** 0.5830 Gold 0.2500 oz. AGW

Date	Mintage	MS-63	Proof
1987 Proof	Inc. above	—	350
Note: plain edge			
1987 Proof	142,750	—	215
Note: lettered edge			

KM# 162   Subject: Bowhead Whales, balaera mysticetus **Rev:** Whales left, date below, within circle, denomination below **Rev. Designer:** Robert R. Carmichael **Weight:** 13.3375 g. **Composition:** 0.5830 Gold 0.2500 oz. AGW

Date	Mintage	MS-63	Proof
1988 Proof	52,594	—	215

KM# 169   Subject: Sainte-Marie **Obv:** Young bust right **Rev:** Huron Indian, Missionary and Mission building, denomination below, dates above **Rev. Designer:** D. J. Craig **Weight:** 13.3375 g. **Composition:** 0.5830 Gold 0.2500 oz. AGW

Date	Mintage	MS-63	Proof
ND(1989) Proof	59,657	—	215

100 DOLLARS

KM# 171 Subject: International Literacy Year **Obv:** Crowned head right, date below **Rev:** Woman with children, denomination below **Rev. Designer:** John Mardon **Weight:** 13.3375 g. **Composition:** 0.5830 Gold 0.2500 oz. AGW

Date	Mintage	MS-63	Proof
1990 Proof	49,940	—	215

KM# 180 Subject: S.S. Empress of India **Obv:** Crowned head right, date below **Rev:** Ship, "SS Empress", denomination below **Rev. Designer:** Karsten Smith **Weight:** 13.3375 g. **Composition:** 0.5830 Gold 0.2500 oz. AGW

Date	Mintage	MS-63	Proof
1991 Proof	33,966	—	215

KM# 211 Subject: Montreal **Obv:** Crowned head right, date below **Rev:** Half figure in foreground with paper, buildings in back, denomination below **Rev. Designer:** Stewart Sherwood **Weight:** 13.3375 g. **Composition:** 0.5830 Gold 0.2500 oz. AGW

Date	Mintage	MS-63	Proof
1992 Proof	28,162	—	215

KM# 245 Subject: Antique Automobiles **Obv:** Crowned head right, date below **Rev:** German Bene Victoria; Simmonds Steam Carriage; French Panhard-Levassor's Daimler; American Duryea; Canadian Featherston Haugh in center, denomination below **Rev. Designer:** John Mardon **Weight:** 13.3375 g. **Composition:** 0.5830 Gold 0.2500 oz. AGW

Date	Mintage	MS-63	Proof
1993 Proof	25,971	—	215

KM# 249 Subject: World War II Home Front **Obv:** Crowned head right, date below **Rev:** Kneeling figure working on plane, denomination below **Rev. Designer:** Paraskeva Clark **Weight:** 13.3375 g. **Composition:** 0.5830 Gold 0.2500 oz. AGW

Date	Mintage	MS-63	Proof
1994 Proof	16,201	—	215

KM# 260 Subject: Louisbourg **Obv:** Crowned head right, date below **Rev:** Ship and buildings, dates and denomination above **Rev. Designer:** Lewis Parker **Weight:** 13.3375 g. **Composition:** 0.5830 Gold 0.2500 oz. AGW

Date	Mintage	MS-63	Proof
1995 Proof	16,916	—	215

KM# 273 Subject: Klondike Gold Rush Centennial **Obv:** Crowned head right, date below **Rev:** Scene of Kate Carmack panning for gold, dates above, denomination lower left **Rev. Designer:** John Mantha **Weight:** 13.3375 g. **Composition:** 0.5830 Gold 0.2500 oz. AGW

Date	Mintage	MS-63	Proof
ND(1996) Proof	17,973	—	215

KM# 287 Subject: Alexander Graham Bell **Obv:** Crowned head right, date below **Rev:** A. G. Bell head right, globe and telephone, denomination upper right **Rev. Designer:** Donald H. Carley **Weight:** 13.3375 g. **Comp:** 0.5830 Gold 0.2500 oz. AGW

Date	Mintage	MS-63	Proof
1997 Proof	14,775	—	215

KM# 307 Subject: Discovery of Insulin **Obv:** Crowned head right, date below **Rev:** Nobel prize award figurine, dates at left, denomination at right **Rev. Designer:** Robert R. Carmichael **Weight:** 13.3375 g. **Comp:** 0.5830 Gold 0.2500 oz. AGW

Date	Mintage	MS-63	Proof
1998 Proof	11,220	—	215

KM# 452 Subject: Discovery of Oil in Alberta **Obv:** Crowned head right **Rev:** Oil well with black oil spill on ground **Rev. Designer:** John Marden **Edge:** Reeded **Weight:** 13.3375 g. **Composition:** 0.5830 Gold 0.2500 oz. AGW **Size:** 27 mm.

Date	Mintage	MS-63	Proof
2002 Proof	9,994	—	250

KM# 341 Subject: 50th Anniversary Newfoundland Unity With Canada **Obv:** Crowned head right, date below **Rev:** Two designs at front, mountains in back, denomination below **Rev. Designer:** Jackie Gale-Vaillancourt **Weight:** 13.3375 g. **Comp:** 0.5830 Gold 0.2500 oz. AGW

Date	Mintage	MS-63	Proof
1999 Proof	10,242	—	215

KM# 486 Subject: 100th Anniversary of the Discovery of Marquis Wheat **Obv:** Head right **Weight:** 13.3375 g. **Composition:** 0.5830 Gold 0.2500 oz. AGW

Date	Mintage	MS-63	Proof
2003 Proof	9,993	—	230

KM# 528 Subject: St. Lawrence Seaway, 50th Anniversary **Obv:** Head right **Weight:** 12.0000 g. **Composition:** 0.5830 Gold 0.2249 oz. AGW

Date	Mintage	MS-63	Proof
2004 Proof	7,454	—	215

KM# 616 Subject: Supreme Court **Obv:** Head right **Rev:** Draped figure with sword **Weight:** 12.0000 g. **Composition:** 0.5833 Gold 0.2250 oz. AGW

Date	Mintage	MS-63	Proof
2005 Proof	5,092	—	225

KM# 591 Subject: 75th Anniversary, Hockey Classic between Royal Military College and U.S. Military Academy **Obv:** Head right **Weight:** 12.0000 g. **Composition:** 0.5833 Gold 0.2250 oz. AGW

Date	Mintage	MS-63	Proof
2006 Proof	5,402	—	225

KM# 593 Subject: 130th Anniversary, Supreme Court **Obv:** Head right **Weight:** 12.0000 g. **Composition:** 0.5833 Gold 0.2250 oz. AGW

Date	Mintage	MS-63	Proof
2006 Proof	5,092	—	420

KM# 689 Subject: 140th Anniversary Dominion **Obv:** Head right **Weight:** 12.0000 g. **Composition:** 0.5833 Gold 0.2250 oz. AGW

Date	Mintage	MS-63	Proof
2007 Proof	5,000	—	225

KM# 402 Subject: McClure's Arctic expedition **Obv:** Crowned head right, date below **Rev:** Six men pulling supply sled to an icebound ship, denomination below **Rev. Designer:** John Mardon **Edge:** Reeded **Weight:** 13.3375 g. **Composition:** 0.5830 Gold 0.2500 oz. AGW **Size:** 27 mm.

Date	Mintage	MS-63	Proof
2000 Proof	9,767	—	215

150 DOLLARS

KM# 388 Subject: Year of the Dragon **Obv:** Crowned head right **Rev. Designer:** Harvey Chan **Weight:** 13.6100 g. **Composition:** 0.7500 Gold 0.3282 oz. AGW

Date	Mintage	MS-63	Proof
2000 Proof	8,851	—	650

KM# 416 Subject: Library of Parliament **Obv:** Crowned head right **Obv. Designer:** Dora dePedery-Hunt **Rev:** Statue in domed building **Rev. Designer:** Robert R. Carmichael **Edge:** Reeded **Weight:** 13.3375 g. **Composition:** 0.5830 Gold 0.2500 oz. AGW **Size:** 27 mm.

Date	Mintage	MS-63	Proof
2001 Proof	8,080	—	235

KM# 417 Subject: Year of the Snake **Obv:** Crowned head right **Obv. Designer:** Dora dePedery-Hunt **Rev:** Multicolor snake hologram **Edge:** Reeded **Weight:** 13.6100 g. **Composition:** 0.7500 Gold 0.3282 oz. AGW **Size:** 28 mm.

Date	Mintage	MS-63	Proof
2001 Proof	6,571	—	300

KM# 604 Obv: Head right **Rev:** Stylized horse left **Weight:** 13.6100 g. **Composition:** 0.7500 Gold 0.3282 oz. AGW

Date	Mintage	MS-63	Proof
2002 Proof	6,843	—	320

KM# 487 Subject: Year of the Ram **Obv:** Crowned head right **Rev:** Stylized ram left **Rev. Designer:** Harvey Chan **Weight:** 13.6100 g. **Composition:** 0.7500 Gold 0.3282 oz. AGW

Date	Mintage	MS-63	Proof
2003 Proof	3,927	—	325

KM# 614 Obv: Head right **Rev:** Year of the Monkey, hologram **Weight:** 13.6100 g. **Composition:** 0.7500 Gold 0.3282 oz. AGW

Date	Mintage	MS-63	Proof
2004 Proof	3,392	—	345

KM# 568 Subject: Year of the Rooster **Obv:** Head right **Rev:** Rooster left **Weight:** 13.6100 g. **Composition:** 0.7500 Gold 0.3282 oz. AGW

Date	Mintage	MS-63	Proof
2005 Proof	3,731	—	350

KM# 592 Subject: Year of the Dog, hologram **Obv:** Head right **Rev:** Stylized dog left **Weight:** 13.6100 g. **Comp:** 0.7500 Gold 0.3282 oz. AGW

Date	Mintage	MS-63	Proof
2006 Proof	2,604	—	350

KM# 690 Subject: Year of the Pig **Obv:** Head right **Rev:** Pig in center with Chinese lunar calendar around **Weight:** 13.6100 g. **Composition:** 0.7500 Gold 0.3282 oz. AGW

Date	Mintage	MS-63	Proof
2007 Proof	4,888	—	350

175 DOLLARS

KM# 217 Subject: 1992 Olympics **Obv:** Crowned head right, date at left, denomination below **Rev:** Passing the torch **Rev. Designer:** Stewart Sherwood **Edge:** Lettered **Weight:** 16.9700 g. **Composition:** 0.9170 Gold 0.5003 oz. AGW

Date	Mintage	MS-63	Proof
1992 Proof	22,092	—	425

200 DOLLARS

KM# 178 Subject: Canadian flag silver jubilee **Obv:** Crowned head right, date below **Rev:** People with flag, denomination above **Rev. Designer:** Stewart Sherwood **Weight:** 17.1350 g. **Comp:** 0.9166 Gold 0.5049 oz. AGW **Size:** 29 mm.

Date	Mintage	MS-63	Proof
1990 Proof	20,980	—	425

KM# 202 Subject: Hockey **Obv:** Crowned head right **Rev:** Hockey players, denomination above **Rev. Designer:** Stewart Sherwood **Weight:** 17.1350 g. **Composition:** 0.9166 Gold 0.5049 oz. AGW **Size:** 29 mm.

Date	Mintage	MS-63	Proof
1991 Proof	10,215	—	425

KM# 230 Subject: Niagara Falls **Obv:** Crowned head right **Rev:** Niagara Falls, denomination above **Rev. Designer:** John Mardon **Weight:** 17.1350 g. **Comp:** 0.9166 Gold 0.5049 oz. AGW **Size:** 29 mm.

Date	Mintage	MS-63	Proof
1992 Proof	9,465	—	425

KM# 244 Subject: Mounted police **Obv:** Crowned head right, date below **Rev:** Mountie with children, denomination above **Rev. Designer:** Stewart Sherwood **Weight:** 17.1350 g. **Composition:** 0.9166 Gold 0.5049 oz. AGW **Size:** 29 mm.

Date	Mintage	MS-63	Proof
1993 Proof	10,807	—	350

200 DOLLARS

KM# 250 Subject: Interpretation of 1908 novel by Lucy Maud Montgomery, 1874-1942, Anne of Green Gables **Obv:** Crowned head right **Rev:** Figure sitting in window, denomination above **Rev. Designer:** Phoebe Gilman **Weight:** 17.1350 g. **Composition:** 0.9166 Gold 0.5049 oz. AGW **Size:** 29 mm.

Date	Mintage	MS-63	Proof
1994 Proof	10,655	—	425

KM# 265 Subject: Maple-syrup production **Obv:** Crowned head right, date below **Rev:** Maple syrup making, denomination at right **Rev. Designer:** J. D. Mantha **Weight:** 17.1350 g. **Composition:** 0.9166 Gold 0.5049 oz. AGW **Size:** 29 mm.

Date	Mintage	MS-63	Proof
1995 Proof	6,579	—	425

KM# 275 Subject: Transcontinental Canadian Railway **Obv:** Crowned head right, date below **Rev:** Train going through mountains, denomination below **Rev. Designer:** Suzanne Duranceau **Weight:** 17.1350 g. **Composition:** 0.9166 Gold 0.5049 oz. AGW **Size:** 29 mm.

Date	Mintage	MS-63	Proof
1996 Proof	8,047	—	425

KM# 288 Subject: Haida mask **Obv:** Crowned head right, date below **Rev:** Haida mask **Rev. Designer:** Robert Davidson **Weight:**

17.1350 g. **Composition:** 0.9166 Gold 0.5049 oz. AGW **Size:** 29 mm.

Date	Mintage	MS-63	Proof
1997 Proof	11,610	—	450

KM# 317 Subject: Legendary white buffalo **Obv:** Crowned head right, date below **Rev:** Buffalo **Rev. Designer:** Alex Janvler **Weight:** 17.1350 g. **Comp:** 0.9166 Gold 0.5049 oz. AGW **Size:** 29 mm.

Date	Mintage	MS-63	Proof
1998 Proof	7,149	—	425

KM# 358 Subject: Mikmaq butterfly **Obv:** Crowned head right **Rev:** Butterfly within design **Rev. Designer:** Alan Syliboy **Weight:** 17.1350 g. **Comp:** 0.9166 Gold 0.5049 oz. AGW **Size:** 29 mm.

Date	Mintage	MS-63	Proof
1999 Proof	6,510	—	425

KM# 403 Subject: Motherhood **Obv:** Crowned head right, date above, denomination at right **Rev:** Inuit mother with infant **Rev. Designer:** Germaine Arnaktauyak **Edge:** Reeded **Weight:** 17.1350 g. **Comp:** 0.9166 Gold 0.5049 oz. AGW **Size:** 29 mm.

Date	Mintage	MS-63	Proof
2000 Proof	6,284	—	425

KM# 418 Subject: Cornelius D. Krieghoff's "The Habitant farm" **Obv:** Queens head right **Edge:** Reeded **Weight:** 17.1350 g. **Composition:** 0.9166 Gold 0.5049 oz. AGW **Size:** 29 mm.

Date	Mintage	MS-63	Proof
2001 Proof	5,406	—	445

KM# 466 Subject: Thomas Thompson "The Jack Pine" (1916-17) **Obv:** Crowned head right **Weight:** 17.1350 g. **Composition:** 0.9166 Gold 0.5049 oz. AGW **Size:** 29 mm.

Date	Mintage	MS-63	Proof
2002 Proof	5,264	—	450

KM# 488 Subject: Fitzgerald's "Houses" (1929) **Obv:** Crowned head right **Rev:** House with trees **Weight:** 17.1350 g. **Composition:** 0.9166 Gold 0.5049 oz. AGW

Date	Mintage	MS-63	Proof
2003 Proof	4,118	—	460

KM# 516 Subject: "Fragments" **Obv:** Crowned head right **Rev:** Fragmented face **Edge:** Reeded **Weight:** 16.0000 g. **Composition:** 0.9166 Gold 0.4715 oz. AGW **Size:** 29 mm.

Date	Mintage	MS-63	Proof
2004 Proof	3,917	—	425

KM# 569 Subject: Fur traders **Obv:** Head right **Rev:** Men in canoe riding wave **Weight:** 16.0000 g. **Composition:** 0.9166 Gold 0.4715 oz. AGW

Date	Mintage	MS-63	Proof
2005 Proof	3,669	—	425

KM# 594 Subject: Timber trade **Obv:** Head right **Rev:** Lumberjacks felling tree **Weight:** 16.0000 g. **Composition:** 0.9166 Gold 0.4715 oz. AGW

Date	Mintage	MS-63	Proof
2006 Proof	3,185	—	425

KM# 691 Subject: Fishing Trade **Obv:** Head right **Weight:** 16.0000 g. **Composition:** 0.9166 Gold 0.4715 oz. AGW

Date	Mintage	MS-63	Proof
2007 Proof	4,000	—	425

250 DOLLARS

KM# 677 Subject: Dog Sled Team **Weight:** 45.0000 g. **Composition:** 0.5833 Gold 0.8439 oz. AGW

Date	Mintage	MS-63	Proof
2006 Proof	900	—	775

300 DOLLARS

KM# 501 Obv: Triple cameo portraits of Queen Elizabeth II by Gillick, Machin and de Pedery-Hunt, each in 14K gold, rose in center **Rev:** Dates "1952-2002" and denomination in legend, rose in center **Weight:** 60.0000 g. **Composition:** 0.5833 Gold 1.1252 oz. AGW **Size:** 50 mm. **Note:** Housed in anodized gold-colored aluminum box with cherrywood stained siding

Date	Mintage	MS-63	Proof
ND(2002) Proof	999	—	1,050

KM# 517 Obv: Four coinage portraits of Elizabeth II **Rev:** Canadian arms above value **Edge:** Plain **Weight:** 60.0000 g. **Composition:** 0.5833 Gold 1.1252 oz. AGW **Size:** 50 mm.

Date	Mintage	MS-63	Proof
2004 Proof	1,000	—	1,075

KM# 570 Subject: Standard Time **Obv:** Head right **Rev:** Roman numeral clock with world inside **Weight:** 60.0000 g. **Composition:** 0.5833 Gold 1.1252 oz. AGW

Date	Mintage	MS-63	Proof
2005 Proof	—	—	1,000

KM# 596 Subject: Shinplaster **Obv:** Head right **Rev:** Britannia bust, spear over shoulder **Weight:** 60.0000 g. **Comp:** 0.5833 Gold 1.1252 oz. AGW

Date	Mintage	MS-63	Proof
2005 Proof	994	—	1,075

KM# 600 Subject: Welcome Figure Totem Pole **Obv:** Head right **Rev:** Men with totem pole **Weight:** 60.0000 g. **Comp:** 0.5833 Gold 1.1252 oz. AGW

Date	Mintage	MS-63	Proof
2005 Proof	948	—	1,000

KM# 595 Subject: The Shinplaster **Obv:** Head right **Rev:** Seated Britannia with shield **Weight:** 60.0000 g. **Comp:** 0.5833 Gold 1.1252 oz. AGW

Date	Mintage	MS-63	Proof
2006 Proof	940	—	1,075

KM# 678 Subject: Canadam and Col. C. Hadfield **Rev:** Hologram of Canadarm **Weight:** 45.0000 g. **Composition:** 0.5833 Gold 0.8439 oz. AGW

Date	Mintage	MS-63	Proof
2006 Proof	565	—	775

KM# 679 Subject: Queen Elizabeth's 80th Birthday **Rev:** State Crown, colorized **Weight:** 60.0000 g. **Composition:** 0.5833 Gold 1.1252 oz. AGW

Date	Mintage	MS-63	Proof
2006 Proof	996	—	1,050

KM# 680 Subject: Crystal Snowflake **Weight:** 60.0000 g. **Composition:** 0.5833 Gold 1.1252 oz. AGW

Date	Mintage	MS-63	Proof
2006 Proof	861	—	1,050

KM# 692 Subject: 1923 25 Cent Banknote **Weight:** 60.0000 g. **Composition:** 0.5833 Gold 1.1252 oz. AGW

Date	Mintage	MS-63	Proof
2007 Proof	1,250	—	1,050

350 DOLLARS

KM# 308   Subject: Flowers of Canada's Coat of Arms **Obv:** Crowned head right, date behind, denomination at bottom **Rev:** Flowers **Rev. Designer:** Pierre Leduc **Weight:** 38.0500 g. **Composition:** 0.9999 Gold 1.2232 oz. AGW

Date	Mintage	MS-63	Proof
1998 Proof	664	—	1,050

KM# 370   Rev: Lady's slipper **Rev. Designer:** Henry Purdy **Weight:** 38.0500 g. **Composition:** 0.9999 Gold 1.2232 oz. AGW

Date	Mintage	MS-63	Proof
1999 Proof	1,990	—	1,050

KM# 404   Obv: Crowned head right **Rev:** Three Pacific Dogwood flowers **Rev. Designer:** Caren Heine **Edge:** Reeded **Weight:** 38.0500 g. **Composition:** 0.9999 Gold 1.2232 oz. AGW **Size:** 34 mm.

Date	Mintage	MS-63	Proof
2000 Proof	1,506	—	1,050

KM# 433   Subject: The Mayflower Flower **Obv:** Crowned head right **Rev:** Two flowers **Rev. Designer:** Bonnie Ross **Edge:** Reeded **Weight:** 38.0500 g. **Composition:** 0.9999 Gold 1.2232 oz. AGW **Size:** 34 mm.

Date	Mintage	MS-63	Proof
2001 Proof	1,988	—	1,150

KM# 502   Subject: The Wild Rose **Obv:** Crowned head right **Obv. Designer:** Dora de Pedery-Hunt **Rev:** Wild rose plant **Rev. Designer:** Dr. Andreas Kare Hellum **Weight:** 38.0500 g. **Composition:** 0.9999 Gold 1.2232 oz. AGW **Size:** 34 mm.

Date	Mintage	MS-63	Proof
2002 Proof	2,001	—	1,150

KM# 504   Subject: The White Trillium **Obv:** Crowned head right **Obv. Designer:** Dora de Pedery-Hunt **Rev:** White Trillium **Weight:** 38.0500 g. **Composition:** 0.9999 Gold 1.2232 oz. AGW **Size:** 34 mm.

Date	Mintage	MS-63	Proof
2003 Proof	1,865	—	1,150

KM# 601   Subject: Western Red Lilly **Obv:** Head right **Rev:** Western Red Lilies **Weight:** 38.0500 g. **Composition:** 0.9999 Gold 1.2232 oz. AGW

Date	Mintage	MS-63	Proof
2005 Proof	1,634	—	1,150

KM# 626   Subject: Iris Vericolor **Obv:** Crowned head right **Rev:** Iris **Weight:** 38.0500 g. **Composition:** 0.9999 Gold 1.2232 oz. AGW **Size:** 34 mm.

Date	Mintage	MS-63	Proof
2006 Proof	1,969	—	1,150

SILVER BULLION COINAGE

DOLLAR

KM# 617   Obv: Crowned head right **Rev:** Holographic Maple leaf **Edge:** Reeded **Weight:** 1.5550 g. **Composition:** 0.9999 Silver 0.0500 oz. ASW **Size:** 16 mm.

Date	Mintage	MS-63	Proof
2003 Proof	—	—	4.50

KM# 621   Obv: Crowned head right **Rev:** Maple leaf and mint logo privy mark **Edge:** Reeded **Weight:** 1.5550 g. **Composition:** 0.9999 Silver 0.0500 oz. ASW **Size:** 17 mm.

Date	Mintage	MS-63	Proof
2004 Proof	25,000	—	4.50

2 DOLLARS

KM# 618 Obv: Crowned head right **Rev:** Holographic Maple leaf **Edge:** Reeded **Weight:** 3.1100 g. **Composition:** 0.9999 Silver 0.1000 oz. ASW **Size:** 20.1 mm.

Date	Mintage	MS-63	Proof
2003 Proof	—	—	7.50

KM# 622 Obv: Crowned head right **Rev:** Maple leaf and mint logo privy mark **Edge:** Reeded **Weight:** 3.1100 g. **Composition:** 0.9999 Silver 0.1000 oz. ASW **Size:** 21 mm.

Date	Mintage	MS-63	Proof
2004 Proof	25,000	—	7.50

KM# 571 Obv: Head right **Rev:** Lynx **Weight:** 3.1050 g. **Comp:** 0.9999 Silver 0.0998 oz. ASW

Date	Mintage	MS-63	Proof
2005 Proof	—	—	7.50

3 DOLLARS

KM# 619 Obv: Crowned head right **Rev:** Holographic Maple leaf **Edge:** Reeded **Weight:** 7.7760 g. **Composition:** 0.9999 Silver 0.2500 oz. ASW **Size:** 26.9 mm.

Date	Mintage	MS-63	Proof
2003 Proof	—	—	15.00

KM# 623 Obv: Crowned head right **Rev:** Maple leaf and mint logo privy mark **Edge:** Reeded **Weight:** 7.7760 g. **Composition:** 0.9999 Silver 0.2500 oz. ASW **Size:** 27 mm.

Date	Mintage	MS-63	Proof
2004 Proof	25,000	—	12.50

KM# 572 Obv: Head right **Rev:** Lynx **Weight:** 7.7760 g. **Comp:** 0.9999 Silver 0.2500 oz. ASW

Date	Mintage	MS-63	Proof
2005 Proof	—	—	12.50

4 DOLLARS

KM# 620 Obv: Crowned head right **Rev:** Holographic Maple leaf **Edge:** Reeded **Weight:** 15.5500 g. **Composition:** 0.9999 Silver 0.4999 oz. ASW **Size:** 33.9 mm.

Date	Mintage	MS-63	Proof
2003 Proof	—	—	30.00

KM# 624 Obv: Crowned head right **Rev:** Maple leaf and mint logo privy mark **Edge:** Reeded **Weight:** 15.5500 g. **Composition:** 0.9999 Silver 0.4999 oz. ASW **Size:** 34 mm.

Date	Mintage	MS-63	Proof
2004 Proof	25,000	—	25.00

KM# 573 Obv: Head right **Rev:** Lynx **Weight:** 15.5500 g. **Comp:** 0.9999 Silver 0.4999 oz. ASW

Date	Mintage	MS-63	Proof
2005 Proof	—	—	22.50

5 DOLLARS

KM# 163 Obv: Young bust right, denomination and date below **Obv. Designer:** Arnold Machin **Rev:** Maple leaf flanked by 9999 **Weight:** 31.1000 g. **Composition:** 0.9999 Silver 0.9997 oz. ASW

Date	Mintage	MS-63	Proof
1988	1,155,931	16.00	—
1989	3,332,200	16.00	—
1989 Proof	29,999	—	30.00

KM# 187 Obv: Crowned head right, date and denomination below **Obv. Designer:** Dora de Pedery-Hunt **Rev:** Maple leaf flanked by 9999 **Weight:** 31.1000 g. **Composition:** 0.9999 Silver 0.9997 oz. ASW

Date	Mintage	MS-63	Proof
1990	1,708,800	16.00	—
1991	644,300	16.50	—
1992	343,800	16.50	—
1993	889,946	16.00	—
1994	1,133,900	16.00	—
1995	326,244	16.00	—
1996	250,445	32.50	—
1997	100,970	17.50	—
1998 Tiger privy mark	25,000	18.50	—
1998	591,359	16.50	—
1998 Titanic privy mark	26,000	75.00	—
1998 R.C.M.P. privy mark	25,000	32.50	—
1998 90th Anniversary R.C.M. privy mark	13,025	18.50	—
1999	1,229,442	16.00	—
1999 Rabbit privy mark	25,000	21.50	—
1999 "Y2K" privy mark	9,999	27.50	—
2000 Dragon privy mark	25,000	22.50	—
2000 Expo Hanover privy mark	—	35.00	—
2000	403,652	16.00	—
2001	398,563	16.00	—
2001 Snake privy mark	25,000	22.00	—
2002	576,196	16.00	—
2002 Horse privy mark	25,000	22.00	—
2003	—	16.00	—
2003 Sheep privy mark	25,000	18.00	—

KM# 363 Obv: Crowned head right, date and denomination below **Rev:** Maple leaf flanked by

9999 **Weight:** 31.1000 g. **Composition:** 0.9999 Silver 0.9997 oz. ASW

Date	Mintage	MS-63	Proof
1999/2000	298,775	17.50	—

Note: Fireworks privy mark

KM# 436 Obv: Crowned head right, date and denomination below **Rev:** Three maple leaves in autumn colors, 9999 flanks **Rev. Designer:** Debbie Adams **Edge:** Reeded **Weight:** 31.1035 g. **Composition:** 0.9999 Silver 0.9999 oz. ASW **Size:** 38 mm.

Date	Mintage	MS-63	Proof
2001 Proof	49,900	—	32.50

KM# 437 Subject: Multicolor Holographic Maple Leaf **Obv:** Crowned head right, date and denomination below **Rev:** Radiant maple leaf hologram with date privy mark **Edge:** Reeded **Weight:** 31.1035 g. **Composition:** 0.9999 Silver 0.9999 oz. ASW **Size:** 38 mm.

Date	Mintage	MS-63	Proof
2001	29,906	75.00	—

KM# 505 Obv: Crowned head right, date and denomination below **Rev:** Two maple leaves in spring color (green) **Edge:** Reeded **Weight:** 31.1035 g. **Composition:** 0.9999 Silver 0.9999 oz. ASW **Size:** 38 mm.

Date	Mintage	MS-63	Proof
2002 Proof	—	—	35.00

KM# 603 Subject: Loon, hologram **Obv:** Head right **Composition:** 0.9999 Silver

Date	Mintage	MS-63	Proof
2002 Satin Proof	30,000	—	45.00

KM# 522 Subject: Colorized maple leaf **Obv:** Head right **Weight:** 31.1050 g. **Composition:** 0.9999 Silver 0.9999 oz. ASW

Date	Mintage	MS-63	Proof
2003	—	32.50	—

KM# 521 Obv: Head right **Rev:** Maple leaf, summer colors **Weight:** 31.1035 g. **Composition:** 0.9999 Silver 0.9999 oz. ASW

Date	Mintage	MS-63	Proof
2003 Proof	—	—	30.00

KM# 508 Obv: Crowned head right, date and denomination below **Obv. Designer:** Dora de Pedery-Hunt **Rev:** Holographic Maple leaf flanked by 9999 **Edge:** Reeded **Weight:** 31.1035 g. **Comp:** 0.9999 Silver 0.9999 oz. ASW **Size:** 38 mm.

Date	Mintage	MS-63	Proof
2003 Proof	—	—	35.00

KM# 625 Obv: Crowned head right **Rev:** Maple leaf and mint logo privy mark **Edge:** Reeded **Weight:** 31.1035 g. **Composition:** 0.9999 Silver 0.9999 oz. ASW **Size:** 38 mm.

Date	Mintage	MS-63	Proof
2004 Proof	25,000	—	35.00

KM# 550 Subject: Big Leaf Maple, colorized **Obv:** Head right **Weight:** 31.1035 g. **Composition:** 0.9999 Silver 0.9999 oz. ASW

Date	Mintage	MS-63	Proof
2005	25,000	30.00	—

KM# 574 Obv: Head right **Rev:** Lynx **Weight:** 1.1035 g. **Composition:** 0.9999 Silver 0.0355 oz. ASW

Date	Mintage	MS-63	Proof
2005 Proof	—	—	35.00

KM# 660 Subject: Silver Maple **Rev:** Colorized **Weight:** 31.1035 g. **Composition:** Silver

Date	Mintage	MS-63	Proof
2006 Proof	—	—	35.00

50 DOLLARS

KM# 326 Subject: 10th Anniversary Silver Maple Leaf **Obv:** Crowned head right **Rev:** Maple leaf flanked by 9999 **Edge:** 10th ANNIVERSARY 10e ANNIVERSAIRE **Weight:** 311.0350 g. **Composition:** 0.9999 Silver 9.9986 oz. ASW

Date	Mintage	MS-63	Proof
1998 Proof	25,000	—	165

250 DOLLARS

KM# 676 Subject: Kilo **Weight:** 1000.0000 g. **Composition:** 0.9999 Silver 32.146 oz. ASW

Date	Mintage	MS-63	Proof
2006	—	550	—

SILVER BULLION

GOLD BULLION COINAGE

DOLLAR

KM# 238 Obv: Crowned head right, denomination and date below **Rev:** Maple leaf flanked by 9999 **Weight:** 1.5551 g. **Composition:** 0.9999 Gold 0.0500 oz. AGW

Date	Mintage	MS-63	Proof
1993	37,080	BV+37%	—
1994	78,860	BV+37%	—
1995	85,920	BV+37%	—
1996	56,520	BV+37%	—
1997	59,720	BV+37%	—
1998	44,260	BV+37%	—
1999	—	BV+46%	—

Note: Maple leaf with oval "20 YEARS ANS" privy mark.

2000	—	—	—

Note: Maple leaf with oval "2000" privy mark.

KM# 365 Obv: Crowned head right **Rev:** Maple leaf hologram **Weight:** 1.5551 g. **Composition:** 0.9999 Gold 0.0500 oz. AGW

Date	Mintage	MS-63	Proof
1999	500	90.00	—

2 DOLLARS

KM# 256 Obv: Crowned head right, denomination and date below **Rev:** Maple leaf flanked by 9999 **Weight:** 2.0735 g. **Composition:** 0.9999 Gold 0.0667 oz. AGW

Date	Mintage	MS-63	Proof
1994	5,493	85.00	—

5 DOLLARS

KM# 135 Obv: Young bust right, date and denomination below **Obv. Designer:** Arnold Machin **Rev:** Maple leaf flanked by 9999 **Weight:** 3.1200 g. **Comp:** 0.9999 Gold 0.1003 oz. AGW

Date	Mintage	MS-63	Proof
1982	246,000	BV+14%	—
1983	304,000	BV+14%	—
1984	262,000	BV+14%	—
1985	398,000	BV+14%	—
1986	529,516	BV+14%	—
1987	459,000	BV+14%	—
1988	506,500	BV+14%	—
1989	539,000	BV+14%	—
1989 Proof	16,992	—	90.00

KM# 188 Obv: Elizabeth II effigy **Obv. Designer:** Dora dePedery-Hunt **Rev:** Maple leaf **Weight:** 3.1200 g. **Comp:** 0.9999 Gold 0.1003 oz. AGW

Date	Mintage	MS-63	Proof
1990	476,000	BV+14%	—
1991	322,000	BV+14%	—
1992	384,000	BV+14%	—
1993	248,630	BV+14%	—
1994	313,150	BV+14%	—
1995	294,890	BV+14%	—
1996	179,220	BV+14%	—
1997	188,540	BV+14%	—
1998	301,940	BV+14%	—
1999	—	BV+19%	—

Note: Maple leaf with oval "20 Years ANS" privy mark

2000	—	BV+19%	—

KM# 366 Rev: Maple leaf hologram **Weight:** 3.1200 g. **Comp:** 0.9999 Gold 0.1003 oz. AGW

Date	Mintage	MS-63	Proof
1999	500	160	—

KM# 439 Subject: Holographic Maple Leaves **Obv:** Crowned head right **Rev:** Three maple leaves multicolor hologram **Edge:** Reeded **Weight:** 3.1310 g. **Composition:** 0.9999 Gold 0.1006 oz. AGW **Size:** 16 mm.

Date	Mintage	MS-63	Proof
2001 in sets only	600	150	—

10 DOLLARS

KM# 136 Obv: Young bust right, date and denomination below **Obv. Designer:** Arnold Machin **Rev:** Maple leaf flanked by 9999 **Weight:** 7.7850 g. **Comp:** 0.9999 Gold 0.2503 oz. AGW

Date	Mintage	MS-63	Proof
1982	184,000	BV+10%	—
1983	308,800	BV+10%	—
1984	242,400	BV+10%	—
1985	620,000	BV+10%	—
1986	915,200	BV+10%	—
1987	376,000	BV+10%	—
1988	436,000	BV+10%	—
1989	328,800	BV+10%	—
1989 Proof	6,998	—	250

KM# 189 Obv: Crowned head right, date and denomination below **Obv. Designer:** Dora dePedery-Hunt **Rev:** Maple leaf flanked by 9999 **Weight:** 7.7850 g. **Composition:** 0.9999 Gold 0.2503 oz. AGW

Date	Mintage	MS-63	Proof
1990	253,600	BV+10%	—
1991	166,400	BV+10%	—
1992	179,600	BV+10%	—
1993	158,452	BV+10%	—
1994	148,792	BV+10%	—
1995	127,596	BV+10%	—
1996	89,148	BV+10%	—
1997	98,104	BV+10%	—
1998	85,472	BV+10%	—

Date	Mintage	MS-63	Proof
1999	—	BV+15%	—

Note: Maple leaf with oval "20 Years ANS" privy mark

Date	Mintage	MS-63	Proof
2000	—	BV+15%	—

Note: Maple leaf with oval "2000" privy mark

KM# 367 Rev: Maple leaf hologram **Weight:** 7.7850 g. **Comp:** 0.9999 Gold 0.2503 oz. AGW

Date	Mintage	MS-63	Proof
1999	—	325	—

KM# 440 Subject: Holographic Maples Leaves **Obv:** Crowned head right **Rev:** Three maple leaves multicolor hologram **Edge:** Reeded **Weight:** 7.7970 g. **Composition:** 0.9999 Gold 0.2506 oz. AGW **Size:** 20 mm.

Date	Mintage	MS-63	Proof
2001	15,000	225	—

20 DOLLARS

KM# 190 Obv: Crowned head right, date and denomination below **Obv. Designer:** Dora dePedery-Hunt **Rev:** Maple leaf flanked by 9999 **Weight:** 15.5515 g. **Composition:** 0.9999 Gold 0.4999 oz. AGW

Date	Mintage	MS-63	Proof
1990	174,400	BV+7%	—
1991	96,200	BV+7%	—
1992	108,000	BV+7%	—
1993	99,492	BV+7%	—
1994	104,766	BV+7%	—
1995	103,162	BV+7%	—
1996	66,246	BV+7%	—
1997	63,354	BV+7%	—
1998	65,366	BV+7%	—
1999	—	BV+12%	—

Note: Maple leaf with oval "20 Years ANS" privy mark

Date	Mintage	MS-63	Proof
2000	—	BV+12%	—

Note: Maple leaf with oval "2000" privy mark.

KM# 153 Obv: Young bust right, date and denomination below **Obv. Designer:** Arnold Machin **Rev:** Maple leaf flanked by 9999 **Weight:** 15.5515 g. **Composition:** 0.9999 Gold 0.4999 oz. AGW **Size:** 32 mm.

Date	Mintage	MS-63	Proof
1986	529,200	BV+7%	—
1987	332,800	BV+7%	—

Date	Mintage	MS-63	Proof
1988	538,400	BV+7%	—
1989	259,200	BV+7%	—
1989 Proof	6,998	—	450

KM# 368 Rev: Maple leaf hologram **Weight:** 15.5515 g. **Comp:** 0.9999 Gold 0.4999 oz. AGW

Date	Mintage	MS-63	Proof
1999	500	700	—

KM# 441 Subject: Holographic Maples Leaves **Obv:** Crowned head right **Rev:** Three maple leaves multicolor hologram **Edge:** Reeded **Weight:** 15.5840 g. **Composition:** 0.9999 Gold 0.5010 oz. AGW **Size:** 25 mm.

Date	Mintage	MS-63	Proof
2001 in sets only	600	675	—

50 DOLLARS

KM# 125.1 Obv: Young bust right, denomination and date below **Rev:** Maple leaf flanked by .999 **Weight:** 31.1030 g. **Composition:** 0.9990 Gold 0.9989 oz. AGW

Date	Mintage	MS-63	Proof
1979	1,000,000	BV+4%	—
1980	1,251,500	BV+4%	—
1981	863,000	BV+4%	—
1982	883,000	BV+4%	—

KM# 125.2 Obv: Young bust right, date and denomination below **Rev:** Maple leaf flanked by .9999 **Weight:** 31.1030 g. **Composition:** 0.9999 Gold 0.9998 oz. AGW

Date	Mintage	MS-63	Proof
1983	843,000	BV+4%	—
1984	1,067,500	BV+4%	—
1985	1,908,000	BV+4%	—
1986	779,115	BV+4%	—
1987	978,000	BV+4%	—
1988	826,500	BV+4%	—
1989	856,000	BV+4%	—
1989 Proof	17,781	—	875

KM# 191 Obv: Crowned head right, date and denomination below **Obv. Designer:** Dora dePedery-Hunt **Rev:** Maple leaf flanked by .9999 **Weight:** 31.1030 g. **Composition:** 0.9999 Gold 0.9998 oz. AGW

Date	Mintage	MS-63	Proof
1990	815,000	BV+4%	—
1991	290,000	BV+4%	—
1992	368,900	BV+4%	—
1993	321,413	BV+4%	—
1994	180,357	BV+4%	—
1995	208,729	BV+4%	—
1996	143,682	BV+4%	—
1997	478,211	BV+4%	—
1998	593,704	BV+4%	—
1999	—	BV+7%	—

Note: Maple leaf with oval "20 Years ANS" privy mark

| 2000 | — | BV+7% | — |

Note: Maple leaf with oval

KM# 305 Obv: Crowned head denomination below, within circle, dates below **Rev:** Mountie at gallop right, within circle **Rev. Designer:** Ago Aarand **Weight:** 31.1030 g. **Composition:** 0.9999 Gold 0.9998 oz. AGW **Shape:** 10-sided

Date	Mintage	MS-63	Proof
1997	12,913	850	—

KM# 369 Obv: Crowned head right, date and denomination below **Rev:** Maple leaf hologram flanked by 9999, with fireworks privy mark **Weight:** 31.1030 g. **Comp:** 0.9999 Gold 0.9998 oz. AGW

Date	Mintage	MS-63	Proof
2000	500	1,400	—

KM# 364 Obv: Crowned head right, denomination and date below **Rev:** Maple leaf flanked by 9999, with fireworks privy mark **Weight:** 31.1030 g. **Composition:** 0.9999 Gold 0.9998 oz. AGW

Date	Mintage	MS-63	Proof
2000	—	850	—

KM# 442 Subject: Holographic Maples Leaves **Obv:** Crowned head right **Rev:** Three maple leaves multicolor hologram **Edge:** Reeded **Weight:** 31.1500 g. **Composition:** 0.9999 Gold 1.0014 oz. AGW **Size:** 30 mm.

Date	Mintage	MS-63	Proof
2001 in sets only	600	1,350	—

2500 DOLLARS

KM# 681 Subject: Kilo **Rev:** Common Characters, Early Canada **Weight:** 1000.0000 g. **Composition:** 0.9999 Gold 32.146 oz. AGW

Date	Mintage	MS-63	Proof
2007	20	29,500	—

PLATINUM BULLION COINAGE

DOLLAR

KM# 239 Obv: Crowned head right, date and denomination below **Rev:** Maple leaf flanked by 9995 **Weight:** 1.5552 g. **Composition:** 0.9995 Platinum 0.0500 oz. APW

Date	Mintage	MS-63	Proof
1993	2,120	BV+35%	—
1994	4,260	BV+35%	—
1995	460	135	—
1996	1,640	BV+35%	—
1997	1,340	BV+35%	—
1998	2,000	BV+35%	—
1999	2,000	BV+35%	—

2 DOLLARS

KM# 257 Obv: Crowned head right, date and denomination below **Rev:** Maple leaf flanked by 9995 **Weight:** 2.0735 g. **Composition:** 0.9995 Platinum 0.0666 oz. APW

Date	Mintage	MS-63	Proof
1994	1,470	235	—

5 DOLLARS

KM# 164 Obv: Young bust right, date and denomination below **Obv. Designer:** Arnold Machin **Rev:** Maple leaf flanked by 9995 **Weight:** 3.1203 g. **Composition:** 0.9995 Platinum 0.1003 oz. APW

Date	Mintage	MS-63	Proof
1988	74,000	BV+18%	—
1989	18,000	BV+18%	—
1989 Proof	11,999	—	165

KM# 192 Obv. Designer: dePedery-Hunt **Rev:** Maple leaf **Weight:** 3.1203 g. **Composition:** 0.9995 Platinum 0.1003 oz. APW

Date	Mintage	MS-63	Proof
1990	9,000	BV+18%	—
1991	13,000	BV+18%	—
1992	16,000	BV+18%	—
1993	14,020	BV+18%	—
1994	19,190	BV+18%	—
1995	8,940	BV+18%	—
1996	8,820	BV+18%	—
1997	7,050	BV+18%	—
1998	5,710	BV+18%	—
1999	2,000	BV+18%	—

10 DOLLARS

KM# 165 Obv: Young bust right, date and denomination below **Obv. Designer:** Machin **Rev:** Maple leaf flanked by 9995 **Weight:** 7.7857 g. **Composition:** 0.9995 Platinum 0.2502 oz. APW

Date	Mintage	MS-63	Proof
1988	93,600	BV+13%	—
1989	3,200	BV+13%	—
1989 Proof	1,999	—	400

KM# 193 Obv. Designer: dePedery-Hunt **Rev:** Maple leaf **Weight:** 7.7857 g. **Composition:** 0.9995 Platinum 0.2502 oz. APW

Date	Mintage	MS-63	Proof
1990	1,600	BV+13%	—
1991	7,200	BV+13%	—
1992	11,600	BV+13%	—
1993	8,048	BV+13%	—
1994	9,456	BV+13%	—
1995	6,524	BV+13%	—
1996	6,160	BV+13%	—
1997	4,552	BV+13%	—
1998	3,816	BV+13%	—
1999	2,000	BV+13%	—

20 DOLLARS

KM#166 Obv: Young bust right, denomination and date below **Obv. Designer:** Machin **Rev:** Maple leaf flanked by 9995 **Weight:** 15.5519 g. **Composition:** 0.9995 Platinum 0.4997 oz. APW

Date	Mintage	MS-63	Proof
1988	23,600	BV+9%	—
1989	4,800	BV+9%	—
1989 Proof	1,999	—	800

KM# 194 Obv. Designer: dePedery-Hunt **Rev:** Maple leaf **Weight:** 15.5519 g. **Composition:** 0.9995 Platinum 0.4997 oz. APW

Date	Mintage	MS-63	Proof
1990	2,600	BV+9%	—
1991	5,600	BV+9%	—
1992	12,800	BV+9%	—
1993	6,022	BV+9%	—
1994	6,710	BV+9%	—
1995	6,308	BV+9%	—
1996	5,490	BV+9%	—
1997	3,990	BV+9%	—
1998	5,486	BV+9%	—
1999	500	BV+15%	—

30 DOLLARS

KM# 174 Obv: Crowned head right **Rev:** Polar bear swimming, denomination below **Rev. Designer:** Robert Bateman **Weight:** 3.1100 g. **Composition:** 0.9990 Platinum 0.0999 oz. APW

Date	Mintage	MS-63	Proof
1990 Proof	2,629	—	165

KM# 198 Obv: Crowned head right **Rev:** Snowy owl, denomination below **Rev. Designer:** Glen Loates **Weight:** 3.1100 g. **Composition:** 0.9990 Platinum 0.0999 oz. APW

Date	Mintage	MS-63	Proof
1991 Proof	3,500	—	165

KM# 226 Obv: Crowned head right **Rev:** Cougar head and shoulders, denomination below **Rev. Designer:** George McLean **Weight:** 3.1100 g. **Composition:** 0.9990 Platinum 0.0999 oz. APW

Date	Mintage	MS-63	Proof
1992 Proof	3,500	—	165

PLATINUM BULLION

KM# 240 Obv: Crowned head right **Rev:** Arctic fox, denomination below **Rev. Designer:** Claude D'Angelo **Weight:** 3.1100 g. **Composition:** 0.9990 Platinum 0.0999 oz. APW

Date	Mintage	MS-63	Proof
1993 Proof	3,500	—	165

KM# 252 Obv: Crowned head right, date below **Rev:** Sea otter, denomination below **Rev. Designer:** Ron S. Parker **Weight:** 3.1100 g. **Composition:** 0.9990 Platinum 0.0999 oz. APW

Date	Mintage	MS-63	Proof
1994 Proof	1,500	—	165

KM# 266 Obv: Crowned head right, date below **Rev:** Canadian lynx, denomination below **Rev. Designer:** Michael Dumas **Weight:** 3.1100 g. **Composition:** 0.9990 Platinum 0.0999 oz. APW

Date	Mintage	MS-63	Proof
1995 Proof	620	—	165

KM# 278 Obv: Crowned head right, date below **Rev:** Falcon portrait, denomination below **Rev. Designer:** Dwayne Harty **Weight:** 3.1100 g. **Composition:** 0.9990 Platinum 0.0999 oz. APW

Date	Mintage	MS-63	Proof
1996 Proof	489	—	165

KM# 300 Obv: Crowned head right, date below **Rev:** Bison head, denomination below **Rev. Designer:** Chris Bacon **Weight:** 3.1100 g. **Composition:** 0.9995 Platinum 0.0999 oz. APW

Date	Mintage	MS-63	Proof
1997 Proof	5,000	—	165

KM# 322 Obv: Crowned head right, date below **Rev:** Grey wolf **Rev. Designer:** Kerr Burnett **Weight:** 3.1100 g. **Composition:** 0.9990 Platinum 0.0999 oz. APW

Date	Mintage	MS-63	Proof
ND(1998) Proof	2,000	—	165

KM# 359 Obv: Crowned head right, date below **Rev:** Musk ox **Rev. Designer:** Mark Hobson **Weight:** 3.1100 g. **Composition:** 0.9995 Platinum 0.0999 oz. APW

Date	Mintage	MS-63	Proof
1999 Proof	1,500	—	165

KM# 405 Obv: Crowned head right, date below **Rev:** Pronghorn antelope head, denomination below **Rev. Designer:** Mark Hobson **Edge:** Reeded **Weight:** 3.1100 g. **Composition:** 0.9995 Platinum 0.0999 oz. APW **Size:** 16 mm.

Date	Mintage	MS-63	Proof
2000 Proof	600	—	165

KM# 429 Obv: Crowned head right **Rev:** Harlequin duck's head **Rev. Designer:** Cosme Saffioti and Susan Taylor **Edge:** Reeded **Weight:** 3.1100 g. **Composition:** 0.9995 Platinum 0.0999 oz. APW **Size:** 16 mm.

Date	Mintage	MS-63	Proof
2001 Proof	448	—	165

50 DOLLARS

KM# 167 Obv: Young bust right, denomination and date below **Obv. Designer:** Machin **Rev:** Maple leaf flanked by 9995 **Weight:** 31.1030 g. **Composition:** 0.9995 Platinum 0.9994 oz. APW

Date	Mintage	MS-63	Proof
1988	37,500	BV+4%	—
1989	10,000	BV+4%	—
1989 Proof	5,965	—	1,500

KM# 195 Obv. Designer: dePedery-Hunt **Rev:** Maple leaf **Weight:** 31.1030 g. **Composition:** 0.9995 Platinum 0.9994 oz. APW

Date	Mintage	MS-63	Proof
1990	15,100	BV+4%	—
1991	31,900	BV+4%	—
1992	40,500	BV+4%	—
1993	17,666	BV+4%	—
1994	36,245	BV+4%	—
1995	25,829	BV+4%	—
1996	62,273	BV+4%	—
1997	25,480	BV+4%	—
1998	10,403	BV+4%	—
1999	1,300	BV+10%	—

75 DOLLARS

KM# 175 Obv: Crowned head right **Rev:** Polar bear resting, denomination below **Rev. Designer:** Robert Bateman **Weight:** 7.7760 g. **Composition:** 0.9990 Platinum 0.2497 oz. APW

Date	Mintage	MS-63	Proof
1990 Proof	2,629	—	380

KM# 199 Obv: Crowned head right **Rev:** Snowy owls perched on branch, denomination below **Rev. Designer:** Glen Loates **Weight:** 7.7760 g. **Composition:** 0.9990 Platinum 0.2497 oz. APW

Date	Mintage	MS-63	Proof
1991 Proof	3,500	—	380

KM# 227 Obv: Crowned head right **Rev:** Cougar prowling, denomination below **Rev. Designer:** George McLean **Weight:** 7.7760 g. **Composition:** 0.9990 Platinum 0.2497 oz. APW

Date	Mintage	MS-63	Proof
1992 Proof	3,500	—	380

KM# 241 Obv: Crowned head right **Rev:** Two Arctic foxes, denomination below **Rev. Designer:** Claude D'Angelo **Weight:** 7.7760 g. **Composition:** 0.9990 Platinum 0.2497 oz. APW

Date	Mintage	MS-63	Proof
1993 Proof	3,500	—	380

KM# 253 Obv: Crowned head right, date below **Rev:** Sea otter eating urchin, denomination below **Rev. Designer:** Ron S. Parker **Weight:** 7.7760 g. **Composition:** 0.9990 Platinum 0.2497 oz. APW

Date	Mintage	MS-63	Proof
1994 Proof	1,500	—	380

KM# 267 Obv: Crowned head right, date below **Rev:** Two lynx kittens, denomination below **Rev. Designer:** Michael Dumas **Weight:** 7.7760 g. **Composition:** 0.9990 Platinum 0.2497 oz. APW

Date	Mintage	MS-63	Proof
1995 Proof	1,500	—	380

KM# 279 Obv: Crowned head right, date below **Rev:** Peregrine falcon, denomination below **Rev. Designer:** Dwayne Harty **Weight:** 7.7760 g. **Composition:** 0.9990 Platinum 0.2497 oz. APW

Date	Mintage	MS-63	Proof
1996 Proof	1,500	—	380

KM# 301 Obv: Crowned head right, date below **Rev:** Two bison calves, denomination below **Rev. Designer:** Chris Bacon **Weight:** 7.7760 g. **Composition:** 0.9990 Platinum 0.2497 oz. APW

Date	Mintage	MS-63	Proof
1997 Proof	1,500	—	380

KM# 323 Obv: Crowned head right, date below **Rev:** Gray wolf **Rev. Designer:** Kerr Burnett **Weight:** 7.7760 g. **Composition:** 0.9990 Platinum 0.2497 oz. APW

Date	Mintage	MS-63	Proof
1998 Proof	1,000	—	380

KM# 360 Obv: Crowned head right, date below **Rev:** Musk ox **Rev. Designer:** Mark Hobson **Weight:** 7.7760 g. **Composition:** 0.9990 Platinum 0.2497 oz. APW

Date	Mintage	MS-63	Proof
1999 Proof	500	—	380

KM# 406 Obv: Crowned head right **Rev:** Standing pronghorn antelope, denomination below **Rev. Designer:** Mark Hobson **Edge:** Reeded **Weight:** 7.7760 g. **Composition:** 0.9990 Platinum 0.2497 oz. APW **Size:** 20 mm.

Date	Mintage	MS-63	Proof
2000 Proof	600	—	380

PLATINUM BULLION

KM# 430 Obv: Crowned head right **Rev:** Harlequin duck in flight **Rev. Des:** Cosme Saffioti and Susan Taylor **Edge:** Reeded **Weight:** 7.7760 g. **Comp:** 0.9995 Platinum 0.2499 oz. APW **Size:** 20 mm.

Date	Mintage	MS-63	Proof
2001 Proof	448	—	400

150 DOLLARS

KM# 176 Obv: Crowned head right **Rev:** Polar bear walking, denomination below **Rev. Designer:** Robert Bateman **Weight:** 15.5520 g. **Composition:** 0.9990 Platinum 0.4995 oz. APW

Date	Mintage	MS-63	Proof
1990 Proof	2,629	—	725

KM# 200 Obv: Crowned head right **Rev:** Snowy owl flying, denomination below **Rev. Designer:** Glen Loates **Weight:** 15.5520 g. **Composition:** 0.9990 Platinum 0.4995 oz. APW

Date	Mintage	MS-63	Proof
1991 Proof	3,500	—	725

KM# 228 Obv: Crowned head right **Rev:** Cougar mother and cub, denomination below **Rev. Designer:** George McLean **Weight:** 15.5520 g. **Composition:** 0.9990 Platinum 0.4995 oz. APW

Date	Mintage	MS-63	Proof
1992 Proof	3,500	—	725

KM# 242 Obv: Crowned head right **Rev:** Arctic fox by lake, denomination below **Rev. Designer:** Claude D'Angelo **Weight:** 15.5520 g. **Composition:** 0.9990 Platinum 0.4995 oz. APW

Date	Mintage	MS-63	Proof
1993 Proof	3,500	—	725

KM# 254 Obv: Crowned head right, date below **Rev:** Sea otter mother carrying pup, denomination below **Rev. Designer:** Ron S. Parker **Weight:** 15.5520 g. **Composition:** 0.9990 Platinum 0.4995 oz. APW

Date	Mintage	MS-63	Proof
1994 Proof	—	—	725

KM# 268 Obv: Crowned head right, date below **Rev:** Prowling lynx, denomination below **Rev. Designer:** Michael Dumas **Weight:** 15.5520 g. **Composition:** 0.9990 Platinum 0.4995 oz. APW

Date	Mintage	MS-63	Proof
1995 Proof	226	—	725

KM# 280 Obv: Crowned head right, date below **Rev:** Peregrine falcon on branch, denomination below **Rev. Designer:** Dwayne Harty **Weight:** 15.5520 g. **Composition:** 0.9990 Platinum 0.4995 oz. APW

Date	Mintage	MS-63	Proof
1996 Proof	100	—	725

KM# 302 Obv: Crowned head right, date below **Rev:** Bison bull, denomination below **Rev. Designer:** Chris Bacon **Weight:** 15.5520 g. **Composition:** 0.9990 Platinum 0.4995 oz. APW

Date	Mintage	MS-63	Proof
1997 Proof	4,000	—	725

KM# 324 Obv: Crowned head right, date below
Rev: Two gray wolf cubs, denomination below
Rev. Designer: Kerr Burnett **Weight:** 15.5520 g.
Composition: 0.9990 Platinum 0.4995 oz. APW

Date	Mintage	MS-63	Proof
1998 Proof	2,000	—	725

KM# 361 Obv: Crowned head right **Rev:** Musk ox,
denomination below **Rev. Designer:** Mark Hobson
Weight: 15.5520 g. **Composition:** 0.9990
Platinum 0.4995 oz. APW

Date	Mintage	MS-63	Proof
1999 Proof	500	—	725

KM# 407 Obv: Crowned head right **Rev:** Two
pronghorn antelope, denomination below
Rev. Designer: Mark Hobson **Edge:** Reeded
Weight: 15.5500 g. **Composition:** 0.9990
Platinum 0.4994 oz. APW **Size:** 25 mm.

Date	Mintage	MS-63	Proof
2000 Proof	600	—	725

KM# 431 Obv: Crowned head right **Rev:** Two
harlequin ducks **Rev. Designer:** Cosme Saffioti and
Susan Taylor **Edge:** Reeded **Weight:** 15.5500 g.
Composition: 0.9995 Platinum 0.4997 oz. APW
Size: 25 mm.

Date	Mintage	MS-63	Proof
2001 Proof	448	—	800

300 DOLLARS

KM# 177 Obv: Crowned head right **Rev:** Polar
bear mother and cub, denomination below **Rev.
Designer:** Robert Bateman **Weight:** 31.1035 g.
Composition: 0.9990 Platinum 0.9990 oz. APW

Date	Mintage	MS-63	Proof
1990 Proof	2,629	—	1,450

KM# 201 Obv: Crowned head right **Rev:** Snowy
owl with chicks, denomination below
Rev. Designer: Glen Loates **Weight:** 31.1035 g.
Composition: 0.9990 Platinum 0.9990 oz. APW

Date	Mintage	MS-63	Proof
1991 Proof	3,500	—	1,450

KM# 229 Obv: Crowned head right **Rev:** Cougar
resting in tree, denomination below **Rev. Designer:**
George McLean **Weight:** 31.1035 g. **Composition:**
0.9990 Platinum 0.9990 oz. APW

Date	Mintage	MS-63	Proof
1992 Proof	3,500	—	1,450

KM# 243 Obv: Crowned head right **Rev:** Mother
fox and three kits, denomination below **Rev.
Designer:** Claude D'Angelo **Weight:** 31.1035 g.
Composition: 0.9990 Platinum 0.9990 oz. APW

Date	Mintage	MS-63	Proof
1993 Proof	3,500	—	1,450

KM# 255 Obv: Crowned head right, date below
Rev: Two otters swimming, denomination below
Rev. Designer: Ron S. Parker **Weight:** 31.1035 g.
Composition: 0.9990 Platinum 0.9990 oz. APW

Date	Mintage	MS-63	Proof
1994 Proof	—	—	1,450

KM# 269 Obv: Crowned head right, date below
Rev: Female lynx and three kittens, denomination
below **Rev. Designer:** Michael Dumas **Weight:**
31.1035 g. **Composition:** 0.9990 Platinum
0.9990 oz. APW

Date	Mintage	MS-63	Proof
1995 Proof	1,500	—	1,450

KM# 281 Obv: Crowned head right, date below
Rev: Peregrine falcon feeding nestlings,
denomination below **Rev. Designer:** Dwayne Harty
Weight: 31.1035 g. **Composition:** 0.9990
Platinum 0.9990 oz. APW

Date	Mintage	MS-63	Proof
1996 Proof	1,500	—	1,450

KM# 303 Obv: Crowned head right, date below
Rev: Bison family, denomination below
Rev. Designer: Chris Bacon **Weight:** 31.1035 g.
Composition: 0.9990 Platinum 0.9990 oz. APW

Date	Mintage	MS-63	Proof
1997 Proof	1,500	—	1,450

KM# 325 Obv: Crowned head right, date below
Rev: Gray wolf and two cubs, denomination below
Rev. Designer: Kerr Burnett **Weight:** 31.1035 g.
Composition: 0.9990 Platinum 0.9990 oz. APW

Date	Mintage	MS-63	Proof
1998 Proof	—	—	1,450

KM# 362 Obv: Crowned head right, date below
Rev: Musk ox **Rev. Designer:** Mark Hobson
Weight: 31.1035 g. **Composition:** 0.9990
Platinum 0.9990 oz. APW

Date	Mintage	MS-63	Proof
1999 Proof	500	—	1,450

KM# 408 Obv: Crowned head right, date below
Rev: Four pronghorn antelope, denomination below
Rev. Designer: Mark Hobson **Edge:** Reeded
Weight: 31.1035 g. **Composition:** 0.9990
Platinum 0.9990 oz. APW **Size:** 30 mm.

Date	Mintage	MS-63	Proof
2000 Proof	600	—	1,450

KM# 432 Obv: Crowned head right **Rev:** Two
standing harlequin ducks **Rev. Designer:** Cosme
Saffioti and Susan Taylor **Edge:** Reeded **Weight:**
31.1035 g. **Composition:** 0.9995 Platinum
0.9995 oz. APW **Size:** 30 mm.

Date	Mintage	MS-63	Proof
2001 Proof	448	—	1,600

SETS

Custom Proof-Like Sets (CPL)

KM#	Date	Mintage	Identification	Issue Price	Mkt. Value
CPL1	1971 (6)	33,517	KM59.1 (2 pcs.), 60.1, 62b-75.1, 77.1 ,79	6.50	5.00
CPL2	1971 (5)	38,198	KM59.1 (2 pcs.), 60.1, 62b, 75.1-77.1	6.50	5.00
CPL3	1973 (5)	35,676	KM59.1 (2 pcs.), 60.1, 75.1, 77.1, 81.1 obv. 120 beads, 82	6.50	6.50
CPL4	1973 (5)	Inc. above	KM59.1 (2 pcs.), 60.1, 75.1, 77.1, 81.1 obv. 132 beads, 82	6.50	200
CPL5	1974 (5)	44,296	KM59.1 (2 pcs.), 60.1, 62b-75.1, 88	8.00	5.00
CPL6	1975 (6)	36,851	KM59.1 (2 pcs.), 60.1, 62b-75.1, 76.2, 77.1	8.00	5.00
CPL7	1976 (6)	28,162	KM59.1 (2 pcs.), 60.1, 62b-75.1, 76.2, 77.1	8.00	5.50
CPL8	1977 (6)	44,198	KM59.1 (2 pcs.), 60.1, 62b-75.2, 77.1, 117	8.15	5.00
CPL9	1978 (6)	41,000	KM59.1 (2 pcs.), 60.1, 62b-75.3, 77.1, 120.1	—	5.00
CPL10	1979 (6)	31,174	KM59.2 (2 pcs.), 60.2, 74, 75.3, 77.2, 120.1	10.75	5.00
CPL11	1980 (7)	41,447	KM60.2, 74, 75.3, 77.2, 120.1, 127 (2 pcs.)	10.75	6.00

Mint Sets

KM#	Date	Mintage	Identification	Issue Price	Mkt. Value
MS1	1973 (4)	Inc. above	KM84-85, 86.1, 87; Olympic Commemoratives, Series I	45.00	70.00
MS2	1974 (4)	Inc. above	KM89-90, 93-94; Olympic Commemoratives, Series II	48.00	70.00
MS3	1974 (4)	Inc. above	KM91-92, 95-96; Olympic Commemorative, Series III	48.00	70.00
MS4	1975 (4)	Inc. above	KM98-99, 102-103; Olympic Commemoratives, Series IV	48.00	70.00
MS5	1975 (4)	Inc. above	KM100-101, 104-105; Olympic Commemoratives, Series V	60.00	70.00
MS6	1976 (4)	Inc. above	KM107-108, 111-112; Olympic Commemoratives, Series VI	60.00	70.00
MS7	1976 (4)	Inc. above	KM109-110, 113-114; Olympic Commemoratives, Series VII	60.00	70.00
MS8	2001 (5)	600	KM438-442	1,996	2,450
MS12	2003 (7)	135,000	KM#289, 182b, 183b, 184b, 290, 186, 270	12.00	12.00
MS13	2003 (7)	75,000	KM#490-496	13.25	14.00

Olympic Commemoratives (OCP)

KM#	Date	Mintage	Identification	Issue Price	Mkt. Value
OCP1	1973 (4)	Inc. above	KM84-87, Series I	78.50	70.00
OCP2	1974 (4)	Inc. above	KM89-90, 93-94, Series II	88.50	70.00
OCP3	1974 (4)	Inc. above	KM91-92, 95-96, Series III	88.50	70.00
OCP4	1975 (4)	Inc. above	KM98-99, 102-103, Series IV	88.50	70.00
OCP5	1975 (4)	Inc. above	KM100-101, 104-105, Series V	88.50	70.00
OCP6	1976 (4)	Inc. above	KM107-108, 111-112, Series VI	88.50	70.00
OCP7	1976 (4)	Inc. above	KM109-110, 113-114, Series VII	88.50	70.00

Proof Sets

KM#	Date	Mintage	Identification	Issue Price	Mkt. Value
XPS1	1952 (6)	—	X#MB41-MB46	—	—
XPS2	1979 (5)	100	X#Tn1a-Tn5a	—	40.00
XPS3	1980 (6)	1,500	X#MB51-MB56	—	110
PS1	1981 (7)	199,000	KM60.2, 74, 75.3, 77.2, 120.1, 127, 130	36.00	17.50
PS2	1982 (7)	180,908	KM60.2a, 74, 75.3, 77.2, 120.1, 132-133	36.00	14.00
PS3	1983 (7)	166,779	KM60.2a, 74, 75.3, 77.2, 120.1, 132, 138	36.00	14.00
PS4	1984 (7)	161,602	KM60.2a, 74, 75.3, 77.2, 120.1, 132, 140	30.00	17.00
PS5	1985 (7)	157,037	KM60.2a, 74, 75.3, 77.2, 120.1, 132, 143	30.00	18.00
PS6	1986 (7)	175,745	KM60.2a, 74, 75.3, 77.2, 120.1, 132, 149	30.00	18.00
PS7	1987 (7)	179,004	KM60.2a, 74, 75.3, 77.2, 120.1, 132, 154	34.00	18.00
PS8	1988 (7)	175,259	KM60.2a, 74, 75.3, 77.2, 132, 157, 161	37.50	23.00
PS10	1989 (4)	6,823	KM125.2, 135-136, 153	1,190	1,100
PS11	1989 (4)	1,995	KM164-167	1,700	2,100
PS12	1989 (3)	2,550	KM125.2, 163, 167	1,530	1,775
PS13	1989 (3)	9,979	KM135, 163-164	165	225
PS9	1989 (7)	170,928	KM60.2a, 74, 75.3, 77.2, 132, 157, 168	40.00	24.00
PS14	1990 (7)	158,068	KM170, 181, 182, 183, 184, 185, 186	41.00	24.00
PS15	1990 (4)	2,629	KM174-177	1,720	2,475
PS16	1991 (7)	14,629	KM179, 181, 182, 183, 184, 185, 186	—	45.00
PS17	1991 (4)	873	KM198-201	1,760	2,475
PS18	1992 (11)	84,397	KM203a, 212a-214a, 218, 220a-223a, 231a-234a	—	90.00
PS19	1992 (7)	147,061	KM204-210	42.75	30.00
PS20	1992 (4)	3,500	KM226-229	1,680	2,500
PS21	1993 (7)	143,065	KM181, 182, 183, 184, 185, 186, 235	42.75	20.00
PS22	1993 (4)	3,500	KM240-243	1,329	2,500
PS23	1994 (7)	47,303	KM181-186, 248	47.50	28.00
PS24	1994 (7)	99,121	KM181, 182, 183, 184, 185, 186, 251	43.00	28.00
PS25	1994 (4)	1,500	KM252-255	915	2,520
PS26	1995 (7)	Inc. above	KM181, 182, 183, 184, 185, 186, 259	37.45	25.00
PS27	1995 (7)	50,000	KM181, 182, 183, 184, 185, 258-259	49.45	22.00
PS28	1995 (4)	Inc. above	KM261-264	42.00	60.00
PS29	1995 (4)	682	KM266-269	1,555	2,500
PS30	1995 (2)	Inc. above	KM261-262	22.00	21.00
PS31	1995 (2)	Inc. above	KM263-264	22.00	30.00
PS32	1996 (4)	423	KM278-281	1,555	2,500
PS33	1996 (7)	Inc. above	KM181a, 182a, 183a, 184a, 185a, 186, 274	49.00	35.00
PS34	1996 (4)	Inc. above	KM283-286	44.45	45.00
PS35	1997 (6)	Inc. above	KM182a, 183a, 184a, 209, 270c, 282, 289,	60.00	45.00
PS36	1997 (4)	Inc. above	KM292-295	44.45	35.00

KM#	Date	Mintage	Identification	Issue Price	Mkt. Value
PS37	1997 (4)	Inc. above	KM300-303	1,530	2,485
PS38	1998 (8)	Inc. above	KM182a, 183a, 184a, 186, 270b, 289, 290a, 306	59.45	50.00
PS39	1998 (5)	25,000	KM309-313	73.50	55.00
PS40	1998 (0)	61,000	KM316 w/China Y-727	72.50	30.00
PS41	1998 (4)	Inc. above	KM318-321	44.45	38.00
PS42	1998 (4)	1,000	KM322-325	1,552	2,500
PS43	1998 (5)	25,000	KM310-313, 332	73.50	30.00
PS44	1999 (7)	Inc. above	KM182a-184a, 186, 270c, 289, 290a,	59.45	90.00
PS45	1999 (4)	Inc. above	KM335-338	39.95	40.00
PS46	1999 (12)	Inc. above	KM342a-353a	99.45	75.00
PS47	1999 (4)	Inc. above	KM359-362	1,425	2,520
PS48	2000 (12)	—	KM373a, 374a, 375a, 376a, 377a, 378a, 379a, 380a, 381a, 382a, 383a, 384.2a	101	90.00
PS49	2000 (4)	—	KM389-392	44.00	40.00
PS50	2000 (4)	600	KM405-408	1,416	2,520
PS51	2001 (4)	—	KM429, 430, 431, 432	—	2,300
PS54	2002 (2)	—	KM#519, 520	750	725
PS57	2004 (8)	—	KM#490, 491a-494a, 495, 496a, 512	—	85.00
PS58	2004 (5)	25,000	KM#621-625	—	125

Proof-Like Dollars

KM#	Date	Mintage	Identification	Issue Price	Mkt. Value
D1.1	1951 (0)	Inc. above	KM46, Canoe		250
D1.2	1951 (0)	Inc. above	KM46, Arnprior		700
D2.1	1952 (1)	Inc. above	KM46, water lines		1,100
D2.2	1952 (1)	Inc. above	KM46, without water lines		350
D3	1953 (1)	1,200	KM54, Canoe w/shoulder fold	—	325
D4	1954 (1)	5,300	KM54, Canoe	1.25	150
D5	1955 (1)	7,950	KM54, Canoe	1.25	125
D5a	1955 (1)	Inc. above	KM54, Arnprior	1.25	175
D6	1956 (0)	10,212	KM54, Canoe	1.25	70.00
D7	1957 (1)	16,241	KM54, Canoe	1.25	40.00
D8	1958 (1)	33,237	KM55, British Columbia	1.25	25.00
D9	1959 (1)	45,160	KM54, Canoe	1.25	15.00
D10	1960 (1)	82,728	KM54, Canoe	1.25	10.00
D11	1961 (1)	120,928	KM54, Canoe	1.25	9.50
D12	1962 (1)	248,901	KM54, Canoe	1.25	9.50
D13	1963 (1)	963,525	KM54, Canoe	1.25	9.50
D14	1964 (1)	2,862,441	KM58, Charlottetown	1.25	9.50
D15	1965 (1)	2,904,352	KM64.1, Canoe	—	9.50
D16	1966 (1)	672,514	KM64.1, Canoe	—	9.50
D17	1967 (1)	1,036,176	KM70, Confederation	—	9.50

Proof-Like Sets (PL)

KM#	Date	Mintage	Identification	Issue Price	Mkt. Value
PL1	1953 (6)	1,200	KM49 w/o shoulder fold, 50-54	2.20	1,250
PL3	1954 (6)	3,000	KM49-54	2.50	450
PL4	1954 (6)	Inc. above	KM49 w/o shoulder fold, 50-54	2.50	1,100
PL5	1955 (6)	6,300	KM49, 50a, 51-54	2.50	375
PL6	1955 (6)	Inc. above	KM49, 50a, 51-54, Arnprior	2.50	500
PL7	1956 (6)	6,500	KM49, 50a, 51-54	2.50	225
PL8	1957 (6)	11,862	KM49, 50a, 51-54	2.50	150
PL9	1958 (6)	18,259	KM49, 50a, 51-53, 55	2.50	100.00
PL10	1959 (6)	31,577	KM49, 50a, 51, 52, 54, 56	2.50	45.00
PL11	1960 (6)	64,097	KM49, 50a, 51, 52, 54, 56	3.00	35.00
PL12	1961 (6)	98,373	KM49, 50a, 51, 52, 54, 56	3.00	30.00
PL13	1962 (6)	200,950	KM49, 50a, 51, 52, 54, 56	3.00	17.50
PL14	1963 (6)	673,006	KM49, 51, 52, 54, 56, 57	3.00	17.00
PL15	1964 (5)	1,653,162	KM49, 51, 52, 56-58	3.00	17.00
PL16	1965 (6)	2,904,352	KM59.1-60.1, 61-63, 64.1	4.00	17.00
PL17	1966 (5)	672,514	KM59.1-60.1, 61-63, 64.1	4.00	17.00
PL18	1967 (6)	961,887	KM65-70 (pliofilm flat pack)	4.00	17.00
PL18A	1967 (6)	70,583	KM65-70 and Silver Medal (red box)	12.00	29.00
PL18B	1967 (7)	337,688	KM65-71 (black box)	40.00	475
PL19	1968 (6)	521,641	KM59.1-60.1, 62b, 72a, 75.1-76.1	4.00	2.25
PL20	1969 (6)	326,203	KM59.1-60.1, 62b, 75.1-77.1	4.00	2.75
PL21	1970 (6)	349,120	KM59.1-60.1, 62b, 75.1, 77.1, 78	4.00	3.25
PL22	1971 (6)	253,311	KM59.1-60.1, 62b, 75.1, 77.1, 79	4.00	2.75
PL23	1972 (6)	224,275	KM59.1-60.1, 62b-77.1	4.00	2.75
PL24	1973 (6)	243,695	KM59.1-60.1, 62b-75.1 obv. 120 beads, 77.1, 81.1, 82	4.00	4.00
PL25	1973 (3)	Inc. above	KM59.1-60.1, 62b-75.1 obv. 132 beads, 77.1, 81.2, 82	4.00	250
PL26	1974 (6)	213,589	KM59.1-60.1, 62b-75.1, 77.1, 88	5.00	3.00
PL27.1	1975 (4)	197,372	KM59.1, 60.1, 62b-75.1, 76.2, 77.1	5.00	3.50
PL27.2	1975 (6)	Inc. above	KM59.1, 60.1, 62b-75.1, 76.3, 77.1	5.00	5.00
PL28	1976 (6)	171,737	KM59.1, 60.1, 62b-75.1, 76.2, 77.1	5.15	2.75
PL29	1977 (6)	225,307	KM59.1, 60.1, 62b, 75.2, 77.1, 117.1	5.15	2.75
PL30	1978 (6)	260,000	KM59.1-60.1, 62b, 75.3, 77.1, 120.1	5.25	2.75
PL31	1979 (6)	187,624	KM59.2-60.2, 74, 75.3, 77.2, 120.1	6.25	2.75
PL32	1980 (6)	410,842	KM60.2, 74, 75.3, 77.2, 120.1, 127	6.50	4.50

KM#	Date	Mintage	Identification	Issue Price	Mkt. Value
PL33	1981 (6)	186,250	KM60.2, 74, 75.3, 77.2, 120.1, 123	5.00	3.25
PL34	1982 (5)	203,287	KM60.2, 74, 75.3, 77.2, 120.1, 123	6.00	3.50
PL36	1983 (6)	190,838	KM60.2a, 74, 75.3, 77.2, 120.1, 132	5.00	5.00
PL36.1	1983 (6)	Inc. above	KM60.2a, 74, 75.3, 77.2, 120.1, 132; set in folder packaged by British Royal Mint Coin Club	—	—
PL37	1984 (6)	181,249	KM60.2a, 74, 75.3, 77.2, 120.1, 132	5.25	5.00
PL38	1985 (6)	173,924	KM60.2a, 74, 75.3, 77.2, 120.1, 132	5.25	6.00
PL39	1986 (6)	167,338	KM60.2a, 74, 75.3, 77.2, 120.1, 132	5.25	6.50
PL40	1987 (6)	212,136	KM60.2a, 74, 75.3, 77.2, 120.1, 132	5.25	5.00
PL41	1988 (6)	182,048	KM60.2a, 74, 75.3, 77.2, 132, 157	6.05	5.00
PL42	1989 (6)	173,622	KM60.2a, 74, 75.3, 77.2, 132, 157	6.60	8.00
PL43	1990 (6)	170,791	KM181-186	7.40	8.00
PL44	1991 (6)	147,814	KM181-186	7.40	25.00
PL45	1992 (6)	217,597	KM204-209	8.25	11.00
PL46	1993 (6)	171,680	KM181-186	8.25	4.00
PL47	1994 (6)	141,676	KM181-185, 258	8.50	5.50
PL48	1994 (6)	18,794	KM181-185, 258 (Oh Canada holder)	—	8.50
PL49	1995 (6)	143,892	KM181-186	6.95	6.00
PL50	1995 (6)	50,927	KM181-186 (Oh Canada holder)	14.65	8.50
PL51	1995 (6)	36,443	KM181-186 (Baby Gift holder)	—	9.00
PL52	1996 (4)	116,736	KM181-186	—	27.00
PL53	1996 (6)	29,747	KM181-186 (Baby Gift holder)	—	14.00
PL54	1996 (6)	Inc. above	KM181a-185a, 186	8.95	16.00
PL55	1996 (6)	Inc. above	KM181a-185a, 186 (Oh Canada holder)	14.65	12.00
PL56	1996 (6)	Inc. above	KM181a-185a, 186 (Baby Gift holder)	—	12.00
PL57	1997 (7)	Inc. above	KM182a-184a, 209, 270, 289-290	10.45	8.00
PL58	1997 (7)	Inc. above	KM182a-184a, 270, 289-291 (Oh Canada holder)	16.45	30.00
PL59	1997 (7)	Inc. above	KM182a-184a, 209, 270, 289-290 (Baby Gift holder)	18.50	9.50
PL60	1998 (7)	Inc. above	KM182-184, 186, 270, 289-290	10.45	15.00
PL61	1998 (7)	Inc. above	KM182-184, 186, 270, 289-290 (Oh Canada holder)	16.45	17.00
PL62	1998 (7)	Inc. above	KM182-184, 186, 270, 289-290 (Tiny Treasures holder)	16.45	17.00
PL63	1999 (12)	Inc. above	KM342-353	16.95	10.00
PL64	2000 (12)	—	KM373-384	16.95	10.00

Specimen Sets (SS)

KM#	Date	Mintage	Identification	Issue Price	Mkt. Value
SS1	1858 (4)	Inc. above	KM1-4, Reeded edge	—	9,000
SS2	1858 (4)	Inc. above	KM1-4, Plain edge	—	6,000
SS3	1858 (8)	Inc. above	KM1-4; Double Set	—	15,000
SS4	1858 (8)	Inc. above	KM1 (overdate), 2-4; Double Set	—	15,000
SS5	1870 (4)	100	KM2, 3, 5, 6 (reeded edges)	—	28,500
SS6	1870 (8)	Inc. above	KM2, 3, 5, 6; Double Set (plain edges)	—	55,000
SS7	1872 (4)	Inc. above	KM2, 3, 5, 6	—	12,500
SS8	1875 (3)	Inc. above	KM2 (Large date), 3, 5	—	65,000
SS9	1880 (3)	Inc. above	KM2, 3, 5 (Narrow 0)	—	35,000
SS10	1881 (5)	Inc. above	KM7, 2, 3, 5, 6	—	26,500
SS11	1892 (2)	Inc. above	KM3, 5	—	10,000
SS12	1902 (5)	100	KM8-12	—	25,000
SS13	1902 (3)	Inc. above	KM9 (Large H), 10, 11	—	6,500
SS14	1903 (3)	Inc. above	KM10, 12, 13	—	7,000
SS15	1908 (5)	1,000	KM8, 10-13	—	2,200
SS16	1911 (5)	1,000	KM15-19	—	5,500
SS17	1911/12 (0)	5	KM15-20, 26-27	—	52,250
SS18	1921 (5)	Inc. above	KM22-25, 28	—	120,000
SS19	1922 (2)	Inc. above	KM28, 29	—	2,500
SS20	1923 (2)	Inc. above	KM28, 29	—	5,000
SS21	1924 (2)	Inc. above	KM28, 29	—	4,000
SS22	1925 (2)	Inc. above	KM28, 29	—	7,000
SS23	1926 (2)	Inc. above	KM28, 29 (Near 6)	—	5,000
SS24	1927 (3)	Inc. above	KM24a, 28, 29	—	8,000
SS25	1928 (4)	Inc. above	KM23a, 24a, 28, 29	—	12,000
SS26	1929 (5)	Inc. above	KM23a,-25a, 28, 29	—	22,500
SS27	1930 (4)	Inc. above	KM23a, 24a. 28, 29	—	16,000
SS28	1931 (5)	Inc. above	KM23a-25a, 28, 29	—	26,500
SS29	1932 (5)	Inc. above	KM23a-25a, 28, 29	—	20,000
SS30	1934 (5)	Inc. above	KM23-25, 28, 29	—	23,000
SS31	1936 (5)	Inc. above	KM23-25, 28, 29	—	12,000
SS32	1936 (6)	Inc. above	KM23a(dot), 24a(dot), 25a, 28(dot), 29, 30	—	400,000
SS33	1937 (6)	1,025	KM32-37, Matte Finish	—	750
SS34	1937 (4)	Inc. above	KM32-35, Mirror Fields	—	1,350
SS35	1937 (6)	75	KM32-37, Mirror Fields	—	3,900
SS36	1938 (6)	Inc. above	KM32-37	—	18,250
SS-A36	1939 (6)	Inc. above	KM32-35, 38, Matte Finish	—	—
SS-B36	1939 (6)	Inc. above	KM32-35, 38, Mirror Fields	—	—
SS-C36	1942 (2)	Inc. above	KM32, 33	—	1,000
SS-D36	1943 (2)	Inc. above	KM32, 40	—	1,000
SS-A37	1944 (2)	Inc. above	KM32, 40a	—	1,000
SS37	1944 (5)	3	KM32, 34-37, 40a	—	11,300
SS-A38	1945 (2)	Inc. above	KM32, 40a	—	1,000

SETS

KM#	Date	Mintage	Identification	Issue Price	Mkt. Value
SS38	1945 (6)	6	KM32, 34-37, 40a	—	4,650
SS39	1946 (6)	15	KM32, 34-37, 39a	—	4,000
SS40	1947 (6)	Inc. above	KM32, 34-37(7 curved), 37(7 pointed),	—	8,500
SS41	1947 (6)	Inc. above	KM32, 34-36(7 curved), 37(blunt 7), 39a	—	6,200
SS42	1947 (6)	Inc. above	KM32, 34-36(7 curved right), 37, 39a	—	4,250
SS43	1948 (6)	30	KM41-46	—	6,000
SS44	1949 (6)	20	KM41-45, 47	—	6,400
SS44A	1949 (2)	Inc. above	KM47	—	1,550
SS45	1950 (6)	12	KM41-46	—	1,650
SS46	1950 (6)	Inc. above	KM41-45, 46 (Amprior)	—	3,175
SS47	1951 (7)	12	KM41, 48, 42a, 43-46 (w/water lines)	—	2,725
SS48	1952 (6)	2,317	KM41, 42a, 43-46 (water lines)	—	3,175
SS48A	1952 (6)	Inc. above	KM41, 42a, 43-46 (w/o water lines)	—	3,175
SS49	1953 (6)	28	KM49 w/o straps, 50-54	—	1,850
SS50	1953 (6)	Inc. above	KM49 w/ straps, 50-54	—	875
SS51	1964 (6)	Inc. above	KM49, 51, 52, 56-58	—	850
SS52	1965 (6)	Inc. above	KM59.1-60.1, 61-63, 64.1	—	850
SS56	1971 (6)	66,860	KM59.1-60.1, 62b-75.1, 77.1, 79 (2 pcs.); Double Dollar Prestige Sets	12.00	14.50
SS57	1972 (7)	36,349	KM59.1,-60.1, 62b-75.1, 76.1 (2 pcs.), 77; Double Dollar Prestige Sets	12.00	18.00
SS58	1973 (6)	119,819	KM59.1-60.1, 75.1, 77.1, 81.1, 82, 83; Double Dollar Prestige Sets	12.00	16.00
SS59	1973 (6)	Inc. above	KM59.1-60.1, 75.1, 77.1, 81.2, 82, 83; Double Dollar Prestige Sets	—	225
SS60	1974 (7)	85,230	KM59.1-60.1, 62b-75.1, 77.1, 88, 88a; Double Dollar Prestige Sets	15.00	10.00
SS61	1975 (7)	97,263	KM59.1-60.1, 62b-75.1, 76.2, 77.1, 97; Double Dollar Prestige Sets	15.00	10.00
SS62	1976 (7)	87,744	KM59.1-60, 62b-75.1, 76.2, 77.1, 106; Double Dollar Prestige Sets	16.00	10.00
SS63	1977 (7)	142,577	KM59.1-60.1, 62b, 75.2, 77.1, 117.1, 118; Double Dollar Prestige Sets	16.50	10.00
SS64	1978 (7)	147,000	KM59.1-60.1, 62b, 75.3, 77.1, 120.1, 121; Double Dollar Prestige Sets	16.50	10.00
SS65	1979 (7)	155,698	KM59.2-60.2, 74, 75.3, 77.2, 120, 124; Double Dollar Prestige Sets	18.50	11.50
SS66	1980 (7)	162,875	KM60.2, 74-75.3, 77.2, 120, 127, 128; Double Dollar Prestige Sets	30.50	22.50
SS67	1981 (6)	71,300	KM60.2, 74, 75.3, 77.2, 120.1, 127; Regular Specimen Sets Resumed	10.00	5.50
SS68	1982 (6)	62,298	KM60.2a, 74, 75.3, 77.2, 120.1, 132; Regular Specimen Sets Resumed	11.50	5.50
SS69	1983 (6)	60,329	KM60.2a, 74, 75.3, 77.2, 120.1, 132; Regular Specimen Sets Resumed	12.75	5.50
SS70	1984 (6)	60,400	KM60.2a, 74, 75.3, 77.2, 120.1, 132; Regular Specimen Sets Resumed	10.00	5.50
SS71	1985 (6)	61,553	KM60.2a, 74, 75.3, 77.2, 120.1, 132; Regular Specimen Sets Resumed	10.00	6.00
SS72	1986 (6)	67,152	KM60.2a, 74, 75.3, 77.2, 120.1, 132; Regular Specimen Sets Resumed	10.00	9.00
SS72A	1987 (6)	75,194	KM60.2a, 74, 75.3, 77.2, 120.1, 132; Regular Specimen Sets Resumed	11.00	6.50
SS73	1988 (6)	70,205	KM60.2a, 74, 75.3, 77.2, 132, 157; Regular Specimen Sets Resumed	12.30	6.50
SS74	1989 (6)	75,306	KM60.2a, 74, 75.3, 77.2, 132, 157; Regular Specimen Sets Resumed	14.50	8.50
SS75	1990 (6)	76,611	KM181-186; Regular Specimen Sets Resumed	15.50	8.50
SS76	1991 (6)	68,552	KM181-186; Regular Specimen Sets Resumed	15.50	30.00
SS77	1992 (6)	78,328	KM204-209; Regular Specimen Sets Resumed	16.25	13.00
SS78	1993 (6)	77,351	KM181-186; Regular Specimen Sets Resumed	16.25	13.00
SS79	1994 (6)	77,349	KM181-186; Regular Specimen Sets Resumed	16.50	9.50
SS80	1995 (6)	Inc. above	KM181-186; Regular Specimen Sets Resumed	13.95	9.50
SS82	1996 (4)	Inc. above	KM181a-185a, 186; Regular Specimen Sets Resumed	18.95	19.00
SS83	1997 (7)	Inc. above	KM182a-184a, 270, 289-291; Regular Specimen Sets Resumed	19.95	25.00
SS84	1998 (7)	Inc. above	KM182-184, 186, 270, 289, 290; Regular Specimen Sets Resumed	19.95	18.00
SS85	1999 (7)	Inc. above	KM182-184, 186, 270, 289a, 290; Regular Specimen Sets Resumed	19.95	11.00
SS91	2003 (7)	75,000	KM#182-184, 186, 270, 289, 290	30.00	27.50

V.I.P. Specimen Sets (VS)

KM#	Date	Mintage	Identification	Issue Price	Mkt. Value
VS1	1969 (0)	4		—	2,000
VS2	1970 (0)	100	KM59.1-60.1, 74.1-75.1, 77.1, 78	—	525
VS3	1971 (0)	69	KM59.1-60.1, 74.1-75.1, 77.1, 79(2 pcs.)	—	525
VS4	1972 (0)	25	KM59.1-60.1, 74.1-75.1, 76.1, (2 pcs.), 77.1	—	650
VS5	1973 (0)	26	KM59.1-60.1, 75.1, 77.1, 81.1, 82, 83	—	650
VS6	1974 (0)	72	KM59.1-60.1, 74.1-75.1, 77.1, 88, 88a	—	525
VS7	1975 (0)	94	KM59.1-60.1, 74.1-75.1, 76.2, 77.1, 97	—	525
VS8	1976 (0)	Inc. above	KM59.1-60.1, 74.1-75.1, 76.2, 77.1, 106	—	525

SETS

NEW BRUNSWICK

PROVINCE

STERLING COINAGE

HALFPENNY TOKEN

KM# 1 **Obv:** Crowned head left **Obv. Legend:** VICTORIA DEI GRATIA REGINA **Rev:** Three masted ship
Rev. Legend: NEW BRUNSWICK **Composition:** Copper

Date	Mintage	VG-8	F-12	VF-20	XF-40	MS-60	MS-63	Proof
1843	480,000	4.00	6.00	11.50	30.00	250	400	—
1843 Proof	—	—	—	—	—	—	—	750

KM# 3 **Obv:** Head left **Obv. Legend:** VICTORIA DEI GRATIA REGINA **Rev:** Three masted ship
Rev. Legend: NEW BRUNSWICK **Composition:** Copper

Date	Mintage	VG-8	F-12	VF-20	XF-40	MS-60	MS-63	Proof
1854	864,000	4.00	6.00	11.50	30.00	225	350	—

KM# 3a **Obv:** Head left **Obv. Legend:** VICTORIA DEI GRATIA REGINA **Rev:** Three masted ship
Rev. Legend: NEW BRUNSWICK **Composition:** Bronze

Date	Mintage	VG-8	F-12	VF-20	XF-40	MS-60	MS-63	Proof
1854 Proof	—	—	—	—	—	—	—	400

1 PENNY TOKEN

KM# 2 **Obv:** Crowned head left **Obv. Legend:** VICTORIA DEI GRATIA REGINA **Rev:** Three masted ship
Rev. Legend: NEW BRUNSWICK **Composition:** Copper

Date	Mintage	VG-8	F-12	VF-20	XF-40	MS-60	MS-63	Proof
1843	480,000	3.75	7.50	15.00	45.00	165	325	—
1843 Proof	—	—	—	—	—	—	—	800

KM# 4   Obv: Head left **Obv. Legend:** VICTORIA DEI GRATIA REGINA **Rev:** Three masted ship **Rev. Legend:** NEW BRUNSWICK **Composition:** Copper

Date	Mintage	VG-8	F-12	VF-20	XF-40	MS-60	MS-63	Proof
1854	432,000	3.75	7.50	15.00	50.00	250	400	—

DECIMAL COINAGE

HALF CENT

KM# 5   Obv: Laureate bust left **Obv. Legend:** VICTORIA D:G: BRITT: REG: F:D: **Rev:** Crown and date within beaded circle, wreath surrounds **Composition:** Bronze

Date	Mintage	VG-8	F-12	VF-20	XF-40	MS-60	MS-63	Proof
1861	222,800	100.00	150	225	350	650	1,500	—
1861 Proof	—	—	—	—	—	—	—	2,200

CENT

KM# 6   Obv: Laureate bust left **Obv. Legend:** VICTORIA D:G: BRITT: REG: F:D: **Rev:** Crown and date within beaded circle, wreath surrounds **Rev. Legend:** NEW BRUNSWICK **Composition:** Bronze

Date	Mintage	VG-8	F-12	VF-20	XF-40	MS-60	MS-63	Proof
1861	1,000,000	3.50	6.00	9.00	14.00	100.00	450	—
1861 Proof	—	—	—	—	—	—	—	450
1864 short 6	1,000,000	3.50	6.00	9.00	20.00	110	550	—
1864 long 6	Inc. above	4.00	6.50	13.00	24.00	175	650	—

5 CENTS

KM# 7   Obv: Laureate head left **Obv. Legend:** VICTORIA D: G: REG: NEW BRUNSWICK **Rev:** Denomination and date within wreath, crown above **Weight:** 1.1620 g. **Composition:** 0.9250 Silver 0.0346 oz. ASW

Date	Mintage	VG-8	F-12	VF-20	XF-40	MS-60	MS-63	Proof
1862	100,000	65.00	100.00	175	375	1,700	3,200	—
1862 Proof	—	—	—	—	—	—	—	3,500

Date	Mintage	VG-8	F-12	VF-20	XF-40	MS-60	MS-63	Proof
1864 small 6	100,000	65.00	100.00	175	375	1,700	4,900	—
1864 large 6	Inc. above	45.00	80.00	175	375	1,700	3,200	—

10 CENTS

KM# 8 Obv: Laureate head left **Obv. Legend:** VICTORIA D: G: REG: NEW BRUNSWICK **Rev:** Denomination and date within wreath, crown above **Weight:** 2.3240 g. **Composition:** 0.9250 Silver 0.0691 oz. ASW

Date	Mintage	VG-8	F-12	VF-20	XF-40	MS-60	MS-63	Proof
1862	150,000	65.00	100.00	175	350	1,200	2,450	—
1862 recut 2	Inc. above	95.00	175	275	550	2,200	6,700	—
1862 Proof	—	—	—	—	—	—	—	2,850
1864	100,000	65.00	100.00	175	350	2,700	6,300	—

20 CENTS

KM# 9 Obv: Laureate head left **Obv. Legend:** VICTORIA D: G: REG: NEW BRUNSWICK **Rev:** Denomination and date within wreath, crown above **Weight:** 4.6480 g. **Composition:** 0.9250 Silver 0.1382 oz. ASW

Date	Mintage	VG-8	F-12	VF-20	XF-40	MS-60	MS-63	Proof
1862	150,000	29.00	50.00	80.00	225	1,050	4,400	—
1862 Proof	—	—	—	—	—	—	—	2,850
1864	150,000	29.00	50.00	80.00	225	1,600	4,600	—

NEWFOUNDLAND

PROVINCE

CIRCULATION COINAGE

LARGE CENT

KM# 1 Obv: Laureate bust left **Obv. Legend:** VICTORIA D:G: BRITT: REG:F:D: **Rev:** Crown and date within circle, florals surround **Rev. Legend:** NEWFOUNDLAND **Composition:** Bronze

Date	Mintage	VG-8	F-12	VF-20	XF-40	MS-60	MS-63	Proof
1865	240,000	3.50	5.50	12.00	30.00	175	550	—
1872H	200,000	2.50	4.00	7.00	17.00	70.00	160	—
1872H Proof	—	—	—	—	—	—	—	800
1873	200,025	4.00	6.50	20.00	40.00	300	1,600	—
1873 Proof	—	—	—	—	—	—	—	3,000
1876H	200,000	3.50	7.00	15.00	60.00	300	1,100	—
1876H Proof, reported not confirmed	—	—	—	—	—	—	—	—
1880 round O, even date	400,000	3.00	3.50	7.00	20.00	125	500	—
1880 round O, low O	Inc. above	4.50	12.00	20.00	50.00	400	2,600	—

Date	Mintage	VG-8	F-12	VF-20	XF-40	MS-60	MS-63	Proof
1880 oval 0	Inc. above	125	225	325	500	2,000	4,500	—
1880 oval O Proof	—	—	—	—	—	—	—	2,500
1885	40,000	27.50	50.00	75.00	125	500	1,800	—
1885 Proof	—	—	—	—	—	—	—	2,500
1888	50,000	30.00	55.00	80.00	175	750	4,800	—
1890	200,000	3.00	6.00	15.00	45.00	300	1,100	—
1894	200,000	3.00	5.00	10.00	25.00	140	700	—
1894 Proof	—	—	—	—	—	—	—	1,500
1896	200,000	3.00	3.50	7.00	27.00	120	500	—
1896 Proof	—	—	—	—	—	—	—	1,500

KM# 9 Obv: Crowned bust right **Obv. Designer:** G.W. DeSaulles **Rev:** Crown and date within center circle, wreath surrounds, denomination above **Rev. Designer:** Horace Morehen **Composition:** Bronze

Date	Mintage	VG-8	F-12	VF-20	XF-40	MS-60	MS-63	Proof
1904H	100,000	7.00	14.00	20.00	55.00	300	700	—
1904H Proof	—	—	—	—	—	—	—	4,000
1907	200,000	2.00	4.00	8.00	30.00	220	650	—
1909 Proof	—	—	—	—	—	—	—	400
1909	200,000	2.00	4.00	7.00	19.00	100.00	150	—

KM# 16 Obv: Crowned bust left **Obv. Designer:** E.B. MacKennal **Rev:** Crown and date within center circle, wreath surrounds, denomination above **Rev. Designer:** Horace Morehen **Composition:** Bronze

Date	Mintage	VG-8	F-12	VF-20	XF-40	MS-60	MS-63	Proof
1913	400,000	1.00	1.50	3.00	7.00	40.00	75.00	—
1917C	702,350	1.00	1.50	3.00	6.00	75.00	200	—
1917C Proof	—	—	—	—	—	—	—	800
1919C	300,000	1.00	2.00	3.00	10.00	175	300	—
1919C Proof	—	—	—	—	—	—	—	1,000
1920C	302,184	1.00	2.00	5.00	18.00	300	1,000	—
1929	300,000	1.00	1.50	3.00	6.00	55.00	100.00	—
1929C Proof	—	—	—	—	—	—	—	1,000
1936	300,000	1.00	1.25	1.75	4.00	28.00	75.00	—

SMALL CENT

KM# 18 Obv: Crowned head left **Obv. Designer:** Percy Metcalfe **Rev:** Pitcher plant divides date, denomination below **Rev. Designer:** Walter J. Newman **Weight:** 3.2000 g. **Composition:** Bronze **Size:** 19 mm.

Date	Mintage	VG-8	F-12	VF-20	XF-40	MS-60	MS-63	Proof
1938	500,000	0.50	0.75	1.50	2.50	16.00	40.00	—
1938 Proof	—	—	—	—	—	—	—	1,000
1940	300,000	1.25	2.00	3.00	10.00	75.00	250	—
1940 Proof	—	—	—	—	—	—	—	1,000
1940 Re-engraved date	—	30.00	40.00	125	70.00	500	900	—
1941C	827,662	0.35	0.45	0.70	2.00	20.00	120	—
1941C Re-engraved date	—	9.00	13.00	30.00	65.00	250	700	—
1942	1,996,889	0.35	0.45	0.70	2.00	30.00	125	—
1943C	1,239,732	0.35	0.45	0.70	2.00	13.50	70.00	—
1944C	1,328,776	1.00	2.00	10.00	30.00	250	550	—
1947C	313,772	0.90	1.65	5.00	12.00	80.00	200	—
1947C Proof	—	—	—	—	—	—	—	2,000

5 CENTS

KM# 2 Obv: Laureate head left **Obv. Legend:** VICTORIA D: G: REG: NEWFOUNDLAND **Rev:** Denomination and date within ornamental circle **Weight:** 1.1782 g. **Composition:** 0.9250 Silver 0.0350 oz. ASW

Date	Mintage	VG-8	F-12	VF-20	XF-40	MS-60	MS-63	Proof
1865	80,000	35.00	50.00	150	300	1,200	2,300	—
1865 Proof	—	—	—	—	—	—	—	4,000
1870	40,000	65.00	125	225	500	1,900	3,000	—
1870 Proof	—	—	—	—	—	—	—	4,000
1872H	40,000	40.00	70.00	125	175	600	1,400	—
1873	44,260	125	200	450	800	4,600	—	—

Date	Mintage	VG-8	F-12	VF-20	XF-40	MS-60	MS-63	Proof
1873H	Inc. above	750	1,100	2,000	3,700	9,700	22,000	—
1873 Proof	—	—	—	—	—	—	—	10,000
1876H	20,000	125	200	350	650	1,200	2,750	—
1880	40,000	45.00	65.00	150	300	1,600	2,400	—
1880 Proof	—	—	—	—	—	—	—	5,000
1881	40,000	45.00	65.00	150	300	1,900	2,500	—
1881 Proof	—	—	—	—	—	—	—	5,000
1882H	60,000	23.00	45.00	90.00	200	800	1,500	—
1882H Proof	—	—	—	—	—	—	—	2,000
1885	16,000	130	210	335	750	2,400	4,500	—
1885 Proof	—	—	—	—	—	—	—	7,500
1888	40,000	40.00	75.00	225	375	1,900	4,900	—
1888 Proof	—	—	—	—	—	—	—	7,500
1890	160,000	11.00	21.00	45.00	125	800	1,500	—
1890 Proof	—	—	—	—	—	—	—	5,000
1894	160,000	10.00	19.00	30.00	100.00	800	2,500	—
1894 Proof	—	—	—	—	—	—	—	5,000
1896	400,000	4.00	8.00	20.00	50.00	700	2,700	—
1896 Proof	—	—	—	—	—	—	—	5,000

KM# 7 **Obv:** Crowned bust right **Rev:** Denomination and date within circle **Designer:** G.W. DeSaulles **Weight:** 1.1782 g. **Composition:** 0.9250 Silver 0.0350 oz. ASW

Date	Mintage	VG-8	F-12	VF-20	XF-40	MS-60	MS-63	Proof
1903	100,000	4.00	9.00	18.00	45.00	435	1,350	—
1903 Proof	—	—	—	—	—	—	—	2,000
1904H	100,000	3.00	5.00	14.00	35.00	160	285	—
1904H Proof	—	—	—	—	—	—	—	1,200
1908	400,000	3.00	6.00	11.50	30.00	260	750	—

KM# 13 **Obv:** Crowned bust left **Obv. Designer:** E.B. MacKennal **Rev:** Denomination and date within circle **Rev. Designer:** G.W. DeSaulles **Weight:** 1.1782 g. **Composition:** 0.9250 Silver 0.0350 oz. ASW

Date	Mintage	VG-8	F-12	VF-20	XF-40	MS-60	MS-63	Proof
1912	300,000	1.50	2.00	5.00	20.00	125	275	—
1912 Proof	—	—	—	—	—	—	—	2,000
1917C	300,319	1.50	3.00	7.00	25.00	250	650	—
1917C Proof	—	—	—	—	—	—	—	2,000
1919C	100,844	5.00	9.00	25.00	100.00	950	2,800	—
1919C Proof	—	—	—	—	—	—	—	2,000
1929	300,000	1.50	2.50	3.25	12.00	165	350	—

KM# 19 **Obv:** Crowned head left **Obv. Designer:** Percy Metcalfe **Rev:** Denomination and date within circle **Rev. Designer:** G.W. DeSaulles **Weight:** 1.1782 g. **Composition:** 0.9250 Silver 0.0350 oz. ASW

Date	Mintage	VG-8	F-12	VF-20	XF-40	MS-60	MS-63	Proof
1938	100,000	0.85	1.50	2.00	7.00	70.00	225	—
1938 Proof	—	—	—	—	—	—	—	1,000
1940C	200,000	0.85	1.50	2.00	7.00	85.00	300	—
1940C Proof	—	—	—	—	—	—	—	2,000
1941C	621,641	0.65	1.50	2.00	4.00	15.00	35.00	—
1942C	298,348	0.85	1.50	2.00	4.00	17.50	40.00	—
1943C	351,666	0.65	1.00	2.00	4.00	15.00	30.00	—

NEWFOUNDLAND

KM# 19a Obv: Crowned head left **Obv. Designer:** Percy Metcalfe **Rev:** Denomination and date within circle
Rev. Designer: G.W. DeSaulles **Weight:** 1.1664 g. **Composition:** 0.8000 Silver 0.0300 oz. ASW

Date	Mintage	VG-8	F-12	VF-20	XF-40	MS-60	MS-63	Proof
1944C	286,504	1.25	1.75	3.00	7.00	50.00	120	—
1945C	203,828	0.65	1.00	2.00	4.00	14.00	32.00	—
1946C	2,041	200	300	350	400	1,200	1,900	—
1946C Prooflike	—	—	—	—	—	—	2,500	—
1947C	38,400	2.00	3.00	5.00	17.00	65.00	200	—
1947C Prooflike	—	—	—	—	—	—	375	—

10 CENTS

KM# 3 Obv: Laureate head left **Obv. Legend:** VICTORIA D: G: REG: NEWFOUNDLAND **Rev:** Denomination
and date within ornamental circle **Weight:** 2.3564 g. **Composition:** 0.9250 Silver 0.0701 oz. ASW

Date	Mintage	VG-8	F-12	VF-20	XF-40	MS-60	MS-63	Proof
1865	80,000	27.00	45.00	75.00	250	1,100	2,250	—
1865 plain edge, Proof	—	—	—	—	—	—	—	5,500
1870	30,000	120	190	335	725	2,350	5,000	—
1870 Proof	—	—	—	—	—	—	—	10,000
1872H	40,000	22.00	35.00	80.00	200	800	1,700	—
1873 flat 3	23,614	55.00	70.00	250	650	2,750	4,750	—
1873 round 3	Inc. above	55.00	70.00	250	650	2,750	4,750	—
1873 Proof	—	—	—	—	—	—	—	12,000
1876H	10,000	55.00	70.00	225	350	1,400	2,500	—
1880/70	10,000	55.00	70.00	250	400	1,800	2,950	—
1880 Proof	—	—	—	—	—	—	—	7,500
1882H	20,000	30.00	55.00	150	475	2,200	6,700	—
1882H Proof	—	—	—	—	—	—	—	3,000
1885	8,000	70.00	130	300	800	2,200	4,250	—
1885 Proof	—	—	—	—	—	—	—	8,000
1888	30,000	35.00	70.00	200	700	2,600	4,600	—
1888 Proof	—	—	—	—	—	—	—	8,000
1890	100,000	9.00	19.00	35.00	150	1,100	3,200	—
1890 Proof	—	—	—	—	—	—	—	5,000
1894	100,000	8.50	12.00	25.00	125	1,200	3,000	—
1894 Proof	—	—	—	—	—	—	—	5,000
1896	230,000	5.00	10.00	25.00	90.00	1,200	3,200	—
1896 Proof	—	—	—	—	—	—	—	5,000

KM# 8 Obv: Crowned bust right **Rev:** Denomination and date within circle **Designer:** G.W. DeSaulles **Weight:**
2.3564 g. **Composition:** 0.9250 Silver 0.0701 oz. ASW

Date	Mintage	VG-8	F-12	VF-20	XF-40	MS-60	MS-63	Proof
1903 Proof	—	—	—	—	—	—	—	2,500
1903	100,000	8.00	25.00	70.00	200	1,200	4,400	—
1904H	100,000	4.00	10.00	30.00	90.00	200	350	—
1904H Proof	—	—	—	—	—	—	—	1,500

KM# 14 Obv: Crowned bust left **Obv. Designer:** E.B. MacKennal **Rev. Designer:** G.W. DeSaulles **Weight:** 2.3564 g. **Composition:** 0.9250 Silver 0.0701 oz. ASW

Date	Mintage	VG-8	F-12	VF-20	XF-40	MS-60	MS-63	Proof
1912	150,000	1.20	3.00	10.00	40.00	165	300	—
1917C	250,805	1.20	3.00	11.00	40.00	400	1,500	—
1919C	54,342	2.00	6.00	18.00	55.00	175	350	—

KM# 20 Obv: Crowned head left **Obv. Designer:** Percy Metcalfe **Rev:** Denomination and date within circle **Rev. Designer:** G.W. DeSaulles **Weight:** 2.3564 g. **Composition:** 0.9250 Silver 0.0701 oz. ASW

Date	Mintage	VG-8	F-12	VF-20	XF-40	MS-60	MS-63	Proof
1938	100,000	1.10	1.75	3.00	11.00	80.00	300	—
1938 Proof	—	—	—	—	—	—	—	2,000
1940	100,000	1.10	1.50	3.00	10.00	80.00	300	—
1940 Proof	—	—	—	—	—	—	—	2,500
1941C	483,630	1.10	1.50	2.20	5.00	40.00	125	—
1942C	293,736	1.10	1.50	2.20	5.00	50.00	130	—
1943C	104,706	1.10	1.50	2.50	6.00	60.00	200	—
1944C	151,471	2.50	3.50	10.00	20.00	200	800	—

KM# 20a Obv: Crowned head left **Obv. Designer:** Percy Metcalfe **Rev. Designer:** G.W. DeSaulles **Weight:** 2.3328 g. **Composition:** 0.8000 Silver 0.0600 oz. ASW

Date	Mintage	VG-8	F-12	VF-20	XF-40	MS-60	MS-63	Proof
1945C	175,833	1.00	1.35	2.25	4.50	45.00	225	—
1946C Proof	—	—	—	—	—	—	—	750
1946C	38,400	2.00	4.00	10.00	25.00	100.00	275	—
1947C	61,988	1.50	3.00	4.50	14.00	65.00	275	—

20 CENTS

KM# 4 Obv: Laureate head left **Rev:** Denomination and date within ornamental circle **Weight:** 4.7127 g. **Composition:** 0.9250 Silver 0.1401 oz. ASW

Date	Mintage	VG-8	F-12	VF-20	XF-40	MS-60	MS-63	Proof
1865	100,000	16.00	30.00	60.00	225	950	2,000	—
1865 plain edge, Proof	—	—	—	—	—	—	—	6,500
1865 reeded edge, Proof	—	—	—	—	—	—	—	10,000
1870	50,000	21.00	45.00	100.00	250	1,250	2,500	—
1870 plain edge, Proof	—	—	—	—	—	—	—	6,500
1870 reeded edge, Proof	—	—	—	—	—	—	—	6,500
1872H	90,000	12.00	25.00	60.00	140	750	1,800	—
1873	45,797	21.00	65.00	175	550	5,400	8,000	—
1873 Proof	—	—	—	—	—	—	—	12,000
1876H	50,000	25.00	50.00	80.00	300	1,350	2,700	—
1880/70	30,000	27.00	55.00	100.00	350	2,000	3,000	—
1880 Proof	—	—	—	—	—	—	—	8,000
1881	60,000	12.00	25.00	80.00	300	1,200	2,900	—
1881 Proof	—	—	—	—	—	—	—	8,000

Date	Mintage	VG-8	F-12	VF-20	XF-40	MS-60	MS-63	Proof
1882H	100,000	9.00	19.00	50.00	140	1,000	3,400	—
1882H Proof	—	—	—	—	—	—	—	3,500
1885	40,000	14.00	30.00	80.00	300	2,900	4,500	—
1885 Proof	—	—	—	—	—	—	—	10,000
1888	75,000	12.00	25.00	70.00	225	1,400	4,200	—
1888 Proof	—	—	—	—	—	—	—	10,000
1890	100,000	9.00	15.00	45.00	225	1,400	3,500	—
1890 Proof	—	—	—	—	—	—	—	6,500
1894	100,000	15.00	30.00	100.00	300	1,200	—	—
1894 Proof	—	—	—	—	—	—	—	6,500
1896 small 96	125,000	6.00	12.00	35.00	150	1,400	3,600	—
1896 large 96	Inc. above	7.00	15.00	50.00	200	1,700	4,500	—
1896 large 96, Proof	—	—	—	—	—	—	—	6,500
1899 hook 99	125,000	27.00	50.00	125	350	1,800	4,900	—
1899 large 99	Inc. above	5.00	12.00	30.00	125	1,400	3,600	—
1900	125,000	5.00	8.00	25.00	80.00	1,100	3,400	—
1900 Proof	—	—	—	—	—	—	—	6,500

KM# 10 Obv: Crowned bust right **Obv. Designer:** G.W. DeSaulles **Rev:** Denomination and date within circle **Rev. Designer:** W.H.J. Blakemore **Weight:** 4.7127 g. **Composition:** 0.9250 Silver 0.1401 oz. ASW

Date	Mintage	VG-8	F-12	VF-20	XF-40	MS-60	MS-63	Proof
1904H	75,000	10.00	30.00	55.00	275	2,500	6,000	—
1904H Proof	—	—	—	—	—	—	—	1,850

KM# 15 Obv: Crowned bust left **Obv. Designer:** E.B. MacKennal **Rev:** Denomination and date within circle **Rev. Designer:** W.H.J. Blakemore **Weight:** 4.7127 g. **Composition:** 0.9250 Silver 0.1401 oz. ASW

Date	Mintage	VG-8	F-12	VF-20	XF-40	MS-60	MS-63	Proof
1912 Proof	—	—	—	—	—	—	—	2,500
1912	350,000	2.50	5.00	14.00	55.00	325	850	—

25 CENTS

KM# 17 Obv: Crowned bust left **Obv. Designer:** E.B. MacKennal **Rev:** Denomination and date within circle **Rev. Designer:** W.H.J. Blakemore **Weight:** 5.8319 g. **Composition:** 0.9250 Silver 0.1734 oz. ASW

Date	Mintage	VG-8	F-12	VF-20	XF-40	MS-60	MS-63	Proof
1917C	464,779	3.00	4.00	7.00	17.00	145	300	—
1917C Proof	—	—	—	—	—	—	—	2,500
1919C	163,939	3.00	5.00	14.00	25.00	350	1,250	—
1919C Proof	—	—	—	—	—	—	—	2,500

50 CENTS

KM# 6 Obv: Laureate head left **Obv. Legend:** VICTORIA DEI GRATIA REGINA NEWFOUNDLAND **Rev:** Denomination and date within ornamental circle **Weight:** 11.7818 g. **Composition:** 0.9250 Silver 0.3504 oz. ASW

Date	Mintage	VG-8	F-12	VF-20	XF-40	MS-60	MS-63	Proof
1870	50,000	26.00	50.00	150	600	3,500	8,500	—
1870 plain edge, Proof	—	—	—	—	—	—	—	25,000
1870 reeded edge, Proof	—	—	—	—	—	—	—	25,000
1872H	48,000	18.00	35.00	90.00	400	1,600	3,600	—
1873	37,675	40.00	75.00	200	650	9,600	10,000	—
1873 Proof	—	—	—	—	—	—	—	40,000
1874	80,000	25.00	45.00	125	550	8,900	8,000	—
1874 Proof	—	—	—	—	—	—	—	40,000
1876H	28,000	35.00	85.00	150	450	2,250	5,250	—
1880	24,000	45.00	95.00	250	900	6,500	16,000	—
1880 Proof	—	—	—	—	—	—	—	40,000
1881	50,000	20.00	35.00	135	400	3,300	9,300	—
1881 Proof	—	—	—	—	—	—	—	40,000
1882H	100,000	12.00	30.00	95.00	350	1,600	5,400	—
1882H Proof	—	—	—	—	—	—	—	8,000
1885	40,000	30.00	60.00	175	650	2,800	7,100	—
1885 Proof	—	—	—	—	—	—	—	40,000
1888	20,000	50.00	90.00	250	925	11,000	12,000	—
1888 Proof	—	—	—	—	—	—	—	40,000
1894	40,000	12.00	28.00	75.00	300	3,700	9,700	—
1896	60,000	8.50	16.00	65.00	300	3,000	8,100	—
1896 Proof	—	—	—	—	—	—	—	25,000
1898	76,607	8.50	13.00	60.00	200	3,100	8,100	—
1899 narrow 9's	Inc. above	8.50	13.00	45.00	150	2,600	7,700	—
1899 wide 9's	150,000	8.50	13.00	60.00	200	2,800	7,200	—
1900	150,000	8.50	13.00	45.00	175	2,600	7,200	—

KM# 11 Obv: Crowned bust right **Obv. Designer:** G.W. DeSaulles **Rev. Designer:** W.H.J. Blakemore **Weight:** 11.7800 g. **Composition:** 0.9250 Silver 0.3503 oz. ASW **Size:** 30 mm.

Date	Mintage	VG-8	F-12	VF-20	XF-40	MS-60	MS-63	Proof
1904H	140,000	5.00	6.00	14.00	55.00	275	850	—
1904H Proof	—	—	—	—	—	—	—	5,000
1907	100,000	5.00	6.00	22.00	65.00	350	1,000	—
1908	160,000	5.00	6.00	13.50	50.00	225	700	—
1909	200,000	5.00	12.00	21.00	55.00	300	800	—

NEWFOUNDLAND

KM# 12 Obv: Crowned bust left **Obv. Designer:** E.B. MacKennal **Rev:** Denomination and date within circle
Rev. Designer: W.H.J. Blakemore **Weight:** 11.7800 g. **Comp:** 0.9250 Silver 0.3503 oz. ASW **Size:** 30 mm.

Date	Mintage	VG-8	F-12	VF-20	XF-40	MS-60	MS-63	Proof
1911	200,000	5.00	6.00	11.00	35.00	200	550	—
1917C	375,560	5.00	6.00	11.00	28.00	145	350	—
1917C Proof	—	—	—	—	—	—	—	2,500
1918C	294,824	5.00	6.00	11.00	28.00	145	350	—
1919C	306,267	5.00	6.00	11.00	30.00	325	1,150	—
1919C Proof	—	—	—	—	—	—	—	2,500

2 DOLLARS

KM# 5 Obv: Laureate head left **Obv. Legend:** VICTORIA D: G: REG: NEWFOUNDLAND **Rev:** Denomination
and date within circle **Weight:** 3.3284 g. **Composition:** 0.9170 Gold 0.0981 oz. AGW

Date	Mintage	F-12	VF-20	XF-40	AU-50	MS-60	MS-63
1865	10,000	150	175	300	375	1,100	5,000
1865 plain edge, Specimen-63, $15,000.	Est. 10	—	—	—	—	—	—
1870	10,000	150	175	300	375	1,100	5,850
1870 reeded edge, Specimen-63 $20,000.	Est. 5	—	—	—	—	—	—
1872	6,050	175	300	375	700	2,200	8,800
1872 Specimen-63 $12,500.	Est. 10	—	—	—	—	—	—
1880	2,500	800	1,000	1,200	2,300	4,650	14,250
1880/70	—	—	—	—	—	—	—
Note: Specimen. Bowers and Merena Norweb sale 11-96, specimen 64 realized $70,400.							
1881 Specimen; Rare	—	—	—	—	—	—	—
1881	10,000	130	150	200	325	1,200	5,400
1882H	25,000	130	150	200	225	425	1,600
1882H Specimen $4,250.	—	—	—	—	—	—	—
1885	10,000	130	150	200	225	700	2,700
1885 Specimen	—	—	—	—	—	—	—
Note: Bowers and Merena Norweb sale 11-96, specimen 66 realized $44,000							
1888	25,000	115	140	175	200	365	1,550
1888 Specimen; Rare	—	—	—	—	—	—	—

NOVA SCOTIA
PROVINCE

DECIMAL COINAGE

HALF CENT

KM# 7 Obv: Laureate bust left **Obv. Legend:** VICTORIA D:G: BRITT: REG:F:D: **Rev:** Crown and date within beaded circle, wreath of roses surrounds **Rev. Legend:** NOVA SCOTIA **Composition:** Bronze

Date	Mintage	VG-8	F-12	VF-20	XF-40	MS-60	MS-63	Proof
1861	400,000	5.00	5.00	8.00	13.00	60.00	300	—
1864	400,000	5.00	5.00	8.00	13.00	55.00	250	—
1864 Proof	—	—	—	—	—	—	—	300

CENT

KM# 8.2 Obv: Laureate bust left **Obv. Legend:** VICTORIA D:G: BRITT: REG:F:D: **Rev:** Crown and date within beaded circle, wreath of roses surrounds **Rev. Legend:** NOVA SCOTIA **Composition:** Bronze **Note:** Prev. KM#8. Small rosebud right of SCOTIA. The Royal Mint report records mintage of 1 million for 1862, which is considered incorrect.

Date	Mintage	VG-8	F-12	VF-20	XF-40	MS-60	MS-63	Proof
1861	800,000	3.00	4.50	5.00	11.00	125	400	—
1862	Est. 1,000,000	45.00	75.00	150	300	1,300	—	—
1864	800,000	3.00	4.50	5.00	16.00	150	450	—

STERLING COINAGE

HALFPENNY TOKEN

KM# 1a Obv: Laureate head left, draped collar **Obv. Legend:** PROVINCE OF NOVA SCOTIA **Rev:** Thistle **Composition:** Copper

Date	Mintage	VG-8	F-12	VF-20	XF-40	MS-60	MS-63	Proof
1382 1382 (error)	—	500	700	1,650	—	—	—	—
1832 (imitation)	—	3.00	9.00	27.00	75.00	125	200	—
1832/1382	—	6.00	15.00	50.00	100.00	—	—	—

KM# 1 Obv: Laureate head left **Obv. Legend:** PROVINCE OF NOVA SCOTIA **Rev:** Thistle **Comp:** Copper

Date	Mintage	VG-8	F-12	VF-20	XF-40	MS-60	MS-63	Proof
1823 without hyphen	Inc. above	5.00	10.00	35.00	90.00	325	—	—

Date	Mintage	VG-8	F-12	VF-20	XF-40	MS-60	MS-63	Proof
1823	400,000	3.00	6.00	13.00	60.00	275	—	—
1824	118,636	6.00	12.00	27.00	65.00	300	—	—
1832	800,000	3.00	5.00	7.50	21.00	150	—	—

KM# 3 Obv: Head left **Obv. Legend:** PROVINCE OF NOVA SCOTIA **Rev:** Thistle **Composition:** Copper

Date	Mintage	VG-8	F-12	VF-20	XF-40	MS-60	MS-63	Proof
1840 medium 0	Inc. above	3.50	9.00	14.00	45.00	150	—	—
1840 large 0	Inc. above	4.00	10.00	27.00	85.00	225	—	—
1840 small 0	300,000	3.50	10.00	25.00	60.00	175	—	—
1843	300,000	3.00	6.00	16.00	60.00	175	—	—

KM# 5 Composition: Copper

Date	Mintage	VG-8	F-12	VF-20	XF-40	MS-60	MS-63	Proof
1856 without LCW, Proof	—	—	—	—	—	—	—	600
1856 without LCW, inverted A for V in PROVINCE, Proof	—	—	—	—	—	—	—	600
1856 without LCW	720,000	2.00	4.00	7.50	15.00	125	—	—

KM# 5a Composition: Bronze

Date	Mintage	VG-8	F-12	VF-20	XF-40	MS-60	MS-63	Proof
1856 with LCW, Proof	—	—	—	—	—	—	—	600

1 PENNY TOKEN

KM# 2 Obv: Laureate head left **Obv. Legend:** PROVINCE OF NOVA SCOTIA **Rev:** Thistle **Composition:** Copper

Date	Mintage	VG-8	F-12	VF-20	XF-40	MS-60	MS-63	Proof
1824	217,776	4.00	10.00	26.00	85.00	300	—	—
1832	200,000	4.00	8.00	15.00	35.00	225	—	—

KM# 2a Obv: Laureate head left **Obv. Legend:** PROVINCE OF NOVA SCOTIA **Rev:** Thistle **Composition:** Copper

Date	Mintage	VG-8	F-12	VF-20	XF-40	MS-60	MS-63	Proof
1832 (imitation)	—	3.75	7.50	22.50	85.00	—	—	—

KM# 4 Obv: Head left **Obv. Legend:** PROVINCE OF NOVA SCOTIA **Rev:** Thistle **Comp:** Copper **Size:** 32 mm.

Date	Mintage	VG-8	F-12	VF-20	XF-40	MS-60	MS-63	Proof
1840	150,000	3.50	6.00	14.00	60.00	300	—	—
1843/0	150,000	45.00	75.00	175	—	—	—	—
1843	Inc. above	4.00	12.00	23.00	60.00	300	—	—

KM# 6 Obv: Crowned head left **Obv. Legend:** VICTORIA D: G: BRITANNIA R: REG: F: D: **Rev:** Plant
Rev. Legend: PROVINCE OF NOVA SCOTIA **Composition:** Copper

Date	Mintage	VG-8	F-12	VF-20	XF-40	MS-60	MS-63	Proof
1856 without LCW	360,000	4.00	7.50	13.00	35.00	225	—	—
1856 with LCW	Inc. above	2.50	5.00	12.00	35.00	200	—	—

KM# 6a Obv: Crowned head left **Obv. Legend:** VICTORIA D: G: BRITANNIA R: REG: F: D: **Rev:** Plant
Rev. Legend: PROVINCE OF NOVA SCOTIA **Composition:** Bronze

Date	Mintage	VG-8	F-12	VF-20	XF-40	MS-60	MS-63	Proof
1856 Proof	—	—	—	—	—	—	—	400

PRINCE EDWARD ISLAND

PROVINCE

CUT & COUNTERMARKED COINAGE

CA. 1813

SHILLING

KM# 1 Composition: Silver **Note:** Countermark on center plug of Spanish or Spanish Colonial 8 Reales.

Date	Mintage	VG-8	F-12	VF-20	XF-40	MS-60	MS-63	Proof
ND	1,000	2,000	3,000	5,000	—	—	—	—

5 SHILLING

KM# 3 Composition: Silver **Note:** Countermark on holed Lima 8 Reales, KM#106.2.

Date	Mintage	VG-8	F-12	VF-20	XF-40	MS-60	MS-63	Proof
ND1809-11	1,000	2,000	3,000	5,000	—	—	—	—

KM# 2.1 Composition: Silver **Note:** Countermark on holed Mexico City 8 Reales, KM#109.

Date	Mintage	VG-8	F-12	VF-20	XF-40	MS-60	MS-63	Proof
1791-1808	—	800	1,350	2,250	—	—	—	—

PRINCE EDWARD ISLAND

KM# 2.2 Composition: Silver **Note:** Countermark on holed Mexico City 8 Reales, KM#110.

Date	Mintage	VG-8	F-12	VF-20	XF-40	MS-60	MS-63	Proof
ND1808-11	—	800	1,350	2,250	—	—	—	—

DECIMAL COINAGE

CENT

KM# 4 Obv: Crowned head left within beaded circle **Obv. Legend:** VICTORIA QUEEN **Rev:** Trees within beaded circle **Rev. Legend:** PRINCE EDWARD ISLAND **Composition:** Bronze

Date	Mintage	VG-8	F-12	VF-20	XF-40	MS-60	MS-63	Proof
1871	2,000,000	2.50	4.00	6.50	16.00	75.00	185	—
1871 Proof	—	—	—	—	—	—	—	2,000

MEXICO

The United States of Mexico, located immediately south of the United States has an area of 759,529 sq. mi. (1,967,183 sq. km.) and an estimated population of 100 million. Capital: Mexico City. The economy is based on agriculture, manufacturing and mining. Oil, cotton, silver, coffee, and shrimp are exported.

Mexico was the site of highly advanced Indian civilizations 1,500 years before conquistador Hernando Cortes conquered the wealthy Aztec empire of Montezuma, 1519-21, and founded a Spanish colony, which lasted for nearly 300 years. During the Spanish period, Mexico, then called New Spain, stretched from Guatemala to the present states of Wyoming and California, its present northern boundary having been established by the secession of Texas during 1836 and the war of 1846-48 with the United States.

Independence from Spain was declared by Father Miguel Hidalgo on Sept. 16, 1810, (Mexican Independence Day) and was achieved by General Agustin de Iturbide in1821. Iturbide became emperor in 1822 but was deposed when a republic was established a year later. For more than fifty years following the birth of the republic, the political scene of Mexico was characterized by turmoil, which saw two emperors (including the unfortunate Maximilian), several dictators and an average of one new government every nine months passing swiftly from obscurity to oblivion. The land, social, economic and labor reforms promulgated by the Reform Constitution of Feb. 5, 1917 established the basis for sustained economic development and participative democracy that have made Mexico one of the most politically stable countries of modern Latin America.

SPANISH COLONY

COB COINAGE

KM# 24   1/2 REAL
1.6900 g., 0.9310 Silver 0.0506 oz. ASW **Ruler:**
Philip V **Obv:** Legend around crowned PHILIPVS monogram **Rev:** Legend around cross, lions and castles **Note:** Mint mark M, Mo.

Date	Mintage	Good	VG	F	VF	XF
ND(1701-28)	—	—	25.00	40.00	65.00	—
Date off flan						
1701 L	—	—	100	125	225	—
1702 L	—	—	100	125	225	—
1703 L	—	—	100	125	225	—
1704 L	—	—	100	125	225	—
1705 L	—	—	100	125	225	—
1706 J	—	—	100	125	225	—
1707 J	—	—	100	125	225	—
1708 J	—	—	100	125	175	—
1709 J	—	—	100	125	175	—
1710 J	—	—	100	125	175	—
1711 J	—	—	100	125	175	—
1712 J	—	—	100	125	175	—
1713 J	—	—	100	125	175	—
1714 J	—	—	100	125	175	—
1715 J	—	—	100	125	175	—
1716 J	—	—	100	125	175	—
1717 J	—	—	100	125	175	—
1718 J	—	—	100	125	175	—
1719 J	—	—	100	125	175	—
1720 J	—	—	100	125	175	—
1721 J	—	—	100	125	175	—
1722 J	—	—	100	125	175	—
1723 J	—	—	100	125	175	—
1724 J	—	—	100	125	175	—
1724 D	—	—	100	125	175	—
1725 D	—	—	100	125	175	—
1726 D	—	—	100	125	175	—
1727 D	—	—	100	125	175	—
1728 D	—	—	100	125	175	—

KM# 25   1/2 REAL
1.6900 g., 0.9310 Silver 0.0506 oz. ASW **Ruler:**
Luis I **Obv:** Legend around crowned LVDOVICVS

monogram **Rev:** Legend around cross, lions and castles **Note:** Mint mark M, Mo.

Date	Mintage	Good	VG	F	VF	XF
ND(1724-25)	—	—	125	200	250	—
Date off flan						
1724 D	—	—	325	450	550	—
1725 D	—	—	325	450	550	—

KM# 24a   1/2 REAL
1.6900 g., 0.9160 Silver 0.0498 oz. ASW **Ruler:**
Philip V **Obv:** Legend around crowned PHILIPVS monogram **Rev:** Legend around cross, lions and castles **Note:** Mint mark M, Mo.

Date	Mintage	Good	VG	F	VF	XF
ND(1729-33)	—	—	25.00	40.00	65.00	—
Date off flan						
1729 R	—	—	90.00	120	150	—
1730 R	—	—	90.00	120	150	—
1731 F	—	—	90.00	120	150	—
1732/1 F	—	—	90.00	120	150	—
1732 F	—	—	90.00	120	150	—
1733/2 F	—	—	90.00	120	150	—
1733 F	—	—	90.00	120	150	—

KM# 30   REAL
3.3800 g., 0.9310 Silver 0.1012 oz. ASW **Ruler:**
Philip V **Obv:** Legend and date around crowned arms **Obv. Legend:** PHILIPVS V DEI G **Rev:** Lions and castles in angles of cross **Note:** Mint mark M, Mo.

Date	Mintage	Good	VG	F	VF	XF
ND(1701-28)	—	—	35.00	55.00	75.00	—
Date off flan						
1701 L	—	—	125	175	275	—
1702 L	—	—	125	175	275	—
1703 L	—	—	125	175	275	—

Date	Mintage	Good	VG	F	VF	XF
1704 L	—	—	125	175	275	—
1705 L	—	—	125	175	275	—
1706 J	—	—	125	175	275	—
1707 J	—	—	125	175	275	—
1708 J	—	—	125	175	275	—
1709 J	—	—	125	175	275	—
1710 J	—	—	125	175	275	—
1711 J	—	—	125	175	275	—
1712 J	—	—	125	175	275	—
1713 J	—	—	125	175	275	—
1714 J	—	—	125	175	275	—
1715 J	—	—	100	175	275	—
1716 J	—	—	100	175	275	—
1717 J	—	—	100	175	275	—
1718 J	—	—	100	175	275	—
1719 J	—	—	100	175	275	—
1720/19 J	—	—	100	175	275	—
1720 J	—	—	100	175	275	—
1721 J	—	—	100	175	275	—
1722 J	—	—	100	175	275	—
1723 J	—	—	100	175	275	—
1726 D	—	—	100	175	275	—
1727 D	—	—	100	175	275	—
1728 D	—	—	100	175	275	—

KM# A31   REAL
3.3834 g., 0.9310 Silver 0.1013 oz. ASW **Ruler:**
Luis I **Note:** A significant portion of the legend must
be visibile for proper attribution. Mint mark M, Mo.

Date	Mintage	Good	VG	F	VF	XF
1724 D Rare	—	—	—	—	—	—
1725 D Rare	—	—	—	—	—	—

KM# 30a   REAL
3.3800 g., 0.9160 Silver 0.0995 oz. ASW **Ruler:**
Philip V **Obv:** Legend and date around crowned arms
Obv. Legend: PHILIPVS V DEI G **Rev:** Lions and
castles in angles of cross **Note:** Mint mark M, Mo.

Date	Mintage	Good	VG	F	VF	XF
ND(1729-32)	—	—	30.00	50.00	70.00	—
Date off flan						
1729 R	—	—	90.00	125	175	—
1730 R	—	—	90.00	125	175	—
1730 F	—	—	90.00	125	175	—
1730 G	—	—	90.00	125	175	—
1731 F	—	—	90.00	125	175	—
1732 F	—	—	90.00	125	175	—

KM# 35   2 REALES
6.7700 g., 0.9310 Silver 0.2026 oz. ASW **Ruler:**
Philip V **Obv:** Legend and date around crowned arms
Obv. Legend: PHILIPVS V DEI G **Rev:** Lions and
castles in angles of cross **Note:** Mint mark M, Mo.

Date	Mintage	Good	VG	F	VF	XF
ND(1701-28)	—	—	45.00	65.00	90.00	—
Date off flan						
1701 L	—	—	125	150	250	—
1702 L	—	—	125	150	250	—
1703 L	—	—	125	150	250	—
1704 L	—	—	125	150	250	—
1705 L	—	—	125	150	250	—
1706 J	—	—	125	150	250	—
1707 J	—	—	125	150	250	—
1708 J	—	—	125	150	250	—
1710 J	—	—	125	150	250	—
1711 J	—	—	125	150	250	—
1712 J	—	—	125	150	250	—
1713 J	—	—	125	150	250	—
1714 J	—	—	150	185	300	—
1715 J	—	—	150	185	300	—
1716 J	—	—	150	185	300	—
1717 J	—	—	150	185	300	—
1718 J	—	—	150	185	300	—
1719 J	—	—	150	185	300	—
1720 J	—	—	150	185	300	—
1721 J	—	—	150	185	300	—
1722 J	—	—	150	185	300	—
1723 J	—	—	150	185	300	—
1724 J	—	—	150	185	300	—
1725 D Rare	—	—	—	—	—	—

Date	Mintage	Good	VG	F	VF	XF
1726 D	—	—	150	185	300	—
1727 D	—	—	150	185	300	—
1728 D	—	—	150	185	300	—

KM# 35a   2 REALES
6.7700 g., 0.9160 Silver 0.1994 oz. ASW **Ruler:**
Philip V **Obv:** Legend and date around crowned arms
Obv. Legend: PHILIPVS V DEI G **Rev:** Lions and
castles in angles of cross **Note:** Mint mark M, Mo.

Date	Mintage	Good	VG	F	VF	XF
ND(1729-32)	—	—	40.00	60.00	90.00	—
Date off flan						
1729 R	—	—	100	125	150	—
1730 R	—	—	100	125	150	—
1731 F	—	—	100	125	150	—
1731/0 F	—	—	100	125	150	—
1732 F	—	—	100	125	150	—
1733 F Rare	—	—	—	—	—	—

KM# 40   4 REALES
13.5400 g., 0.9310 Silver 0.4053 oz. ASW **Ruler:**
Philip V **Obv:** Legend and date around crowned arms
Obv. Legend: PHILIPVS V DEI G **Rev:** Lions and
castles in angles of cross **Note:** Mint mark M, Mo.

Date	Mintage	Good	VG	F	VF	XF
ND (1701-28)	—	—	50.00	75.00	100	—
Date off flan						
1701 L	—	—	175	250	375	—
1702 L	—	—	175	250	375	—
1703 L	—	—	175	250	375	—
1704 L	—	—	175	250	375	—
1705 L	—	—	175	250	375	—
1706 J	—	—	175	250	375	—
1707 J	—	—	175	250	375	—
1708 J	—	—	175	250	375	—
1709 J	—	—	175	250	375	—
1710 J	—	—	175	250	375	—
1711 J	—	—	150	200	300	—
1712 J	—	—	150	200	300	—
1713 J	—	—	150	200	300	—
1714 J	—	—	150	200	300	—
1715 J	—	—	125	225	375	—
1716 J	—	—	200	300	500	—
1717 J	—	—	200	300	500	—
1718 J	—	—	200	300	500	—
1719 J	—	—	200	300	500	—
1720 J	—	—	200	300	500	—
1721 J	—	—	200	300	500	—
1722 J	—	—	200	300	500	—
1723 J	—	—	200	300	500	—
1726 D	—	—	200	300	500	—
1727 D	—	—	200	300	500	—
1728 D	—	—	200	300	500	—

KM# 42   4 REALES
13.5400 g., 0.9310 Silver 0.4053 oz. ASW **Ruler:** Luis I **Obv:** Legend around crowned arms **Obv. Legend:** LVDOVICVS I DEI G **Rev:** Lions and castles in angles of cross, legend around **Note:** A significant portion of the legend must be visible for proper attribution. Mint mark M, Mo.

Date	Mintage	Good	VG	F	VF	XF
1724 D Rare	—	—	—	—	—	—
1725 D Rare	—	—	—	—	—	—

KM# 40a   4 REALES
13.5400 g., 0.9160 Silver 0.3987 oz. ASW **Ruler:** Philip V **Obv:** Legend and date around crowned arms **Obv. Legend:** PHILIPVS V DEI G **Rev:** Lions and castles in angles of cross **Note:** Mint mark M, Mo.

Date	Mintage	Good	VG	F	VF	XF
ND(1729-33) Date off flan	—	—	50.00	75.00	100	—
1729 D	—	—	125	200	275	—
1730 R	—	—	125	200	275	—
1730 G	—	—	125	200	275	—
1731 F	—	—	125	200	275	—
1732/1 F	—	—	125	175	250	—
1732 F	—	—	125	175	250	—
1733/2 F	—	—	125	175	250	—
1733 F	—	—	200	300	400	—

KM# 41   4 REALES
13.5400 g., 0.9160 Silver 0.3987 oz. ASW **Ruler:** Philip V **Obv:** Legend and date around crowned arms **Obv. Legend:** PHILIPVS V DEI G **Rev:** Lions and castles in angles of cross, legend around **Note:** Klippe. Similar to KM#40a. Mint mark M, Mo.

Date	Mintage	Good	VG	F	VF	XF
1733 F	—	—	450	600	750	—
1733 MF	—	—	450	600	750	—
1734/3 MF	—	—	450	600	750	—

KM# 47   8 REALES
27.0700 g., 0.9310 Silver 0.8102 oz. ASW **Ruler:** Philip V **Obv:** Legend and date around crowned arms **Obv. Legend:** PHILIPVS V DEI G **Rev:** Lions and castles in angles of cross, legend around **Note:** Mint mark M, Mo.

Date	Mintage	Good	VG	F	VF	XF
1701 L	—	—	200	350	500	—
ND(1701-28) Date off flan	—	—	70.00	90.00	120	—
1702 L	—	—	200	350	500	—
1703 L	—	—	200	350	500	—
1704 L Rare	—	—	—	—	—	—
1705 L	—	—	200	350	600	—
1706 J	—	—	200	350	600	—
1707 J	—	—	200	350	500	—
1708 J	—	—	200	350	500	—
1709 J	—	—	200	350	500	—
1710 J	—	—	200	350	500	—
1711 J	—	—	175	275	400	—
1712 J	—	—	175	275	400	—
1713 J	—	—	175	275	400	—
1714 J	—	—	175	275	400	—
1715 J	—	—	175	300	450	—
1716 J	—	—	375	575	800	—
1717 J	—	—	375	575	800	—
1718/7 J	—	—	375	575	800	—
1718 J	—	—	350	500	800	—
1719 J	—	—	350	500	800	—
1720 J	—	—	350	500	800	—
1721 J	—	—	350	500	800	—
1722 J	—	—	350	500	800	—
1723 J	—	—	350	500	800	—
1724 D	—	—	350	500	800	—
1725 D	—	—	350	500	800	—
1726 D	—	—	350	500	800	—
1727 D	—	—	350	500	800	—
1728 D	—	—	400	600	1,000	—

Date	Mintage	Good	VG	F	VF	XF
1729 R	—	—	150	225	350	—
1730 G/R	—	—	150	225	350	—
1730 R	—	—	150	225	350	—
1730 G	—	—	150	225	350	—
1730 F	—	—	150	225	350	—
1731/0 F	—	—	150	225	350	—
1731 F	—	—	135	210	325	—
1732/1 F	—	—	135	210	325	—
1732 F	—	—	135	210	350	—
1733/2 F	—	—	200	300	400	—
1733 F	—	—	200	300	400	—

KM# 46   8 REALES
27.0700 g., 0.9310 Silver 0.8102 oz. ASW   **Ruler:** Charles II **Obv:** Legend and date around crowned arms **Obv. Legend:** CAROLVS II DEI G **Rev:** Legend around cross, lions and castles **Note:** Struck at Mexico City Mint, mint mark M, Mo.

Date	Mintage	Good	VG	F	VF	XF
1701 L	—	—	700	1,000	1,700	—

KM# 49   8 REALES
27.0700 g., 0.9310 Silver 0.8102 oz. ASW   **Ruler:** Luis I **Obv:** Legend and date around crowned arms **Obv. Legend:** LVDOVICVS I DEI G **Rev:** Lions and castles in angles of cross, legend around **Rev. Legend:** INDIARVM * REX HISPANIARV ... **Note:** A significant portion of the legend must be visible for proper attribution. Mint mark M, Mo.

Date	Mintage	Good	VG	F	VF	XF
ND(1724-25) Date off flan; Rare	—	—	—	—	—	—
1724 D Rare	—	—	—	—	—	—
1725 D Rare	—	—	—	—	—	—

KM# 48   8 REALES
0.9160 g., Silver   **Ruler:** Philip V **Obv:** Legend around crowned arms **Rev:** Lions and castles in angles of cross, legend around **Note:** Klippe. Similar to KM#47a. Mint mark M, Mo.

Date	Mintage	Good	VG	F	VF	XF
ND(1733-34) Date off flan	—	—	200	350	500	—
1733 F	—	—	550	750	1,150	—
1733 MF	—	—	450	600	750	—
1734/3 MF	—	—	500	750	1,000	—
1734 MF	—	—	500	750	1,000	—

KM# 47a   8 REALES
27.0700 g., 0.9160 Silver 0.7972 oz. ASW   **Ruler:** Philip V **Obv:** Legend and date around crowned arms **Obv. Legend:** PHILIPVS V DEI G **Rev:** Lions and castles in angles of cross, legend around **Note:** Mint mark M, Mo.

Date	Mintage	Good	VG	F	VF	XF
ND(1729-33) Date off flan	—	—	70.00	90.00	110	—

KM# 50   ESCUDO
3.3800 g., 0.9170 Gold 0.0996 oz. AGW   **Ruler:** Charles II **Obv:** Legend and date around crowned arms **Obv. Legend:** CAROLVS II DEI G **Rev:** Lions and castles in angles of cross, legend around **Note:** Mint mark MXo.

Date	Mintage	VG	F	VF	XF	Unc
1701/0MXo L	—	—	3,000	4,000	5,000	—

KM# 51.1 ESCUDO

3.3800 g., 0.9170 Gold 0.0996 oz. AGW **Ruler:** Philip V **Obv:** Legend and date around crowned arms **Obv. Legend:** PHILIPVS V DEI G **Rev:** Lions and castles in angles of cross, legend around **Note:** Mint mark MXo.

Date	Mintage	VG	F	VF	XF	Unc
ND(1702-13) Date off flan	—	—	1,000	1,350	1,500	—
1702MXo L	—	—	1,500	2,500	3,500	—
1703/2MXo L	—	—	1,500	2,500	3,500	—
1704MXo L	—	—	1,500	2,500	3,500	—
1707MXo J	—	—	1,500	2,500	3,500	—
1708MXo J	—	—	1,500	2,500	3,500	—
1709MXo J	—	—	1,500	2,500	3,500	—
1710MXo J	—	—	1,500	2,500	3,500	—
1711MXo J	—	—	1,500	2,500	3,500	—
1712MXo J	—	—	1,500	2,500	3,500	—
1713MXo J	—	—	1,500	2,500	3,500	—

KM# 51.2 ESCUDO

3.3800 g., 0.9170 Gold 0.0996 oz. AGW **Ruler:** Philip V **Obv:** Legend and date around crowned arms **Obv. Legend:** PHILIPVS V DEI G **Rev:** Lions and castles in angles of cross, legend around **Note:** Mint mark Mo.

Date	Mintage	VG	F	VF	XF	Unc
1712Mo J	—	—	2,000	3,000	4,000	—
1714Mo J	—	—	1,400	2,000	3,000	—
1714Mo J J's 1's (J7J4J) Rare	—	—	—	—	—	—
1715Mo J	—	—	2,000	3,000	4,000	—
1727Mo J Rare	—	—	—	—	—	—
1728Mo J Rare	—	—	—	—	—	—

Note: Die-struck counterfeits of 1731 F exist

KM# 52 2 ESCUDOS

6.7700 g., 0.9170 Gold 0.1996 oz. AGW **Ruler:** Philip V **Obv:** Legend and date around crowned arms **Obv. Legend:** CAROLVS II DEI G **Rev:** Legend around cross **Note:** Mint mark MXo.

Date	Mintage	VG	F	VF	XF	Unc
1701MXo L	—	—	4,000	2,200	6,000	—

KM# 53.1 2 ESCUDOS

6.7700 g., 0.9170 Gold 0.1996 oz. AGW **Ruler:** Philip V **Obv:** Legend and date around crowned arms

Obv. Legend: PHILIPVS V DEI G **Rev:** Legend around cross **Note:** Mint mark MXo.

Date	Mintage	VG	F	VF	XF	Unc
ND(1704-13) Date off flan	—	—	1,500	2,000	2,500	—
1704MXo L	—	—	2,750	3,750	4,750	—
1708MXo J	—	—	2,750	3,750	4,750	—
1710MXo J	—	—	2,750	3,750	4,750	—
1711MXo J	—	—	2,750	3,750	4,750	—
1712MXo J	—	—	2,750	3,750	4,750	—
1713MXo J	—	—	2,750	3,750	4,750	—

KM# 53.2 2 ESCUDOS

6.7700 g., 0.9170 Gold 0.1996 oz. AGW **Ruler:** Philip V **Obv:** Legend and date around crowned arms **Obv. Legend:** PHILIPVS V DEI G **Rev:** Legend around cross **Note:** Struck counterfeits exist for 1731. Mint mark Mo.

Date	Mintage	VG	F	VF	XF	Unc
ND(1714-31) Date off flan	—	—	1,500	1,750	2,500	—
1714Mo J	—	—	—	2,500	3,500	—
1715Mo J	—	—	—	3,000	4,000	—
1717Mo J Rare	—	—	—	—	—	—
1722Mo J Rare	—	—	—	—	—	—
1729Mo R Rare	—	—	—	—	—	—
1731Mo F Rare	—	—	—	—	—	—

KM# A54 2 ESCUDOS

6.7700 g., 0.9170 Gold 0.1996 oz. AGW **Ruler:** Luis I **Obv:** Legend and date around crowned arms **Obv. Legend:** LVDOVICVS I DEI G. **Rev:** Legend around cross **Note:** A significant portion of the legend must be visible for proper attribution. Mint mark MXo.

Date	Mintage	VG	F	VF	XF	Unc
NDMo D Rare	—	—	—	—	—	—

KM# 55.1 4 ESCUDOS

13.5400 g., 0.9170 Gold 0.3992 oz. AGW **Ruler:** Philip V **Obv:** Legend and date around crowned arms **Obv. Legend:** PHILIPVS V DEI G **Rev:** Legend around cross **Note:** Mint mark MXo.

Date	Mintage	VG	F	VF	XF	Unc
ND(1705-13) Date off flan	—	—	2,500	3,000	4,000	—
1705MXo J	—	—	4,000	5,750	6,750	—
1706MXo L	—	—	4,000	5,750	6,750	—
1711MXo J	—	—	4,000	5,750	6,750	—
1712MXo J	—	—	4,000	5,750	6,750	—
1713MXo J	—	—	4,000	5,750	6,750	—

KM# 55.2   4 ESCUDOS
13.5400 g., 0.9170 Gold 0.3992 oz. AGW **Ruler:**
Philip V **Obv:** Legend and date around crowned arms
Obv. Legend: PHILIPVS V DEI G **Rev:** Legend
around cross **Note:** Mint mark Mo.

Date	Mintage	VG	F	VF	XF	Unc
ND(1714-20)	—	—	2,500	3,750	5,000	—
Date off flan						
1714Mo J	—	—	—	5,750	7,500	—
1715Mo J	—	—	—	5,750	7,500	—
1720Mo J Rare	—	—	—	—	—	—

KM# 57.1   8 ESCUDOS
27.0700 g., 0.9170 Gold 0.7981 oz. AGW **Ruler:**
Philip V **Obv:** Legend and date around crowned arms
Obv. Legend: PHILIPVS V DEI G **Rev:** Legend
around cross **Note:** Mint mark MXo.

Date	Mintage	VG	F	VF	XF	Unc
ND(1701-13)	—	—	2,000	3,000	4,000	—
Date off flan						
1701MXo L	—	—	6,000	7,500	9,000	—
1703MXo L	—	—	6,000	7,500	9,000	—
1706MXo J	—	—	6,000	7,500	9,000	—
1708MXo J	—	—	6,000	7,500	9,000	—
1709MXo J	—	—	6,000	7,500	9,000	—
1710MXo J	—	—	6,000	7,500	9,000	—
1711MXo J	—	—	3,500	4,000	5,750	—
1712MXo J	—	—	3,500	4,000	5,750	—
1713MXo J	—	—	3,500	4,000	5,750	—

KM# 57.2   8 ESCUDOS
27.0700 g., 0.9170 Gold 0.7981 oz. AGW **Ruler:**
Philip V **Obv:** Legend and date around crowned arms
Obv. Legend: PHILIPVS V DEI G **Rev:** Legend
around cross **Note:** Mint mark Mo.

Date	Mintage	VG	F	VF	XF	Unc
ND(1714-32)Mo	—	—	2,750	3,750	4,750	—
Date off flan						
1714Mo J	—	—	5,000	6,000	7,500	—
1714Mo Date over	—	—	6,000	7,500	9,000	—
GRAT on obverse						

Date	Mintage	VG	F	VF	XF	Unc
1715Mo J	—	—	5,000	6,500	8,000	—
1717/6Mo J Rare	—	—	—	—	—	—
1720/19Mo J Rare	—	—	—	—	—	—
1723Mo J Rare	—	—	—	—	—	—
1727/6Mo D Rare	—	—	—	—	—	—
1728/7Mo D Rare	—	—	—	—	—	—
1729Mo R Rare	—	—	—	—	—	—
1730Mo R Rare	—	—	—	—	—	—
1730Mo F Rare	—	—	—	—	—	—
1731Mo F Rare	—	—	—	—	—	—
1732Mo F Rare	—	—	—	—	—	—

KM# 57.3   8 ESCUDOS
27.0700 g., 0.9170 Gold 0.7981 oz. AGW **Ruler:**
Philip V **Obv:** Date around crowned arms **Obv.**
Legend: PHILIPVS V DEI G **Rev:** Legend and date
around cross **Note:** Mint mark Mo.

Date	Mintage	VG	F	VF	XF	Unc
1714Mo J Date	—	—	6,000	7,500	9,000	—
on reverse						

KM# 58   8 ESCUDOS
27.0700 g., 0.9170 Gold 0.7981 oz. AGW **Ruler:**
Luis I **Obv:** Legend and date around crowned arms
Obv. Legend: LVDOVICVS I DEI G **Rev:** Legend
around cross **Note:** A significant portion of the legend
must be visible for proper attribution. Mint mark Mo.

Date	Mintage	VG	F	VF	XF	Unc
ND(1724-25)Mo	—	—	—	—	—	—
D Rare						

ROYAL COINAGE

Struck on specially prepared round planchets
using well centered dies in excellent condition to
prove the quality of the minting to the Viceroy or
even to the King.

KM# R24   1/2 REAL
1.6917 g., 0.9310 Silver 0.0506 oz. ASW **Ruler:**
Philip V **Note:** Normally found holed. Mint mark Mo.

Date	Mintage	Good	VG	F	VF	XF
1715Mo J	—	—	250	500	750	—
1719Mo J	—	—	250	500	750	—
1721Mo J	—	—	250	500	750	—
1722Mo J	—	—	250	500	750	—
1726Mo D	—	—	250	500	750	—
1727Mo D	—	—	250	500	750	—

KM# R25   1/2 REAL
1.6917 g., 0.9310 Silver 0.0506 oz. ASW **Ruler:**
Luis I **Obv:** Legend around crowned LVDOVICVS
monogram **Rev:** Lions and castles in angles of cross,
legend around **Note:** Mint mark Mo.

Date	Mintage	Good	VG	F	VF	XF
1724Mo D Rare	—	—	—	—	—	—

KM# R24a   1/2 REAL
1.6917 g., 0.9170 Silver 0.0499 oz. ASW **Ruler:**
Philip V **Note:** Normally found holed. Mint mark Mo.

Date	Mintage	Good	VG	F	VF	XF
1730Mo D	—	—	250	500	750	—

KM# R30   REAL
3.3834 g., 0.9310 Silver 0.1013 oz. ASW **Ruler:**
Philip V **Obv. Legend:** PHILIPVS V DEI G **Note:** Mint
mark Mo.

Date	Mintage	Good	VG	F	VF	XF
1715Mo J Rare	—	—	—	—	—	—
1716Mo J Rare	—	—	—	—	—	—
1718Mo J Rare	—	—	—	—	—	—

KM# R35 2 REALES
6.7668 g., 0.9310 Silver 0.2025 oz. ASW **Ruler:** Philip V **Obv. Legend:** PHILIPVS V DEI G **Note:** Mint mark Mo.

Date	Mintage	Good	VG	F	VF	XF
1715Mo J Rare	—	—	—	—	—	—

KM# R35a 2 REALES
6.7668 g., 0.9170 Silver 0.1995 oz. ASW **Ruler:** Philip V **Note:** Mint mark Mo.

Date	Mintage	Good	VG	F	VF	XF
1730Mo R Rare	—	—	—	—	—	—

KM# R40 4 REALES
13.5337 g., 0.9310 Silver 0.4051 oz. ASW **Ruler:** Philip V **Obv. Legend:** PHILIPVS V DEI G **Note:** Mint mark Mo.

Date	Mintage	Good	VG	F	VF	XF
1716Mo J Rare	—	—	—	—	—	—
1719Mo J Rare	—	—	—	—	—	—
1721Mo J Rare	—	—	—	—	—	—
1722Mo J Rare	—	—	—	—	—	—
1723Mo J Rare	—	—	—	—	—	—

KM# R47 8 REALES
27.0674 g., 0.9310 Silver 0.8102 oz. ASW **Ruler:** Philip V **Obv. Legend:** PHILIPVS V DEI G **Note:** Struck at Mexico City Mint, mint mark Mo.

Date	Mintage	Good	VG	F	VF	XF
1702Mo L Rare	—	—	—	—	—	—
1703Mo L Rare	—	—	—	—	—	—
1705Mo J Rare	—	—	—	—	—	—
1706Mo J Rare	—	—	—	—	—	—
1709Mo J Rare	—	—	—	—	—	—
1711Mo J Rare	—	—	—	—	—	—
1714Mo J Rare	—	—	—	—	—	—
1715Mo J Rare	—	—	—	—	—	—
1716Mo J Rare	—	—	—	—	—	—
1717Mo J Rare	—	—	—	—	—	—
1719Mo J Rare	—	—	—	—	—	—
1721Mo J Rare	—	—	—	—	—	—
1722Mo J Rare	—	—	—	—	—	—
1723Mo J Rare	—	—	—	—	—	—
1724Mo D Rare	—	—	—	—	—	—
1725Mo D Rare	—	—	—	—	—	—
1726/5Mo D Rare	—	—	—	—	—	—
1726Mo D Rare	—	—	—	—	—	—
1727Mo D Rare	—	—	—	—	—	—

KM# R49 8 REALES
27.0674 g., 0.9310 Silver 0.8102 oz. ASW **Ruler:** Luis I **Note:** Mint mark Mo.

Date	Mintage	Good	VG	F	VF	XF
1724 D Rare	—	—	—	—	—	—
1725 D Rare	—	—	—	—	—	—

KM# R47a 8 REALES
27.0674 g., 0.9170 Silver 0.7980 oz. ASW **Ruler:** Philip V **Note:** Mint mark Mo.

Date	Mintage	Good	VG	F	VF	XF
1729Mo R Rare	—	—	—	—	—	—
1730Mo R/D Rare	—	—	—	—	—	—
1730Mo G Rare	—	—	—	—	—	—

KM# R51.2 ESCUDO
3.3834 g., 0.9170 Gold 0.0997 oz. AGW **Ruler:** Philip V **Note:** Mint mark Mo.

Date	Mintage	Good	VG	F	VF	XF
1714Mo J Rare	—	—	—	—	—	—
1715Mo J Rare	—	—	—	—	—	—

KM# R53.1 2 ESCUDOS
6.7668 g., 0.9170 Gold 0.1995 oz. AGW **Ruler:** Philip V **Note:** Mint mark MXo.

Date	Mintage	Good	VG	F	VF	XF
1711MXo J Rare	—	—	—	—	—	—
1712MXo J Rare	—	—	—	—	—	—

KM# R55.1 4 ESCUDOS
13.5337 g., 0.9170 Gold 0.3990 oz. AGW **Ruler:** Philip V **Note:** Mint mark M, Mo.

Date	Mintage	Good	VG	F	VF	XF
1711 Rare	—	—	—	—	—	—

KM# R55.2 4 ESCUDOS
13.5337 g., 0.9170 Gold 0.3990 oz. AGW **Ruler:** Philip V **Note:** Mint mark M, Mo.

Date	Mintage	Good	VG	F	VF	XF
1714 Rare	—	—	—	—	—	—

KM# R57.1 8 ESCUDOS
27.0674 g., 0.9170 Gold 0.7980 oz. AGW **Ruler:** Philip V **Note:** Mint mark MXo.

Date	Mintage	Good	VG	F	VF	XF
1702MXo L Rare	—	—	—	—	—	—
1711MXo J Rare	—	—	—	—	—	—
1712MXo J Rare	—	—	—	—	—	—
1713MXo J Rare	—	—	—	—	—	—

KM# R57.3 8 ESCUDOS
27.0674 g., 0.9170 Gold 0.7980 oz. AGW **Ruler:** Philip V **Note:** Mint mark Mo.

Date	Mintage	Good	VG	F	VF	XF
1714Mo J Rare	—	—	—	—	—	—
1715Mo J Rare	—	—	—	—	—	—
1717Mo J Rare	—	—	—	—	—	—
1718Mo J Rare	—	—	—	—	—	—
1723Mo J Rare	—	—	—	—	—	—

MILLED COINAGE

100 Centavos = 1 Peso

KM# 59 1/8 PILON (1/16 Real)
Copper **Ruler:** Ferdinand VII **Obv:** Crowned monogram **Rev:** Castles and lions in wreath **Note:** Mint mark Mo.

Date	Mintage	VG	F	VF	XF	Unc
1814	—	10.00	20.00	45.00	120	—
1815	—	10.00	20.00	45.00	120	—

SPANISH COLONIAL - COB

KM# 63   1/4 TLACO (1/8 Real)
Copper   **Ruler:** Ferdinand VII **Obv:** Crowned monogram flanked by value and mint mark **Obv. Legend:** FERDIN. VII... **Rev:** Arms without shield within wreath **Note:** Mint mark Mo.

Date	Mintage	VG	F	VF	XF	Unc
1814	—	12.00	25.00	50.00	150	—
1815	—	12.00	25.00	50.00	150	—
1816	—	12.00	25.00	50.00	150	—

KM# 62   1/4 REAL
0.8458 g., 0.8960 Silver 0.0244 oz. ASW   **Ruler:** Charles IV **Obv:** Crowned rampant lion, left **Rev:** Castle **Note:** Mint mark Mo.

Date	Mintage	VG	F	VF	XF	Unc
1796	—	15.00	30.00	55.00	90.00	—
1797	—	15.00	30.00	55.00	90.00	—
1798	—	12.50	22.00	50.00	75.00	—
1799/8	—	12.50	22.00	50.00	75.00	—
1799	—	10.00	20.00	40.00	70.00	—
1800	—	10.00	25.00	55.00	90.00	—
1801/0	—	10.00	20.00	40.00	70.00	—
1801	—	10.00	20.00	40.00	70.00	—
1802	—	10.00	20.00	40.00	70.00	—
1803	—	10.00	20.00	40.00	70.00	—
1804	—	10.00	20.00	40.00	75.00	—
1805/4	—	12.50	25.00	55.00	85.00	—
1805	—	10.00	22.00	50.00	75.00	—
1806	—	10.00	22.00	50.00	80.00	—
1807/797	—	15.00	30.00	55.00	85.00	—
1807	—	12.50	25.00	50.00	80.00	—
1808	—	12.50	25.00	50.00	80.00	—
1809/8	—	12.50	25.00	50.00	80.00	—
1809	—	12.50	25.00	50.00	80.00	—
1810	—	12.50	25.00	50.00	75.00	—
1811	—	12.50	25.00	50.00	75.00	—
1812	—	12.50	25.00	50.00	75.00	—
1813	—	10.00	20.00	40.00	70.00	—
1815	—	12.50	22.00	50.00	75.00	—
1816	—	10.00	20.00	40.00	70.00	—

KM# 64   2/4 SENAL (1/4 Real)
Copper   **Ruler:** Ferdinand VII **Obv:** Legend around crowned monogram flanked by mint mark and value **Obv. Legend:** FERDIN. VII... **Rev:** Arms without shield within wreath **Note:** Mint mark Mo.

Date	Mintage	VG	F	VF	XF	Unc
1814	—	12.00	25.00	50.00	150	—
1815/4	—	15.00	30.00	60.00	165	—
1815	—	12.00	25.00	50.00	150	—
1816	—	12.00	25.00	50.00	150	—
1821	—	20.00	40.00	75.00	200	—

KM# 65   1/2 REAL
1.6917 g., 0.9170 Silver 0.0499 oz. ASW   **Ruler:** Philip V **Obv:** Crowned shield flanked by M F, rosettes and small cross **Obv. Legend:** PHILIP • V • D • G • HISPAN • ET IND • REX **Rev:** Crowned globes flanked by crowned pillars with banner, date below **Note:** Mint mark M, Mo, MX.

Date	Mintage	VG	F	VF	XF	Unc
1732 Rare	—	—	—	—	—	—
1732 F	—	500	800	1,200	2,000	—
1733 MF (MX)	—	400	600	1,000	1,500	—
1733 F	—	200	325	550	800	—
1733/2 MF	—	300	400	600	800	—
1733 MF	—	300	400	600	800	—

Date	Mintage	VG	F	VF	XF	Unc
1734/3 MF	—	12.00	25.00	45.00	85.00	—
1734 MF	—	12.00	25.00	45.00	85.00	—
1735/4 MF	—	10.00	20.00	45.00	85.00	—
1735 MF	—	10.00	20.00	45.00	85.00	—
1736/5 MF	—	10.00	20.00	45.00	85.00	—
1736 MF	—	10.00	20.00	45.00	85.00	—
1737/6 MF	—	10.00	20.00	45.00	85.00	—
1737 MF	—	10.00	20.00	45.00	85.00	—
1738/7 MF	—	10.00	20.00	45.00	85.00	—
1738 MF	—	10.00	20.00	45.00	85.00	—
1739 MF	—	10.00	20.00	45.00	85.00	—
1740/30 MF	—	8.00	18.00	40.00	75.00	—
1740 MF	—	8.00	18.00	40.00	75.00	—
1741 MF	—	8.00	18.00	40.00	75.00	—

KM# 66   1/2 REAL
1.6900 g., 0.9170 Silver 0.0498 oz. ASW   **Ruler:** Philip V **Obv:** Crowned shield flanked by stars **Obv. Legend:** PHS • V • D • G • HISP • ET IND • R **Rev:** Crowned globes flanked by crowned pillars with banner, date below **Note:** Mint mark M, Mo.

Date	Mintage	VG	F	VF	XF	Unc
1742 M	—	8.00	18.00	40.00	75.00	—
1743 M	—	8.00	18.00	40.00	75.00	—
1744/3 M	—	8.00	18.00	40.00	75.00	—
1744 M	—	8.00	18.00	40.00	75.00	—
1745 M Rare	—	—	—	—	—	—

Note: Legend variation: PHS. V. D. G. HISP. EST IND. R

Date	Mintage	VG	F	VF	XF	Unc
1745 M	—	8.00	18.00	40.00	75.00	—
1746/5 M	—	8.00	18.00	40.00	75.00	—
1746 M	—	8.00	18.00	40.00	75.00	—
1747 M	—	8.00	18.00	40.00	75.00	—

KM# 67.1   1/2 REAL
1.6900 g., 0.9170 Silver 0.0498 oz. ASW   **Ruler:** Ferdinand VI **Obv:** Royal crown **Obv. Legend:** FRD • VI • D • G • HIPS • ET IND • R **Note:** Mint mark M, Mo.

Date	Mintage	VG	F	VF	XF	Unc
1747/6 M	—	—	—	—	—	—
1747 M	—	8.00	18.00	40.00	75.00	—
1748/7 M	—	8.00	18.00	40.00	75.00	—
1748 M	—	8.00	18.00	40.00	75.00	—
1749 M	—	8.00	18.00	40.00	75.00	—
1750 M	—	8.00	18.00	40.00	75.00	—
1751 M	—	10.00	20.00	45.00	85.00	—
1752 M	—	8.00	18.00	40.00	75.00	—
1753 M	—	8.00	18.00	40.00	75.00	—
1754 M	—	12.00	25.00	55.00	100	—
1755/6 M	—	12.00	25.00	55.00	100	—
1755 M	—	8.00	18.00	40.00	75.00	—
1756/5 M	—	8.00	18.00	40.00	75.00	—
1756 M	—	8.00	18.00	40.00	75.00	—
1757/6 M	—	8.00	18.00	40.00	75.00	—
1757 M	—	8.00	18.00	40.00	75.00	—

KM# 67.2   1/2 REAL
1.6917 g., 0.9170 Silver 0.0499 oz. ASW   **Ruler:** Ferdinand VI **Obv:** Different crown **Note:** Mint mark M, Mo.

Date	Mintage	VG	F	VF	XF	Unc
1757 M	—	8.00	18.00	40.00	75.00	—
1758/7 M	—	8.00	18.00	40.00	75.00	—
1758 M	—	8.00	18.00	40.00	75.00	—
1759 M	—	8.00	18.00	40.00	75.00	—
1760/59 M	—	8.00	18.00	40.00	75.00	—
1760 M	—	8.00	18.00	40.00	75.00	—

KM# 68   1/2 REAL
1.6900 g., 0.9170 Silver 0.0498 oz. ASW   **Ruler:**
Charles III **Obv:** Crowned shield flanked by stars
Obv. Legend: CAR • III • D • G • HISP • ET IND • R
Rev: Crowned globes flanked by crowned pillars with
banner, date below **Note:** Mint mark M, Mo.

Date	Mintage	VG	F	VF	XF	Unc
1760/59 M	—	8.00	18.00	40.00	75.00	—
1760 M	—	8.00	18.00	40.00	75.00	—
1761 M	—	8.00	18.00	40.00	75.00	—
1762 M	—	8.00	18.00	40.00	75.00	—
1763/2 M	—	8.00	18.00	40.00	75.00	—
1763 M	—	8.00	18.00	40.00	75.00	—
1764 M	—	8.00	18.00	40.00	75.00	—
1765/4 M	—	10.00	20.00	42.00	80.00	—
1765 M	—	8.00	18.00	40.00	75.00	—
1766 M	—	8.00	18.00	40.00	75.00	—
1767 M	—	10.00	20.00	45.00	85.00	—
1768/6 M	—	10.00	20.00	42.00	80.00	—
1768 M	—	8.00	18.00	40.00	75.00	—
1769 M	—	10.00	20.00	42.00	80.00	—
1770 M	—	10.00	20.00	42.00	80.00	—
1770 F	—	15.00	30.00	60.00	100	—
1771 F	—	10.00	20.00	42.00	80.00	—

KM# 69.2   1/2 REAL
1.6917 g., 0.9030 Silver 0.0491 oz. ASW   **Ruler:**
Charles III **Obv:** Armored bust of Charles III, right
Obv. Legend: CAROLUS • III • DEI • GRATIA **Rev:**
Crown above shield flanked by pillars with banner,
normal initials and mint mark **Note:** Mint mark Mo.

Date	Mintage	VG	F	VF	XF	Unc
1772Mo FF	—	9.00	18.00	35.00	80.00	—
1773Mo FM	—	4.50	10.00	25.00	60.00	—
1773Mo FM CAROLS (error)	—	75.00	150	250	400	—
1774Mo FM	—	4.50	10.00	25.00	55.00	—
1775Mo FM	—	4.50	10.00	25.00	55.00	—
1776Mo FM	—	4.50	10.00	25.00	55.00	—
1777/6Mo FM	—	10.00	18.00	35.00	75.00	—
1777Mo FM	—	7.00	15.00	30.00	65.00	—
1778Mo FF	—	4.50	10.00	25.00	55.00	—
1779Mo FF	—	4.50	10.00	25.00	55.00	—
1780/79Mo FF	—	6.00	12.50	30.00	75.00	—
1780Mo FF	—	4.50	10.00	25.00	55.00	—
1781Mo FF	—	4.50	10.00	25.00	55.00	—
1782/1Mo FF	—	6.00	12.50	30.00	75.00	—
1782Mo FF	—	4.50	10.00	25.00	55.00	—
1783Mo FF	—	4.50	10.00	25.00	55.00	—
1783Mo FM	—	125	300	450	—	—
1784Mo FF	—	4.50	10.00	25.00	55.00	—
1784Mo FM	—	7.00	15.00	35.00	80.00	—

KM# 69.1   1/2 REAL
1.6900 g., 0.9030 Silver 0.0491 oz. ASW   **Ruler:**
Charles III **Obv. Legend:** CAROLUS • III • DEI •
GRATIA **Rev:** Inverted FM and mint mark **Note:** Mint
mark Mo.

Date	Mintage	VG	F	VF	XF	Unc
1772Mo FM	—	5.00	12.00	27.00	65.00	—
1773Mo FM	—	4.50	10.00	25.00	55.00	—

KM# 69.2a   1/2 REAL
1.6917 g., 0.8960 Silver 0.0487 oz. ASW   **Ruler:**
Charles III **Rev:** Normal initials and mint mark **Note:**
Mint mark M, Mo.

Date	Mintage	VG	F	VF	XF	Unc
1785/4 FM	—	7.00	15.00	35.00	80.00	—
1785 FM	—	5.00	12.00	27.00	60.00	—
1786 FM	—	4.50	10.00	25.00	55.00	—
1787 FM	—	4.50	10.00	25.00	55.00	—
1788 FM	—	4.50	10.00	25.00	55.00	—
1789 FM	—	8.00	16.00	40.00	100	—

KM# 70   1/2 REAL
1.6917 g., 0.8960 Silver 0.0487 oz. ASW   **Ruler:**
Charles IV **Obv:** Armored bust of Charles IV, right
Obv. Legend: CAROLUS ? IV ? ... **Rev:** Crown
above shield flanked by pillars with banner **Note:** Mint
mark M, Mo.

Date	Mintage	VG	F	VF	XF	Unc
1789 FM	—	12.00	25.00	50.00	100	—
1790 FM	—	12.00	25.00	50.00	100	—

KM# 71   1/2 REAL
1.6917 g., 0.8960 Silver 0.0487 oz. ASW   **Ruler:**
Charles IV **Obv:** Armored bust of Charles IIII, right
Obv. Legend: CAROLUS ? IIII ? ... **Rev:** Crown
above shield flanked by pillars with banner **Note:** Mint
mark M, Mo.

Date	Mintage	VG	F	VF	XF	Unc
1790 FM	—	12.00	25.00	50.00	100	—

KM# 72   1/2 REAL
1.6900 g., 0.9030 Silver 0.0491 oz. ASW   **Ruler:**
Charles IV **Obv:** Armored bust of Charles IIII, right
Obv. Legend: CAROLUS • IIII • ... **Rev:** Crowned
shield flanked by pillars with banner **Rev. Legend:**
IND • R • .... **Note:** Mint mark Mo.

Date	Mintage	VG	F	VF	XF	Unc
1792 FM	—	6.00	12.00	25.00	50.00	—
1793 FM	—	6.00	12.00	25.00	50.00	—
1794/3 FM	—	7.50	15.00	30.00	75.00	—
1794 FM	—	5.00	10.00	22.00	45.00	—
1795 FM	—	4.00	10.00	22.00	45.00	—
1796 FM	—	4.00	10.00	22.00	45.00	—
1797 FM	—	4.00	10.00	22.00	45.00	—
1798/7 FM	—	5.00	11.50	25.00	50.00	—
1798 FM	—	4.00	10.00	22.00	45.00	—
1799 FM	—	4.00	10.00	22.00	45.00	—
1800/799 FM	—	5.00	11.50	25.00	50.00	—
1800 FM	—	4.00	10.00	22.00	45.00	—
1801 FM	—	7.50	15.00	30.00	80.00	—
1801 FT	—	4.00	10.00	22.00	45.00	—
1802 FT	—	4.00	10.00	22.00	45.00	—
1803 FT	—	5.00	11.50	25.00	50.00	—
1804 TH	—	4.00	10.00	22.00	45.00	—
1805 TH	—	4.00	10.00	22.00	45.00	—

SPANISH COLONIAL · MILLED

Date	Mintage	VG	F	VF	XF	Unc
1806 TH	—	4.00	10.00	22.00	45.00	—
1807/6 TH	—	5.00	11.50	25.00	50.00	—
1807 TH	—	4.00	10.00	22.00	45.00	—
1808/7 TH	—	5.00	11.50	25.00	50.00	—
1808 TH	—	4.00	10.00	22.00	45.00	—

KM# 73   1/2 REAL
1.6900 g., 0.9030 Silver 0.0491 oz. ASW **Ruler:**
Ferdinand VII **Obv:** Armored laureate bust right **Obv.**
Legend: FERDIN.VII... **Rev:** Crowned shield flanked
by pillars **Rev. Legend:** IND.R.... **Note:** Mint mark Mo.

Date	Mintage	VG	F	VF	XF	Unc
1808 TH	—	3.50	8.00	20.00	35.00	—
1809 TH	—	3.50	8.00	20.00	35.00	—
1810 TH	—	5.00	10.00	22.00	45.00	—
1810 HJ	—	3.50	8.00	20.00	35.00	—
1811 HJ	—	3.50	8.00	20.00	35.00	—
1812/1 HJ	—	7.50	15.00	35.00	80.00	—
1812 HJ	—	3.50	8.00	20.00	35.00	—
1812 JJ	—	12.00	25.00	45.00	100	—
1813/2 JJ	—	12.00	25.00	45.00	100	—
1813 TH	—	3.50	8.00	20.00	35.00	—
1813 JJ	—	6.00	12.00	25.00	75.00	—
1813 HJ	—	7.50	15.00	35.00	90.00	—
1814/3 JJ	—	7.50	15.00	35.00	90.00	—
1814 JJ	—	5.00	10.00	22.00	45.00	—

KM# 74   1/2 REAL
1.6900 g., 0.9030 Silver 0.0491 oz. ASW **Ruler:**
Ferdinand VII **Obv:** Draped laureate bust right **Obv.**
Legend: FERDIN.VII.... **Rev:** Crowned shield
flanked by pillars **Rev. Legend:** IND.R.... **Note:** Mint
mark Mo.

Date	Mintage	VG	F	VF	XF	Unc
1815 JJ	—	3.50	8.00	20.00	40.00	—
1816 JJ	—	3.50	8.00	20.00	40.00	—
1817/6 JJ	—	12.00	25.00	50.00	120	—
1817 JJ	—	3.50	8.00	28.00	45.00	—
1818/7 JJ	—	3.50	8.00	25.00	50.00	—
1818 JJ	—	3.50	8.00	25.00	50.00	—
1819/8 JJ	—	6.00	12.00	35.00	90.00	—
1819 JJ	—	3.50	8.00	20.00	40.00	—
1820 JJ	—	3.50	8.00	25.00	50.00	—
1821 JJ	—	3.50	8.00	20.00	40.00	—

KM# 75.1   REAL
3.3834 g., 0.9170 Silver 0.0997 oz. ASW **Ruler:**
Philip V **Obv:** Crowned shleld flanked by MF I ** **Obv.**
Legend: PHILIP • V • D • G • HISPAN • ET IND •
REX **Rev:** Crowned globes flanked by crowned
pillars with banner, date below **Note:** Mint mark M,
Mo, (MX).

Date	Mintage	VG	F	VF	XF	Unc
1732 Rare	—	—	—	—	—	—
1732 F	—	—	—	—	—	—

Date	Mintage	VG	F	VF	XF	Unc
1733 F (MX)	—	150	350	425	750	—
1733 MF (MX)	—	150	350	425	750	—
1733 F Rare	—	—	—	—	—	—
1733 MF	—	100	200	300	500	—
1734/3 MF	—	15.00	30.00	65.00	150	—
1734 MF	—	12.00	25.00	60.00	140	—
1735 MF	—	12.00	25.00	60.00	140	—
1736 MF	—	12.00	25.00	60.00	140	—
1737 MF	—	12.00	25.00	60.00	140	—
1738 MF	—	12.00	25.00	60.00	140	—
1739 MF	—	12.00	25.00	60.00	140	—
1740 MF	—	12.00	25.00	60.00	140	—
1741 MF	—	12.00	25.00	60.00	140	—

KM# 75.2   REAL
3.3834 g., 0.9170 Silver 0.0997 oz. ASW **Ruler:**
Philip V **Obv. Legend:** PHS ? V ? D ? G ? HISP ?
ET ? IND ? R **Note:** Mint mark M, Mo.

Date	Mintage	VG	F	VF	XF	Unc
1742 M	—	10.00	20.00	50.00	120	—
1743 M	—	10.00	20.00	50.00	120	—
1744/3 M	—	10.00	20.00	50.00	120	—
1744 M	—	10.00	20.00	50.00	120	—
1745 M	—	8.00	18.00	50.00	120	—
1746/5 M	—	12.00	25.00	75.00	200	—
1746 M	—	10.00	20.00	55.00	125	—
1747 M	—	10.00	20.00	55.00	125	—

KM# 76.1   REAL
3.3800 g., 0.9170 Silver 0.0996 oz. ASW **Ruler:**
Ferdinand VI **Obv:** Crowned shield flanked by R I
Obv. Legend: FRD • VI • D • G • HISP • ET IND • R
Rev: Crowned globes flanked by crowned pillars with
banner, date below **Note:** Mint mark M, Mo.

Date	Mintage	VG	F	VF	XF	Unc
1747 M	—	10.00	20.00	50.00	100	—
1748/7 M	—	10.00	20.00	50.00	100	—
1748 M	—	10.00	20.00	50.00	100	—
1749 M	—	10.00	20.00	50.00	100	—
1750/40 M	—	10.00	20.00	50.00	100	—
1750 M	—	10.00	20.00	50.00	100	—
1751 M	—	10.00	20.00	55.00	110	—
1752 M	—	10.00	20.00	50.00	100	—
1753 M	—	10.00	20.00	50.00	100	—
1754 M	—	10.00	20.00	55.00	110	—
1755/4 M	—	10.00	20.00	50.00	100	—
1755 M	—	10.00	20.00	50.00	100	—
1756 M	—	10.00	20.00	55.00	110	—
1757 M	—	10.00	20.00	55.00	110	—
1758/5 M	—	10.00	20.00	50.00	100	—
1758 M	—	10.00	20.00	50.00	100	—

KM# 76.2   REAL
3.3834 g., 0.9170 Silver 0.0997 oz. ASW **Ruler:**
Ferdinand VI **Obv:** Royal and Imperial crowns **Note:**
Mint mark M, Mo.

Date	Mintage	VG	F	VF	XF	Unc
1757 M	—	10.00	20.00	50.00	100	—
1758/7 M	—	10.00	20.00	50.00	100	—
1758 M	—	10.00	20.00	50.00	100	—
1759 M	—	10.00	20.00	55.00	110	—
1760 M	—	15.00	30.00	70.00	140	—

SPANISH COLONIAL · MILLED

KM# 77 REAL
3.3800 g., 0.9170 Silver 0.0996 oz. ASW **Ruler:**
Charles III **Obv:** Crowned shield flanked by R I **Obv.**
Legend: CAR • III • D • G • HISP • ET IND • R **Rev:**
Crowned globes flanked by crowned pillars with
banner, date below **Note:** Mint mark M, Mo.

Date	Mintage	VG	F	VF	XF	Unc
1760 M	—	10.00	20.00	50.00	100	—
1761/0 M	—	10.00	20.00	55.00	125	—
1761 M	—	10.00	20.00	50.00	100	—
1762 M	—	10.00	20.00	50.00	100	—
1763/2 M	—	12.00	25.00	60.00	120	—
1763 M	—	10.00	20.00	50.00	100	—
1764 M	—	10.00	20.00	55.00	110	—
1765 M	—	10.00	20.00	50.00	110	—
1766 M	—	10.00	20.00	50.00	100	—
1767 M	—	10.00	20.00	55.00	110	—
1768 M	—	10.00	20.00	50.00	100	—
1769 M	—	10.00	20.00	50.00	100	—
1769/70 M	—	10.00	20.00	50.00	125	—
1770 M	—	10.00	20.00	55.00	125	—
1770 F	—	20.00	40.00	90.00	250	—
1771 F	—	20.00	40.00	90.00	250	—

KM# 78.1 REAL
3.3834 g., 0.9030 Silver 0.0982 oz. ASW **Ruler:**
Charles III **Obv. Legend:** CAROLUS ? III ? DEI ?
GRATIA **Rev:** Inverted FM and mint mark **Note:** Mint
mark M, Mo.

Date	Mintage	VG	F	VF	XF	Unc
1772 FM	—	5.00	10.00	25.00	60.00	—
1773 FM	—	5.00	10.00	25.00	60.00	—

KM# 78.2 REAL
3.3800 g., 0.9030 Silver 0.0981 oz. ASW **Ruler:**
Charles III **Obv:** Armored bust of Charles III, right
Obv. Legend: CAROLUS • III • DEI • GRATIA **Rev.**
Legend: Crowned shield flanked by pillars with
banner, normal initials and mint mark **Note:** Mint
mark M, Mo.

Date	Mintage	VG	F	VF	XF	Unc
1774 FM	—	5.00	10.00	25.00	60.00	—
1775/4 FM	—	6.00	12.00	28.00	75.00	—
1775 FM	—	5.00	10.00	25.00	60.00	—
1776 FM	—	5.00	10.00	25.00	60.00	—
1777 FM	—	5.00	10.00	25.00	60.00	—
1778 FF/M	—	6.00	12.00	28.00	75.00	—
1778 FF	—	5.00	10.00	25.00	60.00	—
1779 FF	—	5.00	10.00	25.00	60.00	—
1780 FF	—	5.00	10.00	25.00	60.00	—
1780 F F/M	—	5.00	10.00	25.00	60.00	—
1781 FF	—	5.00	10.00	25.00	60.00	—
1782 FF	—	5.00	10.00	25.00	60.00	—
1783 FF	—	5.00	10.00	25.00	60.00	—
1784 FF	—	5.00	10.00	25.00	60.00	—

KM# 78.2a REAL
3.3834 g., 0.8960 Silver 0.0975 oz. ASW **Ruler:**
Charles III **Rev:** Normal initials and mint mark **Note:**
Mint mark M, Mo.

Date	Mintage	VG	F	VF	XF	Unc
1785 FF	—	6.00	12.00	28.00	75.00	—
1785 FM	—	6.00	12.00	28.00	75.00	—
1786 FM	—	6.00	12.00	28.00	75.00	—
1787 FF	—	15.00	30.00	60.00	125	—
1787 FM	—	12.00	25.00	50.00	100	—
1788 FF	—	50.00	100	200	—	—
1788 FM	—	5.00	10.00	25.00	60.00	—
1789 FM	—	6.00	12.00	28.00	75.00	—

KM# 79 REAL
3.3800 g., 0.9030 Silver 0.0981 oz. ASW **Ruler:**
Charles IV **Obv:** Armored bust of Charles III, right
Obv. Legend: CAROLUS • IV • ... **Rev:** Crown above
shield flanked by pillars with banner **Note:** Mint mark
M, Mo.

Date	Mintage	VG	F	VF	XF	Unc
1789 FM	—	15.00	30.00	60.00	150	—
1790 FM	—	15.00	30.00	60.00	150	—

KM# 80 REAL
3.3800 g., 0.9030 Silver 0.0981 oz. ASW **Ruler:**
Charles IV **Obv:** Armored bust of Charles IIII, right
Obv. Legend: CAROLUS • IIII • ... **Rev:** Crowned
shield flanked by pillars with banner **Note:** Mint mark
M, Mo.

Date	Mintage	VG	F	VF	XF	Unc
1790 FM	—	17.00	35.00	70.00	165	—

KM# 81 REAL
3.3834 g., 0.8960 Silver 0.0975 oz. ASW **Ruler:**
Charles IV **Obv:** Armored bust of Charles IIII, right
Obv. Legend: CAROLUS • IIII • ... **Rev:** Crowned
shield flanked by pillars with banner **Rev. Legend:**
IND • REX ... **Note:** Mint mark Mo.

Date	Mintage	VG	F	VF	XF	Unc
1792 FM	—	10.00	20.00	35.00	90.00	—
1793 FM	—	15.00	30.00	60.00	150	—
1794 FM	—	25.00	50.00	100	250	—
1795 FM	—	15.00	30.00	60.00	150	—
1796 FM	—	5.00	10.00	25.00	65.00	—
1797/6 FM	—	8.00	15.00	28.00	80.00	—
1797 FM	—	5.00	10.00	25.00	60.00	—
1798/7 FM	—	5.00	10.00	25.00	65.00	—
1798 FM	—	5.00	10.00	25.00	60.00	—
1799 FM	—	5.00	10.00	25.00	60.00	—
1800 FM	—	5.00	10.00	25.00	60.00	—
1801 FT/M	—	5.00	10.00	25.00	60.00	—
1801 FM	—	8.00	15.00	28.00	80.00	—
1801 FT	—	5.00	10.00	25.00	60.00	—
1802 FM	—	5.00	10.00	25.00	60.00	—
1802/1 FT	—	5.00	10.00	25.00	60.00	—
1802 FT	—	5.00	10.00	25.00	60.00	—

Date	Mintage	VG	F	VF	XF	Unc
1802 FT/M	—	5.00	10.00	25.00	60.00	—
1803 FT	—	5.00	10.00	25.00	60.00	—
1804 TH	—	5.00	10.00	25.00	60.00	—
1805 TH	—	5.00	10.00	25.00	60.00	—
1806 TH	—	5.00	10.00	25.00	60.00	—
1807/6 TH	—	5.00	10.00	25.00	65.00	—
1807 TH	—	5.00	10.00	25.00	60.00	—
1808/7 TH	—	5.00	10.00	25.00	65.00	—
1808 FM	—	5.00	10.00	25.00	60.00	—

KM# 82 REAL
3.3800 g., 0.9030 Silver 0.0981 oz. ASW **Ruler:**
Ferdinand VII **Obv:** Armored laureate bust right **Obv.**
Legend: FERDIN.VII... **Rev:** Crowned shield flanked
by pillars **Rev. Legend:** IND.REX.... **Note:** Mint mark
Mo.

Date	Mintage	VG	F	VF	XF	Unc
1809 TH	—	8.00	15.00	28.00	90.00	—
1810/09 TH	—	8.00	15.00	28.00	90.00	—
1810 TH	—	8.00	15.00	28.00	90.00	—
1811 TH	—	25.00	35.00	60.00	250	—
1811 HJ	—	8.00	15.00	28.00	90.00	—
1812 HJ	—	4.00	9.00	28.00	80.00	—
1812 JJ	—	10.00	20.00	40.00	120	—
1813 HJ	—	10.00	20.00	40.00	120	—
1813 JJ	—	50.00	100	150	250	—
1814 HJ	—	15.00	30.00	150	150	—
1814 JJ	—	50.00	100	175	300	—

KM# 83 REAL
3.3800 g., 0.9030 Silver 0.0981 oz. ASW **Ruler:**
Ferdinand VII **Obv:** Draped laureate bust right **Obv.**
Legend: FERDIN.VII... **Rev:** Crowned shield flanked
by pillars **Rev. Legend:** IND.REX... **Note:** Mint mark
Mo.

Date	Mintage	VG	F	VF	XF	Unc
1814 JJ	—	25.00	50.00	100	350	—
1815 HJ	—	15.00	30.00	60.00	150	—
1815 JJ	—	10.00	20.00	40.00	120	—
1816 JJ	—	5.00	10.00	25.00	70.00	—
1817 JJ	—	5.00	10.00	25.00	70.00	—
1818 JJ	—	30.00	60.00	125	500	—
1819 JJ	—	5.00	10.00	25.00	70.00	—
1820 JJ	—	5.00	10.00	25.00	70.00	—
1821/0 JJ	—	8.00	15.00	30.00	110	—
1821 JJ	—	5.00	10.00	25.00	50.00	—

KM# 84 2 REALES
6.7668 g., 0.9170 Silver 0.1995 oz. ASW **Ruler:**

Philip V **Obv:** Crowned shield flanked by M F 2 **Obv.**
Legend: PHILIP • V • D • G • HISPAN • ET IND •
REX **Rev:** Crowned globes flanked by crowned
pillars with banner, date below **Rev. Legend:**
VTRAQUE VNUM **Note:** Mint mark M, Mo, (MX).

Date	Mintage	VG	F	VF	XF	Unc
1732 Rare	—	—	—	—	—	—
1732 F	—	800	1,300	1,750	2,750	—
1733 F	—	600	800	1,350	2,250	—
1733 MF (MX)	—	350	600	1,000	1,650	—
1733 MF	—	600	900	1,500	2,500	—
1734/3 MF	—	20.00	40.00	85.00	170	—
1734 MF	—	20.00	40.00	85.00	170	—
1735/3 MF	—	15.00	30.00	75.00	150	—
1735/4 MF	—	15.00	30.00	75.00	150	—
1735 MF	—	15.00	30.00	75.00	150	—
1736/3 MF	—	18.00	35.00	80.00	160	—
1736/4 MF	—	18.00	35.00	80.00	160	—
1736/5 MF	—	18.00	35.00	80.00	160	—
1736 MF	—	18.00	35.00	80.00	160	—
1737/3 MF	—	18.00	35.00	80.00	160	—
1737 MF	—	18.00	35.00	80.00	160	—
1738/7 MF	—	18.00	35.00	80.00	160	—
1738 MF	—	18.00	35.00	80.00	160	—
1739 MF	—	18.00	35.00	80.00	160	—
1740/30 MF	—	18.00	35.00	80.00	160	—
1740 MF	—	18.00	35.00	80.00	160	—
1741 MF	—	18.00	35.00	80.00	160	—

KM# 85 2 REALES
6.7700 g., 0.9170 Silver 0.1996 oz. ASW **Ruler:**
Philip V **Obv:** Crowned shield flanked by R 2 **Obv.**
Legend: PHS • V • D • G • HISP • ET IND • R * **Rev:**
Crowned globes flanked by crowned pillars with
banner, date below **Rev. Legend:** VTRA QUE
VNUM **Note:** Mint mark M, Mo.

Date	Mintage	F	VF	XF	Unc	BU
1742 M	—	30.00	75.00	125	—	—
1743/2 M	—	30.00	75.00	125	—	—
1743 M	—	30.00	75.00	125	—	—
1744/3 M	—	30.00	75.00	125	—	—
1744 M	—	30.00	75.00	125	—	—
1745/4 M	—	30.00	75.00	125	—	—
1745 M	—	30.00	75.00	125	—	—
1745 M HIP	—	400	—	—	—	—
1746/5 M	—	30.00	75.00	125	—	—
1746 M	—	30.00	75.00	125	—	—
1747 M	—	30.00	75.00	125	—	—
1750 M	—	450	650	1,000	—	—

KM# 86.1 2 REALES
6.7668 g., 0.9170 Silver 0.1995 oz. ASW **Ruler:**
Ferdinand VI **Obv:** Crowned shield flanked by R 2
Obv. Legend: FRD • VI • D • G • HISP • ET IND • R
Rev: Crowned globes flanked by crowned pillars with

banner, date below **Rev. Legend:** VTRA QUE VNUM
Note: Mint mark M, Mo.

Date	Mintage	VG	F	VF	XF	Unc
1747 M	—	16.00	32.00	78.00	135	—
1748/7 M	—	16.00	32.00	78.00	135	—
1748 M	—	15.00	30.00	75.00	125	—
1749 M	—	15.00	30.00	75.00	125	—
1750 M	—	15.00	30.00	75.00	125	—
1751/41 M	—	18.00	35.00	80.00	150	—
1751 M	—	15.00	30.00	75.00	125	—
1752 M	—	15.00	30.00	75.00	125	—
1753/2 M	—	18.00	35.00	80.00	150	—
1753 M	—	18.00	35.00	80.00	150	—
1754 M	—	18.00	35.00	80.00	150	—
1755/4 M	—	18.00	35.00	80.00	150	—
1755 M	—	18.00	35.00	80.00	150	—
1756/55 M	—	18.00	35.00	80.00	150	—
1756 M	—	18.00	35.00	80.00	140	—
1757/6 M	—	15.00	30.00	75.00	125	—
1757 M	—	18.00	35.00	80.00	150	—

KM# 86.2 2 REALES
6.7668 g., 0.9170 Silver 0.1995 oz. ASW **Ruler:**
Ferdinand VI **Obv:** Royal and Imperial crowns **Note:**
Mint mark M, Mo.

Date	Mintage	VG	F	VF	XF	Unc
1757 M	—	15.00	30.00	75.00	125	—
1758 M	—	15.00	30.00	75.00	125	—
1759/8 M	—	15.00	30.00	75.00	125	—
1759 M	—	20.00	40.00	90.00	175	—
1760 M	—	20.00	40.00	90.00	175	—

KM# 87 2 REALES
6.7700 g., 0.9170 Silver 0.1996 oz. ASW **Ruler:**
Charles III **Obv:** Crowned shield flanked by R 2 **Obv.
Legend:** CAR • III • D • G • HISP • ET IND • R **Rev:**
Crowned globes flanked by crowned pillars with
banner, date below **Rev. Legend:** VTRA QUE VNUM
Note: Mint mark M, Mo.

Date	Mintage	VG	F	VF	XF	Unc
1760 M	—	15.00	30.00	75.00	125	—
1761 M	—	15.00	30.00	75.00	125	—
1762/1 M	—	15.00	30.00	75.00	125	—
1762 M	—	15.00	30.00	75.00	125	—
1763/2 M	—	15.00	30.00	75.00	125	—
1763 M	—	15.00	30.00	75.00	125	—
1764 M	—	15.00	30.00	75.00	125	—
1765 M	—	15.00	30.00	75.00	125	—
1766 M	—	12.00	35.00	80.00	160	—
1767 M	—	15.00	30.00	75.00	125	—
1768/6 M	—	15.00	30.00	75.00	125	—
1768 M	—	15.00	30.00	75.00	125	—
1769 M	—	15.00	30.00	75.00	125	—
1770 M	—	350	550	—	—	—
1770 F Rare	—	—	—	—	—	—
1771 F	—	15.00	30.00	75.00	125	—

KM# 88.1 2 REALES
6.7668 g., 0.9030 Silver 0.1964 oz. ASW **Ruler:**
Charles III **Obv:** Armored bust of Charles III, right
Obv. Legend: CAROLUS • III • DEI • GRATIA **Rev:**
Inverted FM and mint mark **Note:** Mint mark M, Mo.

Date	Mintage	VG	F	VF	XF	Unc
1772 FM	—	7.00	15.00	30.00	100	—
1773 FM	—	7.00	15.00	30.00	100	—

KM# 88.2 2 REALES
6.7700 g., 0.9030 Silver 0.1965 oz. ASW **Ruler:**
Charles III **Obv:** Armored bust od Charles III, right
Obv. Legend: CAROLUS • III • DEI • GRATIA • **Rev:**
Crowned shield flanked by pillars with banner, normal
initials and mint mark **Rev. Legend:** • HISPAN • ET
IND • REX • ... **Note:** Mint mark M, Mo.

Date	Mintage	VG	F	VF	XF	Unc
1773 FM	—	7.00	15.00	30.00	100	—
1774 FM	—	7.00	15.00	30.00	100	—
1775 FM	—	7.00	15.00	30.00	100	—
1776 FM	—	7.00	15.00	30.00	100	—
1777 FM	—	7.00	15.00	30.00	100	—
1770/7 FF	—	7.00	15.00	30.00	100	—
1778 F F/M	—	7.00	15.00	30.00	100	—
1778 FF	—	7.00	15.00	30.00	100	—
1779/8 FF	—	7.00	15.00	30.00	100	—
1779 FF	—	7.00	15.00	30.00	100	—
1780 FF	—	7.00	15.00	30.00	100	—
1781 FF	—	7.00	15.00	30.00	100	—
1782/1 FF	—	7.00	15.00	30.00	100	—
1782 FF	—	7.00	15.00	30.00	100	—
1783 FF	—	7.00	15.00	30.00	100	—
1784 FF	—	7.00	15.00	30.00	100	—
1784 FF DEI GRTIA (error)	—	100	150	250	600	—
1784 FM	—	70.00	120	225	575	—

KM# 88.2a 2 REALES
6.7668 g., 0.8960 Silver 0.1949 oz. ASW **Ruler:**
Charles III **Obv:** Armored bust of Charles III, right
Rev: Crowned shield flanked by pillars with banner
Note: Mint mark Mo.

Date	Mintage	VG	F	VF	XF	Unc
1785Mo FM	—	7.00	15.00	30.00	100	—
1786Mo FF	—	200	350	550	950	—
1786Mo FM	—	7.00	15.00	30.00	100	—
1787Mo FM	—	7.00	15.00	30.00	100	—
1788/98Mo FM	—	7.00	15.00	30.00	100	—
1788Mo FM	—	7.00	15.00	30.00	100	—
1789Mo FM	—	12.00	25.00	50.00	150	—

KM# 89 2 REALES
6.7700 g., 0.9030 Silver 0.1965 oz. ASW **Ruler:**
Charles IV **Obv:** Armored bust of Charles IV, right
Obv. Legend: CAROLUS • IV • DEI • GRATIA • **Rev:**

Crowned shield flanked by pillars with banner **Rev. Legend:** • HISPAN • ET IND • REX • ... **Note:** Mint mark M, Mo.

Date	Mintage	VG	F	VF	XF	Unc
1789 FM	—	15.00	30.00	75.00	200	—
1790 FM	—	15.00	30.00	75.00	200	—

KM# 90 2 REALES
6.7700 g., 0.9030 Silver 0.1965 oz. ASW **Ruler:** Charles IV **Obv:** Armored bust of Charles IIII, right **Obv. Legend:** CAROLUS • IIII • DEI • GRATIA • **Rev:** Crowned shield flanked by pillars with banner **Rev. Legend:** • HISPAN • ET IND REX • ... **Note:** Mint mark M, Mo.

Date	Mintage	VG	F	VF	XF	Unc
1790 FM	—	17.00	35.00	80.00	200	—

KM# 91 2 REALES
6.7668 g., 0.8960 Silver 0.1949 oz. ASW **Ruler:** Charles III **Obv:** Armored bust of Charles IIII, right **Obv. Legend:** CAROLUS • IIII • DEI • GRATIA • **Rev:** Crowned shield flanked by pillars with banner **Rev. Legend:** • HISPAN • ET IND REX • ... **Note:** Mint mark Mo.

Date	Mintage	VG	F	VF	XF	Unc
1792 FM	—	15.00	30.00	60.00	200	—
1793 FM	—	15.00	30.00	60.00	200	—
1794/3 FM	—	50.00	100	200	450	—
1794 FM	—	40.00	75.00	150	400	—
1795 FM	—	7.00	15.00	30.00	85.00	—
1796 FM	—	7.00	15.00	30.00	85.00	—
1797 FM	—	7.00	15.00	30.00	85.00	—
1798 FM	—	7.00	15.00	30.00	85.00	—
1799/8 FM	—	7.00	15.00	32.00	90.00	—
1799 FM	—	7.00	15.00	30.00	85.00	—
1800 FM	—	7.00	15.00	30.00	85.00	—
1801 FT/M	—	7.00	15.00	30.00	85.00	—
1801 FM	—	20.00	40.00	75.00	250	—
1801 FT	—	7.00	15.00	30.00	85.00	—
1802 FT	—	7.00	15.00	30.00	85.00	—
1803 FT	—	7.00	15.00	30.00	85.00	—
1804/3 TH	—	7.00	15.00	30.00	85.00	—
1804 TH	—	7.00	15.00	30.00	85.00	—
1805 TH	—	7.00	15.00	30.00	85.00	—
1806/5 TH	—	7.00	15.00	32.00	90.00	—
1806 TH	—	7.00	15.00	30.00	85.00	—
1807/5 TH	—	7.00	15.00	32.00	90.00	—
1807/6 TH	—	15.00	30.00	60.00	200	—
1807 TH	—	7.00	15.00	30.00	85.00	—
1808/7 TH	—	7.00	15.00	32.00	90.00	—
1808 TH	—	7.00	15.00	30.00	85.00	—

KM# 92 2 REALES
6.7700 g., 0.9030 Silver 0.1965 oz. ASW **Ruler:** Ferdinand VII **Obv:** Armored laureate bust right **Obv. Legend:** FERDIN.VII... **Rev:** Crowned shield flanked by pillars **Rev. Legend:** IND.REX... **Note:** Mint mark Mo.

Date	Mintage	VG	F	VF	XF	Unc
1809 TH	—	15.00	30.00	75.00	200	—
181/00 TH	—	15.00	30.00	75.00	200	—
1810 TH	—	15.00	30.00	75.00	200	—
181/00 HJ	—	15.00	30.00	75.00	200	—
181/00 HJ/TH	—	15.00	30.00	75.00	200	—
1810 HJ	—	15.00	30.00	75.00	200	—
1811 TH	—	150	250	350	750	—
1811/0 HJ/TH	—	40.00	80.00	150	300	—
1811 HJ	—	15.00	30.00	75.00	200	—
1811 HJ/TH	—	40.00	80.00	150	300	—

KM# 93 2 REALES
6.7700 g., 0.9030 Silver 0.1965 oz. ASW **Ruler:** Ferdinand VII **Obv:** Draped laureate bust right **Obv. Legend:** FERDIN.VII... **Rev:** Crowned shield flanked by pillars **Rev. Legend:** IND.REX... **Note:** Mint mark Mo.

Date	Mintage	VG	F	VF	XF	Unc
1812 TH	—	60.00	125	250	550	—
1812 HJ	—	40.00	100	200	500	—
1812 JJ	—	10.00	20.00	60.00	200	—
1813 TH	—	15.00	30.00	100	400	—
1813 JJ	—	20.00	60.00	125	350	—
1813 HJ	—	40.00	100	200	500	—
1814/3 JJ	—	15.00	30.00	100	400	—
1814/2 JJ	—	15.00	30.00	100	400	—
1814 JJ	—	15.00	30.00	100	400	—
1815 JJ	—	6.00	12.00	28.00	85.00	—
1816 JJ	—	6.00	12.00	28.00	85.00	—
1817 JJ	—	6.00	12.00	28.00	85.00	—
1818 JJ	—	6.00	12.00	28.00	85.00	—
1819/8 JJ	—	5.50	12.00	30.00	85.00	—
1819 JJ	—	6.00	12.00	28.00	85.00	—
1820 JJ	—	175	—	—	—	—
1821/0 JJ	—	7.00	15.00	30.00	90.00	—
1821 JJ	—	6.00	12.00	28.00	85.00	—

KM# 94 4 REALES
13.5337 g., 0.9170 Silver 0.3990 oz. ASW **Ruler:**
Philip V **Obv:** Crowned shield flanked by F 4 **Obv.**
Legend: PHILLIP • V • D • G • HISPAN • ET IND •
REX **Rev:** Crowned globes flanked by crowned
pillars with banner, date below **Rev. Legend:**
VTRAQUE VNUM **Note:** Mint mark M, Mo, MX.

Date	Mintage	VG	F	VF	XF	Unc
1732 Rare; Specimen	—	—	—	—	—	—
1732 F	—	2,000	3,000	5,000	10,000	—
1733/2 F	—	1,500	2,000	4,000	6,500	—
1733 MF	—	1,100	1,650	2,250	4,250	—
1733 MF (MX)	—	1,500	2,200	3,250	5,500	—
1733 MX/XM	—	1,500	2,200	3,250	5,500	—
1734/3 MF	—	150	300	600	1,200	—
1734 MF	—	150	300	600	1,200	—
1735/4 MF	—	100	175	300	600	—
1735 MF	—	100	175	300	600	—
1736 MF	—	100	175	300	600	—
1737 MF	—	100	175	300	600	—
1738/7 MF	—	100	175	300	600	—
1738 MF	—	100	175	300	600	—
1739 MF	—	100	175	300	600	—
1740/30 MF	—	100	200	325	625	—
1740 MF	—	100	175	300	600	—
1741 MF	—	100	175	300	600	—
1742/32 MF	—	100	175	300	600	—
1742/1 MF	—	100	175	300	600	—
1742 MF	—	100	175	300	600	—
1743 MF	—	100	175	300	600	—
1744/3 MF	—	100	200	325	625	—
1744 MF	—	100	175	300	600	—
1745 MF	—	100	175	300	600	—
1746 MF	—	100	175	300	600	—
1747 MF	—	150	275	400	650	—

KM# 95 4 REALES
13.5400 g., 0.9170 Silver 0.3992 oz. ASW **Ruler:**
Ferdinand VI **Obv:** Crowned shield flanked by M F 4
Obv. Legend: FERDND • VI • D • G • HISPAN • ET
IND • REX **Rev:** Crowned globes flanked by crowned
pillars with banner, date below **Rev. Legend:** ....QUE
VNUM **Note:** Struck at Mexico City Mint, mint mark
M, Mo.

Date	Mintage	VG	F	VF	XF	Unc
1747 MF	—	100	150	300	550	—
1748/7 MF	—	100	150	300	550	—
1748 MF	—	100	125	250	500	—
1749 MF	—	150	225	350	650	—

Date	Mintage	VG	F	VF	XF	Unc
1750/40 MF	—	100	125	250	500	—
1751/41 MF	—	100	125	250	500	—
1751 MF	—	100	125	250	500	—
1752 MF	—	100	125	250	500	—
1753 MF	—	100	125	300	550	—
1754 MF	—	250	375	500	850	—
1755 MM	—	100	125	250	500	—
1756 MM	—	100	150	300	550	—
1757 MM	—	100	150	300	550	—
1758 MM	—	100	125	250	500	—
1759 MM	—	100	125	250	500	—
1760/59 MM	—	100	175	350	600	—
1760 MM	—	100	175	350	600	—

KM# 96 4 REALES
13.5400 g., 0.9170 Silver 0.3992 oz. ASW **Ruler:**
Charles III **Obv:** Crowned shield flanked by F M 4
Obv. Legend: CAROLVS • III • D • G • HISPAN • ET
IND • REX **Rev:** Crowned globes flanked by crowned
pillars with banner, date below **Rev. Legend:**
...AQUE VNUM **Note:** Mint mark M, Mo.

Date	Mintage	VG	F	VF	XF	Unc
1760 MM	—	100	150	250	900	—
1761 MM	—	100	150	250	900	—
1761 MM Cross between H and I	—	100	150	250	900	—
1762 MM	—	75.00	125	250	500	—
1763/1 MM	—	100	150	300	600	—
1763 MM	—	100	150	300	600	—
1764 MM	—	400	600	1,000	2,000	—
1764 MF	—	350	500	1,000	2,000	—
1765 MF	—	350	500	1,000	2,000	—
1766 MF	—	250	350	550	1,250	—
1767 MF	—	100	150	300	600	—
1768 MF	—	75.00	125	250	500	—
1769 MF	—	75.00	125	250	500	—
1770 MF	—	75.00	125	250	500	—
1771 MF	—	125	200	325	700	—

KM# 97.1 4 REALES
13.5337 g., 0.9030 Silver 0.3929 oz. ASW **Ruler:**
Charles III **Obv:** Armored bust of Charles III, right
Obv. Legend: CAROLUS • III • DEI • GRATIA • **Rev:**
Crowned shield flanked by pillars with banner,
inverted FM and mint mark **Rev. Legend:** • HISPAN
• ET IND REX • ... **Note:** Mint mark M, Mo.

Date	Mintage	VG	F	VF	XF	Unc
1772 FM	—	90.00	125	250	500	—
1773 FM	—	100	175	300	650	—

KM# 97.2   4 REALES

13.5400 g., 0.9030 Silver 0.3931 oz. ASW **Ruler:**
Charles III **Obv:** Armored bust of Charles III, right
Obv. Legend: CAROLUS • III • DEI • GRATIA • **Rev:**
Crowned shield flanked by pillars with banner, normal
initials and mint mark **Rev. Legend:** • HISPAN • ET
IND REX • ... **Note:** Mint mark M, Mo.

Date	Mintage	VG	F	VF	XF	Unc
1774 FM	—	50.00	100	200	500	—
1775 FM	—	50.00	100	200	500	—
1776 FM	—	50.00	100	200	500	—
1777 FM	—	50.00	100	200	500	—
1778 FF	—	50.00	100	200	500	—
1779 FF	—	50.00	100	200	500	—
1780 FF	—	50.00	100	200	500	—
1781 FF	—	50.00	100	200	500	—
1782 FF	—	50.00	100	200	500	—
1783 FF	—	50.00	100	200	500	—
1784 FF	—	50.00	100	200	500	—
1784 FM	—	100	200	350	600	—

KM# 97.2a   4 REALES

13.5337 g., 0.8960 Silver 0.3898 oz. ASW **Ruler:**
Charles III **Obv:** Armored bust of Charles III, right
Obv. Legend: CAROLUS • III • DEI • GRATIA • **Rev:**
Crowned shield flanked by pillars with banner, normal
initials and mint mark **Rev. Legend:** • HISPAN • ET
IND REX • ... **Note:** Mint mark M, Mo.

Date	Mintage	VG	F	VF	XF	Unc
1785 FM	—	100	200	350	600	—
1786 FM	—	50.00	100	200	500	—
1787 FM	—	50.00	100	200	500	—
1788 FM	—	50.00	100	200	500	—
1789 FM	—	50.00	100	200	500	—

KM# 98   4 REALES

13.5400 g., 0.9030 Silver 0.3931 oz. ASW **Ruler:**
Charles III **Obv:** Armored bust of Charles III, right
Obv. Legend: CAROLUS • IV • DEI • GRATIA • **Rev:**
Crowned shield flanked by pillars with banner **Rev.
Legend:** • HISPAN • ET IND REX • ... **Note:** Mintint
mark M, Mo, using old bust punch.

Date	Mintage	VG	F	VF	XF	Unc
1789 FM	—	65.00	125	250	550	—
1790 FM	—	50.00	100	200	500	—

KM# 99   4 REALES

13.5400 g., 0.9030 Silver 0.3931 oz. ASW **Ruler:**
Charles IV **Obv:** Armored bust of Charles III, right
Obv. Legend: CAROLUS • IIII • DEI • GRATIA • **Rev:**
Crowned shield flanked by pillars with banner **Rev.
Legend:** • HISPAN • ET IND • REX • ... **Note:** Mint
mark M, Mo, using old bust punch.

Date	Mintage	VG	F	VF	XF	Unc
1790 FM	—	65.00	125	250	550	—

KM# 100   4 REALES

13.5337 g., 0.8960 Silver 0.3898 oz. ASW **Ruler:**
Charles IV **Obv:** Armored bust of Charles IIII, right
Obv. Legend: CAROLUS • IIII • DEI • GRATIA • **Rev:**
Crowned shield flanked by pillars with banner **Rev.
Legend:** • HISPAN • ET IND • REX • ... **Note:** Mint
mark Mo.

Date	Mintage	VG	F	VF	XF	Unc
1792 FM	—	35.00	65.00	150	400	—
1793 FM	—	75.00	125	200	500	—
1794/3 FM	—	35.00	65.00	150	400	—
1794 FM	—	35.00	65.00	150	400	—
1795 FM	—	35.00	65.00	150	400	—
1796 FM	—	150	250	400	800	—
1797 FM	—	60.00	120	200	500	—
1798/7 FM	—	35.00	65.00	150	400	—
1798 FM	—	35.00	65.00	150	400	—
1799 FM	—	35.00	65.00	150	400	—
1800 FM	—	35.00	65.00	150	400	—
1801 FM	—	35.00	65.00	150	400	—
1801 FT	—	60.00	120	200	500	—
1802 FT	—	200	300	500	1,000	—
1803 FT	—	75.00	135	225	550	—
1803 FM	—	200	300	500	1,000	—
1804 TH	—	40.00	75.00	175	450	—
1805 TH	—	35.00	65.00	150	400	—
1806 TH	—	35.00	65.00	150	400	—
1807 TH	—	35.00	65.00	150	400	—
1808/7 TH	—	40.00	75.00	175	450	—
1808 TH	—	40.00	75.00	175	450	—

KM# 101 4 REALES
13.5400 g., 0.9030 Silver 0.3931 oz. ASW **Ruler:**
Ferdinand VII **Obv:** Armored laureate bust right **Obv.**
Legend: FERDIN.VII... **Rev:** Crowned shield flanked
by pillars **Rev. Legend:** IND.REX... **Note:** Mint mark
Mo.

Date	Mintage	VG	F	VF	XF	Unc
1809 HJ	—	75.00	135	250	750	—
1810 HJ	—	75.00	135	250	750	—
1811 HJ	—	75.00	135	250	750	—
1812 HJ	—	400	650	900	1,850	—

KM# 102 4 REALES
13.5400 g., 0.9030 Silver 0.3931 oz. ASW **Ruler:**
Ferdinand VII **Obv:** Draped laureate bust right **Obv.**
Legend: FERDIN.VII... **Rev:** Crowned shield flanked
by pillars **Rev. Legend:** IND.REX... **Note:** Mint mark
Mo.

Date	Mintage	VG	F	VF	XF	Unc
1816 JJ	—	150	200	325	700	—
1817 JJ	—	250	400	500	1,000	—
1818/7 JJ	—	250	400	500	1,000	—
1819 JJ	—	175	250	325	700	—
1820 JJ	—	175	250	325	700	—
1821 JJ	—	75.00	135	250	650	—

KM# 103 8 REALES
27.0674 g., 0.9170 Silver 0.7980 oz. ASW **Ruler:**

Philip V **Obv:** Crowned shield flanked by M F 8 **Obv.**
Legend: PHILIP ? V ? D ? G ? HISPAN ? ET IND
? REX **Rev:** Crowned globes flanked by crowned
pillars with banner, date below **Rev. Legend:**
...VNUM **Note:** Mint mark M, Mo, MX.

Date	Mintage	VG	F	VF	XF	Unc
1732 F	—	2,750	4,750	8,000	—	—
1733/2 F (MX)	—	3,000	5,250	9,000	—	—
1733 F	—	2,000	3,000	5,000	9,000	—
1733 MF Large crown; Rare	—	—	—	—	—	—
1733 F (MX) Rare	—	—	—	—	—	—

Note: Bonhams Patterson sale 7-96 VF 1733 F (MX) realized $11,710

Date	Mintage	VG	F	VF	XF	Unc
1733 MF (MX) Rare	—	—	—	—	—	—
1733 MF Small crown	—	700	1,500	2,500	4,250	—
1734/3 MF	—	100	150	275	575	—
1734 MF	—	100	150	250	450	—
1735 MF	—	100	150	250	450	—
1736/5 MF	—	100	150	275	575	—
1736 MF Small planchet	—	100	150	250	450	—
1736 MF	—	100	150	250	450	—
1737 MF	—	65.00	100	200	400	—
1738/6 MF	—	65.00	100	200	400	—
1738/7 MF	—	65.00	100	200	400	—
1738 MF	—	65.00	100	200	400	—
1739 MF	—	65.00	100	200	400	—
1739/6 MF 9 over inverted 6	—	65.00	100	200	400	—
1740/30 MF	—	100	150	275	500	—
1740/39 MF	—	100	150	275	500	—
1740 MF	—	65.00	100	200	400	—
1741/31 MF	—	65.00	100	200	400	—
1741 MF	—	65.00	100	200	400	—
1742/32 MF	—	75.00	125	220	500	—
1742/1 MF	—	65.00	100	200	400	—
1742 MF	—	65.00	100	200	400	—
1743/2 MF	—	65.00	100	200	400	—
1743 MF	—	65.00	100	200	400	—
1744/34 MF	—	65.00	100	200	400	—
1744/3 MF	—	65.00	100	200	400	—
1744 MF	—	65.00	100	200	400	—
1745/4 MF	—	65.00	100	200	425	—
1745 MF	—	65.00	100	200	400	—
1746/5 MF	—	100	150	275	575	—
1746 MF	—	65.00	100	200	400	—
1747 MF	—	65.00	100	200	400	—

KM# 104.1 8 REALES
27.0674 g., 0.9170 Silver 0.7980 oz. ASW **Ruler:**
Ferdinand VI **Obv:** Crowned shield flaned by M F 8
Obv. Legend: FERDND • VI • D • G • HISPAN • ET

IND • REX **Rev:** Crowned globes flanked by crowned pillars with banner, date below **Rev. Legend:** ...VNUM M **Note:** Mint mark M, Mo.

Date	Mintage	VG	F	VF	XF	Unc
1747 MF	—	55.00	100	175	300	—
1748/7 MF	—	60.00	120	250	450	—
1748 MF	—	50.00	75.00	125	250	—
1749/8 MF	—	50.00	75.00	125	250	—
1749 MF	—	50.00	75.00	125	250	—
1750 MF	—	50.00	75.00	125	250	—
1751/0 MF	—	55.00	100	165	275	—
1751 MF	—	50.00	75.00	125	250	—
1752/1 MF	—	55.00	100	165	275	—
1752 MF	—	50.00	75.00	125	250	—
1753/2 MF	—	50.00	75.00	125	250	—
1753 MF	—	55.00	100	165	275	—
1754/3 MF	—	55.00	100	185	325	—
1754 MF	—	50.00	75.00	125	250	—
1754 MM/MF	—	300	700	1,500	3,500	—
1754 MM	—	300	700	1,500	3,500	—

KM# 104.2   8 REALES
27.0674 g., 0.9170 Silver 0.7980 oz. ASW   **Ruler:** Ferdinand VI **Obv:** Crowned shield flanked by M M 8 **Obv. Legend:** FERDND • VI • D • G • HISPAN • ET IND • REX **Rev:** Imperial crown on left pillar **Rev. Legend:** ...VNUM M **Note:** Mint mark M, Mo.

Date	Mintage	VG	F	VF	XF	Unc
1754 MM/MF	—	75.00	125	250	500	—
1754 MM	—	60.00	110	200	375	—
1754 MF	—	150	285	550	950	—
1755/4 MM	—	55.00	100	185	325	—
1755 MM	—	50.00	75.00	125	250	—
1756/5 MM	—	55.00	100	165	275	—
1756 MM	—	50.00	75.00	125	250	—
1757/6 MM	—	50.00	75.00	125	250	—
1757 MM	—	55.00	100	185	325	—
1758 MM	—	50.00	75.00	125	250	—
1759 MM	—	50.00	75.00	125	250	—
1760/59 MM	—	55.00	100	165	275	—
1760 MM	—	50.00	75.00	125	250	—

KM# 105   8 REALES
27.0674 g., 0.9170 Silver 0.7980 oz. ASW   **Ruler:** Charles III **Obv:** Crowned shield flanked by M M 8 **Obv. Legend:** CAROLUS • III • D • G • HISPAN • ET IND • REX **Rev:** Crowned globes flanked by crowned pillars with banner, date below **Rev. Legend:** ...E VNUM M **Note:** Mint mark M, Mo.

Date	Mintage	VG	F	VF	XF	Unc
1760/59 MM	—	450	700	—	—	—
Note: CAROLUS. III/Ferdin. Vi						
1760 MM	—	60.00	100	150	325	—
Note: CAROLUS. III/FERDIN. VI. recut die						
1760 MM	—	60.00	100	150	300	—
1761/50 MM	—	65.00	110	165	325	—
Note: Tip of cross between I and S in legend						
1761/51 MM	—	65.00	110	165	325	—
Note: Tip of cross between I and S in legend						
1761/0 MM	—	65.00	110	165	325	—
Note: Tip of cross between H and I in legend						
1761 MM	—	60.00	100	150	275	—
Note: Cross under I in legend						
1761 MM	—	60.00	100	150	275	—
Note: Tip of cross between H and I in legend						
1761 MM	—	65.00	110	165	325	—
Note: Tip of cross between I and S in legend						
1762/1 MM	—	70.00	120	175	450	—
Note: Tip of cross between H and I in legend						
1762/1 MM	—	70.00	120	175	450	—
1762 MM	—	60.00	100	150	275	—
Note: Tip of cross between H and I in legend						
1762 MM	—	50.00	75.00	125	250	—
Note: Tip of cross between I and S in legend						
1762 MF	—	500	750	1,250	2,300	—
1763/2 MM	—	300	450	750	1,350	—
1763 MM	—	450	650	1,150	2,250	—
1763/1 MF	—	50.00	75.00	125	250	—
1763/2 MF	—	50.00	75.00	125	250	—
1763 MF	—	50.00	75.00	125	250	—
1764 MF	—	50.00	75.00	125	250	—
Note: CAR/CRA						
1764 MF	—	50.00	75.00	125	250	—
1765 MF	—	50.00	75.00	125	250	—
1766/5 MF	—	75.00	150	225	575	—
1766 MF	—	50.00	75.00	125	250	—
1767/6 MF	—	50.00	75.00	125	250	—
1767 MF	—	50.00	75.00	125	250	—
1768/7 MF	—	85.00	165	250	600	—
1768 MF	—	50.00	75.00	125	250	—
1769 MF	—	50.00	75.00	125	250	—
1770/60 MF	—	100	185	300	650	—
1770 MF	—	50.00	75.00	125	250	—
1770/60 FM	—	100	185	300	650	—
1770/69 FM	—	100	185	300	650	—
1770 FM/F	—	50.00	75.00	125	250	—
1770 FM	—	50.00	75.00	125	250	—
1771/0 FM	—	50.00	75.00	125	250	—
1771 FM	—	50.00	75.00	125	250	—

Date	Mintage	VG	F	VF	XF	Unc
Note: Superior Casterline sale 5-89 VF realized $17,600						
1778/7 FF	—	25.00	45.00	75.00	150	—
1778 FF	—	25.00	45.00	75.00	150	—
1779 FF	—	25.00	45.00	75.00	150	—
1780 FF	—	25.00	45.00	75.00	150	—
1781 FF	—	25.00	45.00	75.00	150	—
1782 FF	—	25.00	45.00	75.00	150	—
1783 FF	—	25.00	45.00	75.00	150	—
1783 FM	—	4,000	6,000	9,000	—	—
1784 FF	—	150	300	500	1,250	—
1784 FM	—	25.00	45.00	75.00	150	—

KM# 106.1   8 REALES
27.0674 g., 0.9030 Silver 0.7858 oz. ASW **Ruler:**
Charles III **Obv:** Armored bust of Charles III, right
Obv. Legend: CAROLUS • III • DEI • GRATIA • **Rev:**
Crowned shield flanked by pillars with banner,
inverted initials and mint mark **Rev. Legend:** •
HISPAN • ET IND • REX • ... **Note:** Two varieties
exist, one with inverted initials "F.M." (left), and one
with normal presentation (right). Mint mark M, Mo.

Date	Mintage	VG	F	VF	XF	Unc
1772 FM	—	25.00	50.00	120	250	—
1772 FM Inverted	—	150	350	750	1,250	—
1773 FM	—	25.00	50.00	100	175	—

KM# 106.2a   8 REALES
27.0674 g., 0.8960 Silver 0.7797 oz. ASW **Ruler:**
Charles III **Obv:** Armored bust of Charles III, right
Obv. Legend: CAROLUS • III • DEI • GRATIA • **Rev:**
Crowned shield flanked by pillars with banner, normal
initials and mint mark **Rev. Legend:** • HISPAN • ET
IND • REX • ... **Note:** Mint mark M, Mo.

Date	Mintage	VG	F	VF	XF	Unc
1785 FM	—	25.00	45.00	75.00	150	—
1786/5 FM	—	50.00	100	200	400	—
1786 FM	—	25.00	45.00	75.00	150	—
1787/6 FM	—	100	250	450	1,200	—
1787 FM	—	25.00	45.00	75.00	150	—
1788 FM	—	25.00	45.00	75.00	150	—
1789 FM	—	50.00	100	150	225	—

KM# 106.2   8 REALES
27.0674 g., 0.9030 Silver 0.7858 oz. ASW **Ruler:**
Charles III **Obv:** Armored bust of Charles III, right
Obv. Legend: CAROLUS • III • DEI • GRATIA • **Rev:**
Crowned shield flanked by pillars with banner, normal
initials and mint mark **Rev. Legend:** • HISPAN • ET
IND • REX • ... **Note:** Mint mark M, Mo.

Date	Mintage	VG	F	VF	XF	Unc
1773 FM	—	25.00	50.00	80.00	160	—
1774 FM	—	25.00	45.00	75.00	150	—
1775 FM	—	25.00	45.00	75.00	150	—
1776 FM	—	25.00	45.00	75.00	150	—
1777/6 FM	—	35.00	65.00	180	300	—
1777 FM	—	25.00	45.00	75.00	150	—
1777 FF	—	35.00	50.00	100	250	—
1778 FM	—	—	—	—	—	—

KM# 107   8 REALES
27.0674 g., 0.9030 Silver 0.7858 oz. ASW **Ruler:**
Charles IV **Obv:** Armored bust of Charles III, right
Obv. Legend: CAROLUS • IV • DEI • GRATIA • **Rev:**
Crowned shield flanked by pillars with banner **Rev.**

Legend: • HISPAN • ET IND • REX • ... **Note:** Mint mark M, Mo, using old bust punch.

Date	Mintage	VG	F	VF	XF	Unc
1789 FM	—	40.00	65.00	120	250	—
1790 FM	—	30.00	50.00	100	200	—

KM# 108   8 REALES
27.0674 g., 0.9030 Silver 0.7858 oz. ASW **Ruler:**
Charles IV **Obv:** Armored bust of Charles III, right
Obv. Legend: CAROLUS • IIII • DEI • GRATIA • **Rev:**
Crowned shield flanked by pillars with banner **Rev.
Legend:** • HISPAN • ET IND • REX • ... **Note:** Mint
mark M, Mo, using old portait punch.

Date	Mintage	VG	F	VF	XF	Unc
1790 FM	—	30.00	50.00	100	200	—

KM# 109   8 REALES
27.0674 g., 0.8960 Silver 0.7797 oz. ASW **Ruler:**
Charles IV **Obv:** Armored bust of Charles IIII, right
Obv. Inscription: CAROLUS • IIII • DEI • GRATIA •
Rev: Crowned shield flanked by pillars with banner
Rev. Legend: • HISPAN • ET IND • REX • ... **Note:**
Mint mark Mo.

Date	Mintage	VG	F	VF	XF	Unc
1791 FM	—	20.00	35.00	50.00	100	—
1792 FM	—	20.00	35.00	50.00	100	—
1793 FM	—	20.00	35.00	50.00	100	—
1794 FM	—	20.00	35.00	50.00	100	—
1795/4 FM	—	20.00	35.00	50.00	100	—
1795 FM	—	20.00	35.00	50.00	100	—
1796 FM	—	20.00	35.00	50.00	100	—

Date	Mintage	VG	F	VF	XF	Unc
1797 FM	—	20.00	35.00	50.00	100	—
1798 FM	—	20.00	35.00	50.00	100	—
1799 FM	—	20.00	35.00	50.00	100	—
1800/700 FM	—	20.00	35.00	50.00	100	—
1800 FM	—	20.00	35.00	50.00	100	—
1801/0 FT/FM	—	20.00	35.00	50.00	100	—
1801/791 FM	—	35.00	60.00	100	250	—
1801/0 FM	—	35.00	60.00	100	250	—
1801 FM	—	20.00	40.00	100	250	—
1801 FT/M	—	35.00	60.00	100	250	—
1801 FT	—	20.00	35.00	50.00	100	—
1802/1 FT	—	35.00	60.00	100	250	—
1802 FT	—	20.00	35.00	50.00	100	—
1802 FT/M	—	20.00	35.00	50.00	100	—
1803 FT	—	20.00	35.00	50.00	110	—
1803 FT/M	—	20.00	35.00	50.00	100	—
1803 TH	—	75.00	150	250	500	—
1804/3 TH	—	35.00	60.00	100	250	—
1804 TH	—	20.00	35.00	50.00	100	—
Note: CARLUS (error)						
1805/4 TH	—	40.00	80.00	125	275	—
1805 TH	—	20.00	35.00	50.00	100	—
Note: Narrow date						
1805 TH	—	20.00	35.00	50.00	100	—
Note: Wide date						
1806 TH	—	20.00	35.00	50.00	100	—
1807/6 TH	—	150	250	350	700	—
1807 TH	—	20.00	35.00	50.00	100	—
1808/7 TH	—	20.00	35.00	50.00	100	—
1808 TH	—	20.00	35.00	50.00	100	—

KM# 110   8 REALES
27.0674 g., 0.8960 Silver 0.7797 oz. ASW **Ruler:**
Ferdinand VII **Obv:** Armored laureate bust right **Obv.
Legend:** FERDIN . VII... **Rev:** Crowned shield
flanked by pillars **Rev. Legend:** IND.REX... **Note:**
Mint mark Mo.

Date	Mintage	VG	F	VF	XF	Unc
1808 TH	—	25.00	40.00	75.00	145	—
1809/8 TH	—	25.00	40.00	75.00	145	—
1809 TH	—	20.00	35.00	55.00	120	—
1809 HJ	—	25.00	40.00	75.00	145	—
1809 HJ/TH	—	20.00	35.00	55.00	120	—
1810/09 HJ	—	25.00	40.00	75.00	145	—
1810 TH	—	75.00	150	300	600	—
1810 HJ/TH	—	25.00	40.00	75.00	145	—
1810 HJ	—	25.00	40.00	75.00	145	—
1811/0 HJ	—	20.00	35.00	55.00	120	—
1811 HJ	—	20.00	35.00	55.00	120	—
1811 HJ/TH	—	20.00	35.00	50.00	100	—

KM# 111 8 REALES

27.0700 g., 0.9030 Silver 0.7859 oz. ASW **Ruler:**
Ferdinand VII **Obv:** Draped laureate bust right **Obv.
Legend:** FERDIN.VII... **Rev:** Crowned shield flanked
by pillars **Rev. Legend:** IND.REX... **Note:** Mint mark
Mo.

Date	Mintage	VG	F	VF	XF	Unc
1811 HJ	—	20.00	40.00	60.00	125	—
1812 HJ	—	50.00	75.00	125	250	—
1812 JJ/HJ	—	20.00	35.00	50.00	100	—
1812 JJ	—	20.00	35.00	50.00	100	—
1813 HJ	—	50.00	75.00	125	250	—
1813 JJ	—	20.00	35.00	50.00	100	—
1814/3 HJ	—	1,200	2,500	5,000	—	—
1814/3 JJ	—	20.00	35.00	50.00	100	—
1814 JJ	—	20.00	35.00	50.00	100	—
1815/4 JJ	—	20.00	35.00	50.00	100	—
1815 JJ	—	20.00	35.00	50.00	100	—
1816/5 JJ	—	20.00	35.00	50.00	90.00	—
1816 JJ	—	20.00	35.00	50.00	90.00	—
1817 JJ	—	20.00	35.00	50.00	90.00	—
1818 JJ	—	20.00	35.00	50.00	90.00	—
1819 JJ	—	20.00	35.00	50.00	90.00	—
1820 JJ	—	20.00	35.00	50.00	90.00	—
1821 JJ	—	20.00	35.00	50.00	90.00	—

KM# 112 1/2 ESCUDO

1.6917 g., 0.8750 Gold 0.0476 oz. AGW **Ruler:**
Ferdinand VII **Obv:** Laureate head right **Obv.
Legend:** FERD. VII. D. G. HISP. ET IND **Rev:**
Crowned oval shield **Note:** Mint mark Mo.

Date	Mintage	VG	F	VF	XF	Unc
1814 JJ	—	100	150	225	375	525
1815/4 JJ	—	150	200	250	400	875
1815 JJ	—	150	200	250	400	—
1816 JJ	—	100	150	225	375	—
1817 JJ	—	150	200	250	400	—
1818 JJ	—	150	200	250	400	—
1819 JJ	—	150	200	250	400	—
1820 JJ	—	200	300	400	550	—

KM# 113 ESCUDO

3.3834 g., 0.9170 Gold 0.0997 oz. AGW **Ruler:**
Philip V **Obv:** Armored bust right **Obv. Legend:**
PHILIP • V • D • G • HISPAN • ET IND • REX **Rev:**
Crowned shield flanked by M F I **Note:** Mint mark M,
Mo.

Date	Mintage	VG	F	VF	XF	Unc
1732 F	—	1,000	2,000	3,000	4,000	—
1733/2 F	—	1,000	2,000	3,000	4,000	—
1734/3 MF	—	150	250	400	850	—
1735/4 MF	—	150	250	400	850	—
1735 MF	—	150	250	400	850	—
1736/5 MF	—	150	250	400	850	—
1736 MF	—	150	250	400	850	—
1737 MF	—	200	300	600	1,200	—
1738/7 MF	—	200	300	600	1,200	—
1738 MF	—	200	300	600	1,200	—
1739 MF	—	200	300	600	1,200	—
1740/30 MF	—	200	300	600	1,200	—
1741 MF	—	200	300	600	1,200	—
1742 MF	—	200	300	600	1,200	—
1743/2 MF	—	150	275	450	800	—
1743 MF	—	150	250	400	700	—
1744/3 MF	—	150	250	400	700	—
1744 MF	—	150	250	400	700	—
1745 MF	—	150	250	400	700	—
1746/5 MF	—	150	250	400	700	—
1747 MF Rare	—	—	—	—	—	—

KM# 114 ESCUDO

3.3834 g., 0.9170 Gold 0.0997 oz. AGW **Ruler:**
Ferdinand VI **Obv:** Armored bust right **Obv.
Legend:** FERD • VI • D • G • HISPAN • ET IND •
REX **Rev:** Crowned shield flanked by M F I **Note:**
Mint mark M, Mo.

Date	Mintage	VG	F	VF	XF	Unc
1747 MF	—	1,650	3,000	5,000	7,500	—

KM# 115.1 ESCUDO

3.3834 g., 0.9170 Gold 0.0997 oz. AGW **Ruler:**
Ferdinand VI **Obv:** Short armored bust right **Obv.
Legend:** FERD • VI • D • G • HISPAN • ET IND •
REX **Rev:** Crowned shield **Note:** Mint mark M, Mo.

Date	Mintage	VG	F	VF	XF	Unc
1748 MF	—	250	350	550	950	—
1749 MF	—	300	450	700	1,150	—
1750 MF	—	150	250	400	800	—
1751 MF	—	150	250	400	800	—

KM# 115.2   ESCUDO
3.3834 g., 0.9170 Gold 0.0997 oz. AGW   **Ruler:**
Ferdinand VI **Obv:** Short armored bust right **Obv.**
Legend: FERD • VI • D • G • HISPAN • ET IND •
REX **Rev:** Without 1 S flanking crowned shield **Note:**
Mint mark M, Mo.

Date	Mintage	VG	F	VF	XF	Unc
1752 MF	—	125	225	375	750	—
1753/2 MF	—	150	250	400	800	—
1753 MF	—	150	250	400	800	—
1754 MF	—	150	250	400	800	—
1755 MM	—	150	250	400	800	—
1756 MM	—	150	250	400	800	—

KM# A116   ESCUDO
3.3834 g., 0.9170 Gold 0.0997 oz. AGW   **Ruler:**
Ferdinand VI **Obv:** Armored bust right **Obv. Legend:**
FERDIND • VI • D • G • HISPAN • ETIND • REX •
Rev: Crowned shield **Rev. Legend:** M • NOMINA
MAGNA SEQUOR • M **Note:** Mint mark M, Mo.

Date	Mintage	VG	F	VF	XF	Unc
1757 MM	—	150	250	400	800	—
1759 MM	—	150	250	400	800	—

KM# 116   ESCUDO
3.3834 g., 0.9170 Gold 0.0997 oz. AGW   **Ruler:**
Charles III **Obv:** Armored bust right **Obv. Legend:**
CAROLVS • III • D • G • HISPAN • ET IND • REX
Rev: Crowned shield **Rev. Legend:** M • NOMINA
MAGNA SEQUOR • M • **Note:** Mint mark M, Mo.

Date	Mintage	VG	F	VF	XF	Unc
1760 MM	—	400	800	1,500	2,500	—
1761/0 MM	—	400	800	1,500	2,500	—
1761 MM	—	400	800	1,500	2,500	—

KM# 117   ESCUDO
3.3834 g., 0.9170 Gold 0.0997 oz. AGW   **Ruler:**
Charles III **Obv:** Large armored bust right **Obv.**
Legend: CAR • III • D • G • HISP • ET IND • R **Rev:**
Crowned shield **Rev. Legend:** IN • UTROQ • FELIX
• **Note:** Mint mark M, Mo.

Date	Mintage	VG	F	VF	XF	Unc
1762 MM	—	250	375	600	1,000	—
1763 MM	—	275	425	700	1,100	—
1764 MM	—	250	375	600	1,000	—
1765 MM	—	250	375	600	1,000	—
1766 MF	—	250	375	600	1,000	—
1767 MF	—	250	375	600	1,000	—

Date	Mintage	VG	F	VF	XF	Unc
1768 MF	—	250	375	600	1,000	—
1769 MF	—	250	375	600	1,000	—
1770 MF	—	250	375	600	1,000	—
1771 MF	—	250	375	600	1,000	—

KM# 118.1   ESCUDO
3.3834 g., 0.9010 Gold 0.0980 oz. AGW   **Ruler:**
Charles III **Obv:** Large armored bust right **Obv.**
Legend: CAROL • III • D • G • HISPAN • ET IND •
R **Rev:** Crowned shield flanked by 1 S within order
chain **Rev. Legend:** FELIX • A • D • ... **Note:** Mint
mark M, Mo.

Date	Mintage	VG	F	VF	XF	Unc
1772 MF	—	125	150	275	475	—
1772 FM	—	125	150	275	475	—
1773 FM	—	125	150	275	475	—

KM# 118.2   ESCUDO
3.3834 g., 0.9010 Gold 0.0980 oz. AGW   **Ruler:**
Charles III **Obv:** Large armored bust right **Obv.**
Legend: CAROL • III • D • G • HISPAN • ET IND •
R **Rev:** crowned shield in order chain, initials and
mint mark inverted **Rev. Legend:** FELIX • A • D • ...
Note: Mint mark M, Mo.

Date	Mintage	VG	F	VF	XF	Unc
1773 FM	—	125	150	275	475	—
1774 FM	—	125	150	275	475	—
1775 FM	—	125	150	275	475	—
1776 FM	—	125	150	275	475	—
1777 FM	—	125	150	275	475	—
1778 FF	—	125	150	275	475	—
1779 FF	—	125	150	275	475	—
1780 FF	—	125	150	275	475	—
1781 FF	—	125	150	275	475	—
1782 FF	—	125	150	275	475	—
1783/2 FF	—	125	150	275	475	—
1783 FF	—	125	150	275	475	—
1784/3 FF	—	125	150	275	475	—
1784/3 FM/F	—	125	150	275	475	—

KM# 118.2a   ESCUDO
3.3800 g., 0.8750 Gold 0.0951 oz. AGW   **Ruler:**
Charles III **Obv:** Large armored bust right **Obv.**
Legend: CAROL • III • D • G • HISPAN • ET IND •
R • **Rev:** Crowned shield in order chain, initials and
mint mark inverted **Rev. Legend:** FELIX • A • D • ...
Note: Mint mark M, Mo.

Date	Mintage	VG	F	VF	XF	Unc
1785 FM	—	125	150	275	475	—
1786 FM	—	125	150	275	475	—
1787 FM	—	125	150	275	475	—
1788 FM	—	125	150	275	475	—

KM# 118.1a ESCUDO
3.3834 g., 0.8750 Gold 0.0952 oz. AGW **Ruler:**
Charles III **Obv:** Large armored bust right **Obv.**
Legend: CAROL • III • D • G • HISPAN • ET IND •
R **Rev:** Crowned shield in order chain, initial letters
and mint mark upright **Rev. Legend:** FELIX • A • D
• ... **Note:** Mint mark M, Mo.

Date	Mintage	VG	F	VF	XF	Unc
1788 FM	—	125	150	275	475	—

KM# 119 ESCUDO
3.3834 g., 0.8750 Gold 0.0952 oz. AGW **Ruler:**
Charles IV **Obv:** Armored bust of Charles III, right
Obv. Legend: CAROL • IV • D • G • ... **Rev:** Crowned
shield in order chain, initial letters and mint mark
upright **Rev. Legend:** FELIX • A • D • ... **Note:** Mint
mark M, Mo, using old portrait punch.

Date	Mintage	VG	F	VF	XF	Unc
1789 FM	—	300	550	1,000	2,000	—
1790 FM	—	300	550	1,000	2,000	—

KM# 120 ESCUDO
3.3834 g., 0.8750 Gold 0.0952 oz. AGW **Ruler:**
Charles IV **Obv:** Armored bust right **Obv. Legend:**
CAROL • IIII • D • G • ... **Rev:** Crowned shield in order
chain, initial letters and mint mark upright **Rev.**
Legend: FELIX • A • D • ... **Note:** Mint mark Mo.

Date	Mintage	VG	F	VF	XF	Unc
1792 MF	—	125	165	235	345	—
1793 FM	—	125	165	235	345	—
1794 FM	—	125	165	235	345	—
1795 FM	—	125	165	235	345	—
1796 FM	—	125	165	235	345	—
1797 FM	—	125	165	235	345	—
1798 FM	—	125	165	235	345	—
1799 FM	—	125	165	235	345	—
1800 FM	—	125	165	235	345	—
1801 FM	—	125	165	235	345	—
1801 FT	—	125	165	235	345	650
1802 FT	—	125	165	235	345	—
1803 FT	—	125	165	235	345	—
1804/3 TH	—	125	165	235	345	750
1804 TH	—	125	165	235	345	—
1805 TH	—	125	165	235	345	—
1806/5 TH	—	125	165	235	345	—
1806 TH	—	125	165	235	345	—
1807 TH	—	125	165	235	345	—
1808 TH	—	125	165	235	345	—

KM# 121 ESCUDO
3.3834 g., 0.8750 Gold 0.0952 oz. AGW **Ruler:**
Ferdinand VII **Obv:** Armored bust right **Obv.**
Legend: FERDIN.VII... **Rev:** Crowned shield divides

designed wreath **Rev. Legend:** FELIX. A. D, initial
letters and mint mark upright **Note:** Mint mark Mo.

Date	Mintage	VG	F	VF	XF	Unc
1809 HJ/TH	—	125	165	235	400	—
1809 HJ	—	125	165	235	400	1,150
1811/0 HJ	—	125	165	235	400	—
1812 HJ	—	150	250	300	500	—

KM# 122 ESCUDO
3.3834 g., 0.8750 Gold 0.0952 oz. AGW **Ruler:**
Ferdinand VII **Obv:** Laureate head right **Obv. Legend:**
FERDIN. VII. D. G... **Rev:** Crowned shield divides
designed wreath **Rev. Legend:** FELIX. A. D, initial
letters and mint mark upright **Note:** Mint mark Mo.

Date	Mintage	VG	F	VF	XF	Unc
1814 HJ	—	150	250	300	500	—
1815 HJ	—	150	250	300	500	—
1815 JJ	—	150	250	300	500	—
1816 JJ	—	175	275	325	550	—
1817 JJ	—	150	250	300	500	—
1818 JJ	—	150	250	300	500	—
1819 JJ	—	150	250	300	500	—
1820 JJ	—	150	250	300	500	—

KM# 124 2 ESCUDOS
6.7660 g., 0.9170 Gold 0.1995 oz. AGW **Ruler:**
Philip V **Obv:** Armored bust right **Obv. Legend:**
PHILIP • V • D • G • HISPAN • ET IND • REX **Rev:**
Crowned shield flanked by M F 2 **Rev. Legend:**
INITIUM SAPIENTIAE TIMOR DOMINI **Note:** Mint
mark M, Mo.

Date	Mintage	VG	F	VF	XF	Unc
1732 F	—	1,000	1,500	2,000	3,000	—
1733 F	—	750	1,000	1,500	2,500	—
1734/3 MF	—	400	500	900	1,400	—
1735 MF	—	400	500	900	1,400	—
1736/5 MF	—	400	500	900	1,400	—
1736 MF	—	400	500	900	1,400	—
1737 MF	—	400	500	900	1,400	—
1738/7 MF	—	400	500	900	1,400	—
1739 MF	—	400	500	900	1,400	—
1740/30 MF	—	400	500	900	1,400	—
1741 MF	—	400	500	900	1,400	—
1742 MF	—	400	500	900	1,400	—
1743 MF	—	400	500	900	1,400	—
1744/2 MF	—	400	500	900	1,400	—
1744 MF	—	400	500	900	1,400	—
1745 MF	—	400	500	900	1,400	—
1746/5 MF	—	400	500	900	1,400	—
1747 MF	—	400	500	900	1,400	—

SPANISH COLONIAL - MILLED

KM# 125   2 ESCUDOS
6.7660 g., 0.9170 Gold 0.1995 oz. AGW **Ruler:**
Ferdinand VI **Obv:** Large armored bust right **Obv.**
Legend: FERD • VI • D • G • ... **Rev:** Crowned shield
flanked by M F 2 **Rev. Legend:** INITIUM... **Note:** Mint
mark M, Mo.

Date	Mintage	VG	F	VF	XF	Unc
1747 MF	—	3,000	5,500	9,000	15,000	—

KM# 126.1   2 ESCUDOS
6.7660 g., 0.9170 Gold 0.1995 oz. AGW **Ruler:**
Ferdinand VI **Obv:** Head right **Obv. Legend:** FERD
• VI • D • G • ... **Rev:** Crowned shield **Rev. Legend:**
NOMINA MAGNA SEQUOR **Note:** Mint mark M, Mo.

Date	Mintage	VG	F	VF	XF	Unc
1748 MF	—	450	750	1,500	3,000	—
1749/8 MF	—	450	750	1,500	3,000	—
1750 MF	—	400	700	1,400	2,850	—
1751 MF	—	400	700	1,400	2,850	—

KM# 126.2   2 ESCUDOS
6.7660 g., 0.9170 Gold 0.1995 oz. AGW **Ruler:**
Ferdinand VI **Obv:** Head right **Obv. Legend:** FERD
• VI • D • G • ... **Rev:** Without 2 S by crowned shield
Rev. Legend: NOMINA MAGNA SEQUOR **Note:**
Mint mark M, Mo.

Date	Mintage	VG	F	VF	XF	Unc
1752 MF	—	400	700	1,400	2,850	—
1753 MF	—	400	700	1,400	2,850	—
1754 MF	—	600	850	1,750	3,500	—
1755 MM	—	400	700	1,400	2,850	—
1756 MM	—	600	850	1,750	3,500	—

KM# 127   2 ESCUDOS
6.7660 g., 0.9170 Gold 0.1995 oz. AGW **Ruler:**
Ferdinand VI **Obv:** Armored bust right **Obv. Legend:**
FERDIND • VI • D • G • ... **Rev:** Without 2 S by crowned

shield **Rev. Legend:** NOMINA MAGNA SEQUOR
Note: Mint mark M, Mo.

Date	Mintage	VG	F	VF	XF	Unc
1757 MM	—	450	750	1,500	3,000	—
1759 MM	—	450	750	1,500	3,000	—

KM# 128   2 ESCUDOS
6.7660 g., 0.9170 Gold 0.1995 oz. AGW **Ruler:**
Charles III **Obv:** Armored bust right **Obv. Legend:**
CAROLVS • III • D • G • ... **Rev:** Without 2 S by
crowned shield **Rev. Legend:** NOMINA MAGNA
SEQUOR **Note:** Mint mark M, Mo.

Date	Mintage	VG	F	VF	XF	Unc
1760 MM	—	550	1,000	2,000	4,000	—
1761 MM	—	550	1,000	2,000	4,000	—

KM# 129   2 ESCUDOS
6.7668 g., 0.9170 Gold 0.1995 oz. AGW **Ruler:**
Charles III **Obv:** Large armored bust right **Obv.**
Legend: CAROLUS • III • D • G • ... **Rev:** Without 2
S by crowned shield **Rev. Legend:** IN • UTROQ •
FELIX • AUSPICE • DEO **Note:** Mint mark M, Mo.

Date	Mintage	VG	F	VF	XF	Unc
1762 MF	—	500	900	1,850	3,750	—
1763 MF	—	500	900	1,850	3,750	—
1764/3 MF	—	500	900	1,850	3,750	—
1765 MF	—	500	900	1,850	3,750	—
1766 MF	—	500	900	1,850	3,750	—
1767 MF	—	500	900	1,850	3,750	—
1768 MF	—	500	900	1,850	3,750	—
1769 MF	—	500	900	1,850	3,750	—
1770 MF	—	500	900	1,850	3,750	—
1771 MF	—	500	900	1,850	3,750	—

KM# 130.1   2 ESCUDOS
6.7668 g., 0.9010 Gold 0.1960 oz. AGW **Ruler:**
Charles III **Obv:** Older, armored bust right **Obv.**
Legend: CAROLUS • III • D • G • ... **Rev:** Crowned
shield in order chain, initials and mint mark upright
Rev. Legend: IN • UTROQ • FELIX • AUSPICE •
DEO **Note:** Mint mark M, Mo.

Date	Mintage	VG	F	VF	XF	Unc
1772 FM	—	200	375	550	1,000	—
1773 FM	—	200	375	550	1,000	—

KM# 130.2   2 ESCUDOS
6.7668 g., 0.9010 Gold 0.1960 oz. AGW **Ruler:**
Charles III **Obv:** Older, armored bust right **Obv.**
Legend: CAROLUS • III • D • G • ... **Rev:** Crowned
shield in order chain, initials and mint mark inverted
Rev. Legend: IN • UTROQ • FELIX • AUSPICE •
DEO **Note:** Mint mark M, Mo.

Date	Mintage	VG	F	VF	XF	Unc
1773 FM	—	200	375	550	1,000	—
1774 FM	—	200	375	550	1,000	—
1775 FM	—	200	375	550	1,000	—
1776 FM	—	200	375	550	1,000	—
1777 FM	—	175	300	450	900	—
1778 FF	—	175	300	450	900	—

Date	Mintage	VG	F	VF	XF	Unc
1779 FF	—	175	300	450	900	—
1780 FF	—	175	300	450	900	—
1781 FM/M	—	175	300	450	900	—
1781 FF	—	175	300	450	900	—
1782 FF	—	175	300	450	900	—
1783 FF	—	175	300	450	900	—
1784 FF	—	175	300	450	900	—
1784 FM/F	—	175	300	450	900	—

KM# 130.2a 2 ESCUDOS
6.7668 g., 0.8750 Gold 0.1904 oz. AGW **Ruler:**
Charles III **Obv:** Older, armored bust right **Obv.**
Legend: CAROLUS • III • D • G • ... **Rev:** Crowned
shield in order chain, initials and mint mark inverted
Rev. Legend: IN • UTROQ • FELIX • AUSPICE •
DEO **Note:** Mint mark M, Mo.

Date	Mintage	VG	F	VF	XF	Unc
1785 FM	—	175	300	450	900	—
1786 FM	—	175	300	450	900	—
1787 FM	—	175	300	450	900	—
1788 FM	—	175	300	450	900	—

KM# 130.1a 2 ESCUDOS
6.7668 g., 0.8750 Gold 0.1904 oz. AGW **Ruler:**
Charles III **Obv:** Older, armored bust right **Obv.**
Legend: CAROLUS • III • D • G • ... **Rev:** Crowned
shield in order chain, initials and mint mark upright
Rev. Legend: IN • UTROQ • FELIX • AUSPICE •
DEO **Note:** Mint mark M, Mo.

Date	Mintage	VG	F	VF	XF	Unc
1788 FM	—	175	300	450	900	—

KM# 131 2 ESCUDOS
6.7668 g., 0.8750 Gold 0.1904 oz. AGW **Ruler:**
Charles IV **Obv:** Armored bust of Charles III, right
Obv. Legend: CAROL • IV • D • G • ... **Rev:** Crowned
shield in order chain, initials and mint mark upright
Rev. Legend: IN • UTROQ • FELIX • AUSPICE •
DEO **Note:** Mint mark M, Mo, using old portrait punch.

Date	Mintage	VG	F	VF	XF	Unc
1789 FM	—	650	1,200	2,000	3,500	—
1790 FM	—	650	1,200	2,000	3,500	—

KM# 132 2 ESCUDOS
6.7668 g., 0.8750 Gold 0.1904 oz. AGW **Ruler:**
Charles IV **Obv:** Armored bust of Charles IIII, right
Obv. Legend: CAROL • IIII • D • G • ... **Rev:** Crowned
shield flanked by 2 S in order chain **Rev. Legend:**
IN • UTROQ • FELIX • AUSPICE • DEO; initials and
mint mark upright **Note:** Mint mark Mo.

Date	Mintage	VG	F	VF	XF	Unc
1791 FM Mo over inverted Mo	—	300	375	600	950	—
1792 FM	—	125	225	350	575	—
1793 FM	—	125	225	350	575	—
1794 FM	—	125	225	350	575	—
1795 FM	—	125	225	350	575	—
1796 FM	—	125	225	350	575	—

Date	Mintage	VG	F	VF	XF	Unc
1797 FM	—	125	225	350	575	—
1798 FM	—	125	225	350	575	—
1799 FM	—	125	225	350	575	—
1800 FM	—	125	225	350	575	—
1801 FT	—	125	225	350	575	—
1802 FT	—	125	225	350	575	—
1803 FT	—	125	225	350	575	—
1804 TH	—	125	225	350	575	—
1805 TH	—	125	225	350	575	—
1806/5 TH	—	125	225	350	575	—
1807 TH	—	125	225	350	575	—
1808 TH	—	125	225	350	575	1,500

KM# 134 2 ESCUDOS
6.7668 g., 0.8750 Gold 0.1904 oz. AGW **Ruler:**
Ferdinand VII **Obv:** Laureate head right **Obv.**
Legend: FERDIN. VII. D. G... **Rev:** Crowned shield
divides designed wreath **Rev. Legend:** IN. UTROQ.
FELIX. AUSPICE. DEO; initials and mint mark
upright **Note:** Mint mark Mo.

Date	Mintage	VG	F	VF	XF	Unc
1814Mo HJ	—	250	425	700	1,150	—
1815 JJ	—	250	425	700	1,150	—
1816 JJ	—	250	425	700	1,150	—
1817 JJ	—	250	425	700	1,150	—
1818 JJ	—	250	425	700	1,150	3,750
1819 JJ	—	250	425	700	1,150	—
1820 JJ	—	250	425	700	1,150	—
1821 JJ	—	250	425	700	1,150	—

KM# 135 4 ESCUDOS
13.5337 g., 0.9170 Gold 0.3990 oz. AGW **Ruler:**
Philip V **Obv:** Armored bust right **Obv. Legend:**
PHILIP • V • D • G • HISPAN • ET IND • REX **Rev:**
Crowned shield flanked by F 4 **Rev. Legend:**
INITIUM SAPIENTIAE TIMOR DOMINI **Note:** Mint
mark M, Mo.

Date	Mintage	VG	F	VF	XF	Unc
1732 Rare	—	—	—	—	—	—
1732 F Rare	—	—	—	—	—	—
1733 F Rare	—	—	—	—	—	—
1734/3 F	—	1,000	1,500	2,800	4,500	—
1734 MF	—	850	1,350	2,500	4,250	—
1735 MF	—	850	1,350	2,500	4,500	—
1736 MF	—	850	1,350	2,500	4,500	—
1737 MF	—	750	1,250	2,400	4,000	—
1738/7 MF	—	750	1,250	2,400	4,000	—
1738 MF	—	750	1,250	2,400	4,000	—
1739 MF	—	750	1,250	2,400	4,000	—
1740/30 MF	—	750	1,250	2,400	4,000	—
1740 MF	—	750	1,250	2,400	4,000	—
1741 MF	—	750	1,250	2,400	4,000	—
1742/32 MF	—	750	1,250	2,400	4,000	—
1743 MF	—	750	1,250	2,400	4,000	—
1744 MD	—	750	1,250	2,400	4,000	—

Date	Mintage	VG	F	VF	XF	Unc
1745 MF	—	750	1,250	2,400	4,000	—
1746 MF	—	750	1,250	2,400	4,000	—
1747 MF	—	750	1,250	2,400	4,000	—
1746/5 MF	—	750	1,250	2,400	4,000	—

KM# 136   4 ESCUDOS
13.5337 g., 0.9170 Gold 0.3990 oz. AGW   **Ruler:**
Ferdinand VI **Obv:** Large, armored bust right **Obv.**
Legend: FERDND • VI • D • G • ... **Rev:** Crowned shield
flanked by F 4 **Rev. Legend:** INITIUM SAPIENTIAE
TIMOR DOMINI **Note:** Mint mark M, Mo.

Date	Mintage	VG	F	VF	XF	Unc
1747 MF	—	7,500	13,500	20,000	30,000	—

KM# 137   4 ESCUDOS
13.5337 g., 0.9170 Gold 0.3990 oz. AGW   **Ruler:**
Ferdinand VI **Obv:** Armored bust right **Obv. Legend:**
FERDND • VI • D • G • ... **Rev:** Crowned shield flanked
by 4 S **Rev. Legend:** NOMINA MAGNA SEQUOR
Note: Mint mark M, Mo.

Date	Mintage	VG	F	VF	XF	Unc
1748 MF	—	1,500	3,000	5,000	8,000	—
1749 MF	—	1,500	3,000	5,000	8,000	—
1750/48 MF	—	1,500	3,000	5,000	8,000	—
1750 MF	—	1,500	3,000	5,000	8,000	—
1751 MF	—	1,500	3,000	5,000	8,000	—

KM# 138   4 ESCUDOS
13.5337 g., 0.9170 Gold 0.3990 oz. AGW   **Ruler:**
Ferdinand VI **Obv:** Small, armored bust right **Obv.**
Legend: FERDND • VI • D • G • ... **Rev:** Crowned
shield, without value **Rev. Legend:** NOMINA
MAGNA... **Note:** Mint mark M, Mo.

Date	Mintage	VG	F	VF	XF	Unc
1752 MF	—	1,000	2,000	3,500	6,000	—
1753 MF	—	1,000	2,000	3,500	6,000	—
1754 MF	—	1,000	2,000	3,500	6,000	—
1755 MM	—	1,000	2,000	3,500	6,000	—
1756 MM	—	1,000	2,000	3,500	6,000	—

KM# 139   4 ESCUDOS
13.5337 g., 0.9170 Gold 0.3990 oz. AGW   **Ruler:**
Ferdinand VI **Obv:** Armored bust right **Obv. Legend:**
FERDND • VI • D • G • ... **Rev:** Crowned shield, without
value **Rev. Legend:** NOMINA MAGNA... **Note:** Mint
mark M, Mo.

Date	Mintage	VG	F	VF	XF	Unc
1757 MM	—	1,250	2,500	4,000	6,500	—
1759 MM	—	1,250	2,500	4,000	6,500	—

KM# 140   4 ESCUDOS
13.5337 g., 0.9170 Gold 0.3990 oz. AGW   **Ruler:**
Charles III **Obv:** Armored bust right **Obv. Legend:**
CAROLVS • III • D • G • ... **Rev:** Crowned shield,
without value **Rev. Legend:** NOMINA MAGNA
SEQUOR **Note:** Mint mark M, Mo.

Date	Mintage	VG	F	VF	XF	Unc
1760 MM	—	3,500	6,500	10,000	20,000	—
1761 MM	—	3,500	6,500	10,000	20,000	—

KM# 141   4 ESCUDOS
13.5337 g., 0.9170 Gold 0.3990 oz. AGW   **Ruler:**
Charles III **Obv:** Large, armored bust right **Obv.**
Legend: CAROLUS • III • D • G • ... **Rev:** Crowned shield
in order chain, without value **Rev. Legend:** IN • UTROQ
• FELIX • AUSPICE • DEO **Note:** Mint mark M, Mo.

Date	Mintage	VG	F	VF	XF	Unc
1762 MF	—	2,500	4,500	7,500	15,000	—
1763 MF	—	2,500	4,500	7,500	15,000	—
1764 MF	—	2,500	4,500	7,500	15,000	—
1765 MF	—	2,500	4,500	7,500	15,000	—
1766/5 MF	—	2,500	4,500	7,500	15,000	—
1767 MF	—	2,500	4,500	7,500	15,000	—
1768 MF	—	2,500	4,500	7,500	15,000	—
1769 MF	—	2,500	4,500	7,500	15,000	—
1770 MF	—	2,500	4,500	7,500	15,000	—
1771 MF	—	2,500	4,500	7,500	15,000	—

KM# 142.1 4 ESCUDOS
13.5337 g., 0.9010 Gold 0.3920 oz. AGW **Ruler:**
Charles III **Obv:** Large, armored bust right **Obv.**
Legend: CAROL • III • D • G • ... **Rev:** Crowned shield
in order chain, initials and mint mark upright **Rev.**
Legend: IN • UTROQ • FELIX • AUSPICE • DEO
Note: Mint mark M, Mo.

Date	Mintage	VG	F	VF	XF	Unc
1772 FM	—	400	650	1,000	2,000	—
1773 FM	—	400	650	1,000	2,000	—

KM# 142.2 4 ESCUDOS
13.5337 g., 0.9010 Gold 0.3920 oz. AGW **Ruler:**
Charles III **Obv:** Large, armored bust right **Obv.**
Legend: CAROL • III • D • G • ... **Rev:** Crowned shield
flanked by 4 S in order chain, initials and mint mark
inverted **Rev. Legend:** IN • UTROQ • FELIX •
AUSPICE • DEO **Note:** Mint mark M, Mo.

Date	Mintage	VG	F	VF	XF	Unc
1773 FM	—	400	600	900	1,850	—
1774 FM	—	400	600	900	1,850	—
1775 FM	—	400	600	900	1,850	—
1776 FM	—	400	600	900	1,850	—
1777 FM	—	400	600	900	1,850	—
1778 FM	—	400	600	900	1,850	—
1779 FF	—	400	600	900	1,850	—
1780 FF	—	400	600	900	1,850	—
1781 FF	—	400	600	900	1,850	—
1782 FF	—	400	600	900	1,850	—
1783 FF	—	400	600	900	1,850	—
1784 FF	—	400	600	900	1,850	—
1784/3 FM/F	—	400	600	900	1,850	—

KM# 142.2a 4 ESCUDOS
13.5337 g., 0.8750 Gold 0.3807 oz. AGW **Ruler:**
Charles III **Obv:** Large, armored bust right **Obv.**
Legend: CAROL • III • D • G • ... **Rev:** Crowned shield
in order chain, initials and mint mark inverted **Rev.**
Legend: IN • UTROQ • FELIX • AUSPICE • DEO
Note: Mint mark M, Mo.

Date	Mintage	VG	F	VF	XF	Unc
1785 FM	—	400	600	900	1,850	—
1786 FM/F	—	400	600	900	1,850	—
1786 FM	—	400	600	900	1,850	—
1787 FM	—	400	600	900	1,850	—
1788 FM	—	400	600	900	1,850	—

KM# 142.1a 4 ESCUDOS
13.5337 g., 0.8750 Gold 0.3807 oz. AGW **Ruler:**
Charles III **Obv:** Large, armored bust right **Obv.**
Legend: CAROL • III • D • G • ... **Rev:** Crowned shield
in order chain, initials and mint mark upright **Rev.**
Legend: IN • UTROQ • FELIX • AUSPICE • DEO
Note: Mint mark M, Mo.

Date	Mintage	VG	F	VF	XF	Unc
1788 FM	—	400	650	1,000	2,000	—

KM# 143.1 4 ESCUDOS
13.5337 g., 0.8750 Gold 0.3807 oz. AGW **Ruler:**
Charles IV **Obv:** Armored bust of Charles III, right
Obv. Legend: CAROL • IV • D • G • ... **Rev:** Crowned
shield in order chain, initials and mint mark upright
Rev. Legend: IN • UTROQ • FELIX • AUSPICE •
DEO **Note:** Mint mark M, Mo, using old portrait punch.

Date	Mintage	VG	F	VF	XF	Unc
1789 FM	—	500	700	1,100	2,150	—
1790 FM	—	500	700	1,100	2,150	—

KM# 143.2 4 ESCUDOS
13.5337 g., 0.8750 Gold 0.3807 oz. AGW **Ruler:**
Charles IV **Obv:** Armored bust of Charles III, right
Obv. Legend: CAROL • IIII • D • G • ... **Rev:** Crowned
shield in order chain, initials and mint mark upright
Rev. Legend: IN • UTROQ • FELIX • AUSPICE •
DEO **Note:** Mint mark M, Mo, using old portrait punch.

Date	Mintage	VG	F	VF	XF	Unc
1790 FM	—	600	1,000	1,800	3,000	—

KM# 144 4 ESCUDOS
13.5337 g., 0.8750 Gold 0.3807 oz. AGW **Ruler:**
Charles IV **Obv:** Armored bust of Charles IIII, right
Obv. Legend: CAROL • IIII • D • G • ... **Rev:** Crowned
shield flanked by 4 S in order chain **Rev. Legend:**
IN • UTROQ • FELIX • AUSPICE • DEO; initials and
mint mark upright **Note:** Mint mark Mo.

Date	Mintage	VG	F	VF	XF	Unc
1792 FM	—	335	500	750	1,500	—
1793 FM	—	335	500	750	1,500	—
1794/3 FM	—	335	500	750	1,500	—
1795 FM	—	335	500	750	1,500	—
1796 FM	—	335	500	750	1,500	—
1797 FM	—	335	500	750	1,500	—
1798/7 FM	—	335	500	750	1,500	—
1798 FM	—	335	500	750	1,500	—
1799 FM	—	335	500	750	1,500	—
1800 FM	—	335	500	750	1,500	—
1801 FM	—	335	500	750	1,500	—
1801 FT	—	335	500	750	1,500	—
1802 FT	—	365	600	850	1,650	—
1803 FT	—	335	500	750	1,500	—
1804/3 TH	—	335	500	750	1,500	—
1804 TH	—	335	500	750	1,500	—
1805 TH	—	335	500	750	1,500	—
1806/5 TH	—	335	500	750	1,500	—
1807 TH	—	365	600	850	1,650	—
1808/0 TH	—	335	500	750	1,500	—
1808 TH	—	335	500	750	1,500	—

KM# 145   4 ESCUDOS
13.5337 g., 0.8750 Gold 0.3807 oz. AGW   **Ruler:**
Ferdinand VII **Obv:** Armored bust right **Obv.**
Legend: FERDIN. VII D. G... **Rev:** Crowned shield
divides designed wreath **Rev. Legend:** IN. UTROQ.
FELIX. AUSPICE. DEO; initials and mint mark
upright **Note:** Mint mark Mo.

Date	Mintage	VG	F	VF	XF	Unc
1810 HJ	—	365	500	900	1,850	—
1811 HJ	—	365	500	900	1,850	—
1812 HJ	—	365	500	900	1,850	—

KM# 146   4 ESCUDOS
13.5337 g., 0.8750 Gold 0.3807 oz. AGW   **Ruler:**
Ferdinand VII **Obv:** Laureate head right **Obv.**
Legend: FERDIN. VII D. G... **Rev:** Crowned shield
divides designed wreath **Rev. Legend:** IN. UTROQ.
FELIX. AUSPICE. DEO; initials and mint mark
upright **Note:** Mint mark Mo.

Date	Mintage	VG	F	VF	XF	Unc
1814 HJ	—	400	700	1,150	2,500	—
1815 HJ	—	400	700	1,150	2,500	—
1815 JJ	—	400	700	1,150	2,500	—
1816 JJ	—	400	700	1,150	2,500	—
1817 JJ	—	400	700	1,150	2,500	—
1818 JJ	—	400	700	1,150	2,500	—
1819 JJ	—	400	700	1,150	2,500	—
1820 JJ	—	400	700	1,150	2,500	—

KM# 148   8 ESCUDOS
27.0674 g., 0.9170 Gold 0.7980 oz. AGW   **Ruler:**
Philip V **Obv:** Large, armored bust right **Obv.**

Legend: PHILIP • V • D • G • HISPAN • ET IND •
REX **Rev:** Crowned shield flanked by M F 8 in order
chain **Rev. Legend:** INITIUM SAPIENTIAE TIMOR
DOMINI **Note:** Mint mark M, Mo.

Date	Mintage	VG	F	VF	XF	Unc
1732 Rare	—	—	—	—	—	—
1732 F Rare	—	—	—	—	—	—
1733 F Rare	—	—	—	—	—	—
1734 MF/F	—	1,000	1,650	2,750	4,850	—
1734 MF	—	1,000	1,650	2,750	4,850	—
1735 MF	—	1,000	1,500	2,500	4,500	—
1736 MF	—	1,000	1,500	2,500	4,500	—
1737 MF	—	1,000	1,500	2,500	4,500	—
1738/7 MF	—	1,000	1,500	2,500	4,500	—
1738 MF	—	1,000	1,500	2,500	4,500	—
1739 MF	—	1,000	1,500	2,500	4,500	—
1740/30 MF	—	1,000	1,500	2,500	4,500	—
1740 MF	—	1,000	1,500	2,500	4,500	—
1741 MF	—	1,000	1,500	2,500	4,500	—
1742 MF	—	1,000	1,500	2,500	4,500	—
1743 MF	—	1,000	1,500	2,500	4,500	—
1744/3 MF	—	1,000	1,500	2,500	4,500	—
1744 MF	—	1,000	1,500	2,500	4,500	—
1745 MF	—	1,000	1,500	2,500	4,500	—
1745/4 MF	—	1,000	1,500	2,500	4,500	—
1746/5 MF	—	1,000	1,500	2,500	4,500	—
1746 MF	—	1,000	1,500	2,500	4,500	—
1747 MF	—	1,100	1,750	2,850	5,000	—

KM# 149   8 ESCUDOS
27.0674 g., 0.9170 Gold 0.7980 oz. AGW   **Ruler:**
Ferdinand VI **Obv:** Large, armored bust right **Obv.**
Legend: FERDND • VI • D • G • ... **Rev:** Crowned
shield flanked by M F 8 in order chain **Rev. Legend:**
INITIUM SAPIENTIAE TIMOR DOMINI **Note:** Mint
mark M, Mo.

Date	Mintage	VG	F	VF	XF	Unc
1747 MF	—	9,000	15,000	22,000	35,000	—

KM# 150 8 ESCUDOS

27.0674 g., 0.9170 Gold 0.7980 oz. AGW **Ruler:** Ferdinand VI **Obv:** Small, armored bust right **Obv. Legend:** FERDND • VI • D • G • ... **Rev:** Crowned shield flanked by 8 S in order chain **Rev. Legend:** NOMINA MAGNA SEQUOR **Note:** Mint mark M, Mo.

Date	Mintage	VG	F	VF	XF	Unc
1748 MF	—	1,200	2,000	3,500	6,000	—
1749/8 MF	—	1,200	2,000	3,500	6,000	—
1749 MF	—	1,200	2,000	3,500	6,000	—
1750 MF	—	1,200	2,000	3,500	6,000	—
1751/0 MF	—	1,500	2,000	3,500	6,000	—
1751 MF	—	1,200	2,000	3,500	6,000	—

KM# 152 8 ESCUDOS

27.0674 g., 0.9170 Gold 0.7980 oz. AGW **Ruler:** Ferdinand VI **Obv:** Armored bust right **Obv. Legend:** FERDND • VI • D • G • ... **Rev:** Crowned shield in order chain **Rev. Legend:** NOMINA MAGNA SEQUOR **Note:** Mint mark M, Mo.

Date	Mintage	VG	F	VF	XF	Unc
1757 MM	—	1,200	2,000	3,500	6,000	—
1758 MM	—	1,200	2,000	3,500	6,000	—
1759 MM	—	1,200	2,000	3,500	6,000	—

KM# 151 8 ESCUDOS

27.0674 g., 0.9170 Gold 0.7980 oz. AGW **Ruler:** Ferdinand VI **Obv:** Armored bust right **Obv. Legend:** FERDND • VI • D • G • ... **Rev:** Crowned shield in order chain **Rev. Legend:** NOMINA MAGNA SEQUOR **Note:** Mint mark M, Mo.

Date	Mintage	VG	F	VF	XF	Unc
1752 MF	—	1,200	2,000	3,500	6,000	—
1753 MF	—	1,200	2,000	3,500	6,000	—
1754 MF	—	1,200	2,000	3,500	6,000	—
1755 MM	—	1,200	2,000	3,500	6,000	—
1756 MM	—	1,200	2,000	3,500	6,000	—

KM# 153 8 ESCUDOS

27.0674 g., 0.9170 Gold 0.7980 oz. AGW **Ruler:** Charles III **Obv:** Armored bust right **Obv. Legend:** CAROLVS • III • D • G • ... **Rev:** Crowned shield in order chain **Rev. Legend:** NOMINA MAGNA SEQUOR **Note:** Mint mark M, Mo.

Date	Mintage	VG	F	VF	XF	Unc
1760 MM	—	1,750	3,000	5,000	9,000	—
1761/0 MM	—	2,000	3,500	5,500	10,000	—
1761 MM	—	2,000	3,500	5,500	10,000	—

SPANISH COLONIAL · MILLED

KM# 154   8 ESCUDOS
27.0674 g., 0.9170 Gold 0.7980 oz. AGW   **Ruler:**
Charles III **Obv:** Armored bust right **Obv. Legend:**
CAROLVS • III • D • G • ... **Rev:** Crowned shield in
order chain **Rev. Legend:** NOMINA MAGNA
SEQUOR **Note:** Mint mark M, Mo.

Date	Mintage	VG	F	VF	XF	Unc
1761 MM	—	1,750	3,000	5,250	9,500	—

KM# 156.1   8 ESCUDOS
27.0674 g., 0.9010 Gold 0.7841 oz. AGW   **Ruler:**
Charles III **Obv:** Large, armored bust right **Obv.
Legend:** CAROL • III • D • G • ... **Rev:** Crowned shield
flanked by 8 S in order chain, initials and mint mark
upright **Rev. Legend:** ... AUSPICE • DEO • **Note:**
Mint mark M, Mo.

Date	Mintage	VG	F	VF	XF	Unc
1772 FM	—	675	775	1,250	2,000	—
1773 FM	—	700	900	1,350	2,250	—

KM# 155   8 ESCUDOS
27.0674 g., 0.9170 Gold 0.7980 oz. AGW   **Ruler:**
Charles III **Obv:** Large, armored bust right **Obv.
Legend:** CAROLUS • III • D • G • ... **Rev:** Crowned
shield in order chain **Rev. Legend:** IN • UTROQ •
FELIX • AUSPICE • DEO • **Note:** Mint mark M, Mo.

Date	Mintage	VG	F	VF	XF	Unc
1762 MM	—	1,600	2,750	4,500	8,500	—
1763 MM	—	1,600	2,750	4,500	8,500	—
1764 MF	—	1,750	3,000	5,000	9,000	—
1764/2 MF	—	1,750	3,000	5,000	9,000	—
1764 MM	—	1,750	3,000	5,000	9,000	—
1765/4 MM	—	1,750	3,000	5,000	9,000	—
1765/4 MF	—	1,750	3,000	5,000	9,000	—
1765 MF	—	1,750	3,000	5,000	9,000	—
1765 MM	—	1,500	2,500	4,000	7,500	—
1766 MF	—	1,500	2,500	4,000	7,500	—
1767/6 MF	—	1,500	2,500	4,000	7,500	—
1767 MF	—	1,500	2,500	4,000	7,500	—
1768/7 MF	—	1,500	2,500	4,000	7,500	—
1768 MF	—	1,500	2,500	4,000	7,500	—
1769 MF	—	1,500	2,500	4,000	7,500	—
1770 MF	—	1,500	2,500	4,000	7,500	—
1771 MF	—	1,750	3,000	5,000	9,000	—

KM# 156.2   8 ESCUDOS
27.0674 g., 0.9010 Gold 0.7841 oz. AGW   **Ruler:**
Charles III **Obv:** Large, armored bust right **Obv.
Legend:** CAROL • III • D • G • ... **Rev:** Crowned shield
flanked by 8 S in order chain, initials and mint mark
inverted **Rev. Legend:** ... AUSPICE • DEO • **Note:**
Mint mark M, Mo.

Date	Mintage	VG	F	VF	XF	Unc
1773 FM	—	675	750	1,100	1,650	—
1774 FM	—	675	750	1,100	1,650	—
1775 FM	—	675	750	1,100	1,650	—
1776 FM	—	675	750	1,100	1,650	—
1777/6 FM	—	675	750	1,100	1,650	—
1777 FM	—	675	750	1,100	1,650	—
1778 FF	—	675	750	1,100	1,650	—
1779 FF	—	675	750	1,100	1,650	—
1780 FF	—	675	750	1,100	1,650	—
1781 FF	—	675	750	1,100	1,650	—
1782 FF	—	675	750	1,100	1,650	—
1783 FF	—	675	750	1,100	1,650	—
1784 FF	—	675	750	1,100	1,650	—
1784 FM/F	—	675	750	1,100	1,650	—
1784 FM	—	675	750	1,100	1,650	—
1785 FM	—	675	750	1,100	1,650	—

KM# 156.2a 8 ESCUDOS

27.0674 g., 0.8750 Gold 0.7614 oz. AGW **Ruler:** Charles III **Obv:** Large, armored bust right **Obv. Legend:** CAROL • III • D • G • ... **Rev:** Crowned shield flanked by 8 S in order chain, initials and mint mark inverted **Rev. Legend:** ... AUSPICE • DEO • **Note:** Mint mark M, Mo.

Date	Mintage	VG	F	VF	XF	Unc
1786 FM	—	675	750	1,100	1,650	—
1787 FM	—	675	750	1,100	1,650	—
1788 FM	—	675	750	1,100	1,650	—

KM# 157 8 ESCUDOS

27.0674 g., 0.8750 Gold 0.7614 oz. AGW **Ruler:** Charles IV **Obv:** Armored bust of Charles III, right **Obv. Legend:** CAROL • IV • D • G • ... **Rev:** Crowned shield flanked by 8 S in order chain **Rev. Legend:** IN • UTROQ • ... **Note:** Mint mark M, Mo, using old portrait punch.

Date	Mintage	VG	F	VF	XF	Unc
1789 FM	—	675	750	1,150	2,000	—
1790 FM	—	675	750	1,150	2,000	—

KM# 156.1a 8 ESCUDOS

27.0674 g., 0.8750 Gold 0.7614 oz. AGW **Ruler:** Charles III **Obv:** Large, armored bust right **Obv. Legend:** CAROL • III • D • G • ... **Rev:** Crowned shield flanked by 8 S in order chain, initials and mint mark upright **Rev. Legend:** ... AUSPICE • DEO • **Note:** Mint mark M, Mo.

Date	Mintage	VG	F	VF	XF	Unc
1788 FM	—	675	750	1,100	1,650	—

KM# 158 8 ESCUDOS

27.0674 g., 0.8750 Gold 0.7614 oz. AGW **Ruler:** Charles IV **Obv:** Armored bust of Charles III, right **Obv. Legend:** CAROL • IIII • D • G • ... **Rev:** Crowned shield flanked by 8 S in order chain **Rev. Legend:** IN • UTROQ • ... **Note:** Mint mark M, Mo, using old portrait punch.

Date	Mintage	VG	F	VF	XF	Unc
1790 FM	—	675	750	1,150	2,000	—

KM# 159 8 ESCUDOS

27.0674 g., 0.8750 Gold 0.7614 oz. AGW **Ruler:**
Charles IV **Obv:** Armored bust right **Obv. Legend:**
CAROL • IIII • D • G • ... **Rev:** Crowned shield flanked
by 8 S in order chain **Rev. Legend:** IN • UTROQ • ...
Note: Mint mark Mo.

Date	Mintage	VG	F	VF	XF	Unc
1791 FM	—	665	690	700	1,000	—
1792 FM	—	665	690	700	1,000	—
1793 FM	—	665	690	700	1,000	—
1794 FM	—	665	690	700	1,000	—
1795 FM	—	665	690	700	1,000	—
1796/5 FM	—	675	690	700	1,150	—
1796 FM	—	665	690	700	1,000	—
1797 FM	—	665	675	700	1,000	—
1797 FM EPLIX	—	675	690	750	1,150	—
1798 FM	—	665	675	700	1,000	—
1799 FM	—	665	675	700	1,000	—
1800 FM	—	665	675	700	1,000	—
1801/0 FT	—	675	690	775	1,150	—
1801 FM	—	675	690	700	1,000	—
1801 FT	—	675	690	700	1,000	—
1802 FT	—	675	690	700	1,000	—
1803 FT	—	675	700	725	1,000	—
1804/3 TH	—	675	700	750	1,150	—
1804 TH	—	675	690	700	1,000	3,500
1805 TH	—	675	690	700	1,000	—
1806 TH	—	675	690	700	1,000	3,500
1807 TH Mo over inverted Mo	—	675	700	750	1,150	—
1807/6 TH	—	675	700	750	1,150	—
1808/7 TH	—	675	690	700	1,250	—
1807 TH	—	690	700	875	1,000	—
1808 TH	—	690	700	875	1,250	—

KM# 160 8 ESCUDOS

27.0674 g., 0.8750 Gold 0.7614 oz. AGW **Ruler:**
Ferdinand VII **Obv:** Armored bust right **Obv.
Legend:** FERDIN. VII. D. G... **Rev:** Crowned shield
divides designed wreath **Rev. Legend:** IN UTROQ.
FELIX **Note:** Mint mark Mo.

Date	Mintage	VG	F	VF	XF	Unc
1808 TH	—	675	700	800	1,250	—
1809 HJ	—	675	700	800	1,350	—
1810 HJ	—	675	700	775	1,200	—
1811/0 HJ	—	675	700	850	1,350	—
1811 HJ H/T	—	675	700	850	1,350	—
1811 HJ	—	675	700	850	1,350	—

Date	Mintage	VG	F	VF	XF	Unc
1811 JJ	—	675	700	775	1,200	—
1812 JJ	—	675	700	775	1,200	—

KM# 161 8 ESCUDOS

27.0674 g., 0.8750 Gold 0.7614 oz. AGW **Ruler:**
Ferdinand VII **Obv:** Laureate head right **Obv.
Legend:** FERDIN. VII. D. G... **Rev:** Crowned shield
divides designed wreath **Rev. Legend:** IN UTROQ.
FELIX **Note:** Mint mark Mo.

Date	Mintage	VG	F	VF	XF	Unc
1814 JJ	—	675	700	775	1,000	—
1815/4 JJ	—	675	700	800	1,150	—
1815/4 HJ	—	675	700	800	1,150	—
1815 JJ	—	675	700	775	1,000	—
1815 HJ	—	675	700	775	1,000	—
1816 JJ	—	675	700	775	1,000	—
1817 JJ	—	675	700	775	1,150	—
1818/7 JJ	—	675	700	775	1,100	—
1818 JJ	—	675	700	775	1,100	—
1819 JJ	—	675	700	775	1,100	—
1820 JJ	—	675	700	775	1,100	—
1821 JJ	—	675	700	800	1,300	—

PROCLAMATION MEDALLIC COINAGE

The Q used in the following listings refer to
Standard Catalog of Mexican Coins, Paper Money,
Stocks, Bonds, and Medals by Krause Publications,
Inc., ©1981.

KM# Q22 1/2 REAL

1.6000 g., Silver **Issuer:** Mexico City **Obv:** Crowned
shield flanked by crowned pillars with banner **Obv.
Legend:** A CARLOS IV REY DE ESPANA Y DE LAS
YNDIAS **Rev:** Legend, date within wreath **Rev.
Legend:** PROCLAMADO EN MEXICO ANO DE 1789

Date	Mintage	F	VF	XF	Unc	BU
1789	—	20.00	28.50	40.00	—	—

KM# Q22a 1/2 REAL

Bronze **Issuer:** Mexico City **Obv:** Crowned shield
flanked by crowned pillars with banner **Obv. Legend:**
A CARLOS IV REY DE ESPANA Y DE LAS YNDIAS
Rev: Legend, date within wreath **Rev. Legend:**
PROCLAMADO EN MEXICO ANO DE 1789

Date	Mintage	F	VF	XF	Unc	BU
1789	—	22.50	35.00	50.00	—	—

KM# Q23   1/2 REAL
Silver **Issuer:** Mexico City **Obv:** Crowned arms in double-lined circle **Obv. Legend:** A CARLOS IV REY DE ESPANA Y DE LAS YNDIAS **Rev. Legend:** PROCLAMADO EN MEXICO ANO DE 1789

Date	Mintage	F	VF	XF	Unc	BU
1789	—	20.00	28.50	40.00	—	—

KM# Q23a   1/2 REAL
Bronze **Issuer:** Mexico City **Obv:** Crowned arms in double-lined circle **Obv. Legend:** A CARLOS IV REY DE ESPANA Y DE LAS YNDIAS **Rev. Legend:** PROCLAMADO EN MEXICO ANO DE 1789

Date	Mintage	F	VF	XF	Unc	BU
1789	—	22.50	35.00	50.00	—	—

KM# Q24   REAL
Silver **Issuer:** Mexico City **Obv:** Crowned shield flanked by crowned pillars with banner **Obv. Legend:** A CARLOS IV REY DE ESPANA Y DE LAS YNDIAS **Rev:** Legend, date, value within wreath **Rev. Legend:** PROCLAMADO EN MEXICO ANO DE 1789

Date	Mintage	F	VF	XF	Unc	BU
1789	—	20.00	28.50	40.00	—	—

KM# Q24a   REAL
Bronze **Issuer:** Mexico City **Obv:** Crowned shield flanked by crowned pillars with banner **Obv. Legend:** A CARLOS IV REY DE ESPANA Y DE LAS YNDIAS **Rev:** Legend, date, value within wreath **Rev. Legend:** PROCLAMADO EN MEXICO ANO DE 1789

Date	Mintage	F	VF	XF	Unc	BU
1789	—	22.50	35.00	50.00	—	—

KM# Q-A24   REAL
Silver **Issuer:** Mexico City **Obv:** Crowned arms in double-lined circle **Obv. Legend:** A CARLOS IV REY DE ESPANA Y DE LAS YNDIAS **Rev. Legend:** PROCLAMADO EN MEXICO ANO DE 1789

Date	Mintage	F	VF	XF	Unc	BU
1789	—	20.00	28.50	40.00	—	—

KM# Q-A24a   REAL
Copper **Issuer:** Mexico City **Obv:** Crowned arms in double-lined circle **Obv. Legend:** A CARLOS IV REY DE ESPANA Y DE LAS YNDIAS **Rev. Legend:** PROCLAMADO EN MEXICO ANO DE 1789

Date	Mintage	F	VF	XF	Unc	BU
1789	—	22.50	35.00	50.00	—	—

KM# Q8   REAL
Silver **Issuer:** Chiapa **Obv:** Crowned shield flanked by pillars **Obv. Legend:** FERNANDO. VII. REY DE ESPAÑA. Y DE SUS IND. **Rev:** Legend within wreath **Rev. Legend:** PROCLA/MADO ENCUID•R•DE/ CHIAPA•/•A1808•

Date	Mintage	F	VF	XF	Unc	BU
1808	—	20.00	32.50	47.50	75.00	—

KM# Q25   2 REALES
6.7000 g., Silver **Issuer:** Mexico City **Obv:** Crowned shield flanked by crowned pillars with banner **Obv. Legend:** A CARLOS IV REY DE ESPANA Y DE LAS YNDIAS **Rev:** Legend, date, value within wreath **Rev. Legend:** PROCLAMADO EN MEXICO ANO DE 1789

Date	Mintage	F	VF	XF	Unc	BU
1789	—	35.00	50.00	75.00	—	—

KM# Q25a   2 REALES
6.7000 g., Bronze **Issuer:** Mexico City **Obv:** Crowned shield flanked by crowned pillars with banner **Obv. Legend:** A CARLOS IV REY DE ESPANA Y DE LAS YNDIAS **Rev:** Legend, date, value within wreath **Rev. Legend:** PROCLAMADO EN MEXICO ANO DE 1789

Date	Mintage	F	VF	XF	Unc	BU
1789	—	30.00	45.00	60.00	—	—

KM# Q64   2 REALES
Silver **Issuer:** Queretaro **Obv:** Crowned shield flanked by pillars **Obv. Legend:** FERNANDO VII REY DE ESPANA **Rev:** Legend, date within wreath

Date	Mintage	F	VF	XF	Unc	BU
1808	—	20.00	37.50	67.50	100	—

KM# Q10   2 REALES
Silver **Issuer:** Chiapa **Obv:** Crowned shield flanked by pillars **Obv. Legend:** FERNANDO VII REY DE ESPANA Y DE SUS INDIAS **Rev:** Legend, date within wreath

Date	Mintage	F	VF	XF	Unc	BU
1808	—	37.50	57.50	78.50	115	—

KM# Q27　4 REALES
13.6000 g., Silver **Issuer:** Mexico City **Obv:**
Crowned shield flanked by crowned pillars with
banner **Obv. Legend:** A CARLOS IV REY DE
ESPANA Y DE LAS YNDIAS **Rev:** Legend date,
value within wreath **Rev. Legend:** PROCLAMADO
EN MEXICO ANO DE 1789

Date	Mintage	F	VF	XF	Unc	BU
1789	—	100	150	225	—	—

KM# Q27a　4 REALES
13.6000 g., Bronze **Issuer:** Mexico City **Obv:**
Crowned shield flanked by crowned pillars with
banner **Obv. Legend:** A CARLOS IV REY DE
ESPANA Y DE LAS YNDIAS **Rev:** Legend, date,
value within wreath **Rev. Legend:** PROCLAMADO
EN MEXICO ANO DE 1789

Date	Mintage	F	VF	XF	Unc	BU
1789	—	70.00	100	150	—	—

KM# Q28　8 REALES
27.0000 g., Silver **Issuer:** Mexico City **Obv:**
Crowned shield flanked by crowned pillars with
banner **Obv. Legend:** A CARLOS IV REY DE
ESPANA Y DE LAS YNDIAS **Rev:** Legend, date,
value within wreath **Rev. Legend:** PROCLAMADO
EN MEXICO ANO DE 1789

Date	Mintage	F	VF	XF	Unc	BU
1789	—	200	275	400	—	—

KM# Q28a　8 REALES
27.0000 g., Bronze **Issuer:** Mexico City **Obv:**
Crowned shield flanked by crowned pillars with
banner **Obv. Legend:** A CARLOS IV REY DE
ESPANA Y DE LAS YNDIAS **Rev:** Legend, date,
value within wreath **Rev. Legend:** PROCLAMADO
EN MEXICO ANO DE 1789

Date	Mintage	F	VF	XF	Unc	BU
1789	—	70.00	100	150	—	—

KM# Q-A66　4 REALES
Silver **Issuer:** Queretaro **Obv:** Crowned shield
flanked by pillars **Obv. Legend:** FERNANDO VII
REY DE ESPANA **Rev:** Legend, date within wreath

Date	Mintage	F	VF	XF	Unc	BU
1808	—	85.00	135	200	325	—

KM# Q68　8 REALES
Silver **Issuer:** Queretaro **Obv:** Crowned shield
flanked by pillars **Obv. Legend:** FERNANDO VII
REY DE ESPANA **Rev:** Legend, date within wreath

Date	Mintage	F	VF	XF	Unc	BU
1808	—	185	350	475	625	—

WAR OF INDEPENDENCE

CHIHUAHUA

The Chihuahua Mint was established by a decree of October 8, 1810 as a temporary mint. Their first coins were cast 8 Reales using Mexico City coins as patterns and obliterating/changing the mint mark and moneyer initials. Two c/m were placed on the obverse - on the left, a T designating receipt by the Royal Treasurer, crowned pillars of Hercules on the right with pomegranate beneath, the comptrollers symbol.

In 1814, standard dies were made available, thus machine struck 8 Reales were produced until 1822. Only the one denomination was made at Chihuahua.

Mint mark: CA.

ROYALIST COINAGE

KM# 123   8 REALES
Cast Silver   **Ruler:** Ferdinand VII **Countermark:** T at left, pillars at right, pomegranate below **Obv:** Armored bust right **Obv. Legend:** FERDIN. VII. DEI. GRATIA **Rev:** Crowned shield flanked by pillars

Date	Mintage	Good	VG	F	VF	XF
1810CA RP Rare	—	—	—	—	—	—
1811CA RP	—	45.00	60.00	100	150	—
1812CA RP	—	30.00	40.00	60.00	90.00	—
1813CA RP	—	30.00	40.00	60.00	90.00	—

KM# 111.1   8 REALES
27.0700 g., 0.9030 Silver 0.7859 oz. ASW   **Ruler:** Ferdinand VII **Obv:** Draped bust right **Obv. Legend:** FERDIN. VII. DEI. GRATIA **Rev:** Crowned shield flanked by pillars

Date	Mintage	VG	F	VF	XF	Unc
1815CA RP	—	200	275	350	500	—
1816CA RP	—	80.00	125	150	275	—
1817CA RP	—	100	150	185	275	—
1818CA RP	—	100	150	185	275	—
1819/8 RP	—	125	175	250	350	—
1819CA RP	—	125	175	250	350	—
1820CA RP	—	200	275	350	500	—
1821CA RP	—	200	275	350	500	—
1822CA RP	—	400	600	800	1,100	—

Note: KM#111.1 is normally found struck over earlier cast 8 Reales, KM#123 and Monclova (MVA) 1812 cast countermark 8 Reales, KM#202 and Zacatecas 8 Reales, KM#190

DURANGO

The Durango mint was authorized as a temporary mint on the same day as the Chihuahua Mint, October 8, 1810. The mint opened in 1811 and made coins of 6 denominations between 1811 and 1822.

Mint mark: D.

ROYALIST COINAGE

KM# 60   1/8 REAL
Copper   **Ruler:** Ferdinand VII **Obv:** Crowned monogram **Rev:** EN DURANGO, value, date

Date	Mintage	VG	F	VF	XF	Unc
1812D	—	40.00	75.00	125	250	—
1813D	—	65.00	135	185	375	—
1814D Rare	—	—	—	—	—	—

KM# 61   1/8 REAL
Copper   **Ruler:** Ferdinand VII **Obv:** Crowned monogram **Rev:** Value within spray, date below **Rev. Legend:** ENDURANGO.

Date	Mintage	VG	F	VF	XF	Unc
1814D	—	18.00	32.50	55.00	90.00	—
1815D	—	18.00	35.00	60.00	100	—
1816D	—	18.00	35.00	60.00	100	—
1817D	—	15.00	30.00	50.00	90.00	—
1818D	—	15.00	30.00	50.00	90.00	—
1818D	—	45.00	80.00	125	225	—

Note: OCTAVO DD REAL, error

KM# 74.1   1/2 REAL
1.6900 g., 0.9030 Silver 0.0491 oz. ASW   **Ruler:** Ferdinand VII **Obv:** Draped laureate bust right **Rev:** Crowned shield flanked by pillars

Date	Mintage	VG	F	VF	XF	Unc
1813D RM	—	250	450	750	1,800	—
1814D MZ	—	250	450	750	1,850	—
1816D MZ	—	250	450	750	1,850	—

KM# 83.1   REAL
3.3800 g., 0.9030 Silver 0.0981 oz. ASW   **Ruler:** Ferdinand VII **Obv:** Draped laureate bust right **Obv. Legend:** FERDIN.VII... **Rev:** Crowned shield flanked by pillars **Rev. Legend:** IND.REX...

Date	Mintage	VG	F	VF	XF	Unc
1813D RM	—	250	450	650	1,650	—
1814D MZ	—	250	450	650	1,650	—
1815D MZ	—	250	450	650	1,650	—

KM# 92.2   2 REALES
6.7700 g., 0.9030 Silver 0.1965 oz. ASW   **Ruler:** Ferdinand VII **Obv:** Armored bust right **Rev:** Crowned shield flanked by pillars **Rev. Legend:** MON PROV DE DURANGO...

Date	Mintage	VG	F	VF	XF	Unc
1811D RM	—	375	450	850	1,750	—

KM# 92.3   2 REALES
6.7700 g., 0.9030 Silver 0.1965 oz. ASW   **Ruler:** Ferdinand VII **Obv:** Armored bust right **Rev:** Crowned shield flanked by pillars **Rev. Legend:** HISPAN ET IND REX...

Date	Mintage	VG	F	VF	XF	Unc
1812 RM	—	250	400	750	1,650	—

KM# 93.1   2 REALES
6.7700 g., 0.9030 Silver 0.1965 oz. ASW   **Ruler:** Ferdinand VII **Obv:** Draped laureate bust right **Obv. Legend:** FERDIN.VII... **Rev:** Crowned shield flanked by pillars **Rev. Legend:** IND.REX...

Date	Mintage	VG	F	VF	XF	Unc
1812D RM	—	250	400	750	1,650	—
1813D RM	—	300	600	1,000	2,750	—
1813D MZ	—	300	600	1,000	2,750	—
1814D MZ	—	300	600	1,000	2,750	—
1815D MZ	—	300	600	1,000	2,750	—
1816D MZ	—	300	600	1,000	2,750	—
1817D MZ	—	300	600	1,000	2,750	—

KM# 102.1   4 REALES
13.5400 g., 0.9030 Silver 0.3931 oz. ASW   **Ruler:** Ferdinand VII **Obv:** Draped laureate bust right **Obv. Legend:** FERDIN.VII... **Rev:** Crowned shield flanked by pillars **Rev. Legend:** IND.REX...

Date	Mintage	VG	F	VF	XF	Unc
1814D MZ	—	550	1,000	1,650	4,500	—
1816D MZ	—	450	900	1,400	4,000	—
1817D MZ	—	450	900	1,400	4,000	—

KM# 110.1   8 REALES
27.0700 g., 0.9030 Silver 0.7859 oz. ASW   **Ruler:**

Ferdinand VII **Obv:** Armored bust right **Obv.**
Legend: FERD.VII... **Rev:** Crowned shield flanked
by pillars **Rev. Legend:** DURANGO.8R R.M...

Date	Mintage	VG	F	VF	XF	Unc
1811D RM	—	600	1,000	1,750	5,000	—
1812D RM	—	350	650	1,000	3,500	—
1814D MZ	—	350	650	1,000	3,500	—

KM# 111.2   8 REALES
27.0700 g., 0.9030 Silver 0.7859 oz. ASW   **Ruler:**
Ferdinand VII **Obv:** Draped laureate bust right **Obv.**
Legend: FERDIN.VII... **Rev:** Crowned shield flanked
by pillars **Rev. Legend:** IND.REX...

Date	Mintage	VG	F	VF	XF	Unc
1812D RM	—	125	175	275	800	—
1813D RM	—	150	200	325	850	—
1813D MZ	—	125	175	275	750	—
1814/2D MZ	—	150	200	300	750	—
1814D MZ	—	150	200	300	750	—
1815D MZ	—	75.00	125	225	600	—
1816D MZ	—	50.00	75.00	125	325	—
1817D MZ	—	30.00	50.00	90.00	250	—
1818D MZ	—	50.00	75.00	125	350	—
1818D RM	—	50.00	75.00	125	325	—
1818D CG/RM	—	100	125	150	350	—
1818D CG	—	50.00	75.00	125	325	—
1819D CG/RM	—	50.00	100	150	300	—
1819D CG	—	30.00	60.00	100	250	—
1820D CG	—	30.00	60.00	100	250	—
1821D CG	—	30.00	40.00	80.00	200	—
1822D CG	—	30.00	50.00	90.00	240	—

Note: Occasionally these are found struck over cast Chihuahua 8 reales and are very rare in general, specimens dated prior to 1816 are rather crudely struck

GUADALAJARA

GUADALAJARA

The Guadalajara Mint made its first coins in
1812 and the mint operated until April 30, 1815. It
was to reopen in 1818 and continue operations until
1822. It was the only Royalist mint to strike gold
coins, both 4 and 8 Escudos. In addition to these it
struck the standard 5 denominations in silver.
Mint mark: GA.

ROYALIST COINAGE

KM# 74.2   1/2 REAL
1.6900 g., 0.9030 Silver 0.0491 oz. ASW   **Ruler:**
Ferdinand VII **Obv:** Draped laureate bust right **Obv.**
Legend: FERDIN.VII... **Rev:** Crowned shield flanked
by pillars **Rev. Legend:** IND...

Date	Mintage	VG	F	VF	XF	Unc
1812GA MR Rare	—	—	—	—	—	—
1814GA MR	—	40.00	100	200	300	—
1815GA MR	—	200	350	500	1,000	—

KM# 83.2   REAL
3.3800 g., 0.9030 Silver 0.0981 oz. ASW   **Ruler:**
Ferdinand VII **Obv:** Draped laureate bust right **Obv.**
Legend: FERDIN.VII... **Rev:** Crowned shield flanked
by pillars **Rev. Legend:** IND.REX...

Date	Mintage	VG	F	VF	XF	Unc
1813GA MR	—	300	500	800	—	—
1814GA MR	—	150	200	350	650	—
1815GA MR	—	300	500	800	—	—

KM# 93.2   2 REALES
6.7700 g., 0.9030 Silver 0.1965 oz. ASW   **Ruler:**
Ferdinand VII **Obv:** Draped laureate bust right **Obv.**
Legend: FERDIN.VII... **Rev:** Crowned shield flanked
by pillars **Rev. Legend:** IND.REX....

Date	Mintage	VG	F	VF	XF	Unc
1812GA MR	—	300	500	800	2,500	—
1814/2GA MR	—	75.00	125	250	600	—
1814GA MR	—	75.00	125	250	600	—
1815/4GA MR	—	425	725	1,100	3,600	—
1815GA MR	—	400	700	1,000	3,500	—
1821GA FS	—	200	250	350	900	—

KM# 102.2   4 REALES
13.5400 g., 0.9030 Silver 0.3931 oz. ASW **Ruler:**
Ferdinand VII **Obv:** Draped laureate bust right **Obv.**
Legend: FERDIN.VII... **Rev:** Crowned shield flanked
by pillars **Rev. Legend:** IND.REX...

Date	Mintage	VG	F	VF	XF	Unc
1814GA MR	—	40.00	65.00	150	250	—
1815GA MR	—	80.00	150	300	500	—

KM# 102.3   4 REALES
13.5400 g., 0.9030 Silver 0.3931 oz. ASW **Ruler:**
Ferdinand VII **Obv:** Draped laureate bust right **Obv.**
Legend: FERDIN.VII... **Rev:** Crowned shield flanked
by pillars **Rev. Legend:** IND.REX...

Date	Mintage	VG	F	VF	XF	Unc
1814GA MR	—	50.00	100	200	400	—

KM# 102.4   4 REALES
13.5400 g., 0.9030 Silver 0.3931 oz. ASW **Ruler:**
Ferdinand VII **Obv:** Draped laureate bust right **Obv.**
Legend: FERDIN.VII... **Rev:** Crowned shield flanked
by pillars **Rev. Legend:** IND.REX...

Date	Mintage	VG	F	VF	XF	Unc
1814GA MR	—	60.00	120	250	450	—

KM# 111.3   8 REALES
27.0700 g., 0.9030 Silver 0.7859 oz. ASW **Ruler:**
Ferdinand VII **Obv:** Draped laureate bust right **Obv.**
Legend: FERDIN.VII... **Rev:** Crowned shield flanked
by pillars **Rev. Legend:** IND.REX...

Date	Mintage	VG	F	VF	XF	Unc
1812GA MR	—	2,000	3,500	5,000	7,000	—
1813/2GA MR	—	60.00	100	150	400	—
1813GA MR	—	60.00	100	150	400	—
1814GA MR	—	20.00	35.00	60.00	180	—
Note: Several bust varieties exist for the 1814 issue						
1815GA MR	—	150	200	350	750	—
1818GA FS	—	30.00	50.00	75.00	200	—
1821/18GA FS	—	30.00	50.00	75.00	200	—
1821GA FS	—	25.00	35.00	60.00	165	—
1821/2GA FS	—	30.00	50.00	75.00	200	—
1822/1GA FS	—	30.00	50.00	75.00	200	—
1822GA FS	—	30.00	50.00	75.00	200	—

Note: Die varieties exist. Early dates are also encountered
struck over other types

KM# 147   4 ESCUDOS
13.5400 g., 0.8750 Gold 0.3809 oz. AGW **Ruler:**
Ferdinand VII **Obv:** Uniformed bust right **Rev:**
Crowned shield divides designed wreath

Date	Mintage	VG	F	VF	XF	Unc
1812GA MR Rare	—	—	—	—	—	—

KM# 162   8 ESCUDOS
27.0700 g., 0.8750 Gold 0.7615 oz. AGW **Ruler:**
Ferdinand VII **Obv:** Large uniformed bust right **Obv.**
Legend: FERDIN.VII.D.G... **Rev:** Crowned shield
divides designed wreath **Rev. Legend:**
UTROQ.FELIX...

Date	Mintage	VG	F	VF	XF	Unc
1812GA MR Rare	—	—	—	—	—	—
1813GA MR	—	600	900	15,000	25,000	—

Note: American Numismatic Rarities Eliasberg sale 4-05,
VF-30 realized $23,000.

KM# 163   8 ESCUDOS
27.0700 g., 0.8750 Gold 0.7615 oz. AGW   **Ruler:**
Ferdinand VII **Obv:** Small uniformed bust right **Obv.**
Legend: FERDIN.VII... **Rev:** Crowned shield divides
designed wreath **Rev. Legend:** UTROQ.FELIX...

Date	Mintage	VG	F	VF	XF	Unc
1813GA MR	—	10,000	16,000	30,000	45,000	—

Note: Spink America Gerber sale 6-96 VF or better realized
$46,200

KM# 161.1   8 ESCUDOS
27.0700 g., 0.8750 Gold 0.7615 oz. AGW   **Ruler:**
Ferdinand VII **Obv:** Laureate head right **Obv.**
Legend: FERDIN.VII.D.G... **Rev:** Crowned shield
divides designed wreath **Rev. Legend:**
UTROQ.FELIX...

Date	Mintage	VG	F	VF	XF	Unc
1821GA FS	—	1,500	2,500	5,000	8,500	—

Note: American Numismatic Rarities Eliasberg sale 4-05,
AU-55 realized $20,700.

KM# 164   8 ESCUDOS
27.0700 g., 0.8750 Gold 0.7615 oz. AGW   **Ruler:**
Ferdinand VII **Obv:** Draped laureate bust right **Rev:**
Crowned shield flanked by pillars

Date	Mintage	VG	F	VF	XF	Unc
1821GA FS	—	5,500	8,000	14,500	23,500	—

GUANAJUATO

The Guanajuato Mint was authorized December 24, 1812 and started production shortly thereafter; closing for unknown reasons on May 15, 1813.
The mint was reopened in April, 1821 by the insurgents, who struck coins of the old royal Spanish
design to pay their army, even after independence,
well into 1822.
Only the 2 and 8 Reales coins were made.
Mint mark: Go.

ROYALIST COINAGE

KM# 93.3   2 REALES
6.7700 g., 0.9030 Silver 0.1965 oz. ASW   **Ruler:**
Ferdinand VII **Obv:** Draped laureate bust right **Obv.**
Legend: FERDIN.VII... **Rev:** Crowned shield flanked
bu pillars **Rev. Legend:** IND.REX...

Date	Mintage	VG	F	VF	XF	Unc
1821Go JM	—	35.00	65.00	100	185	—
1822Go JM	—	30.00	50.00	75.00	145	—

KM# 111.4   8 REALES
27.0700 g., 0.9030 Silver 0.7859 oz. ASW   **Ruler:**
Ferdinand VII **Obv:** Draped laureate bust right **Obv.**
Legend: FERDIN.VII... **Rev:** Crowned shield flanked
by pillars **Rev. Legend:** IND.REX...

Date	Mintage	VG	F	VF	XF	Unc
1812Go JJ	—	3,000	5,000	—	—	—
1813Go JJ	—	125	175	275	600	—
1821Go JM	—	25.00	50.00	75.00	200	—
1822Go JM	—	20.00	35.00	60.00	185	—

NUEVA GALICIA

(Later became Jalisco State)

In early colonial times, Nueva Galicia was an extensive province which substantially combined later provinces of Zacatecas and Jalisco. These are states of Mexico today although the name was revived during the War of Independence. The only issue was 2 Reales of rather enigmatic origin. No decrees or other authorization to strike this coin has yet been located or reported.

INSURGENT COINAGE

KM# 218   2 REALES
0.9030 Silver **Obv:** N. G. in center, date **Obv. Legend:** PROVYCIONAL... **Rev:** 2R in center **Rev. Legend:** ... A. JUNIANA...

Date	Mintage	Good	VG	F	VF	XF
1813	—	1,000	2,500	4,500	—	—

Note: Excellent struck counterfeits exist

NUEVA VISCAYA

(Later became Durango State)

This 8 Reales, intended for the province of Nueva Viscaya, was minted in the newly-opened Durango Mint during February and March of 1811, before the regular coinage of Durango was started.

ROYALIST COINAGE

KM# 181   8 REALES
27.0700 g., 0.9030 Silver 0.7859 oz. ASW **Ruler:** Ferdinand VII **Obv:** Crowned shield within sprays **Obv. Legend:** MON. PROV. DE NUEV. VIZCAYA **Rev:** Crowned shield flanked by pillars

Date	Mintage	Good	VG	F	VF	XF
1811 RM	—	1,000	2,250	2,850	5,500	—

Note: Several varieties exist.

OAXACA

The city of Oaxaca was in the midst of a coin shortage when it became apparent the city would be taken by the Insurgents. Royalist forces under Lt. Gen. Saravia had coins made. They were cast in a blacksmith shop. 1/2, 1, and 8 Reales were made only briefly in 1812 before the Royalists surrendered the city.

ROYALIST COINAGE

KM# 166   1/2 REAL
0.9030 Silver **Ruler:** Ferdinand VII **Obv:** Cross separating castle, lion, Fo, 7o **Rev:** Legend around shield **Rev. Legend:** PROV. D. OAXACA

Date	Mintage	Good	VG	F	VF	XF
1812	—	1,000	1,500	2,500	3,500	—

KM# 167   REAL
0.9030 Silver **Ruler:** Ferdinand VII **Obv:** Cross separating castle, lion, Fo, 7o **Rev:** Legend around shield **Rev. Legend:** PROV. D. OAXACA

Date	Mintage	Good	VG	F	VF	XF
1812	—	350	650	1,200	2,500	—

KM# 168   8 REALES
0.9030 Silver **Obv:** Cross separating castle, lion, Fo, 7o **Obv. Legend:** OAXACA 1812... **Rev:** Shield, authorization mark above **Note:** These issues usually display a second mark 'O' between the

crowned pillars on the obverse. Varieties of large and small lion in shield also exist.

Date	Mintage	Good	VG	F	VF	XF
1812 "A"	—	1,300	1,900	3,300	5,500	—
1812 "B"	—	1,300	1,900	3,300	5,500	—
1812 "C"	—	1,300	1,900	3,300	5,500	—
1812 "D"	—	1,300	1,900	3,300	5,500	—
1812 "K"	—	1,300	1,900	3,300	5,500	—
1812 "L"	—	1,300	1,900	3,300	5,500	—
1812 "Mo"	—	1,300	1,900	3,300	5,500	—
1812 "N"	—	1,300	1,900	3,300	5,500	—
1812 "O"	—	1,300	1,900	3,300	5,500	—
1812 "R"	—	1,300	1,900	3,300	5,500	—
1812 "V"	—	1,300	1,900	3,300	5,500	—
1812 "Z"	—	1,300	1,900	3,300	5,500	—

INSURGENT COINAGE

Oaxaca was the hub of Insurgent activity in the south where coinage started in July 1811 and continued until October 1814. The Oaxaca issues represent episodic strikings, usually under dire circumstances by various individuals. Coins were commonly made of copper due to urgency and were intended to be redeemed at face value in gold or silver once silver was available to the Insurgents. Some were later made in silver, but most appear to be of more recent origin, to satisfy collectors.

KM# 219 1/2 REAL
Struck Copper **Issuer:** SUD, Under General Morelos **Obv:** Bow, arrow, SUD **Rev:** Morelos monogram Mo, date

Date	Mintage	Good	VG	F	VF	XF
1811	—	6.75	11.50	20.00	35.00	—
1812	—	6.75	11.50	20.00	35.00	—
1813	—	5.50	9.00	17.50	30.00	—
1814	—	9.00	16.50	25.00	40.00	—

Note: Uniface strikes exist of #219

KM# 220.1 1/2 REAL
Struck Silver **Issuer:** SUD, Under General Morelos **Obv:** Bow, arrow, SUD **Rev:** Morelos monogram Mo, date

Date	Mintage	Good	VG	F	VF	XF
1811	—	—	—	—	—	—
1812	—	—	—	—	—	—
1813	—	—	—	—	—	—

KM# 220.2 1/2 REAL
Struck Silver **Issuer:** SUD, Under General Morelos **Obv:** Bow, arrow, SUD **Rev:** Morelos monogram Mo, date

Date	Mintage	Good	VG	F	VF	XF
1811	—	—	—	—	—	—
1812	—	—	—	—	—	—
1813	—	25.00	50.00	100	150	—

Note: Use caution as silver specimens appear questionable and may be considered spurious

KM# 221 1/2 REAL
Struck Silver **Issuer:** SUD, Under General Morelos **Obv:** Bow, arrow **Obv. Legend:** PROVICIONAL DE OAXACA **Rev:** Lion **Rev. Legend:** AMERICA MORELOS

Date	Mintage	Good	VG	F	VF	XF
1812	—	35.00	60.00	100	150	—
1813	—	35.00	60.00	100	150	—

KM# 221a 1/2 REAL
Struck Copper **Issuer:** SUD, Under General Morelos **Obv:** Bow, arrow **Obv. Legend:** PROVICIONAL DE OAXACA **Rev:** Lion **Rev. Legend:** AMERICA MORELOS

Date	Mintage	Good	VG	F	VF	XF
1812	—	27.50	42.50	70.00	100	—
1813	—	20.00	35.00	60.00	85.00	—

KM# A222 1/2 REAL
Struck Copper **Issuer:** SUD, Under General Morelos **Obv:** Similar to KM#220 **Rev:** Similar to KM#221 but with 1/2 at left of lion **Rev. Legend:** AMERICA MORELOS

Date	Mintage	Good	VG	F	VF	XF
1813	—	27.50	42.50	70.00	100	—

KM# 243 1/2 REAL
Struck Copper **Issuer:** Tierra Caliente (Hot Country), Under General Morelos **Obv:** Bow, T.C., SUD **Rev:** Morelos monogram, value, date

Date	Mintage	Good	VG	F	VF	XF
1813	—	37.50	70.00	125	200	—

KM# 222 REAL
Struck Copper **Issuer:** SUD, Under General Morelos **Obv:** Bow, arrow, SUD **Rev:** Morelos monogram, 1 R., date

Date	Mintage	Good	VG	F	VF	XF
1811	—	4.75	9.00	18.00	38.00	—
1812	—	3.75	7.00	14.00	30.00	—
1813	—	3.75	7.00	14.00	30.00	—

KM# 222a REAL
Struck Silver **Issuer:** SUD, Under General Morelos **Obv:** Bow, arrow, SUD **Rev:** Morelos monogram, 1 R., date

Date	Mintage	Good	VG	F	VF	XF
1812	—	—	—	—	—	—
1813	—	—	—	—	—	—

KM# 223   REAL
Cast Silver **Issuer:** SUD, Under General Morelos
Obv: Bow, arrow, SUD with floral ornaments **Rev:**
Morelos monogram, 1 R., date

Date	Mintage	Good	VG	F	VF	XF
1812	—	—	—	—	—	—
1813	—	27.50	60.00	115	160	—

Note: Use caution as many silver specimens appear questionable and may be considered spurious

KM# 224   REAL
Struck Copper **Issuer:** SUD, Under General Morelos
Obv: Bow, arrow/SUD **Rev:** Lion **Rev. Legend:**
AMERICA MORELOS

Date	Mintage	Good	VG	F	VF	XF
1813	—	27.50	42.50	75.00	110	—

KM# 225   REAL
Silver **Issuer:** SUD, Under General Morelos **Obv:**
Bow, arrow/SUD **Rev:** Lion **Rev. Legend:** AMERICA
MORELOS

Date	Mintage	Good	VG	F	VF	XF
1813 Rare	—	—	—	—	—	—

KM# 244   REAL
Struck Copper **Issuer:** Tierra Caliente (Hot
Country), Under General Morelos **Obv:** Bow, T.C.,
SUD **Rev:** Morelos monogram, value, date

Date	Mintage	Good	VG	F	VF	XF
1813	—	13.50	25.00	50.00	80.00	—

KM# 226.1   2 REALES
Struck Copper **Issuer:** SUD, Under General Morelos
Obv: Bow, arrow/SUD **Rev:** Morelos monogram,
.2.R., date

Date	Mintage	Good	VG	F	VF	XF
1811	—	12.50	25.00	55.00	100	—
1811 inverted 2	—	15.00	30.00	60.00	120	—
1812	—	2.50	4.00	6.50	12.00	—
1813	—	3.00	5.00	8.00	15.00	—
1814	—	13.50	28.00	65.00	120	—

KM# 226.1a   2 REALES
Struck Silver **Issuer:** SUD, Under General Morelos
Obv: Bow, arrow/SUD **Rev:** Morelos monogram,
.2.R., date

Date	Mintage	Good	VG	F	VF	XF
1812	—	175	300	500	750	—

KM# 229   2 REALES
Cast Silver **Issuer:** SUD, Under General Morelos
Obv: Bow, arrow, SUD **Rev:** Morelos monogram,
value, date in center with ornamentation around

Date	Mintage	Good	VG	F	VF	XF
1812 Filled in D in SUD	—	60.00	100	150	225	—

Note: Use caution as many silver specimens appear questionable and may be considered spurious

Date	Mintage	Good	VG	F	VF	XF
1812	—	60.00	100	150	225	—

KM# 245   2 REALES
Struck Copper **Issuer:** Tierra Caliente (Hot
Country), Under General Morelos **Obv:** Bow, T.C.,
SUD **Rev:** Morelos monogram, value, date

Date	Mintage	Good	VG	F	VF	XF
1813	—	9.00	22.50	35.00	50.00	—

KM# 227   2 REALES
Struck Silver **Issuer:** SUD, Under General Morelos
Obv: Bow, arrow **Obv. Legend:** SUD-OXA **Rev:**
Morelos monogram, value, date

Date	Mintage	Good	VG	F	VF	XF
1813	—	60.00	100	200	300	—
1814	—	60.00	100	200	300	—

KM# 228   2 REALES
Struck Silver **Issuer:** SUD, Under General Morelos
Obv: Bow, arrow **Obv. Legend:** SUD. OAXACA
Rev: Morelos monogram, value, date

Date	Mintage	Good	VG	F	VF	XF
1814	—	60.00	100	200	325	—

KM# 226.2   2 REALES
Struck Silver **Issuer:** SUD, Under General Morelos
Obv: Three large stars added **Rev:** Morelos
monogram, .2.R., date

Date	Mintage	Good	VG	F	VF	XF
1814	—	10.00	20.00	40.00	60.00	—

KM# 246   2 REALES
Struck Copper **Issuer:** Tierra Caliente (Hot
Country), Under General Morelos **Obv:** Bow, T.C.,
SUD **Rev:** Morelos monogram, value, date

Date	Mintage	Good	VG	F	VF	XF
1814	—	22.50	50.00	100	175	—

KM# 234 8 REALES
Copper **Issuer:** SUD, Under General Morelos **Obv:** Bow, arrow, SUD in floral ornamentation **Rev:** Morelos monogram, .8.R., date surrounded by ornate flowery fields

Date	Mintage	Good	VG	F	VF	XF
1811	—	75.00	125	150	225	—
1812	—	4.00	6.00	10.00	20.00	—
1813	—	4.00	6.00	10.00	20.00	—
1814	—	10.00	15.00	25.00	50.00	—

KM# 234a 8 REALES
Struck Silver **Issuer:** SUD, under General Morelos **Obv:** Bow, arrow, SUD in floral ornamentation **Rev:** Morelos monogram, .8.R., date surrounded by ornate flowery fields

Date	Mintage	Good	VG	F	VF	XF
1811	—	—	—	2,500	4,000	—
1812	—	—	—	1,200	2,000	—

KM# 235 8 REALES
Cast Silver **Issuer:** SUD, Under General Morelos **Obv:** Bow, arrow, SUD in floral ornamentation **Rev:** Morelos monogram, value, date surrounded by ornate flowery fields

Date	Mintage	Good	VG	F	VF	XF
1811	—	—	—	—	—	—
1812	—	75.00	125	200	350	—
1813	—	60.00	100	175	300	—
1814	—	—	—	—	—	—

Note: Most silver specimens available in today's market are considered spurious

KM# 233.5a 8 REALES
Silver **Issuer:** SUD, Under General Morelos **Obv:** 8 dots below bow, SUD, plain fields **Rev:** Morelos monogram, 8.R., date

Date	Mintage	Good	VG	F	VF	XF
1812	—	—	—	1,200	2,000	—

KM# 236 8 REALES
0.9030 Struck Silver **Issuer:** SUD, Under General Morelos **Obv:** M monogram **Obv. Legend:** PROV. D. OAXACA **Rev:** Lion shield with or without bow above

Date	Mintage	Good	VG	F	VF	XF
1812 Rare	—	—	—	—	—	—

KM# 233.1   8 REALES
Copper **Issuer:** SUD, Under General Morelos **Obv:**
Bow, arrow, SUD **Rev:** Morelos monogram, 8.R.,
date, plain fields

Date	Mintage	Good	VG	F	VF	XF
1812	—	15.00	30.00	60.00	90.00	—

KM# 233.1a   8 REALES
Struck Silver **Issuer:** SUD, Under General Morelos
Obv: Bow, arrow, SUD **Rev:** Morelos monogram,
8.R., date, plain fields

Date	Mintage	Good	VG	F	VF	XF
1812	—	100	150	250	450	—

KM# 233.2   8 REALES
Copper **Issuer:** SUD, Under General Morelos **Obv:**
Bow, arrow, SUD **Rev:** Morelos monogram, 8 R,
date, plain fields

Date	Mintage	Good	VG	F	VF	XF
1812	—	6.00	8.00	12.00	15.00	—
1813	—	6.00	8.00	12.00	15.00	—
1814	—	10.00	12.00	15.00	20.00	—

Note: Similar to KM#233.4 but lines below bow slant left

KM# 242   8 REALES
Copper **Issuer:** Huautla, Under General Morelos

Obv: Legend around bow, arrow/SUD **Obv. Legend:**
MONEDA PROVI. CIONAL PS. ES. **Rev. Legend:**
FABRICADO EN HUAUTLA

Date	Mintage	Good	VG	F	VF	XF
1812	—	1,000	1,500	2,000	—	—

KM# 248   8 REALES
Struck Copper **Issuer:** Tierra Caliente (Hot
Country), Under General Morelos **Obv:** Bow, T.C.,
SUD **Rev:** Morelos monogram, value, date

Date	Mintage	Good	VG	F	VF	XF
1813	—	9.00	20.00	40.00	75.00	—

KM# 249   8 REALES
Cast Silver **Issuer:** Tierra Caliente (Hot Country),
Under General Morelos **Obv:** Bow, T.C., SUD **Rev:**
Morelos monogram, value, date

Date	Mintage	Good	VG	F	VF	XF
1813	—	—	—	—	—	—

Note: Use caution as many silver specimens appear questionable and may be considered spurious

KM# 233.2a   8 REALES
Silver **Issuer:** SUD, Under General Morelos **Obv:**
bow, arrow, SUD **Rev:** Morelos monogram, 8R, date,
plain fields

Date	Mintage	Good	VG	F	VF	XF
1813	—	—	—	1,200	2,000	—

KM# 233.3   8 REALES
Struck Copper **Issuer:** SUD, Under General Morelos
Obv: Bow, arrow, SUD, with left slant lines below
bow **Rev:** Morelos monogram, 8.R., date, plain fields

Date	Mintage	Good	VG	F	VF	XF
1813	—	10.00	17.50	30.00	50.00	—

KM# 233.4   8 REALES
Struck Copper **Issuer:** SUD, Under General Morelos
Obv: Bow, arrow, SUD, with right slant lines below
bow **Rev:** Morelos monogram, 8.R., date, plain fields

Date	Mintage	Good	VG	F	VF	XF
1813	—	10.00	17.50	30.00	50.00	—

KM# 237   8 REALES
0.9030 Sterling Silver **Issuer:** SUD, Under General
Morelos **Obv:** M monogram, without legend **Rev:**
Lion shield with or without bow above

Date	Mintage	Good	VG	F	VF	XF
1813 Rare	—	—	—	—	—	—

KM# 238   8 REALES
0.9030 Struck Silver **Issuer:** SUD, Under General
Morelos **Obv:** Bow/M/SUD **Rev:** PROV. DE. ... arms

Date	Mintage	Good	VG	F	VF	XF
1813 Rare	—	—	—	—	—	—

KM# 239   8 REALES
Cast Silver **Issuer:** SUD, Under General Morelos
Obv: Bow, arrow **Obv. Legend:** SUD-OXA **Rev:**
Morelos monogram

Date	Mintage	Good	VG	F	VF	XF
1814 Rare	—	—	—	—	—	—

KM# 240   8 REALES
Copper **Issuer:** SUD, Under General Morelos **Obv:**
Bow, arrow **Obv. Legend:** SUD-OXA **Rev:** Morelos
monogram, 8.R., date

Date	Mintage	Good	VG	F	VF	XF
1814	—	35.00	70.00	150	250	—

KM# 241   8 REALES
Copper **Issuer:** SUD, Under General Morelos **Obv:**
Bow, arrow **Obv. Legend:** SUD-OAXACA **Rev:**
Morelos monogram, 8.R., date

Date	Mintage	Good	VG	F	VF	XF
1814	—	100	200	350	550	—

PUEBLA

INSURGENT COINAGE

KM# 250   1/2 REAL
Copper **Issuer:** Zacatlan, struck by General Osorno
Obv: Osorno monogram, ZACATLAN, date **Rev:**
Crossed arrows, wreath, value

Date	Mintage	Good	VG	F	VF	XF
1813 Rare	—	—	—	—	—	—

KM# 251   REAL
Copper **Issuer:** Zacatlan, struck by General Osorno
Obv: Osorno monogram, ZACATLAN, date **Rev:**
Crossed arrows, wreath, value

Date	Mintage	Good	VG	F	VF	XF
1813	—	100	150	225	450	—

KM# 252   2 REALES
Copper **Issuer:** Zacatlan, struck by General Osorno
Obv: Osorno monogram, ZACATLAN, date **Rev:**
Crossed arrows, wreath, value

Date	Mintage	Good	VG	F	VF	XF
1813	—	125	175	275	500	—

WAR OF INDEPENDENCE

REAL DEL CATORCE

(City in San Luis Potosi)

Real del Catorce is an important mining center in the Province of San Luis Potosi. In 1811 an 8 Reales coin was issued under very primitive conditions while the city was still in Royalist hands. Few survive.

ROYALIST COINAGE

KM# 169   8 REALES
0.9030 Silver **Ruler:** Ferdinand VII **Obv. Legend:** EL R. D. CATORC. POR FERNA. VII **Rev. Legend:** MONEDA. PROVISIONAL. VALE. 8R

Date	Mintage	VG	F	VF	XF	Unc
1811	—	7,000	15,000	35,000	65,000	—

Note: Spink America Gerber Sale 6-96 VF or XF realized $63,800

SAN FERNANDO DE BEXAR

TOKEN COINAGE

KM# Tn1   1/2 REAL (Jola)
Copper **Ruler:** Ferdinand VII **Note:** Prev. KM#170.

Date	Mintage	Good	VG	F	VF	XF
1818	8,000	—	—	—	25,000	30,000

KM# Tn2   1/2 REAL (Jola)
Copper **Ruler:** Ferdinand VII **Note:** Prev. KM#171.

Date	Mintage	Good	VG	F	VF	XF
1818	Inc. above	—	—	—	22,500	27,500

SAN LUIS POTOSI

Sierra de Pinos

ROYALIST COINAGE

KM# A172   1/4 REAL
Copper **Ruler:** Ferdinand VII **Issuer:** Sierra de Pinos, Villa

Date	Mintage	Good	VG	F	VF	XF
1814	—	75.00	125	200	350	—

KM# A172a   1/4 REAL
Silver **Ruler:** Ferdinand VII

Date	Mintage	Good	VG	F	VF	XF
1814 Rare	—	—	—	—	—	—

SOMBRERETE

(Under Royalist Vargas)

The Sombrerete Mint opened on October 8, 1810 in an area that boasted some of the richest mines in Mexico. The mint operated only until July 16, 1811, only to reopen in 1812 and finally close for good at the end of the year. Mines Administrator Fernando Vargas, was also in charge of the coining, all coins bear his name.

ROYALIST COINAGE

KM# 172   1/2 REAL
0.9030 Silver **Ruler:** Ferdinand VII **Obv:** Legend around crowned globes **Obv. Legend:** FERDIN. VII. SOMBRERETE... **Rev:** Legend above lys in oval, sprays, date below **Rev. Legend:** VARGAS

Date	Mintage	Good	VG	F	VF	XF
1811	—	45.00	70.00	150	250	—
1812	—	50.00	90.00	175	275	—

KM# 173 REAL
0.9030 Silver **Ruler:** Ferdinand VII **Obv:** Legend around crowned globes **Obv. Legend:** FERDIN. VII. SOMBRERETE... **Rev:** Legend above lys in oval with denomination flanking, sprays, date below **Rev. Legend:** VARGAS

Date	Mintage	Good	VG	F	VF	XF
1811	—	45.00	70.00	150	250	—

Note: For 1811, denomination reads as '1R' or 'R1'

Date	Mintage	Good	VG	F	VF	XF
1812	—	50.00	90.00	175	275	—

KM# 174 2 REALES
0.9030 Silver **Ruler:** Ferdinand VII **Countermark:** VARGAS **Obv:** Royal arms **Obv. Legend:** R.CAXA. DE. SOMBRERETE **Rev:** 1811, S between crowned pillars

Date	Mintage	Good	VG	F	VF	XF
1811 SE	—	100	250	450	700	—

KM# 175 4 REALES
0.9030 Silver **Ruler:** Ferdinand VII **Obv:** Crowned Royal arms **Obv. Legend:** R. CAXA. DE. SOMBRERETE **Rev:** Large legend **Rev. Legend:** VARGAS/1812 **Note:** Prev. KM#172.

Date	Mintage	Good	VG	F	VF	XF
1812	—	50.00	100	200	450	—

KM# 176 8 REALES
0.9030 Silver **Ruler:** Ferdinand VII **Countermark:** VARGAS, date, S **Obv:** Royal arms **Obv. Legend:** R. CAXA. DE SOMBRERETE **Rev:** Several countermarks between crowned pillars

Date	Mintage	Good	VG	F	VF	XF
1810	—	1,000	1,750	2,750	4,000	—
1811	—	225	325	450	600	—

KM# 177 8 REALES
0.9030 Silver **Ruler:** Ferdinand VII **Obv:** Crowned Royal arms **Obv. Legend:** R. CAXA. DE SOMBRETE **Rev. Legend:** VARGAS/date/3, S between crowned pillars

Date	Mintage	Good	VG	F	VF	XF
1811	—	125	185	245	500	—
1812	—	125	175	225	475	—

VALLADOLID MICHOACAN

ROYALIST COINAGE

KM# 178 8 REALES
0.9030 Silver **Ruler:** Ferdinand VII **Obv:** Royal arms in wreath, value at sides **Rev:** PROVISIONAL/DE VALLADOLID/1813

Date	Mintage	Good	VG	F	VF	XF
1813 Rare	—	—	—	—	—	—

KM# 179 8 REALES
0.9030 Silver **Ruler:** Ferdinand VII **Obv:** Draped laureate bust right **Obv. Legend:** FERDIN. VII. **Rev:** Crowned shield flanked by pillars, P. D. V. in legend **Rev. Legend:** REX.P.D.V...

Date	Mintage	Good	VG	F	VF	XF
1813 Rare	—	—	—	—	—	—

Note: Spink America Gerber sale 6-96 good realized $23,100

VERACRUZ

In Zongolica, in the province of Veracruz, 2 priests and a lawyer decided to raise an army to fight for independence. Due to isolation from other Insurgent forces, they decided to make their own coins. Records show that they intended to mint coins of 1/2, 1, 2, 4, and 8 Reales, but specimens are extant of only the three higher denominations.

INSURGENT COINAGE

KM# 253   2 REALES
0.9030 Silver **Issuer:** Zongolica **Obv:** Bow and arrow **Obv. Legend:** VIVA FERNANDO VII Y AMERICA **Rev:** Value, crossed palm branch, sword, date **Rev. Legend:** ZONGOLICA

Date	Mintage	Good	VG	F	VF	XF
1812	—	85.00	175	300	500	—

KM# 255   8 REALES
0.9030 Silver **Issuer:** Zongolica **Obv:** Bow and arrow **Obv. Legend:** VIVA FERNANDO VII Y AMERICA **Rev:** Value, crossed palm branch, sword, date **Rev. Legend:** ZONGOLICA **Note:** Similar to 2 Reales, KM#253.

Date	Mintage	Good	VG	F	VF	XF
1812 Rare	—	—	—	—	—	—

Note: Spink America Gerber sale 6-96 VF to XF realized $57,200

INSURGENT COUNTERMARKED COINAGE

CONGRESS OF CHILPANZINGO

Type A: Hand holding bow and arrow between quiver with arrows, sword and bow.

Type B: Crowned eagle on bridge.

KM# 256.1   1/2 REAL
Silver **Issuer:** Congress of Chilpanzingo **Countermark:** Type A hand holding bow and arrow between quiver with arrows, sword and bow **Note:** Countermark on cast Mexico City KM#72.

CM Date	Host Date	Good	VG	F	VF	XF
ND	1812	42.50	70.00	90.00	120	—

KM# 256.2   1/2 REAL
Silver **Issuer:** Congress of Chilpanzingo **Countermark:** Type A hand holding bow and arrow between quiver with arrows, sword and bow **Note:** Countermark on Zacatecas KM#181.

CM Date	Host Date	Good	VG	F	VF	XF
ND	1811	50.00	75.00	100	125	—

KM# A257   REAL
Cast Silver **Issuer:** Congress of Chilpanzingo **Countermark:** Type A hand holding bow and arrow between quiver with arrows, sword and bow **Note:** Countermark on cast Mexico City KM#81.

CM Date	Host Date	Good	VG	F	VF	XF
ND	1803	18.50	30.00	50.00	80.00	—

KM# 257.1   2 REALES
Silver **Issuer:** Congress of Chilpanzingo **Countermark:** Type B crowned eagle on bridge **Note:** Countermark on 1/4 cut of 8 Reales.

CM Date	Host Date	Good	VG	F	VF	XF
ND Unique	—	—	—	—	—	—

KM# 257.2   2 REALES
Silver   **Issuer:** Congress of Chilpanzingo
Countermark: Type B crowned eagle on bridge
Note: Countermark on Zacatecas KM#186.

CM Date	Host Date	Good	VG	F	VF	XF
ND	1811 Unique	—	—	—	—	—

KM# 258.1   8 REALES
Silver   **Issuer:** Congress of Chilpanzingo
Countermark: Type A hand holding bow and arrow
between quiver with arrows, sword and bow **Note:**
Countermark on cast Mexico City KM#109.

CM Date	Host Date	Good	VG	F	VF	XF
ND	1805	45.00	65.00	85.00	125	—

Note: A countermark appears on coins dated 1805 TH

KM# 258.2   8 REALES
Silver   **Issuer:** Congress of Chilpanzingo
Countermark: Type A hand holding bow and arrow
between quiver with arrows, sword and bow **Note:**
Countermark on cast Mexico City KM#110.

CM Date	Host Date	Good	VG	F	VF	XF
ND	1810 HJ	50.00	75.00	100	150	—

KM# 258.3   8 REALES
Silver   **Issuer:** Congress of Chilpanzingo
Countermark: Type A hand holding bow and arrow
between quiver with arrows, sword and bow **Note:**
Countermark on cast Mexico City KM#111.

CM Date	Host Date	Good	VG	F	VF	XF
ND	1811 HJ	45.00	65.00	85.00	125	—
ND	1812 HJ	100	125	175	275	—

KM# 259.1   8 REALES
Silver   **Issuer:** Congress of Chilpanzingo
Countermark: Type B crowned eagle on bridge
Note: Countermark on Chihuahua KM#111.1.

CM Date	Host Date	Good	VG	F	VF	XF
ND	1816 RP	200	250	300	350	—

KM# 259.2   8 REALES
Silver   **Issuer:** Congress of Chilpanzingo
Countermark: Type B crowned eagle on bridge
Note: Countermark on cast Mexico City KM#111.

CM Date	Host Date	Good	VG	F	VF	XF
ND	1811 HJ	130	140	150	175	—

KM# 259.3   8 REALES
Silver   **Issuer:** Congress of Chilpanzingo
Countermark: Type B crowned eagle on bridge
Note: Countermark on Valladolid KM#178.

CM Date	Host Date	Good	VG	F	VF	XF
ND	1813	1,000	2,000	3,000	5,000	—

KM# 259.4   8 REALES
Silver   **Issuer:** Congress of Chilpanzingo
Countermark: Type B crowned eagle on bridge
Note: Countermark on Zacatecas KM#190.

CM Date	Host Date	Good	VG	F	VF	XF
ND	1810	400	500	600	750	—

DON JOSE MARIA DE LINARES

KM# 263.1   8 REALES
Silver   **Issuer:** Don Jose Maria De Linares
Countermark: LINA/RES* **Note:** Countermark on
Mexico City KM#110.

CM Date	Host Date	Good	VG	F	VF	XF
ND	1808 TH	250	300	375	500	—

KM# 263.2   8 REALES
Silver **Issuer:** Don Jose Maria De Linares
Countermark: LINA/RES * **Note:** Countermark on
Zacatecas KM#190.

CM Date	Host Date	Good	VG	F	VF	XF
ND	1811	300	375	450	575	—

KM# 263.3   8 REALES
Silver **Issuer:** Don Jose Maria De Linares
Countermark: LINA/RES* **Note:** Countermark on
Zacatecas KM#191.

CM Date	Host Date	Good	VG	F	VF	XF
ND	1812	250	300	375	500	—

GENERAL VICENTE GUERRERO

The countermark of an eagle facing left within a
pearled oval has been attributed by some authors as
that of General Vicente Guerrero, a leader of the
insurgents in the south, 1816-1821.

KM# 276   1/2 REAL
Silver **Issuer:** General Vicente Guerrero
Countermark: Eagle **Note:** Countermark on Mexico
City KM#72.

CM Date	Host Date	Good	VG	F	VF	XF
ND	ND	40.00	60.00	80.00	175	—

KM# 277   REAL
Silver **Issuer:** General Vicente Guerrero
Countermark: Eagle **Note:** Countermark on Mexico
City KM#78.

CM Date	Host Date	Good	VG	F	VF	XF
ND	1772 FM	35.00	50.00	75.00	165	—

KM# 278.1   2 REALES
Silver **Issuer:** General Vicente Guerrero
Countermark: Eagle **Note:** Countermark on Mexico
City KM#88.

CM Date	Host Date	Good	VG	F	VF	XF
ND	1784 FM	40.00	60.00	100	225	—
ND	1798	40.00	60.00	100	225	—

KM# 278.2   2 REALES
Silver **Issuer:** General Vicente Guerrero
Countermark: Eagle **Note:** Countermark on Mexico
City KM#91.

CM Date	Host Date	Good	VG	F	VF	XF
ND	1807 PJ	30.00	50.00	80.00	200	—

KM# 279   8 REALES
Silver **Issuer:** General Vicente Guerrero
Countermark: Eagle **Note:** Countermark on
Zacatecas KM#191.

CM Date	Host Date	Good	VG	F	VF	XF
ND	1811	100	150	200	350	—

ENSAIE

KM# 260.3   8 REALES
Silver **Issuer:** Ensaie **Countermark:** Eagle over
ENSAIE, crude sling below **Note:** Countermark on
Zacatecas KM#190.

CM Date	Host Date	Good	VG	F	VF	XF
ND	1810	—	—	—	—	—
ND	1811	100	150	200	300	—

KM# 260.4   8 REALES
Silver **Issuer:** Ensaie **Countermark:** Eagle over
ENSAIE, crude sling below **Note:** Countermark on
Zacatecas KM#191.

CM Date	Host Date	Good	VG	F	VF	XF
ND	1810	500	700	900	1,200	—
ND	1811	250	300	375	500	—
ND	1812	200	250	285	400	—

WAR OF INDEPENDENCE

KM# 260.1 8 REALES

Silver **Issuer:** Ensaie **Countermark:** Eagle over ENSAIE, crude sling below **Note:** Countermark on Mexico City KM#110.

CM Date	Host Date	Good	VG	F	VF	XF
ND	1811 HJ	150	200	275	350	—

KM# 260.2 8 REALES

Silver **Issuer:** Ensaie **Countermark:** Eagle over ENSAIE, crude sling below **Note:** Countermark on Zacatecas KM#189.

CM Date	Host Date	Good	VG	F	VF	XF
ND	1811	200	400	600	800	—

JOSE MARIA LICEAGA

J.M.L. with banner on cross, crossed olive branches.

(J.M.L./V., D.s, S.M., S.Y.S.L., Ve, A.P., s.r.a., Sea, P.G., S., S.M., El)

KM# A260 1/2 REAL

Silver **Issuer:** Jose Maria Liceaga **Countermark:** JML/SM with banner on cross, crossed olive branches **Note:** Countermark on cast Mexico City 1/ 2 Real.

CM Date	Host Date	Good	VG	F	VF	XF
ND	ND	100	150	200	275	—

KM# 261.6 2 REALES

Silver **Issuer:** Jose Maria Liceaga **Countermark:** J.M.L./V. with banner on cross, crossed olive branches **Note:** Countermark on Zacatecas KM#187.

CM Date	Host Date	Good	VG	F	VF	XF
ND	1811	200	225	250	300	—

KM# 261.7 2 REALES

Silver **Issuer:** Jose Maria Liceaga **Countermark:** J.M.L./DS with banner on cross, crossed olive branches **Note:** Countermark on Zacatecas KM#187.

CM Date	Host Date	Good	VG	F	VF	XF
ND	1811	200	235	275	325	—

KM# 261.8 2 REALES

Silver **Issuer:** Jose Maria Liceaga **Countermark:** J.M.L./S.M. with banner on cross, crossed olive branches **Note:** Countermark on Zacatecas KM#187.

CM Date	Host Date	Good	VG	F	VF	XF
ND	1811	200	235	275	325	—

KM# 261.9 2 REALES

Silver **Issuer:** Jose Maria Liceaga **Countermark:** J.M.L./S.Y. with banner on cross, crossed olive branches **Note:** Countermark on Zacatecas KM#187.

CM Date	Host Date	Good	VG	F	VF	XF
ND	1811	200	235	275	325	—

KM# 261.1 2 REALES

Silver **Issuer:** Jose Maria Liceaga **Countermark:** J.M.L./Ve with banner on cross, crossed olive branches **Note:** Countermark on 1/4 cut of 8 Reales.

CM Date	Host Date	Good	VG	F	VF	XF
ND	ND	175	225	300	—	—

KM# 261.2 2 REALES

Silver **Issuer:** Jose Maria Liceaga **Countermark:** J.M.L./V with banner on cross, crossed olive branchs **Note:** Countermark on Zacatecas KM#186.

CM Date	Host Date	Good	VG	F	VF	XF
ND	1811	200	225	250	300	—

KM# 261.3 2 REALES

Silver **Issuer:** Jose Maria Liceaga **Countermark:** J.M.L./DS with banner on cross, crossed olive branches **Note:** Countermark on Zacatecas KM#186.

CM Date	Host Date	Good	VG	F	VF	XF
ND	1811	200	235	275	325	—

KM# 261.4 2 REALES

Silver **Issuer:** Jose Maria Liceaga **Countermark:** J.M.L./S.M. with banner on cross, crossed olive branches **Note:** Countermark on Zacatecas KM#186.

CM Date	Host Date	Good	VG	F	VF	XF
ND	1811	200	235	275	325	—

KM# 261.5 2 REALES

Silver **Issuer:** Jose Maria Liceaga **Countermark:** J.M.L./S.Y. with banner on cross, crossed olive branches **Note:** Countermark on Zacatecas KM#186.

CM Date	Host Date	Good	VG	F	VF	XF
ND	1811	200	235	275	325	—

KM# 262.1 8 REALES
Silver **Issuer:** Jose Maria Liceaga **Countermark:**
J.M.L./D.S. with banner on cross, crossed olive
branches **Note:** Countermark on Zacatecas
KM#190.

CM Date	Host Date	Good	VG	F	VF	XF
ND	1811	250	325	425	550	—

KM# 262.4 8 REALES
Silver **Issuer:** Jose Maria Liceaga **Countermark:**
J.M.L./S.F. with banner on cross, crossed olive
branches **Note:** Countermark on Zacatecas
KM#190.

CM Date	Host Date	Good	VG	F	VF	XF
ND	1811	200	275	375	525	—

KM# 262.5 8 REALES
Silver **Issuer:** Jose Maria Liceaga **Countermark:**
J.M.L./S.M. with banner on cross, crossed olive
branches **Note:** Countermark on Zacatecas
KM#190.

CM Date	Host Date	Good	VG	F	VF	XF
ND	1811	200	275	375	525	—

KM# 262.10 8 REALES
Silver **Issuer:** Jose Maria Liceaga, J.M.L. with
banner on cross, crossed olive branches. (J.M.L./V.
D.s., S.M., S.Y.S.L.,Ve, A.P., s.r.a., Sea, P.G., S.,
S.M., E.) **Countermark:** J.M.L./S.M. **Note:**
Countermark on Zacatecas KM#190.

CM Date	Host Date	Good	VG	F	VF	XF
ND	1811	—	—	—	—	—

KM# 262.2 8 REALES
Silver **Issuer:** Jose Maria Liceaga **Countermark:**
J.M.L./E with banner on cross, crossed olive
branches **Note:** Countermark on Zacatecas
KM#190.

CM Date	Host Date	Good	VG	F	VF	XF
ND	1811	225	300	400	550	—

KM# 262.3 8 REALES
Silver **Issuer:** Jose Maria Liceaga **Countermark:**
J.M.L./P.G. with banner on cross, crossed olive
branches **Note:** Countermark on Durango
KM#111.2.

CM Date	Host Date	Good	VG	F	VF	XF
ND	1813 RM	200	275	375	525	—

KM# 262.6 8 REALES
Silver **Issuer:** Jose Maria Liceaga **Countermark:**
J.M.L./V.E. with banner on cross, cross olive
branches **Note:** Countermark on Zacatecas
KM#190.

CM Date	Host Date	Good	VG	F	VF	XF
ND	1811	200	275	375	525	—

KM# 262.12 8 REALES
Silver **Issuer:** Jose Maria Liceaga, Banner on cross, crossed olive branches **Countermark:** J.M.L. / P.G. **Note:** Countermark on Guanajuato 8 Reales, KM#111.4.

CM Date	Host Date	Good	VG	F	VF	XF
ND	ND1813	150	250	425	—	—

KM# 262.7 8 REALES
Silver **Issuer:** Jose Maria Liceaga, J.M.L with banner on cross, crossed olive branches. (J.M.L./V., D.s, S.M., S.Y.S.L., Ve, A.P., s.r.a., Sea, P.G., S., S.M., E.) **Countermark:** J.M.L./D.S. **Note:** Countermark on Zacatecas KM#190.

CM Date	Host Date	Good	VG	F	VF	XF
ND	1811	—	—	—	—	—

KM# 262.9 8 REALES
Silver **Issuer:** Jose Maria Liceaga, J.M.L. with banner on cross, crossed olive branches. (J.M.L./V. D.s., S.M., S.Y.S.L.,Ve, A.P., s.r.a., Sea, P.G., S., S.M., E.) **Countermark:** J.M.L./S.F. **Note:** Countermark on Zacatecas KM#190.

CM Date	Host Date	Good	VG	F	VF	XF
ND	1811	—	—	—	—	—

KM# 262.11 8 REALES
Silver **Issuer:** Jose Maria Liceaga, J.M.L. with banner on cross, crossed olive branches. (J.M.L./V. D.s., S.M., S.Y.S.L.,Ve, A.P., s.r.a., Sea, P.G., S., S.M., E.) **Countermark:** J.M.L./V.E. **Note:** Countermark on Zacatecas KM#190.

CM Date	Host Date	Good	VG	F	VF	XF
ND	1811	—	—	—	—	—

KM# 262.8 8 REALES
Silver **Issuer:** Jose Maria Liceaga , J.M.L. with banner on cross, crossed olive branches. (J.M.L./V. D.s., S.M., S.Y.S.L.,Ve, A.P., s.r.a., Sea, P.G., S., S.M., E.) **Countermark:** J.M.L./E **Note:** Countermark on Zacatecas KM#190.

CM Date	Host Date	Good	VG	F	VF	XF
ND	1811	—	—	—	—	—

L.V.S. - LABOR VINCIT SEMPER
Some authorities believe L.V.S. is for La Villa de Sombrerete.

KM# 264.1 8 REALES
Cast Silver **Issuer:** Labor Vincit Semper, Some authorities believe L.V.S. is for "La Villa de Sombrerete" **Countermark:** L.V.S. **Note:** Countermark on Chihuahua KM#123.

CM Date	Host Date	Good	VG	F	VF	XF
ND	1811 RP	275	350	450	550	—
ND	1812 RP	200	250	300	375	—

KM# 264.2 8 REALES
Silver **Issuer:** Labor Vincit Semper, Some authorities believe L.V.S. is for "La Villa de Sombrerete" **Countermark:** L.V.S. **Note:** Countermark on Chihuahua KM#111.1 overstruck on KM#123.

CM Date	Host Date	Good	VG	F	VF	XF
ND	1816 RP	250	300	325	375	—
ND	1817 RP	250	300	325	375	—
ND	1818 RP	250	300	325	375	—
ND	1819 RP	400	450	500	600	—
ND	1820 RP	450	500	550	650	—

KM# 264.3 8 REALES
Silver **Issuer:** Labor Vincit Semper, Some authorities believe L.V.S. is for "La Villa de Sombrerete" **Countermark:** L.V.S. **Note:** Countermark on Guadalajara KM#111.3.

CM Date	Host Date	Good	VG	F	VF	XF
ND	1817	185	220	250	310	—

KM# 264.4 8 REALES
Silver **Issuer:** Labor Vincit Semper, Some authorities believe L.V.S. is for "La Villa de Sombrerete" **Countermark:** L.V.S. **Note:** Countermark on Nueva Vizcaya KM#165.

CM Date	Host Date	Good	VG	F	VF	XF
ND	1811 RM	1,150	3,150	5,250	8,250	—

KM# 264.5 8 REALES
Silver **Issuer:** Labor Vincit Semper, Some authorities believe L.V.S. is for "La Villa de Sombrerete" **Countermark:** L.V.S. **Note:** Countermark on Sombrerete KM#177.

CM Date	Host Date	Good	VG	F	VF	XF
ND	1811	300	350	450	550	—
ND	1812	300	350	450	550	—

KM# 264.6 8 REALES
Silver **Issuer:** Labor Vincit Semper, Some authorities believe L.V.S. is for "La Villa de Sombrerete" **Countermark:** L.V.S. **Note:** Countermark on Zacatecas KM#190.

CM Date	Host Date	Good	VG	F	VF	XF
ND	1811	350	400	450	550	—

KM# 264.7 8 REALES
Silver **Issuer:** Labor Vincit Semper, Some authorities believe L.V.S. is for "La Villa de Sombrerete" **Countermark:** L.V.S. **Note:** Countermark on Zacatecas KM#192.

CM Date	Host Date	Good	VG	F	VF	XF
ND	1813	350	400	450	550	—

MORELOS

Morelos monogram

Type A: Stars above and below monogram in circle.

Type B: Dots above and below monogram in oval.

Type C: Monogram in rectangle.

Note: Many specimens of Type C available in todays market are considered spurious.

KM# A265 2 REALES
Copper **Issuer:** Morelos **Countermark:** Type A stars above and below monogram in circle **Note:** Countermark on Oaxaca Sud, KM#226.1.

CM Date	Host Date	Good	VG	F	VF	XF
ND	1812	—	—	—	—	—

KM# A267 8 REALES
Silver **Note:** Countermark Type C on Zacatecas KM#190.

CM Date	Host Date	Good	VG	F	VF	XF
ND	1811	300	350	425	650	—

KM# 265.1 8 REALES
Silver **Issuer:** Morelos **Countermark:** Type A star above and below monogram in circle **Note:** Countermark on Mexico City KM#109.

CM Date	Host Date	Good	VG	F	VF	XF
ND	1797 FM	45.00	50.00	60.00	85.00	—
ND	1798 FM	45.00	50.00	60.00	85.00	—
ND	1800 FM	45.00	50.00	60.00	85.00	—
ND	1807 TH	45.00	50.00	60.00	85.00	—

KM# 265.2   8 REALES
Silver **Issuer:** Morelos **Countermark:** Type A stars above and below monogram in circle **Note:** Countermark on Mexico City KM#110.

CM Date	Host Date	Good	VG	F	VF	XF
ND	1809 TH	55.00	65.00	85.00	120	—
ND	1811 HJ	55.00	65.00	85.00	120	—

KM# 265.3   8 REALES
Silver **Issuer:** Morelos **Countermark:** Type A stars above and below monogram in circle **Note:** Countermark on Mexico City KM#111.

CM Date	Host Date	Good	VG	F	VF	XF
ND	1812 JJ	50.00	60.00	75.00	110	—

KM# 265.5   8 REALES
Cast Silver **Issuer:** Morelos **Countermark:** Type A stars above and below monogram in circle **Note:** Countermark on Supreme National Congress KM#206.

CM Date	Host Date	Good	VG	F	VF	XF
ND	1811	200	250	375	600	—

KM# 266.1   8 REALES
Silver **Issuer:** Morelos **Countermark:** Type B dots above and below monogram in oval **Note:** Countermark on Guatamala 8 Reales, C#67.

CM Date	Host Date	Good	VG	F	VF	XF
ND	1810 M Rare	—	—	—	—	—

KM# 266.2   8 REALES
Silver **Issuer:** Morelos **Countermark:** Type B dots above and below monogram in oval **Note:** Countermark on Mexico City KM#110.

CM Date	Host Date	Good	VG	F	VF	XF
ND	1809 TH	45.00	55.00	65.00	90.00	—

KM# 267.1   8 REALES
Silver **Issuer:** Morelos **Countermark:** Type C monogram in rectangle **Note:** Countermark on Zacatecas KM#189. Many specimens of Type C available in today's market are considered spurious.

CM Date	Host Date	Good	VG	F	VF	XF
ND	1811	300	350	425	650	—

KM# 265.4   8 REALES
Copper **Issuer:** Morelos **Countermark:** Type A stars above and below monogram in circle **Note:** Countermark on Oaxaca Sud KM#233.2.

CM Date	Host Date	Good	VG	F	VF	XF
ND	1812	12.50	17.50	25.00	40.00	—
ND	1813	12.50	17.50	25.00	40.00	—
ND	1814	12.50	17.50	25.00	40.00	—

KM# 265.6   8 REALES
Silver **Issuer:** Morelos **Countermark:** Type A stars above and below monogram in circle **Note:** Countermark on Zacatecas KM#190.

CM Date	Host Date	Good	VG	F	VF	XF
ND	1811	375	625	900	—	—

WAR OF INDEPENDENCE

KM# 265.7   8 REALES
Silver **Issuer:** Morelos **Countermark:** Type A stars
above and below monogram in circle **Note:**
Countermark on Zacatecas KM#191.

CM Date	Host Date	Good	VG	F	VF	XF
ND	1811	200	250	375	600	—

KM# 267.2   8 REALES
Silver **Issuer:** Morelos **Countermark:** Type C:
monogram in rectangle **Note:** Countermark Type C
on Zacatecas KM#190. Many specimens of Type C
available in today's market are considered spurious.

CM Date	Host Date	Good	VG	F	VF	XF
ND	1811	300	350	425	650	—

NORTE

Issued by the Supreme National Congress and
the Army of the North.

Countermark: Eagle on cactus; star to left;
NORTE below.

KM# 268   1/2 REAL
Silver **Issuer:** Supreme National Congress and the
Army of the North **Countermark:** Eagle on cactus;
star to left; NORTE below **Note:** Countermark on
Zacatecas KM#180.

CM Date	Host Date	Good	VG	F	VF	XF
ND	1811	250	300	375	450	—

KM# 269   2 REALES
Silver **Issuer:** Supreme National Congress and the
Army of the North **Countermark:** Eagle on cactus;
star to left; NORTE below **Note:** Countermark on
Zacatecas KM#187.

CM Date	Host Date	Good	VG	F	VF	XF
ND	1811	225	275	325	400	—

KM# A269   2 REALES
Silver **Issuer:** Supreme National Congress and the
Army of the North **Countermark:** Eagle on cactus;
star to left; NORTE below **Note:** Countermark on
Zacatecas KM#188.

CM Date	Host Date	Good	VG	F	VF	XF
ND	1812	—	—	—	—	—

KM# B269   4 REALES
Silver **Issuer:** Supreme National Congress and the
Army of the North **Countermark:** Eagle on cactus;
star to left; NORTE below **Note:** Countermark on
Sombrerete KM#175.

CM Date	Host Date	Good	VG	F	VF	XF
ND	1812	100	150	200	275	—

KM# 270.4   8 REALES
Silver **Issuer:** Supreme National Congress and the
Army of the North **Countermark:** Eagle on cactus;
star to left; NORTE below **Note:** Countermark on
Zacatecas KM#191.

CM Date	Host Date	Good	VG	F	VF	XF
ND	1811	200	300	400	550	—
ND	1811	200	300	400	550	—
ND	1812	200	300	400	550	—

KM# 270.1   8 REALES
Silver **Issuer:** Supreme National Congress and the
Army of the North **Countermark:** Eagle on cactus;
star to left; NORTE below **Note:** Countermark on
Chihuahua KM#111.1.

CM Date	Host Date	Good	VG	F	VF	XF
ND	1813 RP	250	350	450	550	—

KM# 270.2   8 REALES
Silver **Issuer:** Supreme National Congress and the
Army of the North **Countermark:** Eagle on cactus;
star to left; NORTE below **Note:** Countermark on
Guanajuato KM#111.4.

CM Date	Host Date	Good	VG	F	VF	XF
ND	1813 JM	400	550	700	800	—

KM# 270.3 8 REALES
Silver **Issuer:** Supreme National Congress and the Army of the North **Countermark:** Eagle on cactus; star to left; NORTE below **Note:** Countermark on Zacatecas KM#190.

CM Date	Host Date	Good	VG	F	VF	XF
ND	1811	300	400	500	650	—

OSORNO

Countermark: Osorno monogram. (Jose Francisco Osorno)

KM# 271.1 1/2 REAL
Silver **Issuer:** Jose Francisco Osorno **Countermark:** Osorno monogram **Note:** Countermark on Mexico City KM#72.

CM Date	Host Date	Good	VG	F	VF	XF
ND	1798 FM	65.00	100	150	200	—
ND	1802 FT	65.00	100	150	200	—
ND	1806	65.00	100	150	200	—

KM# 271.2 1/2 REAL
Silver **Issuer:** Jose Francisco Osorno **Countermark:** Osorno monogram **Note:** Countermark on Mexico City KM#73.

CM Date	Host Date	Good	VG	F	VF	XF
ND	1809 TH	65.00	100	150	200	—

KM# 272.1 REAL
Silver **Issuer:** Jose Francisco Osorno **Countermark:** Osorno monogram **Note:** Countermark on Mexico City KM#81.

CM Date	Host Date	Good	VG	F	VF	XF
ND	1803 FT	65.00	100	150	200	—

KM# 272.2 REAL
Silver **Issuer:** Jose Francisco Osorno **Countermark:** Osorno monogram **Note:** Countermark on Potosi KM#70.

CM Date	Host Date	Good	VG	F	VF	XF
ND	ND	75.00	115	175	250	—

KM# 272.3 REAL
Silver **Issuer:** Jose Francisco Osorno **Countermark:** Osorno monogram **Note:** Countermark on Guatemala KM#54.

CM Date	Host Date	Good	VG	F	VF	XF
ND	1804	75.00	115	175	250	—

KM# A272.1 2 REALES
Silver **Issuer:** Jose Francisco Osorno **Countermark:** Osorno monogram **Note:** Countermark on Mexico City KM#88.2.

CM Date	Host Date	Good	VG	F	VF	XF
ND	1788 FM	75.00	125	175	250	—

KM# A272.2 2 REALES
Silver **Issuer:** Jose Francisco Osorno **Countermark:** Osorno monogram **Note:** Countermark on Mexico City KM#91.

CM Date	Host Date	Good	VG	F	VF	XF
ND	1808 TH	75.00	125	175	250	—

KM# A272.3 2 REALES
Silver **Issuer:** Jose Francisco Osorno **Countermark:** Osorno monogram **Note:** Countermark on Mexico City KM#92.

CM Date	Host Date	Good	VG	F	VF	XF
ND	1809 TH	75.00	125	175	250	—

KM# A272.4 2 REALES
Silver **Issuer:** Jose Francisco Osorno **Countermark:** Osorno monogram **Note:** Countermark on Zacatlian KM#252.

CM Date	Host Date	Good	VG	F	VF	XF
ND	1813	150	200	300	400	—

WAR OF INDEPENDENCE

KM# 273.1   4 REALES
Silver **Issuer:** Jose Francisco Osorno
Countermark: Osorno monogram **Note:**
Countermark on Mexico City KM#97.2.

CM Date	Host Date	Good	VG	F	VF	XF
ND	1782 FF	85.00	150	200	275	—

KM# 273.2   4 REALES
Silver **Issuer:** Jose Francisco Osorno
Countermark: Osorno monogram **Note:**
Countermark on Mexico City KM#100.

CM Date	Host Date	Good	VG	F	VF	XF
ND	1799 FM	85.00	150	200	275	—

KM# 274.1   8 REALES
Silver **Issuer:** Jose Francisco Osorno
Countermark: Osorno monogram **Note:**
Countermark on Lima 8 Reales, C#101.

CM Date	Host Date	Good	VG	F	VF	XF
ND	1811 JP	200	225	250	300	—

KM# 274.2   8 REALES
Silver **Issuer:** Jose Francisco Osorno
Countermark: Osorno monogram **Note:**
Countermark on Mexico City KM#110.

CM Date	Host Date	Good	VG	F	VF	XF
ND	1809 TH	125	150	225	300	—
ND	1810 HJ	125	150	225	300	—
ND	1811 HJ	125	150	225	300	—

VILLA / GRAN

(Julian Villagran)

KM# 298   2 REALES
Cast Silver , Julian Villagran **Countermark:** VILLA/
GRAN **Note:** Countermark on cast Mexico City
KM#91.

CM Date	Host Date	Good	VG	F	VF	XF
ND	1799 FM	150	200	250	350	—
ND	1802 FT	150	200	250	350	—

KM# 275   8 REALES
Cast Silver **Issuer:** Julian Villagran **Countermark:**
VILLA/GRAN **Note:** Countermark on cast Mexico
City KM#109.

CM Date	Host Date	Good	VG	F	VF	XF
ND	1796 FM	200	250	300	400	—
ND	1806 TH	200	250	300	400	—

ZMY

KM# 286   8 REALES
Silver **Issuer:** Unknown, presumed insurgent
Countermark: ZMY **Note:** Countermark on
Zacatecas KM#191.

CM Date	Host Date	Good	VG	F	VF	XF
ND	1812	100	150	200	350	—

COUNTERMARKED COINAGE

KM# 263.4   8 REALES
Silver **Issuer:** Don Jose Maria De Linares
Countermark: LINA/RES * **Note:** Countermark on
Zacatecas KM#190.

CM Date	Host Date	Good	VG	F	VF	XF
ND	1811	—	—	—	—	—

KM# 263.5   8 REALES
Silver **Issuer:** Don Jose Maria De Linares
Countermark: LINA/RES* **Note:** Countermark on
Zacatecas KM#192.

CM Date	Host Date	Good	VG	F	VF	XF
ND	1812	—	—	—	—	—

KM# 270.5   8 REALES
Silver **Issuer:** Norte, Issued by the Supreme
National Congress and the Army of the North
Countermark: Eagle on cactus; star to left; NORTE
below **Note:** Countermark on Zacatecas KM#190.

CM Date	Host Date	Good	VG	F	VF	XF
ND	1811	—	—	—	—	—

KM# 265.8   8 REALES
Silver **Issuer:** Morelos, Type A: Stars above and
below monogram in circle. Type B: Dots above and
below monogram in oval. Type C: Monogram in
rectangle. Many specimens of Type C available in
today's market are considered spurious.
Countermark: Type A **Note:** Countermark on
Zacatecas KM#190.

CM Date	Host Date	Good	VG	F	VF	XF
ND	1811	—	—	—	—	—

KM# 264.8   8 REALES
Cast Silver **Issuer:** Labor Vincit Semper, L.V.S.;
Some authorities believe L.V.S. is for "La Villa de
Sombrerete" **Countermark:** L.V.S. **Note:**
Countermark on Zacatecas KM#190.

CM Date	Host Date	Good	VG	F	VF	XF
ND	1811	—	—	—	—	—

MULTIPLE COUNTERMARKS

Many combinations of Royalist and Insurgent
countermarks are usually found on the cast copies
produced by Chihuahua and Mexico City and on the
other crude provisional issues of this period. Struck
Mexico City coins were used to make molds for
casting necessity issues and countermarked
afterwards to show issuing authority. Some were
marked again by either both or separate opposing
friendly forces to authorize circulation in their areas
of occupation.   Some countermarks are only
obtainable with companion markings.

KM# 289   2 REALES
Silver **Issuer:** C.M.S. and S.C.M. **Countermark:**
C.M.S. (Comandancia Militar Suriana) and eagle with
S.C.M. (Soberano Congreso Mexicano) **Note:**
Countermark on Mexico City KM#91.

CM Date	Host Date	Good	VG	F	VF	XF
ND	ND	—	—	—	—	—

KM# 295   2 REALES
Silver **Issuer:** Militar del Sur and Soberano
Congreso Mexicano **Countermark:** M.d.S. and
eagle with S.C.M **Note:** Countermark on Mexico City
KM#91.

CM Date	Host Date	Good	VG	F	VF	XF
ND	ND	150	250	450	—	—

KM# 296   2 REALES
Silver **Issuer:** Jose Francisco Osorno and Julian
Villagran **Countermark:** Osorno monogram and
VILLA/GRAN **Note:** Countermark on cast Mexico
City KM#110.

CM Date	Host Date	Good	VG	F	VF	XF
ND	1809 TH	—	—	—	—	—

KM# A286   2 REALES
Silver **Issuer:** Jose Maria Liceaga and VTIL
Countermark: J.M.L./D.S. AND VTIL **Note:**
Countermark on Zacatecas KM#186.

CM Date	Host Date	Good	VG	F	VF	XF
ND	1811	75.00	125	175	250	—

KM# B286   2 REALES
Silver **Issuer:** Jose Maria Liceaga and VTIL
Countermark: J.M.L./V.E. and VTIL **Note:**
Countermark on Zacatecas KM#186.

CM Date	Host Date	Good	VG	F	VF	XF
ND	1810	75.00	125	175	250	—
ND	1811	75.00	125	175	250	—

KM# 285.2   8 REALES
Silver **Issuer:** Chilpanzingo and Morelos
Countermark: Chilpanzingo Type A and Morelos

monogram Type A **Note:** Countermark on cast
Mexico City KM#110.

CM Date	Host Date	Good	VG	F	VF	XF
ND	1810 HJ	35.00	45.00	60.00	140	—
ND	1811 HJ	35.00	45.00	60.00	140	—

KM# 281   8 REALES
Silver **Issuer:** Chilpanzingo and LVS **Countermark:**
Chilpanzingo Type A and script LVS **Note:**
Countermark on cast Mexico City KM#110.

CM Date	Host Date	Good	VG	F	VF	XF
ND	1809 HJ	45.00	65.00	135	250	—

KM# C286   8 REALES
Silver **Issuer:** Chilpanzingo and Morelos and LVS
Countermark: Chilpanzingo Type A, Morelos Type
A and LVS monogram on cast Mexico City KM#110

CM Date	Host Date	Good	VG	F	VF	XF
ND	1809 HJ	50.00	75.00	125	275	—

KM# 288.2   8 REALES
Silver **Issuer:** Chilpanzingo and Suprema Junta
Nacional Gubernativa **Countermark:** Chilpanzingo
Type B **Note:** Countermark on Zacatecas KM#190.
Prev. KM#288.

CM Date	Host Date	Good	VG	F	VF	XF
ND	1811	—	—	—	—	—

KM# A298   8 REALES
Silver **Issuer:** S.J.N.G. and VTIL **Countermark:**
S.J.N.G and VTIL on Zacatecas KM#191

CM Date	Host Date	Good	VG	F	VF	XF
ND	ND	35.00	50.00	75.00	200	—

KM# A297   8 REALES
Silver **Issuer:** Chilpanzingo and ENSAIE
Countermark: Chilpanzingo Type B and ENSAIE
Note: Countermark on Zacatecas KM#189.

CM Date	Host Date	Good	VG	F	VF	XF
ND	ND	175	250	350	—	—

KM# 297   8 REALES
Silver **Issuer:** Chilpanzingo and LVA **Countermark:**
Chilpanzingo Type A and LVA **Note:** Countermark
on Mexico City KM#109.

CM Date	Host Date	Good	VG	F	VF	XF
ND	1805 TH	45.00	75.00	145	250	—

KM# 290.2   8 REALES
Silver **Issuer:** ENSAIE and VTIL **Countermark:**
ENSAIE and VTIL **Note:** Countermark on Zacatecas
KM#190. Prev. KM#290.

CM Date	Host Date	Good	VG	F	VF	XF
ND	1811	100	175	275	350	—

KM# 291 8 REALES
Silver **Issuer:** Jose Maria Liceaga and VTIL
Countermark: J.M.L./D.S. and VTIL **Note:**
Countermark on Mexico City KM#110.

CM Date	Host Date	Good	VG	F	VF	XF
ND	1810 HJ	85.00	150	250	400	—

KM# 282 8 REALES
Silver **Issuer:** La Comandancia Militar and Morelos
Countermark: L.C.M and Morelos monogram Type
A **Note:** Countermark on cast Mexico City KM#109.

CM Date	Host Date	Good	VG	F	VF	XF
ND	1792 FM	—	—	—	—	—

KM# 283 8 REALES
Silver **Issuer:** Morelos and Morelos **Countermark:**
Morelos Type A and C **Note:** Countermark on cast
Mexico City KM#109.

CM Date	Host Date	Good	VG	F	VF	XF
ND	1806 TH	—	—	—	—	—

KM# 284 8 REALES
Silver **Issuer:** Chilpanzingo and Morelos
Countermark: Chilpanzingo Type A and Morelos
monogram Type A **Note:** Countermark on cast
Mexico City KM#109.

CM Date	Host Date	Good	VG	F	VF	XF
ND	1806 TH	35.00	50.00	100	200	—
ND	1807 TH	35.00	50.00	100	200	—

KM# 285.1 8 REALES
Silver **Issuer:** Chilpanzingo and Morelos
Countermark: Chilpanzingo Type A and Morelos
monogram Type A **Note:** Countermark on struck
Mexico City KM#110.

CM Date	Host Date	Good	VG	F	VF	XF
ND	1809 TH	45.00	65.00	135	250	—

KM# 285.3 8 REALES
Silver **Issuer:** Chilpanzingo and Morelos
Countermark: Chilpanzingo Type A and Morelos
monogram Type A **Note:** Countermark on cast
Mexico City KM#111.

CM Date	Host Date	Good	VG	F	VF	XF
ND	1811 HJ	75.00	120	175	275	—

KM# A290 8 REALES
Silver **Issuer:** ENSAIE and Jose Maria Liceaga
Countermark: ENSAIE and J.M.L. **Note:**
Countermark on Zacatecas KM#190.

CM Date	Host Date	Good	VG	F	VF	XF
ND	1811	100	175	275	350	—

KM# 294 8 REALES
Silver **Issuer:** L.V.A. and Morelos **Countermark:**
Script LVA and Morelos monogram Type A **Note:**
Countermark on cast Mexico City KM#110.

CM Date	Host Date	Good	VG	F	VF	XF
ND	ND HJ	45.00	75.00	135	250	—

KM# 288.1 8 REALES
Silver **Issuer:** Chilpanzingo and Suprema Junta
Nacional Gubernativa **Countermark:** Chilpanzingo
Type B and S.J.N.G **Note:** Countermark on
Zacatecas KM#189.

CM Date	Host Date	Good	VG	F	VF	XF
ND	1811	—	—	—	—	—

KM# 290.1 8 REALES
Silver **Issuer:** ENSAIE and VTIL **Countermark:**
ENSAIE and VTIL **Note:** Countermark on Zacatecas
KM#189.

CM Date	Host Date	Good	VG	F	VF	XF
ND	1811	100	175	275	350	—

KM# 280.1 8 REALES
Silver **Issuer:** Chilpanzingo and Crown and flag
Countermark: Chilpanzingo Type B and Crown and
flag **Note:** Countermark on Zacatecas KM#189.

CM Date	Host Date	Good	VG	F	VF	XF
ND	1811	—	—	—	—	—

KM# 280.2 8 REALES
Silver **Issuer:** Chilpanzingo and crown and flag
Countermark: Chilpanzingo Type B and crown and
flag **Note:** Countermark on Zacatecas KM#190.

CM Date	Host Date	Good	VG	F	VF	XF
ND	1811	—	—	—	—	—

WAR OF INDEPENDENCE

KM# 287   8 REALES
Silver   **Issuer:** Chilpanzingo - Provisional De Valladolid **Countermark:** Chilpanzingo Type B and P.D.V **Note:** Countermark on Valladolid KM#178.

CM Date	Host Date	Good	VG	F	VF	XF
ND	1813	—	—	—	—	—

ZACATECAS

The city of Zacatecas, in a rich mining region has provided silver for the world since mid-1500. On November 14, 1810 a mint began production for the Royalist cause. Zacatecas was the most prolific during the War of Independence. Four of the 5 standard silver denominations were made here, 4 Reales were not. The first, a local type showing mountains of silver on the coins were made only in 1810 and 1811. Some 1811 coins were made by the Insurgents who took the city on April 15, 1811, later retaken by the Royalists on May 21, 1811. Zacatecas struck the standard Ferdinand VII bust type until 1922.
Mint marks: Z, ZS, Zs.

ROYALIST COINAGE

KM# 180   1/2 REAL
0.9030 Silver   **Ruler:** Ferdinand VII **Obv:** Crowned shield flanked by pillars **Obv. Legend:** FERDIN.VII... **Rev:** Mountain within beaded circle **Note:** Mint marks: Z, ZS, Zs.

Date	Mintage	Good	VG	F	VF	XF
1810	—	75.00	125	200	400	—
1811	—	30.00	50.00	90.00	175	—

Note: Date aligned with legend

KM# 181   1/2 REAL
0.9030 Silver   **Ruler:** Ferdinand VII **Obv:** Crowned shield flanked by pillars **Rev:** Mountain within beaded circle **Rev. Legend:** MONEDA PROVISIONAL DE ZACATECAS **Note:** Mint marks: Z, ZS, Zs.

Date	Mintage	Good	VG	F	VF	XF
1811	—	30.00	50.00	90.00	175	—

KM# 182   1/2 REAL
0.9030 Silver   **Ruler:** Ferdinand VII **Obv:** Provincial bust right **Obv. Legend:** FERDIN. VII **Rev:** Crowned shield flanked by pillars **Rev. Legend:** MONEDA PROVISIONAL DE ZACATECAS **Note:** Mint marks: Z, ZS, Zs.

Date	Mintage	Good	VG	F	VF	XF
1811	—	30.00	40.00	65.00	135	—
1812	—	25.00	35.00	60.00	120	—

KM# 73.1   1/2 REAL
1.6900 g., 0.9030 Silver 0.0491 oz. ASW   **Ruler:** Ferdinand VII **Obv:** Armored laureate bust right **Obv. Legend:** FERDIN.VII... **Rev:** Crowned shield flanked by pillars **Rev. Legend:** IND.... **Note:** Mint marks: Z, ZS, Zs.

Date	Mintage	Good	VG	F	VF	XF
1813 AG	—	20.00	40.00	60.00	100	—
1813 FP	—	25.00	45.00	85.00	175	—
1814 AG	—	15.00	30.00	60.00	100	—
1815 AG	—	12.50	25.00	40.00	60.00	—
1816 AG	—	10.00	15.00	25.00	50.00	—
1817 AG	—	10.00	15.00	25.00	50.00	—
1818 AG	—	10.00	15.00	25.00	50.00	—
1819 AG	—	10.00	15.00	25.00	50.00	—

KM# 74.3   1/2 REAL
1.6900 g., 0.9030 Silver 0.0491 oz. ASW   **Ruler:** Ferdinand VII **Obv:** Draped laureate bust right **Obv. Legend:** FERDIN.VII... **Rev:** Crowned shield flanked by pillars **Rev. Legend:** IND.... **Note:** Mint marks: Z, ZS, Zs.

Date	Mintage	VG	F	VF	XF	Unc
1819 AG	—	8.00	12.00	25.00	50.00	—
1820 AG	—	8.00	12.00	25.00	50.00	—
1820 RG	—	5.00	10.00	20.00	45.00	—
1821 AG	—	150	250	450	850	—
1821 RG	—	5.00	10.00	20.00	45.00	—

KM# 183   REAL
0.9030 Silver   **Ruler:** Ferdinand VII **Obv:** Crowned shield flanked by pillars **Rev:** Mountain within beaded circle **Note:** Mint marks: Z, ZS, Zs.

Date	Mintage	Good	VG	F	VF	XF
1810	—	100	150	300	500	—
1811	—	20.00	40.00	75.00	150	—

Note: Date aligned with legend

KM# 184 REAL
0.9030 Silver **Ruler:** Ferdinand VII **Obv:** Crowned shield flanked by pillars **Rev:** Mountain within beaded circle **Rev. Legend:** MONEDA PROVISIONAL DE ZACATECAS **Note:** Mint marks: Z, ZS, Zs.

Date	Mintage	Good	VG	F	VF	XF
1811	—	15.00	30.00	60.00	135	—

KM# 185 REAL
0.9030 Silver **Ruler:** Ferdinand VII **Obv:** Provincial bust right **Obv. Legend:** FERDIN. VII. **Rev:** Crowned shield flanked by pillars **Rev. Legend:** MONEDA PROVISIONAL DE ZACATECAS **Note:** Mint marks: Z, ZS, Zs.

Date	Mintage	Good	VG	F	VF	XF
1811	—	50.00	85.00	120	200	—
1812	—	40.00	70.00	100	175	—

KM# 82.1 REAL
3.3800 g., 0.9030 Silver 0.0981 oz. ASW **Ruler:** Ferdinand VII **Obv:** Armored laureate bust right **Obv. Legend:** FERDIN. VII. **Rev:** Crowned shield flanked by pillars **Rev. Legend:** IND.REX... **Note:** Mint marks: Z, ZS, Zs.

Date	Mintage	Good	VG	F	VF	XF
1813 FP	—	50.00	100	150	250	—
1814 FP	—	20.00	35.00	50.00	85.00	—
1814 AG	—	20.00	35.00	50.00	85.00	—
1815 AG	—	20.00	35.00	50.00	85.00	—
1816 AG	—	10.00	20.00	30.00	65.00	—
1817 AG	—	6.50	12.50	20.00	45.00	—
1818 AG	—	6.50	12.50	20.00	45.00	—
1819 AG	—	5.00	9.00	15.00	35.00	—

KM# 83.3 REAL
3.3800 g., 0.9030 Silver 0.0981 oz. ASW **Ruler:** Ferdinand VII **Obv:** Draped laureate bust right **Obv. Legend:** FERDIN. VII. **Rev:** Crowned shield flanked by pillars **Rev. Legend:** REX.Z... **Note:** Mint marks: Z, ZS, Zs.

Date	Mintage	VG	F	VF	XF	Unc
1820 AG	—	5.00	10.00	20.00	60.00	—
1820 RG	—	5.00	10.00	20.00	60.00	—
1821 AG	—	15.00	30.00	45.00	90.00	—
1821 AZ	—	10.00	20.00	40.00	85.00	—
1821 RG	—	6.00	12.00	25.00	65.00	—
1822 AZ	—	6.00	12.00	25.00	65.00	—
1822 RG	—	15.00	30.00	45.00	90.00	—

KM# 186 2 REALES

0.9030 Silver **Ruler:** Ferdinand VII **Obv:** Crowned shield flanked by pillars **Obv. Legend:** FERDIN.VII... **Rev:** Mountain within beaded circle **Rev. Legend:** MONEDA.PROVISION... **Note:** Mint marks: Z, ZS, Zs.

Date	Mintage	Good	VG	F	VF	XF
1810 Rare	—	—	—	—	—	—
1811	—	25.00	40.00	70.00	120	—

Note: Date aligned with legend

KM# 187 2 REALES
0.9030 Silver **Ruler:** Ferdinand VII **Obv:** Crowned shield flanked by pillars **Rev:** Mountain above L. V. O within beaded circle **Rev. Legend:** MONEDA PROVISIONAL DE ZACATECAS **Note:** Mint marks: Z, ZS, Zs.

Date	Mintage	Good	VG	F	VF	XF
1811	—	15.00	30.00	60.00	100	—

KM# 188 2 REALES
0.9030 Silver **Ruler:** Ferdinand VII **Obv:** Armored bust right **Obv. Legend:** FERDIN. VII **Rev:** Crowned shield flanked by pillars **Rev. Legend:** MONEDA PROVISIONAL DE ZACATECAS **Note:** Mint marks: Z, ZS, Zs.

Date	Mintage	Good	VG	F	VF	XF
1811	—	35.00	65.00	135	225	—
1812	—	30.00	60.00	125	200	—

KM# 92.1 2 REALES
6.7700 g., 0.9030 Silver 0.1965 oz. ASW **Ruler:** Ferdinand VII **Obv:** Large armored bust right **Obv. Legend:** FERDIN. VII **Rev:** Crowned shield flanked by pillars **Rev. Inscription:** MONEDA. PROVISION... **Note:** Mint marks: Z, ZS, Zs.

Date	Mintage	Good	VG	F	VF	XF
1813 FP	—	35.00	50.00	75.00	125	—
1814 FP	—	35.00	50.00	75.00	125	—
1814 AG	—	35.00	50.00	75.00	125	—
1815 AG	—	6.50	12.50	25.00	55.00	—
1816 AG	—	6.50	12.50	25.00	55.00	—
1817 AG	—	6.50	12.50	25.00	55.00	—
1818 AG	—	6.50	12.50	25.00	55.00	—

WAR OF INDEPENDENCE

KM# 93.4   2 REALES
6.7700 g., 0.9030 Silver 0.1965 oz. ASW **Ruler:** Ferdinand VII **Obv:** Draped laureate bust right **Obv. Legend:** FERDIN. VII **Rev:** Crowned shield flanked by pillars **Rev. Legend:** IND.REX... **Note:** Mint marks: Z, ZS, Zs.

Date	Mintage	VG	F	VF	XF	Unc
1818 AG	—	6.50	12.50	25.00	50.00	—
1819 AG	—	10.00	20.00	40.00	85.00	—
1819 AG	—	10.00	20.00	40.00	85.00	—
Note: Reversed 'S' in HISPAN						
1820 AG	—	10.00	20.00	40.00	85.00	—
1820 RG	—	10.00	20.00	40.00	85.00	—
1821 AG	—	10.00	20.00	40.00	85.00	—
1821 AZ/RG	—	10.00	20.00	40.00	85.00	—
1821 AZ	—	10.00	20.00	40.00	85.00	—
1821 RG	—	10.00	20.00	40.00	85.00	—
1822 AG	—	10.00	20.00	40.00	85.00	—
1822 RG	—	10.00	20.00	40.00	85.00	—

KM# A92   2 REALES
6.7700 g., 0.9030 Silver 0.1965 oz. ASW **Ruler:** Ferdinand VII **Obv:** Small armored bust right **Obv. Legend:** FERDIN. VII **Rev:** Crowned shield flanked by pillars **Rev. Inscription:** IND.REX... **Note:** Mint marks: Z, ZS, Zs.

Date	Mintage	Good	VG	F	VF	XF
1819 AG	—	45.00	100	200	400	—

KM# 189   8 REALES
0.9030 Silver **Ruler:** Ferdinand VII **Obv:** Crowned shield flanked by pillars **Rev:** Mountain above L.V.O. within beaded circle **Rev. Legend:** MONEDA.PROVISION... **Note:** Mint Zacatecas.

Date	Mintage	Good	VG	F	VF	XF
1810	—	300	500	750	1,250	—
1811	—	100	150	225	350	—

Note: Date aligned with legend. Also exists with incomplete date

KM# 190   8 REALES
0.9030 Silver **Ruler:** Ferdinand VII **Obv:** Crowned shield flanked by pillars **Obv. Legend:** FERDIN. VII. DEI... **Rev:** Mountain above L. V. O within beaded circle **Rev. Legend:** MONEDA PROVISIONAL DE ZACATECAS

Date	Mintage	Good	VG	F	VF	XF
1811	—	65.00	100	135	220	—

Note: Date aligned with legend

KM# 191   8 REALES
0.9030 Silver **Ruler:** Ferdinand VII **Obv:** Armored bust right **Obv. Legend:** FERDIN. VII. 8.R. DEI... **Rev:** Crowned shield flanked by pillars **Rev. Legend:** MONEDA PROVISIONAL DE ZACATECAS

Date	Mintage	Good	VG	F	VF	XF
1811	—	45.00	75.00	145	275	—
1812	—	50.00	85.00	160	300	—

KM# 192   8 REALES
0.9030 Silver **Ruler:** Ferdinand VII **Obv:** Draped laureate bust right **Obv. Legend:** FERDIN. VII. DEI... **Rev:** Crowned shield flanked by pillars **Rev. Legend:** MONEDA PROVISIONAL DE ZACATECAS

Date	Mintage	Good	VG	F	VF	XF
1812	—	75.00	150	275	450	—

KM# 111.5   8 REALES
27.0700 g., 0.9030 Silver 0.7859 oz. ASW   **Ruler:**
Ferdinand VII **Obv:** Draped laureate bust right **Obv.**
Legend: FERDIN. VII. DEI. GRATIA **Rev:** Crowned
shield flanked by pillars **Rev. Legend:** HISPAN. ET
IND. REX **Note:** Mint mark: Zs. Several bust types
exist for the 1821 issues.

Date	Mintage	VG	F	VF	XF	Unc
1813 FP	—	75.00	125	175	275	—
1814 FP	—	150	250	350	450	—
1814 AG	—	100	150	200	300	—
1814 AG	—	125	175	225	325	—
Note: D over horizontal D in IND						
1814 AG/FP	—	100	150	200	300	—
1815 AG	—	50.00	100	150	250	—
1816 AG	—	35.00	50.00	65.00	125	—
1817 AG	—	35.00	50.00	65.00	125	—
1818 AG	—	30.00	40.00	50.00	100	—
1819 AG	—	30.00	40.00	50.00	100	—
1819 AG 'GRATIA' error	—	100	200	300	400	—
1820 AG 18/11 error	—	100	200	300	400	—
1820 AG	—	30.00	40.00	50.00	100	—
1820 RG	—	30.00	40.00	50.00	100	—
1821/81 RG	—	75.00	150	225	300	—
1821 RG	—	15.00	25.00	35.00	65.00	—
1821 AZ/RG	—	50.00	100	150	200	—
1821 AZ	—	50.00	100	150	200	—
1822 RG	—	40.00	60.00	100	175	—

KM# 111.6   8 REALES
27.0700 g., 0.9030 Silver 0.7859 oz. ASW   **Ruler:**
Ferdinand VII **Obv:** Draped laureate bust right **Obv.**
Legend: FERDIN. VII. DEI. GRATIA **Rev:** Crowned
shield flanked by pillars **Rev. Legend:** HISAV. ET
IND. REX

Date	Mintage	VG	F	VF	XF	Unc
1821Zs	—	160	320	550	750	—

ROYALIST COUNTERMARKED COINAGE

LCM - LA COMANDANCIA MILITAR

Crown and Flag

This countermark exists in 15 various sizes.

KM# 193.1   2 REALES
0.9030 Silver   **Issuer:** La Comandancia Militar
Countermark: LCM **Note:** Countermark on Mexico
KM#92.

CM Date	Host Date	Good	VG	F	VF	XF
ND	1809 TH	85.00	165	250	400	—

KM# 193.2   2 REALES
0.9030 Silver   **Issuer:** La Comandancia Militar, (The
LCM countermark exists in 15 various sizes)
Countermark: LCM **Note:** Countermark on Mexico
KM#186.

CM Date	Host Date	Good	VG	F	VF	XF
ND	1811	85.00	165	250	400	—

KM# 194.1   8 REALES
Cast Silver   **Issuer:** La Comandancia Militar, (The
LCM countermark exists in 15 various sizes)
Countermark: LCM **Note:** Countermark on
Chihuahua KM#123.

CM Date	Host Date	Good	VG	F	VF	XF
ND	1811 RP	100	200	300	450	—
ND	1812 RP	100	200	300	450	—

KM# 194.2   8 REALES
0.9030 Silver **Issuer:** La Comandancia Militar, The LCM countermark exists in 15 different sizes
Countermark: LCM **Note:** Countermark on Chihuahua KM#111.1 struck over KM#123.

CM Date	Host Date	Good	VG	F	VF	XF
ND	1815 RP	200	275	400	550	—
ND	1817 RP	125	175	225	300	—
ND	1820 RP	125	175	225	300	—
ND	1821 RP	125	175	225	300	—

KM# 194.3   8 REALES
0.9030 Silver **Issuer:** La Comandancia Militar, The LCM countermark exists in 15 different sizes
Countermark: LCM **Note:** Countermark on Durango KM#111.2.

CM Date	Host Date	Good	VG	F	VF	XF
ND	1812 RM	70.00	125	190	250	—
ND	1821 CG	70.00	125	190	250	—

KM# 194.4   8 REALES
0.9030 Silver **Issuer:** La Comandancia Militar, The LCM countermark exists in 15 different sizes
Countermark: LCM **Note:** Countermark on Guadalajara KM#111.3.

CM Date	Host Date	Good	VG	F	VF	XF
ND	1813 MR	150	225	300	475	—

KM# 194.5   8 REALES
0.9030 Silver **Issuer:** La Comandancia Militar, The LCM countermark exists in 15 different sizes
Countermark: LCM **Note:** Countermark on Guanajuato KM#111.4.

CM Date	Host Date	Good	VG	F	VF	XF
ND	1813 JJ	225	350	475	650	—

KM# 194.6   8 REALES
0.9030 Silver **Issuer:** La Comandancia Militar, The LCM countermark exists in 15 different sizes
Countermark: LCM **Note:** Countermark on Nueva Viscaya KM#165.

CM Date	Host Date	Good	VG	F	VF	XF
ND	1811 RM Rare	—	—	—	—	—

KM# 194.7   8 REALES
0.9030 Silver **Issuer:** La Comandancia Militar, The LCM countermark exists in 15 different sizes
Countermark: LCM **Note:** Countermark on Mexico KM#111.

CM Date	Host Date	Good	VG	F	VF	XF
ND	1811 HJ	125	225	350	600	—
ND	1812 JJ	110	135	190	325	—
ND	1817 JJ	50.00	65.00	85.00	125	—
ND	1818 JJ	50.00	65.00	85.00	125	—
ND	1820 JJ	—	—	—	—	—

KM# 194.8   8 REALES
0.9030 Silver **Issuer:** La Comandancia Militar, The LCM countermark exists in 15 different sizes
Countermark: LCM **Note:** Countermark on Sombrerete KM#176.

CM Date	Host Date	Good	VG	F	VF	XF
ND	1811 Rare	—	—	—	—	—
ND	1812 Rare	—	—	—	—	—

KM# 194.9 8 REALES
0.9030 Silver **Issuer:** La Comandancia Militar, The LCM countermark exists in 15 different sizes **Countermark:** LCM **Note:** Countermark on Zacatecas KM#190.

CM Date	Host Date	Good	VG	F	VF	XF
ND	1811	225	350	450	—	—

KM# 194.10 8 REALES
0.9030 Silver **Issuer:** La Comandancia Militar, The LCM countermark exists in 15 different sizes **Countermark:** LCM **Note:** Countermark on Zacatecas KM#111.5.

CM Date	Host Date	Good	VG	F	VF	XF
ND	1813 FP	—	—	—	—	—
ND	1814 AG	—	—	—	—	—
ND	1822 RG	—	—	—	—	—

LCV - LAS CAJAS DE VERACRUZ

The Royal Treasury of the City of Veracruz

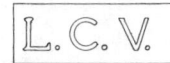

KM# 195 7 REALES
Silver **Issuer:** Las Cajas de Veracruz, The Royal Treasury of the City of Veracruz **Countermark:** LCV **Note:** Countermark and 7 on underweight 8 Reales.

CM Date	Host Date	Good	VG	F	VF	XF
ND	ND Rare	—	—	—	—	—

Note: Most examples are counterfeit

KM# 196 7-1/4 REALES
Silver **Issuer:** Las Cajas de Veracruz, The Royal Treasury of the City of Veracruz **Countermark:** LCV **Note:** Countermark and 7-1/4 on underweight 8 Reales.

CM Date	Host Date	Good	VG	F	VF	XF
ND	ND Rare	—	—	—	—	—

Note: Most examples are counterfeit

KM# 197 7-1/2 REALES
Silver **Issuer:** Las Cajas de Veracruz, The Royal Treasury of the City of Veracruz **Countermark:** LCV **Note:** Countermark and 7-1/2 on underweight 8 Reales.

CM Date	Host Date	Good	VG	F	VF	XF
ND	ND Rare	—	—	—	—	—

Note: Most examples are counterfeit

KM# 198 7-3/4 REALES
Silver **Issuer:** Las Cajas de Veracruz, The Royal Treasury of the City of Veracruz **Countermark:** LCV **Note:** Countermark and 7-3/4 on underweight 8 Reales.

CM Date	Host Date	Good	VG	F	VF	XF
ND	ND	300	375	450	600	—

Note: Many examples are counterfeit

KM# A198 8 REALES
Cast Silver **Issuer:** Las Cajas de Veracruz, The Royal Treasury of the City of Veracruz **Countermark:** LCV **Note:** Countermark on Chihuahua KM#123.

CM Date	Host Date	Good	VG	F	VF	XF
ND	1811 RP	150	250	400	500	—

MVA - MONCLOVA

KM# 199   8 REALES
Silver   **Issuer:** Las Cajas de Veracruz, The Royal Treasury of the City of Veracruz **Countermark:** LCV **Note:** Countermark on Zacatecas KM#191.

CM Date	Host Date	Good	VG	F	VF	XF
ND	1811	175	225	275	350	—
ND	1812	175	225	275	350	—

MS (MONOGRAM) - MANUEL SALCEDO

KM# 202.3   8 REALES
Silver   **Issuer:** Monclova, MVA **Countermark:** MVA/1812 **Note:** Countermark on cast Mexico KM#110.

CM Date	Host Date	Good	VG	F	VF	XF
1812	1809 HJ	100	150	250	350	—
1812	1809 TH	100	150	250	350	—
1812	1810 HJ	100	150	250	350	—

KM# 201   8 REALES
Silver   **Issuer:** Monclova, MVA **Countermark:** MVA/1811 **Note:** Countermark on Chihuahua KM#111.1; struck over cast Mexico KM#110.

CM Date	Host Date	Good	VG	F	VF	XF
ND	1809	250	450	700	1,000	—
ND	1816 RP	250	450	700	1,000	—
ND	1821 RP	250	450	700	1,000	—

KM# 202.5   8 REALES
Silver   **Issuer:** Monclova, MVA **Countermark:** MVA/1812 **Note:** Countermark on Zacatecas KM#189.

CM Date	Host Date	Good	VG	F	VF	XF
1812	1813	300	350	450	550	—

KM# 200   8 REALES
Silver   **Issuer:** Manuel Salcedo **Countermark:** MS monogram **Note:** Countermark on Mexico KM#110.

CM Date	Host Date	Good	VG	F	VF	XF
ND	1809 TH	150	250	400	500	—
ND	1810 HJ	150	250	400	500	—
ND	1811 HJ	150	250	400	500	—

KM# 202.1   8 REALES
Silver   **Issuer:** Monclova, MVA **Countermark:** MVA/1812 **Note:** Countermark on Chihuahua KM#111.1; struck over cast Mexico KM#109.

CM Date	Host Date	Good	VG	F	VF	XF
1812	1810	125	1/5	250	350	—

KM# 202.2 8 REALES

Silver **Issuer:** Monclova, MVA **Countermark:** MVA/ 1812 **Note:** Countermark on cast Mexico KM#109.

CM Date	Host Date	Good	VG	F	VF	XF
1812	1798 FM	100	150	250	350	—
1812	1802 FT	100	150	250	350	—

INSURGENT COINAGE

AMERICAN CONGRESS

KM# 216 REAL

0.9030 Silver **Issuer:** American Congress **Obv:** Eagle on cactus **Obv. Legend:** CONGRESO AMERICANO **Rev:** F. 7 on spread mantle **Rev. Legend:** DEPOSIT D.L. AUCTORI J

Date	Mintage	Good	VG	F	VF	XF
ND(1813)	—	35.00	75.00	120	200	—

KM# 217 REAL

0.9030 Silver **Issuer:** American Congress **Obv:** Eagle on cactus **Obv. Legend:** CONGR. AMER. **Rev:** F. 7 on spread mantle **Rev. Legend:** DEPOS. D. L. AUT. D.

Date	Mintage	Good	VG	F	VF	XF
ND(1813)	—	35.00	75.00	120	200	—

NATIONAL CONGRESS

KM# 209 1/2 REAL

Struck Copper **Issuer:** National Congress **Obv:** Eagle on bridge **Obv. Legend:** VICE FERD. VII DEI GRATIA ET **Rev:** Value, bow quiver, etc **Rev. Legend:** S. P. CONG. NAT. IND.

Date	Mintage	Good	VG	F	VF	XF
1811	—	45.00	85.00	150	200	—

Date	Mintage	Good	VG	F	VF	XF
1812	—	27.50	60.00	100	150	—
1813	—	27.50	60.00	100	150	—
1814	—	45.00	85.00	150	200	—

KM# 210 1/2 REAL

0.9030 Silver **Issuer:** National Congress **Obv:** Eagle on bridge **Obv. Legend:** VICE FERD. VII DEI GRATIA ET **Rev:** Value, bow quiver, etc **Rev. Legend:** S. P. CONG. NAT. IND.

Date	Mintage	Good	VG	F	VF	XF
1812	—	27.50	60.00	100	150	—
1813	—	45.00	90.00	175	275	—

Note: 1812 exists with the date reading inwards and outwards

KM# 211 REAL

0.9030 Silver **Issuer:** National Congress **Obv:** Eagle on bridge **Obv. Legend:** VICE FERD. VII DEI GRATIA ET **Rev:** Value, bow quiver, etc **Rev. Legend:** S. P. CONG. NAT. IND.

Date	Mintage	Good	VG	F	VF	XF
1812	—	22.50	45.00	80.00	125	—
1813	—	22.50	45.00	80.00	125	—

Note: 1812 exists with the date reading either inward or outward

KM# 212 2 REALES

Struck Copper **Issuer:** National Congress **Obv:** Eagle on bridge **Obv. Legend:** VICE FERD. VII DEI GRATIA ET **Rev:** Value, bow quiver, etc **Rev. Legend:** S. P. CONG. NAT. IND.

Date	Mintage	Good	VG	F	VF	XF
1812	—	100	150	200	275	—
1813	—	23.50	50.00	75.00	120	—
1814	—	32.50	75.00	110	165	—

KM# A213 2 REALES

Struck Silver **Issuer:** National Congress **Obv:** Eagle on bridge **Obv. Legend:** VICE FERD. VII DEI GRATIA ET **Rev:** Value, bow, quiver, etc **Rev. Legend:** S. P. CONG. NAT. IND.

Date	Mintage	Good	VG	F	VF	XF
1813	—	950	1,750	3,000	4,850	—

KM# 213   2 REALES
0.9030 Silver **Issuer:** National Congress **Obv:** Eagle on bridge in shield, denomination at sides **Obv. Legend:** VICE FERD. VII DEI GRATIA ET **Rev:** Canon, quiver, arm, etc

Date	Mintage	Good	VG	F	VF	XF
1813	—	75.00	155	265	375	—

Note: These dies were believed to be intended for the striking of 2 Escudos

KM# 214   4 REALES
0.9030 Silver **Issuer:** National Congress **Obv:** Eagle on bridge **Obv. Legend:** VICE FERD. VII DEI GRATIA ET **Rev:** Value, bow, quiver, etc **Rev. Legend:** S. P. CONG. NAT. IND.

Date	Mintage	Good	VG	F	VF	XF
1813	—	600	1,200	2,450	4,400	—

KM# 215.1   8 REALES
0.9030 Silver **Issuer:** National Congress **Obv:** Small crowned eagle **Obv. Legend:** VICE FERD. VII DEI GRATIA ET **Rev:** Value, bow, quiver, etc **Rev. Legend:** S. P. CONG. NAT. IND.

Date	Mintage	Good	VG	F	VF	XF
1812Mo	—	600	1,150	2,350	4,250	—

KM# 215.2   8 REALES
0.9030 Silver **Issuer:** National Congress **Obv:** Large crowned eagle **Obv. Legend:** VICE FERD. VII DEI GRATIA ET **Rev:** Value, bow, quiver, etc **Rev. Legend:** S. P. CONG. NAT. IND.

Date	Mintage	Good	VG	F	VF	XF
1813Mo	—	600	1,150	2,350	4,250	—

SUPREME NATIONAL CONGRESS OF AMERICA

PDV - Provisional de Valladolid

VTIL - Util = useful

(Refer to Multiple countermarks)

KM# 203   1/2 REAL
Struck Copper **Issuer:** Supreme National Congress of America **Obv:** Eagle on bridge **Obv. Legend:** FERDIN. VII DEI GRATIA **Rev:** Value, bow, quiver, etc **Rev. Legend:** S. P. CONG. NAT. IND. GUV.T.

Date	Mintage	Good	VG	F	VF	XF
1811	—	27.50	45.00	60.00	100	—
1812	—	27.50	45.00	60.00	100	—
1813	—	27.50	45.00	60.00	100	—
1814	—	27.50	45.00	60.00	100	—

KM# 204   REAL
Struck Copper **Issuer:** Supreme National Congress of America **Obv:** Eagle on bridge **Obv. Legend:** FERDIN. VII DEI GRATIA **Rev:** Value, bow, quiver, etc **Rev. Legend:** S. P. CONG. NAT. IND. GUV.T.

Date	Mintage	Good	VG	F	VF	XF
1811	—	45.00	75.00	125	200	—

KM# 205   2 REALES
Struck Copper **Issuer:** Supreme National Congress of America **Obv:** Eagle on bridge **Obv. Legend:** FERDIN. VII DEI GRATIA **Rev:** Value, bow, quiver, etc

Date	Mintage	Good	VG	F	VF	XF
1812	—	225	325	475	750	—

KM# 206 8 REALES
Cast Silver **Issuer:** Supreme National Congress of America **Obv:** Eagle on bridge **Obv. Legend:** FERDIN. VII DEI GRATIA **Rev:** Value, bow, quiver, etc

Date	Mintage	Good	VG	F	VF	XF
1811	—	150	250	350	500	—
1812	—	150	250	350	500	—

KM# 207 8 REALES
Struck Silver **Issuer:** Supreme National Congress of America **Obv:** Eagle on bridge **Obv. Legend:** FERDIN. VII DEI GRATIA **Rev:** Value, bow, quiver, etc

Date	Mintage	Good	VG	F	VF	XF
1811	—	—	—	—	—	—
1812	—	300	600	1,000	1,500	—

KM# 208 8 REALES
Struck Copper **Issuer:** Supreme National Congress of America **Obv:** Eagle on bridge **Obv. Legend:** FERDIN. VII... **Rev:** Bow, sword and quiver **Rev. Legend:** PROVICIONAL POR LA SUPREMA JUNTA DE AMERICA

Date	Mintage	Good	VG	F	VF	XF
1811	—	100	150	225	450	—
1812	—	100	150	225	450	—

EMPIRE OF ITURBIDE

RULER
Augustin I Iturbide, 1822-1823
MINT MARK
Mo - Mexico City
ASSAYERS' INITIALS
JA - Jose Garcia Ansaldo, 1812-1833
JM - Joaquin Davila Madrid, 1809-1833

MILLED COINAGE

100 Centavos = 1 Peso

KM# 299 1/8 REAL
Copper **Ruler:** Augustin I Iturbide **Obv:** Crowned shield within sprays **Rev:** Inscription, date **Rev. Inscription:** DE LA PROVINCIA DE NUEVA VISCAYA

Date	Mintage	Good	VG	F	VF	XF
1821D	—	22.50	50.00	85.00	150	—
1822D	—	7.50	13.50	28.50	60.00	—
1823D	—	9.00	13.50	26.50	55.00	—

KM# 300 1/4 REAL
Copper **Ruler:** Augustin I Iturbide **Obv:** Crowned shield within sprays **Rev:** Inscription, date **Rev. Inscription:** DE LA PROVINCIA DE NUEVA VISCAYA

Date	Mintage	Good	VG	F	VF	XF
1822D	—	160	275	400	550	—

KM# 301 1/2 REAL
0.9030 Silver **Ruler:** Augustin I Iturbide **Obv:** Head right **Obv. Legend:** AUGUSTINUS DEI... **Rev:** Crowned eagle **Rev. Legend:** I.M.E.X.I...

Date	Mintage	F	VF	XF	Unc	BU
1822Mo JM	—	20.00	40.00	80.00	325	—
1823Mo JM	—	15.00	30.00	60.00	275	—

KM# 302 REAL
0.9030 Silver **Ruler:** Augustin I Iturbide **Obv:** Head right **Obv. Legend:** AUGUSTINUS DEI... **Rev:** Crowned eagle **Rev. Legend:** MEX.I.IMPERATOR...

Date	Mintage	VG	F	VF	XF	Unc
1822Mo JM	—	100	175	350	550	1,050

KM# 303   2 REALES
6.7667 g., 0.9030 Silver 0.1964 oz. ASW **Ruler:**
Augustin I Iturbide **Obv:** Head right **Obv. Legend:**
AUGUSTINUS DEI... **Rev:** Crowned eagle **Rev.**
Legend: MEX.I.IMPERATOR...

Date	Mintage	F	VF	XF	Unc	BU
1822Mo JM	—	50.00	100	350	1,000	—
1823Mo JM	—	40.00	80.00	250	850	—

KM# 304   8 REALES
27.0674 g., 0.9030 Silver 0.7858 oz. ASW **Ruler:**
Augustin I Iturbide **Obv:** Head right **Obv. Legend:**
AUGUST.... **Rev:** Crowned eagle **Rev. Legend:**
...MEX.I.IMPERATOR...

Date	Mintage	F	VF	XF	Unc	BU
1822Mo JM	—	75.00	150	300	1,050	—
1822Mo JM	—	—	—	—	—	—
Proof, 3 known						

Note: Ponterio & Associates Sale #86, 04-97, choice AU
Proof realized $12,650

KM# 305   8 REALES
0.9030 Silver **Ruler:** Augustin I Iturbide **Obv:** Bust
similar to 8 Escudos, KM#131 **Rev:** Crowned eagle

Date	Mintage	F	VF	XF	Unc	BU
1822Mo JM Rare	—	—	—	—	—	—

KM# 306.1   8 REALES
0.9030 Silver **Ruler:** Augustin I Iturbide **Obv:** Head
right **Obv. Legend:** AUGUST... **Rev:** Crowned
eagle, 8 R.J.M. at upper left of eagle **Rev. Legend:**
MEX.I.IMPERATOR... **Note:** Type I.

Date	Mintage	F	VF	XF	Unc	BU
1822Mo JM	—	90.00	170	450	1,500	—

KM# 306.2   8 REALES
0.9030 Silver **Ruler:** Augustin I Iturbide **Obv:** Head
right **Rev:** Cross on crown **Note:** Type I.

Date	Mintage	F	VF	XF	Unc	BU
1822Mo JM	—	650	1,000	—	—	—

KM# 307   8 REALES
0.9030 Silver **Ruler:** Augustin I Iturbide **Obv:** Head
right **Rev:** Crowned eagle **Note:** Type II.

Date	Mintage	F	VF	XF	Unc	BU
1822Mo JM	—	150	350	650	2,500	—

KM# 308   8 REALES
0.9030 Silver **Ruler:** Augustin I Iturbide **Obv:** Head
right, continuous legend with long smooth truncation
Obv. Legend: AUGUSTINUS DEI... **Rev:** Crowned
eagle **Note:** Type III.

Date	Mintage	F	VF	XF	Unc	BU
1822Mo JM	—	175	500	950	2,500	—

Note: Variety with long, straight truncation is valued at
$5,000 in uncirculated condition

KM# 309 8 REALES

0.9030 Silver **Ruler:** Augustin I Iturbide **Obv:** Head right **Obv. Legend:** AUGUSTINUS DEI... **Rev:** Crowned eagle **Rev. Legend:** MEX.I.IMPERATOR... **Note:** Type IV.

Date	Mintage	F	VF	XF	Unc	BU
1822Mo JM	—	50.00	120	250	850	—

KM# 310 8 REALES

0.9030 Silver **Ruler:** Augustin I Iturbide **Obv:** Head right, continuous legend with short irregular truncation **Obv. Legend:** AUGUSTINUS DEI... **Rev:** Crowned eagle, 8 R.J.M. below eagle **Rev. Legend:** MEX.I.IMPERATOR... **Note:** Type V.

Date	Mintage	F	VF	XF	Unc	BU
1822Mo JM	—	50.00	120	225	1,000	—
1823Mo JM	—	50.00	120	225	1,000	—

KM# 311 8 REALES

0.9030 Silver **Ruler:** Augustin I Iturbide **Obv:** Head right,long truncation **Rev:** Crowned eagle **Note:** Type VI.

Date	Mintage	F	VF	XF	Unc	BU
1822Mo JM Rare	—	—	—	—	—	—

KM# 312 4 SCUDOS

13.5334 g., 0.8750 Gold 0.3807 oz. AGW **Ruler:** Augustin I Iturbide **Obv:** Head right **Obv. Legend:** AUGUSTINUS DEI... **Rev:** Crowned eagle within ornate shield **Rev. Legend:** CONSTITUT.4.S.I.M...

Date	Mintage	F	VF	XF	Unc	BU
1823Mo JM	—	1,000	1,850	3,750	7,000	—

KM# 313.1 8 SCUDOS

27.0674 g., 0.8750 Gold 0.7614 oz. AGW **Ruler:** Augustin I Iturbide **Obv:** Head right **Obv. Legend:** AUGUSTINUS . DEI... **Rev:** Crowned eagle **Rev. Legend:** CONSTITUT.8.S.I.M...

Date	Mintage	F	VF	XF	Unc	BU
1822Mo JM	—	1,200	2,000	4,000	—	—

Note: American Numismatic Rarities Eliasberg sale 4-05, MS-62 realized $20,700. Superior Casterline sale 5-89 choice AU realized $11,000

KM# 313.2 8 SCUDOS

0.8750 Gold **Ruler:** Augustin I Iturbide **Obv:** Head right, error in legend **Obv. Legend:** AUGSTINUS . DEI... **Rev:** Crowned eagle **Rev. Legend:** CONSTITUT.8.S.I.M...

Date	Mintage	F	VF	XF	Unc	BU
1822Mo JM	—	1,250	2,250	4,500	—	—

KM# 314   8 SCUDOS
0.8750 Gold **Ruler:** Augustin I Iturbide **Obv:** Head
right **Obv. Legend:** AUGUSTINUS DEI... **Rev:**
Crowned eagle within ornate shield **Rev. Legend:**
CONSTITUT.8.S.I.M...

Date	Mintage	F	VF	XF	Unc	BU
1823Mo JM	—	1,000	1,800	3,500	6,500	—

LOCAL COINAGE

AHUALULCO

KM# L2   1/8 REAL (Octavo)
Copper **Issuer:** Ahualulco **Obv:** Script AHO, 1/8
below **Note:** Uniface.

Date	Mintage	Good	VG	F	VF	XF
ND	—	10.00	17.50	25.00	40.00	—

KM# L1   1/8 REAL (Octavo)
Copper **Issuer:** Ahualulco **Obv:** AHUALULCO and
1813 arfound 1/8 in circle **Note:** Uniface.

Date	Mintage	Good	VG	F	VF	XF
1813	—	15.00	25.00	35.00	55.00	—

AMECA

KM# L10   1/8 REAL (Octavo)
Copper **Issuer:** Ameca **Obv:** F 1/8 Z within wavy
circle **Note:** Octagonal planchet.

Date	Mintage	Good	VG	F	VF	XF
ND	—	16.50	25.00	33.50	57.50	—

KM# L9   1/8 REAL (Octavo)
Copper **Issuer:** Ameca **Obv:** AME/CA 1811 in circle
Note: Octagonal planchet.

Date	Mintage	Good	VG	F	VF	XF
1811	—	16.50	27.50	38.50	65.00	—

KM# L8   1/8 REAL (Octavo)
Copper **Issuer:** Ameca **Obv:** AME/CA 1811 in circle
Note: Uniface.

Date	Mintage	Good	VG	F	VF	XF
1811	—	15.00	25.00	35.00	55.00	—

KM# L7   1/8 REAL (Octavo)
Copper **Issuer:** Ameca **Obv:** QTG monogram in
toothed circle **Obv. Legend:** TLACO DE AMECA

Date	Mintage	Good	VG	F	VF	XF
ND(1812)	—	10.00	17.50	25.00	40.00	—

KM# L6   1/8 REAL (Octavo)
Copper **Issuer:** Ameca **Obv:** Church flanked by
trees **Note:** Uniface.

Date	Mintage	Good	VG	F	VF	XF
1824	—	10.00	17.50	25.00	40.00	—

KM# L11   1/8 REAL (Octavo)
Copper **Issuer:** Ameca **Obv:** T.Z. AMECA 1833
around value **Note:** Octagonal planchet.

Date	Mintage	Good	VG	F	VF	XF
1833	—	10.00	15.00	22.50	35.00	—

KM# L12   1/8 REAL (Octavo)
Copper **Issuer:** Ameca **Obv:** V.F AMECA 1858
below value **Note:** Octagonal planchet.

Date	Mintage	Good	VG	F	VF	XF
1858	—	12.50	17.50	25.00	40.00	—

AMESCUA

KM# L15   1/8 REAL (Octavo)
Copper **Issuer:** Amescua **Obv:** Mexican eagle

Date	Mintage	Good	VG	F	VF	XF
1828	—	10.00	15.00	22.50	35.00	—

KM# L16   1/8 REAL (Octavo)
Copper **Issuer:** Amescua **Obv:** Darte below eagle

Date	Mintage	Good	VG	F	VF	XF
1838	—	13.50	20.00	28.50	45.00	—

ATENCINCO

KM# L19   1/8 REAL (Octavo)
Copper **Issuer:** Atencinco **Obv:** ATENCINCO in
outer border, 8-leaved rosette above branch in center

Date	Mintage	Good	VG	F	VF	XF
ND	—	13.50	20.00	28.00	45.00	—

ATOTONILCO

KM# L23   1/4 REAL (Octavo)
Copper **Issuer:** Atotonilco **Obv:** Legend in outer
border, 1821 in center **Obv. Legend:** ATOTONILCO
ANO DE **Rev:** Legend around outer border **Rev.
Legend:** V.F.7.q.D.C...

Date	Mintage	Good	VG	F	VF	XF
1821	—	15.00	25.00	35.00	55.00	—

KM# L22   1/8 REAL (Octavo)
Copper **Issuer:** Atotonilco **Obv:** ATOTONILCO
ANO DE 1808 in outer border, L. S. S. / JUSU/ESES
in circle

Date	Mintage	Good	VG	F	VF	XF
1808	—	25.00	37.50	55.00	80.00	—

KM# L24 1/8 REAL (Octavo)
Copper **Issuer:** Atotonilco **Obv:** Legend in outer border, 1826 in center **Obv. Legend:** VILL ATOTONILCO **Rev:** Legend in center, stars in outer border **Rev. Legend:** 1/8

Date	Mintage	Good	VG	F	VF	XF
1826	—	15.00	25.00	35.00	55.00	—

CAMPECHE

KM# L27 CENTAVO
Brass **Issuer:** Campeche

Date	Mintage	Good	VG	F	VF	XF
1861	—	7.00	10.00	17.50	27.50	—

CATORCE

KM# L30 1/4 REAL
Copper **Issuer:** Catorce **Obv:** Legend around border, 1/4 below flower and raised rectangle **Obv. Legend:** FONDOS PUBLICOS **Rev:** Legend around border, eagle on cactus **Rev. Legend:** DE CATORCE 1822

Date	Mintage	Good	VG	F	VF	XF
1822	—	12.00	18.50	30.00	45.00	—

CELAYA

KM# L33 1/8 REAL (Octavo)
Copper **Issuer:** Celaya **Obv. Legend:** EN/CELAYA/DE/1803 **Rev:** Branches below legend, flower above **Rev. Legend:** LUIS/VASQUE S

Date	Mintage	Good	VG	F	VF	XF
1803	—	25.00	37.50	55.00	80.00	—

KM# L34 1/8 REAL (Octavo)
Copper **Issuer:** Celaya **Obv. Legend:** VIDERI/QUE/CELALLA/1808 **Rev:** Branches below legend, flower above **Rev. Legend:** LUIS/VASQUE S **Note:** Uniface.

Date	Mintage	Good	VG	F	VF	XF
1808	—	25.00	37.50	55.00	80.00	—

KM# L35 1/8 REAL (Octavo)
Copper **Issuer:** Celaya **Obv. Legend:** VISCARA/CELAYA/1814 with ornament above **Rev:** Branches below legend, flower above **Rev. Legend:** LUIS/VASQUE S **Note:** Uniface.

Date	Mintage	Good	VG	F	VF	XF
1814	—	17.50	25.00	35.00	55.00	—

CHILCHOTA

KM# L38 1/8 REAL (Octavo)
Copper **Issuer:** Chilchota **Obv:** Head to right, date below legend **Obv. Legend:** CHILCHOTA UN OCTAVO **Rev:** Wreath in center **Rev. Legend:** RESPONSAVILIDAD DE MURGVIA

Date	Mintage	Good	VG	F	VF	XF
1858	—	15.00	25.00	35.00	55.00	—

COLIMA

KM# L41 1/8 REAL (Octavo)
Copper **Issuer:** Colima **Obv:** Legend around border as continuos legend **Obv. Legend:** VILLA DE COLIMA **Rev:** Blank

Date	Mintage	Good	VG	F	VF	XF
1813	—	12.50	17.50	25.00	42.50	—

KM# L42 1/8 REAL (Octavo)
Copper **Issuer:** Colima **Obv:** Legend and date in three lines **Obv. Legend:** VILLA DE COLIMA **Rev:** Blank

Date	Mintage	Good	VG	F	VF	XF
1814	—	12.50	17.50	25.00	42.50	—

KM# L44 1/8 REAL (Octavo)
Copper **Issuer:** Colima **Obv:** Legend and date in three lines **Obv. Legend:** OCT. DE COLI **Rev:** Date

Date	Mintage	Good	VG	F	VF	XF
1819	—	15.00	22.50	30.00	50.00	—

KM# L46 1/8 REAL (Octavo)
Copper **Issuer:** Colima **Obv:** Legend around border, date in center circle **Obv. Legend:** OCTO DE COLIMA **Rev:** Legend within wreath, pellet in center **Rev. Legend:** OCTAVO

Date	Mintage	Good	VG	F	VF	XF
1824	—	13.50	17.50	25.00	42.00	—

KM# L47 1/8 REAL (Octavo)
Copper **Issuer:** Colima **Obv:** Legend in three lines **Obv. Legend:** OCTO DE COLA **Rev:** Legend within wreath, pellet in center **Rev. Legend:** OCTAVO

Date	Mintage	Good	VG	F	VF	XF
1824	—	13.50	17.50	25.00	42.50	—
1828	—	13.50	17.50	25.00	42.50	—

KM# L48 1/8 REAL (Octavo)
Copper **Issuer:** Colima **Obv:** Legend in three lines **Obv. Legend:** OCTO DE COLIMA **Rev:** Legend in three lines **Rev. Legend:** ANO DE 1830

Date	Mintage	Good	VG	F	VF	XF
1830	—	13.50	17.50	25.00	42.50	—

KM# L43 1/4 REAL (Quarto)
Copper **Issuer:** Colima **Obv:** Legend in three lines in wreath **Obv. Legend:** QUART COLIMA 1816 **Rev:** Colima monogram in wreath

Date	Mintage	Good	VG	F	VF	XF
1816	—	10.00	16.50	22.50	40.00	—

KM# L45 1/4 REAL (Quarto)
Copper **Issuer:** Colima **Obv:** Legend around border, date in center circle **Obv. Legend:** QUARTo DE COLIMA **Rev:** Colima monogram in wreath

Date	Mintage	Good	VG	F	VF	XF
1824	—	12.50	16.50	22.50	40.00	—

COTIJA

KM# L51 1/4 REAL (Quarto)
Copper **Issuer:** Cotija **Obv:** Seated Liberty with staff and liberty cap **Obv. Legend:** DE. D. JOSE NUNES **Rev:** Value and date in wreath **Rev. Legend:** COMMERCIO. D. COTIJA

Date	Mintage	Good	VG	F	VF	XF
ND	—	12.50	18.50	25.00	42.50	—

CUIDO

KM# L52 1/8 REAL (Octavo)
Copper **Issuer:** Cuido **Note:** Uniface. "CUIDO" above "1/8" in spray.

Date	Mintage	Good	VG	F	VF	XF
ND	—	12.50	20.00	28.50	45.00	—

GUADALAJARA

KM# L57 1/8 REAL (Octavo)
Copper **Issuer:** Guadalajara **Obv:** Eagle with wings spread **Obv. Legend:** GUADALAXARA **Note:** Uniface.

Date	Mintage	Good	VG	F	VF	XF
ND	—	27.50	37.50	55.00	80.00	—

LAGOS

KM# L59 1/4 REAL
Bronze **Issuer:** Lagos **Obv:** 2 globes with crown above, wreath and 1/4 below **Rev:** Coat of arms of Lagos

Date	Mintage	Good	VG	F	VF	XF
ND	—	60.00	75.00	120	185	—

KM# L59a 1/4 REAL
Silver **Issuer:** Lagos **Obv:** 2 globes with crown above, wreath and 1/4 below **Rev:** Coat of arms of Lagos

Date	Mintage	Good	VG	F	VF	XF
ND	—	150	200	300	500	—

MERIDA

KM# L60 1/2 GRANO
Lead **Issuer:** Merida **Obv:** First part of legend in center, second part of legend around border, 1859 below **Obv. Legend:** PART/DE LA SO/CIED • MERIDADE YUCATAN **Rev. Legend:** 1/2/GRANO/ DE PESO/FUERTE

Date	Mintage	Good	VG	F	VF	XF
1859	—	10.00	16.00	32.50	55.00	—

PAZCUARO

KM# L63 1/8 REAL (Octavo)
Copper **Issuer:** Pazcuaro **Obv:** Town at base of mountains, lake in foreground, value 1/8 above **Rev:** Woman walking right, carrying bag, fish net and fish

Date	Mintage	Good	VG	F	VF	XF
ND	—	11.00	16.50	22.50	35.00	—

Note: Also in brass and cast in bronze; minor die varieties have been observed

KM# L64 1/8 REAL (Octavo)
Copper **Issuer:** Pazcuaro **Obv:** 1/8 PAZCUARO
Rev: Crude rendering of Woman walking right,
carrying bag, fish net and fish.

Date	Mintage	Good	VG	F	VF	XF
ND	—	12.50	17.50	25.00	40.00	—

PROGRESO

KM# L66 1/8 REAL (Octavo)
Copper **Issuer:** Progreso **Obv:** Radiant star above
open book **Rev:** Value 1/8 in double wreath

Date	Mintage	Good	VG	F	VF	XF
1858	—	15.00	22.50	35.00	55.00	—

KM# L67 CENTAVO
Lead **Issuer:** Progreso **Obv:** Legend and 1873 in
center **Obv. Legend:** MUNICIPALIDAD DE
PROGRESO UN CENT **Rev:** Flank in oval band

Date	Mintage	Good	VG	F	VF	XF
1873	—	12.50	20.00	30.00	50.00	—

QUITUPAN

KM# L69 1/8 REAL (Octavo)
Copper **Issuer:** Quitupan **Obv:** Bow and two arrows
in center **Obv. Legend:** QUITUPAN ... 1854 **Rev:** 1/
8 in center, mongram countermark **Rev. Legend:**
YGNACIO BUENROSTRO

Date	Mintage	Good	VG	F	VF	XF
1854	—	15.00	22.50	32.50	55.00	—

TACAMBARO

KM# L72 1/8 REAL (Octavo)
Copper **Issuer:** Tacambaro **Obv:** Winged caduceus
in sprays **Rev:** Value 1/8 in sprays

Date	Mintage	Good	VG	F	VF	XF
ND	—	12.50	18.50	25.00	40.00	—

TARETAN

KM# L75 1/8 REAL (Octavo)
Copper **Issuer:** Taretan **Obv:** Head of man right
Rev: Tree

Date	Mintage	Good	VG	F	VF	XF
1858	—	15.00	25.00	37.50	60.00	—

TLAZASALCA

KM# L78 1/8 REAL (Octavo)
Copper **Issuer:** Tlazasalca **Obv:** Two mountains,
date below **Rev:** Value 1/8 in wreath

Date	Mintage	Good	VG	F	VF	XF
1853	—	16.50	25.00	35.00	55.00	—

XALOSTOTITLAN

KM# L54 1/8 REAL (Octavo)
Copper **Issuer:** Xalostotitlan **Obv:** Crown in center
Obv. Legend: ILVSTRE AYVNTAMIENTO **Rev:** 4
in center **Rev. Legend:** DE XALOS.TOTITAN. 1820

Date	Mintage	Good	VG	F	VF	XF
1820	—	22.50	35.00	55.00	80.00	—

ZAMORA

KM# L80 1/8 REAL (Octavo)
Copper **Issuer:** Zamora

Date	Mintage	Good	VG	F	VF	XF
1842	—	6.00	12.50	22.50	37.50	—
1848	—	6.00	12.50	22.50	37.50	—
1854	—	6.00	12.50	22.50	37.50	—
1858	—	6.00	12.50	22.50	37.50	—

KM# L81 1/8 REAL (Octavo)
Copper Or Bronze **Issuer:** Zamora **Obv:** Eagle on
cactus above sprays **Rev:** Liberty cap, bow and arrows
above sprays. With or without various countermarks

Date	Mintage	Good	VG	F	VF	XF
1852	—	6.00	12.50	22.50	37.50	—
1853	—	6.00	12.50	22.50	37.50	—
1854	—	6.00	12.50	22.50	37.50	—
1856	—	6.00	12.50	22.50	37.50	—
1857	—	6.00	12.50	22.50	37.50	—
1858	—	6.00	12.50	22.50	37.50	—

Note: These pieces are also found with various countermarks; "Za" in a dentilated circle is the most common; "1/8"
in a circular countermark is also encountered

ZAPOTLAN

KM# L84 1/8 REAL (Octavo)
Copper **Issuer:** Zapotlan **Obv. Legend:** ZAPO/
TLAN/1813

Date	Mintage	Good	VG	F	VF	XF
1813	—	17.50	27.50	40.00	60.00	—

REPUBLIC
FIRST

MINT MARKS
A, AS - Alamos
CE - Real de Catorce
CA,CH - Chihuahua
C, Cn, Gn(error) - Culiacan
D, Do - Durango
EoMo - Estado de Mexico
Ga - Guadalajara
GC - Guadalupe y Calvo
G, Go - Guanajuato
H, Ho - Hermosillo
M, Mo - Mexico City
O, OA - Oaxaca
SLP, PI, P, I/P - San Luis Potosi
Z, Zs – Zacatecas

ASSAYERS' INITIALS

ALAMOS MINT

PG	1862-68	Pascual Gaxiola
DL, L	1866-79	Domingo Larraguibel
AM	1872-74	Antonio Moreno
ML, L	1878-95	Manuel Larraguibel

REAL DE CATORCE MINT

ML	1863	Mariano Cristobal Ramirez

CHIHUAHUA MINT

MR	1831-34	Mariano Cristobal Ramirez
AM	1833-39	Jose Antonio Mucharraz
MJ	1832	Jose Mariano Jimenez
RG	1839-56	Rodrigo Garcia
JC	1856-65	Joaquin Campa
BA	1858	Bruno Arriada
FP	1866	Francisco Potts
JC	1866-1868	Jose Maria Gomez del Campo
MM, M	1868-95	Manuel Merino
AV	1873-80	Antonio Valero
EA	1877	Eduardo Avila
JM	1877	Jacobo Mucharraz
GR	1877	Guadalupe Rocha
MG	1880-82	Manuel Gameros

CULIACAN MINT

CE	1846-70	Clemente Espinosa de los Monteros
C	1870	???
PV	1860-61	Pablo Viruega
MP, P	1871-76	Manuel Onofre Parodi
GP	1876	Celso Gaxiola & Manuel Onofre Parodi
CG, G	1876-78	Celso Gaxiola
JD, D	1878-82	Juan Dominguez
AM, M	1882-1899	Antonio Moreno
F	1870	Fernando Ferrari
JQ, Q	1899-1903	Jesus S. Quiroz

DURANGO MINT

RL	1825-1832	???
RM	1830-48	Ramon Mascarenas
OMC	1840	Octavio Martinez de Castro
CM	1848-76	Clemente Moron
JMR	1849-52	Jose Maria Ramirez
CP, P	1853-64, 1867-73	Carlos Leon de la Pena
LT	1864-65	???
JMP, P	1877	Carlos Miguel de la Palma
PE, E	1878	Pedro Espejo
TB, B	1878-80	Trinidad Barrera
JP	1880-94	J. Miguel Palma
MC, C,	1882-90	Manuel M. Canseco or Melchor Calderon
JB	1885	Jocobo Blanco
ND, D	1892-95	Norberto Dominguez

ESTADO DE MEXICO MINT

L	1828-30	Luis Valazquez de la Cadena
F	1828-30	Francisco Parodi

GUADALAJARA MINT

FS	1818-35	Francisco Suarez
JM	1830-32	???
JG	1836-39, 1842-67	Juan de Dios Guzman
MC	1839-46	Manuel Cueras
JM	1867-69	Jesus P. Manzano
IC, C	1869-77	Ignacio Canizo y Soto
MC	1874-75	Manuel Contreras
JA, A	1877-81	Julio Arancivia
FS, S	1880-82	Fernando Sayago
TB, B	1883-84	Trinidad Barrera
AH, H	1884-85	Antonio Hernandez y Prado
JS, S	1885-95	Jose S. Schiafino

GUADALUPE Y CALVO MINT

MP	1844-52	Manuel Onofre Parodi

GUANAJUATO MINT

JJ	1825-26	Jose Mariano Jimenez
MJ, MR, JM, PG, PJ, PF		???
PM	1841-48, 1853-61	Patrick Murphy
YF	1862-68	Yldefonso Flores
YE	1862-63	Ynocencio Espinoza
FR	1870-78	Faustino Ramirez
SB, RR		???
RS	1891-1900	Rosendo Sandoval

HERMOSILLO MINT

PP	1835-36	Pedro Peimbert
FM	1871-76	Florencio Monteverde
MP	1866	Manuel Onofre Parodi
PR	1866-75	Pablo Rubio
R	1874-75	Pablo Rubio
GR	1877	Guadalupe Rocha
AF, F	1876-77	Alejandro Fourcade
JA, A	1877-83	Jesus Acosta
FM, M	1883-86	Fernando Mendez
FG, G	1886-95	Fausto Gaxiola

MEXICO CITY MINT

Because of the great number of assayers for this mint (Mexico City is a much larger mint than any of the others)there is much confusion as to which initial stands for which assayer at any one time. Therefore we feel that it would be of no value to list the assayers.

OAXACA MINT

AE	1859-91	Agustin Endner
E	1889-90	Agustin Endner
FR	1861-64	Francisco de la Rosa
EN	1890	Eduardo Navarro Luna
N	1890	Eduardo Navarro Luna

POTOSI MINT

JS	1827-42	Juan Sanabria
AM	1838, 1843-49	Jose Antonio Mucharraz
PS	1842-43, 1848-49, 1857-61, 1867-70	Pompaso Sanabria
S	1869-70	Pomposo Sanabria
MC	1849-59	Mariano Catano
RO	1859-65	Romualdo Obregon
MH, H	1870-85	Manuel Herrera Razo
O	1870-73	Juan R. Ochoa
CA, G	1867-70	Carlos Aguirre Gomez
BE, E	1879-81	Blas Escontria
LC, C	1885-86	Luis Cuevas
MR, R	1886-93	Mariano Reyes

ZACATECAS MINT

A	1825-29	Adalco
Z	1825-26	Mariano Zaldivar
V	1824-31	Jose Mariano Vela
O	1829-67	Manuel Ochoa
M	1831-67	Manuel Miner
VL	1860-66	Vicente Larranaga
JS	1867-68, 1876-86	J.S. de Santa Ana
YH	1868-74	Ygnacio Hierro
JA	1874-76	Juan H. Acuna
FZ	18861905	Francisco de P. Zarate

DIE VARIETIES

Similar basic designs were utilized by all the Mexican mints, but many variations are noticeable, particularly in the eagle, cactus and sprays.

1835 Durango, 8 Escudos
Illustration enlarged.
A large winged eagle was portrayed on the earlier coinage of the new republic.

1849 Mexico City, 8 Escudos
Illustration enlarged.
The later eagle featured undersized wings.

1844 Durango, 8 Escudos
Illustration enlarged.
The early renditions of the hand held Liberty cap over open book were massive in the gold escudo series.

1864 Durango, 8 Escudos
Illustration enlarged.
A finer, more petite style was adopted later on in the gold escudo series.

PROFILE EAGLE COINAGE

The first coins of the Republic were of the distinctive Profile Eagle style, sometimes called the "Hooked Neck Eagle". They were struck first in Mexico City in 1823 in denominations of eight reales and eight escudos. In 1824, they were produced at the Durango and Guanajuato mints in addition to Mexico City. Denominations included the one half, one, two and eight reales. No gold escudos of this design were struck in 1824. In 1825, only the eight reales were struck briefly at the Guanajuato mint.

NOTE: For a more extensive examination of Profile Eagle Coinage, please refer to Hookneck - El Aguila de Perfil by Clyde Hubbard and David O Harrow.

KM# 369   1/2 REAL
1.6900 g., 0.9030 Silver 0.0491 oz. ASW **Obv:** Full
breast Profile eagle **Rev:** Cap and rays **Note:** Die
varieties exist.

Date	Mintage	F	VF	XF	Unc	BU
1824Mo JM	—	45.00	75.00	150	750	—

KM# 371.1   REAL
3.3800 g., 0.9030 Silver 0.0981 oz. ASW **Obv:** Thin
Profile eagle **Rev:** Superscript S reversed

Date	Mintage	F	VF	XF	Unc	BU
1824Do RL	—	5,500	9,500	13,000	—	—

KM# 371.2   REAL
3.3800 g., 0.9030 Silver 0.0981 oz. ASW **Obv:** Thin
Profile eagle **Rev:** Superscript S normal

Date	Mintage	F	VF	XF	Unc	BU
1824Do RL 3 known	—	—	—	—	—	—

Mint mark: Do

KM# 373.1   2 REALES
6.7600 g., 0.9030 Silver 0.1962 oz. ASW **Obv:**
Profile eagle, snake in beak **Obv. Legend:**
REPUBLICA.MEXICANA **Rev:** Radiant cap **Note:**
Die varieties exist.

Date	Mintage	F	VF	XF	Unc	BU
1824Do RL	—	50.00	125	850	2,200	—

KM# 373.2   2 REALES
6.7600 g., 0.9030 Silver 0.1962 oz. ASW **Obv:**
Profile eagle, snake in beak **Obv. Legend:** Thin
profile **Rev:** Radiant cap **Rev. Legend:** Type 1, dot
before 2R in legend

Date	Mintage	F	VF	XF	Unc	BU
1824D RL	—	100	200	1,000	3,000	—

KM# 373.3   2 REALES
6.7600 g., 0.9030 Silver 0.1962 oz. ASW **Obv:**
Profile eagle, snake in beak **Obv. Legend:** Thin
profile **Rev:** Radiant cap **Rev. Legend:** Type II, no
dot before 2R in legend

Date	Mintage	F	VF	XF	Unc	BU
1824D RL	—	100	200	1,000	3,000	—

KM# 373.4   2 REALES
Obv: Profile eagle, snake in beak **Obv. Legend:**
REPUBLICA.MEXICANA **Rev:** Radiant cap **Note:**
Varieties exist.

Date	Mintage	F	VF	XF	Unc	BU
1824Mo JM	—	30.00	70.00	450	2,000	—

Note: No coins are known with visible feather details on the
eagle's breast

KM# A376.2   8 REALES
27.0700 g., 0.9030 Silver 0.7859 oz. ASW **Obv:** Full
breast profile eagle, snake in beak **Obv. Legend:**
REPUBLICA MEXICANA **Rev:** Radiant cap **Edge:**
Standard or Republic

Date	Mintage	F	VF	XF	Unc	BU
1823Mo JM	—	150	300	800	4,500	—
1824Mo JM	—	125	250	700	4,000	—

KM# A376.1   8 REALES
27.0700 g., 0.9030 Silver 0.7859 oz. ASW **Obv:** Full breast profile eagle, snake in beak **Obv. Legend:** REPUBLICA MEXICANA. **Rev:** Radiant cap

Date	Mintage	F	VF	XF	Unc	BU
1824Go JM	—	250	400	1,100	3,500	—
1825/4Go JJ	—	600	1,200	2,750	7,000	—
1825Go JJ	—	500	750	1,400	5,500	—

KM# A376.3   8 REALES
27.0700 g., 0.9030 Silver 0.7859 oz. ASW **Obv:** Full breast profile eagle, snake in beak **Rev:** Radiant cap **Edge:** Colonial or circle and rectangle

Date	Mintage	F	VF	XF	Unc	BU
1823Mo JM Rare	—	—	—	—	—	—

The Round-Topped Three

KM# A376.4   8 REALES
27.0700 g., 0.9030 Silver 0.7859 oz. ASW **Obv:** Full breast profile eagle, snake in beak **Rev:** Radiant cap, round topped three **Edge:** Standard or Republic

Date	Mintage	F	VF	XF	Unc	BU
1823Mo JM	—	2,000	4,000	6,000	8,000	—

Note: Many die varieties exist; Illustrations of one of the die differences is the size of the snake loop at the eagle's beak; This difference is not apparent except on the 1824 Mo 8 Reales

Typical Submissive Snake Obverse

KM# A376.5   8 REALES
27.0700 g., 0.9030 Silver 0.7859 oz. ASW **Obv:** Full breast profile eagle, snake in beak, REPULICA (error) **Rev:** Radiant cap

Date	Mintage	F	VF	XF	Unc	BU
1824Mo JM	—	6,000	9,000	11,000	—	—

Note: Legible Libertads on the cap are not as prevalent on the Mexico City 8 Reales as on the Durango 8 Reales; They are much more numerous than on the Guanajuato 8 Reales

Typical Folded Snake Obverse

NOTE: Legible Libertads on the Cap are common Durango eight reales.

Med. Libertad **Small Libertad** **Large Libertad**
Cap Reverse **Cap Reverse** **Cap Reverse**

NOTE: The three styles of obverses and the three styles of reverses were combined   to make six distinct varieties of coins.

KM# 376.1   8 REALES
27.0700 g., 0.9030 Silver 0.7859 oz. ASW   **Obv:** Thin profile eagle, defiant snake **Rev:** Radiant cap, medium Libertad

Date	Mintage	F	VF	XF	Unc	BU
1824Do RL	—	500	1,200	4,500	7,000	—

Note: Five die varieties are known, all are rare

KM# 376.2   8 REALES
27.0700 g., 0.9030 Silver 0.7859 oz. ASW   **Obv:** Thin profile eagle, defiant snake **Obv. Legend:** REPUBLICA MEXICANA **Rev:** Radiant cap, small Libertad

Date	Mintage	F	VF	XF	Unc	BU
1824Do RL	—	300	400	1,600	3,500	—

Note: Eleven die varieties are known, some are rare

KM# 376.3   8 REALES
27.0700 g., 0.9030 Silver 0.7859 oz. ASW   **Obv:** Thin profile eagle, submissive snake **Obv. Legend:** REPUBLICA.MEXICANA **Rev:** Radiant cap, small Libertad

Date	Mintage	F	VF	XF	Unc	BU
1824Do RL	—	200	350	1,250	2,750	—

Note: Seven die varieties are known, some are rare

KM# 376.4   8 REALES
27.0700 g., 0.9030 Silver 0.7859 oz. ASW   **Obv:** Thin profile eagle, submissive snake **Rev:** Radiant cap, large Libertad

Date	Mintage	F	VF	XF	Unc	BU
1824Do RL	—	200	350	1,250	2,750	—

Note: Twelve die varieties known, some are rare

KM# 376.5   8 REALES
27.0700 g., 0.9030 Silver 0.7859 oz. ASW   **Obv:** Thin profile eagle, folded snake **Rev:** Radiant cap, small Libertad

Date	Mintage	F	VF	XF	Unc	BU
1824Do RL	—	200	350	1,200	2,500	—

Note: Only one die variety is known

KM# 376.6   8 REALES
27.0700 g., 0.9030 Silver 0.7859 oz. ASW   **Obv:** Thin profile eagle, folded snake **Rev:** Radiant cap, large Libertad

Date	Mintage	F	VF	XF	Unc	BU
1824Do RL	—	200	400	1,500	3,000	—

Note: Eleven die varieties known, some are rare

Type I Obverse/Reverse

NOTE: The cap on the reverse of the curved tail Type I points to the "A" of LIBERTAD.

KM# 382.1 8 ESCUDOS

27.0700 g., 0.8750 Gold 0.7615 oz. AGW **Obv:** Profile eagle, snake's tail curved **Obv. Legend:** REPUBLICA MEXICANA **Rev:** Open book, hand holding stick with cap, cap points to "A" of LIBERTAD **Rev. Legend:** LIBERTAD EN...

Date	Mintage	F	VF	XF	Unc	BU
1823Mo JM	—	7,000	10,000	20,000	—	—

Note: American Numismatic Rarities Eliasberg sale 4-05, MS-61 realized $55,200.

Type II Obverse/Reverse

NOTE: The cap on the reverse of the looped tail Type II points to the "T" of LIBERTAD.

KM# 382.2 8 ESCUDOS

27.0700 g., 0.8750 Gold 0.7615 oz. AGW **Obv:** Profile eagle, snake's tail looped **Obv. Legend:** REPUBLICA MEXICANA **Rev:** Open book, hand holding stick with cap, cap points to "T" of LIBERTAD **Rev. Legend:** LIBERTAD EN...

Date	Mintage	F	VF	XF	Unc	BU
1823Mo JM	—	6,000	9,000	18,000	—	—

Note: The quality of the strikes of Type I coins is almost always superior to that of the Type II; Details of the eagle feathers, cactus and lettering on the open book are better on most Type I coins but the Type II coins are scarcer; Type I coins outnumber Type II coins by about two to one

STATE COINAGE

KM# 316 1/16 REAL (Medio Octavo)

4.7500 g., Copper, 21 mm. **Obv:** Bow, quiver and flag **Obv. Legend:** DEPARTAMENTO DE JALISCO **Rev:** Seated figure, left, cap on pole **Edge:** Oblique reeding

Date	Mintage	Good	VG	F	VF	XF
1860	—	3.00	8.00	17.50	55.00	—

KM# 317 1/16 REAL (Medio Octavo)

4.7500 g., Copper, 21 mm. **Obv. Legend:** ESTADO LIBRE DE JALISCO **Edge:** Oblique reeding

Date	Mintage	Good	VG	F	VF	XF
1861	—	2.50	6.00	13.50	32.50	—

KM# 320 1/8 REAL (Octavo Real)

Copper **Obv:** Facing eagle, snake in beak, value at lower left **Rev:** Radiant Libertad above date within wreath **Rev. Legend:** LIBERTAD **Edge:** Oblique reeding **Note:** Size varies 17-18mm. Weight varies 2.5-4 g. These pieces were frequently struck over 1/8 Real, dated 1821-23 of Nueva Vizcaya. All known examples struck over these coins are believed to be contemporary counterfeits.

Date	Mintage	Good	VG	F	VF	XF
1824D	—	5.00	12.50	35.00	85.00	—
1828D	—	150	250	400	1,000	—

KM# 338 1/8 REAL (Octavo Real)

4.0000 g., Brass, 21 mm. **Obv:** Monument **Obv. Legend:** ESTo LIBe FEDo DE ZACATECAS **Rev:** Floating angel holding radiant cap **Edge:** Oblique reeding

Date	Mintage	Good	VG	F	VF	XF
1825	—	3.00	5.50	12.00	25.00	—
1827	—	3.00	5.50	12.00	25.00	—
1827	—	12.00	20.00	40.00	100	—
Note: Inverted A for V in OCTAVO						
1827	—	15.00	25.00	50.00	120	—
Note: OCTAVA (error)						
1827 Inverted 1	—	12.00	20.00	40.00	100	—
1829 Rare	—	—	—	—	—	—
1830	—	2.75	5.00	8.00	20.00	—
1831	—	4.50	6.75	13.50	27.50	—
1832	—	2.75	5.00	8.00	20.00	—
1833	—	2.75	5.00	8.00	20.00	—
1835	—	3.50	6.00	10.00	25.00	—
1846	—	3.50	6.00	10.00	25.00	—
1851	—	38.00	70.00	115	220	—
1852	—	3.50	6.00	10.00	25.00	—
1858	—	2.75	5.00	8.00	20.00	—
1859	—	2.75	5.00	8.00	20.00	—
1862	—	2.75	5.00	8.00	20.00	—
1863 Reversed 6 in date	—	2.75	5.00	8.00	20.00	—

KM# 321 1/8 REAL (Octavo Real)

3.3000 g., Copper **Obv:** Child holding bow, right, small tree **Rev:** Radiant cap **Rev. Legend:** OCTo. DE. R. DE DO **Edge:** Oblique reeding **Note:** Size varies 18-19mm.

Date	Mintage	Good	VG	F	VF	XF
1828D	—	7.50	18.50	40.00	115	—

KM# 335   1/8 REAL (Octavo Real)
Copper   **Obv. Legend:** ESTADO DE OCCIDENTE
Edge: Oblique reeding **Note:** Size varies: 17-18mm,
weight varies: 2-3 g. The C before date on reverse
may be a mint mark standing for Concepcion de
Alamos.

Date	Mintage	Good	VG	F	VF	XF
1828 Reverse S	—	35.00	65.00	120	—	—
1829	—	30.00	60.00	110	—	—

KM# 329   1/8 REAL (Octavo Real)
4.8000 g., Copper, 21 mm.   **Obv:** Bow, quiver and
flag **Obv. Legend:** ESTADO LIBRE DE JALISCO
Rev: Seated figure, left, cap on pole **Edge:** Oblique
reeding

Date	Mintage	Good	VG	F	VF	XF
1828	—	3.00	5.00	8.00	22.50	—
1831	—	62.50	100	185	275	—
1832/28	—	4.50	6.50	11.00	27.50	—
1832	—	4.50	6.00	10.00	25.00	—
1833	—	3.50	5.50	9.00	23.50	—
1834	—	37.50	80.00	150	235	—

KM# 326   1/8 REAL (Octavo Real)
3.5000 g., Copper, 21 mm.   **Obv:** Seated figure **Obv.
Legend:** ESTADO LIBRE DE GUANAJUATO **Rev:**
Cap within center wreath of stylized rays, date below
Edge: Ornamented with incuse dots

Date	Mintage	Good	VG	F	VF	XF
1829	—	3.00	5.00	10.00	26.50	—
1829	—	4.00	6.50	12.50	28.50	—
Note: Error with GUANJUATO						
1830	—	8.00	13.50	28.50	62.50	—

KM# 336   1/8 REAL (Octavo Real)
Copper, 21 mm.   **Obv:** Value above divides wreath,
open book within **Obv. Legend:** ESTADO LIBRE DE
SAN LUIS POTOSI **Rev:** Seated figure **Edge:**
Oblique reeding **Note:** Weight varies (1829-31) 4.5-
5.5 g; (1859) 4-4.5 g.

Date	Mintage	Good	VG	F	VF	XF
1829	—	6.00	11.00	26.50	62.50	—
1830	—	8.50	15.00	30.00	70.00	—
1831	—	6.00	9.50	18.50	47.50	—
1859	—	5.00	8.00	16.50	45.00	—
1865/1	—	—	—	—	—	—
Note: Reported, not confirmed						

KM# 318   1/8 REAL (Octavo Real)
3.5400 g., Copper, 20 mm.   **Obv. Legend:** ESTADO
SOBERANO DE CHIHUAHUA **Edge:** Plain

Date	Mintage	Good	VG	F	VF	XF
1833	—	350	750	—	—	—
1834	—	350	750	—	—	—
1835/3	—	350	750	—	—	—

KM# 322   1/8 REAL (Octavo Real)
3.5000 g., Copper, 20 mm.   **Obv:** Profile eagle, snake
in beak **Obv. Legend:** ESTADO DE DURANGO **Rev:**
Value and date within circle and wreath

Date	Mintage	Good	VG	F	VF	XF
1833 Rare	—	—	—	—	—	—

KM# 339   1/8 REAL (Octavo Real)
4.0000 g., Copper, 21 mm.   **Obv:** Monument **Obv.
Legend:** DEPARTAMENTO DE ZACATECAS **Rev:**
Floating angel holding radiant cap **Edge:** Oblique
reeding

Date	Mintage	Good	VG	F	VF	XF
1836	—	5.00	8.50	17.50	40.00	—
1845	—	7.50	12.50	22.50	50.00	—
1846	—	8.50	10.00	20.00	45.00	—

KM# 323   1/8 REAL (Octavo Real)
3.5000 g., Copper   **Obv:** Facing eagle, snake in beak
Obv. Legend: REPUBLICA MEXICANA **Rev:** Value
and date within circle and wreath **Note:** Size varies:
19-23mm.

Date	Mintage	Good	VG	F	VF	XF
1842/33	—	12.50	22.50	42.50	115	—
1842	—	8.50	15.00	32.50	100	—

KM# 324   1/8 REAL (Octavo Real)
Copper, 19 mm.   **Obv:** Facing eagle, snake in beak
Obv. Legend: REPUBLICA MEXICANA **Rev:** Value
within circle **Rev. Legend:** DEPARTAMENTO DE
DURANGO **Edge:** Ornamented with arc and dot
pattern **Note:** Weight varies: 3.5-3.8 g.

Date	Mintage	Good	VG	F	VF	XF
1845	—	22.50	55.00	115	250	—
1846 Rare	—	—	—	—	—	—
1847	—	3.50	7.50	17.50	37.50	—

KM# 325 1/8 REAL (Octavo Real)
Copper, 19 mm. **Obv:** Facing eagle, snake in beak **Obv. Legend:** REPUBLICA MEXICANA **Rev:** Value within circle **Rev. Legend:** ESTADO DE DURANGO **Edge:** Ornamented with arc and dot pattern **Note:** Weight varies: 3.5-3.8 g.

Date	Mintage	Good	VG	F	VF	XF
1851	—	3.50	8.00	12.50	33.50	—
1852/1	—	3.50	6.50	11.00	33.50	—
1852	—	3.00	5.00	8.00	30.00	—
1854	—	7.00	13.50	28.50	62.50	—

KM# 319 1/8 REAL (Octavo Real)
3.5400 g., Copper, 20 mm. **Obv:** Standing figure facing holding bow and arrow **Obv. Legend:** ESTADO DE CHIHUAHUA **Rev:** Date and value within wreath **Edge:** Plain

Date	Mintage	Good	VG	F	VF	XF
1855	—	5.00	8.50	25.00	75.00	—

KM# 327 1/8 REAL (Octavo Real)
7.2000 g., Brass, 29 mm. **Obv:** Facing eagle, snake in beak **Obv. Legend:** ESTADO LIBRE DE GUANAJUATO **Rev:** Oval arms within sprays below radiant cap **Edge:** Plain

Date	Mintage	Good	VG	F	VF	XF
1856	—	7.50	12.00	20.00	75.00	—

KM# 330 1/8 REAL (Octavo Real)
9.5000 g., Copper, 28 mm. **Obv. Legend:** ESTADO LIBRE DE JALISCO **Rev:** Seated figure, left, cap on pole **Edge:** Oblique reeding

Date	Mintage	Good	VG	F	VF	XF
1856	—	3.00	6.00	9.00	18.50	—
1857	—	3.00	6.00	9.00	18.50	—
1858	—	3.00	6.00	9.00	18.50	—
1861	—	75.00	135	200	300	—
1862/1	—	4.00	7.00	10.00	22.50	—
1862	—	4.00	7.00	10.00	22.50	—

KM# 328 1/8 REAL (Octavo Real)
Brass, 25 mm. **Obv:** Facing eagle, snake in beak **Obv. Legend:** ESTADO LIBRE DE GUANAJUATO **Rev:** Oval arms within sprays below radiant cap **Edge:** Plain **Note:** Weight varies: 7.1-7.2 g.

Date	Mintage	Good	VG	F	VF	XF
1856	—	4.00	7.50	12.50	35.00	—
1857	—	3.50	6.00	10.00	30.00	—

KM# 328a 1/8 REAL (Octavo Real)
Copper, 25 mm. **Obv:** Facing eagle, snake in beak **Obv. Legend:** ESTADO LIBRE DE GUANAJUATO **Rev:** Oval arms within sprays below radiant cap **Edge:** Plain **Note:** Weight varies: 7.1-7.2 g.

Date	Mintage	Good	VG	F	VF	XF
1857	—	7.00	16.50	32.50	55.00	—

KM# 331 1/8 REAL (Octavo Real)
9.5000 g., Copper, 28 mm. **Obv:** Bow, quiver and flag **Obv. Legend:** DEPARTAMENTO DE JALISCO **Edge:** Oblique reeding

Date	Mintage	Good	VG	F	VF	XF
1858	—	4.00	7.00	13.50	28.50	—
1859	—	3.00	5.75	8.00	20.00	—
1860/59	—	3.25	6.00	9.00	22.50	—
1860	—	3.25	6.00	9.00	22.50	—
1862	—	4.00	8.00	17.50	37.50	—

KM# 337 1/8 REAL (Octavo Real)
6.7000 g., Copper, 28 mm. **Obv. Legend:** ESTO LIBE Y SOBO DE SONORA **Edge:** Reeded

Date	Mintage	Good	VG	F	VF	XF
1859 Rare	—	—	—	—	—	—

KM# 366 1/4 REAL (Un Quarto/Una Quartilla)
8.0000 g., Brass **Obv:** Monument **Obv. Legend:** ESTO LIBE FEDO DE ZACATECAS **Rev:** Floating angel with radiant cap on tip of arrow **Edge:** Oblique reeding **Note:** Size varies: 28-29mm.

Date	Mintage	Good	VG	F	VF	XF
1824 Rare	—	—	—	—	—	—
1825	—	2.50	5.00	10.00	20.00	—
1826	—	75.00	130	220	325	—
1827/17	—	2.50	5.00	9.00	20.00	—
1829	—	2.50	5.00	9.00	20.00	—

Date	Mintage	Good	VG	F	VF	XF
1830	—	2.50	5.00	8.50	20.00	—
1831	—	40.00	85.00	140	220	—
1832	—	2.50	5.00	9.00	20.00	—
1833	—	2.50	5.00	9.00	20.00	—
1834 Rare	—	—	—	—	—	—
1835	—	2.50	5.00	9.00	20.00	—
1846	—	2.50	5.00	8.50	20.00	—
1847	—	2.50	5.00	8.50	20.00	—
1852	—	2.50	5.00	8.50	20.00	—
1853	—	2.50	5.00	8.50	20.00	—
1855	—	4.50	10.00	25.00	65.00	—
1858	—	2.50	5.00	8.50	20.00	—
1859	—	2.50	5.00	8.50	20.00	—
1860	—	75.00	125	200	310	—
1862/57	—	2.50	5.00	8.00	20.00	—
1862/59/7	—	8.00	18.00	37.50	75.00	—
1862	—	2.50	5.00	8.00	20.00	—
1863/2	—	2.50	5.00	8.00	20.00	—
1863	—	2.50	5.00	8.00	20.00	—
1864	—	4.00	11.00	25.00	60.00	—

KM# 359   1/4 REAL (Un Quarto/Una Quartilla)
Copper   **Obv:** Value above divides wreath, open book within **Obv. Legend:** ESTADO LIBRE DE SAN LUIS POTOSI **Rev:** Seated figure with cap on tip of arrow **Rev. Legend:** MEXICO LIBRE **Edge:** Oblique reeding **Note:** Size varies: 25-31mm, weight varies: (1828-32) 9-10 g.; (1859-60) 8-9 g.

Date	Mintage	Good	VG	F	VF	XF
1828	—	2.00	3.50	8.00	17.50	—
1829	—	3.00	4.50	8.50	18.50	—
1830	—	2.00	3.50	7.00	15.00	—
1832	—	3.25	5.00	9.00	20.00	—
1859 Large LIBRE	—	2.50	4.00	7.50	16.50	—
1859 Small LIBRE	—	2.50	4.00	7.50	16.50	—
1860	—	2.50	4.00	7.00	16.50	—

KM# 351   1/4 REAL (Un Quarto/Una Quartilla)
7.0000 g., Copper, 27 mm.   **Obv:** Seated figure with head right **Obv. Legend:** ESTADO LIBRE DE GUANAJUATO **Rev:** Cap within radiant wreath **Edge:** Ornamented with incuse dots

Date	Mintage	Good	VG	F	VF	XF
1828	—	3.75	8.00	18.50	40.00	—
1828	—	4.00	9.00	20.00	42.50	—
Note: Error with GUANJUATO						
1829	—	5.50	12.00	22.50	47.50	—

KM# 353   1/4 REAL (Un Quarto/Una Quartilla)
9.3500 g., Copper, 28 mm.   **Obv:** Oblique reeding **Obv. Legend:** ESTADO LIBRE DE JALISCO **Rev:** Seated figure, left, cap on pole

Date	Mintage	Good	VG	F	VF	XF
1828	—	3.75	7.00	15.00	37.50	—
1829/8	—	3.00	6.00	13.00	33.00	—
1829	—	3.00	6.00	13.00	33.00	—
1830/20	—	3.00	5.00	10.00	28.50	—
1830/29	—	3.00	5.00	10.00	28.50	—
1830	—	3.00	5.00	10.00	28.50	—
1831 Rare	—	—	—	—	—	—
1832/20	—	3.00	5.00	10.00	28.50	—
1832/28	—	3.00	5.00	10.00	28.50	—
1832	—	2.50	5.00	9.00	27.50	—
1833/2	—	3.00	5.00	9.00	27.50	—
1834	—	2.50	5.00	9.00	27.50	—
1835/3	—	3.00	5.00	9.00	27.50	—
1835	—	2.50	5.00	9.00	27.50	—
1836 Rare	—	—	—	—	—	—

KM# 364   1/4 REAL (Un Quarto/Una Quartilla)
Copper   **Obv:** Arrow divides quivers **Obv. Legend:** EST. D. SONORA UNA CUART **Rev:** Stylized radiant cap **Edge:** Oblique reeding **Note:** Size varies: 21-22mm. Weight varies: 2.3-5.5 g.

Date	Mintage	Good	VG	F	VF	XF
1831 L.S. Rare	—	—	—	—	—	—
1832 L.S.	—	2.75	5.50	15.00	50.00	—
1833/2 L.S.	—	2.00	4.00	12.50	37.50	—
1833 L.S.	—	2.00	4.00	12.50	37.50	—
1834 L.S.	—	2.00	4.00	12.50	37.50	—
1835/3 L.S.	—	2.50	5.50	15.00	40.00	—
1835 L.S.	—	2.00	4.00	12.50	37.50	—
1836 L.S.	—	2.00	4.00	12.50	37.50	—

KM# 340   1/4 REAL (Un Quarto/Una Quartilla)
Copper, 27 mm.   **Obv:** Child facing, holding bow and arrow **Obv. Legend:** ESTADO SOBERANO DE CHIHUAHUA **Rev:** Value and date within palm wreath **Edge:** Herringbone pattern

Date	Mintage	Good	VG	F	VF	XF
1833	—	7.50	16.50	37.50	85.00	—
1834	—	6.50	13.50	28.00	55.00	—
1835	—	5.00	10.00	22.00	50.00	—
1835 Plain edge	—	5.00	8.00	12.00	50.00	—

KM# 354   1/4 REAL (Un Quarto/Una Quartilla)
9.3500 g., Copper, 28 mm.   **Obv. Legend:**
DEPARTAMENTO DE JALISCO **Edge:** Oblique
reeding

Date	Mintage	Good	VG	F	VF	XF
1836	—	120	200	300	—	—

KM# 367   1/4 REAL (Un Quarto/Una Quartilla)
8.0000 g., Brass   **Obv:** Monument **Obv. Legend:**
DEPARTAMENTO DE ZACATECAS **Rev:** Floating
angel with radiant cap on tip of arrow **Edge:** Oblique
reeding **Note:** Size varies: 28-29mm.

Date	Mintage	Good	VG	F	VF	XF
1836	—	4.00	8.50	13.50	25.00	—
1845 Rare	—	—	—	—	—	—
1846	—	3.50	6.75	9.00	20.00	—

KM# 345   1/4 REAL (Un Quarto/Una Quartilla)
7.0000 g., Copper, 27 mm.   **Obv:** Facing eagle,
snake in beak **Obv. Legend:** REPUBLICA
MEXICANA **Rev:** Value and date within circle,
DURANGO above in wreath

Date	Mintage	Good	VG	F	VF	XF
1845 Rare	—	—	—	—	—	—

KM# 341   1/4 REAL (Un Quarto/Una Quartilla)
7.0800 g., Copper, 27 mm.   **Obv:** Stylized figure
facing, holding bow and arrow **Obv. Legend:**
ESTADO LIBRE DE CHIHUAHUA **Rev:** Value and
date within designed wreath **Edge:** Plain

Date	Mintage	Good	VG	F	VF	XF
1846	—	3.50	6.00	12.00	37.50	—
Note: With fraction bar						
1846	—	5.00	8.50	15.00	45.00	—
Note: Without fraction bar						

KM# 363   1/4 REAL (Un Quarto/Una Quartilla)
27.0000 g., Copper, 27 mm.   **Obv:** Head left within
wreath **Obv. Legend:** ESTADO LIBRE Y
SOBERANO DE SINALOA **Rev:** Value and date
within wreath **Edge:** Reeded

Date	Mintage	Good	VG	F	VF	XF
1847	—	3.50	5.50	12.00	23.50	—
1848	—	3.50	5.50	11.00	22.00	—
1859	—	3.00	4.50	7.50	16.50	—
1861	—	1.75	3.00	4.00	10.00	—
1862	—	1.75	3.00	4.00	11.00	—
1863	—	2.50	4.00	5.00	11.00	—
1864/3	—	2.50	4.00	5.00	11.00	—
1864	—	1.75	3.00	4.75	10.00	—
1865	—	3.00	5.50	8.50	18.50	—
1866/5	7,401,000	2.50	3.50	5.00	11.00	—
1866	Inc. above	1.75	3.00	4.00	10.00	—

KM# 363a   1/4 REAL (Un Quarto/Una Quartilla)
7.0000 g., Brass, 27 mm.   **Obv:** Head left within
wreath **Obv. Legend:** ESTADO LIBRE Y
SOBERANO DE SINALOA **Rev:** Value and date
within wreath **Edge:** Reeded

Date	Mintage	Good	VG	F	VF	XF
1847	—	5.00	10.00	18.50	40.00	—

KM# 342   1/4 REAL (Un Quarto/Una Quartilla)
7.0800 g., Copper, 27 mm.   **Obv:** Stylized figure
facing, holding bow and arrow **Obv. Legend:**
ESTADO DE CHIHUAHUA **Rev:** Value and date
within designed wreath **Edge:** Plain

Date	Mintage	Good	VG	F	VF	XF
1855	—	2.50	5.75	13.50	40.00	—
1856	—	2.50	5.75	13.50	40.00	—

KM# 343   1/4 REAL (Un Quarto/Una Quartilla)
7.0800 g., Copper, 27 mm.   **Obv:** Stylized figure
facing, holding bow and arrow **Obv. Legend:**
DEPARTAMENTO DE CHIHUAHUA **Rev:** Value
and date within designed wreath **Edge:** Plain

Date	Mintage	Good	VG	F	VF	XF
1855	—	3.00	5.75	13.00	36.50	—
1855 DE	—	4.50	8.50	17.50	40.00	—
(reversed D)						

KM# 352 1/4 REAL (Un Quarto/Una Quartilla)
14.0000 g., Copper, 32 mm. **Obv:** Facing eagle, snake in beak **Obv. Legend:** EST. LIB. DE GUANAXUATO **Rev:** Oval arms within sprays below radiant cap **Rev. Legend:** OMNIA VINCIT LABOR **Edge:** Plain

Date	Mintage	Good	VG	F	VF	XF
1856	—	7.50	18.50	37.50	65.00	—
1857	—	6.50	13.50	27.50	48.00	—

KM# 352a 1/4 REAL (Un Quarto/Una Quartilla)
14.0000 g., Brass, 32 mm. **Obv:** Facing eagle, snake in beak **Obv. Legend:** EST. LIB. DE GUANAXUATO **Rev:** Oval arms within sprays below radiant cap **Rev. Legend:** OMNIA VINCIT LABOR **Edge:** Plain

Date	Mintage	Good	VG	F	VF	XF
1856	—	3.25	6.75	13.50	30.00	—
1857	—	3.25	6.75	13.50	30.00	—

KM# 346 1/4 REAL (Un Quarto/Una Quartilla)
7.5000 g., Copper, 27 mm. **Obv:** Facing eagle, snake in beak **Obv. Legend:** REPUBLICA MEXICANA **Rev:** Date, value **Rev. Legend:** DURANGO **Edge:** Ornamented with arc and dot pattern

Date	Mintage	Good	VG	F	VF	XF
1858 Rare	—	—	—	—	—	—

KM# 347 1/4 REAL (Un Quarto/Una Quartilla)
7.5000 g., Copper, 27 mm. **Obv:** Facing eagle, snake in beak **Obv. Legend:** ESTADO DE DURANGO **Rev:** Radiant cap above value and date within stylized sprays **Rev. Legend:** CONSTITUCION **Edge:** Ornamented with arc and dot pattern **Note:** Brass examples have been reported, but not confirmed.

Date	Mintage	Good	VG	F	VF	XF
1858	—	4.00	8.50	22.00	50.00	—

KM# 355 1/4 REAL (Un Quarto/Una Quartilla)
19.0000 g., Copper, 32 mm. **Obv:** Bow, quiver and flag **Obv. Legend:** ESTADO LIBRE DE JALISCO **Rev:** Seated figure, left, cap on pole **Edge:** Oblique reeding

Date	Mintage	Good	VG	F	VF	XF
1858	—	3.00	5.50	10.00	22.50	—
1861	—	3.50	7.50	15.00	30.00	—
1862	—	3.00	5.50	10.00	22.50	—

KM# 356 1/4 REAL (Un Quarto/Una Quartilla)
19.0000 g., Copper, 32 mm. **Obv:** Bow, quiver and flag **Obv. Legend:** DEPARTAMENTO DE JALISCO **Rev:** Seated figure, left, cap on pole **Edge:** Oblique reeding

Date	Mintage	Good	VG	F	VF	XF
1858	—	2.75	5.00	8.50	18.50	—
1859/8	—	2.75	5.00	8.50	18.50	—
1859	—	2.75	5.00	8.50	18.50	—
1860	—	2.75	5.00	8.50	18.50	—

KM# 365 1/4 REAL (Un Quarto/Una Quartilla)
14.3000 g., Copper, 32 mm. **Obv:** Facing eagle, snake in beak **Obv. Legend:** ESTO. LIBE. Y SOBO. DE SONORA **Rev:** Seated figure, left, cap on pole **Edge:** Reeded

Date	Mintage	Good	VG	F	VF	XF
1859	—	2.00	5.00	8.00	20.00	—
1861/59	—	2.75	6.50	11.00	25.00	—
1861	—	2.00	5.00	8.00	20.00	—
1862	—	2.00	5.00	8.00	20.00	—
1863/2	—	5.00	12.50	25.00	55.00	—

KM# 344 1/4 REAL (Un Quarto/Una Quartilla)
Copper, 28 mm. **Obv:** Seated figure, right **Obv. Legend:** E. CHIHA LIBERTAD **Rev:** Value and date within wreath **Edge:** Plain **Note:** Weight varies 11-11.5 g.

Date	Mintage	Good	VG	F	VF	XF
1860	—	2.00	4.00	11.00	25.00	—
1861	—	2.00	4.00	11.00	25.00	—
1865/1	—	2.50	5.50	13.50	30.00	—
1865	—	6.00	14.00	28.50	65.00	—
1866/5	—	5.00	9.50	25.00	60.00	—
1866	—	2.00	4.00	11.00	25.00	—
Note: Coin rotation						
1866	—	2.00	4.00	11.00	25.00	—
Note: Medal rotation						

KM# 348 1/4 REAL (Un Quarto/Una Quartilla)
Copper, 27 mm. **Obv:** Facing eagle, snake in beak **Obv. Legend:** DEPARTAMENTO DE DURANGO **Rev:** Value and date within circular legend and wreath **Rev. Legend:** LIBERTAD EN EL ORDEN **Edge:** Ornamented with arc and dot pattern **Note:** Weight varies: 7-7.5 g.

Date	Mintage	Good	VG	F	VF	XF
1860	—	2.25	6.00	15.00	38.50	—
1866	—	3.00	7.50	16.50	42.50	—

KM# 360 1/4 REAL (Un Quarto/Una Quartilla)
Copper **Obv:** Value above divides wreath, open book within **Obv. Legend:** ESTADO LIBRE DE SAN LUIS POTOSI **Rev:** Seated figure with cap on tip of arrow **Rev. Legend:** REPUBLICA MEXICANA **Edge:** Oblique reeding **Note:** Size varies: 25-31mm.

Date	Mintage	Good	VG	F	VF	XF
1862	1,367	2.50	4.00	7.00	15.00	—
1862 LIBR	Inc. above	3.25	5.00	8.00	16.50	—

KM# 349 1/4 REAL (Un Quarto/Una Quartilla)
7.0000 g., Copper **Obv:** Facing eagle, snake in beak **Obv. Legend:** ESTADO DE DURANGO **Rev:** Value and date above sprays **Rev. Legend:** INDEPENDENCIA Y LIBERTAD **Edge:** Ornamented with arc and dot pattern **Note:** Size varies: 26-27mm.

Date	Mintage	Good	VG	F	VF	XF
1866	—	3.75	8.50	22.00	50.00	—

KM# 361 1/4 REAL (Un Quarto/Una Quartilla)
Copper **Obv. Legend:** ESTADO LIBRE Y SOBERANO DE S.L. POTOSI **Rev:** Radiant cap and value within wrath, date below **Rev. Legend:** LIBERTAD Y REFORMA **Edge:** Reeded or plain **Note:** Size varies: 27-28mm. Weight varies: 9-10 g.

Date	Mintage	Good	VG	F	VF	XF
1867	3,177,000	2.50	3.75	6.50	15.00	—
1867 AFG	Inc. above	2.50	3.75	6.50	15.00	—
Note: "AFG" are the coin designer/engraver initials						

KM# 362 1/4 REAL (Un Quarto/Una Quartilla)
Copper **Obv. Legend:** ESTADO LIBRE Y SOBERANO DE S.L. POTOSI **Rev. Legend:** LIBERTAD Y REFORMA **Edge:** Plain

Date	Mintage	Good	VG	F	VF	XF
1867	Inc. above	2.50	3.75	6.50	15.00	—
1867 AFG	Inc. above	2.50	3.75	6.50	15.00	—
Note: "AFG" are the coin designer/engraver initials						

KM# 350 1/4 REAL (Un Quarto/Una Quartilla)
7.5000 g., Copper, 27 mm. **Obv:** Facing eagle, snake in beak **Obv. Legend:** ESTADO DE DURANGO **Rev:** Date and circular legend, value within **Rev. Legend:** SUFRAGIO LIBRE **Edge:** Ornamented with arc and dot pattern **Note:** Brass examples have been reported, but not confirmed.

Date	Mintage	Good	VG	F	VF	XF
1872	—	2.00	3.75	8.50	18.50	—

FEDERAL COINAGE

KM# 315   1/16 REAL (Medio Octavo)
1.7500 g., Copper, 17 mm. **Obv. Legend:**
REPUBLICA MEXICANA **Edge:** Ornamented with
small incuse rectangles

Date	Mintage	VG	F	VF	XF	Unc
1831	—	10.00	20.00	50.00	100	—
1832/1	—	12.00	22.00	55.00	125	—
1832	—	10.00	20.00	50.00	100	—
1833	—	10.00	20.00	50.00	100	—

KM# 315a   1/16 REAL (Medio Octavo)
1.7500 g., Brass, 17 mm. **Obv. Legend:**
REPUBLICA MEXICANA **Edge:** Ornamented with
small incuse rectangles

Date	Mintage	VG	F	VF	XF	Unc
1832	—	13.50	22.50	60.00	165	—
1833	—	10.00	17.50	50.00	135	—
1835	—	400	800	1,250	2,500	—

KM# 333   1/8 REAL (Octavo Real)
3.5000 g., Copper, 21 mm. **Obv:** Facing eagle,
snake in beak **Obv. Legend:** REPUBLICA
MEXICANA **Rev:** Value and date within wreath
Edge: Ornamented with small incuse rectangles

Date	Mintage	Good	VG	F	VF	XF
1829	—	7.50	12.00	25.00	55.00	—
1830	—	1.00	2.00	6.00	25.00	—
1831	—	1.50	3.50	7.00	25.00	—
1832	—	1.50	3.50	7.00	25.00	—
1833/2	—	1.50	3.50	7.00	25.00	—
1833	—	1.50	2.75	6.00	20.00	—
1834	—	1.50	2.75	6.00	20.00	—
1835	—	1.50	2.75	6.00	20.00	—
1835/4	—	1.75	3.50	7.00	25.00	—

KM# 332   1/8 REAL (Octavo Real)
7.0000 g., Copper, 27 mm. **Obv. Legend:**
REPUBLICA MEXICANA **Edge:** Ornamented with
small incuse rectangles

Date	Mintage	VG	F	VF	XF	Unc
1829	—	450	900	1,500	2,500	—

KM# 334   1/8 REAL (Octavo Real)
14.0000 g., Copper **Obv:** Seated figure, right **Obv.
Legend:** LIBERTAD **Rev:** Value and date within
wreath **Edge:** Lettered (1841-42); Plain (1850-61)
Edge Lettering: REPUBLICA MEXICANA **Note:**
Size varies: 29-30mm.

Date	Mintage	Good	VG	F	VF	XF
1841	—	6.00	15.00	30.00	75.00	—
1842	—	2.50	5.00	10.00	30.00	—
1850	—	12.50	20.00	30.00	80.00	—
1861	—	5.00	12.00	25.00	70.00	—

KM# 357   1/4 REAL (Un Quarto/Una Quartilla)
14.0000 g., Copper, 33 mm. **Obv:** Facing eagle,
snake in beak **Obv. Legend:** REPUBLICA
MEXICANA **Rev:** Value and date within wreath
Edge: Ornamented with small incuse rectangles

Date	Mintage	VG	F	VF	XF	Unc
1829	—	8.00	30.00	75.00	250	—

KM# 358   1/4 REAL (Un Quarto/Una Quartilla)
7.0000 g., Copper, 27 mm. **Obv:** Facing eagle,
snake in beak **Obv. Legend:** REPUBLICA
MEXICANA **Rev:** Value and date within wreath
Edge: Ornamented with small incuse rectangles
Note: Reduced size.

Date	Mintage	VG	F	VF	XF	Unc
1829	—	12.00	25.00	50.00	150	—
1830	—	1.50	2.75	5.00	10.00	—
1831	—	1.50	2.75	5.00	10.00	—
1832	—	5.50	10.00	20.00	35.00	—
1833	—	1.50	2.75	5.00	10.00	—
1834/3	—	1.75	3.00	6.00	12.00	—
1834	—	1.50	2.75	5.00	10.00	—
1835	—	1.50	2.75	5.00	10.00	—
1836/5	—	1.75	3.00	6.00	12.00	—
1836	—	1.50	2.75	5.00	10.00	—
1837	—	6.50	13.50	22.50	45.00	—

KM# 358a.1   1/4 REAL (Un Quarto/Una Quartilla)
7.0000 g., Brass, 27 mm. **Countermark:** JM **Obv.
Legend:** REPUBLICA MEXICANA **Edge:**
Ornamented with small incuse rectangles **Note:**
Reduced size.

Date	Mintage	VG	F	VF	XF	Unc
1831	—	8.00	13.50	27.50	50.00	—

KM# 358a.2   1/4 REAL (Un Quarto/Una Quartilla)
7.0000 g., Brass, 27 mm. **Obv. Legend:**
REPUBLICA MEXICANA **Edge:** Ornamented with
small incuse rectangles **Note:** Without countermark.

Date	Mintage	VG	F	VF	XF	Unc
1831	—	—	—	—	—	—

KM# 368.2   1/4 REAL (Un Quarto/Una Quartilla)
0.8450 g., 0.9030 Silver 0.0245 oz. ASW **Note:**
Struck at Durango Mint, mint mark Do.

Date	Mintage	VG	F	VF	XF	Unc
1842Do LR	—	12.00	20.00	40.00	125	—
1843Do	—	20.00	40.00	90.00	200	—

KM# 368 1/4 REAL (Un Quarto/Una Quartilla)
0.8450 g., 0.9030 Silver 0.0245 oz. ASW **Obv:** Head left **Rev:** Value **Note:** Mint mark CA.

Date	Mintage	VG	F	VF	XF	Unc
1843CA RG	—	75.00	125	300	500	—

KM# 368.3 1/4 REAL (Un Quarto/Una Quartilla)
0.8450 g., 0.9030 Silver 0.0245 oz. ASW **Note:** Mint mark Ga.

Date	Mintage	VG	F	VF	XF	Unc
1842Ga JG	—	2.50	5.50	8.00	20.00	—
1843/2Ga JG	—	—	—	—	—	—
1843Ga JG	—	6.00	9.00	12.50	30.00	—
1843Ga MC	—	4.00	6.50	9.00	25.00	—
1844Ga MC	—	4.00	6.50	9.00	25.00	—
1844Ga LR	—	2.50	5.00	10.00	20.00	—
1845Ga LR	—	8.00	20.00	40.00	75.00	—
1846Ga LR	—	10.00	25.00	40.00	60.00	—
1847Ga LR	—	8.00	20.00	40.00	60.00	—
1848Ga LR Rare	—	—	—	—	—	—
1850Ga LR Rare	—	—	—	—	—	—
1851Ga LR	—	6.00	10.00	20.00	50.00	—
1852Ga LR	—	50.00	100	135	200	—
1854/3Ga LR	—	50.00	100	135	200	—
1854Ga LR	—	10.00	20.00	50.00	100	—
1855Ga LR	—	10.00	20.00	50.00	100	—
1857Ga LR	—	10.00	20.00	50.00	100	—
1862Ga LR	—	10.00	20.00	50.00	100	—

KM# 368.5 1/4 REAL (Un Quarto/Una Quartilla)
0.8450 g., 0.9030 Silver 0.0245 oz. ASW **Note:** Mint mark Go.

Date	Mintage	VG	F	VF	XF	Unc
1842Go PM	—	5.00	15.00	35.00	75.00	—
1842Go LR	—	2.00	4.00	8.00	15.00	—
1843/2Go LR	—	4.00	6.00	10.00	20.00	—
1843Go LR	—	2.00	4.00	8.00	15.00	—
1844/3Go LR	—	—	—	—	—	—
1844Go LR	—	10.00	25.00	60.00	125	—
1845Go LR	—	8.00	17.00	40.00	80.00	—
1846/5Go LR	—	—	—	—	—	—
1846Go LR	—	6.00	15.00	30.00	60.00	—
1847Go LR	—	2.00	4.00	8.00	15.00	—
1848/7Go LR	—	2.00	4.00	8.00	15.00	—
1848Go LR	—	2.00	4.00	8.00	15.00	—
1849/7Go LR	—	8.00	15.00	30.00	60.00	—
1849Go LR	—	2.00	4.00	8.00	15.00	—
1850Go LR	—	2.00	4.00	8.00	15.00	—
1851Go LR	—	2.00	4.00	8.00	15.00	—
1852Go LR	—	2.00	4.00	8.00	15.00	—
1853Go LR	—	2.00	4.00	8.00	15.00	—
1855Go LR	—	4.00	8.00	15.00	30.00	—
1856/4Go LR	—	20.00	40.00	60.00	100	—
1856Go LR	—	5.00	10.00	20.00	35.00	—
1862/1Go LR	—	3.00	5.00	10.00	20.00	—
1862Go LR	—	2.00	4.00	8.00	15.00	—
1863Go	—	2.00	4.00	8.00	15.00	—

KM# 368.6 1/4 REAL (Un Quarto/Una Quartilla)
0.8450 g., 0.9030 Silver 0.0245 oz. ASW **Note:** Mint mark Mo.

Date	Mintage	VG	F	VF	XF	Unc
1842Mo LR	—	2.00	4.00	8.00	15.00	—
1843Mo LR	—	2.00	4.00	8.00	15.00	—
1844/3Mo LR	—	20.00	30.00	75.00	125	—
1844Mo LR	—	4.00	6.00	10.00	20.00	—
1845Mo LR	—	6.00	15.00	35.00	70.00	—
1846Mo LR	—	10.00	20.00	35.00	65.00	—
1850Mo LR Rare	—	—	—	—	—	—
1858Mo LR	—	4.00	8.00	15.00	30.00	—
1859Mo LR	—	4.00	6.00	10.00	20.00	—
1860Mo LR	—	4.00	6.00	10.00	20.00	—
1861Mo LR	—	4.00	6.00	10.00	20.00	—
1862Mo LR	—	4.00	6.00	10.00	20.00	—
1863/53Mo LR	—	4.00	6.00	10.00	20.00	—
1863Mo LR	—	4.00	6.00	10.00	20.00	—

KM# 368.7 1/4 REAL (Un Quarto/Una Quartilla)
0.8450 g., 0.9030 Silver 0.0245 oz. ASW **Note:** Mint mark SLP, PI, P, I/P.

Date	Mintage	VG	F	VF	XF	Unc
1842S.L.Pi	—	2.00	5.00	10.00	20.00	—
1843/2S.L.Pi	—	4.00	6.00	10.00	20.00	—
1843S.L.Pi	—	2.00	4.00	8.00	20.00	—
1844S.L.Pi	—	2.00	4.00	8.00	20.00	—
1845/3S.L.Pi	—	4.00	6.00	10.00	25.00	—
1845/4S.L.Pi	—	4.00	6.00	10.00	25.00	—
1845S.L.Pi	—	2.00	4.00	8.00	20.00	—
1847/5S.L.Pi	—	4.00	9.00	20.00	40.00	—
1847S.L.Pi	—	3.00	6.00	12.00	25.00	—
1851/47S.L.Pi	—	10.00	20.00	35.00	60.00	—
1854S.L.Pi	—	125	200	275	400	—
1856S.L.Pi	—	10.00	20.00	35.00	60.00	—
1857S.L.Pi	—	30.00	60.00	100	175	—
1862/57S.L.Pi	—	10.00	20.00	40.00	85.00	—

KM# 368.1 1/4 REAL (Un Quarto/Una Quartilla)
0.8450 g., 0.9030 Silver 0.0245 oz. ASW **Note:** Mint mark C.

Date	Mintage	VG	F	VF	XF	Unc
1855C LR	—	50.00	100	225	475	—

KM# 368.4 1/4 REAL (Un Quarto/Una Quartilla)
0.8450 g., 0.9030 Silver 0.0245 oz. ASW **Note:** Mint mark GC.

Date	Mintage	VG	F	VF	XF	Unc
1844GC LR	—	50.00	75.00	200	450	—

KM# 368.8 1/4 REAL (Un Quarto/Una Quartilla)
0.8450 g., 0.9030 Silver 0.0245 oz. ASW **Note:** Mint mark Zs.

Date	Mintage	VG	F	VF	XF	Unc
1842/1Zs LR	—	4.00	8.00	15.00	30.00	—
1842Zs LR	—	4.00	8.00	15.00	30.00	—

KM# 370.5 1/2 REAL
1.6900 g., 0.9030 Silver 0.0491 oz. ASW **Obv:** Facing eagle, snake in beak

Date	Mintage	F	VF	XF	Unc	BU
1825Ga FS	—	25.00	40.00	75.00	200	—
1826Ga FS	—	10.00	15.00	35.00	80.00	—
1828/7Ga FS	—	12.50	20.00	40.00	90.00	—
1829Ga FS	—	7.50	15.00	30.00	70.00	—
1830/29Ga FS	—	40.00	60.00	100	200	—
1831Ga LP	—	350	—	—	—	—
1832Ga FS	—	10.00	20.00	35.00	80.00	—
1834/3Ga FS	—	65.00	100	175	250	—
1834Ga FS	—	10.00	20.00	35.00	80.00	—
1835/4/3Ga FS/LP	—	15.00	25.00	40.00	90.00	—
1837/6Ga JG	—	100	250	500	1,000	—
1838/7Ga JG	—	15.00	25.00	40.00	90.00	—
1839/8Ga JG/FS	—	35.00	75.00	150	250	—
1839Ga MC	—	10.00	20.00	35.00	80.00	—
1840/39Ga MC/JG	—	—	—	—	—	—
1840Ga MC	—	15.00	25.00	40.00	90.00	—
1841Ga MC	—	20.00	35.00	50.00	100	—
1842/1Ga JG	—	15.00	25.00	40.00	90.00	—
1842Ga JG	—	10.00	20.00	35.00	80.00	—
1843/2Ga JG	—	15.00	30.00	50.00	100	—
1843Ga JG	—	10.00	20.00	35.00	80.00	—
1843Ga MC/JG	—	10.00	20.00	35.00	80.00	—
1843Ga MC	—	10.00	20.00	35.00	80.00	—
1844Ga MC	—	10.00	20.00	35.00	80.00	—
1845Ga MC	—	10.00	20.00	35.00	80.00	—
1845Ga JG	—	10.00	20.00	35.00	80.00	—
1846Ga MC	—	10.00	20.00	35.00	80.00	—
1846Ga JG	—	10.00	20.00	35.00	80.00	—
1847Ga JG	—	10.00	20.00	35.00	80.00	—
1848/7Ga JG	—	10.00	20.00	35.00	80.00	—
1849Ga JG	—	10.00	20.00	35.00	80.00	—
1850/49Ga JG	—	—	—	—	—	—
1850Ga JG	—	10.00	20.00	35.00	80.00	—
1851/0Ga JG	—	10.00	20.00	35.00	80.00	—
1852Ga JG	—	10.00	20.00	35.00	80.00	—
1853Ga JG	—	10.00	20.00	35.00	80.00	—
1854Ga JG	—	10.00	20.00	35.00	80.00	—
1855/4Ga JG	—	10.00	20.00	35.00	80.00	—
1855Ga JG	—	10.00	20.00	35.00	80.00	—

FIRST REPUBLIC - FEDERAL

Date	Mintage	F	VF	XF	Unc	BU
1856Ga JG	—	10.00	20.00	35.00	80.00	—
1857Ga JG	—	10.00	20.00	35.00	80.00	—
1858/7Ga JG	—	10.00	20.00	35.00	80.00	—
1858Ga JG	—	10.00	20.00	35.00	80.00	—
1859/7Ga JG	—	10.00	20.00	35.00	80.00	—
1860/59Ga JG	—	10.00	20.00	35.00	80.00	—
1861Ga JG	—	5.00	12.50	25.00	60.00	—
1862/1Ga JG	—	15.00	25.00	40.00	90.00	—

KM# 370.6 1/2 REAL
1.6900 g., 0.9030 Silver 0.0491 oz. ASW **Obv:** Facing eagle, snake in beak

Date	Mintage	F	VF	XF	Unc	BU
1844GC MP	—	50.00	100	150	350	—
1845GC MP	—	25.00	50.00	100	200	—
1846GC MP	—	25.00	50.00	100	200	—
1847GC MP	—	25.00	50.00	100	300	—
1848GC MP	—	20.00	40.00	75.00	150	—
1849GC MP	—	25.00	50.00	100	200	—
1850GC MP	—	30.00	60.00	125	250	—
1851GC MP	—	25.00	50.00	100	200	—

KM# 370.8 1/2 REAL
1.6900 g., 0.9030 Silver 0.0491 oz. ASW **Obv:** Facing eagle, snake in beak

Date	Mintage	F	VF	XF	Unc	BU
1839Ho PP Unique	—	—	—	—	—	—
1862Ho FM	—	500	650	1,000	—	—
1867Ho PR/FM Inverted 6, and 7/1	—	100	175	250	500	—

KM# 370.9 1/2 REAL
1.6900 g., 0.9030 Silver 0.0491 oz. ASW **Obv:** Facing eagle, snake in beak

Date	Mintage	F	VF	XF	Unc	BU
1825Mo JM Short top 5	—	10.00	20.00	40.00	80.00	—
1825Mo JM Long top 5	—	10.00	20.00	40.00	80.00	—
1826/5Mo JM	—	10.00	20.00	40.00	80.00	—
1826Mo JM	—	5.00	10.00	20.00	60.00	—
1827/6Mo JM	—	5.00	10.00	20.00	60.00	—
1827Mo JM	—	5.00	10.00	20.00	60.00	—
1828/7Mo JM	—	7.50	15.00	25.00	85.00	—
1828Mo JM	—	10.00	20.00	40.00	90.00	—
1829Mo JM	—	7.50	15.00	25.00	75.00	—
1830Mo JM	—	5.00	10.00	20.00	60.00	—
1831Mo JM	—	5.00	10.00	20.00	60.00	—
1832Mo JM	—	7.50	12.50	27.50	60.00	—
1833Mo MJ	—	7.50	12.50	27.50	60.00	—
1834Mo ML	—	5.00	10.00	20.00	60.00	—
1835Mo ML	—	5.00	10.00	20.00	60.00	—
1836/5Mo ML/MF	—	7.50	15.00	25.00	65.00	—
1836Mo ML	—	7.50	15.00	25.00	65.00	—
1838Mo ML	—	5.00	10.00	20.00	60.00	—
1839/8Mo ML	—	5.00	10.00	25.00	65.00	—
1839Mo ML	—	5.00	10.00	20.00	50.00	—
1840Mo ML	—	5.00	10.00	20.00	50.00	—
1841Mo ML	—	5.00	10.00	20.00	50.00	—
1842Mo ML	—	15.00	35.00	80.00	200	—
1842Mo MM	—	5.00	10.00	20.00	50.00	—
1843Mo MM	—	10.00	20.00	40.00	80.00	—
1844Mo MF	—	5.00	10.00	20.00	50.00	—
1845/4Mo MF	—	5.00	10.00	25.00	60.00	—
1845Mo MF	—	5.00	10.00	20.00	50.00	—
1846Mo MF	—	5.00	10.00	20.00	50.00	—
1847Mo RC	—	10.00	20.00	40.00	80.00	—
1847Mo RC R/M	—	10.00	20.00	40.00	80.00	—
1848/7Mo GC/RC	—	5.00	10.00	20.00	50.00	—
1849Mo GC	—	5.00	10.00	20.00	50.00	—
1850Mo GC	—	5.00	10.00	20.00	50.00	—
1851Mo GC	—	5.00	10.00	20.00	50.00	—
1852Mo GC	—	5.00	10.00	20.00	50.00	—
1853Mo GC	—	5.00	10.00	20.00	50.00	—
1854Mo GC	—	5.00	10.00	20.00	50.00	—
1855Mo GC	—	5.00	10.00	20.00	50.00	—
1855Mo GF/GC	—	7.50	12.50	25.00	65.00	—
1856/5Mo GF	—	7.50	12.50	25.00	65.00	—
1857Mo GF	—	5.00	10.00	20.00	50.00	—
1858Mo FH	—	3.00	5.00	12.50	40.00	—
1858Mo FH F/G	—	5.00	10.00	20.00	50.00	—

Date	Mintage	F	VF	XF	Unc	BU
1858/9Mo FH	—	5.00	10.00	20.00	50.00	—
1859Mo FH/GC	—	5.00	10.00	20.00	50.00	—
1859Mo FH	—	3.00	6.00	15.00	50.00	—
1860Mo FH/GC	—	5.00	10.00	20.00	50.00	—
1860Mo FH	—	3.00	6.00	15.00	50.00	—
1860Mo TH	—	25.00	50.00	100	200	—
1860/59Mo FH	—	7.50	12.50	25.00	65.00	—
1861Mo CH	—	3.00	6.00	15.00	45.00	—
1862/52Mo CH	—	5.00	10.00	20.00	45.00	—
1862Mo CH	—	3.00	6.00	15.00	45.00	—
1863/55Mo TH/GC	—	5.00	10.00	20.00	50.00	—
1863Mo CH/GC	—	5.00	10.00	20.00	50.00	—
1863Mo CH	—	3.00	6.00	15.00	45.00	—

KM# 370.10 1/2 REAL
1.6900 g., 0.9030 Silver 0.0491 oz. ASW **Obv:** Facing eagle, snake in beak

Date	Mintage	F	VF	XF	Unc	BU
1831Pi JS	—	7.50	12.50	25.00	65.00	—
1841/36Pi JS	—	20.00	40.00	75.00	125	—
1842/1Pi PS	—	20.00	40.00	75.00	125	—
1842/1Pi PS P/J	—	60.00	80.00	150	300	—
1842Pi PS/PJ	—	50.00	75.00	125	250	—
1842 PS	—	60.00	80.00	150	300	—
1842Pi JS	—	20.00	40.00	75.00	125	—
1843/2Pi PS	—	17.50	25.00	40.00	80.00	—
1843Pi PS	—	15.00	25.00	35.00	70.00	—
1843Pi AM	—	10.00	15.00	25.00	60.00	—
1844Pi AM	—	10.00	15.00	30.00	65.00	—
1845Pi AM	—	250	375	500	1,500	—
1846/5Pi AM	—	40.00	75.00	125	200	—
1847/6Pi AM	—	15.00	25.00	40.00	80.00	—
1848Pi AM	—	15.00	25.00	40.00	80.00	—
1849Pi MC/AM	—	15.00	25.00	40.00	80.00	—
1849Pi MC	—	12.50	20.00	35.00	70.00	—
1850/49Pi MC	—	—	—	—	—	—
1850Pi MC	—	10.00	15.00	25.00	60.00	—
1850P MC	—	—	—	—	—	—
1851Pi MC	—	10.00	15.00	25.00	60.00	—
1852Pi MC	—	10.00	20.00	30.00	65.00	—
1853Pi MC	—	7.50	12.50	20.00	60.00	—
1854Pi MC	—	7.50	12.50	20.00	60.00	—
1855Pi MC	—	15.00	20.00	35.00	70.00	—
1856Pi MC	—	15.00	25.00	50.00	100	—
1856PI (no I)	—	—	—	—	—	—
1857Pi MC	—	7.50	12.50	20.00	60.00	—
1857Pi PS	—	10.00	15.00	30.00	65.00	—
1858Pi MC	—	12.50	20.00	35.00	70.00	—
1858Pi PS	—	12.50	20.00	35.00	70.00	—
1859Pi MC Rare	—	—	—	—	—	—
1860/59Pi PS	—	125	200	600	—	—
1861Pi RO	—	10.00	15.00	30.00	60.00	—
1862/1Pi RO	—	15.00	25.00	50.00	125	—
1862Pi RO	—	15.00	25.00	50.00	125	—
1863/2Pi RO	—	15.00	25.00	45.00	100	—

KM# 370.2 1/2 REAL
1.6900 g., 0.9030 Silver 0.0491 oz. ASW **Obv:** Facing eagle, snake in beak **Obv. Legend:** REPUBLICA MEXICANA **Rev:** Radiant cap **Note:** Mint mark C.

Date	Mintage	F	VF	XF	Unc	BU
1846 CE	—	30.00	50.00	75.00	150	—
1848/7 CE	—	15.00	25.00	45.00	90.00	—
1049/8 CE	—	15.00	25.00	45.00	90.00	—
1849 CE	—	—	—	—	—	—
1852 CE	—	12.50	20.00	40.00	80.00	—
1853/1 CE	—	12.50	20.00	40.00	80.00	—
1854 CE	—	20.00	35.00	50.00	100	—
1856 CE	—	12.50	20.00	40.00	80.00	—
1057/6 CE	—	20.00	35.00	50.00	100	—
1857 CE	—	15.00	25.00	45.00	90.00	—

Date	Mintage	F	VF	XF	Unc	BU
1858 CE Error 1 for 1/2	—	12.50	20.00	40.00	80.00	—
1860/59 PV	—	20.00	35.00	50.00	100	—
1860 PV	—	12.50	20.00	40.00	80.00	—
1861 PV	—	12.50	20.00	40.00	80.00	—
1863 CE Error 1 for 1/2	—	15.00	25.00	45.00	90.00	—
1867 CE	—	12.50	20.00	40.00	80.00	—
1869 6/5 CE Error 1 for 1/2	—	12.50	20.00	40.00	80.00	—

KM# 370.3 1/2 REAL
1.6900 g., 0.9030 Silver 0.0491 oz. ASW **Obv:** Facing eagle, snake in beak **Note:** Mint mark D, Do.

Date	Mintage	F	VF	XF	Unc	BU
1832 RM	—	125	225	350	600	—
1832 RM/L	—	—	—	—	—	—
1833/2 RM/L	—	75.00	100	150	225	—
1833/1 RM/L	—	12.50	20.00	40.00	80.00	—
1833 RM	—	25.00	40.00	75.00	150	—
1834/1 RM	—	25.00	40.00	75.00	150	—
1834 RM	—	12.50	20.00	40.00	80.00	—
1837/1 RM	—	12.50	30.00	60.00	200	—
1837/4 RM	—	12.50	30.00	60.00	200	—
1837/6 RM	—	12.50	30.00	60.00	200	—
1841/33 RM	—	15.00	30.00	60.00	250	—
1842/32 RM	—	12.50	20.00	40.00	80.00	—
1842 RM	—	12.50	20.00	40.00	80.00	—
1842 8R RM Error	—	12.50	20.00	40.00	80.00	—
1842 1/2/8R RM	—	12.50	20.00	40.00	80.00	—
1843/33 RM	—	15.00	25.00	50.00	100	—
1843 RM	—	15.00	25.00	50.00	100	—
1845/31 RM	—	12.50	20.00	40.00	80.00	—
1845/34 RM	—	12.50	20.00	40.00	80.00	—
1845/35 RM	—	12.50	20.00	40.00	80.00	—
1845 RM	—	15.00	25.00	50.00	100	—
1846 RM	—	30.00	50.00	80.00	200	—
1848/5 RM	—	35.00	55.00	110	250	—
1848/36 RM	—	25.00	40.00	75.00	200	—
1849 JMR	—	25.00	40.00	75.00	200	—
1850 RM Rare	—	—	—	—	—	—
1850 JMR	—	25.00	40.00	75.00	200	—
1851 JMR	—	20.00	35.00	50.00	100	—
1852/1 JMR	—	65.00	125	250	600	—
1852 JMR	—	30.00	50.00	80.00	200	—
1853 CP	—	12.50	20.00	40.00	80.00	—
1854 CP	—	25.00	40.00	75.00	200	—
1855 CP	—	25.00	40.00	60.00	150	—
1856/5 CP	—	20.00	35.00	50.00	100	—
1857 CP	—	20.00	35.00	50.00	100	—
1858/7 CP	—	20.00	35.00	50.00	100	—
1859 CP	—	20.00	35.00	50.00	100	—
1860/59 CP	—	40.00	65.00	135	300	—
1861 CP	—	125	250	400	700	—
1862 CP	—	25.00	40.00	60.00	125	—
1864 LT	—	100	300	500	1,000	—
1869 CP	—	40.00	65.00	125	275	—

KM# 370.11 1/2 REAL
1.6900 g., 0.9030 Silver 0.0491 oz. ASW **Obv:** Facing eagle, snake in beak **Note:** Mint mark Z, Zs.

Date	Mintage	F	VF	XF	Unc	BU
1826 AZ	—	5.00	10.00	20.00	60.00	—
1826 AO	—	5.00	10.00	20.00	60.00	—
1827 AO	—	5.00	10.00	20.00	60.00	—

Date	Mintage	F	VF	XF	Unc	BU
1828/7 AO	—	5.00	10.00	20.00	60.00	—
1829 AO	—	5.00	10.00	20.00	60.00	—
1830 OV	—	5.00	10.00	20.00	60.00	—
1831 OV	—	25.00	50.00	75.00	150	—
1831 OM	—	5.00	10.00	20.00	60.00	—
1832 OM	—	5.00	10.00	20.00	60.00	—
1833 OM	—	5.00	10.00	20.00	60.00	—
1834 OM	—	5.00	10.00	20.00	60.00	—
1835/4 OM	—	5.00	10.00	20.00	60.00	—
1835 OM	—	5.00	10.00	20.00	60.00	—
1836 OM	—	5.00	10.00	20.00	60.00	—
1837 OM	—	10.00	20.00	40.00	80.00	—
1838 OM	—	5.00	10.00	20.00	60.00	—
1839 OM	—	7.50	15.00	30.00	65.00	—
1840 OM	—	10.00	25.00	45.00	90.00	—
1841 OM	—	10.00	25.00	45.00	90.00	—
1842/1 OM	—	5.00	10.00	20.00	60.00	—
1842 OM	—	5.00	10.00	20.00	60.00	—
1843 OM	—	40.00	75.00	115	250	—
1844 OM	—	5.00	10.00	20.00	60.00	—
1845 OM	—	5.00	10.00	20.00	60.00	—
1846 OM	—	7.50	15.00	30.00	65.00	—
1847 OM	—	5.00	10.00	20.00	60.00	—
1848 OM	—	5.00	10.00	20.00	50.00	—
1849 OM	—	5.00	10.00	20.00	50.00	—
1850 OM	—	5.00	10.00	20.00	50.00	—
1851 OM	—	5.00	10.00	20.00	50.00	—
1852 OM	—	5.00	10.00	20.00	50.00	—
1853 OM	—	5.00	10.00	20.00	50.00	—
1854/3 OM	—	5.00	10.00	20.00	50.00	—
1854 OM	—	5.00	10.00	20.00	50.00	—
1855/3 OM	—	7.50	15.00	30.00	65.00	—
1855 OM	—	5.00	10.00	20.00	50.00	—
1856 OM	—	5.00	10.00	20.00	50.00	—
1857 MO	—	5.00	10.00	20.00	50.00	—
1858 MO	—	5.00	10.00	20.00	50.00	—
1859 MO	—	6.00	8.50	17.50	35.00	—
1859 VL	—	6.00	8.50	17.50	40.00	—
1860/50 VL Inverted A for V	—	5.00	10.00	20.00	50.00	—
1860/59 VL Inverted A for V	—	5.00	10.00	20.00	50.00	—
1860 MO	—	5.00	10.00	20.00	50.00	—
1860 VL	—	5.00	10.00	20.00	50.00	—
1861/0 VL	—	7.50	15.00	30.00	65.00	—
1861 VL Inverted A for V	—	5.00	10.00	20.00	50.00	—
1862 VL Inverted A for V	—	5.00	10.00	20.00	50.00	—
1863 VL Inverted A for V	—	5.00	10.00	20.00	50.00	—
1863/1 VL Inverted A for V	—	7.50	15.00	30.00	65.00	—
1869 YH	—	5.00	10.00	20.00	50.00	—

KM# 370.7 1/2 REAL
1.6900 g., 0.9030 Silver 0.0491 oz. ASW **Obv:** Facing eagle, snake in beak **Note:** Varieties exist.

Date	Mintage	F	VF	XF	Unc	BU
1826Go MJ	—	125	250	400	1,000	—
1827/6Go MJ	—	7.50	15.00	30.00	75.00	—
1828/7Go MJ	—	7.50	15.00	30.00	75.00	—
1828Go MJ	—	—	—	—	—	—
Note: Denomination 2/1						
1828Go JG	—	—	—	—	—	—
1828Go MR	—	50.00	100	150	250	—
1829/8Go MJ	—	5.00	10.00	25.00	50.00	—
1829Go MJ	—	5.00	10.00	25.00	50.00	—
Note: Reversed N in MEXICANA						
1830Go MJ	—	5.00	10.00	25.00	50.00	—
1831/29Go MJ	—	15.00	30.00	60.00	150	—
1831Go MJ	—	10.00	20.00	40.00	80.00	—
1832/1Go MJ	—	7.50	15.00	30.00	75.00	—
1832Go MJ	—	7.50	15.00	30.00	75.00	—
1833Go MJ Round top 3	—	10.00	20.00	40.00	80.00	—
1833Go MJ Flat top 3	—	10.00	20.00	40.00	80.00	—
1834Go PJ	—	5.00	10.00	25.00	50.00	—

Date	Mintage	F	VF	XF	Unc	BU
1835Go PJ	—	5.00	10.00	25.00	50.00	—
1836/5Go PJ	—	7.50	15.00	30.00	75.00	—
1836Go PJ	—	5.00	10.00	25.00	50.00	—
1837Go PJ	—	5.00	10.00	25.00	50.00	—
1838/7Go PJ	—	5.00	10.00	25.00	50.00	—
1839Go PJ	—	5.00	10.00	25.00	50.00	—
1839Go PJ	—	5.00	10.00	25.00	50.00	—
Note: Error: REPUBLIGA						
1840/39Go PJ	—	7.50	10.00	25.00	75.00	—
1840Go PJ Straight J	—	5.00	10.00	25.00	50.00	—
1840Go PJ Curved J	—	5.00	10.00	25.00	50.00	—
1841/31Go PJ	—	5.00	10.00	25.00	50.00	—
1841Go PJ	—	5.00	10.00	25.00	50.00	—
1842/1Go PJ	—	5.00	10.00	25.00	50.00	—
1842/1Go PM	—	5.00	10.00	25.00	50.00	—
1842Go PM/J	—	5.00	10.00	25.00	50.00	—
1842Go PJ	—	5.00	10.00	25.00	50.00	—
1842Go PM	—	5.00	10.00	25.00	50.00	—
1843/33Go PM 1/2 over 8	—	5.00	10.00	25.00	50.00	—
1843Go PM	—	5.00	10.00	25.00	50.00	—
Note: Convex wings						
1843Go PM	—	5.00	10.00	25.00	50.00	—
Note: Concave wings						
1844/3Go PM	—	5.00	10.00	25.00	50.00	—
1844Go PM	—	10.00	20.00	40.00	90.00	—
1845/4Go PM	—	5.00	10.00	25.00	50.00	—
1845Go PM	—	5.00	10.00	25.00	50.00	—
1846/4Go PM	—	5.00	10.00	25.00	50.00	—
1846/5Go PM	—	5.00	10.00	25.00	50.00	—
1846Go PM	—	5.00	10.00	25.00	50.00	—
1847/6Go PM	—	7.50	15.00	30.00	60.00	—
1847Go PM	—	7.50	15.00	30.00	60.00	—
1848/35Go PM	—	5.00	10.00	25.00	50.00	—
1848Go PM	—	5.00	10.00	25.00	50.00	—
1848Go PF/M	—	5.00	10.00	25.00	50.00	—
1849/39Go PF	—	5.00	10.00	25.00	50.00	—
1849Go PF	—	5.00	10.00	25.00	50.00	—
1849Go PF	—	5.00	10.00	25.00	50.00	—
Note: Error: MEXCANA						
1850Go PF	—	5.00	10.00	25.00	50.00	—
1851Go PF	—	5.00	10.00	25.00	50.00	—
1852/1Go PF	—	5.00	10.00	25.00	50.00	—
1852Go PF	—	2.50	7.50	17.50	40.00	—
1853Go PF/R	—	5.00	10.00	25.00	50.00	—
1853Go PF	—	5.00	10.00	25.00	50.00	—
1854Go PF	—	5.00	10.00	25.00	50.00	—
1855Go PF	—	5.00	10.00	25.00	50.00	—
1856/4Go PF	—	5.00	10.00	25.00	50.00	—
1856/5Go PF	—	5.00	10.00	25.00	50.00	—
1856Go PF	—	5.00	10.00	25.00	50.00	—
1857/6Go PF	—	5.00	10.00	25.00	50.00	—
1857Go PF	—	5.00	10.00	25.00	50.00	—
1858/7Go PF	—	7.50	15.00	30.00	60.00	—
1858Go PF	—	5.00	10.00	25.00	50.00	—
1859Go PF	—	5.00	10.00	25.00	50.00	—
1860Go PF Small 1/2	—	5.00	10.00	25.00	50.00	—
1860Go PF Large 1/2	—	5.00	10.00	25.00	50.00	—
1860/59Go PF	—	5.00	10.00	25.00	50.00	—
1861Go PF Small 1/2	—	5.00	10.00	25.00	50.00	—
1861Go PF Large 1/2	—	5.00	10.00	25.00	50.00	—
1862/1Go YE	—	5.00	10.00	25.00	50.00	—
1862Go YE	—	2.50	7.50	17.50	40.00	—
1862Go YF	—	5.00	10.00	25.00	50.00	—
1867Go YF	—	2.50	7.50	17.50	40.00	—
1868Go YF	—	2.50	7.50	17.50	40.00	—

KM# 370.1   1/2 REAL
1.6900 g., 0.9030 Silver 0.0491 oz. ASW   **Obv:** Facing eagle

Date	Mintage	F	VF	XF	Unc	BU
1844Ca RG	—	75.00	125	175	275	—
1845Ca RG	—	75.00	125	150	250	—

KM# 370   1/2 REAL
1.6900 g., 0.9030 Silver 0.0491 oz. ASW   **Obv:** Hooked-neck eagle

Date	Mintage	F	VF	XF	Unc	BU
1862A PG Rare	—	—	—	—	—	—

KM# 370.4   1/2 REAL
1.6900 g., 0.9030 Silver 0.0491 oz. ASW   **Obv:** Facing eagle, snake in beak

Date	Mintage	F	VF	XF	Unc	BU
1829EoMo LF	—	175	300	500	1,400	—

KM# 372   REAL
3.3800 g., 0.9030 Silver 0.0981 oz. ASW   **Obv:** Facing eagle, snake in beak

Date	Mintage	F	VF	XF	Unc	BU
1844Ca RG	—	500	1,000	1,500	2,750	—
1845Ca RG	—	500	1,000	1,500	2,750	—
1855Ca RG	—	100	150	225	450	—

KM# 372.1   REAL
3.3800 g., 0.9030 Silver 0.0981 oz. ASW   **Obv:** Facing eagle, snake in beak

Date	Mintage	F	VF	XF	Unc	BU
1846C CE	—	12.50	25.00	40.00	110	—
1848C CE	—	12.50	25.00	40.00	110	—
1850C CE	—	12.50	25.00	40.00	110	—
1851/0C CE	—	12.50	25.00	40.00	110	—
1852/1C CE	—	7.50	15.00	30.00	100	—
1853/2C CE	—	7.50	15.00	30.00	100	—
1854C CE	—	7.50	15.00	30.00	100	—
1856C CE	—	40.00	65.00	100	225	—
1857/4C CE	—	10.00	20.00	35.00	100	—
1857/6C CE	—	10.00	20.00	35.00	100	—
1858C CE	—	5.00	7.50	15.00	100	—
1859C CE	—	—	—	—	—	—
1860/9C PV/N	—	6.00	10.00	17.50	120	—
1860C PV	—	5.00	7.50	15.00	100	—
1861C PV	—	5.00	7.50	15.00	100	—
1863C CE	—	—	—	1,650	2,250	—
Note: 3 known						
1869C CE	—	—	7.50	15.00	100	—

KM# 372.2   REAL
3.3800 g., 0.9030 Silver 0.0981 oz. ASW   **Obv:** Facing eagle, snake in beak

Date	Mintage	F	VF	XF	Unc	BU
1832/1Do RM	—	5.00	10.00	20.00	90.00	—
1832Do RM/RL	—	10.00	15.00	30.00	100	—
1832Do RM	—	5.00	10.00	20.00	100	—
1834/24Do RM/RL	—	15.00	25.00	50.00	150	—
1834/3Do RM/RL	—	15.00	25.00	50.00	150	—
1834Do RM	—	10.00	20.00	40.00	110	—
1836/4Do RM	—	5.00	7.50	15.00	100	—
1836Do RM	—	5.00	7.50	15.00	100	—
1837Do RM 3/2	—	12.50	20.00	40.00	110	—
1837Do RM	—	12.50	20.00	40.00	110	—
1841Do RM	—	7.50	15.00	30.00	100	—
1842/32Do RM	—	10.00	20.00	40.00	110	—
1842Do RM	—	7.50	15.00	30.00	100	—
1843/37Do RM	—	10.00	20.00	40.00	110	—
1843Do RM	—	5.00	7.50	15.00	100	—
1844/34Do RM	—	15.00	25.00	45.00	125	—
1845Do RM	—	5.00	7.50	15.00	100	—
1846Do RM	—	7.50	15.00	30.00	100	—
1847Do RM	—	10.00	15.00	35.00	100	—
1848/31Do RM	—	10.00	15.00	35.00	100	—
1848/33Do RM	—	10.00	15.00	35.00	100	—
1848/5Do RM	—	10.00	15.00	35.00	100	—
1848Do RM	—	7.50	12.50	20.00	100	—
1849/8Do CM	—	5.00	10.00	30.00	100	—
1850Do JMR	—	20.00	40.00	75.00	175	—
1851Do JMR	—	20.00	40.00	75.00	175	—
1852Do JMR	—	20.00	40.00	75.00	175	—
1853Do CP	—	12.50	20.00	35.00	100	—
1854/1Do CP	—	10.00	15.00	25.00	100	—
1854Do CP	—	7.50	12.50	20.00	100	—
1855Do CP	—	10.00	15.00	25.00	100	—
1856Do CP	—	12.50	20.00	35.00	100	—
1857Do CP	—	12.50	20.00	35.00	100	—
1858Do CP		12.50	20.00	35.00	100	—

Date	Mintage	F	VF	XF	Unc	BU
1859Do CP	—	7.50	12.50	20.00	100	—
1860/59Do CP	—	10.00	15.00	25.00	100	—
1861Do CP	—	15.00	25.00	40.00	110	—
1862/1Do CP	—	225	300	450	1,250	—
1864Do LT	—	15.00	25.00	40.00	110	—

KM# 372.4 REAL
3.3800 g., 0.9030 Silver 0.0981 oz. ASW **Obv:** Facing eagle, snake in beak

Date	Mintage	F	VF	XF	Unc	BU
1826Ga FS	—	15.00	30.00	50.00	125	—
1828/7Ga FS	—	15.00	30.00	50.00	125	—
1829/8/7Ga FS	—	—	—	—	—	—
1829Ga FS	—	15.00	30.00	50.00	125	—
1830Ga FS	—	250	425	600	—	—
1831Ga LP	—	15.00	30.00	50.00	125	—
1831Ga LP/FS	—	300	450	600	—	—
1832Ga FS	—	250	350	500	—	—
1833/2Ga G FS	—	100	150	275	550	—
1833Ga FS	—	75.00	125	225	500	—
1834/3Ga FS	—	75.00	125	225	500	—
1835Ga FS	—	—	—	—	—	—
1837/6Ga JG/FS	—	12.50	20.00	35.00	100	—
1838/7Ga JG/FS	—	100	200	400	—	—
1839Ga JG	—	250	350	500	—	—
1840Ga JG	—	12.50	20.00	35.00	100	—
1840Ga MC	—	7.50	12.50	25.00	70.00	—
1841Ga MC	—	50.00	75.00	125	250	—
1842/0Ga JG/MC	—	10.00	15.00	30.00	100	—
1842Ga JG	—	7.50	12.50	20.00	100	—
1843Ga JG	—	150	200	300	750	—
1843Ga MC	—	5.00	7.50	15.00	100	—
1844Ga MC	—	7.50	12.50	20.00	100	—
1845Ga MC	—	10.00	15.00	25.00	100	—
1845Ga JG	—	5.00	7.50	20.00	100	—
1846Ga JG	—	12.50	20.00	35.00	100	—
1847/6Ga JG	—	10.00	15.00	25.00	100	—
1847Ga JG	—	10.00	15.00	25.00	100	—
1848Ga JG	—	400	550	700	—	—
1849Ga JG	—	7.50	12.50	20.00	100	—
1850Ga JG	—	175	275	400	—	—
1851Ga JG	—	10.00	15.00	25.00	100	—
1852Ga JG	—	10.00	15.00	25.00	100	—
1853/2Ga JG	—	10.00	15.00	25.00	100	—
1854Ga JG	—	10.00	15.00	25.00	100	—
1855Ga JG	—	15.00	25.00	40.00	100	—
1856Ga JG	—	7.50	12.50	20.00	100	—
1857/6Ga JG	—	12.50	20.00	35.00	100	—
1858/7Ga JG	—	15.00	25.00	40.00	110	—
1859/8Ga JG	—	25.00	50.00	75.00	150	—
1860/59Ga JG	—	30.00	60.00	90.00	225	—
1861/0Ga JG	—	20.00	30.00	50.00	125	—
1861Ga JG	—	25.00	50.00	100	250	—
1862Ga JG	—	7.50	12.50	20.00	100	—

KM# 372.5 REAL
3.3800 g., 0.9030 Silver 0.0981 oz. ASW **Obv:** Facing eagle, snake in beak **Obv. Legend:** REPUBLICA MEXICANA **Rev:** Radiant cap

Date	Mintage	F	VF	XF	Unc	BU
1844GC MP	—	40.00	60.00	100	300	—
1845GC MP	—	40.00	60.00	100	300	—
1846GC MP	—	40.00	60.00	100	300	—
1847GC MP	—	40.00	60.00	100	300	—
1848GC MP	—	40.00	60.00	100	300	—
1849/7GC MP	—	40.00	60.00	100	300	—
1849/8GC MP	—	40.00	60.00	100	300	—
1849GC MP	—	40.00	60.00	100	300	—
1850GC MP	—	40.00	60.00	100	300	—
1851GC MP	—	40.00	60.00	100	300	—

KM# 372.6 REAL
3.3800 g., 0.9030 Silver 0.0981 oz. ASW **Obv:** Facing eagle, snake in beak

Date	Mintage	F	VF	XF	Unc	BU
1826/5Go JJ	—	5.00	7.50	15.00	85.00	—
1826Go MJ	—	4.00	6.00	15.00	85.00	—
1827Go MJ	—	4.00	6.00	15.00	65.00	—
1827Go JM	—	10.00	15.00	25.00	75.00	—
1828/7Go MR	—	4.00	6.00	15.00	85.00	—
1828Go MJ	—	4.00	6.00	15.00	85.00	—

Note: Straight J, small 8

Date	Mintage	F	VF	XF	Unc	BU
1828Go MJ	—	4.00	6.00	15.00	85.00	—

Note: Full J, large 8

Date	Mintage	F	VF	XF	Unc	BU
1828/6G MR/JJ	—	4.00	6.00	15.00	85.00	—
1828G MR/JJ	—	4.00	6.00	15.00	85.00	—
1828G MR	—	4.00	6.00	15.00	85.00	—
1829/8Go MG Small eagle	—	4.00	6.00	15.00	85.00	—
1829Go MJ Small eagle	—	4.00	6.00	15.00	85.00	—
1829Go MJ Large eagle	—	4.00	6.00	15.00	85.00	—
1830Go MJ Small initials	—	4.00	6.00	15.00	85.00	—
1830Go MJ Medium initials	—	4.00	6.00	15.00	85.00	—
1830Go MJ Large initials	—	4.00	6.00	15.00	85.00	—
1830Go MJ	—	4.00	6.00	15.00	85.00	—

Note: Reversed N in MEXICANA

Date	Mintage	F	VF	XF	Unc	BU
1830GC MJ 3/2	—	4.00	6.00	15.00	85.00	—
1831/0Go MJ	—	4.00	6.00	15.00	85.00	—

Note: Reversed N in MEXICANA

Date	Mintage	F	VF	XF	Unc	BU
1831Go MJ	—	4.00	6.00	15.00	85.00	—
1832/1Go MJ	—	15.00	30.00	50.00	125	—
1832Go MJ	—	15.00	30.00	50.00	125	—
1833Go MJ Top of 3 round	—	4.00	6.00	15.00	85.00	—
1833Go MJ Top of 3 flat	—	4.00	6.00	15.00	85.00	—
1834Go PJ	—	4.00	6.00	15.00	85.00	—
1835Go PJ	—	7.50	12.50	20.00	85.00	—
1836Go PJ	—	4.00	6.00	15.00	85.00	—
1837Go PJ	—	15.00	30.00	50.00	125	—
1838/7Go PJ	—	10.00	20.00	35.00	85.00	—
1839Go PJ	—	4.00	6.00	15.00	85.00	—
1840/39Go PJ	—	4.00	6.00	15.00	85.00	—
1840Go PJ	—	4.00	6.00	15.00	85.00	—
1841/31Go PJ	—	10.00	20.00	35.00	85.00	—
1841Go PJ	—	4.00	6.00	15.00	85.00	—
1842Go PJ	—	4.00	6.00	15.00	85.00	—
1842Go PM	—	4.00	6.00	15.00	85.00	—
1843Go PM Convex wings	—	4.00	6.00	15.00	85.00	—
1843Go PM Concave wings	—	4.00	6.00	15.00	85.00	—
1844Go PM	—	4.00	6.00	15.00	85.00	—
1845/4Go PM	—	4.00	6.00	15.00	85.00	—
1845Go PM	—	4.00	6.00	15.00	85.00	—
1846/5Go PM	—	7.50	12.50	20.00	85.00	—
1846Go PM	—	4.00	6.00	15.00	85.00	—
1847/6Go PM	—	4.00	6.00	15.00	85.00	—
1847Go PM	—	4.00	6.00	15.00	85.00	—
1848Go PM	—	4.00	6.00	15.00	85.00	—
1849Go PF	—	10.00	20.00	35.00	85.00	—
1850Go PF	—	4.00	6.00	15.00	85.00	—
1851Go PF	—	10.00	20.00	35.00	100	—
1853/2Go PF	—	7.50	12.50	20.00	75.00	—
1853Go PF	—	4.00	6.00	15.00	75.00	—
1853Go PF/M 5/4	—	7.50	12.50	20.00	75.00	—
1854/3Go PF	—	4.00	6.00	15.00	75.00	—
1854Go PF Large eagle	—	4.00	6.00	15.00	75.00	—
1854Go PF Small eagle	—	4.00	6.00	15.00	75.00	—
1855/3Go PF	—	4.00	6.00	15.00	75.00	—
1855/4Go PF	—	4.00	6.00	15.00	75.00	—
1855Go PF	—	4.00	6.00	15.00	75.00	—
1856/5Go PF	—	4.00	6.00	15.00	75.00	—
1856Go PF	—	4.00	6.00	15.00	75.00	—
1857/6Go PF	—	4.00	6.00	15.00	75.00	—

Date	Mintage	F	VF	XF	Unc	BU
1857Go PF	—	4.00	6.00	15.00	75.00	—
1858Go PF	—	4.00	6.00	15.00	75.00	—
1859Go PF	—	4.00	6.00	15.00	75.00	—
1860/50Go PF	—	4.00	6.00	15.00	75.00	—
1860Go PF	—	4.00	6.00	15.00	75.00	—
1861Go PF	—	4.00	6.00	15.00	75.00	—
1862Go YE	—	4.00	6.00	15.00	75.00	—
1862/1Go YF	—	7.50	12.50	20.00	75.00	—
1862Go YF	—	4.00	6.00	15.00	75.00	—
1867Go YF	—	4.00	6.00	15.00	75.00	—
1868/7Go YF	—	4.00	6.00	15.00	75.00	—

KM# 372.7   REAL
3.3800 g., 0.9030 Silver 0.0981 oz. ASW **Obv:** Facing eagle, snake in beak

Date	Mintage	F	VF	XF	Unc	BU
1867Ho PR	—	38.50	75.00	120	250	—
Note: Small 7/1						
1867Ho PR	—	38.50	75.00	120	250	—
Note: Large 7/ small 7						
1868Ho PR	—	38.50	75.00	120	250	—

KM# 372.8   REAL
3.3800 g., 0.9030 Silver 0.0981 oz. ASW **Obv:** Facing eagle, snake in beak

Date	Mintage	F	VF	XF	Unc	BU
1825Mo JM	—	10.00	20.00	40.00	125	—
1826Mo JM	—	7.50	15.00	30.00	115	—
1827/6Mo JM	—	7.50	15.00	30.00	85.00	—
1827Mo JM	—	5.00	10.00	20.00	80.00	—
1828Mo JM	—	7.50	15.00	30.00	110	—
1830/29Mo JM	—	5.00	10.00	20.00	110	—
1830Mo JM	—	5.00	12.50	25.00	110	—
1831Mo JM	—	100	200	300	800	—
1832Mo JM	—	5.00	10.00	20.00	110	—
1833/2Mo MJ	—	5.00	10.00	20.00	110	—
1850Mo GC	—	5.00	10.00	20.00	110	—
1852Mo GC	—	275	425	575	—	—
1854Mo GC	—	10.00	20.00	40.00	110	—
1855Mo GF	—	5.00	10.00	20.00	90.00	—
1856Mo GF	—	100	200	400	1,000	—
1857Mo GF	—	5.00	10.00	20.00	90.00	—
1858Mo FH	—	5.00	10.00	20.00	90.00	—
1859Mo FH	—	5.00	10.00	20.00	90.00	—
1861Mo CH	—	5.00	10.00	20.00	90.00	—
1862Mo CH	—	5.00	10.00	20.00	90.00	—
1863/2Mo CH	—	7.50	12.50	25.00	90.00	—

KM# 372.9   REAL
3.3800 g., 0.9030 Silver 0.0981 oz. ASW **Obv:** Facing eagle, snake in beak

Date	Mintage	F	VF	XF	Unc	BU
1831Pi JS	—	5.00	10.00	20.00	125	—
1837Pi JS	—	600	750	1,000	—	—
1838/7Pi JS	—	250	300	375	—	—
1838Pi JS	—	20.00	35.00	60.00	125	—
1840/39Pi JS	—	7.50	15.00	30.00	125	—
1840Pi JS	—	7.50	15.00	30.00	125	—
1841Pi JS	—	7.50	15.00	30.00	125	—
1842Pi JS	—	15.00	30.00	55.00	150	—
1842Pi PS	—	5.00	10.00	20.00	125	—
1843Pi PS	—	12.50	20.00	35.00	125	—
1843Pi AM	—	40.00	60.00	80.00	150	—
1844Pi AM	—	40.00	60.00	80.00	150	—
1845Pi AM	—	7.50	15.00	30.00	125	—
1846/5Pi AM	—	7.50	15.00	30.00	125	—
1847/6Pi AM	—	7.50	15.00	30.00	125	—
1847Pi AM	—	7.50	15.00	30.00	125	—
1848/7Pi AM	—	7.50	15.00	30.00	125	—
1849Pi PS	—	7.50	15.00	30.00	125	—
1849/8Pi SP	—	60.00	100	150	—	—
1849Pi SP	—	15.00	25.00	40.00	125	—
1850Pi MC	—	5.00	10.00	20.00	125	—
1851/0Pi MC	—	7.50	15.00	30.00	125	—
1851Pi MC	—	7.50	15.00	30.00	125	—
1852/1/0Pi MC	—	10.00	20.00	35.00	125	—
1852Pi MC	—	7.50	15.00	30.00	125	—
1853/1Pi MC	—	12.50	20.00	35.00	125	—
1853Pi MC	—	10.00	20.00	35.00	125	—
1854/2Pi MO	—	30.00	60.00	100	—	—

Date	Mintage	F	VF	XF	Unc	BU
1854/3Pi MC	—	20.00	40.00	60.00	150	—
1855/4Pi MC	—	20.00	40.00	60.00	150	—
1855Pi MC	—	15.00	25.00	45.00	125	—
1856Pi MC	—	15.00	25.00	45.00	125	—
1857Pi PS	—	20.00	35.00	55.00	135	—
1857Pi MC	—	20.00	40.00	60.00	150	—
1858Pi MC	—	12.50	20.00	35.00	125	—
1859Pi PS	—	10.00	15.00	30.00	125	—
1860/59Pi PS	—	10.00	15.00	30.00	125	—
1861Pi PS	—	7.50	12.50	20.00	125	—
1861Pi RO	—	12.50	20.00	35.00	125	—
1862/1Pi RO	—	12.50	20.00	35.00	90.00	—
1862Pi RO	—	7.50	12.50	20.00	125	—

KM# 372.10   REAL
3.3800 g., 0.9030 Silver 0.0981 oz. ASW **Obv:** Facing eagle, snake in beak

Date	Mintage	F	VF	XF	Unc	BU
1826Zs AZ	—	5.00	12.50	35.00	120	—
1826Zs AO	—	5.00	12.50	35.00	120	—
1827Zs AO	—	5.00	12.50	35.00	120	—
1828/7Zs AO	—	5.00	12.50	35.00	120	—
1828Zs AO	—	5.00	12.50	35.00	120	—
1828Zs AO Inverted V for A	—	5.00	12.50	35.00	120	—
1829Zs AO	—	5.00	12.50	35.00	120	—
1830Zs ZsOV	—	5.00	12.50	35.00	120	—
1830Zs ZOV	—	5.00	12.50	35.00	120	—
1831Zs OV	—	5.00	12.50	35.00	120	—
1831Zs OM	—	5.00	12.50	30.00	120	—
1832Zs OM	—	5.00	12.50	30.00	120	—
1833/2Zs OM	—	5.00	12.50	30.00	120	—
1833/2Zs OM/V	—	5.00	12.50	30.00	120	—
1833Zs OM	—	5.00	12.50	30.00	120	—
1834/3Zs OM	—	5.00	12.50	30.00	120	—
1834Zs OM	—	5.00	12.50	30.00	120	—
1835/4Zs OM	—	20.00	35.00	60.00	150	—
1835Zs OM	—	4.00	8.00	20.00	65.00	—
1836/5Zs OM	—	4.00	8.00	20.00	85.00	—
1836Zs OM	—	4.00	8.00	20.00	85.00	—
1837Zs OM	—	4.00	8.00	20.00	85.00	—
1838Zs OM	—	4.00	8.00	20.00	85.00	—
1839Zs OM	—	4.00	8.00	20.00	85.00	—
1840Zs OM	—	4.00	8.00	20.00	85.00	—
1841Zs OM	—	20.00	40.00	60.00	150	—
1842/1Zs OM	—	4.00	8.00	20.00	85.00	—
1842Zs OM	—	4.00	8.00	20.00	85.00	—
1843Zs OM	—	4.00	8.00	20.00	85.00	—
1844Zs OM	—	4.00	8.00	20.00	85.00	—
1845/4Zs OM	—	5.00	12.50	30.00	100	—
1845Zs OM	—	4.00	8.00	20.00	85.00	—
1846Zs OM	—	4.00	8.00	20.00	85.00	—
Note: Old font and obverse						
1846Zs OM	—	4.00	8.00	20.00	85.00	—
Note: New font and obverse						
1847Zs OM	—	4.00	8.00	20.00	85.00	—
1848Zs OM	—	4.00	8.00	20.00	85.00	—
1849Zs OM	—	10.00	25.00	50.00	125	—
1850Zs OM	—	4.00	6.00	15.00	85.00	—
1851Zs OM	—	4.00	6.00	15.00	85.00	—
1852Zs OM	—	4.00	6.00	15.00	85.00	—
1853Zs OM	—	4.00	6.00	15.00	85.00	—
1854/2Zs OM	—	4.00	6.00	15.00	85.00	—
1854/3Zs OM	—	4.00	6.00	15.00	85.00	—
1854Zs OM	—	4.00	6.00	15.00	85.00	—
1855/4Zs OM	—	4.00	6.00	15.00	85.00	—
1855Zs OM	—	4.00	6.00	15.00	85.00	—
1855Zs MO	—	4.00	6.00	15.00	85.00	—
1856Zs MO	—	4.00	6.00	15.00	85.00	—
1856Zs MO/OM	—	4.00	6.00	15.00	85.00	—
1857Zs MO	—	4.00	6.00	15.00	85.00	—
1858Zs MO	—	4.00	6.00	15.00	85.00	—
1859Zs MO	—	4.00	6.00	15.00	75.00	—
1860 MO	—	250	—	—	—	—
1860Zs VL	—	4.00	6.00	15.00	75.00	—
1860Zs VL Inverted A for V	—	4.00	6.00	15.00	75.00	—
1861Zs VL	—	4.00	6.00	15.00	75.00	—
1061Zs VL Inverted A for V	—	4.00	6.00	15.00	75.00	—

Date	Mintage	F	VF	XF	Unc	BU
1862Zs VL	—	5.00	12.50	30.00	100	—
1868Zs JS	—	25.00	45.00	90.00	175	—
1869Zs YH	—	4.00	8.00	20.00	75.00	—

KM# 372.3 REAL
3.3800 g., 0.9030 Silver 0.0981 oz. ASW **Obv:**
Facing eagle, snake in beak

Date	Mintage	F	VF	XF	Unc	BU
1828EoMo LF	—	200	300	450	1,500	—

KM# 374.2 2 REALES
6.7600 g., 0.9030 Silver 0.1962 oz. ASW **Obv:**
Facing eagle, snake in beak **Edge:** Reeded

Date	Mintage	F	VF	XF	Unc	BU
1832Ca MR	—	30.00	60.00	100	200	—
1833Ca MR	—	30.00	60.00	125	500	—
1834Ca MR	—	35.00	75.00	125	500	—
1834Ca AM	—	35.00	75.00	125	500	—
1835Ca AM	—	35.00	75.00	125	500	—
1836Ca AM	—	20.00	40.00	80.00	200	—
1844Ca AM Rare	—	—	—	—	—	—
1844Ca RG Unique	—	—	—	—	—	—
1845Ca RG	—	20.00	40.00	80.00	200	—
1855Ca RG	—	20.00	40.00	80.00	200	—

KM# 374.3 2 REALES
6.7600 g., 0.9030 Silver 0.1962 oz. ASW **Obv:**
Facing eagle, snake in beak **Edge:** Reeded

Date	Mintage	F	VF	XF	Unc	BU
1846/1146C CE	—	25.00	50.00	100	225	—
1847C CE	—	12.50	20.00	40.00	200	—
1848C CE	—	12.50	20.00	40.00	200	—
1850C CE	—	25.00	50.00	75.00	200	—
1851C CE	—	12.50	20.00	40.00	200	—
1852/1C CE	—	12.50	20.00	40.00	200	—
1853/2C CE	—	12.50	20.00	40.00	200	—
1854C CE	—	15.00	30.00	50.00	200	—
1856C CE	—	20.00	35.00	70.00	200	—
1857C CE	—	12.50	20.00	40.00	200	—
1860C PV	—	12.50	20.00	40.00	200	—
1861C PV	—	12.50	20.00	40.00	200	—
1869C CE	—	12.50	20.00	40.00	200	—

KM# 374.4 2 REALES
6.7600 g., 0.9030 Silver 0.1962 oz. ASW **Obv:**
Facing eagle, snake in beak **Edge:** Reeded

Date	Mintage	F	VF	XF	Unc	BU
1826Do RL	—	20.00	40.00	60.00	200	—
1832Do RM	—	20.00	40.00	60.00	200	—
Note: Style of pre-1832						
1832Do RM	—	20.00	40.00	60.00	200	—
Note: Style of post-1832						
1834/2Do RM	—	20.00	40.00	60.00	200	—
1834/3Do RM	—	20.00	40.00	60.00	200	—
1835/4Do RM/RL	—	200	300	500	—	—
1841/31Do RM	—	50.00	75.00	125	250	—
1841Do RM	—	50.00	75.00	125	250	—
1842/32Do RM	—	12.50	20.00	40.00	200	—
1843Do RM/RL	—	12.50	20.00	40.00	200	—
1844Do RM	—	35.00	50.00	80.00	200	—
1845/34Do RM/RL	—	12.50	20.00	40.00	200	—
1846/36Do RM	—	100	150	200	350	—
1848/36Do RM	—	12.50	20.00	40.00	200	—
1848/37Do RM	—	12.50	20.00	40.00	200	—
1848/7Do RM	—	12.50	20.00	40.00	200	—
1848Do RM	—	12.50	20.00	40.00	200	—
1849Do CM/RM	—	12.50	20.00	40.00	200	—
1849Do CM	—	12.50	20.00	40.00	200	—
1851Do JMR/RL	—	12.50	20.00	40.00	200	—
1852Do JMR	—	12.50	20.00	40.00	200	—
1854Do CP/CR	—	30.00	50.00	80.00	200	—
1855Do CP	—	250	350	500	—	—
1856Do CP	—	100	150	250	500	—
1858Do CP	—	12.50	20.00	40.00	200	—
1859/8Do CP	—	12.50	20.00	40.00	200	—
1861Do CP	—	12.50	20.00	40.00	200	—

KM# 374.6 2 REALES
6.7600 g., 0.9030 Silver 0.1962 oz. ASW **Obv:**
Facing eagle, snake in beak **Edge:** Reeded

Date	Mintage	F	VF	XF	Unc	BU
1825Ga FS	—	20.00	40.00	80.00	200	—
1826Ga FS	—	20.00	40.00	80.00	200	—
1828/7Ga FS	—	100	150	225	400	—
1829Ga FS Rare	—	—	—	—	—	—
1832/0Ga FS/LP	—	100	150	225	350	—
1832Ga FS	—	12.50	20.00	40.00	200	—
1833/2Ga FS/LP	—	12.50	20.00	40.00	200	—
1834/27Ga FS Rare	—	—	—	—	—	—
1834Ga FS	—	12.50	20.00	40.00	200	—
1835Ga FS	—	2,100	—	—	—	—
1837Ga JG	—	12.50	20.00	40.00	200	—
1838Ga JG	—	12.50	20.00	40.00	200	—
1840/30Ga MC	—	12.50	20.00	40.00	200	—
1841Ga MC	—	30.00	50.00	200	500	—
1842/32Ga JG/MC	—	35.00	50.00	100	200	—
1842Ga JG	—	20.00	40.00	80.00	200	—
1843Ga JG	—	12.50	20.00	40.00	200	—
1843Ga MC/JG	—	12.50	20.00	40.00	200	—
1844Ga MC	—	12.50	20.00	40.00	200	—
1845/3Ga MC/JG	—	12.50	20.00	40.00	200	—
1845/4Ga MC/JG	—	12.50	20.00	40.00	200	—
1845Ga JG	—	12.50	20.00	40.00	200	—
1846Ga JG	—	12.50	20.00	40.00	200	—
1847/6Ga JG	—	25.00	40.00	80.00	200	—
1848/7Ga JG	—	12.50	20.00	40.00	200	—
1849Ga JG	—	12.50	20.00	40.00	200	—
1850/40Ga JG	—	12.50	20.00	40.00	200	—
1851Ga JG	—	250	350	500	—	—
1852Ga JG	—	12.50	20.00	40.00	200	—
1853/1Ga JG	—	12.50	20.00	40.00	200	—
1854/3Ga JG	—	250	350	500	—	—
1855Ga JG	—	35.00	50.00	80.00	200	—
1856Ga JG	—	12.50	20.00	40.00	200	—
1857Ga JG	—	250	350	500	—	—
1859/8Ga JG	—	12.50	20.00	40.00	200	—
1859Ga JG	—	12.50	20.00	40.00	200	—
1862/1Ga JG	—	12.50	20.00	40.00	200	—

KM# 374.7 2 REALES
6.7600 g., 0.9030 Silver 0.1962 oz. ASW **Obv:**
Facing eagle, snake in beak **Edge:** Reeded

Date	Mintage	F	VF	XF	Unc	BU
1844GC MP	—	40.00	60.00	125	275	—
1845GC MP	—	40.00	60.00	125	275	—
1846GC MP	—	50.00	100	150	300	—
1847GC MP	—	35.00	50.00	100	250	—
1848GC MP	—	50.00	100	150	300	—
1849GC MP	—	50.00	100	150	300	—
1850GC MP	—	125	250	—	—	—
1851/0GC MP	—	50.00	100	150	300	—
1851GC MP	—	50.00	100	150	300	—

KM# 374.9 2 REALES
6.7600 g., 0.9030 Silver 0.1962 oz. ASW **Obv:**
Facing eagle, snake in beak **Edge:** Reeded

Date	Mintage	F	VF	XF	Unc
1861Ho FM	—	200	300	400	650
1862/52Ho FM/C. CE	—	250	350	500	—
1867/1Ho PR/FM	—	75.00	150	250	500

KM# 374.11 2 REALES
6.7600 g., 0.9030 Silver 0.1962 oz. ASW **Obv:**
Facing eagle, snake in beak **Edge:** Reeded

Date	Mintage	F	VF	XF	Unc	BU
1829Pi JS	—	10.00	15.00	30.00	200	—
1830/20Pi JS	—	20.00	30.00	60.00	200	—
1837Pi JS	—	10.00	15.00	30.00	200	—
1841Pi JS	—	10.00	15.00	30.00	200	—
1842/1Pi JS	—	10.00	15.00	30.00	200	—
1842Pi JS	—	10.00	15.00	30.00	200	—
1842Pi PS	—	20.00	35.00	60.00	200	—
1843Pi PS	—	12.50	20.00	40.00	200	—
1843Pi AM	—	10.00	15.00	30.00	200	—
1844Pi AM	—	10.00	15.00	30.00	200	—
1845Pi AM	—	10.00	15.00	30.00	200	—
1846Pi AM	—	10.00	15.00	30.00	200	—

Date	Mintage	F	VF	XF	Unc	BU
1849Pi MC	—	10.00	15.00	30.00	200	—
1850Pi MC	—	10.00	15.00	30.00	200	—
1856Pi MC	—	40.00	60.00	125	250	—
1857Pi MC	—	—	—	—	—	—
1858Pi MC	—	12.50	20.00	40.00	200	—
1859Pi MC	—	50.00	70.00	100	200	—
1861Pi PS	—	10.00	15.00	30.00	200	—
1862Pi RO	—	12.50	20.00	40.00	200	—
1863Pi RO	—	100	250	350	500	—
1868Pi PS	—	10.00	15.00	30.00	200	—
1869/8Pi PS	—	10.00	15.00	30.00	200	—
1869Pi PS	—	10.00	15.00	30.00	200	—

KM# 374.8 2 REALES
6.7600 g., 0.9030 Silver 0.1962 oz. ASW **Obv:** Facing eagle, snake in beak **Edge:** Reeded **Note:** Varieties exist.

Date	Mintage	F	VF	XF	Unc	BU
1825Go JJ	—	7.50	15.00	30.00	150	—
1826/5Go JJ	—	7.50	15.00	30.00	150	—
1826Go JJ	—	7.50	10.00	25.00	150	—
1826Go MJ	—	7.50	10.00	25.00	150	—
1827/6Go MJ	—	7.50	10.00	25.00	150	—
1827Go MJ	—	7.50	10.00	25.00	150	—
1828/7Go MR	—	7.50	15.00	30.00	150	—
1828Go MJ	—	7.50	10.00	20.00	150	—
1828Go JM	—	7.50	10.00	20.00	150	—
1829Go MJ	—	7.50	10.00	20.00	150	—
1831Go MJ	—	7.50	10.00	20.00	150	—
1832Go MJ	—	7.50	10.00	20.00	150	—
1833Go MJ	—	7.50	10.00	20.00	150	—
1834Go PJ	—	7.50	10.00	20.00	150	—
1835/4Go PJ	—	7.50	15.00	30.00	150	—
1835Go PJ	—	7.50	10.00	20.00	150	—
1836Go PJ	—	7.50	10.00	20.00	150	—
1837/6Go PJ	—	7.50	10.00	20.00	150	—
1837Go PJ	—	7.50	10.00	20.00	150	—
1838/7Go PJ	—	7.50	10.00	20.00	150	—
1838Go PJ	—	7.50	10.00	20.00	150	—
1839/8Go PJ	—	7.50	15.00	30.00	150	—
1839Go PJ	—	7.50	10.00	20.00	150	—
1840Go PJ	—	7.50	10.00	20.00	150	—
1841Go PJ	—	7.50	10.00	20.00	150	—
1842Go PJ	—	7.50	10.00	20.00	150	—
1842Go PM/PJ	—	7.50	10.00	20.00	150	—
1842Go PM	—	7.50	10.00	20.00	150	—
1843/2Go PM	—	7.50	10.00	20.00	150	—

Note: Concave wings, thin rays, small letters

| 1843Go PM | — | 7.50 | 10.00 | 20.00 | 150 | — |

Note: Convex wings, thick rays, large letters

1844Go PM	—	7.50	10.00	20.00	150	—
1845/4Go PM	—	7.50	10.00	20.00	150	—
1845Go PM	—	7.50	10.00	20.00	150	—
1846/5Go PM	—	10.00	15.00	35.00	150	—
1846Go PM	—	7.50	10.00	20.00	150	—
1847Go PM	—	7.50	10.00	20.00	150	—
1848/7Go PM	—	7.50	15.00	30.00	150	—
1848Go PM	—	7.50	15.00	30.00	150	—
1848Go PF	—	100	150	250	500	—
1849/8Go PF/PM	—	7.50	10.00	20.00	150	—
1849Go PF	—	7.50	10.00	20.00	150	—
1850/40Go PF	—	7.50	10.00	20.00	150	—
1850Go PF	—	7.50	10.00	20.00	150	—
1851Go PF	—	7.50	10.00	20.00	150	—
1852/1Go PF	—	7.50	10.00	20.00	150	—
1852Go PF	—	7.50	10.00	20.00	150	—
1853Go PF	—	7.50	10.00	20.00	150	—
1854/3Go PF	—	7.50	10.00	20.00	150	—
1854Go PF	—	7.50	10.00	20.00	150	—

Note: Old font and obverse

| 1854Go PF | — | 7.50 | 10.00 | 20.00 | 150 | — |

Note: New font and obverse

| 1855Go PF | — | 7.50 | 10.00 | 20.00 | 150 | — |
| 1855Go PF | — | 7.50 | 10.00 | 20.00 | 150 | — |

Note: Star in G of mint mark

1856/5Go PF	—	10.00	15.00	35.00	150	—
1856Go PF	—	10.00	15.00	25.00	150	—
1857/6Go PF	—	7.50	10.00	20.00	150	—
1857Go PF	—	7.50	10.00	20.00	150	—

Date	Mintage	F	VF	XF	Unc	BU
1858/7Go PF	—	7.50	10.00	20.00	150	—
1858Go PF	—	7.50	10.00	20.00	150	—
1859/7Go PF	—	7.50	10.00	20.00	150	—
1859Go PF	—	7.50	10.00	20.00	150	—
1860/7Go PF	—	7.50	10.00	20.00	150	—
1860/50Go PF	—	7.50	10.00	20.00	150	—
1860/59Go PF	—	7.50	10.00	20.00	150	—
1860Go PF	—	7.50	10.00	20.00	150	—
1861/51Go PF	—	7.50	10.00	20.00	150	—
1861/57Go PF	—	7.50	10.00	20.00	150	—
1861/0Go PF	—	7.50	10.00	20.00	150	—
1861Go PF	—	7.50	10.00	20.00	150	—
1862/1Go YE	—	7.50	10.00	20.00	125	—
1862Go YE	—	7.50	10.00	20.00	125	—
1862/57Go YE	—	7.50	10.00	20.00	125	—
1862Go YE/PF	—	7.50	10.00	20.00	125	—
1862/57Go YF/E	—	7.50	10.00	20.00	125	—
1862/57Go YF	—	7.50	10.00	20.00	125	—
1862Go YF	—	7.50	10.00	20.00	125	—
1863/52Go YF/PE	—	7.50	10.00	20.00	125	—
1863/52Go YF	—	7.50	10.00	20.00	125	—
1863Go YF	—	7.50	10.00	20.00	125	—
1867/57Go YF	—	7.50	10.00	20.00	125	—
1868/57Go YF	—	10.00	15.00	25.00	125	—

KM# 374.10 2 REALES
6.7600 g., 0.9030 Silver 0.1962 oz. ASW **Obv:** Facing eagle, snake in beak **Obv. Legend:** REPUBLICA MEXICANA. **Rev:** Radiant cap **Edge:** Reeded **Note:** Varieties exist.

Date	Mintage	F	VF	XF	Unc	BU
1825Mo JM	—	10.00	15.00	30.00	175	—
1826Mo JM	—	10.00	15.00	30.00	175	—
1827Mo JM	—	10.00	15.00	30.00	175	—
1828Mo JM	—	10.00	15.00	30.00	175	—
1829/8Mo JM	—	10.00	15.00	30.00	175	—
1829Mo JM	—	10.00	15.00	30.00	175	—
1830Mo JM	—	40.00	60.00	125	250	—
1831Mo JM	—	10.00	15.00	30.00	175	—
1832Mo JM	—	100	200	400	—	—
1833/2Mo MJ/JM	—	10.00	15.00	30.00	175	—
1834Mo ML	—	50.00	100	200	400	—
1836Mo MF	—	10.00	15.00	30.00	175	—
1837Mo ML	—	10.00	15.00	30.00	175	—
1840/7Mo ML	—	150	225	350	—	—
1840Mo ML	—	150	225	350	—	—
1841Mo ML	—	15.00	40.00	100	250	—
1842 ML Rare	—	—	—	—	—	—
1847Mo RC Narrow date	—	10.00	15.00	30.00	175	—
1847Mo RC Wide date	—	10.00	15.00	30.00	175	—
1848Mo GC	—	10.00	15.00	30.00	175	—
1849Mo GC	—	10.00	15.00	30.00	175	—
1850Mo GC	—	10.00	15.00	30.00	175	—
1851Mo GC	—	40.00	60.00	125	250	—
1852Mo GC	—	10.00	15.00	30.00	175	—
1853Mo GC	—	10.00	15.00	30.00	175	—
1854/44Mo GC	—	10.00	15.00	30.00	175	—
1855Mo GC	—	10.00	15.00	30.00	175	—
1855Mo GF/GC	—	10.00	15.00	30.00	175	—
1855Mo GF	—	10.00	15.00	30.00	175	—
1856/5Mo GF/GC	—	10.00	15.00	30.00	175	—
1857Mo GF	—	10.00	15.00	30.00	175	—
1858Mo FH	—	7.50	12.50	25.00	150	—
1858Mo FH/GF	—	7.50	12.50	25.00	150	—
1859Mo FH	—	7.50	12.50	25.00	150	—

Date	Mintage	F	VF	XF	Unc	BU
1860Mo FH	—	7.50	12.50	25.00	150	—
1860Mo TH	—	7.50	12.50	25.00	150	—
1861Mo CH	—	7.50	12.50	25.00	150	—
1862Mo CH	—	7.50	12.50	25.00	150	—
1863Mo CH	—	7.50	12.50	25.00	150	—
1863Mo TH	—	7.50	12.50	25.00	150	—
1867Mo CH	—	7.50	12.50	25.00	150	—
1868Mo CH	—	10.00	15.00	30.00	150	—
1868Mo PH	—	7.50	12.50	25.00	150	—

KM# 374.12 2 REALES
6.7600 g., 0.9030 Silver 0.1962 oz. ASW **Obv:** Facing eagle, snake in beak **Edge:** Reeded **Note:** Varieties exist.

Date	Mintage	F	VF	XF	Unc	BU
1825Zs AZ	—	10.00	15.00	30.00	150	—
1826Zs AV	—	7.50	10.00	25.00	150	—
Note: A is inverted V						
1826Zs AZ	—	7.50	10.00	25.00	150	—
Note: A is inverted V						
1826Zs AO	—	10.00	15.00	30.00	150	—
1827Zs AO	—	6.00	8.00	12.00	150	—
Note: A is inverted V						
1827Zs AO	—	6.00	8.00	12.00	150	—
1828/7Zs AO	—	15.00	30.00	60.00	175	—
1828Zs AO	—	7.50	10.00	25.00	100	—
1828Zs AO	—	7.50	10.00	25.00	150	—
Note: A is inverted V						
1829Zs AO	—	7.50	10.00	25.00	150	—
1829Zs OV	—	7.50	10.00	25.00	150	—
1830Zs OV	—	7.50	10.00	25.00	150	—
1831Zs OV	—	7.50	10.00	25.00	150	—
1831Zs OM/OV	—	7.50	10.00	25.00	150	—
1831Zs OM	—	7.50	10.00	25.00	150	—
1832/1Zs OM	—	15.00	30.00	60.00	150	—
1832Zs OM	—	7.50	10.00	25.00	150	—
1833/27Zs OM	—	7.50	10.00	25.00	150	—
1833/2Zs OM	—	7.50	10.00	25.00	150	—
1833Zs OM	—	7.50	10.00	25.00	150	—
1834Zs OM	—	40.00	60.00	125	200	—
1835Zs OM	—	7.50	10.00	25.00	150	—
1836Zs OM	—	7.50	10.00	25.00	150	—
1837Zs OM	—	7.50	10.00	25.00	150	—
1838Zs OM	—	15.00	30.00	60.00	150	—
1839Zs OM	—	7.50	10.00	20.00	150	—
1840Zs OM	—	7.50	10.00	20.00	150	—
1841/0Zs OM	—	7.50	10.00	20.00	150	—
1841Zs OM	—	7.50	10.00	20.00	150	—
1842Zs OM	—	7.50	10.00	20.00	150	—
Narrow date						
1842Zs OM	—	7.50	10.00	20.00	150	—
Wide date						
1843Zs OM	—	7.50	10.00	20.00	150	—
1844Zs OM	—	7.50	10.00	20.00	150	—
1845Zs OM	—	7.50	10.00	20.00	150	—
Note: Small letters with leaves						
1845Zs OM	—	7.50	10.00	20.00	150	—
Note: Large letters with leaves						
1846Zs OM	—	7.50	10.00	20.00	150	—
1847Zs OM	—	7.50	10.00	20.00	150	—
1848Zs OM	—	7.50	10.00	20.00	150	—
1849Zs OM	—	7.50	10.00	20.00	150	—
1850Zs OM	—	7.50	10.00	20.00	150	—
1851Zs OM	—	7.50	10.00	20.00	150	—
1852Zs OM	—	7.50	10.00	20.00	150	—
1853Zs OM	—	7.50	10.00	20.00	150	—
1854/3Zs OM	—	7.50	10.00	20.00	150	—
1854Zs OM	—	7.50	10.00	20.00	150	—
1855/4Zs OM	—	7.50	10.00	20.00	150	—
1855Zs OM	—	7.50	10.00	20.00	150	—
1855Zs MO	—	7.50	10.00	20.00	150	—
1856/5Zs MO	—	7.50	10.00	20.00	150	—
1856Zs MO	—	7.50	10.00	20.00	150	—
1857Zs MO	—	7.50	10.00	20.00	150	—
1858Zs MO	—	7.50	10.00	20.00	150	—
1859Zs MO	—	7.50	10.00	20.00	150	—
1860/59Zs MO	—	7.50	10.00	20.00	150	—
1860Zs MO	—	7.50	10.00	20.00	100	—
1860Zs VL	—	7.50	10.00	20.00	150	—

Date	Mintage	F	VF	XF	Unc	BU
1861Zs VL	—	7.50	10.00	20.00	150	—
1862Zs VL	—	7.50	10.00	20.00	100	—
1863Zs MO	—	12.50	20.00	40.00	150	—
1863Zs VL	—	7.50	10.00	20.00	150	—
1864Zs MO	—	7.50	10.00	20.00	150	—
1864Zs VL	—	7.50	10.00	20.00	150	—
1865Zs MO	—	7.50	10.00	20.00	150	—
1867Zs JS	—	7.50	10.00	20.00	150	—
1868Zs JS	—	10.00	15.00	35.00	150	—
1868Zs YH	—	7.50	10.00	20.00	150	—
1869Zs YH	—	7.50	10.00	20.00	150	—
1870Zs YH	—	7.50	10.00	20.00	150	—

KM# 374 2 REALES
6.7600 g., 0.9030 Silver 0.1962 oz. ASW **Obv:** Facing eagle, snake in beak **Edge:** Reeded

Date	Mintage	F	VF	XF	Unc	BU
1872A AM	15,000	50.00	115	225	550	—

KM# 374.1 2 REALES
6.7600 g., 0.9030 Silver 0.1962 oz. ASW **Obv:** Facing eagle, snake in beak **Edge:** Reeded

Date	Mintage	F	VF	XF	Unc	BU
1863Ce ML	—	125	200	325	675	—

KM# 374.5 2 REALES
6.7600 g., 0.9030 Silver 0.1962 oz. ASW **Obv:** Facing eagle, snake in beak **Edge:** Reeded

Date	Mintage	F	VF	XF	Unc	BU
1828EoMo LF	—	325	525	900	2,500	—

KM# 375.1 4 REALES
13.5400 g., 0.9030 Silver 0.3931 oz. ASW **Obv:** Facing eagle, snake in beak

Date	Mintage	F	VF	XF	Unc	BU
1846C CE	—	400	550	900	—	—
1850C CE	—	75.00	125	250	—	—
1852C CE	—	200	300	500	—	—
1857C CE Rare	—	—	—	—	—	—
1858C CE	—	100	200	350	—	—
1860C PV	—	25.00	50.00	125	—	—

KM# 375.2 4 REALES
13.5400 g., 0.9030 Silver 0.3931 oz. ASW **Obv:** Facing eagle, snake in beak

Date	Mintage	F	VF	XF	Unc	BU
1843Ga MC	—	20.00	40.00	80.00	—	—
1844/3Ga MC	—	30.00	60.00	125	—	—
1844Ga MC	—	20.00	40.00	80.00	—	—
1845Ga MC	—	20.00	40.00	80.00	—	—
1845Ga JG	—	20.00	40.00	80.00	—	—
1846Ga JG	—	20.00	40.00	80.00	—	—
1847Ga JG	—	40.00	80.00	150	—	—
1848/7Ga JG	—	40.00	80.00	150	—	—
1849Ga JG	—	40.00	80.00	150	—	—
1850Ga JG	—	65.00	125	250	—	—
1852Ga JG Rare	—	—	—	—	—	—
1854Ga JG Rare	—	—	—	—	—	—
1855Ga JG	—	100	200	400	—	—
1856Ga JG Rare	—	—	—	—	—	—
1857/6Ga JG	—	65.00	125	250	—	—
1858Ga JG	—	125	250	450	—	—
1859/8Ga JG	—	125	250	450	—	—
1860Ga JG	—	850	1,450	—	—	—
1863/2Ga JG	—	150	300	1,250	—	—
1863Ga JG	—	150	300	1,250	—	—

KM# 375.3 4 REALES
13.5400 g., 0.9030 Silver 0.3931 oz. ASW **Obv:** Facing eagle, snake in beak

Date	Mintage	F	VF	XF	Unc	BU
1844GC MP	—	3,000	5,000	—	—	—
1845GC MP	—	6,500	8,000	—	—	—
1846GC MP	—	1,700	2,800	—	—	—
1847GC MP	—	1,500	2,500	—	—	—
1849GC MP	—	3,000	4,000	—	—	—
1850GC MP	—	1,500	2,500	—	—	—

KM# 375.5 4 REALES
13.5400 g., 0.9030 Silver 0.3931 oz. ASW **Obv:** Facing eagle, snake in beak

Date	Mintage	F	VF	XF	Unc	BU
1861Ho FM	—	200	350	500	—	—
1867/1Ho PR/FM	—	150	275	400	—	—

KM# 375.6 4 REALES
13.5400 g., 0.9030 Silver 0.3931 oz. ASW **Obv:** Facing eagle, snake in beak

Date	Mintage	F	VF	XF	Unc	BU
1827/6Mo JM	—	200	400	800	—	—
1850Mo GC Rare	—	—	—	—	—	—
1852Mo GC Rare	—	—	—	—	—	—
1854Mo GC Rare	—	—	—	—	—	—
1855Mo GF	—	100	200	350	—	—
1855Mo GF/GC	—	50.00	100	200	—	—
1856Mo GF/GC	—	50.00	125	400	—	—
1856Mo GF Rare	—	—	—	—	—	—
1859Mo FH	—	20.00	50.00	150	—	—
1861Mo CH	—	15.00	35.00	125	—	—
1862Mo CH	—	20.00	50.00	150	—	—
1863/2Mo CH	—	20.00	50.00	150	—	—
1863Mo CH	—	75.00	150	300	—	—
1867Mo CH	—	20.00	50.00	150	—	—
1868Mo CH/PH	—	30.00	75.00	150	—	—
1868Mo CH	—	20.00	50.00	150	—	—
1868Mo PH	—	30.00	75.00	200	—	—

KM# 375.8 4 REALES
13.5400 g., 0.9030 Silver 0.3931 oz. ASW **Obv:** Facing eagle, snake in beak

Date	Mintage	F	VF	XF	Unc	BU
1837Pi JS	—	200	350	—	—	—
1838Pi JS	—	150	250	400	—	—
1842Pi PS	—	50.00	100	200	—	—

Date	Mintage	F	VF	XF	Unc	BU
1843/2Pi PS	—	50.00	100	200	—	—
1843/2Pi PS	—	50.00	100	200	—	—
Note: 3 cut from 8 punch						
1843Pi AM	—	30.00	75.00	150	—	—
1843Pi PS	—	50.00	100	200	—	—
1844Pi AM	—	30.00	75.00	150	—	—
1845/4Pi AM	—	20.00	50.00	100	—	—
1845Pi AM	—	20.00	50.00	100	—	—
1846Pi AM	—	20.00	50.00	100	—	—
1847Pi AM	—	75.00	150	250	—	—
1848Pi AM Rare	—	—	—	—	—	—
1849Pi MC/AM	—	20.00	50.00	100	—	—
1849Pi MC	—	20.00	50.00	100	—	—
1849Pi PS	—	20.00	50.00	100	—	—
1850Pi MC	—	20.00	50.00	100	—	—
1851Pi MC	—	20.00	50.00	100	—	—
1852Pi MC	—	20.00	50.00	100	—	—
1853Pi MC	—	20.00	50.00	100	—	—
1854Pi MC	—	100	200	400	—	—
1855Pi MC	—	175	300	750	—	—
1856Pi MC	—	250	400	700	—	—
1857Pi MC Rare	—	—	—	—	—	—
1857Pi PS Rare	—	—	—	—	—	—
1858Pi MC	—	100	200	400	—	—
1859Pi MC	—	2,000	3,000	—	—	—
1860Pi PS	—	300	450	700	—	—
1861/0Pi PS	—	300	600	—	—	—
1861Pi PS	—	150	300	600	—	—
1861Pi RO/PS	—	30.00	75.00	150	—	—
1861Pi RO	—	50.00	100	200	—	—
1862Pi RO	—	30.00	75.00	150	—	—
1863Pi RO	—	30.00	75.00	150	—	—
1864Pi RO	—	2,500	3,500	—	—	—
1868Pi PS	—	30.00	75.00	150	—	—
1869/8Pi PS	—	30.00	75.00	150	—	—
1869Pi PS	—	30.00	75.00	150	—	—

KM# 375.9 4 REALES
13.5400 g., 0.9030 Silver 0.3931 oz. ASW **Obv:** Facing eagle, snake in beak

Date	Mintage	F	VF	XF	Unc	BU
1830Zs OM	—	20.00	50.00	100	—	—
1831Zs OM	—	15.00	30.00	75.00	—	—
1832/1Zs OM	—	20.00	50.00	100	—	—
1832Zs OM	—	20.00	50.00	100	—	—
1833/2Zs OM	—	20.00	50.00	100	—	—
1833/27Zs OM	—	15.00	30.00	75.00	—	—
1833Zs OM	—	15.00	30.00	75.00	—	—
1834/3Zs OM	—	20.00	50.00	100	—	—
1834Zs OM	—	15.00	30.00	75.00	—	—
1835Zs OM	—	15.00	30.00	75.00	—	—
1836Zs OM	—	15.00	30.00	75.00	—	—
1837/5Zs OM	—	20.00	50.00	100	—	—
1837/6Zs OM	—	20.00	50.00	100	—	—
1837Zs OM	—	20.00	50.00	100	—	—
1838/7Zs OM	—	15.00	30.00	75.00	—	—
1839Zs OM	—	250	375	500	—	—
1840Zs OM	—	500	1,300	—	—	—
1841Zs OM	—	15.00	30.00	75.00	—	—
1842Zs OM	—	15.00	40.00	85.00	—	—
1842Zs OM Small letters	—	15.00	30.00	75.00	—	—
1842Zs OM Large letters						
1843Zs OM	—	15.00	30.00	75.00	—	—
1844Zs OM	—	20.00	50.00	100	—	—
1845Zs OM	—	20.00	50.00	100	—	—
1846/5Zs OM	—	25.00	60.00	125	—	—
1846Zs OM	—	20.00	50.00	100	—	—
1847Zs OM	—	15.00	30.00	75.00	—	—
1848/6Zs OM	—	50.00	75.00	125	—	—
1848Zs OM	—	20.00	50.00	100	—	—
1849Zs OM	—	20.00	50.00	100	—	—
1850Zs OM	—	20.00	50.00	100	—	—
1851Zs OM	—	15.00	30.00	75.00	—	—
1852Zs OM	—	15.00	30.00	75.00	—	—
1853Zs OM	—	20.00	50.00	100	—	—
1854/3Zs OM	—	30.00	75.00	150	—	—
1855/4Zs OM	—	20.00	50.00	100	—	—
1855Zs OM	—	15.00	30.00	75.00	—	—
1856Zs OM	—	15.00	30.00	75.00	—	—

Date	Mintage	F	VF	XF	Unc	BU
1856Zs MO	—	20.00	50.00	100	—	—
1857/5Zs MO	—	20.00	50.00	100	—	—
1857Zs O/M	—	20.00	50.00	100	—	—
1857Zs MO	—	15.00	30.00	75.00	—	—
1858Zs MO	—	20.00	50.00	100	—	—
1859Zs MO	—	15.00	30.00	75.00	—	—
1860/59Zs MO	—	20.00	50.00	100	—	—
1860Zs MO	—	15.00	30.00	75.00	—	—
1860Zs VL	—	20.00	50.00	100	—	—
1861/0Zs VL	—	20.00	50.00	100	—	—
1861Zs VL	—	15.00	30.00	75.00	—	—
1861Zs VL 6/5	—	20.00	50.00	100	—	—
1862/1Zs VL	—	20.00	50.00	100	—	—
1862Zs VL	—	20.00	50.00	100	—	—
1863Zs VL	—	20.00	50.00	100	—	—
1863Zs MO	—	20.00	50.00	100	—	—
1864Zs VL	—	15.00	30.00	75.00	—	—
1868Zs JS	—	20.00	50.00	100	—	—
1868Zs YH	—	15.00	30.00	75.00	—	—
1869Zs YH	—	15.00	30.00	75.00	—	—
1870Zs YH	—	15.00	30.00	75.00	—	—

Date	Mintage	F	VF	XF	Unc	BU
Note: Small eagle						
1855/4Go PF	—	15.00	30.00	75.00	—	—
1855Go PF	—	12.50	25.00	60.00	—	—
1856Go PF	—	12.50	25.00	60.00	—	—
1857Go PF	—	20.00	50.00	100	—	—
1858Go PF	—	20.00	50.00	100	—	—
1859Go PF	—	20.00	50.00	100	—	—
1860/59Go PF	—	15.00	30.00	75.00	—	—
1860Go PF	—	15.00	30.00	75.00	—	—
1861/51Go PF	—	15.00	30.00	75.00	—	—
1861Go PF	—	20.00	50.00	100	—	—
1862/1Go YE	—	15.00	30.00	75.00	—	—
1862/1Go YF	—	15.00	30.00	75.00	—	—
1862Go YE/PF	—	15.00	30.00	75.00	—	—
1862Go YE	—	15.00	30.00	75.00	—	—
1862Go YF	—	15.00	30.00	75.00	—	—
1863/53Go YF	—	15.00	30.00	75.00	—	—
1863Go YF/PF	—	15.00	30.00	75.00	—	—
186/53Go YF	—	15.00	30.00	75.00	—	—
1863Go YF	—	15.00	30.00	75.00	—	—
1867/57Go YF/PF	—	15.00	30.00	75.00	—	—
1868/58Go YF/PF	—	15.00	30.00	75.00	—	—
1870Go FR	—	15.00	30.00	75.00	—	—

KM# 375.4 4 REALES
13.5400 g., 0.9030 Silver 0.3931 oz. ASW **Obv:**
Facing eagle, snake in beak **Obv. Legend:**
REPUBLICA MEXICANA **Rev:** Radiant cap **Note:**
Varieties exist. Some 1862 dates appear to be 1869
because of weak dies.

Date	Mintage	F	VF	XF	Unc	BU
1835Go PJ	—	12.50	25.00	60.00	—	—
1836/5Go PJ	—	15.00	30.00	75.00	—	—
1836Go PJ	—	15.00	30.00	75.00	—	—
1837Go PJ	—	12.50	25.00	60.00	—	—
1838/7Go PJ	—	15.00	30.00	75.00	—	—
1838Go PJ	—	12.50	30.00	75.00	—	—
1839Go PJ	—	12.50	25.00	60.00	—	—
1840/30Go PJ	—	20.00	50.00	100	—	—
1840 PJ	—	20.00	50.00	100	—	—
1841/30 PJ	—	200	325	600	—	—
1841/31Go PJ	—	150	250	450	—	—
1842Go PJ Rare	—	—	—	—	—	—
1842Go PM	—	15.00	30.00	75.00	—	—
1843/2Go PM	—	12.50	25.00	60.00	—	—
Note: Eagle with convex wings, thick rays						
1843Go PM	—	12.50	25.00	60.00	—	—
Note: Eagle with concave wings, thin rays						
1844/3Go PM	—	15.00	30.00	75.00	—	—
1844Go PM	—	20.00	50.00	100	—	—
1845/4Go PM	—	20.00	50.00	100	—	—
1845Go PM	—	20.00	50.00	100	—	—
1846/5Go PM	—	15.00	30.00	75.00	—	—
1846Go PM	—	15.00	30.00	75.00	—	—
1847/6Go PM	—	15.00	30.00	75.00	—	—
1847Go PM	—	15.00	30.00	75.00	—	—
1848/7Go PM	—	20.00	50.00	100	—	—
1848Go PM	—	20.00	50.00	100	—	—
1849Go PF	—	20.00	50.00	100	—	—
1850Go PF	—	12.50	25.00	60.00	—	—
1851Go PF	—	12.50	25.00	60.00	—	—
1852Go PF	—	15.00	30.00	75.00	—	—
1852Go PF 5/4	—	20.00	50.00	100	—	—
1853Go PF	—	15.00	30.00	75.00	—	—
1854Go PF	—	15.00	30.00	75.00	—	—
Note: Large eagle						
1854Go PF	—	15.00	30.00	75.00	—	—

KM# 375 4 REALES
13.5400 g., 0.9030 Silver 0.3931 oz. ASW **Obv:**
Facing eagle, snake in beak **Obv. Legend:**
REPUBLICA MEXICANA. **Rev:** Radiant cap

Date	Mintage	F	VF	XF	Unc	BU
1863Ce ML Large C	—	200	500	850	—	—
1863Ce ML Small C	—	225	650	1,500	—	—

KM# 375.7 4 REALES
13.5400 g., 0.9030 Silver 0.3931 oz. ASW **Obv:**
Facing eagle, snake in beak **Obv. Legend:**
REPUBLICA MEXICANA **Rev:** Radiant cap

Date	Mintage	F	VF	XF	Unc	BU
1861O FR	—	225	450	750	—	—
Note: Ornamental edge						
1861O FR	—	300	550	850	—	—
Note: Herringbone edge						
1861O FR	—	200	400	700	—	—
Note: Obliquely reeded edge						

KM# 377.5   8 REALES
27.0700 g., 0.9030 Silver 0.7859 oz. ASW **Obv:**
Facing eagle, snake in beak **Rev:** Radiant cap

Date	Mintage	F	VF	XF	Unc	BU
1828EoMo LF/LP	—	350	850	2,150	—	—
1828EoMo LF	—	350	850	2,150	6,000	—
1829EoMo LF	—	300	750	1,850	4,800	—
1830/20EoMo LF	—	1,250	2,750	4,250	—	—
1830EoMo LF	—	1,000	2,000	3,250	6,500	—

KM# 377.7   8 REALES
27.0700 g., 0.9030 Silver 0.7859 oz. ASW **Obv:**
Facing eagle, snake in beak **Obv. Legend:**
REPUBLICA MEXICANA. **Rev:** Radiant cap

Date	Mintage	F	VF	XF	Unc	BU
1844GC MP	—	350	500	1,000	2,000	—
1844GC MP	—	400	600	1,200	2,250	—
Note: Error, reversed S in Ds, Gs						
1845GC MP	—	125	200	325	700	—
Note: Eagle's tail square						
1845GC MP	—	175	350	650	1,200	—
Note: Eagle's tail round						
1846GC MP	—	175	350	750	1,650	—
Note: Eagle's tail square						
1846GC MP	—	125	200	350	750	—
Note: Eagle's tail round						
1847GC MP	—	150	250	400	800	—
1848GC MP	—	175	300	500	900	—
1849GC MP	—	175	300	525	1,000	—
1850GC MP	—	175	300	575	1,100	—
1851GC MP	—	300	500	900	1,600	—
1852GC MP	—	350	600	1,250	2,500	—

KM# 377   8 REALES
27.0700 g., 0.9030 Silver 0.7859 oz. ASW **Obv:**
Facing eagle, snake in beak **Obv. Legend:**
REPUBLICA MEXICANA. **Rev:** Radiant cap **Note:**
Mint mark A, As. Varieties exist.

Date	Mintage	F	VF	XF	Unc	BU
1864 PG	—	750	1,250	2,000	—	—
1865/4 PG Rare	—	—	—	—	—	—
1865 PG	—	500	750	1,000	—	—
1866/5 PG Rare	—	—	—	—	—	—
1866 PG	—	1,250	2,250	—	—	—
1866 DL Rare	—	—	—	—	—	—
1867 DL	—	1,150	2,150	—	—	—
1868 DL	—	50.00	90.00	150	300	—
1869/8 DL	—	50.00	90.00	150	—	—
1869 DL	—	50.00	80.00	120	300	—
1870 DL	—	30.00	60.00	120	300	—
1871 DL	—	20.00	35.00	75.00	200	—
1872 AM/DL	—	25.00	50.00	100	300	—
1872 AM	—	25.00	50.00	100	250	—
1873 AM	509,000	15.00	25.00	50.00	150	—
1874/3As DL	—	25.00	50.00	100	250	—
1874 DL	—	15.00	25.00	50.00	150	—
1875A DL 7/7	—	40.00	80.00	120	300	—
1875A DL	—	15.00	25.00	50.00	150	—
1875As DL	—	30.00	60.00	110	250	—
1876 DL	—	15.00	25.00	50.00	150	—
1877 DL	515,000	15.00	25.00	50.00	150	—
1878 DL	513,000	15.00	25.00	50.00	150	—
1879 DL	—	20.00	35.00	75.00	175	—
1879 ML	—	30.00	60.00	—	125	350
1880 ML	—	12.00	15.00	30.00	140	—
1881 ML	966,000	12.00	15.00	30.00	140	—
1882 ML	480,000	12.00	15.00	30.00	140	—
1883 ML	464,000	12.00	15.00	30.00	140	—
1884 ML	—	12.00	15.00	30.00	140	—
1885 ML	280,000	12.00	15.00	30.00	140	—
1886 ML	857,000	12.00	15.00	25.00	115	—
1886/0As/Cn ML/JD	Inc. above	15.00	20.00	35.00	160	—
1887 ML	650,000	12.00	15.00	25.00	115	—
1888/7 ML	508,000	30.00	60.00	100	400	—
1888 ML	Inc. above	12.00	15.00	25.00	115	—
1889 ML	427,000	12.00	15.00	25.00	115	—
1890 ML	450,000	12.00	15.00	25.00	115	—
1891 ML	533,000	12.00	15.00	25.00	115	—
1892/0 ML	—	20.00	30.00	60.00	160	—
1892 ML	465,000	12.00	15.00	25.00	115	—
1893 ML	734,000	10.00	12.00	22.00	95.00	—
1894 ML	725,000	10.00	12.00	22.00	95.00	—
1895 ML	477,000	10.00	12.00	22.00	95.00	—

KM# 377.3 8 REALES
27.0700 g., 0.9030 Silver 0.7859 oz. ASW **Obv:**
Facing eagle, snake in beak **Obv. Legend:**
REPUBLICA MEXICANA **Rev:** Radiant cap **Note:**
Mint mark C, Cn. Varieties exist.

Date	Mintage	F	VF	XF	Unc	BU
1846 CE	—	150	300	800	1,500	—
1846 CE	—	175	385	900	1,650	—
Note: Dot after G						
1846 CE	—	125	265	750	1,450	—
Note: No dot after G						
1847 CE	—	400	700	1,500	—	—
1848 CE	—	125	250	450	1,000	—
1849 CE C/G	—	75.00	125	200	400	—
1849 CE	—	75.00	125	200	400	—
1850 CE	—	75.00	125	200	400	—
1851 CE	—	125	250	450	1,000	—
1852/1 CE	—	100	150	250	500	—
1852 CE	—	100	200	300	600	—
1853/0 CE	—	200	350	700	1,300	—
1853/2/0	—	200	400	750	1,400	—
1853 CE	—	100	175	300	600	—
Note: Thick rays						
1853 CE	—	200	350	650	—	—
Note: Error: MEXIGANA						
1854 CE	—	750	1,250	—	—	—
1854 CE	—	175	350	750	1,200	—
Note: Large eagle and hat						
1855/6 CE	—	40.00	60.00	100	200	—
1855 CE	—	25.00	40.00	75.00	150	—
1856 CE	—	50.00	100	175	350	—
1857 CE	—	20.00	35.00	75.00	160	—
1858 CE	—	30.00	40.00	75.00	160	—
1859 CE	—	20.00	35.00	75.00	160	—
1860/9 PV/CV	—	50.00	70.00	100	200	—
1860/9 PV/E	—	50.00	70.00	100	200	—
1860 CE	—	25.00	40.00	75.00	160	—
1860/9 PV	—	40.00	60.00	90.00	175	—
1860 PV	—	40.00	60.00	90.00	175	—
1861/0 CE	—	50.00	80.00	120	250	—
1861 PV/CE	—	75.00	125	200	350	—
1861 CE	—	20.00	35.00	60.00	150	—
1862 CE	—	20.00	35.00	60.00	150	—
1863/2 CE	—	30.00	50.00	75.00	200	—
1863 CE	—	20.00	30.00	60.00	150	—
1864 CE	—	30.00	60.00	100	300	—
1865 CE	—	125	200	325	650	—
1866 CE	—	400	750	1,250	2,250	—
1867 CE	—	125	200	350	700	—
1868/7 CE	—	30.00	40.00	75.00	160	—
1868/8	—	50.00	100	150	300	—
1868 CE	—	30.00	40.00	75.00	160	—
1869 CE	—	30.00	40.00	75.00	175	—
1870 CE	—	50.00	100	150	350	—
1873 MP	—	50.00	100	150	300	—

Date	Mintage	F	VF	XF	Unc	BU
1874/3 MP	—	30.00	40.00	75.00	160	—
1874C MP	—	20.00	30.00	45.00	125	—
1874CN MP	—	125	200	300	600	—
1875 MP	—	12.00	15.00	22.00	95.00	—
1876 GP	—	12.00	15.00	30.00	100	—
1876 CG	—	12.00	15.00	22.00	95.00	—
1877 CG	339,000	12.00	15.00	22.00	95.00	—
1877Gn CG Error	—	65.00	125	200	400	—
1877 JA	Inc. above	35.00	75.00	125	250	—
1878/7 CG	483,000	35.00	75.00	125	250	—
1878 CG	Inc. above	15.00	25.00	35.00	125	—
1878 JD/CG	—	25.00	35.00	50.00	150	—
1878 JD	Inc. above	15.00	20.00	30.00	125	—
1878 JD	Inc. above	20.00	30.00	40.00	150	—
Note: D over retrograde D						
1879 JD	—	12.00	15.00	30.00	135	—
1880/70 JD	—	15.00	20.00	30.00	100	—
1880 JD	—	12.00	15.00	22.00	120	—
1881/0 JD	1,032,000	15.00	20.00	30.00	100	—
1881C JD	Inc. above	12.00	15.00	22.00	95.00	—
1881Cn JD	Inc. above	40.00	60.00	90.00	150	—
1882 JD	397,000	12.00	15.00	22.00	95.00	—
1882 AM	Inc. above	12.00	15.00	22.00	95.00	—
1883 AM	333,000	12.00	15.00	22.00	125	—
1884 AM	—	12.00	15.00	22.00	95.00	—
1885/6 AM	227,000	20.00	30.00	45.00	125	—
1885C AM	Inc. above	35.00	70.00	150	350	—
1885Cn AM	Inc. above	12.00	15.00	22.00	95.00	—
1885Gn AM Error	Inc. above	25.00	50.00	100	275	—
1886 AM	571,000	12.00	15.00	22.00	95.00	—
1887 AM	732,000	12.00	15.00	22.00	95.00	—
1888 AM	768,000	12.00	15.00	22.00	95.00	—
1889 AM	1,075,000	12.00	15.00	22.00	95.00	500
1890 AM	074,000	10.00	12.00	20.00	90.00	—
1891 AM	777,000	10.00	12.00	20.00	90.00	—
1892 AM	681,000	10.00	12.00	20.00	90.00	—
1893 AM	1,144,000	10.00	12.00	20.00	90.00	—
1894 AM	2,118,000	10.00	12.00	20.00	90.00	—
1895 AM	1,834,000	10.00	12.00	20.00	90.00	—
1896 AM	2,134,000	10.00	12.00	20.00	90.00	—
1897 AM	1,580,000	10.00	12.00	20.00	90.00	—

KM# 377.11 8 REALES
27.0700 g., 0.9030 Silver 0.7859 oz. ASW **Obv:**
Facing eagle, snake in beak **Rev:** Radiant cap **Note:**
Mint mark O, Oa. Varieties exist.

Date	Mintage	F	VF	XF	Unc	BU
1858O AE	—	2,500	4,000	—	—	—
1858Oa AE Unique	—	—	—	—	—	—
1859 AE	—	500	900	1,750	—	—
Note: A in O of mint mark						
1860 AE	—	200	450	800	—	—
Note: A in O of mint mark						
1861O FR	—	125	250	550	1,350	—

Date	Mintage	F	VF	XF	Unc	BU
1861Oa FR	—	150	350	700	—	—
1862O FR	—	40.00	80.00	200	375	—
1862Oa FR	—	65.00	125	250	450	—
1863O FR	—	30.00	60.00	100	250	—
1863O AE	—	30.00	60.00	100	250	—
1863Oa AE	—	100	150	250	450	—
Note: A in O of mint mark						
1863Oa AE	—	1,000	1,750	2,750	—	—
Note: A above O in mint mark						
1864 FR	—	25.00	50.00	75.00	200	—
1865 AE	—	1,850	3,000	—	—	—
1867 AE	—	40.00	80.00	150	400	—
1868 AE	—	40.00	80.00	150	400	—
1869 AE	—	30.00	60.00	100	250	—
1873 AE	—	200	300	550	1,350	—
1874 AE	142,000	15.00	30.00	50.00	200	—
1875/4 AE	131,000	25.00	50.00	75.00	200	—
1875 AE	Inc. above	15.00	30.00	40.00	135	—
1876 AE	140,000	20.00	35.00	55.00	200	—
1877 AE	139,000	20.00	30.00	50.00	200	—
1878 AE	125,000	20.00	30.00	50.00	200	—
1879 AE	153,000	20.00	30.00	50.00	200	—
1880 AE	143,000	15.00	30.00	45.00	150	—
1881 AE	134,000	20.00	35.00	60.00	150	—
1882 AE	100,000	20.00	35.00	60.00	150	—
1883 AE	122,000	15.00	30.00	45.00	150	—
1884 AE	142,000	15.00	30.00	50.00	150	—
1885 AE	158,000	15.00	25.00	40.00	135	—
1886 AE	120,000	15.00	30.00	45.00	150	—
1887/6 AE	115,000	25.00	50.00	80.00	200	—
1887 AE	Inc. above	15.00	25.00	40.00	135	—
1888 AE	145,000	15.00	25.00	40.00	135	—
1889 AE	150,000	20.00	30.00	60.00	175	—
1890 AE	181,000	20.00	30.00	60.00	175	—
1891 EN	160,000	15.00	25.00	40.00	135	—
1892 EN	120,000	15.00	25.00	40.00	135	—
1893 EN	66,000	45.00	75.00	115	300	—

Date	Mintage	F	VF	XF	Unc
1831Do RM	—	20.00	30.00	60.00	150
Note: B on eagle's claw					
1832Do RM	—	35.00	60.00	120	300
Note: Mexican dies, B on eagle's claw					
1832/1Do RM/RL	—	25.00	35.00	75.00	165
Note: French dies, REPUB MEX spaced					
1833/2Do RM/RL	—	20.00	35.00	75.00	165
1833Do RM	—	15.00	30.00	60.00	150
1834/3/2Do RM/RL	—	20.00	35.00	75.00	165
1834Do RM	—	15.00	25.00	50.00	150
1835/4Do RM/RL	—	20.00	35.00	65.00	150
1835Do RM	—	20.00	35.00	65.00	150
Note: Mexican dies, REPUBMEX not spaced					
1836/1Do RM	—	20.00	35.00	65.00	150
1836/4Do RM	—	20.00	35.00	65.00	150
1836/5/4Do RM/RL	—	75.00	150	250	500
1836Do RM	—	20.00	30.00	55.00	150
1836Do RM	—	20.00	30.00	55.00	150
Note: M on snake					
1837/1Do RM	—	20.00	30.00	55.00	150
1837Do RM	—	20.00	30.00	55.00	150
1838/1Do RM	—	20.00	30.00	60.00	165
1838/7Do RM	—	20.00	30.00	60.00	165
1838Do RM	—	20.00	30.00	55.00	150
1839/1Do RM/RL	—	20.00	30.00	55.00	150
1839/1Do RM	—	20.00	30.00	55.00	150
1839Do RM	—	20.00	30.00	55.00	150
1840/38/31Do RM	—	20.00	30.00	55.00	150
1840/39Do RM	—	20.00	30.00	55.00	150
1840Do RM	—	20.00	30.00	55.00	150
1841/31Do RM	—	65.00	125	275	450
1841/39Do RM/L	—	25.00	50.00	85.00	200
1841/39Do RM	—	25.00	50.00	85.00	200
1842/31Do RM	—	125	250	400	750
Note: B below cactus					
1842/31Do RM	—	40.00	80.00	125	250
1842/32Do RM	—	40.00	80.00	125	250
1842Do RM	—	20.00	30.00	55.00	150
Note: Eagle of 1832-41					
1842Do RM	—	20.00	30.00	55.00	150
Note: Pre-1832 eagle resumed					
1842Do RM	—	40.00	80.00	125	250
1843/33Do RM	—	50.00	90.00	150	250
1843Do RM	—	50.00	90.00	150	250
1844/34Do RM	—	100	200	300	500
1844/35Do RM	—	100	200	300	500
1844/43Do RM	—	60.00	120	220	425
1845/31Do RM	—	100	200	300	500
1845/34Do RM	—	35.00	75.00	125	250
1845/35Do RM	—	35.00	75.00	125	250
1845Do RM	—	20.00	30.00	55.00	150
1846/31Do RM	—	20.00	30.00	55.00	150
1846/36Do RM	—	20.00	30.00	55.00	150
1846Do RM	—	20.00	30.00	55.00	150
1847Do RM	—	25.00	50.00	80.00	185
1848/7Do RM	—	125	250	400	750
1848/7Do CM/RM	—	100	200	350	700
1848Do CM/RM	—	100	200	350	700
1848Do RM	—	100	200	300	600
1848Du CM	—	50.00	100	200	400
1849/39Do CM	—	100	200	350	700
1849Do CM	—	65.00	125	250	550
1849Do JMR/CM Oval 0	—	200	400	450	800
1849Do JMR Oval 0	—	200	325	450	800
1849Do JMR Round 0	—	200	400	600	1,000
1850Do JMR	—	100	150	250	500
1851/0Do JMR	—	65.00	125	225	475
1851Do JMR	—	100	150	250	500
1852Do CP/JMR	—	450	800	1,500	—
1852Do CP	—	750	1,200	2,250	—
1852Do JMR	—	175	250	375	650
1853Do CP/JMR	—	125	235	350	600
1853Do CP	—	200	350	600	1,200
1854Do CP	—	25.00	35.00	65.00	300
1855Do CP	—	50.00	100	175	350
Note: Eagle type of 1854					
1855Do CP	—	50.00	100	175	350
Note: Eagle type of 1856					
1856Do CP	—	50.00	100	175	350

KM# 377.4   8 REALES
27.0700 g., 0.9030 Silver 0.7859 oz. ASW **Obv:**
Facing eagle, snake in beak **Note:** Varieties exist.

Date	Mintage	F	VF	XF	Unc
1825Do RL	—	30.00	65.00	150	375
1826Do RL	—	40.00	85.00	200	475
1827/6Do RL	—	35.00	60.00	85.00	200
1827/8Do RL	—	150	275	500	—
1827Do RL	—	30.00	50.00	90.00	200
1828/7Do RL	—	35.00	60.00	90.00	200
1828Do RL	—	25.00	50.00	80.00	175
1829Do RL	—	25.00	50.00	80.00	175
1830Do RM	—	25.00	50.00	90.00	200
Note: B on eagle's claw					

Date	Mintage	F	VF	XF	Unc
1857Do CP	—	35.00	65.00	125	250
1858/7Do CP	—	25.00	35.00	70.00	165
1858Do CP	—	20.00	30.00	60.00	165
1859Do CP	—	20.00	30.00	60.00	165
1860/59Do CP	—	30.00	50.00	100	200
1860Do CP	—	20.00	30.00	60.00	165
1861/0Do CP	—	20.00	30.00	60.00	165
1861Do CP	—	20.00	30.00	50.00	125
1862/1Do CP	—	25.00	35.00	60.00	125
1862Do CP	—	20.00	30.00	60.00	175
1863/1Do CP	—	30.00	60.00	90.00	200
1863/2Do CP	—	25.00	50.00	75.00	175
1863/53Do CP	—	30.00	60.00	90.00	200
1863Do CP	—	25.00	50.00	75.00	175
1864Do CP	—	100	150	250	500
1864Do LT	—	25.00	40.00	80.00	175
1864Do LT/T	—	25.00	40.00	80.00	175
1864Do LT/CP	—	50.00	100	175	350
1865Do LT Rare	—	—	—	—	—
1866/4Do CM	—	2,750	5,500	—	—
1866Do CM	—	1,750	3,250	5,500	8,500
1867Do CM	—	3,500	—	—	—
1867/6Do CP	—	200	400	600	1,200
1867Do CP	—	175	300	500	1,000
1867Do CP/CM	—	125	250	400	900
1867Do CP/LT	—	200	400	650	1,250
1868Do CP	—	25.00	40.00	80.00	175
1869Do CP	—	20.00	30.00	50.00	135
1870/69Do CP	—	20.00	30.00	50.00	125
1870/9Do CP	—	20.00	30.00	50.00	125
1870Do CP	—	20.00	30.00	50.00	125
1873Do CP	—	125	225	325	600
1873Do CM	—	30.00	50.00	100	200
1874/3Do CM	—	12.00	15.00	22.00	125
1874Do CM	—	10.00	15.00	22.00	125
1874Do JH	—	1,150	1,750	2,750	—
1875Do CM	—	10.00	15.00	22.00	125
1875Do JH	—	80.00	150	250	450
1876Do CM	—	10.00	15.00	22.00	125
1877Do CM	431,000	1,450	2,500	—	—
1877Do CP	Inc. above	10.00	15.00	22.00	125
1877Do JMP	Inc. above	750	1,250	2,000	—
1878Do PE	409,000	15.00	25.00	40.00	125
1878Do TB	Inc. above	10.00	15.00	25.00	125
1879Do TB	—	10.00	15.00	22.00	125
1880/70Do TB	—	60.00	100	175	350
1880/70Do TB/JP	—	150	250	375	650
1880/70Do JP	—	15.00	25.00	40.00	125
1880Do TB	—	150	250	375	650
1880Do JP	—	10.00	15.00	22.00	125
1881Do JP	928,000	10.00	15.00	25.00	125
1882Do JP	414,000	10.00	15.00	22.00	125
1882Do MC/JP	Inc. above	30.00	60.00	100	200
1882Do MC	Inc. above	25.00	50.00	75.00	150
1883/73Do MC	452,000	15.00	25.00	40.00	125
1883Do MC	Inc. above	10.00	15.00	22.00	125
1884/3Do MC	—	15.00	25.00	40.00	125
1884Do MC	—	10.00	15.00	22.00	125
1885Do MC M/J	—	15.00	25.00	40.00	125
1885Do JB	Inc. above	25.00	35.00	50.00	135
1885Do MC	547,000	10.00	12.00	20.00	125
1886/5Do MC	—	15.00	25.00	40.00	100
1886/3Do MC	955,000	15.00	25.00	40.00	100
1886Do MC	Inc. above	10.00	12.00	20.00	90.00
1887Do MC	1,004,000	10.00	12.00	20.00	90.00
1888/7Do MC	—	65.00	125	250	450
1888Do MC	996,000	10.00	12.00	20.00	90.00
1889Do MC	874,000	10.00	12.00	20.00	90.00
1890Do MC	1,119,000	10.00	12.00	20.00	90.00
1890Do JP	Inc. above	10.00	12.00	20.00	90.00
1891Do JP	1,487,000	10.00	12.00	20.00	90.00
1892Do JP	1,597,000	10.00	12.00	20.00	90.00
1892Do ND	Inc. above	25.00	50.00	100	200
1893Do ND	1,617,000	10.00	12.00	20.00	90.00
1894Do ND	1,537,000	10.00	12.00	20.00	90.00
1895/3Do ND	761,000	15.00	25.00	40.00	100
1895Do ND	Inc. above	10.00	12.00	20.00	90.00
1895Do ND/P	—	15.00	25.00	40.00	100

KM# 377.6   8 REALES

27.0700 g., 0.9030 Silver 0.7859 oz. ASW **Obv:** Facing eagle, snake in beak **Obv. Legend:** REPUBLICA MEXICANA. **Rev:** Radiant cap **Note:** Varieties exist.

Date	Mintage	F	VF	XF	Unc	BU
1825Ga FS	—	150	275	475	1,000	—
1826/5Ga FS	—	125	250	450	1,000	—
1826Ga FS	—	125	250	450	1,000	—
1827/87Ga FS	—	125	250	450	1,000	—
1827Ga FS	—	125	250	450	1,000	—
1287Ga FS Error	—	8,500	9,500	—	—	—
1828Ga FS	—	200	375	550	1,200	—
1829/8Ga FS	—	200	375	550	1,200	—
1829Ga FS	—	175	325	475	950	—
1830/29Ga FS	—	100	175	300	600	—
1830Ga FS	—	100	175	300	600	—
1830Ga LP/FS	—	800	1,450	—	—	—

Note: The 1830 LP/FS is currently only known with a Philippine countermark

Date	Mintage	F	VF	XF	Unc	BU
1831Ga LP	—	200	400	600	1,200	—
1831Ga FS/LP	—	300	500	750	1,500	—
1831Ga FS	—	125	275	400	—	—
1832/1Ga FS	—	50.00	100	175	300	—
1832/1Ga FS/LP	—	50.00	100	175	300	—
1832Ga FS/LP	—	75.00	150	285	550	—
1832Ga FS	—	25.00	50.00	100	225	—
1833/2/1Ga FS/LP	—	45.00	75.00	125	250	—
1833/2Ga FS	—	25.00	50.00	100	225	—
1834/2Ga FS	—	60.00	125	200	350	—
1834/3Ga FS	—	60.00	125	200	350	—
1834/0Ga FS	—	50.00	100	150	300	—
1834Ga FS	—	50.00	100	150	300	—
1835Ga FS	—	25.00	50.00	100	225	—
1836/5Ga FS	—	175	350	—	—	—
1836/1Ga JG/FS	—	40.00	80.00	125	250	—
1836Ga FS	—	275	450	750	—	—
1836Ga JG/FS	—	25.00	50.00	100	225	—
1836Ga JG	—	25.00	50.00	100	225	—
1837/6Ga JG/FS	—	50.00	100	175	300	—
1837/6Ga JG	—	45.00	90.00	160	285	—
1837Ga JG	—	40.00	80.00	125	250	—
1838/7Ga JG	—	100	175	300	550	—
1838Ga JG	—	100	150	275	500	—
1839Ga MC	—	100	200	350	600	—
1839Ga MC/JG	—	100	200	300	550	—
1839Ga JG	—	60.00	125	200	350	—
1840/30Ga MC	—	50.00	75.00	150	275	—
1840Ga MC	—	30.00	60.00	125	250	—
1841Ga MC	—	30.00	60.00	125	250	—
1842/1Ga JG/MG	—	100	150	250	450	—
1842/1Ga JG/MC	—	100	150	250	450	—

Date	Mintage	F	VF	XF	Unc	BU
1842Ga JG	—	25.00	50.00	100	225	—
1842Ga JG/MG	—	25.00	50.00	100	225	—
1843/2Ga MC/JG	—	25.00	50.00	100	225	—
1843Ga MC/JG	—	25.00	50.00	100	225	—
1843Ga JG	—	400	600	900	1,800	—
1843Ga MC	—	50.00	100	150	300	—
1844Ga MC	—	50.00	100	150	300	—
1845Ga MC	—	75.00	150	300	700	—
1845Ga JG	—	500	850	1,250	1,850	—
1846Ga JG	—	40.00	80.00	150	300	—
1847Ga JG	—	100	150	225	400	—
1848/7Ga JG	—	55.00	85.00	125	250	—
1848Ga JG	—	50.00	75.00	100	225	—
1849Ga JG	—	90.00	125	175	325	—
1849/39Ga JG	—	250	500	—	—	—
1850Ga JG	—	50.00	100	150	300	—
1851Ga JG	—	125	200	350	650	—
1852Ga JG	—	100	150	250	450	—
1853/2Ga JG	—	125	175	250	475	—
1853Ga JG	—	90.00	125	175	300	—
1854/3Ga JG	—	65.00	90.00	125	250	—
1854Ga JG	—	50.00	75.00	110	225	—
1855/4Ga JG	—	50.00	100	150	275	—
1855Ga JG	—	25.00	50.00	100	225	—
1856/4Ga JG	—	60.00	125	175	300	—
1856/5Ga 56	—	60.00	125	175	300	—
1856Ga JG	—	50.00	100	150	275	—
1857Ga JG	—	50.00	100	225	450	—
1858Ga JG	—	100	150	300	500	—
1859/7Ga JG	—	25.00	50.00	110	225	—
1859/8Ga JG	—	25.00	50.00	100	200	—
1859Ga JG	—	20.00	40.00	80.00	175	—
1860Ga JG	—	350	750	1,200	2,250	—
1860Ga JG Without dot						

Note: Dot in loop of snake's tail, base alloy

Date	Mintage	F	VF	XF	Unc	BU
1861Ga JG	—	2,000	3,250	4,500	—	—
1862Ga JG	—	2,200	5,750	—	—	—
1863/52Ga JG	—	850	1,350	2,750	4,500	—
1863/59Ga JG	—	—	—	—	—	—
1863/2Ga JG	—	45.00	50.00	85.00	145	—
1863/4Ga JG	—	30.00	50.00	90.00	175	—
1863Ga JG	—	40.00	75.00	150	250	—
1863Ga FV Rare	—	25.00	45.00	75.00	150	—
1867Ga JM Rare	—	—	—	—	—	—
1868/7Ga JM	—	—	—	—	—	—
1868Ga JM	—	50.00	75.00	125	200	—
1869Ga JM	—	50.00	75.00	125	200	—
1869Ga IC	—	50.00	75.00	125	200	—
1870/60Ga IC	—	75.00	125	200	375	—
1870Ga IC	—	60.00	90.00	150	275	—
1873Ga IC	—	60.00	90.00	150	275	—
1874Ga IC	—	15.00	25.00	50.00	135	—
1874Ga MC	—	10.00	15.00	22.00	90.00	—
1875Ga IC	—	25.00	50.00	100	200	—
1875Ga MC	—	15.00	30.00	60.00	135	—
1876Ga IC	559,000	10.00	15.00	22.00	125	—
1876Ga MC	Inc. above	15.00	30.00	50.00	125	—
1877Ga IC	928,000	125	175	250	375	—
1877/6Ga JA	—	10.00	15.00	22.00	125	—
1877Ga JA	Inc. above	10.00	15.00	22.00	125	—
1878Ga JA	764,000	10.00	15.00	22.00	125	—
1879Ga JA	—	10.00	15.00	22.00	125	—
1880/70Ga FS	—	15.00	25.00	50.00	135	—
1880Ga JA	—	10.00	15.00	22.00	125	—
1880Ga FS	—	10.00	15.00	22.00	125	—
1881Ga FS	1,300,000	10.00	15.00	22.00	125	—
1882/1Ga FS	537,000	15.00	25.00	50.00	135	—
1882Ga FS	Inc. above	10.00	15.00	22.00	125	—
1882Ga TB/FS	Inc. above	50.00	100	175	300	—
1882Ga TB	Inc. above	50.00	100	175	300	—
1883Ga TB	561,000	15.00	25.00	40.00	135	—
1884Ga TB	—	10.00	12.00	20.00	125	—
1884Ga AH	—	10.00	12.00	20.00	125	—
1885Ga AH	443,000	10.00	12.00	20.00	125	—
1885Ga JS	Inc. above	30.00	60.00	100	200	—
1886Ga JS/H	—	10.00	12.00	20.00	125	—
1886Ga JS	1,038,999	10.00	12.00	20.00	125	—
1887Ga JS	878,000	10.00	12.00	20.00	125	—

Date	Mintage	F	VF	XF	Unc	BU
1888Ga JS	1,159,000	10.00	12.00	20.00	125	—
1889Ga JS	1,583,000	10.00	12.00	20.00	125	—
1890Ga JS	1,658,000	10.00	12.00	20.00	110	—
1891Ga JS	1,507,000	10.00	12.00	20.00	110	—
1892/1Ga JS	1,627,000	15.00	25.00	50.00	125	—
1892Ga JS	Inc. above	10.00	12.00	20.00	110	—
1893Ga JS	1,952,000	10.00	12.00	20.00	110	—
1894Ga JS	2,045,999	10.00	12.00	20.00	110	—
1895/3Ga JS	—	12.00	20.00	35.00	115	—
1895Ga JS	1,146,000	10.00	12.00	20.00	110	—

KM# 377.8   8 REALES

27.0700 g., 0.9030 Silver 0.7859 oz. ASW   **Obv:** Facing eagle, snake in beak **Obv. Legend:** REPUBLICA MEXICANA. **Rev:** Radiant cap **Note:** Varieties exist.

Date	Mintage	F	VF	XF	Unc	BU
1825Go JJ	—	40.00	70.00	150	300	—
1825G JJ	—	1,250	1,650	—	—	—
Note: Error mint mark G						
1826Go JJ	—	40.00	80.00	175	350	—
Note: Straight J's						
1826Go JJ	—	30.00	60.00	125	250	—
Note: Full J's						
1826Go MJ	—	250	450	850	—	—
1827Go MJ	—	40.00	75.00	125	250	—
1827Go MJ/JJ	—	—	—	—	—	—
1827Go MR	—	100	200	350	600	—
1828Go MJ	—	—	—	—	—	—
Note: Error mint mark Goo						
1828Go MJ	—	30.00	60.00	125	250	—
1828/7Go MR	—	150	300	600	1,200	—
1828Go MR	—	150	300	600	1,200	—
1829Go MJ	—	20.00	35.00	55.00	165	—
1830Go MJ	—	20.00	30.00	55.00	165	—
Note: Oblong beading and narrow J						
1830Go MJ	—	20.00	30.00	55.00	165	—
Note: Regular beading and wide J						
1831Go MJ	—	12.00	20.00	40.00	150	—
Note: Colon after date						
1831Go MJ	—	12.00	20.00	40.00	150	—
Note: 2 stars after date						
1832Go MJ	—	12.00	20.00	40.00	150	—
1832Go MJ	—	20.00	35.00	65.00	175	—
Note: 1 of date over inverted 1						
1833Go MJ/1	—	20.00	35.00	65.00	175	—
1833Go MJ	—	12.00	20.00	40.00	150	—
1833Go JM	—	400	750	1,250	2,500	—
1834Go PJ	—	12.00	20.00	40.00	150	—
1835Go PJ	—	12.00	20.00	40.00	150	—

Date	Mintage	F	VF	XF	Unc	BU
Note: Star on cap						
1835Go PJ	—	12.00	20.00	40.00	150	—
Note: Dot on cap						
1836Go PJ	—	12.00	20.00	40.00	150	—
1837Go PJ	—	12.00	20.00	40.00	150	—
1838Go PJ	—	12.00	20.00	40.00	150	—
1839Go PJ/JJ	—	12.00	20.00	40.00	150	—
1839Go PJ	—	12.00	20.00	40.00	150	—
1840/30Go PJ	—	20.00	30.00	50.00	150	—
1840Go PJ	—	12.00	20.00	35.00	125	—
1841/31Go PJ	—	12.00	20.00	35.00	125	—
1841Go PJ	—	12.00	20.00	35.00	125	—
1842/1Go PM	—	20.00	30.00	50.00	125	—
1842/31Go PM/PJ	—	25.00	35.00	60.00	150	—
1842/1Go PJ	—	20.00	30.00	50.00	125	—
1842Go PJ	—	20.00	30.00	50.00	125	—
1842Go PM/PJ	—	12.00	20.00	35.00	125	—
1842Go PM	—	12.00	20.00	35.00	125	—
1843Go PM	—	12.00	20.00	35.00	125	—
Note: Dot after date						
1843Go PM	—	12.00	20.00	35.00	125	—
Note: Triangle of dots after date						
1844Go PM	—	12.00	20.00	35.00	125	—
1845Go PM	—	12.00	20.00	35.00	125	—
1846/5Go PM	—	20.00	30.00	50.00	150	—
Note: Eagle type of 1845						
1846Go PM	—	20.00	30.00	50.00	150	—
Note: Eagle type of 1845						
1846Go PM	—	15.00	25.00	40.00	135	—
Note: Eagle type of 1847						
1847Go PM Narrow date	—	12.00	20.00	35.00	125	—
1847Go PM Wide date	—	12.00	20.00	35.00	125	—
1848/7Go PM	—	20.00	35.00	65.00	150	—
1848Go PM	—	20.00	35.00	65.00	150	—
1848Go PF	—	12.00	20.00	35.00	125	—
1849Go PF	—	12.00	20.00	35.00	125	—
1850Go PF	—	12.00	20.00	35.00	125	—
1851/0Go PF	—	20.00	30.00	50.00	150	—
1851Go PF	—	12.00	20.00	35.00	125	—
1852/1Go PF	—	20.00	30.00	50.00	150	—
1852Go PF	—	12.00	20.00	35.00	125	—
1853/2Go PF	—	20.00	30.00	50.00	150	—
1853Go PF	—	12.00	20.00	35.00	125	—
1854Go PF	—	12.00	20.00	35.00	125	—
1855Go PF Large letters	—	12.00	20.00	35.00	125	—
1855Go PF Small letters	—	12.00	20.00	35.00	125	—
1856/5Go PF	—	20.00	30.00	50.00	150	—
1856Go PF	—	12.00	20.00	35.00	125	—
1857/5Go PF	—	20.00	30.00	50.00	150	—
1857/6Go PF	—	20.00	35.00	70.00	200	—
1857Go PF	—	12.00	15.00	20.00	90.00	—
1858/7Go PI Narrow date	—	12.00	20.00	35.00	125	—
1858Go PF Wide date	—	12.00	20.00	35.00	125	—
1859/7Go PF	—	12.00	20.00	35.00	125	—
1859/8Go PF	—	20.00	30.00	50.00	150	—
1859Go PF	—	12.00	20.00	35.00	125	—
1860/50Go PF	—	20.00	30.00	50.00	150	—
1860/59Go PF	—	12.00	18.00	25.00	95.00	—
1860Go PF	—	12.00	15.00	20.00	90.00	—
1861/51Go PF	—	15.00	20.00	30.00	100	—
Note: Narrow and wide dates exist						
1861/0Go PF	—	12.00	15.00	20.00	90.00	—
1861Go PF	—	12.00	15.00	20.00	90.00	—
186/52Go YE	—	15.00	20.00	30.00	100	—
1862Go YE/PF	—	12.00	15.00	20.00	90.00	—
186/52Go YF	—	15.00	20.00	30.00	100	—
1862Go YE	—	12.00	15.00	20.00	90.00	—
1862Go YF	—	12.00	15.00	20.00	90.00	—
1862Go YF/PF	—	12.00	15.00	20.00	90.00	—
1863/53Go YF	—	12.00	18.00	25.00	90.00	—
1863/54Go YF	—	15.00	20.00	30.00	100	—
1863Go YE Rare	—	—	—	—	—	—
1863Go YF	—	12.00	15.00	20.00	90.00	—
1867/57Go YF	—	15.00	20.00	30.00	100	—
1867Go YF	—	12.00	15.00	20.00	90.00	—
1868/58Go YF	—	15.00	20.00	30.00	100	—
1868/7Go YF	—	15.00	20.00	30.00	100	—
1868Go YF	—	12.00	15.00	20.00	90.00	—
1870/60Go FR	—	20.00	30.00	50.00	150	—
1870Go YF	—	1,800	3,000	5,000	7,500	—
1870Go FR/YF	—	20.00	35.00	70.00	200	—
1870Go FR	—	12.00	15.00	20.00	90.00	—
1873Go FR	—	12.00	15.00	20.00	90.00	—
1874/3Go FR	—	15.00	20.00	30.00	95.00	—
1874Go FR	—	15.00	25.00	35.00	100	—
1875/3Go FR	—	15.00	20.00	30.00	95.00	—
1875/6Go FR	—	15.00	20.00	30.00	95.00	—
1875Go FR	—	12.00	15.00	20.00	90.00	—
Note: Small circle with dot on eagle						
1876/5Go FR	—	15.00	20.00	30.00	95.00	—
1876Go FR	—	12.00	15.00	20.00	90.00	—
1877Go FR Narrow date	—	12.00	15.00	20.00	90.00	—
1877Go FR Wide date	2,477,000	12.00	15.00	20.00	90.00	—
1878/7Go FR	2,273,000	15.00	20.00	30.00	90.00	—
1878/7Go SM, S/F	—	15.00	20.00	30.00	90.00	—
1878/7Go SM	—	15.00	20.00	30.00	90.00	—
1878Go FR	Inc. above	12.00	15.00	20.00	90.00	—
1878Go SM, S/F	—	15.00	20.00	25.00	90.00	—
1878Go SM	—	12.00	15.00	20.00	90.00	—
1879/7Go SM	—	15.00	20.00	30.00	90.00	—
1879/8Go SM	—	15.00	20.00	30.00	90.00	—
1879/8Go SM/FR	—	15.00	20.00	30.00	90.00	—
1879Go SM	—	12.00	15.00	20.00	90.00	—
1879Go SM/FR	—	15.00	20.00	30.00	90.00	—
1880/70Go SB	—	15.00	20.00	30.00	90.00	—
1880Go SB/SM	—	12.00	15.00	20.00	90.00	—
1880Go SB	—	12.00	15.00	20.00	90.00	—
1881/71Go SD	3,974,000	15.00	20.00	30.00	90.00	—
1881/0Go SB	Inc. above	15.00	20.00	30.00	90.00	—
1881Go SB	Inc. above	12.00	15.00	20.00	90.00	—
1882Go SB	2,015,000	12.00	15.00	20.00	90.00	—
1883Go SB	2,100,000	35.00	75.00	125	250	—
1883Go BR	Inc. above	12.00	15.00	20.00	90.00	—
1883Go BR/SR	—	12.00	15.00	20.00	90.00	—
1883Go BR/SB	Inc. above	12.00	15.00	20.00	90.00	—
1884/73Go BR	—	20.00	30.00	40.00	100	—
1884/74Go BR	—	20.00	30.00	40.00	100	—
1884/3Go BR	—	20.00	30.00	60.00	150	—
1884Go BR	—	12.00	15.00	20.00	90.00	—
1884/74Go RR	—	50.00	100	175	350	—
1884Go RR	—	25.00	50.00	100	250	—
1885/75Go RR/BR	—	15.00	20.00	300	90.00	—
1885/75Go RR	2,363,000	15.00	20.00	30.00	90.00	—
1885Go RR	Inc. above	12.00	15.00	20.00	90.00	—
1886/75Go RR/BR	—	15.00	20.00	25.00	90.00	—
1886/75Go RR	4,127,000	15.00	20.00	25.00	90.00	—
1886/76Go RR/BR	—	12.00	15.00	20.00	90.00	—
1886/76Go RR	Inc. above	12.00	15.00	20.00	90.00	—
1886/5Go RR/BR	Inc. above	12.00	15.00	20.00	90.00	—
1886Go RR	Inc. above	12.00	15.00	20.00	90.00	—
1887Go RR	4,205,000	10.00	15.00	20.00	90.00	—
1888Go RR	3,985,000	10.00	15.00	20.00	90.00	—
1889Go RR	3,646,000	10.00	15.00	20.00	90.00	—
1890Go RR	3,615,000	10.00	15.00	20.00	90.00	—
1891Go RS/R	—	10.00	15.00	20.00	90.00	—
1891Go RS	3,197,000	10.00	15.00	20.00	90.00	—
1892/0Go/A RS	—	10.00	15.00	20.00	90.00	—
1892/0Go RS	—	10.00	15.00	20.00	90.00	—
1892Go RS	3,672,000	10.00	15.00	20.00	90.00	—
1892Go/A RS	—	10.00	15.00	20.00	90.00	—
1893Go RS	3,854,000	10.00	15.00	20.00	90.00	—
1894Go RS	4,127,000	10.00	15.00	20.00	90.00	—
1895/1Go RS	3,768,000	15.00	20.00	25.00	90.00	—
1895/3Go RS	Inc. above	15.00	20.00	25.00	90.00	—
1895Go RS	Inc. above	10.00	15.00	20.00	90.00	—
1896/1Go/As RS/ML	5,229,000	15.00	20.00	25.00	90.00	—
1896/1Go RS	Inc. above	12.00	15.00	20.00	90.00	—
1896Go/Ga RS	Inc. above	—	—	—	—	—
1896Go RS	Inc. above	10.00	12.00	18.00	90.00	—
1897Go RS	4,344,000	10.00	12.00	18.00	90.00	—

Date	Mintage	F	VF	XF	Unc	BU
1886Ho FM	225,000	20.00	30.00	45.00	125	—
1886Ho FG	Inc. above	20.00	30.00	45.00	125	—
1887/6Ho FG	—	20.00	35.00	65.00	150	—
1887Ho FG	150,000	20.00	35.00	65.00	150	—
1888Ho FG	364,000	12.00	18.00	25.00	110	—
1889Ho FG	490,000	12.00	18.00	25.00	110	—
1890Ho FG	565,000	12.00	18.00	25.00	110	—
1891Ho FG	738,000	12.00	18.00	25.00	110	—
1892Ho FG	643,000	12.00	18.00	25.00	110	—
1893Ho FG	518,000	12.00	18.00	25.00	110	—
1894Ho FG	504,000	12.00	18.00	25.00	110	—
1895Ho FG	320,000	12.00	18.00	25.00	110	—

KM# 377.9   8 REALES
27.0700 g., 0.9030 Silver 0.7859 oz. ASW **Obv:** Facing eagle, snake in beak **Rev:** Radiant cap **Note:** Varieties exist.

Date	Mintage	F	VF	XF	Unc	BU
1835Ho PP Rare	—	—	—	—	—	—
1836Ho PP Rare	—	—	—	—	—	—
1839Ho PR Unique	—	—	—	—	—	—
1861Ho FM	—	4,500	7,500	—	—	—
Note: Reeded edge						
1862Ho FM Rare	—	—	—	—	—	—
Note: Plain edge, snakes tail left, long ray over *8R						
1862Ho FM	—	1,550	2,700	—	—	—
Note: Plain edge, snake's tail left						
1862Ho FM	—	1,650	2,750	—	—	—
Note: Reeded edge, snakes tail right						
1863Ho FM	—	150	300	800	—	—
1864Ho FM	—	850	1,650	2,750	—	—
1864Ho PR/FM	—	1,200	2,200	—	—	—
1864Ho FM	—	650	1,250	2,150	3,350	—
1865Ho FM	—	250	500	950	1,850	—
1866Ho FM	—	1,150	2,150	3,500	5,500	—
1866Ho MP	—	950	1,750	3,000	4,650	—
1867Ho PR	—	100	175	275	500	—
1868Ho PR	—	20.00	35.00	65.00	175	—
1869Ho PR	—	40.00	60.00	125	250	—
1870Ho PR	—	100	175	275	550	—
1871/0Ho PR	—	50.00	75.00	125	250	—
1871Ho PR	—	30.00	50.00	90.00	200	—
1872/1Ho PR	—	35.00	60.00	90.00	200	—
1872Ho PR	—	30.00	50.00	75.00	175	—
1873Ho PR	351,000	30.00	50.00	85.00	150	—
1874Ho PR	—	15.00	20.00	40.00	125	—
1875Ho PR	—	15.00	20.00	40.00	125	—
1876Ho AF	—	15.00	20.00	40.00	125	—
1877Ho AF	410,000	20.00	30.00	50.00	150	—
1877Ho GR	Inc. above	100	150	225	400	—
1877Ho JA	Inc. above	25.00	50.00	85.00	175	—
1878Ho JA	451,000	15.00	20.00	40.00	120	—
1879Ho JA	—	15.00	20.00	40.00	120	—
1880Ho JA	—	15.00	20.00	40.00	120	—
1881Ho JA	586,000	15.00	20.00	40.00	120	—
1882Ho JA	240,000	25.00	40.00	65.00	125	—
Note: O above H						
1882Ho JA	Inc. above	25.00	40.00	65.00	125	—
Note: O after H						
1883/2Ho JA	204,000	200	350	500	1,000	—
1883/2Ho FM/JA	Inc. above	25.00	40.00	75.00	150	—
1883Ho FM/JA	—	27.00	45.00	85.00	165	—
1883Ho FM	Inc. above	20.00	30.00	60.00	125	—
1883Ho JA	Inc. above	275	450	800	1,500	—
1884/3Ho FM	—	20.00	25.00	50.00	125	—
1884Ho FM	—	15.00	20.00	40.00	120	—
1885Ho FM	132,000	15.00	20.00	40.00	120	—

KM# 377.12   8 REALES
27.0700 g., 0.9030 Silver 0.7859 oz. ASW **Obv:** Facing eagle, snake in beak **Obv. Legend:** REPUBLICA MEXICANA **Rev:** Radiant cap **Note:** Varieties exist.

Date	Mintage	F	VF	XF	Unc	BU
1827Pi JS	—	3,800	—	—	—	—
1827Pi SA	—	6,000	9,000	—	—	—
1828/7Pi JS	—	275	425	650	1,350	—
1828Pi JS	—	225	375	550	1,200	—
1829Pi JS	—	35.00	65.00	125	250	—
1830Pi JS	—	30.00	50.00	100	200	—
Note: Varities with low cap or centered cap						
1831/0Pi JS	—	35.00	75.00	200	350	—
1831Pi JS	—	25.00	35.00	75.00	200	—
1832/22Pi JS	—	25.00	35.00	65.00	165	—
18/032Pi JS	—	40.00	80.00	175	300	—
1832Pi JS	—	25.00	35.00	65.00	165	—
1833/2Pi JS	—	30.00	45.00	80.00	250	—
1833Pi JS Narrow date	—	20.00	30.00	50.00	150	—
Note: Planchet diameter 37.5 mm						
1833Pi JS Wide date	—	20.00	30.00	50.00	150	—
Note: Planchet diameter 38.5 mm						
1834/3Pi JS	—	35.00	65.00	125	300	—
1834Pi JS	—	15.00	25.00	50.00	150	—
Note: Varieties with low cap or centered cap						
1835/4Pi JS	—	60.00	125	250	500	—
1835Pi JS	—	20.00	30.00	65.00	175	—
Note: Denomination as 8R						
1835Pi JS	—	15.00	25.00	50.00	150	—
Note: Denomination as 8Rs						
1836Pi JS	—	20.00	30.00	55.00	150	—
1837Pi JS	—	30.00	50.00	85.00	200	—
1838Pi JS	—	20.00	30.00	55.00	150	—
1839Pi JS	—	20.00	40.00	70.00	150	—
Note: Varieties with small low cap or large high cap						
1840Pi JS	—	20.00	30.00	60.00	150	—
184/31Pi JS	—	25.00	40.00	85.00	200	—
1841Pi JS	—	25.00	40.00	85.00	200	—
1841iP JS Error	—	200	350	550	—	—

Date	Mintage	F	VF	XF	Unc	BU
1842/1Pi JS	—	40.00	65.00	125	300	—
1842/1Pi JS/PS	—	35.00	55.00	90.00	200	—
1842Pi JS	—	30.00	50.00	80.00	175	—
Note: Eagle type of 1843						
1842Pi PS	—	30.00	50.00	80.00	175	—
1842Pi PS/JS	—	30.00	50.00	80.00	175	—
Note: Eagle type of 1841						
1843/2Pi PS Round-top 3	—	50.00	75.00	150	300	—
1843Pi PS Flat-top 3	—	60.00	100	200	475	—
1843Pi AM Round-top 3	—	20.00	30.00	55.00	150	—
1843Pi AM Flat-top 3	—	20.00	30.00	55.00	150	—
1844Pi AM	—	20.00	30.00	55.00	150	—
1845/4Pi AM	—	35.00	55.00	120	250	—
1845Pi AM	—	25.00	50.00	100	225	—
1846/5Pi AM	—	40.00	65.00	125	300	—
1846Pi AM	—	15.00	25.00	50.00	150	—
1847Pi AM	—	30.00	50.00	85.00	175	—
1848/7Pi AM	—	30.00	60.00	100	200	—
1848Pi AM	—	30.00	50.00	85.00	175	—
1849/8Pi PS/AM	—	950	1,750	—	—	—
1849Pi PS	—	950	1,750	—	—	—
1849Pi MC/PS	—	60.00	125	250	500	—
1849Pi AM	—	1,850	3,250	5,000	—	—
1849Pi MC	—	60.00	125	250	500	—
1850Pi MC	—	40.00	80.00	150	300	—
185/41Pi MC	—	75.00	150	275	550	—
1851Pi MC	—	75.00	150	275	550	—
1852Pi MC	—	75.00	125	200	400	—
1853Pi MC	—	150	275	400	850	—
1854Pi MC	—	100	150	250	500	—
1855Pi MC	—	100	150	250	500	—
1856Pi MC	—	65.00	100	200	400	—
1857Pi MC	—	400	700	1,250	—	—
1857Pi PS/MC	—	150	250	450	1,000	—
1857Pi PS	—	125	200	350	650	—
1858Pi MC/PS	—	250	400	650	1,200	—
1858Pi MC	—	250	400	650	1,200	—
1858Pi PS	—	650	1,150	1,750	—	—
1859/8Pi MC/PS	—	3,650	5,750	—	—	—
1859Pi MC/PS	—	900	1,750	—	—	—
1859Pi MC	—	2,000	3,500	5,000	—	—
1859Pi PS/MC	—	800	1,500	2,500	—	—
1860Pi FC Rare	—	—	—	—	—	—
1860Pi FE Rare	—	—	—	—	—	—
1860Pi MC	—	1,750	2,750	6,000	—	—
1860Pi PS/FE	—	500	1,000	—	—	—
1860Pi RO Rare	—	—	—	—	—	—
Note: Spink America Gerber sale 6-96 cleaned VF or better realized $33,000						
1860Pi PS	—	400	600	900	1,750	—
1861Pi PS	—	30.00	60.00	90.00	175	—
1861Pi RO	—	25.00	35.00	55.00	135	—
1862/1Pi RO	—	20.00	25.00	50.00	135	—
1862Pi RO	—	15.00	20.00	40.00	120	—
Note: Round O/M						
1862Pi RO	—	15.00	20.00	40.00	120	—
Note: Oval O in RO						
1862Pi RO	—	20.00	30.00	50.00	135	—
Note: Round O in RO, 6 is an inverted 9						
1863/2Pi RO	—	25.00	35.00	65.00	150	—
1863Pi RO/MO/FC	—	20.00	30.00	50.00	150	—
1863/5Pi RO	—	18.00	25.00	45.00	150	—
1863Pi RO	—	15.00	20.00	40.00	135	—
1863	—	25.00	35.00	55.00	135	—
Note: 6 over inverted 6						
1863Pi FC	—	2,750	4,750	—	—	—
1864Pi RO Rare	—	—	—	—	—	—
1867Pi CA	—	300	500	—	—	—
1867Pi LR	—	250	400	650	—	—
1867Pi PS/CA	—	850	—	—	—	—
1867Pi PS	—	30.00	60.00	125	275	—
1868/7Pi PS	—	30.00	60.00	125	250	—
1868Pi PS	—	20.00	30.00	50.00	135	—
1869/8Pi PS	—	20.00	25.00	45.00	135	—
1869Pi PS	—	15.00	20.00	40.00	135	—

Date	Mintage	F	VF	XF	Unc	BU
1870/69Pi PS	—	750	1,450	3,500	—	—
1870Pi PS	—	650	1,250	2,500	—	—
1873Pi MH	—	18.00	25.00	45.00	150	—
1874/3Pi MH	—	25.00	50.00	120	250	—
1874Pi MH	—	10.00	12.00	22.00	120	—
1875Pi MH	—	10.00	12.00	22.00	110	—
1876/5Pi MH	—	18.00	25.00	45.00	150	—
1876Pi MH	—	10.00	12.00	22.00	110	—
1877/6Pi MH	—	165	325	550	—	—
1877Pi MH	1,018,000	10.00	12.00	20.00	120	—
1878Pi MH	1,046,000	15.00	30.00	100	225	—
1879/8Pi MH	—	15.00	20.00	30.00	125	—
1879Pi MH	—	10.00	12.00	22.00	110	—
1879Pi BE	—	25.00	50.00	75.00	150	—
1879Pi MR	—	30.00	50.00	100	200	—
1880Pi MR	—	250	375	750	—	—
1880/70Pi MH/R	—	10.00	12.00	22.00	110	—
1880Pi MH/R	—	10.00	12.00	22.00	110	—
1880Pi MH	—	10.00	12.00	22.00	110	—
1881/71Pi MH/R	—	10.00	12.00	22.00	110	—
1881Pi MH/R	—	10.00	12.00	22.00	110	—
1881Pi MH	2,100,000	10.00	12.00	22.00	110	—
1882/1Pi MH	1,602,000	15.00	20.00	30.00	125	—
1882Pi MH	Inc. above	10.00	12.00	22.00	110	—
1883/2Pi MH	—	15.00	20.00	30.00	125	—
1883Pi MH	1,545,000	10.00	12.00	22.00	110	—
1884/3Pi MH	—	15.00	20.00	30.00	125	—
1884Pi MH/MM	—	12.00	15.00	22.00	95.00	—
1884Pi MH	—	10.00	12.00	20.00	90.00	—
1885/4Pi MH	1,736,000	15.00	20.00	30.00	125	—
1885/8Pi MH	Inc. above	15.00	20.00	30.00	125	—
1885Pi MH	Inc. above	10.00	12.00	20.00	90.00	—
1885Pi LC	Inc. above	12.00	18.00	25.00	110	—
1886Pi LC	3,347,000	10.00	12.00	20.00	90.00	—
1886Pi MR	Inc. above	10.00	12.00	20.00	90.00	—
1887Pi MR	2,922,000	10.00	12.00	20.00	90.00	—
1888/7Pi MR	—	15.00	20.00	30.00	125	—
1888Pi MR	2,438,000	10.00	12.00	20.00	90.00	—
1889Pi MR	2,103,000	10.00	12.00	20.00	90.00	—
1890Pi MR	1,562,000	10.00	12.00	20.00	90.00	—
1891Pi MR	1,184,000	10.00	12.00	20.00	90.00	—
1892Pi MR	1,336,000	10.00	12.00	20.00	90.00	—
1893Pi MR	530,000	10.00	12.00	20.00	90.00	—

KM# 377.13   8 REALES
27.0700 g., 0.9030 Silver 0.7859 oz. ASW **Obv:** Facing eagle, snake in beak **Obv. Legend:** REPUBLICA MEXICANA. **Rev:** Radiant cap **Note:** Varieties exist.

Date	Mintage	F	VF	XF	Unc	BU
1825Zs AZ	—	25.00	35.00	65.00	175	—
1826/5Zs AZ	—	25.00	45.00	85.00	200	—
1826Zs AZ	—	100	200	400	800	—
1826Zs AV	—	175	350	600	1,500	—
1826/5Zs AO/AZ	—	300	600	1,000	2,000	—

Date	Mintage	F	VF	XF	Unc	BU
1826Zs AO	—	200	350	750	2,000	—
1827Zs AO/AZ	—	35.00	50.00	125	250	—
1827Zs AO	—	25.00	45.00	85.00	200	—
1828Zs AO	—	15.00	20.00	45.00	165	—
Note: Wide and narrow date varieties exist						
1829Zs AO	—	15.00	20.00	45.00	165	—
1829Zs OV	—	50.00	90.00	150	300	—
1830Zs OM	—	—	—	—	—	—
1830Zs OV	—	15.00	20.00	45.00	165	—
1831Zs OV	—	25.00	50.00	90.00	200	—
1831Zs OM	—	15.00	25.00	55.00	165	—
1832/1Zs OM	—	20.00	25.00	45.00	165	—
1832Zs OM	—	15.00	20.00	40.00	150	—
1833/2Zs OM	—	20.00	30.00	45.00	165	—
1833Zs OM/MM	—	15.00	25.00	40.00	150	—
1833Zs OM	—	15.00	20.00	35.00	150	—
1834Zs OM	—	15.00	20.00	35.00	150	—
Note: Known with large, medium and small "34" in date						
1835Zs OM	—	15.00	20.00	40.00	150	—
1836/4Zs OM	—	20.00	30.00	50.00	165	—
1836/5Zs OM	—	20.00	30.00	50.00	165	—
1836Zs OM	—	15.00	20.00	35.00	150	—
1837Zs OM	—	15.00	20.00	35.00	150	—
1838/7Zs OM	—	20.00	30.00	45.00	165	—
1838Zs OM	—	15.00	20.00	35.00	150	—
1839Zs OM	—	15.00	20.00	35.00	150	—
1840Zs OM	—	15.00	20.00	35.00	150	—
1841Zs OM	—	15.00	20.00	35.00	150	—
1842Zs OM	—	15.00	20.00	35.00	150	—
Note: Eagle type of 1841						
1842Zs OM	—	15.00	20.00	35.00	150	—
Note: Eagle type of 1843						
1843Zs OM	—	15.00	20.00	35.00	150	—
1844Zs OM	—	15.00	20.00	35.00	150	—
1845Zs OM	—	15.00	20.00	35.00	150	—
1846Zs OM	—	15.00	20.00	35.00	150	—
1847Zs OM	—	15.00	20.00	35.00	150	—
1848/7Zs OM	—	20.00	30.00	45.00	165	—
1848Zs OM	—	15.00	20.00	35.00	150	—
1849Zs OM	—	15.00	20.00	35.00	150	—
1850Zs OM	—	15.00	20.00	35.00	150	—
1851Zs OM	—	15.00	20.00	35.00	150	—
1852Zs OM	—	15.00	20.00	35.00	150	—
1853Zs OM	—	30.00	45.00	75.00	200	—
1854/3Zs OM	—	20.00	30.00	60.00	175	—
1854Zs OM	—	15.00	25.00	45.00	165	—
1855Zs OM	—	20.00	30.00	60.00	175	—
1855Zs MO	—	30.00	60.00	90.00	200	—
1856/5Zs MO	—	20.00	30.00	45.00	165	—
1856Zs MO	—	15.00	20.00	35.00	150	—
1857/5Zs MO	—	20.00	30.00	45.00	165	—
1857Zs MO	—	15.00	20.00	35.00	150	—
1858/7Zs MO	—	15.00	20.00	35.00	150	—
1858Zs MO	—	15.00	20.00	35.00	150	—
1859/8Zs MO	—	15.00	20.00	35.00	150	—
1859Zs MO	—	15.00	20.00	35.00	150	—
1859Zs VL/MO	—	25.00	50.00	75.00	175	—
1859Zs VL	—	20.00	40.00	60.00	165	—
1860/50Zs MO	—	10.00	12.00	20.00	90.00	—
1860/59Zs MO	—	10.00	12.00	20.00	90.00	—
1860Zs MO	—	10.00	12.00	20.00	90.00	—
1860Zs VL/MO	—	10.00	12.00	20.00	90.00	—
1860Zs VL	—	10.00	12.00	20.00	90.00	—
1861Zs VL	—	10.00	12.00	20.00	90.00	—
1861/0Zs VL/MO	—	10.00	12.00	20.00	90.00	—
1861/0Zs VL	—	10.00	12.00	20.00	90.00	—
1862/1Zs VL	—	15.00	20.00	35.00	110	—
1862Zs VL	—	10.00	12.00	20.00	90.00	—
1863Zs VL	—	10.00	12.00	20.00	90.00	—
1863Zs MO	—	10.00	12.00	20.00	90.00	—
1864/3Zs VL	—	15.00	20.00	35.00	110	—
1864Zs VL	—	10.00	12.00	20.00	90.00	—
1864Zs MO	—	15.00	20.00	35.00	110	—
1865/4Zs MO	—	200	450	800	1,550	—
1865Zs MO	—	150	300	600	1,250	—
1866Zs VL	—	—	—	—	—	—
Note: Contemporary counterfeit						
1867Zs JS Rare	—	—	—	—	—	—
1868Zs JS	—	10.00	12.00	20.00	90.00	—

Date	Mintage	F	VF	XF	Unc	BU
1868Zs YH	—	10.00	12.00	20.00	90.00	—
1869Zs YH	—	10.00	12.00	20.00	90.00	—
1870Zs YH Rare	—	—	—	—	—	—
1873Zs YH	—	10.00	12.00	20.00	90.00	—
1874Zs YH	—	10.00	12.00	20.00	90.00	—
1874Zs JA/YA	—	10.00	12.00	20.00	90.00	—
1874Zs JA	—	10.00	12.00	20.00	90.00	—
1875Zs JA	—	10.00	12.00	20.00	90.00	—
1876Zs JA	—	10.00	12.00	20.00	90.00	—
1876Zs JS	—	10.00	12.00	20.00	90.00	—
1877Zs JS	2,700,000	10.00	12.00	20.00	90.00	—
1878Zs JS	2,310,000	10.00	12.00	20.00	90.00	—
1879/8Zs JS	—	15.00	20.00	35.00	110	—
1879Zs JS	—	10.00	12.00	20.00	90.00	—
1880Zs JS	—	10.00	12.00	20.00	90.00	—
1881Zs JS	5,592,000	10.00	12.00	20.00	90.00	—
1882/1Zs JS	2,485,000	15.00	20.00	35.00	110	—
1882Zs JS Straight J	Inc. above	10.00	12.00	20.00	90.00	—
1882Zs JS Full J	Inc. above	10.00	12.00	20.00	90.00	—
1883/2Zs JS	2,563,000	15.00	20.00	35.00	110	—
1883Zs JS	Inc. above	10.00	12.00	20.00	90.00	—
1884Zs JS	—	10.00	12.00	20.00	90.00	—
1885Zs JS	2,252,000	10.00	12.00	20.00	90.00	—
1886/5Zs JS	5,303,000	15.00	20.00	35.00	110	—
1886/8Zs JS	Inc. above	15.00	20.00	35.00	110	—
1886Zs JS	Inc. above	10.00	12.00	20.00	90.00	—
1886Zs FZ	Inc. above	10.00	12.00	20.00	90.00	—
1887Zs FZ	4,733,000	10.00	12.00	20.00	90.00	—
1887Z FZ	Inc. above	20.00	30.00	50.00	110	—
1888/7Zs FZ	5,132,000	12.00	15.00	25.00	95.00	—
1888Zs FZ	Inc. above	10.00	12.00	20.00	90.00	—
1889Zs FZ	4,344,000	10.00	12.00	20.00	90.00	—
1890Zs FZ	3,887,000	10.00	12.00	20.00	90.00	—
1891Zs FZ	4,114,000	10.00	12.00	20.00	90.00	—
1892/1Zs FZ	4,238,000	12.00	15.00	25.00	95.00	—
1892Zs FZ Narrow date	Inc. above	10.00	12.00	20.00	90.00	—
1892Zs FZ Wide date	—	10.00	12.00	20.00	90.00	—
1893Zs FZ	3,872,000	10.00	12.00	20.00	90.00	—
1894Zs FZ	3,081,000	10.00	12.00	20.00	90.00	—
1895Zs FZ	4,718,000	10.00	12.00	20.00	90.00	—
1896Zs FZ	4,226,000	10.00	12.00	20.00	90.00	—
1897Zs FZ	4,877,000	10.00	12.00	20.00	90.00	—

KM# 377.10   8 REALES
27.0700 g., 0.9030 Silver 0.7859 oz. ASW   **Obv:**
Facing eagle, snake in beak **Obv. Legend:**
REPUBLICA MEXICANA. **Rev:** Radiant cap **Note:**
Varieties exist. 1874 CP is a die struck counterfeit.

Date	Mintage	F	VF	XF	Unc	BU
1824Mo JM Round tail	—	75.00	125	250	500	—
1824Mo JM Square tail	—	75.00	125	250	500	—

Date	Mintage	F	VF	XF	Unc	BU
1825Mo JM	—	25.00	40.00	75.00	200	—
1826/5Mo JM	—	25.00	40.00	75.00	200	—
1826Mo JM	—	20.00	30.00	55.00	165	—
1827Mo JM	—	25.00	35.00	60.00	175	—
Note: Medal alignment						
1827Mo JM	—	25.00	35.00	60.00	175	—
Note: Coin alignment						
1828Mo JM	—	30.00	60.00	100	250	—
1829Mo JM	—	20.00	30.00	90.00	220	—
1830/20Mo JM	—	35.00	5.00	150	300	—
1830Mo JM	—	30.00	50.00	90.00	220	—
1831Mo JM	—	30.00	50.00	100	240	—
1832/1Mo JM	—	25.00	40.00	65.00	180	—
1832Mo JM	—	20.00	30.00	55.00	165	—
1833Mo MJ	—	25.00	40.00	80.00	200	—
1833Mo ML	—	450	650	950	2,000	—
1834/3Mo ML	—	25.00	35.00	60.00	175	—
1834Mo ML	—	20.00	30.00	55.00	165	—
1835Mo ML Narrow date	—	20.00	30.00	55.00	165	—
1835Mo ML Wide date	—	20.00	30.00	55.00	165	—
1836Mo ML	—	50.00	100	150	325	—
1836Mo ML/MF	—	50.00	100	150	325	—
1836Mo MF	—	30.00	50.00	90.00	220	—
1836Mo MF/ML	—	35.00	60.00	100	240	—
1837/6Mo ML	—	30.00	50.00	80.00	200	—
1837/6Mo MM	—	30.00	50.00	80.00	200	—
1837/6Mo MM/ML	—	30.00	50.00	80.00	200	—
1837/6Mo MM/MF	—	30.00	50.00	80.00	200	—
1837Mo ML	—	30.00	50.00	80.00	200	—
1837Mo MM	—	75.00	125	175	325	—
1838Mo MM	—	30.00	50.00	80.00	200	—
1838Mo ML	—	20.00	35.00	60.00	180	—
1838Mo ML/MM	—	20.00	35.00	60.00	180	—
1839Mo ML Narow date	—	15.00	25.00	50.00	165	—
1839Mo ML Wide date	—	15.00	25.00	50.00	165	—
1840Mo ML	—	15.00	25.00	50.00	165	—
1841Mo ML	—	15.00	25.00	45.00	150	—
1842Mo ML	—	15.00	25.00	45.00	150	—
1842Mo MM	—	15.00	25.00	45.00	150	—
1843Mo MM	—	15.00	25.00	45.00	150	—
1844Mo MF/MM	—	—	—	—	—	—
1844Mo MF	—	15.00	25.00	45.00	150	—
1845/4Mo MF	—	15.00	25.00	45.00	150	—
1845Mo MF	—	15.00	25.00	45.00	150	—
1846/5Mo MF	—	15.00	25.00	50.00	165	—
1846Mo MF	—	15.00	25.00	50.00	165	—
1847/6Mo MF	—	2,000	3,550	—	—	—
1847Mo MF	—	1,500	2,750	5,000	7,500	—
1847Mo RC	—	20.00	30.00	55.00	165	—
1847Mo RC/MF	—	15.00	25.00	45.00	150	—
1848Mo GC	—	15.00	25.00	45.00	150	—
1849Mo GC	—	20.00	35.00	60.00	180	—
1849Mo GC	—	15.00	25.00	45.00	150	—
1850/40Mo GC	—	25.00	50.00	100	240	—
1850/49Mo GC	—	25.00	50.00	100	240	—
1850Mo GC	—	20.00	40.00	75.00	200	—
1851Mo GC	—	20.00	40.00	60.00	175	—
1852Mo GC	—	20.00	40.00	75.00	200	—
1853Mo GC	—	15.00	25.00	50.00	160	—
1854Mo GC	—	12.00	15.00	30.00	125	—
1855Mo GC	—	20.00	35.00	65.00	180	—
1855Mo GF	—	12.00	15.00	30.00	125	—
1855Mo GF/GC	—	12.00	15.00	30.00	125	—
1856/4Mo GF	—	15.00	25.00	45.00	145	—
1856/5Mo GF	—	15.00	25.00	45.00	145	—
1856Mo GF	—	12.00	15.00	30.00	125	—
1857Mo GF	—	10.00	15.00	30.00	125	—
1858/7Mo FH/GF	—	10.00	15.00	30.00	125	—
1858Mo FH Narrow date	—	10.00	15.00	30.00	125	—
1858Mo FH Wide date	—	10.00	15.00	30.00	125	—
1859Mo FH	—	10.00	15.00	30.00	125	—
1859/8Mo FH	—	25.00	50.00	100	240	—
1860/59Mo FH	—	15.00	20.00	30.00	125	—
1860Mo FH	—	10.00	15.00	30.00	125	—
1860Mo TH	—	12.00	18.00	40.00	145	—
1861Mo TH	—	12.00	18.00	40.00	145	—
1861Mo CH	—	10.00	15.00	20.00	90.00	—
1862Mo CH	—	10.00	15.00	20.00	90.00	—
1863Mo CH	—	10.00	15.00	20.00	90.00	—
1863Mo CH/TH	—	10.00	15.00	20.00	90.00	—
1863Mo TH	—	10.00	15.00	20.00	90.00	—
1867Mo CH	—	10.00	15.00	20.00	90.00	—
1867Mo CH/TH	—	20.00	45.00	70.00	185	—
1868Mo CH	—	10.00	15.00	20.00	90.00	—
1868Mo PH	—	10.00	15.00	20.00	90.00	—
1868Mo CH/PH	—	10.00	15.00	20.00	90.00	—
1868Mo PH Narrow date	—	10.00	15.00	20.00	90.00	—
1868Mo PH Wide date	—	10.00	15.00	20.00	90.00	—
1869Mo CH	—	10.00	15.00	20.00	—	—
1873Mo MH	—	10.00	15.00	20.00	90.00	—
1873Mo MH/HH	—	12.00	18.00	25.00	95.00	—
1874/69Mo MH	—	20.00	45.00	70.00	185	—
1874Mo MH	—	12.00	18.00	25.00	95.00	—
1874Mo BH/MH	—	12.00	18.00	25.00	95.00	—
1874Mo BH	—	12.00	18.00	25.00	95.00	—
1875Mo BH	—	10.00	15.00	20.00	90.00	—
1876/4Mo BH	—	12.00	18.00	25.00	95.00	—
1876/5Mo BH	—	12.00	18.00	25.00	95.00	—
1876Mo BH	—	10.00	15.00	20.00	90.00	—
1877Mo MH	898,000	10.00	15.00	20.00	90.00	—
1877Mo MH/BH	Inc. above	12.00	18.00	25.00	95.00	—
1878Mo MH	2,154,000	10.00	15.00	20.00	90.00	—
1879/8Mo MH	—	10.00	15.00	20.00	95.00	—
1879Mo MH	—	10.00	15.00	20.00	90.00	—
1880/79Mo MH	—	15.00	20.00	30.00	100	—
1880Mo MH	—	10.00	15.00	20.00	90.00	—
1881Mo MH	5,712,000	10.00	15.00	20.00	90.00	—
1882/1Mo MH	2,746,000	12.00	15.00	20.00	90.00	—
1882Mo MH	Inc. above	10.00	15.00	20.00	90.00	—
1883/2Mo MH	2,726,000	12.00	18.00	25.00	95.00	—
1883Mo MH Narrow date	Inc. above	10.00	15.00	20.00	90.00	—
1883Mo MH Wide date	—	10.00	15.00	20.00	90.00	—
1884/3Mo MH	—	15.00	20.00	30.00	100	—
1884Mo MH	—	10.00	15.00	20.00	90.00	—
1885Mo MH	3,649,000	10.00	15.00	20.00	90.00	—
1886Mo MH	7,558,000	10.00	12.00	18.00	90.00	—
1887Mo MH	7,681,000	10.00	12.00	18.00	90.00	—
1888Mo MH Narrow date	7,179,000	10.00	12.00	18.00	90.00	—
1888Mo MH Wide date	—	10.00	12.00	18.00	90.00	—
1889Mo MH	7,332,000	10.00	15.00	20.00	90.00	—
1890Mo MH Narrow date	7,412,000	10.00	12.00	18.00	90.00	—
1890Mo AM Wide date	—	10.00	12.00	18.00	90.00	—
1890Mo AM	Inc. above	10.00	12.00	18.00	90.00	—
1891Mo AM	8,076,000	10.00	12.00	18.00	90.00	—
1892Mo AM	9,392,000	10.00	12.00	18.00	90.00	—
1893Mo AM	10,773,000	10.00	12.00	18.00	90.00	—
1894Mo AM	12,394,000	10.00	12.00	18.00	90.00	—
1895Mo AM	10,474,000	10.00	12.00	18.00	90.00	—
1895Mo AB	Inc. above	10.00	12.00	18.00	90.00	—
1896Mo AB	9,327,000	10.00	12.00	18.00	90.00	—
1896Mo AM	Inc. above	10.00	12.00	18.00	90.00	—
1897Mo AM	8,621,000	10.00	12.00	18.00	90.00	—

KM# 377.1   8 REALES
27.0700 g., 0.9030 Silver 0.7859 oz. ASW **Obv:**
Facing eagle, snake in beak **Obv. Legend:**
REPUBLICA MEXICANA. **Rev:** Radiant cap

Date	Mintage	F	VF	XF	Unc	BU
1863Ce ME	—	425	700	1,350	3,000	—
1863Ce /PI ML/ MC	—	425	750	1,500	3,250	—

KM# 377.2   8 REALES
27.0700 g., 0.9030 Silver 0.7859 oz. ASW **Obv:**
Facing eagle, snake in beak **Obv. Legend:**
REPUBLICA MEXICANA. **Rev:** Radiant cap **Note:**
Varieties exist.

Date	Mintage	F	VF	XF	Unc	BU
1831Ca MR	—	1,000	1,750	2,250	3,250	—
1832Ca MR	—	125	200	300	600	—
1833Ca MR	—	250	550	1,000	—	—
1834Ca MR	—	300	600	1,150	—	—
1834Ca AM	—	350	500	700	—	—
1835Ca AM	—	150	250	475	900	—
1836Ca AM	—	100	200	300	600	—
1837Ca AM	—	550	1,150	—	—	—
1838Ca AM	—	100	200	300	600	—
1839Ca RG	—	750	1,250	2,500	—	—
1840Ca RG	—	300	500	800	1,500	—
Note: 1 dot after date						
1840Ca RG	—	300	500	800	1,500	—
Note: 3 dots after date						
1841Ca RG	—	50.00	100	150	300	—
1842Ca RG	—	25.00	40.00	75.00	150	—
1843Ca RG	—	40.00	80.00	125	250	—
1844/1Ca RG	—	35.00	70.00	100	200	—
1844Ca RG	—	25.00	40.00	75.00	160	—
1845Ca RG	—	25.00	40.00	75.00	160	—
1846Ca RG	—	30.00	60.00	100	250	—
1847Ca RG	—	40.00	80.00	125	250	—
1848Ca RG	—	35.00	70.00	125	250	—
1849Ca RG	—	30.00	60.00	100	200	—
1850/40Ca RG	—	40.00	80.00	125	250	—
1850Ca RG	—	30.00	60.00	100	200	—
1851/41Ca RG	—	100	200	300	500	—
1851Ca RG	—	150	250	400	750	—
1852/42Ca RG	—	150	250	400	750	—
1852Ca RG	—	150	250	400	750	—
1853/43Ca RG	—	150	250	400	750	—
1853Ca RG	—	150	250	350	700	—
1854/44Ca RG	—	100	200	300	500	—
1854Ca RG	—	50.00	100	150	300	—
1855/45Ca RG	—	100	200	350	650	—
1855Ca RG	—	50.00	100	150	300	—
1856/45Ca RG	—	275	450	750	1,250	—

Date	Mintage	F	VF	XF	Unc	BU
1856/5Ca RG	—	400	700	1,500	3,500	—
1857Ca JC/RG	—	40.00	80.00	125	250	—
1857Ca JC	—	50.00	100	150	250	—
1858Ca JC	—	35.00	70.00	125	250	—
1858Ca BA	—	2,000	3,500	—	—	—
1859Ca JC	—	40.00	80.00	125	250	—
1860Ca JC	—	20.00	40.00	90.00	175	—
1861Ca JC	—	15.00	25.00	55.00	135	—
1862Ca JC	—	15.00	25.00	55.00	135	—
1863Ca JC	—	20.00	35.00	75.00	150	—
1864Ca JC	—	20.00	35.00	75.00	150	—
1865Ca JC	—	100	200	350	600	—
1865Ca FP	—	1,275	2,150	3,250	—	—
1866Ca JC	—	750	1,150	2,250	—	—
1866Ca FP	—	1,000	2,000	3,250	5,000	—
1866Ca JG	—	850	1,650	2,750	4,250	—
1867Ca JG	—	100	200	350	600	—
1868Ca JG	—	75.00	150	250	400	—
1868Ca MM	—	65.00	125	200	350	—
1869Ca MM	—	20.00	35.00	65.00	145	—
1870Ca MM	—	20.00	35.00	65.00	145	—
1871/0Ca MM	—	15.00	25.00	55.00	135	—
1871Ca MM	—	15.00	25.00	55.00	135	—
1871Ca MM	—	20.00	35.00	65.00	145	—
Note: Known with first M over inverted M and second M over inverted M						
1873/5Ca MM	—	20.00	35.00	65.00	145	—
1873Ca MM	—	20.00	35.00	65.00	145	—
1873Ca MM/T	—	15.00	25.00	55.00	135	—
1874Ca MM	—	12.00	15.00	30.00	110	—
1875Ca MM	—	12.00	15.00	30.00	110	—
1876Ca MM	—	12.00	15.00	30.00	110	—
1877Ca EA E/G	—	20.00	40.00	85.00	200	—
1877Ca EA	472,000	20.00	40.00	85.00	200	—
1877Ca GR	Inc. above	25.00	45.00	65.00	150	—
1877Ca JM	Inc. above	12.00	15.00	30.00	110	—
1877Ca AV	Inc. above	100	200	350	750	—
1878Ca AV	439,000	12.00	15.00	25.00	90.00	—
1879Ca AV	—	12.00	15.00	25.00	90.00	—
1880Ca AV	—	200	350	600	1,250	—
1880Ca PM	—	500	800	1,250	2,500	—
1880Ca MG	—	12.00	15.00	25.00	110	—
Note: Normal initials						
1880Ca MG	—	12.00	15.00	25.00	110	—
Note: Tall initials						
1880Ca MM	—	12.00	15.00	25.00	110	—
1881Ca MG	1,085,000	10.00	12.00	20.00	90.00	—
1882Ca MG	779,000	10.00	12.00	20.00	90.00	—
1882Ca MM	Inc. above	10.00	12.00	20.00	90.00	—
1882Ca MM	Inc. above	20.00	45.00	100	175	—
Note: Second M over sideways M						
1883Ca MM	818,000	—	—	—	—	—
Note: Sideways M						
1883/2Ca MM/G	—	12.00	15.00	30.00	95.00	—
1883Ca MM	Inc. above	10.00	12.00	20.00	90.00	—
1884/3Ca MM	—	12.00	15.00	30.00	90.00	—
1884Ca MM	—	10.00	12.00	20.00	90.00	—
1885/4Ca MM	1,345,000	15.00	25.00	55.00	135	—
1885/6Ca MM	Inc. above	15.00	25.00	55.00	135	—
1885Ca MM	Inc. above	10.00	12.00	20.00	90.00	—
1886Ca MM	2,483,000	10.00	12.00	20.00	90.00	—
1887Ca MM	2,625,000	10.00	12.00	20.00	90.00	—
1888/7Ca MM	2,434,000	15.00	25.00	65.00	145	—
1888Ca MM	Inc. above	10.00	12.00	20.00	90.00	—
1889Ca MM	2,681,000	10.00	12.00	20.00	90.00	—
1890/89Ca MM	—	15.00	25.00	55.00	135	—
1890Ca MM	2,137,000	10.00	12.00	20.00	90.00	—
1891/0Ca MM	2,268,000	15.00	25.00	55.00	135	—
1891Ca MM	Inc. above	10.00	12.00	20.00	95.00	—
1892Ca MM	2,527,000	10.00	12.00	20.00	90.00	—
1893Ca MM	2,632,000	10.00	12.00	20.00	90.00	—
1894Ca MM	2,642,000	10.00	12.00	20.00	90.00	—
1895Ca MM	1,112,000	10.00	12.00	20.00	90.00	—

KM# 378.2 1/2 ESCUDO
1.6900 g., 0.8750 Gold 0.0475 oz. AGW **Obv:**
Facing eagle, snake in beak **Obv. Legend:**
REPUBLICA MEXICANA **Rev:** Hand holding cap on
stick, open book **Rev. Legend:** LIBERTAD...

Date	Mintage	VG	F	VF	XF	Unc
1825Ga FS	—	45.00	60.00	100	175	—
1829Ga FS	—	45.00	60.00	100	175	—
1831Ga FS	—	45.00	60.00	100	175	—
1834Ga FS	—	45.00	60.00	100	175	—
1835Ga FS	—	45.00	60.00	100	175	—
1837Ga JG	—	45.00	60.00	100	175	—
1838Ga JG	—	45.00	60.00	100	175	—
1839Ga JG	—	—	—	—	—	—
1840Ga MC Unique	—	—	—	—	—	—
1842Ga JG	—	—	—	—	—	—
1847Ga JG	—	45.00	60.00	100	175	—
1850Ga JG	—	45.00	65.00	125	225	—
1852Ga JG	—	40.00	65.00	75.00	150	—
1859Ga JG	—	45.00	60.00	100	175	—
1861Ga JG	—	40.00	55.00	75.00	150	—

KM# 378.3 1/2 ESCUDO
1.6900 g., 0.8750 Gold 0.0475 oz. AGW **Obv:**
Facing eagle, snake in beak **Obv. Legend:**
REPUBLICA MEXICANA. **Rev:** Hand holding cap on
stick, open book **Rev. Legend:** LIBERTAD...

Date	Mintage	VG	F	VF	XF	Unc
1846GC MP	—	50.00	75.00	100	175	—
1847GC MP	—	50.00	75.00	100	175	450
1848/7GC MP	—	50.00	75.00	100	200	650
1850GC MP	—	50.00	75.00	100	175	—
1851GC MP Revised eagle	—	50.00	75.00	100	175	—

KM# 378.4 1/2 ESCUDO
1.6900 g., 0.8750 Gold 0.0475 oz. AGW **Obv:**
Facing eagle, snake in beak **Rev:** Hand holding cap
on stick, open book

Date	Mintage	VG	F	VF	XF	Unc
1845Go PM	—	35.00	45.00	65.00	125	—
1849Go PF	—	35.00	50.00	90.00	175	750
1851/41Go PF	—	35.00	45.00	65.00	125	—
1851Go PF	—	35.00	45.00	65.00	125	—
1852Go PF	—	35.00	45.00	65.00	125	—
1852Go PF/FF	—	—	—	—	—	—
1853Go PF	—	35.00	45.00	65.00	125	—
1855Go PF	—	35.00	50.00	80.00	150	—
1857Go PF	—	35.00	45.00	65.00	125	—
1858/7Go PF	—	35.00	45.00	65.00	125	—
1859Go PF	—	35.00	45.00	65.00	125	—
1860Go PF	—	35.00	45.00	65.00	125	—
1861Go PF	—	35.00	45.00	65.00	125	—
1862/1Go YE	—	35.00	45.00	65.00	125	—
1863Go PF	—	35.00	50.00	80.00	150	—
1863Go YF	—	35.00	45.00	65.00	125	—

KM# 378.5 1/2 ESCUDO
1.6900 g., 0.8750 Gold 0.0475 oz. AGW **Obv:**

Facing eagle, snake in beak **Obv. Legend:**
REPUBLICA MEXICANA. **Rev:** Hand holding cap on
stick, open book **Rev. Legend:** LIBERTAD...

Date	Mintage	VG	F	VF	XF	Unc
1825/1Mo JM	—	50.00	75.00	125	200	—
1825/4Mo JM	—	50.00	75.00	125	200	—
1825Mo JM	—	35.00	50.00	80.00	150	350
1827/6Mo JM	—	35.00	50.00	80.00	150	—
1827Mo JM	—	35.00	50.00	80.00	150	350
1829Mo JM	—	35.00	50.00	80.00	150	—
1831/0Mo JM	—	35.00	50.00	80.00	150	—
1831Mo JM	—	35.00	45.00	65.00	125	—
1832Mo	—	35.00	45.00	65.00	125	—
1833Mo MJ	—	35.00	50.00	90.00	175	450
Note: Olive and oak branches reversed						
1834Mo ML	—	35.00	45.00	75.00	150	400
1835Mo ML	—	35.00	45.00	80.00	150	—
1838Mo ML	—	35.00	50.00	90.00	175	—
1839Mo ML	—	35.00	50.00	90.00	175	—
1840Mo ML	—	35.00	45.00	65.00	125	—
1841Mo ML	—	35.00	45.00	65.00	125	—
1842Mo ML	—	35.00	45.00	80.00	150	—
1842Mo MM	—	35.00	45.00	80.00	150	—
1843Mo MM	—	35.00	45.00	65.00	125	—
1844Mo MF	—	35.00	45.00	65.00	125	250
1845Mo MF	—	35.00	45.00	65.00	125	—
1846/5Mo MF	—	35.00	45.00	65.00	125	—
1846Mo MF	—	35.00	45.00	65.00	125	—
1848Mo GC	—	35.00	50.00	90.00	175	450
1850Mo GC	—	35.00	45.00	65.00	125	—
1851Mo GC	—	35.00	45.00	65.00	125	—
1852Mo GC	—	35.00	45.00	65.00	125	—
1853Mo GC	—	40.00	60.00	100	200	650
1854Mo GC	—	35.00	45.00	65.00	125	—
1855Mo GF	—	35.00	45.00	75.00	150	350
1856/4Mo GF	—	35.00	45.00	65.00	125	—
1857Mo GF	—	35.00	45.00	65.00	125	—
1858/7Mo FH/GF	—	35.00	50.00	75.00	150	—
1858Mo FH	—	35.00	45.00	65.00	125	—
1859Mo FH	—	35.00	45.00	65.00	125	—
1860/59Mo FH	—	35.00	45.00	65.00	125	250
1861Mo CH/FH	—	35.00	45.00	80.00	150	—
1862Mo CH	—	35.00	45.00	65.00	125	200
1863/57Mo CH/GF	—	35.00	45.00	65.00	125	250
1868/58Mo PH	—	35.00	45.00	80.00	150	—
1869/59Mo CH	—	35.00	45.00	80.00	150	—

KM# 378.6 1/2 ESCUDO
1.6900 g., 0.8750 Gold 0.0475 oz. AGW **Obv:**
Facing eagle, snake in beak **Obv. Legend:**
REPUBLICA MEXICANA. **Rev:** Hand holding cap on
stick, open book **Rev. Legend:** LIBERTAD...

Date	Mintage	VG	F	VF	XF	Unc
1860Zs VL	—	40.00	50.00	75.00	150	—
1862/1Zs VL	—	40.00	50.00	75.00	150	—
1862Zs VL	—	35.00	45.00	65.00	125	—

KM# 378 1/2 ESCUDO
1.6900 g., 0.8750 Gold 0.0475 oz. AGW **Obv:**
Facing eagle, snake in beak **Obv. Legend:**
REPUBLICA MEXICANA **Rev:** Hand holding cap on
stick, open book **Rev. Legend:** LIBERTAD...

Date	Mintage	VG	F	VF	XF	Unc
1848C CE	—	40.00	50.00	75.00	150	300
1853C CE	—	40.00	50.00	75.00	150	—

Date	Mintage	VG	F	VF	XF	Unc
1854C CE	—	40.00	50.00	75.00	150	—
Revised eagle						

Note: Dates 1854-1870 of this type display the revised eagle

Date	Mintage	VG	F	VF	XF	Unc
1856C CE	—	50.00	100	150	250	—
1857C CE	—	40.00	50.00	75.00	150	—
1859C CE	—	40.00	50.00	75.00	150	—
1860C CE	—	40.00	50.00	75.00	150	—
1862C CE	—	40.00	50.00	75.00	125	—
1863C CE	—	40.00	50.00	75.00	125	300
1866C CE	—	40.00	50.00	75.00	125	—
1867C CE	—	40.00	50.00	75.00	125	250
1870C CE	—	75.00	150	275	450	—

KM# 378.1 1/2 ESCUDO
1.6900 g., 0.8750 Gold 0.0475 oz. AGW **Obv:** Facing eagle, snake in beak **Rev:** Hand holding cap on stick, open book

Date	Mintage	VG	F	VF	XF	Unc
1833Do RM/RL	—	40.00	50.00	75.00	150	—
1834/1Do RM	—	40.00	50.00	75.00	150	—
1834/3Do RM	—	40.00	50.00	75.00	150	—
1835/2Do RM	—	40.00	50.00	75.00	150	—
1835/3Do RM	—	40.00	50.00	75.00	150	—
1835/4Do RM	—	40.00	50.00	75.00	150	—
1836/5/4Do RM/L	—	45.00	60.00	100	175	450
1836/4Do RM	—	40.00	50.00	75.00	150	—
1837Do RM	—	40.00	50.00	75.00	150	—
1838Do RM	—	45.00	60.00	100	175	—
1843Do RM	—	45.00	60.00	100	175	—
1844/33Do RM	—	45.00	60.00	100	175	—
1844/33Do R,/RL	—	65.00	125	275	450	—
1845Do CM	—	45.00	60.00	100	175	—
1846Do RM	—	45.00	60.00	100	175	—
1848Do RM	—	45.00	60.00	100	175	—
1850/33Do JMR	—	45.00	60.00	100	175	475
1851Do JMR	—	45.00	60.00	100	200	—
1852Do JMR	—	45.00	60.00	100	175	—
1853/33Do CP	—	75.00	150	300	500	—
1853Do CP	—	50.00	70.00	150	250	550
1854Do CP	—	40.00	50.00	75.00	150	—
1855Do CP	—	40.00	50.00	75.00	150	—
1859Do CP	—	40.00	50.00	75.00	150	—
1861Do CP	—	40.00	50.00	75.00	150	—
1862Do CP	—	40.00	50.00	75.00	150	—
1864Do LT	—	75.00	125	250	400	—

KM# 379 ESCUDO
3.3800 g., 0.8750 Gold 0.0951 oz. AGW **Obv:** Facing eagle, snake in beak **Rev:** Hand holding cap on stick, open book

Date	Mintage	VG	F	VF	XF	Unc
1846C CE	—	75.00	100	200	350	—
1847C CE	—	60.00	75.00	125	175	—
1848C CE	—	60.00	75.00	125	175	700
1849/8C CE	—	65.00	100	150	225	—
1850C CE	—	60.00	75.00	125	175	—
1851C CE	—	65.00	100	150	225	—
1853/1C CE	—	65.00	100	150	225	—
1854C CE	—	60.00	75.00	125	175	—
1856/5/4C CE	—	65.00	100	150	225	—
1856C CE	—	60.00	75.00	125	175	—
1857/1C CE	—	65.00	100	150	225	—
1857C CE	—	60.00	75.00	125	175	—
1861C PV	—	60.00	75.00	125	175	—
1862C CE	—	60.00	75.00	125	175	—
1863C CE	—	60.00	75.00	125	175	—
1866C CE	—	60.00	75.00	125	175	—
1870C CE	—	60.00	75.00	125	175	—

KM# 379.1 ESCUDO
3.3800 g., 0.8750 Gold 0.0951 oz. AGW **Obv:** Facing eagle, snake in beak **Obv. Legend:** REPUBLICA MEXICANA. **Rev:** Hand holding cap on stick, open book **Rev. Legend:** LIBERTAD...

Date	Mintage	VG	F	VF	XF	Unc
1832Do R.L.	—	—	—	—	—	—
1833/2Do RM/R.L.	—	75.00	125	200	300	—
1834Do RM	—	65.00	100	150	250	—
1835Do RM	—	—	—	—	—	—
1836Do RM/RL	—	65.00	100	150	250	—
1838Do RM	—	65.00	100	150	250	—
1846/38Do RM	—	75.00	125	200	300	—
1850Do JMR	—	75.00	125	175	275	—
1851/31Do JMR	—	75.00	125	200	300	—
1851Do JMR	—	75.00	125	175	275	—
1853Do CP	—	75.00	125	175	275	—
1854/34Do CP	—	75.00	125	175	275	—
1854/44Do CP/RP	—	75.00	125	175	275	—
1855Do CP	—	75.00	125	175	275	—
1859Do CP	—	75.00	125	175	275	—
1861Do CP	—	75.00	125	175	275	—
1864Do LT/CP Rare	—	—	—	—	—	—

KM# 379.2 ESCUDO
3.3800 g., 0.8750 Gold 0.0951 oz. AGW **Obv:** Facing eagle, snake in beak **Obv. Legend:** REPUBLICA MEXICANA. **Rev:** Hand holding cap on stick, open book

Date	Mintage	VG	F	VF	XF	Unc
1825Ga FS	—	65.00	90.00	125	200	—
1826Ga FS	—	65.00	90.00	125	200	—
1829Ga FS	—	—	—	—	—	—
1831Ga FS	—	65.00	90.00	125	200	—
1834Ga FS	—	65.00	90.00	125	200	—
1835Ga JG	—	65.00	90.00	125	200	—
1842Ga JG/MC	—	65.00	90.00	125	200	—
1843Ga MC	—	65.00	90.00	125	200	—
1847Ga JG	—	65.00	90.00	125	200	—
1848/7Ga JG	—	65.00	90.00	125	200	—
1849Ga JG	—	65.00	90.00	125	200	—
1850/40Ga JG	—	70.00	125	225	325	—
1850Ga JG	—	65.00	90.00	125	200	—
1852/1Ga JG	—	65.00	90.00	125	200	900
1856Ga JG	—	65.00	90.00	125	200	—
1857Ga JG	—	65.00	90.00	125	200	—
1859/7Ga JG	—	65.00	90.00	125	200	—
1860/59Ga JG	—	70.00	100	175	275	—
1860Ga	—	65.00	90.00	125	200	—

KM# 379.3 ESCUDO
3.3800 g., 0.8750 Gold 0.0951 oz. AGW **Obv:** Facing eagle, snake in beak **Obv. Legend:**

REPUBLICA MEXICANA. **Rev:** Hand holding cap on stick, open book

Date	Mintage	VG	F	VF	XF	Unc
1844GC MP	—	75.00	100	175	250	—
1845GC MP	—	75.00	100	175	250	—
1846GC MP	—	75.00	100	175	250	—
1847GC MP	—	75.00	100	175	250	—
1848GC MP	—	75.00	100	175	250	—
1849GC MP	—	75.00	100	175	250	—
1850GC MP	—	100	150	250	500	2,000
1851GC MP	—	75.00	100	175	250	—
Revised eagle						

KM# 379.4 ESCUDO
3.3800 g., 0.8750 Gold 0.0951 oz. AGW **Obv:** Facing eagle, snake in beak **Rev:** Hand holding cap on stick, open book

Date	Mintage	VG	F	VF	XF	Unc
1845Go PM	—	65.00	80.00	125	200	—
1849Go PF	—	65.00	80.00	125	200	—
1851Go PF	—	65.00	80.00	125	200	—
1853Go PF	—	65.00	80.00	125	200	—
1860Go PF	—	75.00	125	200	300	—
1862Go YE	—	65.00	80.00	125	200	600

KM# 379.5 ESCUDO
3.3800 g., 0.8750 Gold 0.0951 oz. AGW **Obv:** Facing eagle, snake in beak **Obv. Legend:** REPUBLICA MEXICANA. **Rev:** Hand holding cap on stick, open book

Date	Mintage	VG	F	VF	XF	Unc
1825Mo JM/FM	—	60.00	70.00	100	150	350
1825Mo JM	—	60.00	70.00	100	150	—
1827/6Mo JM	—	60.00	70.00	100	150	—
1827Mo JM	—	60.00	70.00	100	150	—
1830/29Mo JM	—	60.00	70.00	100	150	—
1831Mo JM	—	60.00	75.00	125	175	550
1832Mo JM	—	60.00	75.00	125	175	—
1833Mo MJ	—	60.00	70.00	100	150	—
1834Mo ML	—	60.00	75.00	125	175	—
1841Mo ML	—	60.00	75.00	125	175	—
1843Mo MM	—	60.00	75.00	125	175	875
1845Mo MF	—	60.00	70.00	100	150	—
1846/5Mo MF	—	60.00	70.00	100	150	—
1848Mo GC	—	60.00	75.00	125	175	—
1850Mo GC	—	60.00	75.00	125	175	—
1856/4Mo GF	—	60.00	70.00	100	150	—
1856/5Mo GF	—	60.00	70.00	100	150	—
1856Mo GF	—	60.00	70.00	100	150	—
1858Mo FH	—	60.00	75.00	125	175	—
1859Mo FH	—	60.00	75.00	125	175	750
1860Mo TH	—	60.00	75.00	125	175	—
1861Mo CH	—	60.00	75.00	125	175	1,000
1862Mo CH	—	60.00	75.00	125	175	—
1863Mo TH	—	60.00	70.00	100	150	—
1869Mo CH	—	60.00	75.00	125	175	650

KM# 379.6 ESCUDO
3.3800 g., 0.8750 Gold 0.0951 oz. AGW **Obv:** Facing eagle, snake in beak **Rev:** Hand holding cap on stick, open book **Note:** Struck at Zacatecas Mint, mint mark Zs.

Date	Mintage	VG	F	VF	XF	Unc
1853Zs OM	—	100	125	200	300	—

Date	Mintage	VG	F	VF	XF	Unc
1860/59Zs VL V is inverted A	—	75.00	100	200	350	—
1860Zs VL	—	75.00	100	150	200	—
1862Zs VL	—	75.00	100	150	200	—

KM# 380.3 2 ESCUDOS
6.7700 g., 0.8750 Gold 0.1904 oz. AGW **Obv:** Facing eagle, snake in beak **Obv. Legend:** REPUBLICA MEXICANA. **Rev:** Hand holding cap on stick, open book **Rev. Legend:** LIBERTAD...

Date	Mintage	VG	F	VF	XF	Unc
1835Ga FS	—	125	160	225	325	—
1836/5Ga JG	—	145	200	400	500	—
1839/5Ga JG	—	—	—	—	—	—
1839Ga JG	—	125	150	200	285	—
1840Ga MC	—	125	150	200	285	—
1841Ga MC	—	125	165	250	400	—
1847/6Ga JG	—	125	160	225	300	—
1848/7Ga JG	—	125	160	225	300	—
1850/40Ga JG	—	125	150	200	285	—
1851Ga JG	—	125	150	200	285	—
1852Ga JG	—	125	160	225	325	—
1853Ga JG	—	125	150	200	285	—
1854/2Ga JG	—	—	—	—	—	—
1858Ga JG	—	125	150	200	285	—
1859/8Ga JG	—	125	160	225	300	—
1859Ga JG	—	125	160	225	300	—
1860/50Ga JG	—	125	160	225	300	—
1860Ga JG	—	125	160	225	300	750
1861/59Ga JG	—	125	150	200	285	—
1861/0Ga JG	—	125	150	200	285	—
1863/2Ga JG	—	125	160	225	300	800
1863/1Ga JG	—	125	150	200	285	—
1870Ga IC	—	125	150	200	285	—

KM# 380.4 2 ESCUDOS
6.7700 g., 0.8750 Gold 0.1904 oz. AGW **Obv:** Facing eagle, snake in beak **Rev:** Hand holding cap on stick, open book

Date	Mintage	VG	F	VF	XF	Unc
1844GC MP	—	250	450	1,000	2,000	—
1845GC MP	—	750	1,250	2,000	3,000	—
1846GC MP	—	750	1,250	2,000	3,000	—
1847GC MP	—	500	1,000	2,000	3,000	—
1848GC MP	—	150	200	400	600	—
1849GC MP	—	750	1,250	—	—	—
1850GC MP	—	250	450	1,000	2,000	—

KM# 380.5 2 ESCUDOS
6.7700 g., 0.8750 Gold 0.1904 oz. AGW **Obv:** Facing eagle, snake in beak **Rev:** Hand holding cap on stick, open book

Date	Mintage	VG	F	VF	XF	Unc
1845Go PM	—	125	160	250	400	—
1849Go PF	—	125	160	250	400	—
1853Go PF	—	150	300	650	1,000	—
1856Go PF	—	—	—	—	—	—
1859Go PF	—	150	300	650	1,000	—
1860/59Go PF	—	—	—	—	—	—
1860Go PF	—	125	160	250	400	—
1862Go YE	—	125	160	250	400	—

KM# 380 2 ESCUDOS
6.7700 g., 0.8750 Gold 0.1904 oz. AGW **Obv:**
Facing eagle, snake in beak **Obv. Legend:**
REPUBLICA MEXICANA. **Rev:** Hand holding cap on
stick, open book

Date	Mintage	VG	F	VF	XF	Unc
1846C CE	—	125	160	225	325	—
1847C CE	—	125	160	225	325	—
1848C CE	—	125	160	225	325	—
1852C CE	—	125	160	225	325	—
1854C CE	—	125	175	250	375	—
1856/4C CE	—	125	175	250	375	—
1857C CE	—	125	160	225	325	—

KM# 380.1 2 ESCUDOS
6.7700 g., 0.8750 Gold 0.1904 oz. AGW **Obv:**
Facing eagle, snake in beak **Obv. Legend:**
REPUBLICA MEXICANA. **Rev:** Hand holding cap on
stick, open book **Rev. Legend:** LIBERTAD...

Date	Mintage	VG	F	VF	XF	Unc
1833Do RM	—	300	450	700	1,200	—
1837/4Do RM	—	—	—	—	—	—
1837Do RM	—	—	—	—	—	—
1844Do RM	—	275	400	600	1,000	—

KM# 380.7 2 ESCUDOS
6.7700 g., 0.8750 Gold 0.1904 oz. AGW **Obv:**
Facing eagle, snake in beak **Obv. Legend:**
REPUBLICA MEXICANA **Rev:** Hand holding cap on
stick, open book **Rev. Legend:** LIBERTAD...

Date	Mintage	VG	F	VF	XF	Unc
1825Mo JM	—	125	150	200	285	—
1827/6Mo JM	—	125	150	200	285	—
1827Mo JM	—	125	150	200	285	—
1830/29Mo JM	—	125	150	200	285	—
1831Mo JM	—	125	150	200	285	—
1833Mo ML	—	125	150	200	285	—
1841Mo ML	—	125	150	200	285	—
1844Mo MF	—	125	150	200	285	—
1845Mo MF	—	125	150	200	285	—
1846Mo MF	—	140	200	400	600	—
1848Mo GC	—	125	150	200	285	—
1850Mo GC	—	125	150	200	285	—
1856/5Mo GF	—	125	150	200	285	—
1856Mo GF	—	125	150	200	285	—
1858Mo FH	—	125	150	200	285	—
1859Mo FH	—	125	150	200	285	—
1861Mo TH	—	125	150	200	285	—
1861Mo CH	—	125	150	200	300	—

Date	Mintage	VG	F	VF	XF	Unc
1862Mo CH	—	125	150	200	300	—
1863Mo TH	—	125	150	200	300	750
1868Mo PH	—	125	150	200	300	—
1869Mo CH	—	125	150	200	300	—

KM# 380.8 2 ESCUDOS
6.7700 g., 0.8750 Gold 0.1904 oz. AGW **Obv:**
Facing eagle, snake in beak **Obv. Legend:**
REPUBLICA MEXICANA. **Rev:** Hand holding cap on
stick, open book **Rev. Legend:** LA LIBERTAD...

Date	Mintage	VG	F	VF	XF	Unc
1860Zs VL	—	150	300	600	1,200	—
1862Zs VL	—	250	500	800	1,200	—
1864Zs MO	—	150	300	600	1,200	—

KM# 380.2 2 ESCUDOS
6.7700 g., 0.8750 Gold 0.1904 oz. AGW **Obv:**
Facing eagle, snake in beak **Obv. Legend:**
REPUBLICA MEXICANA. **Rev:** Hand holding cap on
stick, open book **Rev. Legend:** LIBERTAD...

Date	Mintage	VG	F	VF	XF	Unc
1828EoMo LF	—	700	1,000	1,750	3,000	—

KM# 380.6 2 ESCUDOS
6.7700 g., 0.8750 Gold 0.1904 oz. AGW **Obv:**
Facing eagle, snake in beak **Rev:** Hand holding cap
on stick, open book

Date	Mintage	VG	F	VF	XF	Unc
1861Ho FM	—	500	1,000	1,500	2,200	—

KM# 381 4 ESCUDOS
13.5400 g., 0.8750 Gold 0.3809 oz. AGW **Obv:**
Facing eagle, snake in beak **Obv. Legend:**
REPUBLICA MEXICANA. **Rev:** Hand holding cap on
stick, open book **Rev. Legend:** LA LIBERTAD...

Date	Mintage	VG	F	VF	XF	Unc
1846C CE	—	1,200	1,700	—	—	—
1847C CE	—	400	650	850	1,500	—
1848C CE	—	600	900	1,250	2,000	—

KM# 381.1 4 ESCUDOS

13.5400 g., 0.8750 Gold 0.3809 oz. AGW **Obv:**
Facing eagle, snake in beak **Obv. Legend:**
REPUBLICA MEXICANA. **Rev:** Hand holding cap on
stick, open book **Rev. Legend:** LA LIBERTAD....

Date	Mintage	VG	F	VF	XF	Unc
1832Do RM/LR Rare	—	—	—	—	—	—
1832Do RM	—	600	900	1,250	2,000	—
1833Do RM/RL Rare	—	—	—	—	—	—
1852Do JMR Rare	—	—	—	—	—	—

KM# 381.3 4 ESCUDOS

13.5400 g., 0.8750 Gold 0.3809 oz. AGW **Obv:**
Facing eagle, snake in beak **Obv. Legend:**
REPUBLICA MEXICANA **Rev:** Hand holding cap on
stick, open book **Rev. Legend:** LA LIBERTAD...

Date	Mintage	VG	F	VF	XF	Unc
1844GC MP	—	400	650	850	1,350	—
1845GC MP	—	350	500	700	1,000	—
1846GC MP	—	400	650	850	1,350	—
1848GC MP	—	400	650	850	1,350	—
1850GC MP	—	500	750	1,000	1,600	—

KM# 381.4 4 ESCUDOS

13.5400 g., 0.8750 Gold 0.3809 oz. AGW **Obv:**
Facing eagle, snake in beak **Obv. Legend:**
REPUBLICA MEXICANA. **Rev:** Hand holding cap on
stick, open book **Rev. Legend:** LA LIBERTAD...

Date	Mintage	VG	F	VF	XF	Unc
1829/8Go MJ	—	250	300	450	850	—
1829Go JM	—	250	300	450	850	—
1829Go MJ	—	250	300	450	850	—
1831Go MJ	—	250	300	450	850	—
1832Go MJ	—	250	300	450	850	—
1833Go MJ	—	250	325	500	900	—
1834Go PJ	—	265	450	650	1,000	—
1835Go PJ	—	265	450	650	1,000	—
1836Go PJ	—	250	325	500	900	—

Date	Mintage	VG	F	VF	XF	Unc
1837Go PJ	—	250	325	500	900	2,750
1838Go PJ	—	250	325	500	900	—
1839Go PJ	—	265	450	650	1,000	—
1840Go PJ	—	250	325	550	1,000	—
1841Go PJ	—	265	450	650	1,000	—
1845Go PM	—	250	325	500	900	—
1847/5Go YE	—	265	450	650	1,000	—
1847Go PM	—	265	450	650	1,000	—
1849Go PF	—	265	450	650	1,000	—
1851Go PF	—	265	450	650	1,000	—
1852Go PF	—	250	325	500	900	—
1855Go PF	—	250	325	500	900	—
1857/5Go PF	—	250	325	500	900	—
1858/7Go PF	—	250	325	500	900	—
1858Go PF	—	250	325	500	900	—
1859/7Go PF	—	265	450	650	1,000	—
1860Go PF	—	275	475	750	1,200	—
1862Go YE	—	250	325	500	900	—
1863Go YF	—	250	325	500	900	—

KM# 381.6 4 ESCUDOS

13.5400 g., 0.8750 Gold 0.3809 oz. AGW **Obv:**
Facing eagle, snake in beak **Obv. Legend:**
REPUBLICA MEXICANA. **Rev:** Hand holding cap on
stick, open book **Rev. Legend:** LA LIBERTAD...

Date	Mintage	VG	F	VF	XF	Unc
1825Mo JM	—	250	325	525	950	—
1827/6Mo JM	—	250	325	500	900	—
1829Mo JM	—	250	350	650	1,000	—
1831Mo JM	—	250	350	650	1,000	—
1832Mo JM	—	275	475	750	1,200	—
1844Mo MF	—	250	350	650	1,000	—
1850Mo GC	—	250	350	650	1,000	—
1856Mo GF	—	250	325	500	900	—
1857/6Mo GF	—	250	325	500	900	—
1857Mo GF	—	250	325	500	900	—
1858Mo FH	—	250	350	650	1,000	—
1859/8Mo FH	—	250	350	650	1,000	—
1861Mo CH	—	400	800	1,200	1,750	—
1863Mo CH	—	250	350	650	1,000	2,000
1868Mo PH	—	250	325	500	900	—
1869Mo CH	—	250	325	500	900	1,500

KM# 381.8 4 ESCUDOS

13.5400 g., 0.8750 Gold 0.3809 oz. AGW **Obv:**
Facing eagle, snake in beak **Obv. Legend:**
REPUBLICA MEXICANA. **Rev:** Hand holding cap on
stick, open book **Rev. Legend:** LA LIBERTAD...

Date	Mintage	VG	F	VF	XF	Unc
1860Zs VL Rare	—	—	—	—	—	—
1862Zs VL	—	750	1,250	2,250	3,750	—

Note: American Numismatic Rarities Eliasberg sale 4-05,
MS-64 realized $18,400.

KM# 381.2 4 ESCUDOS

13.5400 g., 0.8750 Gold 0.3809 oz. AGW **Obv:**
Facing eagle, snake in beak **Obv. Legend:**
REPUBLICA MEXICANA. **Rev:** Hand holding cap on
stick, open book **Rev. Legend:** LA LIBERTAD...

Date	Mintage	VG	F	VF	XF	Unc
1844Ga MC	—	500	750	1,000	1,600	—
1844Ga JG	—	400	650	850	1,350	—

KM# 381.5 4 ESCUDOS

13.5400 g., 0.8750 Gold 0.3809 oz. AGW **Obv:**
Facing eagle, snake in beak **Rev:** Hand holding cap
on stick, open book

Date	Mintage	VG	F	VF	XF	Unc
1861Ho FM	—	1,000	1,500	2,500	4,000	—

KM# 381.7 4 ESCUDOS

13.5400 g., 0.8750 Gold 0.3809 oz. AGW **Obv:**
Facing eagle, snake in beak **Obv. Legend:**
REPUBLICA MEXICANA. **Rev:** Hand holding cap on
stick, open book **Rev. Legend:** LA LIBERTAD EN
LA LEY... **Note:** Mint mark O, Oa.

Date	Mintage	VG	F	VF	XF	Unc
1861O FR	—	1,500	2,500	4,000	7,000	—

KM# 383 8 ESCUDOS

27.0700 g., 0.8750 Gold 0.7615 oz. AGW **Obv:**
Facing eagle, snake in beak **Obv. Legend:**
REPUBLICA MEXICANA **Rev:** Hand holding cap on
stick, open book **Rev. Legend:** LA LIBERTAD...

Date	Mintage	F	VF	XF	Unc	BU
1864A PG	—	700	1,250	2,500	—	—
1866A DL	—	—	—	7,500	—	—
1868/7A DL	—	2,000	3,500	5,500	—	—
1869A DL	—	—	4,000	6,000	—	—
1870A DL	—	—	2,500	5,000	—	—
1872A AM Rare	—	—	—	—	—	—

KM# 383.1 8 ESCUDOS

27.0700 g., 0.8750 Gold 0.7615 oz. AGW **Obv:**
Facing eagle, snake in beak **Obv. Legend:**
REPUBLICA MEXICANA **Rev:** Hand holding cap on
stick, open book **Rev. Legend:** LA LIBERTAD....

Date	Mintage	F	VF	XF	Unc	BU
1841Ca RG	—	550	750	1,250	1,750	—
1842Ca RG	—	500	600	1,000	1,500	—
1843Ca RG	—	500	600	1,000	1,500	—
1844Ca RG	—	500	600	1,000	1,500	—
1845Ca RG	—	500	600	1,000	1,500	—
1846Ca RG	—	650	1,250	1,500	2,000	—
1847Ca RG	—	1,000	2,500	—	—	—
1848Ca RG	—	500	600	1,000	1,500	—
1849Ca RG	—	500	600	1,000	1,500	—
1850/40Ca RG	—	500	600	1,000	1,500	—
1851/41Ca RG	—	500	600	1,000	1,500	—
1852/42Ca RG	—	500	600	1,000	1,500	—
1853/43Ca RG	—	500	600	1,000	1,500	—
1854/44Ca RG	—	500	600	1,000	1,500	—
1855/43Ca RG	—	500	600	1,000	1,500	—
1856/46Ca RG	—	525	650	1,250	1,750	—
1857Ca JC/RG	—	500	550	800	1,250	—
1858Ca JC	—	500	550	800	1,250	—
1858Ca BA/RG	—	500	550	800	1,250	—
1859Ca JC/RG	—	500	550	800	1,250	—
1860Ca JC/RG	—	500	600	1,000	1,500	—
1861Ca JC	—	500	550	800	1,250	—
1862Ca JC	—	500	550	800	1,250	—
1863Ca JC	—	600	1,000	1,750	2,250	—
1864Ca JC	—	550	750	1,250	1,750	—
1865Ca JC	—	750	1,500	2,500	3,500	—
1866Ca JC	—	500	500	1,000	1,500	—
1866Ca FP	—	650	1,250	2,000	2,500	—
1866Ca JG	—	500	600	1,000	1,500	—
1867Ca JG	—	500	550	800	1,250	—
1868Ca JG Concave wings	—	500	550	800	1,250	—
1869Ca MM Regular eagle	—	500	550	800	1,250	—
1870/60Ca MM	—	500	550	750	1,250	—
1871/61Ca MM	—	500	550	750	1,250	—

KM# 383.2 8 ESCUDOS

27.0700 g., 0.8750 Gold 0.7615 oz. AGW **Obv:**
Facing eagle, snake in beak **Obv. Legend:**
REPUBLICA MEXICANA. **Rev:** Hand holding cap on
stick, open book **Rev. Legend:** LA LIBERTAD...

Date	Mintage	F	VF	XF	Unc	BU
1846C CE	—	500	600	1,000	1,750	—

Date	Mintage	F	VF	XF	Unc	BU
1847C CE	—	500	550	800	1,250	—
1848C CE	—	500	600	1,000	1,750	—
1849C CE	—	500	550	750	1,250	—
1850C CE	—	500	550	750	1,250	—
1851C CE	—	500	550	800	1,250	—
1852C CE	—	500	550	800	1,250	—
1853/1C CE	—	500	550	750	1,200	—
1854C CE	—	500	550	750	1,200	—
1855/4C CE	—	500	500	1,000	1,750	—
1855C CE	—	500	550	800	1,250	—
1856C CE	—	500	550	750	1,200	—
1857C CE	—	500	550	750	1,200	—
1857C CE	—	—	—	—	—	—
Note: Without periods after C's						
1858C CE	—	500	550	750	1,200	—
1859C CE	—	500	550	750	1,200	—
1860/58C CE	—	500	550	800	1,250	—
1860C CE	—	500	550	800	1,250	—
1860C PV	—	500	550	750	1,200	—
1861C PV	—	500	550	800	1,250	—
1861C CE	—	500	550	800	1,250	—
1862C CE	—	500	550	800	1,250	—
1863C CE	—	500	550	800	1,250	—
1864C CE	—	500	550	750	1,200	—
1865C CE	—	500	550	750	1,200	—
1866/5C CE	—	500	550	750	1,200	—
1866C CE	—	500	550	750	1,200	—
1867C CB Error	—	500	550	750	1,200	—
1867C CE/CB	—	500	550	750	1,200	—
1868C CB Error	—	500	550	750	1,200	—
1869C CE	—	500	550	750	1,200	—
1870C CE	—	500	550	800	1,250	—

Date	Mintage	F	VF	XF	Unc	BU
1843/33Do RM	—	550	750	1,250	2,000	—
1843/1Do RM	—	500	550	800	1,250	—
1843Do RM	—	500	550	800	1,250	—
1844/34Do RM/RL	—	600	1,000	1,500	2,500	—
1844Do RM	—	550	800	1,250	2,000	—
1845/36Do RM	—	500	650	1,000	1,750	—
1845Do RM	—	500	650	1,000	1,750	—
1846Do RM	—	500	550	800	1,250	—
1847/37Do RM	—	500	550	800	1,250	—
1848/37Do RM	—	—	—	—	—	—
1848/38Do CM	—	500	550	800	1,250	—
1849/39Do CM	—	500	550	800	1,250	—
1849Do J.M.R. Rare	—	—	—	—	—	—
1850Do .JMR.	—	500	750	1,250	2,000	—
1851Do JMR	—	500	750	1,250	2,000	—
1852/1Do JMR	—	500	800	1,250	2,000	—
1852Do CP	—	500	800	1,250	2,000	—
1853Do CP	—	500	800	1,250	2,000	—
1854Do CP	—	500	650	1,000	1,750	—
1855/4Do CP	—	500	550	800	1,250	—
1855Do CP	—	500	550	800	1,250	—
1856Do CP	—	500	600	900	1,650	—
1857Do CP	—	500	550	800	1,250	—
Note: French style eagle, 1832-57						
1857Do CP	—	500	550	800	1,250	—
Note: Mexican style eagle						
1858Do CP	—	500	600	900	1,650	—
1859Do CP	—	500	550	800	1,250	—
1860/59Do CP	—	500	750	1,250	2,200	—
1861/0Do CP	—	500	650	1,000	1,750	—
1862/52Do CP	—	500	550	800	1,250	—
1862/1Do CP	—	500	550	800	1,250	—
1862Do CP	—	500	550	800	1,250	—
1863/53Do CP	—	500	550	800	1,250	—
1864Do LT	—	500	550	800	1,250	2,000
1865/4Do LT	—	600	1,000	1,650	2,750	—
1866/4Do CM	—	1,250	2,000	2,500	—	—
1866Do CM	—	500	650	1,000	1,750	—
1867/56Do CP	—	500	650	1,000	1,750	—
1867/4Do CP	—	500	550	800	1,250	—
1868/4Do CP/LT	—	—	—	—	—	—
1869Do CP	—	650	1,250	1,750	2,750	—
1870Do CP	—	500	650	1,000	1,750	—

KM# 383.3 8 ESCUDOS
27.0700 g., 0.8750 Gold 0.7615 oz. AGW **Obv:** Facing eagle, snake in beak **Obv. Legend:** REPUBLICA MEXICANA **Rev:** Hand holding cap on stick, open book **Rev. Legend:** LA LIBERTAD....

Date	Mintage	F	VF	XF	Unc	BU
1832Do RM	—	500	1,750	2,000	3,000	—
1833Do RM/RL	—	500	550	800	1,250	—
1834Do RM	—	500	550	800	1,250	—
1835Do RM	—	500	550	800	1,250	—
1836Do RM/RL	—	500	550	800	1,250	—
1836Do RM	—	500	550	800	1,250	—
Note: M on snake						
1837Do RM	—	500	550	800	1,250	—
1838/6Do RM	—	500	550	800	1,250	—
1838Do RM	—	500	550	800	1,250	—
1839Do RM	—	500	550	750	1,250	2,000
1840/30Do RM/RL	—	500	650	1,000	1,750	—
1841/0Do RM	—	500	550	750	1,250	—
1841/30Do RM	—	550	750	1,250	2,000	—
1841/31Do RM	—	500	550	800	1,250	—
1841/34Do RM	—	500	550	800	1,250	—
1841Do RM/RL	—	500	550	800	1,250	—
1842/32Do RM	—	500	550	800	1,250	—

KM# 383.4 8 ESCUDOS
27.0700 g., 0.8750 Gold 0.7615 oz. AGW **Obv:** Facing eagle, snake in beak **Obv. Legend:** REPUBLICA MEXICANA **Rev:** Hand holding cap on stick, open book **Rev. Legend:** LA LIBERTAD...

Date	Mintage	F	VF	XF	Unc	BU
1828EoMo LF Rare	—	—	—	—	—	—
1829EoMo LF	—	3,500	5,500	8,500	—	—

KM# 383.5 8 ESCUDOS
27.0700 g., 0.8750 Gold 0.7615 oz. AGW **Obv:**
Facing eagle, snake in beak **Obv. Legend:**
REPUBLICA MEXICANA **Rev:** Hand holding cap on
stick, open book **Rev. Legend:** LA LIBERTAD...

Date	Mintage	F	VF	XF	Unc	BU
1825Ga FS	—	600	1,000	1,250	1,750	—
1826Ga FS	—	600	1,000	1,250	1,750	—
1830Ga FS	—	600	1,000	1,250	1,750	—
1836Ga FS	—	750	1,500	2,000	3,000	—
1836Ga JG	—	1,000	2,500	3,500	—	—
1837Ga JG	—	1,000	2,500	3,500	—	—
1840Ga MC Rare	—	—	—	—	—	—
1841/31Ga MC	—	1,000	2,500		—	—
1841Ga MC	—	850	1,650	2,250	—	—
1842Ga JG Rare	—	—	3,000	5,000	—	—
1843Ga MC	—	—	2,500	6,500	—	—
1845Ga MC Rare	—	—	—	—	—	—
1847Ga JG	—	2,250	—	—	—	—
1849Ga JG	—	600	1,000	1,250	1,750	—
1850Ga JG	—	550	850	1,100	1,650	—
1851Ga JG	—	1,000	2,500	3,500	—	—
1852/1Ga JG	—	600	1,000	1,250	1,750	—
1855Ga JG	—	1,000	2,500	3,500	—	—
1856Ga JG	—	550	850	1,100	1,650	—
1857Ga JG	—	550	850	1,100	1,650	—
1861/0Ga JG	—	600	1,000	1,250	1,750	—
1861Ga JG	—	500	700	1,200	1,750	—
1863/1Ga JG	—	600	1,000	1,250	1,750	—
1866Ga JG	—	550	850	1,100	1,650	—

KM# 383.6 8 ESCUDOS
27.0700 g., 0.8750 Gold 0.7615 oz. AGW **Obv:**
Facing eagle, snake in beak **Obv. Legend:**
REPUBLICA MEXICANA **Rev:** Hand holding cap on
stick, open book **Rev. Legend:** LA LIBERTAD...

Date	Mintage	F	VF	XF	Unc	BU
1844GC MP	—	550	750	1,250	2,000	—
1845GC MP	—	550	750	1,250	2,000	—
Note: Eagle's tail square						
1845GC MP	—	550	750	1,250	2,000	—
Note: Eagle's tail round						
1846GC MP	—	500	650	1,000	1,750	—
Note: Eagle's tail square						
1846GC MP	—	500	650	1,000	1,750	—
Note: Eagle's tail round						
1847GC MP	—	500	650	1,000	1,750	—
1848GC MP	—	550	750	1,250	2,000	—

Date	Mintage	F	VF	XF	Unc	BU
1849GC MP	—	550	750	1,250	2,000	—
1850GC MP	—	500	650	1,000	1,750	—
1851GC MP	—	500	650	1,000	1,750	—
1852GC MP	—	550	750	1,250	2,000	—

KM# 383.7 8 ESCUDOS
27.0700 g., 0.8750 Gold 0.7615 oz. AGW **Obv:**
Facing eagle, snake in beak **Obv. Legend:**
REPUBLICA MEXICANA **Rev:** Hand holding cap on
stick, open book **Rev. Legend:** LA LIBERTAD...

Date	Mintage	F	VF	XF	Unc	BU
1828Go MJ	—	750	1,750	2,250	3,000	—
1829Go MJ	—	650	1,500	2,000	2,750	—
1830Go MJ	—	500	550	750	1,000	—
1831Go MJ	—	650	1,500	2,000	2,750	—
1832Go MJ	—	550	1,000	1,500	2,500	—
1833Go MJ	—	500	550	700	1,000	—
1834Go PJ	—	500	550	700	1,000	—
1835Go PJ	—	500	550	700	1,000	—
1836Go PJ	—	500	650	900	1,250	—
1837Go PJ	—	500	650	900	1,250	—
1838/7Go PJ	—	500	550	700	1,000	—
1838Go PJ	—	500	550	800	1,200	—
1839/8Go PJ	—	500	550	700	1,000	—
1839Go PJ	—	500	550	800	1,200	—
Note: Regular eagle						
1840Go PJ	—	500	550	700	1,000	—
Note: Concave wings						
1841Go PJ	—	500	550	700	1,000	—
1842Go PJ	—	500	550	600	900	—
1842Go PM	—	500	550	700	1,000	—
1843Go PM	—	500	550	700	1,000	—
Note: Small eagle						
1844/3Go PM	—	500	650	900	1,250	—
1844Go PM	—	500	550	650	1,000	—
1845Go PM	—	500	550	700	1,000	—
1846/5Go PM	—	500	550	800	1,200	—
1846Go PM	—	500	550	700	1,000	—
1847Go PM	—	500	550	900	1,250	—
1848/7Go PM	—	500	550	700	1,000	—
1848Go PM	—	500	550	700	1,000	—
1848Go PF	—	500	550	700	1,000	—
1849Go PF	—	500	550	600	950	—
1850Go PF	—	500	550	600	950	—
1851Go PF	—	500	550	700	1,000	—
1852Go PF	—	500	550	650	1,000	—
1853Go PF	—	500	550	650	1,000	—
1854Go PF	—	500	550	700	1,000	—
Note: Eagle of 1853						
1854Go PF	—	500	550	700	1,000	—
Note: Eagle of 1855						
1855/4Go PF	—	500	550	700	1,000	—
1855Go PF	—	500	550	700	1,000	—
1856Go PF	—	500	550	700	1,000	—
1857Go PF	—	500	550	700	1,000	—
1858Go PF	—	500	550	700	1,000	—
1859Go PF	—	500	550	600	900	—
1860/50Go PF	—	500	550	600	900	—
1860/59Go PF	—	500	550	700	1,100	—
1860Go PF	—	500	550	700	1,100	—
1861/0Go PF	—	500	550	600	850	—
1861Go PF	—	500	550	600	850	—
1862/1Go YE	—	500	550	700	1,000	—
1862Go YE	—	500	550	650	950	—

Date	Mintage	F	VF	XF	Unc	BU
1862Go YF	—	—	—	—	—	—
1863/53Go YF	—	500	550	700	1,000	2,500
1863Go PF	—	500	550	700	1,000	—
1867/57Go YF/PF	—	500	550	700	1,000	—
1867Go YF	—	500	550	650	950	—
1868/58Go YF	—	500	550	700	1,000	1,750
1870Go FR	—	500	550	600	900	—

KM# 383.8   8 ESCUDOS
27.0700 g., 0.8750 Gold 0.7615 oz. AGW **Obv:**
Facing eagle, snake in beak **Obv. Legend:**
REPUBLICA MEXICANA. **Rev:** Hand holding cap on
stick, open book **Rev. Legend:** LA LIBERTAD...

Date	Mintage	F	VF	XF	Unc	BU
1863Ho FM	—	550	700	1,000	2,000	—
1864Ho FM	—	650	1,250	1,750	2,750	—
1864Ho PR/FM	—	550	700	1,000	2,000	—
1865Ho FM/PR	—	600	800	1,250	2,500	—
1867/57Ho PR	—	550	700	1,000	2,500	—
1868Ho PR	—	600	800	1,250	2,500	—
1868Ho PR/FM	—	600	800	1,250	2,500	—
1869Ho PR/FM	—	550	700	1,000	2,000	—
1869Ho PR	—	550	700	1,000	2,000	—
1870Ho PR	—	600	800	1,250	2,750	5,500
1871/0Ho PR	—	600	800	1,250	2,500	—
1871Ho PR	—	600	800	1,250	2,500	—
1872/1Ho PR	—	650	1,250	1,750	2,750	—
1873Ho PR	—	550	700	1,000	2,000	—

KM# 383.10   8 ESCUDOS
27.0700 g., 0.8750 Gold 0.7615 oz. AGW **Obv:**
Facing eagle, snake in beak **Obv. Legend:**
REPUBLICA MEXICANA **Rev:** Hand holding cap on
stick, open book **Rev. Legend:** LA LIBERTAD...

Date	Mintage	F	VF	XF	Unc	BU
1858Oa AE	—	2,000	3,000	4,000	6,000	—
1859O AE	—	1,000	2,500	3,750	5,500	—
1860O AE	—	1,000	2,500	3,750	5,500	—
1861O FR	—	600	850	1,250	2,750	—
1862O FR	—	600	850	1,250	2,750	—
1863O FR	—	600	850	1,250	2,750	—
1864O FR	—	600	850	1,250	2,750	—
1867O AE	—	600	850	1,250	2,750	—
1868O AE	—	600	850	1,250	2,750	—
1869O AE	—	600	850	1,250	2,750	—

KM# 383.11   8 ESCUDOS
27.0700 g., 0.8750 Gold 0.7615 oz. AGW **Obv:**
Facing eagle, snake in beak **Obv. Legend:**
REPUBLICA MEXICANA **Rev:** Hand holding cap on
stick, open book **Rev. Legend:** LA LIBERTAD...

Date	Mintage	F	VF	XF	Unc	BU
1858Zs MO	—	550	750	1,000	2,000	—
1859Zs MO	—	500	550	600	1,000	—
1860/59Zs VL/MO	—	2,000	3,000	4,000	—	—
1860/9Zs MO	—	550	750	1,000	2,000	—
1860Zs MO	—	500	550	700	1,100	—
1861/0Zs VL	—	500	550	700	1,100	—
1861Zs VL	—	500	550	700	1,100	3,000
1862Zs VL	—	500	550	700	1,150	—
1863Zs VL	—	500	550	750	1,200	—
1863Zs MO	—	500	550	700	1,100	—
1864Zs MO	—	750	1,000	1,500	3,500	—
1865Zs MO	—	750	1,000	1,600	3,750	—
1868Zs JS	—	500	600	800	1,250	—
1868Zs YH	—	500	600	800	1,250	—
1869Zs YH	—	500	600	800	1,250	—
1870Zs YH	—	500	600	800	1,250	—
1871Zs YH	—	500	600	800	1,250	—

KM# 383.9   8 ESCUDOS
27.0700 g., 0.8750 Gold 0.7615 oz. AGW **Obv:**
Facing eagle, snake in beak **Obv. Legend:**
REPUBLICA MEXICANA **Rev:** Hand holding cap on
stick, open book **Rev. Legend:** LA LIBERTAD...
Note: Formerly reported 1825/3 JM is merely a
reworked 5.

Date	Mintage	F	VF	XF	Unc	BU
1824Mo JM	—	600	1,000	1,250	2,000	—
Note: Large book reverse						
1825Mo JM	—	500	550	700	1,000	2,000
Note: Small book reverse						
1826/5Mo JM	—	750	1,750	2,250	3,000	—
1827/6Mo JM	—	500	550	700	1,000	—
1827Mo JM	—	500	550	700	1,000	—
1828Mo JM	—	500	550	700	1,000	—
1829Mo JM	—	500	550	700	1,000	—
1830Mo JM	—	500	550	700	1,000	—
1831Mo JM	—	500	550	700	1,000	—
1832/1Mo JM	—	500	550	700	1,000	—
1832Mo JM	—	500	550	700	1,000	—
1833Mo MJ	—	550	750	1,000	1,500	—
1833Mo ML	—	500	550	650	1,000	—
1834Mo ML	—	550	750	1,000	1,500	—

Date	Mintage	F	VF	XF	Unc	BU
1835/4Mo ML	—	600	1,000	1,250	2,000	—
1836Mo ML	—	500	550	650	1,000	—
1836Mo MF	—	550	750	1,200	2,000	—
1837/6Mo ML	—	500	550	650	1,000	—
1838Mo ML	—	500	550	650	1,000	—
1839Mo ML	—	500	550	650	1,000	—
1840Mo ML	—	500	550	650	1,000	—
1841Mo ML	—	500	550	650	1,000	—
1842/1Mo ML	—	—	—	—	—	—
1842Mo ML	—	500	550	650	1,000	—
1842Mo MM	—	—	—	—	—	—
1843Mo MM	—	500	550	650	1,000	—
1844Mo MF	—	500	550	650	1,000	—
1845Mo MF	—	500	550	650	1,000	—
1846Mo MF	—	600	1,000	1,250	2,000	—
1847Mo MF	—	1,000	2,250	—	—	—
1847Mo RC	—	500	600	800	1,250	—
1848Mo GC	—	500	550	650	1,000	—
1849Mo GC	—	500	550	650	1,000	—
1850Mo GC	—	500	550	650	1,000	2,000
1851Mo GC	—	500	550	650	1,000	—
1852Mo GC	—	500	550	650	1,000	—
1853Mo GC	—	500	550	650	1,000	—
1854/44Mo GC	—	500	550	650	1,000	—
1854/3Mo GC	—	500	550	650	1,000	—
1855Mo GF	—	500	550	650	1,000	—
1856/5Mo GF	—	500	550	600	950	—
1856Mo GF	—	500	550	600	950	—
1857Mo GF	—	500	550	600	950	—
1858Mo FH	—	500	550	600	950	—
1859Mo FH	—	550	750	1,000	1,500	—
1860Mo FH	—	500	550	600	950	—
1860Mo TH	—	500	550	600	950	—
1861/51Mo CH	—	500	550	600	950	—
1862Mo CH	—	500	550	600	950	—
1863/53Mo CH	—	500	550	600	950	4,750
1863/53Mo TH	—	500	550	600	950	—
1867Mo CH	—	500	550	600	950	—
1868Mo CH	—	500	550	600	950	—
1868Mo PH	—	500	550	600	950	—
1869Mo CH	—	500	550	600	950	—

EMPIRE OF MAXIMILIAN

RULER
Maximilian, Emperor, 1864-1867
MINT MARKS
Refer To Republic Coinage
MONETARY SYSTEM
100 Centavos = 1 Peso (8 Reales)

MILLED COINAGE

100 Centavos = 1 Peso

KM# 384   CENTAVO
Copper   **Ruler:** Maximilian **Obv:** Crowned facing eagle, snake In beak **Obv. Legend:** IMPERIO MEXICANO **Rev:** Value and date within wreath

Date	Mintage	F	VF	XF	Unc	BU
1864M	—	40.00	75.00	250	1,250	—

KM# 385   5 CENTAVOS
1.3537 g., 0.9030 Silver 0.0393 oz. ASW   **Ruler:** Maximilian

Date	Mintage	F	VF	XF	Unc	BU
1864G	90,000	17.50	35.00	85.00	320	—
1865G	—	20.00	30.00	65.00	300	—
1866G	—	75.00	150	300	2,000	—

KM# 385.1   5 CENTAVOS
1.3537 g., 0.9030 Silver 0.0393 oz. ASW   **Ruler:** Maximilian

Date	Mintage	F	VF	XF	Unc	BU
1864M	—	12.50	20.00	55.00	300	—
1866/4M	—	25.00	40.00	75.00	425	—
1866M	—	20.00	35.00	65.00	400	—

KM# 385.2   5 CENTAVOS
1.3537 g., 0.9030 Silver 0.0393 oz. ASW   **Ruler:** Maximilian

Date	Mintage	F	VF	XF	Unc	BU
1864P	—	150	400	1,500	2,500	—

KM# 385.3   5 CENTAVOS
1.3537 g., 0.9030 Silver 0.0393 oz. ASW   **Ruler:** Maximilian **Obv:** Crowned facing eagle, snake in beak **Obv. Legend:** IMPERIO MEXICANO **Rev:** Value and date within wreath

Date	Mintage	F	VF	XF	Unc	BU
1865Z	—	25.00	45.00	150	450	—

KM# 386   10 CENTAVOS
2.7073 g., 0.9030 Silver 0.0786 oz. ASW   **Ruler:** Maximilian **Obv:** Crowned facing eagle, snake in beak **Obv. Legend:** IMPERIO MEXICANO **Rev:** Value and date within wreath

Date	Mintage	F	VF	XF	Unc	BU
1864G	45,000	20.00	45.00	90.00	325	—
1865G	—	30.00	60.00	110	375	—

KM# 386.1   10 CENTAVOS
2.7073 g., 0.9030 Silver 0.0786 oz. ASW   **Ruler:** Maximilian **Obv:** Crowned facing eagle, snake in beak **Obv. Legend:** IMPERIO MEXICANO **Rev:** Value and date within wreath **Note:** Struck at Mexico City Mint, mint mark M.

Date	Mintage	F	VF	XF	Unc	BU
1864M	—	15.00	25.00	55.00	285	—
1866/4M	—	25.00	35.00	70.00	320	—
1866/5M	—	25.00	40.00	85.00	375	—
1866M	—	25.00	35.00	75.00	375	—

KM# 386.2   10 CENTAVOS
2.7073 g., 0.9030 Silver 0.0786 oz. ASW   **Ruler:** Maximilian

Date	Mintage	F	VF	XF	Unc	BU
1864P	—	70.00	150	300	700	—

KM# 386.3 10 CENTAVOS
2.7073 g., 0.9030 Silver 0.0786 oz. ASW **Ruler:** Maximilian

Date	Mintage	F	VF	XF	Unc	BU
1865Z	—	22.50	55.00	165	525	—

KM# 387 50 CENTAVOS
13.5365 g., 0.9030 Silver 0.3930 oz. ASW **Ruler:** Maximilian **Obv:** Head right, with beard **Obv. Legend:** MAXIMILIANO EMPERADOR **Rev:** Crowned oval shield **Rev. Legend:** IMPERIO MEXICANO

Date	Mintage	F	VF	XF	Unc	BU
1866Mo	31,000	40.00	95.00	200	750	—

KM# 388 PESO
27.0700 g., 0.9030 Silver 0.7859 oz. ASW **Ruler:** Maximilian **Obv:** Head right, with beard **Obv. Legend:** MAXIMILIANO EMPERADOR **Rev:** Crowned arms with supporters

Date	Mintage	F	VF	XF	Unc	BU
1866Go	—	300	450	950	3,500	—

KM# 388.1 PESO
27.0700 g., 0.9030 Silver 0.7859 oz. ASW **Ruler:** Maximilian **Obv:** Head right, with beard **Obv. Legend:** MAXIMILIANO EMPERADOR **Rev:** Crowned arms with supporters

Date	Mintage	F	VF	XF	Unc	BU
1866Mo	2,148,000	30.00	45.00	135	400	—
1867Mo	1,238,000	40.00	65.00	185	450	—

KM# 388.2 PESO
27.0700 g., 0.9030 Silver 0.7859 oz. ASW **Ruler:** Maximilian **Obv:** Head right, with beard **Rev:** Crowned arms with supporters

Date	Mintage	F	VF	XF	Unc	BU
1866Pi	—	45.00	90.00	275	775	—

KM# 389 20 PESOS
33.8400 g., 0.8750 Gold 0.9519 oz. AGW **Ruler:** Maximilian **Obv:** Head right, with beard **Obv. Legend:** MAXIMILIANO EMPERADOR **Rev:** Crowned arms with supporters

Date	Mintage	F	VF	XF	Unc	BU
1866Mo	8,274	500	950	1,450	3,000	—

REPUBLIC
SECOND

DECIMAL COINAGE
100 CENTAVOS = 1 PESO

KM# 390 CENTAVO
Copper, 25 mm. **Obv:** Seated Liberty **Rev:** Thick wreath.

Date	Mintage	F	VF	XF	Unc	BU
1863Mo	—	10.00	30.00	70.00	500	—
Note: Flat-top 3, reeded edge						
1863Mo	—	13.50	32.50	75.00	500	—
Note: Round-top 3, reeded edge						
1863Mo	—	13.50	32.50	75.00	500	—
Note: Round-top 3, plain edge						

KM# 390.1 CENTAVO
Copper, 26.5 mm. **Obv:** Seated liberty **Obv. Legend:** LIBERTAD V REFORMA. **Rev:** Value and date within wreath

Date	Mintage	F	VF	XF	Unc	BU
1863SLP	1,024,999	15.00	32.50	75.00	400	—

KM# 391 CENTAVO
Copper **Obv:** Facing eagle, snake in beak **Rev:** Value and date within wreath **Edge:** Reeded.

Date	Mintage	F	VF	XF	Unc	BU
1875As Rare	—	—	—	—	—	—
1876As	50,000	100	200	300	650	—
1880As	—	25.00	50.00	200	500	—
1881As	—	30.00	60.00	125	350	—

KM# 391.1 CENTAVO
Copper **Obv:** Facing eagle, snake in beak **Obv. Legend:** REPUBLICA MEXICANA **Rev:** Value and date within wreath **Edge:** Plain

Date	Mintage	F	VF	XF	Unc	BU
1874Cn	266,000	12.50	17.50	35.00	250	—
1875/4Cn	153,000	15.00	20.00	45.00	250	—
1875Cn	Inc. above	10.00	15.00	25.00	250	—
1876Cn	154,000	5.00	8.00	15.00	200	—
1877/6Cn	993,000	7.50	11.50	17.50	200	—
1877Cn	Inc. above	6.00	9.00	15.00	200	—
1880Cn	142,000	7.50	10.00	12.50	200	—
1881Cn	167,000	7.50	10.00	25.00	200	—
1897Cn	300,000	2.50	5.00	12.00	50.00	—
Note: Large N in mint mark						
1897Cn	Inc. above	2.50	5.00	9.00	45.00	—
Note: Small N in mint mark						

KM# 391.2 CENTAVO
Copper **Obv:** Facing eagle, snake in beak **Rev:** Value and date within wreath

Date	Mintage	F	VF	XF	Unc	BU
1879Do	110,000	10.00	35.00	60.00	200	—
1880Do	69,000	40.00	90.00	175	500	—
1891Do	—	8.00	25.00	50.00	200	—
1891Do/Mo	—	8.00	25.00	50.00	200	—

KM# 391.3 CENTAVO
Copper **Obv:** Facing eagle, snake in beak **Obv. Legend:** REPUBLICA MEXICANA **Rev:** Value and date within wreath

Date	Mintage	F	VF	XF	Unc	BU
1872Ga	263,000	15.00	30.00	60.00	225	—
1873Ga	333,000	6.00	9.00	25.00	200	—
1874Ga	76,000	15.00	25.00	50.00	200	—
1875Ga	—	10.00	15.00	30.00	200	—
1876Ga	303,000	3.00	6.00	17.50	200	—
1877Ga	108,000	4.00	6.00	20.00	200	—
1878Ga	543,000	4.00	6.00	15.00	200	—
1881/71Ga	975,000	7.00	9.00	20.00	—	—
1881Ga	Inc. above	7.00	9.00	20.00	200	—
1889Ga/Mo	—	3.50	5.00	25.00	200	—
1890Ga	—	4.00	7.50	20.00	200	—

KM# 391.4 CENTAVO
Copper **Obv:** Facing eagle, snake in beak **Rev:** Value and date within wreath

Date	Mintage	F	VF	XF	Unc	BU
1874Go	—	20.00	40.00	80.00	250	—
1875Go	190,000	11.50	20.00	60.00	200	—
18/6Go	—	125	200	350	750	—
1877Go Rare	—	—	—	—	—	—
1878Go	576,000	8.00	11.00	30.00	200	—
1880Go	890,000	6.00	10.00	25.00	200	—

KM# 391.5 CENTAVO
Copper **Obv:** Facing eagle, snake in beak **Obv. Inscription:** REPUBLICA MEXICANA **Rev:** Value and date within wreath

Date	Mintage	F	VF	XF	Unc	BU
1875Ho	3,500	450	—	—	—	—
1876Ho	8,508	50.00	100	225	500	—
1880Ho Short H, round O	102,000	7.50	15.00	50.00	200	—
1880Ho Tall H, oval O	Inc. above	7.50	15.00	50.00	200	—
1881Ho	459,000	5.00	10.00	50.00	200	—

KM# 391.7 CENTAVO
Copper **Obv:** Facing eagle, snake in beak **Obv. Legend:** REPUBLICA MEXICANA **Rev:** Value and date within wreath

Date	Mintage	F	VF	XF	Unc	BU
1872Oa	16,000	300	500	1,200	—	—
1873Oa	11,000	350	600	—	—	—
1874Oa	4,835	450	—	—	—	—
1875Oa	2,860	500	—	—	—	—

KM# 391.8 CENTAVO
Copper **Obv:** Facing eagle, snake in beak **Obv. Legend:** REPUBLICA MEXICANA **Rev:** Value and date within wreath

Date	Mintage	F	VF	XF	Unc	BU
1871Pi Rare	—	—	—	—	—	—
1877Pi	249,000	15.00	50.00	200	—	—
1878Pi	751,000	12.50	25.00	50.00	200	—
1878	—	—	—	—	—	—
Note: Pp error mintmark - rare						
1891Pi/Mo	—	10.00	50.00	150	300	—
1891Pi	—	8.00	25.00	125	250	—

KM# 391.9 CENTAVO
Copper **Obv:** Facing eagle, snake in beak **Rev:** Value and date within wreath **Note:** Struck at Zacatecas Mint, mint mark Zs.

Date	Mintage	F	VF	XF	Unc	BU
1872Zs	55,000	22.50	30.00	100	300	—
1873Zs	1,460,000	4.00	8.00	25.00	150	—
1874/3Zs	685,000	5.50	11.00	30.00	250	—
1874Zs	Inc. above	4.00	8.00	25.00	200	—
1875/4Zs	200,000	8.50	17.00	45.00	250	—
1875Zs	Inc. above	7.00	14.00	35.00	200	—
1876Zs	—	5.00	10.00	25.00	200	—

Date	Mintage	F	VF	XF	Unc	BU
1877Zs	—	50.00	125	300	750	—
1878Zs	—	4.50	9.00	25.00	200	—
1880Zs	100,000	5.00	10.00	30.00	200	—
1881Zs	1,200,000	4.25	8.00	25.00	150	—

KM# 391.6 CENTAVO
7.4000 g., Copper **Obv:** Facing eagle, snake in beak **Obv. Legend:** REPUBLICA MEXICANA **Rev:** Value and date within wreath **Note:** Varieties exist.

Date	Mintage	F	VF	XF	Unc	BU
1869Mo	1,874,000	7.50	25.00	60.00	200	—
1870/69Mo	1,200,000	10.00	25.00	60.00	225	—
1870Mo	Inc. above	8.00	20.00	50.00	200	—
1871Mo	918,000	8.00	15.00	40.00	200	—
1872/1Mo	1,625,000	6.50	10.00	30.00	200	—
1872Mo	Inc. above	6.00	9.00	25.00	200	—
1873Mo	1,605,000	4.00	7.50	20.00	200	—
1874/3Mo	1,700,000	5.00	7.00	15.00	100	—
1874Mo	Inc. above	3.00	5.50	15.00	100	—
1874Mo	Inc. above	5.00	10.00	25.00	200	—
1875Mo	1,495,000	6.00	8.00	30.00	100	—
1876Mo	1,600,000	3.00	5.50	12.50	100	—
1877Mo	1,270,000	3.00	5.50	13.50	100	—
1878/5Mo	1,900,000	7.50	11.00	22.50	125	—
1878/6Mo	Inc. above	7.50	11.00	22.50	125	—
1878/7Mo	Inc. above	7.50	11.00	20.00	125	—
1878Mo	Inc. above	6.00	9.00	13.50	100	—
1879/8Mo	1,505,000	4.50	6.50	13.50	100	—
1879Mo	Inc. above	3.00	5.50	12.50	75.00	—
1880/70Mo	1,130,000	5.50	7.50	15.00	100	—
1880/72Mo	Inc. above	20.00	50.00	100	250	—
1880/79Mo	Inc. above	15.00	35.00	75.00	175	—
1880Mo	Inc. above	4.25	6.00	12.50	75.00	—
1881Mo	1,060,000	4.50	7.00	15.00	75.00	—
1886Mo	12,687,000	1.50	2.00	10.00	40.00	—
1887Mo	7,292,000	1.50	2.00	10.00	35.00	—
1888/78Mo	9,984,000	2.50	3.00	10.00	30.00	—
1888/7Mo	Inc. above	2.50	3.00	10.00	30.00	—
1888Mo	Inc. above	1.50	2.00	10.00	30.00	—
1889Mo	19,970,000	2.00	3.00	10.00	30.00	—
1890/89Mo	18,726,000	2.50	3.00	12.00	40.00	—
1890/990Mo	Inc. above	2.50	3.00	12.00	40.00	—
1890Mo	Inc. above	1.50	2.00	10.00	30.00	—
1891Mo	14,544,000	1.50	2.00	10.00	30.00	—
1892Mo	12,908,000	1.50	2.00	10.00	30.00	—
1893/2Mo	5,078,000	2.50	3.00	12.00	35.00	—
1893Mo	Inc. above	1.50	2.00	10.00	30.00	—
1894/3Mo	1,896,000	3.00	6.00	15.00	50.00	—
1894Mo	Inc. above	2.00	3.00	12.00	35.00	—
1895/3Mo	3,453,000	3.00	4.50	12.50	35.00	—
1895/85Mo	Inc. above	3.00	6.00	15.00	50.00	—
1895Mo	Inc. above	2.00	3.00	10.00	30.00	—
1896Mo	3,075,000	2.00	3.00	10.00	30.00	—
1897Mo	4,150,000	1.50	2.00	10.00	30.00	—

KM# 392 CENTAVO
Copper-Nickel **Obv:** Crossed bow and quiver above date **Obv. Legend:** REPUBLICA MEXICANA **Rev:** Value within wreath

Date	Mintage	F	VF	XF	Unc	BU
1882Mo	99,955,000	7.50	12.50	17.50	35.00	—
1883Mo	Inc. above	0.50	0.75	1.00	1.50	—

KM# 393 CENTAVO
Copper **Obv:** Facing eagle, snake in beak **Obv. Legend:** REPUBLICA MEXICANA **Rev:** Value and date within wreath **Note:** Varieties exist.

Date	Mintage	F	VF	XF	Unc	BU
1898Mo	1,529,000	4.00	6.00	15.00	50.00	—

KM# 394.1 CENTAVO
2.6100 g., Copper **Obv:** Facing eagle, snake in beak **Obv. Legend:** REPUBLICA MEXICANA **Rev:** Value below date within wreath **Note:** Reduced size. Varieties exist.

Date	Mintage	F	VF	XF	Unc	BU
1899M	51,000	150	175	300	800	—
1900M Wide date	4,010,000	2.50	4.00	8.00	28.00	—
1900M Narrow date	Inc. above	2.50	4.00	8.00	28.00	—
1901M	1,494,000	3.00	8.00	17.50	50.00	—
1902/899M	2,090,000	30.00	60.00	125	225	—
1902M	Inc. above	2.25	4.00	10.00	40.00	—
1903M	8,400,000	1.50	3.00	7.00	20.00	—
1904/3M	10,250,000	1.50	10.00	20.00	55.00	—
1904M	Inc. above	1.50	3.00	8.00	25.00	—
1905M	3,643,000	2.25	4.00	10.00	40.00	—

KM# 394 CENTAVO
Copper **Obv:** National arms **Rev:** Value below date within wreath **Note:** Reduced size. Varieties exist.

Date	Mintage	F	VF	XF	Unc	BU
1901C	220,000	15.00	22.50	35.00	65.00	—
1902C	320,000	15.00	22.50	50.00	90.00	—
1903C	536,000	7.50	12.50	20.00	50.00	—
1904/3C	148,000	35.00	50.00	75.00	125	—
1905C	110,000	100	150	300	600	—

KM# 395 2 CENTAVOS
Copper-Nickel **Obv:** Crossed bow and quiver above date **Obv. Legend:** REPUBLICA MEXICANA **Rev:** Value within wreath

Date	Mintage	F	VF	XF	Unc	BU
1882	50,023,000	2.00	3.00	7.50	15.00	—
1883/2	Inc. above	2.00	3.00	7.50	15.00	—
1883	Inc. above	0.50	0.75	1.00	2.50	—

KM# 396.1 5 CENTAVOS
1.3530 g., 0.9030 Silver 0.0393 oz. ASW **Obv:** Facing eagle, snake in beak **Rev:** Value within wreath

Date	Mintage	F	VF	XF	Unc	BU
1863SLP	—	37.50	135	350	1,200	—

KM# 397 5 CENTAVOS
1.3530 g., 0.9030 Silver 0.0393 oz. ASW **Obv:** Facing eagle, snake in beak **Obv. Legend:** REPUBLICA MEXICANA **Rev:** Radiant cap **Note:** Varieties exist.

Date	Mintage	F	VF	XF	Unc	BU
1867Mo	—	20.00	45.00	110	400	—
1867/3Mo	—	22.50	50.00	125	425	—
1868/7Mo	—	22.50	50.00	150	500	—
1868Mo	—	18.50	42.50	100	400	—

KM# 397.1 5 CENTAVOS
1.3530 g., 0.9030 Silver 0.0393 oz. ASW **Obv:** Facing eagle, snake in beak **Rev:** Radiant cap

Date	Mintage	F	VF	XF	Unc	BU
1868P	Inc. above	20.00	45.00	100	400	—
1868/7P	34,000	25.00	50.00	125	450	—
1869P	14,000	150	300	600	—	—

KM# 396 5 CENTAVOS
1.3530 g., 0.9030 Silver 0.0393 oz. ASW **Obv:** Facing eagle, snake in beak **Obv. Legend:** REPUBLICA MEXICANA **Rev:** Value within wreath

Date	Mintage	F	VF	XF	Unc	BU
1868Ca	—	40.00	65.00	125	450	—
1869Ca	30,000	25.00	40.00	100	400	—
1870/69Ca	—	35.00	55.00	120	425	—
1870Ca	35,000	30.00	50.00	100	400	—

KM# 398.7 5 CENTAVOS
1.3530 g., 0.9030 Silver 0.0393 oz. ASW **Obv:** Facing eagle, snake in beak **Obv. Legend:** REPUBLICA MEXICANA **Rev:** Value within 1/2 wreath **Note:** Mint mark Mo. Varieties exist.

Date	Mintage	F	VF	XF	Unc	BU
1869/8Mo C	40,000	8.00	15.00	40.00	120	—
1870Mo C	140,000	4.00	7.00	20.00	60.00	—
1871Mo C	103,000	9.00	20.00	40.00	100	—
1871Mo M	Inc. above	7.50	12.50	25.00	60.00	—
1872Mo M	266,000	5.00	8.00	20.00	55.00	—
1873Mo M	20,000	40.00	60.00	100	225	—
1874/69Mo M	—	7.50	15.00	30.00	75.00	—
1874Mo M	—	4.00	7.00	17.50	50.00	—
1874/3Mo B	—	5.00	8.00	22.50	55.00	—
1874Mo B	—	5.00	8.00	22.50	55.00	—
1875Mo B	—	4.00	7.00	15.00	50.00	—
1875Mo B/M	—	6.00	9.00	17.50	60.00	—
1876/5Mo B	—	4.00	7.00	15.00	50.00	—
1876Mo B	—	4.00	7.00	12.50	50.00	—
1877/6Mo M	80,000	4.00	7.00	15.00	60.00	—
1877Mo M	Inc. above	4.00	7.00	12.50	60.00	—
1878/7Mo M	100,000	4.00	7.00	15.00	55.00	—
1878Mo M	Inc. above	2.50	5.00	12.50	45.00	—
1879/8Mo M	—	8.00	12.50	22.50	55.00	—

Date	Mintage	F	VF	XF	Unc	BU
1879Mo M	—	4.50	7.00	15.00	50.00	—
1879Mo M 9/ inverted 9	—	10.00	15.00	25.00	75.00	—
1880/76Mo M/B	—	5.00	7.50	15.00	50.00	—
1880/76Mo M	—	5.00	7.50	15.00	50.00	—
1880Mo M	—	4.00	6.00	12.00	40.00	—
1881/0Mo M	180,000	4.00	6.00	10.00	35.00	—
1881Mo M	Inc. above	3.00	4.50	9.00	35.00	—
1886/0Mo M	398,000	2.00	2.75	7.50	25.00	—
1886/1Mo M	Inc. above	2.00	2.75	7.50	25.00	—
1886Mo M	Inc. above	1.75	2.25	6.00	20.00	—
1887Mo m	720,000	1.75	2.00	5.00	20.00	—
1887Mo M/m	Inc. above	1.75	2.00	5.00	20.00	—
1888/7Mo M	1,360,000	2.25	2.50	6.00	20.00	—
1888Mo M	Inc. above	1.75	2.00	5.00	20.00	—
1889/8Mo M	1,242,000	2.25	2.50	6.00	20.00	—
1889Mo M	Inc. above	1.75	2.00	5.00	20.00	—
1890/00Mo M	1,694,000	1.75	2.75	6.00	20.00	—
1890Mo M	Inc. above	1.50	2.00	5.00	20.00	—
1891Mo M	1,030,000	1.75	2.00	5.00	20.00	—
1892Mo M	1,400,000	1.75	2.00	5.00	20.00	—
1892Mo M 9/ inverted 9	Inc. above	2.00	2.75	7.50	20.00	—
1893Mo M	220,000	1.75	2.00	5.00	15.00	—
1894Mo M	320,000	1.75	2.00	5.00	15.00	—
1895Mo M	78,000	3.00	5.00	8.00	25.00	—
1896Mo B	80,000	1.75	2.00	5.00	20.00	—
1897Mo B	160,000	1.75	2.00	5.00	15.00	—

KM# 398.1 5 CENTAVOS
1.3530 g., 0.9030 Silver 0.0393 oz. ASW **Obv:** Facing eagle, snake in beak **Rev:** Value within 1/2 wreath **Note:** Mint mark: *Ca or Ch*.

Date	Mintage	F	VF	XF	Unc	BU
1871* M	14,000	20.00	40.00	100	250	—
1873* M Crude date	—	100	150	250	500	—
1874* M Crude date	—	25.00	50.00	75.00	150	—
1886* M	25,000	7.50	15.00	30.00	100	—
1887* M	37,000	7.50	15.00	30.00	100	—
1887* Ca/MoM	Inc. above	10.00	20.00	40.00	125	—
1888* M	145,000	1.50	3.00	6.00	25.00	—
1889* M	44,000	5.00	10.00	20.00	50.00	—
1890* M	102,000	1.50	3.00	6.00	25.00	—
1891* M	164,000	1.50	3.00	6.00	25.00	—
1892* M	85,000	1.50	3.00	6.00	25.00	—
1892* M/U	—	2.00	4.00	7.50	30.00	—
1892* M 9/ inverted 9	Inc. above	2.00	4.00	7.50	30.00	—
1893* M	133,000	1.50	3.00	6.00	25.00	—
1894* M	108,000	1.50	3.00	6.00	25.00	—
1895* M	74,000	2.00	4.00	7.50	30.00	—

KM# 398 5 CENTAVOS
1.3530 g., 0.9030 Silver 0.0393 oz. ASW **Obv:** Facing eagle, snake in beak **Rev:** Value within 1/2 wreath

Date	Mintage	F	VF	XF	Unc	BU
1874As DL	—	10.00	20.00	40.00	150	—
1875As DL	—	10.00	20.00	40.00	150	—
18/6As L	—	22.00	45.00	70.00	160	—
1878As L	—	250	350	650	—	—
Note: Mule, gold peso reverse						
1879As L	—	40.00	65.00	120	275	—
Note: Mule, gold peso obverse						
1880As L	12,000	55.00	85.00	165	325	—
Note: Mule, gold peso obverse						
1886As L	43,000	12.00	25.00	50.00	165	—
1886As L	Inc. above	55.00	85.00	165	300	—
Note: Mule, gold peso obverse						
1887As L	20,000	25.00	50.00	75.00	165	—
1888As L	32,000	12.00	25.00	50.00	125	—
1889As L	16,000	25.00	50.00	100	200	—
1890As L	30,000	25.00	50.00	85.00	175	—
1891As L	8,000	65.00	125	200	400	—
1892As L	13,000	20.00	40.00	60.00	125	—
1893As L	24,000	10.00	20.00	45.00	90.00	—
1895As L	20,000	10.00	20.00	45.00	90.00	—

KM# 398.2 5 CENTAVOS

1.3530 g., 0.9030 Silver 0.0393 oz. ASW **Obv:** Facing eagle, snake in beak **Rev:** Value within 1/2 wreath

Date	Mintage	F	VF	XF	Unc	BU
1871Cn P	—	125	200	350	—	—
1873Cn P	4,992	50.00	100	200	400	—
1874Cn P	—	25.00	50.00	100	200	—
1875Cn P Rare	—	—	—	—	—	—
1876Cn P	—	25.00	50.00	100	200	—
1886Cn M	10,000	25.00	50.00	100	200	—
1887Cn M	10,000	25.00	50.00	100	200	—
1888Cn M	119,000	1.50	3.00	6.00	30.00	—
1889Cn M	66,000	4.00	7.50	15.00	50.00	—
189/80Cn M	—	2.00	4.00	8.00	40.00	—
1890Cn M	180,000	1.50	3.00	6.00	25.00	—
1890/9Cn M	—	2.00	4.00	8.00	40.00	—
1890Cn D Error	Inc. above	125	175	250	—	—
1891Cn M	87,000	2.00	4.00	7.50	25.00	—
1894Cn M	24,000	4.00	7.50	15.00	40.00	—
1896Cn M	16,000	7.50	12.50	25.00	75.00	—
1897Cn M	223,000	1.50	2.50	5.00	20.00	—

KM# 398.3 5 CENTAVOS

1.3530 g., 0.9030 Silver 0.0393 oz. ASW **Obv:** Facing eagle, snake in beak **Rev:** Value within 1/2 wreath

Date	Mintage	F	VF	XF	Unc	BU
1874Do M	—	100	150	225	500	—
1877Do P	4,795	75.00	125	225	450	—
1878/7Do E/P	4,300	200	300	450	—	—
1879Do B	—	125	200	350	—	—
1880Do B Rare	—	—	—	—	—	—
1881Do P	3,020	300	500	800	—	—
1887Do C	42,000	5.00	8.00	17.50	60.00	—
1888/9Do C	91,000	6.00	10.00	20.00	70.00	—
1888Do C	Inc. above	4.00	7.50	15.00	55.00	—
1889Do C	49,000	3.50	6.00	12.50	50.00	—
1890Do C	136,000	4.00	7.50	15.00	55.00	—
1890Do P	Inc. above	5.00	8.00	17.50	60.00	—
1891/0Do P	48,000	3.50	6.00	12.50	50.00	—
1891Do P	Inc. above	3.00	5.00	10.00	45.00	—
1894Do D	38,000	3.50	6.00	12.50	50.00	—

KM# 398.4 5 CENTAVOS

1.3530 g., 0.9030 Silver 0.0393 oz. ASW **Obv:** Facing eagle, snake in beak **Rev:** Value within 1/2 wreath

Date	Mintage	F	VF	XF	Unc	BU
1877Ga A	—	15.00	30.00	60.00	150	—
1881Ga S	156,000	4.00	7.50	15.00	60.00	—
1886Ga S	87,000	2.00	4.00	7.50	25.00	—
1888Ga S Large G	262,000	2.00	4.00	10.00	30.00	—
1888Ga S Small G	Inc. above	2.00	4.00	10.00	30.00	—
1889Ga S	178,000	1.50	3.00	7.50	25.00	—
1890Ga S	68,000	4.00	7.50	12.50	35.00	—
1891Ga S	50,000	4.00	6.50	10.00	35.00	—
1892Ga S	78,000	2.00	4.00	7.50	25.00	—
1893Ga S	44,000	4.00	7.50	14.00	45.00	—

KM# 398.5 5 CENTAVOS

1.3530 g., 0.9030 Silver 0.0393 oz. ASW **Obv:** Facing eagle, snake in beak **Obv. Legend:** REPUBLICA MEXICANA **Rev:** Value within 1/2 wreath

Date	Mintage	F	VF	XF	Unc	BU
1869Go S	80,000	15.00	30.00	75.00	175	—
1871Go S	100,000	5.00	10.00	25.00	75.00	—
1872Go S	30,000	30.00	60.00	125	250	—
1873Go S	40,000	30.00	60.00	125	250	—
1874Go S	—	7.00	12.00	25.00	75.00	—
1875Go S	—	8.00	15.00	30.00	75.00	—
1876Go S	—	8.00	15.00	30.00	75.00	—
1877Go S	—	7.00	12.00	20.00	75.00	—
1878/7Go S	20,000	8.00	15.00	25.00	75.00	—
1879Go S	—	8.00	15.00	25.00	75.00	—

Date	Mintage	F	VF	XF	Unc	BU
1880Go S	55,000	15.00	30.00	60.00	200	—
1881/0Go S	160,000	5.00	8.00	17.50	60.00	—
1881Go S	Inc. above	4.00	6.00	12.00	45.00	—
1886Go R	230,000	1.50	3.00	6.00	30.00	—
1887Go R/S	—	1.50	3.00	6.00	30.00	—
1887Go R	230,000	1.50	2.50	5.00	30.00	—
1888Go R	320,000	1.50	2.50	5.00	20.00	—
1889Go R/S	—	4.00	6.00	12.00	45.00	—
1889Go R	60,000	4.00	6.00	12.00	45.00	—
1890/5Go R/S	—	1.50	3.00	6.00	30.00	—
1890Go R	250,000	1.50	2.50	5.00	20.00	—
1891/0Go R	168,000	1.80	3.00	6.00	30.00	—
1891Go R	Inc. above	1.50	2.50	5.00	20.00	—
1892Go R	138,000	1.50	3.00	6.00	25.00	—
1893Go R	200,000	1.25	2.50	5.00	20.00	—
1894Go R	200,000	1.25	2.50	5.00	20.00	—
1896Go R	525,000	1.25	2.00	4.00	15.00	—
1896Go R/S	—	1.50	3.00	6.00	25.00	—
1897Go R	596,000	1.50	2.00	4.00	15.00	—
1898Go R	—	—	—	—	—	—

KM# 398.6 5 CENTAVOS

1.3530 g., 0.9030 Silver 0.0393 oz. ASW **Obv:** Facing eagle, snake in beak **Rev:** Value within 1/2 wreath

Date	Mintage	F	VF	XF	Unc	BU
1874/69Ho R	—	125	225	350	—	—
1874Ho R	—	100	200	325	—	—
1878/7Ho A Rare	22,000	—	—	—	—	—
1878Ho A	Inc. above	20.00	40.00	80.00	175	—
1878Ho A	Inc. above	40.00	80.00	150	300	—
Note: Mule, gold peso obverse						
1880Ho A	43,000	7.50	15.00	30.00	75.00	—
1886Ho G	44,000	5.00	10.00	20.00	75.00	—
1887Ho G	20,000	5.00	10.00	20.00	75.00	—
1888Ho G	12,000	7.50	15.00	30.00	85.00	—
1889Ho G	67,000	3.00	6.00	12.50	40.00	—
1890Ho G	50,000	3.00	6.00	12.50	40.00	—
1891Ho G	46,000	3.00	6.00	12.50	40.00	—
1893Ho G	84,000	2.50	5.00	10.00	30.00	—
1894Ho G	68,000	2.00	4.00	10.00	30.00	—

KM# 398.9 5 CENTAVOS

1.3530 g., 0.9030 Silver 0.0393 oz. ASW **Obv:** Facing eagle, snake in beak **Rev:** Value within 1/2 wreath **Note:** Varieties exist.

Date	Mintage	F	VF	XF	Unc	BU
1869Pi S	—	300	400	500	—	—
1870Pi G/MoC Rare	20,000	150	250	400	—	—
1870Pi O	Inc. above	200	300	450	—	—
1871Pi O Rare	5,400	—	—	—	—	—
1872Pi O	—	75.00	100	175	400	—
1873Pi Rare	5,000	—	—	—	—	—
1874Pi H	—	30.00	50.00	100	225	—
1875Pi H	—	7.50	12.50	30.00	75.00	—
1876Pi H	—	10.00	20.00	45.00	100	—
1877Pi H	—	7.50	12.50	20.00	60.00	—
1878/7Pi H Rare	—	—	—	—	—	—
1878Pi H	—	60.00	90.00	150	300	—
1879 H	—	200	400	—	—	—
1880Pi H Rare	6,200	—	—	—	—	—
1881Pi H Rare	4,500	—	—	—	—	—
1886Pi R	33,000	12.50	25.00	50.00	125	—
1887/0Pi R	169,000	4.00	7.50	15.00	45.00	—
1887Pi R	Inc. above	3.00	5.00	10.00	32.00	—
1888Pi R	210,000	2.00	4.00	9.00	30.00	—
1889/7Pi R	197,000	2.50	5.00	10.00	32.00	—
1889Pi R	Inc. above	2.00	4.00	9.00	30.00	—
1890Pi R	221,000	2.00	3.00	6.00	25.00	—
1891/89Pi R/B	176,000	2.00	4.00	8.00	25.00	—
1891/0Pi R/B	—	2.00	4.00	8.00	25.00	—
1891Pi R	Inc. above	2.00	3.00	6.00	20.00	—
1892/89Pi R	182,000	2.00	4.00	8.00	25.00	—
1892/0Pi R	Inc. above	2.00	4.00	8.00	25.00	—
1892Pi R	Inc. above	2.00	3.00	6.00	20.00	—
1893Pi R	41,000	5.00	10.00	20.00	60.00	—

KM# 398.10   5 CENTAVOS
1.3530 g., 0.9030 Silver 0.0393 oz. ASW **Obv:** Facing eagle, snake in beak **Rev:** Value within 1/2 wreath

Date	Mintage	F	VF	XF	Unc
1870Zs H	40,000	12.50	25.00	50.00	125
1871Zs H	40,000	12.50	25.00	50.00	125
1872Zs H	40,000	12.50	25.00	50.00	125
1873/2Zs H	20,000	35.00	65.00	125	275
1873Zs H	Inc. above	25.00	50.00	100	250
1874Zs H	—	7.50	12.50	25.00	75.00
1874Zs A	—	40.00	75.00	150	300
1875Zs A	—	7.50	12.50	25.00	75.00
1876Zs A	—	50.00	75.00	150	500
1876/5Zs S	—	15.00	30.00	60.00	150
1876Zs S	—	12.50	25.00	50.00	125
1877Zs S	—	3.00	6.00	12.00	40.00
1878Zs S	60,000	3.00	6.00	12.00	40.00
1879/8Zs S	—	3.00	6.00	15.00	50.00
1879Zs S	—	3.00	6.00	12.00	40.00
1880/79Zs S	130,000	6.00	10.00	20.00	60.00
1880Zs S	Inc. above	5.00	8.00	16.00	45.00
1881Zs S	210,000	2.50	5.00	10.00	35.00
1886/4Zs S	360,000	6.00	10.00	20.00	60.00
1886Zs S	Inc. above	2.00	3.00	6.00	20.00
1886Zs Z	Inc. above	5.00	10.00	25.00	65.00
1887Zs Z	400,000	2.00	3.00	6.00	25.00
1888/7Zs Z	500,000	2.00	3.00	6.00	25.00
1888Zs Z	Inc. above	2.00	3.00	6.00	25.00
1889Zs Z	520,000	2.00	3.00	6.00	25.00
1889Zs Z 9/inverted 9	Inc. above	2.00	3.00	6.00	25.00
1889Zs Z/MoM	Inc. above	2.00	3.00	6.00	25.00
1890Zs Z	580,000	1.75	2.50	5.00	20.00
1890Zs Z/MoM	Inc. above	2.00	3.00	6.00	25.00
1890Zs ZsZ 9/8	—	2.00	3.00	6.00	25.00
1890Zs ZsZ 0/9 Z/M	—	2.00	3.00	6.00	25.00
1891Zs Z	420,000	1.75	2.50	5.00	20.00
1892Zs Z	346,000	1.75	2.50	5.00	20.00
1893Zs Z	258,000	1.75	2.50	5.00	20.00
1894Zs ZoZ Error	Inc. above	2.00	4.00	8.00	30.00
1894Zs Z	228,000	1.75	2.50	5.00	20.00
1895Zs Z	260,000	1.75	2.50	5.00	20.00
1895/4Zs ZsZ	—	2.00	3.00	6.00	25.00
1896Zs Z	200,000	1.75	2.50	5.00	20.00
1896Zs 6/inverted 6	Inc. above	2.00	3.00	6.00	25.00
1897/6Zs Z	200,000	2.00	3.00	6.00	25.00
1897Zs Z	Inc. above	1.75	2.50	5.00	20.00

KM# 398.8   5 CENTAVOS
1.3530 g., 0.9030 Silver 0.0393 oz. ASW **Obv:** Facing eagle, snake in beak **Obv. Legend:** REPUBLICA MEXICANA **Rev:** Value within 1/2 wreath

Date	Mintage	F	VF	XF	Unc	BU
1890Oa E Rare	48,000	—	—	—	—	—
1890Oa N	Inc. above	65.00	125	200	350	—

KM# 399   5 CENTAVOS
Copper-Nickel **Obv:** Crossed bow and quiver above date **Obv. Legend:** REPUBLICA MEXICANA **Rev:** Value within wreath

Date	Mintage	F	VF	XF	Unc	BU
1882	Inc. above	0.50	1.00	2.50	7.50	—
1883	Inc. above	25.00	50.00	80.00	250	—

KM# 400.2   5 CENTAVOS
1.3530 g., 0.9027 Silver 0.0393 oz. ASW **Obv:** Facing eagle, snake in beak **Rev:** Value within 1/2 wreath

Date	Mintage	F	VF	XF	Unc	BU
1898Mo M	80,000	2.00	4.00	7.00	25.00	—
1899Mo M	168,000	1.75	2.50	4.50	15.00	—
1900/800Mo M	300,000	4.50	6.50	10.00	30.00	—
1900Mo M	Inc. above	1.75	2.50	4.50	15.00	—
1901Mo M	100,000	1.75	2.50	4.50	15.00	—
1902Mo M	144,000	1.25	2.00	3.75	12.00	—
1902/1Mo MoM	—	1.75	3.00	7.00	16.50	—
1903Mo M	500,000	1.25	2.00	3.75	12.00	—
1904/804Mo M	1,090,000	1.75	3.50	8.50	16.50	18.50
1904/94Mo M	Inc. above	1.75	3.75	9.00	16.50	18.50
1904Mo M	Inc. above	1.75	3.00	6.00	15.00	—
1905Mo M	344,000	1.75	3.00	7.00	16.50	—

KM# 400.3   5 CENTAVOS
1.3530 g., 0.9027 Silver 0.0393 oz. ASW **Obv:** Facing eagle, snake in beak **Rev:** Value within 1/2 wreath

Date	Mintage	F	VF	XF	Unc	BU
1898Zs Z	100,000	1.75	2.25	4.50	12.50	—
1899Zs Z	50,000	2.00	3.00	7.00	20.00	—
1900Zs Z	55,000	1.75	2.50	5.00	16.50	—
1901Zs Z	40,000	1.75	2.50	5.00	16.50	—
1902/1Zs Z	34,000	2.00	4.50	9.00	22.50	—
1902Zs Z	Inc. above	1.75	3.75	7.50	18.50	—
1903Zs Z	217,000	1.25	2.00	5.00	12.50	—
1904Zs Z	191,000	1.75	2.50	6.00	16.50	—
1904Zs M	Inc. above	1.75	2.50	6.00	16.50	—
1905Zs M	46,000	2.00	4.50	9.00	22.50	—
1905Zs M	Inc. above	—	—	—	—	—
Repullica; Rare						

KM# 400   5 CENTAVOS
1.3530 g., 0.9027 Silver 0.0393 oz. ASW, 14 mm. **Obv:** Facing eagle, snake in beak **Obv. Legend:** REPUBLICA MEXICANA **Rev:** Value within 1/2 wreath **Note:** Varieties exist.

Date	Mintage	F	VF	XF	Unc	BU
1898Cn M	44,000	1.75	4.00	8.00	20.00	—
1899Cn M	111,000	5.50	8.50	20.00	50.00	—
1899Cn Q	Inc. above	1.75	2.50	4.50	15.00	—
1900/800Cn Q	239,000	3.50	5.00	12.50	30.00	—
1900Cn Q	Inc. above	1.75	3.00	6.00	16.50	—
Note: Round Q, single tail						
1900Cn Q	Inc. above	1.75	3.00	6.00	16.50	—
Note: Narrow C, oval Q						
1900Cn Q	Inc. above	1.75	3.00	6.00	16.50	—
Note: Wide C, oval Q						
1901Cn Q	148,000	1.75	2.50	4.50	15.00	—
1902Cn Q	262,000	1.75	3.00	6.00	16.50	—
Note: Narrow C, heavy serifs						
1902Cn Q	Inc. above	1.75	3.00	6.00	16.50	—
Note: Wide C, light serifs						
1903/1Cn Q	331,000	2.00	3.00	6.00	16.50	20.00
1903Cn Q	Inc. above	1.75	2.50	4.50	15.00	18.00
1903/1898Cn V	Inc. above	3.50	4.50	9.00	22.50	—
1903Cn V	Inc. above	1.75	2.50	4.50	15.00	—
1904Cn H	352,000	1.75	2.25	5.00	16.50	—
1904Cn H 0/9	—	1.75	2.50	5.00	16.50	—
1904Cn H/C	—	1.75	2.50	5.00	16.50	—

KM# 400.1   5 CENTAVOS
1.3530 g., 0.9027 Silver 0.0393 oz. ASW **Obv:** Facing eagle, snake in beak **Rev:** Value within 1/2 wreath **Note:** Varieties exist.

Date	Mintage	F	VF	XF	Unc	BU
1898Go R	180,000	7.50	15.00	30.00	75.00	—
Note: Mule, gold peso obverse						
1899Go R	260,000	1.75	2.50	4.50	15.00	—
1900Go R	200,000	1.75	2.50	4.50	15.00	—

KM# 402 10 CENTAVOS
2.7070 g., 0.9030 Silver 0.0786 oz. ASW **Obv:** Facing eagle, snake in beak **Rev:** Radiant cap

Date	Mintage	F	VF	XF	Unc	BU
1867/3Mo	—	50.00	100	200	550	—
1867Mo	—	20.00	50.00	150	450	—
1868/7Mo	—	20.00	50.00	175	500	—
1868Mo	—	20.00	55.00	175	500	—

KM# 402.1 10 CENTAVOS
2.7070 g., 0.9030 Silver 0.0786 oz. ASW **Obv:** Facing eagle, snake in beak **Obv. Legend:** REPUBLICA MEXICANA **Rev:** Radiant cap

Date	Mintage	F	VF	XF	Unc	BU
1868/7P	38,000	45.00	90.00	175	650	—
1868P	Inc. above	20.00	40.00	100	550	—
1869/7P	4,900	55.00	125	250	800	—

KM# 401.1 10 CENTAVOS
2.7070 g., 0.9030 Silver 0.0786 oz. ASW **Obv:** Facing eagle, snake in beak **Rev:** Value within wreath **Note:** Previous KM#401.

Date	Mintage	F	VF	XF	Unc	BU
1868/7Ca	—	30.00	60.00	150	550	—
1868Ca	—	30.00	60.00	150	550	—
1869Ca	15,000	25.00	50.00	125	600	—
1870Ca	17,000	22.50	45.00	100	550	—

KM# 401.2 10 CENTAVOS
2.7070 g., 0.9030 Silver 0.0786 oz. ASW **Obv:** Facing eagle, snake in beak **Obv. Legend:** REPUBLICA MEXICANA **Rev:** Value and date within wreath

Date	Mintage	F	VF	XF	Unc	BU
1863SLP	—	75.00	150	275	900	—

KM# 403 10 CENTAVOS
2.7070 g., 0.9030 Silver 0.0786 oz. ASW **Obv:** Facing eagle, snake in beak **Rev:** Value within 1/2 wreath **Note:** Varieties exist.

Date	Mintage	F	VF	XF	Unc	BU
1874As DL	—	20.00	40.00	80.00	175	—
1875As L	—	5.00	10.00	25.00	90.00	—
1876As L	—	10.00	18.00	40.00	110	—
1878/7As L	—	10.00	18.00	45.00	120	—
1878As L	—	5.00	10.00	30.00	100	—
1879As L	—	10.00	18.00	40.00	110	—
1880As L	13,000	10.00	18.00	40.00	110	—
1882As L	22,000	10.00	18.00	40.00	110	—
1883As L	8,520	25.00	50.00	100	225	—
1884As L	—	7.50	12.50	35.00	100	—
1885As L	15,000	7.50	12.50	35.00	100	—
1886As L	45,000	7.50	12.50	35.00	100	—
1887As L	15,000	7.50	12.50	35.00	100	—
1888As L	38,000	7.50	12.50	35.00	100	—
1889As L	20,000	7.50	12.50	35.00	100	—
1890As L	40,000	7.50	12.50	35.00	100	—
1891As L	38,000	7.50	12.50	35.00	100	—
1892As L	57,000	5.00	10.00	25.00	90.00	—
1893As L	70,000	10.00	18.00	40.00	110	—

Note: An 1891 As L over 1889 HoG exists which was evidently produced at the Alamos Mint using dies sent from the Hermosillo Mint

KM# 403.4 10 CENTAVOS
2.7070 g., 0.9030 Silver 0.0786 oz. ASW **Obv:** Facing eagle, snake in beak **Rev:** Value within 1/2 wreath **Note:** Varieties exist.

Date	Mintage	F	VF	XF	Unc	BU
1871Ga C	4,734	75.00	125	200	500	—
1873/1Ga C	25,000	10.00	15.00	35.00	150	—
1873Ga C	Inc. above	10.00	15.00	35.00	150	—
1874Ga C	—	10.00	15.00	35.00	150	—
1877Ga A	—	10.00	15.00	30.00	150	—
1881Ga S	115,000	5.00	10.00	25.00	150	—
1883Ga B	90,000	4.00	8.00	15.00	90.00	—
1884Ga H	—	3.00	5.00	10.00	90.00	—
1884Ga B/S	—	6.00	12.50	25.00	90.00	—
1884Ga B	—	5.00	10.00	20.00	90.00	—
1885Ga H	93,000	3.00	5.00	10.00	90.00	—
1886Ga S	151,000	2.50	4.00	9.00	90.00	—
1887Ga S	162,000	1.50	3.00	6.00	90.00	—
1888Ga S	225,000	1.50	3.00	6.00	90.00	—
1888Ga GaS/HoG	Inc. above	1.50	3.00	6.00	90.00	—
1889Ga S	310,000	1.50	3.00	6.00	40.00	—
1890Ga S	303,000	1.50	3.00	6.00	40.00	—
1891Ga S	199,000	5.00	10.00	20.00	45.00	—
1892Ga S	329,000	1.50	3.00	6.00	40.00	—
1893Ga S	225,000	1.50	3.00	6.00	40.00	—
1894Ga S	243,000	3.00	6.00	12.00	40.00	—
1895Ga S	150,000	1.50	3.00	6.00	40.00	—

KM# 403.5 10 CENTAVOS
2.7070 g., 0.9030 Silver 0.0786 oz. ASW **Obv:** Facing eagle, snake in beak **Rev:** Value within 1/2 wreath **Note:** Varieties exist.

Date	Mintage	F	VF	XF	Unc	BU
1869Go S	7,000	20.00	40.00	80.00	200	—
1871/0Go S	60,000	15.00	25.00	50.00	125	—
1872Go S	60,000	15.00	25.00	50.00	125	—
1873Go S	50,000	15.00	25.00	50.00	125	—
1874Go S	—	15.00	25.00	50.00	125	—
1875Go S	—	250	350	500	800	—
1876Go S	—	10.00	20.00	40.00	100	—
1877Go S	—	80.00	120	200	400	—
1878/7Go S	10,000	10.00	20.00	45.00	110	—
1878Go S	Inc. above	7.50	12.00	20.00	75.00	—
1879Go S	—	7.50	12.00	20.00	75.00	—
1880Go S	—	100	200	300	450	—
1881/71Go S	100,000	3.00	5.00	10.00	75.00	—
1881/0Go S	Inc. above	3.50	5.00	10.00	75.00	—
1881Go S	Inc. above	3.00	5.00	10.00	75.00	—
1882/1Go S	40,000	3.00	6.00	12.00	75.00	—
1883Go B	—	3.00	5.00	10.00	75.00	—
1884Go B	—	1.50	3.00	6.00	75.00	—
1884Go S	—	6.00	12.50	25.00	90.00	—
1885Go R	100,000	1.50	3.00	6.00	75.00	—
1886Go R	95,000	3.00	5.00	10.00	75.00	—
1887Go R	330,000	2.50	5.00	10.00	75.00	—
1888Go R	270,000	1.50	3.00	6.00	75.00	—
1889Go R	205,000	2.00	4.00	8.00	75.00	—
1889Go GoR/HoG	Inc. above	3.00	5.00	10.00	75.00	—
1890Go R	270,000	1.50	3.00	6.00	35.00	—
1890Go GoR/CnM	Inc. above	1.50	3.00	6.00	35.00	—
1891Go R/G	—	1.50	3.00	6.00	35.00	—
1891Go R	523,000	1.50	3.00	6.00	35.00	—
1891Go GoR/HoG	Inc. above	1.50	3.00	6.00	35.00	—
1892Go R	440,000	1.50	3.00	6.00	35.00	—
1893/1Go R	389,000	3.00	5.00	10.00	35.00	—
1893Go R	Inc. above	1.50	3.00	6.00	35.00	—
1894Go R	400,000	1.50	2.50	5.00	35.00	—
1895Go R	355,000	1.50	2.50	5.00	35.00	—
1896Go R	190,000	1.50	2.50	5.00	35.00	—
1897Go R	205,000	1.50	2.50	5.00	35.00	—

KM# 403.7 10 CENTAVOS
2.7070 g., 0.9020 Silver 0.0785 oz. ASW **Obv:**
Facing eagle, snake in beak **Obv. Legend:**
REPUBLICA MEXICANA **Rev:** Value within 1/2
wreath **Note:** Varieties exist.

Date	Mintage	F	VF	XF	Unc	BU
1869/8Mo C	30,000	10.00	20.00	40.00	100	—
1869Mo C	Inc. above	8.00	17.50	35.00	90.00	—
1870Mo C	110,000	3.00	7.50	15.00	50.00	—
1871Mo C	84,000	50.00	75.00	125	250	—
1871Mo M	Inc. above	12.00	17.50	45.00	125	—
1872/69Mo M	198,000	10.00	20.00	35.00	100	—
1872Mo M	Inc. above	3.00	7.50	15.00	65.00	—
1873Mo M	40,000	10.00	15.00	30.00	75.00	—
1874Mo M	—	5.00	10.00	20.00	65.00	—
1874Mo M/C	—	5.00	10.00	20.00	65.00	—
1874/64Mo B	—	5.00	10.00	20.00	65.00	—
1874Mo B/M	—	20.00	40.00	60.00	125	—
1874Mo B	—	5.00	10.00	15.00	65.00	—
1875Mo B	—	20.00	40.00	60.00	125	—
1876/5Mo B	—	3.00	5.00	9.00	65.00	—
1876/5Mo B/M	—	3.00	5.00	9.00	65.00	—
1877/6Mo M	—	3.00	5.00	9.00	65.00	—
1877/6Mo M/B	—	3.00	5.00	9.00	65.00	—
1877Mo M	—	3.00	5.00	9.00	65.00	—
1878/7Mo M	100,000	3.00	5.00	9.00	65.00	—
1878Mo M	Inc. above	3.00	5.00	9.00	65.00	—
1879/69Mo M	—	3.00	5.00	9.00	65.00	—
1879Mo M/C	—	3.00	5.00	9.00	65.00	—
1880/79Mo M	—	3.00	5.00	9.00	65.00	—
1881/0Mo M	510,000	3.00	5.00	9.00	35.00	—
1881Mo M	Inc. above	3.00	5.00	9.00	35.00	—
1882/1Mo M	550,000	3.00	5.00	9.00	35.00	—
1882Mo M	Inc. above	3.00	5.00	9.00	35.00	—
1883/2Mo M	250,000	3.00	5.00	9.00	35.00	—
1884Mo M	—	3.00	5.00	9.00	35.00	—
1885Mo M	470,000	3.00	5.00	9.00	35.00	—
1886Mo M	603,000	3.00	5.00	9.00	35.00	—
1887/6Mo M	—	3.00	5.00	9.00	35.00	—
1887Mo M	580,000	3.00	5.00	9.00	35.00	—
1888/7Mo MoM	710,000	3.00	5.00	9.00	35.00	—
1888Mo MoM	Inc. above	3.00	5.00	9.00	35.00	—
1888Mo MOM	Inc. above	3.00	5.00	9.00	35.00	—
1889/8Mo M	622,000	3.00	5.00	9.00	35.00	—
1889Mo M	Inc. above	3.00	5.00	9.00	35.00	—
1890/89Mo M	815,000	3.00	5.00	9.00	35.00	—
1890Mo M	Inc. above	3.00	5.00	9.00	35.00	—
1891Mo M	859,000	1.50	2.50	7.00	25.00	—
1892Mo M	1,030,000	1.50	2.50	7.00	25.00	—
1893Mo M	310,000	1.50	2.50	7.00	25.00	—
1893Mo M/C	Inc. above	1.50	2.50	7.00	25.00	—
1893Mo Mo/Ho M/G	—	1.50	2.50	7.00	25.00	—
1894/3Mo M	—	5.00	10.00	20.00	60.00	—
1894Mo M	350,000	5.00	10.00	20.00	60.00	—
1895Mo M	320,000	1.50	2.50	7.00	25.00	—
1896Mo B/G	340,000	1.50	2.50	7.00	25.00	—
1896Mo M	Inc. above	35.00	70.00	100	150	—
1897Mo M	170,000	1.50	2.50	5.00	20.00	—

KM# 403.9 10 CENTAVOS
2.7070 g., 0.9030 Silver 0.0786 oz. ASW **Obv:**
Facing eagle, snake in beak **Rev:** Value within 1/2
wreath **Note:** Varieties exist.

Date	Mintage	F	VF	XF	Unc	BU
1869/8Pi S Rare	4,000	—	—	—	—	—
1870/69Pi O Rare	18,000	—	—	—	—	—
1870Pi G	Inc. above	125	200	325	600	—
1871Pi O	21,000	50.00	100	150	300	—
1872Pi O	16,000	150	225	350	650	—
1873Pi O Rare	4,750	—	—	—	—	—

Date	Mintage	F	VF	XF	Unc	BU
1874Pi H	—	25.00	50.00	100	200	—
1875Pi H	—	75.00	125	200	400	—
1876Pi H	—	75.00	125	200	400	—
1877Pi H	—	75.00	125	200	400	—
1878Pi H	—	250	500	750	—	—
1879Pi H	—	—	—	—	—	—
1880Pi H	—	150	250	350	—	—
1881Pi H	7,600	250	350	500	—	—
1882Pi H Rare	4,000	—	—	—	—	—
1883Pi H	—	125	200	300	500	—
1884Pi H	—	25.00	50.00	100	200	—
1885Pi H	51,000	25.00	50.00	100	200	—
1885Pi C Rare	Inc. above	—	—	—	—	—
1886Pi C	52,000	15.00	30.00	60.00	150	—
1886Pi R	Inc. above	5.00	10.00	20.00	65.00	—
1887Pi R	118,000	2.50	5.00	10.00	50.00	—
1888Pi R	136,000	2.50	5.00	10.00	50.00	—
1889/8Pi R/G	—	7.50	12.50	20.00	60.00	—
1889/7Pi R	131,000	7.50	12.50	20.00	60.00	—
1890Pi R/G	—	2.00	4.00	8.00	40.00	—
1890Pi R	204,000	1.50	3.00	7.50	40.00	—
1891/89Pi R	163,000	2.50	5.00	10.00	40.00	—
1891Pi R	Inc. above	1.50	3.50	6.00	30.00	—
1892/0Pi R/G	—	2.00	4.00	8.00	40.00	—
1892/0Pi R	200,000	2.00	4.00	8.00	40.00	—
1892Pi R	Inc. above	1.50	2.50	5.00	40.00	—
1892Pi R/G	—	2.00	4.00	8.00	40.00	—
1893Pi R/G	—	1.50	10.00	17.50	60.00	—
1893Pi R	48,000	7.50	10.00	17.50	60.00	—

KM# 403.2 10 CENTAVOS
2.7070 g., 0.9030 Silver 0.0786 oz. ASW **Obv:** Facing
eagle, snake in beak **Rev:** Value within 1/2 wreath

Date	Mintage	F	VF	XF	Unc	BU
1871Cn P Rare	—	—	—	—	—	—
1873Cn P	8,732	20.00	50.00	100	225	—
1881Cn D	9,440	75.00	175	325	500	—
1882Cn D	12,000	75.00	125	200	400	—
1885Cn M	18,000	25.00	50.00	100	200	—
Note: Mule, gold 2-1/2 peso obverse						
1886Cn M	13,000	50.00	100	150	300	—
Note: Mule, gold 2-1/2 peso obverse						
1887Cn M	11,000	20.00	40.00	75.00	175	—
1888Cn M	56,000	5.00	10.00	25.00	125	—
1889Cn M	42,000	5.00	10.00	20.00	75.00	—
1890Cn M	132,000	2.00	4.00	7.50	75.00	—
1891Cn M	84,000	5.00	10.00	20.00	75.00	—
1892/1Cn M	37,000	4.00	8.00	15.00	75.00	—
1892Cn M	Inc. above	2.50	5.00	10.00	75.00	—
1894Cn M	43,000	2.50	5.00	10.00	75.00	—
1895Cn M	23,000	2.50	5.00	10.00	60.00	—
1896Cn M	121,000	1.50	2.50	5.00	50.00	—

KM# 403.3 10 CENTAVOS
2.7070 g., 0.9030 Silver 0.0786 oz. ASW **Obv:** Facing
eagle, snake in beak **Rev:** Value within 1/2 wreath

Date	Mintage	F	VF	XF	Unc	BU
1878Do E	2,500	100	175	300	600	—
1879Do B Rare	—	—	—	—	—	—
1880/70Do B Rare	—	—	—	—	—	—
1880/79Do B Rare	—	—	—	—	—	—
1884Do C	—	30.00	60.00	100	225	—
1886Do C	13,000	75.00	150	300	500	—
1887Do C	81,000	4.00	8.00	15.00	100	—
1888Do C	31,000	6.00	12.00	30.00	100	—
1889Do C	55,000	4.00	8.00	15.00	100	—
1890Do C	50,000	4.00	8.00	15.00	100	—
1891Do P	139,000	2.00	4.00	8.00	80.00	—
1892Do P	212,000	2.00	4.00	8.00	80.00	—
1892Do D	Inc. above	2.00	4.00	8.00	80.00	—
1893Do D	258,000	2.00	4.00	8.00	80.00	—
1893Do D/C	Inc. above	2.50	5.00	10.00	80.00	—
1894Do D	184,000	1.50	3.00	6.00	80.00	—
1894Do D/C	Inc. above	2.00	4.00	8.00	80.00	—
1895Do D	142,000	1.50	3.00	6.00	80.00	—

KM# 403.6 10 CENTAVOS
2.7070 g., 0.9030 Silver 0.0786 oz. ASW **Obv:** Facing eagle, snake in beak **Rev:** Value within 1/2 wreath

Date	Mintage	F	VF	XF	Unc	BU
1874Ho R	—	30.00	60.00	100	200	—
1876Ho F	3,140	200	300	450	750	—
1878Ho A	—	5.00	10.00	15.00	85.00	—
1879Ho A	—	25.00	50.00	90.00	175	—
1880Ho A	—	3.00	6.00	12.50	85.00	—
1881Ho A	28,000	4.00	7.00	15.00	85.00	—
1882/1Ho A	25,000	5.00	10.00	20.00	85.00	—
1882/1Ho a	Inc. above	6.00	12.50	25.00	85.00	—
1882Ho A	Inc. above	4.00	7.00	15.00	85.00	—
1883Ho	7,000	65.00	100	200	400	—
1884/3Ho M	—	10.00	20.00	40.00	90.00	—
1884Ho A	—	35.00	75.00	150	300	—
1884/3Ho M	—	7.50	15.00	30.00	85.00	—
1884Ho M	—	7.50	15.00	30.00	85.00	—
1885Ho M	21,000	12.50	25.00	50.00	100	—
1886Ho M Rare	10,000	—	—	—	—	—
1886Ho G	Inc. above	7.50	12.50	25.00	85.00	—
1887Ho G	—	25.00	50.00	75.00	150	—
1888Ho G	25,000	6.00	12.50	25.00	85.00	—
1889Ho G	42,000	3.00	6.00	10.00	85.00	—
1890Ho G	48,000	3.00	6.00	10.00	85.00	—
1891/80Ho G	136,000	3.00	6.00	10.00	85.00	—
1891/0Ho G	Inc. above	3.00	6.00	10.00	85.00	—
1891Ho G	Inc. above	3.00	6.00	10.00	85.00	—
1892Ho G	67,000	3.00	6.00	10.00	85.00	—
1893Ho G	67,000	3.00	6.00	10.00	85.00	—

KM# 403.8 10 CENTAVOS
2.7070 g., 0.9030 Silver 0.0786 oz. ASW **Obv:** Facing eagle, snake in beak **Rev:** Value within 1/2 wreath

Date	Mintage	F	VF	XF	Unc	BU
1889Oa E	21,000	200	400	600	—	—
1890Oa N Rare	Inc. above	—	—	—	—	—
1890Oa E	31,000	100	150	250	500	—

KM# 403.10 10 CENTAVOS
2.7070 g., 0.9030 Silver 0.0786 oz. ASW **Obv:** Facing eagle, snake in beak **Obv. Legend:** REPUBLICA MEXICANA **Rev:** Value within 1/2 wreath **Note:** Varieties exist.

Date	Mintage	F	VF	XF	Unc	BU
1870Zs H	20,000	100	150	200	400	—
1871/0Zs H	10,000	—	—	—	—	—
1871Zs H	Inc. above	—	—	—	—	—
1872Zs H	10,000	150	200	275	500	—
1873Zs H	10,000	250	350	600	—	—
1874Zs A	—	200	300	500	—	—
1874/3Zs H	—	50.00	75.00	150	300	—
1875Zs A	—	5.00	10.00	25.00	100	—
1876Zs S	—	100	200	300	500	—
1876Zs A	—	10.00	25.00	50.00	100	—
1877Zs S Small S	—	7.50	12.50	25.00	100	—
1877Zs Regular S over small S	—	7.50	12.50	25.00	100	—
1877Zs S Regular S	—	7.50	12.50	25.00	100	—
1878/7Zs S	30,000	5.00	10.00	20.00	80.00	—
1878Zs S	Inc. above	5.00	10.00	20.00	80.00	—
1879Zs S	—	5.00	10.00	20.00	80.00	—
1880Zs S	—	5.00	10.00	20.00	80.00	—
1881Zs S	Inc. above	3.00	6.00	12.50	50.00	—
1881/0Zs S	120,000	3.00	6.00	12.50	50.00	—
1882/1Zs S	64,000	12.50	25.00	50.00	125	—
1882Zs S	Inc. above	12.50	25.00	50.00	125	—
1883Zs S	Inc. above	2.00	4.00	8.00	50.00	—
1883/73Zs S	102,000	2.00	4.00	8.00	50.00	—
1884/3Zs S	—	2.00	4.00	8.00	50.00	—
1884Zs S	—	2.00	4.00	8.00	50.00	—
1885Zs S	297,000	1.50	2.50	5.00	50.00	—
1885Zs S Small S in mint mark	Inc. above	2.50	4.00	8.00	50.00	—
1885Zs Z	Inc. above	3.50	7.50	15.00	65.00	—

Note: Without assayers initials, error

Date	Mintage	F	VF	XF	Unc	BU
1886Zs S	274,000	1.50	2.50	5.00	30.00	—
1886Zs Z	Inc. above	12.50	25.00	50.00	125	—
1887Zs Z Z Error	Inc. above	3.50	10.00	25.00	100	—
1887Zs ZsZ	233,000	1.50	2.50	5.00	30.00	—
1888Zs Z Z Error	Inc. above	3.50	10.00	25.00	100	—
1888Zs ZsZ	270,000	1.50	2.50	5.00	30.00	—
1889/7Zs Z/S	240,000	4.00	8.00	12.50	40.00	—
1889Zs ZS	Inc. above	1.50	4.00	8.00	30.00	—
1889Zs Z/G	—	1.50	4.00	8.00	30.00	—
1889Zs Z	Inc. above	1.50	2.50	5.00	30.00	—
1890Zs ZsZ	410,000	1.50	2.50	5.00	30.00	—
1890Zs Z Z Error	Inc. above	3.75	10.00	25.00	100	—
1891Zs ZsZ Double s	Inc. above	2.00	4.00	7.00	30.00	—
1891Zs Z	1,105,000	1.50	2.50	5.00	30.00	—
1892Zs Z	1,102,000	1.50	2.50	5.00	30.00	—
1892Zs Z/G	—	2.00	4.00	7.00	30.00	—
1893/2Zs Z	—	2.00	4.00	8.00	40.00	—
1893Zs Z	1,010,999	1.50	2.50	5.00	25.00	—
1894Zs Z	892,000	1.50	2.50	5.00	30.00	—
1895Zs Z 9/5	—	2.00	4.00	7.00	30.00	—
1895Zs Z	920,000	1.50	2.50	5.00	30.00	—
1896/5Z S/O Z/G	—	2.00	4.00	8.00	30.00	—
1896/5Zs Z/G	—	1.50	2.50	5.00	30.00	—
1896Zs Z/G	—	1.50	2.50	5.00	30.00	—
1896/5Zs ZsZ	700,000	1.50	2.50	5.00	30.00	—
1896Zs ZsZ	Inc. above	1.50	2.50	5.00	30.00	—
1896Zs Z Z Error	Inc. above	3.75	10.00	25.00	100	—
1897Zs Z	Inc. above	1.50	2.50	5.00	30.00	—
1897/6Zs ZsZ	900,000	2.00	5.00	10.00	30.00	—
1897/6Zs Z Z Error	Inc. above	3.75	10.00	25.00	100	—

KM# 403.1 10 CENTAVOS
2.7070 g., 0.9030 Silver 0.0786 oz. ASW **Obv:** Facing eagle, snake in beak **Rev:** Value within 1/2 wreath **Note:** Mint mark CH, Ca. Varieties exist.

Date	Mintage	F	VF	XF	Unc	BU
1871 M	8,150	15.00	30.00	60.00	150	—
1873 M Crude date	—	35.00	75.00	125	175	—
1874 M	—	10.00	17.50	35.00	100	—
1880/70 G	7,620	20.00	40.00	80.00	175	—
1880 G/g	Inc. above	15.00	25.00	50.00	125	—
1881 Rare	340	—	—	—	—	—
1883 M	9,000	10.00	20.00	40.00	125	—
1884/73	—	5.00	30.00	60.00	150	—
1884 M	—	10.00	20.00	40.00	125	—
1886 M	45,000	7.50	12.50	30.00	100	—
1887/3 M/G	96,000	5.00	10.00	20.00	75.00	—
1887 M/G	—	2.00	4.00	8.00	75.00	—
1887 M	Inc. above	2.00	4.00	8.00	75.00	—
1888 M/G	—	2.00	4.00	8.00	75.00	—
1888 M	299,000	1.50	2.50	5.00	75.00	—
1888 Ca/Mo	Inc. above	1.50	2.50	5.00	75.00	—
1889 M	Inc. above	2.00	4.00	8.00	75.00	—

Note: Small 89 (5 Centavo font)

Date	Mintage	F	VF	XF	Unc	BU
1889/8 M	115,000	2.00	4.00	8.00	75.00	—
1890 M	Inc. above	1.50	3.00	7.00	75.00	—
1890/80 M	140,000	2.00	4.00	8.00	75.00	—
1890/89 M	Inc. above	2.00	4.00	8.00	75.00	—
1891 M	163,000	1.50	3.00	7.00	75.00	—
1892 M 9/ inverted 9	Inc. above	2.00	4.00	8.00	75.00	—
1892 M	169,000	1.50	3.00	7.00	75.00	—
1893 M	246,000	1.50	3.00	7.00	75.00	—
1894 M	163,000	1.50	3.00	7.00	75.00	—
1895 M	127,000	1.50	3.00	7.00	75.00	—

SECOND REPUBLIC - EMPIRE OF MAXIMILLIAN

KM# 404   10 CENTAVOS
2.7070 g., 0.9030 Silver 0.0786 oz. ASW **Obv:**
Facing eagle, snake in beak **Obv. Legend:**
REPUBLICA MEXICANA **Rev:** Value within 1/2
wreath **Note:** Varieties exist.

Date	Mintage	F	VF	XF	Unc	BU
1898Cn M	9,870	50.00	100	200	500	—
1899Cn Q Oval Q, double tail	Inc. above	5.00	7.50	25.00	100	—
1899Cn Q Round Q, single tail	80,000	5.00	7.50	25.00	100	—
1900Cn Q	160,000	1.50	2.50	5.00	20.00	—
1901Cn Q	235,000	1.50	2.50	5.00	18.00	20.00
1902Cn Q	186,000	1.50	2.50	5.00	20.00	—
1903Cn Q	256,000	1.50	2.50	6.00	20.00	—
1903Cn V	Inc. above	1.50	2.50	5.00	15.00	—
1904Cn H	307,000	1.50	2.50	5.00	15.00	—

KM# 404.1   10 CENTAVOS
2.7070 g., 0.9030 Silver 0.0786 oz. ASW **Obv:**
Facing eagle, snake in beak **Rev:** Value within 1/2
wreath

Date	Mintage	F	VF	XF	Unc	BU
1898Go R	435,000	1.50	2.50	5.00	20.00	—
1899Go R	270,000	1.50	2.50	5.00	25.00	—
1900Go R	130,000	7.50	12.50	25.00	60.00	—

KM# 404.2   10 CENTAVOS
2.7070 g., 0.9030 Silver 0.0786 oz. ASW **Obv:** Facing
eagle, snake in beak **Obv. Legend:** REPUBLICA
MEXICANA **Rev:** Value within 1/2 wreath

Date	Mintage	F	VF	XF	Unc	BU
1898Mo M	130,000	1.50	2.50	5.00	20.00	—
1899Mo M	190,000	1.50	2.50	5.00	20.00	—
1900Mo M	311,000	1.50	2.50	5.00	20.00	—
1901Mo M	80,000	2.50	3.50	7.00	22.50	—
1902Mo M	181,000	1.50	2.50	6.00	20.00	—
1903Mo M	581,000	1.50	2.50	6.00	20.00	—
1904Mo M	1,266,000	1.25	2.00	4.50	18.00	—
1904Mo MM (Error)	Inc. above	2.50	5.00	10.00	25.00	—
1905Mo M	266,000	2.00	3.75	7.50	20.00	—

KM# 404.3   10 CENTAVOS
2.7070 g., 0.9020 Silver 0.0785 oz. ASW **Obv:** Facing
eagle, snake in beak **Rev:** Value within 1/2 wreath

Date	Mintage	F	VF	XF	Unc	BU
1898Zs Z	240,000	1.50	2.50	7.50	20.00	—
1899Zs Z	105,000	1.50	3.00	10.00	22.00	—
1900Zs Z	219,000	7.50	10.00	20.00	45.00	—
1901Zs Z	70,000	2.50	5.00	10.00	25.00	—
1902Zs Z	120,000	2.50	5.00	10.00	25.00	—
1903Zs Z	228,000	1.50	3.00	9.00	18.00	20.00
1904Zs Z	368,000	1.50	3.00	9.00	18.00	20.00
1904Zs M	Inc. above	1.50	3.00	9.00	22.00	25.00
1905Zs M	66,000	7.50	20.00	50.00	200	—

KM# 405   20 CENTAVOS
5.4150 g., 0.9030 Silver 0.1572 oz. ASW **Obv:** Facing
eagle, snake in beak **Rev:** Value within 1/2 wreath

Date	Mintage	F	VF	XF	Unc	BU
1898Cn M	114,000	5.00	12.50	35.00	140	—
1899Cn M	44,000	12.00	20.00	45.00	225	—
1899Cn Q	Inc. above	20.00	35.00	100	250	—
1900Cn Q	68,000	6.50	12.50	35.00	140	—
1901Cn Q	185,000	5.00	10.00	30.00	120	—
1902/802Cn Q	98,000	6.00	10.00	30.00	120	—
1902Cn Q	Inc. above	4.00	9.00	30.00	120	—
1903Cn Q	93,000	4.00	9.00	30.00	120	—
1904/3Cn H	258,000	—	—	—	—	—
1904Cn H	Inc. above	5.00	10.00	30.00	120	—

KM# 405.1   20 CENTAVOS
5.4150 g., 0.9027 Silver 0.1572 oz. ASW **Obv:** Facing
eagle, snake in beak **Obv. Legend:** REPUBLICA
MEXICANA **Rev:** Value within 1/2 wreath

Date	Mintage	F	VF	XF	Unc	BU
1898Go R	135,000	4.00	8.00	20.00	100	—
1899Go R	215,000	4.00	8.00	20.00	100	—
1900/800Go R	38,000	10.00	20.00	60.00	250	—

KM# 405.3   20 CENTAVOS
5.4150 g., 0.9027 Silver 0.1572 oz. ASW **Obv:** Facing
eagle, snake in beak **Obv. Legend:** REPUBLICA
MEXICANA **Rev:** Value within 1/2 wreath

Date	Mintage	F	VF	XF	Unc	BU
1898Zs Z	195,000	5.00	10.00	20.00	100	—
1899Zs Z	210,000	5.00	10.00	20.00	100	—
1900/800Zs Z	97,000	5.00	10.00	40.00	200	—
1901Zs Z	Inc. above	5.00	10.00	20.00	100	—
1901/0Zs Z	130,000	25.00	50.00	100	250	—
1902Zs Z	105,000	5.00	10.00	20.00	100	—
1903Zs Z	143,000	5.00	10.00	20.00	100	—
1904Zs M	Inc. above	5.00	10.00	50.00	300	—
1904Zs Z	246,000	5.00	10.00	20.00	100	—
1905Zs M	59,000	10.00	70.00	50.00	400	—

KM# 405.2   20 CENTAVOS
5.4150 g., 0.9030 Silver 0.1572 oz. ASW **Obv:**
Facing eagle, snake in beak **Rev:** Value within 1/2
wreath **Note:** Varieties exist.

Date	Mintage	F	VF	XF	Unc	BU
1898Mo M	150,000	4.00	8.00	20.00	125	—
1899Mo M	425,000	4.00	8.00	20.00	125	—
1900/800Mo M	295,000	4.00	8.00	20.00	125	—
1901Mo M	110,000	4.00	8.00	20.00	90.00	—
1902Mo M	120,000	4.00	8.00	20.00	90.00	—
1903Mo M	213,000	4.00	8.00	20.00	90.00	—
1904Mo M	276,000	4.00	8.00	20.00	90.00	—
1905Mo M	117,000	6.50	20.00	50.00	150	—

KM# 406.2   25 CENTAVOS
6.7680 g., 0.9030 Silver 0.1965 oz. ASW **Obv:** Facing
eagle, snake in beak **Rev:** Radiant cap above scales

Date	Mintage	F	VF	XF	Unc	BU
1871Cn P	—	250	500	750	—	—
1872Cn P	2,780	300	550	800	—	—
1873Cn P	20,000	100	150	250	500	—
1874Cn P	—	20.00	50.00	125	250	—
1875Cn P	—	250	500	750	—	—
1876Cn P Rare	—	—	—	—	—	—
1878Cn Cn/Go D/S	—	100	150	250	500	—
1878/7Cn D/S	—	100	150	250	500	—
1878Cn D	—	100	150	250	500	—
1879Cn D	—	15.00	35.00	70.00	175	—
1880Cn D	—	250	500	750	—	—
1881/0Cn D	18,000	15.00	30.00	60.00	175	—
1882Cn D	—	200	350	600	—	—
1882Cn M Rare	—	—	—	—	—	—
1883Cn M	15,000	50.00	100	150	300	—
1884Cn M	—	20.00	40.00	80.00	175	—

Date	Mintage	F	VF	XF	Unc	BU
1885/4Cn M	19,000	20.00	40.00	80.00	175	—
1886Cn M	22,000	12.50	20.00	50.00	175	—
1887Cn M	32,000	12.50	20.00	50.00	175	—
1888Cn M	86,000	7.50	15.00	30.00	175	—
1888Cn M Cn/ Mo	—	—	—	—	—	—
1889Cn M	50,000	10.00	25.00	50.00	175	—
1890Cn M 9/8	—	7.50	17.50	40.00	175	—
1890Cn M	91,000	7.50	17.50	40.00	175	—
1892/0Cn M	16,000	20.00	40.00	80.00	200	—
1892Cn M	Inc. above	20.00	40.00	80.00	200	—

KM# 406.3   25 CENTAVOS
6.7680 g., 0.9030 Silver 0.1965 oz. ASW **Obv:** Facing eagle, snake in beak **Rev:** Radiant cap above scales

Date	Mintage	F	VF	XF	Unc	BU
1873Do P Rare	892	—	—	—	—	—
1877Do P	—	25.00	50.00	100	200	—
1878/7Do E	—	250	500	750	—	—
1878Do B Rare	—	—	—	—	—	—
1879Do B	—	50.00	75.00	125	250	—
1880Do B Rare	—	—	—	—	—	—
1882Do C	17,000	25.00	50.00	100	225	—
1884/3Do C	—	25.00	50.00	100	200	—
1885Do C/S	—	20.00	40.00	80.00	200	—
1885Do C	15,000	20.00	40.00	80.00	200	—
1886Do C	33,000	15.00	30.00	60.00	200	—
1887Do C	27,000	10.00	20.00	50.00	200	—
1888Do C	25,000	10.00	20.00	50.00	200	—
1889Do C	29,000	10.00	20.00	50.00	200	—
1890Do C	68,000	7.50	15.00	40.00	200	—

KM# 406.4   25 CENTAVOS
6.7680 g., 0.9030 Silver 0.1965 oz. ASW **Obv:** Facing eagle, snake in beak **Rev:** Radiant cap above scales

Date	Mintage	F	VF	XF	Unc	BU
1880Ga A	38,000	25.00	50.00	100	200	—
1881/0Ga S	39,000	25.00	50.00	100	200	—
1881Ga S	Inc. above	25.00	50.00	100	200	—
1882Ga S	18,000	25.00	50.00	100	200	—
1883/2Ga B/S	—	50.00	100	150	300	—
1884Ga B	—	20.00	40.00	80.00	150	—
1889Ga S	30,000	20.00	40.00	80.00	150	—

KM# 406   25 CENTAVOS
6.7680 g., 0.9030 Silver 0.1965 oz. ASW **Obv:** Facing eagle, snake in beak **Rev:** Radiant cap above scales **Note:** Mint mark A, As.

Date	Mintage	F	VF	XF	Unc	BU
1874 L	—	20.00	40.00	90.00	200	—
1875 L	—	15.00	30.00	70.00	200	—
1876 L	—	30.00	50.00	100	200	—
1877 L	11,000	200	300	500	—	—
1877.	Inc. above	10.00	25.00	60.00	200	—
1878 L	25,000	10.00	25.00	60.00	200	—
1879 L	—	10.00	25.00	60.00	200	—
1880 L	—	10.00	25.00	60.00	200	—
1880. L	—	10.00	25.00	60.00	200	—
1881 L	8,800	500	700	—	—	—
1882 L	7,777	15.00	35.00	80.00	200	—
1883 L	28,000	10.00	25.00	60.00	200	—
1884 L	—	10.00	25.00	60.00	200	—
1885 L	—	20.00	40.00	90.00	200	—
1886 L	46,000	15.00	30.00	70.00	200	—
1887 L	12,000	12.50	27.50	65.00	200	—
1888 L	20,000	12.50	27.50	65.00	200	—
1889 L	14,000	12.50	27.50	65.00	200	—
1890 L	23,000	10.00	25.00	60.00	200	—

KM# 406.1   25 CENTAVOS
6.7680 g., 0.9030 Silver 0.1965 oz. ASW **Obv:** Facing eagle, snake in beak **Rev:** Radiant cap above scales **Note:** Mint mark CA, CH, Ca.

Date	Mintage	F	VF	XF	Unc	BU
1871 M	18,000	25.00	50.00	100	200	—
1872 M Very crude date	24,000	50.00	100	150	300	—
1883 M	12,000	10.00	25.00	50.00	175	—
1885/3 M	35,000	10.00	25.00	50.00	175	—
1885 M	Inc. above	10.00	25.00	50.00	175	—
1886 M	22,000	10.00	25.00	50.00	175	—
1887/6 M	26,000	10.00	15.00	30.00	175	—
1887 M	Inc. above	10.00	15.00	30.00	175	—
1888 M	14,000	10.00	25.00	50.00	175	—
1889 M	50,000	10.00	15.00	30.00	175	—

KM# 406.5   25 CENTAVOS
6.7680 g., 0.9030 Silver 0.1965 oz. ASW **Obv:** Facing eagle, snake in beak **Rev:** Radiant cap above scales **Note:** Varieties exist.

Date	Mintage	F	VF	XF	Unc	BU
1870Go S	128,000	10.00	20.00	50.00	125	—
1871Go S	172,000	10.00	20.00	50.00	125	—
1872/1Go S	178,000	10.00	20.00	50.00	125	—
1872Go S	Inc. above	10.00	20.00	50.00	125	—
1873Go S	120,000	10.00	20.00	50.00	125	—
1874Go S	—	15.00	30.00	60.00	150	—
1875/4Go S	—	15.00	30.00	60.00	150	—
1875Go S	—	10.00	20.00	50.00	125	—
1876Go S	—	20.00	40.00	80.00	175	—
1877Go S	124,000	10.00	20.00	50.00	125	—
1878Go S	146,000	10.00	20.00	50.00	125	—
1879Go S	—	10.00	20.00	50.00	125	—
1880Go S	—	20.00	40.00	80.00	175	—
1881Go S	408,000	7.50	17.50	45.00	125	—
1882Go S	204,000	7.50	17.50	45.00	125	—
1883Go B	168,000	7.50	17.50	45.00	125	—
1884/69Go B	—	7.50	17.50	45.00	125	—
1884/3Go B	—	7.50	17.50	45.00	125	—
1884/3Go B/R	—	7.50	17.50	45.00	125	—
1884Go B	—	7.50	17.50	45.00	125	—
1885/65Go R	300,000	7.50	17.50	45.00	125	—
1885/69Go R	Inc. above	7.50	17.50	45.00	125	—
1885Go R	Inc. above	7.50	17.50	45.00	125	—
1886/65Go R	—	7.50	17.50	45.00	125	—
1886/66Go R	322,000	7.50	17.50	45.00	125	—
1886/69Go R/S	Inc. above	7.50	17.50	45.00	125	—
1886/5/69Go R	Inc. above	7.50	15.00	45.00	125	—
1886Go R	Inc. above	7.50	15.00	45.00	125	—
1887Go R	254,000	7.50	15.00	45.00	125	—
1887Go/Cn R/D	Inc. above	7.50	15.00	45.00	125	—
1888Go R	312,000	7.50	15.00	45.00	125	—
1889/8Go R RS inverted B	—	—	—	—	—	—
1889/8Go R	304,000	7.50	15.00	45.00	125	—
1889/8Go/Cn R/ D	Inc. above	7.50	15.00	45.00	125	—
1889Go R	Inc. above	7.50	15.00	45.00	125	—
1890Go R	236,000	7.50	15.00	45.00	125	—

KM# 406.6   25 CENTAVOS
6.7680 g., 0.9030 Silver 0.1965 oz. ASW **Obv:** Facing eagle, snake in beak **Rev:** Radiant cap above scales **Note:** Varieties exist.

Date	Mintage	F	VF	XF	Unc	BU
1874/64Ho R	Inc. above	10.00	20.00	40.00	125	—
1874/69Ho R	—	10.00	20.00	40.00	125	—
1874Ho R	23,000	10.00	20.00	40.00	125	—
1875Ho R Rare	—	—	—	—	—	—
1876/4Ho F/R	34,000	10.00	20.00	50.00	150	—
1876Ho F/R	Inc. above	10.00	25.00	60.00	150	—
1876Ho F	Inc. above	10.00	25.00	55.00	135	—
1877Ho F	—	10.00	20.00	50.00	125	—
1878Ho A	23,000	10.00	20.00	50.00	125	—
1879Ho A	—	10.00	20.00	50.00	125	—
1880Ho A	—	15.00	30.00	60.00	125	—
1881Ho A	19,000	15.00	30.00	60.00	125	—
1882Ho A	8,120	20.00	40.00	80.00	150	—
1883Ho M	2,000	100	200	300	600	—
1884Ho M	—	12.50	25.00	50.00	150	—

Date	Mintage	F	VF	XF	Unc	BU
1885Ho M	—	10.00	20.00	50.00	125	—
1886Ho G	6,400	30.00	60.00	125	250	—
1887Ho G	12,000	10.00	20.00	40.00	125	—
1888Ho G	20,000	10.00	20.00	40.00	125	—
1889Ho G	28,000	10.00	20.00	40.00	125	—
1890/80Ho G	18,000	25.00	50.00	100	125	—
1890Ho G	Inc. above	25.00	50.00	100	125	—

KM# 406.7   25 CENTAVOS
6.7680 g., 0.9027 Silver 0.1964 oz. ASW **Obv:** Facing eagle, snake in beak **Obv. Legend:** REPUBLICA MEXICANA **Rev:** Radiant cap above scales **Note:** Varieties exist.

Date	Mintage	F	VF	XF	Unc	BU
1869Mo C	76,000	10.00	25.00	50.00	125	—
1870/69Mo C	—	6.00	12.00	30.00	125	—
1870/9Mo C	136,000	6.00	12.00	30.00	125	—
1870Mo C	Inc. above	6.00	12.00	30.00	125	—
1871Mo M	138,000	6.00	12.00	30.00	125	—
1872Mo M	220,000	6.00	12.00	30.00	125	—
1873/1Mo M	48,000	10.00	25.00	50.00	125	—
1873Mo M	Inc. above	10.00	25.00	50.00	125	—
1874/69Mo B/M	—	10.00	25.00	50.00	125	—
1874/3Mo M	—	10.00	25.00	50.00	125	—
1874/3Mo B	—	10.00	25.00	50.00	125	—
1874/3Mo B/M	—	10.00	25.00	50.00	125	—
1874Mo M	—	6.00	12.00	30.00	125	—
1874Mo B/M	—	10.00	25.00	50.00	125	—
1875Mo B	—	6.00	12.00	30.00	125	—
1876/5Mo B	—	7.50	15.00	40.00	125	—
1876Mo B	—	6.00	12.00	30.00	125	—
1877Mo M	56,000	10.00	25.00	50.00	125	—
1878/1Mo M	120,000	10.00	25.00	50.00	125	—
1878/7Mo M	Inc. above	10.00	25.00	50.00	125	—
1878Mo M	Inc. above	6.00	12.00	30.00	125	—
1879Mo M	—	10.00	20.00	40.00	125	—
1880Mo M	—	7.50	15.00	35.00	125	—
1881/0Mo M	300,000	10.00	25.00	50.00	125	—
1881Mo M	Inc. above	10.00	25.00	50.00	125	—
1882Mo M	212,000	7.50	15.00	35.00	125	—
1883Mo M	108,000	7.50	15.00	35.00	125	—
1884/3Mo M	—	10.00	25.00	50.00	125	—
1884Mo M	—	10.00	20.00	40.00	125	—
1885Mo M	—	10.00	20.00	40.00	125	—
1886/5Mo M	436,000	7.50	15.00	35.00	125	—
1886Mo M	Inc. above	7.50	15.00	35.00	125	—
1887Mo M	376,000	7.50	15.00	35.00	125	—
1888Mo M	192,000	7.50	15.00	35.00	125	—
1889Mo M	132,000	7.50	15.00	35.00	125	—
1890Mo M	60,000	10.00	20.00	40.00	125	—

KM# 406.8   25 CENTAVOS
6.7680 g., 0.9030 Silver 0.1965 oz. ASW **Obv:** Facing eagle, snake in beak **Rev:** Radiant cap above scales **Note:** Varieties exist.

Date	Mintage	F	VF	XF	Unc	BU
1869Pi S	—	25.00	75.00	150	300	—
1870Pi G	50,000	10.00	30.00	75.00	150	—
1870Pi O	Inc. above	15.00	35.00	85.00	175	—
1871Pi O	30,000	10.00	30.00	75.00	150	—
1872Pi O	46,000	10.00	30.00	75.00	150	—
1873Pi O	13,000	15.00	40.00	90.00	175	—
1874Pi H	—	15.00	40.00	90.00	200	—
1875Pi H	—	10.00	20.00	60.00	150	—
1876/5Pi H	—	15.00	30.00	80.00	175	—
1876Pi H	—	10.00	25.00	65.00	150	—
1877Pi H	19,000	10.00	25.00	65.00	150	—
1878Pi H	—	15.00	30.00	60.00	150	—

Date	Mintage	F	VF	XF	Unc	BU
1879/8Pi H	—	10.00	25.00	60.00	150	—
1879Pi H	—	10.00	25.00	60.00	150	—
1879Pi E	—	100	200	300	600	—
1880Pi H	—	20.00	40.00	100	200	—
1880Pi H/M	—	20.00	40.00	100	200	—
1881Pi H	50,000	20.00	40.00	80.00	175	—
1881Pi E Rare	Inc. above	—	—	—	—	—
1882Pi H	20,000	10.00	20.00	60.00	150	—
1883Pi H	17,000	10.00	25.00	65.00	150	—
1884Pi H	—	10.00	25.00	65.00	150	—
1885/4Pi H	—	10.00	20.00	60.00	150	—
1885Pi H	43,000	10.00	20.00	60.00	150	—
1886Pi C	78,000	10.00	25.00	65.00	150	—
1886Pi R	Inc. above	7.50	20.00	50.00	150	—
1886Pi R 6/ inverted 6	Inc. above	7.50	20.00	50.00	150	—
1887Pi/ZsR	92,000	7.50	20.00	50.00	150	—
1887Pi/ZsB	Inc. above	100	150	300	500	—
1887Pi R	—	7.50	20.00	50.00	150	—
1888Pi R	106,000	7.50	20.00	50.00	150	—
1888Pi/ZsR	Inc. above	10.00	20.00	50.00	150	—
1888Pi R/B	Inc. above	10.00	20.00	50.00	150	—
1889Pi R	115,000	7.50	15.00	40.00	150	—
1889Pi/ZsR	Inc. above	10.00	20.00	50.00	150	—
1889Pi R/B	Inc. above	10.00	20.00	50.00	150	—
1890Pi R	64,000	10.00	20.00	50.00	150	—
1890Pi/ZsR/B	Inc. above	7.50	15.00	50.00	150	—
1890Pi R/B	Inc. above	10.00	20.00	50.00	150	—

KM# 406.9   25 CENTAVOS
6.7680 g., 0.9030 Silver 0.1965 oz. ASW **Obv:** Facing eagle, snake in beak **Rev:** Radiant cap above scales **Note:** Varieties exist.

Date	Mintage	F	VF	XF	Unc	BU
1870Zs H	152,000	6.00	15.00	50.00	125	—
1871Zs H	250,000	6.00	15.00	50.00	125	—
1872Zs H	260,000	6.00	15.00	50.00	125	—
1872Zs/Cn H	—	—	—	—	—	—
1872Zs H	—	—	—	—	—	—
1873Zs H	132,000	6.00	15.00	50.00	125	—
1874Zs H	—	10.00	20.00	60.00	125	—
1874Zs A	—	10.00	20.00	60.00	125	—
1875Zs A	—	7.00	20.00	60.00	125	—
1876Zs A	—	6.00	15.00	50.00	125	—
1876Zs S	—	6.00	15.00	50.00	125	—
1877Zs S	350,000	6.00	15.00	50.00	125	—
1878Zs S	252,000	6.00	15.00	50.00	125	—
1878/7Zs S	—	7.00	20.00	60.00	125	—
1878/1Zs S	—	7.00	20.00	60.00	125	—
1879Zs S	—	6.00	15.00	50.00	125	—
1880Zs S	—	6.00	15.00	50.00	125	—
1881/0Zs S	570,000	6.00	15.00	50.00	125	—
1881Zs S	Inc. above	6.00	15.00	50.00	125	—
1882/1Zs S	300,000	10.00	17.50	55.00	125	—
1882Zs S	Inc. above	6.00	15.00	50.00	125	—
1883/2Zs S	193,000	10.00	17.50	55.00	125	—
1883Zs S	Inc. above	6.00	15.00	50.00	125	—
1884/3Zs S	—	10.00	17.50	55.00	125	—
1884Zs S	—	6.00	15.00	50.00	125	—
1885Zs S	309,000	6.00	15.00	50.00	125	—
1886/2Zs S	—	10.00	17.50	55.00	125	—
1886/5Zs S	613,000	6.00	15.00	50.00	125	—
1886Zs S	Inc. above	6.00	15.00	50.00	125	—
1886Zs Z	Inc. above	6.00	15.00	55.00	125	—
1887Zs Z	389,000	6.00	15.00	50.00	125	—
1888Zs Z	408,000	6.00	15.00	50.00	125	—
1889Zs Z	400,000	6.00	15.00	50.00	125	—
1890Zs Z	269,000	6.00	15.00	50.00	125	—

KM# 407.7   50 CENTAVOS
13.5360 g., 0.9030 Silver 0.3930 oz. ASW **Obv:** Facing eagle, snake in beak **Rev:** Radiant cap above scales

Date	Mintage	F	VF	XF	Unc	BU
1870Pi G	Inc. above	20.00	40.00	100	450	—
1870/780Pi G	50,000	25.00	45.00	110	500	—
1870Pi O	Inc. above	20.00	40.00	100	450	—
1871Pi O	—	15.00	30.00	80.00	400	—
1871Pi O/G	64,000	15.00	30.00	80.00	400	—
1872Pi O/G	Inc. above	15.00	30.00	80.00	400	—

Date	Mintage	F	VF	XF	Unc	BU
1872Pi O	52,000	15.00	30.00	80.00	400	—
1873Pi O	32,000	20.00	40.00	100	450	—
1873Pi H	Inc. above	25.00	50.00	125	550	—
1874Pi H/O	—	15.00	30.00	80.00	400	—
1875/3Pi H	—	15.00	30.00	80.00	400	—
1875Pi H	—	15.00	30.00	80.00	400	—
1876Pi H	—	30.00	60.00	150	700	—
1877Pi H	34,000	20.00	40.00	100	450	—
1878Pi H	9,700	20.00	40.00	100	450	—
1879/7Pi H	—	15.00	35.00	90.00	450	—
1879Pi H	—	15.00	35.00	90.00	400	—
1880Pi H	—	20.00	40.00	100	450	—
1881Pi H	28,000	20.00	40.00	100	450	—
1882Pi H	22,000	15.00	30.00	80.00	400	—
1883Pi H 8/8	29,000	50.00	100	200	750	—
1883Pi H	Inc. above	15.00	30.00	80.00	400	—
1884Pi H	—	50.00	100	175	600	—
1885/3Pi H	—	20.00	40.00	100	450	—
1885/0Pi H	45,000	20.00	40.00	100	450	—
1885/4Pi H	Inc. above	20.00	40.00	100	450	—
1885Pi H	Inc. above	25.00	50.00	125	450	—
1885Pi C	Inc. above	15.00	30.00	80.00	400	—
1886/1Pi R	92,000	50.00	100	175	600	—
1886/1Pi C	—	25.00	40.00	100	450	—
1886Pi C	Inc. above	15.00	30.00	80.00	400	—
1886Pi R	Inc. above	15.00	30.00	80.00	400	—
1887Pi R	32,000	15.00	30.00	90.00	450	—

KM# 407 50 CENTAVOS
13.5360 g., 0.9030 Silver 0.3930 oz. ASW **Obv:**
Facing eagle, snake in beak **Rev:** Radiant cap above
scales **Note:** Mint mark A, As.

Date	Mintage	F	VF	XF	Unc	BU
1875 L	—	12.00	25.00	70.00	400	—
1876/5 L	—	25.00	50.00	120	450	—
1876 L	—	12.00	25.00	70.00	400	—
1876. L	—	—	—	—	—	—
1877 L	26,000	15.00	30.00	85.00	450	—
1878 L	—	12.00	25.00	70.00	400	—
1879 L	—	25.00	50.00	120	450	—
1880 L	57,000	12.00	25.00	70.00	400	—
1881 L	18,000	15.00	30.00	80.00	450	—
1884 L	6,286	65.00	120	250	650	—
1885As/HoL	21,000	15.00	35.00	90.00	450	—
1888 L	—	4,000	5,000	7,000	—	—

KM# 407.1 50 CENTAVOS
13.5360 g., 0.9030 Silver 0.3930 oz. ASW **Obv:**
Facing eagle, snake in beak **Rev:** Radiant cap above
scales **Note:** Mint mark Ca, CHa.

Date	Mintage	F	VF	XF	Unc	BU
1883 M	12,000	30.00	60.00	125	500	—
1884 M	—	25.00	50.00	125	500	—
1885 M	13,000	15.00	35.00	90.00	400	—
1886 M	18,000	20.00	40.00	100	450	—
1887 M	26,000	25.00	65.00	150	500	—

KM# 407.4 50 CENTAVOS
13.5360 g., 0.9030 Silver 0.3930 oz. ASW **Obv:**
Facing eagle, snake in beak **Rev:** Radiant cap above
scales **Note:** Struck at Guanajuato Mint, mitn mark
Go. Varieties exist.

Date	Mintage	F	VF	XF	Unc	BU
1869Go S	—	15.00	35.00	75.00	550	—
1870Go S	166,000	12.00	25.00	50.00	450	—
1871Go S	148,000	12.00	25.00	50.00	450	—
1872/1Go S	144,000	15.00	30.00	60.00	500	—
1872Go S	Inc. above	12.00	25.00	50.00	450	—
1873Go S	50,000	12.00	25.00	50.00	450	—
1874Go S	—	12.00	25.00	50.00	450	—
1875Go S	—	15.00	35.00	75.00	450	—
1876/5Go S	—	12.00	25.00	50.00	450	—
1877Go S	76,000	12.00	25.00	60.00	450	—
1878Go S	37,000	15.00	30.00	75.00	550	—
1879/8Go S	—	15.00	30.00	60.00	500	—
1879Go S	—	12.00	25.00	50.00	450	—
1880Go S	—	12.00	25.00	50.00	450	—
1881/79Go S	32,000	15.00	30.00	60.00	500	—
1881Go S	Inc. above	12.00	25.00	50.00	450	—
1882Go S	18,000	12.00	25.00	50.00	450	—

Date	Mintage	F	VF	XF	Unc	BU
1883/2Go B/S	—	15.00	30.00	60.00	500	—
1883Go B	—	12.00	25.00	50.00	450	—
1883Go S Rare	—	—	—	—	—	—
1884Go B/S	—	15.00	30.00	60.00	500	—
1885/4Go R/B	—	15.00	30.00	60.00	500	—
1885Go R	53,000	12.00	25.00	50.00	450	—
1886/5Go R/B	59,000	15.00	30.00	60.00	500	—
1886/5Go R/S	Inc. above	20.00	40.00	75.00	500	—
1886Go R	Inc. above	20.00	40.00	75.00	500	—
1887Go R	18,000	20.00	40.00	75.00	550	—
1888Go R 1	—	—	—	—	—	—
known; Rare						

KM# 407.8 50 CENTAVOS
13.5360 g., 0.9030 Silver 0.3930 oz. ASW **Obv:**
Facing eagle, snake in beak **Rev:** Radiant cap above
scales **Note:** Varieties exist.

Date	Mintage	F	VF	XF	Unc	BU
1870Zs H	86,000	12.00	25.00	60.00	450	—
1871Zs H	146,000	12.00	25.00	50.00	400	—
1872Zs H	132,000	12.00	25.00	50.00	400	—
1873Zs H	56,000	12.00	25.00	50.00	400	—
1874Zs A Rare	—	—	—	—	—	—
1874Zs H	—	12.00	25.00	50.00	400	—
1875Zs A	—	12.00	25.00	50.00	400	—
1876Zs S	—	100	200	350	750	—
1876Zs A	—	12.00	25.00	50.00	400	—
1876/5Zs A	—	15.00	30.00	60.00	450	—
1877Zs S	100,000	12.00	25.00	50.00	400	—
1878Zs S	Inc. above	15.00	30.00	60.00	400	—
1878/7Zs S	254,000	15.00	30.00	50.00	450	—
1879Zs S	—	12.00	25.00	50.00	400	—
1880Zs S	—	12.00	25.00	50.00	400	—
1881Zs S	201,000	12.00	25.00	50.00	400	—
1882/1Zs S	2,000	50.00	100	250	650	—
1882Zs S	Inc. above	50.00	100	250	650	—
1883Zs S	Inc. above	25.00	50.00	100	450	—
1883Zs/Za S	31,000	30.00	60.00	100	450	—
1884/3Zs S	—	15.00	30.00	60.00	450	—
1884Zs S	—	12.00	25.00	50.00	400	—
1885/4Zs S	2,000	25.00	50.00	125	450	—
1885Zs S	Inc. above	25.00	50.00	125	450	—
1886Zs Z	2,000	150	275	400	1,000	—
1887Zs Z	63,000	30.00	60.00	125	450	—

KM# 407.5 50 CENTAVOS
13.5360 g., 0.9030 Silver 0.3930 oz. ASW **Obv:**
Facing eagle, snake in beak **Rev:** Radiant cap above
scales **Note:** With and without dot after 50 of
denomination, in medal and coin alignment.

Date	Mintage	F	VF	XF	Unc	BU
1874Ho R	—	20.00	40.00	100	600	—
1875/4Ho R	—	20.00	50.00	125	600	—
1875Ho R	—	20.00	50.00	125	600	—
1876/5Ho F/R	—	15.00	35.00	100	550	—
1876Ho F	—	15.00	35.00	100	550	—
1877Ho F	—	50.00	75.00	150	650	—
1880/70Ho A	—	15.00	35.00	100	550	—
1880Ho A	—	15.00	35.00	100	550	—
1881Ho A	13,000	15.00	35.00	100	550	—
1882Ho A	—	75.00	150	250	750	—
1888Ho G	—	2,000	3,000	6,000	—	—
1894Ho G	59,000	15.00	30.00	100	450	—
1895Ho G	8,000	250	350	700	1,500	—

SECOND REPUBLIC - EMPIRE OF MAXIMILLIAN

Date	Mintage	F	VF	XF	Unc	BU
1884Do C	—	—	—	—	—	—
1885Do B/P	—	15.00	40.00	100	500	—
1885Do B	—	15.00	40.00	100	500	—
1886Do C	16,000	15.00	40.00	100	500	—
1887Do/Mo C	28,000	15.00	40.00	100	500	—
1887Do C	—	15.00	40.00	100	500	—

KM# 407.2　50 CENTAVOS
13.5360 g., 0.9030 Silver 0.3930 oz. ASW **Obv:** Facing eagle, snake in beak **Obv. Legend:** REPUBLICA MEXICANA **Rev:** Radiant cap above scales

Date	Mintage	F	VF	XF	Unc	BU
1871Cn P	—	400	550	750	1,500	—
1873Cn P	—	400	550	750	1,500	—
1874Cn P	—	200	300	500	1,000	—
1875/4Cn P	—	20.00	40.00	75.00	450	—
1875Cn P	—	12.00	25.00	50.00	450	—
1876Cn P	—	15.00	30.00	60.00	450	—
1877/6Cn G	—	15.00	30.00	60.00	450	—
1877Cn G	—	12.00	25.00	50.00	450	—
1878Cn G	18,000	20.00	40.00	75.00	450	—
1878Cn/Mo D	Inc. above	30.00	60.00	100	450	—
1878Cn D	Inc. above	15.00	35.00	75.00	450	—
1879Cn D	—	12.00	25.00	50.00	450	—
1879Cn D/G	—	12.00	25.00	50.00	450	—
1880/8Cn D	—	15.00	30.00	60.00	450	—
1880Cn D	—	15.00	30.00	60.00	450	—
1881/0Cn D	188,000	15.00	30.00	60.00	450	—
1881Cn D	Inc. above	15.00	30.00	60.00	450	—
1881Cn G	Inc. above	125	175	275	550	—
1882Cn D	—	175	300	500	2,000	—
1882Gn G	—	100	250	300	1,000	—
1883 D	19,000	25.00	50.00	100	500	—
1885Cn M/M/G	—	30.00	60.00	100	500	—
1885/3Cn M/H	9,254	30.00	60.00	100	500	—
1886Cn M/G	7,030	50.00	100	300	1,500	—
1886Cn M	Inc. above	40.00	80.00	150	800	—
1887Cn M	76,000	20.00	40.00	100	450	—
1888Cn M	—	4,000	6,000	—	—	—
1892Cn M	8,200	40.00	80.00	150	650	—

KM# 407.3　50 CENTAVOS
13.5360 g., 0.9030 Silver 0.3930 oz. ASW **Obv:** Facing eagle, snake in beak **Obv. Legend:** REPUBLICA MEXICANA **Rev:** Radiant cap above scales

Date	Mintage	F	VF	XF	Unc	BU
1871Do P Rare	591	—	—	—	—	—
1873Do P	4,010	150	250	500	1,250	—
1873Do M/P	Inc. above	150	250	500	1,250	—
1874Do M	—	20.00	40.00	175	750	—
1875Do M	—	20.00	40.00	80.00	350	—
1875Do H	—	150	250	450	1,000	—
1876/5Do M	—	35.00	70.00	150	500	—
1876Do M	—	35.00	70.00	150	500	—
1877Do P	2,000	30.00	45.00	150	1,250	—
1878Do B Rare	—	—	—	—	—	—
1879Do B Rare	—	—	—	—	—	—
1880Do P	—	30.00	60.00	125	500	—
1881Do P	10,000	40.00	80.00	150	550	—
1882Do C	8,957	30.00	75.00	200	800	—
1884/2Do C	—	20.00	50.00	125	600	—

KM# 407.6　50 CENTAVOS
13.5360 g., 0.9027 Silver 0.3928 oz. ASW **Obv:** Facing eagle, snake in beak **Obv. Legend:** REPUBLICA MEXICANA **Rev:** Radiant cap above scales

Date	Mintage	F	VF	XF	Unc	BU
1869Mo C	46,000	15.00	35.00	95.00	600	—
1870Mo C	52,000	15.00	30.00	90.00	550	—
1871Mo M/C	Inc. above	35.00	75.00	150	600	—
1871Mo C	14,000	40.00	75.00	150	650	—
1872/1Mo M	60,000	35.00	75.00	150	550	—
1872Mo M	Inc. above	35.00	75.00	150	550	—
1873Mo M	6,000	35.00	75.00	150	600	—
1874/3Mo M	—	200	400	600	1,250	—
1874/2Mo B	—	15.00	30.00	75.00	500	—
1874/2Mo B/M	—	15.00	30.00	75.00	500	—
1874/3Mo B/M	—	15.00	30.00	75.00	500	—
1874Mo B	—	15.00	30.00	75.00	500	—
1875Mo B	—	15.00	30.00	75.00	550	—
1876Mo B	—	12.00	25.00	75.00	500	—
1876/5Mo B	—	15.00	30.00	75.00	500	—
1877/2Mo M	—	20.00	40.00	100	550	—
1877Mo M	—	15.00	30.00	90.00	500	—
1878Mo M	Inc. above	15.00	35.00	100	550	—
1878/7Mo M	8,000	25.00	50.00	125	600	—
1879Mo M	—	25.00	50.00	125	550	—
1880Mo M	—	100	150	250	750	—
1881Mo M	16,000	25.00	50.00	125	600	—
1881/0Mo M	—	30.00	50.00	125	600	—
1882/1Mo M	2,000	30.00	60.00	150	750	—
1883/2Mo M	4,000	150	225	350	1,000	—
1884Mo M	—	150	225	350	1,000	—
1885Mo M	12,000	30.00	60.00	150	600	—
1886Mo M	Inc. above	12.00	25.00	75.00	450	—
1886/5Mo M	66,000	15.00	35.00	90.00	475	—
1887/6Mo M	88,000	15.00	35.00	90.00	475	—
1887Mo M	Inc. above	15.00	35.00	75.00	475	—
1888Mo M	—	3,000	4,000	6,000	—	—

KM# 408　PESO
27.0730 g., 0.9030 Silver 0.7860 oz. ASW **Obv:** Facing eagle, snake in beak **Rev:** Radiant cap above scales

Date	Mintage	F	VF	XF	Unc	BU
1872CH P/M	747,000	750	1,500	3,500	—	—
1872CH P	Inc. above	350	700	1,500	—	—
1872/1CH M	Inc. above	25.00	40.00	75.00	400	—
1872CH M	Inc. above	17.50	25.00	50.00	250	—
1873CH M	320,000	20.00	30.00	60.00	265	—
1873CH M/P	Inc. above	25.00	40.00	75.00	350	—

KM# 408.1　PESO
27.0730 g., 0.9030 Silver 0.7860 oz. ASW **Obv:** Facing eagle, snake in beak **Rev:** Radiant cap above scales

Date	Mintage	F	VF	XF	Unc
1870Cn E	—	40.00	80.00	150	500
1871Cn P	Inc. above	20.00	40.00	75.00	300
1871/11Cn P	478,000	25.00	45.00	100	450
1872/1Cn P	—	20.00	40.00	75.00	300
1872Cn P	209,000	20.00	40.00	75.00	300
1873Cn P Narrow date	527,000	20.00	40.00	75.00	300
1873Cn P Wide date	Inc. above	20.00	40.00	75.00	300

KM# 408.2 PESO

27.0730 g., 0.9027 Silver 0.7857 oz. ASW **Obv:** Facing eagle, snake in beak **Obv. Legend:** REPUBLICA MEXICANA **Rev:** Radiant cap above scales

Date	Mintage	F	VF	XF	Unc	BU
1870Do P	—	50.00	100	175	450	—
1871Do P	427,000	25.00	50.00	75.00	300	—
1872Do P	296,000	20.00	40.00	75.00	350	—
1872Do PT	Inc. above	100	175	250	850	—
1873Do P	203,000	25.00	45.00	85.00	350	—

KM# 408.3 PESO

27.0730 g., 0.9030 Silver 0.7860 oz. ASW **Obv:** Facing eagle, snake in beak **Obv. Legend:** REPUBLICA MEXICANA **Rev:** Radiant cap above scales

Date	Mintage	F	VF	XF	Unc	BU
1870Ga C	—	650	850	—	—	—
1871Ga C	829,000	25.00	65.00	135	600	—
1872Ga C	485,000	40.00	90.00	175	650	—
1873/2Ga C	277,000	40.00	90.00	175	700	—
1873Ga C	Inc. above	25.00	65.00	135	600	—

KM# 408.4 PESO

27.0730 g., 0.9027 Silver 0.7857 oz. ASW **Obv:** Facing eagle, snake in beak **Obv. Legend:** REPUBLICA MEXICANA **Rev:** Radiant cap above scales

Date	Mintage	F	VF	XF	Unc	BU
1871/0Go S	3,946,000	30.00	50.00	90.00	350	—
1871/3Go S	Inc. above	20.00	35.00	70.00	275	—
1871Go S	Inc. above	12.00	20.00	40.00	220	—
1872Go S	4,067,000	12.00	20.00	40.00	250	—
1873/2Go S	1,560,000	15.00	25.00	50.00	250	—
1873Go S	Inc. above	12.00	20.00	45.00	250	—
1873Go/Mo/S/M	Inc. above	12.00	20.00	45.00	250	—

KM# 408.5 PESO

27.0730 g., 0.9030 Silver 0.7860 oz. ASW **Obv:** Facing eagle, snake in beak **Rev:** Radiant cap above scales

Date	Mintage	F	VF	XF	Unc	BU
1869Mo C	—	35.00	65.00	135	600	—
1870Mo C	Inc. above	12.00	20.00	40.00	250	—
1870Mo M/C	Inc. above	18.00	30.00	60.00	275	—
1870/69Mo C	5,115,000	15.00	25.00	55.00	275	—
1870Mo M	Inc. above	18.00	30.00	60.00	275	—
1871Mo M	Inc. above	12.00	20.00	40.00	250	—
1871/0Mo M	6,974,000	15.00	25.00	55.00	275	—
1872/1Mo M	—	15.00	25.00	50.00	275	—
1872/1Mo M/C	4,801,000	15.00	25.00	50.00	275	—
1872Mo M	Inc. above	12.00	20.00	40.00	250	—
1873Mo M	1,765,000	12.00	20.00	40.00	250	—

Note: The 1869 C with large LEY on the scroll is a pattern

KM# 408.6 PESO

27.0730 g., 0.9030 Silver 0.7860 oz. ASW **Obv:** Facing eagle, snake in beak **Obv. Legend:** REPUBLICA MEXICANA **Rev:** Radiant cap above scales

Date	Mintage	F	VF	XF	Unc	BU
1869Oa E	—	275	400	600	2,000	—
1870Oa E Small A	Inc. above	15.00	30.00	75.00	400	—
1870OA E Large A	Inc. above	100	150	300	900	—
1871/69Oa E	140,000	30.00	50.00	125	550	—
1871Oa E Small A	Inc. above	15.00	30.00	60.00	300	—
1871Oa E Large A	Inc. above	15.00	30.00	75.00	400	—
1872Oa E Small A	180,000	15.00	30.00	75.00	400	—
1872Oa E Large A	Inc. above	50.00	100	200	450	—
1873Oa E	105,000	15.00	30.00	75.00	350	—

Date	Mintage	F	VF	XF	Unc	BU
1904Cn/Mo/ H	Inc. above	65.00	100	150	250	—
1905Cn P	1,000	—	—	—	—	—

Note: Reported, not confirmed

KM# 410.3   PESO
1.6920 g., 0.8750 Gold 0.0476 oz. AGW **Obv:** Facing eagle, snake in beak **Obv. Legend:** REPUBLICA MEXICANA **Rev:** Value within 1/2 wreath

Date	Mintage	F	VF	XF	Unc	BU
1870Go S	—	100	125	150	265	—
1871Go S	500	100	175	225	475	—
1888Go R	210	125	200	250	550	—
1890Go R	1,916	75.00	100	150	265	—
1892Go R	533	100	150	175	350	—
1894Go R	180	150	200	250	550	—
1895Go R	676	100	150	175	325	—
1896/5Go R	4,671	65.00	100	150	250	—
1897/6Go R	4,280	65.00	100	150	250	—
1897Go R	Inc. above	65.00	100	150	250	—
1898Go R	5,193	65.00	100	150	250	750

Note: Regular obverse

Date	Mintage	F	VF	XF	Unc	BU
1898Go R	Inc. above	75.00	100	150	250	750

Note: Mule, 5 Centavos obverse, normal reverse

Date	Mintage	F	VF	XF	Unc	BU
1899Go R	2,748	65.00	100	150	250	—
1900/800Go R	864	75.00	125	150	285	—

KM# 410.4   PESO
1.6920 g., 0.8750 Gold 0.0476 oz. AGW **Obv:** Facing eagle, snake in beak **Obv. Legend:** REPUBLICA MEXICANA **Rev:** Value within 1/2 wreath

Date	Mintage	F	VF	XF	Unc	BU
1875Ho R Rare	310	—	—	—	—	—
1876Ho F Rare	—	—	—	—	—	—
1888Ho G/MoM Rare	—	—	—	—	—	—

KM# 410.5   PESO
1.6920 g., 0.8750 Gold 0.0476 oz. AGW **Obv:** Facing eagle, snake in beak **Obv. Legend:** REPUBLICA MEXICANA **Rev:** Value within 1/2 wreath

Date	Mintage	F	VF	XF	Unc	BU
1870Mo C	2,540	45.00	65.00	95.00	185	—
1871Mo M/C	1,000	55.00	100	150	250	—
1872Mo M/C	3,000	45.00	65.00	95.00	185	—
1873/1Mo M	2,900	45.00	65.00	100	200	—
1873Mo M	Inc. above	45.00	65.00	95.00	185	—
1874Mo M	—	45.00	65.00	95.00	185	—
1875Mo B/M	—	45.00	65.00	95.00	185	250
1876/5Mo B/M	—	45.00	65.00	95.00	185	—
1877Mo M	—	45.00	65.00	95.00	185	—
1878Mo M	2,000	45.00	65.00	95.00	185	—
1879Mo M	—	45.00	65.00	95.00	185	—
1880/70Mo M	—	45.00	65.00	95.00	185	—
1881/71Mo M	1,000	45.00	65.00	95.00	185	—
1882/72Mo M	—	45.00	65.00	95.00	185	—
1883/72Mo M	1,000	45.00	65.00	95.00	185	—
1884Mo M	—	45.00	65.00	95.00	185	—
1885/71Mo M	—	45.00	65.00	95.00	185	—
1885Mo M	—	45.00	65.00	95.00	185	—
1886Mo M	1,700	45.00	65.00	95.00	185	—

KM# 409   PESO
27.0730 g., 0.9030 Silver 0.7860 oz. ASW **Obv:** Facing eagle, snake in beak **Rev:** Radiant cap

Date	Mintage	F	VF	XF	Unc	BU
1898Cn AM	1,720,000	12.00	15.00	25.00	65.00	—
1898Cn/MoAM	Inc. above	15.00	30.00	90.00	150	—
1899Cn AM	1,722,000	25.00	50.00	90.00	175	—
1899Cn JQ	Inc. above	12.00	15.00	50.00	125	—
1900Cn JQ	1,804,000	12.00	15.00	25.00	75.00	—
1901Cn JQ	1,473,000	12.00	15.00	25.00	75.00	—
1902Cn JQ	1,194,000	12.00	15.00	45.00	125	—
1903Cn JQ	1,514,000	12.00	15.00	30.00	85.00	—
1903Cn FV	Inc. above	25.00	50.00	100	225	—
1904Cn MH	1,554,000	12.00	15.00	25.00	75.00	—
1904Cn RP	Inc. above	50.00	100	150	350	—
1905Cn RP	598,000	25.00	50.00	100	250	—

KM# 410.2   PESO
1.6920 g., 0.8750 Gold 0.0476 oz. AGW **Obv:** Facing eagle, snake in beak **Obv. Legend:** REPUBLICA MEXICANA **Rev:** Value within 1/2 wreath

Date	Mintage	F	VF	XF	Unc	BU
1873Cn P	1,221	75.00	100	150	250	—
1875Cn P	—	85.00	125	150	250	—
1878Cn G	248	100	175	225	500	—
1879Cn D	—	100	150	200	475	—
1881/0Cn D	338	100	150	200	475	—
1882Cn D	340	100	150	200	475	—
1883Cn D	—	100	150	200	475	—
1884Cn M	—	100	150	200	475	—
1886/4Cn M	277	100	150	225	500	—
1888/7Cn M	2,586	100	175	225	450	—
1888Cn M	Inc. above	65.00	100	150	265	—
1889Cn M Rare	—	—	—	—	—	—
1891/89Cn M	969	75.00	100	150	275	—
1892Cn M	780	75.00	100	150	275	—
1893Cn M	498	85.00	125	150	275	—
1894Cn M	493	80.00	125	150	275	—
1895Cn M	1,143	65.00	100	150	250	300
1896/5Cn M	1,028	65.00	100	150	250	—
1897Cn M	785	65.00	100	150	250	325
1898Cn M	3,521	65.00	100	150	225	—
1898Cn/MoM	Inc. above	65.00	100	150	250	—
1899Cn Q	2,000	65.00	100	150	225	—
1901Cn Q	Inc. above	65.00	100	150	225	—
1901/0Cn Q	2,350	65.00	100	150	225	—
1902Cn Q	2,480	65.00	100	150	225	—
1902Cn/MoQ/C	Inc. above	65.00	100	150	225	—
1904Cn H	3,614	65.00	100	150	225	—

Date	Mintage	F	VF	XF	Unc	BU
1887Mo M	2,200	45.00	65.00	95.00	185	—
1888Mo M	1,000	45.00	65.00	95.00	185	—
1889Mo M	500	100	150	200	285	—
1890Mo M	570	100	150	200	285	—
1891Mo M	746	100	150	200	285	—
1892/0Mo M	2,895	45.00	65.00	95.00	185	—
1893Mo M	5,917	45.00	65.00	95.00	185	—
1894/3MMo	—	45.00	65.00	95.00	185	—
1894Mo M	6,244	45.00	65.00	95.00	185	—
1895Mo M	8,994	45.00	65.00	95.00	185	—
1895Mo B	Inc. above	45.00	65.00	95.00	185	—
1896Mo B	7,166	45.00	65.00	95.00	185	—
1896Mo M	Inc. above	45.00	65.00	95.00	185	—
1897Mo M	5,131	45.00	65.00	95.00	185	—
1898/7Mo M	5,368	45.00	65.00	95.00	185	—
1899Mo M	9,515	45.00	65.00	95.00	185	—
1900/800Mo M	9,301	45.00	65.00	95.00	185	—
1900/880Mo M	Inc. above	45.00	65.00	95.00	185	—
1900/890Mo M	Inc. above	45.00	65.00	95.00	185	—
1900Mo M	Inc. above	45.00	65.00	95.00	185	—
1901Mo M Small date	Inc. above	45.00	65.00	95.00	185	—
1901/801Mo M Large date	8,293	45.00	65.00	95.00	185	—
1902Mo M Large date	11,000	45.00	65.00	95.00	185	—
1902Mo M Small date	Inc. above	45.00	65.00	95.00	185	—
1903Mo M Large date	10,000	45.00	65.00	95.00	185	—
1903Mo M Small date	Inc. above	55.00	85.00	125	200	—
1904Mo M	9,845	45.00	65.00	95.00	185	—
1905Mo M	3,429	45.00	65.00	95.00	185	—

KM# 410.6 PESO

1.6920 g., 0.8750 Gold 0.0476 oz. AGW **Obv:** Facing eagle, snake in beak **Obv. Legend:** REPUBLICA MEXICANA **Rev:** Value within 1/2 wreath

Date	Mintage	F	VF	XF	Unc	BU
1872Zs H	2,024	125	150	175	275	—
1875/3Zs A	—	125	150	200	325	—
1878Zs S	—	125	150	175	275	—
1888Zs Z	280	175	225	325	700	—
1889Zs Z	492	150	175	225	450	—
1890Zs Z	738	150	175	225	450	—

KM# 409.3 PESO

27.0730 g., 0.9030 Silver 0.7860 oz. ASW **Obv:** Facing eagle, snake in beak **Rev:** Radiant cap **Note:** Mint mark Zs. Varieties exist.

Date	Mintage	F	VF	XF	Unc	BU
1898Zs FZ	5,714,000	11.50	13.50	20.00	60.00	—

Date	Mintage	F	VF	XF	Unc	BU
1899Zs FZ	5,618,000	11.50	13.50	20.00	65.00	—
1900Zs FZ	5,357,000	11.50	13.50	20.00	65.00	—
1901Zs FZ	Inc. above	11.50	13.50	20.00	55.00	—
1901Zs AZ	5,706,000	4,000	6,500	10,000	—	—
1902Zs FZ	7,134,000	11.50	13.50	20.00	55.00	—
1903/2Zs FZ	3,080,000	12.50	15.00	50.00	125	—
1903Zs FZ	Inc. above	11.50	13.50	20.00	65.00	—
1904Zs FZ	2,423,000	12.00	15.00	25.00	85.00	—
1904Zs FM	Inc. above	12.00	15.00	25.00	75.00	—
1905Zs FM	995,000	20.00	40.00	60.00	150	—

KM# 408.7 PESO

27.0730 g., 0.9030 Silver 0.7860 oz. ASW **Obv:** Facing eagle, snake in beak **Rev:** Radiant cap above scales **Note:** Varieties exist.

Date	Mintage	F	VF	XF	Unc	BU
1870Pi S	1,967,000	200	350	500	1,000	—
1870Pi S/A	Inc. above	200	350	550	1,200	—
1870Pi G	Inc. above	25.00	40.00	75.00	550	—
1870Pi H	Inc. above	—	—	—	—	—

Note: Contemporary counterfeits

Date	Mintage	F	VF	XF	Unc	BU
1870Pi O/G	Inc. above	25.00	40.00	75.00	550	—
1870Pi O	Inc. above	20.00	30.00	100	400	—
1871/69Pi O	2,103,000	75.00	100	200	500	—
1871Pi O	—	15.00	30.00	60.00	500	—
1871Pi O/G	Inc. above	15.00	30.00	60.00	500	—
1872Pi O	1,873,000	15.00	30.00	60.00	500	—
1873Pi O	893,000	15.00	30.00	60.00	500	—
1873Pi H	Inc. above	15.00	30.00	60.00	500	—

KM# 408.8 PESO

27.0730 g., 0.9030 Silver 0.7860 oz. ASW **Obv:** Facing eagle, snake in beak **Rev:** Radiant cap above scales **Note:** Varieties exist.

Date	Mintage	F	VF	XF	Unc	BU
1870Zs H	4,519,000	12.00	30.00	40.00	220	—
1871Zs H	4,459,000	12.00	20.00	40.00	220	—
1872Zs H	4,039,000	12.00	20.00	40.00	220	—
1873/1Zs H	Inc. above	12.00	20.00	40.00	220	—
1873Zs H	1,782,000	12.00	20.00	40.00	220	—

KM# 409.1 PESO

27.0730 g., 0.9030 Silver 0.7860 oz. ASW **Obv:** Facing eagle, snake in beak **Rev:** Radiant cap **Note:** Varieties exist.

Date	Mintage	F	VF	XF	Unc	BU
1898Go RS	4,256,000	11.50	16.00	35.00	75.00	—
1898Go/MoRS	Inc. above	20.00	30.00	60.00	125	—
1899Go RS	3,207,000	11.50	16.00	30.00	75.00	—
1900Go RS	1,489,000	25.00	50.00	100	250	—

KM# 409.2 PESO

27.0730 g., 0.9027 Silver 0.7857 oz. ASW **Obv:** Facing eagle, snake in beak **Obv. Legend:** REPUBLICA MEXICANA **Rev:** Radiant cap **Note:** Varieties exist.

Date	Mintage	F	VF	XF	Unc	BU
1898Mo AM	10,156,000	11.50	13.50	18.50	60.00	—

Date	Mintage	F	VF	XF	Unc	BU
Note: Original strike - reverse with 139 beads						
1898Mo AM	10,250,000	11.50	13.50	16.50	40.00	—
Note: Restrike (1949) - reverse with 134 beads						
1899Mo AM	7,930,000	11.50	13.50	20.00	70.00	—
1900Mo AM	8,226,000	11.50	13.50	20.00	70.00	—
1901Mo AM	14,505,000	11.50	13.50	20.00	70.00	—
1902/1Mo AM	16,224,000	150	300	500	950	—
1902Mo AM	Inc. above	11.50	13.50	20.00	70.00	—
1903Mo AM	22,396,000	11.50	13.50	20.00	70.00	—
1903Mo MA (Error)	Inc. above	1,500	2,500	3,500	7,500	—
1904Mo AM	14,935,000	11.50	13.50	20.00	70.00	—
1905Mo AM	3,557,000	15.00	25.00	55.00	125	—
1908Mo AM	7,575,000	11.50	13.50	20.00	60.00	—
1908Mo GV	Inc. above	11.50	13.50	18.50	40.00	—
1909Mo GV	2,924,000	11.50	13.50	18.50	40.00	—

KM# 410 PESO
1.6920 g., 0.8750 Gold 0.0476 oz. AGW **Obv:** Facing eagle, snake in beak **Obv. Legend:** REPUBLICA MEXICANA **Rev:** Value within 1/2 wreath

Date	Mintage	F	VF	XF	Unc	BU
1888AsL/MoM Rare	—	—	—	—	—	—
1888As L Rare	—	—	—	—	—	—

KM# 410.1 PESO
1.6920 g., 0.8750 Gold 0.0476 oz. AGW **Obv:** Facing eagle, snake in beak **Obv. Legend:** REPUBLICA MEXICANA **Rev:** Value within 1/2 wreath

Date	Mintage	F	VF	XF	Unc	BU
1888Ca/MoM Rare	104	—	—	—	—	—

KM# 411.3 2-1/2 PESOS
4.2300 g., 0.8750 Gold 0.1190 oz. AGW **Obv:** Facing eagle, snake in beak **Obv. Legend:** REPUBLICA MEXICANA **Rev:** Value within 1/2 wreath

Date	Mintage	F	VF	XF	Unc	BU
1871Go S	600	1,250	2,000	2,500	3,250	—
1888Go/MoR	110	1,750	2,250	2,750	3,500	—

KM# 411.4 2-1/2 PESOS
4.2300 g., 0.8750 Gold 0.1190 oz. AGW **Obv:** Facing eagle, snake in beak **Obv. Legend:** REPUBLICA MEXICANA **Rev:** Value within 1/2 wreath

Date	Mintage	F	VF	XF	Unc	BU
1874Ho R Rare	—	—	—	—	—	—
1888Ho G Rare	—	—	—	—	—	—

KM# 411.5 2-1/2 PESOS
4.2300 g., 0.8750 Gold 0.1190 oz. AGW **Obv:** Facing eagle, snake in beak **Rev:** Value within 1/2 wreath

Date	Mintage	F	VF	XF	Unc	BU
1870Mo C	820	150	250	350	750	—
1872Mo M/C	800	150	250	350	750	—
1873/2Mo M	—	200	350	750	1,350	—
1874Mo M	—	200	350	750	1,350	—
1874Mo B/M	—	200	350	750	1,350	—
1875Mo B	—	200	350	750	1,350	—
1876Mo B	—	250	500	1,000	1,850	—
1877Mo M	—	200	350	750	1,350	—
1878Mo M	400	200	350	750	1,350	—
1879Mo M	—	200	350	750	1,350	—
1880/79Mo M	—	200	350	750	1,350	—
1881Mo M	400	200	350	750	1,350	—
1882Mo M	—	225	400	850	1,500	2,000
1883/73Mo M	400	200	350	750	1,350	—
1884Mo M	—	250	500	1,000	1,600	—
1885Mo M	—	400	850	1,750	3,000	—
1886Mo M	400	200	350	750	1,350	—
1887Mo M	400	200	350	750	1,350	—
1888Mo M	540	200	350	750	1,350	—
1889Mo M	240	150	300	525	950	—
1890Mo M	420	200	350	750	1,350	—
1891Mo M	188	200	350	750	1,350	—
1892Mo M	240	200	350	750	1,350	—

KM# 411.6 2-1/2 PESOS
4.2300 g., 0.8750 Gold 0.1190 oz. AGW **Obv:** Facing eagle, snake in beak **Obv. Legend:** REPUBLICA MEXICANA **Rev:** Value within 1/2 wreath

Date	Mintage	F	VF	XF	Unc	BU
1872Zs H	1,300	200	350	500	1,200	—
1873Zs H	—	175	325	475	900	—
1875/3Zs A	—	200	350	750	1,350	—
1877Zs S	—	200	350	750	1,350	—
1878Zs S	300	200	350	750	1,350	—
1888Zs/MoS	80	300	500	1,000	1,800	—
1889Zs/Mo Z	184	250	450	950	1,600	—
1890Zs Z	326	200	350	750	1,350	—

KM# 411 2-1/2 PESOS
4.2300 g., 0.8750 Gold 0.1190 oz. AGW **Obv:** Facing eagle, snake in beak **Obv. Legend:** REPUBLICA MEXICANA **Rev:** Value within 1/2 wreath

Date	Mintage	F	VF	XF	Unc	BU
1888As/MoL Rare	—	—	—	—	—	—

KM# 411.1 2-1/2 PESOS
4.2300 g., 0.8750 Gold 0.1190 oz. AGW **Obv:** Facing eagle, snake in beak **Rev:** Value within 1/2 wreath

Date	Mintage	F	VF	XF	Unc	BU
1893Cn M	141	1,500	2,000	2,500	3,500	—

KM# 411.2 2-1/2 PESOS
4.2300 g., 0.8750 Gold 0.1190 oz. AGW **Obv:** Facing eagle, snake in beak **Rev:** Value within 1/2 wreath

Date	Mintage	F	VF	XF	Unc	BU
1888Do C Rare	—	—	—	—	—	—

KM# 412.2 5 PESOS
8.4600 g., 0.8750 Gold 0.2380 oz. AGW **Obv:** Facing eagle, snake in beak **Obv. Legend:** REPUBLICA MEXICANA **Rev:** Radiant cap above scales

Date	Mintage	F	VF	XF	Unc	BU
1873Cn P	—	300	600	1,000	2,000	—
1874Cn P	—	—	—	—	—	—
1875Cn P	—	300	500	800	1,750	—
1876Cn P	—	300	500	800	1,750	—
1877Cn G	—	300	500	800	1,750	—
1882Cn Rare	174	—	—	—	—	—
1888Cn M	—	500	1,000	1,350	2,000	—
1890Cn M	435	250	500	750	1,600	—
1891Cn M	1,390	250	400	500	1,000	—
1894Cn M	484	250	500	750	1,600	—
1895Cn M	142	500	750	1,500	2,500	—
1900Cn Q	1,536	230	300	400	900	—
1903Cn Q	1,000	230	300	400	750	—

KM# 412.3 5 PESOS
8.4600 g., 0.8750 Gold 0.2380 oz. AGW **Obv:** Facing eagle, snake in beak **Obv. Legend:** REPUBLICA MEXICANA **Rev:** Radiant cap above scales

Date	Mintage	F	VF	XF	Unc	BU
1873/2Do P	—	700	1,250	1,800	3,000	—
1877Do P	—	700	1,250	1,800	3,000	—
1878Do E	—	700	1,250	1,800	3,000	—
1879Do B	—	700	1,250	1,800	3,000	—
1879/7Do B	—	700	1,250	1,800	3,000	—

KM# 412.4 5 PESOS
8.4600 g., 0.8750 Gold 0.2380 oz. AGW **Obv:** Facing eagle, snake in beak **Obv. Legend:** REPUBLICA MEXICANA **Rev:** Radiant cap above scales

Date	Mintage	F	VF	XF	Unc	BU
1871Go S	1,600	400	800	1,250	2,250	—
1887Go R	140	600	1,200	1,600	3,000	—
1888Go R Rare	65	—	—	—	—	—
1893Go R Rare	16	—	—	—	—	—

KM# 412 5 PESOS
8.4600 g., 0.8750 Gold 0.2380 oz. AGW **Obv:** Facing eagle, snake in beak **Obv. Legend:** REPUBLICA MEXICANA **Rev:** Radiant cap above scales

Date	Mintage	F	VF	XF	Unc	BU
1875As L	—	—	—	—	—	—
1878As L	383	900	1,700	3,000	4,500	—

KM# 412.6 5 PESOS
8.4600 g., 0.8750 Gold 0.2380 oz. AGW **Obv:** Facing eagle, snake in beak **Obv. Legend:** REPUBLICA MEXICANA **Rev:** Radiant cap above scales

Date	Mintage	F	VF	XF	Unc	BU
1870Mo C	550	230	400	600	1,500	—
1871/69Mo M	1,600	230	300	400	650	—
1871Mo M	Inc. above	230	300	400	650	—
1872Mo M	1,600	230	300	400	650	—
1873/2Mo M	—	230	400	550	850	—
1874Mo M	—	230	400	550	850	—
1875/3Mo B/M	—	230	400	550	950	—
1875Mo B	—	230	400	550	950	—
1876/5Mo B/M	—	230	400	550	1,000	—
1877Mo M	—	250	450	750	1,650	—
1878/7Mo M	400	230	400	550	1,250	—
1878Mo M	Inc. above	230	400	550	1,250	—
1879/8Mo M	—	230	400	550	1,250	—
1880Mo M	—	230	400	550	1,250	—
1881Mo M	—	230	400	550	1,250	—
1882Mo M	200	250	450	750	1,650	—
1883Mo M	200	250	450	750	1,650	—
1884Mo M	—	250	450	750	1,650	—
1886Mo M	200	250	450	750	1,650	—
1887Mo M	200	250	450	750	1,650	—
1888Mo M	250	230	400	550	1,650	—
1889Mo M	190	250	450	750	1,650	—
1890Mo M	149	250	450	750	1,650	—
1891Mo M	156	250	450	750	1,650	—
1892Mo M	214	250	450	750	1,650	—
1893Mo M	1,058	230	400	500	800	—
1897Mo M	370	230	400	550	1,000	—
1898Mo M	376	230	400	550	1,000	—
1900Mo M	1,014	230	300	400	650	1,000
1901Mo M	1,071	230	300	400	650	—
1902Mo M	1,478	230	300	400	650	—
1903Mo M	1,162	230	300	400	650	—
1904Mo M	1,415	230	300	400	650	—
1905Mo M	563	230	400	550	1,500	—

KM# 412.7 5 PESOS
8.4600 g., 0.8750 Gold 0.2380 oz. AGW **Obv:** Facing eagle, snake in beak **Obv. Legend:** REPUBLICA MEXICANA **Rev:** Radiant cap above scales

Date	Mintage	F	VF	XF	Unc	BU
1874Zs A	—	250	500	750	1,500	—
1875Zs A	—	200	400	500	1,000	—
1877Zs S/A	—	200	400	550	1,000	—
1878/7Zs S/A	—	200	400	550	1,000	—
1883Zs S	—	175	300	450	700	—
1888Zs Z	70	1,000	1,500	2,000	3,000	—
1889Zs Z	373	200	300	500	850	—
1892Zs Z	1,229	175	300	450	700	—

KM# 412.1   5 PESOS
8.4600 g., 0.8750 Gold 0.2380 oz. AGW **Obv:** Facing
eagle, snake in beak **Obv. Legend:** REPUBLICA
MEXICANA **Rev:** Radiant cap above scales

Date	Mintage	F	VF	XF	Unc	BU
1888Ca M Rare	120	—	—	—	—	—

KM# 412.5   5 PESOS
8.4600 g., 0.8750 Gold 0.2380 oz. AGW **Obv:** Facing
eagle, snake in beak **Obv. Legend:** REPUBLICA
MEXICANA **Rev:** Radiant cap above scales

Date	Mintage	F	VF	XF	Unc	BU
1874Ho R	—	1,750	2,500	3,000	4,500	—
1877Ho A	Inc. above	650	1,100	1,750	2,750	—
1877Ho R	990	750	1,250	2,000	3,000	—
1888Ho G Rare	—	—	—	—	—	—

KM# 413.2   10 PESOS
16.9200 g., 0.8750 Gold 0.4760 oz. AGW **Obv:** Facing
eagle, snake in beak **Obv. Legend:** REPUBLICA
MEXICANA **Rev:** Radiant cap above scales

Date	Mintage	F	VF	XF	Unc	BU
1881Cn D	—	450	600	1,000	1,750	—
1882Cn D	874	450	600	1,000	1,750	—
1882Cn E	Inc. above	450	600	1,000	1,750	—
1883Cn D	221	—	—	—	—	—
1883Cn M	Inc. above	450	600	1,000	1,750	—
1884Cn D	—	450	600	1,000	1,750	—
1884Cn M	—	450	600	1,000	1,750	—
1885Cn M	1,235	450	600	1,000	1,750	—
1886Cn M	981	450	600	1,000	1,750	—
1887Cn M	2,289	450	600	1,000	1,750	—
1888Cn M	767	450	600	1,000	1,750	—
1889Cn M	859	450	600	1,000	1,750	—
1890Cn M	1,427	450	600	1,000	1,750	—
1891Cn M	670	450	600	1,000	1,750	—
1892Cn M	379	450	600	1,000	1,750	—
1893Cn M	1,806	450	600	1,000	1,750	—
1895Cn M	179	500	1,000	1,500	2,500	—
1903Cn Q	774	450	600	1,000	1,750	—

KM# 413.3   10 PESOS
16.9200 g., 0.8750 Gold 0.4760 oz. AGW **Obv:** Facing
eagle, snake in beak **Obv. Legend:** REPUBLICA
MEXICANA **Rev:** Radiant cap above scales

Date	Mintage	F	VF	XF	Unc	BU
1872Do P	1,755	350	500	800	1,250	—
1873/2Do P	1,091	350	500	850	1,350	—
1873/2Do M/P	Inc. above	350	550	900	1,450	—
1874Do M	—	350	550	900	1,450	—
1875Do M	—	350	550	900	1,450	—
1876Do M	—	450	750	1,250	2,000	—
1877Do P	—	350	550	900	1,450	—
1878Do E	582	350	550	900	1,450	—
1879/8Do B	—	350	550	900	1,450	—
1879Do B	—	350	550	900	1,450	—
1880Do P	2,030	350	550	900	1,450	3,750
1881/79Do P	2,617	350	550	900	1,450	—
1882Do P Rare	1,528	—	—	—	—	—
1882Do C	Inc. above	350	550	900	1,450	—
1883Do C	793	450	750	1,250	2,000	—
1884Do C	108	450	750	1,250	2,000	—

KM# 413.4   10 PESOS
16.9200 g., 0.8750 Gold 0.4760 oz. AGW **Obv:**
Facing eagle, snake in beak **Obv. Legend:**
REPUBLICA MEXICANA **Rev:** Radiant cap above
scales

Date	Mintage	F	VF	XF	Unc	BU
1870Ga C	490	500	800	1,000	1,750	—
1871Ga C	1,910	400	800	1,250	2,250	—
1872Ga C	780	500	1,000	2,000	2,500	—
1873Ga C	422	500	1,000	2,000	3,000	—
1874/3Ga C	477	500	1,000	2,000	3,000	—
1875Ga C	710	500	1,000	2,000	3,000	—
1878Ga A	183	600	1,200	2,500	3,500	—
1879Ga A	200	600	1,200	2,500	3,500	—
1880Ga S	404	500	1,000	2,000	3,000	—
1881Ga S	239	600	1,200	2,500	3,500	—
1891Ga S	196	600	1,200	2,500	3,500	—

KM# 413.5   10 PESOS
16.9200 g., 0.8750 Gold 0.4760 oz. AGW **Obv:** Facing
eagle, snake in beak **Obv. Legend:** REPUBLICA
MEXICANA **Rev:** Radiant cap above scales

Date	Mintage	F	VF	XF	Unc	BU
1872Go S	1,400	2,000	4,000	6,500	10,000	—
1887Go R Rare	80	—	—	—	—	—

Note: Stack's Rio Grande Sale 6-93, P/L AU realized, $12,650

Date	Mintage	F	VF	XF	Unc	BU
1888Go R Rare	68	—	—	—	—	—

KM# 413.6 10 PESOS
16.9200 g., 0.8750 Gold 0.4760 oz. AGW **Obv:** Facing eagle, snake in beak **Obv. Legend:** REPUBLICA MEXICANA **Rev:** Radiant cap above scales

Date	Mintage	F	VF	XF	Unc	BU
1874Ho R Rare	—	—	—	—	—	—
1876Ho F Rare	357	—	—	—	—	—
1878Ho A	814	1,750	3,000	3,500	5,500	—
1879Ho A	—	1,000	2,000	2,500	4,000	—
1880Ho A	—	1,000	2,000	2,500	4,000	—
1881Ho A Rare	—	—	—	—	—	—

Note: American Numismatic Rarities Eliasberg sale 4-05, MS-62 realized $34,500.

KM# 413.7 10 PESOS
16.9200 g., 0.8750 Gold 0.4760 oz. AGW **Obv:** Facing eagle, snake in beak **Obv. Legend:** REPUBLICA MEXICANA **Rev:** Radiant cap above scales

Date	Mintage	F	VF	XF	Unc	BU
1870Mo C	480	500	900	1,200	2,000	—
1872/1Mo M/C	2,100	450	550	900	1,350	—
1873Mo M	—	450	600	950	1,450	—
1874/3Mo M	—	450	600	950	1,450	—
1875Mo B/M	—	450	600	950	1,450	—
1876Mo B Rare	—	—	—	—	—	—
1878Mo M	300	450	600	950	1,450	—
1879Mo M	—	—	—	—	—	—
1881Mo M	100	500	1,000	1,600	2,500	—
1882Mo M	—	450	600	950	1,450	—
1883Mo M	100	600	1,000	1,600	2,500	—
1884Mo M	—	600	1,000	1,600	2,500	—
1885Mo M	—	450	600	950	1,450	—
1886Mo M	100	600	1,000	1,600	2,500	—
1887Mo M	100	600	1,000	1,625	2,750	—
1888Mo M	144	450	750	1,200	2,000	—
1889Mo M	88	600	1,000	1,600	2,500	—
1890Mo M	137	600	1,000	1,600	2,500	—
1891Mo M	133	600	1,000	1,600	2,500	—
1892Mo M	45	600	1,000	1,600	2,500	—
1893Mo M	1,361	450	550	900	1,350	—
1897Mo M	239	450	600	950	1,450	—
1898/7Mo M	244	450	625	1,000	1,750	—
1900Mo M	733	450	600	950	1,450	—
1901Mo M	562	450	500	800	1,250	—
1902Mo M	719	450	500	800	1,250	—
1903Mo M	713	450	500	800	1,250	—
1904Mo M	694	450	500	800	1,250	—
1905Mo M	401	450	600	950	1,500	—

KM# 413.8 10 PESOS
16.9200 g., 0.8750 Gold 0.4760 oz. AGW **Obv:** Facing eagle, snake in beak **Obv. Legend:** REPUBLICA MEXICANA **Rev:** Radiant cap above scales

Date	Mintage	F	VF	XF	Unc	BU
1870oa E	4,614	400	600	900	1,600	—
1871oa E	2,705	400	600	950	1,650	—
1872oa E	5,897	400	600	850	1,500	—
1873oa E	3,537	400	600	850	1,500	—
1874oa E	2,205	400	600	1,200	1,850	—
1875oa E	312	450	750	1,400	2,250	—
1876oa E	766	450	750	1,400	2,250	—
1877oa E	463	450	750	1,400	2,250	—
1878oa E	229	450	750	1,400	2,250	—
1879oa E	210	450	750	1,400	2,250	—
1880oa E	238	450	750	1,400	2,250	—
1881oa E	961	400	600	1,200	2,000	—
1882oa E	170	600	1,000	1,500	2,500	—
1883oa E	111	600	1,000	1,500	2,500	—
1884oa E	325	450	750	1,400	2,250	—
1885oa E	370	450	750	1,400	2,250	—
1886oa E	400	450	750	1,400	2,250	—
1887oa E	—	700	1,250	2,250	4,000	—
1888oa F	—	—	—	—	—	—

KM# 413.9 10 PESOS
16.9200 g., 0.8750 Gold 0.4760 oz. AGW **Obv:** Facing eagle, snake in beak **Obv. Legend:** REPUBLICA MEXICANA **Rev:** Radiant cap above scales

Date	Mintage	F	VF	XF	Unc	BU
1871Zs H	2,000	350	500	800	1,250	—
1872Zs H	3,092	325	500	750	1,150	—
1873Zs H	936	400	600	950	1,450	—
1874Zs H	—	400	600	950	1,450	—
1875/3Zs A	—	400	600	1,000	1,750	—
1876/5Zs S	—	400	600	1,000	1,750	—
1877Zs S/H	506	400	600	1,000	1,750	—
1878Zs S	711	400	600	1,000	1,750	—
1879/8Zs S	—	450	750	1,400	2,250	—
1879Zs S	—	450	750	1,400	2,250	—
1880Zs S	2,089	350	550	950	1,450	—
1881Zs S	736	400	600	1,000	1,750	—
1882/1Zs Z	—	400	600	1,000	1,750	2,500
1882Zs S	1,599	350	550	950	1,450	—
1883/2Zs S	256	400	600	1,000	1,750	—
1884/3Zs S	—	350	550	950	1,600	—
1884Zs S	—	350	550	950	1,600	—
1885Zs S	1,588	350	550	950	1,450	—
1886Zs S	5,364	350	550	950	1,450	—
1887Zs Z	2,330	350	550	950	1,450	—
1888Zs Z	4,810	350	550	950	1,450	—
1889Zs Z	6,154	300	500	750	1,250	—
1890Zs Z	1,321	350	550	950	1,450	—
1891Zs Z	1,930	350	550	950	1,450	—
1892Zs Z	1,882	350	550	950	1,450	—
1893Zs Z	2,899	350	550	950	1,450	—
1894Zs Z	2,501	350	550	950	1,450	—
1895Zs Z	1,217	350	550	950	1,450	—

KM# 413   10 PESOS
16.9200 g., 0.8750 Gold 0.4760 oz. AGW **Obv:** Facing
eagle, snake in beak **Obv. Legend:** REPUBLICA
MEXICANA **Rev:** Radiant cap above scales

Date	Mintage	F	VF	XF	Unc	BU
1874As DL Rare	—	—	—	—	—	—
1875As L	642	600	1,250	2,500	3,500	—
1878As L	977	500	1,000	2,000	3,000	—
1879As L	1,078	500	1,000	2,000	3,000	—
1880As L	2,629	500	1,000	2,000	3,000	—
1881As L	2,574	500	1,000	2,000	3,000	—
1882As L	3,403	500	1,000	2,000	3,000	—
1883As L	3,597	500	1,000	2,000	3,000	—
1884As L Rare	—	—	—	—	—	—
1885As L	4,562	500	1,000	2,000	3,000	—
1886As L	4,643	500	1,000	2,000	3,000	—
1887As L	3,667	500	1,000	2,000	3,000	—
1888As L	4,521	500	1,000	2,000	3,000	—
1889As L	5,615	500	1,000	2,000	3,000	—
1890As L	4,920	500	1,000	2,000	3,000	—
1891As L	568	500	1,000	2,000	3,000	—
1892As L	—	—	—	—	—	—
1893As L	817	500	1,000	2,000	3,000	—
1894/3As L	1,658	—	—	—	—	—
1894As L	Inc. above	500	1,000	2,000	3,000	—
1895As L	1,237	500	1,000	2,000	3,000	—

KM# 413.1   10 PESOS
16.9200 g., 0.8750 Gold 0.4760 oz. AGW **Obv:** Facing
eagle, snake in beak **Obv. Legend:** REPUBLICA
MEXICANA **Rev:** Radiant cap above scales

Date	Mintage	F	VF	XF	Unc	BU
1888Ca M	175	—	—	7,500	—	—

KM# 414   20 PESOS
33.8400 g., 0.8750 Gold 0.9519 oz. AGW **Obv:** Facing
eagle, snake in beak **Rev:** Radiant cap above scales

Date	Mintage	F	VF	XF	Unc	BU
1876As L Rare	276	—	—	—	—	—
1877As L Rare	166	—	—	—	—	—
1878As L	—	—	—	—	—	—
1888As L Rare	—	—	—	—	—	—

KM# 414.2   20 PESOS
33.8400 g., 0.8750 Gold 0.9519 oz. AGW **Obv:** Facing
eagle, snake in beak **Obv. Legend:** REPUBLICA
MEXICANA **Rev:** Radiant cap above scales

Date	Mintage	F	VF	XF	Unc	BU
1870Cn E	3,749	BV	685	950	2,000	—
1871Cn P	3,046	BV	685	950	2,000	—
1872Cn P	972	BV	685	950	2,000	—
1873Cn P	1,317	BV	685	950	2,000	—
1874Cn P	—	BV	685	950	2,000	—
1875Cn P	—	600	1,200	1,800	2,500	—
1876Cn P	—	BV	685	950	2,000	—
1876Cn G	—	BV	685	950	2,000	—
1877Cn G	167	600	1,000	1,500	3,000	—
1878Cn Rare	842	—	—	—	—	—
1881/0Cn D	2,039	—	—	—	—	—
1881Cn D	Inc. above	BV	685	950	2,000	—
1882/1Cn D	736	BV	685	950	2,000	—
1883Cn M	1,836	BV	685	950	2,000	—
1884Cn M	—	BV	685	950	2,000	—
1885Cn M	544	BV	685	950	2,000	—
1886Cn M	882	BV	685	950	2,000	—
1887Cn M	837	BV	685	950	2,000	—
1888Cn M	473	BV	685	950	2,000	—
1889Cn M	1,376	BV	685	950	2,000	—
1890Cn M	—	800	1,750	3,500	8,750	—
1891Cn M	237	BV	900	1,200	2,250	—
1892Cn M	526	BV	685	950	2,000	—
1893Cn M	2,062	BV	685	950	2,000	—
1894Cn M	4,516	BV	685	950	2,000	—
1895Cn M	3,193	BV	685	950	2,000	—
1896Cn M	4,072	BV	685	950	2,000	—
1897/6Cn M	959	BV	685	950	2,000	—
1897Cn M	Inc. above	BV	685	950	2,000	—
1898Cn M	1,660	BV	685	950	2,000	—
1899Cn M	1,243	BV	685	950	2,000	—
1899Cn Q	Inc. above	BV	900	1,200	2,250	—
1900Cn Q	1,558	BV	685	950	2,000	—
1901Cn Q	Inc. above	BV	685	950	2,000	—
1901/0Cn Q	1,496	—	—	—	—	—
1902Cn Q	1,059	BV	685	950	2,000	—
1903Cn Q	1,121	BV	685	950	2,000	—
1904Cn H	4,646	BV	685	950	2,000	—
1905Cn P	1,738	BV	900	1,200	2,250	—

KM# 414.3   20 PESOS
33.8400 g., 0.8750 Gold 0.9519 oz. AGW **Obv:** Facing
eagle, snake in beak **Obv. Legend:** REPUBLICA
MEXICANA **Rev:** Radiant cap above scales

Date	Mintage	F	VF	XF	Unc	BU
1870Do P	416	1,000	1,500	2,000	2,500	—
1871/0Do P	1,073	1,000	1,750	2,250	2,750	—
1871Do P	Inc. above	1,000	1,500	2,000	2,500	—
1872/1Do PT	—	1,500	3,000	4,500	7,000	—
1876Do M	—	1,000	1,500	2,000	2,500	—
1877Do P	94	1,500	2,250	2,750	3,250	—
1878Do Rare	258	—	—	—	—	—

KM# 414.4   20 PESOS
33.8400 g., 0.8750 Gold 0.9519 oz. AGW **Obv:** Facing eagle, snake in beak **Obv. Legend:** REPUBLICA MEXICANA **Rev:** Radiant cap above scales

Date	Mintage	F	VF	XF	Unc	BU
1870Go S	3,250	BV	665	900	1,500	—
1871Go S	20,000	BV	665	900	1,500	2,200
1872Go S	18,000	BV	665	900	1,500	—
1873Go S	7,000	BV	665	900	1,500	—
1874Go S	—	BV	665	900	1,500	—
1875Go S	—	BV	665	900	1,500	—
1876Go S	—	BV	665	900	1,500	—
1876Go M/S	—	—	—	—	—	—
1877Go M/S Rare	15,000	—	—	—	—	—
1877Go R	Inc. above	BV	665	900	1,500	—
1877Go S Rare	Inc. above	—	—	—	—	—
1878/7Go M/S	13,000	675	1,250	2,000	2,800	—
1878Go M	Inc. above	675	1,250	2,000	2,800	—
1878Go S	Inc. above	BV	665	900	1,500	—
1879Go S	8,202	BV	800	1,200	2,300	—
1880Go S	7,375	BV	665	900	1,500	—
1881Go S	4,909	BV	665	900	1,500	—
1882Go S	4,020	BV	665	900	1,500	—
1883/2Go B	3,705	BV	750	1,150	2,250	—
1883Go B	Inc. above	BV	665	900	1,500	—
1884Go B	1,798	BV	665	900	1,500	—
1885Go R	2,660	BV	665	900	1,500	—
1886Go R	1,090	625	800	1,250	2,500	—
1887Go R	1,009	625	800	1,250	2,500	—
1888Go R	1,011	625	800	1,250	2,500	—
1889Go R	956	625	800	1,250	2,500	—
1890Go R	879	625	800	1,250	2,500	—
1891Go R	818	625	800	1,250	2,500	—
1892Go R	730	625	800	1,250	2,500	—
1893Go R	3,343	BV	665	1,000	2,000	—
1894/3Go R	6,734	BV	665	900	1,500	—
1894Go R	Inc. above	BV	665	900	1,500	—
1895/3Go R	7,118	BV	665	900	1,500	—
1895Go R	Inc. above	BV	665	900	1,500	—
1896Go R	9,219	BV	665	900	1,500	5,750
1897/6Go R	6,781	BV	665	900	1,500	—
1897Go R	Inc. above	BV	665	900	1,500	—
1898Go R	7,710	BV	665	900	1,500	—
1899Go R	8,527	BV	665	900	1,500	—
1900Go R	4,512	550	800	1,250	2,350	—

KM# 414.5   20 PESOS
33.8400 g., 0.8750 Gold 0.9519 oz. AGW **Obv:** Facing eagle, snake in beak **Obv. Legend:** REPUBLICA MEXICANA **Rev:** Radiant cap above scales

Date	Mintage	F	VF	XF	Unc	BU
1874Ho R Rare	—	—	—	—	—	—
1875Ho R Rare	—	—	—	—	—	—
1876Ho F Rare	—	—	—	—	—	—
1888Ho g Rare	—	—	—	—	—	—

KM# 414.6   20 PESOS
33.8400 g., 0.8750 Gold 0.9519 oz. AGW **Obv:** Facing eagle, snake in beak **Obv. Legend:** REPUBLICA MEXICANA **Rev:** Radiant cap above scales

Date	Mintage	F	VF	XF	Unc	BU
1870Mo C	14,000	BV	BV	900	1,500	—
1871Mo M	21,000	BV	BV	900	1,500	—
1872/1Mo M	11,000	BV	BV	900	1,650	—
1872Mo M	Inc. above	BV	BV	900	1,500	—
1873Mo M	5,600	BV	BV	900	1,500	—
1874/2Mo M	—	BV	BV	900	1,500	—
1874/2Mo B	—	BV	BV	1,000	1,650	—
1875Mo B	—	BV	BV	900	1,600	—
1876Mo B	—	BV	BV	900	1,600	—
1876Mo M	—	—	—	—	—	—

Note: Reported, not confirmed

Date	Mintage	F	VF	XF	Unc	BU
1877Mo M	2,000	BV	900	1,100	2,000	—
1878Mo M	7,000	BV	BV	900	1,600	—
1879Mo M	—	BV	BV	900	1,750	—
1880Mo M	—	BV	BV	900	1,750	—
1881/0Mo M	11,000	BV	BV	900	1,500	—
1881Mo M	Inc. above	BV	BV	900	1,500	—
1882/1Mo M	5,800	BV	BV	900	1,500	—
1882Mo M	Inc. above	BV	BV	900	1,500	—
1883/1Mo M	4,000	BV	BV	900	1,500	—
1883Mo M	Inc. above	BV	BV	900	1,500	—
1884/3Mo M	—	BV	BV	900	1,600	—
1884Mo M	—	BV	BV	900	1,600	—
1885Mo M	6,000	BV	BV	900	1,750	—
1886Mo M	10,000	BV	BV	900	1,500	—
1887Mo M	12,000	BV	900	1,500	2,500	—
1888Mo M	7,300	BV	BV	900	1,450	—
1889Mo M	6,477	BV	900	1,650	3,750	—
1890Mo M	7,852	BV	BV	900	1,550	—
1891/0Mo M	8,725	BV	BV	900	1,550	—
1891Mo M	Inc. above	BV	BV	900	1,550	—
1892Mo M	11,000	BV	BV	900	1,500	—
1893Mo M	15,000	BV	BV	900	1,500	—
1894Mo M	14,000	BV	BV	900	1,500	—
1895Mo M	13,000	BV	BV	900	1,500	—

Date	Mintage	F	VF	XF	Unc	BU
1896Mo B	14,000	BV	BV	900	1,500	—
1897/6Mo M	12,000	BV	BV	900	1,500	—
1897Mo M	Inc. above	BV	BV	900	1,500	—
1898Mo M	20,000	BV	BV	900	1,500	—
1899Mo M	23,000	BV	BV	900	1,500	—
1900Mo M	21,000	BV	BV	900	1,500	—
1901Mo M	29,000	BV	BV	900	1,500	—
1902Mo M	38,000	BV	BV	900	1,500	—
1903/2Mo M	31,000	BV	BV	900	1,500	—
1903Mo M	Inc. above	BV	BV	900	1,500	—
1904Mo M	52,000	BV	BV	900	1,500	—
1905Mo M	9,757	BV	BV	900	1,500	—

KM# 414.7   20 PESOS
33.8400 g., 0.8750 Gold 0.9519 oz. AGW **Obv:** Facing
eagle, snake in beak **Obv. Legend:** REPUBLICA
MEXICANA **Rev:** Radiant cap above scales

Date	Mintage	F	VF	XF	Unc	BU
1870oa E	1,131	750	1,500	2,500	5,000	—
1871oa E	1,591	750	1,500	2,500	5,000	—
1872oa E	255	1,000	1,750	3,000	7,000	—
1888oa E	170	2,000	3,000	5,000	—	—

KM# 414.8   20 PESOS
33.8400 g., 0.8750 Gold 0.9519 oz. AGW **Obv:** Facing
eagle, snake in beak **Rev:** Radiant cap above scales

Date	Mintage	F	VF	XF	Unc	BU
1871Zs H	1,000	3,500	6,500	7,000	9,000	—
1875Zs A	—	4,000	6,000	7,500	9,500	—
1878Zs S	441	4,000	6,000	7,500	9,500	—
1888Zs Z Rare	50	—	—	—	—	—
1889Zs Z	640	3,500	5,500	7,000	9,000	—

KM# 414.1   20 PESOS
33.8400 g., 0.8750 Gold 0.9519 oz. AGW **Obv:**
Facing eagle, snake in beak **Rev:** Radiant cap above
scales **Note:** Mint mark CH, Ca.

Date	Mintage	F	VF	XF	Unc	BU
1872CH M	995	BV	700	1,000	2,500	—
1873CH M	950	BV	700	1,000	2,500	—
1874CH M	1,116	BV	685	950	2,500	—
1875CH M	750	BV	700	1,000	2,500	—
1876CH M	600	BV	800	1,250	2,750	—
1877CH Rare	55	—	—	—	—	—
1882CH M	1,758	BV	685	950	2,500	—
1883CH M	161	700	1,000	1,500	3,000	—
1884CH M	496	BV	700	1,000	2,500	—
1885CH M	122	700	1,000	1,500	3,000	—
1887Ca M	550	BV	700	1,000	2,500	—
1888Ca M	351	BV	700	1,000	2,500	—
1889Ca M	464	BV	700	1,000	2,500	—
1890Ca M	1,209	BV	685	950	2,500	—
1891Ca M	2,004	BV	665	900	2,250	—
1893Ca M	418	BV	700	950	2,500	—
1895Ca M	133	700	1,000	1,500	3,000	—

UNITED STATES

DECIMAL COINAGE

100 Centavos = 1 Peso

KM# 415   CENTAVO
3.0000 g., Bronze, 20 mm. **Obv:** National arms **Rev:**
Value below date within wreath **Note:** Mint mark Mo.

Date	Mintage	F	VF	XF	Unc	BU
1905 Narrow date	6,040,000	4.00	6.50	14.00	90.00	—
1905 Wide date	—	4.00	6.50	14.00	90.00	—
1906 Narrow date	Est. 67,505,000	0.50	0.75	1.25	14.00	—

Note: 50,000,000 pcs. were struck at the Birmingham Mint

Date	Mintage	F	VF	XF	Unc	BU
1906 Wide date	Inc. above	0.75	1.50	2.50	20.00	—
1910 Narrow date	8,700,000	2.00	3.00	6.50	85.00	—
1910 Wide date	—	2.00	3.00	6.50	85.00	—
1911 Narrow date	16,450,000	0.60	1.00	2.75	22.50	—
1911 Wide date	Inc. above	0.75	1.00	4.00	32.00	—
1912	12,650,000	1.00	1.35	3.25	32.00	—
1913	12,850,000	0.75	1.25	3.00	35.00	—
1914 Narrow date	17,350,000	0.75	1.00	3.00	13.50	18.00
1914 Wide date	Inc. above	0.75	1.00	3.00	13.50	18.00
1915	2,277,000	11.00	25.00	67.50	250	—
1916	500,000	45.00	80.00	170	1,200	—
1920	1,433,000	22.00	50.00	110	400	—
1921	3,470,000	5.50	15.50	47.00	275	—
1922	1,880,000	9.00	17.00	50.00	250	—
1923	4,800,000	0.75	1.25	1.75	13.50	—
1924/3	2,000,000	65.00	170	285	525	—
1924	Inc. above	4.50	11.00	22.00	235	275
1925	1,550,000	4.50	10.00	25.00	220	—
1926	5,000,000	1.00	2.00	4.00	26.00	30.00
1927/6	6,000,000	30.00	45.00	70.00	150	—
1927	Inc. above	0.75	1.25	4.50	36.00	—
1928	5,000,000	0.75	1.00	3.25	16.50	25.00
1929	4,500,000	0.75	1.00	1.75	17.00	25.00
1930	7,000,000	0.75	1.00	2.50	19.00	—
1933	10,000,000	0.25	0.35	1.75	16.50	—
1934	7,500,000	0.25	0.95	3.25	30.00	—
1935	12,400,000	0.15	0.25	0.40	11.50	—
1936	20,100,000	0.15	0.20	0.30	8.00	—
1937	20,000,000	0.15	0.25	0.35	3.25	5.00
1938	10,000,000	0.10	0.15	0.30	2.00	2.75
1939	30,000,000	0.10	0.20	0.30	1.00	1.50
1940	10,000,000	0.20	0.30	0.60	5.50	7.50
1941	15,800,000	0.15	0.25	0.35	2.00	3.00
1942	30,400,000	0.15	0.20	0.30	1.25	2.00
1943	4,310,000	0.30	0.50	0.75	8.00	10.00
1944	5,645,000	0.15	0.25	0.50	6.00	7.50
1945	26,375,000	0.10	0.15	0.25	1.00	1.25
1946	42,135,000	—	0.15	0.20	0.60	1.00
1947	13,445,000	—	0.10	0.15	0.80	1.25
1948	20,040,000	0.10	0.15	0.30	1.10	2.00
1949	6,235,000	0.10	0.15	0.30	1.25	2.00

Note: Varieties exist

KM# 416   CENTAVO
Bronze, 16 mm. **Obv:** National arms **Rev:** Value

below date within wreath **Note:** Zapata issue. Struck at Mexico City Mint, mint mark Mo. Reduced size. Weight varies 1.39-1.5g.

Date	Mintage	F	VF	XF	Unc	BU
1915	179,000	18.00	30.00	50.00	75.00	—

KM# 417   CENTAVO
2.0000 g., Brass, 16 mm. **Obv:** National arms, eagle left **Rev:** Oat sprigs **Note:** Mint mark Mo.

Date	Mintage	F	VF	XF	Unc	BU
1950	12,815,000	—	0.15	0.35	1.65	2.00
1951	25,740,000	—	0.15	0.35	0.65	1.00
1952	24,610,000	—	0.10	0.25	0.40	0.75
1953	21,160,000	—	0.10	0.25	0.40	0.85
1954	25,675,000	—	0.10	0.15	0.85	1.20
1955	9,820,000	—	0.15	0.25	0.85	1.50
1956	11,285,000	—	0.15	0.25	0.80	1.25
1957	9,805,000	—	0.15	0.25	0.85	1.35
1958	12,155,000	—	0.10	0.25	0.45	0.75
1959	11,875,000	—	0.10	0.25	0.75	1.25
1960	10,360,000	—	0.10	0.15	0.40	0.65
1961	6,385,000	—	0.10	0.15	0.45	0.85
1962	4,850,000	—	0.10	0.15	0.55	0.90
1963	7,775,000	—	0.10	0.15	0.25	0.45
1964	4,280,000	—	0.10	0.15	0.20	0.30
1965	2,255,000	—	0.10	0.15	0.25	0.40
1966	1,760,000	—	0.10	0.25	0.60	0.75
1967	1,290,000	—	0.10	0.15	0.40	0.60
1968	1,000,000	—	0.10	0.20	0.85	1.25
1969	1,000,000	—	0.10	0.15	0.65	0.85

KM# 418   CENTAVO
1.5000 g., Brass, 13 mm. **Obv:** National arms, eagle left **Rev:** Oat sprigs **Note:** Reduced size.

Date	Mintage	F	VF	XF	Unc	BU
1970	1,000,000	—	0.20	0.40	1.45	1.75
1972	1,000,000	—	0.20	0.45	2.50	3.25
1972/2	—	—	0.50	1.25	3.50	5.00
1973	1,000,000	—	1.65	2.75	8.50	12.00

KM# 419   2 CENTAVOS
6.0000 g., Bronze, 25 mm. **Obv:** National arms **Rev:** Value below date within wreath **Note:** Mint mark Mo.

Date	Mintage	F	VF	XF	Unc	BU
1905	50,000	150	300	500	1,200	1,350
1906 Inverted 6	9,998,000	30.00	55.00	120	375	—
1906 Wide date	Inc. above	5.00	11.00	23.00	80.00	—
1906 Narrow date	Inc. above	6.50	14.00	28.00	85.00	—

Note: 5,000,000 pieces were struck at the Birmingham Mint

Date	Mintage	F	VF	XF	Unc	BU
1920	1,325,000	6.50	17.50	35.00	350	—
1921	4,275,000	2.50	4.75	10.00	90.00	—
1922	—	225	550	1,350	4,000	—
1924	750,000	8.50	22.50	55.00	450	—
1925	3,650,000	2.50	3.50	7.50	38.00	—
1926	4,750,000	1.00	2.25	5.50	35.00	—
1927	7,250,000	0.60	1.00	4.50	22.00	—
1928	3,250,000	0.75	1.50	4.75	30.00	—

Date	Mintage	F	VF	XF	Unc	BU
1929	250,000	65.00	180	500	1,000	—
1935	1,250,000	4.25	9.25	22.50	200	—
1939	5,000,000	0.60	0.90	2.25	20.00	22.00
1941	3,550,000	0.45	0.60	1.25	18.00	20.00

KM# 420   2 CENTAVOS
Bronze, 20 mm. **Obv:** National arms **Rev:** Value below date within wreath **Note:** Zapata issue. Mint mark Mo. Reduced size. Weight varies 3-3.03g.

Date	Mintage	F	VF	XF	Unc	BU
1915	487,000	7.50	9.00	17.50	75.00	—

KM# 421   5 CENTAVOS
5.0000 g., Nickel, 20 mm. **Obv:** National arms **Rev:** Value and date within beaded circle **Note:** Mint mark Mo. Varieties exist.

Date	Mintage	F	VF	XF	Unc	BU
1905	1,420,000	7.00	10.00	25.00	300	375
1906/5	10,615,000	13.00	30.00	70.00	375	—
1906	Inc. above	0.75	1.35	3.25	55.00	75.00
1907	4,000,000	1.25	4.00	12.00	350	—
1909	2,052,000	3.25	10.00	48.00	360	—
1910	6,181,000	1.30	3.50	6.00	78.00	115
1911 Narrow date	4,487,000	1.00	3.00	5.00	85.00	125
1911 Wide date	Inc. above	2.50	5.00	9.00	110	160
1912 Small mint mark	420,000	90.00	100	230	725	—
1912 Large mint mark	Inc. above	70.00	95.00	175	575	—
1913	2,035,000	1.75	4.25	9.00	100	150

Note: Wide and narrow dates exist for 1913

1914	2,000,000	1.00	2.00	3.50	70.00	95.00

Note: 5,000,000 pieces appear to have been struck at the Birmingham Mint in 1914 and all of 1909-1911. The Mexican Mint report does not mention receiving the 1914 dated coins

KM# 422   5 CENTAVOS
9.0000 g., Bronze, 28 mm. **Obv:** National arms **Rev:** Value below date within wreath

Date	Mintage	F	VF	XF	Unc	BU
1914Mo	2,500,000	10.00	23.00	50.00	240	—
1915Mo	11,424,000	3.00	5.00	20.00	145	—
1916Mo	2,860,000	15.00	35.00	150	645	—
1917Mo	800,000	75.00	195	375	825	—
1918Mo	1,332,000	35.00	90.00	200	625	—
1919Mo	400,000	115	225	360	925	—
1920Mo	5,920,000	3.00	8.00	40.00	265	—
1921Mo	2,080,000	10.00	24.00	75.00	275	—
1924Mo	780,000	40.00	95.00	260	625	—

Date	Mintage	F	VF	XF	Unc	BU
1925Mo	4,040,000	5.50	11.00	47.50	200	—
1926Mo	3,160,000	5.50	11.00	48.00	300	—
1927Mo	3,600,000	4.00	7.00	30.00	215	250
1928Mo Large date	1,740,000	11.00	18.00	65.00	250	—
1928Mo Small date	Inc. above	30.00	45.00	95.00	385	—
1929Mo	2,400,000	5.50	11.00	48.00	195	—
1930Mo	2,600,000	5.00	8.00	27.50	210	—
Note: Large oval O in date						
1930Mo	Inc. above	60.00	125	250	565	—
Note: Small square O in date						
1931Mo	—	475	750	1,150	3,000	—
1933Mo	8,000,000	1.50	2.25	3.50	27.50	35.00
1934Mo	10,000,000	1.25	1.75	2.75	25.00	40.00
1935Mo	21,980,000	0.75	1.20	2.50	22.50	30.00

KM# 423   5 CENTAVOS
4.0000 g., Copper-Nickel, 20.5 mm. **Obv:** National arms, eagle left **Rev:** Value and date within circle

Date	Mintage	F	VF	XF	Unc	BU
1936M	46,700,000	—	0.65	1.25	6.50	7.50
1937M	49,060,000	—	0.50	1.00	6.00	7.00
1938M	3,340,000	—	4.00	10.00	75.00	250
1940M	22,800,000	—	0.75	1.25	8.00	10.00
1942M	7,100,000	—	1.50	3.00	35.00	45.00

KM# 424   5 CENTAVOS
6.5000 g., Bronze, 25.5 mm. **Obv:** National arms, eagle left **Rev:** Head left

Date	Mintage	F	VF	XF	Unc	BU
1942Mo	900,000	—	25.00	75.00	375	550
1943Mo	54,660,000	—	0.50	0.75	2.50	3.50
1944Mo	53,463,000	—	0.25	0.35	0.75	1.00
1945Mo	44,262,000	—	0.25	0.35	0.75	1.25
1946Mo	49,054,000	—	0.50	1.00	2.00	3.00
1951Mo	50,758,000	—	0.75	0.90	3.00	5.00
1952Mo	17,674,000	—	1.50	2.50	9.50	11.50
1953Mo	31,568,000	—	1.25	2.00	6.00	9.00
1954Mo	58,680,000	—	0.40	1.00	2.75	4.00
1955Mo	31,114,000	—	2.00	3.00	11.00	14.00

KM# 425   5 CENTAVOS
4.0000 g., Copper-Nickel, 20.5 mm. **Obv:** National arms, eagle left **Rev:** Bust right flanked by date and value

Date	Mintage	F	VF	XF	Unc	BU
1950Mo	5,700,000	—	0.75	1.50	6.00	7.00
Note: 5,600,000 pieces struck at Connecticut melted						

KM# 426   5 CENTAVOS
4.0000 g., Brass, 20.5 mm. **Obv:** National arms, eagle left **Rev:** Bust right

Date	Mintage	VF	XF	Unc	BU
1954Mo Dot	—	10.00	45.00	300	375
1954Mo Without dot	—	15.00	30.00	250	290
1955Mo	12,136,000	0.75	1.50	9.00	12.50
1956Mo	60,216,000	0.20	0.30	0.75	1.25
1957Mo	55,288,000	0.15	0.20	0.90	1.50
1958Mo	104,624,000	0.15	0.20	0.60	1.00
1959Mo	106,000,000	0.15	0.25	0.75	1.25
1960Mo	99,144,000	0.10	0.15	0.50	0.75
1961Mo	61,136,000	0.10	0.15	0.50	0.75
1962Mo	47,232,000	0.10	0.15	0.25	0.35
1963Mo	156,680,000	—	0.15	0.25	0.40
1964Mo	71,168,000	—	0.15	0.20	0.40
1965Mo	155,720,000	—	0.15	0.25	0.35
1966Mo	124,944,000	—	0.15	0.40	0.65
1967Mo	118,816,000	—	0.15	0.25	0.40
1968Mo	189,588,000	—	0.15	0.50	0.75
1969Mo	210,492,000	—	0.15	0.55	0.80

KM# 426a   5 CENTAVOS
Copper-Nickel, 20.5 mm. **Obv:** National arms, eagle left **Rev:** Bust right

Date	Mintage	F	VF	XF	Unc	BU
1960Mo	—	—	250	300	350	—
1962Mo	19	—	250	300	350	—
1965Mo	—	—	250	300	350	—

KM# 427   5 CENTAVOS
2.7500 g., Brass, 18 mm. **Obv:** National arms, eagle left **Rev:** Bust right **Note:** Due to some minor alloy variations this type is often encountered with a bronze-color toning. Reduced size.

Date	Mintage	VF	XF	Unc	BU
1970	163,368,000	0.10	0.15	0.35	0.45
1971	198,844,000	0.10	0.15	0.25	0.30
1972	225,000,000	0.10	0.15	0.25	0.30
1973 Flat top 3	595,070,000	0.10	0.15	0.25	0.40
1973 Round top 3	Inc. above	0.10	0.15	0.20	0.30
1974	401,584,000	0.10	0.15	0.30	0.40
1975	342,308,000	0.10	0.15	0.25	0.35
1976	367,524,000	0.10	0.15	0.40	0.60

KM# 428   10 CENTAVOS
2.5000 g., 0.8000 Silver 0.0643 oz. ASW, 18 mm. **Obv:** National arms **Rev:** Value and date within 3/4 wreath with Liberty cap above **Note:** Mint mark Mo.

Date	Mintage	VF	XF	Unc	BU
1905	3,920,000	6.00	8.00	40.00	50.00
1906	8,410,000	5.50	7.50	27.00	35.00
1907/6	5,950,000	50.00	135	275	350
1907	Inc. above	5.50	6.25	35.00	42.50
1909	2,620,000	8.50	13.00	70.00	85.00

Date	Mintage	VF	XF	Unc	BU
1910/00	3,450,000	10.00	40.00	75.00	85.00
1910	Inc. above	7.00	15.00	25.00	30.00
1911 Narrow date	2,550,000	11.00	17.00	88.00	125
1911 Wide date	Inc. above	7.50	10.00	42.00	60.00
1912	1,350,000	10.00	18.00	130	160
1912 Low 2	Inc. above	10.00	18.00	115	140
1913/2	1,990,000	10.00	25.00	40.00	70.00
1913	Inc. above	7.00	10.00	33.00	40.00
1914	3,110,000	5.50	7.00	15.00	20.00

Note: Wide and narrow dates exist for 1914

KM# 429   10 CENTAVOS
1.8125 g., 0.8000 Silver 0.0466 oz. ASW, 15 mm.
Obv: National arms **Rev:** Value and date within 3/4
wreath with Liberty cap above **Note:** Mint mark Mo.
Reduced size.

Date	Mintage	F	VF	XF	Unc	BU
1919	8,360,000	—	10.00	15.00	85.00	110

KM# 430   10 CENTAVOS
12.0000 g., Bronze, 30.5 mm. **Obv:** National arms
Rev: Value below date within wreath **Note:** Mint
mark Mo.

Date	Mintage	F	VF	XF	Unc	BU
1919	1,232,000	—	25.00	70.00	450	525
1920	6,612,000	—	15.00	50.00	400	475
1921	2,255,000	—	35.00	80.00	650	800
1935	5,970,000	—	14.00	30.00	120	175

KM# 431   10 CENTAVOS
1.6600 g., 0.7200 Silver 0.0384 oz. ASW, 15 mm.
Obv: National arms **Rev:** Value and date within
wreath with Liberty cap above **Note:** Mint mark Mo.

Date	Mintage	F	VF	XF	Unc	BU
1925/15	5,350,000	—	30.00	75.00	125	175
1925/3	Inc. above	—	20.00	40.00	125	150
1925	Inc. above	—	2.00	5.00	40.00	45.00
1926/16	2,650,000	—	30.00	75.00	125	175
1926	Inc. above	—	3.50	7.50	65.00	85.00
1927	2,810,000	—	2.25	3.00	17.50	22.50
1928	5,270,000	—	2.00	2.75	13.50	16.50
1930	2,000,000	—	3.75	5.00	18.75	25.00
1933	5,000,000	—	1.50	3.00	10.00	11.50
1934	8,000,000	—	1.75	2.50	8.00	10.00
1935	3,500,000	—	2.75	5.00	11.00	12.50

KM# 432   10 CENTAVOS
5.5000 g., Copper-Nickel, 23.5 mm. **Obv:** National
arms, eagle left **Rev:** Value and date within circle
Note: Mint mark Mo.

Date	Mintage	F	VF	XF	Unc	BU
1936	33,030,000	—	0.75	2.50	9.00	10.00
1937	3,000,000	—	8.00	45.00	215	250
1938	3,650,000	1.25	2.00	7.00	60.00	75.00
1939	6,920,000	—	1.00	3.50	27.50	30.00
1940	12,300,000	—	0.40	1.25	5.00	6.00
1942	14,380,000	—	0.60	1.50	7.00	9.00
1945	9,558,000	—	0.40	0.70	3.50	4.00
1946	46,230,000	—	0.40	0.60	2.50	3.00

KM# 433   10 CENTAVOS
5.5000 g., Bronze, 23.5 mm. **Obv:** National arms,
eagle left **Rev:** Bust left **Note:** Mint mark Mo.

Date	Mintage	F	VF	XF	Unc	BU
1955	1,818,000	—	0.75	3.25	23.00	30.00
1956	5,255,000	—	0.75	3.25	23.00	28.00
1957	11,925,000	—	0.20	0.40	5.50	8.00
1959	26,140,000	—	0.30	0.45	0.75	1.25
1966	5,873,000	—	0.15	0.25	0.60	1.75
1967	32,318,000	—	0.10	0.15	0.30	0.40

Sharp stem

KM# 434.1   10 CENTAVOS
1.5200 g., Copper-Nickel **Obv:** National arms, eagle
left **Rev:** Upright ear of corn **Note:** Variety I- Sharp
stem and wide date

Date	Mintage	F	VF	XF	Unc	BU
1974	6,000,000	—	—	0.35	0.75	1.00
1975	5,550,000	—	0.10	0.35	0.75	1.00
1976	7,680,000	—	0.10	0.20	0.30	0.40
1977	144,650,000	—	1.25	2.25	3.00	3.50
1978	271,870,000	—	—	1.00	1.50	2.25
1979	375,660,000	—	—	0.50	1.00	1.75
1980/79	21,290,000	—	2.45	3.75	6.00	7.00
1980	Inc. above	—	1.50	2.00	4.50	5.50

Blunt stem

KM# 434.2   10 CENTAVOS
1.5600 g., Copper-Nickel **Obv:** National arms, eagle
left **Rev:** Upright ear of corn **Note:** Variety II- Blunt
stem and narrow date

Date	Mintage	F	VF	XF	Unc	BU
1974	Inc. above	—	—	0.10	0.20	0.30
1977	Inc. above	—	0.15	0.50	1.25	2.25
1978	Inc. above	—	—	0.10	0.30	0.40
1979	Inc. above	—	0.15	0.35	0.85	1.50
1980	Inc. above	—	—	0.10	0.20	0.30

KM# 434.4   10 CENTAVOS
Copper-Nickel **Obv:** National arms, eagle left **Rev:** Upright ear of corn **Note:** Variety IV- Sharp stem and narrow date

Date	Mintage	F	VF	XF	Unc	BU
1974	—	—	—	—	1.50	2.50
1979	—	—	—	—	1.50	2.50

KM# 434.3   10 CENTAVOS
Copper-Nickel **Obv:** National arms, eagle left **Rev:** Upright ear of corn **Note:** Variety III- Blunt stem and wide date

Date	Mintage	F	VF	XF	Unc	BU
1980/79	—	—	—	—	5.00	6.00

KM# 435   20 CENTAVOS
5.0000 g., 0.8000 Silver 0.1286 oz. ASW, 22 mm.
Obv: National arms **Rev:** Value and date within wreath with Liberty cap above **Note:** Mint mark Mo.

Date	Mintage	F	VF	XF	Unc	BU
1905	2,565,000	—	12.00	20.00	145	175
1906	6,860,000	—	9.00	16.50	60.00	80.00
1907 Straight 7	4,000,000	—	11.50	20.00	70.00	100
1907 Curved 7	5,435,000	—	7.50	13.50	65.00	90.00
1908	350,000	50.00	90.00	225	1,500	—
1910	1,135,000	—	11.00	16.00	80.00	95.00
1911	1,150,000	12.00	15.00	35.00	125	150
1912	625,000	20.00	40.00	70.00	335	375
1913	1,000,000	—	14.50	30.00	95.00	115
1914	1,500,000	—	10.00	21.50	62.50	75.00

KM# 436   20 CENTAVOS
3.6250 g., 0.8000 Silver 0.0932 oz. ASW, 19 mm.
Obv: National arms **Rev:** Value and date within wreath with Liberty cap above **Note:** Mint mark Mo. Reduced size.

Date	Mintage	F	VF	XF	Unc	BU
1919	4,155,000	—	30.00	55.00	190	225

KM# 437   20 CENTAVOS
15.0000 g., Bronze, 32.5 mm. **Obv:** National arms

Rev: Value below date within wreath **Note:** Mint mark Mo.

Date	Mintage	F	VF	XF	Unc	BU
1920	4,835,000	—	45.00	140	650	750
1935	20,000,000	—	6.00	10.00	80.00	125

KM# 438   20 CENTAVOS
3.3333 g., 0.7200 Silver 0.0772 oz. ASW, 19 mm.
Obv: National arms **Rev:** Value and date within wreath with Liberty cap above **Note:** Mint mark Mo.

Date	Mintage	F	VF	XF	Unc	BU
1920	3,710,000	—	6.00	17.50	165	200
1921	6,160,000	—	6.00	14.00	100	145
1925	1,450,000	—	12.00	20.00	125	150
1926/5	1,465,000	—	20.00	65.00	325	375
1926	Inc. above	—	3.25	7.50	80.00	110
1927	1,405,000	—	3.50	8.00	85.00	115
1928	3,630,000	—	4.00	5.25	14.50	19.50
1930	1,000,000	—	5.00	8.00	25.00	35.00
1933	2,500,000	—	2.25	3.00	10.00	11.50
1934	2,500,000	—	2.25	4.00	11.00	12.50
1935	2,460,000	—	2.25	4.00	11.00	12.50
1937	10,000,000	—	1.75	2.25	4.00	5.00
1939	8,800,000	—	1.75	2.25	4.00	5.00
1940	3,000,000	—	1.75	2.25	3.50	5.00
1941	5,740,000	—	1.50	2.25	3.00	4.00
1942	12,460,000	—	1.50	2.25	3.25	3.75
1943	3,955,000	—	2.00	2.50	3.50	4.25

KM# 439   20 CENTAVOS
Bronze, 28.5 mm. **Obv:** National arms, eagle left **Rev:** Liberty cap divides value above Pyramid of the Sun at Teotihuacán, volcanos Ixtaccihuatl and Popocatepetl in background **Edge:** Plain **Note:** Mint mark Mo.

Date	Mintage	F	VF	XF	Unc	BU
1943	46,350,000	—	1.25	3.00	18.00	25.00
1944	83,650,000	—	0.40	0.65	8.00	10.00
1945	26,801,000	—	1.25	3.50	9.50	12.00
1946	25,695,000	—	1.10	2.25	6.00	8.25
1951	11,385,000	—	3.00	8.75	90.00	110
1952	6,560,000	—	3.00	5.00	25.00	32.00
1953	26,948,000	—	0.35	0.80	8.25	12.00
1954	40,108,000	—	0.35	0.80	8.00	11.50
1955	16,950,000	—	2.75	7.00	60.00	75.00

KM# 440   20 CENTAVOS
Bronze, 28.5 mm. **Obv:** National arms, eagle left **Rev:** Liberty cap divides value above Pyramid of the Sun at Teotihuacán, volcanos Ixtaccihuatl and Popocatepetl in background **Edge:** Plain **Note:** Mint mark Mo.

Date	Mintage	VF	XF	Unc	BU
1955 Inc. KM#439	Inc. above	0.75	1.75	17.00	22.00
1956	22,431,000	0.30	0.35	3.00	4.00

Date	Mintage	VF	XF	Unc	BU
1957	13,455,000	0.45	1.25	9.00	12.00
1959	6,017,000	4.50	9.00	75.00	100
1960	39,756,000	0.15	0.25	0.75	1.00
1963	14,869,000	0.25	0.35	0.80	1.00
1964	28,654,000	0.25	0.40	0.90	1.25
1965	74,162,000	0.20	0.35	0.80	1.00
1966	43,745,000	0.15	0.25	0.75	1.00
1967	46,487,000	0.20	0.50	1.00	1.25
1968	15,477,000	0.30	0.55	1.35	1.65
1969	63,647,000	0.20	0.35	0.80	1.00
1970	76,287,000	0.15	0.20	0.90	1.30
1971	49,892,000	0.30	0.50	1.25	1.50

KM# 441 20 CENTAVOS
Bronze, 28.5 mm. **Obv:** National arms, eagle left **Rev:** Liberty cap divides value above Pyramid of the Sun at Teotihuacán, volcanos Ixtaccihuatl and Popocatepet in background **Edge:** Plain

Date	Mintage	VF	XF	Unc	BU
1971 Inc. KM#440	Inc. above	0.20	0.35	1.85	2.35
1973	78,398,000	0.25	0.35	0.95	1.50
1974	34,200,000	0.20	0.35	1.25	1.75

KM# 442 20 CENTAVOS
3.0600 g., Copper-Nickel, 20 mm. **Obv:** National arms, eagle left **Rev:** Bust 3/4 facing flanked by value and date

Date	Mintage	VF	XF	Unc	BU
1974	112,000,000	0.10	0.15	0.25	0.30
1975	611,000,000	0.10	0.15	0.30	0.35
1976	394,000,000	0.10	0.15	0.35	0.45
1977	394,350,000	0.10	0.15	0.40	0.45
1978	527,950,000	0.10	0.15	0.25	0.30
1979	524,615,000	0.10	0.15	0.25	0.30
1979	—	1.25	2.00	4.00	8.00
Note: Doubled die obv. small letters					
1979	—	1.25	2.00	4.00	8.00
Note: Doubled die obv. large letters					
1980	326,500,000	0.15	0.20	0.30	0.40
1981 Open 8	106,205,000	0.30	0.50	1.00	2.00
1981 Closed 8, high date	248,500,000	0.30	0.50	1.00	2.00
1981 Closed 8, low date	—	1.00	1.50	3.50	4.25
1981/1982	—	40.00	75.00	175	195
Note: The 1981/1982 overdate is often mistaken as 1982/1981					
1982	286,855,000	0.40	0.60	0.90	1.10
1983 Round top 3	100,930,000	0.25	0.40	1.75	2.25
1983 Flat top 3	Inc. above	0.25	0.50	1.25	1.75
1983 Proof	998				

KM# 491 20 CENTAVOS
3.0000 g., Bronze, 20 mm. **Subject:** Olmec Culture **Obv:** National arms, eagle left **Rev:** Mask 3/4 right with value below

Date	Mintage	F	VF	XF	Unc	BU
1983 Proof	53	Value: 185				

Date	Mintage	F	VF	XF	Unc	BU
1983	260,000,000	—	0.20	0.25	1.25	1.75
1984	180,320,000	—	0.20	0.35	1.85	2.25

KM# 443 25 CENTAVOS
3.3330 g., 0.3000 Silver 0.0321 oz. ASW, 21.5 mm. **Obv:** National arms, eagle left **Rev:** Scale below Liberty cap **Note:** Mint mark Mo.

Date	Mintage	F	VF	XF	Unc	BU
1950	77,060,000	—	0.60	0.80	1.60	2.00
1951	41,172,000	—	0.60	0.80	1.60	2.00
1952	29,264,000	—	0.75	1.10	1.75	2.25
1953	38,144,000	—	0.65	0.85	1.60	2.00

KM# 444 25 CENTAVOS
5.5000 g., Copper-Nickel, 23 mm. **Obv:** National arms, eagle left **Rev:** Bust 3/4 facing

Date	Mintage	F	VF	XF	Unc	BU
1964	20,686,000	—	—	0.15	0.20	0.30
1966 Closed beak	180,000	—	0.65	1.00	2.25	2.50
1966 Open beak	Inc. above	—	1.75	3.50	10.00	13.50

KM# 445 50 CENTAVOS
12.5000 g., 0.8000 Silver 0.3215 oz. ASW, 30 mm. **Obv:** National arms **Rev:** Value and date within 3/4 wreath with Liberty cap above **Note:** Mint mark Mo.

Date	Mintage	F	VF	XF	Unc	BU
1905	2,446,000	12.50	20.00	30.00	150	225
1906 Open 9	16,966,000	—	6.00	10.00	40.00	60.00
1906 Closed 9	Inc. above	—	5.00	9.00	35.00	50.00
1907 Straight 7	18,920,000	—	5.00	9.00	25.00	28.50
1907 Curved 7	14,841,000	—	5.25	9.00	25.00	32.00
1908	488,000	—	80.00	190	545	650
1912	3,736,000	—	11.00	14.00	45.00	60.00
1913/07	10,510,000	—	40.00	90.00	240	275
1913/2	Inc. above	—	20.00	27.50	65.00	85.00
1913	Inc. above	—	5.50	8.50	27.50	35.00
1914	7,710,000	—	6.75	13.50	32.00	45.00
1916 Narrow date	480,000	—	60.00	85.00	200	290
1916 Wide date	Inc. above	—	60.00	85.00	200	290
1917	37,112,000	—	6.00	9.50	20.00	22.50
1918	1,320,000	—	70.00	135	250	335

KM# 446 50 CENTAVOS
9.0625 g., 0.8000 Silver 0.2331 oz. ASW, 27 mm.
Obv: National arms **Rev:** Value and date within 3/4
wreath with Liberty cap above **Note:** Mint mark Mo.
Reduced size.

Date	Mintage	F	VF	XF	Unc	BU
1918/7	2,760,000	—	525	675	1,250	—
1918	Inc. above	—	17.50	55.00	300	385
1919	29,670,000	—	9.50	22.50	95.00	125

KM# 447 50 CENTAVOS
8.3333 g., 0.7200 Silver 0.1929 oz. ASW, 27 mm.
Obv: National arms **Rev:** Value and date within 3/4
wreath with Liberty cap above **Note:** Mint mark Mo.

Date	Mintage	F	VF	XF	Unc	BU
1919	10,200,000	—	10.00	20.00	90.00	110
1920	27,166,000	—	8.00	14.00	70.00	80.00
1921	21,864,000	—	8.00	14.00	85.00	100
1925	3,280,000	—	17.50	30.00	125	160
1937	20,000,000	—	4.25	5.50	7.50	8.50
1938	100,000	—	50.00	85.00	225	300
1939	10,440,000	—	6.00	8.00	15.00	18.50
1942	800,000	—	6.00	9.00	16.00	20.00
1943	41,512,000	—	3.25	4.25	5.50	6.50
1944	55,806,000	—	3.25	4.25	5.50	6.50
1945	56,766,000	—	3.25	4.25	5.50	6.50

KM# 448 50 CENTAVOS
7.9730 g., 0.4200 Silver 0.1077 oz. ASW, 27 mm.
Obv: National arms **Rev:** Value and date within 3/4
wreath with Liberty cap above **Note:** Mint mark Mo.

Date	Mintage	F	VF	XF	Unc	BU
1935	70,800,000	—	2.50	3.25	5.50	7.00

KM# 449 50 CENTAVOS
6.6600 g., 0.3000 Silver 0.0642 oz. ASW, 26 mm.
Obv: National arms, eagle left **Rev:** Head with head
covering right **Note:** Mint mark Mo.

Date	Mintage	F	VF	XF	Unc	BU
1950	13,570,000	—	1.50	1.85	3.00	4.50
1951	3,650,000	—	2.00	2.50	3.75	5.75

KM# 450 50 CENTAVOS
14.0000 g., Bronze, 33 mm. **Obv:** National arms,
eagle left **Rev:** Head with headdress left **Note:** Mint
mark Mo.

Date	Mintage	F	VF	XF	Unc	BU
1955	3,502,000	—	1.50	3.00	29.00	35.00
1956	34,643,000	—	0.75	1.50	3.75	4.50
1957	9,675,000	—	1.00	2.00	6.50	7.50
1959	4,540,000	—	0.50	0.75	2.00	2.75

KM# 451 50 CENTAVOS
6.5000 g., Copper-Nickel, 25 mm. **Obv:** National
arms, eagle left **Rev:** Head with headdress left

Date	Mintage	F	VF	XF	Unc	BU
1964	43,806,000	—	0.15	0.20	0.40	0.60
1965	14,326,000	—	0.20	0.25	0.45	0.65
1966	1,726,000	—	0.20	0.40	1.30	1.75
1967	55,144,000	—	0.20	0.30	0.65	1.00
1968	80,438,000	—	0.15	0.30	0.65	0.90
1969	87,640,000	—	0.20	0.35	0.80	1.00

KM# 452 50 CENTAVOS
6.5000 g., Copper-Nickel, 25 mm. **Obv:** National
arms, eagle left **Rev:** Head with headdress left **Note:**
Coins dated 1975 and 1976 exlst wlth and without
dots in centers of three circles on plumage on
reverse. Edge varieties exist.

Date	Mintage	VF	XF	Unc	BU
1970	76,236,000	0.15	0.20	0.80	1.00
1971	125,288,000	0.15	0.20	0.90	1.30
1972	16,000,000	1.25	2.00	3.00	4.75
1975 Dots	177,958,000	0.60	1.25	3.50	6.00
1975 No dots	Inc. above	0.15	0.20	0.75	1.00
1976 Dots	37,480,000	0.75	1.25	5.00	6.00
1976 No dots	Inc. above	0.15	0.20	0.50	0.75
1977	12,410,000	6.50	10.00	32.50	42.50
1978	85,400,000	0.15	0.25	0.50	0.75
1979 Round 2nd 9 in date	229,000,000	0.15	0.25	0.50	0.65
1979 Square 9's in date	Inc. above	0.20	0.40	1.60	2.00
1980 Narrow date, square 9	89,978,000	0.45	0.75	1.75	2.50
1980 Wide date, round 9	178,188,000	0.20	0.25	1.00	1.15

Date	Mintage	VF	XF	Unc	BU
1981 Rectangular 9, narrow date	142,212,000	0.50	0.75	1.75	2.50
1981 Round 9, wide date	Inc. above	0.30	0.50	1.25	1.75
1982	45,474,000	0.20	0.40	1.00	1.25
1983	90,318,000	0.50	0.75	2.00	2.50
1983 Proof	998				

KM# 492   50 CENTAVOS
Stainless Steel, 22 mm. **Subject:** Palenque Culture
Obv: National arms, eagle left **Rev:** Head with
headdress 3/4 left

Date	Mintage	F	VF	XF	Unc	BU
1983	99,540,000	—	—	0.30	1.50	2.50
1983 Proof	53	Value: 195				

KM# 453   PESO
27.0700 g., 0.9030 Silver 0.7859 oz. ASW, 39 mm.
Subject: Caballito **Obv:** National arms **Rev:** Horse
and rider facing left among sun rays **Designer:**
Charles Pillet **Note:** Mint mark Mo.

Date	Mintage	F	VF	XF	Unc	BU
1910	3,814,000	—	45.00	50.00	160	250
1911	1,227,000	—	45.00	75.00	200	275
Note: Long lower left ray on reverse						
1911	Inc. above	—	145	210	650	800
Note: Short lower left ray on reverse						
1912	322,000	—	100	210	365	500
1913/2	2,880,000	—	45.00	75.00	270	400
1913	Inc. above	—	45.00	70.00	175	250
Note: 1913 coins exist with even and unevenly spaced date						
1914	120,000	—	600	950	2,800	—

KM# 454   PESO
18.1300 g., 0.8000 Silver 0.4663 oz. ASW, 34 mm.
Obv: National arms **Rev:** Value and date within 3/4
wreath with Liberty cap above **Note:** Mint mark Mo.

Date	Mintage	F	VF	XF	Unc	BU
1918	3,050,000	—	35.00	125	1,350	2,100
1919	6,151,000	—	20.00	50.00	900	1,600

KM# 455   PESO
16.6600 g., 0.7200 Silver 0.3856 oz. ASW, 34 mm.
Obv: National arms **Rev:** Value and date within 3/4
wreath with Liberty cap above **Note:** Mint mark Mo.

Date	Mintage	F	VF	XF	Unc	BU
1920/10	8,830,000	—	50.00	90.00	325	—
1920	Inc. above	—	8.00	25.00	185	300
1921	5,480,000	—	8.00	25.00	155	200
1922	33,620,000	—	BV	6.00	20.00	26.00
1923	35,280,000	—	BV	6.00	20.00	28.00
1924	33,060,000	—	BV	6.00	20.00	26.00
1925	9,160,000	—	4.50	10.00	60.00	75.00
1926	28,840,000	—	BV	6.00	20.00	25.00
1927	5,060,000	—	7.00	10.00	70.00	85.00
1932 Open 9	50,770,000	—	—	BV	6.00	7.50
1932 Closed 9	Inc. above	—	—	BV	6.00	7.50
1933/2	43,920,000	—	15.00	25.00	85.00	—
1933	Inc. above	—	—	BV	6.50	8.50
1934	22,070,000	—	—	BV	8.00	10.00
1935	8,050,000	—	BV	6.00	11.50	13.50
1938	30,000,000	—	—	BV	6.00	7.50
1940	20,000,000	—	—	BV	6.50	8.00
1943	47,662,000	—	—	BV	5.75	6.50
1944	39,522,000	—	—	BV	6.00	7.00
1945	37,300,000	—	—	BV	6.00	7.00

KM# 456   PESO
14.0000 g., 0.5000 Silver 0.2250 oz. ASW, 32 mm.
Obv: National arms, eagle left **Rev:** Head with
headcovering right **Note:** Mint mark Mo.

Date	Mintage	F	VF	XF	Unc	BU
1947	61,460,000	—	BV	3.50	4.50	5.50
1948	22,915,000	—	3.50	4.50	5.50	6.50
1949	4,000,000	—	—	1,200	1,600	2,500
Note: Not released for circulation						
1949 Proof	—	Value: 4,000				

Date	Mintage	F	VF	XF	Unc	BU
1962	61,094,000	—	BV	0.80	1.75	2.25
1963	26,394,000	—	BV	0.80	1.75	2.00
1964	15,615,000	—	BV	0.80	2.00	2.40
1965	5,004,000	—	—	0.80	1.85	2.00
1966	30,998,000	—	—	0.75	1.35	1.85
1967	9,308,000	—	—	0.85	2.75	3.50

KM# 457 PESO
13.3300 g., 0.3000 Silver 0.1286 oz. ASW, 32 mm.
Obv: National arms, eagle left **Rev:** Armored bust 3/4 left **Note:** Mint mark Mo.

Date	Mintage	F	VF	XF	Unc	BU
1950	3,287,000	—	2.50	4.00	7.00	8.50

Tall date	Short date

KM# 460 PESO
9.0000 g., Copper-Nickel, 29 mm. **Obv:** National arms, eagle left **Rev:** Head left

Date	Mintage	VF	XF	Unc	BU
1970 Narrow date	102,715,000	0.25	0.35	0.65	0.80
1970 Wide date	Inc. above	1.25	2.50	7.50	9.00
1971	426,222,000	0.20	0.25	0.55	0.75
1972	120,000,000	0.20	0.25	0.40	0.65
1974	63,700,000	0.20	0.25	0.65	0.90
1975 Tall narrow date	205,979,000	0.25	0.45	1.00	1.35
1975 Short wide date	Inc. above	0.30	0.40	0.75	1.00
1976	94,489,000	0.15	0.20	0.50	0.75
1977 Thick date close to rim	94,364,000	0.25	0.45	1.00	1.25
1977 Thin date, space between sideburns and collar	Inc. above	1.00	2.00	6.50	13.50
1978 Closed 8	208,300,000	0.20	0.30	1.00	1.50
1978 Open 8	55,140,000	0.75	1.75	12.00	15.00
1979 Thin date	117,884,000	0.20	0.30	1.15	1.50
1979 Thick date	Inc. above	0.20	0.30	1.25	1.75
1980 Closed 8	318,800,000	0.25	0.35	1.00	1.25
1980 Open 8	23,865,000	0.75	1.50	8.00	12.00
1981 Closed 8	413,349,000	0.20	0.30	0.75	0.90
1981 Open 8	58,616,000	0.50	1.25	6.50	8.00
1982 Closed 8	235,000,000	0.25	0.75	2.25	2.50
1982 Open 8	—	0.75	1.50	8.00	12.00
1983 Wide date	100,000,000	0.30	0.45	3.00	3.50
1983 Narrow date	Inc. above	0.30	0.45	3.00	3.50
1983 Proof	1,051,000				

KM# 458 PESO
16.0000 g., 0.1000 Silver 0.0514 oz. ASW, 34.5 mm.
Subject: 100th Anniversary of Constitution **Obv:** National arms, eagle left within wreath **Obv. Designer:** Manuel L. Negrete **Rev:** Head left **Edge Lettering:** INDEPENDENCIA Y LIBERTAD **Note:** Mint mark Mo.

Date	Mintage	F	VF	XF	Unc	BU
1957	500,000	—	3.50	5.00	12.50	15.00

KM# 459 PESO
16.0000 g., 0.1000 Silver 0.0514 oz. ASW, 34.5 mm. **Obv:** National arms, eagle left within wreath **Rev:** Armored bust right within wreath **Edge Lettering:** INDEPENDENCIA Y LIBERTAD **Note:** Mint mark Mo.

Date	Mintage	F	VF	XF	Unc	BU
1957	28,273,000	—	0.75	1.00	2.50	10.00
1958	41,899,000	—	BV	0.80	1.65	2.00
1959	27,369,000	—	1.25	2.00	5.50	8.00
1960	26,259,000	—	0.75	1.10	3.25	4.50
1961	52,601,000	—	BV	0.90	2.25	3.00

KM# 496 PESO
Stainless Steel, 24.5 mm. **Obv:** National arms, eagle left **Rev:** Armored bust right

Date	Mintage	VF	XF	Unc	BU
1984	722,802,000	0.10	0.25	0.65	1.00
1985	985,000,000	0.10	0.25	0.50	0.75
1986	740,000,000	0.10	0.25	0.50	0.75
1987	250,000,000	—	0.25	0.50	0.80
1987 Proof; 2 known	—				

KM# 461 2 PESOS
1.6666 g., 0.9000 Gold 0.0482 oz. AGW, 13 mm.
Obv: National arms **Rev:** Date above value within wreath **Note:** Mint mark Mo.

Date	Mintage	F	VF	XF	Unc
1919	1,670,000	—	BV	47.50	65.00
1920/10	—	BV	47.50	55.00	100
1920	4,282,000	—	BV	47.50	50.00
1944	10,000	BV	47.50	50.00	70.00
1945	Est. 140,000	—	—	—	BV+20%
1946	168,000	BV	47.50	50.00	100
1947	25,000	BV	47.50	50.00	75.00
1948 No specimens known	45,000	—	—	—	—

Note: During 1951-1972 a total of 4,590,493 pieces were restruck, most likely dated 1945. In 1996 matte restrikes were produced

KM# 462 2 PESOS
26.6667 g., 0.9000 Silver 0.7716 oz. ASW, 39 mm.
Subject: Centennial of Independence **Obv:** National arms, eagle left within wreath **Rev:** Winged Victory **Designer:** Emilio del Moral **Note:** Mint mark Mo.

Date	Mintage	F	VF	XF	Unc	BU
1921	1,278,000	—	40.00	55.00	325	450

KM# 463 2-1/2 PESOS
2.0833 g., 0.9000 Gold 0.0603 oz. AGW, 15.5 mm.
Obv: National arms **Rev:** Miguel Hidalgo y Costilla **Note:** Mint mark Mo.

Date	Mintage	F	VF	XF	Unc
1918	1,704,000	—	BV	60.00	80.00
1919	984,000	—	BV	60.00	80.00
1920/10	607,000	—	BV	60.00	130
1920	Inc. above	—	BV	60.00	65.00
1944	20,000	—	BV	60.00	65.00

Date	Mintage	F	VF	XF	Unc
1945	Est. 180,000	—	—	—	BV+18%
1946	163,000	—	BV	60.00	65.00
1947	24,000	200	265	325	500
1948	63,000	—	BV	60.00	70.00

Note: During 1951-1972 a total of 5,025,087 pieces were restruck, most likely dated 1945. In 1996 matte restrikes were produced

KM# 464 5 PESOS
4.1666 g., 0.9000 Gold 0.1206 oz. AGW, 19 mm.
Obv: National arms **Rev:** Miguel Hidalgo y Costilla **Note:** Mint mark Mo.

Date	Mintage	F	VF	XF	Unc
1905	18,000	120	175	245	600
1906	4,638,000	—	—	BV	115
1907/6	—	—	—	—	—
1907	1,088,000	—	—	BV	115
1910	100,000	—	—	BV	150
1918/7	609,000	—	—	BV	200
1918	Inc. above	—	—	BV	115
1919	506,000	—	—	BV	115
1920	2,385,000	—	—	BV	115
1955	Est. 48,000	—	—	—	BV+12%

Note: During 1955-1972 a total of 1,767,645 pieces were restruck, most likely dated 1955. In 1996 matte restrikes were produced

KM# 465 5 PESOS
30.0000 g., 0.9000 Silver 0.8680 oz. ASW, 40 mm.
Obv: National arms, eagle left **Rev:** Head with headdress left **Note:** Mint mark Mo.

Date	Mintage	F	VF	XF	Unc	BU
1947	5,110,000	—	—	BV	12.75	14.50
1948	26,740,000	—	—	BV	12.50	13.50

KM# 466 5 PESOS

27.7800 g., 0.7200 Silver 0.6430 oz. ASW, 40 mm.
Subject: Opening of Southern Railroad **Obv:**
National arms, eagle left **Rev:** Radiant sun flanked
by palm trees above train **Edge Lettering:**
COMERCIO - AGRICULTURA - INDUSTRIA
Designer: Manuel L. Negrete **Note:** Mint mark Mo.

Date	Mintage	F	VF	XF	Unc	BU
1950	200,000	—	22.50	40.00	50.00	55.00

Note: It is recorded that 100,000 pieces were melted to be
used for the 1968 Mexican Olympic 25 Pesos

KM# 467 5 PESOS

27.7800 g., 0.7200 Silver 0.6430 oz. ASW, 40 mm.
Obv: National arms, eagle left **Rev:** Head left within
wreath **Edge Lettering:** COMERCIO -
AGRICULTURA - INDUSTRIA **Note:** Mint mark Mo.

Date	Mintage	F	VF	XF	Unc	BU
1951	4,958,000	—	—	BV	10.00	12.00
1952	9,595,000	—	—	BV	9.50	11.00
1953	20,376,000	—	—	BV	9.50	11.00
1954	30,000	—	30.00	60.00	70.00	85.00

KM# 468 5 PESOS

27.7800 g., 0.7200 Silver 0.6430 oz. ASW, 40 mm.
Subject: Bicentennial of Hidalgo's Birth **Obv:**
National arms, eagle left **Rev:** Half-length figure
facing to right of building and dates **Edge Lettering:**
COMERCIO - AGRICULTURA - INDUSTRIA
Designer: Manuel L. Negrete **Note:** Mint mark Mo.

Date	Mintage	F	VF	XF	Unc	BU
1953	1,000,000	—	BV	9.50	11.00	13.50

KM# 469 5 PESOS

18.0500 g., 0.7200 Silver 0.4178 oz. ASW, 36 mm.
Obv: National arms, eagle left **Rev:** Head left **Note:**
Mint mark Mo.

Date	Mintage	F	VF	XF	Unc	BU
1955	4,271,000	—	BV	6.25	7.00	8.50
1956	4,596,000	—	BV	6.25	7.00	8.50
1957	3,464,000	—	BV	6.25	7.00	8.50

KM# 470 5 PESOS

18.0500 g., 0.7200 Silver 0.4178 oz. ASW, 36 mm.
Subject: 100th Anniversary of Constitution **Obv:**
National arms, eagle left **Rev:** Head left **Edge
Lettering:** INDEPENDENCIA Y LIBERTAD
Designer: Manuel L. Negrete **Note:** Mint mark Mo.

Date	Mintage	F	VF	XF	Unc	BU
1957	200,000	—	6.50	7.50	13.50	15.50

KM# 471 5 PESOS
18.0500 g., 0.7200 Silver 0.4178 oz. ASW, 36 mm.
Subject: Centennial of Carranza's Birth **Obv:**
National arms, eagle left **Rev:** Head left **Edge:** Plain
Designer: Manuel L. Negrete **Note:** Mint mark Mo.

Date	Mintage	F	VF	XF	Unc	BU
1959	1,000,000	—	—	BV	7.00	9.00

Small date   Large date

KM# 472 5 PESOS
14.0000 g., Copper-Nickel, 33 mm. **Obv:** National
arms, eagle left **Rev:** Armored bust right **Edge
Lettering:** INDEPENDENCIA Y LIBERTAD **Note:**
Small date, large date varieties.

Date	Mintage	VF	XF	Unc	BU
1971	28,457,000	0.50	0.95	2.50	3.25
1972	75,000,000	0.60	1.25	2.00	2.50
1973	19,405,000	1.25	2.00	4.50	5.50
1974	34,500,000	0.50	0.80	1.75	2.25
1976 Small date	26,121,000	0.75	1.45	3.25	4.00
1976 Large date	121,550,000	0.35	0.50	1.50	1.75
1977	102,000,000	0.35	0.50	1.50	1.75
1978	25,700,000	1.00	1.50	4.50	6.25

KM# 485 5 PESOS
Copper-Nickel, 27 mm. **Subject:** Quetzalcoatl **Obv:**
National arms, eagle left **Rev:** Native sculpture to
lower right of value and dollar sign **Edge Lettering:**
LIBERTAD Y INDEPENDENCIA **Note:** Inverted and
normal edge legend varieties exist for the 1980 and
1981 dates.

Date	Mintage	VF	XF	Unc	BU
1980	266,899,999	0.25	0.50	1.75	2.25
1981	30,500,000	0.45	0.65	2.75	3.25

Date	Mintage	VF	XF	Unc	BU
1982	20,000,000	1.50	2.35	4.25	5.25
1982 Proof	1,051				
1983 Proof; 7 known	—				
1984	16,300,000	1.25	2.00	4.75	6.00
1985	76,900,000	2.00	3.25	4.25	5.00

KM# 502 5 PESOS
Brass, 17 mm. **Subject:** Quetzalcoatl **Obv:** National
arms, eagle left **Rev:** Date and value **Note:**
Circulation coinage.

Date	Mintage	VF	XF	Unc	BU
1985	30,000,000	—	0.15	0.35	0.50
1987	81,900,000	8.00	9.50	12.50	15.00
1988	76,600,000	—	0.10	0.25	0.35
1988 Proof; 2 known	—				

KM# 473 10 PESOS
8.3333 g., 0.9000 Gold 0.2411 oz. AGW, 22.5 mm.
Obv: National arms **Rev:** Miguel Hidalgo y Costilla
Note: Mint mark Mo.

Date	Mintage	F	VF	XF	Unc	BU
1905	39,000	—	BV	170	225	—
1906	2,949,000	—	BV	165	185	—
1907	1,589,000	—	BV	165	185	—
1908	890,000	—	BV	165	185	—
1910	451,000	—	BV	165	185	—
1916	26,000	—	BV	175	350	—
1917	1,967,000	—	BV	165	185	—
1919	266,000	—	BV	165	200	—
1920	12,000	—	BV	425	700	—
1959	Est. 50,000	—	—	—	BV+7%	—

Note: *During 1961-1972 a total of 954,983 pieces were
restruck, most likely dated 1959. In 1996 matte restrikes
were produced

KM# 474 10 PESOS
28.8800 g., 0.9000 Silver 0.8356 oz. ASW, 40 mm.
Obv: National arms **Rev:** Head left **Note:** Mint mark
Mo.

Date	Mintage	F	VF	XF	Unc	BU
1955	585,000	—	—	BV	12.50	14.50
1956	3,535,000	—	—	BV	12.25	13.50

KM# 475   10 PESOS
28.8800 g., 0.9000 Silver 0.8356 oz. ASW, 40 mm.
Subject: 100th Anniversary of Constitution **Obv:**
National arms, eagle left **Rev:** Head left **Edge
Lettering:** INDEPENDENCIA Y LIBERTAD
Designer: Manuel L. Negrete **Note:** Mint mark Mo.

Date	Mintage	F	VF	XF	Unc	BU
1957	100,000	—	13.50	27.50	45.00	50.00

KM# 476   10 PESOS
28.8800 g., 0.9000 Silver 0.8356 oz. ASW, 40 mm.
Subject: 150th Anniversary - War of Independence
Obv: National arms, eagle left **Rev:** Conjoined busts
facing flanked by dates **Designer:** Manuel L. Negrete
Note: Mint mark Mo.

Date	Mintage	F	VF	XF	Unc	BU
1960	1,000,000	—	—	BV	12.50	15.00

KM# 477.1   10 PESOS
Copper-Nickel, 30.5 mm. **Obv:** National arms, eagle
left **Rev:** Miguel Hidalgo y Costilla **Shape:** 7-sided
Note: Thin flan - 1.6mm

Date	Mintage	F	VF	XF	Unc	BU
1974	3,900,000	—	0.50	1.00	3.00	4.00
1974 Proof	—	Value: 625				
1975	1,000,000	—	2.25	3.25	7.50	8.50
1976	74,500,000	—	0.25	0.75	1.75	2.25
1977	79,620,000	—	0.50	1.00	2.00	3.00

KM# 477.2   10 PESOS
Copper-Nickel, 30.5 mm. **Obv:** National arms, eagle
left **Rev:** Head left **Shape:** 7-sided **Note:** Thick flan
- 2.3mm

Date	Mintage	VF	XF	Unc	BU
1978	124,850,000	0.50	0.75	2.50	2.75
1979	57,200,000	0.50	0.75	2.25	2.50
1980	55,200,000	0.50	0.75	2.50	3.75
1981	222,768,000	0.40	0.60	2.25	2.65
1982 Proof	1,051				
1982	151,770,000	0.50	0.80	2.50	3.50
1983 Proof; 3 known	—				
1985	58,000,000	1.25	1.75	5.75	7.50

KM# 512   10 PESOS
3.8400 g., Stainless Steel, 19 mm. **Obv:** National
arms, eagle left **Rev:** Head facing with diagonal value
at left **Note:** Date varieties exist.

Date	Mintage	VF	XF	Unc	BU
1985	257,000,000	—	0.15	0.50	0.75
1986	392,000,000	—	0.15	0.50	1.50
1987	305,000,000	—	0.15	0.35	0.50
1988	500,300,000	—	0.15	0.25	0.35
1989	—	0.20	0.25	0.75	1.50
1990	—	—	0.25	0.75	1.25
1990 Proof; 2 known	—				

KM# 478 20 PESOS
16.6666 g., 0.9000 Gold 0.4822 oz. AGW, 27.5 mm.
Obv: National arms, eagle left **Rev:** Aztec Sunstone
with denomination below **Edge:** Lettered **Edge
Lettering:** INDEPEDENCIA Y LIBERTAD **Note:**
Mint mark Mo.

Date	Mintage	F	VF	XF	Unc	BU
1917	852,000	—	—	BV	450	—
1918	2,831,000	—	—	BV	450	—
1919	1,094,000	—	—	BV	450	—
1920/10	462,000	—	—	BV	450	—
1920	Inc. above	—	—	BV	450	—
1921/11	922,000	—	—	BV	450	—
1921/10		—	—	—	—	—
1921	Inc. above	—	—	BV	450	—
1959	Est. 13,000	—	—	—	—	—

Note: During 1960-1971 a total of 1,158,414 pieces were
restruck, most likely dated 1959. In 1996 matte restrikes
were produced

KM# 486 20 PESOS
Copper-Nickel, 32 mm. **Obv:** National arms, eagle
left **Rev:** Figure with headdress facing left within
circle

Date	Mintage	VF	XF	Unc	BU
1980	84,900,000	0.50	0.85	2.25	3.00
1981	250,573,000	0.60	0.80	2.25	3.25
1982	236,892,000	1.00	1.75	2.50	3.50
1982 Proof	1,051				
1983 Proof; 3 known	—				
1984	55,000,000	1.00	1.50	2.50	4.75

KM# 508 20 PESOS
6.0000 g., Brass, 21 mm. **Obv:** National arms, eagle
left **Rev:** Bust facing with diagonal value at left

Date	Mintage	VF	XF	Unc	BU
1985 Wide date	25,000,000	0.10	0.20	1.00	1.25
1985 Narrow date	Inc. above	0.10	0.25	1.50	2.00
1986	10,000,000	1.00	1.75	5.00	5.50
1988	355,200,000	0.10	0.20	0.45	0.75
1989	—	0.15	0.30	1.50	2.00
1990	—	0.15	0.30	1.50	2.50
1990 Proof; 3 known	—				

Snake's tongue straight

KM# 479.1 25 PESOS
22.5000 g., 0.7200 Silver 0.5208 oz. ASW, 38 mm.
Obv: National arms, eagle left **Rev:** Olympic rings
below dancing native left, numeral design in
background **Designer:** Lorenzo Rafael **Note:** Type
I, Rings aligned.

Date	Mintage	F	VF	XF	Unc	BU
1968	27,182,000	—	—	BV	7.50	8.00

KM# 479.2 25 PESOS
22.5000 g., 0.7200 Silver 0.5208 oz. ASW, 38 mm.
Subject: Summer Olympics - Mexico City **Obv:**
National arms, eagle left **Rev:** Olympic rings below
dancing native left, numeral design in background
Note: Type II, center ring low.

Date	Mintage	F	VF	XF	Unc	BU
1968	Inc. above	—	BV	7.50	8.50	10.00

Snake's tongue curved

KM# 479.3 25 PESOS
22.5000 g., 0.7200 Silver 0.5208 oz. ASW, 38 mm.
Subject: Summer Olympics - Mexico City **Obv:**
National arms, eagle left **Rev:** Olympic rings below
dancing native left, numeral design in background
Note: Snake with long curved or normal tongue. Type
III, center rings low.

Date	Mintage	F	VF	XF	Unc	BU
1968	Inc. above	—	BV	7.50	9.50	11.00

UNITED STATES OF MEXICO 1905-1992

KM# 480   25 PESOS
22.5000 g., 0.7200 Silver 0.5208 oz. ASW, 38 mm.
Obv: National arms, eagle left **Rev:** Bust facing

Date	Mintage	F	VF	XF	Unc	BU
1972	2,000,000	—	—	BV	7.50	8.50

KM# 497   25 PESOS
7.7760 g., 0.7200 Silver 0.1800 oz. ASW **Subject:**
1986 World Cup Soccer Games **Obv:** National arms,
eagle left **Rev:** Value above soccer ball with date
below

Date	Mintage	F	VF	XF	Unc	BU
1985	354,000	—	—	—	—	7.50

KM# 503   25 PESOS
8.4060 g., 0.9250 Silver 0.2500 oz. ASW **Subject:**
1986 World Cup Soccer Games **Obv:** National arms,
eagle left **Rev:** Pre-Columbian hieroglyphs, ojo de
buey, and soccer ball

Date	Mintage	F	VF	XF	Unc	BU
1985 Proof	277,000	Value: 12.00				

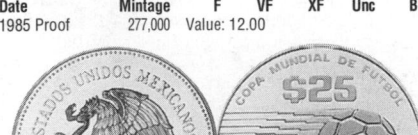

KM# 514   25 PESOS
8.4060 g., 0.9250 Silver 0.2500 oz. ASW **Subject:**
1986 World Cup Soccer Games **Obv:** National arms,
eagle left **Rev:** Value above soccer ball

Date	Mintage	F	VF	XF	Unc	BU
1985 Proof	234,000	Value: 12.00				

KM# 519   25 PESOS
8.4060 g., 0.9250 Silver 0.2500 oz. ASW **Subject:**
1986 World Cup Soccer Games **Obv:** National
arms, eagle left **Rev:** Soccer ball within net, date
and value to left

Date	Mintage	F	VF	XF	Unc	BU
1986 Proof	—	Value: 12.00				

KM# 497a   25 PESOS
8.4060 g., 0.9250 Silver 0.2500 oz. ASW **Subject:**
1986 World Cup Soccer Games **Obv:** National arms,
eagle left **Rev:** Value above soccerball with date below
Note: Without finess statement- reverse description

Date	Mintage	F	VF	XF	Unc	BU
1986 Proof	—	Value: 12.00				

KM# 481   50 PESOS
41.6666 g., 0.9000 Gold 1.2056 oz. AGW, 37 mm.
Subject: Centennial of Independence **Obv:** National
arms **Rev:** Winged Victory **Edge:** Reeded **Designer:**
Emilio del Moral **Note:** During 1949-1972 a total of
3,975,654 pieces were restruck, most likely dated 1947.
In 1996 matte restrikes were produced. Mint mark Mo.

Date	Mintage	F	VF	XF	Unc	BU
1921	180,000	—	—	BV	1,075	1,125
1922	463,000	—	—	BV	1,075	1,125
1923	432,000	—	—	BV	1,075	1,125
1924	439,000	—	—	BV	1,075	1,125
1925	716,000	—	—	BV	1,075	1,125
1926	600,000	—	—	BV	1,075	1,125
1927	606,000	—	—	BV	1,075	1,125
1928	538,000	—	—	BV	1,075	1,125
1929	458,000	—	—	BV	1,075	1,125
1930	372,000	—	—	BV	1,075	1,125
1931	137,000	—	—	BV	1,075	1,125
1944	593,000	—	—	BV	1,075	1,125
1945	1,012,000	—	—	BV	1,075	1,125
1946	1,588,000	—	—	BV	1,075	1,125
1947	309,000	—	—	— BV+3%	—
1947 Specimen	—	—	—	—	—	—

Note: Value, $6,500

KM# 482 50 PESOS

41.6666 g., 0.9000 Gold 1.2056 oz. AGW, 39 mm.
Obv: National arms **Rev:** Winged Victory

Date	Mintage	F	VF	XF	Unc	BU
1943	89,000	—	—	—	BV	1,075

KM# 490 50 PESOS

19.8400 g., Copper-Nickel, 35 mm. **Subject:**
Coyolxauhqui **Obv:** National arms, eagle left **Rev:**
Value to right of artistic designs **Edge:** Reeded **Note:**
Doubled die examples of 1982 and 1983 dates exist.

Date	Mintage	VF	XF	Unc	BU
1982	222,890,000	1.00	2.50	5.00	6.00
1983	45,000,000	1.50	3.00	6.00	6.50
1983 Proof	1,051				
1984	73,537,000	1.00	1.35	3.50	4.00
1984 Proof; 4 known	—				

KM# 495 50 PESOS

Copper-Nickel, 23.5 mm. **Subject:** Benito Juarez
Obv: National arms, eagle left **Rev:** Bust 1/4 left with
diagonal value at left **Edge:** Reeded

Date	Mintage	F	VF	XF	Unc	BU
1984	94,216,000	—	0.65	1.25	2.70	3.00
1985	296,000,000	—	0.25	0.45	1.25	2.00
1986	50,000,000	—	6.00	10.00	12.00	14.00
1987	210,000,000	—	0.25	0.45	1.00	1.25
1988	80,200,000	—	6.25	9.00	13.50	15.50

KM# 495a 50 PESOS

Stainless Steel, 23.5 mm. **Subject:** Benito Juarez
Obv: National arms, eagle left **Rev:** Bust 1/4 left with
diagonal value at left **Edge:** Plain

Date	Mintage	F	VF	XF	Unc	BU
1988	353,300,000	—	—	0.20	1.25	1.75
1990	—	—	—	0.30	1.00	2.00
1992	—	—	—	0.25	1.00	2.75

KM# 498 50 PESOS

15.5520 g., 0.7200 Silver 0.3600 oz. ASW **Subject:**
1986 World Cup Soccer Games **Obv:** National arms,
eagle left **Rev:** Pair of feet and soccer ball

Date	Mintage	F	VF	XF	Unc	BU
1985	347,000	—	—	—	—	6.50

KM# 504 50 PESOS

16.8310 g., 0.9250 Silver 0.5005 oz. ASW **Subject:**
1986 World Cup Soccer Games **Obv:** National arms,
eagle left **Rev:** Stylized athlete as soccer forerunner

Date	Mintage	F	VF	XF	Unc	BU
1985 Proof	347,000	Value: 20.00				

KM# 515 50 PESOS

16.8310 g., 0.9250 Silver 0.5005 oz. ASW **Subject:**
1986 World Cup Soccer Games **Obv:** National arms,
eagle left **Rev:** Value to right of soccer player

Date	Mintage	F	VF	XF	Unc	BU
1985 Proof	234,000	Value: 20.00				

KM# 523 50 PESOS

16.8310 g., 0.9250 Silver 0.5005 oz. ASW **Subject:**

1986 World Cup Soccer Games **Obv:** National arms,
eagle left **Rev:** Value to left of soccer balls

Date	Mintage	F	VF	XF	Unc	BU
1986 Proof	190,000	Value: 20.00				

KM# 498a   50 PESOS
16.8310 g., 0.9250 Silver 0.5005 oz. ASW **Subject:**
1986 World Cup Soccer Games **Obv:** National arms,
eagle left **Rev:** Without fineness statement

Date	Mintage	F	VF	XF	Unc	BU
1986 Proof	10,000	Value: 20.00				

KM# 532   50 PESOS
15.5500 g., 0.9990 Silver 0.4994 oz. ASW **Subject:**
50th Anniversary - Nationalization of Oil Industry
Obv: National arms, eagle left **Rev:** Monument

Date	Mintage	F	VF	XF	Unc	BU
ND(1988)	30,000	—	—	—	20.00	22.00

Low 7's

KM# 483.1   100 PESOS
27.7700 g., 0.7200 Silver 0.6428 oz. ASW, 39 mm.
Obv: National arms, eagle left **Rev:** Bust facing,
sloping right shoulder, round left shoulder with no
clothing folds **Edge:** Reeded

Date	Mintage	F	VF	XF	Unc	BU
1977 Low 7's	5,225,000	—	—	BV	9.50	11.50
1977 High 7's	Inc. above	—	—	BV	9.50	12.00

High 7's

KM# 483.2   100 PESOS
27.7700 g., 0.7200 Silver 0.6428 oz. ASW, 39 mm.
Obv: National arms, eagle left **Rev:** Bust facing,
higher right shoulder, left shoulder with clothing folds.
Note: Mintage inc. KM#483.1

Date	Mintage	F	VF	XF	Unc	BU
1977 Date in line	—	—	—	BV	9.25	10.00
1978	9,879,000	—	—	BV	9.50	11.50
1979	784,000	—	—	BV	9.50	11.50
1979 Proof	—	Value: 650				

KM# 493   100 PESOS
Aluminum-Bronze, 26.5 mm.   **Obv:** National arms,
eagle left **Rev:** Head 1/4 right with diagonal value at
right

Date	Mintage	VF	XF	Unc	BU
1984	227,809,000	0.45	0.60	2.50	4.00
1985	377,423,000	0.30	0.50	2.00	3.00
1986	43,000,000	1.00	2.50	4.75	7.50
1987	165,000,000	0.60	1.25	2.25	3.00
1988	433,100,000	0.30	0.50	2.00	2.75
1989	—	0.35	0.65	2.00	2.75
1990	—	0.15	0.40	1.50	2.50
1990 Proof; 1 known	—				
1991	—	0.15	0.25	1.00	2.50
1992	—	0.30	0.75	1.75	3.00

KM# 499 100 PESOS
31.1030 g., 0.7200 Silver 0.7200 oz. ASW **Subject:**
1986 World Cup Soccer Games **Obv:** National arms,
eagle left **Rev:** Value above artistic designs and
soccer ball

Date	Mintage	F	VF	XF	Unc	BU
1985	302,000	—	—	—	—	15.00

KM# 499a 100 PESOS
32.6250 g., 0.9250 Silver 0.9702 oz. ASW **Subject:**
1986 World Cup Soccer Games **Obv:** National arms,
eagle left **Rev:** Without fineness statement

Date	Mintage	F	VF	XF	Unc	BU
1985 Proof	9,006	Value: 30.00				

KM# 505 100 PESOS
32.6250 g., 0.9250 Silver 0.9702 oz. ASW, 38 mm.
Subject: 1986 World Cup Soccer Games **Obv:**
National arms, eagle left **Rev:** Without fineness
statement

Date	Mintage	F	VF	XF	Unc	BU
1985 Proof	9,006	Value: 30.00				

KM# 521 100 PESOS
32.6250 g., 0.9250 Silver 0.9702 oz. ASW **Subject:**
1986 World Cup Soccer Games **Obv:** National arms,
eagle left **Rev:** Without fineness statement

Date	Mintage	F	VF	XF	Unc	BU
1986 Proof	208,000	Value: 30.00				

KM# 524 100 PESOS
32.6250 g., 0.9250 Silver 0.9702 oz. ASW **Subject:**
1986 World Cup Soccer Games **Obv:** National arms,
eagle left **Rev:** Without fineness statement

Date	Mintage	F	VF	XF	Unc	BU
1986 Proof	190,000	Value: 30.00				

KM# 537 100 PESOS
32.6250 g., 0.7200 Silver 0.7552 oz. ASW **Subject:**
World Wildlife Fund **Obv:** National arms, eagle left
Rev: Monarch butterflies

Date	Mintage	F	VF	XF	Unc	BU
1987 Proof	Est. 30,000	Value: 50.00				

KM# 533   100 PESOS
31.1030 g., 0.9990 Silver 0.9989 oz. ASW **Subject:**
50th Anniversary - Nationalization of Oil Industry
Obv: National arms, eagle left **Rev:** Bust facing
above sprigs and dates

Date	Mintage	F	VF	XF	Unc	BU
1988	10,000	—	—	—	28.00	40.00

KM# 539   100 PESOS
33.6250 g., 0.9250 Silver 0.9999 oz. ASW **Subject:**
Save the Children **Obv:** National arms, eagle left
Rev: Child flying kite, two others sitting and playing

Date	Mintage	F	VF	XF	Unc	BU
1991 Proof	30,000	Value: 45.00				

KM# 540   100 PESOS
27.0000 g., 0.9250 Silver 0.8029 oz. ASW **Subject:**
Ibero - American Series **Obv:** National arms, eagle

left within center of assorted arms **Rev:** Maps within
circles flanked by pillars above sailboats

Date	Mintage	F	VF	XF	Unc	BU
1991 Proof	50,000	Value: 55.00				
1992 Proof	75,000	Value: 45.00				

KM# 566   100 PESOS
31.1035 g., 0.9990 Silver 0.9990 oz. ASW **Subject:**
Save the Vaquita Porpoise **Obv:** National arms,
eagle left **Rev:** Swimming vaquita porpoise

Date	Mintage	F	VF	XF	Unc	BU
1992 Proof	—	Value: 45.00				

KM# 509   200 PESOS
Copper-Nickel, 29.5 mm. **Subject:** 175th
Anniversary of Independence **Obv:** National arms,
eagle left **Rev:** Conjoined busts left

Date	Mintage	F	VF	XF	Unc	BU
1985	75,000,000	—	—	0.25	3.00	4.00

KM# 510   200 PESOS
Copper-Nickel, 29.5 mm. **Subject:** 75th
Anniversary of 1910 Revolution **Obv:** National arms,
eagle left **Rev:** Conjoined heads left below building

Date	Mintage	F	VF	XF	Unc	BU
1985	98,590,000	—	—	0.25	3.25	4.50

KM# 525 200 PESOS
Copper-Nickel, 29.5 mm. **Subject:** 1986 World Cup Soccer Games **Obv:** National arms, eagle left **Rev:** Soccer players **Edge:** Reeded

Date	Mintage	F	VF	XF	Unc	BU
1986	50,000,000	—	—	1.00	3.50	4.50

KM# 526 200 PESOS
62.2060 g., 0.9990 Silver 1.9979 oz. ASW **Subject:** 1986 World Cup Soccer Games **Obv:** National arms, eagle left **Rev:** Value above 3 soccer balls

Date	Mintage	F	VF	XF	Unc	BU
1986	50,000	—	—	—	40.00	50.00

KM# 500.1 250 PESOS
8.6400 g., 0.9000 Gold 0.2500 oz. AGW **Subject:** 1986 World Cup Soccer Games **Obv:** National arms, eagle left **Rev:** Soccer ball within top 1/2 of design with value, date, and state below

Date	Mintage	F	VF	XF	Unc	BU
1985	100,000	—	—	—	—	250
1986	—	—	—	—	—	250

KM# 500.2 250 PESOS
8.6400 g., 0.9000 Gold 0.2500 oz. AGW **Subject:** 1986 World Cup Soccer Games **Obv:** National arms, eagle left **Rev:** Without fineness statement

Date	Mintage	F	VF	XF	Unc	BU
1985 Proof	4,506	Value: 250				
1986 Proof	—	Value: 250				

KM# 506.1 250 PESOS
8.6400 g., 0.9000 Gold 0.2500 oz. AGW **Subject:** 1986 World Cup Soccer Games **Obv:** National arms, eagle left **Rev:** Equestrian left within circle

Date	Mintage	F	VF	XF	Unc	BU
1985	88,000	—	—	—	—	245

KM# 506.2 250 PESOS
8.6400 g., 0.9000 Gold 0.2500 oz. AGW **Subject:** 1986 World Cup Soccer Games **Obv:** National arms, eagle left **Rev:** Without fineness statement

Date	Mintage	F	VF	XF	Unc	BU
1985 Proof	Est. 80,000	Value: 245				

KM# 501.1 500 PESOS
17.2800 g., 0.9000 Gold 0.5000 oz. AGW **Subject:** 1986 World Cup Soccer Games **Obv:** National arms, eagle left **Rev:** Soccer player to right within emblem

Date	Mintage	F	VF	XF	Unc	BU
1985	102,000	—	—	—	—	475
1986	—	—	—	—	—	475

KM# 501.2 500 PESOS
17.2800 g., 0.9000 Gold 0.5000 oz. AGW **Subject:** 1986 World Cup Soccer Games **Obv:** National arms, eagle left **Rev:** Without fineness statement

Date	Mintage	F	VF	XF	Unc	BU
1985 Proof	5,506	Value: 475				
1986 Proof	—	Value: 475				

KM# 507.1 500 PESOS
17.2800 g., 0.9000 Gold 0.5000 oz. AGW **Subject:** 1986 World Cup Soccer Games **Obv:** National arms, eagle left **Rev:** Soccer ball within emblem flanked by value and date

Date	Mintage	F	VF	XF	Unc	BU
1985	—	—	—	—	—	475

KM# 507.2 500 PESOS
17.2800 g., 0.9000 Gold 0.5000 oz. AGW **Subject:** 1986 World Cup Soccer Games **Obv:** National arms, eagle left **Rev:** Without fineness statement

Date	Mintage	F	VF	XF	Unc	BU
1985 Proof	—	Value: 475				

KM# 511   500 PESOS
33.4500 g., 0.9250 Silver 0.9947 oz. ASW **Subject:**
75th Anniversary of 1910 Revolution **Obv:** National
arms, eagle left **Rev:** Conjoined heads left below
building

Date	Mintage	F	VF	XF	Unc	BU
1985 Proof	40,000	Value: 35.00				

KM# 529   500 PESOS
Copper-Nickel, 28.5 mm. **Obv:** National arms, eagle
left **Rev:** Head 1/4 right

Date	Mintage	VF	XF	Unc	BU
1986	20,000,000	—	1.00	3.25	3.50
1987	180,000,000	—	0.75	2.25	2.50
1988	230,000,000	—	0.50	2.25	2.50
1988 Proof; 2 known	—				
1989	—	—	0.75	2.25	3.00
1992	—	—	1.00	2.25	3.50

KM# 534   500 PESOS
17.2800 g., 0.9000 Gold 0.5000 oz. AGW **Subject:**
50th Anniversary - Nationalization of Oil Industry
Obv: National arms, eagle left **Rev:** Monument **Note:**
Similar to 5000 Pesos, KM#531.

Date	Mintage	F	VF	XF	Unc	BU
1988	—	—	—	—	—	475

KM# 513   1000 PESOS
17.2800 g., 0.9000 Gold 0.5000 oz. AGW **Subject:**
175th Anniversary of Independence **Obv:** National
arms, eagle left **Rev:** Conjoined heads left below
value

Date	Mintage	F	VF	XF	Unc	BU
1985 Proof	—	Value: 475				

KM# 527   1000 PESOS
31.1050 g., 0.9990 Gold 0.9990 oz. AGW **Subject:**
1986 World Cup Soccer Games **Obv:** National arms,
eagle left **Rev:** Value above soccer ball and two
hemispheres

Date	Mintage	F	VF	XF	Unc	BU
1986	—	—	—	—	—	925

KM# 536   1000 PESOS
15.0000 g., Aluminum-Bronze, 30.5 mm. **Obv:**
National arms, eagle left **Rev:** Bust 1/4 left with
diagonal value at left **Note:** Juana de Asbaje

Date	Mintage	VF	XF	Unc	BU
1988	229,300,000	0.85	2.00	4.25	5.75
1989	—	0.85	2.00	4.25	5.75
1990	—	0.85	2.00	4.00	5.50
1990 Proof; 2 known	—				
1991	—	1.00	2.00	3.00	7.00
1992	—	1.00	2.00	3.00	7.00

KM# 535   1000 PESOS
34.5590 g., 0.9000 Gold 0.9999 oz. AGW **Subject:**
50th Anniversary - Nationalization of Oil Industry
Obv: National arms, eagle left **Rev:** Portrait of
Cardenas **Note:** Similar to 5000 Pesos, KM#531.

Date	Mintage	F	VF	XF	Unc	BU
1988 Proof	—	Value: 925				

KM# 643   1000 PESOS
Aluminum-Bronze, 22 mm. **Obv:** National arms,
eagle left **Rev:** Stylized boat and "ATLAN" above
denomination **Note:** Unissued type due to currency
reform.

Date	Mintage	F	VF	XF	Unc	BU
1991 Mo	—	—	—	—	15.00	—

KM# 528   2000 PESOS
62.2000 g., 0.9990 Gold 1.9977 oz. AGW **Subject:**

1986 World Cup Soccer Games **Obv:** National arms, eagle left **Rev:** Value above soccer ball and two hemispheres

Date	Mintage	F	VF	XF	Unc	BU
1986	—	—	—	—	—	1,850

KM# 531   5000 PESOS
Copper-Nickel, 33.5 mm. **Subject:** 50th Anniversary - Nationalization of Oil Industry **Obv:** National arms, eagle left **Rev:** Monument above dates with diagonal value at left

Date	Mintage	F	VF	XF	Unc	BU
ND(1988)	50,000,000	—	—	4.75	7.75	10.00

REFORM COINAGE
1 New Peso = 1000 Old Pesos

KM# 546   5 CENTAVOS
1.5900 g., Stainless Steel, 15.58 mm. **Obv:** National arms **Rev:** Large value **Edge:** Plain

Date	Mintage	VF	XF	Unc	BU
1992	136,800,000	—	0.15	0.20	0.25
1993	234,000,000	—	0.15	0.20	0.25
1994	125,000,000	—	0.15	0.20	0.25
1995	195,000,000	—	0.15	0.20	0.25
1995 Proof	6,981				
1996	104,831,000	—	0.15	0.20	0.25
1997	153,675,000	—	0.15	0.20	0.25
1998	64,417,000	—	0.15	0.20	0.25
1999	9,949,000	—	0.15	0.20	0.25
2000Mo	10,871,000	—	0.15	0.20	0.25
2001Mo	34,811,000	—	0.15	0.20	0.25
2002Mo	14,901,000	—	0.15	0.20	0.25

KM# 547   10 CENTAVOS
2.0300 g., Stainless Steel, 17 mm. **Obv:** National arms, eagle left **Rev:** Value

Date	Mintage	F	VF	XF	Unc	BU
1992	121,250,000	—	—	0.20	0.30	0.35
1993	755,000,000	—	—	0.20	0.25	0.30
1994	557,000,000	—	—	0.20	0.25	0.30
1995	560,000,000	—	—	0.20	0.25	0.30
1995 Proof	6,981	Value: 0.50				
1996	594,216,000	—	—	0.20	0.25	0.30
1997	581,622,000	—	—	0.20	0.25	0.30
1998	602,667,000	—	—	0.20	0.25	0.30
1999	488,346,000	—	—	0.20	0.25	0.30
2000	577,546,000	—	—	0.20	0.30	0.35
2001	618,061,000	—	—	0.20	0.25	0.30

Date	Mintage	F	VF	XF	Unc	BU
2002	463,968,000	—	—	0.20	0.25	0.30
2003Mo	378,938,000	—	—	0.20	0.25	0.30
2004	393,705,000	—	—	0.20	0.25	0.30
2005	488,773,000	—	—	0.20	0.25	0.30
2006	473,104,000	—	—	0.20	0.25	0.30

KM# 548   20 CENTAVOS
Aluminum-Bronze, 19 mm. **Obv:** National arms, eagle left **Rev:** Value and date within 3/4 wreath **Shape:** 12-sided

Date	Mintage	F	VF	XF	Unc	BU
1992	95,000,000	—	—	0.25	0.35	0.40
1993	95,000,000	—	—	0.25	0.35	0.40
1994	105,000,000	—	—	0.25	0.35	0.40
1995	180,000,000	—	—	0.25	0.35	0.40
1995 Proof	6,981	Value: 0.75				
1996	54,896,000	—	—	0.25	0.35	0.40
1997	178,807,000	—	—	0.25	0.35	0.40
1998	223,847,000	—	—	0.25	0.35	0.40
1999	233,753,000	—	—	0.25	0.35	0.40
2000	223,973,000	—	—	0.25	0.35	0.40
2001	234,360,000	—	—	0.25	0.35	0.40
2002Mo	229,256,000	—	—	0.25	0.35	0.40
2003Mo	149,518,000	—	—	0.25	0.35	0.40
2004	174,351,000	—	—	0.25	0.35	0.40
2005	204,444,000	—	—	0.25	0.35	0.40
2006	233,989,000	—	—	0.25	0.35	0.40

KM# 549   50 CENTAVOS
Aluminum-Bronze, 22 mm. **Obv:** National arms, eagle left **Rev:** Value and date within 1/2 designed wreath **Shape:** 12-sided

Date	Mintage	VF	XF	Unc	BU
1992	120,150,000	—	0.45	0.85	1.00
1993	330,000,000	—	0.45	0.75	1.00
1994	100,000,000	—	0.45	0.75	1.00
1995	60,000,000	—	0.45	0.75	1.00
1995 Proof	6,981				
1996	69,956,000	—	0.45	0.75	1.00
1997	129,029,000	—	0.45	0.75	1.00
1998	223,605,000	—	0.45	0.75	1.00
1999	89,516,000	—	0.45	0.75	1.00
2000	135,112,000	—	0.45	0.75	1.00
2001	199,006,000	—	0.45	0.75	1.00
2002	94,552,000	—	0.45	0.75	1.00
2003Mo	124,522,000	—	0.45	0.75	1.00
2004	154,434,000	—	0.45	0.75	1.00
2005	179,304,000	—	0.45	0.75	1.00
2006	233,786,000	—	0.45	0.75	1.00

KM# 550   NUEVO PESO
3.9400 g., Bi-Metallic Aluminum-Bronze center in

Stainless Steel ring, 22 mm. **Obv:** National arms, eagle left **Rev:** Value

Date	Mintage	VF	XF	Unc	BU
1992	144,000,000	—	0.60	1.50	2.25
1993	329,860,000	—	0.60	1.50	2.25
1994	221,000,000	—	0.60	1.50	2.25
1995 Small date	125,000,000	—	0.60	1.50	2.25
1995 Large date	Inc. above	—	0.60	1.50	2.25
1995 Proof	6,981				

KM# 603   PESO
3.9500 g., Bi-Metallic Stainless-steel ring in Aluminum Bronze center, 21 mm. **Obv:** National arms, eagle left within circle **Rev:** Value and date within circle **Note:** Similar to KM#550 but without N.

Date	Mintage	VF	XF	Unc	BU
1996Mo	169,510,000	—	—	1.25	2.25
1997Mo	222,870,000	—	—	1.25	2.25
1998Mo	261,942,000	—	—	1.25	2.25
1999Mo	99,168,000	—	—	1.25	2.25
2000Mo	158,379,000	—	—	1.25	2.25
2001Mo	208,576,000	—	—	1.25	2.25
2002Mo	119,541,000	—	—	1.25	2.25
2003Mo	169,320,000	—	—	1.25	2.25
2004	208,611,000	—	—	1.25	2.25
2005	253,924,000	—	—	1.25	2.25
2006	289,717,000	—	—	1.25	2.25

KM# 551   2 NUEVO PESOS
Bi-Metallic Aluminum-Bronze center in Stainless Steel ring, 23 mm. **Obv:** National arms, eagle left within circle **Rev:** Value and date within circle with assorted emblems around border

Date	Mintage	F	VF	XF	Unc	BU
1992	60,000,000	—	—	1.00	2.35	2.50
1993	77,000,000	—	—	1.00	2.35	2.50
1994	44,000,000	—	—	1.00	2.35	2.50
1995	20,000,000	—	—	1.00	2.35	2.50
1995 Proof	6,981	Value: 4.50				

KM# 604   2 PESOS
5.2100 g., Bi-Metallic Aluminum-Bronze center in Stainless Steel ring, 23 mm. **Obv:** National arms, eagle left within circle **Rev:** Value and date within center circle of assorted emblems **Note:** Similar to KM#551, but denomination without N.

Date	Mintage	VF	XF	Unc	BU
1996Mo	24,902,000	—	—	2.35	2.50
1997Mo	34,560,000	—	—	2.35	2.50
1998Mo	104,138,000	—	—	2.35	2.50
1999Mo	34,713,000	—	—	2.35	2.50
2000Mo	69,322,000	—	—	2.35	2.50
2001Mo	74,563,000	—	—	2.35	2.50
2002Mo	74,547,000	—	—	2.35	2.50
2003Mo	39,814,000	—	—	2.35	2.50
2004	89,496,000	—	—	2.35	2.50
2005	94,532,000	—	—	2.35	2.50
2006	143,919,000	—	—	2.35	2.50

KM# 552   5 NUEVO PESOS
Bi-Metallic Aluminum-Bronze center in Stainless Steel ring, 25.5 mm. **Obv:** National arms, eagle left within circle **Rev:** Value and date within circle with bow below

Date	Mintage	VF	XF	Unc	BU
1992	70,000,000	—	2.00	4.00	4.50
1993	168,240,000	—	2.00	4.00	4.50
1994	58,000,000	—	2.00	4.00	4.50
1995 Proof	6,981				

KM# 588   5 NUEVO PESOS
27.0000 g., 0.9250 Silver 0.8029 oz. ASW **Subject:** Environmental Protection **Obv:** National arms, eagle left within center of past and present arms **Rev:** Pacific Ridley Sea Turtle

Date	Mintage	F	VF	XF	Unc	BU
1994 Proof	20,000	Value: 50.00				

KM# 629   5 PESOS
27.0000 g., 0.9250 Silver 0.8029 oz. ASW **Subject:** Jarabe Tapatio **Obv:** National arms, eagle left within center of assorted arms **Rev:** Mexican dancers

Date	Mintage	F	VF	XF	Unc	BU
1997 Proof	20,000	Value: 275				
1998 Proof	—	Value: 275				

KM# 605   5 PESOS
Bi-Metallic Aluminum-Bronze center in Stainless Steel ring, 25.5 mm. **Obv:** National arms, eagle left within circle **Rev:** Value within circle **Note:** Similar to KM#552 but denomination without N.

Date	Mintage	F	VF	XF	Unc	BU
1997Mo	39,468,000	—	—	3.00	4.00	5.00
1998Mo	103,729,000	—	—	3.00	4.00	5.00
1999Mo	59,427,000	—	—	3.00	4.00	5.00
2000Mo	20,869,000	—	—	3.00	4.00	5.00
2001Mo	79,169,000	—	—	3.00	4.00	5.00
2002Mo	34,754,000	—	—	3.00	4.00	5.00
2003Mo	54,676,000	—	—	3.00	4.00	5.00
2004	89,518,000	—	—	3.00	4.00	5.00

Date	Mintage	F	VF	XF	Unc	BU
2005	94,482,000	—	—	3.00	4.00	5.00
2006	89,189,000	—	—	3.00	4.00	5.00

KM# 627 5 PESOS
31.1035 g., 0.9990 Silver 0.9990 oz. ASW **Subject:** World Wildlife Fund **Obv:** National arms, eagle left **Rev:** Wolf with pup

Date	Mintage	F	VF	XF	Unc	BU
1998 Proof	Est. 15,000	Value: 75.00				

KM# 630 5 PESOS
31.1800 g., 0.9990 Silver 1.0014 oz. ASW **Subject:** Millennium Series **Obv:** National arms, eagle left within center of past and present arms **Rev:** Butterfly flanked by sprigs above hands **Rev. Designer:** Francisco Ortega Romero

Date	Mintage	F	VF	XF	Unc	BU
1999-2000 Proof	75,000	Value: 45.00				

KM# 631 5 PESOS
31.1800 g., 0.9990 Silver 1.0014 oz. ASW **Subject:** Millennium Series **Obv:** National arms, eagle left within center of past and present arms **Rev:** Stylized dove as hand of peace **Rev. Designer:** Omar Jiminez Torres

Date	Mintage	VF	XF	Unc	BU
1999-2000 Proof	75,000				

KM# 632 5 PESOS
31.1800 g., 0.9990 Silver 1.0014 oz. ASW **Subject:** Millennium Series **Obv:** National arms, eagle left within center of past and present arms **Rev:** Aztec bird design and value

Date	Mintage	F	VF	XF	Unc	BU
1999-2000 Proof	75,000	Value: 40.00				

KM# 635 5 PESOS
19.6000 g., 0.9250 Silver 0.5829 oz. ASW **Subject:** Millennium Series **Obv:** National arms, eagle left **Rev:** Naval training ship Cuauhtemoc sailing into world globe

Date	Mintage	F	VF	XF	Unc	BU
1999	—	Value: 35.00				

KM# 640 5 PESOS
31.1030 g., 0.9990 Silver 0.9989 oz. ASW, 40 mm. **Subject:** UNICEF **Obv:** National arms, eagle left **Rev:** Two children flying kite **Edge:** Reeded

Date	Mintage	F	VF	XF	Unc	BU
1999 Proof	—	Value: 45.00				

KM# 655 5 PESOS
31.1710 g., 0.9990 Silver 1.0011 oz. ASW, 40 mm. **Series:** Endangered Wildlife **Subject:** Cocodrilo de Rio **Obv:** National arms, eagle left within center of past and present arms **Rev:** American Crocodile

Date	Mintage	F	VF	XF	Unc	BU
2000	50,000	—	—	—	32.50	—

KM# 656   5 PESOS
31.1710 g., 0.9990 Silver 1.0011 oz. ASW, 40 mm.
Series: Endangered Wildlife **Subject:** Nutria de Rio
Obv: National arms, eagle left within center of past
and present arms **Rev:** Neotropical River Otter

Date	Mintage	F	VF	XF	Unc	BU
2000	50,000	—	—	—	32.50	—

KM# 657   5 PESOS
31.1710 g., 0.9990 Silver 1.0011 oz. ASW, 40 mm.
Series: Endangered Wildlife - Berrendo **Obv:**
National arms, eagle left within center of past and
present arms **Rev:** Peninsular Pronghorn, giant
cardon cactus in back

Date	Mintage	F	VF	XF	Unc	BU
2000	50,000	—	—	—	32.50	—

KM# 652   5 PESOS
31.1710 g., 0.9990 Silver 1.0011 oz. ASW, 40 mm.
Series: Endangered Wildlife **Subject:** Aguila Real
Obv: National arms, eagle left within center of past
and present arms **Rev:** Golden Eagle on branch

Date	Mintage	F	VF	XF	Unc	BU
2000	50,000	—	—	—	32.50	—

KM# 670   5 PESOS
27.0000 g., 0.9250 Silver 0.8029 oz. ASW, 40 mm.
Series: Ibero-America **Obv:** National arms, eagle left
within center of past and present arms **Rev:** Cowboy
trick riding two horses **Edge:** Reeded

Date	Mintage	F	VF	XF	Unc	BU
2000 Proof	—	Value: 45.00				

KM# 653   5 PESOS
31.1710 g., 0.9990 Silver 1.0011 oz. ASW, 40 mm.
Subject: Aguila Arpia **Obv:** National arms in center
of past and present arms **Rev:** Crowned Harpy Eagle
perched on branch

Date	Mintage	F	VF	XF	Unc	BU
2001	50,000	—	—	—	35.00	—

KM# 654   5 PESOS
31.1710 g., 0.9990 Silver 1.0011 oz. ASW, 40 mm.
Series: Endangered Wildlife **Subject:** Oso Negro
Obv: National arms in center of past and present
arms **Rev:** Black bear, value and date

Date	Mintage	F	VF	XF	Unc	BU
2001	50,000	—	—	—	35.00	—

KM# 658   5 PESOS
31.1710 g., 0.9990 Silver 1.0011 oz. ASW, 40 mm.
Series: Endangered Wildlife **Obv:** National arms in
center of past and present arms **Rev:** Jaguar, value
and date

Date	Mintage	F	VF	XF	Unc	BU
2001	50,000	—	—	—	35.00	—

KM# 659   5 PESOS
31.1710 g., 0.9990 Silver 1.0011 oz. ASW, 40 mm.
Series: Endangered Wildlife **Obv:** National arms in
center of past and present arms **Rev:** Prairie dog,
value and date

Date	Mintage	F	VF	XF	Unc	BU
2001	50,000	—	—	—	35.00	—

KM# 660   5 PESOS
31.1710 g., 0.9990 Silver 1.0011 oz. ASW, 40 mm.
Series: Endangered Wildlife **Obv:** National arms in
center of past and present arms **Rev:** Volcano rabbit,
value and date

Date	Mintage	F	VF	XF	Unc	BU
2001	50,000	—	—	—	35.00	—

KM# 651   5 PESOS
31.1710 g., 0.9990 Silver 1.0011 oz. ASW, 40 mm.
Series: Endangered Wildlife **Obv:** National arms in
center of past and present arms **Rev:** Manatee, value
and date **Edge:** Reeded

Date	Mintage	F	VF	XF	Unc	BU
2001	50,000	—	—	—	35.00	—

KM# 678   5 PESOS
27.0000 g., 0.9250 Silver 0.8029 oz. ASW, 40 mm.
Subject: Ibero-America: Acapulco Galleon **Obv:**
National arms in center of past and present arms
Rev: Spanish galleon with Pacific Ocean background
and trading scene in foreground **Edge:** Reeded

Date	Mintage	F	VF	XF	Unc	BU
2003Mo Proof	5,000	Value: 65.00				

KM# 765   5 PESOS
31.1035 g., 0.9250 Silver 0.9250 oz. ASW, 40 mm.
Subject: Palacio de Bellas Artes **Obv:** Mexican
Eagle and Snake **Rev:** Palace of Fine Arts **Edge:**
Reeded

Date	Mintage	F	VF	XF	Unc	BU
2005Mo Proof	—	Value: 40.00				

KM# 769   5 PESOS
15.5518 g., 0.9990 Silver 0.4995 oz. ASW, 33 mm.
Subject: Monetary Reform of 1905 **Obv:** Mexican
Eagle and Snake **Rev:** Cap and rays coin design

Date	Mintage	F	VF	XF	Unc	BU
2005Mo Proof	—	Value: 30.00				

KM# 770   5 PESOS
31.1035 g., 0.9990 Silver 0.9990 oz. ASW, 40 mm.
Subject: World Cup Soccer **Obv:** Mexican Eagle and
Snake **Rev:** Mayan Pelota player and soccer ball

Date	Mintage	F	VF	XF	Unc	BU
2006Mo Proof	40,000	Value: 40.00				

KM# 805   5 PESOS
Silver **Obv:** Eagle on cactus **Rev:** Mayan ball game

Date	Mintage	F	VF	XF	Unc	BU
2006 Proof	—	Value: 55.00				

KM# 553 10 NUEVO PESOS
11.1300 g., Bi-Metallic 0.925 Silver center, .1667 oz.
ASW within Aluminum-Bronze ring, 27.95 mm. **Obv:**
National arms **Obv. Legend:** Estados Unidos
Mexicanos **Rev:** Assorted shields within circle **Edge:**
Reeded

Date	Mintage	F	VF	XF	Unc	BU
1992	20,000,000	—	—	—	7.50	8.50
1993	47,981,000	—	—	—	7.50	8.50
1994	15,000,000	—	—	—	7.50	8.50
1995 Proof	6,981	Value: 15.00				
1995	15,000,000	—	—	—	7.50	8.50

KM# 616 10 PESOS
10.3500 g., Bi-Metallic Copper-Nickel-Brass center
within Brass ring, 27.95 mm. **Obv:** National arms
Obv. Legend: ESTADOS UNIDOS MEXICANOS
Rev: Aztec design

Date	Mintage	F	VF	XF	Unc	BU
1997Mo	44,837,000	—	—	—	5.00	6.50
1998Mo	203,735,000	—	—	—	5.00	6.50
1999Mo	29,842,000	—	—	—	5.00	6.50

KM# 633 10 PESOS
62.0300 g., 0.9990 Silver 1.9922 oz. ASW **Subject:**
Millennium Series **Obv:** National arms, eagle left
within center of past and present arms **Rev:** Ancient
and modern buildings within circle

Date	Mintage	F	VF	XF	Unc	BU
1999-2000 Proof	75,000	Value: 47.50				

KM# 636 10 PESOS
10.3500 g., Bi-Metallic Copper-Nickel center in
Brass ring, 28 mm. **Series:** Millennium **Obv:**

National arms **Obv. Legend:** ESTADOS UNIDOS
MEXICANOS **Rev:** Aztec carving **Edge:** Lettered
Edge Lettering: ANO and date repeated 3 times

Date	Mintage	F	VF	XF	Unc	BU
2000Mo	24,839,000	—	—	—	5.00	6.50
2001Mo	44,768,000	—	—	—	5.00	6.50
2002Mo	44,721,000	—	—	—	5.00	6.50
2004Mo	74,739,000	—	—	—	5.00	6.50
2005Mo	64,635,000	—	—	—	5.00	6.50
2006Mo	84,480,000	—	—	—	5.00	6.50

KM# 739 10 PESOS
31.1040 g., 0.9990 Bi-Metallic 0.9990 oz., 39.9 mm.
Series: First **Subject:** 180th Anniversary of
Federation **Obv:** National arms **Obv. Legend:**
ESTADOS UNIDOS MEXICANOS **Rev:** State arms
Rev. Legend: ESTADO DE OAXACA **Edge:**
Reeded

Date	Mintage	F	VF	XF	Unc	BU
2004Mo Proof	10,000	Value: 75.00				

KM# 766 10 PESOS
31.1035 g., 0.9990 Silver 0.9990 oz. ASW, 40 mm.
Subject: Cervantes Festival **Obv:** Mexican Eagle
and Snake **Rev:** Don Quixote **Edge:** Reeded

Date	Mintage	F	VF	XF	Unc	BU
2005Mo Proof	—	Value: 55.00				

KM# 768 10 PESOS
31.1035 g., 0.9990 Silver 0.9990 oz. ASW, 40 mm.
Subject: 470th Anniversary -   Mexico City Mint
Obv: Mexican Eagle and Snake **Rev:** Antique coin
press

Date	Mintage	F	VF	XF	Unc	BU
2005Mo Proof	—	Value: 45.00				

KM# 755 10 PESOS
31.1040 g., 0.9990 Silver 0.9990 oz. ASW, 40 mm.
Obv: National arms **Rev:** Baja California del Norte
arms

Date	Mintage	F	VF	XF	Unc	BU
2005 Proof	—	Value: 55.00				

KM# 763 10 PESOS
31.1040 g., 0.9990 Silver 0.9990 oz. ASW, 40 mm.
Obv: National arms **Rev:** Benito Juarez **Edge:**
Reeded

Date	Mintage	F	VF	XF	Unc	BU
2006Mo Proof	—	Value: 55.00				

KM# 561   20 NUEVO PESOS
16.9200 g., Bi-Metallic 0.925 Silver 16.9g, (.2500 oz. ASW) center within Aluminum-Bronze ring, 31.86 mm.   **Obv:** National arms **Obv. Legend:** ESTADOS UNIDOS MEXICANOS **Rev:** Head of Hidalgo left within wreath **Edge:** Reeded

Date	Mintage	F	VF	XF	Unc	BU
1993Mo	25,000,000	—	—	—	12.00	15.00
1994Mo	5,000,000	—	—	—	12.00	15.00
1995Mo	5,000,000	—	—	—	12.00	15.00

KM# 641   20 PESOS
6.2210 g., 0.9990 Gold 0.1998 oz. AGW, 21.9 mm. **Subject:** UNICEF **Obv:** National arms, eagle left **Rev:** Child playing with lasso **Edge:** Reeded

Date	Mintage	F	VF	XF	Unc	BU
1999 Proof	—	Value: 275				

KM# 637   20 PESOS
Bi-Metallic Copper-Nickel center within Brass ring, 32 mm.   **Subject:** Xiuhtecuhtli **Obv:** National arms, eagle left within circle **Rev:** Aztec with torch within spiked circle

Date	Mintage	F	VF	XF	Unc	BU
2000	14,890,000	—	—	—	15.00	17.50
2001	2,478,000	—	—	—	15.00	17.50

KM# 638   20 PESOS
Bi-Metallic Copper-Nickel center within Brass ring,

---

32 mm.   **Obv:** National arms, eagle left within circle
Rev: Head 1/4 right within circle

Date	Mintage	F	VF	XF	Unc	BU
2000	14,943,000	—	—	—	15.00	17.50
2001	2,515,000	—	—	—	15.00	17.50

KM# 704   20 PESOS
62.4000 g., 0.9990 Silver 2.0041 oz. ASW, 48.1 mm. **Subject:** 400th Anniversary of Don Quijote de la Manchia **Obv:** National arms **Rev:** Skeletal figure horseback with spear galloping right **Edge:** Plain

Date	Mintage	F	VF	XF	Unc	BU
ND(2005)Mo Proof	10,000	Value: 85.00				

KM# 767   20 PESOS
62.4000 g., 0.9990 Silver 2.0041 oz. ASW, 48 mm. **Subject:** 80th Anniversary - Bank of Mexico **Obv:** National arms **Rev:** 100 Peso banknote design of 1925

Date	Mintage	F	VF	XF	Unc	BU
2005Mo	—	—	—	—	—	45.00
2005Mo Proof	—	Value: 90.00				

KM# 571   50 NUEVO PESOS
34.1100 g., Bi-Metallic 0.925 Silver .5000 ASW center within Brass ring, 38.87 mm.   **Subject:** Nino Heroes **Obv:** National arms **Obv. Legend:** ESTADOS UNIDOS MEXICANOS **Rev:** Six heads facing with date at upper right, all within circle and 1/2 wreath **Edge:** Reeded

Date	Mintage	F	VF	XF	Unc	BU
1993Mo	2,000,000	—	—	—	25.00	28.00
1994Mo	1,500,000	—	—	—	25.00	28.00
1995Mo	1,500,000	—	—	—	25.00	28.00

KM# 705   100 PESOS
33.7400 g., Bi-Metallic .925 Silver center in Aluminum-Bronze ring, 39 mm. **Subject:** 400th Anniversary of Don Quijote de la Manchia **Obv:** National arms **Obv. Legend:** ESTADOS UNIDOS MEXICANOS **Rev:** Sekeletal figure Horseback with spear galloping right **Edge:** Segmented reeding

Date	Mintage	F	VF	XF	Unc	BU
2005Mo	726,833	—	—	—	35.00	45.00
2005Mo Proof	3,761	Value: 75.00				

KM# 730   100 PESOS
33.8250 g., Bi-Metallic .925 Silver 20.1753g center in Aluminum-Bronze ring, 39.9 mm. **Subject:** Monetary Reform Centennial **Obv:** National arms **Rev:** Radiant Liberty Cap divides date above value within circle **Edge:** Segmented reeding

Date	Mintage	F	VF	XF	Unc	BU
2005Mo	49,716	—	—	—	35.00	45.00

KM# 731   100 PESOS
33.8250 g., Bi-Metallic .925 Silver 20.1753g center in Aluminum-Bronze ring, 39.9 mm. **Subject:** Mexico City Mint's 470th Anniversary **Obv:** National arms **Rev:** Screw press, value and date within circle **Edge:** Segmented reeding

Date	Mintage	F	VF	XF	Unc	BU
2005Mo	49,895	—	—	—	35.00	45.00

KM# 732   100 PESOS
33.8250 g., Bi-Metallic .925 Silver 20.1753g center in Aluminum-Bronze ring, 39.9 mm. **Subject:** Bank of Mexico's 80th Anniversary **Obv:** National arms **Rev:** Back design of the 1925 hundred peso note **Edge:** Segmented reeding

Date	Mintage	F	VF	XF	Unc	BU
2005Mo	49,712	—	—	—	35.00	45.00

KM# 764   100 PESOS
33.7000 g., Bi-Metallic .925 Silver 20.1753g center in Aluminum-Bronze ring **Subject:** 200th Anniversary Birth of Benito Juarez Garcia **Obv:** National arms **Rev:** Bust 1/4 left within circle

Date	Mintage	F	VF	XF	Unc	BU
2006Mo	49,913	—	—	—	35.00	45.00

KM# 771   50000 PESOS
0.9990 Gold, 23 mm. **Subject:** World Cup Soccer **Obv:** Mexican Eagle and Snake **Rev:** Kneeling Mayan Pelota player and soccer ball

Date	Mintage	F	VF	XF	Unc	BU
2006Mo Proof	—	Value: 600				

REFORM COINAGE
STATE COMMEMORATIVES

KM# 679   10 PESOS
31.1040 g., 0.9990 Silver 0.9990 oz. ASW, 39.9 mm. **Series:** First **Subject:** 180th Anniversary of Federation **Obv:** National arms **Obv. Legend:** ESTADOS UNIDOS MEXICANOS **Rev:** State Arms **Rev. Legend:** ESTADO DE ZACATECAS **Edge:** Reeded

Date	Mintage	F	VF	XF	Unc	BU
2003Mo Proof	10,000	Value: 75.00				

KM# 680   10 PESOS
31.1040 g., 0.9990 Silver 0.9990 oz. ASW, 39.9 mm.
Series: First **Subject:** 180th Anniversary of Federation
Obv: National arms **Obv. Legend:** ESTADO UNIDOS
MEXICANOS **Rev:** State arms **Rev. Legend:**
ESTADO DE YUCATÁN **Edge:** Reeded

Date	Mintage	F	VF	XF	Unc	BU
2003Mo Proof	10,000	Value: 75.00				

KM# 681   10 PESOS
31.1040 g., 0.9990 Silver 0.9990 oz. ASW, 39.9 mm.
Series: First **Subject:** 180th Anniversary of
Federation **Obv:** National arms **Obv. Legend:**
ESTADOS UNIDOS MEXICANOS **Rev:** State arms
Rev. Legend: ESTADO DE VERACRUZ-LLAVE
Edge: Reeded

Date	Mintage	F	VF	XF	Unc	BU
2003Mo Proof	10,000	Value: 75.00				

KM# 682   10 PESOS
31.1040 g., 0.9990 Silver 0.9990 oz. ASW, 39.9 mm.
Series: First **Subject:** 180th Anniversary of Frederation
Obv: National arms **Obv. Legend:** ESTADOS
UNIDOS MEXICANOS **Rev:** State arms **Rev. Legend:**
ESTADO DE TLAXCALA **Edge:** Reeded

Date	Mintage	F	VF	XF	Unc	BU
2003Mo Proof	10,000	Value: 75.00				

KM# 683   10 PESOS
31.1040 g., 0.9990 Silver 0.9990 oz. ASW, 39.9 mm.
Series: First **Subject:** 180th Anniversary of Federation
Obv: National arms **Obv. Legend:** ESTADOS
UNIDOS MEXICANOS **Rev:** State arms **Rev.
Legend:** ESTADO DE TAMAULIPAS **Edge:** Reeded

Date	Mintage	F	VF	XF	Unc	BU
2004Mo Proof	10,000	Value: 75.00				

KM# 684   10 PESOS
31.1040 g., 0.9990 Silver 0.9990 oz. ASW, 39.9 mm.
Series: First **Subject:** 180th Anniversary of Federation
Obv: National arms **Obv. Legend:** ESTADOS
UNIDOS DE MEXICANOS **Rev:** State arms **Rev.
Legend:** ESTADO DE TABASCO **Edge:** Reeded

Date	Mintage	F	VF	XF	Unc	BU
2004Mo Proof	10,000	Value: 75.00				

KM# 685   10 PESOS
31.1040 g., 0.9990 Silver 0.9990 oz. ASW, 39.9 mm.
Series: First **Subject:** 180th Anniversary of
Federation **Obv:** National arms **Obv. Legend:**
ESTADOS UNIDOS MEXICANOS **Rev:** State arms
Rev. Legend: ESTADO DE SONORA **Edge:**
Reeded **Note:** Mexican States: Sonora

Date	Mintage	F	VF	XF	Unc	BU
2004Mo Proof	10,000	Value: 75.00				

KM# 686   10 PESOS
31.1040 g., 0.9990 Silver 0.9990 oz. ASW, 39.9 mm.
Series: First **Subject:** 180th Anniversary of
Federation **Obv:** National arms **Obv. Legend:**
ESTADOS UNIDOS DE MEXICANOS **Rev:** State
arms **Rev. Legend:** ESTADO DE SINALOA **Edge:**
Reeded **Note:** Mexican States: Sinaloa

Date	Mintage	F	VF	XF	Unc	BU
2004Mo Proof	10,000	Value: 75.00				

KM# 687   10 PESOS
31.1040 g., 0.9990 Silver 0.9990 oz. ASW, 39.9 mm.
Series: First **Subject:** 180th Anniversary of
Federation **Obv:** National arms **Obv. Legend:**
ESTADOS UNIDOS MEXICANOS **Rev:** State arms
Rev. Legend: ESTADO DE SAN LUIS POTOSÍ
Edge: Reeded

Date	Mintage	F	VF	XF	Unc	BU
2004Mo Proof	10,000	Value: 75.00				

KM# 735   10 PESOS
31.1040 g., 0.9990 Silver 0.9990 oz. ASW, 39.9 mm.
Series: First **Subject:** 180th Anniversary of
Federation **Obv:** National arms **Obv. Legend:**
ESTADOS UNIDOS MEXICANOS **Rev:** State arms
Rev. Legend: ESTADO DE QUINTANA ROO

Date	Mintage	F	VF	XF	Unc	BU
2004 Proof	10,000	Value: 75.00				

KM# 733   10 PESOS
31.1040 g., 0.9990 Silver 0.9990 oz. ASW, 39.9 mm.
Series: First **Subject:** 180th Anniversary of
Federation **Obv:** National arms **Obv. Legend:**
ESTADOS UNIDOS MEXICANOS **Rev:** State arms
Rev. Legend: ESTADO DE QUERÉTARO
ARTEAGA **Edge:** Reeded

Date	Mintage	F	VF	XF	Unc	BU
2004 Proof	10,000	Value: 75.00				

KM# 737   10 PESOS
31.1040 g., 0.9990 Silver 0.9990 oz. ASW, 39.9 mm.
Series: First **Subject:** 180th Anniversary of
Federation **Obv:** National arms **Obv. Legend:**
ESTADOS UNIDOS MEXICANOS **Rev:** State arms
Rev. Legend: ESTADO DE PUEBLA **Edge:** Reeded

Date	Mintage	F	VF	XF	Unc	BU
2004Mo Proof	10,000	Value: 75.00				

KM# 741 10 PESOS
31.1040 g., 0.9990 Silver 0.9990 oz. ASW, 39.9 mm.
Series: First **Subject:** 180th Anniversary of
Federation **Obv:** National arms **Obv. Legend:**
ESTADOS UNIDOS MEXICANOS **Rev:** State arms
Rev. Legend: ESTADO DE NUEVO LEÓN **Edge:**
Reeded

Date	Mintage	F	VF	XF	Unc	BU
2004Mo Proof	10,000	Value: 75.00				

KM# 743 10 PESOS
31.1040 g., 0.9990 Silver 0.9990 oz. ASW, 39.9 mm.
Series: First **Subject:** 180th Anniversary of
Federation **Obv:** National arms **Obv. Legend:**
ESTADOS UNIDOS MEXICANOS **Rev:** State arms
Rev. Legend: ESTADO DE NAYARIT **Edge:**
Reeded

Date	Mintage	F	VF	XF	Unc	BU
2004Mo Proof	10,000	Value: 75.00				

KM# 745 10 PESOS
31.1040 g., 0.9990 Silver 0.9990 oz. ASW, 39.9 mm.
Series: First **Subject:** 180th Anniversary of Federation
Obv: National arms **Obv. Legend:** ESTADOS
UNIDOS MEXICANOS **Rev:** State arms **Rev.
Legend:** ESTADO DE MORELOS **Edge:** Reeded

Date	Mintage	F	VF	XF	Unc	BU
2004Mo Proof	10,000	Value: 75.00				

KM# 796 10 PESOS
31.1040 g., 0.9990 Silver 0.9990 oz. ASW, 39.9 mm.
Series: First **Subject:** 180th Anniversary of
Federation **Obv:** National arms **Obv. Legend:**
ESTADOS UNIDOS MEXICANOS **Rev:** State arms
Rev. Legend: ESTADO DE MICHOACÁN DE
OCAMPO **Edge:** Reeded

Date	Mintage	F	VF	XF	Unc	BU
2004Mo Proof	10,000	Value: 75.00				

KM# 747 10 PESOS
31.1040 g., 0.9990 Silver 0.9990 oz. ASW, 39.9 mm.
Series: First **Subject:** 180th Anniversary of
Federation **Obv:** National arms **Obv. Legend:**
ESTADOS UNIDOS MEXICANOS **Rev:** State arms
Rev. Legend: ESTADO DE MÉXICO **Edge:** Reeded

Date	Mintage	F	VF	XF	Unc	BU
2004Mo Proof	10,000	Value: 75.00				

KM# 749 10 PESOS
31.1040 g., 0.9990 Silver 0.9990 oz. ASW, 39.9 mm.
Series: First **Subject:** 180th Anniversary of Federation
Obv: National arms **Obv. Legend:** ESTADOS
UNIDOS MEXICANOS **Rev:** State arms **Rev.
Legend:** ESTADO DE JALISCO **Edge:** Reeded

Date	Mintage	F	VF	XF	Unc	BU
2004Mo Proof	10,000	Value: 75.00				

KM# 711 10 PESOS
31.1040 g., 0.9990 Silver 0.9990 oz. ASW, 39.9 mm.
Series: First **Subject:** 180th Anniversary of Federation
Obv: National arms **Obv. Legend:** ESTADOS
UNIDOS MEXICANOS **Rev:** State arms **Rev.
Legend:** ESTADO DE HIDALGO **Edge:** Reeded

Date	Mintage	F	VF	XF	Unc	BU
2005Mo Proof	10,000	Value: 75.00				

KM# 710 10 PESOS
31.1040 g., 0.9990 Silver 0.9990 oz. ASW, 39.9 mm.
Series: First **Subject:** 180th Anniversary of Federation
Obv: National arms **Obv. Legend:** ESTADOS
UNIDOS MEXICANOS **Rev:** State arms **Rev.
Legend:** ESTADO DE GUERRERO **Edge:** Reeded

Date	Mintage	F	VF	XF	Unc	BU
2005Mo Proof	10,000	Value: 75.00				

KM# 709 10 PESOS
31.1040 g., 0.9990 Silver 0.9990 oz. ASW, 39.9 mm.
Series: First **Subject:** 180th Anniversary of Federation
Obv: National arms **Obv. Legend:** ESTADOS
UNIDOS MEXICANOS **Rev:** State arms **Rev.
Legend:** ESTADO DE GUANAJUATO **Edge:** Reeded

Date	Mintage	F	VF	XF	Unc	BU
2005Mo Proof	10,000	Value: 75.00				

KM# 708   10 PESOS
31.1040 g., 0.9990 Silver 0.9990 oz. ASW, 39.9 mm.
Series: First **Subject:** 180th Anniversary of Federation
Obv: National arms **Obv. Legend:** ESTADOS
UNIDOS MEXICANOS **Rev:** State arms **Rev.**
Legend: ESTADO DE DURANGO **Edge:** Reeded

Date	Mintage	F	VF	XF	Unc	BU
2005Mo Proof	10,000	Value: 75.00				

KM# 707   10 PESOS
31.1040 g., 0.9990 Silver 0.9990 oz. ASW, 39.9 mm.
Series: First **Subject:** 180th Anniversary of
Federation **Obv:** National arms **Obv. Legend:**
ESTADOS UNIDOS MEXICANOS **Rev:** Federal
District arms **Rev. Legend:** DISTRITO FEDERAL
Edge: Reeded

Date	Mintage	F	VF	XF	Unc	BU
2005Mo Proof	10,000	Value: 75.00				

KM# 753   10 PESOS
31.1040 g., 0.9990 Silver 0.9990 oz. ASW, 39.9 mm.
Series: First **Subject:** 180th Anniversary of Federation
Obv: National arms **Obv. Legend:** ESTADOS
UNIDOS MEXICANOS **Rev:** State arms **Rev.**
Legend: ESTADO DE CHIHUAHUA **Edge:** Reeded

Date	Mintage	F	VF	XF	Unc	BU
2005Mo Proof	10,000	Value: 75.00				

KM# 706   10 PESOS
31.1040 g., 0.9990 Silver 0.9990 oz. ASW, 39.9 mm.
Series: First **Subject:** 180th Anniversary of Federation
Obv: National arms **Obv. Legend:** ESTADOS
UNIDOS MEXICANOS **Rev:** State arms **Rev.**
Legend: ESTADO DE CHIAPAS **Edge:** Reeded

Date	Mintage	F	VF	XF	Unc	BU
2005Mo Proof	10,000	Value: 75.00				

KM# 728   10 PESOS
31.1040 g., 0.9990 Silver 0.9990 oz. ASW, 39.9 mm.
Series: First **Subject:** 180th Anniversary of Federation
Obv: National arms **Obv. Legend:** ESTADOS
UNIDOS MEXICANOS **Rev:** State arms **Rev.**
Legend: ESTADO DE COLIMA **Edge:** Reeded

Date	Mintage	F	VF	XF	Unc	BU
2005Mo Proof	10,000	Value: 75.00				

KM# 751   10 PESOS
31.1040 g., 0.9990 Silver 0.9990 oz. ASW, 39.9 mm.
Series: First **Subject:** 180th Anniversary of
Federation **Obv:** National arms **Obv. Legend:**
ESTADOS UNIDOS MEXICANOS **Rev:** State arms
Rev. Legend: ESTADO DE COAHUILA DE
ZARAGOZA **Edge:** Reeded

Date	Mintage	F	VF	XF	Unc	BU
2005Mo Proof	10,000	Value: 75.00				

KM# 726   10 PESOS
31.1040 g., 0.9990 Silver 0.9990 oz. ASW, 39.9 mm.
Series: First **Subject:** 180th Anniversary of Federation
Obv: National arms **Obv. Legend:** ESTADOS
UNIDOS MEXICANOS **Rev:** State arms **Rev. Legend:**
ESTADO DE CAMPECHE **Edge:** Reeded

Date	Mintage	F	VF	XF	Unc	BU
2005Mo Proof	10,000	Value: 75.00				

KM# 724   10 PESOS
31.1040 g., 0.9990 Silver 0.9990 oz. ASW, 39.9 mm.
Series: First **Subject:** 180th Anniversary of
Federation **Obv:** National arms **Obv. Legend:**
ESTADOS UNIDOS MEXICANOS **Rev:** State arms
Rev. Legend: ESTADO DE BAJA CALIFORNIA
SUR **Edge:** Reeded

Date	Mintage	F	VF	XF	Unc	BU
2005Mo Proof	10,000	Value: 75.00				

KM# 722   10 PESOS
31.1040 g., 0.9990 Silver 0.9990 oz. ASW, 39.9 mm.
Series: First **Subject:** 180th Anniversary of Federation
Obv: National arms **Obv. Legend:** ESTADOS
UNIDOS MEXICANOS **Rev:** State arms **Rev. Legend:**
ESTADO DE BAJA CALIFORNIA **Edge:** Reeded

Date	Mintage	F	VF	XF	Unc	BU
2005Mo Proof	10,000	Value: 75.00				

KM# 720   10 PESOS
31.1040 g., 0.9990 Silver 0.9990 oz. ASW, 39.9 mm.
Series: First **Subject:** 180th Anniversary of
Federation **Obv:** National arms **Obv. Legend:**
ESTADOS UNIDOS MEXICANOS **Rev:** State arms
Rev. Legend: ESTADO DE AGUASCALIENTES
Edge: Reeded

Date	Mintage	F	VF	XF	Unc	BU
2005Mo Proof	10,000	Value: 75.00				

KM# 718   10 PESOS
31.1040 g., 0.9990 Silver 0.9990 oz. ASW, 40 mm.
Series: Second **Obv:** National arms **Obv. Legend:**
ESTADOS UNIDOS MEXICANOS **Rev:** Facade of
the San Marcos garden above sculpture of national
emblem at left, San Antonio Temple at right **Rev.**
Legend: AGUASCALIENTES **Edge:** Reeded

Date	Mintage	F	VF	XF	Unc	BU
2005Mo Proof	6,000	Value: 75.00				

KM# 757 10 PESOS
31.1040 g., 0.9990 Silver 0.9990 oz. ASW, 40 mm.
Series: Second **Obv:** National arms **Obv. Legend:**
ESTADOS UNIDOS MEXICANOS **Rev:** Rams head,
mountain outline in background **Rev. Legend:** BAJA
CALIFORNIA - GOBIERNO DEL ESTADO **Edge:**
Reeded

Date	Mintage	F	VF	XF	Unc	BU
2005Mo Proof	6,000	Value: 75.00				

KM# 761 10 PESOS
31.1040 g., 0.9990 Silver 0.9990 oz. ASW, 40 mm.
Series: Second **Obv:** National arms **Obv. Legend:**
ESTADOS UNIDOS MEXICANOS **Rev:** Outlined
map of peninsula at center, cave painting of deer
behind, cactus at right **Rev. Legend:** ESTADO DE
BAJA CALIFORNIA SUR **Edge:** Reeded

Date	Mintage	F	VF	XF	Unc	BU
2006Mo Proof	6,000	Value: 75.00				

KM# 759 10 PESOS
31.1040 g., 0.9990 Silver 0.9990 oz. ASW, 40 mm.
Series: Second **Obv:** National arms **Obv. Legend:**
ESTADOS UNIDOS MEXICANOS **Rev:** Jade mask
- Calakmul, Campeche **Rev. Legend:** ESTADO DE
CAMPECHE **Edge:** Reeded

Date	Mintage	F	VF	XF	Unc	BU
2006Mo Proof	6,000	Value: 75.00				

KM# 780 10 PESOS
31.1040 g., 0.9990 Silver 0.9990 oz. ASW, 40 mm.
Series: Second **Obv:** National arms **Obv. Legend:**
ESTADOS UNIDOS MEXICANOS **Rev:** Outlined
map with turtle, mine cart above grapes at center,
Friendship dam above Christ of the Nodas at left,
chimneys above crucibles and bell tower of
Santiago's cathedral at right **Rev. Inscription:**
COAHUILA DE ZARAGOZA **Edge:** Reeded

Date	Mintage	F	VF	XF	Unc	BU
2006Mo Proof	6,000	Value: 75.00				

KM# 776 10 PESOS
31.1040 g., 0.9990 Silver 0.9990 oz. ASW, 40 mm.
Series: Second **Obv:** National arms **Obv. Legend:**
ESTADOS UNIDOS MEXICANOS **Rev:** State arms at
lower center, Nevado de Colima and Volcan de Fuego
volcanos in background **Rev. Legend:** *Colima* **Rev.
Inscription:** GENEROSO **Edge:** Reeded

Date	Mintage	F	VF	XF	Unc	BU
2006Mo Proof	6,000	Value: 75.00				

KM# 772 10 PESOS
31.1040 g., 0.9990 Silver 0.9990 oz. ASW, 40 mm.
Series: Second **Obv:** National arms **Obv. Legend:**
ESTADOS UNIDOS MEXICANOS **Rev:** Head of
Pakal, ancient Mayan king, Palenque **Rev. Legend:**
ESTADO DE CHIAPAS - CABEZA MAYA DEL REY
PAKAL, PALENQUE **Edge:** Reeded

Date	Mintage	F	VF	XF	Unc	BU
2006Mo Proof	6,000	Value: 75.00				

KM# 774 10 PESOS
31.1040 g., 0.9990 Silver 0.9990 oz. ASW, 40 mm.
Series: Second **Obv:** National arms **Obv. Legend:**
ESTADOS UNIDOS MEXICANOS **Rev:** Angel of
Liberty **Rev. Legend:** MÉXICO - ANGEL DE LA
LIBERTAD, CHIHUAHUA **Edge:** Reeded

Date	Mintage	F	VF	XF	Unc	BU
2006Mo Proof	6,000	Value: 75.00				

KM# 778 10 PESOS
31.1040 g., 0.9990 Silver 0.9990 oz. ASW, 40 mm.
Series: Second **Obv:** National arms **Obv. Legend:**
ESTADOS UNIDOS MEXICANOS **Rev:** National
Palace **Rev. Legend:** DISTRITO FEDERAL -
ANTIGUO AYUNTAMIENTO **Edge:** Reeded

Date	Mintage	F	VF	XF	Unc	BU
2006Mo Proof	6,000	Value: 75.00				

KM# 786 10 PESOS
31.1040 g., 0.9990 Silver 0.9990 oz. ASW, 40 mm.
Series: Second **Obv:** National arms **Obv. Legend:**
ESTADOS UNIDOS MEXICANOS **Rev:** Tree **Rev.
Legend:** PRIMERA RESERVA NACIONAL
FORESTAL - DURANGO **Edge:** Reeded

Date	Mintage	F	VF	XF	Unc	BU
2006Mo Proof	6,000	Value: 75.00				

KM# 788 10 PESOS
31.1040 g., 0.9990 Silver 0.9990 oz. ASW, 40 mm.
Series: Second **Obv:** National arms **Obv. Legend:**
ESTADOS UNIDOS MEXICANOS **Rev:** State arms at
center, statue of Miguel Hidalgo at left, monument to
Pípila at lower right **Rev. Inscription:** *Guanajuato*
Edge: Reeded

Date	Mintage	F	VF	XF	Unc	BU
2006Mo Proof	6,000	Value: 75.00				

KM# 790   10 PESOS
31.1040 g., 0.9990 Silver 0.9990 oz. ASW, 40 mm.
Series: Second **Obv:** National arms **Obv. Legend:**
ESTADOS UNIDOS MEXICANOS **Rev:** Stylized
portrait of Vicente Guerrero at left, church of Taxco
at upper center, Acapulco's la Quebrada with diver
above Christmas Eve flower and mask **Rev. Legend:**
GUERRERO **Edge:** Reeded

Date	Mintage	F	VF	XF	Unc	BU
2006Mo Proof	6,000	Value: 75.00				

KM# 792   10 PESOS
31.1040 g., 0.9990 Silver 0.9990 oz. ASW, 40 mm.
Series: Second **Obv:** National arms **Obv. Legend:**
ESTADOS UNIDOS MEXICANOS **Rev:** Monument
of Pachuca Hidalgo **Rev. Inscription:** *RELOJ /
MONUMENTAL / DE / PACHUCA / HIDALGO - La
/ Bella / Airosa* **Edge:** Reeded

Date	Mintage	F	VF	XF	Unc	BU
2006Mo Proof	6,000	Value: 75.00				

KM# 794   10 PESOS
31.1040 g., 0.9990 Silver 0.9990 oz. ASW, 40 mm.
Series: Second **Obv:** National arms **Obv. Legend:**
ESTADOS UNIDOS MEXICANOS **Rev:** Hospicio
Cabañas orphanage **Rev. Legend:** ESTADO DE
JALISCCO **Edge:** Reeded

Date	Mintage	F	VF	XF	Unc	BU
2006Mo Proof	6,000	Value: 75.00				

KM# 830   10 PESOS
31.1040 g., 0.9990 Silver 0.9990 oz. ASW, 40 mm.
Series: Second **Obv:** National arms **Obv. Legend:**
ESTADOS UNIDOS MEXICANOS **Rev:** Pyramid de
la Loona (Moon) **Rev. Legend:** ESTADO DE
MÉXICO **Edge:** Reeded

Date	Mintage	F	VF	XF	Unc	BU
2006Mo Proof	6,000	Value: 75.00				

KM# 831   10 PESOS
31.1040 g., 0.9990 Silver 0.9990 oz. ASW, 40 mm.
Series: Second **Obv:** National arms **Obv. Legend:**
ESTADOS UNIDOS MEXICANOS **Rev:** Four
Monarch butterflies **Rev. Legend:** ESTADO DE
MICHOACÁN **Edge:** Reeded

Date	Mintage	F	VF	XF	Unc	BU
2006Mo Proof	6,000	Value: 75.00				

KM# 832   10 PESOS
31.1040 g., 0.9990 Silver 0.9990 oz. ASW, 40 mm.
Series: Second **Obv:** National arms **Obv. Legend:**
ESTADOS UNIDOS MEXICANOS **Rev:** 1/2 length
figure of Chinelo (local dancer) at right, Palacio de
Cortes in background **Rev. Inscription:** ESTADO
DE / MORELOS **Edge:** Reeded

Date	Mintage	F	VF	XF	Unc	BU
2006Mo Proof	6,000	Value: 75.00				

KM# 833   10 PESOS
31.1040 g., 0.9990 Silver 0.9990 oz. ASW, 40 mm.
Series: Second **Obv:** National arms **Obv. Legend:**
ESTADOS UNIDOS MEXICANOS **Rev:** Isle de
Mexcaltitlán **Rev. Legend:** ESTADO DE NAYARIT
Edge: Reeded

Date	Mintage	F	VF	XF	Unc	BU
2007Mo Proof	6,000	Value: 75.00				

KM# 834   10 PESOS
31.1040 g., 0.9990 Silver 0.9990 oz. ASW, 40 mm.
Series: Second **Obv:** National arms **Obv. Legend:**
ESTADOS UNIDOS MEXICANOS **Rev:** Old foundry
in Pargue Fundidora (public park) at right, Cerro de
la Silla (Saddle Hill) in background **Rev. Legend:**
ESTADO DE NUEVO LEÓN **Edge:** Reeded

Date	Mintage	F	VF	XF	Unc	BU
2007Mo Proof	6,000	Value: 75.00				

KM# 835   10 PESOS
31.1040 g., 0.9990 Silver 0.9990 oz. ASW, 40 mm.
Series: Second **Obv:** National arms **Obv. Legend:**
ESTADOS UNIDOS MEXICANOS **Rev:** Teatro
Macedonio Alcala (theater) **Rev. Legend:** OAXACA
Edge: Reeded

Date	Mintage	F	VF	XF	Unc	BU
2007Mo Proof	6,000	Value: 75.00				

KM# 836   10 PESOS
31.1040 g., 0.9990 Silver 0.9990 oz. ASW, 40 mm.
Series: Second **Obv:** National arms **Obv. Legend:**
ESTADOS UNIDOS MEXICANOS **Rev:** Talavera
porcelain dish **Rev. Legend:** ESTADO DE PUEBLA
Edge: Reeded

Date	Mintage	F	VF	XF	Unc	BU
2007Mo Proof	6,000	Value: 75.00				

KM# 837   10 PESOS
31.1040 g., 0.9990 Silver 0.9990 oz. ASW, 40 mm.
Series: Second **Obv:** National arms **Obv. Legend:**
ESTADOS UNIDOS MEXICANOS **Rev:** Mask at left,
rays above state arms at center, Mayan ruins at right
Rev. Legend: QUINTANA ROO **Edge:** Reeded

Date	Mintage	F	VF	XF	Unc	BU
2007Mo Proof	6,000	Value: 75.00				

KM# 838   10 PESOS
31.1040 g., 0.9990 Silver 0.9990 oz. ASW, 40 mm.
Series: Second **Obv:** National arms **Obv. Legend:**
ESTADOS UNIDOS MEXICANOS **Rev:** Acueduct of
Querétaro at left, church of Santa Rosa de Viterbo
at right **Rev. Legend:** ESTADO DE QUERÉTARO
ARTEAGA **Edge:** Reeded

Date	Mintage	F	VF	XF	Unc	BU
2007Mo Proof	6,000	Value: 75.00				

KM# 839   10 PESOS
31.1040 g., Silver, 40 mm. **Series:** Second **Obv:**
National arms **Obv. Legend:** ESTADOS UNIDOS
MEXICANOS **Rev:** Facade of Caja Real **Rev.
Legend:** • SAN LUIS POTOSÍ • **Edge:** Reeded

Date	Mintage	F	VF	XF	Unc	BU
2007Mo Proof	6,000	Value: 75.00				

KM# 840 10 PESOS
31.1040 g., 0.9990 Silver 0.9990 oz. ASW, 40 mm.
Series: Second **Obv:** National arms **Obv. Legend:**
ESTADOS UNIDOS MEXICANOS **Rev:** Shield on
pile of cactus fruits **Rev. Legend:** ESTADO DE
SINALOA - LUGAR DE PITAHAYAS **Edge:** Reeded

Date	Mintage	F	VF	XF	Unc	BU
2007Mo Proof	6,000	Value: 75.00				

KM# 841 10 PESOS
31.1040 g., 0.9990 Silver 0.9990 oz. ASW, 40 mm.
Series: Second **Obv:** National arms **Obv. Legend:**
ESTADOS UNIDOS MEXICANOS **Rev:** Local in
Dance of the Deer at left, cactus at right, mountains
in background **Rev. Legend:** ESTADO DE SONORA
Edge: Reeded

Date	Mintage	F	VF	XF	Unc	BU
2007Mo Proof	6,000	Value: 75.00				

KM# 842 10 PESOS
31.1040 g., 0.9990 Silver 0.9990 oz. ASW, 40 mm.
Series: Second **Obv:** National arms **Obv. Legend:**
ESTADOS UNIDOS MEXICANOS **Rev:** Fuente de
los Pescadores (fisherman fountain) at lower left,
giant head from the Olmec-pre-Hispanic culture at
right, Planetario Tabasco in background **Rev.
Legend:** TABASCO **Edge:** Reeded

Date	Mintage	F	VF	XF	Unc	BU
2007Mo Proof	6,000	Value: 75.00				

KM# 843 10 PESOS
31.1040 g., 0.9990 Silver 0.9990 oz. ASW, 40 mm.
Series: Second **Obv:** National arms **Obv. Legend:**
ESTADOS UNIDOS MEXICANOS **Rev:** Ridge -
Cerro Del Bernal, Gonzáles **Rev. Legend:**
TAMAULIPAS **Edge:** Reeded

Date	Mintage	F	VF	XF	Unc	BU
2007Mo Proof	6,000	Value: 75.00				

KM# 844 10 PESOS
31.1040 g., 0.9990 Silver 0.9990 oz. ASW, 40 mm.
Series: Second **Obv:** National arms **Obv. Legend:**
ESTADOS UNIDOS MEXICANOS **Rev:** Basilica de
Ocotlán at left, state arms above Capilla Abierta,
Plaza de Toros Ranchero Aguilar below, Exconvento
de San Francisco at right **Rev. Legend:** ESTADO
DE TLAXCALA **Edge:** Reeded

Date	Mintage	F	VF	XF	Unc	BU
2007Mo Proof	6,000	Value: 75.00				

KM# 845 10 PESOS
31.1040 g., 0.9990 Silver 0.9990 oz. ASW, 40 mm.
Series: Second **Obv:** National arms **Obv. Legend:**
ESTADOS UNIDOS MEXICANOS **Rev:** Pyramid of
El Tajín **Rev. Legend:** • VERACRUZ • - • DE
IGNACIO DE LA LLAVE • **Edge:** Reeded

Date	Mintage	F	VF	XF	Unc	BU
2007Mo Proof	6,000	Value: 75.00				

KM# 846 10 PESOS
31.1030 g., 0.9990 Silver 0.9989 oz. ASW, 40 mm.
Series: Second **Obv:** National arms **Obv. Legend:**
ESTADOS UNIDOS MEXICANOS **Rev:** Stylized
pyramid of Chichén-Itzá **Rev. Legend:** Castillo de
Chichén Itzá **Rev. Inscription:** YUCATÁN **Edge:**
Reeded

Date	Mintage	F	VF	XF	Unc	BU
2007Mo Proof	6,000	Value: 75.00				

KM# 847 10 PESOS
31.1040 g., 0.9990 Silver 0.9990 oz. ASW, 40 mm.
Series: Second **Obv:** National arms **Obv. Legend:**
ESTADOS UNIDOS MEXICANOS **Rev:** Cable car
above Monumento al Minero at left, Catedral de
Zacatecas at center right **Rev. Legend:** Zacatecas
Edge: Reeded

Date	Mintage	F	VF	XF	Unc	BU
2007Mo Proof	6,000	Value: 75.00				

KM# 688 100 PESOS
33.9400 g., Bi-Metallic .925 Silver 20.1753g center
in Aluminum-Bronze ring, 39.04 mm. **Series:** First
Subject: 180th Anniversary of Federation **Obv:**
National arms **Obv. Legend:** ESTADOS UNIDOS
MEXICANOS **Rev:** State arms **Rev. Legend:**
ESTADO DE ZACATECAS **Edge:** Segmented
reeding

Date	Mintage	F	VF	XF	Unc	BU
2003Mo	244,900	—	—	—	35.00	45.00

KM# 696   100 PESOS
29.1690 g., Bi-Metallic .999 Gold 17.154g center in .999 Silver 12.015g ring, 34.5 mm. **Series:** First **Subject:** 180th Anniversary of Federation **Obv:** National arms **Obv. Legend:** ESTADOS UNIDOS MEXICANOS **Rev:** State arms **Rev. Legend:** ESTADO DE ZACATECAS **Edge:** Segmented reeding

Date	Mintage	F	VF	XF	Unc	BU
2003Mo Proof	1,000	Value: 775				

KM# 689   100 PESOS
33.9400 g., Bi-Metallic .925 Silver 20.1753g center in Aluminum-Bronze ring, 39.04 mm. **Series:** First **Subject:** 180th Anniversary of Federation **Obv:** National arms **Obv. Legend:** ESTADOS UNIDOS MEXICANOS **Rev:** State arms **Rev. Legend:** ESTADO DE YUCATÁN **Edge:** Segmented reeding

Date	Mintage	F	VF	XF	Unc	BU
2003Mo	235,763	—	—	—	35.00	45.00

KM# 697   100 PESOS
29.1690 g., Bi-Metallic .999 Gold 17.154g center in .999 Silver 12.015g ring, 34.5 mm. **Series:** First **Subject:** 180th Anniversary of Federation **Obv:** National arms **Obv. Legend:** ESTADOS UNIDOS MEXICANOS **Rev:** State arms **Rev. Legend:** ESTADO DE YUCATÁN **Edge:** Segmented reeding

Date	Mintage	F	VF	XF	Unc	BU
2003Mo Proof	1,000	Value: 775				

KM# 690   100 PESOS
33.9400 g., Bi-Metallic .925 Silver 20.1753g center in Aluminum-Bronze ring, 39.04 mm. **Series:** First **Subject:** 180th Anniversary of Federation **Obv:** National arms **Obv. Legend:** ESTADOS UNIDOS MEXICANOS **Rev:** State arms **Rev. Legend:** ESTADO DE VERACRUZ-LLAVE **Edge:** Segmented reeding

Date	Mintage	F	VF	XF	Unc	BU
2003Mo	248,810	—	—	—	35.00	45.00

KM# 698   100 PESOS
29.1690 g., Bi-Metallic .999 Gold 17.154g center in .999 Silver 12.015g ring, 34.5 mm. **Series:** First **Subject:** 180th Anniversary of Federation **Obv:** National arms **Obv. Legend:** ESTADOS UNIDOS MEXICANOS **Rev:** State arms **Rev. Legend:** ESTADO DE VERACRUZ-LLAVE **Edge:** Segmented reeding

Date	Mintage	F	VF	XF	Unc	BU
2003Mo Proof	1,000	Value: 775				

KM# 691   100 PESOS
33.9400 g., Bi-Metallic .925 Silver 20.1753g center in Aluminum-Bronze ring, 39.9 mm. **Series:** First **Subject:** 180th Anniversary of Federation **Obv:** National arms **Obv. Legend:** ESTADOS UNIDOS MEXICANOS **Rev:** State arms **Rev. Legend:** ESTADO DE TLAXCALA **Edge:** Segmented reeding

Date	Mintage	F	VF	XF	Unc	BU
2003Mo	248,976	—	—	—	35.00	45.00

KM# 699   100 PESOS
29.1690 g., Bi-Metallic .999 Gold 17.154g center in .999 Silver 12.015g ring, 34.5 mm. **Series:** First **Subject:** 180th Anniversary of Federation **Obv:** National arms **Obv. Legend:** ESTADOS UNIDOS MEXICANOS **Rev:** State arms **Rev. Legend:** ESTADO DE TLAXCALA **Edge:** Segmented reeding

Date	Mintage	F	VF	XF	Unc	BU
2003Mo Proof	1,000	Value: 775				

KM# 692   100 PESOS
33.9400 g., Bi-Metallic .925 Silver 20.1753g center in Aluminum-Bronze ring, 39.04 mm. **Series:** First **Subject:** 180th Anniversary of Federation **Obv:** National arms **Obv. Legend:** ESTADOS UNIDOS MEXICANOS **Rev:** State arms **Rev. Legend:** ESTADO DE TAMAULIPAS **Edge:** Segmented reeding

Date	Mintage	F	VF	XF	Unc	BU
2004Mo	249,398	—	—	—	35.00	45.00

KM# 700   100 PESOS
29.1690 g., Bi-Metallic .999 Gold 17.154g center in .999 Silver 12.015g ring, 34.5 mm. **Series:** First **Subject:** 180th Anniversary of Federation **Obv:** National arms **Obv. Legend:** ESTADOS UNIDOS MEXICANOS **Rev:** State arms **Rev. Legend:** ESTADO DE TAMAULIPAS **Edge:** Segmented reeding

Date	Mintage	F	VF	XF	Unc	BU
2004Mo Proof	1,000	Value: 775				

KM# 693   100 PESOS
33.9400 g., Bi-Metallic .925 Silver 20.1753g center in Aluminum-Bronze ring, 39.04 mm. **Series:** First **Subject:** 180th Anniversary of Federation **Obv:** National arms **Obv. Legend:** ESTADOS UNIDOS MEXICANOS **Rev:** State arms **Rev. Legend:** ESTADO DE TABASCO **Edge:** Segmented reeding

Date	Mintage	F	VF	XF	Unc	BU
2004Mo	249,318	—	—	—	35.00	45.00

KM# 701   100 PESOS
29.1690 g., Bi-Metallic .999 Gold 17.154g center in .999 Silver 12.015g ring, 34.5 mm. **Series:** First **Subject:** 180th Anniversary of Federation **Obv:** National arms **Obv. Legend:** ESTADOS UNIDOS MEXICANOS **Rev:** State arms **Rev. Legend:** ESTADO DE TABASCO **Edge:** Segmented reeding

Date	Mintage	F	VF	XF	Unc	BU
2004Mo Proof	1,000	Value: 775				

KM# 694   100 PESOS
33.9400 g., Bi-Metallic .925 Silver 20.1753g center in Aluminum-Bronze ring, 39.04 mm. **Series:** First **Subject:** 180th Anniversary of Federation **Obv:** National arms **Obv. Legend:** ESTADOS UNIDOS MEXICANOS **Rev:** State arms **Rev. Legend:** ESTADO DE SONORA **Edge:** Segmented reeding

Date	Mintage	F	VF	XF	Unc	BU
2004Mo	249,300	—	—	—	—	30.00

KM# 702 100 PESOS
29.1690 g., Bi-Metallic .999 Gold 17.154g center in
.999 Silver 12.015g ring, 34.5 mm. **Series:** First
Subject: 180th Anniversary of Federation **Obv:**
National arms **Obv. Legend:** ESTADOS UNIDOS
MEXICANOS **Rev:** State arms **Rev. Legend:**
ESTADO DE SONORA **Edge:** Segmented reeding

Date	Mintage	F	VF	XF	Unc	BU
2004Mo Proof	1,000	Value: 775				

KM# 695 100 PESOS
33.9400 g., Bi-Metallic .925 Silver 20.1753g center
in Aluminum-Bronze ring, 39.04 mm. **Series:** First
Subject: 180th Anniversary of Federation **Obv:**
National arms **Obv. Legend:** ESTADOS UNIDOS
MEXICANOS **Rev:** State arms **Rev. Legend:**
ESTADO DE SINALOA **Edge:** Segmented reeding

Date	Mintage	F	VF	XF	Unc	BU
2004Mo	244,722	—	—	—	35.00	45.00

KM# 703 100 PESOS
29.1690 g., Bi-Metallic .999 Gold 17.154g center in
.999 Silver 12.015g ring, 34.5 mm. **Series:** First
Subject: 180th Anniversary of Federation **Obv:**
National arms **Obv. Legend:** ESTADOS UNIDOS
MEXICANOS **Rev:** State arms **Rev. Legend:**
ESTADO DE SINALOA **Edge:** Segmented reeding

Date	Mintage	F	VF	XF	Unc	BU
2004Mo Proof	1,000	Value: 775				

KM# 803 100 PESOS
33.9400 g., Bi-Metallic .925 Silver 20.1753g center
in Aluminum-Bronze ring, 39.04 mm. **Series:** First
Subject: 180th Anniversary of Federation **Obv:**
National arms **Obv. Legend:** ESTADOS UNIDOS
MEXICANOS **Rev:** State arms **Rev. Legend:**
ESTADO DE SAN LUIS POTOSÍ **Edge:** Segmented
reeding

Date	Mintage	F	VF	XF	Unc	BU
2004Mo	249,662	—	—	—	35.00	45.00

KM# 806 100 PESOS
29.1690 g., Bi-Metallic .999 Gold 17.154g center in
.999 silver 12.015 ring, 34.5 mm. **Series:** First
Subject: 180th Anniversary of Federation **Obv:**
National arms **Obv. Legend:** ESTADOS UNIDOS
MEXICANOS **Rev:** State arms **Rev. Legend:**
ESTADO DE SAN LUIS POTOSÍ **Edge:** Segmented
reeding

Date	Mintage	F	VF	XF	Unc	BU
2004Mo Proof	1,000	Value: 775				

KM# 736 100 PESOS
33.9400 g., Bi-Metallic .925 Silver 20.1753g center
in Aluminum-Bronze ring, 39.04 mm. **Series:** First
Subject: 180th Anniversary of Federation **Obv:**
National arms **Obv. Legend:** ESTADOS UNIDOS
MEXICANOS **Rev:** State arms **Rev. Legend:**
ESTADO DE QUINTANA ROO **Edge:** Segmented
reeding

Date	Mintage	F	VF	XF	Unc	BU
2004Mo	249,134	—	—	—	35.00	45.00

KM# 807 100 PESOS
29.1690 g., Bi-Metallic .999 Gold 17.154g center in
.999 Silver 12.015g ring, 34.5 mm. **Series:** First
Subject: 180th Anniversary of Federation **Obv:**
National arms **Obv. Legend:** ESTADOS UNIDOS
MEXICANOS **Rev:** State arms **Rev. Legend:**
ESTADO DE QUINTANA ROO **Edge:** Segmented
reeding

Date	Mintage	F	VF	XF	Unc	BU
2004Mo Proof	1,000	Value: 775				

KM# 734 100 PESOS
33.9400 g., Bi-Metallic .925 Silver 20.1753g center
in Aluminum-Bronze ring, 39.04 mm. **Series:** First
Subject: 180th Anniversary of Federation **Obv:**
National arms **Obv. Legend:** ESTADOS UNIDOS
MEXICANOS **Rev:** State arms **Rev. Legend:**
ESTADO DE QUERÉTARO ARTEAGA **Edge:**
Segmented reeding

Date	Mintage	F	VF	XF	Unc	BU
2004Mo	249,263	—	—	—	35.00	45.00

KM# 808 100 PESOS
29.1690 g., Bi-Metallic .999 Gold 17.154g center in
.999 Silver 12.015g ring, 34.5 mm. **Series:** First
Subject: 180th Anniversary of Federation **Obv:**
National arms **Obv. Legend:** ESTADOS UNIDOS
MEXICANOS **Rev:** State arms **Rev. Legend:**
ESTADO DE QUERÉTARO ARTEAGA **Edge:**
Segmented reeding

Date	Mintage	F	VF	XF	Unc	BU
2004Mo Proof	1,000	Value: 775				

KM# 738 100 PESOS
33.9400 g., Bi-Metallic .925 Silver 20.1753g center
in Aluminum-Bronze ring, 39.04 mm. **Series:** First
Subject: 180th Anniversary of Federation **Obv:**
National arms **Obv. Legend:** ESTADOS UNIDOS
MEXICANOS **Rev:** State arms **Rev. Legend:**
ESTADO DE PUEBLA **Edge:** Segmented reeding

Date	Mintage	F	VF	XF	Unc	BU
2004Mo	248,850	—	—	—	35.00	45.00

KM# 809 100 PESOS
Bi-Metallic .999 Gold 17.154g center in .999 Silver
12.015g ring, 34.5 mm. **Series:** First **Subject:** 180th
Anniversary of Federation **Obv:** National arms **Obv.
Legend:** ESTADOS UNIDOS MEXICANOS **Rev:**
State arms **Rev. Legend:** ESTADO DE PUEBLA
Edge: Segmented reeding

Date	Mintage	F	VF	XF	Unc	BU
2004Mo Proof	1,000	Value: 775				

KM# 740   100 PESOS
33.9400 g., Bi-Metallic .925 Silver 20.1753g center in Aluminum-Bronze ring, 39.04 mm. **Series:** First **Subject:** 180th Anniversary of Federation **Obv:** National arms **Obv. Legend:** ESTADOS UNIDOS MEXICANOS **Rev:** State arms **Rev. Legend:** ESTADO DE OAXACA **Edge:** Segmented reeding

Date	Mintage	F	VF	XF	Unc	BU
2004Mo	249,589	—	—	—	35.00	45.00

KM# 810   100 PESOS
29.1690 g., Bi-Metallic .999 Gold 17.154g center in .999 Silver 12.015g ring, 34.5 mm. **Series:** First **Subject:** 180th Anniversary of Federation **Obv:** National arms **Obv. Legend:** ESTADOS UNIDOS MEXICANOS **Rev:** State arms **Rev. Legend:** ESTADO DE OAXACA **Edge:** Segmented reeding

Date	Mintage	F	VF	XF	Unc	BU
2004Mo Proof	1,000	Value: 775				

KM# 742   100 PESOS
33.9400 g., Bi-Metallic .925 Silver 20.1753g center in Aluminum-Bronze ring, 39.04 mm. **Series:** First **Subject:** 180th Anniversary of Federation **Obv:** National arms **Obv. Legend:** ESTADOS UNIDOS MEXICANOS **Rev:** State arms **Rev. Legend:** ESTADO DE NUEVO LEÓN **Edge:** Segmented reeding

Date	Mintage	F	VF	XF	Unc	BU
2004Mo	249,199	—	—	—	35.00	45.00

KM# 811   100 PESOS
29.1690 g., Bi-Metallic .999 Gold 17.154g center in .999 Silver 12.015g ring, 34.5 mm. **Series:** First **Subject:** 180th Anniversary of Federation **Obv:** National arms **Obv. Legend:** ESTADOS UNIDOS MEXICANOS **Rev:** State arms **Rev. Legend:** ESTADO DE NUEVO LEÓN **Edge:** Segmented reeding

Date	Mintage	F	VF	XF	Unc	BU
2004Mo Proof	1,000	Value: 775				

KM# 744   100 PESOS
33.9400 g., Bi-Metallic .925 Silver 20.1753g center

in Aluminum-Bronze ring, 39.04 mm. **Series:** First **Subject:** 180th Anniversary of Federation **Obv:** National arms **Obv. Legend:** ESTADOS UNIDOS MEXICANOS **Rev:** State arms **Rev. Legend:** ESTADO DE NAYARIT **Edge:** Segmented reeding

Date	Mintage	F	VF	XF	Unc	BU
2004Mo	248,305	—	—	—	35.00	45.00

KM# 812   100 PESOS
29.1690 g., Bi-Metallic .999 Gold 17.154g center in .999 Silver 12.015g ring, 34.5 mm. **Series:** First **Subject:** 180th Anniversary of Federation **Obv:** National arms **Obv. Legend:** ESTADOS UNIDOS MEXICANOS **Rev:** State arms **Rev. Legend:** ESTADO DE NAYARIT **Edge:** Segmented reeding

Date	Mintage	F	VF	XF	Unc	BU
2004Mo Proof	1,000	Value: 775				

KM# 746   100 PESOS
33.9400 g., Bi-Metallic .925 Silver 20.1753g center in Aluminum-Bronze ring, 39.04 mm. **Series:** First **Subject:** 180th Anniversary of Federation **Obv:** National arms **Obv. Legend:** ESTADOS UNIDOS MEXICANOS **Rev:** State arms **Rev. Legend:** ESTADO DE MORELOS **Edge:** Segmented reeding

Date	Mintage	F	VF	XF	Unc	BU
2004Mo	249,260	—	—	—	35.00	45.00

KM# 813   100 PESOS
29.1690 g., Bi-Metallic .999 Gold 17.154g center in .999 Silver 12.015g ring, 34.5 mm. **Series:** First **Subject:** 180th Anniversary of Federation **Obv:** National arms **Obv. Legend:** ESTADOS UNIDOS MEXICANOS **Rev:** State arms **Rev. Legend:** ESTADO DE MORELOS **Edge:** Segmented reeding

Date	Mintage	F	VF	XF	Unc	BU
2004Mo Proof	1,000	Value: 775				

KM# 804   100 PESOS
33.9400 g., Bi-Metallic o.925 Silver 20.1763g center in Aluminum-Bronze ring, 39.04 mm. **Series:** First **Subject:** 180th Anniversary of Federation **Obv:** National arms **Obv. Legend:** ESTADOS UNIDOS MEXICANOS **Rev:** State arms **Rev. Legend:** ESTADO DE MICHOACÁN DE OCAMPO **Edge:** Segmented reeding

Date	Mintage	F	VF	XF	Unc	BU
2004Mo	249,492	—	—	—	35.00	45.00

KM# 814   100 PESOS
29.1690 g., Bi-Metallic .999 Gold 17.154g center in .999 12.015g ring, 34.5 mm. **Series:** First **Subject:** 180th Anniversary of Federation **Obv:** National arms **Obv. Legend:** ESTADOS UNIDOS MEXICANOS **Rev:** State arms **Rev. Legend:** ESTADO DE MICHOACÁN DE OCAMPO **Edge:** Segmented reeding

Date	Mintage	F	VF	XF	Unc	BU
2004Mo Proof	1,000	Value: 775				

KM# 748   100 PESOS
33.9400 g., Bi-Metallic .925 Silver 20.1753g center in Aluminum-Bronze ring, 39.04 mm. **Series:** First **Subject:** 180th Anniversary of Federation **Obv:** National arms **Obv. Legend:** ESTADOS UNIDOS MEXICANOS **Rev:** State arms **Rev. Legend:** ESTADO DE MÉXICO **Edge:** Segmented reeding

Date	Mintage	F	VF	XF	Unc	BU
2004Mo	249,800	—	—	—	35.00	45.00

KM# 815   100 PESOS
29.1690 g., Bi-Metallic .999 Gold 17.154 center in .999 Silver 12.015 ring, 34.5 mm. **Series:** First **Subject:** 180th Anniversary of Federation **Obv:** National arms **Obv. Legend:** ESTADOS UNIDOS MEXICANOS **Rev:** State arms **Rev. Legend:** ESTADO DE MÉXICO **Edge:** Segmented reeding

Date	Mintage	F	VF	XF	Unc	BU
2004Mo Proof	1,000	Value: 775				

KM# 750 100 PESOS
33.9400 g., Bi-Metallic .925 Silver 20.1753g center
in Aluminum-Bronze ring, 39.04 mm. **Series:** First
Subject: 180th Anniversary of Federation **Obv:**
National arms **Obv. Legend:** ESTADOS UNIDOS
MEXICANOS **Rev:** State arms **Rev. Legend:**
ESTADO DE JALISCO **Edge:** Segmented reeding

Date	Mintage	F	VF	XF	Unc	BU
2004Mo	249,115	—	—	—	35.00	45.00

KM# 816 100 PESOS
29.1690 g., Bi-Metallic .999 Gold 17.154g center in
.999 Silver 12.015g ring, 34.5 mm. **Series:** First
Subject: 180th Anniversary of Federation **Obv:**
National arms **Obv. Legend:** ESTADOS UNIDOS
MEXICANOS **Rev:** State arms **Rev. Legend:**
ESTADO DE JALISCO **Edge:** Segmented reeding

Date	Mintage	F	VF	XF	Unc	BU
2004Mo Proof	1,000	Value: 775				

KM# 717 100 PESOS
33.9400 g., Bi-Metallic .925 Silver center in Brass
ring, 39.04 mm. **Series:** First **Subject:** 180th
Anniversary of Federation **Obv:** National arms **Obv.
Legend:** ESTADOS UNIDOS MEXICANOS **Rev:**
State arms **Rev. Legend:** ESTADO DE HIDALGO
Edge: Segmented reeding

Date	Mintage	F	VF	XF	Unc	BU
2005Mo	249,820	—	—	—	35.00	45.00

KM# 817 100 PESOS
29.1690 g., Bi-Metallic .999 Gold 17.154g center in
.999 Silver 12.015g ring, 34.5 mm. **Series:** First
Subject: 180th Anniversary of Federation **Obv:**
National arms **Obv. Legend:** ESTADOS UNIDOS
MEXICANOS **Rev:** State arms **Rev. Legend:**
ESTADO DE HIDALGO **Edge:** Segmented reeding

Date	Mintage	F	VF	XF	Unc	BU
2005Mo Proof	1,000	Value: 775				

KM# 716 100 PESOS
33.9400 g., Bi-Metallic .925 Silver center in Brass
ring, 39.04 mm. **Series:** First **Subject:** 180th
Anniversary of Federation **Obv:** National arms **Obv.
Legend:** ESTADOS UNIDOS MEXICANOS **Rev:**
State arms **Rev. Legend:** ESTADO DE GUERRERO
Edge: Segmented reeding

Date	Mintage	F	VF	XF	Unc	BU
2005Mo	248,850	—	—	—	35.00	45.00

KM# 818 100 PESOS
29.1690 g., Bi-Metallic .999 Gold 17.154g center in
.999 Silver 12.015 ring, 34.5 mm. **Series:** First
Subject: 180th Anniversary of Federation **Obv:**
National arms **Obv. Legend:** ESTADOS UNIDOS
MEXICANOS **Rev:** State arms **Rev. Legend:**
ESTADO DE GUERRERO **Edge:** Segmented
reeding

Date	Mintage	F	VF	XF	Unc	BU
2005Mo Proof	1,000	Value: 775				

KM# 715 100 PESOS
33.9400 g., Bi-Metallic .925 Silver center in Brass
ring, 39.04 mm. **Series:** First **Subject:** 180th
Anniversary of Federation **Obv:** National arms **Obv.
Legend:** ESTADOS UNIDOS MEXICANOS **Rev:**
State arms **Rev. Legend:** ESTADO DE
GUANAJUATO **Edge:** Segmented reeding

Date	Mintage	F	VF	XF	Unc	BU
2005Mo	249,489	—	—	—	35.00	45.00

KM# 819 100 PESOS
29.1690 g., Bi-Metallic .999 Gold 17.154g center in
.999 Silver 12.015g ring, 34.5 mm. **Series:** First
Subject: 180th Anniversary of Federation **Obv:**
National arms **Obv. Legend:** ESTADOS UNIDOS
MEXICANOS **Rev:** State arms **Rev. Legend:**
ESTADO DE GUANAJUATO **Edge:** Segmented
reeding

Date	Mintage	F	VF	XF	Unc	BU
2005Mo Proof	1,000	Value: 775				

KM# 714 100 PESOS
33.9400 g., Bi-Metallic .925 Silver center in Brass
ring, 39.04 mm. **Series:** First **Subject:** 180th
Anniversary of Federation **Obv:** National arms **Obv.
Legend:** ESTADOS UNIDOS MEXICANOS **Rev:**
State arms **Rev. Legend:** ESTADO DE DURANGO
Edge: Segmented reeding

Date	Mintage	F	VF	XF	Unc	BU
2005Mo	249,774	—	—	—	35.00	45.00

KM# 820 100 PESOS
29.1690 g., Bi-Metallic .999 Gold 17.154g center in
.999 silver 12.015g ring, 34.5 mm. **Series:** First
Subject: 180th Anniversary of Federation **Obv:**
National arms **Obv. Legend:** ESTADOS UNIDOS
MEXICANOS **Rev:** State arms **Rev. Legend:**
ESTADO DE DURANGO **Edge:** Segmented reeding

Date	Mintage	F	VF	XF	Unc	BU
2005Mo Proof	1,000	Value: 775				

KM# 713 100 PESOS
33.9400 g., Bi-Metallic .925 Silver 20.1753g center

in Brass ring, 39.04 mm. **Series:** First **Subject:** 180th Anniversary of Federation **Obv:** National arms **Obv. Legend:** ESTADOS UNIDOS MEXICANOS **Rev:** Federal District arms **Rev. Legend:** DISTRITO FEDERAL **Edge:** Segmented reeding

Date	Mintage	F	VF	XF	Unc	BU
2005Mo	249,461	—	—	—	35.00	45.00

KM# 821 100 PESOS
29.1690 g., Bi-Metallic .999 Gold 17.154g center in .999 Silver 12.015g ring, 34.5 mm. **Series:** First **Subject:** 180th Anniversary of Federation **Obv:** National arms **Obv. Legend:** ESTADOS UNIDOS MEXICANOS **Rev:** Federal District arms **Rev. Legend:** DISTRITO FEDERAL **Edge:** Segmented reeding

Date	Mintage	F	VF	XF	Unc	BU
2005Mo Proof	1,000	Value: 775				

KM# 754 100 PESOS
33.9400 g., Bi-Metallic .925 Silver 20.1753g center in Aluminum-Bronze ring, 39.04 mm. **Series:** First **Subject:** 180th Anniversary of Federation **Obv:** National arms **Obv. Legend:** ESTADOS UNIDOS MEXICANOS **Rev:** State arms **Rev. Legend:** ESTADO DE CHIHUAHUA **Edge:** Segmented reeding

Date	Mintage	F	VF	XF	Unc	BU
2005Mo	249,102	—	—	—	35.00	45.00

KM# 822 100 PESOS
29.1690 g., Bi-Metallic .999 Gold 17.154g center in .999 Silver 12.015g ring, 34.5 mm. **Series:** First **Subject:** 180th Anniversary of Federation **Obv:** National arms **Obv. Legend:** ESTADOS UNIDOS MEXICANOS **Rev:** State arms **Rev. Legend:** ESTADO DE CHIHUAHUA **Edge:** Segmented reeding

Date	Mintage	F	VF	XF	Unc	BU
2005Mo Proof	1,000	Value: 775				

KM# 712 100 PESOS
33.9400 g., Bi-Metallic .925 Silver 20.1753g center in Brass ring, 39.04 mm. **Series:** First **Subject:** 180th Anniversary of Federation **Obv:** National arms **Obv. Legend:** ESTADOS UNIDOS MEXICANOS **Rev:** State arms **Rev. Legend:** ESTADO DE CHIAPAS **Edge:** Segmented reeding

Date	Mintage	F	VF	XF	Unc	BU
2005Mo	249,417	—	—	—	35.00	45.00

KM# 823 100 PESOS
29.1690 g., Bi-Metallic .999 Gold 17.154g center in .999 Silver 12.015g ring, 34.5 mm. **Series:** First **Subject:** 180th Anniversary of Federation **Obv:** National arms **Obv. Legend:** ESTADOS UNIDOS MEXICANOS **Rev:** State arms **Rev. Legend:** ESTADO DE CHIAPAS **Edge:** Segmented reeding

Date	Mintage	F	VF	XF	Unc	BU
2005Mo Proof	1,000	Value: 775				

KM# 729 100 PESOS
33.8250 g., Bi-Metallic .925 Silver 20.1753g center

in Aluminum-Bronze ring, 39.04 mm. **Series:** First **Subject:** 180th Anniversary of Federation **Obv:** National arms **Obv. Legend:** ESTADOS UNIDOS MEXICANOS **Rev:** State arms **Rev. Legend:** ESTADO DE COLIMA **Edge:** Segmented reeding

Date	Mintage	F	VF	XF	Unc	BU
2005Mo	248,850	—	—	—	35.00	45.00

KM# 824 100 PESOS
29.1690 g., Bi-Metallic .999 Gold 17.154g center in .999 Silver 12.015g ring, 34.5 mm. **Series:** First **Subject:** 180th Anniversary of Federation **Obv:** National arms **Obv. Legend:** ESTADOS UNIDOS MEXICANOS **Rev:** State arms **Rev. Legend:** ESTADO DE COLIMA **Edge:** Segmented reeding

Date	Mintage	F	VF	XF	Unc	BU
2005Mo Proof	1,000	Value: 775				

KM# 752 100 PESOS
33.9400 g., Bi-Metallic .925 Silver 20.1753g center in Aluminum-Bronze ring, 39.04 mm. **Series:** First **Subject:** 180th Anniversary of Federation **Obv:** National arms **Obv. Legend:** ESTADOS UNIDOS MEXICANOS **Rev:** State arms **Rev. Legend:** ESTADO DE COAHUILA DE ZARAGOZA **Edge:** Segmented reeding

Date	Mintage	F	VF	XF	Unc	BU
2005Mo	247,991	—	—	—	35.00	45.00

KM# 825 100 PESOS
29.1690 g., Bi-Metallic .999 Gold 17.154g center in .999 Silver 12.015g ring, 34.5 mm. **Series:** First **Subject:** 180th Anniversary of Federation **Obv:** National arms **Obv. Legend:** ESTADOS UNIDOS MEXICANOS **Rev:** State arms **Rev. Legend:** ESTADO DE COAHUILA DE ZARAGOZA **Edge:** Segmented reeding

Date	Mintage	F	VF	XF	Unc	BU
2005Mo Proof	1,000	Value: 775				

KM# 727 100 PESOS
33.9400 g., Bi-Metallic .925 Silver 20.1753g center in Aluminum-Bronze ring, 39.04 mm. **Series:** First **Subject:** 180th Anniversary of Federation **Obv:** National arms **Obv. Legend:** ESTADOS UNIDOS MEXICANOS **Rev:** State arms **Rev. Legend:** ESTADO DE CAMPECHE **Edge:** Segmented reeding

Date	Mintage	F	VF	XF	Unc	BU
2005Mo	249,040	—	—	—	35.00	45.00

KM# 826 100 PESOS
29.1690 g., Bi-Metallic .999 Gold 17.154g center in .999 Silver 12.015g ring, 34.5 mm. **Series:** First **Subject:** 180th Anniversary of Federation **Obv:** National arms **Obv. Legend:** ESTADOS UNIDOS MEXICANOS **Rev:** State arms **Rev. Legend:** ESTADO DE CAMPECHE **Edge:** Segmented reeding

Date	Mintage	F	VF	XF	Unc	BU
2005Mo Proof	1,000	Value: 775				

KM# 725 100 PESOS
33.9400 g., Bi-Metallic .925 Silver 20.1753g center in Aluminum-Bronze ring, 39.04 mm. **Series:** First **Subject:** 180th Anniversary of Federation **Obv:** National arms **Obv. Legend:** ESTADOS UNIDOS MEXICANOS **Rev:** State arms **Rev. Legend:** ESTADO DE BAJA CALIFORNIA SUR **Edge:** Segmented reeding

Date	Mintage	F	VF	XF	Unc	BU
2005Mo	249,585	—	—	—	35.00	45.00

KM# 827 100 PESOS
29.1690 g., Bi-Metallic .999 Gold 17.154g center in .999 Silver 12.015g ring, 34.5 mm. **Series:** First **Subject:** 180th Anniversary of Federation **Obv:** National arms **Obv. Legend:** ESTADOS UNIDOS MEXICANOS **Rev:** State arms **Rev. Legend:** ESTADO DE BAJA CALIFORNIA SUR **Edge:** Segmented reeding

Date	Mintage	F	VF	XF	Unc	BU
2005Mo Proof	—	Value: 775				

KM# 723 100 PESOS
33.9400 g., Bi-Metallic .925 Silver 20.1753g center in Aluminum-Bronze ring, 39.04 mm. **Series:** First **Subject:** 180th Anniversary of Federation **Obv:** National arms **Obv. Legend:** ESTADOS UNIDOS MEXICANOS **Rev:** State arms **Rev. Legend:** ESTADO DE BAJA CALIFORNIA **Edge:** Segmented reeding

Date	Mintage	F	VF	XF	Unc	BU
2005Mo	249,263	—	—	—	35.00	45.00

KM# 828 100 PESOS
29.1690 g., Bi-Metallic .999 Gold 17.154g center in .999 Silver 12.015g ring, 34.5 mm. **Series:** First **Subject:** 180th Anniversary of Federation **Obv:** National arms **Obv. Legend:** ESTADOS UNIDOS MEXICANOS **Rev:** State arms **Rev. Legend:** ESTADO DE BAJA CALIFORNIA **Edge:** Segmented reeding

Date	Mintage	F	VF	XF	Unc	BU
2005Mo Proof	1,000	Value: 775				

KM# 721 100 PESOS
33.9400 g., Bi-Metallic .925 Silver 20.1753g center in Aluminum-Bronze ring, 39.04 mm. **Series:** First **Subject:** 180th Anniversary of Federation **Obv:** National arms **Obv. Legend:** ESTADOS UNIDOS MEXICANOS **Rev:** Estados de Aguascalientes state arms **Rev. Legend:** ESTADO DE AGUASCALIENTES **Edge:** Segmented reeding

Date	Mintage	F	VF	XF	Unc	BU
2005Mo	248,410	—	—	—	35.00	45.00

KM# 829 100 PESOS
29.1690 g., Bi-Metallic .999 Gold 17.154g center in .999 Silver 12.015g ring, 34.5 mm. **Series:** First **Subject:** 180th Anniversary of Federation **Obv:** National arms **Obv. Legend:** ESTADOS UNIDOS MEXICANOS **Rev:** State arms **Rev. Legend:** ESTADO DE AGUASCALIENTES **Edge:** Segmented reeding

Date	Mintage	F	VF	XF	Unc	BU
2005Mo Proof	1,000	Value: 775				

KM# 719 100 PESOS
33.8250 g., Bi-Metallic .925 Silver 20.1753g center in Aluminum-Bronze ring, 39.04 mm. **Series:** Second **Obv:** National arms **Obv. Legend:** ESTADOS UNIDOS MEXICANOS **Rev:** Facade of the San Marcos garden above sculpture of national emblem at left, San Antonio Temple at right **Rev. Legend:** AGUASCALIENTES **Edge:** Segmented reeding

Date	Mintage	F	VF	XF	Unc	BU
2005Mo	149,705	—	—	—	35.00	45.00

KM# 862 100 PESOS
29.1690 g., Bi-Metallic .999 Gold 17.154g center in .999 Silver 12.015g ring, 34.5 mm. **Series:** Second **Obv:** National arms **Obv. Legend:** ESTADOS UNIDOS MEXICANOS **Rev:** Facade of the San

Marcos garden above sculpture of national emblem at left, San Antonio temple at right **Rev. Legend:** AGUASCALUENTES **Edge:** Segmented reeding

Date	Mintage	F	VF	XF	Unc	BU
2005Mo Proof	600	Value: 775				

KM# 758 100 PESOS
33.9400 g., Bi-Metallic .925 Silver 20.1753g center in Aluminum-Bronze ring, 39.04 mm. **Series:** Second **Obv:** National arms **Obv. Legend:** ESTADOS UNIDOS MEXICANOS **Rev:** Ram's head and value within circle **Rev. Legend:** BAJA CALIFORNIA - GOBIERNO DEL ESTADO **Edge:** Segmented reeding

Date	Mintage	F	VF	XF	Unc	BU
2005Mo	—	—	—	—	25.00	30.00

KM# 863 100 PESOS
29.1690 g., Bi-Metallic .999 Gold 17.154g center in .999 Silver 12.015g ring, 34.5 mm. **Series:** Second **Obv:** National arms **Obv. Legend:** ESTTADOS UNIDOS MEXICANOS **Rev:** Ram's head, mountain outline in background **Rev. Legend:** BAJA CALIFORNIA - GOBIERNO DEL ESTADO **Edge:** Segmented reeding

Date	Mintage	F	VF	XF	Unc	BU
2005Mo Proof	600	Value: 775				

KM# 762 100 PESOS
33.9400 g., Bi-Metallic .925 Silver 20.175g center in Aluminum-Bronze ring, 39.04 mm. **Series:** Second **Obv:** National arms **Obv. Legend:** ESTADOS UNIDOS MEXICANOS **Rev:** Outlined map of peninsula at center, cave painting of deer behind, cactus at right **Rev. Legend:** ESTADO DE BAJA CALIFORNIA SUR **Edge:** Segmented reeding

Date	Mintage	F	VF	XF	Unc	BU
2005Mo	149,152	—	—	—	—	25.00

KM# 864 100 PESOS
29.1690 g., Bi-Metallic .999 Gold 17.154g center in .999 Silver 12.015g ring, 34.5 mm. **Series:** Second **Obv:** National arms **Obv. Legend:** ESTADOS UNIDOS MEXICANOS **Rev:** Outlined map of peninsula at center, cave painting of deer behind, cactus at right **Rev. Legend:** ESTADO DE BAJA CALIFORNIA SUR **Edge:** Segmented reeding

Date	Mintage	F	VF	XF	Unc	BU
2006Mo Proof	600	Value: 775				

KM# 760 100 PESOS
33.9400 g., Bi-Metallic .925 Silver 20.1753g center in Aluminum-Bronze ring, 39.04 mm. **Series:** Second **Subject:** Estado de Campeche **Obv:** National arms **Obv. Legend:** ESTADOS UNIDOS MEXICANOS **Rev:** Jade mask - Calakmul, Campeche **Rev. Legend:** ESTADO DE CAMPECHE **Edge:** Segmented reeding

Date	Mintage	F	VF	XF	Unc	BU
2006Mo	—	—	—	—	—	25.00

KM# 865   100 PESOS
29.1690 g., Bi-Metallic .999 Gold 17.154g center in
.999 Silver 12.015g ring, 34.5 mm.   **Series:** Second
Obv: National arms **Obv. Legend:** ESTADOS
UNIDOS MEXICANOS **Rev:** Jade mask - Calakmul,
Campeche **Rev. Legend:** ESTADO DE CAMPECHE
Edge: Segmented reeding

Date	Mintage	F	VF	XF	Unc	BU
2006Mo Proof	600	Value: 775				

KM# 781   100 PESOS
33.7000 g., Bi-Metallic .925 Silver 20.1753g center in
Aluminum-Bronze ring, 39.04 mm.   **Series:** Second
Obv: National arms **Obv. Legend:** ESTADOS
UNIDOS MEXICANOS **Rev:** Outlined map with turtle,
mine cart above grapes at center, Friendship Dam
above Christ of the Nodas at left, chimneys above
crucibles and bell tower of Santiago's cathedral at right
Rev. Legend: COAHUILA DE ZARAGOZA **Edge:**
Segmented reeding

Date	Mintage	F	VF	XF	Unc	BU
2006Mo	—	—	—	—	35.00	45.00

KM# 866   100 PESOS
29.1690 g., Bi-Metallic .999 Gold 17.154g center in
.999 Silver 12.015g ring, 34.5 mm.   **Series:** Second
Obv: National arms **Obv. Legend:** ESTADOS
UNIDOS MEXICANOS **Rev:** Outlined map with
turtle, mine cart above grapes at center, Friendship
dam above Christ of the Nodas at left, chimneys
above crucibles and bell tower of Santiago's
cathedral at right **Rev. Inscription:** COAHUILA DE
ZARAGOZA **Edge:** Segmented reeding

Date	Mintage	F	VF	XF	Unc	BU
2006Mo Proof	600	Value: 775				

KM# 777   100 PESOS
33.9400 g., Bi-Metallic .925 Silver 20.1753g center in
Aluminum-Bronze ring, 39.04 mm.   **Series:** Second
Obv: National arms **Obv. Legend:** ESTADOS
UNIDOS MEXICANOS **Rev:** State arms at lower
center, Nevado de Colima and Volcan de Fuego
volcanos in background **Rev. Legend:** *Colima* **Rev.
Inscription:** GENEROSO **Edge:** Segmented reeding

Date	Mintage	F	VF	XF	Unc	BU
2006Mo	149,041	—	—	—	35.00	45.00

KM# 867   100 PESOS
29.1690 g., Bi-Metallic .999 Gold 17.154g center in
.999 Silver 12.015 ring, 34.5 mm.   **Series:** Second
Obv: National arms **Obv. Legend:** ESTADOS
UNIDOS MEXICANOS **Rev:** State arms at lower
center, Nevado de Colima and Volcan de Fuego
volcanos in background **Rev. Legend:** *Colima* **Rev.
Inscription:** GENEROSO **Edge:** Segmented reeding

Date	Mintage	F	VF	XF	Unc	BU
2006Mo Proof	600	Value: 775				

KM# 773   100 PESOS
33.9400 g., Bi-Metallic .925 Silver 20.1753g center
in Aluminum-Bronze ring, 39.04 mm.   **Series:**
Second **Obv:** National arms **Obv. Legend:**
ESTADOS UNIDOS MEXICANOS **Rev:** Head of

Pakal, ancient Mayan king, Palenque **Rev. Legend:**
ESTADO DE CHIAPAS - CABEZA MAYA DEL REY
PAKAL, PALENQUE **Edge:** Segmented reeding

Date	Mintage	F	VF	XF	Unc	BU
2006Mo	149,491	—	—	—	35.00	45.00

KM# 868   100 PESOS
29.1690 g., Bi-Metallic .999 Gold 17.154g center in
.999 Silver 12.015g ring, 34.5 mm.   **Series:** Second
Obv: National arms **Obv. Legend:** ESTADOS
UNIDOS MEXICANOS **Rev:** Head of Pakal, ancient
Mayan king, Palenque **Rev. Legend:** ESTADO DE
CHIAPAS - CABEZA MAYA DEL REY PAKAL,
PALENQUE **Edge:** Segmented reeding

Date	Mintage	F	VF	XF	Unc	BU
2006Mo Proof	600	Value: 775				

KM# 775   100 PESOS
33.9400 g., Bi-Metallic .925 Silver 20.1753g center in
Aluminum-Bronze ring, 39.04 mm.   **Series:** Second
Obv: National arms **Obv. Legend:** ESTADOS
UNIDOS MEXICANOS **Rev:** Angel of Liberty **Rev.
Legend:** MÉXICO - ANGEL DE LA LIBERTAD,
CHIHUAHUA **Edge:** Segmented reeding

Date	Mintage	F	VF	XF	Unc	BU
2006Mo	149,557	—	—	—	35.00	45.00

KM# 869   100 PESOS
29.1690 g., Bi-Metallic .999 Gold 17.154g center in
.999 Silver 12.015g ring, 34.5 mm.   **Series:** Second
Obv: National arms **Obv. Legend:** ESTADOS
UNIDOS MEXICANOS **Rev:** Angel of Liberty **Rev.
Legend:** MÉXICO - ANGEL DE LA LIBERTAD,
CHIHUAHUA **Edge:** Segmented reeding

Date	Mintage	F	VF	XF	Unc	BU
2006Mo Proof	600	Value: 775				

KM# 779   100 PESOS
33.9400 g., Bi-Metallic .925 Silver 20.1753g center in
Aluminum-Bronze ring, 39.04 mm.   **Series:** Second
Obv: National arms **Obv. Legend:** ESTADOS
UNIDOS MEXICANOS **Rev:** National Palace **Rev.
Legend:** DISTRITO FEDERAL - ANTIGUO
AYUNTAMIENTO **Edge:** Segmented reeding

Date	Mintage	F	VF	XF	Unc	BU
2006Mo	149,525	—	—	—	35.00	45.00

KM# 870   100 PESOS
29.1690 g., Bi-Metallic .999 Gold 17.154g center in
.999 Silver 12.015g ring, 34.5 mm.   **Series:** Second
Obv: National arms **Obv. Legend:** ESTADOS
UNIDOS MEXICANOS **Rev:** National palace **Rev.
Legend:** DISTRITO FEDERAL - ANTIGUO
AYUNTAMIENTO **Edge:** Segmented reeding

Date	Mintage	F	VF	XF	Unc	BU
2006Mo Proof	600	Value: 775				

KM# 787   100 PESOS
33.9400 g., Bi-Metallic .925 Silver 20.1753g center
in Brass ring, 39.04 mm.   **Series:** Second **Obv:**
National arms **Obv. Legend:** ESTADOS UNIDOS
MEXICANOS **Rev:** Tree **Rev. Legend:** PRIMERA

RESERVA NACIONAL FORESTAL - DURANGO
Edge: Segmented reeding

Date	Mintage	F	VF	XF	Unc	BU
2006Mo	149,034	—	—	—	35.00	45.00

KM# 871 100 PESOS
29.1690 g., Bi-Metallic .999 Gold 17.154g center in .999 Silver 12.015g ring, 34.5 mm. **Series:** Second **Obv:** National arms **Obv. Legend:** ESYADOS UNIDOS MEXICANOS **Rev:** Tree **Rev. Legend:** PRIMERA RESERVA NACIONAL RORESTAL - DURANGO **Edge:** Segmented reeding

Date	Mintage	F	VF	XF	Unc	BU
2006Mo Proof	600	Value: 775				

KM# 789 100 PESOS
33.9400 g., Bi-Metallic .925 Silver 20.1753g center in Brass ring, 39.04 mm. **Series:** Second **Obv:** National arms **Obv. Legend:** ESTADOS UNIDOS MEXICANOS **Rev:** State arms at center, statue of Miguel Hidalgo at left, monument to Pipla at lower right **Rev. Inscription:** *Guanajuato* **Edge:** Segmented reeding

Date	Mintage	F	VF	XF	Unc	BU
2006Mo	149,921	—	—	—	—	25.00

KM# 872 100 PESOS
29.1690 g., Bi-Metallic .999 Gold 17.154g center in .999 Silver 12.015g ring, 34.50 mm. **Series:** Second **Obv:** National arms **Obv. Legend:** ESTADOS UNIDOS MEXICANOS **Rev:** State arms at lower center, statue of Miguel Hidalgo at left, monument to Pipila at lower right **Rev. Inscription:** *Guanajauto* **Edge:** Segmented reeding

Date	Mintage	F	VF	XF	Unc	BU
2006Mo Proof	600	Value: 775				

KM# 791 100 PESOS
33.9400 g., Bi-Metallic .925 Silver 20.1753g center in Brass ring, 39.04 mm. **Series:** Second **Obv:** National arms **Obv. Legend:** ESTADOS UNIDOS MEXICANOS **Rev:** Stylized portrait of Vicente Guerrero at left, church of Taxco at upper center, Acapulco's la Quebrada with diver above Christmas Eve flower and mask **Rev. Legend:** GUERRERO **Edge:** Segmented reeding

Date	Mintage	F	VF	XF	Unc	BU
2006Mo	149,675	—	—	—	35.00	45.00

KM# 873 100 PESOS
29.1690 g., Bi-Metallic .999 Gold 17.154g center in .999 Silver 12.015g ring, 34.5 mm. **Series:** Second **Obv:** National arms **Obv. Legend:** ESTADOS UNIDOS MEXICANOS **Rev:** Stylized portrait of Vicente Guerrero at left, church of Taxco at upper center, Acapulco's la Quebrada with diver over Christmas Eve flower and mask **Rev. Legend:** GUERRERO **Edge:** Segmented reeding

Date	Mintage	F	VF	XF	Unc	BU
2006Mo Proof	600	Value: 775				

KM# 793 100 PESOS
33.9400 g., Bi-Metallic .925 Silver 20.1753g center in Aluminum-Bronze ring, 39.04 mm. **Series:** Second **Obv:** National arms **Obv. Legend:** ESTADOS UNIDOS MEXICANOS **Rev:** Monument of Pachuca Hidalgo **Rev. Inscription:** *RELOJ / MONUMENTAL / DE / PACHUCA / HIDALGO - La / Bella / Airosa* **Edge:** Segmented reeding

Date	Mintage	F	VF	XF	Unc	BU
2006Mo	149,273	—	—	—	35.00	45.00

KM# 874 100 PESOS
29.1690 g., Bi-Metallic .999 Gold 17.154g center in .999 Silver 12.015g ring, 34.5 mm. **Series:** Second **Obv:** National arms **Obv. Legend:** ESTADOS UNIDOS MEXICANOS **Rev:** Monument of Pachuca Hidalgo **Rev. Inscription:** *RELOJ / MONUMENTAL / DE / PACHUCA / HIDALGO* **Edge:** Segmented reeding

Date	Mintage	F	VF	XF	Unc	BU
2006Mo Proof	600	Value: 775				

KM# 795 100 PESOS
33.9400 g., Bi-Metallic .925 Silver 20.1753g center in Brass ring, 39.04 mm. **Series:** Second **Obv:** National arms **Obv. Legend:** ESTADOS UNIDOS MEXICANOS **Rev:** Hospicio Cabañas orphanage **Rev. Legend:** ESTADO DE JALISCO **Edge:** Segmented reeding

Date	Mintage	F	VF	XF	Unc	BU
2006Mo	149,750	—	—	—	—	25.00

KM# 875 100 PESOS
29.1690 g., Bi-Metallic .999 Gold 17.154g center in .999 Silver 12.015g ring, 34.5 mm. **Series:** Second **Obv:** National arms **Obv. Legend:** ESTADOS UNIDOS MEXICANOS **Rev:** Hospicio Cabañas orphanage **Rev. Legend:** ESTADO DE JALISCO **Edge:** Segmented reeding

Date	Mintage	F	VF	XF	Unc	BU
2006Mo Proof	600	Value: 775				

KM# 802 100 PESOS
33.9400 g., Bi-Metallic .925 Silver 20.1753g center in Aluminum-Bronze ring, 33.7, 39.04 mm. **Series:** Second **Obv:** National arms **Obv. Legend:** ESTADOS UNIDOS MEXICANOS **Rev:** Pyramid de la Loona (moon) **Rev. Legend:** ESTADO DE MÉXICO **Edge:** Segmented reeding

Date	Mintage	F	VF	XF	Unc	BU
2006Mo	149,377	—	—	—	—	25.00

KM# 876 100 PESOS
29.1690 g., Bi-Metallic .999 Gold 17.154g center in .999 Silver 12.015g ring, 34.5 mm. **Series:** Second **Obv:** National arms **Obv. Legend:** ESTADOS UNIDOS MEXICANOS **Rev:** Pyramid de la Looona (moon) **Rev. Legend:** ESTADO DE MÉXICO **Edge:** Segmented reeding

Date	Mintage	F	VF	XF	Unc	BU
2006Mo Proof	600	Value: 775				

KM# 785 100 PESOS
33.9400 g., Bi-Metallic .925 Silver 20.1753g center

in Aluminum-Bronze ring, 33.7, 39.04 mm. **Series:** Second **Obv:** National arms **Obv. Legend:** ESTADOS UNIDOS MEXICANOS **Rev:** Four Monarch butterflies **Rev. Legend:** ESTADO DE MICHOACÁN **Edge:** Segmented reeding

Date	Mintage	F	VF	XF	Unc	BU
2006Mo	149,730	—	—	—	—	25.00

KM# 877   100 PESOS
29.1690 g., Bi-Metallic .999 Gold 17.154g center in .999 Silver 12.015g ring, 34.5 mm. **Series:** Second **Obv:** National arms **Obv. Legend:** ESTADOS UNIDOS MEXICANOS **Rev:** Four Monarch butterflies **Rev. Legend:** ESTADO DE MICHOACÁN **Edge:** Segmented reeding

Date	Mintage	F	VF	XF	Unc	BU
2006Mo Proof	600	Value: 775				

KM# 800   100 PESOS
33.9400 g., Bi-Metallic .925 Silver 20.1753g center in Aluminum-Bronze ring, 33.7, 39.04 mm. **Series:** Second **Obv:** National arms **Obv. Legend:** ESTADOS UNIDOS MEXICANOS **Rev:** 1/2 length figure of Chinelo (local dancer) at right, Palacio de Cortes in background **Rev. Inscription:** ESTADO DE / MORELOS **Edge:** Segmented reeding

Date	Mintage	F	VF	XF	Unc	BU
2006Mo	149,648	—	—	—	—	25.00

KM# 878   100 PESOS
29.1690 g., Bi-Metallic .999 Gold 17.154g center in .999 Silver 12.015g ring, 34.5 mm. **Series:** Second **Obv:** National arms **Obv. Legend:** ESTADOS UNIDOS MEXICANOS **Rev:** 1/2 length figure of Chinelo (local dancer) at right, Palacio de Cortes in background **Rev. Inscription:** ESTADO DE / MORELOS **Edge:** Segmented reeding

Date	Mintage	F	VF	XF	Unc	BU
2006Mo Proof	600	Value: 775				

KM# 798   100 PESOS
33.9400 g., 33.8250 Bi-Metallic 0.925 Silver 20.1753g center in Aluminum-Bronze ring 36.908 oz., 39.04 mm. **Series:** Second **Obv:** National arms **Obv. Legend:** ESTADOS UNIDOS MEXICANOS **Rev:** Isle de Mexcaltitlán **Rev. Legend:** ESTADO DE NAYARIT **Edge:** Segmented reeding

Date	Mintage	F	VF	XF	Unc	BU
2007Mo	149,560	—	—	—	—	25.00

KM# 879   100 PESOS
29.1690 g., Bi-Metallic .999 Gold 17.154g center in .999 12.015g ring, 34.5 mm. **Series:** Second **Obv:** National arms **Obv. Legend:** ESTADOS UNIDOS MEXICANOS **Rev:** Isle de Mexcaltitlán **Rev. Legend:** ESTADO DE NAYARIT **Edge:** Segmented reeding

Date	Mintage	F	VF	XF	Unc	BU
2007Mo Proof	600	Value: 775				

KM# 848   100 PESOS
33.9400 g., Bi-Metallic .925 Silver 20.1753 center in Aluminum Bronze ring, 39.04 mm. **Series:** Second **Obv:** National arms **Obv. Legend:** ESTADOS

UNIDOS MEXICANOE **Rev:** Old foundry in Parque Fundidora (public park) at right, Cerro de la Silla (Saddle Hill) in background **Rev. Legend:** ESTADO DE NUEVO LÉON **Edge:** Segmented reeding

Date	Mintage	F	VF	XF	Unc	BU
2007Mo	—	—	—	—	—	25.00

KM# 880   100 PESOS
29.1690 g., Bi-Metallic .999 Gold 17.154g center in .999 Silver 12.015g ring, 34.5 mm. **Series:** Second **Obv:** National arms **Obv. Legend:** ESTADOS UNIDOS MEXICANOS **Rev:** Old foundry in Parque Fundidora (public park) at right, Cerro de la Silla (Saddle hill) in background **Rev. Legend:** ESTADO DE NUEVO LEÓN **Edge:** Segmented reeding

Date	Mintage	F	VF	XF	Unc	BU
2007Mo Proof	600	Value: 775				

KM# 849   100 PESOS
33.9400 g., Bi-Metallic .925 Silver 20.1753g center in Aluminum-Bronze ring, 39.04 mm. **Series:** Second **Obv:** National arms **Obv. Legend:** ESTADOS UNIDOS MEXICANOS **Rev:** Teatro Macedonio Alcala (theater) **Rev. Legend:** OAXACA **Edge:** Segmented reeding

Date	Mintage	F	VF	XF	Unc	BU
2007Mo	—	—	—	—	—	25.00

KM# 881   100 PESOS
29.1690 g., Bi-Metallic .999 Gold 17.154g center in .999 Silver 12.015g ring, 34.50 mm. **Series:** Second **Obv:** National arms **Obv. Legend:** ESTADOS UNIDOS MEXICANOS **Rev:** Teatro Macedonio Alcala (theater) **Rev. Legend:** OAXACA **Edge:** Segmented reeding

Date	Mintage	F	VF	XF	Unc	BU
2007Mo Proof	600	Value: 775				

KM# 850   100 PESOS
33.9400 g., Bi-Metallic .925 Silver 20.1753g center in Aluminum-Bronze ring, 39.04 mm. **Series:** Second **Obv:** National arms **Obv. Legend:** ESTADOS UNIDOS MEXICANOS **Rev:** Talavera porcelain dish **Rev. Legend:** ESTADO DE PUEBLA **Edge:** Segmented reeding

Date	Mintage	F	VF	XF	Unc	BU
2007Mo	—	—	—	—	—	25.00

KM# 882   100 PESOS
29.1690 g., Bi-Metallic .999 Gold 17.154g center in .999 Silver 12.015g ring, 34.5 mm. **Series:** Second **Obv:** National arms **Obv. Legend:** ESTADOS UNIDOS MEXICANOS **Rev:** Talavera porcelain dish **Rev. Legend:** ESTADO DE PUEBLA **Edge:** Segmented reeding

Date	Mintage	F	VF	XF	Unc	BU
2007Mo Proof	600	Value: 775				

KM# 851   100 PESOS
33.9400 g., Bi-Metallic .925 Silver 20.1753g center in Aluminum-Bronze ring, 39.04 mm. **Series:** Second **Obv:** National arms **Obv. Legend:**

ESTADOS UNIDOS MEXICANOS **Rev:** Mask at left, rays above state arms at center, Mayan ruins at right **Rev. Legend:** QUINTANA ROO **Edge:** Segmented reeding

Date	Mintage	F	VF	XF	Unc	BU
2007Mo	—	—	—	—	—	25.00

KM# 883   100 PESOS
29.1690 g., Gold .999 Gold 17.154g center in .999 Silver 12.015g ring, 34.5 mm. **Series:** Second **Obv:** National arms **Obv. Legend:** ESTADOS UNIDOS MEXICANOS **Rev:** Mask at left, rays above state arms at center, Mayan ruins at right **Rev. Legend:** QUINTANA ROO **Edge:** Segmented reeding

Date	Mintage	F	VF	XF	Unc	BU
2007Mo Proof	600	Value: 775				

KM# 852   100 PESOS
33.9400 g., Bi-Metallic .925 Silver 20.1753 center in Aluminum-Bronze ring, 39.04 mm. **Series:** Second **Obv:** National arms **Obv. Legend:** ESTADOS UNIDOS MEXICANOS **Rev:** Acueduct of Querétaro at left, church of Santa Rosa de Viterbo at right **Rev. Legend:** ESTADO DE QUERÉTARO ARTEAGA **Edge:** Segmented reeding

Date	Mintage	F	VF	XF	Unc	BU
2007Mo	—	—	—	—	—	25.00

KM# 884   100 PESOS
29.1690 g., Bi-Metallic .999 Gold 17.154g center in .999 Silver 12.015g ring, 34.5 mm. **Series:** Second **Obv:** National arms **Obv. Legend:** ESTADOS UNIDOS MEXICANOS **Rev:** Acueduct of Querétaro at left, church of Santa Rosa de Viterbo at right **Rev. Legend:** ESTADO DE QUERÉTARO ARTEAGA **Edge:** Segmented reeding

Date	Mintage	F	VF	XF	Unc	BU
2007Mo Proof	600	—	—	—	—	775

KM# 853   100 PESOS
33.9400 g., Bi-Metallic .925 Silver 20.1753g center in Aluminum-Bronze ring, 39.04 mm. **Series:** Second **Obv:** National arms **Obv. Legend:** ESRADOS UNIDOS MEXICANOS **Rev:** Facade of Caja Real **Rev. Legend:** • SAN LUIS POTOSÍ • **Edge:** Segmented reeding

Date	Mintage	F	VF	XF	Unc	BU
2007Mo	—	—	—	—	—	25.00

KM# 885   100 PESOS
29.1690 g., Bi-Metallic .999 Gold 17.154g center in .999 Silver 12.015 ring, 34.5 mm. **Series:** Second **Obv:** National arms **Obv. Legend:** ESTADOS UNIDOS MEXICANOS **Rev:** Facade of Caja Real **Rev. Legend:** • SAN LUIS POTOSÍ • **Edge:** Segmented reeding

Date	Mintage	F	VF	XF	Unc	BU
2007Mo Proof	600	Value: 775				

KM# 854   100 PESOS
33.9400 g., Bi-Metallic .925 Silver 20.1753g center in Aluminum-Bronze ring, 39.04 mm. **Series:** Second **Obv:** National arms **Obv. Legend:** ESTADOS UNIDOS MEXICANOS **Rev:** Shield on pile of cactus fruits **Rev. Legend:** ESTADO DE SINALOA - LUGAR DE PITAHAYAS **Edge:** Segmented reeding

Date	Mintage	F	VF	XF	Unc	BU
2007Mo	—	—	—	—	—	25.00

KM# 886   100 PESOS
29.1690 g., Bi-Metallic .999 Gold 17.154 center in .999 Silver 12.015g ring, 34.5 mm. **Series:** Second **Obv:** National arms **Obv. Legend:** ESTADOS UNIDOS MEXICANOS **Rev:** Shield on pile of cactus fruits **Rev. Legend:** ESTADO DE SINALOA - LUGAR DE PITAHAYAS **Edge:** Segmented reeding

Date	Mintage	F	VF	XF	Unc	BU
2007Mo Proof	600	Value: 775				

KM# 855   100 PESOS
33.9400 g., Bi-Metallic .925 Silver 20.1753g center in Aluminum-Bronze ring, 39.04 mm. **Series:** Second **Obv:** National arms **Obv. Legend:** ESTADOS UNIDOS MEXICANOS **Rev:** Local in Dance of the Deer at left, cactus at right, mountains in background **Rev. Legend:** ESTADO DE SONORA **Edge:** Segmented reeding

Date	Mintage	F	VF	XF	Unc	BU
2007Mo	—	—	—	—	—	25.00

KM# 887   100 PESOS
29.1690 g., Bi-Metallic .999 Gold 17.154g center in .999 Silver 12.015g ring, 34.5 mm. **Series:** Second **Obv:** National arms **Obv. Legend:** ESTADOS UNIDOS MEXICANOS **Rev:** Local in Dance of the Deer at left, cactus at right, mountains in background **Rev. Legend:** ESTADO DE SONORA **Edge:** Segmented reeding

Date	Mintage	F	VF	XF	Unc	BU
2007Mo Proof	600	Value: 775				

KM# 856   100 PESOS
33.9400 g., Bi-Metallic .925 Silver 20.1753 center in Aluminum-Bronze ring, 39.04 mm. **Series:** Second **Obv:** National arms **Obv. Legend:** ESTADOS UNIDOS MEXICANOS **Rev:** Fuente de los Pescadores (fisherman fountain) at lower left, giant head from the Olmec-pre-Hispanic culture at right, Planetario Tabasco in background **Rev. Legend:** TABASCO **Edge:** Segmented reeding

Date	Mintage	F	VF	XF	Unc	BU
2007Mo	—	—	—	—	—	25.00

KM# 888   100 PESOS
29.1690 g., Bi-Metallic .999 Gold 17.154g center in .999 Silver 12.015g ring, 34.5 mm. **Series:** Second **Obv:** National arms **Obv. Legend:** ESTADOS UNIDOS MEXICANOS **Rev:** Fuente de los Pescadores (fisherman fountain) at lower left, giant head from the Olmec-pre-Hispanic culture at right, Planetario Tabasco in background **Rev. Legend:** TABASCO **Edge:** Segmented reeding

Date	Mintage	F	VF	XF	Unc	BU
2007Mo Proof	600	Value: 775				

KM# 857   100 PESOS
33.9400 g., Bi-Metallic .925 Silver 20.1753g center in Aluminum-Bronze ring, 39.04 mm. **Series:** Second **Obv:** National arms **Obv. Legend:** ESTADOS UNIDOS MEXICANOS **Rev:** Ridge - Cerro Del Bermal, Gonzáles **Rev. Legend:** TAMAULIPAS **Edge:** Segmented reeding

Date	Mintage	F	VF	XF	Unc	BU
2007Mo	—	—	—	—	—	25.00

KM# 889   100 PESOS
29.1690 g., Bi-Metallic .999 Gold 17.154g center in .999 Silver 12.015g ring, 34.5 mm. **Series:** Second **Obv:** National arms **Obv. Legend:** ESTADOS DE MEXICANOS **Rev:** Ridge - Cerro Del Bemal, Gonzáles **Rev. Legend:** TAMAULIPAS **Edge:** Segmented reeding

Date	Mintage	F	VF	XF	Unc	BU
2007Mo Proof	600	Value: 775				

KM# 858   100 PESOS
33.9400 g., Bi-Metallic .925 Silver 20.1753g center in Aluminum-Bronze ring, 39.04 mm. **Series:** Second **Obv:** National arms **Obv. Legend:** ESTADOS UNIDOS MEXICANOS **Rev:** Basilica de Ocotlán at left, state arms above Capilla Abierta, Plaza de Toros Ranchero Aguilar below, Exconvento de San Francisco at right **Rev. Legend:** ESTADO DE TLAXCALA **Edge:** Segmented reeding

Date	Mintage	F	VF	XF	Unc	BU
2007Mo	—	—	—	—	—	25.00

KM# 890   100 PESOS
29.1690 g., Bi-Metallic .999 Gold 17.154g center in .999 Silver 12.015g ring, 34.5 mm. **Series:** Second **Obv:** National arms **Obv. Legend:** ESTADOS UNIDOS MEXICANOS **Rev:** Basilica de Ocotlán at left, state arms above Capilla Abierta, Plaza de Toros Ranchero Aguilar below, Exconvento de San Francisco at right **Rev. Legend:** ESTADO DE TLAXCALA **Edge:** Segmented reeding

Date	Mintage	F	VF	XF	Unc	BU
2007Mo Proof	600	Value: 775				

KM# 859   100 PESOS
33.9400 g., Bi-Metallic .912 Silver 20.1753g center in Aluminum-Bronze ring, 39.04 mm. **Series:** Second **Obv:** National arms **Obv. Legend:** ESTADOS UNIDOS MEXICANOS **Rev:** Pyramid of El Tajín **Rev. Legend:** • VERACRUZ • - • DE IGNACIO DE LA LLAVE • **Edge:** Segmented reeding

Date	Mintage	F	VF	XF	Unc	BU
2007Mo	—	—	—	—	—	25.00

KM# 891   100 PESOS
29.1690 g., Bi-Metallic .999 Gold 17.154g center in .999 Silver 12.015g ring, 34.5 mm. **Series:** Second **Obv:** National arms **Obv. Legend:** ESTADOS UNIDOS MEXICANOS **Rev:** Pyramid of El Tajin **Rev. Legend:** • VERACRUZ • - • DE IGNACIO DE LA LLAVE • **Edge:** Segmented reeding

Date	Mintage	F	VF	XF	Unc	BU
2007Mo Proof	600	Value: 775				

KM# 860   100 PESOS
33.9400 g., Bi-Metallic .925 Silver 20.1753 center in Aluminum-Bronze ring, 39.04 mm. **Series:** Second **Obv:** National arms **Obv. Legend:** ESTADOS UNIDOS MEXICANOS **Rev:** Stylized pryamid of Chichén Itzá **Rev. Legend:** Castillo de Chichén Itzá **Edge:** Segmented reeding

Date	Mintage	F	VF	XF	Unc	BU
2007Mo	—	—	—	—	—	25.00

KM# 892   100 PESOS
29.1690 g., Bi-Metallic .999 Gold 17.154g center in .999 Silver 12.015g ring, 34.5 mm. **Series:** Second **Obv:** National arms **Obv. Legend:** ESTADOS UNIDOS MEXICANOS **Rev:** Stylized pyramid of Chichén-Itzá **Rev. Inscription:** YUCATÁN **Edge:** Segmented reeding

Date	Mintage	F	VF	XF	Unc	BU
2007Mo Proof	600	Value: 775				

KM# 861   100 PESOS
33.9400 g., Bi-Metallic .925 Silver 20.1753g center in Aluminum-Bronze ring, 39.04 mm. **Series:** Second **Obv:** National arms **Obv. Legend:** ESTADOS UNIDOS MEXICANOS **Rev:** Cable car above Monumento al Minero at left, Catedral de Zacatecas at center right **Rev. Legend:** ZACATEXAS **Edge:** Segmented reeding

Date	Mintage	F	VF	XF	Unc	BU
2007Mo	—	—	—	—	—	25.00

KM# 893   100 PESOS
29.1690 g., Bi-Metallic .999 Gold 17.154g center in .999 Silver 12.015g ring, 34.5 mm. **Series:** Second **Obv:** National arms **Obv. Legend:** ESTADOS UNIDOS MEXICANOS **Rev:** Cable car above Monumento al Minero at left, Catedral de Zacatecas at center right **Rev. Legend:** Zacatecas **Edge:** Segmented reeding

Date	Mintage	F	VF	XF	Unc	BU
2007Mo Proof	600	Value: 775				

SILVER BULLION COINAGE
LIBERTAD SERIES

KM# 542   1/20 ONZA (1/20 Troy Ounce of Silver)
1.5551 g., 0.9990 Silver 0.0499 oz. ASW **Obv:**
National arms, eagle left **Rev:** Winged Victory

Date	Mintage	F	VF	XF	Unc	BU
1991Mo	50,017	—	—	—	—	5.50
1992Mo	295,783	—	—	—	—	4.50
1992Mo Proof	5,000	Value: 10.00				
1993Mo	100,000	—	—	—	—	4.50
1993Mo Proof	—	Value: 10.00				
1994Mo	90,100	—	—	—	—	4.50
1994Mo Proof	10,000	Value: 10.00				
1995Mo	50,000	—	—	—	—	5.50
1995Mo Proof	2,000	Value: 12.00				

KM# 609   1/20 ONZA (1/20 Troy Ounce of Silver)
1.5551 g., 0.9990 Silver 0.0499 oz. ASW **Obv:**
National arms, eagle left **Rev:** Winged Victory

Date	Mintage	F	VF	XF	Unc	BU
1996Mo	50,000	—	—	—	—	10.00
1996Mo Proof	1,000	Value: 15.00				
1997Mo	20,000	—	—	—	—	10.00
1997Mo Proof	800	Value: 15.00				
1998Mo	6,400	—	—	—	—	10.00
1998Mo Proof	300	Value: 18.50				
1999Mo	8,001	—	—	—	—	12.00
1999Mo Proof	600	Value: 16.50				
2000Mo	57,500	—	—	—	—	12.00
2000Mo Proof	900	Value: 16.50				
2001Mo	25,000	—	—	—	—	12.00
2001Mo Proof	1,500	Value: 15.00				
2002Mo	45,000	—	—	—	—	8.00
2002Mo Proof	2,800	Value: 13.00				
2003Mo Proof	3,015	Value: 13.00				
2003Mo	35,000	—	—	—	—	8.00
2004Mo Proof	5,285	Value: 13.00				
2004Mo	35,000	—	—	—	—	8.00
2005Mo	16,525	—	—	—	—	8.00
2005Mo Proof	1,500	Value: 12.00				
2006Mo	20,000	—	—	—	—	8.00
2006Mo Proof	3,300	Value: 12.00				
2007Mo	—	—	—	—	—	8.00
2007Mo Proof	—	Value: 12.00				

KM# 543   1/10 ONZA (1/10 Troy Ounce of Silver)
3.1103 g., 0.9990 Silver 0.0999 oz. ASW **Obv:**
National arms, eagle left **Rev:** Winged Victory

Date	Mintage	F	VF	XF	Unc	BU
1991Mo	50,017	—	—	—	—	7.50
1992Mo	299,983	—	—	—	—	6.50
1992Mo Proof	5,000	Value: 12.00				
1993Mo	100,000	—	—	—	—	6.50
1993Mo Proof	—	Value: 12.00				
1994Mo	90,100	—	—	—	—	6.50

Date	Mintage	F	VF	XF	Unc	BU
1994Mo Proof	10,000	Value: 12.00				
1995Mo	50,000	—	—	—	—	7.50
1995Mo Proof	2,000	Value: 13.50				

KM# 610   1/10 ONZA (1/10 Troy Ounce of Silver)
3.1103 g., 0.9990 Silver 0.0999 oz. ASW **Obv:**
National arms, eagle left **Rev:** Winged Victory

Date	Mintage	F	VF	XF	Unc	BU
1996Mo	50,000	—	—	—	—	12.00
1996Mo Proof	1,000	Value: 17.50				
1997Mo	20,000	—	—	—	—	12.00
1997Mo Proof	800	Value: 17.50				
1998Mo	6,400	—	—	—	—	12.00
1998Mo Proof	300	Value: 22.50				
1999Mo	8,000	—	—	—	—	14.00
1999Mo Proof	600	Value: 20.00				
2000Mo	27,500	—	—	—	—	14.00
2000Mo Proof	1,000	Value: 20.00				
2001Mo	25,000	—	—	—	—	14.00
2001Mo Proof	1,500	Value: 18.00				
2002Mo	35,000	—	—	—	—	10.00
2002Mo Proof	2,800	Value: 15.00				
2003Mo	5,000	—	—	—	—	10.00
2003Mo Proof	4,500	Value: 15.00				
2004Mo	22,277	—	—	—	—	10.00
2004Mo Proof	3,500	Value: 15.00				
2005Mo	7,086	—	—	—	—	10.00
2005Mo Proof	2,500	Value: 14.00				
2006Mo	15,000	—	—	—	—	10.00
2006Mo Proof	3,000	Value: 14.00				
2007Mo	—	—	—	—	—	10.00
2007Mo Proof	—	Value: 14.00				

KM# 544   1/4 ONZA (1/4 Troy Ounce of Silver)
7.7758 g., 0.9990 Silver 0.2497 oz. ASW **Obv:**
National arms, eagle left **Rev:** Winged Victory

Date	Mintage	F	VF	XF	Unc	BU
1991Mo	50,017	—	—	—	—	9.00
1992Mo	104,000	—	—	—	—	7.50
1992Mo Proof	5,000	Value: 15.00				
1993Mo	86,500	—	—	—	—	7.50
1993Mo Proof	—	Value: 15.00				
1994Mo	90,100	—	—	—	—	7.50
1994Mo Proof	15,000	Value: 15.00				
1995Mo	50,000	—	—	—	—	9.00
1995Mo Proof	2,000	Value: 16.50				

KM# 611   1/4 ONZA (1/4 Troy Ounce of Silver)
7.7758 g., 0.9990 Silver 0.2497 oz. ASW **Obv:**
National arms, eagle left **Rev:** Winged Victory

Date	Mintage	F	VF	XF	Unc	BU
1996Mo	50,000	—	—	—	—	15.00
1996Mo Proof	1,000	Value: 20.00				
1997Mo	20,000	—	—	—	—	15.00
1997Mo Proof	800	Value: 20.00				
1998Mo	6,400	—	—	—	—	15.00
1998Mo Proof	300	Value: 32.50				
1999Mo	7,000	—	—	—	—	18.00
1999Mo Proof	600	Value: 25.00				
2000Mo	21,000	—	—	—	—	18.00

Date	Mintage	F	VF	XF	Unc	BU
2000Mo Proof	700	Value: 25.00				
2001Mo	25,000	—	—	—	—	18.00
2001Mo Proof	1,000	Value: 22.00				
2002Mo	35,000	—	—	—	—	13.50
2002Mo Proof	2,800	Value: 20.00				
2003Mo Proof	3,500	Value: 20.00				
2003Mo	7,000	—	—	—	—	13.50
2004Mo	30,000	—	—	—	—	13.50
2004Mo Proof	3,900	Value: 20.00				
2005Mo	1,901	—	—	—	—	13.50
2005Mo Proof	1,500	Value: 18.50				
2006Mo	15,000	—	—	—	—	13.00
2006Mo Proof	3,000	Value: 18.50				
2007Mo	—	—	—	—	—	13.00
2007Mo Proof	—	Value: 18.50				

KM# 545   1/2 ONZA (1/2 Troy Ounce of Silver)
15.5517 g., 0.9990 Silver 0.4995 oz. ASW **Obv:**
National arms, eagle left **Rev:** Winged Victory

Date	Mintage	F	VF	XF	Unc	BU
1991Mo	50,618	—	—	—	—	12.00
1992Mo	119,000	—	—	—	—	10.00
1992Mo Proof	5,000	Value: 17.50				
1993Mo	71,500	—	—	—	—	10.00
1993Mo Proof	—	Value: 17.50				
1994Mo	90,100	—	—	—	—	10.00
1994Mo Proof	15,000	Value: 17.50				
1995Mo	50,000	—	—	—	—	10.00
1995Mo Proof	2,000	Value: 18.50				

KM# 612   1/2 ONZA (1/2 Troy Ounce of Silver)
15.5517 g., 0.9990 Silver 0.4995 oz. ASW **Obv:**
National arms, eagle left **Rev:** Winged Victory

Date	Mintage	F	VF	XF	Unc	BU
1996Mo	50,000	—	—	—	—	20.00
1996Mo Proof	1,000	Value: 30.00				
1997Mo	20,000	—	—	—	—	20.00
1997Mo Proof	800	Value: 30.00				
1998Mo	6,400	—	—	—	—	22.00
1998Mo Proof	300	Value: 45.00				
1999Mo	7,000	—	—	—	—	22.00
1999Mo Proof	600	Value: 35.00				
2000Mo	20,000	—	—	—	—	22.00
2000Mo Proof	700	Value: 35.00				
2001Mo	20,000	—	—	—	—	22.00
2001Mo Proof	1,000	Value: 30.00				
2002Mo	35,000	—	—	—	—	18.00
2002Mo Proof	2,800	Value: 25.00				
2003Mo Proof	3,000	Value: 25.00				
2003Mo	13,000	—	—	—	—	18.00
2004Mo	24,000	—	—	—	—	18.00
2004Mo Proof	4,300	Value: 25.00				
2005Mo	8,126	—	—	—	—	18.00
2005Mo Proof	1,500	Value: 22.00				
2006Mo	15,000	—	—	—	—	18.00
2006Mo Proof	2,900	Value: 22.00				
2007Mo	—	—	—	—	—	18.00
2007Mo Proof	—	Value: 22.00				

KM# 494.1   ONZA (Troy Ounce of Silver)
31.1000 g., 0.9990 Silver 0.9988 oz. ASW **Subject:**
Libertad **Obv:** National arms, eagle left **Rev:** Winged
Victory

Date	Mintage	F	VF	XF	Unc	BU
1982Mo	1,049,680	—	—	—	BV	17.50
1983Mo	1,001,768	—	—	—	BV	17.50
1983Mo Proof	998	Value: 225				
1984Mo	1,014,000	—	—	—	BV	17.50
1985Mo	2,017,000	—	—	—	BV	17.50
1986Mo	1,699,426	—	—	—	BV	17.50
1986Mo Proof	30,006	Value: 30.00				
1987Mo	500,000	—	—	—	BV	50.00
1987Mo Proof	12,000	Value: 38.00				
1987Mo Proof doubled date	Inc. above	Value: 45.00				
1988Mo	1,500,500	—	—	—	BV	47.00
1989Mo	1,396,500	—	—	—	BV	27.00
1989Mo Proof	10,000	Value: 70.00				

KM# 494.2   ONZA (Troy Ounce of Silver)
31.1000 g., 0.9990 Silver 0.9988 oz. ASW **Obv:**
National arms, eagle left **Rev:** Winged Victory **Edge:**
Reeded

Date	Mintage	F	VF	XF	Unc	BU
1988Mo Proof	10,000	Value: 75.00				
1990Mo	1,200,000	—	—	—	BV	17.50
1990Mo Proof	10,000	Value: 63.00				
1991Mo	1,650,518	—	—	—	BV	30.00

KM# 494.5   ONZA (Troy Ounce of Silver)
31.1000 g., 0.9990 Silver 0.9988 oz. ASW **Subject:**
Libertad **Obv:** National arms, eagle left **Rev:** Winged
Victory **Edge:** Reeded edge **Note:** Mule

Date	Mintage	F	VF	XF	Unc	BU
1991Mo Proof	10,000	Value: 57.00				

KM# 494.3   ONZA (Troy Ounce of Silver)
31.1000 g., 0.9990 Silver 0.9988 oz. ASW **Subject:**
Libertad **Obv:** National arms **Rev:** Winged Victory
with revised design and lettering **Edge:** Reeded edge
Note: Mule

Date	Mintage	F	VF	XF	Unc	BU
1991Mo	Inc. above	—	—	—	BV	45.00
1991Mo Proof	10,000	Value: 53.00				
1992Mo	2,458,000	—	—	—	BV	30.00
1992Mo Proof	10,000	Value: 53.00				

KM# 494.4   ONZA (Troy Ounce of Silver)
31.1000 g., 0.9990 Silver 0.9988 oz. ASW **Subject:**
Libertad **Obv:** National arms, eagle left **Rev:** Winged
Victory with revised design and lettering **Edge:**
Reeded edge **Note:** Mule

Date	Mintage	F	VF	XF	Unc	BU
1993Mo	1,000,000	—	—	—	BV	20.00
1993Mo Proof	—	Value: 57.00				
1994Mo	400,000	—	—	—	BV	25.00
1994Mo Proof	10,000	Value: 57.00				
1995Mo	500,000	—	—	—	BV	25.00
1995Mo Proof	2,000	Value: 57.00				

KM# 613   ONZA (Troy Ounce of Silver)
33.6250 g., 0.9250 Silver 0.9999 oz. ASW **Obv:** National arms, eagle left **Rev:** Winged Victory

Date	Mintage	F	VF	XF	Unc	BU
1996Mo	300,000	—	—	—	—	27.00
1996Mo Proof	2,000	Value: 60.00				
1997Mo	100,000	—	—	—	—	27.00
1997Mo Proof	1,500	Value: 60.00				
1998Mo	67,000	—	—	—	—	42.00
1998Mo Proof	500	Value: 85.00				
1999Mo	95,000	—	—	—	—	27.00
1999Mo Proof	600	Value: 70.00				

KM# 639   ONZA (Troy Ounce of Silver)
31.1000 g., 0.9990 Silver 0.9988 oz. ASW **Subject:** Libertad **Obv:** National arms, eagle left within center of past and present arms **Rev:** Winged Victory **Edge:** Reeded

Date	Mintage	F	VF	XF	Unc	BU
2000Mo	340,000	—	—	—	—	28.00
2000Mo Proof	1,600	Value: 60.00				
2001Mo	650,000	—	—	—	—	28.00
2001Mo Proof	2,000	Value: 60.00				
2002Mo	850,000	—	—	—	—	28.00
2002Mo Proof	3,800	Value: 60.00				
2003Mo	678,869	—	—	—	—	28.00
2003Mo Proof	5,000	Value: 60.00				
2004Mo	560,412	—	—	—	—	35.00
2004Mo Proof	5,300	Value: 60.00				
2005Mo	300,000	—	—	—	—	45.00
2005Mo Proof	4,000	Value: 60.00				
2006Mo	—	—	—	—	—	28.00
2006Mo Proof	—	Value: 60.00				
2007Mo	—	—	—	—	—	28.00
2007Mo Proof	—	Value: 60.00				

KM# 614   2 ONZAS (2 Troy Ounces of Silver)
62.2070 g., 0.9990 Silver 1.9979 oz. ASW, 48 mm. **Subject:** Libertad **Obv:** National arms, eagle left within center of past and present arms **Rev:** Winged Victory **Edge:** Reeded

Date	Mintage	F	VF	XF	Unc	BU
1996Mo	50,000	—	—	—	—	35.00
1996Mo Proof	1,200	Value: 65.00				
1997Mo	15,000	—	—	—	—	35.00
1997Mo Proof	1,300	Value: 70.00				
1998Mo	7,000	—	—	—	—	45.00
1998Mo Proof	400	Value: 100				
1999Mo	5,000	—	—	—	—	60.00
1999Mo Proof	280	Value: 175				
2000Mo	7,500	—	—	—	—	60.00
2000Mo Proof	500	Value: 75.00				
2001Mo	1,700	—	—	—	—	60.00
2001Mo Proof	500	Value: 75.00				
2002Mo	8,700	—	—	—	—	55.00
2002Mo Proof	1,000	Value: 70.00				
2003Mo Proof	400	Value: 70.00				
2003Mo	9,000	—	—	—	—	55.00
2004Mo	11,349	—	—	—	—	45.00
2004Mo Proof	1,360	Value: 70.00				
2005Mo	1,200	—	—	—	—	45.00
2005Mo Proof	740	Value: 70.00				
2006Mo	5,800	—	—	—	—	45.00
2006Mo Proof	1,100	Value: 70.00				
2007Mo	—	—	—	—	—	45.00
2007Mo Proof	—	Value: 70.00				

KM# 615   5 ONZAS (5 Troy Ounces of Silver)
155.5175 g., 0.9990 Silver 4.9948 oz. ASW, 65 mm. **Subject:** Libertad **Obv:** National arms, eagle left within center of past and present arms **Rev:** Winged Victory **Edge:** Reeded **Note:** Illustration reduced.

Date	Mintage	F	VF	XF	Unc	BU
1996Mo	20,000	—	—	—	—	120
1996Mo Proof	1,200	Value: 200				
1997Mo	10,000	—	—	—	—	120
1997Mo Proof	1,300	Value: 200				
1998Mo	3,500	—	—	—	—	220
1998Mo Proof	400	Value: 400				
1999Mo	2,800	—	—	—	—	110
1999Mo Proof	100	Value: 500				
2000Mo	4,000	—	—	—	—	110
2000Mo Proof	500	Value: 200				
2001Mo	4,000	—	—	—	—	110
2001Mo Proof	600	Value: 200				
2002Mo	5,200	—	—	—	—	110
2002Mo Proof	1,000	Value: 200				
2003Mo	5,500	—	—	—	—	100
2003Mo Proof	495	Value: 115				
2004Mo	6,324	—	—	—	—	100
2004Mo Proof	1,805	Value: 135				
2005Mo Proof	900	Value: 125				
2005Mo	790	—	—	—	—	100
2006Mo	3,000	—	—	—	—	100
2006Mo Proof	1,000	Value: 125				
2007Mo	—	—	—	—	—	100
2007Mo Proof	—	Value: 125				

KM# 677   KILO (32.15 Troy Ounces of Silver)
999.9775 g., 0.9990 Silver 32.116 oz. ASW, 110 mm. **Subject:** Collector Bullion **Obv:** National arms in center of past and present arms **Rev:** Winged Victory **Edge:** Reeded

Date	Mintage	VF	XF	Unc	BU
2002Mo Prooflike	1,100	—	—	—	750
2003Mo Proof	2,234				
2004Mo Prooflike	500	—	—	—	650
2005Mo Proof	874				

GOLD BULLION COINAGE

KM# 530   1/20 ONZA (1/20 Ounce of Pure Gold)
1.7500 g., 0.9000 Gold 0.0506 oz. AGW   **Obv:**
Winged Victory **Rev:** Calendar stone

Date	Mintage	F	VF	XF	Unc	BU
1987Mo	—	—	—	—	—	275
1988Mo						

KM# 589   1/20 ONZA (1/20 Ounce of Pure Gold)
1.5551 g., 0.9990 Gold 0.0499 oz. AGW   **Obv:**
Winged Victory **Rev:** National arms, eagle left

Date	Mintage	F	VF	XF	Unc	BU
1991Mo	10,000	—	—	—	—	BV+30%
1992Mo	65,225	—	—	—	—	BV+30%
1993Mo	10,000	—	—	—	—	BV+30%
1994Mo	10,000	—	—	—	—	BV+30%

KM# 642   1/20 ONZA (1/20 Ounce of Pure Gold)
1.5551 g., 0.9990 Gold 0.0499 oz. AGW   **Obv:**
National arms, eagle left **Rev:** Native working

Date	Mintage	F	VF	XF	Unc	BU
2000Mo Proof	—	Value: 50.00				

KM# 671   1/20 ONZA (1/20 Ounce of Pure Gold)
1.5551 g., 0.9990 Gold 0.0499 oz. AGW, 16 mm.
Obv: National arms, eagle left **Rev:** Winged Victory
Edge: Reeded **Note:** Design similar to KM#609.
Value estimates do not include the high taxes and
surcharges added to the issue prices by the Mexican
Government.

Date	Mintage	F	VF	XF	Unc	BU
Mo	—	—	—	—	—	
2000Mo	5,300	—	—	—	—	BV+30%
2002Mo	5,000	—	—	—	—	BV+30%
2004Mo		—	—	—	—	BV+30%
2005Mo		—	—	—	—	BV+30%
2006Mo		—	—	—	—	BV+30%
2007Mo		—	—	—	—	

KM# 628   1/15 ONZA (1/15 Ounce of Pure Gold)
0.9990 Gold   **Obv:** Winged Victory above legend
Rev: National arms, eagle left within circle

Date	Mintage	F	VF	XF	Unc	BU
1987Mo	—	—	—	—	—	275

KM# 541   1/10 ONZA (1/10 Ounce of Pure Gold)
3.1103 g., 0.9990 Gold 0.0999 oz. AGW   **Obv:**
National arms, eagle left **Rev:** Winged Victory

Date	Mintage	F	VF	XF	Unc	BU
1991Mo	10,000	—	—	—	—	BV+20%
1992Mo	50,777	—	—	—	—	BV+20%
1993Mo	10,000	—	—	—	—	BV+20%
1994Mo	10,000	—	—	—	—	BV+20%

KM# 672   1/10 ONZA (1/10 Ounce of Pure Gold)
3.1103 g., 0.9990 Gold 0.0999 oz. AGW, 20 mm.
Obv: National arms, eagle left **Rev:** Winged Victory
Edge: Reeded **Note:** Design similar to KM#610.
Value estimates do not include the high taxes and
surcharges added to the issue prices by the Mexican
Government.

Date	Mintage	F	VF	XF	Unc	BU
2000Mo	3,500	—	—	—	—	BV+20%
2002Mo	5,000	—	—	—	—	BV+20%
2004Mo	—	—	—	—	—	BV+20%
2005Mo	—	—	—	—	—	BV+20%

Date	Mintage	F	VF	XF	Unc	BU
2006Mo Proof	—	BV+22%				
2006Mo	—	—	—	—	—	BV+20%
2007Mo	—	—	—	—	—	BV+20%

KM# 487   1/4 ONZA (1/4 Ounce of Pure Gold)
8.6396 g., 0.9000 Gold 0.2500 oz. AGW   **Obv:**
National arms, eagle left **Rev:** Winged Victory **Note:**
Similar to KM#488.

Date	Mintage	F	VF	XF	Unc	BU
1981Mo	313,000	—	—	—	—	BV+11%
1982Mo	—	—	—	—	—	BV+11%

KM# 590   1/4 ONZA (1/4 Ounce of Pure Gold)
7.7758 g., 0.9990 Gold 0.2497 oz. AGW   **Obv:**
Winged Victory above legend **Rev:** National arms,
eagle left

Date	Mintage	F	VF	XF	Unc	BU
1991Mo	10,000	—	—	—	—	BV+11%
1992Mo	28,106	—	—	—	—	BV+11%
1993Mo	2,500	—	—	—	—	BV+11%
1994Mo	2,500	—	—	—	—	BV+11%

KM# 673   1/4 ONZA (1/4 Ounce of Pure Gold)
7.7758 g., 0.9990 Gold 0.2497 oz. AGW, 26.9 mm.
Obv: National arms, eagle left **Rev:** Winged Victory
Edge: Reeded **Note:** Design similar to KM#611.
Value estimates do not include the high taxes and
surcharges added to the issue prices by the Mexican
Government.

Date	Mintage	F	VF	XF	Unc	BU
2000Mo	2,500	—	—	—	—	BV+12%
2002Mo	—	—	—	—	—	BV+12%
2004Mo	—	—	—	—	—	BV+12%
2004Mo Proof	—	BV+15%				
2005Mo Proof	—	BV+15%				
2005Mo	—	—	—	—	—	BV+12%
2006Mo Proof	—	BV+12%				
2006Mo	—	—	—	—	—	BV+12%
2007Mo	—	—	—	—	—	BV+12%

KM# 488   1/2 ONZA (1/2 Ounce of Pure Gold)
17.2792 g., 0.9000 Gold 0.5000 oz. AGW   **Obv:**
National arms, eagle left **Rev:** Winged Victory

Date	Mintage	F	VF	XF	Unc	BU
1981Mo	193,000	—	—	—	—	BV+8%
1982Mo	—	—	—	—	—	BV+8%
1989Mo Proof	704	Value: 500				

KM# 591   1/2 ONZA (1/2 Ounce of Pure Gold)
15.5517 g., 0.9990 Gold 0.4995 oz. AGW   **Obv:**
Winged Victory above legend **Rev:** National arms,
eagle left

Date	Mintage	F	VF	XF	Unc	BU
1991Mo	10,000	—	—	—	—	BV+8%
1992Mo	25,220	—	—	—	—	BV+8%
1993Mo	2,500	—	—	—	—	BV+8%
1994Mo	2,500	—	—	—	—	BV+8%

KM# 674   1/2 ONZA (1/2 Ounce of Pure Gold)
15.5517 g., 0.9990 Gold 0.4995 oz. AGW, 32.9 mm.
Obv: National arms, eagle left **Rev:** Winged Victory
Edge: Reeded **Note:** Design similar to KM#612.
Value estimates do not include the high taxes and
surcharges added to the issue prices by the Mexican
Government.

Date	Mintage	F	VF	XF	Unc	BU
2000Mo	1,500	—	—	—	—	BV+8%

Date	Mintage	F	VF	XF	Unc	BU
2002Mo	—	—	—	—	—	BV+8%
2004Mo	—	—	—	—	—	BV+8%
2005Mo	—	—	—	—	—	BV+8%
2005Mo Proof	—	BV+12%				
2006Mo	—	—	—	—	—	BV+8%
2006Mo Proof	—	BV+12%				
2007Mo	—	—	—	—	—	BV+8%

KM# 489   ONZA (Ounce of Pure Gold)
34.5585 g., 0.9000 Gold 0.9999 oz. AGW **Obv:**
National arms, eagle left **Rev:** Winged Victory **Note:**
Similar to KM#488.

Date	Mintage	F	VF	XF	Unc	BU
1981Mo	596,000	—	—	—	—	BV+3%
1985Mo	—	—	—	—	—	BV+3%
1988Mo	—	—	—	—	—	BV+3%

KM# 592   ONZA (Ounce of Pure Gold)
31.1035 g., 0.9990 Gold 0.9990 oz. AGW **Obv:**
Winged Victory above legend **Rev:** National arms,
eagle left

Date	Mintage	F	VF	XF	Unc	BU
1991Mo	109,193	—	—	—	—	BV+3%
1992Mo	46,281	—	—	—	—	BV+3%
1993Mo	10,000	—	—	—	—	BV+3%
1994Mo	1,000	—	—	—	—	BV+3%

KM# 675   ONZA (Ounce of Pure Gold)
31.1035 g., 0.9990 Gold 0.9990 oz. AGW, 40 mm.
Obv: National arms, eagle left **Rev:** Winged Victory
Edge: Reeded **Note:** Design similar to KM#639.
Value estimates do not include the high taxes and
surcharges added to the issue prices by the Mexican
Government.

Date	Mintage	F	VF	XF	Unc	BU
2000Mo	2,730	—	—	—	—	BV+3%
2002Mo	—	—	—	—	—	BV+3%
2004Mo	—	—	—	—	—	BV+3%
2005Mo	—	—	—	—	—	BV+3%
2005Mo Proof	—	BV+5%				
2006Mo Proof	—	BV+5%				
2006Mo	—	—	—	—	—	BV+3%

PLATINUM BULLION COINAGE

KM# 538   1/4 ONZA (1/4 Ounce)
7.7775 g., 0.9990 Platinum 0.2498 oz. APW **Obv:**
National arms, eagle left **Rev:** Winged Victory

Date	Mintage	F	VF	XF	Unc	BU
1989Mo	704	Value: 450				

BULLION COINAGE PRE-COLUMBIAN • AZTECA SERIES

KM# 644   NUEVO PESO

7.7700 g., 0.9990 Silver 0.2496 oz. ASW, 26.8 mm.
Subject: Eagle Warrior **Obv:** National arms, eagle
left within D-shaped circle and dotted border **Rev:**
Eagle warrior within D-shaped circle and dotted
border **Edge:** Reeded

Date	Mintage	F	VF	XF	Unc	BU
1993Mo	1,500	—	—	—	—	15.00
1993 Proof	900	Value: 22.50				

KM# 645   2 NUEVO PESOS
15.4200 g., 0.9990 Silver 0.4952 oz. ASW, 32.9 mm.
Subject: Eagle Warrior **Obv:** National arms, eagle
left **Rev:** Eagle warrior **Edge:** Reeded

Date	Mintage	F	VF	XF	Unc	BU
1993Mo	1,500	—	—	—	—	15.00
1993 Proof	800	Value: 25.00				

KM# 646   5 NUEVO PESOS
31.0500 g., 0.9990 Silver 0.9972 oz. ASW, 40 mm.
Subject: Eagle Warrior **Obv:** National arms, eagle
left **Rev:** Eagle warrior **Edge:** Reeded

Date	Mintage	F	VF	XF	Unc	BU
1993	2,000	—	—	—	—	22.00
1993 Proof	1,000	Value: 50.00				

KM# 647   5 NUEVO PESOS
31.0000 g., 0.9990 Silver 0.9956 oz. ASW, 40 mm.
Subject: Xochipilli **Obv:** National arms, eagle left
within D-shaped circle and flower blossom border
Rev: Seated figure sculpture within D-shaped circle
and flower blossom border **Edge:** Reeded

Date	Mintage	F	VF	XF	Unc	BU
1993	2,000	—	—	—	—	25.00
1993 Proof	800	Value: 60.00				

KM# 649   5 NUEVO PESOS
31.0000 g., 0.9990 Silver 0.9956 oz. ASW, 40 mm.
Subject: Huchucteotl **Obv:** National arms, eagle left
within D-shaped circle and designed border **Rev:**
Aztec sculpture within D-shaped circle and designed
border **Edge:** Reeded

Date	Mintage	F	VF	XF	Unc	BU
1993	5,000	—	—	—	—	20.00
1993 Proof	800	Value: 65.00				

KM# 648   5 NUEVO PESOS
31.0000 g., 0.9990 Silver 0.9956 oz. ASW, 40 mm.
Subject: Brasco Efigie **Obv:** National arms, eagle
left within D-shaped circle and designed border **Rev:**
Sculpture within D-shaped circle and designed
border **Edge:** Reeded

Date	Mintage	F	VF	XF	Unc	BU
1993	2,000	—	—	—	—	25.00
1993 Proof	500	Value: 55.00				

KM# 650   10 NUEVO PESOS
155.3100 g., 0.9990 Silver 4.9881 oz. ASW, 64 mm.
Subject: Piedra de Tizoc **Obv:** National arms, eagle left
Rev: Warrior capturing woman **Edge:** Reeded **Note:**
Illustration reduced, similar to 100 Pesos, KM# 557

Date	Mintage	F	VF	XF	Unc	BU
1992 Proof	—	Value: 150				
1993 Proof	1,000	Value: 120				
1993	1,000	—	—	—	—	90.00

KM# 554   25 PESOS
7.7758 g., 0.9990 Silver 0.2497 oz. ASW **Obv:**
National arms, eagle left within D-shaped circle and
designed border **Rev:** Eagle warrior right within D-
shaped circle and a designed border

Date	Mintage	F	VF	XF	Unc	BU
1992	50,000	—	—	—	14.00	—
1992 Proof	3,000	Value: 22.50				

KM# 555   50 PESOS
15.5517 g., 0.9990 Silver 0.4995 oz. ASW **Obv:**
National arms, eagle left within D-shaped circle
designed border **Rev:** Eagle warrior right within D-
shaped circle and designed border

Date	Mintage	F	VF	XF	Unc	BU
1992	50,000	—	—	—	20.00	—
1992 Proof	3,000	Value: 25.00				

KM# 556   100 PESOS
31.1035 g., 0.9990 Silver 0.9990 oz. ASW **Obv:**
National arms, eagle left **Rev:** Eagle warrior

Date	Mintage	F	VF	XF	Unc	BU
1992	205,000	—	—	—	22.00	—
1992	4,000	Value: 50.00				

KM# 562   100 PESOS
31.1035 g., 0.9990 Silver 0.9990 oz. ASW **Obv:**
National arms, eagle left within D-shaped circle and
designed border **Rev:** Seated figure sculpture within
D-shaped circle and designed border

Date	Mintage	F	VF	XF	Unc	BU
1992 Proof	4,000	Value: 60.00				

KM# 563   100 PESOS
31.1035 g., 0.9990 Silver 0.9990 oz. ASW **Obv:**
National arms, eagle left within D-shaped circle and
designed border **Rev:** Brasero Efigie - The God of
Rain within D-shaped circle and designed border

Date	Mintage	F	VF	XF	Unc	BU
1992 Proof	4,000	Value: 65.00				

KM# 564   100 PESOS
31.1035 g., 0.9990 Silver 0.9990 oz. ASW **Obv:**
National arms, eagle left within D-shaped circle and
designed border **Rev:** Huehueteotl - The God of Fire
within D-shaped circle and designed border

Date	Mintage	F	VF	XF	Unc	BU
1992 Proof	4,000	Value: 50.00				

KM# 558   250 PESOS
7.7758 g., 0.9990 Gold 0.2497 oz. AGW **Subject:**
Native Culture **Obv:** National arms, eagle left within
D-shaped circle and designed border **Rev:** Sculpture
of Jaguar head within D-shaped circle and designed
border

Date	Mintage	F	VF	XF	Unc	BU
1992	10,000	—	—	—	—	240
1992 Proof	2,000	Value: 285				

KM# 559   500 PESOS
15.5517 g., 0.9990 Gold 0.4995 oz. AGW **Subject:**
Native Culture **Obv:** National arms, eagle left within
D-shaped circle and designed border **Rev:**
Sculpture of Jaguar head within D-shaped circle and
designed border

Date	Mintage	F	VF	XF	Unc	BU
1992	10,000	—	—	—	—	475
1992 Proof	2,000	Value: 485				

KM# 560   1000 PESOS
31.1035 g., 0.9990 Gold 0.9990 oz. AGW **Subject:**
Native Culture **Obv:** National arms, eagle left within
D-shaped circle and designed border **Rev:**
Sculpture of Jaguar head within D-shaped circle and
designed border

Date	Mintage	F	VF	XF	Unc	BU
1992	17,850	—	—	—	—	925
1992 Proof	2,000	Value: 950				

KM# 557   10000 PESOS
155.5175 g., 0.9990 Silver 4.9948 oz. ASW, 64 mm.
Subject: Pieora De Tizoc **Obv:** National arms, eagle
left within D-shaped circle and designed border **Rev:**
Native warriors within D-shaped circle and designed
border **Note:** Similar to 10 Nuevo Pesos, KM#650

Date	Mintage	F	VF	XF	Unc	BU
1992	51,900	—	—	—	—	80.00
1992 Proof	3,300	Value: 160				

BULLION COINAGE
PRE-COLUMBIAN •
CENTRAL VERACRUZ SERIES

KM# 567 NUEVO PESO
7.7601 g., 0.9990 Silver 0.2492 oz. ASW **Subject:** Bajo relieve de el Tajin **Obv:** National arms, eagle left within D-shaped circle and designed border **Rev:** Design within D-shaped circle and designed border

Date	Mintage	F	VF	XF	Unc	BU
1993	100,000	—	—	—	—	13.50
1993 Proof	3,300	Value: 25.00				

KM# 568 2 NUEVO PESOS
15.5516 g., 0.9990 Silver 0.4995 oz. ASW **Subject:** Bajo relieve de el Tajin **Obv:** National arms, eagle left within D-shaped circle and designed border **Rev:** Design within D-shaped circle and designed border

Date	Mintage	F	VF	XF	Unc	BU
1993	100,000	—	—	—	—	16.50
1993 Proof	3,000	Value: 25.00				

KM# 569 5 NUEVO PESOS
31.1035 g., 0.9990 Silver 0.9990 oz. ASW **Subject:** Bajo relieve de el Tajin **Obv:** National arms, eagle left within D-shaped circle and designed border **Rev:** Design within D-shaped circle and designed border

Date	Mintage	F	VF	XF	Unc	BU
1993	100,000	—	—	—	—	20.00
1993 Proof	3,000	Value: 50.00				

KM# 582 5 NUEVO PESOS
31.1035 g., 0.9990 Silver 0.9990 oz. ASW **Subject:** Palma Con Cocodrilo **Obv:** National arms, eagle left within D-shaped circle and designed border **Rev:** Aerial view of crocodile within D-shaped circle and designed border

Date	Mintage	F	VF	XF	Unc	BU
1993	4,500	—	—	—	—	20.00
1993 Proof	2,650	Value: 50.00				

KM# 583 5 NUEVO PESOS
31.1035 g., 0.9990 Silver 0.9990 oz. ASW **Subject:** Anciano Con Brasero **Obv:** National arms, eagle left within D-shaped circle and designed border **Rev:** Kneeling figure sculpture within D-shaped circle and designed border

Date	Mintage	F	VF	XF	Unc	BU
1993	2,650	—	—	—	—	25.00
1993 Proof	1,500	Value: 50.00				

KM# 584 5 NUEVO PESOS
31.1035 g., 0.9990 Silver 0.9990 oz. ASW **Subject:** Carita Sonriente **Obv:** National arms, eagle left **Rev:** Sculptured head

Date	Mintage	F	VF	XF	Unc	BU
1993	4,500	—	—	—	—	20.00
1993 Proof	3,300	Value: 50.00				

KM# 570 10 NUEVO PESOS
Center Weight: 115.5175 g. **Center Composition:** 0.9990 Silver 3.7101 oz. ASW , 64 mm. **Subject:** Piramide Del El Tajin **Obv:** National arms, eagle left within flat shaped circle and designed border **Rev:** Pyramid within flat shaped circle and designed border **Note:** Illustration reduced.

Date	Mintage	F	VF	XF	Unc	BU
1993	50,000	—	—	—	—	80.00
1993 Proof	3,100	Value: 160				

KM# 585 25 NUEVO PESOS
7.7758 g., 0.9990 Gold 0.2497 oz. AGW **Subject:** Hacha Ceremonial **Obv:** National arms, eagle left **Rev:** Mask left **Note:** Similar to 100 New Pesos, KM#587.

Date	Mintage	F	VF	XF	Unc	BU
1993 Proof	800	Value: 285				
1993	15,500	—	—	—	—	240

KM# 586 50 NUEVO PESOS
15.5517 g., 0.9990 Gold 0.4995 oz. AGW **Subject:** Hacha Ceremonial **Obv:** National arms, eagle left **Rev:** Mask left **Note:** Similar to 100 New Pesos, KM#587.

Date	Mintage	F	VF	XF	Unc	BU
1993	15,500	—	—	—	—	475
1993 Proof	500	Value: 485				

KM# 587 100 NUEVO PESOS
31.1035 g., 0.9990 Gold 0.9990 oz. AGW **Subject:** Hacha Ceremonial **Obv:** National arms, eagle left **Rev:** Mask left

Date	Mintage	F	VF	XF	Unc	BU
1993	7,150	—	—	—	—	940
1993 Proof	500	Value: 950				

BULLION COINAGE
PRE-COLUMBIAN •
MAYAN SERIES

KM# 572 NUEVO PESO
7.7601 g., 0.9990 Silver 0.2492 oz. ASW **Subject:** Chaac Mool **Obv:** National arms, eagle left within six sided shield and designed border **Rev:** Reclining figure within six sided shield and designed border

Date	Mintage	F	VF	XF	Unc	BU
1994 Matte	30,000	—	—	—	—	13.50
1994 Proof	2,500	Value: 25.00				

KM# 573 2 NUEVO PESOS
15.5516 g., 0.9990 Silver 0.4995 oz. ASW **Subject:** Chaac Mool **Obv:** National arms, eagle left within six sided shield and designed border **Rev:** Reclining figure within six sided shield and designed border

Date	Mintage	F	VF	XF	Unc	BU
1994 Matte	30,000	—	—	—	—	16.50
1994 Proof	2,500	Value: 25.00				

KM# 574 5 NUEVO PESOS
31.1035 g., 0.9990 Silver 0.9990 oz. ASW **Subject:** Chaac Mool **Obv:** National arms, eagle left within six sided shield and designed border **Rev:** Reclining figure within six sided shield and designed border

Date	Mintage	F	VF	XF	Unc	BU
1994 Matte	50,000	—	—	—	—	20.00
1994 Proof	3,000	Value: 50.00				

KM# 575   5 NUEVO PESOS
31.1035 g., 0.9990 Silver 0.9990 oz. ASW **Subject:** Chaac Mool **Obv:** National arms, eagle left within six sided shield and designed border **Rev:** Tomb of Palenque Memorial Stone within six sided shield and designed border

Date	Mintage	F	VF	XF	Unc	BU
1994	4,500	—	—	—	—	20.00
1994 Proof	2,800	Value: 50.00				

KM# 577   5 NUEVO PESOS
31.1035 g., 0.9990 Silver 0.9990 oz. ASW **Subject:** Mascaron Del Dios Chaac **Rev:** Elaborately carved wall segment

Date	Mintage	F	VF	XF	Unc	BU
1994	4,500	—	—	—	—	20.00
1994 Proof	2,500	Value: 50.00				

KM# 578   5 NUEVO PESOS
31.1035 g., 0.9990 Silver 0.9990 oz. ASW **Subject:** Dintel 26 **Obv:** National arms, eagle left within six sided shield and designed border **Rev:** Two seated figures wall carving within six sided shield and designed border

Date	Mintage	F	VF	XF	Unc	BU
1994	4,500	—	—	—	—	20.00
1994 Proof	2,600	Value: 50.00				

KM# 676   10 NUEVO PESOS
155.5175 g., 0.9990 Silver 4.9948 oz. ASW, 65 mm. **Subject:** Piramide Del Castillo **Obv:** National arms, eagle left above metal content statement **Rev:** Pyramid above two-line inscription **Rev. Inscription:** PIRAMIDE DEL CASTILLO / CHICHEN-ITZA **Edge:** Reeded

Date	Mintage	F	VF	XF	Unc	BU
1993Mo Proof	—	Value: 325				

KM# 576   10 NUEVO PESOS
Center Weight: 115.5175 g. **Center Composition:** 0.9990 Silver 3.7101 oz. ASW , 64 mm. **Subject:** Piramide del Castillo **Obv:** National arms, eagle left **Rev:** Pyramid **Note:** Illustration reduced.

Date	Mintage	F	VF	XF	Unc	BU
1994	20,000	—	—	—	—	85.00
1994 Proof	2,100	Value: 165				

KM# 579   25 NUEVO PESOS
7.7758 g., 0.9990 Gold 0.2497 oz. AGW **Subject:** Personaje de Jaina **Rev:** Seated figure

Date	Mintage	F	VF	XF	Unc	BU
1994	2,000	—	—	—	—	250
1994 Proof	500	Value: 285				

KM# 580   50 NUEVO PESOS
15.5517 g., 0.9990 Gold 0.4995 oz. AGW **Subject:** Personaje de Jaina **Rev:** Seated figure

Date	Mintage	F	VF	XF	Unc	BU
1994	1,000	—	—	—	—	475
1994 Proof	500	Value: 485				

KM# 581   100 NUEVO PESOS
31.1035 g., 0.9990 Gold 0.9990 oz. AGW **Subject:** Personaje de Jaina **Obv:** National arms, eagle left within six sided shield and designed border **Rev:** Seated figure within six sided shield and designed border

Date	Mintage	F	VF	XF	Unc	BU
1994	1,000	—	—	—	—	940
1994 Proof	500	Value: 950				

BULLION COINAGE
PRE-COLUMBIAN •
OLMEC SERIES

KM# 593   PESO
7.7750 g., 0.9990 Silver 0.2497 oz. ASW **Subject:** Senor De Las Limas **Obv:** National arms, eagle left within square and designed border **Rev:** Sitting figure facing within square and designed border **Note:** Similar to 5 Pesos, KM#595.

Date	Mintage	F	VF	XF	Unc	BU
1996	4,000	—	—	—	—	13.50
1996 Proof	2,200	Value: 25.00				
1998 Matte	2,400	—	—	—	—	15.00

KM# 594   2 PESOS
15.5517 g., 0.9990 Silver 0.4995 oz. ASW **Subject:** Senor De Las Limas **Obv:** National arms, eagle left within square and designed border **Rev:** Sitting figure facing within square and designed border **Note:** Similar to 5 Pesos, KM#595.

Date	Mintage	F	VF	XF	Unc	BU
1996	4,000	—	—	—	—	16.50
1996 Proof	2,200	Value: 25.00				
1998 Matte	2,400	—	—	—	—	18.00

KM# 596   5 PESOS
31.1035 g., 0.9990 Silver 0.9990 oz. ASW **Subject:** Hombre Jaguar **Obv:** National arms, eagle left within square and designed border **Rev:** Statue facing within square and designed border

Date	Mintage	F	VF	XF	Unc	BU
1996	1,500	—	—	—	—	85.00
1996 Proof	2,800	Value: 50.00				
1998 Matte	6,000	—	—	—	—	25.00
1998 Proof	4,800	Value: 50.00				

KM# 595   5 PESOS
31.1035 g., 0.9990 Silver 0.9990 oz. ASW **Subject:** Senor De Las Limas **Obv:** National arms, eagle left within square and designed border **Rev:** Seated figure facing within square and designed border

Date	Mintage	F	VF	XF	Unc	BU
1996	4,000	—	—	—	—	20.00
1996 Proof	3,000	Value: 50.00				
1998 Matte	3,400	—	—	—	—	22.00

KM# 597   5 PESOS
31.1035 g., 0.9990 Silver 0.9990 oz. ASW **Subject:** El Luchador **Obv:** National arms, eagle left **Rev:** El Luchador

Date	Mintage	F	VF	XF	Unc	BU
1996	4,500	—	—	—	—	20.00
1996 Proof	2,700	Value: 50.00				
1998 Matte	2,000	—	—	—	—	25.00

KM# 598   5 PESOS
31.1035 g., 0.9990 Silver 0.9990 oz. ASW **Subject:** Hacha Ceremonial **Obv:** National arms, eagle left within square and designed border **Rev:** Statue within square and designed border

Date	Mintage	F	VF	XF	Unc	BU
1996	4,500	—	—	—	—	20.00
1996 Proof	2,700	Value: 50.00				
1998 Matte	2,000	—	—	—	—	25.00

KM# 599   10 PESOS
Center Weight: 155.5175 g. **Center Composition:** 0.9990 Silver 4.9948 oz. ASW , 64 mm. **Subject:** Cabeza Olmeca **Obv:** National arms, eagle left **Rev:** Native mask **Note:** Illustration reduced.

Date	Mintage	F	VF	XF	Unc	BU
1996	2,000	—	—	—	—	85.00
1996 Proof	2,750	Value: 110				
1998 Matte	2,150	—	—	—	—	85.00

KM# 600   25 PESOS
7.7758 g., 0.9990 Gold 0.2497 oz. AGW **Subject:** Sacerdote **Obv:** National arms, eagle left **Rev:** Sculpture **Note:** Similar to 100 Pesos, KM#602.

Date	Mintage	F	VF	XF	Unc	BU
1996	500	—	—	—	—	275
1996 Proof	750	Value: 285				

KM# 601   50 PESOS
15.5517 g., 0.9990 Gold 0.4995 oz. AGW **Subject:** Sacerdote **Obv:** National arms, eagle left **Rev:** Sculpture **Note:** Similar to 100 Pesos, KM#602.

Date	Mintage	F	VF	XF	Unc	BU
1996	500	—	—	—	—	475
1996 Proof	500	Value: 485				

KM# 602   100 PESOS
31.1035 g., 0.9990 Gold 0.9990 oz. AGW **Subject:** Sacerdote **Obv:** National arms, eagle left within square and designed border **Rev:** Sculpture within square and designed border

Date	Mintage	F	VF	XF	Unc	BU
1996	500	—	—	—	—	925
1996 Proof	500	Value: 950				

BULLION COINAGE PRE-COLUMBIAN • TEOTIHUACAN SERIES

KM# 617   PESO
7.7759 g., 0.9990 Silver 0.2497 oz. ASW **Subject:** Disco De La Muerte **Obv:** National arms, eagle left within oblong circle and designed border **Rev:** Sculpture within oblong circle and designed border

Date	Mintage	F	VF	XF	Unc	BU
1997	3,000	—	—	—	—	13.50
1997 Proof	1,600	Value: 25.00				
1998 Matte	2,400	—	—	—	—	15.00
1998 Proof	500	Value: 30.00				

KM# 618   2 PESOS
15.5517 g., 0.9990 Silver 0.4995 oz. ASW **Subject:** Disco De La Muerte **Obv:** National arms, eagle left within oblong circle and designed border **Rev:** Sculpture within oblong circle and designed border

Date	Mintage	F	VF	XF	Unc	BU
1997	3,000	—	—	—	—	16.50
1997 Proof	1,600	Value: 25.00				
1998 Proof	500	Value: 30.00				
1998	2,400	—	—	—	—	18.00

KM# 621   5 PESOS
31.1035 g., 0.9990 Silver 0.9990 oz. ASW **Subject:** Teotihuacan - Vasija **Obv:** National arms, eagle left within oval and designed border **Rev:** Seated woman joined to pottery vase within oval and designed border

Date	Mintage	F	VF	XF	Unc	BU
1997	4,500	—	—	—	—	20.00
1997 Proof	Est. 1,800	Value: 50.00				
1998 Proof	500	Value: 60.00				
1998 Matte	2,000	—	—	—	—	25.00

KM# 622   5 PESOS
31.1035 g., 0.9990 Silver 0.9990 oz. ASW **Subject:** Teotihuacan - Jugador de Pelota **Obv:** National arms, eagle left

Date	Mintage	F	VF	XF	Unc	BU
1997 Proof	Est. 1,800	Value: 50.00				
1997	4,500	—	—	—	—	20.00
1998 Proof	500	Value: 60.00				
1998 Matte	2,000	—	—	—	—	25.00

KM# 619   5 PESOS
31.1035 g., 0.9990 Silver 0.9990 oz. ASW **Subject:** Teotihuacan - Disco de la Muerte **Obv:** National arms, eagle left within oblong circle and designed border **Rev:** Sculpture within oblong circle and designed border

Date	Mintage	F	VF	XF	Unc	BU
1997	3,500	—	—	—	—	20.00
1997 Proof	Est. 1,800	Value: 50.00				
1998	3,400	—	—	—	—	22.00
1998 Proof	500	Value: 60.00				

KM# 620   5 PESOS
31.1035 g., 0.9990 Silver 0.9990 oz. ASW **Subject:** Teotihuacan - Mascara **Obv:** National arms, eagle left within oblong circle and designed border **Rev:** Face sculpture within oblong circle and designed border

Date	Mintage	F	VF	XF	Unc	BU
1997	4,500	—	—	—	—	20.00
1997 Proof	Est. 1,800	Value: 60.00				
1998	2,000	—	—	—	—	25.00
1998 Proof	500	Value: 65.00				

KM# 623   10 PESOS
155.5175 g., 0.9990 Silver 4.9948 oz. ASW, 64 mm. **Subject:** Piramide Del Sol **Obv:** National arms, eagle left within oblong circle and designed border **Rev:**

Pyramid within oblong circle and designed border **Note:** Illustration reduced.

Date	Mintage	F	VF	XF	Unc	BU
1997 Proof	2,100	Value: 165				
1997	1,500	—	—	—	—	85.00
1998 Matte	2,150	—	—	—	—	85.00

KM# 624   25 PESOS
7.7758 g., 0.9990 Gold 0.2497 oz. AGW **Subject:** Serpiente Emplumada **Obv:** National arms, eagle left **Note:** Similar to 100 Pesos, KM#626.

Date	Mintage	F	VF	XF	Unc	BU
1997	500	—	—	—	—	250
1997 Proof	200	Value: 300				

KM# 625   50 PESOS
15.5517 g., 0.9990 Gold 0.4995 oz. AGW **Subject:** Serpiente Emplumada **Obv:** National arms, eagle left **Note:** Similar to 100 Pesos, KM#626.

Date	Mintage	F	VF	XF	Unc	BU
1997 Proof	200	Value: 500				
1997	500	—	—	—	—	475

KM# 626   100 PESOS
31.1035 g., 0.9990 Gold 0.9990 oz. AGW **Subject:** Teotihuacan - Serpiente Emplumada **Obv:** National arms, eagle left

Date	Mintage	F	VF	XF	Unc	BU
1997 Proof	Est. 200	Value: 950				
1997	500	—	—	—	—	925

BULLION COINAGE
PRE-COLUMBIAN •
TOLTECA SERIES

KM# 661   PESO
7.7759 g., 0.9990 Silver 0.2497 oz. ASW, 27 mm. **Subject:** Jaguar **Obv:** National arms, eagle left **Rev:** Jaguar carving **Edge:** Reeded

Date	Mintage	F	VF	XF	Unc	BU
1998	6,000	—	—	—	—	13.50
1998 Proof	4,800	Value: 25.00				

KM# 662   2 PESOS
15.5517 g., 0.9990 Silver 0.4995 oz. ASW, 33 mm. **Subject:** Jaguar **Obv:** National arms, eagle left **Rev:** Jaguar carving **Edge:** Reeded

Date	Mintage	F	VF	XF	Unc	BU
1998	6,000	—	—	—	—	16.50
1998 Proof	4,800	Value: 30.00				

KM# 663   5 PESOS
31.1035 g., 0.9990 Silver 0.9990 oz. ASW, 40 mm. **Subject:** Jaguar **Obv:** National arms, eagle left within shield and designed border **Rev:** Jaguar carving within shield and designed border **Edge:** Reeded

Date	Mintage	F	VF	XF	Unc	BU
1998	6,000	—	—	—	—	20.00
1998 Proof	4,800	Value: 50.00				

KM# 664 5 PESOS
31.1035 g., 0.9990 Silver 0.9990 oz. ASW, 40 mm.
Obv: National arms, eagle left **Rev:** Sacerdote
sculpture **Edge:** Reeded

Date	Mintage	F	VF	XF	Unc	BU
1998	5,000	—	—	—	—	20.00
1998 Proof	4,800	Value: 50.00				

KM# 666 5 PESOS
31.1035 g., 0.9990 Silver 0.9990 oz. ASW, 40 mm.
Subject: Serpiente con Craneo **Obv:** National arms,
eagle left **Rev:** Large sculpture **Edge:** Reeded

Date	Mintage	F	VF	XF	Unc	BU
1998	5,000	—	—	—	—	20.00
1998 Proof	4,800	Value: 50.00				

KM# 665 5 PESOS
31.1035 g., 0.9990 Silver 0.9990 oz. ASW, 40 mm.
Subject: Quetzalcoatl **Obv:** National arms, eagle left
Rev: Quetzalcoatl sculpture **Edge:** Reeded

Date	Mintage	F	VF	XF	Unc	BU
1998	5,000	—	—	—	—	20.00
1998 Proof	4,800	Value: 50.00				

KM# 634 10 PESOS
155.7300 g., 0.9990 Silver 5.0016 oz. ASW
Subject: Atlantes **Obv:** National arms, eagle left
within shield and designed border **Rev:** Three carved
statues within shield and designed border

Date	Mintage	F	VF	XF	Unc	BU
1998	3,500	—	—	—	—	85.00
1998 Proof	4,200	Value: 135				

KM# 667 25 PESOS
7.7759 g., 0.9990 Gold 0.2497 oz. AGW, 23 mm.
Subject: Aguila **Obv:** National arms, eagle left **Rev:**
Eagle sculpture **Edge:** Reeded

Date	Mintage	F	VF	XF	Unc	BU
1998	300	—	—	—	—	250
1998 Proof	300	Value: 300				

KM# 668 50 PESOS
15.5517 g., 0.9990 Gold 0.4995 oz. AGW, 29 mm.
Subject: Aguila **Obv:** National arms, eagle left **Rev:**
Eagle sculpture **Edge:** Reeded

Date	Mintage	F	VF	XF	Unc	BU
1998 Proof	300	Value: 500				
1998	300	—	—	—	—	475

KM# 669 100 PESOS
31.1035 g., 0.9990 Gold 0.9990 oz. AGW, 34.5 mm.
Subject: Aguila **Obv:** National arms, eagle left within
designed shield **Rev:** Eagle sculpture within
designed shield **Edge:** Reeded

Date	Mintage	F	VF	XF	Unc	BU
1998 Proof	300	Value: 950				
1998	300	—	—	—	—	925

MEDALLIC
SILVER BULLION COINAGE

KM# M49a ONZA
33.6250 g., 0.9250 Silver 0.9999 oz. ASW **Obv:**
Mint mark above coin press

Date	Mintage	F	VF	XF	Unc	BU
1949	1,000,000	—	12.00	13.50	17.50	27.50

KM# M49b.1   ONZA
33.6250 g., 0.9250 Silver 0.9999 oz. ASW   **Obv:**
Wide spacing between DE MONEDA **Rev:** Mint mark
below balance scale **Note:** Type I

Date	Mintage	F	VF	XF	Unc	BU
1978Mo	280,000	—	—	BV	11.50	13.50

KM# M49b.2   ONZA
33.6250 g., 0.9250 Silver 0.9999 oz. ASW   **Obv:**
Close spacing between DE MONEDA **Rev:** Mint
mark below balance scale **Note:** Type II

Date	Mintage	F	VF	XF	Unc	BU
1978Mo	Inc. above	—	—	BV	17.50	22.50

KM# M49b.4   ONZA
33.6250 g., 0.9250 Silver 0.9999 oz. ASW   **Obv:**
Close spacing between DE MONEDA **Rev:** Left scale
pan points between U and N of UNA **Note:** Type IV

Date	Mintage	F	VF	XF	Unc	BU
1979Mo	Inc. above	—	—	BV	16.50	20.00

KM# M49b.3   ONZA
33.6250 g., 0.9250 Silver 0.9999 oz. ASW   **Obv:**
Close spacing between DE MONEDA **Rev:** Left scale
pan points to U in UNA **Note:** Type III

Date	Mintage	F	VF	XF	Unc	BU
1979Mo	4,508,000	—	—	BV	16.50	20.00

KM# M49b.5   ONZA
33.6250 g., 0.9250 Silver 0.9999 oz. ASW   **Obv:**
Close spacing between DE MONEDA **Rev:** Left scale
pan points between U and N of UNA **Note:** Type V

Date	Mintage	F	VF	XF	Unc	BU
1980Mo	6,104,000	—	—	BV	16.50	20.00
1980/70Mo	Inc. above	—	—	BV	16.50	25.00

BANK SETS

Hard Case Sets unless otherwise noted.

KM#	Date	Mintage	Identification	Issue Price	Mkt Val
BS1	1972 (6)	—	KM#418, 427, 452, 460, 472, 480	—	30.00
BS2	1973 (5)	—	KM#418, 427 (2), 441, 472	—	20.00
BS3	1974 (7)	—	KM#427, 434.4, 441, 442, 460, 472, 477.1	—	30.00
BS4	1975 (7)	—	KM#427, 434.1, 442, 452, 460 (2), 477.1	—	20.00
BS5	1976 (9)	—	KM#427, 434.1, 442, 452 (2), 460, 472(2), 477.1	—	15.00
BS6	1977 (9)	—	KM#434.1, 434.2, 442, 452, 460 (2), 472, 477.1, 483.1	—	35.00
BS7	1977 (9)	—	KM#434.1, 434.2, 442, 452, 460 (2), 472, 477.1, 483.2 Type II for 3-ring binder	—	—
BS8	1978 (9)	500	KM#434.1, 434.2, 442, 452, 460 (2), 472, 477.2, 483.2, Type I, flat pack	—	35.00
BS9	1978 (9)	—	KM#434.1, 434.2, 442, 452, 460 (2), 472, 477.2, 483.2 Type II for 3-ring binder,	—	15.00
BS10	1979 (9)	—	KM#434.1, 434.4, 442, 452 (2), 460 (2), 477.2, 483.2 Type I flat pack	11.00	25.00
BS11	1979 (8)	—	KM#434.1, 434.2, 442, 452 (2), 460, 477.2, 483.2 Type II for 3-ring binder	11.00	15.00
BS12	1980 (9)	—	KM#434.2, 442, 452 (2), 460 (2), 485, 486, 477.2	4.20	25.00
BS13	1981 (9)	—	KM#442 (2), 452 (2), 460 (2), 477.2, 485, 486	4.20	25.00
BS14	1982 (7)	—	KM#442, 452, 460, 477.2, 485, 486, 490	—	20.00
BS15	1983 (11)	—	KM#442 (2), 452 (2), 460 (2), 490, 491 (2), 492 (2)	—	20.00
BS16	1983 (11)	—	KM#442 (2), 452 (2), 460 (2), 490, 491 (2), 492 (2) 3-ring plastic page	—	12.50
BS17	1984 (8)	—	KM#485, 486, 490, 491, 493, 495 (2), 496,	—	25.00
BS22	1988 (8)	—	KM#493, 495a, 502, 508, 512, 529, 531, 536	—	20.00
BS18	1985 (12)	—	KM#477.2, 485, 493 (2), 495 (2), 496, 502, 508, 509, 510, 512	—	30.00
BS19	1985 (12)	—	KM#477.2, 485, 493 (2), 495 (2), 496, 502, 508, 509, 510, 512 3-ring plastic page	—	20.00
BS20	1986 (7)	—	KM#493, 495, 496, 508, 512, 525, 529 3-ring plastic page	—	20.00
BS21	1987 (9)	—	KM#493, 495 (2), 496, 502 (2), 512, 529 (2)	—	20.00
BS23	1989 (10)	—	KM#493 (3), 508 (3), 512, 529, 536 (2)	—	20.00
BS24	1990 (8)	—	KM#493 (2), 495a, 509 (2), 512, 536 (2)	—	20.00
BS25	1991 (4)	—	KM#493 (2), 536 (2)	—	15.00
BS26	1992 (5)	—	KM#493 (2), 495a, 529, 536	—	15.00
BS27	1992 (8)	—	KM#546-553	—	30.00
BSA28	1992-93 (9)	—	KM#546-553, 561 in heavy wooden case	—	125
BS28	1993 (7)	—	KM#546-552	—	18.00
BS29	1993 (3)	—	KM#553, 561, 571	—	35.00
BS30	1994 (7)	—	KM#546-552	—	18.00
BS31	1994 (3)	—	KM#553, 561, 571	—	35.00
BS32	1995 (9)	—	KM#546-551, 553, 561, 571	—	45.00
BS33	1996 (6)	—	KM#546-549, 603, 604	12.00	30.00
BS34	1997 (8)	—	KM#546-549, 603-605, 616	—	30.00
BS35	1998 (8)	—	KM#546-549, 603-605, 616	—	30.00
BS36	1999 (8)	—	KM#546-549, 603-605, 616	—	35.00
BS37	2000 (7)	—	KM#547-549, 603-605, 636 Set in folder	—	30.00
BS38	2001 (10)	—	KM#546-549, 603-605, 636-638 Set in folder	—	30.00
BS39	2002 (8)	—	KM#546-549, 603-605, 616 Set in folder	—	30.00
BS40	2003 (6)	—	KM#547-549, 603-605 Set in folder	—	30.00

PROOF SETS

KM#	Date	Mintage	Identification	Issue Price	Mkt Val
XPS2	1988Mo (5)	—	X#MB45-MB49	—	300
XPS3	1988Mo (5)	—	X#MB57-MB61	—	—
PS1	1982/1983 (8)	998	KM442, 452, 460, 485, 477.2, 486, 490, 494.1	495	325
PS2	1982/1983 (8)	—	KM460, 477.2, 485, 486, 490, 491, 492, PnB169 (in white box with Mo. in gold)	—	—
PS3	1982/1983 (7)	23	KM460, 477.2, 485, 486, 490, 491, 492 (in white box with Mo in gold)	—	500
PS4	1982/1983 (7)	17	KM460, 477.2, 485, 486, 490, 491, 492 (in white box)	—	500
PS5	1982/1983 (7)	8	KM460, 477.2, 485, 486, 490, 491, 492 (in white box)	—	500
PS6	1983 (7)	3	KM460, 477.2, 485, 486, 490, 491, 492	—	—
PS10	1985 (3)	—	KM503-505 (in blue box)	—	60.00
PS11	1985 (2)	—	KM511, 513	—	350
PS7	1985/1986 (12)	—	KM497a-499a, 503-505, 514-515, 519, 521, 523-524	—	250
PS8	1985 (4)	—	KM500.2-501.2, 506.2, 507.2	—	700
PS9	1985 (3)	—	KM499a, 514, 515 (in blue box)	—	60.00
XPS1	1987Mo (2)	—	X#MB34, 35	—	—
PS12	1989 (3)	704	KM488, 494.1, 538, Rainbow	730	850
PS13	1992 (5)	5,000	KM494.3, 542-545	—	87.50
PS14	1993 (5)	5,000	KM494.4, 542-545	—	87.50
PS15	1994 (5)	5,000	KM494.4, 542-545	—	85.00
PS16	1995 (7)	—	KM546-550, 552, 553, 555	45.00	48.00

UNITED STATES OF MEXICO · SETS

MEXICO-REVOLUTIONARY

AGUASCALIENTES

Aguascalientes is a state in central Mexico. Its coin issues, struck by authority of Pancho Villa, represent his deepest penetration into the Mexican heartland. Lack of silver made it necessary to make all denominations in copper.

FRANCISCO PANCHO VILLA

REVOLUTIONARY COINAGE

KM# 601   CENTAVO
Copper, 17 mm. **Obv:** Liberty cap **Rev:** Value within 3/4 wreath below date **Note:** Large date weight 3.55g.

Date	Mintage	VG	F	VF	XF	Unc
1915	—	30.00	60.00	100	130	—
Note: Small date, plain edge						
1915	—	30.00	60.00	100	200	—
Note: Large date, reeded edge						
1915	—	250	350	450	—	—
Note: Large date, plain edge						
1915	—	30.00	60.00	80.00	120	—
Note: Small date, reeded edge						

KM# 602.1   2 CENTAVOS
4.2800 g., Copper **Obv:** Liberty cap **Rev:** Value within 3/4 wreath below date

Date	Mintage	VG	F	VF	XF	Unc
1915	—	40.00	100	200	350	—
Note: Round front 2, plain edge						

KM# 602.2   2 CENTAVOS
3.3500 g., Copper, 19 mm. **Obv:** Liberty cap **Rev:** Value within 1/2 wreath below date

Date	Mintage	VG	F	VF	XF	Unc
1915	—	35.00	60.00	85.00	200	—
Note: Square front 2, reeded edge						
1915 Plain edge	—	50.00	90.00	200	300	—
Note: Square front 2						

KM# 603   5 CENTAVOS
Copper, 25 mm. **Obv:** National arms **Rev:** Liberty cap and value above sprigs

Date	Mintage	VG	F	VF	XF	Unc
1915 Plain edge; Rare	—	—	—	—	—	—
1915 Reeded edge	—	10.00	20.00	30.00	45.00	—

KM# 604.1   5 CENTAVOS
7.1300 g., Copper, 25 mm. **Obv:** National arms **Rev:** Vertically shaded 5 within sprigs

Date	Mintage	VG	F	VF	XF	Unc
1915	—	20.00	40.00	50.00	100	—
Note: Reeded edge						
1915	—	100	150	225	325	—
Note: Plain edge						

KM# 604.2   5 CENTAVOS
Copper, 25 mm. **Obv:** National arms **Rev:** Horizontally shaded 5 within sprigs

Date	Mintage	VG	F	VF	XF	Unc
1915	—	25.00	40.00	65.00	125	—
Note: Reeded edge						
1915	—	30.00	50.00	80.00	150	—
Note: Plain edge						

KM# 606   20 CENTAVOS
Copper, 29 mm. **Obv:** National arms **Rev:** Value below Liberty cap within sprigs

Date	Mintage	VG	F	VF	XF	Unc
1915 Reeded edge	—	10.00	20.00	50.00	80.00	—

KM# 605   20 CENTAVOS
Copper, 29 mm. **Obv:** National arms **Rev:** Value below Liberty cap within sprigs

Date	Mintage	VG	F	VF	XF	Unc
1915 Reeded edge	—	10.00	20.00	50.00	80.00	—

KM# 600   20 CENTAVOS
Copper **Obv:** National arms **Rev:** Value below Liberty cap within sprigs **Edge:** Reeded

Date	Mintage	VG	F	VF	XF	Unc
1915	—	15.00	20.00	35.00	60.00	—

Note: Varieties exist with both plain and milled edges and many variations in the shading of the numerals

PIEFORTS

KM#	Date	Mintage	Identification	Mkt Val
P1	1915	50	Centavo. Silver. Large date. Prev. KM#601a.	650
P2	1915	—	Centavo. Silver. Small date. Prev. KM#601a.	650
P4	1915	50	5 Centavos. Silver. Prev. KM#604a.	3,500
P5	1915	50	20 Centavos. Silver. Plain edge. Prev. KM#605a.	3,800
P6	1915	—	20 Centavos. Silver. Prev. KM#600a.	3,000
P3	1915	50	2 Centavos. Silver. Prev. KM#602a.	1,200

CHIHUAHUA

Chihuahua is a northern state of Mexico bordering the U.S. It was the arena that introduced Pancho Villa to the world. Villa, an outlaw, was given a title when asked by Madero to participate in maintaining order during Madero's presidency. After Madero's death in February 1913, Villa became a persuasive leader. Chihuahua was where he made his first coins - the Parral series. The *Army of the North* pesos also came from this state. This coin helped Villa recruit soldiers because of his ability to pay in silver while others were paying in worthless paper money.

HIDALGO DEL PARRAL

Fuerzas Constitucionalistas

REVOLUTIONARY COINAGE

KM# 607 2 CENTAVOS
6.8500 g., Copper, 25 mm. **Obv:** Liberty cap within circle flanked by sprigs **Rev:** Value flanked by sprigs within circle

Date	Mintage	VG	F	VF	XF	Unc
1913	—	5.00	10.00	15.00	25.00	—

KM# 607a 2 CENTAVOS
Brass **Obv:** Liberty cap within circle flanked by sprigs **Rev:** Value flanked by sprigs within circle

Date	Mintage	VG	F	VF	XF	Unc
1913	—	95.00	150	200	350	—

KM# 608 50 CENTAVOS

12.6500 g., Silver **Obv:** Liberty cap **Rev:** Value flanked by sprigs below Liberty cap **Edge:** Reeded

Date	Mintage	VG	F	VF	XF	Unc
1913	—	15.00	40.00	60.00	85.00	—

KM# 609 50 CENTAVOS
12.1700 g., Silver, 30 mm. **Edge:** Plain

Date	Mintage	VG	F	VF	XF	Unc
1913	—	50.00	70.00	95.00	125	—

KM# 609a 50 CENTAVOS
Copper **Edge:** Plain

Date	Mintage	VG	F	VF	XF	Unc
1913 rare	—	200	400	525	800	—

KM# 610 PESO
Silver **Obv:** Inscription **Rev:** 1 through PESO and small circle above sprigs **Note:** Weight varies 29.18-30.9g.

Date	Mintage	VG	F	VF	XF	Unc
1913	—	1,200	2,000	3,000	4,000	—

KM# 611 PESO
Silver, 38 mm. **Obv:** Inscription **Rev:** Value above sprigs **Note:** Well struck counterfeits of this coin exist with the dot at the end of the word Peso even with the bottom of the O. On legitimate pieces the dot is slightly higher. Weight varies 27.3-28.85g.

Date	Mintage	VG	F	VF	XF	Unc
1913	—	35.00	40.00	100	200	400

CONSTITUTIONALIST ARMY
Ejercito Constitucionalista

REVOLUTIONARY COINAGE

KM# 612   5 CENTAVOS
Copper **Obv:** Liberty cap **Rev:** Value above date

Date	Mintage	VG	F	VF	XF	Unc
1914	—	25.00	45.00	80.00	125	—

KM# 613   5 CENTAVOS
Copper, 25.36 mm. **Obv:** Liberty cap **Rev:** Value above date **Note:** Numerous varieties exist. Weight varies 6.3-6.93g.

Date	Mintage	VG	F	VF	XF	Unc
1914	—	1.00	2.50	4.00	10.00	—
1915	—	1.00	2.50	4.00	10.00	—

KM# 613a   5 CENTAVOS
Brass **Obv:** Liberty cap **Rev:** Value above date **Note:** Numerous varieties exist.

Date	Mintage	VG	F	VF	XF	Unc
1914	—	2.00	3.00	8.00	10.00	—
1915	—	2.00	3.00	8.00	10.00	—

KM# 613b   5 CENTAVOS
Cast Copper **Obv:** Liberty cap **Rev:** Value above date

Date	Mintage	VG	F	VF	XF	Unc
1914	—	75.00	200	300	400	—

KM# 614a   5 CENTAVOS
Copper **Obv:** National arms **Rev:** Value below date within sprigs with solid V

Date	Mintage	VG	F	VF	XF	Unc
1915 Rare	—	—	—	—	—	—

KM# 614b   5 CENTAVOS
Copper **Obv:** National arms **Rev:** Value above date **Note:** Mule.

Date	Mintage	VG	F	VF	XF	Unc
1915	—	—	350	—	—	—

KM# 614c   5 CENTAVOS
Copper **Obv:** National arms **Rev:** Liberty cap **Note:** Mule.

Date	Mintage	VG	F	VF	XF	Unc
1915 Rare	—	—	—	—	—	—

KM# 614   5 CENTAVOS
Copper **Obv:** National arms **Rev:** Value below date within sprigs with double-lined V

Date	Mintage	VG	F	VF	XF	Unc
1915 SS Unique	—	—	—	—	—	—

KM# 615   10 CENTAVOS
8.7900 g., Copper, 27.5 mm. **Obv:** Liberty cap **Rev:** Value above date

Date	Mintage	VG	F	VF	XF	Unc
1915	—	1.25	2.50	3.50	5.00	—

KM# 615a   10 CENTAVOS
8.8900 g., Brass, 27.5 mm. **Obv:** Liberty cap **Rev:** Value above date

Date	Mintage	VG	F	VF	XF	Unc
1915	—	5.00	10.00	30.00	40.00	—

Note: Many varieties exist

ARMY OF THE NORTH
Ejercito Del Norte

REVOLUTIONARY COINAGE

KM# 619   PESO
29.2700 g., Silver **Obv:** National arms **Rev:** Liberty cap

Date	Mintage	VG	F	VF	XF	Unc
1915	—	20.00	30.00	40.00	150	300

KM# 619a   PESO
Copper **Obv:** National arms **Rev:** Liberty cap

Date	Mintage	VG	F	VF	XF	Unc
1915	—	500	1,000	1,500	2,200	—

KM# 619b   PESO
Brass **Obv:** National arms **Rev:** Liberty cap **Note:** Uniface obverse

Date	Mintage	VG	F	VF	XF	Unc
1915 Rare	—	—	—	—	—	—

PATTERNS
CONSTITUTIONALIST ARMY

KM#	Date	Mintage Identification	Mkt Val

Pn1	1913	— Peso. Silver.	15,000
	1913	— Peso. Silver.	15,000
	1913	— Peso. Silver.	15,000
Pn3	1914	— Peso. Copper.	3,500
Pn2.1	1914	— 50 Centavos. Copper. 12.1800 g. 30 mm. Reeded edge.	3,500
Pn2.2	1914	— 50 Centavos. Copper. Plain edge.	3,000

Note: Specimens exist in silver plated copper

| | 1914 | — 50 Centavos. Copper. Plain edge. | 3,000 |

Note: Specimens exist in silver plated copper

| Pn3 | 1914 | — Peso. Copper. | 3,500 |
| Pn4 | 1914 | — Peso. Silver. | 3,500 |

Note: Silver or silver-plated copper pieces are modern fantasies

| | 1914 | — Peso. Silver. | 3,500 |

Note: Silver or silver-plated copper pieces are modern fantasies

| Pn2.1 | 1914 | — 50 Centavos. Copper. 12.1800 g. 30 mm. Reeded edge. | 3,500 |
| Pn2.2 | 1914 | — 50 Centavos. Copper. Plain edge. | 3,000 |

Note: Specimens exist in silver plated copper

| Pn3 | 1914 | — Peso. Copper. | 3,500 |
| Pn4 | 1914 | — Peso. Silver. | 3,500 |

Note: Silver or silver-plated copper pieces are modern fantasies

| Pn2.1 | 1914 | — 50 Centavos. Copper. 12.1800 g. 30 mm. Reeded edge. | 3,500 |
| Pn5 | 1915 MS | — 5 Centavos. Copper. Prev. KM#614. | 600 |

DURANGO

A state in north central Mexico. Another area of operation for Pancho Villa. The *Muera Huerta* peso originates in this state. The coins were made in Cuencame under the orders of Generals Cemceros and Contreras.

CUENCAME
Muera Huerta (Death to Huerta)

REVOLUTIONARY COINAGE

KM# 620 PESO
Silver **Obv:** National arms **Rev:** Liberty cap with written value flanked by stars

Date	Mintage	VG	F	VF	XF	Unc
1914	—	1,000	2,000	3,000	5,000	—

KM# 621 PESO
23.2000 g., Silver, 39 mm. **Obv:** National arms with continuous border **Rev:** Liberty cap with continuous border

Date	Mintage	VG	F	VF	XF	Unc
1914	—	75.00	125	250	500	800

KM# 621a   PESO
Copper **Obv:** National arms with continuous border
Rev: Liberty cap with continuous border **Note:**
Varieties exist.

Date	Mintage	VG	F	VF	XF	Unc
1914	—	400	600	1,000	2,000	—

KM# 621b   PESO
Brass **Obv:** National arms **Rev:** Liberty cap

Date	Mintage	VG	F	VF	XF	Unc
1914	—	—	1,000	2,000	3,500	—

KM# 622   PESO
23.4000 g., Silver, 38.5 mm. **Obv:** National arms
with dot and dash border **Rev:** Liberty cap with
continuous border **Note:** The so-called 20 Pesos
gold Muera Huerta pieces are modern fantasies.
Refer to Unusual World Coins, 4th edition, ©2005,
KP Books, Inc.

Date	Mintage	VG	F	VF	XF	Unc
1914	—	60.00	100	300	450	800

ESTADO DE DURANGO

REVOLUTIONARY COINAGE

KM# 625   CENTAVO
3.2900 g., Copper, 20 mm. **Obv:** Large date in
center **Rev:** Value within wreath

Date	Mintage	VG	F	VF	XF	Unc
1914	—	2.00	4.00	8.00	12.00	—

KM# 625a   CENTAVO
Brass **Obv:** Large date in center **Rev:** Value within
wreath

Date	Mintage	VG	F	VF	XF	Unc
1914	—	75.00	150	300	400	—

KM# 625b   CENTAVO
Lead **Obv:** Large date in center **Rev:** Value within
wreath

Date	Mintage	VG	F	VF	XF	Unc
1914	—	20.00	40.00	65.00	90.00	—

KM# 625c   CENTAVO
Copper **Obv:** Large date in center **Rev:** Value within
wreath

Date	Mintage	VG	F	VF	XF	Unc
1914	—	25.00	50.00	80.00	125	—

KM# 624   CENTAVO
Cast Lead **Obv:** Date **Rev:** Value within wreath

Date	Mintage	VG	F	VF	XF	Unc
1914	—	45.00	75.00	100	200	—

KM# 626a   CENTAVO
Brass **Obv:** Date **Rev:** Value within wreath

Date	Mintage	VG	F	VF	XF	Unc
1914	—	75.00	100	200	350	—

KM# 626b   CENTAVO
Lead **Obv:** Date **Rev:** Value within wreath

Date	Mintage	VG	F	VF	XF	Unc
1914	—	20.00	25.00	40.00	60.00	—

Note: Varieties in size exist

KM# 627   CENTAVO
Copper, 20 mm. **Obv:** Stars below date **Rev:** Value
with retrograde N

Date	Mintage	VG	F	VF	XF	Unc
1914	—	6.00	10.00	20.00	30.00	—

KM# 627a   CENTAVO
Lead, 20 mm. **Obv:** Stars below date **Rev:** Value
with retrograde N

Date	Mintage	VG	F	VF	XF	Unc
1914	—	20.00	30.00	40.00	50.00	—

KM# 628   CENTAVO
Aluminum **Obv:** National arms within sprigs **Rev:**
Value

Date	Mintage	VG	F	VF	XF	Unc
1914	—	0.65	1.00	2.00	4.00	10.00

KM# 626   CENTAVO
Copper, 20 mm. **Obv:** Date **Rev:** Value within
wreath **Note:** Weight varies 2.46-2.78g.

Date	Mintage	VG	F	VF	XF	Unc
1914	—	15.00	20.00	35.00	45.00	—

KM# 634b   5 CENTAVOS
6.8900 g., Copper-Nickel, 25.53 mm. **Obv:** National
arms above sprigs **Obv. Legend:** REPUBLICA
MEXICANA **Rev:** Value **Rev. Legend:** ESTADO DE
DURANGO **Edge:** Plain

Date	Mintage	F	VF	XF	Unc	BU
1914	—	25.00	50.00	85.00	135	175

KM# 629   5 CENTAVOS
6.2000 g., Copper, 24 mm. **Obv:** Date above sprigs
Obv. Legend: ESTADO DE DURANGO **Rev:** Value
within designed wreath

Date	Mintage	VG	F	VF	XF	Unc
1914	—	2.00	3.00	6.00	12.00	—

KM# 630   5 CENTAVOS

Copper **Obv:** Date above sprigs **Obv. Legend:** E. DE DURANGO **Rev:** Value within designed wreath

Date	Mintage	VG	F	VF	XF	Unc
1914	—	125	275	375	600	—

KM# 631   5 CENTAVOS

5.0500 g., Copper, 23.5 mm. **Obv:** Date above sprigs **Obv. Legend:** E. DE DURANGO **Rev:** Value within designed wreath

Date	Mintage	VG	F	VF	XF	Unc
1914	—	1.25	3.00	6.00	15.00	—

KM# 631a   5 CENTAVOS

Brass **Obv:** Date above sprigs **Obv. Legend:** E. DE DURANGO **Rev:** Value within designed wreath

Date	Mintage	VG	F	VF	XF	Unc
1914	—	30.00	40.00	50.00	85.00	—

KM# 631b   5 CENTAVOS

Lead **Obv:** Date above sprigs **Obv. Legend:** E. DE DURANGO **Rev:** Value within designed wreath

Date	Mintage	VG	F	VF	XF	Unc
1914	—	45.00	70.00	100	180	—

KM# 632   5 CENTAVOS

4.6100 g., Copper, 23.5 mm. **Obv:** Date above sprigs **Obv. Legend:** E. DE DURANGO **Rev:** Roman numeral value

Date	Mintage	VG	F	VF	XF	Unc
1914	—	4.00	8.00	15.00	35.00	—

KM# 632a   5 CENTAVOS

Lead **Obv:** Date above sprigs **Obv. Legend:** E. DE DURANGO **Rev:** Roman numeral value

Date	Mintage	VG	F	VF	XF	Unc
1914	—	50.00	75.00	100	150	—

KM# 634   5 CENTAVOS

Brass **Obv:** National arms above sprigs **Obv. Legend:** REPUBLICA MEXICANA **Rev:** Value **Rev. Legend:** ESTADO DE DURANGO

Date	Mintage	VG	F	VF	XF	Unc
1914	—	0.50	1.00	2.50	5.00	—

KM# 633   5 CENTAVOS

Lead **Obv:** Three stars below 1914 **Rev:** 5 CVS **Note:** Counterfeits are prevalent in the market

Date	Mintage	VG	F	VF	XF	Unc
1914	—	—	600	2,000	—	—

KM# 634a   5 CENTAVOS

Copper **Obv:** National arms above sprigs **Obv. Legend:** REPUBLICA MEXICANA **Rev:** Value **Rev. Legend:** ESTADO DE DURANGO **Note:** There are numerous varieties of these general types of the Durango 1 and 5 Centavo pieces.

Date	Mintage	VG	F	VF	XF	Unc
1914	—	75.00	125	175	250	—

GUERRERO

Guerrero is a state on the southwestern coast of Mexico. It was one of the areas of operation of Zapata and his forces in the south of Mexico. The Zapata forces operated seven different mints in this state. The date ranges were from 1914 to 1917 and denominations from 2 Centavos to 2 Pesos. Some were cast but most were struck and the rarest coin of the group is the Suriana 1915 2 Pesos.

EMILIANO ZAPATA
(General Salgado)

REVOLUTIONARY COINAGE

KM# 638   2 CENTAVOS

Copper, 22 mm. **Obv:** National arms **Rev:** Value within wreath **Note:** Weight varies 5.4-6.03g.

Date	Mintage	VG	F	VF	XF	Unc
1915	—	75.00	125	175	250	—

KM# 635   3 CENTAVOS

Copper, 25 mm. **Obv:** National arms **Rev:** Value within wreath **Note:** Weight varies 4.63-6.87g.

Date	Mintage	VG	F	VF	XF	Unc
1915	—	500	1,500	2,000	3,000	—

KM# 636   5 CENTAVOS

Copper, 26 mm. **Obv:** National arms **Rev:** Value within wreath

Date	Mintage	VG	F	VF	XF	Unc
1915GRO	—	800	1,200	2,000	3,000	—

KM# 637.1   10 CENTAVOS

Copper, 27-28.5 mm. **Obv:** National arms **Rev:** Date and value within wreath **Note:** Size varies.

Date	Mintage	VG	F	VF	XF	Unc
1915GRO	—	600	1,000	1,500	2,000	—

KM# 637.2   10 CENTAVOS
Copper, 27-28.5 mm.   **Obv:** National arms **Rev:** Value within wreath **Note:** Size varies.

Date	Mintage	VG	F	VF	XF	Unc
1915GRO	—	3.00	5.00	8.00	15.00	—

KM# 637.2a   10 CENTAVOS
8.2300 g., Brass, 26 mm.   **Obv:** Snake head ends at C in REPUBLICA **Rev:** Value within wreath

Date	Mintage	VG	F	VF	XF	Unc
1915GRO	—	8.00	15.00	25.00	50.00	—

KM# 637.2b   10 CENTAVOS
Lead   **Obv:** Snake head ends at C in REPUBLICA **Rev:** Value within wreath

Date	Mintage	VG	F	VF	XF	Unc
1915GRO	—	50.00	75.00	175	275	—

KM# 637.3   10 CENTAVOS
Copper   **Obv:** National arms **Rev:** Date and value within wreath

Date	Mintage	VG	F	VF	XF	Unc
1915GRO	—	3.00	5.00	8.00	15.00	—

KM# 637.3a   10 CENTAVOS
Brass   **Obv:** Snake head ends before A in REPUBLICA **Rev:** Value and date within wreath with dot after date

Date	Mintage	VG	F	VF	XF	Unc
1915GRO	—	12.00	20.00	50.00	100	—

KM# 639   25 CENTAVOS
Silver, 25 mm.   **Obv:** Liberty cap **Rev:** Value above date **Note:** Weight varies 7.41-7.5g.

Date	Mintage	VG	F	VF	XF	Unc
1915	—	125	300	500	900	—

KM# 640   50 CENTAVOS
Silver, 34 mm.   **Obv:** Liberty cap **Rev:** Date and value within beaded border **Note:** Weight varies 14.5-14.8g.

Date	Mintage	VG	F	VF	XF	Unc
1915	—	1,000	2,000	3,500	5,000	—

KM# 641a   PESO (UN)
Copper   **Obv:** National arms **Rev:** Liberty cap within sprigs

Date	Mintage	Good	VG	F	VF	XF
1914	—	—	100	200	300	1,500

KM# 641   PESO (UN)
Gold-Silver, 29-31 mm.   **Obv:** National arms **Rev:** Liberty cap within sprigs **Rev. Inscription:** Oro:0,300 **Note:** Many die varieties exist. Size varies. Weight varies 10.28-14.84g. Coin is 0.30g fine Gold.

Date	Mintage	VG	F	VF	XF	Unc
1914	—	15.00	25.00	35.00	65.00	—

KM# 642   PESO (UN)
Gold-Silver, 30.5-31 mm.   **Obv:** National arms **Rev:** Liberty cap within sprigs **Rev. Inscription:** Oro:0,300 **Note:** Weight varies 12.93-14.66g. Coin is 0.300g fine Gold.

Date	Mintage	VG	F	VF	XF	Unc
1914	—	50.00	75.00	100	150	—
1915	—	600	1,000	1,500	1,800	—

KM# 643   2 PESOS (Dos)
Gold-Silver, 38.25-39.6 mm.   **Obv:** National arms **Rev:** Radiant sun face above mountains **Rev. Inscription:** Oro:0,595 **Note:** Many varieties exist. Coin is 0.595g fine Gold.

Date	Mintage	VG	F	VF	XF	Unc
1914GRO	—	12.00	30.00	40.00	80.00	—

KM# 643a 2 PESOS (Dos)
Copper, 38-38.5 mm. **Obv:** National arms **Rev:**
Radiant sun face above mountains **Note:** Size varies.

Date	Mintage	Good	VG	F	VF	XF
1914	—	—	—	1,200	1,400	2,000

KM# 644a 2 PESOS (Dos)
Copper **Obv:** National arms **Rev:** Radiant sun and
mountains

Date	Mintage	VG	F	VF	XF	Unc
1915GRO	—	400	1,000	1,200	1,800	—

KM# 644 2 PESOS (Dos)
Gold-Silver, 39-40 mm. **Obv:** National arms **Rev:**
Radiant sun and mountains **Rev. Inscription:**
Oro:0,595 **Note:** Weight varies 21.71-26.54g. Coin
is 0.595g fine Gold.

Date	Mintage	VG	F	VF	XF	Unc
1915GRO	—	65.00	85.00	160	200	—

ATLIXTAC

REVOLUTIONARY COINAGE

KM# 645 10 CENTAVOS
Copper, 27.5-28 mm. **Obv:** National arms **Rev:**
Value within sprigs **Note:** Size varies. Weight varies
4.76-9.74g.

Date	Mintage	VG	F	VF	XF	Unc
1915	—	3.00	5.00	8.00	15.00	—

KM# 646 10 CENTAVOS
Copper, 27.55-28 mm. **Obv:** National arms **Rev:**
Value within sprigs **Note:** Size varies. Weight varies
6.13-7.94g.

Date	Mintage	VG	F	VF	XF	Unc
1915	—	3.00	5.00	8.00	15.00	—

CACAHUATEPEC

REVOLUTIONARY COINAGE

KM# 648 5 CENTAVOS
12.1900 g., Copper, 28 mm. **Obv:** National arms
Rev: Value within wreath

Date	Mintage	VG	F	VF	XF	Unc
1917	—	12.00	25.00	40.00	75.00	—

KM# 649 20 CENTAVOS
Silver, 21-23.8 mm. **Obv:** National arms **Rev:** Value
within sprigs below liberty cap **Note:** Size varies.
Weight varies 3.99-6.2g.

Date	Mintage	VG	F	VF	XF	Unc
1917	—	100	200	350	400	—

KM# 650 50 CENTAVOS
Silver, 30-30.3 mm. **Obv:** National arms **Rev:** Value
and date within sprigs below Liberty cap **Note:** Size
varies. Weight varies 13.45-13.78g.

Date	Mintage	VG	F	VF	XF	Unc
1917	—	10.00	30.00	45.00	90.00	—

KM# 651 PESO (UN)
Silver, 38 mm. **Obv:** National arms **Rev:** Liberty cap
Note: Weight varies 26.81-32.05g.

Date	Mintage	VG	F	VF	XF	Unc
1917 L.V. Go	—	2,000	4,000	6,000	8,000	—

CACALOTEPEC

REVOLUTIONARY COINAGE

KM# 652 20 CENTAVOS
Silver, 22.5 mm. **Obv:** National arms **Rev:** Date and

value within sprigs below Liberty cap **Note:** Weight varies 3.89-5.73g.

Date	Mintage	VG	F	VF	XF	Unc
1917	—	1,000	1,800	3,000	4,000	—

CHILPANCINGO

REVOLUTIONARY COINAGE

KM# 663   10 CENTAVOS
2.5200 g., Cast Silver, 18 mm. **Obv:** National arms **Rev:** Sun above value and sprigs

Date	Mintage	VG	F	VF	XF	Unc
1914	—	700	1,000	1,200	1,500	—

Note: Many counterfeits exist

KM# 664   20 CENTAVOS
4.9400 g., Cast Silver, 21.5 mm. **Obv:** National arms **Rev:** Sun above value and sprigs

Date	Mintage	VG	F	VF	XF	Unc
1914	—	700	1,000	1,200	1,500	—

Note: Many counterfeits exist

CAMPO MORADO

REVOLUTIONARY COINAGE

KM# 653   5 CENTAVOS
4.3700 g., Copper, 23.5-24 mm. **Obv:** National arms **Rev:** Value within wreath **Note:** Size varies.

Date	Mintage	VG	F	VF	XF	Unc
1915 C.M.	—	9.00	15.00	22.50	35.00	—

KM# 654   10 CENTAVOS
Copper, 25.25-26 mm. **Obv:** National arms **Rev:**

Value and date within wreath **Note:** Size varies. Weight varies. 4.48-8.77g.

Date	Mintage	VG	F	VF	XF	Unc
1915 C.M. GRO	—	6.00	10.00	20.00	30.00	—

KM# 655   20 CENTAVOS
Copper, 28 mm. **Obv:** National arms **Rev:** Date above star and value within wreath **Note:** Weight varies 4.48-9g.

Date	Mintage	VG	F	VF	XF	Unc
1915 C.M. GRO	—	15.00	25.00	35.00	50.00	—

KM# 657a   50 CENTAVOS
Base Silver **Obv:** National arms **Rev:** Date and value within wreath **Note:** Regular obverse.

Date	Mintage	VG	F	VF	XF	Unc
1915 C.M. GRO	—	200	300	500	1,000	—

KM# 657   50 CENTAVOS
Copper, 30-31 mm. **Obv:** National arms **Rev:** Date and value within wreath **Note:** Regular obverse. Size varies. Weight varies 6.49-13.19g.

Date	Mintage	VG	F	VF	XF	Unc
1915 C.M. GRO	—	6.00	10.00	15.00	25.00	—

KM# 656   50 CENTAVOS
Copper, 29-31 mm. **Obv:** National arms **Rev:** Date and value within wreath **Note:** Size varies. Weight varies 9.81-16.77g.

Date	Mintage	VG	F	VF	XF	Unc
1915 C.M. GRO	—	12.00	20.00	30.00	60.00	—

KM# 658a   PESO (UN)
Brass **Obv:** National arms **Rev:** Liberty cap

Date	Mintage	VG	F	VF	XF	Unc
1914 Co Mo Gro Unique	—	—	—	—	—	—

KM# 659   PESO (UN)
Gold-Silver, 30-31 mm. **Obv:** National arms **Rev:** Liberty cap within sprigs **Rev. Inscription:** Oro:0,300 **Note:** Weight varies 12.26-15.81g. Coin is 0.300g fine Gold.

Date	Mintage	VG	F	VF	XF	Unc
1914 CAMPO Mo	—	15.00	30.00	45.00	60.00	—

KM# 658 PESO (UN)
Gold-Silver, 32-32.5 mm. **Obv:** National arms **Rev:**
Liberty cap **Rev. Inscription:** Oro:0,300 **Note:**
Weight varies 12.42-16.5g. Coin is 0.300g fine Gold.

Date	Mintage	VG	F	VF	XF	Unc
1914 Co Mo Gro	—	500	600	1,000	1,200	—

KM# 660a 2 PESOS (Dos)
Copper **Obv:** National arms **Rev:** Sun over
mountains

Date	Mintage	VG	F	VF	XF	Unc
1915 Co. Mo.	—	—	800	1,000	1,200	—

KM# 662a.1 2 PESOS (Dos)
Copper **Obv:** National arms **Rev:** Liberty cap

Date	Mintage	VG	F	VF	XF	Unc
1915 C. M. GRO	—	—	—	—	1,200	—

KM# 662a.2 2 PESOS (Dos)
Copper **Obv:** National arms **Rev:** Liberty cap

Date	Mintage	VG	F	VF	XF	Unc
1915 C. M. GRO Unique	—	—	—	—	—	—

KM# 661 2 PESOS (Dos)
29.4400 g., Gold-Silver, 39 mm. **Obv:** National arms
Rev: Sun and mountains **Rev. Inscription:**
Oro:0,595 **Note:** Coin is 0.595g fine Gold.

Date	Mintage	VG	F	VF	XF	Unc
1915 Co. Mo.	—	2,000	4,000	8,000	10,000	—

KM# 662 2 PESOS (Dos)
0.5950 g., 1.0000 Gold-Silver 0.0191 oz., 34.5-
35 mm. **Obv:** National arms **Rev:** Liberty cap **Note:**
Size varies. Weight varies 18.27-20.08g.

Date	Mintage	VG	F	VF	XF	Unc
1915 C. M. GRO	—	20.00	30.00	45.00	85.00	—

KM# 660 2 PESOS (Dos)
Gold-Silver, 38.9-39 mm. **Obv:** National arms **Rev:**
Sun over mountains **Rev. Inscription:** Oro:0,595
Note: Weight varies 20.6-26.02g. Coin is 0.595g fine
Gold.

Date	Mintage	VG	F	VF	XF	Unc
1915 Co. Mo.	—	12.00	20.00	30.00	50.00	—

TAXCO

REVOLUTIONARY COINAGE

KM# 667 2 CENTAVOS
Copper, 25.25-26 mm. **Obv:** National arms **Obv.
Legend:** EDO.DE.GRO **Rev:** Value within sprigs
Note: Size varies. Weight varies 6.81-8.55g.

Date	Mintage	VG	F	VF	XF	Unc
1915 O/T	—	25.00	40.00	60.00	90.00	—

KM# 668 5 CENTAVOS
Copper **Obv:** National arms **Rev:** Value within sprigs
Note: Weight varies 7.13-7.39g.

Date	Mintage	VG	F	VF	XF	Unc
1915	—	10.00	20.00	30.00	50.00	—

KM# 669   10 CENTAVOS
Copper, 27-28 mm. **Obv:** National arms **Rev:** Date and value within sprigs **Note:** Size varies. Weight varies 7.51-8.67g.

Date	Mintage	VG	F	VF	XF	Unc
1915	—	9.00	20.00	35.00	50.00	—

KM# 670   50 CENTAVOS
5.4500 g., Copper, 27-28 mm. **Obv:** National arms with legend in large letters **Rev:** Value within sprigs **Note:** Size varies.

Date	Mintage	VG	F	VF	XF	Unc
1915	—	15.00	25.00	50.00	65.00	—

KM# 671   50 CENTAVOS
Silver, 27.6-28 mm. **Obv:** National arms **Rev:** Sun above value and sprigs **Note:** Size varies. Weight varies 8.95-10.85g.

Date	Mintage	VG	F	VF	XF	Unc
1915	—	25.00	40.00	60.00	100	—

KM# 672a   PESO (UN)
Brass **Obv:** National arms **Rev:** Liberty cap within sprigs

Date	Mintage	VG	F	VF	XF	Unc
1915	—	200	300	450	600	—

KM# 672b   PESO (UN)
Lead **Obv:** National arms **Rev:** Liberty cap within sprigs

Date	Mintage	VG	F	VF	XF	Unc
1915	—	50.00	100	200	350	—

KM# 672c   PESO (UN)
Copper **Obv:** National arms **Rev:** Liberty cap within sprigs

Date	Mintage	VG	F	VF	XF	Unc
1915	—	200	300	400	650	—

KM# 673   PESO (UN)
11.6000 g., Gold-Silver, 30 mm. **Obv:** National arms **Rev:** Liberty cap within sprigs **Rev. Inscription:** Oro:0,300 **Note:** Coin is 0.300g fine Gold.

Date	Mintage	VG	F	VF	XF	Unc
1915	—	250	400	500	800	—

KM# 674   PESO (UN)
Gold-Silver, 30 mm. **Obv:** National arms **Rev:** Liberty cap within sprigs **Rev. Inscription:** Oro:0,300 **Note:** Weight varies 10.51-12.79g. Coin is 0.300g fine Gold.

Date	Mintage	VG	F	VF	XF	Unc
1915	—	100	200	300	500	—

KM# 672   PESO (UN)
Gold-Silver, 30-31 mm. **Obv:** National arms **Rev:** Liberty cap within sprigs **Rev. Inscription:** Oro:0,300 **Note:** Weight varies 30-31g. Coin is 0.300g fine Gold.

Date	Mintage	VG	F	VF	XF	Unc
1915	—	12.00	20.00	30.00	45.00	—

SURIANA

REVOLUTIONARY COINAGE

KM# 665   2 PESOS (Dos)
22.9300 g., Gold-Silver, 39 mm. **Obv:** National arms **Rev:** Sun over mountains **Rev. Inscription:** Oro:0,595 **Note:** Coin is 0.595g fine Gold.

Date	Mintage	VG	F	VF	XF	Unc
1915 Rare	—	—	—	20,000	28,000	—

Note: Spink America Gerber sale part 2, 6-96 VF realized $16,500

PATTERNS
Includng Off Metal Strikes

KM#	Date	Mintage	Identification	Mkt Val
Pn674	1914	—	2 Pesos. 1.0000 Gold-Silver.	—
	1914	—	2 Pesos. 1.0000 Gold-Silver.	—
Pn647	1914	—	2 Pesos. Gold-Silver. 0.3000 g. Atlixtac.	—
	1914	—	2 Pesos. Gold-Silver. 0.3000 g. Atlixtac.	—
	1914	—	2 Pesos. Gold-Silver. 0.3000 g. Atlixtac.	—
Pn674	1914	—	2 Pesos. 1.0000 Gold-Silver.	—
Pn647	1914	—	2 Pesos. Gold-Silver. 0.3000 g. Atlixtac.	—

JALISCO

Jalisco is a state on the west coast of Mexico. The few coins made for this state show that the *Army of the North* did not restrict their operations to the northern border states. The coins were made in Guadalajara under the watchful eye of General Dieguez, commander of this segment of Villa's forces.

GUADALAJARA

REVOLUTIONARY COINAGE

KM# 675   CENTAVO
Copper   Obv: Liberty cap Rev: Value

Date	Mintage	VG	F	VF	XF	Unc
1915	—	9.50	15.00	20.00	30.00	—

KM# 675a   CENTAVO
Brass   Obv: Liberty cap Rev: Value

Date	Mintage	VG	F	VF	XF	Unc
1915	—	—	—	300	450	—

KM# A676   CENTAVO
Copper   Obv: Liberty cap Rev: Retrograde value
Note: Varieties exist.

Date	Mintage	VG	F	VF	XF	Unc
1915	—	100	300	600	1,000	—

KM# 676.1   2 CENTAVOS
Copper, 20 mm.   Obv: Liberty cap Rev: Value

Date	Mintage	VG	F	VF	XF	Unc
1915	—	10.00	18.00	20.00	35.00	—

Note: Varieties exist.

KM# 676.2   2 CENTAVOS
Copper   Obv: Liberty cap Rev: Value

Date	Mintage	VG	F	VF	XF	Unc
1915	—	200	300	500	800	—

KM# 677   5 CENTAVOS
Copper, 24 mm.   Obv: Liberty cap Rev: Value

Date	Mintage	VG	F	VF	XF	Unc
1915	—	6.50	12.00	15.00	25.00	—

KM# 677a   5 CENTAVOS
Brass   Obv: Liberty cap Rev: Value

Date	Mintage	VG	F	VF	XF	Unc
1915 rare	—	—	—	—	—	—

KM# 678   10 CENTAVOS
Copper Obv: Liberty cap above value and date Rev: Crowned shield

Date	Mintage	VG	F	VF	XF	Unc
1915	—	—	—	3,000	5,000	—

KM# A678   PESO
Copper Obv: Liberty cap above value and date Rev: Crowned shield

Date	Mintage	VG	F	VF	XF	Unc
1915	—	—	—	17,000		—

MEXICO, ESTADO DE

Estado de Mexico is a state in central Mexico that surrounds the Federal District on three sides. The issues by the Zapata forces in this state have two distinctions – the Amecameca pieces are the crudest and the Toluca cardboard piece is the most unusual. General Tenorio authorized the crude incuse Amecameca pieces.

TENANCINGO, TOWN
(Distrito Federal Mexico)

REVOLUTIONARY COINAGE

KM# 688.1   2 CENTAVOS
Copper   Obv: National arms Rev: Value within wreath without TM below value

Date	Mintage	VG	F	VF	XF	Unc
1915	—	—	—	800	2,000	—

KM# 688.2 2 CENTAVOS
Copper **Obv:** National arms **Rev:** Value within
wreath with TM below value

Date	Mintage	VG	F	VF	XF	Unc
1915	—	—	400	800	2,000	—

KM# 689.1 5 CENTAVOS
Copper, 19 mm. **Obv:** National arms **Rev:** Numeral
value over lined C within wreath **Note:** Weight varies
2.83-2.84g.

Date	Mintage	VG	F	VF	XF	Unc
1915	—	10.00	20.00	30.00	50.00	—

KM# 689.2 5 CENTAVOS
Copper, 19 mm. **Obv:** National arms **Rev:** Numeral
value over lined C within wreath **Note:** Weight varies
2.83-2.84g.

Date	Mintage	VG	F	VF	XF	Unc
1915	—	100	300	500	800	—

KM# 690.1 10 CENTAVOS
Copper, 25.25 mm. **Obv:** National arms **Rev:** Value
over lined C within wreath below date **Note:** Weight
varies 4.27-5.64g.

Date	Mintage	VG	F	VF	XF	Unc
1916	—	10.00	20.00	40.00	60.00	—

KM# 690.2 10 CENTAVOS
Copper, 25.25 mm. **Obv:** National arms **Rev:** Value
over lined C within wreath **Note:** Weight varies 4.27-
5.64g.

Date	Mintage	VG	F	VF	XF	Unc
1916	—	100	200	400	500	—

KM# 691 20 CENTAVOS
Copper, 27.5-28 mm. **Obv:** National arms **Rev:**
Value and date above sprigs **Note:** Size varies.
Weight varies 8.51-11.39g.

Date	Mintage	VG	F	VF	XF	Unc
1915	—	25.00	40.00	55.00	75.00	—

TOLUCA, CITY
(Distrito Federal Mexico)

REVOLUTIONARY COINAGE

KM# 692.1 5 CENTAVOS
Grey Cardboard, 27-28 mm. **Obv:** Crowned shield
within sprigs **Rev:** Banner accross large numeral
value **Note:** Size varies. Weight varies 1.04-1.16g.

Date	Mintage	VG	F	VF	XF	Unc
1915	—	15.00	30.00	50.00	75.00	—

KM# 692.2 5 CENTAVOS
Grey Cardboard, 27-28 mm. **Obv:** Crowned shield
within sprigs **Rev:** Banner accross large numeral
value **Note:** Size varies. Weight varies 1.04-1.16g.

Date	Mintage	VG	F	VF	XF	Unc
1915	—	15.00	30.00	50.00	75.00	—

COUNTERMARKED COINAGE

KM# 693.1 20 CENTAVOS
Copper, 20 mm. **Countermark:** 20 within C **Obv:**
National arms **Rev:** Numeral 20 within C and inner
circle within sprigs **Note:** Countermark on 1 Centavo,
KM#415. Varieties exist. Weight varies 2.65-2.95g.

CM Date	Host Date	Good	VG	F	VF	XF
ND(1915)	ND	—	20.00	40.00	55.00	80.00

KM# 693.2 20 CENTAVOS
Copper, 20 mm. **Countermark:** 20 within C **Obv:**
National arms **Rev:** Numeral 20 within C and inner
circle within 3/4 wreath **Note:** Countermark on 1
Centavo, KM#394.1. Weight varies 2.65-2.95g.

CM Date	Host Date	Good	VG	F	VF	XF
ND(1915)	1904	—	30.00	50.00	90.00	150

KM# 694 40 CENTAVOS
5.8600 g., Copper, 24.75-25 mm. **Countermark:**
40 within C **Obv:** National arms **Rev:** Numeral 40
within C and inner circle within wreath **Note:**
Countermark on 2 Centavos, KM#419. Varieties
exist. Size varies.

CM Date	Host Date	Good	VG	F	VF	XF
ND(1915)	ND	—	25.00	40.00	60.00	80.00

AMECAMECA

REVOLUTIONARY COINAGE

KM# 679 5 CENTAVOS
12.5500 g., Brass, 24.5 mm. **Obv:** Legend **Obv.**
Legend: EJERCITO CONVENCIONISTA **Rev:**
Value above cent sign

Date	Mintage	VG	F	VF	XF	Unc
ND unique	—	—	—	—	—	—

KM# 680 5 CENTAVOS
12.7700 g., Brass, 24.6 mm. **Obv:** National arms
above RM **Rev:** Value above cent sign **Note:** Hand
stamped.

Date	Mintage	VG	F	VF	XF	Unc
ND	—	300	400	600	800	—

KM# 681a 10 CENTAVOS
Copper **Obv:** National arms above RM **Rev:** Value
above cent sign **Note:** Hand stamped.

Date	Mintage	VG	F	VF	XF	Unc
ND	—	75.00	125	225	350	—

KM# 681 10 CENTAVOS
15.0000 g., Brass, 24.5-24.8 mm. **Obv:** National
arms above RM **Rev:** Value above cent sign **Note:**
Hand stamped. Varieties exist. Size varies.

Date	Mintage	VG	F	VF	XF	Unc
ND	—	60.00	90.00	150	200	—

KM# 682 20 CENTAVOS
Brass, 24-25 mm. **Obv:** National arms above RM
Rev: Value above cent sign **Note:** Hand stamped.
Varieties exist. Size varies. Weight varies 11.34-
12.86g.

Date	Mintage	VG	F	VF	XF	Unc
ND	—	15.00	22.50	35.00	60.00	—

KM# 682a 20 CENTAVOS
Copper **Obv:** National arms above RM **Rev:** Value
above cent sign **Note:** Hand stamped.

Date	Mintage	VG	F	VF	XF	Unc
ND	—	25.00	50.00	175	250	—

KM# 683 20 CENTAVOS
Copper, 19-20 mm. **Obv:** National arms above A.
D. J. **Rev:** Value **Note:** Size varies. Weight varies
3.99-5.35g.

Date	Mintage	VG	F	VF	XF	Unc
ND	—	7.50	12.50	20.00	35.00	—

KM# 683a 20 CENTAVOS
Brass **Obv:** National arms above A. D. J. **Rev:** Value

Date	Mintage	VG	F	VF	XF	Unc
ND	—	—	—	300	500	—

KM# 684 25 CENTAVOS
Brass **Obv:** Legend **Obv. Legend:** EJERCITO
CONVENCIONISTA **Rev:** Value above cent sign

Date	Mintage	VG	F	VF	XF	Unc
ND unique	—	—	—	—	—	—

KM# 685   25 CENTAVOS
Copper, 25 mm. **Obv:** National arms above sprigs
Rev: Large numeral value **Note:** Hand stamped.
Many modern counterfeits exist in all metals. Weight
varies 6.32-6.99g.

Date	Mintage	VG	F	VF	XF	Unc
ND	—	15.00	20.00	30.00	40.00	—

KM# 685a   25 CENTAVOS
7.9200 g., Brass, 25 mm. **Obv:** National arms above
sprigs **Rev:** Large numeral value **Note:** Hand
stamped.

Date	Mintage	VG	F	VF	XF	Unc
ND	—	—	—	100	300	—

KM# 685b   25 CENTAVOS
Silver **Obv:** National arms above sprigs **Rev:** Large
numeral value **Note:** Hand stamped.

Date	Mintage	VG	F	VF	XF	Unc
ND	—	—	—	250	400	—

KM# 687   50 CENTAVOS
Copper, 23.5-29 mm.   **Obv:** National arms above
sprigs **Rev:** Large numeral value **Note:**
Contemporary counterfeit, hand engraved. Size
varies. Weight varies 8.8-10.8g.

Date	Mintage	VG	F	VF	XF	Unc
ND	—	12.00	30.00	50.00	80.00	—

Note: "¢" clears top of 5

KM# 686a   50 CENTAVOS
16.0400 g., Brass, 28.5 mm. **Obv:** National arms
above sprigs **Rev:** Large numeral value **Note:** Hand
stamped.

Date	Mintage	VG	F	VF	XF	Unc
ND	—	100	200	300	400	—

Note: Stem of "¢" above the 5

MORELOS

Morelos is a state in south central Mexico,
adjoining the federal district on the south. It was
the headquarters of Emiliano Zapata. His personal
quarters were at Tlatizapan in Morelos. The Morelos coins from 2 Centavos to 1 Peso were all copper except one type of 1 Peso in silver. The two
operating Zapatista mints in Morelos were Atlihua-
yan and Tlaltizapan.

EMILIANO ZAPATA
(Zapatista)

REVOLUTIONARY COINAGE

KM# 695   2 CENTAVOS
Copper, 23 mm. **Obv:** National arms **Obv. Legend:**
E.L. DE MORELOS **Rev:** Value within wreath

Date	Mintage	VG	F	VF	XF	Unc
1915	—	1,000	1,400	1,800	2,250	—

KM# 696   5 CENTAVOS
9.0000 g., Copper, 25.9 mm. **Obv:** National arms
Rev: Value within 3/4 wreath **Rev. Legend:** E. DE
MOR. 1915

Date	Mintage	VG	F	VF	XF	Unc
1915	—	300	500	1,000	3,500	—

KM# 697   10 CENTAVOS
8.6900 g., Copper, 24 mm. **Obv:** National arms
Rev: Value within lined C and wreath

Date	Mintage	VG	F	VF	XF	Unc
1915	—	12.00	20.00	30.00	40.00	—

KM# 699   10 CENTAVOS
Copper **Obv:** National arms **Rev:** Date and value
within wreath **Rev. Legend:** E. DE MOR

Date	Mintage	VG	F	VF	XF	Unc
1915	—	1,000	2,000	2,500	3,000	—

KM# 698   10 CENTAVOS
Copper, 24-24.5 mm. **Obv:** National arms **Rev:**
Value within lined C and wreath with date effaced
from die **Note:** Size varies. Weight varies 4.83-6.8g.

Date	Mintage	VG	F	VF	XF	Unc
ND	—	12.00	20.00	35.00	55.00	—

KM# 700   10 CENTAVOS
Copper, 28 mm. **Obv:** National arms **Rev:** Date and
value within wreath **Rev. Legend:** MOR **Note:**
Weight varies 5.56-8.36g.

Date	Mintage	VG	F	VF	XF	Unc
1916	—	5.00	20.00	30.00	50.00	—

KM# 701   20 CENTAVOS
Copper, 23.75-24.75 mm. **Obv:** National arms **Rev:**
Value within lined C and 3/4 wreath **Note:** Size varies.
Weight varies 3.88-4.15g.

Date	Mintage	VG	F	VF	XF	Unc
1915	—	9.00	15.00	25.00	35.00	—

KM# 702   50 CENTAVOS
Copper, 28.8 mm. **Obv:** National arms with MOR
beneath eagle **Rev:** 50C monogram

Date	Mintage	VG	F	VF	XF	Unc
1915	—	300	500	900	1,300	—

KM# 703a   50 CENTAVOS
Brass   **Obv:** National arms above sprigs **Rev:** 50C
monogram

Date	Mintage	VG	F	VF	XF	Unc
1915	—	100	200	400	600	—

KM# 706   50 CENTAVOS
Copper, 28 mm. **Obv:** National arms **Rev:** Date
above large numeral value **Rev. Legend:**
REFORMA LIBERTAD JUSTICIA Y LEY

Date	Mintage	VG	F	VF	XF	Unc
1915	—	350	500	800	1,000	—

KM# 703   50 CENTAVOS
Copper, 28-29.5 mm. **Obv:** National arms **Rev:**
Numeral value within lined C and 1/2 wreath **Note:**
This coin exists with a silver and also a brass wash.
Size varies. Weight varies 5.73-13.77g.

Date	Mintage	VG	F	VF	XF	Unc
1915	—	12.50	17.50	30.00	42.00	—

KM# 704   50 CENTAVOS
Copper, 29-30 mm. **Obv:** National arms with
Morelos written below **Rev:** Value within wreath
Note: Size varies. Weight varies 8.56-11.47g.

Date	Mintage	VG	F	VF	XF	Unc
1916	—	12.50	20.00	30.00	50.00	—

KM# 708   PESO (UN)
Silver   **Obv:** National arms **Rev:** Liberty cap within
wreath

Date	Mintage	VG	F	VF	XF	Unc
1916	—	450	750	1,000	1,500	—

KM# 708a   PESO (UN)
10.0000 g., Copper, 30 mm. **Obv:** National arms
Rev: Liberty cap within wreath

Date	Mintage	VG	F	VF	XF	Unc
1916	—	500	1,000	1,200	2,000	—

PATTERNS
Including Off Metal Strikes

KM#	Date	Mintage	Identification	Mkt Val
Pn1	1915	—	50 Centavos. Silver. 12.0000 g. 29.3 mm. KM#705.	1,500
	1915	—	50 Centavos. Silver. 12.0000 g. 29.3 mm. KM#705.	1,500
	1915	—	50 Centavos. Silver. 12.0000 g. 29.3 mm. KM#705.	1,500
Pn2	1915	—	50 Centavos. Copper. KM#705.	1,500
	1915	—	50 Centavos. Copper. KM#705.	1,500
	1915	—	50 Centavos. Copper. KM#705.	1,500
Pn3	191x	—	Peso. Silver. KM#707.	8,000
	191x	—	Peso. Silver. KM#707.	8,000
	191x	—	Peso. Silver. KM#707.	8,000
Pn4	191x	—	Peso. Copper. KM#707a.	8,000
	191x	—	Peso. Copper. KM#707a.	8,000
	191x	—	Peso. Copper. KM#707a.	8,000
Pn5	1916	—	Peso. Copper. KM#707b.	6,500
	1916	—	Peso. Copper. KM#707b.	6,500
	1916	—	Peso. Copper. KM#707b.	6,500

OAXACA

Oaxaca is one of the southern states in Mexico. The coins issued in this state represent the most prolific series of the Revolution. Most of the coins bear the portrait of Benito Juarez, have corded or plain edges and were issued by a provisional government in the state. The exceptions are the rectangular 1 and 3 Centavos pieces that begin the series.

PROVISIONAL GOVERNMENT

REVOLUTIONARY COINAGE

KM# 709 CENTAVO (UN)
Copper, 19 mm. **Obv:** Legend within beaded rectangle **Rev:** Legend within beaded rectangle **Note:** Rectangular flan.

Date	Mintage	VG	F	VF	XF	Unc
1915	—	90.00	125	400	600	—

KM# 710 CENTAVO (UN)
Copper, 18 mm. **Obv:** Bust left with date flanked by stars below **Rev:** Value within lined C and 1/2 wreath

Date	Mintage	VG	F	VF	XF	Unc
1915	—	12.00	17.50	25.00	40.00	—

KM# 710a CENTAVO (UN)
Brass **Obv:** Head left with date flanked by stars below **Rev:** Value within lined C and 1/2 wreath

Date	Mintage	VG	F	VF	XF	Unc
1915	—	50.00	100	200	300	—

KM# 711 3 CENTAVOS (Tres)
Copper, 24 mm. **Obv:** Legend within rectangle with date below, stars in corners **Rev:** Legend within rectangle with stars in corners **Rev. Legend:** PROVISIO... **Note:** Rectangular flan.

Date	Mintage	VG	F	VF	XF	Unc
1915	—	100	200	400	500	—

KM# 712 3 CENTAVOS (Tres)
Copper **Obv:** Legend within rectangle with date below, stars in corners **Rev:** Legend within rectangle

with stars in corners **Rev. Legend:** PROVISI... **Note:** Rectangular flan.

Date	Mintage	VG	F	VF	XF	Unc
1915	—	1,000	3,000	4,000	8,000	—

KM# 713.1 3 CENTAVOS (Tres)
2.2500 g., Copper, 20 mm. **Obv:** Bust left flanked by stars below **Rev:** Value above sprigs **Note:** Without TM below value

Date	Mintage	VG	F	VF	XF	Unc
1915	—	3.00	5.00	12.00	25.00	—

KM# 713.2 3 CENTAVOS (Tres)
2.2500 g., Copper, 20 mm. **Obv:** Bust left flanked by stars below **Rev:** Value above sprigs **Edge:** Plain **Note:** Without TM below value

Date	Mintage	VG	F	VF	XF	Unc
1915	—	—	—	70.00	100	—

KM# 713.3 3 CENTAVOS (Tres)
2.2500 g., Copper, 20 mm. **Obv:** Bust left flanked by stars below **Rev:** Value above sprigs **Note:** With TM below value

Date	Mintage	VG	F	VF	XF	Unc
1915	—	100	200	400	500	—

KM# 714 3 CENTAVOS (Tres)
Copper, 20 mm. **Obv:** Bust left **Rev:** Value above sprigs **Note:** Small 3

Date	Mintage	VG	F	VF	XF	Unc
1915	—	6.00	10.00	15.00	30.00	—

KM# 715 5 CENTAVOS
Copper **Note:** JAN. 15 1915. incuse lettering

Date	Mintage	VG	F	VF	XF	Unc
1915 Rare	—	—	—	—	—	—

KM# 716 5 CENTAVOS
Copper **Obv:** Bust facing within circle **Rev:** Value above sprigs

Date	Mintage	VG	F	VF	XF	Unc
1915	—	—	—	—	8,000	—

KM# 717 5 CENTAVOS
Copper, 22 mm. **Obv:** Low relief bust left with date flanked by stars below **Rev:** Value above sprigs **Note:** Low relief with long, pointed truncation

Date	Mintage	VG	F	VF	XF	Unc
1915	—	1.50	3.00	4.50	10.00	—

KM# 718 5 CENTAVOS
Copper, 22 mm. **Obv:** Raised bust left with date flanked by stars below **Rev:** Value above sprigs **Note:** Heavy with short unfinished lapels

Date	Mintage	VG	F	VF	XF	Unc
1915	—	1.50	2.50	4.00	10.00	—

KM# 719 5 CENTAVOS
Copper, 22 mm. **Obv:** Raised bust left with date flanked by stars below **Rev:** Value above sprigs **Note:** Curved bottom

Date	Mintage	VG	F	VF	XF	Unc
1915	—	1.50	2.50	4.00	10.00	—

KM# 720 5 CENTAVOS
Copper, 22 mm. **Obv:** Bust left with date flanked by stars below **Rev:** Value above sprigs **Note:** Short truncation with closed lapels

Date	Mintage	VG	F	VF	XF	Unc
1915	—	1.50	3.00	4.50	10.00	—

KM# 721 5 CENTAVOS
Copper, 22 mm. **Obv:** Bust left with date flanked by stars below **Rev:** Value above sprigs **Note:** Short curved truncation

Date	Mintage	VG	F	VF	XF	Unc
1915	—	1.50	2.50	5.00	10.00	—

KM# 722 10 CENTAVOS
Copper **Obv:** Low relief bust left with date flanked by stars below **Rev:** Value above sprigs **Note:** Low relief with long pointed truncation

Date	Mintage	VG	F	VF	XF	Unc
1915	—	1.50	2.50	5.00	10.00	—

KM# 723 10 CENTAVOS
Copper **Obv:** Bust left with date flanked by stars below **Rev:** Value above sprigs **Note:** Obverse and reverse legend retrograde.

Date	Mintage	VG	F	VF	XF	Unc
1915 Rare	—	—	—	—	—	—

KM# 724 10 CENTAVOS
Copper, 26.5 mm. **Obv:** Raised bust left with date flanked by stars below **Rev:** Value above sprigs **Note:** Bold and unfinished truncation using 1 peso obverse die of km#740

Date	Mintage	VG	F	VF	XF	Unc
1915	—	3.00	5.00	7.00	10.00	—

KM# 725 10 CENTAVOS
Copper, 26.5 mm. **Obv:** Bust left with date flanked by stars below **Rev:** Value above sprigs **Note:** Heavy with short unfinished lapels centered high

Date	Mintage	VG	F	VF	XF	Unc
1915	—	1.50	2.50	4.00	10.00	—

KM# 726 10 CENTAVOS
Copper **Obv:** Raised bust left with date flanked by stars below **Rev:** Value above sprigs **Note:** Curved bottom

Date	Mintage	VG	F	VF	XF	Unc
1915	—	1.50	2.50	4.00	10.00	—

KM# 727.1 10 CENTAVOS
Copper **Obv:** Raised bust left with date flanked by stars below **Rev:** Value above sprigs **Note:** Short truncation with closed lapels

Date	Mintage	VG	F	VF	XF	Unc
1915	—	1.50	2.50	4.00	10.00	—

KM# 727.2 10 CENTAVOS
Copper **Obv:** Bust left with date flanked by stars below **Rev:** Value above sprigs **Note:** At present, only four pieces of this type are known. All are VF or better; T below bow with M below first leaf

Date	Mintage	VG	F	VF	XF	Unc
1915	—	—	—	400	550	—

KM# 727.3 10 CENTAVOS
Copper **Obv:** Raised bust left flanked by letters GV with date flanked by stars below **Rev:** Value above sprigs **Note:** This counterstamp appears on several different type host 10 cent coins.

Date	Mintage	VG	F	VF	XF	Unc
1915	—	100	200	300	400	—

Note: Letters GV correspond to General Garcia Vigil

KM# 730 20 CENTAVOS
Copper **Obv:** Bust left with date flanked by stars below **Rev:** Value above sprigs **Note:** 5th bust, heavy with short unfinished lapels using 20 Pesos obverse die

Date	Mintage	VG	F	VF	XF	Unc
1915	—	5.00	7.00	10.00	15.00	—

KM# 729.2   20 CENTAVOS

Copper   **Counterstamp:** Liberty cap **Obv:** Bust left with date flanked by stars below **Rev:** Value above sprigs **Note:** Counterstamp: Liberty cap and rays with bold unfinished truncation using 1 peso obverse die

Date	Mintage	VG	F	VF	XF	Unc
1915	—	100	150	300	350	—

KM# 728   20 CENTAVOS

Silver, 19 mm.   **Obv:** Low relief bust left with date flanked by stars below **Rev:** Value above sprigs **Note:** Low relief with long pointed truncation

Date	Mintage	VG	F	VF	XF	Unc
1915	—	800	2,000	3,000	4,000	—

KM# 728a   20 CENTAVOS

Copper, 19 mm.   **Obv:** Bust left with date flanked by stars below **Rev:** Value above sprigs **Note:** Low relief with long pointed truncation

Date	Mintage	VG	F	VF	XF	Unc
1915 Rare	—	—	—	—	—	—

KM# 729.1   20 CENTAVOS

Copper   **Obv:** Raised bust left with date flanked by stars below **Rev:** Value above sprigs **Note:** Unfinished truncation using 1 peso obverse die

Date	Mintage	VG	F	VF	XF	Unc
1915	—	1.50	3.00	4.50	10.00	—

KM# 731.1   20 CENTAVOS

Copper, 31 mm.   **Obv:** Raised bust left with date flanked by stars below **Rev:** Value above sprigs **Note:** Curved bottom

Date	Mintage	VG	F	VF	XF	Unc
1915	—	1.50	2.50	5.00	10.00	—

KM# 731.2   20 CENTAVOS

Copper   **Obv:** Raised bust left with date flanked by stars below **Rev:** Value above sprigs **Note:** Similar to KM#731.1 but with fourth bust.

Date	Mintage	VG	F	VF	XF	Unc
1915 Unique	—	—	—	—	—	—

KM# 732   20 CENTAVOS

Copper   **Obv:** Raised bust left with date flanked by stars below **Rev:** Value above sprigs

Date	Mintage	VG	F	VF	XF	Unc
1915	—	1.50	2.50	4.00	10.00	—

KM# 733   20 CENTAVOS

Copper   **Obv:** Bust left with date flanked by stars below **Rev:** Value above sprigs **Note:** 7th bust, short truncation with closed lapels

Date	Mintage	VG	F	VF	XF	Unc
1915	—	1.50	3.00	4.50	10.00	—

KM# 735   50 CENTAVOS

Silver, 22 mm.   **Obv:** Raised bust left with date flanked by stars below **Rev:** Value above sprigs **Note:** Curved bottom

Date	Mintage	VG	F	VF	XF	Unc
1915	—	8.00	15.00	30.00	50.00	—

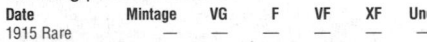

KM# 734   50 CENTAVOS

4.0700 g., Silver, 22 mm.   **Obv:** Raised bust left with date flanked by stars below **Rev:** Value above sprigs **Note:** Heavy with short unfinished lapels

Date	Mintage	VG	F	VF	XF	Unc
1915	—	10.00	20.00	50.00	100	—

KM# 739   50 CENTAVOS

Billon   **Obv:** Raised bust left with date flanked by stars below **Rev:** Value above sprigs **Note:** Ninth bust, high nearly straight truncation

Date	Mintage	VG	F	VF	XF	Unc
1915	—	—	—	—	4,000	—

KM# 739a   50 CENTAVOS

Copper   **Obv:** Raised bust left with date flanked by stars below **Rev:** Value above sprigs **Note:** Ninth bust, high nearly straight truncation

Date	Mintage	VG	F	VF	XF	Unc
1915	—	—	—	—	—	—

KM# 736   50 CENTAVOS

Silver   **Obv:** Bust left with date flanked by stars below **Rev:** Value above sprigs **Note:** Short truncation with closed lapels

Date	Mintage	VG	F	VF	XF	Unc
1915	—	8.00	15.00	30.00	50.00	—

KM# 737   50 CENTAVOS

4.5400 g., Silver, 22 mm.   **Obv:** Bust left with date flanked by stars below **Rev:** Value above sprigs **Note:** Short truncation with pronounced curve

Date	Mintage	VG	F	VF	XF	Unc
1915	—	10.00	15.00	25.00	40.00	—

KM# 741 PESO (UN)
Silver **Obv:** Raised bust with date flanked by stars below **Rev:** Value above sprigs **Note:** Fifth bust, heavy with short unfinished lapels, centered high

Date	Mintage	VG	F	VF	XF	Unc
1915	—	8.00	10.00	25.00	35.00	—

KM# 740.1 PESO (UN)
Silver, 26 mm. **Obv:** Raised bust left with date flanked by stars below **Rev:** Written value above sprigs **Note:** Fourth bust with heavy unfinished truncation

Date	Mintage	VG	F	VF	XF	Unc
1915	—	5.00	10.00	20.00	35.00	—

KM# 740.2 PESO (UN)
Silver, 26 mm. **Obv:** Raised bust left with date flanked by stars below **Rev:** Written value above sprigs **Note:** Fourth bust with heavy unfinished truncation w/TM.

Date	Mintage	VG	F	VF	XF	Unc
1915	—	150	300	400	600	—

KM# 743 PESO (UN)
Silver **Obv:** Low relief bust left with date flanked by stars below **Rev:** Value above sprigs **Note:** Seventh bust, short truncation with closed lapels

Date	Mintage	VG	F	VF	XF	Unc
1915	—	10.00	20.00	30.00	50.00	—

KM# 743a PESO (UN)
Silver **Obv:** Low relief bust left with date flanked by stars below **Rev:** Value above sprigs **Note:** Seventh bust, short truncation with closed lapels

Date	Mintage	VG	F	VF	XF	Unc
1915	—	35.00	75.00	150	200	—

KM# 742 PESO (UN)
Silver **Obv:** Low relief bust left with date flanked by stars below **Rev:** Value above sprigs **Note:** Sixth bust; Curved bottom line

Date	Mintage	VG	F	VF	XF	Unc
1915	—	10.00	15.00	30.00	50.00	—

KM# 742a PESO (UN)
Copper **Obv:** Low relief bust left with date flanked by stars below **Rev:** Value above sprigs **Note:** Sixth bust; Curved bottom line

Date	Mintage	VG	F	VF	XF	Unc
1915	—	—	—	—	500	—

KM# 744 2 PESOS (Dos)
Silver, 30 mm. **Obv:** Raised bust left with date flanked by stars below **Rev:** Value above sprigs **Note:** Fourth bust, using 1 peso obverse die

Date	Mintage	VG	F	VF	XF	Unc
1915	—	15.00	25.00	40.00	65.00	—

KM# 744a 2 PESOS (Dos)
Copper **Obv:** Raised bust left with date flanked by stars below **Rev:** Value above sprigs **Note:** Fourth bust, using 1 peso obverse die

Date	Mintage	VG	F	VF	XF	Unc
1915 Rare	—	—	—	—	—	—

KM# 745 2 PESOS (Dos)
Gold-Silver, 22 mm. **Obv:** Low relief bust left with date flanked by stars below **Rev:** Value above sprigs **Note:** 0.9020 Silver, 0.0100 Gold. Fifth bust, curved bottom 2 over pesos

Date	Mintage	VG	F	VF	XF	Unc
1915	—	12.00	20.00	40.00	60.00	—

KM# 745a 2 PESOS (Dos)
Copper **Obv:** Low relief bust left with date flanked by stars below **Rev:** Value above sprigs **Note:** Fifth bust, curved bottom 2 over pesos

Date	Mintage	VG	F	VF	XF	Unc
1915	—	75.00	100	150	200	—

KM# A746 2 PESOS (Dos)
Copper **Obv:** Raised bust left with date flanked by stars below **Rev:** Balance scale below liberty cap **Note:** Seventh bust, short truncation with closed lapels

Date	Mintage	VG	F	VF	XF	Unc
1915 Unique	—	—	—	—	—	—

KM# 746 2 PESOS (Dos)
Silver **Obv:** Raised bust left with date flanked by stars below **Rev:** Balance scale below liberty cap

Date	Mintage	VG	F	VF	XF	Unc
1915	—	20.00	25.00	50.00	75.00	—

KM# A747 2 PESOS (Dos)
Silver **Obv:** Bust left with date flanked by stars below **Rev:** Balance scale below liberty cap **Note:** Obverse die is free hand engraved

Date	Mintage	VG	F	VF	XF	Unc
1915	—	—	—	185	275	—

KM# 746a 2 PESOS (Dos)
Copper **Obv:** Bust left with date flanked by stars below **Rev:** Balance scale below liberty cap

Date	Mintage	Good	VG	F	VF	XF
1915	—	—	150	200	600	900

KM# 747.1 2 PESOS (Dos)
13.4400 g., Silver, 33 mm. **Obv:** Bust left with date flanked by stars below **Rev:** Balance scale below liberty cap

Date	Mintage	VG	F	VF	XF	Unc
1915	—	15.00	20.00	50.00	80.00	—

KM# 747.2 2 PESOS (Dos)
13.4400 g., Silver, 33 mm. **Obv:** Bust left with date flanked by stars below **Rev:** Balance scale below liberty cap

Date	Mintage	VG	F	VF	XF	Unc
1915	—	20.00	25.00	50.00	80.00	—

KM# 747.3 2 PESOS (Dos)
13.4400 g., Silver, 33 mm. **Obv:** Bust left with date flanked by stars below **Rev:** Balance scale below liberty cap

Date	Mintage	VG	F	VF	XF	Unc
1915	—	15.00	30.00	50.00	80.00	—

KM# 748 2 PESOS (Dos)
0.9020 Silver, 22 mm. **Obv:** Bust left with date flanked by stars below **Rev:** Value above sprigs

Date	Mintage	VG	F	VF	XF	Unc
1915	—	15.00	30.00	50.00	80.00	—

KM# 749 2 PESOS (Dos)
Silver **Obv:** Head left with date flanked by stars below **Rev:** Value above sprigs

Date	Mintage	VG	F	VF	XF	Unc
1915 Unique	—	—	—	3,000	—

KM# 751 5 PESOS
16.7700 g., Silver, 30 mm. **Obv:** Low relief bust left with date flanked by stars below **Rev:** Value above sprigs **Note:** Seventh bust, short truncation with closed lapels

Date	Mintage	VG	F	VF	XF	Unc
1915	—	50.00	100	200	250	—

KM# 751a 5 PESOS
Copper **Obv:** Low relief bust left with date flanked by stars below **Rev:** Value above sprigs **Note:** Seventh bust, short truncation with closed lapels

Date	Mintage	VG	F	VF	XF	Unc
1915	—	125	200	300	800	—

KM# 750 5 PESOS
0.1750 Gold, 19 mm. **Obv:** Bust left **Rev:** Value above sprigs **Note:** Third bust, heavy, with short unfinished lapels

Date	Mintage	VG	F	VF	XF	Unc
1915	—	150	200	300	450	—

KM# 750a 5 PESOS
Copper **Obv:** Bust left **Rev:** Value above sprigs **Note:** Third bust, heavy, with short unfinished lapels

Date	Mintage	VG	F	VF	XF	Unc
1915 Unique	—	—	—	—	—	—

KM# A752 10 PESOS
0.1500 Gold **Obv:** Bust left with date flanked by stars below **Rev:** Value above sprigs

Date	Mintage	VG	F	VF	XF	Unc
1915 Rare	—	—	—	—	—	—

KM# 752 10 PESOS
0.1750 Gold, 23 mm. **Obv:** Bust left with date flanked by stars below **Rev:** Value above sprigs

Date	Mintage	VG	F	VF	XF	Unc
1915	—	200	300	400	600	—

KM# 752a 10 PESOS
Copper **Obv:** Bust left with date flanked by stars below **Rev:** Value above sprigs

Date	Mintage	VG	F	VF	XF	Unc
1915	—	800	1,500	2,000	4,000	—

KM# 753 20 PESOS
0.1750 Gold **Obv:** Bust left with date flanked by stars below **Rev:** Value above sprigs

Date	Mintage	VG	F	VF	XF	Unc
1915	—	400	500	800	1,000	—

KM# 754 20 PESOS
0.1750 Gold, 27 mm. **Obv:** Bust left with date flanked by stars below **Rev:** Value above sprigs

Date	Mintage	VG	F	VF	XF	Unc
1915	—	200	400	600	900	—

MEXICO- REVOLUTIONARY

KM# A753   20 PESOS
0.1500 Gold   **Obv:** Bust left with date flanked by
stars below **Rev:** Value above sprigs **Note:** Fourth
bust

Date	Mintage	VG	F	VF	XF	Unc
1915 Unique	—	—	—	—	—	—

KM# 755   60 PESOS
50.0000 g., 0.8590 Gold 1.3808 oz. AGW   **Obv:**
Head left within 3/4 wreath **Rev:** Balance scale below
liberty cap **Edge:** Reeded

Date	Mintage	F	VF	XF	Unc	BU
1916 Rare	—	—	8,000	15,000	22,000	—

KM# 755a   60 PESOS
Silver **Obv:** Head left within 3/4 wreath **Rev:** Balance
scales below liberty cap **Edge:** Reeded

Date	Mintage	F	VF	XF	Unc	BU
1916	—	—	—	—	1,800	—

KM# 755b   60 PESOS
Copper **Obv:** Head left within 3/4 wreath **Rev:**
Balance scales below liberty cap **Edge:** Plain

Date	Mintage	F	VF	XF	Unc	BU
1916	—	—	—	—	1,000	1,800	—

PUEBLA

A state of central Mexico. Puebla was a state
that occasionally saw Zapata forces active within its
boundaries. Also active, and an issuer of coins, was
the Madero brigade who issued coins with their
name two years after Madero's death. The state
issue of 2, 5, 10 and 20 Centavos saw limited circulation and recent hoards have been found of some
values.

CHICONCUAUTLA
Madero Brigade

REVOLUTIONARY COINAGE

KM# 756   10 CENTAVOS
6.7300 g., Copper, 27 mm.   **Obv:** Date below
national arms **Rev:** Letters X and C entwined

Date	Mintage	VG	F	VF	XF	Unc
1915	—	7.50	12.50	17.50	25.00	—

KM# 758   20 CENTAVOS
Copper, 28 mm.   **Obv:** Date below national arms
Rev: Value

Date	Mintage	VG	F	VF	XF	Unc
1915	—	2.50	4.00	6.50	12.00	—

KM# 757   20 CENTAVOS
Copper, 28 mm.   **Obv:** Date below national arms
Rev: Value **Note:** Varieties exist.

Date	Mintage	VG	F	VF	XF	Unc
1915	—	2.50	4.00	6.50	12.00	—

TETELA DEL ORO Y OCAMPO

REVOLUTIONARY COINAGE

KM# 759   2 CENTAVOS
Copper, 16 mm.   **Obv:** National arms above date
Rev: Value

Date	Mintage	VG	F	VF	XF	Unc
1915	—	12.50	20.00	28.00	45.00	—
1915 Restrikes	—	—	1.00	1.50	2.00	—

KM# 760   2 CENTAVOS
Copper, 20 mm.   **Obv:** National arms within beaded circle **Rev:** Value within beaded circle **Rev. Legend:** E. DE PU.

Date	Mintage	VG	F	VF	XF	Unc
1915	—	15.00	25.00	35.00	75.00	—

KM# 761   2 CENTAVOS
Copper, 20 mm.   **Obv:** National arms within beaded circle **Rev:** Value within beaded circle **Rev. Legend:** E. DE PUE.

Date	Mintage	VG	F	VF	XF	Unc
1915	—	9.00	20.00	25.00	50.00	—

KM# 762   5 CENTAVOS
Copper, 21 mm.   **Obv:** National arms within beaded circle **Rev:** Value within beaded circle

Date	Mintage	VG	F	VF	XF	Unc
1915	—	100	200	300	400	—

KM# 764   20 CENTAVOS
Copper, 24 mm.   **Obv:** National arms **Rev:** Value above sprigs

Date	Mintage	VG	F	VF	XF	Unc
1915	—	50.00	100	150	225	—

TRIAL STRIKES

KM#	Date	Mintage	Identification	Mkt Val
TS1	1915	—	10 Centavos. Copper. Uniface, KM#763.	475
	1915	—	10 Centavos. Copper. Uniface, KM#763.	475
	1915	—	10 Centavos. Copper. Uniface, KM#763.	475
TS2	1915	—	10 Centavos. Brass. Uniface, KM#763.	750
	1915	—	10 Centavos. Brass. Uniface, KM#763.	750
	1915	—	10 Centavos. Brass. Uniface, KM#763.	750
TS3	1915	—	10 Centavos. Copper. KM#761. Eagle.	1,600
	1915	—	10 Centavos. Copper. KM#761. Eagle.	1,600
	1915	—	10 Centavos. Copper. KM#761. Eagle.	1,600

SINALOA

A state along the west coast of Mexico. The cast pieces of this state have been attributed to two people - Generals Rafael Buelna and Juan Carrasco. The cap and rays 8 Reales is usually attributed to General Buelna and the rest of the series to Carrasco. Because of their crude nature it is questionable whether separate series or mints can be determined.

BUELNA / CARRASCO

CAST COINAGE REVOLUTIONARY

KM# 766   50 CENTAVOS
Cast Silver, 29-31 mm.   **Obv:** National arms **Rev:** Numeral value within wreath **Note:** Sand molded using regular 50 Centavos, KM#445. Size varies. Weight varies 12.81-14.8g.

Date	Mintage	Good	VG	F	VF	XF
ND(1905-1918)	—	200	300	—	—	—

COUNTERMARKED COINAGE
REVOLUTIONARY COINAGE

These are all crude sand cast coins using regular coins to prepare the mold. Prices below give a range for how much of the original coin from which the mold was prepared is visible.

KM# 765   20 CENTAVOS
Cast Silver **Obv:** National arms within beaded circle **Rev:** Value within beaded circle **Note:** Sand molded using regular 20 Centavos.

CM Date	Host Date	Good	VG	F	VF
ND(ca.1915)	ND(1898-1905)	200	300	—	—

KM# 767   50 CENTAVOS
Cast Silver **Countermark:** G.C. **Obv:** National arms with additional countermark **Rev:** Value and date within wreath with liberty cap above **Note:** Sand molded using regular 50 Centavos, KM#445.

CM Date	Host Date	Good	VG	F	VF	XF
ND	ND(1905-1918)	100	150	200	300	—

KM# 769   PESO
Cast Silver **Note:** Sand molded using regular Peso, KM#409.

CM Date	Host Date	Good	VG	F	VF	XF
	ND(1898-1909)	10.00	20.00	30.00	40.00	—

KM# 768.1   PESO
Cast Silver, 38.8-39 mm. **Note:** Sand molded using regular 8 Reales, KM#377. Size varies. Weight varies 26-33.67g.

CM Date	Host Date	Good	VG	F	VF	XF
ND(ca.1915)	ND(1824-97)	17.50	35.00	45.00	55.00	—

KM# 768.2   PESO
Cast Silver, 38.5-39 mm. **Countermark:** G.C. **Obv:** With additional countermark **Note:** Sand molded using regular 8 Reales, KM#377. Size varies. Weight varies 26-33.67g.

CM Date	Host Date	Good	VG	F	VF	XF
ND(ca.1915)	ND(1824-97)	25.00	45.00	100	150	—

KM# 770   PESO
Cast Silver, 38.5 mm. **Countermark:** G.C **Obv:** National arms with additional countermark **Rev:** Liberty cap with additional countermark **Note:** Sand molded using regular Peso, KM#409.

CM Date	Host Date	Good	VG	F	VF
ND(ca.1915)	ND(1898-1909)	30.00	60.00	140	175

MEXICO- REVOLUTIONARY

Precise Pricing for Your Coins